Aberdour Boat Club
A
B C
99   R
Fife - Scotland

CRUISING
ASSOCIATION
HANDBOOK

"Each petty hand
Can steer a ship becalm'd; but he that will
Govern and carry her to her ends, must know
His tides, his currents; how to shift his sails:
What she will bear in foul, what in fair weather;
What her springs are, her leaks, and how to stop them,
What strands, what shelves, what rocks do threaten her.
The forces and the natures of all winds,
Gusts, storms and tempests; when her keel ploughs hell,
And deck knocks heaven; then to manage her
Becomes the name and office of a pilot."

BEN JONSON.

CRUISING
ASSOCIATION
HANDBOOK

Sixth Edition

CRUISING ASSOCIATION
LONDON

Cruising Association
Ivory House
St Katharine Dock
London E1 9AT

Published in Great Britain
First edition 1920
Fifth edition 1971
Sixth edition 1981

Copyright © Cruising Association 1981

British Library Cataloguing in Publication Data

Cruising Association.
  Cruising Association Handbook. – 6th ed.
  1. Pilot guides – Europe, Western
  2. Harbors – Europe, Western
  I. Title
  623.89′294   VK802

ISBN 0-9503742-1-0

Text set in 12/13 pt Linotron 202 Times, printed and bound in
Great Britain at The Pitman Press, Bath

Other publications by the Cruising Association

Notes on French Inland Waterways
Visiting Yachtsman's Guide to the London River

DISCLAIMER

While every effort has been made to ensure the greatest possible accuracy in the contents of this book, the Cruising Association, the Editor and other members responsible for its compilation accept no responsibility for the results of any errors or omissions. This *Handbook* should only be used in conjunction with the appropriate up-to-date charts and *Notices to Mariners*.

The *Handbook*, as amended by the late Corrections enclosed with each copy sold, is compiled on the basis of information available as at 31 December 1980. After publication, Corrections will be issued annually beginning with a Spring 1982 issue, and the *Handbook* must only be used in conjunction with all current issues of Corrections.

CONTENTS

Acknowledgements   viii
Foreword by the President of the Cruising Association   ix
The Cruising Association   xi
Explanatory Notes to the Text   xiii
List of Abbreviations   xvi

ENGLAND, SOUTH COAST

Scilly Isles to Ramsgate   1

ENGLAND, EAST COAST

North Foreland to Berwick   93

SCOTLAND

East Coast – Eyemouth to Wick   156
Orkney   177
Shetland   181
North Coast of Scotland – Duncansby Head to Cape Wrath   184
Scotland, West Coast   189
West Side of the Minches – Butt of Lewis to Barra Head   192
East Side of the Minches – Isle of Skye (West) and the Small Isles   200
Mainland – Loch Gairloch to Ardnamurchan Point   204

ENGLAND, WEST COAST AND WALES   222

Isle of Man   225
St Bees to Duddon   230
Wales   236
England, West Coast   266

IRELAND 276

Southwest Coast 278
South Coast 284
East Coast 298
North Coast 311
West Coast 317

DENMARK AND THE SOUTHWEST BALTIC 325

Southwest Baltic 327
Denmark, North Sea Coast 335

GERMANY 336

HOLLAND 344

BELGIUM 365

FRANCE 368

French Inland Waterways 370
French Channel Ports 374
Channel Islands 396
France, North Coast – West of Cherbourg 407
France, West Coast – Chenal du Four to Hendaye 438

SPAIN AND PORTUGAL 486

Spain, North Coast 487
Spain, West Coast 493
Portugal 496
Spain, Southwest Coast, to Gibraltar 498

BIBLIOGRAPHY 499

INDEX 501

Index of Passage Notes 509

ACKNOWLEDGEMENTS

The Cruising Association is most grateful for permission to reproduce information from official sources and charts, and wishes to acknowledge the following hydrographic authorities:

The Hydrographer of the Navy
Service Hydrographique et Océanographique de la Marine, France
Deutsches Hydrographisches Institut, Hamburg
Reproduction of parts of Netherlands charts with the permission of the Minister of Defence

The assistance of the following yachting organisations is also gratefully acknowledged:

Clyde Cruising Club
Irish Cruising Club
Bristol Channel Yachting Conference
Royal Northumberland Yacht Club

FOREWORD

By the President of the Cruising Association,
WILLIAM HURST

The production of a new edition of the *Cruising Association Handbook* represents the culmination of many years of dedicated voluntary work by a quite remarkable number of people, of whom Mark Brackenbury, the Honorary Editor of this edition, represents only the tip of the iceberg. Since he took over the editorship several years ago, he has put in an enormous number of hours on preparing the text and plans for publication, but he is the first to point out that his efforts could not have possibly come to fruition without the assistance of the Handbook Committee, other members of the Association, and many more.

For the year before publication, the Chairman of the Handbook Committee, Barrie Johnson, took on the intricate task of bringing the plans up to date and controlling the preparation of the cartography, while another member of the Committee, Phoebe Mason, looked after the technical matters of production and printing. The remainder of the Committee were Sectional Editors, each responsible for a section of the final text. In their efforts, they were in turn helped by the large number of Honorary Local Representatives which the Association has in most of the ports of Britain and numerous foreign ports. Information sent in by other members was also of the greatest value in drawing the editorial team's attention to changes and developments.

Other vital sources of information, without which the quality of the coverage must inevitably have suffered, have been the Royal Northumberland Yacht Club, the Clyde Cruising Club and the Irish Cruising Club, all of which have generously allowed us to make use of plans and information in the sailing directions which they publish for their respective areas. We are also grateful to many yacht clubs and harbourmasters, both at home and overseas, for taking the trouble to supply information or confirm facts.

The unfailing courtesy of the Hydrographer of the Navy and his staff should be mentioned; this is in addition to the formal acknowledgement of permission to base plans on their charts which will be found elsewhere.

Finally, I would like to add a word of thanks to Ted Wilson, the Association's principal cartographer, and the General and Assistant Secretaries of the Association, and the special secretary to the Handbook Editor. They are the paid members of the team, but the quality of the final product owes a great deal to their hard work and dedicated cooperation.

William Hunt

THE CRUISING ASSOCIATION

The Cruising Association was founded in 1908 'to encourage cruising in yachts and boats and to protect the interests of yachtsmen'. It had some 3,500 members in 1980, the majority resident in the British Isles but several hundred living in Europe and other parts of the world. Its club rooms, offices and reference library are at Ivory House, St Katharine Dock, London E1 9AT, tel (01) 481 0881. The Association is fortunate to have its home in such an appropriate building, a beautiful eighteenth century warehouse almost totally surrounded by the pontoons of London's principal marina.

The Library contains some 10,000 books, and may well be the most important collection on sailing and allied subjects in private hands on the eastern side of the Atlantic. There is a large collection of charts for cruise planning purposes, and files of information on cruising areas all over the world are kept, in which news from members and other sources are collated.

Publications   The main one in terms of circulation is of course this *Handbook*, as it is sold to the public as well as members. Members are entitled to buy copies for their own use at a substantially reduced price. The *Handbook* is updated by annual lists of Corrections, available from the Association's headquarters to callers or by post. As noted elsewhere, the *Handbook* should never be used without all current Corrections. Shorter guides to special areas are also published: in print in 1980 were *Notes on French Inland Waterways* and *Visiting Yachtsman's Guide to the London River*.

Turning to publications available to members only, the *Bulletin* is a tri-annual magazine containing news, logs and articles. *Harbour, Anchorage and Navigational Notes* are also tri-annual, circulating the most recent news from members and other sources on ports, harbours and other navigational matters. The *Year Book* is published annually, containing lists of members and boats, Honorary Local Representatives, Association Boatmen, latest Customs regulations for various countries, and much other useful information.

Honorary Local Representatives are yachtsmen, usually members, whose detailed knowledge of the ports they cover is available to other members in the form of advice or assistance.

Association Boatmen are professionals, often organisations rather than individuals, who are recommended as giving reliable and good service at a particular port. They can often arrange moorings, look after boats that are left in their care, and of course provide normal repair and maintenance facilities. The services which they can offer are detailed in the *Year Book*.

Crew List To assist owners and crews to get in touch with each other, the Association provides a service circulating the names and addresses of owners seeking crew and vice versa.

Enquiries on cruising matters The C.A. is associated with numerous cruising clubs in Britain and elsewhere. Full details are to be found in the *Year Book*. It thus has access to an unrivalled body of cruising knowledge, available to members through the secretariat.

Educational and social events The Association organises a full programme of lectures, training and purely social events during the winter, and numerous meets where members gather together in ports in Britain and overseas are held during the sailing season.

Challenge Cups Several Challenge Cups are awarded every year, mainly for logs of cruises in various categories, but also for outstanding cruises or acts of seamanship.

Enquiries about membership should be addressed to the General Secretary, Cruising Association, Ivory House, St Katharine Dock, London E1 9AT.

EXPLANATORY NOTES TO THE TEXT

The sailing directions in this *Handbook* are laid out in a standard form as far as possible. Users will find that the knowledge is presented in the order in which it is required as the port is approached from seaward. Ports in Great Britain are covered anticlockwise from the Scillies, Irish ports similarly from Valentia, and the European coast from north to south of the area covered (SW Baltic to Gibraltar).

Times are given in local time; bearings of lights, transits etc are given from seaward; and all courses and bearings are True unless specifically stated to be otherwise.

On most plans, the only depth contour shown is the 2m line, and in such cases this contour is not marked with its depth, but merely shown as a dotted line. In a few cases, however, depth contours other than the 2m line have had to be used: where this occurs, the depth of the contour line is shown on the plan.

Dredged depths are indicated by the depth followed by **m**, as: 3.5m, meaning 'Dredged to 3.5 metres'.

As colour is not available to indicate lights on buoys, a conventional four-ray light star is used to indicate that a buoy is lit. This precludes the showing of radar reflectors.

Corrections to the *Handbook* are issued annually, and users *must* ensure that they are using it in conjunction with all the relevant Corrections. Every two or three years these Corrections are issued in cumulative form, which enables earlier issues to be discarded. The exact status of each set of Corrections is clearly set out on the cover of the issue concerned. The *Handbook* is designed to supplement, and not replace, Admiralty pilots, charts, light lists, tide tables, and Notices to Mariners, and it is essential that appropriate issues of all these should be carried. Users must always be aware of the possibility of changes having been made or occurred after publication date of the *Handbook* or latest corrections, and should always navigate carefully and with the latest possible information.

IALA Buoyage Changes

At the time when this edition went to press, the changeover of European Buoyage to the IALA system 'A' had not been finally completed. In the British Isles, the Irish coast from Old Head of Kinsale round west to Malin Head, and the Scottish coast north of a line between Malin Head and the Rhinns of Islay, and north of 57°N on the east coast, were not due for completion until the end of 1981. This also applies to parts of the French west coast.

As far as practicable, the proposed changes have been anticipated in the plans of the affected areas and in the text on the basis of published intentions, so users of the *Handbook* during 1981 should be aware that in these areas there is a possibility that some unconverted buoyage may still be in place, and that the actual changes made may in fact not always accord with the published changes to buoyage and lights.

Notes on Tidal Data

(1) DEFINITIONS

Chart Datum is the level from which the depth of water or drying height is measured. With the exception of a few very old editions, datum for British charts and tide tables is now LAT, i.e. Lowest Astronomical Tide, the lowest level which can ever occur as a result of purely astronomical conjunctions, under average meteorological conditions.

The **Height** of the tide is the vertical distance at any one moment between the level of the sea surface and chart datum.

The **Rise** of the tide on a particular day is the height to which High Water will rise above chart datum.

The **Range** of the tide is the difference in height between successive High and Low Waters.

Mean High Water Springs (MHWS) has a highly complicated astronomical definition, but is in effect the average height of the spring tides throughout the year. Similarly for **Mean Low Water Springs (MLWS)**, **Mean High Water Neaps (MHWN)** and **Mean Low Water Neaps (MLWN)**. **Mean Tide Level (MTL)** is the average of these four levels, and knowledge of this figure enables the user who knows the height of the day's tide to calculate the range (twice the difference between the Rise and MTL), which is vital for anchoring, or for calculations involving minimum depths of water.

Explanation of Tidal Data Provided in the *Handbook*

The time of High Water (HW followed by a figure) and the Direction of Stream usually in the offing (DS followed by directions and figures), are based on the times of High Water at Dover. The provision of these figures has been found a useful practice for many years, as the times of Dover tides are readily available aboard most vessels, but it must be most strongly emphasized that these differences are approximations only, and are only intended for cruise planning purposes. Far more accuracy will be obtained by using local tide tables, or applying the appropriate difference to a tide table for a nearby Standard Port. The differences on Dover are the mean of extremes, and in some areas (the Cornish coast and certain parts of west Scotland are two examples) the variation between the constant at spring tides and neap tides can be nearly two hours. It is therefore possible that the actual time of High Water on a particular day can vary by nearly an hour from the figures given in the *Handbook*. Nevertheless, it is felt that the figures are useful as a general guide, when planning a cruise or deciding between alternatives.

The figures provided for the heights of tides at MHWS, etc are, it is hoped, self-explanatory. All figures are in metres. It should be noted, however, that certain tides have been included based on local observation or interpolation. It was felt in these cases that an educated estimate was better than no information at all, but in any case it must always be borne in mind that *all* tidal predictions are approximations, and that tide levels, and the rate and even direction of tidal streams, can be substantially influenced by wind, meteorological conditions and other factors. Even when tidal data are derived from the most impeccable sources, therefore, the prudent navigator will always allow a sensible margin of error in the light of the circumstances.

It may be useful to record that the Mean Spring range at Dover is 5.9 metres, and the Mean Neap range 3.3 metres. The Height of Tide predicted as MHWS will therefore be attained on a day when the Dover range is 5.9 metres, and this will apply (± one day) anywhere in Europe. It is worth pointing out that tides occur substantially outside the mean levels, the predicted range for Dover in 1980 being as much as 6.9 metres on the March spring tide, and as little as 2.8 metres on a February neap. Thus, if the text of this *Handbook* states that 'Streams attain 4 knots at springs', it may well be that they would attain 5 knots or more on a day when the tidal range at Dover was 6.9 metres, i.e. an extreme spring tide. The differences of times of HW compared with Dover are a mean between the differences at these extreme tides, as this ensures that the maximum possible error is kept as low as possible.

Important Note

All depths given in the *Handbook*, except where otherwise stated, refer to the depth at chart datum (usually LAT). Thus, if advice is given to 'Anchor in 3–4m', then if at the time the level of the tide is $2\frac{1}{2}$m above datum ($2\frac{1}{2}$m Height of Tide, see next paragraph), the boat should be anchored in an *actual* depth of $5\frac{1}{2}$ to $6\frac{1}{2}$m. This applies to stated depths in channels and over bars, to soundings at which course should be changed, and to all depths mentioned except where specifically referred to other tide heights. FAILURE TO REMEMBER THIS PRINCIPLE, WHICH APPLIES TO ALL NAVIGATIONAL WORKS, CAN BE DANGEROUS.

Calculation of Height of Tide

For the purposes of most yachtsmen, the Rule of Twelve gives quite enough accuracy. This states that the tide rises or falls 1/12 of its range in the first hour, 2/12 in the second, 3/12 in the third and fourth, 2/12 in the fifth and 1/12 in the sixth. Thus, once the range is known (twice the difference between MTL and the day's rise), 4 hours before HW the tide will be 9/12 ($\frac{3}{4}$) of the range below HW level; 2 hours after, it will be 3/12 ($\frac{1}{4}$) of the range below HW level.

In most ports the error involved in using this rule is unlikely to exceed 5–10 per cent of the range, and weather and other factors mean that the predictions are not much more accurate than this in any case. However the rule is useless in ports with freak tides, such as those in the Solent with double high waters, or the Seine Estuary which has a prolonged HW stand. For these, local advice must be taken: some nautical almanacs give tidal curves enabling these tides to be calculated, and normal tides to be worked out with greater accuracy.

ABBREVIATIONS USED IN THE HANDBOOK

Other than standard Admiralty abbreviations, to be found in Chart BA 5011, and generally known and accepted ones.

Note: In the middle of the year before publication, the Admiralty adopted a revised system of abbreviations for light rhythms, etc. It has been possible to adopt the new standard consistently in the text, but it would have been an impossible task to attempt to alter all the plans, so some of these will show a light flashing twice every five seconds as Gp Fl(2) 5s, and some as Fl(2) 5s, and so on. We do not feel that this can create any serious problems, as throughout the lifetime of this edition BA charts based on both forms will continue to be current.

alt	alternating	Lt Ho	lighthouse
anch	anchor(age)	LV	light vessel
app	approach	LW(S)	Low Water (Springs)
approx	approximately	M	nautical mile(s), *also*
BA	British Admiralty		Mean as in MHWS
bn	beacon	m	metre(s)
br	bridge	Mag	magnetic
C	cape	min	minute(s)
ca	cable(s)	Mo	Morse code
Card	cardinal (buoyage)	NB	noticeboard
ch	church	Oc, Occ	occulting
chan	channel	PO	post office
con	conical	Q, Qk Fl	quick flashing
conspic	conspicuous	R	river, *also* red
EC	early closing	rk(s)	rocks
ent	entrance	Ro Bn	radio beacon
HAT	Highest Astronomical Tide	rly	railway
HM	harbourmaster	s	seconds
ho	house	Sd	sound
hr	harbour, *also* hour	Sig Mst	signal mast
ht	height	Sig Stn	signal station
HW(N)	High Water (Neaps)	spher	spherical
I	île (French), island (plans only)	sq	square
		stb	starboard
Is	islands, isle (text)	T	ton(s)
kn	knot(s)	tel	telephone (number)
L	loch	tr	tower
LAT	Lowest Astronomical Tide	W	white, *also* West
LB	Lifeboat (station)	U	unattended
ldg	leading	v	vertical
lt(s)	light(s)	YC	yacht club

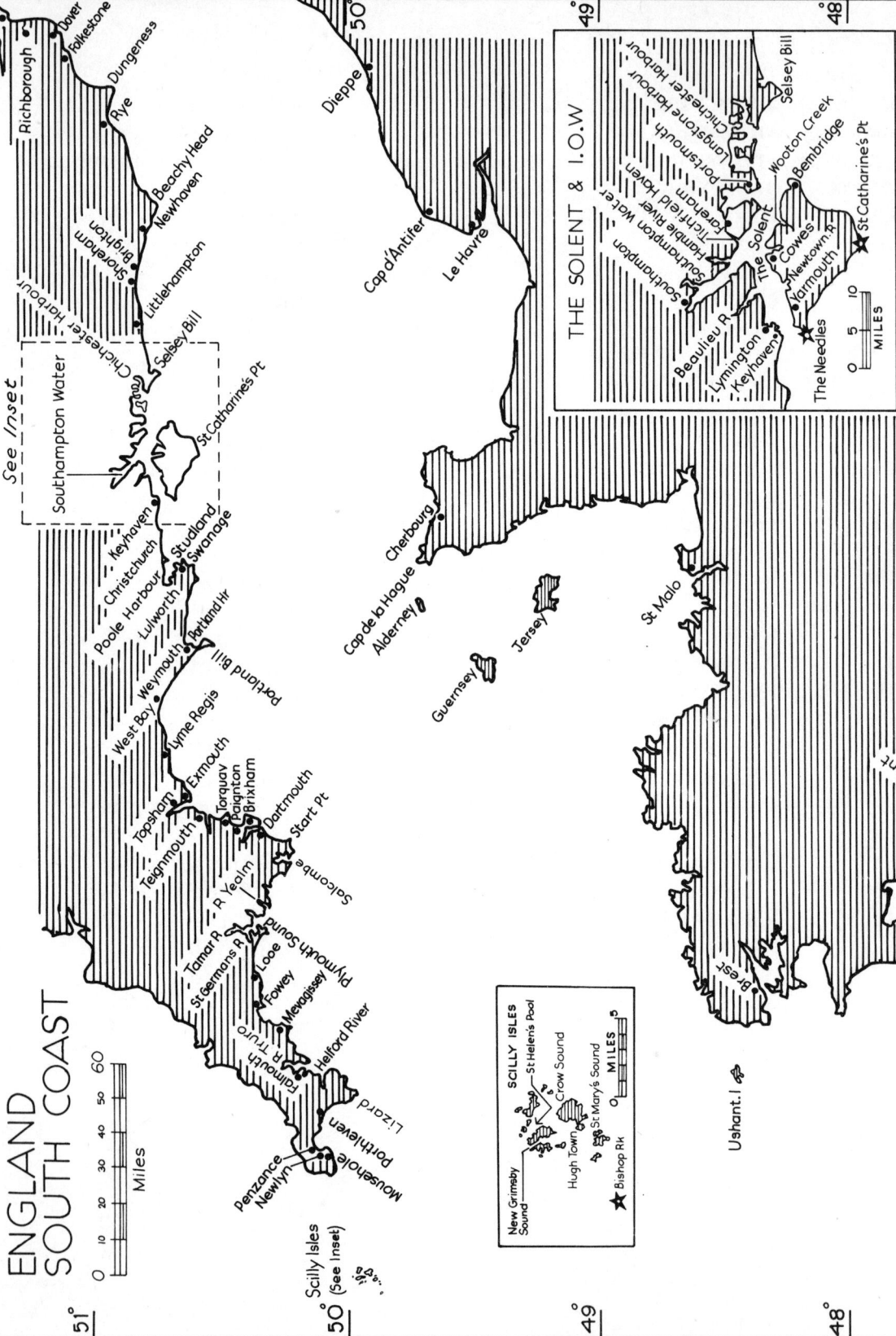

ENGLAND
SOUTH COAST

Miles
0 10 20 30 40 50 60

Ramsgate
Dover
Folkestone
Richborough
Dungeness
Rye
Beachy Head
Newhaven
Brighton
Shoreham
Littlehampton
Chichester Harbour
Selsey Bill
St Catharine's Pt
Southampton Water
See Inset
Keyhaven
Christchurch
Poole Harbour
Studland
Lulworth
Swanage
Portland Bill
Weymouth
West Bay
Lyme Regis
Exmouth
Topsham
Teignmouth
Torquay
Paignton
Brixham
Dartmouth
Start Pt
Salcombe
R Yealm
Tamar R
St Germans R
Plymouth Sound
Looe
Fowey
Mevagissey
Helford River
Falmouth
R Truro
Lizard
Porthleven
Mousehole
Penzance
Newlyn
Scilly Isles
(See Inset)

Dieppe
Cap d'Antifer
Le Havre
Cherbourg
Cap de la Hague
Alderney
Guernsey
Jersey
St Malo
Brest
Lorient
Ushant I.

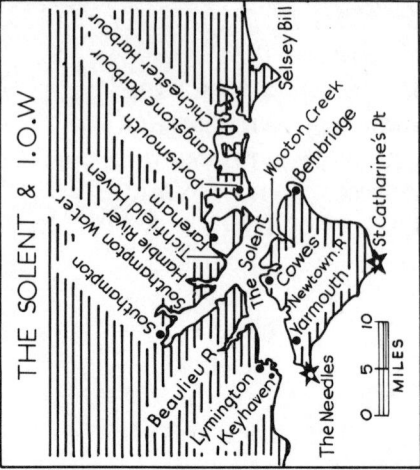

THE SOLENT & I.O.W

Selsey Bill
Chichester Harbour
Langstone Harbour
Portsmouth
Fareham
Titchfield Haven
Southampton Water
Hamble River
The Solent
Cowes
Wootton Creek
Bembridge
Newtown R.
St Catharine's Pt
Beaulieu R.
Lymington
Keyhaven
The Needles
Yarmouth

MILES
0 5 10

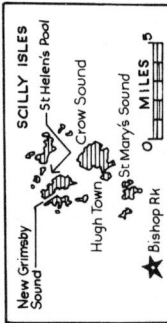

SCILLY ISLES

New Grimsby
Sound
St Helen's Pool
Crow Sound
Hugh Town
St Mary's Sound
Bishop Rk

MILES
0 5

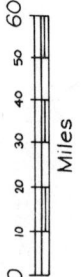

xviii

ENGLAND, SOUTH COAST

Scilly Isles to Ramsgate

Between the Scilly Isles and Land's End tidal streams are rotary clockwise: SSE −3.40; WNW +0.20; N +2.45; ENE +5.45.
Land's End: DS: N HWD; S −5.10. Runnelstone: DS: E −6 for 3h; NW −3 for 9½h.

A falling barometer should be taken as a danger signal whatever the forecast and appearance of the weather at the time.

When proceeding E from the Scillies towards Penzance make for the Wolf Rock Lt Ho. There is deep water up to ½M off the Rock on all sides. Thence head to pass well S of the Runnelstone lt buoy before following the coast to Penzance keeping at least 1M offshore.

SCILLY ISLES   Chart BA 34 (Plans p2,3,4)
The Scilly Isles are situated 21M from Land's End and 43M from Lizard Pt.
HW St Mary's +6.00.
MHWS 5.7; MLWS 0.7; MTL 3.1; MHWN 4.4; MLWN 2.0.
The tidal streams are rotary clockwise ¾ to 1½kn but the rate increases at various pts. Off St Martin's Hd there is a tide rip to S and SE which extends 3M.
DS Off Gilstone: NE +2.15, 1.8kn; SW −4.10, 2.5kn.
St Mary's Road: E +1.45; W (direction varies between SW and NW) −5.40; both about 1kn.
St Mary's Sound: SE +2.45; NW −4.00; both 2kn.
Crow Sound: Weak and irregular except from −1.40 to +5.15 when it runs SE at first, changing through E to N; max 1.4kn NE at +2.45.
New Grimsby Hr: N −4.00; S +4.00; both 1kn. Off the entrance: E +1.15; W −5.10; both 2½kn.
Bar   Crow Sound which gives access from E to St Mary's Road is obstructed by a bar, 0.3 to 1.2m at MLWS. Other approaches from N, S and W are available at all times. Vessels without power should avoid the far W entrances except in clear

The Scilly Isles
Depths in Metres

Based on British Admiralty Charts (nos. in text) with the permission of the Controller of H.M. Stationery Office and the Hydrographer of the Navy, and on other sources.

Tresco
Rushy Pt
Lizard Pt
Great Pool
Abbey Hill Mont=FS
Pentle
Bay
Gt Pentle Rk
Skirt I
Bounty Ledge
Green I
Diamond Ledge
Figtree Ledge
Tobaccomans Ledge
Broad Ledge
Slip
Crow Pt
The Mare
The Pots
Nut Rk

Gt Cheese Rk
Moths Ledge
Broad Ledge
Pigs Ledge
Old Quay
Higher Town Bay
New Quay
English I
Hanjague (24)
Nornour
Cruthers Pt
Wra Ledge
St Martin's Flats
Gt Ganilly
Mouls (7)
Little Innisvouls
Guthers I
Seal Rk
Three Rks
Damasinnas
Little Ganilly
Long Scud
Gt Ganinick
Little Ganinick
Gt Innisvouls
Gt Arthur
Renny Rk
Ragged I
Arthur Hd
Menawethan
Biggal (13)

Craggyelli's
Crow Bar
Queen's Ledge
Hats
Boiler
(I) Biggal
Crow Rk Bn
Bn
Bar Pt
Bns
Hats
Crow Pt in line with NE extreme of Innisidgen 276°
Trinity Rk 5

Crow Sound
Depths in Metres
0 Cables   5   10

St Mary's Road
Creeb
The Cow
Bacon Ledge
Newford I

Bants Carn
TV Mast (118) (conspic)
(R Lts)
Block House Pt
Watermill Cove
Innisidgen
Radio Masts (R Lts)
CG
Radio Mast
Telegraph Tr Carn (conspic) (62)
Morval Pt
Bn
Taylors

Trenears Rk
Vinegar Ledge
Tolls I

St Mary's
FS
Gap
Bn
Deep Pt

49° 56'
49° 53'
49° 54'

N Carn of Serica
Wk
Woolpack Pt
Morning Pt
Porth Hellick
Raveen (5)
Peninnis Hd
Radio Mast FR
Foul
Tolman Pt
Gilstone
Serica Rk 7
Bartholomew Ledges
Mincarlo
Bn (7)
Biggal (2)
The Chair
Inner Hd (18)
St Mary's Sound
Mincarlo in line with W extreme of Gt Minalto 308°

Old Wreck Rk
The Ruddy
Haycocks
Gt Smith (10)
Bristolman
Little Smith
Perconger Ledge
The Cow
The Kittern
The Bow (11)
Spanish Ledges
BY B

Annet
Carnmanuoueth
Burnt I
Pascoe Rk
Porth Coose
Stony I
Kittern Hill
Gugh
Middle Ranneys
Annet Ledge
Menrounds
Hale Rk
Pehny Ledges
Old Lt Ho (conspic)
St Agnes
Long Pt
Jetty
Bn (tr)
Bn
Hoe Pt

Isinvrank
Brothers
Muncoy
Muncoy Neck
Gt Menbean
Flat Carn (4)
Melledgan
Gorregan Neck

Pidney Brow
Lethegus Rks
Wrecks
Great Wingletang
Horse Pt
Wk

Smith Sound
Gap in Gt Smith 351°
Castle Bryher Summit in line with
Gap in Gt Smith

Depths in Metres
0 Cables   5   10

St Mary's and Smith Sounds

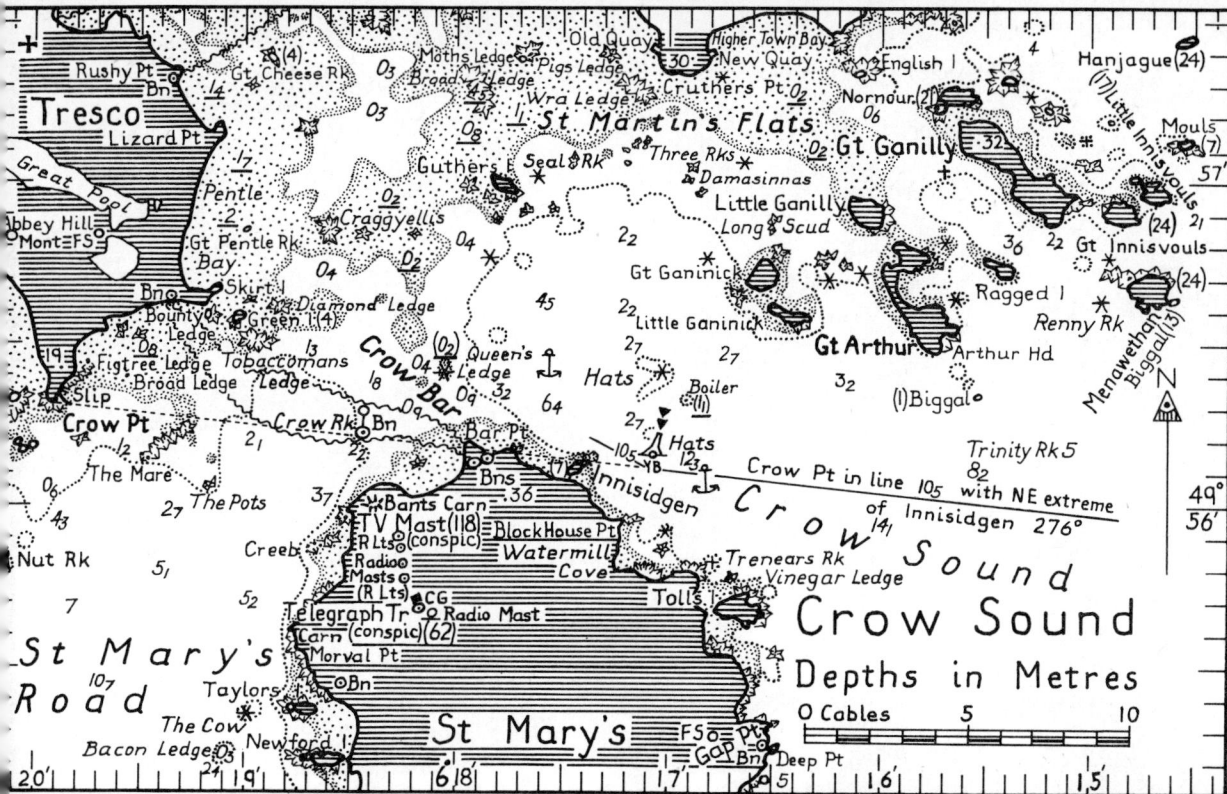

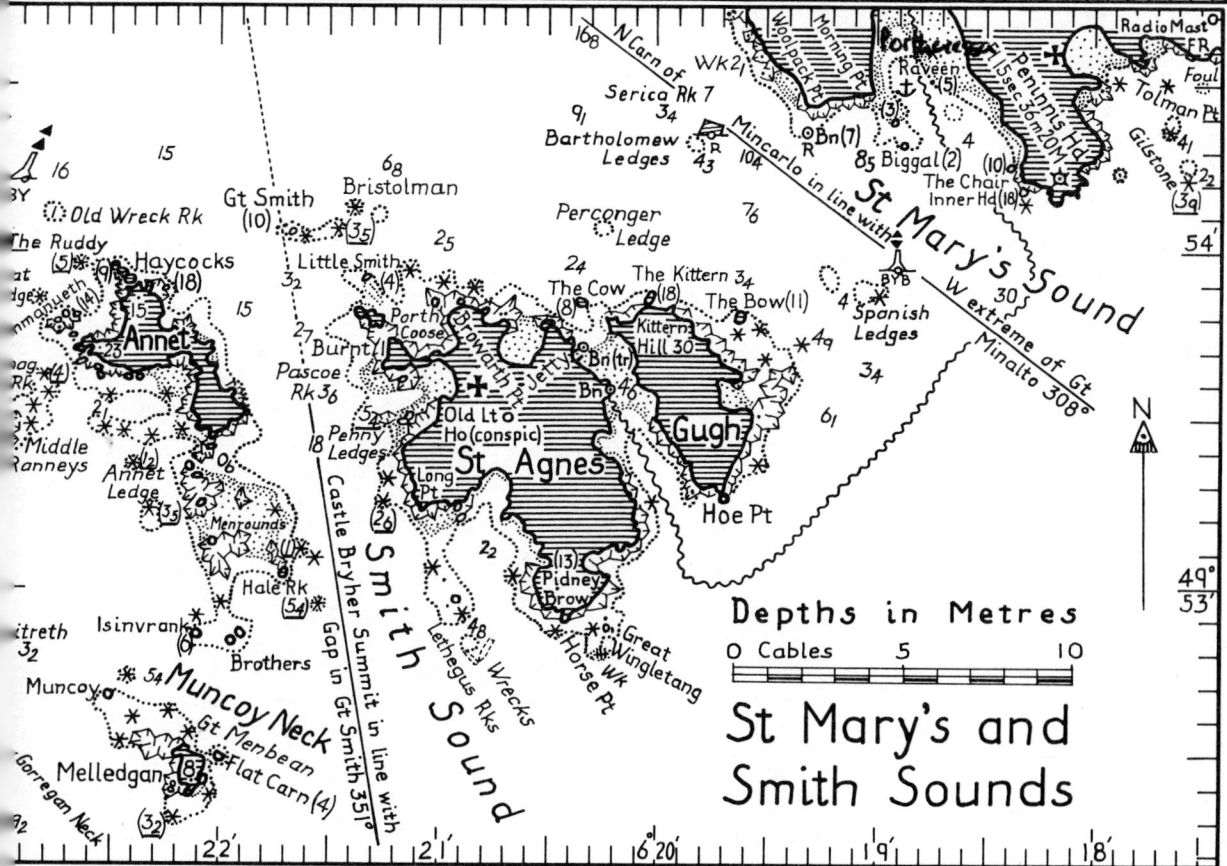

...ed on British Admiralty Charts (nos. in text) with the permission of the Controller of H.M. Stationery Office and of Hydrographer of the Navy, and on other sources.

3

Fl.R 10s 55m 24M
Siren (4) 60s
RC   Round I.

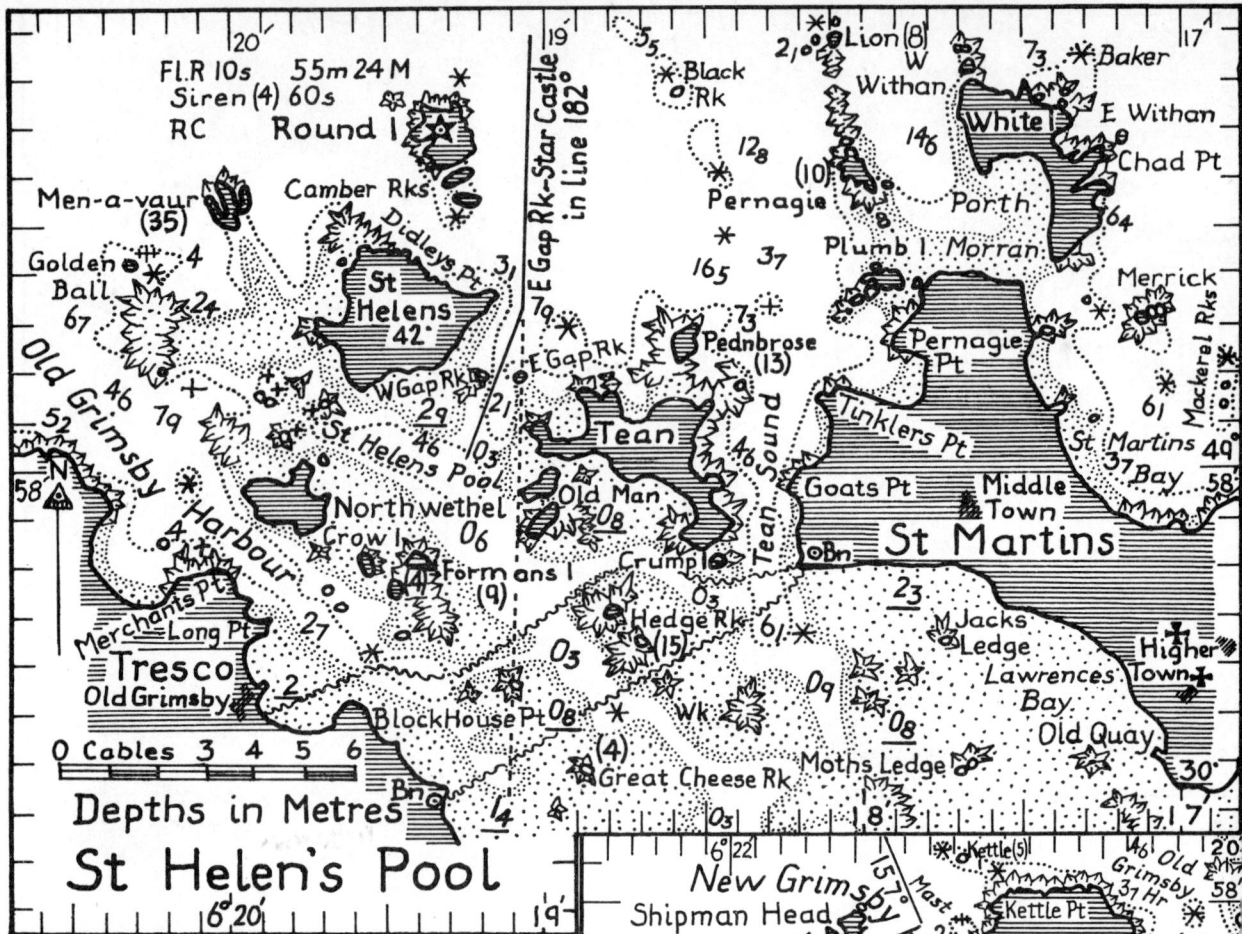

Men-a-vaur (35)
Camber Rks.
Didleys Pt.
Golden Ball
67
St Helens 42
W Gap Rk.
2₉
46 ₀3 21
Old Grimsby Harbour
52
58 N
46 7₉
24
4
St Helens Pool
North wethel 0₆
Crow I.
Formans I. (4) (9)
Merchants Pt. Long Pt.
2₇
Tresco
Old Grimsby
2
BlockHouse Pt 0₈
(4)
Great Cheese Rk.

E Gap Rk-Star Castle in line 182°
7₉
E Gap Rk.
0₃

5₅
Black Rk
Pernagie
12₈
(10)
16₅
37
Pednbrose (13)
Tean
Old Man 0₈
Crumple 0₃
Hedge Rk (15)
0₃
Wk
0₈
Moths Ledge
1·8

Lion (8)
W Withan
14₆
White I.
Porth
Plumb I. Morran
Pernagie Pt
Tunklers Pt
Goats Pt
Middle Town
St Martins
●Bn
2·3
Jacks Ledge
Lawrences Bay
Old Quay
7₃ Baker
E Withan
Chad Pt
64
Merrick
Mackerel Rks
61
St Martins Bay 49
37 58
6₁
0₉
0₈
Higher Town
·30
1·7

0 Cables 3 4 5 6
Depths in Metres
St Helen's Pool
Bn●
·4
6 20' 19'

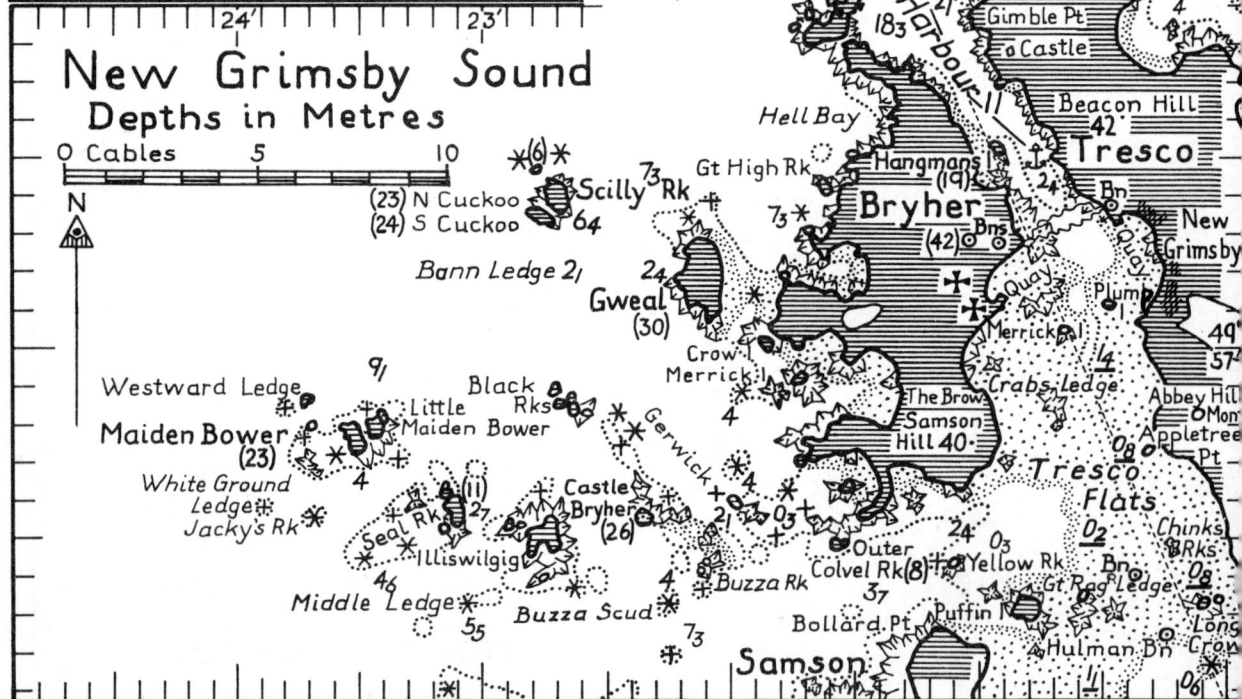

New Grimsby Sound
Depths in Metres
0 Cables 5 10
N

(6)
(23) N Cuckoo
(24) S Cuckoo
Scilly Rk 7₃
64
Bann Ledge 2₁
Gweal (30)
24
Crow I.
Merrick I.

Westward Ledge
9₁
Little Maiden Bower
Black Rks
Maiden Bower (23)
4
White Ground Ledge
Jacky's Rk
Seal Rk 27
Illiswilgig
Middle Ledge
5₅
Buzza Scud
7₃
Samson

New Grimsby Harbour
Shipman Head
157°
Mast
183
2₁
Hell Bay
Gt High Rk
Hangmans (19)
7₃
Bryher (42)
Bns
Crow I.
The Brow
Samson Hill 40
Gerwick
4
Castle Bryher (26)
2₁
0₃
4
Outer Colvel Rk (8)
Yellow Rk
0₃
Buzza Rk
37
Bollard Pt
Puffin I.

Kettle (5)
Old Grimsby Hr
4₆ 37 58
4
Kettle Pt
Gimble Pt
Castle
Beacon Hill 42
Tresco
New Grimsby
Quay
Plumb
4₉
57
Merrick I.
Quay
Crabs Ledge
Tresco Flats
Abbey Hill
Appletree Pt
0₂
Chinks Rks
Gt Rag Ledge
Puffin
Hulman Bn
1
0₆

Based on British Admiralty Charts (nos. in text) with the permission of the Controller of H.M. Stationery Office and of the Hydrographer of the Navy, and on other sources.

4

weather and with a fair wind as the tidal streams run hard across the course and the buoys are over 1M apart while the ldg marks are 8M distant.

Approach   The principal landmarks are as follows: (a) on St Mary's Is at SE of the group, TV tr 62m and radio tr 118m (lts FR) at NW corner of Is; (b) on St Martin's Is at NE of group, R and W con daymark with hor bands, 56m; (c) on Round Is at N centre of group, W circular Lt Ho, 55m; (d) on St Agnes Is at S centre of group, W stone Lt Ho, 23m, lt discontinued; (e) on Bishop Rk, at SW extremity of group, grey circular Lt Ho, 42m; (f) on Peninnis Hd (S corner of St Mary's Is), W circular iron Lt Ho, 36m.

The islands are visible in clear weather 10 to 15M. From E the daymark on St Martin's and Hanjague, a conspic pinnacle rk, 24m about 1M SE of the daymark and 2M NE of St Mary's Is, come above the horizon first; from S, the TV tr on St Mary's. Strangers are recommended to enter for the first time by St Mary's Sound or by New Grimsby Sound.

Entrance   (1) *By St Mary's Sd* at all states of the tide, rounding S of St Mary's keeping ½M off Tolman Pt to clear the Gilstone, dries 3.4m, then close past Peninnis Hd. The ldg line up this chan is 308°. When St Mary's Sd opens out clear of St Agnes Is steer up the W side of the island leaving Spanish Ledges E Card bell buoy to port, Woolpack bn to stb and Bartholomew Ledges R can buoy to port. The ldg marks for this chan are Gt Minalto in line with the N Carn of Mincarlo. When clear of W extreme of St Mary's keep the NW corner of the Is on with St Martin's daymark 040° until St Mary's Pool is open when steer in. A W arrow-shaped mark on E side of St Mary's Hr in line with a large W cross on top of the hill leads in between Bacon Ledge and the pier-head. Airport Lts E of pier-head FG clears ledges at entrance. Anch NE of a line between LB slip and pier-head in 1.8 to 2.5m. Heavy roll in W to NW winds.

(2) *By New Grimsby Sd* between Tresco and Bryher, the two principal Is at the NW of group. From N keep within 1 ca of Bryher, the western of the two Is, and steer in with the W side of Hangman Is (a conspic pinnacle rk 19m) on with Star Castle on the crest of St Mary's Is, 157°. Anch to SE of Hangman Is in 2 to 5½m. Beware of tel cable. This is the best and most sheltered anch for yachts.

(3) *By Crow Sd.* Steer for the TV tr until near approach then round the NE side of St Mary's Is at about 4 ca. Keep N extreme of St Mary's Is about 280° to pass S of the Hats (S Card buoy) and other rks. After passing the buoy round Bar Pt, leave Crow Rk bn ¼ ca on either side and then steer for St Mary's Pool. To pass NE of Bacon Ledge between it and Cow Ledge (dries 0.2m), keep B vert strip on W shelter on promenade in line with Buzza Tr, prominent on skyline, 151°, and so steer into St Mary's Pool. There is water on the bar for 1.8m draft from half flood to half ebb. On port hand, S of Innisidgen Is, is Watermill Cove; good anch in W winds in 5.5m abreast cove, exposed to E. Keeping S end of Innisidgen Is on with Abbey Hill on Tresco, small craft may feel their way nearer to the shore.

(4) *From WSW.* This requires great caution because of the many outlying rks.

(5) *From N by Round Is.* Approach Round Is from N leaving it 1¼ ca to W. Bring Star Castle on St Mary's Is on with E Gap Rk, 2m, 182° and keep it so until past

Didleys Pt, the E extreme of St Helen's Is, whence steer 201° passing between E Gap Rk and W Gap Rk, 1m, over a 0.5m bar into St Helen's Pool. Secure anch in 1½ to 5½m, exposed at HW.

The channels between (a) Tresco, Bryher and Samson; (b) Tresco and St Martin's dry at MLWS and should not be used by boats drawing 1.5m or more below half tide. There is also a variable bar off Appletree Pt in the middle of the Tresco–Bryher chan.

Anchorage (see detailed plans p3,4) (1) In St Mary's Pool NE of line between pier and LBS. (2) New Grimsby. (3) St Helen's Pool. (4) Old Grimsby in 3½ to 9m in fine weather. (5) Porth Cressa, sheltered in winds from NW through N to E.✱ (6) Watermill Bay, sheltered in winds from S through W to NW. If when anchored in St Mary's Pool it comes on to blow from W, at HW vessels can run to shelter over Crow bar behind St Mary's Is or over Tresco Flats (5m MHWS, 3.4m MHWN) into New Grimsby. Going N into New Grimsby leave Nut Rk to port, round Hulman bn leaving it ¼ ca to stb until Merrick Is is in line with Hangman Is, then proceed on this transit keeping Little Rag Ledge bn to port, Chink Rks to stb, Gt Crabs Ledge to port, Plump Rks to stb, Merrick Is to port and Plump Is to stb, direction about 340°. The passage across these flats should not be attempted until 2h after LW for draft of 1.3m, and preferably not before half flood for 1.8m. The chan is narrow.

St Mary's Hr (Hughtown) is owned by the Duchy of Cornwall. Pilot available. HM office (tel Scillonia 22768) is open weekdays and Sunday mornings in season. Anch free outside line Newman Is–Newford Is, small charge inside. Dinghies use steps at junction of Old and New Quays. Showers and water (small charge) at quay between 0830 and 1130, Mon–Fri. Provisions, PO, banks, shipwright, engineer, Customs (tel 22571), CG (tel 22651), hospital. EC Wed.

MOUSEHOLE   Chart BA 2345   (Plan p7)
A small pier hr S of Newlyn; dries, bottom sand and rk with 4m MHWS, 2.6m MHWN. The S approach is preferable. Sheltered from SE by St Clement's Is. In heavy gales from S the entrance is dangerous and should not be attempted. The hr entrance is closed with baulks of timber from the end of Oct to the end of Mar (approx).

NEWLYN   Chart BA 2345   (Plan p7)
HW +6.00.   MHWS 5.6; MLWS 0.8; MTL 3.2; MHWN 4.4; MLWN 2.0.
From last quarter flood to first quarter ebb the tide flows NE in the N part of Mount's Bay.

The hr is available at all states of the tide; 2.1m depth between pier-heads. No dock. Slip, power operated, max draft 3.2m, available approx 1hr before HW; priority to fishing vessels. Hr only suitable for short visits; if more than overnight stay envisaged use Penzance.

Approach When abreast St Clement's Is approach the Lt Ho, Fl 5s, at the end

Newlyn

Tolcarne

Wherry Rks

‡8(5)Bn⊙ Gear Rk (1·8)
B ‑O3
3₁

Lariggan Rks

2₁

2₁

0₆

+ Dog Rk

4

4₆

Depths in Metres
1/3
0 Cables   2   3   4

FS ☆

North

Gwavas
0₉ ⚓ Lake

24

6₄

9₄

3′1′

Newlyn

2₁Ldg FR ☆

Pier 1₅   Custom Ho. 3

FG 4m 2M

2   0₉

2₂

4₉

Fl 5s 10m 9M

FR

Siren 60
South Pier

50°
6′

2F66·5m (vert)

50°
5′

Old Quay

+

4₃

9₄   4₉

Sheerlegs

St Clements
Isle

(0₉)

1₂   4₉   ‑3 2₇

Obelisk
+(0₆)

3·4

S Pier Lt Ho 305°

6₁   2₄

Mousehole

6₁

2₁

Arc. of Visibility

85

33′

Carn Gwavas
Quarry

Carn
Base ·8

9₁

5° 32′

5° 32′

Heliport   Longrock

2₁

2₇

Penzance

2₇

1₂

Long Rk (4₉)

0₉
Red

1₂

2₁
Cressars

2₂

Albert Pier

1₂

2₇

Red

Ryeman
B.Bn(6) 2₁

Western
Cressar

2₃

Dome
(conspic)

2₁

2FG (vert)

3

1·8

24

2FR (vert)

BW Bn(5)

4

4₉   3

7

Swingbridge

18

Oc.(2)WR.15s
11m·9/8M

2₇

50°
7′

Dry Dock

FwG

FS

2₁   7

St Mary's Ch
(conspic)

FwR

H M

South Pier

3₇

5₈

White

Mont

3₇

7

Depths in Metres

Swimming Pool

0 Cables   2   3   4   5

Chimney Rks

2₁

Battery Rks

5₅

7₃

Penzance

herry

1₅

Red

0₃

*

6₄

2₄   Wherry Rks   3

(5)Bn⊛ Gear Rk
B 32   (1·8)

32′   5° 31′   30′

d on British Admiralty Charts (nos. in text) with the permission of the Controller of H.M. Stationery Office and of
Hydrographer of the Navy, and on other sources.

7

of S arm of hr on 305° which will clear Low Lee and Carn Base, two isolated rks off Penlee Pt. Low Lee marked by E Card buoy.

Entrance   Leave the Lt Ho to port, keep close to the N pier and round up to N alongside it or vessels berthed there. The N pier is marked by a FG lt visible to seaward.

Berthing   Lie alongside S half of N pier in 1 to 2m. No room to lie afloat at anch. Two-thirds of hr dries out. Heavy swell in SE winds. Good anch in offshore winds outside hr in Gwavas Lake; keep clear of entrance.

The hr is usually full of fishermen. All facilities including shipwrights and engineers. Bus to Penzance and thence to Land's End and St Ives. Steamer from Penzance to Scilly Is. Hard alongside N end of N pier. EC Wed.

PENZANCE   Chart BA 2345   (Plan p7)
HW +6.00.   MHWS 5.6; MLWS 0.8; MTL 3.2; MHWN 4.4; MLWN 2.0.
From last quarter flood to first quarter ebb the tide flows NE in the N part of Mount's Bay.

The tidal hr dries out. The wet dock is open HW −2 to HW but the gates may occasionally be left open for a tide. There is a ledge round the dock with 1.4m at MLWS except against the quay under the warehouse (immediately to stb on entering) where there is 2.4m. This ledge is about 1m wide and any big ships in dock are kept clear by large floating wooden fenders.

Signals   At night 2 R lts (vert) are shown when the dock gates are open; a R over G indicates that the hr is closed. By day 2 B balls (vert) are shown when the gates are open and a ship is expected. Yachts should wait outside until signalled to proceed by the dockmaster on the quay.

Approach   From the W clear Low Lee and Carn Base, two isolated rks off Penlee Pt, the Gear Rk (bn), and the Battery Rks which extend off the shore to the SW of the S pier. From the Lizard in wind or swell approach on a NNW bearing to avoid the Boa and Iron Gates. At night keep in the W sector of the lt Oc WR (2) 15s on S pier-head. The lts are difficult to distinguish against the shore lts until close in.

Berthing   Anch in offshore winds 2 ca or more off the Lt Ho pier, clear of the fairway, preferably not E of the Lt Ho because of swell, or wait in tidal hr until the gates open into basin, then lie alongside the wall; substantial fenders needed. The Albert N Pier is often used by the Scilly steamship, particularly in bad weather and at weekends. Her normal berth is alongside the Lt Ho pier but this is only occupied from 1900 to 0930 hrs the following morning and additionally on Sat 1230 to 1400 hrs in summer. Hence the Lt Ho pier is usually available while awaiting the opening of the dock gates between 1000 and 1830 hrs. There is 1.8m alongside between the Lt Ho and the ladder halfway along the pier. The S wall is swept by seas in S and SE gales.

All facilities. Rly, buses to Land's End, St Ives. Steamer and helicopter services to Scilly Is. EC Wed (suspended in summer).

Passage notes: Penzance to Falmouth

Chart BA 777

Mount's Bay: The tidal stream is weak (less than 1kn). In the middle of the bay it is rotary clockwise, E −6.00; W +0.30.
Lizard. DS: W −3.30; E +2.00.
Lizard to Falmouth. DS: SW −3.00 to +2.00; NE +3.00 to −4.00.

Bound to Falmouth from Mount's Bay it is desirable to reach the Lizard at the turn of the tide to the E because the ebb stream out of Falmouth makes progress slow. Avoid the Boa, an 11m shoal 3¼M W of the Lizard Lt Ho, in strong SW winds because of breaking seas. Off the Lizard dangers extend ½M to seaward, and a race extends to the S and SE for 3M. The violence of the seas varies with the tide and wind but it is particularly bad in strong westerlies against a down-Channel tide. In bad weather keep at least 3 to 4M offshore. Otherwise, to clear Lizard dangers keep Godolphin Hill open of Rill Hd, 337°, until Lowland Pt opens E of Black Hd, 036°.

Black Head should be cleared by ½M and the Manacles buoy given a wide berth to seaward. In E winds a confused sea builds up between Black Hd and the Manacles and with the flood tide a race may develop which at springs can reach dangerous proportions. In such conditions if heading for Falmouth it is best to make for the lt buoy Fl Y 10s in posn 50°00′N, 05°00′W and not to steer for Falmouth until due S of St Anthony Lt.

From the Manacles to Helford R and Falmouth the passage is straightforward, but there are unlit buoys low in the water off Porthallow which create a special hazard in poor visibility.

Anchorages *Loe Pool.* Good anch ¾M SSW of Pool. There is no navigable water between the sea and the Pool.
Mullion Good anch in E wind NW of the island.
Perran Vose Between the Lizard and Black Hd there are three anch, Housel Bay, Perran Vose and Cadgwith. It is imperative to get out to sea immediately if wind should come onshore.
Porthoustock Anch in 3.7m. Approach by S side of bay: N shore is foul.

PORTHLEVEN
Chart BA 777
HW +6.05. MHWS 5.5; MLWS 0.8; MTL 3.1; MHWN 4.3; MLWN 2.0.
A tidal hr situated 8M N of the Lizard and 1M N of Loe Pool with which it should not be confused. For 1¾M to the N of Porthleven the cliffs rise 46m. To the S the coast is low and sandy to Loe Pool where cliffs rise again from 15 to 61m. The entrance is tricky for a stranger.
Entrance The hr is entered to N of a pier extending 125m to the W and between it and the Deazle Rks which dry 0.8m at MLWS leaving a chan 70m wide exposed to the W. The entrance to the inner hr is 200m within the pier-head and dries at half-tide. There is 3.6m over the sill at MHWS and 2.7m at MHWN. The inner hr is often closed by baulks across the entrance to protect moored vessels in bad

weather. When the baulks are in position a R ball is displayed at the yardarm on the FS by the outer pier by day and at night the F G lt normally shown on the S side of the hr entrance is extinguished.

Berthing   At quayside. All facilities and stores; engine and hull repairs.

HELFORD RIVER   Chart BA 147   (Plan p11)
HW −6.10. MHWS 5.3; MLWS 0.6; MTL 3.0; MHWN 4.2; MLWN 1.9.

Bar   1M inside the river a bar stretches halfway across the chan from Passage Pt leaving 2.7m in the narrow chan along the S side. The hr is available at all times, 3½–11m inside bar. Vessels awaiting the tide to cross the bar can anch off Durgan, a good berth according to wind. Tidal stream turns 1hr after HW and LW.

Approach   To clear the Gedges, keep Pennance Pt well open of Rosemullion Pt until Bosahan Pt on S side of entrance is well open of Mawnan Shear on N side, then steer in. An E Card buoy lies about 1 ca SE of August Rk.

Entrance   Keep Helford Pt open of Bosham Pt to clear a reef lying off the E end of the latter. NW of the Bosahan Narrows a G con buoy is moored on the edge of the N bank.

Berthing   (1) Off Durgan or Grebe Rk, 2½–3½m, disturbed in S to E winds. (2) Off Helford, 5½–11m, strong tide. Edge of mud across Penarvon Cove is very steep-to. The Helford Boat Yard on E shore of Penarvon Cove has a pontoon and can advise on visitors' moorings. (3) Near the entrance to Navas Creek along the N shore, to S of oyster buoys and well out of the tide, 1¾m or more. Uncomfortable if far out in the stream in fresh E or W winds. Quiet anch inside Navas Creek 2m in a pool known as Abraham's Bosom, but there is a 0.9m bar at the entrance which lies on W side and oyster beds to W of moorings in creek. Landing at Helford River Oyster Fisheries' quay. Charge made.

   The river may be explored up to Gweek, Mawnan and Polwheverill. Oyster beds are laid between Bar Beach and Mawgan Creek. At LW land at extreme end of Helford Pt. Provisions, PO, tel, fuel at garage 1M up steep hill or at Port Navas, EC Wed. Water at Durgan, Helford and Port Navas Boatyards. No dues. Beach for laying ashore along N shore E of entrance to Navas Creek. Ferry from Helford Pt to Helford Passage in summer, thence bus to Falmouth.

GILLAN CREEK
To S of Helford River S of Dennis Hd (see plan). Midway between the points of entrance there is a rk which uncovers at MLWS and is marked by a spar buoy with 2 B balls (vert).

Approach   While outside the line of Dennis Hd bring the village of Flushing on the S shore within the creek open S of the N arm of the entrance, when a small Is E of Flushing will be seen near the S shore. Bring this Is to bear 227° and steer in for its N edge, leaving the rk already mentioned to port.

   The passage S of the rk lies in line with S edge of the Is, bearing 243°.

Anchorage   There is a pool carrying 1½ to 2m inside the entrance. No shelter in E winds unless lying on the mud 1M up the creek. A depth of 1½ to 3m will be

Helford River

Depths in Metres

Helford River

N

Rosemullion Head
Prisk Cove
August Rk or The Gedges (PA) (Seasonal)
Shag Rk
Mawnan Rk
Mawnan
Tr
Mawnan Shear
Toll Pt
Porth Saxon
Durgan
Grebe Rk
Polgwidden Cove
Bosahan Pt open of Mawnan Shear 259
The Voose
Bosahan Pt
Bosahan Cove
Badgagarrack Cove
Ponsence Cove
The Gew
Dennis Head
Gillan Hn
St Anthony
Gillan Creek
Gillan Cove
Flushing Cove
Menaver Cove
Parbean Cove
Point
Nare Head
Nare Point
Nare Cove
Fletching's Cove
Porthallow Cove
Porthkerris Pt

Manaccan

Helford
Helford Passage
YCF5
CGF5
The Bar
The Pool
Helford Slip
Bm Landing
Quay
SC

Perran Cove
Pill Cove
Abraham's Bosom
Porth Navas
Quay
Port Navas Creek
Polwheveral Creek
Lower Calamansack
Groyne Pt
Scott's Quay
Range
Butts
Frenchman's Creek
Withan
Tremayne Quay
Boat Ho
Merthen Quay

Continuation

Cables

Merthen Quay
Vallum
Tremayne Creek
Bonallak Barton
Bishops Quay
Boat Ho
Mawgan Creek
Constantine Quay
Polpenwith Creek
Polwheveral Creek
Lower Quay
Gweek
Mawgan

...n British Admiralty Charts (nos. in text) with the permission of the Controller of H.M. Stationery Office and of ...rographer of the Navy, and on other sources.

found on either side of and just beyond the mid-chan rk. The water rapidly shoals to less than 1m.

FALMOUTH

Charts BA 32, 1267   (Plan p14)

HW −6.05.   DS: W −3.00; E +2.00.
MHWS 5.3; MLWS 0.6; MTL 3.0; MHWN 4.2; MLWN 1.9.

Approach   From the E it should be remembered that the St Anthony Lt, Oc WR 15s 14M, Nauto 30s, R sector over Manacles, first appears to NW.

Entrance   The entrance is divided into two chans by Black Rk marked by conspic B bn and an E Card buoy, Q (3) 10s. When this rk is covered there is 2.7m over the banks inside the hr as far as Trelissick. In W-ly winds the direction of wind in the hr is somewhat more N-ly.

When the N arm Q Lt comes on with the R Fl Lt on the E breakwater, 293°, the fairway to Falmouth is open.

Berthing   (1) Anch either side of the fairway to Penryn, keeping fairway clear, i.e. just outside the moorings of RCYC between the tug moorings and yacht moorings or in the Trefusis–Kiln Quay area. (2) In Falmouth Yacht Marina, at North Parade on the NW edge of Falmouth towards Penryn. There is an underwater obstruction (a buried pipeline, dr 1m) across the middle of the basin, so take an outside berth and make enquiries. (3) Moorings are sometimes available, by permission, from the RCYC and from yacht yards. (4) Several Hr Authority buoys for visitors (yellow pick-up buoys) between New Quay, Flushing and Prince of Wales Pier. These may be booked beforehand.

Landing places   Customs House Quay, Fish Quay, Prince of Wales Pier, Green Bank Pier on Falmouth side, Old and New Quay on Flushing side.

All facilities. Fuel and water at Customs House Quay (North Quay) and Falmouth Boat Construction Co. pontoon. Ferry to Flushing and St Mawes, steamer services to Malpas and Truro in summer. Hard at Flushing Quay. Several good hards both sides of hr. EC Wed.

St Just Creek   Good anch in 3m inside Mesack Pt under N shore (sound in).

St Mawes   Leave St Mawes S Card buoy marking Lugo Rk well to port when entering and anch in 2m or more between the two beaches beyond the pier. To pass between Lugo Rk and Castle Pt, bring right-hand end of trees on Amsterdam Pt in line with conspic gap in hedge on skyline behind. At half-tide the depth is not less than 1.8m anywhere between the buoy and Castle Pt, or on the ldg line at MLWN. In SW wind, good shelter is available round Amsterdam Pt in midstream, 5m. Avoid Black Rk close inshore abreast the N end of the wood on the E side. Good hard on the beach. Landing at slipway on St Mawes SC quay at Polvarth except at extreme LWS. There is about 1.2m up to Porthcuel, but chan is tortuous and unmarked. Water from tap adjoining Polvarth Boatyard and at Porthcuel.

RIVER TRURO (Plan p14)

HW (Truro) −5.55. MHWS 5.3; MHWN 4.2

From Cross Road leave St Just R can buoy to port or use E swatch through the bank off Penarrow Pt keeping Vilt buoy on with E extremity of Pendennis Castle astern. From Mesack Pt, keep the MOT buoys to stb until past Pill Creek. When Penarrow Pt comes on with Pendennis Pt steer 024°, keeping Trelissick Ho open of Trelissick Pt to clear Carick Carlys Rk to E. This rk lies just NW of the bend in the main chan and is marked by small B and W poles at its N and S ends. After leaving the buoy off Turnaware Pt to stb, continue in mid-river. There is plenty of water up to Malpas except at Maggoty Bank, marked by a buoy which must be left to stb. There are good anchs above King Harry Ferry off the entrance to Cowlands Creek on the N side. A little further up there is a good anch off the mouth of the River Fal (Ruan Creek) which joins River Truro near Tregothnan.

At Malpas, which is the limit of LW navigation, there is a fair anch in 2–4m. Drawing not more than 2.5m one can reach Truro on the tide following buoyed chan. There is no recommended anch at Truro but a yacht can berth alongside by previous arrangement with HM.

Mylor Creek   Pass through W swatchway through the bank off Penarrow Pt and when Mesack Pt bears E stand in over the bank or from N Bank buoy. Head for boats on outer moorings of Mylor Pool and anch in 2m, just outside the boats. Above the quay the creek dries. Provisions at Mylor Bridge, 1M by dinghy.

Restronguet Creek   Leave the main Truro chan, pass S of Carick Carlys Rk (2 pole bns) in ½m to the entrance. Anch in 3m just within the entrance points. Landing at Ferry Ho and Pt Deveron may be reached by dinghy on the tide, 1½M.

Loe Beach   Good, clean, quiet anch in 2m close inshore off Loe Vean. Summer moorings are laid all the way between Restronguet and Loe Beach. Anch anywhere outside these. Riding lts advisable.

PASSAGE NOTES: FALMOUTH TO PLYMOUTH

Chart BA 1267

Leaving Falmouth bound E, keep at least 1M offshore to clear the Bizzies, a shoal patch off Greeb Pt. The Whelps off Nare Hd should likewise be given a good clearance.

Dodman Pt marked by a conspic stone cross should not be approached closer than 2M in bad weather because of heavy overfalls. If navigating inshore towards Fowey give a wide berth to the Gwineas and Yaw Rks ¾M S of Chapel Pt, and Cannis Rk 4 ca SE of Gribben Hd. E of Fowey bound for Plymouth care should be taken to clear Udder Rk 3M E of Fowey and the Rennies Rks off Looe Is. Rame Hd, marking the W boundary of Plymouth Sound when viewed from seaward, appears conical, and has a small chapel on its summit. There are no offlying dangers.

If bound up-Channel offshore the Eddystone Lt Ho should be given a

Falmouth
Depths in Metres

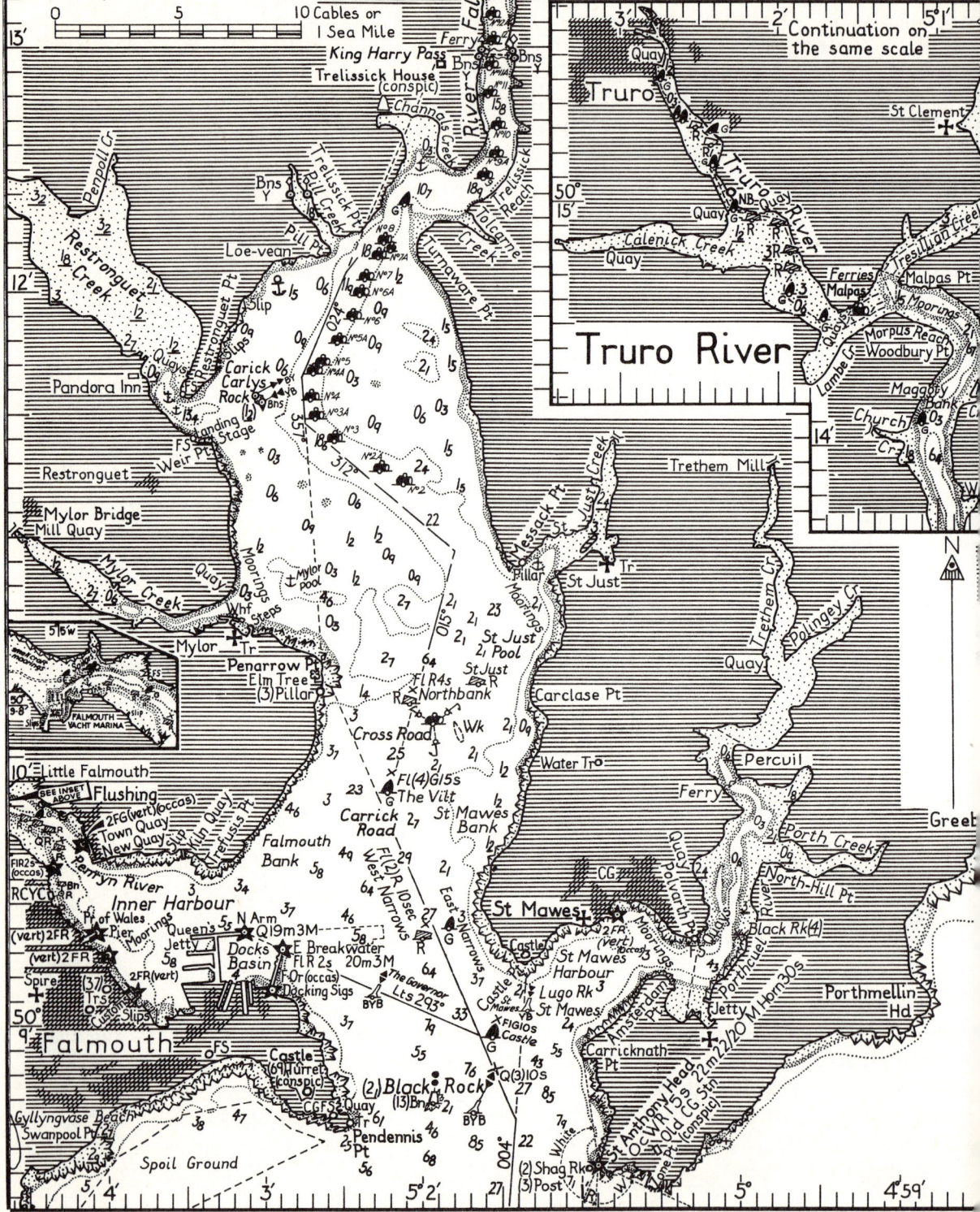

0 ... 5 ... 10 Cables or 1 Sea Mile

13'

Cowlands Cr.
Lamouth Cr.
Wht.
River Truro
River Fal
Ruan Creek
Tolvern Reach
Mills

King Harry Pass
Ferry
Bns
Trelissick House (conspic.)
Channals Creek
River Fal
Bns Y
Trelissick Reach

Continuation on the same scale

Truro
St Clement
Quay
Truro River
Calenick Creek
Quay
Quay
NB Quay
50° 15'
Ferries
Malpas Pt.
Malpas
Moorings
Morpus Reach
Woodbury Pt.
Lambe Cr.
Maggoty Bank
Church
Cr.

Penpoll Cr.
Restronguet Creek
Restronguet Pt.
Loe-vean
Pill Creek
Pill Pt.
Lamorran Creek
Turnaware Pt.
Pandora Inn
Carrick Carlys Rock
Bns Y
Quays
Restronguet
Weir Pt.
Landing Stage
FS

Mylor Bridge
Mill Quay
Mylor Creek
Quay
Mylor Pool
Moorings
Whf
Steps
Mylor
Tr
Penarrow Pt.
Elm Tree
Pillar

St Mick Creek
St Just Creek
Trethem Mill
Pillar
St Just
Tr
St Just Pool
St Just
Carclase Pt.
Messack Pt.
Moorings

Little Falmouth
Flushing
Town Quay
New Quay
Trefusis Pt.
Kiln Quay
Penryn River
Inner Harbour
RCYC
Pr of Wales Pier
Queen's Jetty
N Arm
Docks Basin
E Breakwater
FLR 2s 20m 3M
Docking Sigs
The Governor
Lts 293°
BYB

FALMOUTH YACHT MARINA

Cross Road
Northbank
Fl R 4s
Wk
The Vilt
Fl(4)Gl5s
Carrick Road
St Mawes Bank
Falmouth Bank
Fl(2) R.10sec
West Narrows
East Narrows
Water Tr
Percuil
Ferry
Porth Creek
North-Hill Pt.
Trethem Cr.
Polingey Cr.
Quay
Percuil River
Porth
Greeb

Falmouth
Castle (conspic)
Turret
Gyllyngvase Beach
Swanpool Pt.
Spoil Ground
Pendennis Pt.
Black Rock
(13)Bns
BYB
Q(3)10s
CG FS
Quay

St Mawes
CG
Castle
St Mawes Harbour
Lugo Rk
St Mawes Castle
Figgis
Castle
Carricknath Pt.
Amsterdam Pt.
Jetty
Porthcuel River
Castle
Black Rk(4)
Porthmellin Hd.
Anthony Head
OCWR Old CG Stn (conspic)
M.Horn 30s
Shag Rk
Post
White

N

Based on British Admiralty Charts (nos. in text) with the permission of the Controller of H.M. Stationery Office, the Hydrographer of the Navy, and on other sources.

reasonably wide berth especially in bad weather. Also keep clear of Hurd Deep, some 3¾M to the NW, where overfalls can be dangerous.

Tidal streams are weak (less than 1kn) from Falmouth to Plymouth; rectilinear in the W, rotary clockwise in the E. DS 5M E of St Anthony Pt: NE +2.45; SW −3.30. DS Plymouth: E +4.00; W −2.00. In fine settled weather when the wind is light along the shore it may often be possible to carry a breeze round by the Dodman and Fowey close inshore, while an attempt at a direct course to Plymouth may end in being becalmed.

Bound from Fowey or Plymouth to Falmouth there is a considerable set into the bight N of Falmouth, requiring care in foggy weather. Remember St Anthony Lt first appears when bearing NW.

Anchorages *Gorran:* good anch in W winds, 6m. *Portmellin:* good anch in W winds, 5m. *St Austell Bay:* in S corner, 5m. In SW winds anch off *Rope Hawne*, good holding. *Polkerris:* good anch in E winds, 5m. *Whitesand Bay:* if befogged between the Dodman and Rame Hd, Whitesand Bay offers a long stretch of clear coast with shelving shore in which to close the land in safety, affording good anch in calm weather and offshore winds.

MEVAGISSEY

Chart BA 147   (Plan p16)

HW −5.45. DS: E +2.00; W −3.00
MHWS 5.4; MLWS 0.7; MTL 3.1; MHWN 4.3; MLWN 2.0
The hr is available at all states of the tide. There is 2.7m in the ent and alongside the S pier: further W the outer hr is shoal, and the W part dries. The inner hr dries 1.2m or more, but affords complete shelter to boats taking the ground and has 3.0m at MHWN. There are ledges of rk inside both the N and S walls of the outer hr. Berth as directed. The hr is full of fishing boats in the season. EC Thurs.

Anchorage   Good anch in offshore winds off Porthmellin ½M S of the hr.

FOWEY

Chart BA 31   (Plan p17)

HW −5.45. MHWS 5.4; MLWS 0.6; MTL 3.1; MHWN 4.3; MLWN 2.0
The hr is available at all states of the tide and has 5.5m on the outer bar, 1.8–9m inside. The whole of the main fairway up to Wiseman's Pt is dredged to 6m. There is a W house below the Polruan watch house and a conspic windmill E of Polruan, about 3 ca from the quay.

Approach   *From E:* Approach with RWHS Tr on Gribbin Hd bearing more than 273° to clear the Udder Rk, 3M to E of Fowey, ½M offshore, dries 0.6m, S Card bell buoy. To pass between the Udder and the mainland, keep Looe Is shut in by Nealand Pt. *From SW:* to clear the Cannis Rk, a half-tide rk ¼M SE from Gribbin Hd and marked by a S Card lt buoy, keep Dodman Pt open to seaward of Gwineas until the tr of Fowey Parish ch, square with four pinnacles, comes open of St Catherine Pt. Alternatively, to pass between Cannis Rk and the mainland (1.2m MLWS), keep the old castle on Polruan Pt in line with conspic memorial on Penleath Pt.

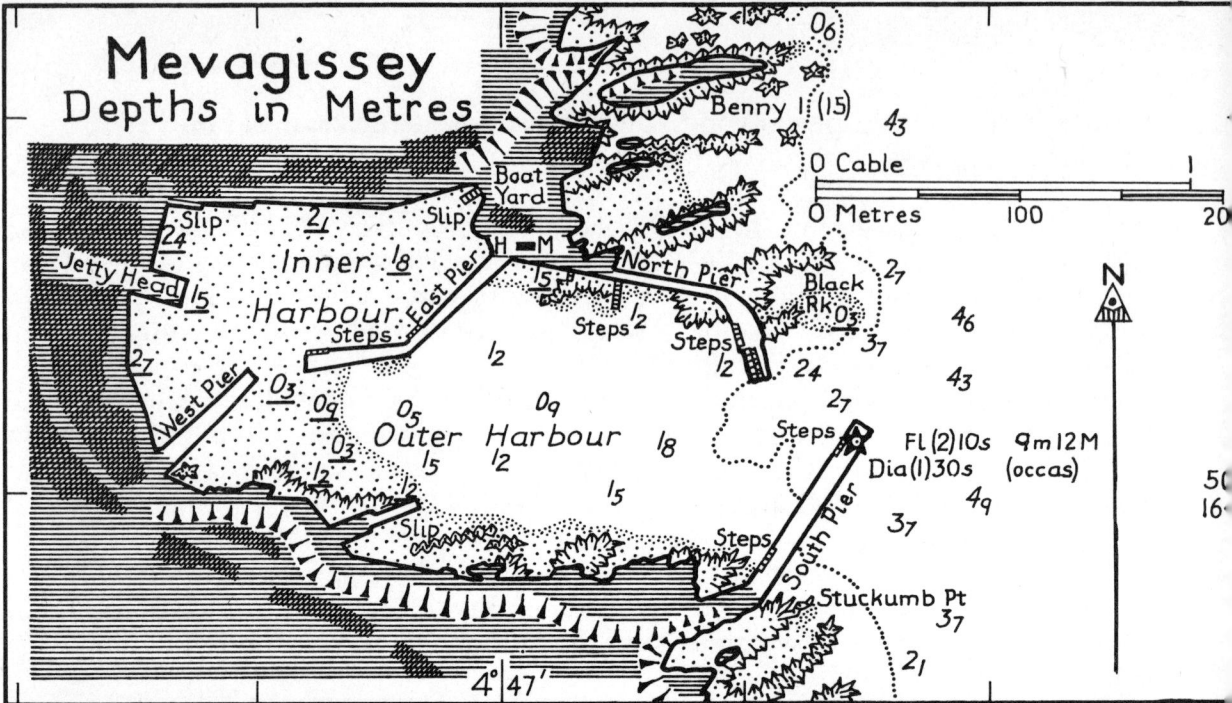

Mevagissey
Depths in Metres

Benny I (15)

0 Cable

0 Metres   100   20

Boat Yard

Slip

H = M

North Pier

Black Rk

Inner Harbour

Slip

Jetty Head

East Pier

Steps

Steps

Steps

West Pier

Outer Harbour

Steps

Fl (2) 10s   9m 12M

Dia (1) 30s   (occas)

Slip

Steps

South Pier

Steps

Stuckumb Pt

4° 47'

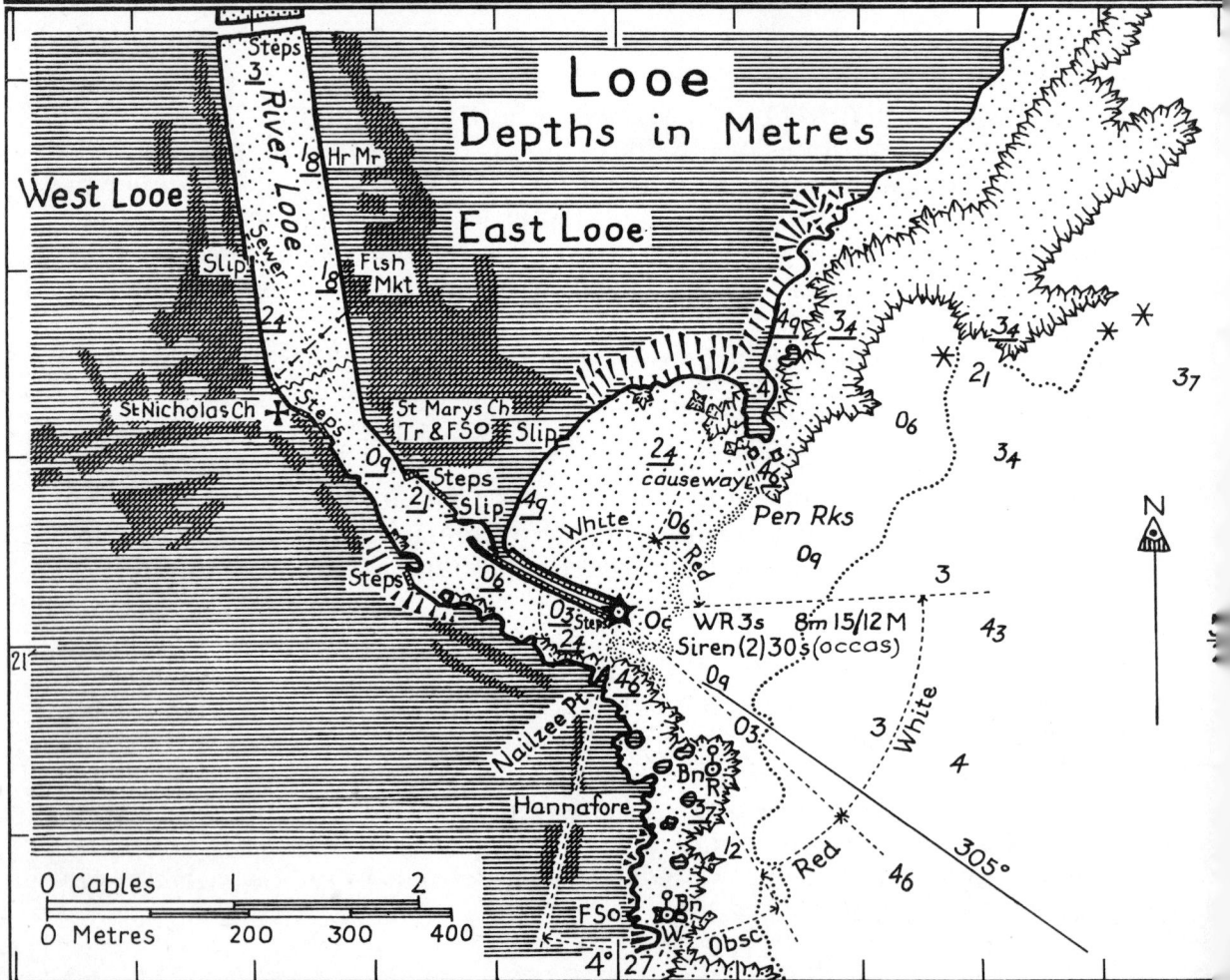

Looe
Depths in Metres

Steps

River Looe

Hr Mr

West Looe

East Looe

Sewer

Slip

Fish Mkt

St Nicholas Ch

St Marys Ch
Tr & FSO

Slip

Steps

Steps

Slip

White

Red

Pen Rks

causeway

WR 3s   8m 15/12M

Siren (2) 30s (occas)

Nailzee Pt

White

Hannafore

Bn R

Red

305°

FSo

Bn W

Obsc

0 Cables   1   2

0 Metres   200   300   400

4° 27'

Lostwithiel
18
HWOS

0 Cables 5 10

Manor Ho
The Channel position above
Golant is liable to vary

Mansion
(ruins)

River Fowey
0°
3'
HWOS 18
St Winnows Ch
Quay
Boat Ho
River Lerryn
Mendy
Pill
HWOS 21
Lerryn
Manely
Pill
37'

Woodgate
Pill
Quay

Boat Hou
HWOS 2N
Cliff
Pill

St Sampson
Golant
Rlwy

2'

40'
39' Quay
Hay Pt

Priory
Hay Pt
St
Cyric's Cr
Penpoll
Quay

Penpoll
Cr
Old Quay
Continuation of R Fowey

50°
4' 37'

21'
Wiseman Pt

Wiseman's Ft Reach
31

No 8
Mixtow
Quays
Wiseman Pt
Slip
Mixtow

Mixtow Pill
Mixtow Reach
63
China Clay Qy
Polmort Pt
64
62

Upper Carn Pt
No 4
Dn
Dn
No 3
Lew Roads
64
Slip &
Quay
76

Lower Carn Pt
Dinghy Park
Slip
Bodinnick
Car Ferry
65

Pottery Corner

Boat Ho
61

Fowey
(conspic)
Custom Ho
Tr
HM Quay
Tr & FS
Town
Quay
6
FS
RFYC
Mont (conspic)
Penleath Pt
Slip
Pont Pill
2
0.6

50°
20'

Fowey
(Lifeboat)
(Pilots)
Fowey
Hall

2 FR (vert)
Swinging
Ground
Swing
Buoy 2s
(RF VC Buoys)
Oq

Whitehouse Pt
Hotel (conspic)
Old Castle
63
Iso WRG 3s
11m 11/8M
7
052°
3
Ferry
Polruan Pool
Polruan Pt
Town Quay
Polruan
River Fowey
Brawn Pt
Patent
Slipway
Hr
Commissioners
Wharf
Dock
Tom's
Boat Yard
Sea Wall

Neptune Pt
Bn
Mundy
Rks (8)
W
76

Readymoney Cove
St Catherine's Pt
Tomb
FS
Coat
45
Lamp Rk
FS
OCGFS
Tr (ruins)
Castle
(ruins)

(conspic) Fowey Lighthouse
Fl WR 5s 28m 11/9M
6
24
3
Punch Cross Rks
46
64
(59)
Lo
Pilots Lookout
CG Lookout
White House (conspic)
O (conspic) Tr (ruins)

Coombe Haven
7
Venture
Cove
88
White
Washing Rks
76
46
49
3
CG Lookout
Wellake
37
Light obscured northward of this line
3
73 Rk
Blackbottle

Wk
0.3
3.4
Red
46
85
White
7
Green
94

Polruan Castle - Penleath
Mont in line 050°
85
Fowey Ch Tr - Whitehouse Pt
in line 028°
Wk
3'9'

Fowey
Depths in Metres
Maximum ebb stream in ship Channel 1¾ kn.

0 Cables 1 2 3 4 5
19'

4' 38'
37'

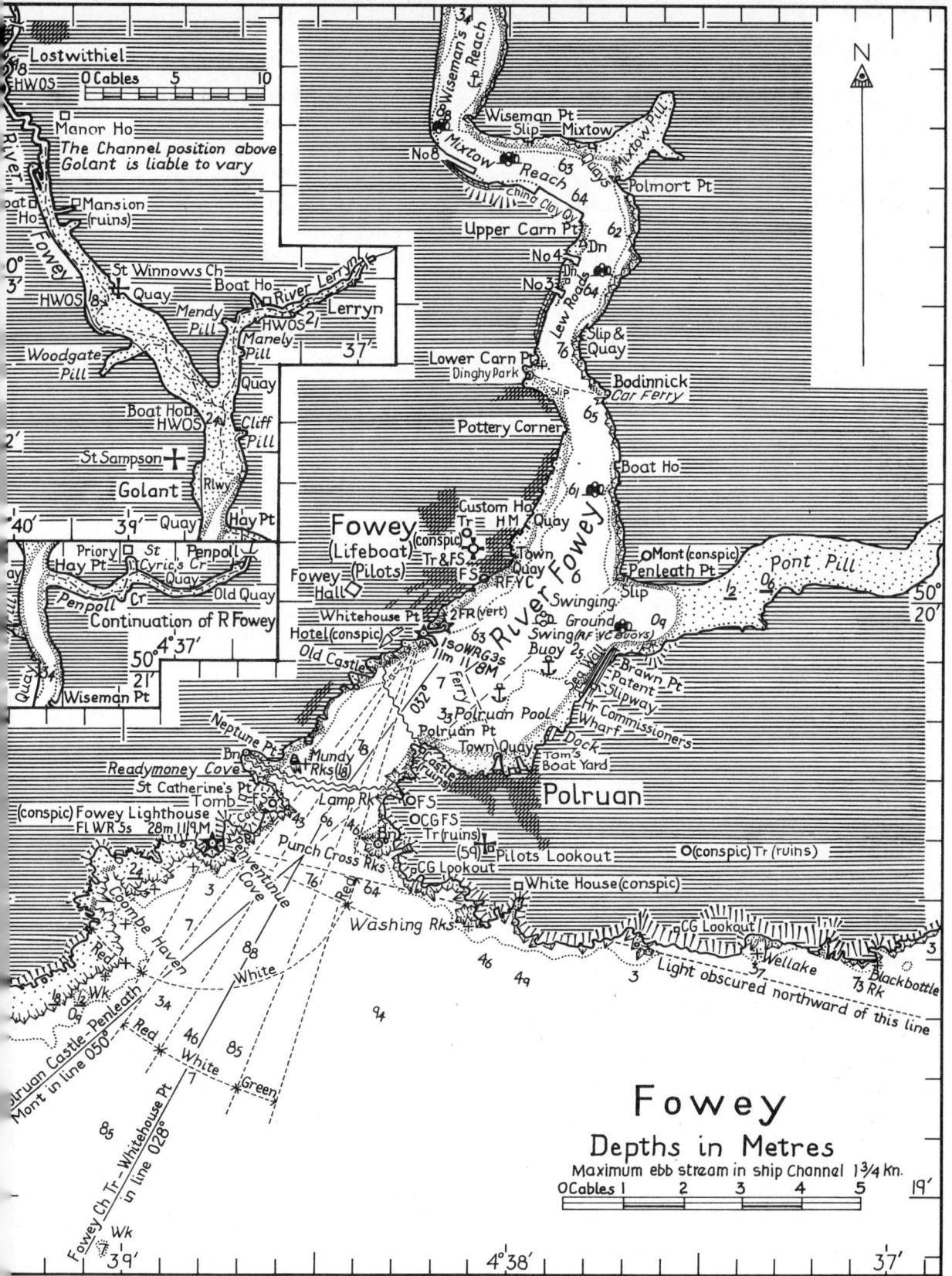

ed on British Admiralty Charts (nos. in text) with the permission of the Controller of H.M. Stationery Office and of
Hydrographer of the Navy, and on other sources.

17

At night keep in the W sector of St Catherine Lt Fl WR 5s, until the W sector of Lt Iso WRG 3s on Whitehouse Pt opens up, then stand in.

Entrance Fowey ch tr in line with Whitehouse Pt, 028°, leads in mid-chan clear of all dangers. To clear Lamp Rk on the E side of the entrance opposite Ready Money Cove, keep the houses at Bodinnick shut in by Fowey Town Quay. To keep clear E of Mundy Rk, on the W side of the entrance N of Ready Money Cove, keep the FS at the YC open of the end of the breakwater at Whitehouse Pt. Polruan Pt is steep-to.

Berthing (1) East of the fairway SW of Penleath Pt. Take one of the RFYC buoys (marked 1–6), or a mooring as directed, going ashore to pay at the Club. (2) Anch in the pool above Wiseman's Pt about 1M from entrance, complete shelter. Tripping line advisable.

Avoid anch between Penleath Pt and Wiseman's Pt, as large ships are swung in the chan. The large can mooring buoy on edge of fairway opposite Pont Pill should be given a berth of 90m when anch. The river is often crowded with shipping, and it is inadvisable to attempt to reach Wiseman's Pt without reliable power. In the upper reaches of the river there are no anchs where vessels can lie afloat even at neaps, but the river is well worth exploring by dinghy to Lostwithiel and Lerryn.

At Fowey, land at one of the numerous steps. All stores. Water at Town Quay (tap), YC and Polruan quay (hose), where there are also fuel pumps. Ferry to Polruan. EC Wed.

POLPERRO   Chart BA 1267

A small drying harbour, with room for only two or three visiting yachts. Approach from SW, as there is a reef projecting offshore to E of the ent. Yachts tie up and dry alongside the wall on the E side of the hr, just inside the lock gate which is closed in bad weather. The hr has over 1½m at half tide. Dangerous in strong onshore winds. Beware numerous sight-seeing launches, which can emerge unexpectedly from behind the pier-heads.

LOOE   Chart BA 147   (Plan p16)

HW −5.45.   DS: W −2.00; E +3.00
MHWS 5.4; MLWS 0.6; MTL 3.0; MHWN 4.2; MLWN 2.0
Hr, which dries out, has 4.0m MHWS, 3m MHWN. It dries 0.3m at pier-head. W quay dries 2.1 to 3m. E quay dries 1.2 to 1.8m.

Approach From the W, to clear the Rennies, keep the mainland showing over the top of Looe Is. When E Looe ch is well open of the W pt of the entrance steer in. At night coming from W, keep in the W sector of pier-head Lt Oc WR which opens on 313°.

Entrance If beating in from the E, remember Longstone Rks run out 1½ ca from the shore, NE of entrance. Beware of an outgoing eddy on the flood alongside E quay. There are overfalls S of the Is: passage between the Is and mainland should not be attempted except at HW and with local knowledge.

Anchorage   Inside the hr lie alongside the W quay between the two sets of steps S of small church, or elsewhere as space permits. The hr is commercial and shark boats do not permit yachts to lie alongside. Outside, bring pier-head on with St Nicholas ch, W Looe, and anch in 3m abreast the white marks on the W shore; sand and mud. Anch open to winds between SE by E and S by W. Sheltered in W winds. The ebb runs at 3kn max through the narrows. There are mooring rings alongside the cliffs on the W side. Hr is crowded when fishermen are in. All facilities, water at quayside. EC Thurs.

PLYMOUTH   Charts BA 1900, 1901, 1902, 1967   (Plan p20)
HW −5.35.   DS: E +4.00; W −2.00
MHWS 5.5; MLWS 0.8; MTL 3.2; MHWN 4.4; MLWN 2.2
Plymouth Sound may be entered W or E of the breakwater. The W entrance is lit.

Approach   *W Entrance:* from the E round the Mewstone and steer 292° with Stock Pt on with the N side of the Mewstone astern until the breakwater Lt Ho comes in line with Mount Batten Tr, or at night until within the W Low Sector Iso 4s of the lt on the W end of the breakwater, when steer to leave the Lt Ho to stb. *E Entrance:* bring the bn (B sph topmark) on the E arm of the breakwater in line with Smeaton's Tr on the Hoe, bearing 355°. Give the breakwater end 1 ca clearance.

   In strong S winds the sea breaks heavily on the Knap and Panther Shoals and on the ebb in the E entrance. The W entrance is then preferable.

   From W, having rounded Rame Hd make the Draystone R can buoy (Fl (2) R 5s), and leaving it to port steer for the breakwater Lt Ho. At night, proceed within the Low W sector Iso 4s of the breakwater Lt and leave the Lt Ho to stb. In calm weather small craft can take a direct course from seaward to W end of the breakwater.

Entrance   Having passed the breakwater Lt Ho, leave the New Grounds R can buoy (Fl R 2s) to stb and Melampus R can buoy (Fl R 4s) to port. Pass ½ ca W of Mount Batten breakwater (2 FG vert) leaving to port the Mallard Shoal, marked by a W Card buoy (Q (9) 15s) on its W side and so into the Cattewater. To pass inside to W of Drake Is over the Bridge, keep to the buoyed chan which is unlit. Remains of dolphins and concrete spikes obstruct the bottom close to the chan. It should be negotiated with especial care in bad weather as the sea breaks heavily in the vicinity.

Berthing   (1) Except in E and SE winds, at Cawsand, 3M from Plymouth, which may be reached by bus and the Cremyl Ferry, both infrequent. Anch close inshore on the S side of the bay. (2) Jenny Cliff Bay, sheltered from the NE through E to SE. (3) Barn Pool, at W end of Drake Chan. Anch in NW corner, bottom very steep-to. Good shelter from W winds. (4) N of Drake Is to E of private pier. Buoy the anch. (5) Sutton Pool. In marina, or alongside temporarily at fish quay or North Quay (somewhat obstructed by marina), or stern to B spher buoy off fish quay, crowded by fishing vessels, and anch to windward. (6) Cattewater. Anch E of RAF moorings off Turnchapel Village or contact yacht

PLYMOUTH SOUND

Depths in Metres

Based on British Admiralty Charts (nos. in text) with the permission of the Controller of H.M. Stationery Office and the Hydrographer of the Navy, and on other sources.

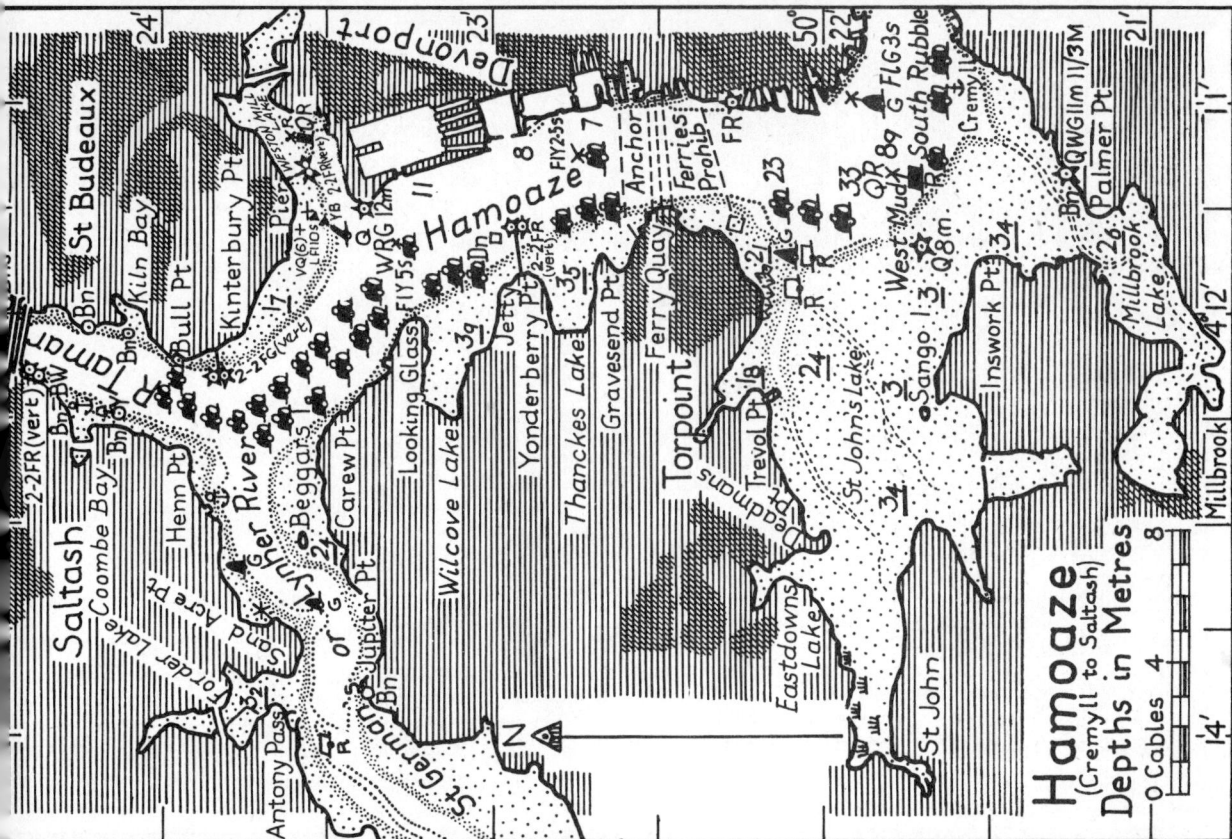

Hamoaze
(Cremyll to Saltash)
Depths in Metres

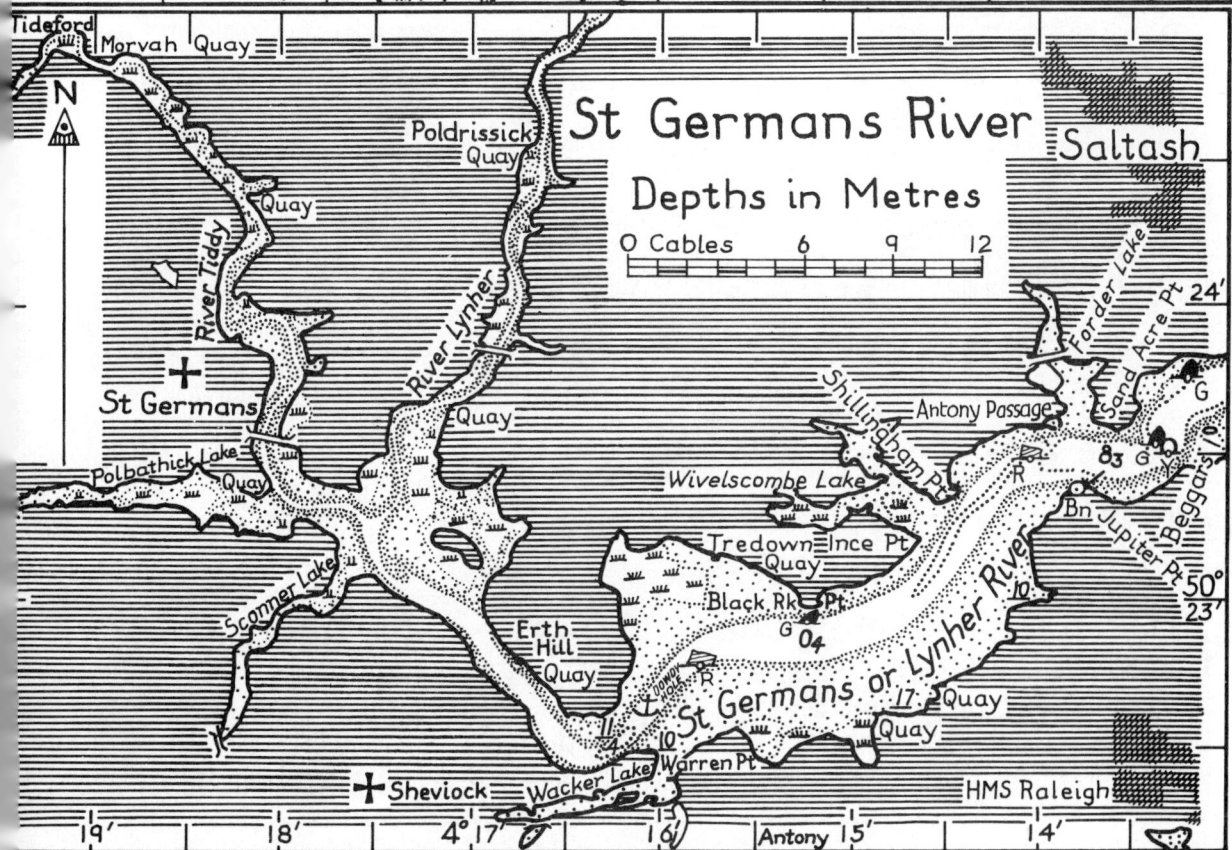

St Germans River

Saltash

Depths in Metres

0 Cables   6   9   12

d on British Admiralty Charts (nos. in text) with the permission of the Controller of H.M. Stationery Office and of
Hydrographer of the Navy, and on other sources.

Tamar River
(Cargreen to Calstock) Depths in Metres

0 Cables 5 10

To Weir Head

Calstock

High Lane Railway Br

Ferry

Bootyard–Calstock Marina

Cotehele House

Quay SLIP

Bere Alston

River Tamar

Weir Quay & Boatyard

Quay

Thorn Pt

MLW

MLW

MLWS

Cargreen

Halton Quay

Pentillie Castle Quay

N

29'

28

50° 27'

Tamar River
(Saltash to Cargreen) Depths in Metres

0 Cables 4 8

10' Weir 2 Cables

Ford

River Tavy MLW

Quay MLW

Bere Ferrers

Pennards Pt

Lime Pt Quay

Power (12m)

Warleigh Pt

Tamerton Lake

Whitleigh

Agaton Fort

Ernesettle

Honicknowle

King's Tamerton

N

Thorn Pt

Cargreen Quay

Weir Pt

Bn

Power (30m)

Neal Pt

0·5

2

0·3

0·5

SMTW

2·8

0·5

1·8

G

QG

Gt Tamar

QG

Warren Pt

Bn

Ernesettle Jetty & Pier

St Budeaux

2 FR (vert)

Fl Y 4s

Kingsmill Lake

Skinham Pt

2·1

SMTW

2·3

2·4

3·4

Saltmill Creek

Wharves

FG

6·7

Saltash

River Tamar

MLW

MLW

Go

50° 26'

25'

11'

12'

27'

27

26

Based on British Admiralty Charts (nos. in text) with the permission of the Controller of H.M. Stationery Office and the Hydrographer of the Navy, and on other sources.

yards for moorings. (7) Millbay Dock. Enter close to E pier-head, ask piermaster for permission (VHF ch 16, 14). Secure fore and aft on E side of outer hr on trots or lie alongside in inner hr. Lock opens about 2h before HW and closes at or just before HW. Apply to the Dock Office at the lock or at Royal Western YC information office a few yards E of the lock. B balls shown at E side of outer entrance when lock is open. (8) Off West Hoe in $3\frac{1}{2}$ to $7\frac{1}{2}$m in all but S winds, very uncomfortable in SE wind. Moorings usually available. Buoy anch. Bottom foul. Continual steamer wash day and night. (9) Stonehouse Pool. Anch clear of moorings and Victualling Yard entrance. Land at Admiral's Hard. Ferry wash. Moorings and services from boatyard adjoining Admiral's Hard; marina off Ocean Quay. Allow for strong tidal set. (10) Millbrook Lake, 3 ca E of Mashford's Yard at Cremyl. (11) Saltash. Coombe Bay or W side in $3\frac{1}{2}$m above the bridge. (12) Anthony Passage. Make the entrance to St Germans (Lynher) River, give S shore a good berth, leaving Beggar's Is to port. The river as far as Dandy Hole is buoyed. Anch off Anthony Village. Continue up river to Dandy Pool off Earth Hill and on the tide to St German's Quay. (13) Cargreen. On W side of Tamar, about $\frac{3}{4}$M above Tavy River entrance. From Saltash bridges keep between moored barges and from last barge make for Neal Pt buoy (G con) then to bn off Weir Pt and thence to Cargreen where there is good holding in 3–$3\frac{1}{2}$m except opposite quays. Also six visitors' buoys owned by the Spaniard Inn. PO and shop. Continue up Tamar on the tide to Calstock. Vessels able to take the mud may proceed to Morwellham and Weir Hd.

W bns 9m high with triangle Or/W daymarks (mostly lit: W on course, alt WR or WG slightly off chan, FR or FG further off chan) in Plymouth Sound and Hamoaze define the track for larger vessels.

Port regulations   See latest notices. Permanent ones include: (1) The chain ferry between Torpoint and Devonport has right of way over small craft. (2) Signals from QHM's Signal Mast just W of Millbay Dock entrance: R flag with W stripe, no ball – no movement to take place in main channels; B ball over R flag with W stripe – HM ship(s) entering; B ball under R flag with W stripe – HM ship(s) leaving. When either of these latter signals is shown, craft are obliged to keep clear of the main channels approaching the Hamoaze. A single RW vert striped flag flown from QHM Signal Stn and other prominent pts indicates wind exceeds 17kn, two flags above 27kn. QHM VHF ch 16, 14, 12: callsign 'Longroom'.

PASSAGE NOTES: PLYMOUTH TO WEYMOUTH

Charts BA 1613, 3315

Between Plymouth and Bolt Tail the coast is broken into numerous coves and rocky ledges forming Bigbury Bay. Although in fine weather the coast may be followed safely $\frac{1}{2}$M offshore, it is wiser to keep well to seaward in strong onshore winds.

Between Bolt Tail and Bolt Hd, a distance of $3\frac{3}{4}$M, rugged cliffs rise to a height of 120m. Radio masts $1\frac{1}{4}$M E of Bolt Tail assist identification. Heavy swell may be met along this section of the coast. Keep at least ½M offshore. DS: E +5.00; W −2.00.

Start point   DS (3M S): ENE +5.00; WSW −1.20, about 2kn in both directions. Nearer the Pt the streams begin ½h earlier and attain a velocity of 4kn at sp. In strong winds a race extends 1M or more SE. In strong SW winds against a weather-going tide this may be severe and extend over 2M. It is less severe when the wind is from the NE.

If bound E direct for Portland Bill there are no further dangers. There is, however, a decided set into West Bay especially in S winds. Tidal streams are very strong towards Portland Bill but midway do not exceed 1½kn.

If bound for Dartmouth or beyond either pass outside the Skerries Bank or take the inner passage between Start Pt and Skerries Bank, which is ¾M wide and provides much smoother water in most conditions. Keep at least 4 ca off the Lt Ho until it bears 320° (a min of 2 ca S of Start Rks), thence pass close to the Point. The southernmost white ho (conspic) at Beesands bearing 320° leads through.

In fog it is inadvisable to try to make the land between Bolt Tail and Start Pt where soundings are irregular and there are offshore dangers. Instead try for Start Bay or Torbay according to the following directions.

(1) *Start Bay*   DS: NE +4.10; SSW −1.20. This may be entered in a calm with no swell, under power, when position is known to within a couple of miles. Approach from SE and aim for Torcross, allowing for the tide. Pass over Skerries Bank: steep-to so sound constantly. There is 40m or more within 5 ca of it, up to 4m on its SW end, up to 6m in the middle and up to 8m on its NE end. Start Pt fog siren often inaudible here. When soundings deepen to 14m you are over the bank and in Start Bay; steer WNW and anch when soundings (reduced) fall to 8 to 9m, sand, and wait for it to clear. Good holding sheltered from all winds between SSW and N, no traffic. If shallow soundings are not met when expected, stand off to the E and either wait for it to clear in Lyme Bay, N of the steamer lane, or try for Torbay. If there is any swell keep away from the Skerries.

(2) *Torbay*   This may be found in nil visibility even if position is only known to within 10M or so. Keep well S of the land until sure of being somewhere off the W half of Lyme Bay. Then steer N made good into 36m (reduced). This puts you E of Torbay. Next steer W made good into 9m. This puts you inside Torbay. If visibility is less than about 2 ca, stand on a short way and anch in 8m to wait for it to clear. Do not go into less than 8m or you may anch on foul ground. Though some way from shore, this anch is sheltered except from winds between NE and SE. If visibility is 2 ca or more, as soon as you get 9m steer S until land is sighted. If cliffs drop into the water you are W of Brixham, deep close in. Follow the land round into the hr fairway. If the shore is shelving rocky beach, steer W at once for the breakwater.

Further E, avoid Nimble Rk least depth 0.9m ¾M NE of E Blackstone on leaving Dartmouth. DS at Berry Hd: N +5.40; S −1.00. N of Torbay keep to seaward of the Ore Stone ½M SE of Hopes Nose. Thereafter as far as

Teignmouth the coast is free of dangers. From Teignmouth to Exmouth the only danger is Dawlish Rk ½M off the town, least depth is 3.5m.

From Exmouth to Portland Bill there are two conspic features, Beer Hd 130m, the W-most chalk cliff on the South Coast, and 3M before Bridport, Golden Cap (186m). Inshore DS: E +6.00; W HWD. Streams weak.

The passage across Lyme Bay can be hazardous. S–SW gales can blow up quickly and there is no place of refuge in onshore winds. Portland Bill causes an eddy in West Bay on the W-going stream producing a N set which is felt as far as 10M W of the Bill and a S set off the Bill which is felt as far as 6M S of the Bill.

Portland Bill The shape of this peninsula causes strong S streams from the bays on either side for 9 or 10h, and these, impinging on the main E–W Channel streams, cause violent turbulence which is aggravated by the sudden changes in depth over Portland Ledge off the pitch of the Bill. The resulting race is dangerous to yachts, and even to small ships in strong winds and should be avoided by passing at least 5M S of the Bill and outside the E Shambles E Card buoy Q(3)10s, Horn(2)30s, Bell, or if conditions permit accurate timing, by using the inshore passage of relatively smooth water about 5 ca wide between the Bill and the Race. The timing is important because the streams are so strong at certain times that they may set a yacht out of this chan and through the Race.

Off the Bill the E-going stream begins about +5.00 and the W-going stream begins about −1.00. At sp the max rate of the E-going stream is 6kn at −5.00; the max rate of the W-going stream is over 7kn at +1.00.

On the W side of the peninsula the stream runs S at 3kn for 9½h from +2.05 to −0.50, and N at 1.1kn from −0.10 to +2.05. On the E side of the peninsula the stream runs S at 4½kn for 10¼h from −5.10 to +5.05 and N at 1.8kn from +5.05 to −5.10.

It follows that bound E the best time for passing the Bill is about +5.00 and it remains practicable up to about −5.00 when the strong S stream from East Bay is about to begin and the E-going stream in the Race is reaching its maximum rate. Between these times the S stream is running out of West Bay and therefore the land must be closed to 1 to 2 ca well N of the pitch of the Bill, which should be rounded at this distance.

Bound W, the best time for passing the Bill is at −1.00 when the main stream is slack and the S stream from West Bay is ending. To arrive earlier would be to risk being set through the last of the E-going Race. The passage westward should be practicable until +2.00 when the S stream from West Bay commences. Throughout this period the yacht will have a strong fair stream down the E side of the peninsula and the land should be kept within 1 to 2 ca down to the pitch of the Bill. If the tide has turned to the W when the pitch of the Bill is reached, steer NW into West Bay to avoid being set into the Race.

Cautions In winds of Force 6 and over and in E winds of less strength the inshore passage ceases to be 'relatively smooth'.

The passage between the Race and the Shambles should not be attempted without local knowledge. Yachts taking the offshore route should pass outside the E Shambles lt buoy.

Lobster pots are a hazard off the Bill and along the E coast of the peninsula.
Anchorages   (1) Borough Is, NE side inshore of Murray Rk, 1 ca E of Is NE of the rk, 2m. Reasonable protection in moderate weather from all but SE winds but exercise great care in approach. (2) Hope Cove, anch in offshore winds only. Holding not good. Beware rk drying 3m ½ ca offshore. (3) Start Bay, in offshore winds off Hall Sands, or Torcross close inshore. Run for Dartmouth if wind backs S. (4) Torbay, Elberry Cove in SW corner of bay in 5m, 3 ca offshore. (5) Babbacombe, in offshore winds off local moorings. (6) Exmouth, outside anch near Fairway buoy if waiting for the tide in fair weather. (7) Beer Roads, E of Beer Hd: good anch in offshore winds through W to WSW in the Bay of Beer.

RIVER YEALM   Chart BA 95   (Plan p27)
HW −5.30 (entrance).
MHWS 5.4; MLWS 0.7; MTL 3.1; MHWN 4.3; MLWN 2.1
Bar   A sand bar runs S from Season Pt leaving a shallow narrow chan close along the S shore. The least depth occurs on the inner line: about 2m at half tide. Further in the river deepens. Entry and exit 2h either side of LW should be attempted with caution having due regard to weather conditions and the tidal level. Speed limit 6kn.
Approach   To clear the outlying rks on E and W of approach, keep Cawsand open of the Mewstone 298° until, coming from W, Wembury ch bears 030°, which clears Slimers Rks on W of approach; or coming from E, Wembury ch appears its own width E inside W edge of Langdon trees which bearing 006° clears Ebb Rks on E of approach. When beating in or out keep Misery Pt well open of Season Pt to clear Church Ledge, which runs from the N shore just below Wembury ch.
Entrance   Stand in between the above limits until the hillcrest on the top of Warren Pt, ½M inside the bar, shows open of Misery Pt, 078°, which bearing clears Mouthstone ledge. BW triangle bns abreast Battery Cottage lead, 089°, into Cellar Bay. Keep the hillcrest above Warren Pt just open of Misery Pt until Mouthstone Pt is abeam. Steer close to S shore, straight in to Cellar Bay, 089°, on a conspic house situated on Misery Pt, then RW triangle bns lead past Misery Pt 045°. From NE end of Cellar Bay follow round the curve of the shore in midstream. Care should be taken to avoid the spit extending S from Warren Pt and marked by a small R can buoy (can topmark). It is not possible to beat in against the ebb, as the wind baffles.
Berthing   Anch in fine weather in Cellar Bay (open from W to NW). Inside, river is crowded with moorings but anch is sometimes possible in pool W of Baring Pt. Visiting yachts moor fore and aft in four trots to buoys on port hand side of chan N of Yealm Hotel, there are also three swinging visitors' moorings: apply to HM. Anch N of line between Madge Pt and Clitters Wood is prohibited owing to oyster beds.

Landing at slip near Yealm Hotel: the slip opposite Spit buoy is private. Public

YEALM RIVER

Depths in Metres

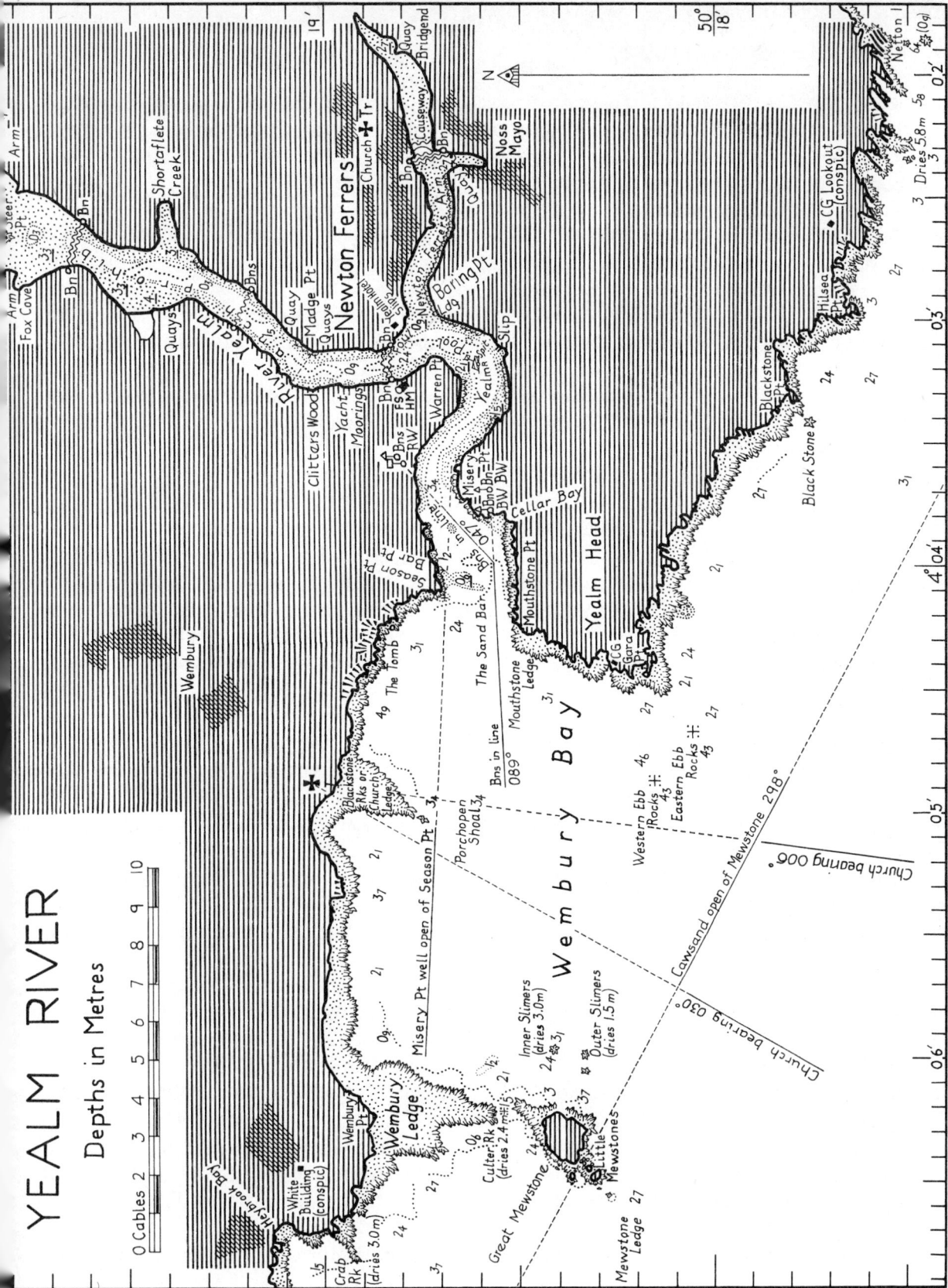

Heybrook Bay

White Building (conspic)

Crab Rk (dries 3.0m)

Wembury Pt

Wembury Ledge

Culver Rk (dries 2.4 m)

Great Mewstone

Little Mewstones

Mewstone Ledge

Outer Slimers (dries 1.5 m)

Inner Slimers (dries 3.0m)

Porchopen Shoal

Blackstone Rks or Church Ledge

Misery Pt well open of Season Pt

The Tomb

Season Pt

Bar Pt

Wembury

Fox Cove

Arm

W. Jeer Pt

Shortaflete Creek

River Yealm

Clittars Wood

Quays

Madge Pt

Quay

Bns

Newton Ferrers

Church

Tr

Quay

Bridgend

Causeway

Noss Mayo

Baring Pt

Arm

Yacht Moorings

Warren Pt

Bns

FS

HM

BW

Misery Pt

Cellar Bay

Mouthstone Pt

Mouthstone Ledge

The Sand Bar

Bns in line 089°

Yealm Head

Gara

CG

Wembury Bay

Western Ebb Rocks 46

Eastern Ebb Rocks

Black Stone

Blackstone

Hilsea Pt

CG Lookout (conspic)

Newton I

Dries 5.8m

Cawsand open of Mewstone 298°

Church bearing 030°

Church bearing 006°

N

50° 18'

19'

on British Admiralty Charts (nos. in text) with the permission of the Controller of H.M. Stationery Office and of
on British Admiralty Charts (nos. in text) with the permission of the Controller of H.M. Stationery Office and of
ydrographer of the Navy, and on other sources.

27

water supply. Newton Ferrers and Noss Mayo dry but can be reached by dinghy at half-tide. A footpath at LW connects Newton with Noss. Shops: Newton – PO, Co-op, butcher, chemist; Noss – PO, grocer-fishmonger. EC Thurs. Yacht repairs further up Newton Ferrers arm. Bus service to Plymouth.

SALCOMBE   Chart BA 28   (Plan p29)
HW −5.30.   DS: W −2.00; E +4.00
MHWS 5.3; MLWS 0.7; MTL 3.0; MHWN 4.1; MLWN 2.1
Bar   The Bar itself (1.5m MLWS) extends SW from Limebury Pt. It is at the inward limit of the gradually shoaling water of the Range; conditions can be hazardous in winds from E through S to SW, and it is dangerous to try to enter against the ebb in strong onshore winds. Inside there is 5m or more up to town.
Approach   Give the Mew Stone and Cadmus Rk clearances of 2 ca and 1 ca respectively. Starhole Bay provides temporary anch in W winds to wait for a suitable time to cross the Bar.

Coming from the E, give Prawle Pt a clearance of 2 ca and steer 298° for the pine-wood S of Bar Lodge, a tall narrow building with a red roof.

From 2 ca off Mew Stone steer N for about 4 ca to a position about 1 ca off the Eelstones; continue 000° with RW bn (R can topmark) on Poundstone Rk in line with the RWHS bn (diamond topmark) on Sandhill Pt to W of red-roofed house. The deepest water is ¾ ca W of the ldg line. Leave Bass Rks to port and Wolf Rk G con buoy to stb, and leaving Blackstone BW triangular bn (triangle topmark) to stb and RW Poundstone bn to port, round up 043° for the anch (two more port bns).

By night a Dir Lt is shown from Sandhill Pt above the ruins of Fort Charles, W sector (Fl 2s) 357½° to 002½°. A G sector lies to the E and a R sector to the W of the correct course. A sectored lt Q WR on Blackstone Rk Bn shows R until the rk is cleared, W up the entrance. An inner lead consists of two ldg lts close N of Scoble Pt in line 042°. The rear Higher Lt is Oc 4½s and the Lower is Q (the latter may be obscured by or confused with anchored vessels). These lead up the hr past Salcombe.
Warning   The ferry boats between Salcombe and Portlemouth have no reverse: pass under their stern.
Berthing   (1) Twenty visitors' moorings, most marked with a 'V' and a number. (2) Off Marine Hotel, although South Pool is crowded with moorings. (3) In settled weather anch in deep water in the fairway to seaward of the first moorings. (4) In settled weather with modest draft, off Sunny Cove on the E side. (5) In the Bag, 2–10m round the corner off Snapes Pt, where a mooring may be available. (6) Frogmore Lake in peace and quiet. (7) Large craft report to HM.

If it comes on to blow from SE to W it is well worth the trouble of running round into the Bag, where there is complete shelter. The tide runs 2½kn max. When bound E remember that the stream in the offing turns to the E 3h after LW by the shore.

Landing at Town Pier, Ferry House, pontoon landing. The upper reaches of

Salcombe
Depths in Metres

0 Cables 2   3   4   5

Salcombe
(Lifeboat)

Slip

Black Knob Pt

Batson Lake
24

Slip   Bns
Lifeboat
Grid
Bn

Snapes Pt

7
3·4
Ox Pt ☆ Fl 3
Ox Rk
☆ Fl 1·5

Boat Pool
2·7

13
3
10·7

FS
Scoble Pt

The Bag

Southpool Lake
0·9

Middle Ground

8·8

Tr & FS ✝
Customs Wharf
H M

Slip
Posts

⚓
9·8

Slip

Slip

FR ☆
Mont FS
FS

FS 14'
Bns
Smalls Cove

Lt's in line 042°

Kingsbridge

Squares Quay

New Quay
Southville
Bns

Balcombe Lake

0 Cables 4   7

17'

High House Pt

Park Bay

Bns
Bns

Charleton 50°

16'

FS
Bn

FS
Bn

Slip (disused)

Mill Bay

White Ho

North Sand Bay

Moult Pt

Dir Fl WRG 2s 27m 10·7·7M

Sandhill Pt

FS
Bns

Bn

Anchor
Prohib

Castle
Bn
Bn WLR

Biddlehead

Sunny Cove

Calliop Lake

Collap Lake

Gerston Pt

Charleton Pt

Frogmore Lake

Ham Pt

Blanks Lake

Rowden Pt

Wareham Pt

Bns

Salt Stone

(4) Bn
Poundstone

Blackstone (1)
Bn Q WR 4m 2M
Wolf Rk
G

Bass Rk

Splat Pt

South Sand Bay

2·4

1·8

Heath Pt
Bns
Slip

Halwell Pt

15'

Tosnos Pt
Mabel Sh

Ox Pt 4·5'
3·46

4·7'

Limebury Pt
Portlemouth Down

2·4
0·9

0·9

3·7

4·3

43

24

Chapple Rks
4·3

27
Rickham Rk

FSO

N
4

50°
13'

4

27

The Bar
0·9
1·2
3·7
4·3
5·2

9·4

7·6

Little Eelstone
Great Eelstone

The Range
⚓
Green

Wk
0·3 Cadmus Rks

Starehole Bay   W
Red

8·8

Bn and Lt. in line 000°

White Ho in line with Poundstone Bn 327°

Mew Stone (19)

Head
Little Mew Stone (5)

4·7'   3·46'   4·5'

ed on British Admiralty Charts (nos. in text) with the permission of the Controller of H.M. Stationery Office and of
Hydrographer of the Navy, and on other sources.

Chy (White) (conspic)

Shows positions of mooring buoys

Continued in Inset

2FG(vert)

The Noss

Noss Marina

OLD MILL CREEK

Bns

Bn

2FG(vert)

Bn

4-2FR(vert)

2FR(vert)

FS

Royal Naval College

Dome & Clock Tr

Dart Marina

Yacht Moorings

Yacht Moorings

Darthaven Marina

FS

FS

2FR (vert)

4-2FG(vert)

50° 21'

FS

HM

Dartmouth YC

Obscd

FlWRG2s5m6M

Kingswear

Tr & FS

Royal Dart YC

FS

Steps

Iso WRG3s 9m 8M

Steps

Ferry

Mooring

Arc of vis

Moorings

R Bn

Moorings

Steps

One Gun Pt

2-FS

Dartmouth Castle

Castle Pt

Checkstone

F5m9M

Kettle Pt

Kingswear Castle

FS

THE RANGE

Wash Pt

Day Beacon (about 170m) (Truncated pyramid)

White cottages (conspic)

FS

2-FS

Blackstone Pt

Western Blackstone

Old Castle Rk

Bears Tail

Castle Ledge

G

The Verticals

West Rk

Inner Froward Pt

Outer Froward Pt

Maw Stone

COMBE BAY

Meg Rks

Combe Pt

Inner Combe Rks

Outer Combe Rks

Homestone

R

Red

White

Green

Warren Pt

Redlap Ho

35

Dancing Beggars

20'

Dittisham

FS

Bn

Lr. Dittisham

Bn

Small Craft Moorings

WK

FERRY

Hard

Ned's Pt

Bn

Vipars Quay

Ancho Stone

Boat House

PARSONS MUD

Pontoon Jetty

Bn G

Grid

Bn G

RIVER DART TO DITTISHAM
Depths in Metres

0   Cables   5

35·5'W

3° 35'

DARTMOUTH HARBOUR
Depths in Metres

0   Cables   7

N

Based on British Admiralty Charts (nos. in text) with the permission of the Controller of H.M. Stationery Office and the Hydrographer of the Navy, and on other sources.

the river afford a fine area for small boat sailing when the tide is up. All facilities, water from water boat, fuel from pontoon. Bus to Kingsbridge. EC Thurs.

DARTMOUTH   Chart BA 2253   (Plan p30)

HW Dartmouth −5.15; Dittisham −5.15; Totnes −5.05.   DS: SW −1.00; NE +5.40

Dartmouth: MHWS 4.8; MLWS 0.4; MTL 2.7; MHWN 3.6; MLWN 1.8

Approaches   A truncated pyramidal stone bn 24m high and 177m above HW is a prominent mark on the E side above Froward Pt.

Approaching from E, Mewstone Rk (38m) is a good mark. Crab pots make it unwise to keep close to this rk, although there is plenty of water. A ledge of rks consisting of the Verticals, West Rk, etc, extending about 3 ca WSW from the Mewstone must also be avoided, by keeping E Blackstone (also called Black Rk) well open E of the Mewstone. After allowing this distance it is safe to make for Castle Ledge G con buoy. Approaching from W, keep outside the Homestone buoy (R can) and E of W Blackstone Rk (2.4m). It is unwise to pass close to Coombe Pt at any time. Approaching from S, Skerries bell buoy, 3½M from the entrance, is an excellent guide.

Entrance   Entrance is easy under power but squalls off the high land on either side of the entrance often make entry under sail difficult particularly with winds from SW through W to NW. Checkstone buoy (R can) is moored just E of a rocky ledge and must be left well to port.

Tides in the offing are weak, not exceeding 1kn, but off Battery and Castle Pts the flood reaches 3½kn and the ebb 4kn at sp. Inside these rates decrease again. Tides in the Homestone and Mewstone area turn 2h later than inside. In the approach a SW set may be experienced on the flood (except near its end) and a NE set on the ebb (except near its end).

At night, first pick up the W sector of Kingswear Lt Iso WRG 3s 26m, 12M and keep in this until within the W sector of the Old Coastguard Lt Fl WRG 2s. Keep in this until the G lts on the Kingswear pontoon are well open. Then course should be altered to pass through the fairway and to the anch E of the main hr buoys.

Note   There is a F W lt NNW of Kettle Pt principally for vessels going out, but it is useful if kept astern when heading for the W sector of Old Coastguard Lt.

Berthing   (1) Anchor E of the town and of the main hr buoys in 4½–7½m. Good holding. Take care not to drag onto chains of mooring buoys. (2) Visitors' buoys; enquire at hr office on South Embankment. (3) Darthaven, pontoon berths on E side of river off Kingswear (tel Kingswear (080 425) 545). (4) Dart Marina, pontoon berths on W side of river above Upper Ferry (floating bridge). All facilities (tel Dartmouth (080 43) 3351). (5) Anchor on W side of river below Anchor Stone (R bn) off Parsons Mud clear of the moorings and off the main channel. (6) Visitors' moorings off Dittisham. (7) For anchorage above Dittisham consult the river officer, generally afloat near Dittisham. When waiting for him best pick up one of the visitors' moorings, each of which will take more

RIVER DART
Dittisham to Totnes

Depths in Metres
one Mile

Continued in Inset

Continuation
On the same scale
(Mill Reach to Totnes)

Totnes

N

3° 40'w

3° 38'w

Mill Reach

Sharpham Pt

The Guc

Quay

Sharpham Reach

Ham Pt

Hackney

Ashprington Pt

Duncannon Reach

Langham Wood Pt

Bow Creek

White Rk

Langham Wood

Langham

Stoke Pt

Duncannon

Small Craft Moorings

Mill Pt

Dam

Mill Pool

Stoke Gabriel

Home Reach

Ship Turning Bay

Steamer Quay

Quay

Lang Stream

MIDDLE BACK

Middle Back

Cross Back

Pighole Pt

Higher Gurrow Pt

Blackness Pt

Dittisham

FLAT OWERS

Galmpton Creek

Fleet Mill Quay

Mill Reach

N

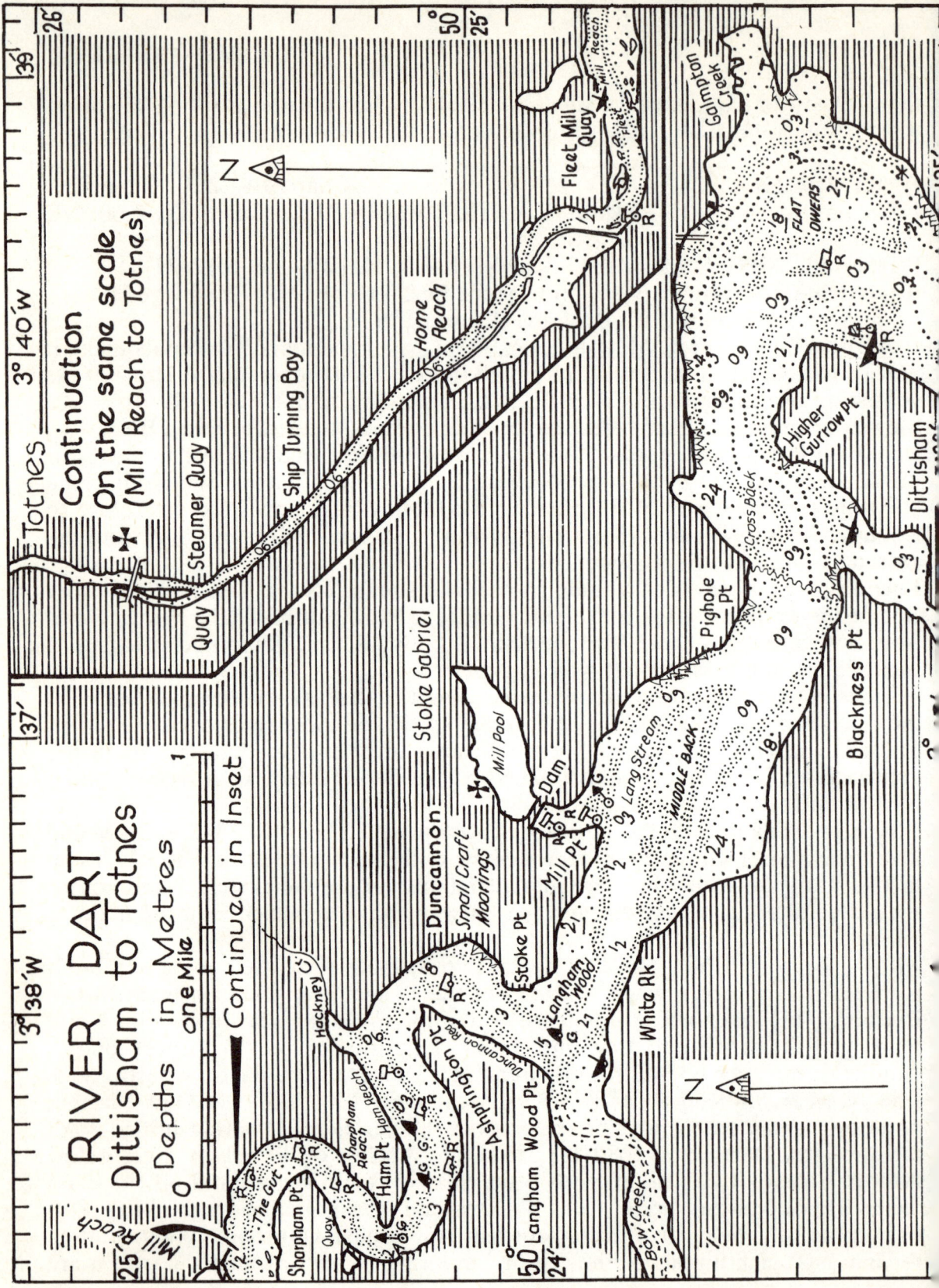

than one yacht. Quite large timber steamers use the fairway W of the Flat Owers and go right up to Totnes.

The whole river is controlled by the Hr Authority at Dartmouth and dues are levied. The Lower Ferry must be given right of way.

Water and stores at Dittisham but no fuel. All facilities at Galmpton. Excellent notes on the hr giving detailed instructions for navigation as far as Totnes are available free from the Dart Hr and Navigation Authority, The Old PO, South Embankment, Dartmouth (tel 2337). EC Wed.

BRIXHAM   Chart BA 26   (Plan p34)

HW −5.05.   DS: SW −1.00, NE +5.00
MHWS 4.8; MLWS 0.6; MTL 2.7; MHWN 3.6; MLWN 1.9
The inner hr dries. There is 1.8–11m inside the breakwater. In NE–E winds the scend in the outer hr is considerable and in these conditions Torquay is preferable.

Approach   Approaching Torbay from S, Hope's Nose open of Berry Hd 359° clears all dangers between the Mewstone and Berry Hd which has over 25m close inshore. From Berry Hd steer 284° for a position off the breakwater lt.

Entrance   The fairway is marked by a G con buoy Q G SW of the Breakwater Lt, Oc R 15s, and an unlit G con buoy 1 ca N of jetty. 3 R balls or lts hoisted at the inner hr ent indicate hr closed.

Berthing   There is no room to anch in the outer hr. Five W visitors' buoys off Upham's Boatyard: contact HM for allocation. Good anch off Elbury Cove. Silver Cove and Fishcombe Cove are both safe with fairly deep water close inshore.

Landing at Brixham YC pier or Breakwater Hard at all states of tide. Trots for dinghies. Water at end of pier, lit at night, and at Breakwater Hard, New Pier and Oil Jetty. Diesel at Oil Jetty, 20 gal minimum; otherwise Torquay or Dartmouth nearest. Good hard at top of inner hr on port hand and grid on E side. Small craft may be launched by crane or on slip on inner hr or on Breakwater Hard. There is a slip off Freshwater Quarry unsuitable at MLWS. All facilities. EC Wed.

PAIGNTON   Chart BA 26

A small pier hr, opening to NE, dries 3.5m at MLWS. Suitable for small boats. E winds send in a swell near HW. The hr is situated on N side of Roundham Pt, 3½M 245° from the Orestone.

Approach   On near approach, to clear the rks which extend about 1 ca eastward from the E wall of the hr, steer to N of Roundham Pt to a position about midway between Paignton pier-head and the hr entrance, thence inside the line of moorings to the entrance. 3 R balls or lts indicate hr closed.

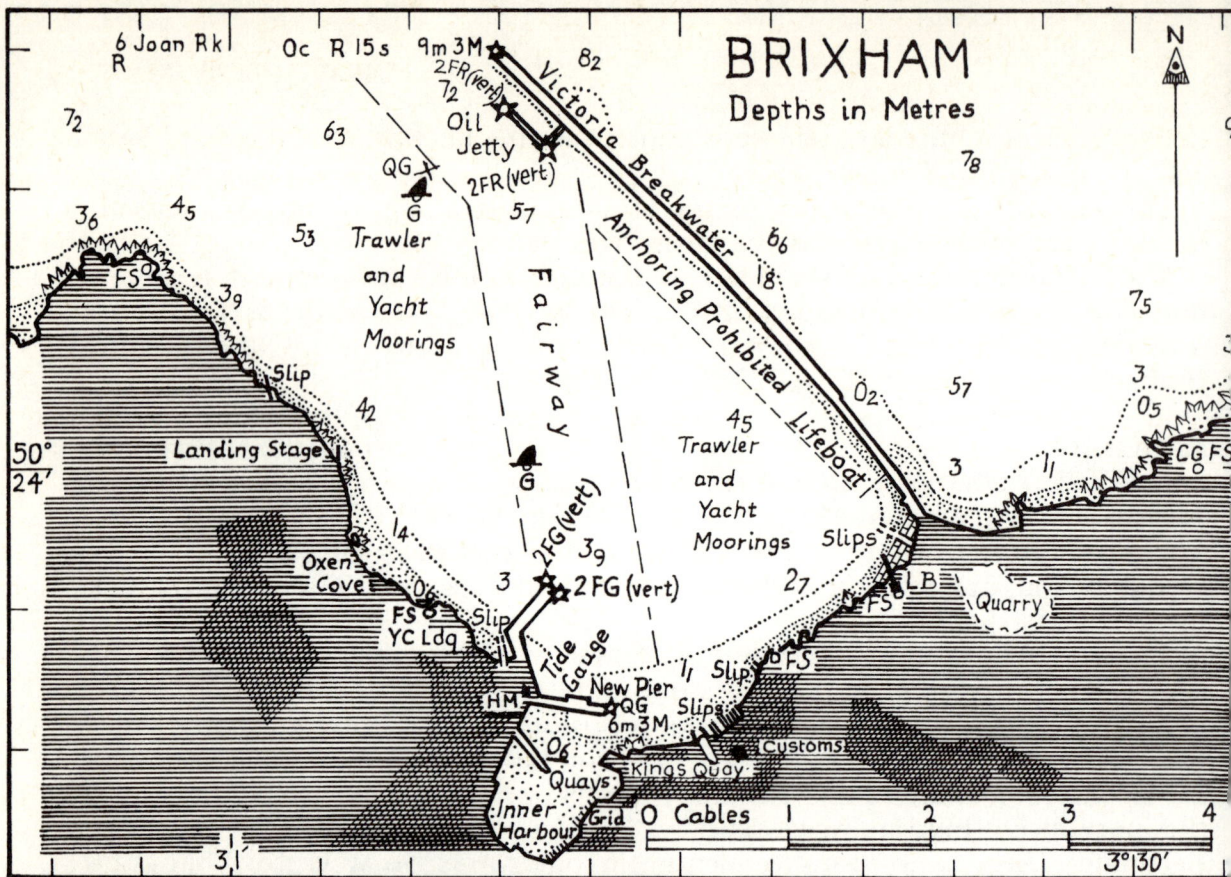

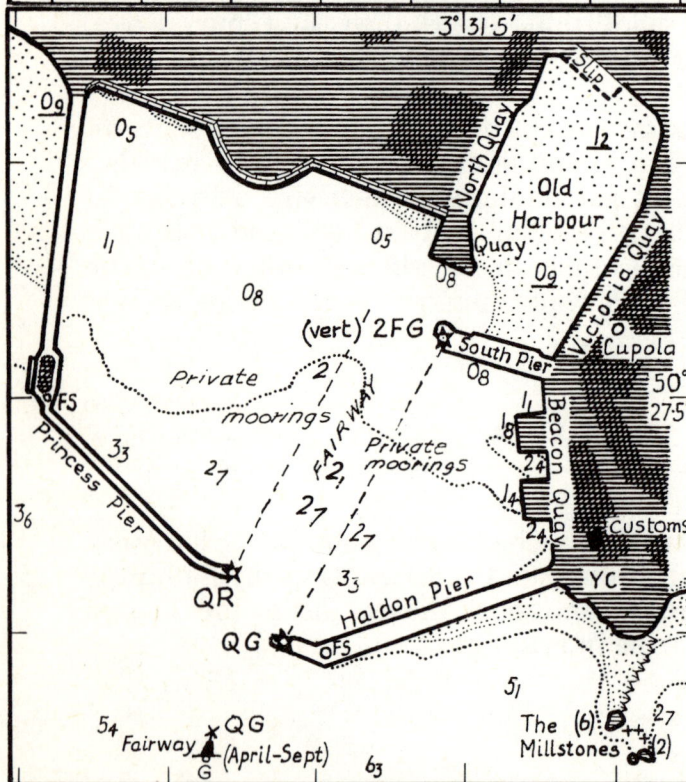

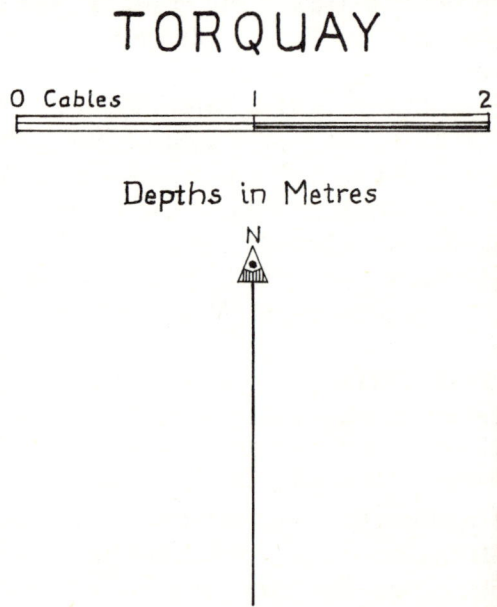

Based on British Admiralty Charts (nos. in text) with the permission of the Controller of H.M. Stationery Office and the Hydrographer of the Navy, and on other sources.

TORQUAY   Chart BA 26   (Plan p34)
HW −5.00.   DS: W −1.00; E +5.00
MHWS 4.9; MLWS 0.7; MTL 2.8; MHWN 3.7; MLWN 2.0
The outer hr is always available, 4–5m shelving to 1m in NE corner. Good shelter with winds from S through W to NE. In strong SE winds there is much scend in the outer hr and Brixham is preferable. The inner hr dries and is only used by small craft and dinghies.
Approach   From E, a ch tr and spire close together stand out on the skyline above Babbacombe. There is safe passage between the Orestone and the Flat Rk off Hope's Nose. Even at HW sp it is unsafe for strangers to attempt to pass inside the Thatcher Rk. The Orestone its own length open of the Thatcher will clear all shoals along N shore of Torbay.
Entrance   Busy. A G con buoy QG marks the approach during the season. 3 R balls or lts indicate hr closed.
Berthing   Outside the hr, anch in good holding, sand, anywhere with sufficient depth, but avoid the buoyed approach fairway.
   Inside the hr, the outer hr is much congested during the season and there is little room to manoeuvre. There is a fairway between the mouth of the outer and that of the inner hr with swinging moorings on trots on either side. All these moorings belong to local craft. Visiting yachts may be allotted a vacant mooring or tie up to pontoons alongside Haldon Pier to the E of the entrance, though all space is frequently occupied by steamers and large craft. If not already contacted by hr staff on arrival, find a space alongside Haldon Pier (or alongside a boat already there) and report to HM's office for directions. Do not anch in, or obstruct, the fairway except in emergency. Yachts from foreign countries should await examination at Haldon Pier or out of hours telephone the Customs.
   Land at steps on either side of hr, preferably on Haldon or South Piers or on Beacon Quay. HM's Office and Custom Ho on Beacon Quay. Tel on Beacon Quay. Royal Torbay YC on Beacon Hill, and premises on Haldon Pier. All facilities. Rly 1M. For scrubbing lay ashore along Victoria Quay in inner hr, one grid available. Fresh water on Haldon Pier, fuel station and also 5-ton hand crane on South Pier. EC Wed and Sat.

TEIGNMOUTH   Chart BA 26   (Plan p37)
HW −5.00.   DS: W −0.30; E +5.10
MHWS 4.8; MLWS 0.6; MTL 2.7; MHWN 3.6; MLWN 1.9
The hr is completely sheltered but is not accessible in strong onshore winds (between NE and S) when there is heavy surf on the bar especially on the ebb. With other winds it is often calm off the entrance and the wind very fluky. The chan over the bar is unlit except in summer months, half-flood to half-ebb, when vessels are expected so the entrance should not be attempted at night. Anchoring anywhere within the hr limits is prohibited and the hr is crowded. Apply to HM for a vacant mooring.
Bar   Depth about ½m MLWS. Frequently shifts.

Approach No firm directions can be given because of the shifting bar, and a pilot is strongly advised. If the entrance is attempted unaided, avoid onshore weather and arrive on a rising tide while the banks are still visible. Local fishermen are often very helpful in giving directions. There are rks off the Ness which should be given a good berth but everywhere else there is sand only. A small B barrel buoy is sometimes moored on the S side of the chan over the bar and this should be rounded close-to. (But approach with caution: sometimes after the chan has changed, the pilots are unable to move the buoy immediately.) Once across the bar, bring the W bn tr on the training wall between two vert W strips on the grey wall on the shore and enter on that line until 50m from the bn. Then keep in the middle of the chan.

Entrance The shoals off Ferry Pt are marked by a small G buoy and the Salty Flat is marked by R buoys, but care is necessary as the flat sometimes extends beyond the line of the buoys. Keep to the stb side of the chan when entering on the flood because of the strong set along the Shaldon shore. Note: (a) the large extent of Salty Flat which dries at half-tide; (b) the shoals above the quay on the stb side which are unmarked. There is a considerable coaster traffic and these vessels must be given right-of-way. The tidal stream runs at 4kn off the Pt and is strong throughout the hr, especially for the last half of the ebb, but above the bridge and outside the Pt it is much easier.

Berthing Enquire of HM for mooring, or better still, write in advance so that he can make arrangements and give assistance as required. Quiet anch above bridge for small motor craft.

Water from quays or boatyards. Hard for scrubbing on S side of New Quay, arrange first with HM. All facilities and stores except diesel in bulk which is better obtained at Brixham. Ferry to Shaldon. Rly. EC Thurs.

EXMOUTH Chart BA 2290 (Plan p38,37)
HW −4.55. DS: E +4.45; W HWD.
MHWS 4.6; MLWS 0.5; MTL 2.5; MHWN 3.4; MLWN 1.7

Bar A long shallow bar with 1.5m of water, rocks on N side and Pole Sand on S side, extends SE as far as Orcombe Pt. The hr, which has $3\frac{1}{2}$–$5\frac{1}{2}$m inside, is easy of access in fine weather but should not be approached in strong winds between S and E. The chan is well buoyed.

Approach From SW steer for Straight Pt, 41m high, until Exmouth ch bears 320°, then make for Exe Fairway bell buoy spher RWVS, $\frac{3}{4}$M S of highest part of cliff. Take care not to confuse this buoy with two spher DZ buoys Fl Y 3s, 147°, 1.37M and Fl Y 5s, 188°, 1.48M from Straight Pt.

From E or W Mamhead Tr (218m) 3M inland in line with Langstone Pt, 269°, will clear Pole Sand and ledges S of Orcombe Pt.

Entrance The chan is tortuous and should not be attempted without local knowledge at night. It is marked by odd-numbered G con buoys to stb and even-numbered R can buoys to port. When past Orcombe Pt, where cliff drops, bring a conspicuous R tr on foreshore at Starcross on with end of pier at NW

Topsham

Whit...
Cust Brdams 1m MLW
West Br 50dams 1m
Pier
Lock Ferry
Slip
Viaduct
Exton
Barracks
No.29
No.27
No.23
Lympstone Pier
Lympstone Lake
Cockle Sand
Kings Lake

G Nob
QR
FlG5s
QG
The Ridge
QG
GNP25
FlG5s BnP
Lympstone Sound2
No.23
MLW
FlG5s G
Starcross Sands
Jetty

Powderham Sand
Powderham Pool
Powderham Pool Landing Stage
River Kenn (Tidal)
River Exe

Starcross

Green Land
Inn
FlG5s MLW
Bn.P5
Perch West
Mud
Perch
Turf Lock
Inn Pier

Exeter Canal Depth 3.3m

The Channel position above Starcross is liable to vary

Depths in Metres
0 Cables 5   10

TEIGNMOUTH
Depths in Metres

3° 30'

(conspic)
Tr & FS

Customs
Quay
2FG(vert) (occas)
Teignmouth
2FG(vert) (occas)
Wks
Swing Bridge 30ft wide
FG (occas)
HM
New Quay
FG (occas)
FS
The Den

Ldg Lts 01°
Salty I
NB
R
The Salty
SSn
Green
R
R
Slips
FR11m 3M (occas)
Bn
FlG5s
FR 10m 6M (occas)
White Red

Slip
Slip
Slip Quay
Shaldon Pool
Shaldon
Ferry
The Point
Bn
Spratt Sand

The Bar

East Pole Sand

Training Wall (dries 1 to 3m)
FWRG 4m 2M Oc
Pole Sand
The Ness (53)
Leading Lights 334°

0 Cables 1   2   3   4

British Admiralty Charts (nos. in text) with the permission of the Controller of H.M. Stationery Office and of ...drographer of the Navy, and on other sources.

37

Exmouth

Depths in Metres

N

Buoyage
The channel into the harbour
is subject to change.
The buoys are moved accordingly.

0 Cables   5   10

Withycombe Raleigh
Tr & FS

Exmouth
Tr & FS
Spire
Tr & FS (conspic)
Clock
Tr
Custom Ho
CG
CG

King's Lake
Cockle Sand
Shelly Bank
The Point
Exe SC
Lifeboat
Posts
Dock
WL
6m
WL

River Exe
Shaggles Sand
Starcross
Moorings
Tr & FS
Inn
Bull Hill Bank
The Bight
Moorings
Salthouse Lake
Landing Inn at HW

Warren
Warren Pt
Checkstone
Sand
Ledge

Sandhills
Days Ledge
Inshore
LB
Sewer
Wall
Page Ledge
Sea Wall
Conger Rks
Double Ledge
Ledge
Orcombe Pt
Orcombe Ledge
Straight Pt
Fl R 10s

Pole Sand

The Warren
Pier (ruins)
Groynes
Ruin
Footbridges
Dawlish Warren
Inn
FS
Langstone Pt (16)
Landing

Exe Fairway Bell
Fl.10s
RW

Lights in line 305°

Based on British Admiralty Charts (nos. in text) with the permission of the Controller of H.M. Stationery Office and the Hydrographer of the Navy, and on other sources.

38

extreme of Exmouth Esplanade, 305°, which will lead between Conger Rks and Pole Sand. Keep close to stb buoys from No. 5 to No. 11 as Pole Sand borrows a little on chan to NE. After passing No. 11, it is advisable if cheating the tide to keep to stb of chan until halfway between No. 10 and shore; thence to avoid shoal patch off Clock Tr steer straight to a point just W of Dock pier-head, when turn up into the Bight. The Western Way dries at LW Neaps.

By night: Straight Point Lt Ho (Fl R 10s) enables course to be shaped for the Fairway Buoy. Leave No. 1 (QG) and No. 7 (Fl G 5s) G con buoys to stb and No. 8 R can buoy to port. Then pick up F Y ldg lts on iron bn on inner end of sea wall and Custom Ho F S leading in 305°.

If proceeding up river follow carefully the curves of the centre of the chan. Do not assume that straight-line courses between buoys are safe: for example Bull Hill obtrudes between Nos. 13 and 15, while Lymstone Sand must be cleared by a curved course leaving Nos. 21, 23, a W perch, and Nos. 25 and 27 to stb. A direct course from No. 23 to No. 25 is liable to put one into a lagoon within the sand.

Berthing   Bring up in the Bight in 3–5½m, sand. Visiting yachts may lie in the dock. There are lay-up berths (2½m) in the canal at Topsham; apply to wharfinger at Exeter. The canal, 5M long, connects Topsham with Exeter.

It is considered dangerous to anch off the Pt close to the dock during spring tides or strong winds between S and E. The flood sets fairly over the bar until the banks cover. The ebb sets over Warren Sand 2½kn over Pole Sand 1kn. These uncover after half ebb.

Land at dock entrance. All facilities. Water from dock. Hard. Rly at Exmouth and Starcross. EC Wed.

LYME REGIS   Chart BA 3315
HW −4.45.   DS: E +4.50; W −1.10.
MHWS 4.3; MLWS 0.6; MTL 2.4; MHWN 3.1; MLWN 1.7.
A drying pier hr with 2½ to 4m at HWS. Hard bottom. Bad shelter in heavy weather.
Approach   To clear the rks (bn) off Outer Cobb, keep the High Lt FR just open E of Low Lt FR sector and give the bn a very good berth.
Entrance   Steer straight in through the entrance from E on the line of the ldg lts, 296°. There is a R can buoy on a plinth at entrance which when awash indicates 1.5m of water.
Berthing   Lie alongside quay abreast the buildings on S wall. A nasty swell runs in with heavy SE winds, and the sea breaks outside the hr in S gales. The stream is slight. Land at the steps.
Stores in the town ½M from hr. Water on quay. EC Thurs.

WEST BAY (BRIDPORT)   Chart BA 3315
HW −5.00.   DS: E +5.10; W HWD.
MHWS 4.1; MLWS 0.6; MTL 2.3; MHWN 3.0; MLWN 1.6.
Bar   The hr ent dries at MLWS. Depth at MHWS 3 to 4m. Except in heavy

weather and strong onshore winds it is safe to enter from 2h before to 2h after HW when there is at least 1.8m of water over the bar, but sea breaks on the bar between the piers below half-tide if there is any swell.

Approach   There are no dangers for craft drawing 1.8m within 1M E and W of entrance beyond ½ ca from the shore. From W to clear High Ground (2.7m), keep E pier-head on with North Hill (115m to E of entrance), 075°. From S to clear Pollock Stone (3.3m) keep W pier on with Down Hall (above Bridport town), 011°. When the sluice gates in the hr can be seen between the piers, steer for the entrance. There is an unlit sewer outfall buoy ¾M S of hr ent.

The hr can be identified at night by a lt Oc 1½s on the roof of the HM's office at the shore end of the W pier. This is not a ldg lt and is to the W of the chan. The lts on the pier-head (E pier FG, W pier FR) are only shown when commercial vessels are due to enter.

Entrance   Enter hr between stone piers by 12m wide chan which runs straight in for nearly 1 ca. Visiting craft should tie up to the quay on the E side of the chan beyond the two projecting stone breakwaters. Outside, in fair weather, anch abreast of the piers 1 ca or more offshore, sand. In heavy weather or if there is any swell the ent is subject to considerable backwash across the channel between the piers. An extension to the E pier and development of the hr to include a marina is planned.

Shops, PO. All stores at Bridport 1½M inland. Hard. EC Thurs.

PORTLAND HARBOUR   Charts BA 2268, 2255   (Plan p41)
HW −4.25.   MHWS 2.1; MLWS 0.2; MTL 1.1; MHWN 1.4; MLWN 0.7.
Tidal currents are imperceptible in the hr but run at rates up to 1kn in the entrances, with eddies. Depths from 2 to 20m.

Entrance   There are three entrances, called the S, E and N Ship Channels respectively. The S Ship Chan is closed: there is a block-ship which uncovers at LW and also wires are stretched across it. There is no difficulty in entering by either of the other two chans. However, vessels are recommended to enter by the E Ship Chan and leave by the N. With VHF, permission to enter should be requested on Chan 13.

Anchorages   (1) Off Castletown Pier in the SW corner of the hr, not too far to the W where kelp makes for bad holding. Landing on beach E of Castletown Pier near HW or at RNSA pontoons near the castle with permission. (2) At Old Castle Cove in NE corner of the hr ½M W of N end of the breakwater in 2 to 3½m, a little more than 1 ca offshore of Castle Cove SC landing stage. It is best to anch outside the yacht moorings.

Entering by the N Ship Chan, the radio mast at Wykes Regis indicates the approx position of the Cove. The landing stage is built over a drain pipe which extends beyond the landing stage and dries at MLWS; the end of the drain is marked by a small bn with a triangle. Holding is good if not too close to shore. This is a pleasant berth in fine weather or in NW gales but it is not so comfortable in SE or SW gales to which it is exposed.

Portland and Weymouth
Depths in Metres

0 Cables   5   10

37'

N

Spire (conspic)

Pier

Melcombe Clock
Regis

Statue

Weir

34

Ldg Lts 237°

Weymouth Harbour

2FG(vert)6M
Bell(occas)

Traffic Sig

Weymouth

5

Ldg FR

42

The Nothe

Q 10m 9M

Explos(3) & Reed(occas)

Fl R 5s   Wks

R

The Mixen

Fl Y 5s

Fl Y 2s

Y   Y

Newton's
Cove

Obscd

Y

Fl Y 10s

7

Cable Area

Y

36'

Northern Arm

Bldgs
(conspic)
Torpedo Pier

Fl G 5s

Bn No 3

C Head
Oc G 10s   11m 5M

Pier

Castle Cove

Bn

North Ship Channel
B Head
Oc R 15s 11m 5M

Castle
(ruins)

Wyke Regis

Bn

QG 2M

7·6

FS & Tr
(obscured from seaward)

North-eastern Breakwater

Bn

0·3

4·9

L Fl 2M

Small Mouth

Portland

Harbour

A Head (conspic)
Fl 10sec 22m 20M Horn

East Ship Channel
Fort Head

QR

50'
35'

(Numerous Moorings)

0·3

Anchor
Prohib

Obscd

Bn E
2F(vert)

7·6

(obscured from seaward)

Anchoring Prohibited

Outer Breakwater
Cable Area

Chesil Beach

Bn

Bn

Fl R
Fl R
Fl G

Dns   QR
(occas)

Chys

Bn

Q Pier

piles

Oc G

coaling
pier

VQ(3)

2FR(vert)
2F(vert)

D Head
Oc R

Naval
Air Station

Castletown

FS

Chy

FS

Inner Breakwater

Obstn
(0·3)

34'

28'   2° 27'   26'   25'

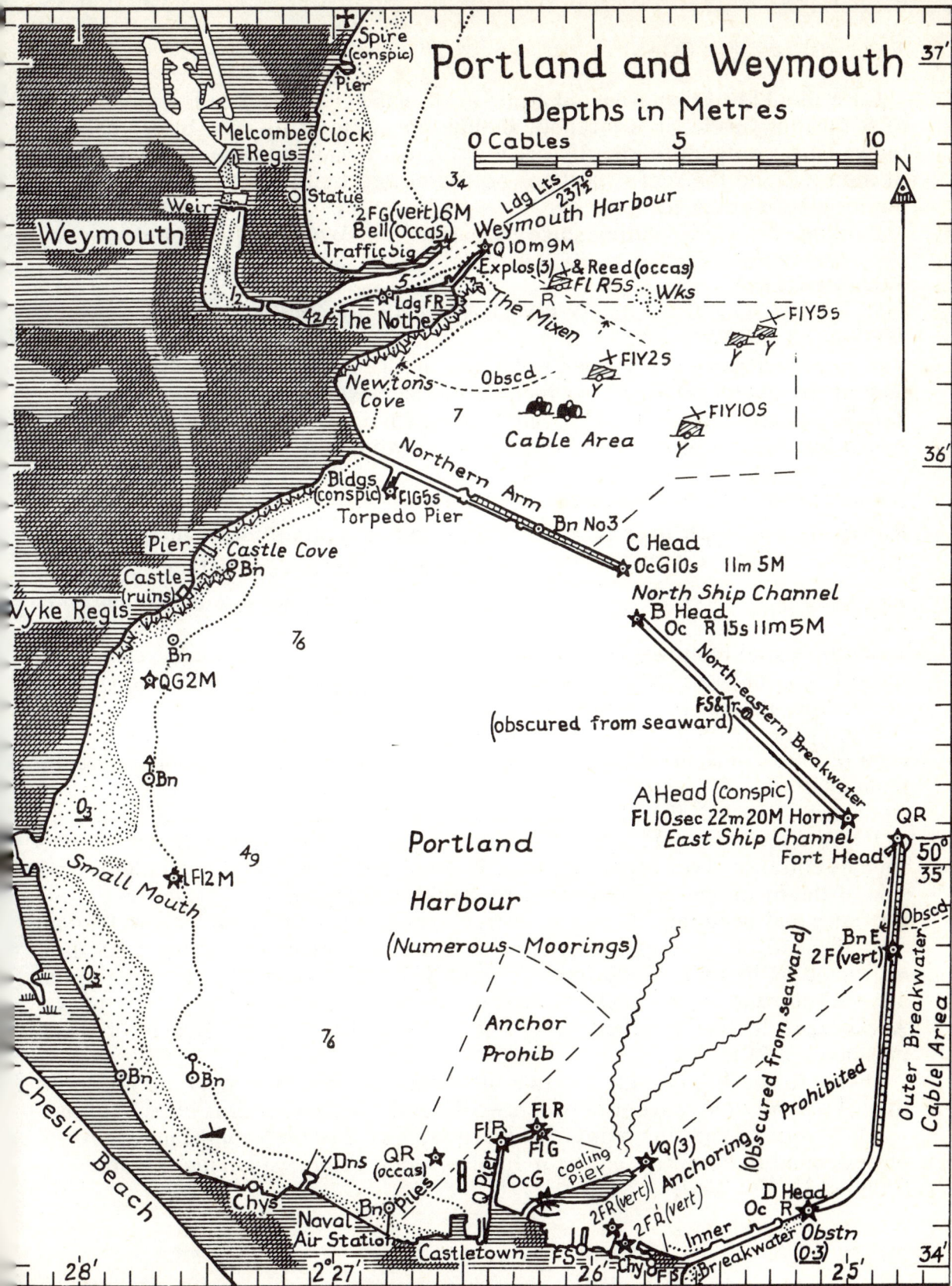

Care should be taken to avoid a reef of rks which extends 1 ca E from the foot of Sandsfoot Castle; it is marked, though not quite at its end, by a small can buoy. This is difficult to identify because there are yacht moorings on either side of the reef, and the reef is perhaps best indicated by the fact that there are no mooring buoys over it.

Landing at the SC landing stage by permission. Water from boatman.

WEYMOUTH   Chart BA 2255   (Plan p41)
HW −4.40.   DS: E +5.45; W HWD. Tides 4h flood 4h ebb 4h LW.
MHWS 2.1; MHWN 1.4.

The hr and entrance which open to NE are dredged to 4½m in mid-chan to within 60m of the town bridge, after which depth decreases to 1.8m.

Traffic signals   The following signals are exhibited from the flagstaff on the North Pier (Pleasure Pier) and are in force throughout the year.

FLAGS BY DAY	LTS BY NIGHT	MEANING
R over G	**2R over G**	Entrance foul, entry or departure forbidden
Two R	**3 R**	Vessel leaving hr: keep entrance clear.
Two G	**3 G**	Vessel arriving: do not attempt to leave hr.

When no signal is shown on the mast, it denotes that the entrance is clear both inward and outward, but a good lookout must be kept by an approaching vessel in case the signal is put against her.

Within the hr limits, all boats whether under oars sails or power must keep clear of the main chan and not obstruct vessels which can navigate only inside the main chan.

Approach   To clear the Mixen keep St John's ch spire at the N end of town open to E of the sewer buoy Fl R 5s off the S stone pier. Leave it to port and steer in as soon as entrance is well open. By day, W posts and triangles (R lts at night) on S side of the hr in line 237° lead directly between the piers.

Entrance and berthing   Berthing instructions are usually given by a watchman near the end of the pier, otherwise berth as convenient above the LBS until instructed by hr staff. Good fenders needed. Anch must not be dropped in the hr. A swell runs up the hr if it is blowing from the E or NE.

Anchorage   In fine weather, good anch outside the hr 3 or 4 ca N of the S pier-head in 2½ to 3½m.

Owing to the E bay eddy the tide in Weymouth Roads is W-going not more than ½kn at all times except between −5.10 and −3.10 when it is imperceptible.

All facilities. Watering point near Piermaster's office on N pier, taps at several places round the hr. Rly 1½M near Jubilee Clock Tr on Esplanade. Steamers to Channel Is. EC Wed.

PASSAGE NOTES: WEYMOUTH TO POOLE

Chart BA 2615

Whether proceeding from S of Portland Race either N to Weymouth or direct up-Channel always pass well to the S of the Shambles. If attempting the deep-water channel between the Shambles and the Race, even in good weather allow for strong current onto Race or the Shambles depending on tidal stream.

If following the coast inshore there is an obstruction, least depth 4m, 3 ca SE of Redcliffe Pt, and a rocky ledge running out 3 ca from Ringstead Pt. Otherwise there are no dangers outside 2 ca as far as Lulworth Cove. Tides do not run strongly on this part of the coast. E of Lulworth Cove to St Albans Hd avoid Kimmeridge Ledge which extends seaward for over $\frac{1}{2}$M.

Caution Beware Lulworth Gunnery Range. See latest Notices to Mariners for times when active. Patrol boats are in the area and small craft are expected to proceed through the area as quickly and directly as possible.

St Albans Hd is easily identified by an ancient chapel and CG hut on its summit. Off this hd there is a dangerous race E on the flood and W on the ebb at spring tides. The race varies considerably in its position and severity; it extends some 3M seaward except during S winds when it lies closer inshore. It may be avoided by giving the Hd a berth of $3\frac{1}{2}$M. DS: E +5.45; W −0.15; 4–5kn at sp. In good weather especially in offshore winds there is a safe inshore passage nearly $\frac{1}{2}$M wide between the Hd and the race. Keep close inshore. This passage has the advantage of an early fair eddy, but a local eddy runs down the W side of the Hd to the SE nearly continuously.

From St Albans Hd to Anvil Pt there is deep water to within a short distance of the shore the whole way. The point is easily identified by a W Lt Ho. There is a local eddy inshore running contrary to the main stream between St Albans Hd and Lulworth. It turns W −2.00 and +5.00, quickly becoming strong. Beyond Anvil Pt there are three conspic headlands before reaching Poole Hr. Under certain conditions rough water may be expected the whole way. Off Durlston Hd, identified by the castellated building on its summit, the stream runs NE +5.30, SW −0.30, 3kn Sp. Off Peveril Pt with its CG and FS there is a rocky ledge extending $\frac{1}{4}$M to seaward. Give this ledge a wide berth by passing well to the E of the buoy marking its extremity as the stream sets towards it. DS: NNE +5.00, $1\frac{1}{2}$kn; SSW −2.15, 3kn. In bad weather a dangerous race runs seaward of the buoy especially to the SE during the W-going stream and even under normal conditions there are numerous eddies and tide-rips. Off Handfast Pt and Old Harry wind against the ebb brings up a nasty lop. Old Harry DS: W −1.15; E +5.00.

Caution Keep a good look out for coasters and fishing boats especially if becalmed at night between Swanage and Poole. Also beware lobster pots up to $\frac{1}{2}$M offshore, often not clearly marked.

Anchorages (1) Worbarrow Bay. 1M E of Lulworth Cove, good anch abreast Arish Mell gap. Sheltered from WNW–ESE. It is, however, within the Sea Area of Lulworth Gunnery Ranges, which extends 5.3M seawards. While vessels in the ordinary course of navigation passing directly through the Sea Area are exempted from the Lulworth Range Byelaws, exemption does not apply to anchoring while the Range is in use. For schedule of closures telephone Range Officer on Bindon Abbey (0929) 462721 Ext 219 or CG. (2) Chapmans Pool, W of St Albans Hd. Only in calm weather to await turn of tide. Swell can cause great discomfort. If necessary to anch because of calm, W of Kimmeridge Ledge clear of rocky bottom may be preferable. (3) Studland Bay. See separate entry below.

LULWORTH COVE   Chart BA 2610
HW −4.40. DS: E +5.45; W HWD.
MHWS 2.3; MLWS 0.3; MTL 1.2; MHWN 1.5; MLWN 0.9.
The cove has 4.8m in entrance, 3 to 3½m in middle inside. It should not be used in bad or unsettled weather. A roll is commonly felt in even fine weather.
Approach From W to clear Ringstead Ledge give shore a berth of ½M. Lulworth lies 3M E of White Nose, where the cliffs change from clay to chalk. Near the hr the shore is steep-to. From E, Arish Mell Gap open of Worbarrow Hd clears Kimmeridge Ledges.
Entrance Have power ready as the wind baffles between the cliffs. Submerged ledges of rock extend into the entrance from both sides; the W ledge is the longer and must be given a berth of 50m. Steer in through the E centre of entrance, heading for the junction of G and W cliffs on N side of hr. When fully halfway across the cove, steer to port or stb and bring up in 3½m, clay and sand, preferably in NW corner. Ledges of rk extend for nearly 120m in NNE direction from the extremity of each arm of entrance leaving a chan 4.8m deep and 80m wide. Heavy S winds send in a severe swell. With proper ground tackle, vessels may ride out bad weather from W safely though uncomfortably, but never from S when conditions may be very dangerous.
   Good hotel. Landing on beach NW side. Stores. Rly at Wool, 5M. PO. Possible to careen on beach.

SWANAGE   Chart BA 2172
Double HW: Springs −2.20 and +0.40; Neaps −5.00 and +1.35.   DS: E +5.00; W −1.00.
MHWS 2.0 and 1.5; MLWS 0.3; MTL 1.5; MHWN 1.4 and 1.6; MLWN 0.3
Approach   From W give Peveril Ledge buoy a good berth as the tide sets across the ledge. There can be a sharp tide-race off Peveril Pt.
Anchorage   Anch in 2½ to 3½m N of the pier, ¼M from the shore. Good shelter in winds between N and SW. Ground foul in places. This is a good berth in fine weather. In unsettled weather it is better to bring up in Studland Bay with Poole under the lee in case of a southerly shift of wind. When anch in Swanage or Studland avoid weed. The clear sandy patches are usually visible. Streams inside the bay are slight. Landing on beach, shops. Water at pier. EC Thurs.

STUDLAND BAY
Chart BA 2172 (Plan p46)

Tidal data approx as Swanage. A good anch with a snug hr (Poole) under the lee if the winds shift. Sheltered from all but NE to ESE winds; good holding in firm sand. Anch where shown on plan about 2 ca E of the S end of the sandy part of the beach and about the same distance N of the W end of the visible cliffs. About 2½m available (or a little more abreast of the Yards, three prominent projections in the cliff), but take care to avoid the small foul patches marked on the plan and chart. This is accepted as a known anch locally, and many yachts do not carry riding lights, so care is needed entering at night. Village with shops up steep hill. Beware Training Bank on W side of Swash Chan and give maximum room to large vessels in the Swash.

POOLE HARBOUR
Chart BA 2611 (Plan p46)

For double HW see next paragraph. LW +5.05 (2hr before LWD).
Entrance: MHWS 2.0 and 1.5; MLWS 0.3; MTL 1.5; MHWN 1.4 and 1.6; MLWN 1.1.
Bridge: MHWS 2.2 and 1.7; MLWS 0.4; MTL 1.5; MHWN 1.5 and 1.8; MLWN 1.0.
DS Handfast Point (Old Harry): E +5.00; W −1.00.
LW can be predicted with reasonable accuracy and is given in the appropriate publications. Local tide tables are available which also give the times of first and second HW daily. If no other information is available, LW at the entrance may be taken as that for the Needles: i.e. Dover −0.45.

When LW occurs between 2.30 and 8.30 am or pm (springs pattern) the highest HW will occur just under 5h after the preceding LW.

When LW occurs between 8.30 and 2.30 am or pm (neaps pattern) the highest HW will occur just over 3h before the succeeding LW. At neaps a first HW may occur 2½ to 4h after LW, or there may be a rise, a stand for 2h, and then a steady rise to Second HW.

HW Full and Change Poole Bridge occurs around 0930 GMT; lowest LW springs around 1730 GMT. HW at entrance approximately 0.35 before Poole Bridge, at Russell Quay approximately 0.40 after Poole Bridge, at Wareham Quay approximately 1.20 after Poole Bridge. Tidal streams run up to 3½kn at sp.
Bar The bar has 3.7m MLWS; 5.8m MHWS; 5.2 MHWN. Strong winds between S and E cause a heavy sea on the bar. The hr is usually easy of access and affords an excellent sailing ground for small craft.
Approach From W, keep Anvil Pt Lt Ho open until you pick up the Poole lts which must not be closed in. Avoid tide-rip off Handfast Pt on the ebb in a breeze. The bar should be approached from the Poole Fairway buoy from which a course may be steered to Bar Buoy No. 1. From Bournemouth, keep Swanage open of Ballard Pt to clear shoal patches 2.4m or more.
Entrance The entrance chan called the Swash lies between two banks of sand and is narrow. It is marked by Poole Bar G con buoy No. 1 (QG) to stb, No. 2 R can buoy (Fl R) to port; halfway up the chan No. 13 Hook Sands buoy (G con Fl G 3s) to stb and No. 12 buoy (R can Fl R 3s) to port.

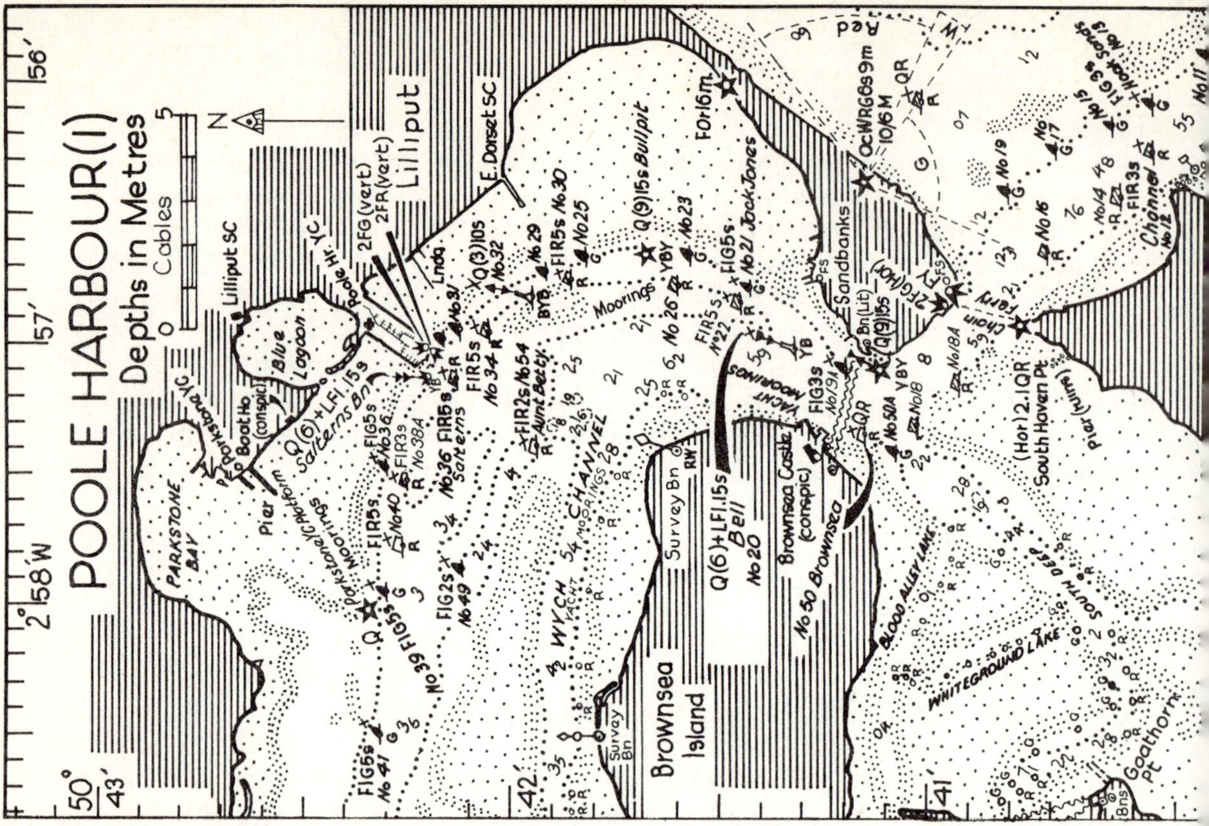

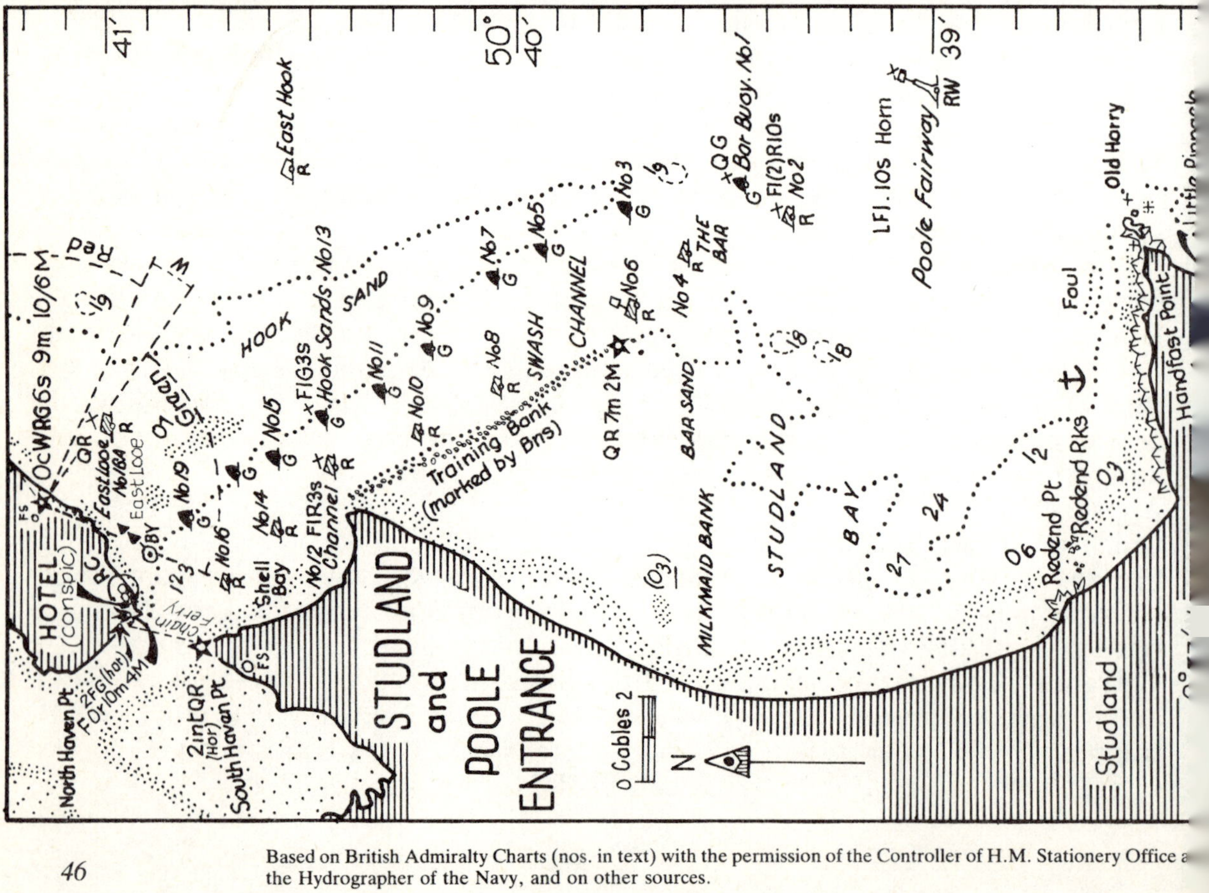

POOLE HARBOUR(I)

Depths in Metres

N

0 Cables 5

Lilliput SC

2FG(vert)
2FR(vert)
Lilliput

E.Dorset SC

Lnd⊙

Q(9)15s Bullpit

FO·16m

OcWRG6s9m
10/6M QR

Red

No11

No19

No16

No17

No14
No18

FIR3s
Channel
No12

Sandbanks

Q(9)15s
Bn(Lit)
2(9)(Hor)
FERRY

No8A

Blue Lagoon

Poole Hr.YC

Boot.Ho
(conspic)

Q(6)+LFI.15s
Salterns Bn

FI(5s
No36

FIR3s
No40

No38A

No36 FIR5s
Salterns

FIR5s
No34

FIR2s No54
Aunt Betty

Q(9)15s Jack Jones

No2 No23
YB Y

No29
FIR5s No30

No25

No26 No32
R Q(3)105

Moorings

FIR3s
No22

FIR3s
No19A
QR

Brownsea Castle
(conspic)

YACHT
MOORINGS

FIG3s
No19A

No50A

South Haven
Point

Pier (ruins)

PARKSTONE BAY

Parkstone YC (conspic)

Parkstone Moorings

Pier

Q.
No39 FIG5s
G

FIG3s
No49

No41
FIG6s

No20

Survey Bn
RW

WYCH CHANNEL

MOORINGS

No50
Brownsea

Q(6)+LFI.15s
No20 Bell

Brownsea Island

Survey Bn

BLOOD ALLEY LAKE

WHITEGROUND LAKE

Goathorn Pt

56' 57' 2°58'W 50°43' 42' 41'

STUDLAND and POOLE ENTRANCE

N

0 Cables 2

East Hook

HOOK SAND

FIG3s
Hook Sands·No13

No15

No11

No9

No10

No7

No8

No5

No6

SWASH CHANNEL

No3

No4
THE BAR

QG
Bar Buoy.No1
G FI(2)R10s
No2

LFI.10s Horn
Poole Fairway
RW

North Haven Pt

OcWRG6s 9m 10/6M

Red
L
T
W

QR

Eastlook

East look

No19

No16

No14

No6

FIR3s
Channel

Shell Bay

No2 FIR3s
Channel

Training Bank
(marked by Bns)

MILKMAID BANK

(O₃)

BAR SAND

STUDLAND BAY

QR 7m 2M

Redend Pt

Redend Rks

Foul

Old Harry

Little Pinnacle

Handfast Point

Studland

HOTEL
(conspic)

2FG(hor)
FOr10m4M

2intQR
(Hor)
South Haven Pt

41' 50°40' 39'

Based on British Admiralty Charts (nos. in text) with the permission of the Controller of H.M. Stationery Office and the Hydrographer of the Navy, and on other sources.

POOLE HARBOUR (2)

Depths in Metres

ased on British Admiralty Charts (nos. in text) with the permission of the Controller of H.M. Stationery Office and of
e Hydrographer of the Navy, and on other sources.

POOLE BAY

POOLE

Poole (Bscule)

Poole (Bscule)

HOLES

Landing

LB

FS

★ Fl(3)G5s

Oyster Bank Bn

Fl(6)+LFl5s

2FG

Cobbs Quay Marina

Customs

Causeway

Chy(99)

Chy(99)(conspic)

Rockley Bridge

Caravan site

Rockley Pt

Sandy cliffs

Rockley Jetty

Power (2m)

LYCHETT BAY

Slip

N

BW Bns

BW

Cablas

Kaysworth Pt

Giggar's I.

R.Frome 2

Bower Pt

Hyde's Quay

WAREHAM CHANNEL

Boundary Stone

Russet Quay

Gold Pt

Lake Pier

2. CHANNEL 13

Landing

Fl G10s No59

OYSTER BEDS

Yacht Mooring

No57

No55

Fl G5s

Hutchins No53

Patchins Pt

POOLE YC

Bns

2FG(Vert)

2FG

2FG(Vert)

MIDDLE MUD

Surrey Bn

Pottery Pier

Furzey I.

Landing (ruin)

Goathorn Pt

Chy

Green I.

SOUTH DEEP

WYCH 3 CHANNEL

UPPER

Long I.

Round I.

Pier Bn

WYCH LAKE

NEWTON BAY

ARNE BAY

Arne

Bn

CONTINUATION OF RIVER FROME

Wareham

R. Frome

Ridge Wharf Yacht Centre

Slip

Quay

Castle (ruin)

Redcliff Yacht Club

N

50° 43'

On the stb side of the chan are nine con buoys with uneven numbers. On the SW side of the chan a RW Dolphin 7.3m, Fl R 3s, marks the outer end of a Training Bank (itself marked by nine bns R can topmarks) awash at HW, which extends along the line of even-numbered R can buoys as far as S Haven Pt and 1 ca to W.

Caution The Sandbanks chain ferry operates continuously between Sandbanks and S Haven Pt between 0600 and 2330.

When within the entrance keep to stb side of centre chan rounding N Haven Dolphin Q (9) 15s, with a good clearance. Having left this well to stb the main chan to Poole Town turns abruptly to NE and is marked by lateral buoys.

Abreast the first R can buoy (No. 22) the main chan turns 010°, and 2½ ca further on is the Bullpit stb bn Q(9)15s, whence the chan turns N then 310° past Poole Hr YC marina and Salterns Bn Q(6) +L Fl 15s and so 280° to the G con Stakes stb buoy, Fl 5s.

Entrance *East Looe* has up to about 1.5m MLWS, variable. Used by local yachtsmen and fishermen but frequently shifts and should be used by strangers only with great caution and careful sounding, and never in heavy swell or fresh onshore winds. Vessels drawing 1.3m can enter on the flood at half-tide. From well offshore to the E steer for the East Looe R can buoy QR. Pass 20m N of it, then steer for the Haven Hotel giving a clearance of about 20m from the shore opposite the Hotel.

Wych Chan To proceed up hr by this chan leave the No. 20 S Card buoy (Q(6) +L Fl 15s) to stb and steer 340° to leave booms off the RW bn on Brownsea to port, when round in, 310°. Wych Chan has booms on both sides: G posts surmounted by G triangle to stb, R posts surmounted by R cans to port as far as Shepstall. Entrance to Wych marked by intersection stake 'Wych' to port and 'New Cut' to stb.

Middle Chan has been dredged and is boomed. It is lit at each end only. Leaving the No. 20 S Card buoy (Q(6) +L Fl 15s) to stb, steer N for 5 ca until No. 54 large R can buoy Fl (2) R 'Aunt Betty' is abeam to port, then alter course to 306° when Bullpit bn (Q(9)15s) will be on with a Y lt on shore astern 117° (ahead the Power Stn Chimneys provide a good mark in daylight), and so proceed to join Main Chan entrance to Middle Chan shown by the Diver buoy.

Anchorages (1) On rounding the N Haven dolphin anch in Brownsea Road between No. 20 buoy and houses on Brownsea in 0.6 to 2m, strong stream. Care should be taken to avoid fouling the telephone and power cables between North Haven and Brownsea Island. (2) In North Haven Lake, 1m, very crowded. (3) Anywhere in South Deep above the line of mooring buoys and below Ramshorn Lake. Good shelter off Goathorn Pt. When entering South Deep by the buoyed chan, give the port-hand buoy a good berth as it dries 0.6m just inside it. If making into South Deep on the flood, keep well in to Stoney Is shore as flood sets towards Brownsea; with the ebb tide bear more towards Brownsea Is. (4) In Wych Chan N of R W bn or higher up, the most sheltered berth in the hr in strong winds; also off Shipstal Pt. (5) Below Lake Pier in 1.8m but very congested.

Buoys in the hr are moored at the edge of channels and may dry out at LW: they should be given a wide berth. No anch is allowed in Main Chan between buoys No. 20 and No. 35.

Berthing (1) Poole Hr YC marina. Berths seldom available for visitors. (2) Poole Quay, very crowded. (3) Above Poole Br, West Quay marina and Cobbs Quay. Follow boomed chan. (4) R Frome at Ridge Wharf and Wareham Quay. See also entry for Studland Bay, above, as an alternative.

Poole Br only opens for pleasure craft at fixed times: weekdays 0930, 1130, 1430, 1630, 1830, 2130; Sat, Sun, Bk holidays 0730, 0930, 1130, 1330, 1530, 1730, 1930, 2130. All times liable to alteration.

Signals for Poole Lifting Bridge Lights visible by day as well as at night are shown from NE and SW trs. Flashing amber when bridge is being opened and vessels may proceed with caution; G when the bridge is fully lifted and the vessel may approach and pass through. R when vessels must not approach close to the bridge: if they do, it is not raised.

Landing at Lilliput YC, Parkstone YC, East Dorset SC, at piers on E side Sandbanks, at S Haven Pt, at Lake and at Poole Town.

Bus from Sandbanks to Poole or Bournemouth. Water and PO at Sandbanks. All facilities and stores at Poole, Sandbanks and Canford Cliffs. EC Wed.

Passage notes: Poole to Chichester

Between Poole and the West Solent the main dangers are Christchurch Ledge, which extends some 2¾M SE from Hengistbury Hd, and the Shingles Bank. Yachts wishing to make Christchurch Hr from the W may either pass around the outer end of the ledge SE of Christchurch Ledge buoy or cross the ledge near its centre. There are overfalls on the sp ebb.

DS Poole Bay (offshore): NE +5.30; SW −0.30. Inshore: E +5.00; W −1.15.

The E stream sets towards Christchurch Ledge and across the Shingles. The W stream sets well S of Durlston Hd and Anvil Pt. Streams are weak inside the line Handfast Pt to Hengistbury Hd and in Christchurch Bay, but they run strongly across Christchurch Ledge and the Shingles. Between Swanage, Poole and the Wight full allowance should be made for the stream which sets strongly into Poole Bay on the flood. In strong onshore winds with a heavy sea rolling in one may need to allow 20° or more for this effect.

Conspic landmarks are Southbourne water tr, three blocks of flats to the W and one ENE of Bournemouth Pier, and Poole power station chimney. Hengistbury Pt is easily distinguished by the lookout hut and FS on Warren Hill close to the W. When approaching the Solent from the W at night in good visibility, the R Fl Lts on the tall chimneys of the oil refinery at Fawley can be seen at a great distance low down on the horizon. This can be of assistance to the navigator if their existence is known, otherwise it can be most confusing.

Entry into the Solent can either be made close inshore of the Shingles Bk through the North Chan and thence past Hurst Pt, or outside the Shingles through the Needles Chan.

DS Needles entrance: E +5.30; W −0.30. DS North Chan, Hurst, Solent (with slight variations): E +5.00; W −1.00.

Needles entrance If fog should come down when approaching the entrance to the Needles Chan from W the posn of the Lt Ho may often be located by knowing that the fog usually lies lightly to the W of the entrance where the coast is low and that it hangs in a dark and heavy patch over the tops of the down which overlooks the Lt Ho, gradually becoming lighter in shade as the land breaks away towards St Catherine's Pt. By steering for this dark patch of fog the Lt Ho will be seen. If the wind should be fresh onshore do not close with the land unless certain of your posn. In fresh onshore weather less sea will be encountered halfway between the Bridge buoy and the Needles Lt than in the main chan between the Bridge and the SW Shingles buoy.

North entrance. North Hd G con buoy Fl (3) G 10s marks the N end of the Shingles Bk.

Spithead. DS on line Gilkicker Ft–Ryde Pier: E +4.15; W −1.25. S coast of Isle of Wight. DS: ENE +5.35; WSW −0.40.

St Catherine's Pt At night rounding the Pt from NW keep Needles W sector in view until St Catherine's Lt bears 064°, when round St Catherine's keeping S of its fixed R sector. St Catherine's race should be avoided. From St Catherine's Pt to Dunnose the streams are strong (up to 5kn at sp) and there is a race off Dunnose.

Anchorages (1) Bournemouth, between Bournemouth pier and Boscombe in offshore winds only. Land lee side of pier. (2) Milford. In offshore winds when awaiting stream to turn into Solent, good anch off Milford in North Channel close inshore. Do not forget to clear the Trap off Hurst when entering Solent. (3) Totland Bay. From E small craft may carry 1.8m over the Warden Ledge instead of rounding the buoy by keeping W of the line Hurst R Lt to the outer end of Totland pier. Good anch in settled weather. Bring up just W of pier opposite a wooden building with FS, inside the pilot boat moorings and clear of the small boat moorings. Buses to Freshwater and Yarmouth. (4) Hurst. A good quiet berth except in E winds may be found inside Hurst Pt off the High Lt. The rotary stream is apt to trip the anch. (5) Yarmouth. Small craft may anch on either side of the pier-head clear of the entrance. The stream runs hard. (6) Lymington Roads. Comfortable anch in fine weather and a good posn from which to start when bound W. A fresh wind against tide makes anch uncomfortable. (7) Beaulieu. Anch anywhere offshore clear of the flats between Lymington and Stansore Pt. (8) Stokes Bay. Good anch in calm weather and offshore winds; excellent holding, but beware of an obstruction, marked by 2 spher buoys, 7 ca W of Gilkicker Fort. (9) Osborne Bay. Good anch in 2½m, holding good, stream little felt. Anch clear of the remains of the causeway. If wind comes round to N cross to Stokes Bay or Southampton Water. (10) Off Wootton. Bottom not so good as Osborne Bay. With fresh wind against tide it can be uncomfortable. (11) Ryde, a poor anch for small craft. Anch clear W of steamer fairway to the pier-head. In any wind, Stokes Bay and Osborne Bay according to direction are preferable. (12) Seaview. Fine weather anch only. A continuous roll sometimes sets in here without any apparent cause. (13) Off Bembridge, a good anch with wind offshore. Get out at once if it comes on to blow from E. (14) Hayling Bay, a pleasant anch in settled weather with offshore wind, ¼M offshore, a little to E of the hotel and a conspic terrace. The bay lies recessed inside extensive banks to E and W over which the stream sets. If wind comes onshore at night care must be exercised.

CHRISTCHURCH   Chart BA 2219   (Plan p52)
Double HW: −2.00 and +1.20 at springs; +1.00 at neaps. DS: E +5.00; W −1.15
MHWS 1.8 (and 1.5); MLWS 0.4; MTL 1; MHWN 1.4; MLWN 0.6.
Tidal streams. Sp: flood 5h, stand 3½h, ebb 4h. Np: flood 5½h, stand 2¾h, ebb 4¼h.

At sp first HW is the higher followed by a moderate fall during the stand and a slight rise to second HW; the tide then ebbs strongly until LW. At high sp the second HW is only a pause in the ebb. At np there is a slow rise from LW through first HW, which is barely noticeable and is ignored in Admiralty Tide Tables, to second HW. The tide then ebbs but not so hard as at sp. Between sp and np the two HWs are equal in height.

The ebb is always fierce and entry should not be attempted more than ½h after second HW. Best times to enter: sp, 2h before first HW to second HW; np, during the stand. Inside the hr and in the Run, the ebb stream does not ease until 1½h of main flood outside has raised the level.

The hr formed by the estuary of the Rivers Avon and Stour, is largely unspoilt and is completely protected from the sea. It is safely accessible to vessels of 1.2m draft except in fresh winds between S and E. At springs vessels of 1.5m draft may enter.

Bar   Normally 0.3 to 0.6m but varies in position and depth. During the season it is clearly marked with about four pairs of buoys, and a spher RWVS fairway buoy further to seaward.

Approach   The entrance lies about ¾M NE of Hengistbury Hd. From W give groyne at Hengistbury Hd a berth of ¾M to clear Beerpan Rks and shallow part of Christchurch Ledge. No dangers from E.

Entrance   After crossing bar the chan turns to port and runs SW parallel to Haven Quay. On stb or N side is the Quay (with a cluster of houses on it), on the port or southern side is the submerged shingle and sand extension of Mudeford Sandspit on which stands Black House.

Boats may lie alongside the quay for short periods but the tide runs hard and it is not comfortable. Immediately past Haven Quay the chan bears sharply to port to run parallel to Mudeford Sandspit. Give first G spher buoy a wide berth to stb.

Inside the hr, the chan is stable and buoyed. Halfway to Christchurch there is a

Christchurch
Depths in Metres

Cables

Barton on Sea

Highcliffe

Castle

Groynes & Bns

Christchurch Airfield

Somerford

Mudeford

Stanpit

Christchurch

Yachtyards

Clay Pool

Stanpit Marsh

Grimbury Pt & Marsh

R Avon

Wick

R Stour

(40) Tr.
(conspic)

Quay

SC

Landing stones & Bns

The Flats

Blackberry Point

Buoyed Channel

Christchurch Harbour

Warren Hill

Warren Bight

Hengistbury Hd.

Post

FS
(conspic)

Hut

Bn

Beerpan Rks

Foul Ground

Sewers

BY

BY

BY

Christchurch Bay

Christchurch Ledge

Buoyed Channel

The Run

Groynes

N

3_7

4

5_5

4

4

6_4

5_2

4_3

3_4

4_3

3

2_7

4_3

3_1

4_9

4

4

2_7

2_7

2_1

0_9

2_1

0_9

0_7

0_1

0_8

0_4

0_9

1_6

0_8

0_6

0_6

7

0_9

7_9

4_6

4

4_6

1_1

1_1

2_3

3_8

3_8

7

Bn

Based on British Admiralty Charts (nos. in text) with the permission of the Controller of H.M. Stationery Office and the Hydrographer of the Navy, and on other sources.

Keyhaven

Hawkers Lake

○Bn

Pennington Spit

43'

Keyhaven Lake

06

Bns ○○

○4 ✕ Bn.
○

○5

○2 Ldg line 66
287°

○4

15

Mount Lake

37
22
11

Rabbit Pt

Low Light
15m 14M

Iso 4 S

Hurst Road
W

High Light (conspic)
Iso WR 6sec 23m 14-11 M

18₄

N

Hurst Fort

○
Hurst Pt

White

The Trap   White

Keyhaven
Depths in Metres

0 Cables   2   4

10₇
✕

042° White

VQ(3)5s

NE Shingles

Ldg Lts 042°

BYB

2₁

50°
42'

1°33'

34'

d on British Admiralty Charts (nos. in text) with the permission of the Controller of H.M. Stationery Office and of Hydrographer of the Navy, and on other sources.

dredged section only 9m wide, and boats drawing 1.2m should keep to the middle. It is well marked. Beware fishermen shooting salmon nets (Mon to Fri in season only) from punts in the Run.

Berthing (1) In reach running SSW from Haven Quay between Black House and concrete jetty, 1.5 to 1.8m on edge of fairway. Use two anchors to restrict swing. (2) In Lob's Hole at W end of reach running W from concrete jetty above moorings. (3) The quietest anch (0.9m) is in unmarked chan close to N side of Hengistbury Hd. Enter from Lob's Hole and sound carefully. (4) Further up at SE end of Steep Bank on W side immediately below port-hand moorings. (5) In Clay Pool at junction of Avon and Stour. (6) Visitors' mooring at Christchurch SC. (7) In River Avon, quiet bankside berths on application to Christchurch Marine, G. Elkins or Purbrook Rossiter.

Land at Haven Quay, ½M to bus for Christchurch; cafe on Mudeford Sandspit, tel, ferry to Christchurch from concrete jetty; at Christchurch SC near Priory, with permission. Provisions and services at Christchurch town. Services, repairs, slip, laying up, water, chandlery at Purbrook Rossiter. Fuel and water at jetty next to Christchurch SC. Crane and laying up at G. Elkins. Rly Christchurch. Frequent buses to Bournemouth. PO Christchurch and Mudeford. EC Wed.

KEYHAVEN   Chart BA 2219   (Plan p53)

Bar Constantly changing. Strangers should not attempt the entrance in strong E winds. Tide remains high for 3h after HW Hurst Pt.

Approach From E, keep Hurst Low Lt open twice its own width S of High Lt. From W, give the Trap off S side of Hurst Castle a berth of 1½ ca.

Entrance When approximately E of the High Lt bring the 2 ldg bns (X topmarks) in line 287°. These marks give the best line of approach, but the chan is ill-defined. A shingle spit forms the port side of the entrance and the point of the spit was in 1980 about 1 ca NW of a conspic B wooden structure which is the Hurst Castle SC starting platform. (The shingle spit is extending year by year.) There is one G buoy outside the entrance and close inside is the first of a number of G spher buoys all of which are stb marks. There are no port-hand marks in the river, and the only other stb mark (G spher) is at the junction of Long Reach and Short Reach. The line of private moorings indicates the best water in Long Reach.

Berthing The river is congested with private moorings, but space for anch may be found in the bay formed by the extending shingle spit on the port side of the entrance. Buoy the anch. Tel cables are laid between Hurst and Keyhaven. Land at Keyhaven hard. Grocer, PO, inn at Keyhaven. EC Thursday. Shops and hotels at Milford, 1M from Keyhaven. Buses to Lymington and Bournemouth.

LYMINGTON   Chart BA 2040   (Plan p56)

HW −0.25 and +1.15 springs; +0.35 neaps. DS: E +4.30; W −1.00.
MHWS 3.0 and 2.9; MLWS 0.5; MTL 1.8; MHWN 2.6; MLWN 1.3.
The river is accessible at all states of tide.

Approach Keep Hurst Low Lt fully twice its own width open S of the High Lt to clear the banks at LW between Hurst and Pitts Deep. Warden Ledge buoy in line with Needles Lt Ho leads to Jack-in-the-Basket, a conspic post with barrel on the end of the mud at the W corner of entrance. By day, the RLYC starting platform on the E corner of the entrance is the most conspic mark. Thence the river is clearly marked.

Entrance All lit river marks operate throughout the year. The lights are Fl R 2s to port and Fl G 2s to stb. In the reach between Tar Barrel and Cocked Hat Bns are two pairs of ldg bns whose purpose is to assist ferries in passing each other: they are not channel marks. The channel bns have topmarks G N cone to stb, R truncated cone to port. The two bns at Harpers Post mark the entrance to the Lymington Yacht Marina.

Berthing Anch in the hr is prohibited. Moorings are available to visitors opposite the Town Quay immediately below the rly br. These dry at LWS but bottom is soft and yachts lie safely. There are a few berths alongside the pontoon at the Town Quay. Marinas: Lymington Marina (Berthon) up to 24m LOA, 2.5m draft (tel Lymington (0590) 3312); Lymington Yacht Haven up to 2.5m (tel Lymington 5999); Town Quay up to 9.1m, not bookable.

YARMOUTH I.o.W. Chart BA 2040 (Plan p58)

HW −0.35 and +1.20 springs; +0.35 neaps. DS: E +5.05; W −1.00.
MHWS 3.1 and 2.8; MLWS 0.6; MTL 2.0; MHWN 2.5; MLWN 1.4.

Tidal streams The Solent stream runs hard outside across the outer half of the pier, but is not felt close to the entrance to the hr where the hr stream takes over. The hr affords complete shelter and comfortable berths and is dredged to between 1.8 and 2.4m. There are 50 piles in five mooring lines with a chan at the NW end.

Owing to increased popularity, the hr sometimes has to be closed and owners of yachts of more than 15m length or 4.2m beam or 2.5m draft are asked to give notice of arrival to the HM (tel Yarmouth (0983 760) 300).

Approach From W: leaving Bank Rk buoy to stb a course may be steered for the pier towards a point about one-third of its length from the pier-head. When the hr ldg marks, two BW diamonds, come into line 187° steer on them.

Entrance Has 2.1m on the ldg line. There is a tide gauge on the end of the jetty which should be read on entering, and another on the dolphin at the breakwater for use when leaving. If beating into the hr near HW the diamonds may be opened somewhat on either side, but it is not advisable to stand in to E under N wall of the castle, as the wind is sure to baffle or fail.

The ldg marks are lit at night. Front 2 FG, rear FG, and on the SW corner of quay a F lt shows W towards the hr, R towards the quay. There are 2 FR lts on the end of the steamer jetty.

Berthing From near the entrance proceed to tie up fore and aft between piles as directed by the HM. Moor to rings provided, use plenty of fenders. A steel training wall extends NNW from the Yarmouth SC clubhouse on the bridge.

Lymington River
Depths in Metres

O Cables   3   6

Mont

Chy

Town Quay

Pile

O3

FSO

Marina

2FG(vert)

DnB

FR

Pontoon

Horn Reach

Ferry Bn

Nash Pt

FSO

Pontoon

Lymington

FR

H M

N

Mag

FS

Yacht Haven

QR

FlG2s

G O2

Post

FlR2s

Bns BW

FlG2s

Pile

O·O

R

FlG2s

G

Pylewell Lake

Bn

G

5

4

FlR 2s

FlG 2s

Bns RW

4

FlG 2s

G

Bn O

R

Lymington River

Long Reach

Bn O·G

·6

FlG2s No3

Sewer Outfall

Oxey Lake

Bn O·8

R

G

FlR2s

No2

FlG2s No1

Bn

Stag

R

G

Y

·6

Jack in the Basket

Bn

R

Fl R 2s

Ldg Lts 318°30'

Oxey Marsh

O·2

3·9

O·5

2·3

Bn

O

1°·31'

32'

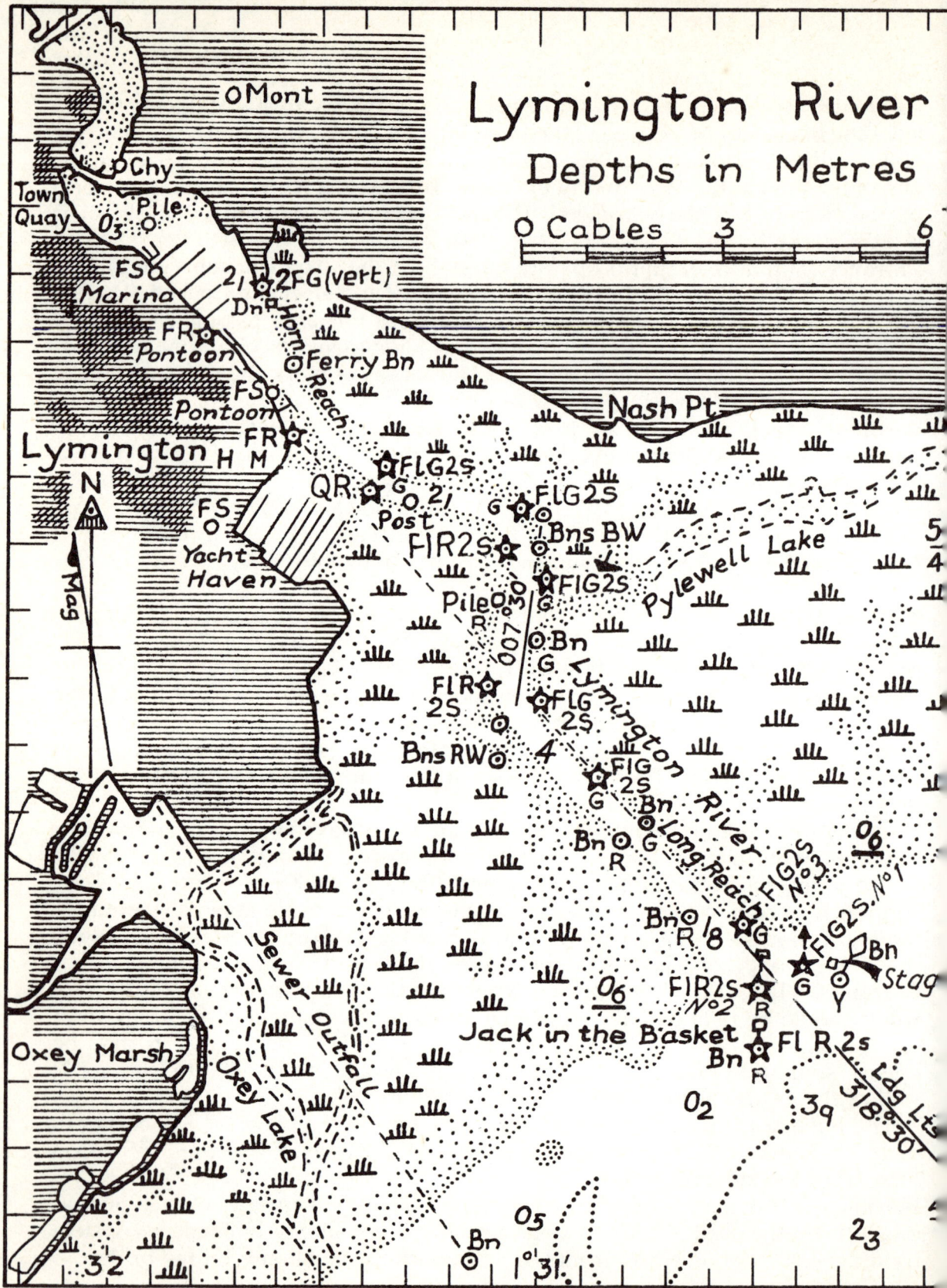

Based on British Admiralty Charts (nos. in text) with the permission of the Controller of H.M. Stationery Office and the Hydrographer of the Navy, and on other sources.

There is a LW landing stage alongside the bridge, and a good hard at W end of hr for those who wish to land on that sandy shore. The ebb runs hard. Two scrubbing berths inside breakwater, at entrance and halfway along. It is a pleasant trip up the river on the flood by dinghy. The road bridge opens on request and gives access to the upper reaches of the river.

Outside, anch in line with the pier-head in 3½m on the W side, or in 2m on the E side. Keep clear of steamer fairway and of moorings. Further out there is 5m and more. Land at pier-head or row to the quay. When it blows, the anch to E of Jack-in-the-Basket off Lymington is more comfortable except in S winds than lying outside the hr.

Landing at the Town Quay. All facilities. Water at the quay; water, fuel and engine repairs at New Quay. Hard. Bus to Freshwater, Cowes. Ferry to Lymington. Customs House above HM office near ferry slipway, entrance in Quay St. Berth alongside New Quay. EC Wed.

NEWTOWN RIVER I.o.W.   Chart BA 2040   (Plan p59)
HW −0.20 sp; +0.40 np.   MHWS 3.1; MHWN 2.1.   DS: E +5.00; W −1.00.
Bar   The bar is situated a few yards SW of the R spher Bar buoy and has 1.5m MLWS. There is 1.8 to 3.6m in the narrow chan inside the buoy.
Approach   The entrance lies 1½M W of Salt Mead G con buoy and ¾M E of Hamstead Ledge G con buoy. From E, Yarmouth Pier open of Hamstead Pt carries 3½m. Steer in leaving Bar buoy to port. Bring ldg marks in line: a 'Y' bn off Fishhouse Pt in line with a W bn with a W disc on Fishhouse Pt bearing 127°. Once past the stb hand buoy almost opposite the RW 'Y' bn steer 159° and leave perches to port.

Inside the entrance there are many perches, and strangers should sound continuously. Off Clamerkin Lake keep to the E side to avoid a gravel spit off the W shore marked by three perches.
Berthing   The usual anch is between the entrance to Clamerkin Lake to the N, and the noticeboard at the junction of Shalfleet Creek and Western Haven to the S. There are moorings laid in this creek in 1.8m. The other anch is in Clamerkin Lake from the entrance as far as the two noticeboards on either side of the chan. The whole peninsula ending at Fishhouse Pt is now a nature reserve, and yachtsmen are asked not to land there in April, May or June. Notices are displayed.

There are oyster beds beyond the noticeboards and anch is prohibited. A fresh breeze from SW blows hard at the anch. Strong SW winds will hold the tide several feet above ordinary LW level and NE winds may lower the level below chart datum.

Excursions may be made by dinghy to Newtown, up Clamerkin Lake, Western Haven and Causeway Lake. At HW the Yarmouth road may be reached in the dinghy, 2M by the W Haven, whence 3M to Yarmouth.

Up Shalfleet Lake there is a public landing whence a footpath leads to the main road. Causeway Lake leads S of Newtown to the road bridge below the Old

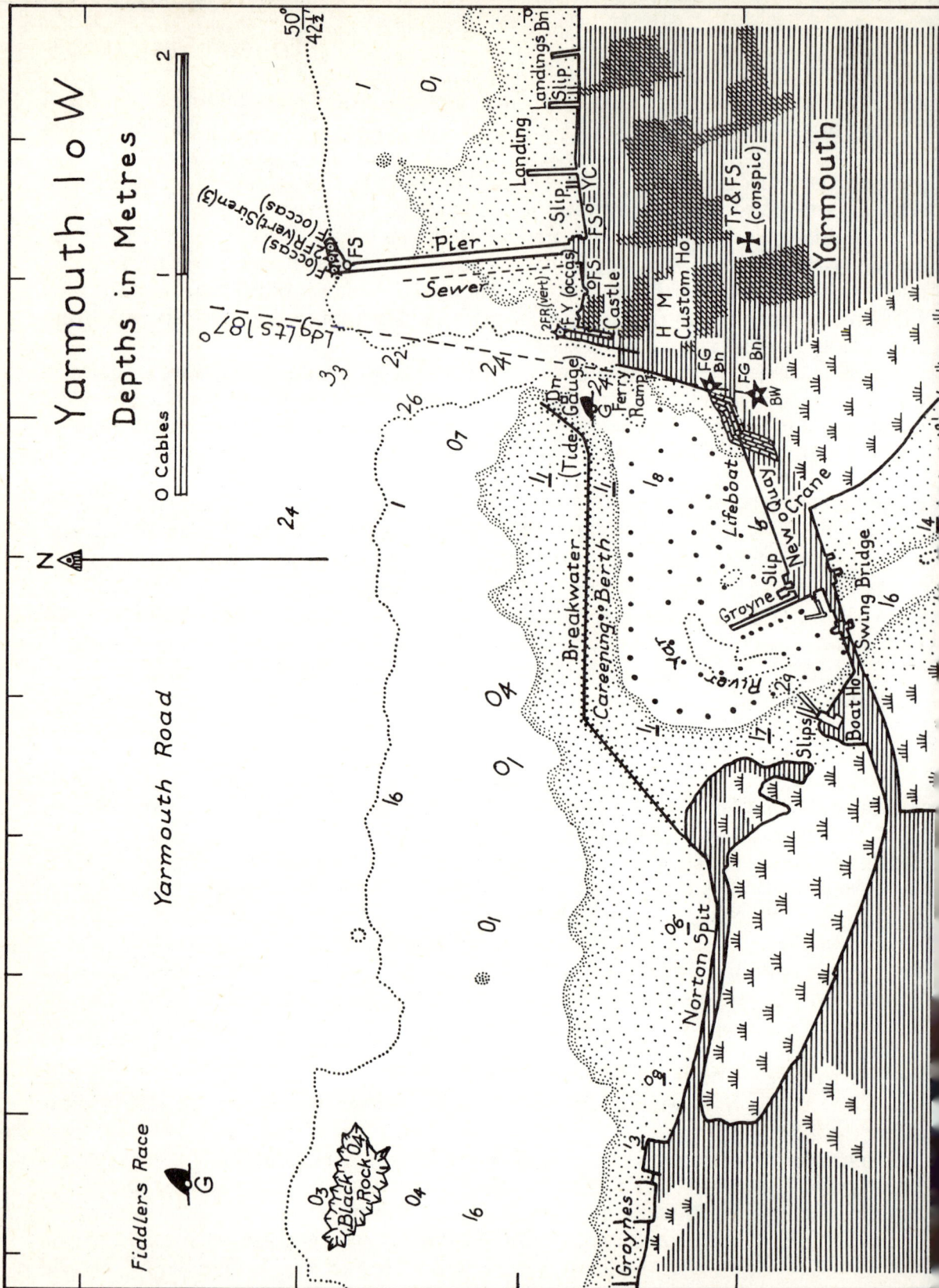

Yarmouth IoW

Depths in Metres

N

Fiddlers Race

Yarmouth Road

Black Rock

Groynes

Norton Spit

Breakwater

Careening Berth

Dn (Tide Gauge)

Ferry Ramp

Castle

2FV (occas)
2FR (vert)

Custom Ho

H M

Pier

Sewer

FS

FGd(occas) FR(vert) Suen(3) (occas)

FS

Slip

FS° = YC

O FS

Landing

Landings Bn

Slip

Tr & FS (conspic)

Yarmouth

FG Bn

FG Bn

BW

Lifeboat

New Crane

Quay

Groyne Slip

River Yar

Swing Bridge

Boat Ho

Slips

0 Cables   1   2

Based on British Admiralty Charts (nos. in text) with the permission of the Controller of H.M. Stationery Office and the Hydrographer of the Navy, and on other sources.

Wootton Creek
Depths in Metres

0 Cables 3 6

N

King's Quay Cr

FSo

Wootton Rks ✳ (2̲1̲)

(2̲7̲)

1̲4

FSo
Wootton Pt

Bn o

QG
No3 ☆

2

2

QYC

Fishbourne

Wootton Creek

Moorings

Moorings

Wootton Bridge

Wharf 1°01' 13'

2̲2 ⚓

Q1M
04 BY

Wooton Bn

3̲2

Wooton Rocks

1̲3

No1 ☆ 1̲6
Fl G 3s

No2 ☆
Fl(2)G 5s 2̲

2

50°
44'

Turret
(conspic)
✝

Quarr Abbey
(ruins)

1̲4

1'4'

1'2'

Newtown
Depths in Metres

0 Cables 3 5 7

N

14̲6 Newtown R

1̲4 07 R

Newtown Gravel
Banks 0̲6

1̲3 oPost

RW
Bn

Bn
▲
o
RW 040
FS

Shepherds
Hill

Y.Bns
o o
G RWoBW

amstead Pt

Fishhouse Pt
NB
Oysters

Spur Lake

Clamerkin Lake

Oyster
Beds

Lower
Hamstead

N Quay

NB o

Newtown
✝

Oysters

Western Haven

Shalfleet Lake

Causeway Lake

50°
43'

25' 1°01' 24' 23'

---

ed on British Admiralty Charts (nos. in text) with the permission of the Controller of H.M. Stationery Office and of
Hydrographer of the Navy, and on other sources.

59

Town Hall. There is a public landing at Newtown. Clamerkin leads to the road to Cowes, 5½M from the bridge. Water and stores at Lower Hampstead Farm.

BEAULIEU RIVER Chart BA 2040 (Plan p61)

HW +0.05 sp; +0.35 np. MHWS 3.4; MHWN 2.7. DS off Egypt Pt: W −0.55; E +5.00.

Note: Beaulieu is pronounced 'Bewly'.

Bar The depth and position of the best water is slightly E of the ldg line. Least depth on the bar at MLWS is usually 1.2m slightly to E of ldg line. Inside the entrance there is from 2½ to 7m except towards Needs Oar Pt where there are 1.5m patches with a further patch 2 ca short of Gins Farm. 2.1m least water to Gilbury Hard, thence 1.2m patches towards Buckler's Hard.

Approach and entrance Give the shore a berth of 3 ca S off Stansore, Stone and Needs Oar Pts. When near East Lepe buoy, a terrace of cottages will be seen to N and a white boathouse on the shore below. The boathouse on with the W-most house of the terrace leads towards the entrance. Ldg marks (339°): rear, a triangle over square topmark is about 1 ca W of the row of cottages, and stands in trees; front, R with W topmark, stands in the water 2½ ca from the shore mark. Close W of the seaward ldg mark and 90m S is a R dolphin marking the E end of Beaulieu Spit. When closing the shore, keep the ldg marks in line until about 1 ca seaward of Beaulieu Spit dolphin, thence keep slightly to E of the line leaving the dolphin about 20m to port. At night the dolphin flashes QR over an arc of 120° centred on 339°. Entrance piles have reflectors, R to port, W to stb.

Follow the pile bns to the W: port hand bns R with R can topmarks, stb hand bns G with G cone topmarks. Upriver the chan is marked with bns and withies; the latter dry at LW. Do not cut corners without local knowledge.

Needs Oar Swatch On a sufficient rise of tide, small craft can enter or leave by the buoyed Swatch to E of Needs Oar Pt. Local knowledge is desirable.

Berthing Anch in the first reach up to Needs Oar Pt. Above this consult the HM (tel Buckler's Hard (059 063) 200). There is a 100 berth marina just upriver from Buckler's Hard, dredged to 2m MLWS, and pile moorings for visitors at Buckler's Hard for up to 100 vessels. Anch prohibited 1M either side of Buckler's Hard. All vessels are requested to keep the fairway clear and there is a 5kn speed limit.

From Buckler's Hard there is a footpath over the fields to Beaulieu Abbey (2M). Landing (1) at the entrance on the beach near the boathouse; (2) at RSYC pontoon at Gin's Farm; (3) at Buckler's Hard. Rly at Brockenhurst, 8M: PO Beaulieu. Buckler's Hard has hotel, restaurant, tel, shop with provisions, maritime museum, water and fuel at jetty, hard, boatyard with lift and all facilities.

COWES, I.o.W. Chart BA 2793 (Plan p63)

HW +0.30. DS: E +4.35; W −1.15.
MHWS 4.2, MLWS 0.6; MTL 2.5; MHWN 3.5; MLWN 1.7.
The hr is available at all states of tide.

Beaulieu River

Depths in Metres

N

Cables 0 5 10

Brick Works

Keeping Marsh

Yacht Harbour

Piles

Quay

Bucklers Hard

Gilbury Hard

Pier

Jetty

Slip (private)

Jetty

YC

Gins Farm Landing

Beaulieu River

Exbury Pt

Quay

Boat Ho (conspic)

Hard

Bn

Bns

Groynes

Stone Pt

QR

Needs Ore Pt

(marked by beacons)

Beaulieu Spit

Bn QR

339°

Arc of visibility

Anchoring prohibited

East Lepe
Fl(2)R10s
Bell(2)20s

Lepe Middle

Warren Flat

Old CG Cottages (conspic)

Great Marsh

Groynes FSo

48' 50 47 46'
21'
22'
23'
24'
25'
26'

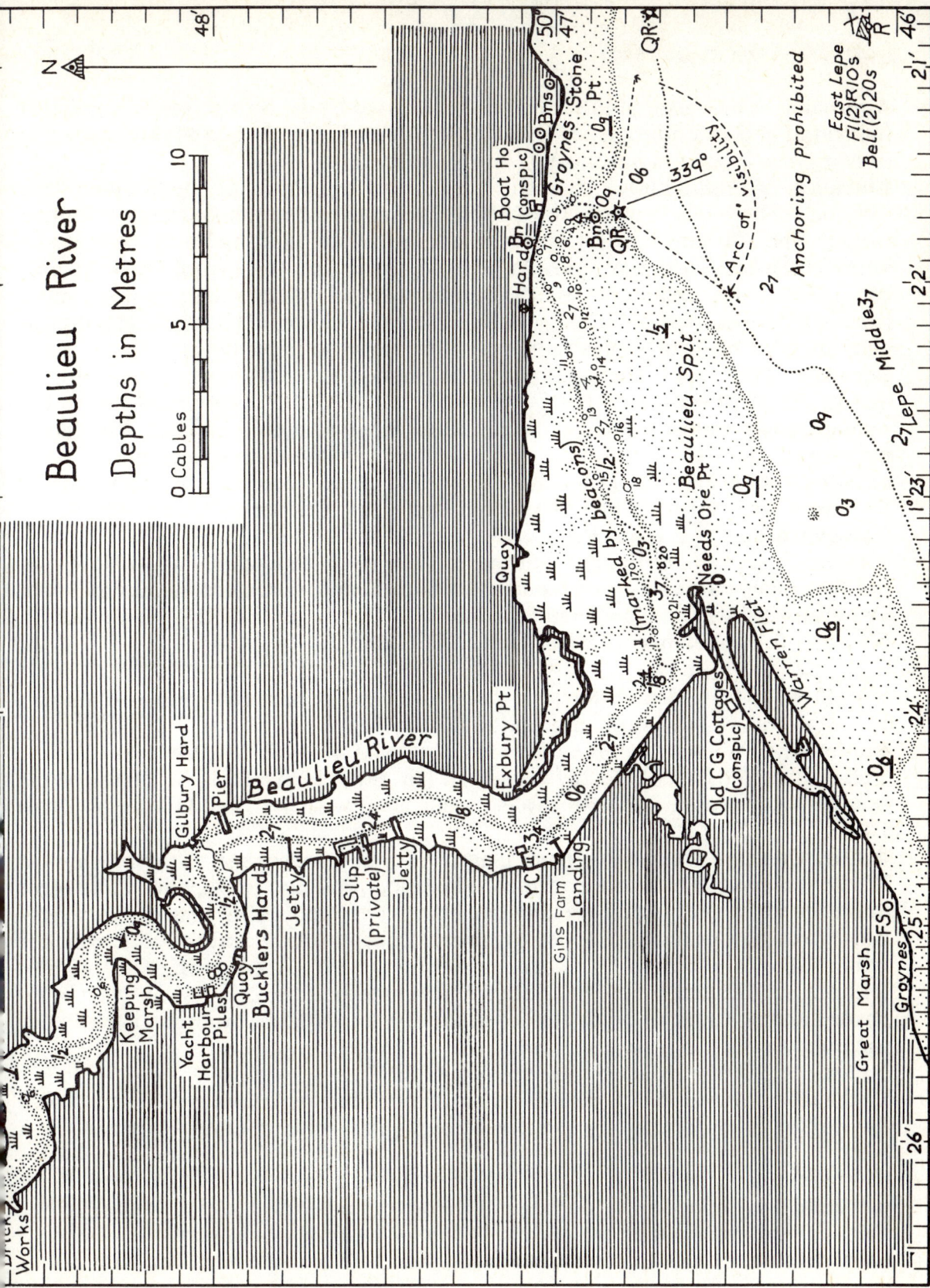

d on British Admiralty Charts (nos. in text) with the permission of the Controller of H.M. Stationery Office and of
Hydrographer of the Navy, and on other sources.

Approach   The E side of the entrance is occupied by the Shrape mud, covered at half-flood and extending from Old Castle Pt and E Cowes across the hr leaving only a narrow chan along the W Cowes shore.

Entrance   A R can buoy marks the E side, and a G con buoy the W side of the entrance. There is a least depth of about 2½m in the channel. Beware of floating bridge. The ebb runs hardest on the E side below the floating bridge, but at and above it hardest on the W side. At night ldg lts in line 164°: front Iso W 2s 6M, rear Iso R 2s 3M. When the W Lt is abeam, a useful mark to steer on is the more S set of 2 FR Lts (vert) on Trinity House Wharf (E Cowes). There is a Hovercraft chan marked by orange plastic buoys at the extreme E of the hr.

Berthing   (1) Cowes Yacht Haven on stb hand. Visitors' berths along outside and inside of breakwater. Tel Cowes (098 382) 5724. (2) About ¼M above the public bridge opposite the National Sailing Centre; public hard at Whitegates between Clark's and National Sailing Centre. (3) Public moorings on stb hand entering. (4) Near the Folly Inn 1.8m. (5) Wight Marina. Visitors usually accommodated up to 27m LOA, 2.5m draft: tel Newport (098 381) 3929. (6) Cowes Marina on E bank ½M above Floating Bridge: tel Cowes 3983.

Dinghies should not be left unattended. The river is navigable up to Newport, but the upper part dries. All facilities at both E and W Cowes. Water at Town Quay and Whitegates pontoon. Steamers to Southampton. BR hovercraft to Portsmouth connecting with fast trains. EC Wed.

SOUTHAMPTON WATER   Chart BA 1905   (Plan p64)

HW Calshot +0.40; Southampton +0.00.
Calshot: MHWS 4.4; MLWS 0.6; MTL 2.6; MHWN 3.7; MLWN 1.8

Tides   The tide flows 1½ to 2h, slacks 1 to 1½h, flows 3⅓h to 1st HW, (the only one now shown in Admiralty Tide Tables), ebbs 1h, flows 1¼h to 2nd HW, ebbs 3¼h to LW.

Ashlett Creek   Lies ¾M 244° from Hamble Pt buoy, very close to the Fawley Oil Wharf and has 0.3m on the bar and 1.8m inside. Pass the Fawley buoy and steer in on the ldg marks (small rectangular boards) erected on the marsh grass. RW can buoys to port and BW spher to stb mark the entrance and the chan which is both shallow and narrow. The creek dries out at LW. All moorings are private. Visitors may anchor below the notice board provided they do not obstruct main chan. Land at Public Quay at HW or at the LW hard, 0.3m. Soft mud berths near the quay to port. All stores. Fawley ½M. EC Wed.

Netley   Anch outside club moorings in about 2m.

Hythe Pier   Anch S of pier-head in about 2m. Ferry every ½h to Town Quay, Southampton. PO, tel. Steps at end and middle of pier. Hythe SC S of pier.

Southampton *River Test*. Anch off, out of the fairway in 2 to 3½m N of pier-head, or opposite, on the edge of the Gymp in 4.5m. Land (1) at the Royal Pier; (2) at Town Quay, crowded with buoys. See note below.

Southampton, River Itchen   The mud dries well outside the bns with spher

Cowes Roads

Arc of visibility

19' 1°18' 17'

X Q
BY

X VQ
Prince Consort
BY

Ldg Lts 164°

Fl Y 2s
Trinity House

Fl R 5s

Egypt Pt
Fl.10s8m18M

Royal Yacht Squadron
Tr & FS
Osborne Court (conspic)

Custom Ho
FS
FS

West Cowes

Iso 2s 3m 6M

Iso R 2s 5m 3M
HM

N°3

N°6
R

QR 3M
Breakwater

E Cowes Pt

East Cowes

6-2FG(vert)

Cowes Yacht Haven

Spire
Cowes Corinthian YC

QR

Hovercraft Slip
2FR(vert)
CAR FERRY SLIP
2FR(vert)
Trinity Wharf

Hovercraft Terminal
Landing
Thetis Whf
Crane (Conspic)

Slip
Falcon yard British Hovercraft Co
Crane
Crane
East Cowes SC
Ramp
Slips

N
↑

Slip
Slip

2FG(vert)

National Sailing Centre

Slip
Slip

2FR(vert)
2FR(vert)

Slip
COWES MARINA

2FR(vert)

Slip

Folly Pt
2FR
FS
QG
S Folly
stakes

Medway Queen Marina

Posts

2FG(vert)
2FG(vert)
FS
Causeway
Tr
(3.5m)
Steps Hard
FS
Tr

Sewage Works

Pump Ho
Tr

50° 45'

50° 43'

2FR(vert)
2FR(vert)

2FG(vert)
Medina Coal Wharf
Jetty
Slip
Oil Tanks
Gas Holders
2FR(vert)
chy
Kingston Quay
Pylon
Pylon
(3.5m)
2-2FR(vert)
Chy (Power Stn)
Southern Electricity Jetty

50° 45'

COWES
&
R. MEDINA
Depths in Metres

R. MEDINA
Depths in Metres

Cables

Cables

2FG(vert)

Ldg Lts 192°15'

FR 7m 2M
FR 11m 2M
Crane
Seaclose Whf
Timber Whf
Hard
Newport
HM
1°17'
Spire

VQ(3)5s
Bn
Medham
MOORING PILES

Folly Works

2FG(vert)
2FR(vert)
Folly Inn
FS
Folly Pt
2FR(vert)

44'

1°18' 17'

SOUTHAMPTON WATER

Depths in Metres

5 Cables 0 Mile 1

Northam Br
Chy
Millstone Pt
FS
Bn
Merry Oak
R Itchen
Southampton
Spire
Post House Hotel (conspic)
Royal Pier
Hovercraft Terminal
FSO (customs)(conspic)
Vane (conspic)
Woolston
Itchen
2FG (vert)
OcR5s
FG3s
Chy
2FR(vert)
Eastern Dks
Weston Jetty (Pontoons)
2FG (vert)
FS
Ocean Dock
Empress Dock
Marchwood
Bn No 4
FS
2FG
FS
QR
R Gymp
2FR (vert)
AFG (vert)
Swinging Ground No 1
Oc4s
Bn
TV Aerial
Bn
Landing
Bn Y
Building (conspic)(70)
Bursledon
Hard
FI(2)R10s
53
Hythe Knock
Fl R3s
FI G(3)15s
Weston Shelf
2FR (vert)
Moorhead
Bn
Slip
FS (Netley Castle)
Netley
Hard
Netley Hard
FS
Badnam Creek
R Hamble
QG
Wooded
52
Chy (79)
2FR (vert)
R Test
FI G7s
NW Netley
OcR4s
Deans Elbow
FI G3s
Netley
Mont
Netley Great Dome
Mercury Yacht Harbour (Marked by Red Lts)
FS
No 1
Hotel (conspic)
FSO
Hythe
FS
Hythe Pier
2FR (vert)
Bn
Aero RC O
FSo
FI(3)G10s
Hound
FI(2)R4s
Lains Lake
After Barn
FI Y 6s 17m 5M
Hard
Port Hamble (Marked by Red Lts)
Hamble
Red Roof (conspic)
FR
Hamble SC
Hard
Rising Sun Bn IsoG6s
Warsash
Deans Lake
Fl 2s14m3M
Fl 2s14m3M
1QG10s
Greenland
QR
Hamble Pt Marina (Marked by Red Lights)
Bns
FR
FS
QG (Warsash YC) Shore Bn
50°
51
Union Carbide Works
Bn
Bns
FI R3s
Cadland
R 6-2FG (vert)
Hamble Bn
(Hamble Bn)
2FR(vert)
Bn
Warsash Jetty
Chy
School of Navigation
International Synthetic Rubber
Chy
24
Bns
Bn
2FR(vert)
Cadland Quay
Cathead (Mar-Oct)
OC(2)R12s
Bn No 6
Warsash Bn
Monsanto Chemical Works
Reservoir
Bn
2FR(vert)
Bn
Spit Pile
Hamble Point
Q(6)+LFl.15s
50°
N
Esso Petroleum Refinery
(101)
QR Lts
Chy
2FR(vert)
Bell(2)20s
Fawley
Lt 326° 01
Lt Lts 327°
Bald Head
Flare(101)
Flare(101)
FS
Posts
254°
Bns Piles
345°
Spit
50'
Tr & FS
Fawley
FSo
Hard
254°
QG Bell.15s
Hook
Tr (conspic)(34)(Red Lt)
Ashlett
Bns
Posts (Mar-Oct) Marn
FI R3s
Coronation
FI Y5s
FI G3s (occas)
Fl(2)R5s (occas)
Fl(3)R7s (occas)
QR (occas)
FR
Fl(2)R4s
Black Jack
49'
Power Stn
Chy (198)(conspic) (QR Lt)
Q (occas)
QR (occas)
Bns
1QR10
Castle Point
Ra Bn
FSo

Based on British Admiralty Charts (nos. in text) with the permission of the Controller of H.M. Stationery Office and the Hydrographer of the Navy, and on other sources.

topmarks on the E bank, which should be given a wide berth. Riding lt essential.
Note Both River Test and River Itchen are commercialised and it is inadvisable
for strangers to use them, but the Itchen has some yards for small boats.

HAMBLE

Chart BA 1905 (Plan p67)

HW +0.30 MHWS (Calshot Cas.), 4.4. MHWN 3.7; MTL 2.6.
DS along N shore, off Hillhead: E +2.30; W −2.00. Along NW side of Bramble
bank: NE +4.30; SW −0.45.

Tides The tide flows for 1½ to 2h, slacks 1 to 1½h, flows 3½h to 1st HW, ebbs 1h,
flows 1¼h to 2nd HW, ebbs 3½h.

Bar 2.2m about 1 ca N of Hamble Spit buoy. The river has 3.6m up to Hamble
Village, 2.1m to Burlesdon Bridge; R perch bns with topmarks mark port and
similar G bns stb hand, standing on LW line. There are visitors' berths between
piles off Port Hamble and Warsash but the number is very small compared with
the demand.

Approach From abreast Calshot Castle, leave the Bald Head buoy to stb.
Thence steer for the Hamble Pt buoy, S Card Q(6) +L Fl 15s which should be
left 50m to port. From this posn steer 345° and proceed between stb and port bns
to bn No. 10. Then leave Warsash Jetty (2 FG vert) to stb. Above the pier are
numerous booms and bns on either side, many mooring buoys, and the RTYC
pier FG lt which is left to stb. Beware the projecting spit on the E side of the chan
between Mercury YH and Crableck bn. When approaching and rounding the
right-angle corner at Swanick Shore, keep over to the E side to avoid the mud
spit (post) on the W Pt which dries.

At night The centre of entrance abreast the Hamble Pt Lt bears 351° from
Calshot Castle. From the W, leave Hamble Pt buoy to port and proceed as
above. Ldg Lts 345°: rear QR, front Oc (2) R 12s to bn No. 4, thence 024°, rear
Iso G6s, front QG, to Warsash jetty 2 FG vert. Great care is necessary,
especially in the reach between No. 6 bn (port) and Warsash Jetty as the chan
winds. Above Warsash some piles are lit, QR or QG as appropriate. All piles
have R or G reflectors clearly visible by hand torch. FR lts on marinas and club
pontoons on port side, FG on stb. Above Warsash the chan lies between lines of
closely moored yachts. If weather permits, a stranger should bring up in the chan
at No. 6 bn and proceed next morning.

Berthing There is no anch in the Hamble River above bns 9 and 10. Visitors'
moorings can usually be obtained on the Hr Board piles. Berths at marinas by
arrangement with berth masters, and sometimes on RAF YC moorings by
arrangement with the Secretary.

Keep clear of the bank which borrows on the chan between the Hamble Pt
buoy and No. 2 port hand bn at the entrance. The stream runs hard for last 2½h
ebb. All piles should be given a good berth.

Landing at Warsash, Hamble, Swanwick Shore and Jolly Sailor Inn below the
station at Bursledon. HM's office in conspic BWHS tr at Warsash (tel Locks
Heath 6387), dinghy landing at HM's jetty. All facilities at Hamble Village and

Swanwick Shore. Provisions at Warsash, Hamble and Swanwick. No dues. Hards at Warsash, Hamble and Bursledon. Public scrubbing berths at Hamble, Warsash, Mercury Hard (above Port Hamble) and Land's End (Bursledon). Fuel and water alongside at Warsash and Port Hamble. A passenger ferry runs between Hamble and Warsash. Rly at Bursledon alongside water. Imray Chart Y35 also recommended. EC Wed.

TITCHFIELD HAVEN   Chart BA 1905
DS: E +2.45; W −2.00

Bar   Dries ¼M offshore. Haven is available for up to 1.8m draft at HW. Entrance dries 1.2m at MLWS.

Entrance   Hillhead SC's large square white clubhouse marks the entrance. Shingle bank on S side: keep close to slipway on N side. Steer between the bns which line the side of the entrance, spher topmarks to port, triangles to stb.

Berthing   There is a small camber inside to W where small craft can lie on soft mud alongside the bank. It should be examined at LW. Apply to SC for mooring. It is not advisable for a stranger to enter the Haven when the tides are taking off. Shops, PO, chandlery in Hillhead village ¼M to E. EC Thurs.

WOOTTON, I.o.W.   Chart BA 394   (Plan p59)
HW +0.25.   DS: E +4.15; W −1.25.   MHWS 3.7; MHWN 2.7.

Approach   Wootton Creek lies S of SE Ryde Middle buoy. From W keep N of a line Old Castle Pt to the second dolphin from seaward to clear Wootton Rks. From E give the shore a wide berth. When Wootton Rks to the W of the booms are covered, there is 0.9m of water over the mud flats.

The approach chan, ½M long, is dredged to a depth of 2.4m for a width of 30m and is marked on the stb hand by four dolphins Fl 6s, WGWG in succession from the entrance. The dredged chan is 6m to port of the dolphins but there is usually 1.8m close to them at LW.

Entrance   It is not advisable to enter when a ferry is approaching or leaving. Strangers should keep close to the E of the dolphins to avoid mud banks to port. If proceeding to the pool, steer for the pier-head keeping close to it. If proceeding up the creek, turn to stb immediately after the fourth dolphin and follow the line of moorings.

Berthing   There are a few moorings for boats of 1.8m draft W of ferry slip, and for shallower draft boats in pool further up river. These moorings are sometimes available for short periods on application to the boatman, usually afloat off the ferry slip. Owing to restricted space and the frequent passage of the ferries, anch should not be attempted below the Fishbourne ferry slip. If necessary, bring up near the moored craft and await instructions from the boatman. The bottom is soft mud.

The creek may be navigated by shallow drafts or in the dinghy as far as Wootton Bridge, about 1M, but the chan is not marked all the way and landing is only possible for 2h on either side of HW. Landing and water at Fishbourne

HAMBLE RIVER
Depths in Metres

1°20'W   19'   18'

53'

Burseldon Bridge →

Bursledon

Swanwick Marina
(Marked by Green Lts)

53'

Hard

QR

21

Bn

FS

Shipyard

QG Crableck Bn

Badnam Creek

Badnam Bn

Mercury Yacht Harbour
(Marked by Red Lts)

Wooded

50

52'

Monument

O Netley Gt Dome (conspic)
Fl Y 6s 17m 5M

Drain

FS

FS O Mercury Hard

FS

HAMBLE RIVER

PILES

3

Fl Y 6s
Bn
HARD
FS

18

G

Fl 2s 14m 3M

2¹

Bn

Fl 2s 14m 3M

Port Hamble
(Marked by Red Lts)
Hamble

FR

Bn

Bn

3

Bn

24

Warsash

1QG 10s
Greenland
G
Fl R 3s
Cadland
R
6-2FG (vert)

FR

FR

Hamble SC

Red roof
(conspic)

FS

HARD

HARD

FERRY

HARD

Bn

Chy
(conspic)

Bns

Hamble Pt Marina
(marked by Red Lts)

Bns

PILES

4

Iso G 6s Rising Sun Bn

2FR (vert)

Fawley Bn (8)
(Tide Guage)

2 FR (vert)

Shell Mex Jetty

QR (HAMBLE Bn)

FS

Chy

FG

FS

QG Warsash Shore Bn

51'

9.6

HAMBLE
SPIT

345°

2.7

Warsash Jetty

Newtown

FS
Chy

Navigation School

2¹

3¹

Ldg Lts 326°

4.3

OC (2) R 12s
No 6

1.8

1.5

Entrance marked by Bns

Ldg Lts 327°

3

Lts 024° 30

0.8

Spit Pile

Warsash Bn (Or)

Esso
Terminal

AGWI Pier

12.9

1.2

Q(6)+LFl
15s
Hamble Point
YB

0.7

1.6

Bns
BY

1°20'W   2FR (vert) Bell (2) 20s   18'

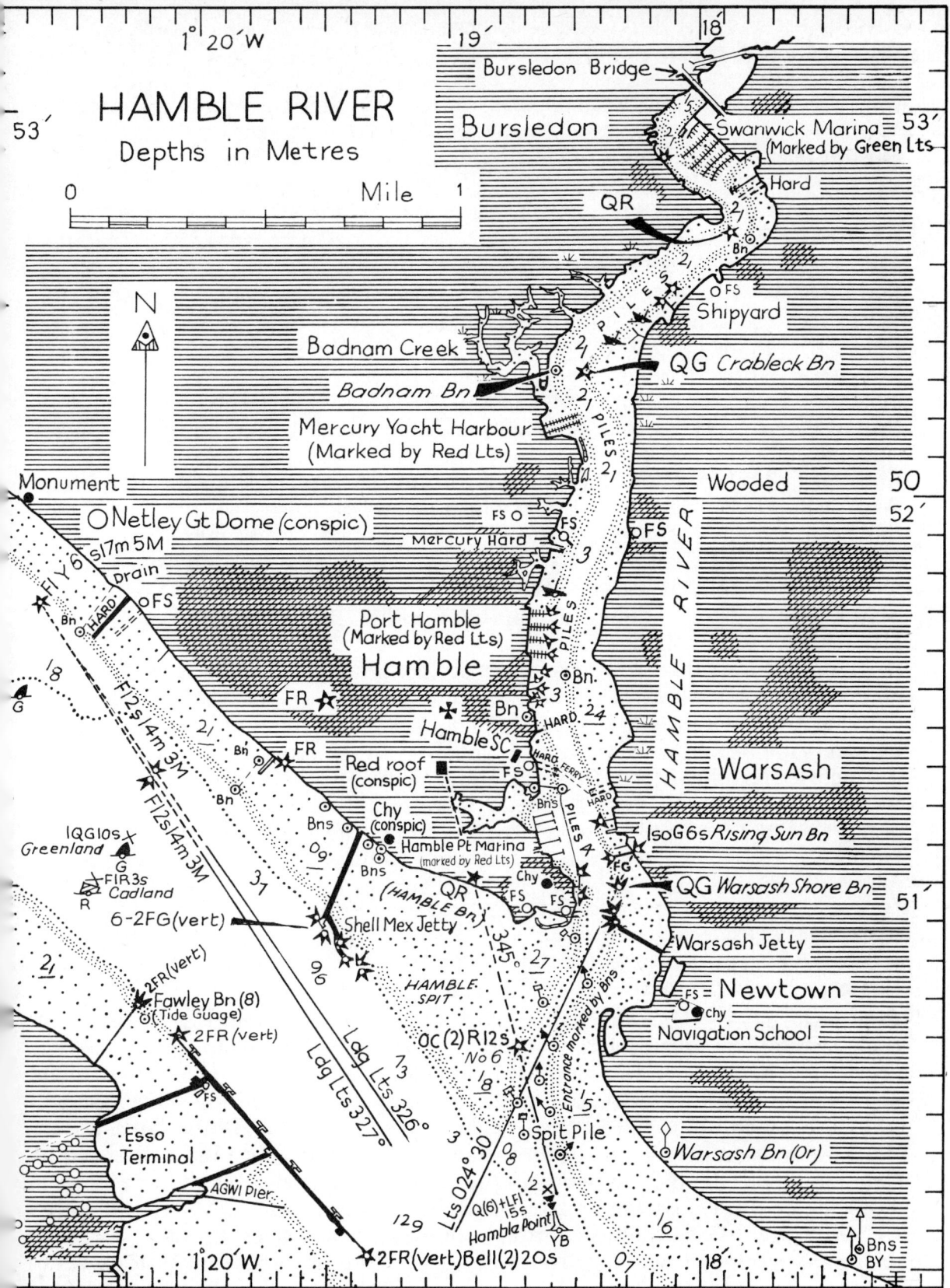

d on British Admiralty Charts (nos. in text) with the permission of the Controller of H.M. Stationery Office and of
Hydrographer of the Navy, and on other sources.

where there is an inn and a small store. Petrol, PO, shops at Wootton Bridge. EC Wed.

Outside anch   Vessels anch offshore will find 2.1 to 2.4m about 3 ca off Wootton Pt.

BEMBRIDGE, I.o.W.   Chart BA 2050   (Plan p69)
HW +0.30.   MHWS 3.1; MHWN 2.3.
DS: tides are weak and variable in St Helen's Road, less than ½kn, except from +3.15 to +4.15 when the rate is 1–1½kn S.
Bar   Dries 0.3m.
Approach   Gravel banks extend from St Helen's Fort to Nodes Pt and on to Seaview. This area should be avoided. St Helen's Fort shows a lt Fl(3)10s through the full 360°. Breakwater Rks and other obstructions lie off its seaward side and it should not be approached nearer than ½ ca.
Entrance   From NW of St Helen's Fort and seamark pick up the Bembridge Approach bn triangle topmark (Q) which lies nearly 2 ca W of the Fort. Leave this bn to stb and keeping close to the stb hand buoys (odd numbers) proceed along the buoyed chan to hr entrance at No. 10. The Approach bn tide gauge indicates the depth of water over the shallowest section between Nos. 6 and 8 buoys. Strangers are advised to approach within 2h of HW. The area S of St Helen's Fort is a prohibited anch.
Berthing   Observe notices displayed at the hr entrance. Anch is forbidden except for yachts which can take the ground. These should keep to port after entering and anch fore and aft in the small sandy bay adjoining Bembridge SC. Others should follow the buoyed chan to St Helen's marina mooring as instructed. Berthing Master tel Bembridge (098 387) 2973.

   Land on the beach near Spithead Hotel or at St Helen's Duver, or with permission at Woodnutt's Yacht Yard pier opposite No. 15 buoy. Water at St Helen's marina. Chandlery and fuel. Laying ashore by arrangement with one of the yards. Buses cover the whole Is. EC Thurs.

PORTSMOUTH   Charts BA 2625, 2631   (Plan p71)
HW +0.30.   DS: E +3.00; W −2.00.
MHWS 4.7; MLWS 0.6; MTL 2.7; MHWN 3.8; MLWN 1.8.
Approach   (1) By the main channel, St Jude's Ch on with Southsea Castle (003°) leads into fairway off the latter. Then steer along buoyed chan for hr entrance (Fort Blockhouse open fine on port bow bearing approximately 325°). At night approach in the FW sector of Southsea Castle Dir Lt bearing 001° past Spit Refuge buoy and then follow the lit chan buoys as above until the Dir FW Fort Blockhouse lt on the W side of hr entrance comes into sight (320°). Proceed up chan parallel to the parade lights on the shore. During the ebb an eddy flows in along the beach. (2) By the Swashway. Keep the war memorial on with St Jude's Church spire (048°) to pass through the Swashway over the Spit Bank in minimum depth of 1.8m. This is not lit. (3) Inshore passage from W is useful to

Bembridge

Depths in Metres

0 Cables 3

0 3 6

St Helen's Road

St Helen's Patch

51 4₆

37

51 5

Nettlestone

Horestone Pt.

N

Priory Bay

17

2·3

Nodes Pt.

0·3

0₁

0₁

2·3

(Tide Gauge)

St Helen's Fort
Fl(3) 10s 6m 8M

4

4

Long Rk 6₁

50° 42′

Ethel Ledge

Cole Rk

Lifeboat Ho

2₁Om (conspic)

FS FS Sewers

0·Brl 4·3

0₁

4

1₃

4

Q No 2

R No 2

No 4

G No 4

No 3

R No 5

G

No 6

G R No 8

Sewer No 7 G

No 9

G

2

3₂

Bn No 10

Groyne

Bembridge Pt.

Hard

Bembridge

Spire (conspic)

0₁

5′

6′

6′

FS

Bn

R

No 10

Quay

Groynes

No 9a

G

G No 11

R No 11

FS

No 13

R No 13

Bn No 12 G

FS YC

No 15

No 15

G

No 14

R

No 17

G

Mill Ponds

(ruins)

Boat Houses

Brading Harbour

Sluice

Quay

St Helens

St Helen's Ch.
(W) Seamark

(ruins)

River Yar

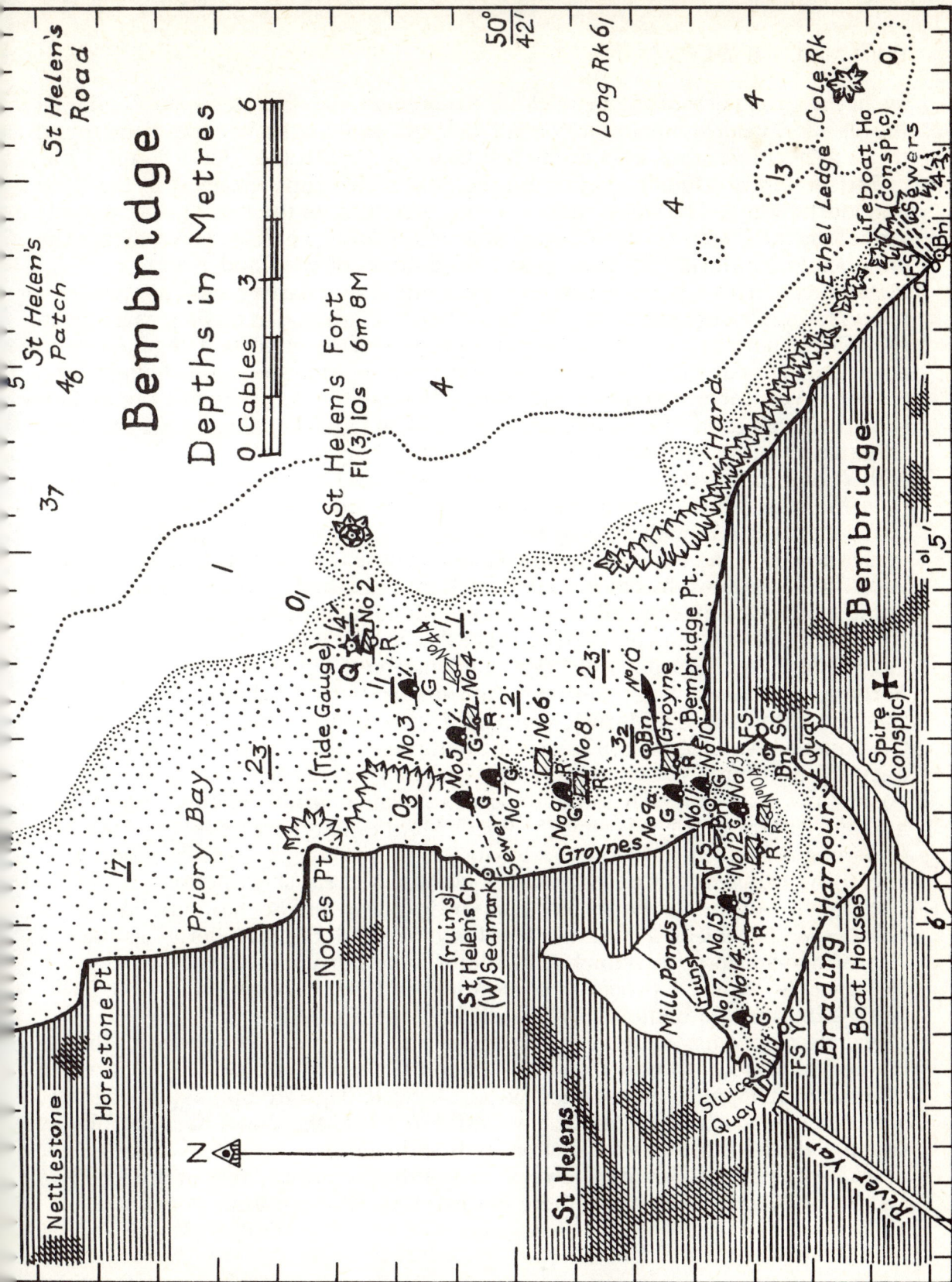

Based on British Admiralty Charts (nos. in text) with the permission of the Controller of H.M. Stationery Office and of Hydrographer of the Navy, and on other sources.

avoid the strong ebb in the main chan. Rounding Gilkicker, keep the W edge of the big conspicuous tank in the Naval Dockyard on with the W edge of the round tower (029°): this leads into main chan near the hr entrance, least depth 0.2m.

Portsmouth is difficult to enter on the ebb, which runs strongest in the third and fourth hours. The flood runs at 4–5kn, strongest in the last 2h, but an eddy runs along the E side of the hr during part of the flood. There is slack water in the entrance for ¾h during the second and third hours of the flood.

Regulations   This is a Naval and ferry port with a very narrow and busy entrance necessitating strict regulations which members are advised to read up carefully in the Pilot. There are penalties for infringement. Two important regulations in particular: (1) All yachts with engines must use them in the main channel from Southsea War Memorial in the S to Ballast buoy in the N. (2) Traffic regulations should be read carefully. Signals are displayed on Gilkicker Central Sig Stn, Fort Blockhouse at the entrance to the hr, and Central Sig Stn in Dockyard: (a) R flag with W diag bar by day, or by night one R over two G lts means no vessels other than those in whose favour the signal is displayed can either leave or enter harbour; (b) R flag with W diag bar with B ball below or W over G lt by night means no vessel can enter the main channel from seaward; (c) R flag with W diag bar with B ball above by day or G over W lt by night means no vessel can leave hr but incoming vessels may enter; (d) International Code pendant above pendant Nine means vessels may proceed in either direction but must give a wide berth to any vessel flying International Code pendant above pendant Zero.

Berthing   This is a large harbour but with restricted berthing facilities. (1) Camper & Nicholson's Marina, Gosport. Convenient, crowded in the summer. CA boatman. (2) Hardway SC, visitors' moorings. (3) Camber Hr, alongside the quay or a fishing vessel. This is only a temporary place to moor. Other possibilities are (but advisable to make advance arrangements): (4) Coldharbour, NW of C & N Marina; (5) Wicor Marine, Fareham Lake; (6) PME Ltd of Fareham Quay, just below the town. Lastly, the use of a vacant mooring in one of the many creeks can sometimes be obtained for short periods.

At night beware of large black mooring buoys in the harbour. Water at Camper & Nicholson's Marina, Hardway SC and the Camber. Customs at Cross-Channel Ferry Terminal at Fountain Lake but yachts cannot lie there. If clearance is required proceed to mooring and tel Portsmouth (0705) 26241 (0700–2200) or Southampton (0703) 29251 (24h). EC Wed.

Portchester Lake has 4.3m at its lower end and 1.8m near Portchester. Chan is marked by R posts to port (Nos. 57–72) and G posts to stb (95–73). There is a rifle range at Tipnor abreast piles 89–92. If the R flags are up pass through the area quickly. Anch near Porchester Castle in 1.8m; there is a hard for dinghy landing; ¼M walk to the village shop, pub and church.

Fareham Lake has 4.3m at its lower end and shores and narrows at Spider Lake and Bomb Ketch Lake where there are many yacht moorings.

PORTSMOUTH HARBOUR

Depths in Metres

Cables
0 — 5

Hardway SC

Pier
1·8 W

Bn
Pile 57
Pile 94
Pile 95
Pile 96
THE NARROWS
Pile 102 103 104
Pile
Whale I.
chy
Pile 107
Pile 106
F1R3S
Pile
Pontoons
2-2FR(vert)
FOUNTAIN LAKE
QR
2-2FG(vert)
Ferry Port & Quay

Hard

2-2FR(vert)
Small Craft Moorings
Q(6)+LF1.15s
F1Y2s
Q
Pile 97
Pile 100
G
Pile 110
2FG(vert)
Fountain Lake Jetty

Pile 15
2-2FR(vert)
YB
Pile 98
YB

Priddy's Hard
2-2FR(vert)
NW Wall
Basin Nº3
Crane (conspic)

FORTON LAKE
Pile 12
Pile 13
Y
TIDAL BASIN
10 4
10 3
9 5

Burrow I.
Posts
Y
R.N. Dockyard
Landport

10 7
Portsea

10 2
2FR(vert)
Y
10 8
Portsea

COLD Hr.
Yacht Marina
2FR(vert)
FS. Central Sig Stn (conspic). Traffic Sigs.

Gosport
2FR(vert)
11 3
12 2
Guildhall Tr
50°
48'

Mill Gate Ho (conspic)

Portsmouth

F1G
2FG(vert)
Hulk
2FG(vert)
FY
2-2FG(vert)
Tank (conspic)
Chy (conspic) (92) Red Lts
Chy (conspic) (92)

2-2FR(vert)
Tr (conspic)
F1R2·5s3 Ballast
9
1QG
ROUND TOWER

QG
Haslar Lake
2FR(vert)
2FG(vert)
St Thomas Cathedral

Gas House Lake
Fort Blockhouse
2FR(vert)
2FG(vert) Victoria Pier

Oyster Pool Lake
Marina
Tr (conspic)(40)
Q
OcG15s
Clarence Esplanade Pier
Southsea

Water Tr (conspic)
Dir WdG6m13/5M
Traffic Sig
F1RW
QG
FS
2-2FG(vert)
Spire

Haslar
Bell Tr
Haslar Bank
F1-+-LF1.G
QG
G
FY(occas)
Hovercraft Terminal
FS
7'

QR
Nº4
War Memorial (conspic)
47'

Spit Sand
YB 26
Southsea Castle
Dir WRG16m13/5M

Bn
RW
Fort Monckton
(Apl-Oct)
W. edge of Tank in line with W. edge of Tr 029°
Iso W
F1(3)G10s Nº1

F1(3)R10s Nº2

Fort Gilkicker
OcG10s7M
Iso W
Castle
F1(2)G6s

Bn.RW
Spire in line with War Memorial 047°
F1(2)R6s Ridge
Alt RW
Alt WG
FG

F1R5s7M
Spit Sand Fort
Spit Refuge
F1R5s
Bell
FR

8'
1° 7'W
6'

Langstone Hr
Depths in Metres

0 Cables 5 10

N

Langstone
Langstone Lake
North Lake
Ldg Bns 340°
FIR 3S
FIG 3S
Broad Lake
Long Lake
Baker
N Binness
S Binness
Duck
Obstn
Pylon

Spire (conspic)
South Hayling
Hayling Island

Hotel (conspic)
Hayling Bay
The Kench
Gunner Pt FS6
Langstone Bar East Winner
Fairway
Langstone R 24
3. Bar
23
R/10s
FI(2)R
Y
BRB
FI(2)5s
West Winner
Wk

Langstone Channel
Sinah Lake
Sinah
QR
FIG 5S
Sword
R Sands
Mallard Sands
Sinah
QR
R
Ferry
FIR
Chy QR
conspic
Bn
Eastney

Langstone Harbour
Farlington
Farlington Marshes
Drayton
Broom
R
Wharf
Hisea Chan
24
R River
Quay
Channel
Portsea Island
Portsmouth Eastney
Fort Cumberland
(conspic)
Water Tr (conspic)
Eastney Pt
Clock & Clock
(conspic)
Bn

PORTSMOUTH HARBOUR
(NORTHERN PART)

Depths in Metres

Cables
0   10

Channels marked by numbered Piles, Green to Starboard, Red to Port, both shown as O

N

SLIP
TOWN QUAY
UPPER QUAY
QUAY
LOWER QUAY
Fareham
QUAY
Pylon (conspic)
Pylon (conspic)
NB (conspic)
Pylon (conspic)
Saltings
HEAVY REACH
Saltings
CAMS BAY
Wicormarine
Wicor Hard
NB
FOXBURY PT
NB
NB
Slip
Jetty
Chy

Boat Yd
FS (conspic)
Catwalk

Portchester

Portchester Castle
SC Hard
Hard
Old Windmill (ruins)
Vane
Hard

NB
Spider Survey Pile

Pylon (conspic)
NB (conspic)
Ship Yd
Fleetlands Pier
2-2FR (vert)
FS
2FR (vert)
2-2FR (vert)

Fareham Lake
Pewit I
Tripod
Spider Lake
Bomb Ketch Lake
Shingle Pile
Frater Lake
Whf
Frater Pt
Tripod
Fort Elson

Portchester Lake

Tipner Lake
Slipway
Stamshaw Pt
FS Tank Butts
FS
Horsea I
Tank
2R
2 Buoys

MOORINGS
THE NARROWS
Hardway SC
2-2FR (vert)
Pile
Dns
Lone (survey) Pile
FIY2s
QR
Bn
Fountain Lake
Whale I
FS (Danger)
Clock Tr

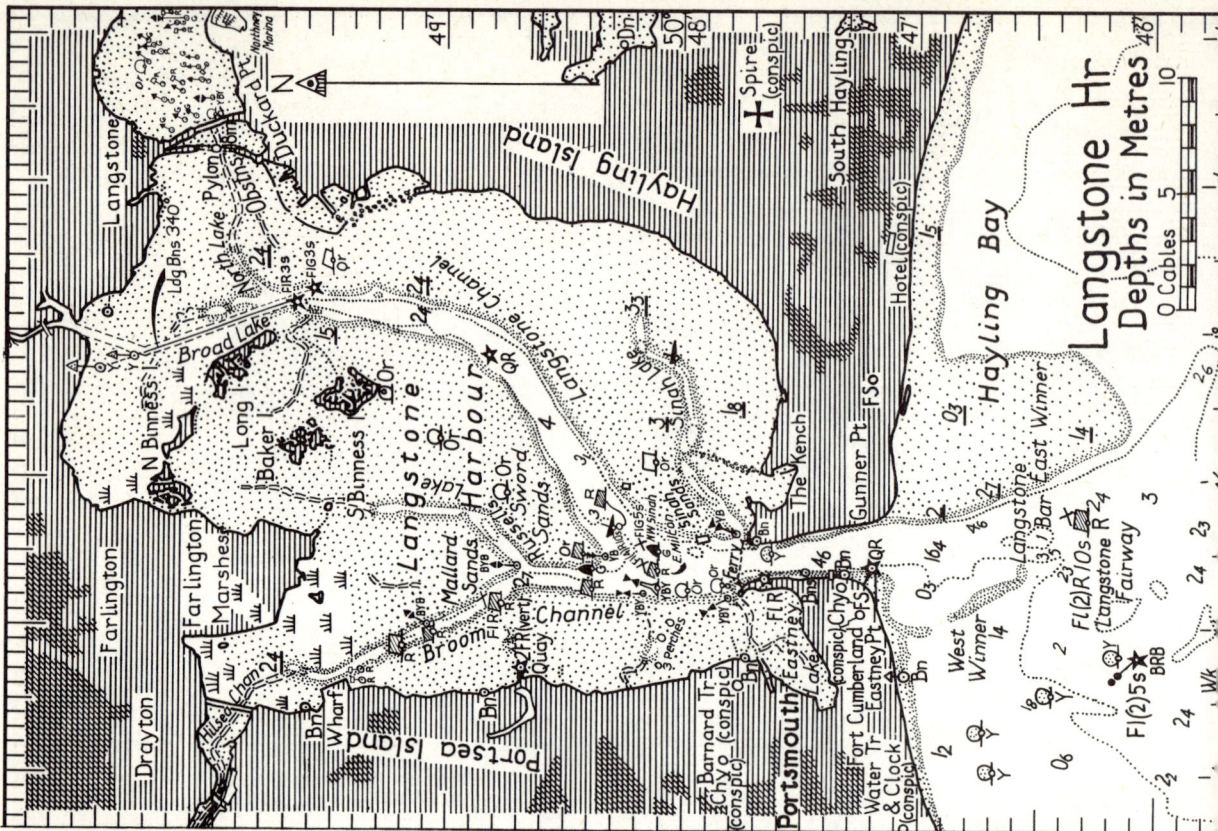

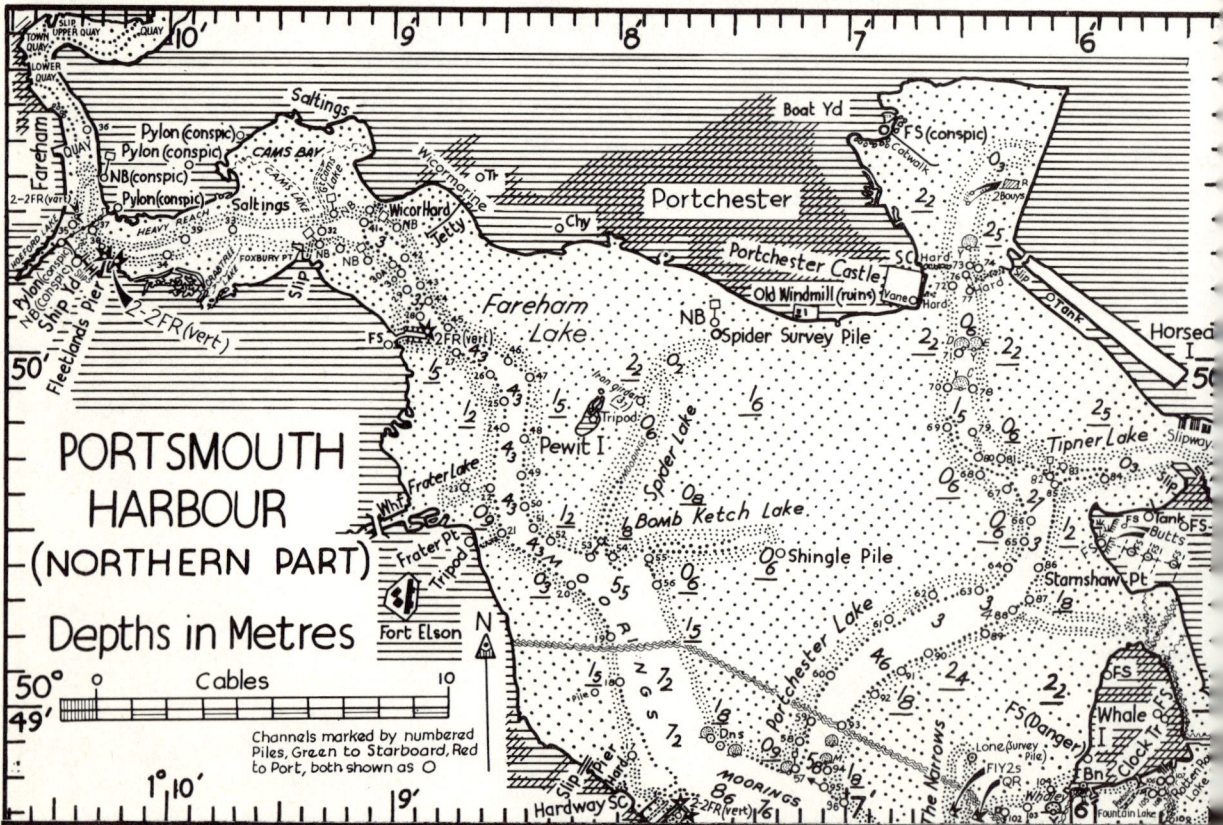

Based on British Admiralty Charts (nos. in text) with the permission of the Controller of H.M. Stationery Office and the Hydrographer of the Navy, and on other sources.

FAREHAM   Chart BA 2631
Entrance   The chan through Fareham Lake to Fareham is marked by R posts to
port and G to stb. The highest LW anch for 1.5m draft is ¾M below the town.
Riding light necessary as there is commercial traffic passing. Small craft can take
the mud at LW on moorings in the upper reaches below the town. Landing by
permission at Fareham SC pontoon. Water from Fareham SC or Portsmouth
Marine Engineering next door or close downstream. Hard for scrubbing at
Portsmouth Marine or just above the lower quay. From the town (2 mins from
SC), buses to Gosport whence ferries to Portsmouth, Southampton, Warsash.
EC Wed.

LANGSTONE HARBOUR   Chart BA 3418   (Plan p72)
HW +0.30.   MHWS 4.1; MHWN 3.2.
Bar   1.5 to 1.8m, 1M offshore. Inside there is always plenty of water in the chan
near the entrance. The hr cannot be approached when a heavy sea is running.
Approach   From the W pass through the gap in the barrier (submerged at HW)
between Southsea Beach and Horse Fort. The passage through the barrier is
marked by a dolphin, QR, on S side and G post on N side; or pass to S of Horse
Fort. To clear the Winner Banks (2.1m MHWS) coming E or W for Langstone
Bar, keep Haslar Tr open S of Southsea Castle until Norman and Horse Forts are
in line, bearing 238°, when stand in with these forts in line astern until the R can
Fairway buoy Fl(2)R 10s on the port hand, is on with the centre of hr entrance,
bearing 354°. Then steer on this bearing for centre entrance, giving the E shore of
the entrance a fair berth and leaving the sewer outfall dolphins to port, or bring
the outer dolphin (QR) in line with the ferry house, a grey building on W side of
entrance; two bns on the W bank are day marks. If beating in or out, while on the
alignment of the Horse and Norman Forts these forts should be just opened of
one another on each tack. After rounding the buoy, in the middle of the fairway,
the chan is steep-to and barely a ca wide.
   Across the Winner Banks the tide sets NW for 2½h until local HW, turning at
local HW by W to SW for 2½h. After 3h flood, −3.15 HWD, there is 1h slack
water, in which vessels may leave the harbour with about 2.7m on the bar before
the main flood makes. Target buoys are moored 1M offshore on the W side of
entrance.
Berthing Six visitors' mooring buoys on stb hand at entrance to Sinah Lake;
virtually no anch space in the Lake. If wishing to stay overnight apply to HM at
the ferry on Hayling Is (tel (07016) 3419). There is only 0.9m of water on bar
abreast of the pontoon at the entrance to this lake. Streams run hard. Good
landing at all states of the tide. Inn with tel close by. Hayling village, shops and
PO 2M by road to E. Bus in summer. Ferry to W side of entrance, whence by
road 1M to bus which runs to Southsea etc. Hard alongside pontoon. No supplies
but water, nearer than the village.
   Vessels up to 2.4m draft may pass up Langstone Hr along the North Lake to
Langstone village. Passage through to Chichester Hr is no longer possible with

fixed masts. North Lake dries, but at half flood a stranger should have no difficulty. All stores may be obtained at Havant, 1M by bus from quay along high road. Dinghies and centreboard craft may pass round Portsea Is from Langstone Hr into Porchester Lake off Portsmouth Hr, passing under low bridges with 1.2m water at HW; mast must be lowered.

CHICHESTER   Chart BA 3418   (Plan p76)

HW (entrance) +0.30.   DS: E +3.30; W −1.15.
MHWS 4.9; MLWS 0.7; MTL 2.8; MHWN 4.0; MLWN 1.8.

Bar   1.4m at MLWS. The entrance lies between Eastoke Pt on Hayling Is on the W, and West Wittering on the E. The chan, about $1\frac{3}{4}$ ca wide, lies close to the W shore. The coast is low and shoal water extends over $1\frac{1}{2}$M offshore. In strong winds between SE and W with ebb tide the seas break over the whole of these shoals and the entrance should not be attempted. On sp tides the outgoing stream can reach $6\frac{1}{2}$kn.

Approach and entrance   Vessels approaching from E or W should keep not less than $1\frac{1}{2}$M (in poor vis the 5m line) offshore until the Nab Tr bears 184°, then identify the Chichester Bar bn (framework tr, R can topmark Fl WR 5s, W 322°–080°, R 080°–322°). Leave this bn about $\frac{1}{4}$ ca to port, then steer 016° to pass between Eastoke bn (positioned on a groyne at Eastoke Hd) and W Winner bn G con daymark. Follow the W shore until abreast of Hayling Is SC when NW Winner buoy (G con Fl G 10s) will be 2 ca away to stb. From this point the chan divides and the directions are continued below under separate headings.

At night the entrance should not be attempted by strangers without favourable weather and plenty of water. Keep well offshore until in the R sector of the Nab Tr. Identify the Chichester Bar bn and taking care to remain in its W sector, steer to leave it $\frac{1}{4}$ ca to port. From here, alter course to pass between Eastoke Pt bn (QR) and the W Winner bn (QG), from which the NW Winner buoy (Fl G 10s) can be picked up. This should be left to stb.

Chichester Bar bn has a Ro Bn, ident CH freq 303.4kHz, range 10M, sequence 1, 4. There is a speed limit of 8kn in the whole of the hr.

Berthing   Anch in Emsworth Chan N of Hayling Is SC and clear to the N and E of their moorings, good holding. Tripping line advisable. The SC maintains a visitors' buoy R barrel with WVS off the club foreshore; it is suitable for yachts up to 10 ton TM.

Chichester Channel   Abreast of Hayling Is SC turn NE leaving NW Winner G con buoy (Fl G 10s), N Winner G con buoy (Fl(2)G 10s), and Mid Winner G con buoy (Fl(3)G 10s) all to stb. From this posn the chan is marked by Stocker R can buoy (Fl(3)R 10s), Sandhead R can (Fl(4)R 10s), and NE Sandhead R can (Fl R 10s) on the port hand, and by East Hd bn G con daymark, tide gauge (Fl(4)G 10s), and Rookwood G con buoy on the stb hand. From abreast NE Sandhead buoy pick up the leading marks: Roman Transit bn, R can topmark, in line with Main Channel bn, W rectangular topmark, bearing 032°. Keep Camber bn S Card Q(6) +L Fl 15s to port and head on transit to leave Chaldock bn (G con daymark

Fl(2)G 10s) to stb, then alter course to Fairway buoy (G con Fl(3)G 10s). Leave it to stb and steer a course through the moorings. A good anch in 4m, mud bottom, exists W of Fairway buoy. Anch prohibited in Itchenor Reach and Bosham Chan. Visitors should either make fast to the two visitors' buoys off Itchenor or go alongside temporarily on the HM's pontoon (2 FG vert) while arranging a berth with the HM at Itchenor (tel Birdham (0243) 512301 by day).

Itchenor Shipyard, water, hotel, HM's office, Customs, YC. Buses to Chichester. Chandlery.

Birdham Pool From Itchenor Fairway follow a course through the moorings, leaving mooring buoys with R reflective patches to port and those with G reflective patches to stb. Then leave Birdham bn (G can topmark Fl(4)G 10s) close to port and G perches con topmark marking the narrow winding chan close to stb, and the R perch rectangular topmark close to port, up to the lock gates of Birdham Pool. The chan dries. Shipyard, fuel, water, provisions, chandlery. Lock open 2–3h either side of HW Chichester Yacht Basin.

Chichester Yacht Basin From Birdham bn steer NE leaving moorings to port and CY bn (G con topmark Fl G 5s) close to stb; then steer for the lock leaving the G bns, triangular topmarks, all close to stb. The dredged channel is 18m wide with 0.5m at MLWS. Lock is manned 0700–2100 on weekdays, 0600–2200 at weekends (BST). All facilities. Visitors accommodated. Tel Birdham (0243) 512731.

Dell Quay Leaving CT bn to stb, the chan is marked by G can buoys to stb and R can buoys to port. Chan dries. Berthing at quay by arrangement with HM Shipyard. Inn, SC.

Bosham Channel Make Deep End S Card bn; leave it 10m to stb and head 352° for Cobnor keeping close to stb of single line of moorings. After passing Cobnor steer 035° for Bosham Ch keeping in mid-chan between double line of moorings; 2 to 4m in channel but depth decreases to 1m in mid-channel opposite the quay and hard. In chan beyond quay there is deeper water for $\frac{1}{4}$M. When visiting quay from main channel at HW alter course only when in line with quay to avoid shoal patch. Yacht yards, rly 1M, buses to Chichester. EC Old Bosham Wed.

Thorney Channel Strangers are advised to navigate at half-flood. Leave Camber bn, S Card Q (6) + L Fl 15s, to stb. Steer to leave Pilsey bn Fl(2)R 10s to port. Anch off Pilsey ($2\frac{1}{2}$m) in W winds. Keep single perch position approx 100m NE of Pilsey bn to stb (owing to soft nature of ground it is liable to disappear during heavy weather). Proceeding up chan steer between the port hand bn and Thorney stb bn Fl G 5s. These mark the passage between line of posts across the channel. The chan is marked by perches. Clear water until Thorney Village is reached. Continuing up chan two smaller creeks appear, Prinsted Chan, full of moorings to port, and Nutbourne Chan to stb. Prinsted Chan leads to the village of that name and care should be taken to keep the perch with can topmark to port. From this point Thornham Boatyard lies to port, the village lies ahead; shops, buses and rly $\frac{3}{4}$M from shore. It is only safe to land between 2h before and after HW; the whole bay dries out. There are six Corporation moorings in the

N. PILSEY
G

Pilsey I.

Chichester Harbour

Pilsey Sands

Stockers Lake

3

37

Rookwood
G

Camber Bn
YB Q(6)+LFl.15s

2½ 58
R

Perch
Y

Y

FIG5s
N.W. PILSEY
R

6₄

0₃

0₉

FlR10s
NE SANDHEAD
R

7₃

1₈

Perches in transit
lead through
swashway

Fl(4)R10s
SANDHEAD
R

Tide Gauge

Fl(2)G10s
N.WINNER
QR

Q(6)+LFl.15s
YB
Y

0₉
VBY

Fl(3)R10s
STOCKER

4₄
Fl(4)G10s
EAST HEAD Bn

Ella Nore

Fl(3)G10s
Mid WINNER

3₄

East Head

Sandy Pt.
Q
Y

F 15

FI G10s
NW WINNER
G

NE WINNER
G

2₄

FSo
West
Wittering
SC

47

F5s
(occas)

9₁

1₈ The Winner

1₂

West Wittering

Landing
slip

Hayling Island SC
CLUB HOUSE
(conspic)
G

G
W.WINNER
QG Tide Gauge

19₂

Spire
(conspic)

R
Bns
QR
EASTOKE Bn
0₄

Eastoke Pt.
Bns
Bn
Bns

7₂

2₇

2₁

OFS

Groynes

Cakeham Tr
(conspic)

2₄
West Pole

1

Red

1₅

3

0₂

2₄

0₉

0₃

2₁

0₃

1₂

MIDDLE
POLE

0₆

Chichester Bar

0₂

0₃

Target
(3)
G
Bn

0₉

1₅

Bracklesham Bay

2

Fl WR 5s 14m
RW CHICHESTER BAR Bn
Tide Gauge

Y

2·5

1₂

0₁

East Pole Sands

2·8

1·4

White

0₇

Bn
G

Approaches to
Chichester Hr
Depths in Metres

1₅

1·4

0₈

50

4

0 Cables   4   8

1₂

5·6'

5·5' YQ

0°54'

4

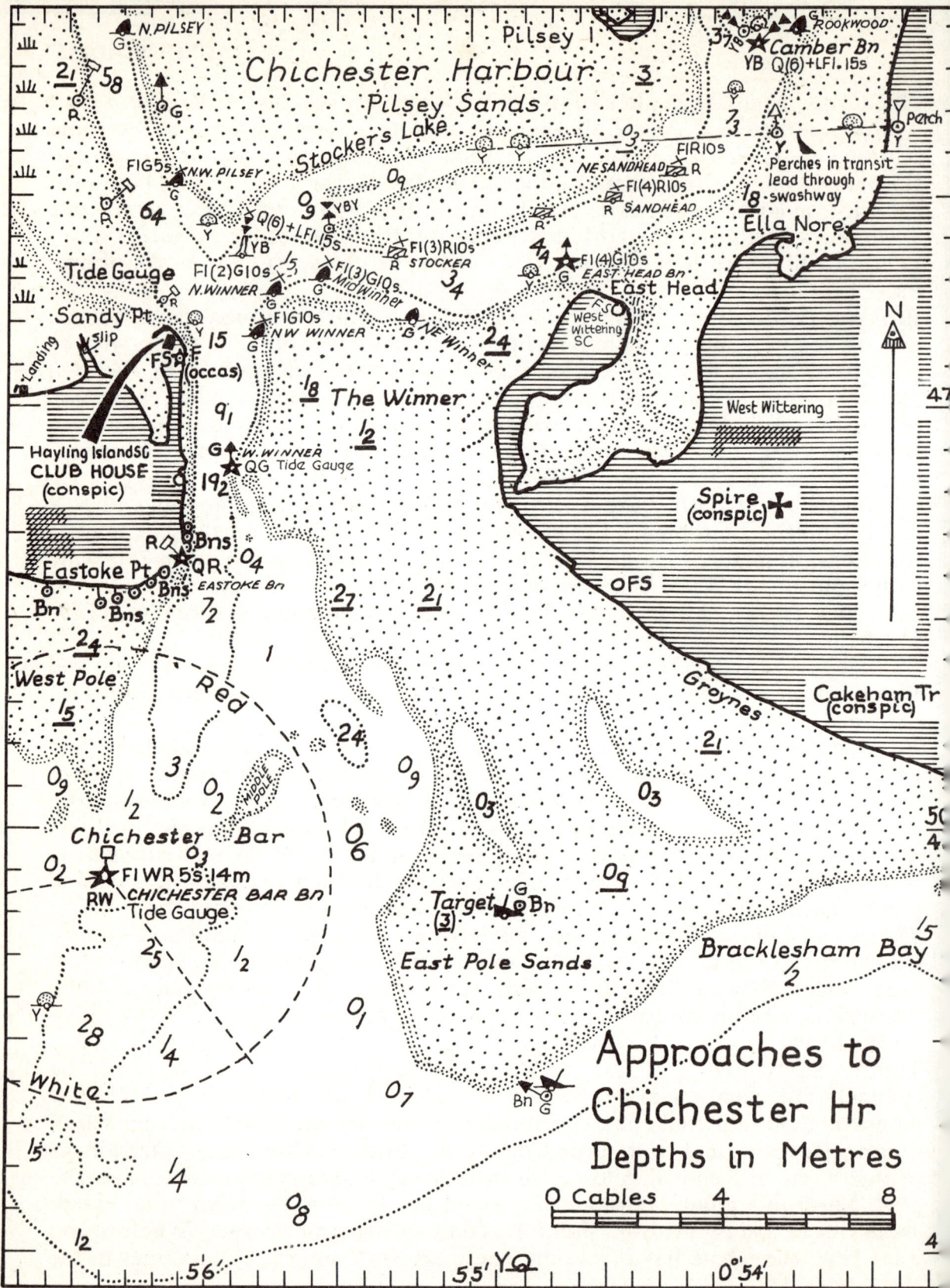

Based on British Admiralty Charts (nos. in text) with the permission of the Controller of H.M. Stationery Office and
the Hydrographer of the Navy, and on other sources.

76

Chichester Harbour
Depths in Metres

N

Fishbourne

Broadbridge

Dell Quay SC

Fishbourne Chan

Copperas Pt

Chichester Lake

Chichester Yacht Basin

Birdham Yacht Basin

Locks

Old Canal

Birdham

Bosham

Quay

Hard

Bosham Chan

Trees lie outside chart

Chidham Pt

Nutbourne

Southbourne

Nutbourne

Itchenor Piers

Longmore Pier

Pier

Hard

Ferry

Chalkdock Pt

Wear Pt

Reach

SC Pier

HM

SC Pier

Jetties

Bns

Cobnor

Channel Bn

Chalkdock Bn

Chichester Channel

Broken piles

Thorney Channel

Nutbourne Chan

Prinsted Channel

Prinsted

Stanbury Pt

Water Tr (conspic)

Marker Pt

West Thorney

Thorney Island

Airfield (disused)

Longmere Pt Broken Piles

Stump

Pilsey I

Pilsey Sands

Stocker's Lake

Chichester Harbour

Sandhead

Lila Nore

East Hd

Spire (conspic)

West Wittering

The Winner

Sandy Pt

Eastoke Pt

Hayling Island SC

CLUB HOUSE (conspic)

Mengham Rythe SC

Groynes

Slip

Emsworth

Yacht Hr

Cobnor Bn

Great Deep

Sweare Deep

Prinsted Pt

Victor Tr

Radio Tr

Fisherman's Beacon

Marina

North Hayling

Emsworth Channel
(marked by perches)

Hayling Island

Landing Stages

Verner

NW Pilsey

NE Sandhead

NE Winner

NW Winner Bn

NW Winner

The Winner

Channel Beacons
Channels marked by Green Bns with triangular topmarks to Stbd. & Red Bns with can topmark to port, indicated by ⊙

0 Cables 5 10 15

52'

53'

54'

55'

56'

57'

58'

50   49   48   47

rather exposed Nutbourne Chan. Nutbourne can be reached on the tide. Rly. Shops.

The chan has 3.7m up to Stanbury Pt and provides useful anch with fair holding.

Thorney Village   A concrete hard runs out from the shore by the ch. To land at Thorney and proceed to the mainland, i.e. Emsworth, it should be remembered that the whole of Is is owned by the Ministry of Defence and is subject to restriction. Thorney Is SC welcomes visitors. Water from Club Ho.

Emsworth Channel is a broad channel running N from Hayling Is SC with 2m at LAT for nearly 3M. Most is free of moorings and provides excellent sailing between drying mud flats marked by stakes. Leave Pilsey Sands to stb, marked by NW Pilsey (Fl G 5s) and N Pilsey (unlit) G con buoys; the W edge of the fairway is marked by lines of mooring trots which stretch N from Sandy Pt. Verner pile bn (R can daymark, Fl R 10s) should be left to port, then Marker Point bn (G con daymark, Fl(2)G 10s) to stb. From here it is less than a mile to the junction of Sweare Deep and Fowley Rythe, marked on the port hand by NE Hayling pile bn (R can topmark, Fl(2)R 10s).

Some 100m to the NE is Emsworth bn (S Card Q(6)+L Fl 5s), the first of a line of pile moorings on the W edge of the chan leading to Emsworth. Sail close to the piles leaving swinging moorings to stb until Fisherman's bn (R can daymark, Fl(3)R 10s) is reached; from here the chan dries. Fisherman's bn leads 020° on Echo pile bn (G con daymark, Fl(3) 10s), leaving Fisherman's Walk (landing at LW) to port marked by perches with red cans. At Echo turn to stb for Emsworth Yacht Hr or port for South Street quay. EYH is accessible to yachts of 1.2m draft at HWN, the sill drying 2.5m above Portsmouth datum. All facilities. Clubs, shipyards.

Sweare Deep is entered between NE Hayling and Emsworth pile bns, running NW towards Hayling road bridge. There are depths of 1–2m for ½M until Sweare Deep port hand bn is reached (Fl(3)R 10s), whence it gradually shallows until Northney port hand bn (Fl(4)R 10s), after which the chan dries as does the entrance to the marina, which runs off to the SW marked by stakes with R can topmarks. Progress to Hayling (fixed) road bridge and Langstone village (SC, inn) is through New Cut, a narrow drying chan well marked by perches.

Two navigable creeks flow into the W side of the main Emsworth Chan, as follows.

Mengham Rythe is entered immediately N of Sandy Pt, leaving the tide gauge to stb. There is a bar at the entrance with only 0.3m at LAT, but within the creek there are pools with 1–3m. Sparkes Boatyard is on the S side at the end of the first reach. The chan soon turns NW and is marked by perches, with moorings in mid-channel (least depth 1m). When the chan turns sharply SW depths decrease and within 50m it dries completely. Strangers should enter on the flood as it is easy to go aground and there is very little room. Dinghies can reach the quay of Mengham Rythe SC. Mengham, 1M inland, has PO, garage and shops.

Mill Rythe is a quiet creek marked by a R can buoy, which should be left to port;

Verner pile bn is located about 1 ca N of the entrance. The chan is marked by perches, and once inside there are depths of 0.3–1.5m until Wall Corner, the first steep-to bank on the port side, where a disused scaffolding pier should be given a reasonable berth. From here the creek dries out, the S arm leading to the slips of the Hayling Is Yacht Co., the N arm to the old stagings at Yachthaven. At MHWS craft of 1.8m draft can reach the head of either arm, but local advice is advised for drafts greater than 1.2m. Vessels not able to take the ground comfortably are not advised to enter without local knowledge.

PASSAGE NOTES: CHICHESTER TO NEWHAVEN

Charts BA 1652, 2045

When rounding Selsey Bill inshore in good conditions it is usual for yachts going up-Channel to take the Looe Channel. However, the distance can be shortened and the tidal stream in the Looe avoided by going close inshore, when circumstances permit. For 2½h either side of HW, the passage of the Bill may be made close inshore. However, good local knowledge and perfect weather conditions are necessary.

From the E the LB Ho may be approached on a bearing of not less than 280°. The line of the Bill may then be followed round approx 46m off the ends of the beaconed groynes until the windmill (conspic) is abeam, when head out for Nab Tr 238°. Care should be taken to keep S of transit of mill with water tr to clear The Hounds. On this passage shallowest water will occur between end of Selsey High St and CG tr. When ½M clear of the shore, if bound for Chichester a course should be laid towards the Chichester bn to clear the old target and the Pole Sand at the W edge of Bracklesham Bay. From the W, head for windmill (conspic) with Nab Tr astern, then follow line of beaconed groynes.

DS the Looe: E +4.45; W −1.20. DS S of Owers: E +5.40; W −0.50.

Note that the direction of the stream changes considerably earlier than in the Looe or offshore, and that on the early sp ebb a current of 6 to 7kn may be met with just to the E and round the pitch of the Bill. If proceeding E the effect of this may be reduced by a wider sweep offshore.

Between Selsey Bill and Beachy Head with a foul tide the full strength of the stream may be escaped by keeping inshore. Care must be exercised between Angmering and Shoreham where shallows extend a considerable distance offshore especially to seaward of Worthing pier. All along this coast the change of direction of the stream may be as much as 1½–2h before the main stream offshore.

Anchorage In W and N weather anch may be obtained in 2 to 3½m in the Run N and S of the LB Ho taking care to avoid fixed moorings. Although marked on BA charts as obstructed, the Park, NE of Selsey Bill, is reported to be clear of obstructions, at least inshore of the bn, and can be a comfortable berth for small craft in offshore weather.

LITTLEHAMPTON
Chart BA 1991 (Plan p81)

HW (ent) +0.20. DS: W −1.00; E +6.00.

MHWS 5.7; MLWS 0.5; MTL 3.1; MHWN 4.6; MLWN 1.7.

Bar Shallowest part dries 0.1m near West Pier. The shoal area extends 3 ca seawards.

Anchorage SE winds send in the largest sea, SW make the most on the bar. Yachts waiting tide to enter should anch due S of hr entrance about ¾M offshore in 2½m. This anchorage gets considerable shelter in W and WSW winds from the Owers shoal.

Approach The entrance lies between a pier on the W side and a pier and Training Wall extension on the E side which runs out 2.3 ca from the shore. The Training Wall is marked by seven perches; a bn stands at its end and has a diamond topmark. The W pier has a round refuge at the outer end.

All craft entering the harbour should keep the leading lts (345°) in line: front, iron column, FR; rear, 9m white concrete tr YW sector Oc 7.5s. These lights lead to the entrance; then proceed up the hr to Fisherman's Quay marked by a FW lt.

Pilot boat with lts or flag signifies commercial vessel is about to enter or leave hr and all craft must keep clear of the narrows.

Entrance The stream is slacker on the W side of the hr on the flood. It rushes round the pier-head from the E and causes an eddy.

Craft should keep to the E centre of fairway entering, to allow for the W-going set of the tide which commences 2h before HW. The spring ebb tide can reach up to 5kn.

Shoal water exists within 25m of the W pier and alongside the Training Wall. Caution should be observed below half-tide.

Berthing All visiting craft should report to the HM at County Wharf on the stb hand when entering; it can be recognised by a conspic R crane. Water available at this berth. Rly. All facilities. EC Wed.

There is a swing bridge ¾M from the entrance which is only opened for commercial shipping. Beware of the swing bridge and its projecting breakwaters. Headroom under the bridge is 1.8m at MHWS. A marina for small craft lies just upstream from the bridge on the port side. No anch in river. The river is navigable for 7M for reasonable draft: boats drawing 1.2m can reach Arundel; dinghies can reach Amberley. Ford bridge is fixed.

SHOREHAM
Chart BA 2044 (Plan p82)

HW +0.10. DS: W −1.40; E +5.30.

MHWS 6.2; MLWS 0.7; MTL 3.4; MHWN 5.0; MLWN 1.9.

Bar About 2.5m between pier-heads but depth varies with weather. Continuous W or SW winds may cause silting. Dredger frequently working in channel.

The hr is available in all weathers. There is 2kn stream into the entrance at sp.

Approach The power station chimneys, lt FR, ¾ to 1M E of entrance, are a good landmark visible for some miles from seaward. At night, Lt Ho shows Fl 10s

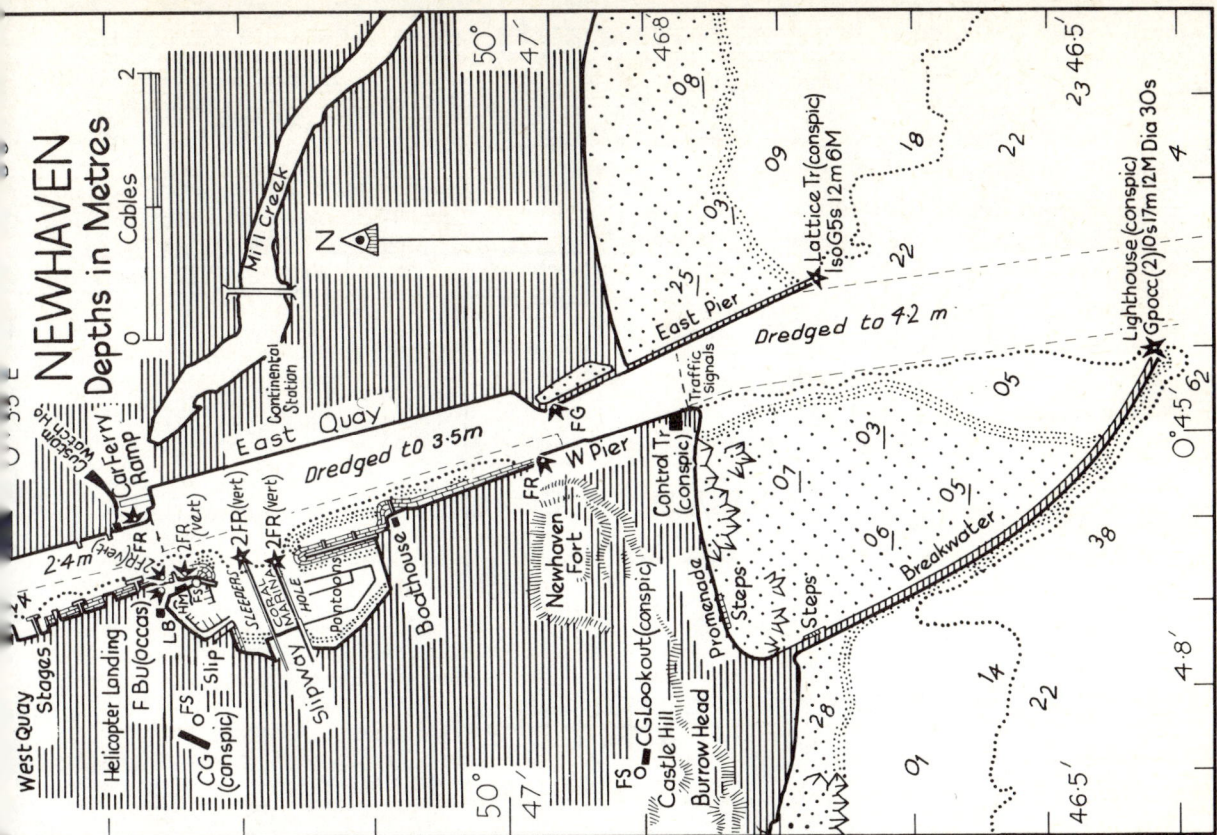

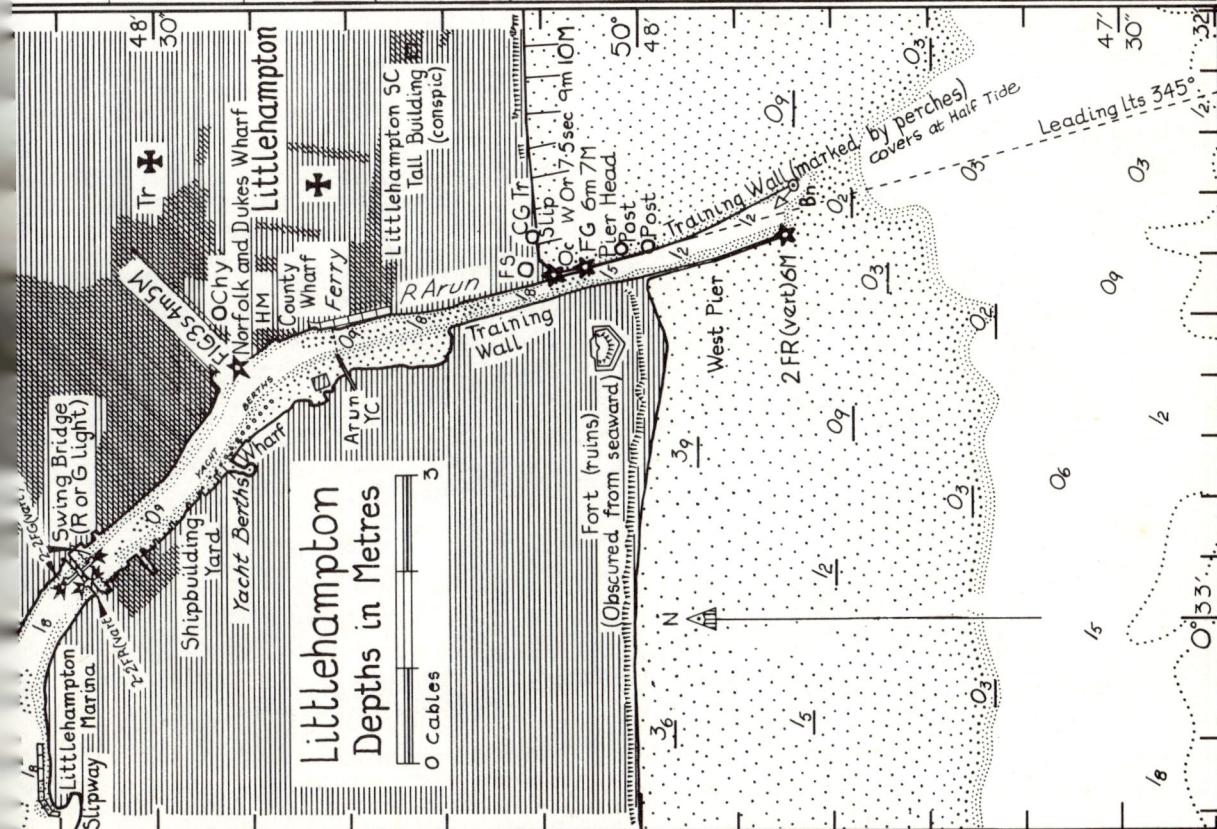

NEWHAVEN Depths in Metres

Cables

Mill Creek

N

Car Ferry Ramp

Customs Ho

Watch Ho

East Quay

Dredged to 3·5m

East Pier

Dredged to 4·2 m

Lattice Tr(conspic) IsoG5s 12m 6M

Lighthouse (conspic) Gpocc(2)10s17m12M Dia 30s

Continental Station

2·4 m

2FR(vert)
2FR(vert)
FR(vert)
FR(vert)
CENTRE FR
F Bu(occas)
LB
FS

SLEEPER
CORAL MARINA
HOLE
Pontoons
Slipway
Boathouse

West Quay
Stages
Helicopter Landing
CG (conspic)
FS

W Pier
FR
FG
FG
Control Tr (conspic)
Traffic Signals

Newhaven Fort
CG Lookout(conspic)
Castle Hill
Burrow Head
Promenade
Steps
Steps
Breakwater

FS

50° 47'
50° 47'

468
08
08
09
03
25
22
22
05
01
03
05
06
38
28
14
22
01
46·5'
46·5'
23 46·5'
4
0°45·6 E
4·8'

Littlehampton Depths in Metres

Tr

Tr

Littlehampton

Norfolk and Dukes Wharf

OChy

Littlehampton SC Tall Building (conspic)

FIG3·5m5M

HM
County Wharf
Ferry
R Arun
FS
CG Tr
Slip
Oc WOr 7·5 sec 9m 10M
FG 6m 7M
Pier Head
Post
Post
Bn

Training Wall (marked by perches)
covers at Half Tide

Leading Lts 345°

West Pier
2 FR (vert) 6M

Swing Bridge (R or G Light)
2FR(vert)

Shipbuilding Yard
Yacht Berths
Arun YC
BERTHS

Wharf

Littlehampton Marina
Slipway

Fort (ruins)
(Obscured from seaward)

N

0 Cables 3

4·8' 30"
50° 48'
4·7' 30"
32'

03
03
03
02
03
03
03
09
09
09
06
09
02
39
36
15
15
12
12
18
18
0°33'

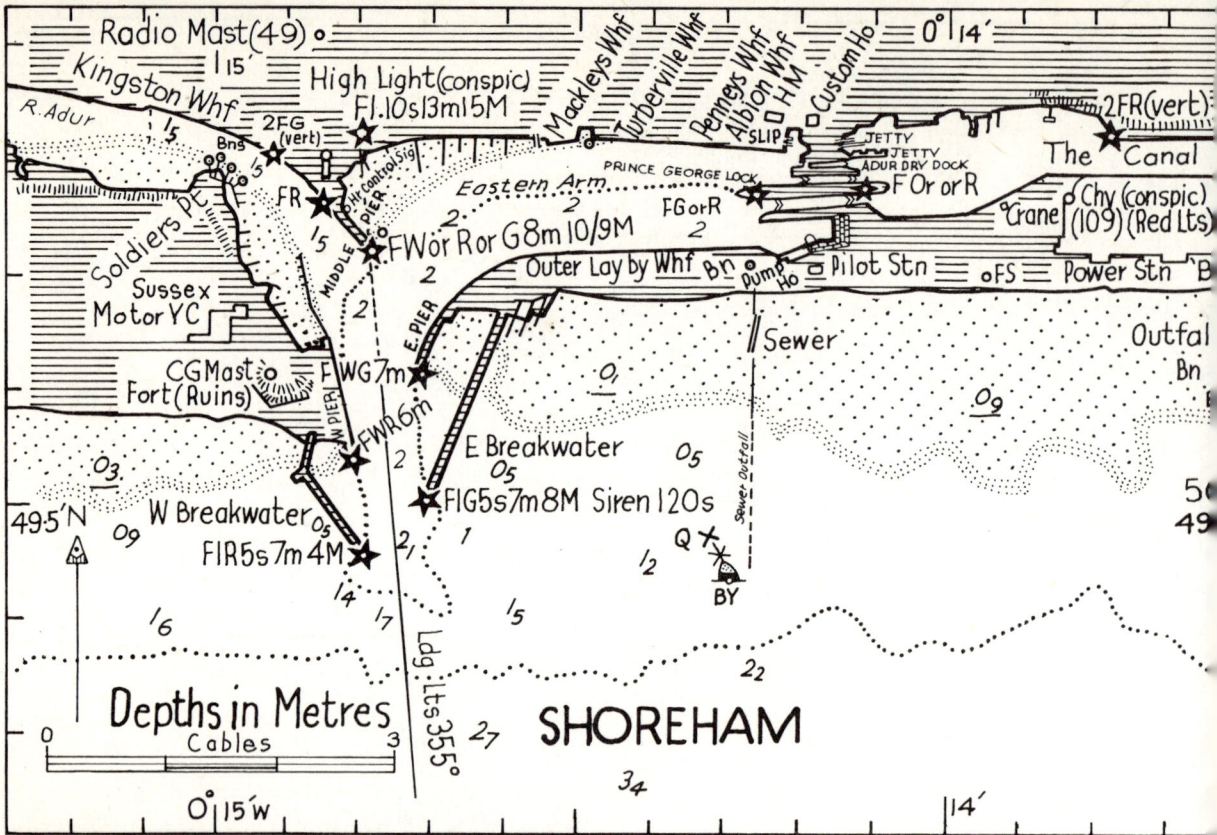

SHOREHAM

Depths in Metres

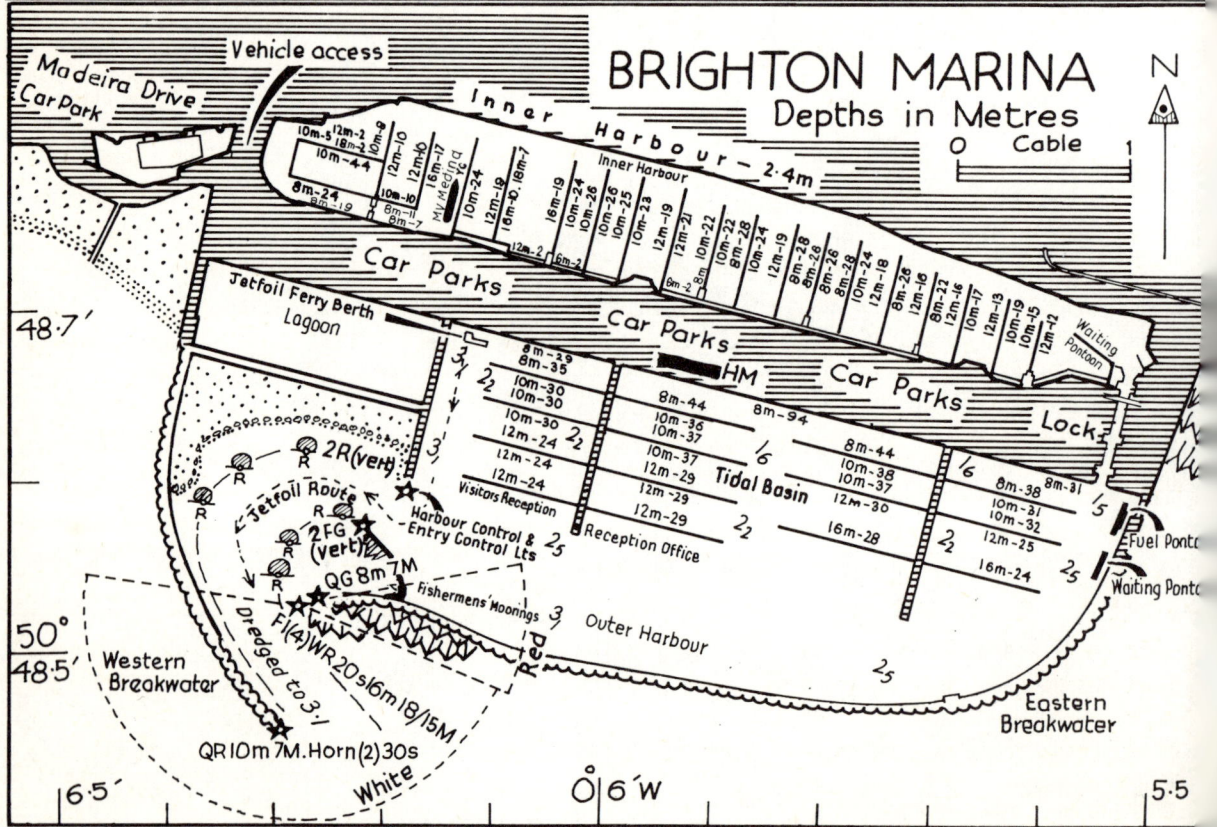

BRIGHTON MARINA
Depths in Metres

12M. Avoid Jenny Ground, 1¼M E of entrance, least depth 1.5m. Church Rks, least depth 0.9m, lie about 1½M W of entrance.

Entrance Lies between E and W breakwaters and further in between E and W piers. Within and opposite the entrance is another pier, known as Middle Pier, which divides the hr into two parts: the Western Arm, which is the main course of the river; and the Eastern Arm, which is an artificial hr the locked portion of which extends about 1½M into Southwick and Portslade and is called the Canal.

When entering, hr signals must be observed. Keep between the breakwater, Fl R 5s to port, G to stb, and the piers, FR to port, G to stb; keeping the front ldg lt on the Middle Pier watch house (FWRG depending on the depth of water) the upper half of which is W, the lower R, in line with the Lt Ho Fl 10s, 355°. Care is necessary at tide times to avoid the eddies along the piers, especially on the flood. Keep to the middle. Yachtsmen are advised not to use the Western Arm unless prepared to take the ground, but in heavy weather it may be the only practicable alternative if access to the Canal is not possible or permitted.

The hr is essentially commercial and yachtsmen must know and strictly obey the current bye-laws and signals.

Anchorage In good settled conditions 1 to 1½M from High Lt, bearing 360°, in about 7m.

Berthing *Western Arm:* avoid the groyne extending N from the W Pier, which is awash at half-tide and is marked with poles with port-hand topmarks. The flood and ebb set against the E end of Kingston Wharf, by the entrance to the river, and past the pt opposite; thereafter the tide sets fairly. Mud berths are sometimes available by arrangement with local yards. All stores and some facilities. Rly, Shoreham-by-Sea (London 1¼h). EC Wed.

Eastern Arm: unless prior arrangements for berthing have been made entry to the Eastern Arm may be forbidden. While awaiting pre-arranged lock opening, recommended anch due S of slipway on Mackley's Wharf just N of 1.5m chan.

Locks are normally manned 4h before to 2h after HW. The Prince George Lock is usually used for yacht traffic. Immediately through the lock on port hand are moorings (only available by prior arrangement) alongside or on mooring buoys.

All facilities and stores. Good laying-up ashore or afloat. YC. Dry dock for vessels up to 50m. Rly Southwick (London 1¼h), 5 min walk. Buses to Brighton (20 min). EC Wed.

BRIGHTON
Chart BA 1652 (Plan p82)
HW +0.05.   DS: W −2.00; E +4.00. Streams weak.
MHWS 6.5; MLWS 0.6; MTL 3.5; MHWN 5.1; MLWN 1.9.

The man-made hr projects from below the first cliffs of Brighton and accommodates many yachts and small fishing boats. There is over 3m in the entrance. Although exposed to SE the entrance is quite easy under power in most conditions. Under sail it is trickier, because of the high breakwaters and the bend in the chan.

Approach   No outlying dangers. Nearby landmarks include Roedean School on clifftops to E, and to W a tall block of flats with conspic W vert stripe. At night a Lt Ho Fl(4) 20s marks the entrance. This Lt Ho stands near W end of E (main) breakwater and has a R sector covering E breakwater; keep in W sector. Breakwater heads have lts Fl R (W breakwater) and Fl G (E breakwater) vis 7M. A Ro Bn ('BM' on 303.4kHz, 10M) is located at the Lt Ho. HM listens on VHF Ch. 37, 24h.

Entrance   Near W end of hr where W breakwater overlaps E breakwater. Avoid shoal obstn adjacent S and N of E breakwater hd. After running NW inside the W breakwater the chan curves steadily to stb beyond the E breakwater and is marked by three Lt buoys (two Fl R and one Fl G) but look out also for small unlit sph R and G buoys. Between dusk and midnight in summer strip-lighting inside W breakwater illuminates the chan. Enter the tidal basin between the inner breakwaters (lts 2 FR (vert) to port, 2 FG (vert) to stb); by this time the heading is roughly E.

Caution: a triangle of three amber Fl Lts on the N inner breakwater warns of Jetfoil manoeuvring: keep clear of the Jetfoil channel along the E side of that breakwater and the buoyed section of ent chan, unless authorised by Hr Control on VHF ch 37.

Berthing   Visitors' reception pontoon, clearly signed, lies immediately inside the tidal basin. Water, toilets, showers, shops, clubhouse (MV *Medina*). Normal lock opening times: 0800–2000 on demand.

Petrol, diesel, bottled gas from pontoon at E end of tidal basin, near lock. For the boatyard, pass through lock. Buses to Brighton town centre and Rly station.

NEWHAVEN   Chart BA 2154   (Plan p81)
HW +0.00.   DS in offing: E −5.35; W −0.15.
MHWS 6.6; MLWS 0.5; MTL 3.6; MHWN 5.2; MLWN 1.9.
The hr is accessible in all weathers. There is 4.2m in the entrance which is protected by a breakwater 715m long. The hr lies immediately E of Burrow Hd which is the E end of the line of cliffs stretching from Brighton to Newhaven. The coast to the E of the hr is low as far as Seaford Hd but the Downs can be seen in the background.

Approach   From the E steer for Burrow Hd until the breakwater is sighted, when steer to leave the Lt Ho at the end (Oc(2) 10s) to port. In heavy weather keep breakwater Lt Ho to stb until E pier lts are open, to clear shallows E of entrance.

From the W, Seaford (with its lts at night and Seaford Hd to S by day) makes a convenient mark to steer on until the breakwater comes in sight.

Entrance   Within the breakwater keep the W side of hr open in order to clear the mud of the W side between the breakwater and the W pier. The wind baffles under Burrow Hd with heavy squalls in a W blow. Traffic signals from W pier must be obeyed by all vessels. A R ball or G over R lt permits entry or exit by small vessels (under 15m) with care; triangle over ball or G lt, entry no exit; ball

over triangle or R lt, exit no entry; ball-triangle-ball or RGR lts, port temporarily closed to all traffic. (Signals other than the first are for commercial shipping.)
Berthing Once inside the piers the East Quay opens up to stb and the marina in Sleepers Hole to port. Just beyond the ferry ramp to stb is the HM's watch ho and berthing instructions will be given from here by loud-hailer.

It is usual to tie up to staging berths, or to other vessels already there. The hr bottom is soft mud.

All facilities. Fuel barge, water from hose at berth. Good hard, apply HM. EC Wed.

PASSAGE NOTES: NEWHAVEN TO RAMSGATE
Charts BA 536, 1892, 1828

Beachy Hd DS(2M S): W +0.15; E −5.20.   Dungeness DS(2M SE): SW +4.30; NE −2.00
With sufficient speed a fair tide can be carried for 10h to N Foreland where it slacks at +4.40. Streams run at 2½kn at sp off Beachy Hd, Royal Sovereign and Dungeness, but only 1kn between Royal Sovereign and Dungeness.
S Foreland to N Foreland DS S Goodwin: SW +4.00; NE −2.00; Gull Stream: SSW +4.35; NNE −1.35; 3M SE of N Foreland lt: SSW +4.40; NE −1.20.
Inshore streams Between S Foreland and Deal: S +4.15; N −1.50. Off Ramsgate Hr: SW +4.00; NE −2.10. Ramsgate to N Foreland: S +4.20; N −1.40.

A vessel passing Dungeness at the beginning of the W-going stream will have a fair stream for only 2h. When bound W it pays to round Dungeness on the last of a fair stream, fight the comparatively slight foul stream between Rye and Hastings, and pick up the next fair stream off Eastbourne.
Anchorages *Seaford Road* Anch off Seaford ¼M offshore abreast the ch. Sheltered from ESE to NNW. Very little stream, good holding ground. If only staying a night and the wind is offshore, some may prefer this anch rather than enter Newhaven. It is possible to run into Newhaven if the wind should come onshore.

Hook Rocks The Fairlight cliffs terminate at their E end in a ledge of rk running down to E, off which is sufficient room for small vessels to shelter with the wind W to SW. Rye fishermen often anch there.

Dungeness, West Road Anch in NE winds, 1M inside the Ness out of strength of the stream. *East Road* Good anch NE of the Ness in 5½m MLWS with Lydd ch on with the CGS and Newcombe buoy bearing about 073°. The holding ground is good and shelter is afforded with the wind as far round as SW by S. Vessels will lie wind-rode, the strength of the stream sweeping round the bay further offshore. This anch may be preferred to a heavy beat to windward down-Channel.

Small Downs Anch about 1M N of Deal Pier off Sandown Castle, rather less than ½M offshore, sheltered from SSW through W to N. Good holding, some stream but much less than further out. If the wind should blow onshore vessels can run through the Ramsgate chan to Ramsgate, get away to the S, or run through the Gull Stream if bound in that direction.

Off Ramsgate In calm weather or with the wind between NW and NE an outside anch may be preferred to lying in the hr. Good anch about 3 ca SW of Ramsgate hr entrance in 2½m. From this position it is easy to slip into the hr if necessary. Good holding. A tidal eddy renders it advisable to moor if staying more than a few hours.

Anch further S in Pegwell Bay is not recommended, as the fetch from the W is too great when Sandwich flats are covered.

RYE
Chart BA 1991 (Plan p87)

HW +0.00. DS: E −4.00; W +3.00.
(Approach) MHWS 7.7; MHWN 6.0. (Harbour) MHWS 5.3; MHWN 3.6.
The hr should be entered 1–1½h before HW. The whole hr dries well before LW even at neaps.

Bar The sands off the hr are flat and shoal gradually to the entrance, drying ½M or more offshore at MLWS. The bar shifts in position and height but is of little consequence around HW.

Approach The hr lies in the apex of Rye Bay, 9M from Dungeness and 4M E of Fairlight Cliffs. From W in hazy weather these cliffs may be identified by CGS and conspic square tr of Fairlight ch on skyline. From E, follow the coast from Dungeness about 1M offshore until the W pier and tripod bn are seen. Approach the entrance from the SE. A clear chan 300m wide is maintained between the Fairway buoy Fl 10s (1.8M from the ent) and the entrance, in which no fishing or anchoring is permitted and no nets may be laid. Vessels should approach by this chan as otherwise they may foul nets.

The head of the W groyne 2½ ca from land has a lt bn Fl R 5s, 7.3m 6M, and the head of the E pier has a lt Fl 2.5s 7m 4M. The ldg lts on E pier are: front Fl G, rear Oc WG 4s, W sector 326° to 331°, in line 329°. Steer 330° on E pier lt and then enter. To await tide, anch 1M offshore with lt on this bearing in 3½–4½m, hard sand, good holding. Three port hand QR lts mark chan to Rye Hr village; three QR lts mark limit of private mooring area on W bank off Rye Hr village. There is a QR lt about 1½ ca below bend into unlit Rock chan below Rye town.

Entrance In normal conditions the entrance is straightforward, but it should not be attempted in strong onshore winds. It lies between a groyne on the W side and a steel and concrete training wall on the E, the whole of the latter covering near MHWS except for the post at the end. The sea piles up the shingle on the W side of the entrance, but otherwise there are no hazards in the chan. There is 5.5m at MHWS in midstream as far as the moorings off Rye Hr village (see below) 1M from the entrance.

Rye town is 1M further upstream, with the Fish Market staging (4.5m MHWS) used only by fishing vessels and the Strand Quay (3.0m MHWS) used by vessels of all types. Those bound for Strand Quay should turn off 90° to port taking a wide sweep into Rock chan before reaching the Fish Market. Rock Chan is

RYE HARBOUR
Depths in Metres

Cables

N

Camber 50°

Channel marked by beacons

R. Rother

STRAND QUAY
Spire & FS (art)
2FR
RYE
Rock
Martello Tr
R. Brede

RYE Quay

3-QR Commercial Quay
Private drying Moorings

Jetty Mooring Stages
FS
HM. Traffic Sigs
OcWG4s7/6M

SLIP
QR

Rye Hr
Enchantress Tr

QR

East Pier

QG3m3M

Training Wall, covers at HW
Marked by Bns

QR
QR

Q(9)15s7m5M

Camber Sand

3. Camber Sand

FlR5s7m6M

Ldg Lts 329°

Training Wall, Covers at HW
Marked by Bns

Camber Castle (ruins)

T H E   G U Y N E S

0₃

0₄

0₅

0₉

1₇

1₃

0°46'

0°48'

0°47'

0°45'

44'

45'

46'

47'

48'

50'

56'

50°

56'

Based on British Admiralty Charts (nos. in text) with the permission of the Controller of H.M. Stationery Office and of the Hydrographer of the Navy, and on other sources.

narrow but marked by bns and there is a sharp bend to stb before the Strand Quay can be seen. There is a slipway for careening only at the seaward end of Strand Quay.

Berthing Instructions should be obtained from HM's office on stb hand opposite Rye Hr village. All craft must be prepared to take the ground. A few berths are available to visitors at seaward end of catwalk extension near HM's office. Alternatively proceed to Strand Quay to berth alongside, soft mud. This is more suitable for deep-keel yachts than the catwalk. Local knowledge should be sought for level bottom.

Tides The flood tide first covers the sand outside, and only commences to enter hr 2½h after LW then setting in rapidly, attaining 3 to 4kn at sp for more than 1h before HW −1. At HW −1 at sp the tide flows over the outer half of E pier as well as over the W retaining wall (both marked by bns), and then the stream in the fairway slackens. This is the best time to enter.

Caution The last hr of flood and first hr of ebb both set diagonally over the outer half of E pier at sp tides only, when great care is required. At neaps the E pier does not cover. There is no absolute slack water. Strong E winds hold the water back, reducing the rise in hr entrance by 0.6m but there is rarely less than 3.3m at MHWN.

Facilities *Rye Hr village* On the opposite side to the HM office are the Rye Hr SC, village stores, inn and PO. Water on both banks. Under HM office is a shower, WC and tel. *Rye town* Several small yards with slipways and chandlery between Fish Market and Strand Quay. All provisions, fuel, water, shops, inns, PO, rly. EC tues.

FOLKESTONE   Chart BA 1991   (Plan p90)
HW −0.15.   DS: E −2.00; W +5.00.
MHWS 7.1; MLWS 0.7; MTL 3.9; MHWN 5.7; MLWN 2.0.
The hr entrance dries at LW. Yachts can lie in shelter of the outer pier at any time of tide.

Approach To clear dangers offshore, keep S Foreland open of Dover cliffs by day and the S Foreland Lt open by night. Approach the pier between the bearings of W by N and ENE. The stream sweeps past the outer pier and leaves an eddy. Do not enter if B flag is flying at pier-head as this indicates a ferry is about to enter or leave.

Berthing The harbour is untenable in very strong winds from the E. For refuge in such conditions anch in shingle just W of pier near Trinity Ho Lookout Stn. In normal conditions if not wishing to take the ground anch just outside entrance to fishing hr (to E of pier), sand. Good holding ground and comfortable in winds of up to F6 from S or W. If prepared to take the ground enter the fishing hr from 2h before to 3h after HW and lie alongside quay in thick mud (beware of muddy gulley a few feet out from quayside). Alternatively lie to own ground tackle (fore and aft) among sailing yachts in the fishing hr.

All facilities. Water from HM. Hard, slip, 5 ton crane. EC Wed.

DOVER Chart BA 1698 (Plan p90)

HW +0.00. DS: E −2.00; W +5.00.

MHWS 6.7; MLWS 0.8; MTL 3.7; MHWN 5.3; MLWN 2.0.

Approach Shallow-draft boats may escape the tide by keeping close inshore when past S Foreland. W gales cause a race off the S breakwater.

Entrance There are two entrances. Traffic control signals are in operation. Vessels intending to enter should carry the complete list of regulations and signals on board, but to summarise for emergency use, vessels with VHF should keep in contact with Port Control while entering or leaving. Working Ch is 74, or call on 16 if not fitted and ask for transfer to Ch 12 (only manned on request). Otherwise 'SV' (· · ·   · · · −) to Port Control by Aldis means 'I wish to enter', 'SW' (· · ·   · − −) 'I wish to leave'. Day signals, both entrances, 3 R balls in triangle, vessels may leave with permission, no entry; 2 R balls vertical, vessels may enter with permission, no exit; 3 R balls vertical (or 3 R lts at night), no entrance or exit. Other night signals: at the E entrance, 2 G lts visible to you means you may proceed through the entrance with permission; at the W entrance, 3 R lts in a triangle permit exit, 3 W lts in a triangle permit entrance, both with permission. A Q Fl lamp from the control tower means keep clear of the entrance you are approaching.

The streams sets from N to S across the E breakwater entrance except from HW −2.00 to +3.00. In strong winds the heaviest sea at the entrance is from HW to HW +4.00: it is advisable to avoid this period during heavy weather. The tidal stream flows in at the W entrance clockwise and into the centre of the hr.

In onshore winds there is a confused sea off the W entrance and especially at LW. The breakwaters obscure vessels about to leave hr. Keep up-tide until traffic signals permit entrance.

Berthing Yachts anch on E side of Prince of Wales Pier, 3½ to 7½m, inshore of the line of Y buoys marking the Hovercraft flight path. Bad swell.

Avoid using the Camber (Eastern Docks); there is heavy car ferry traffic. The old Inner Hr gives access to Wellington Dock. The tidal hr has 0.4m between the piers and a large part dries out. On entering the Inner Hr avoid Mole Head Rks 6m off the N pier and staging on the opposite side. The piers are lit QG and QR.

Entrance to Wellington Dock approx 1½h before HW to HW. As the yacht approaches the dock-head, it will be called alongside Crosswell Quay for berthing instructions.

All facilities. Water from HM at all piers and docks. Boats may be laid ashore on E side of Inner Hr. EC Wed.

RICHBOROUGH

HW +0.20. DS (offing): NE −2.10; SW +4.00.

Richborough Quay is privately owned, and is ½M up the River Stour; small tankers use the Quay.

Bar Dries; 3–4m at HW.

Entrance The entrance to the chan in Pegwell Bay is buoyed. Inside the bar

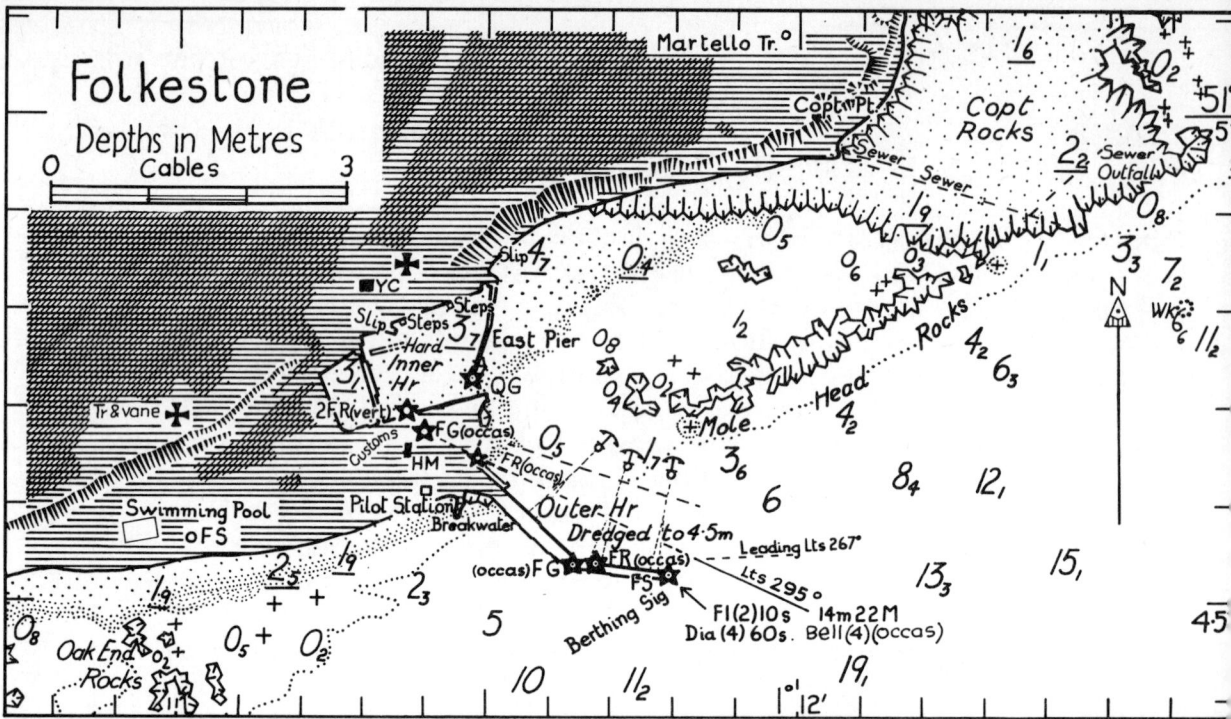

Folkestone
Depths in Metres

Cables

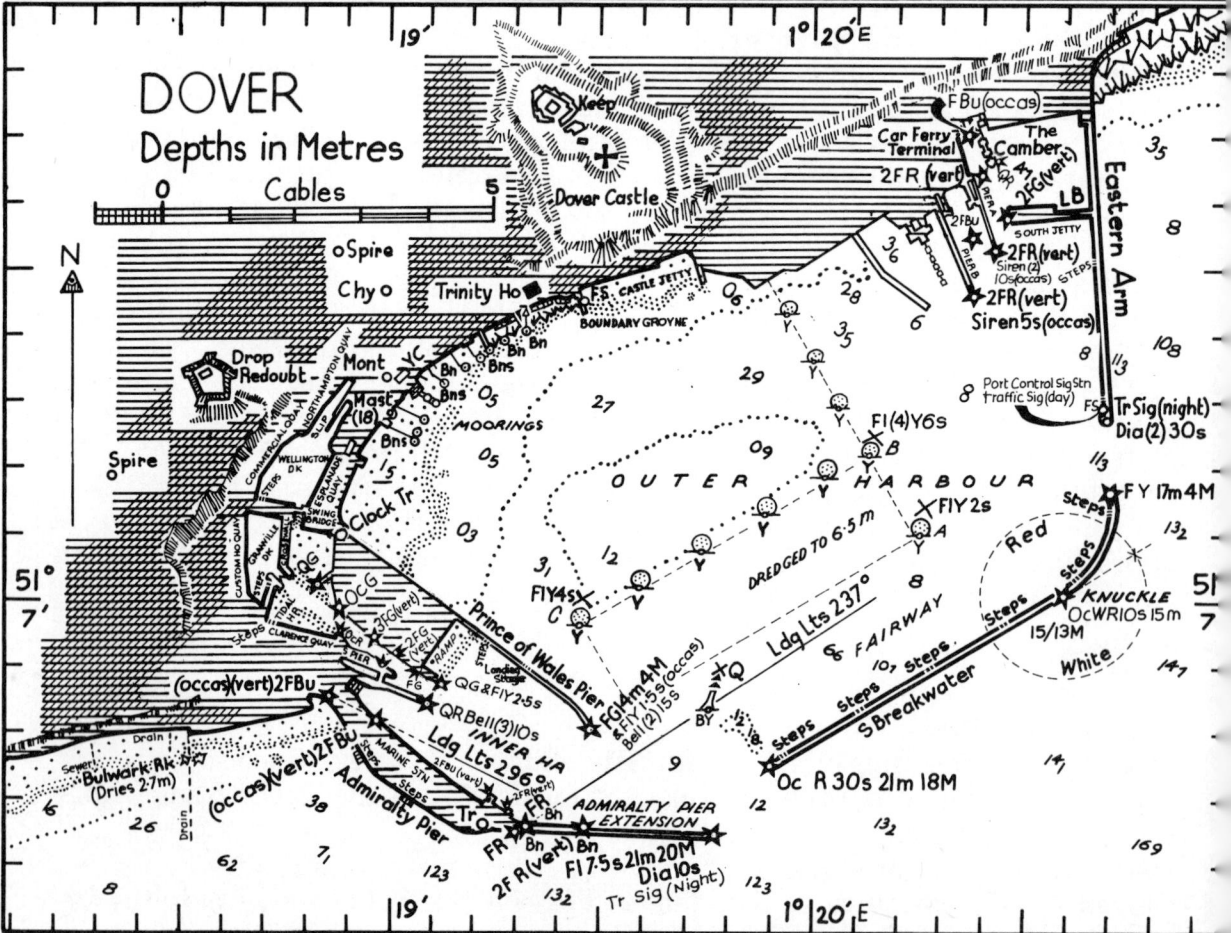

DOVER
Depths in Metres

Cables

Based on British Admiralty Charts (nos. in text) with the permission of the Controller of H.M. Stationery Office and the Hydrographer of the Navy, and on other sources.

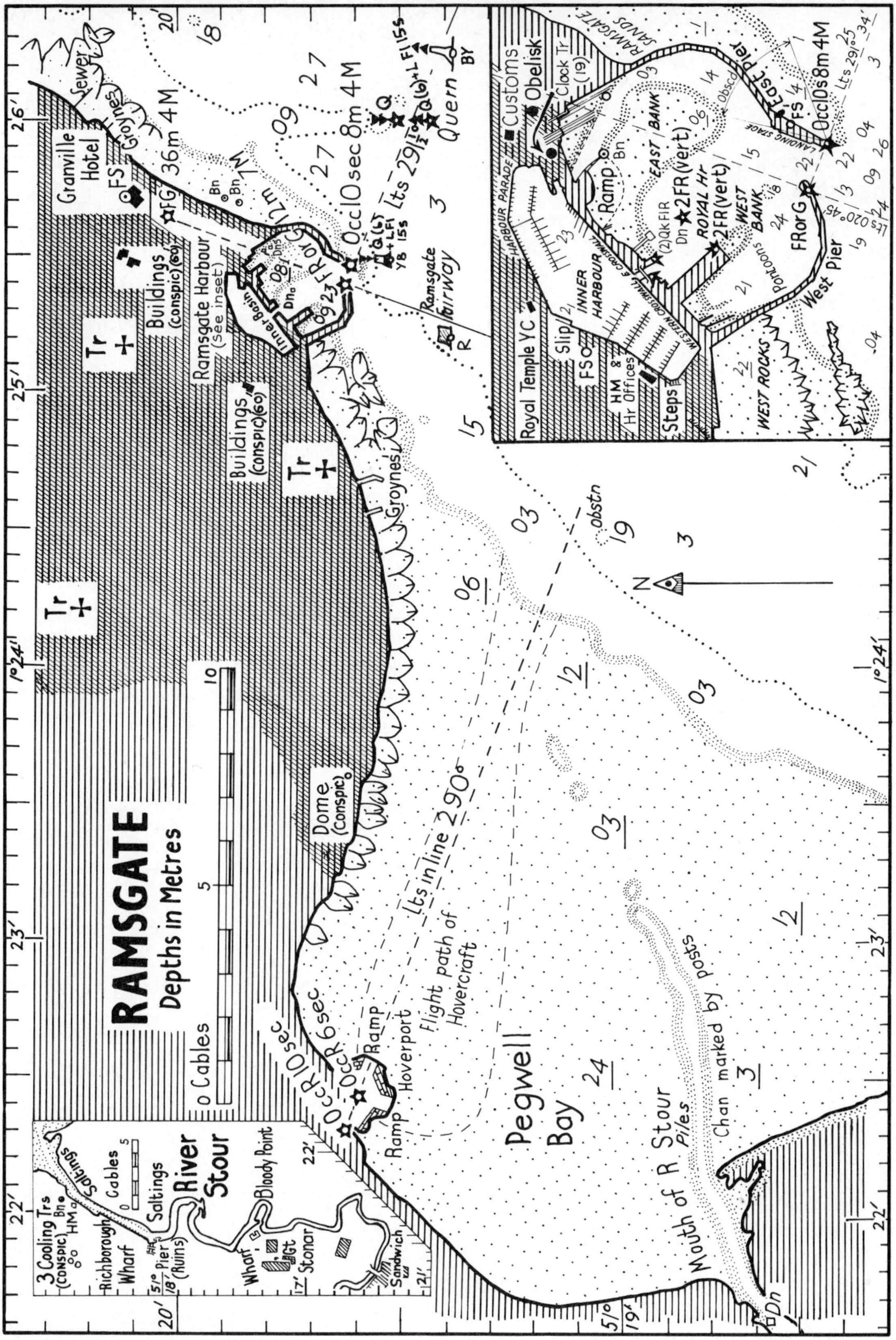

RAMSGATE
Depths in Metres

Main chart labels:

Sewer

Granville Hotel

FS

Groynes

36m 4M

2m

Bn. Bn.

Buildings (conspic)(60)

Tr ✝

Buildings (conspic)(60)

Tr ✝

Ramsgate Harbour (See inset)

Inner basin

FG

Dn

08

0.9 2.3 FR

Tr ✝

Dome (conspic)

Groynes

Occl 10 sec 8m 4M

FL Q(6) + L Fl 15s YB

Lts 29½

L Fl(5) Q(16)

G(5)

+ L Fl

YB 15s

Quern BY

Ramsgate Fairway R

09 27 27

27

09

18 20 20'

26'

26'

25'

1°24'

23'

22'

15

03

06

obstn 19

3

12

03

N

03

12

(Lts in line 290°)

Flight path of Hovercraft

Pegwell Bay

24

Piles

Chan marked by posts

3

12

Mouth of R Stour

Dn

21

Occ R 6 sec

Occ R 10 sec

Ramp Hoverport

Ramp

0 Cables 5 10

River Stour inset (lower left):

River Stour

3 Cooling Trs (conspic)

Bn. HM.

Richborough Wharf

5' Pier

18' Pier (Ruins)

HM.

Saltings

Saltings

Bloody Point

Wharf

Jct

Stonar

Wharf

Sandwich

0 Cables 5

22'

20' 19'

5° 5'

12'

17'

17'

Ramsgate Harbour inset (top right):

RAMSGATE SANDS

Lts 29¼ 25 34

Obelisk

Clock Tr (19)

Customs

Harbour Parade

Ramp

Bn.

EAST BANK

WEST BANK

(2)QkFlR Dn

ROYAL HR

2FR(Vert)

2FR(Vert)

FRorG

FS

Occl 10s 8m 4M

Lts 020° 45

Royal Temple YC

Slip

FSO

Steps

HM & Hr Offices

INNER HARBOUR

Potholcos

West Pier

WEST ROCKS

East Pier

Landing Stage

0.3

0.4

0.5

0.6

0.6

1.5

2.2

2.2

2.1

2.3

2.4

1.8

09 03 03

04 26

25

13

24

2.1

0.4

Based on British Admiralty Charts (nos. in text) with the permission of the Controller of H.M. Stationery Office and of the Hydrographer of the Navy, and on other sources.

there is a min depth of 4.5m at HW for 10 miles. Keep to mid-chan. For a further 12M the river is non-tidal and carries a depth of about 2m.

At Sandwich, about 6M from entrance, there is an opening bridge (no charge). There is little room at the boatyard; slip for up to 12m, water, fuel and electric light available. Berths (dry mud). Sandwich, one of the Cinque Ports, is an interesting old town. Bus to Ramsgate.

RAMSGATE   Chart BA 1827   (Plan p91)

HW +0.20.   DS (offing): NE −2.10; SW +4.00. At Gull buoy: NNE −1.30; SSW +4.40.

MHWS 4.9; MLWS 0.4; MTL 2.6; MHWN 3.8; MLWN 1.2.

Approach   The entrance has 1.8m or less, variable. Tide gauge. Signals from Watch Ho on pier-head: permission to enter, B flag (Q lt at night); permission to leave, 2 B balls (QR at night). The app chan from the E is well marked by lt bns and buoys, and is dredged to 5.2m up to the ferry berth on the outside of the W pier. The ferry must be given right of way if met. Avoid the unlit Quern N Card buoy. From the S, app by the Ramsgate Chan, leaving G con buoys fairly close to stb, or by the Gull Stream and then by the main E app chan.

Entrance   Enter from well W of the E pier-head, as there is often a shallow spit running W from its end, then steer in keeping close to the outside of the W pier.

Berthing   From the hr entrance, steer directly for pontoon at the gate to the inner hr, or turn sharply to port for other pontoons on the inside of the W pier. The whole of the inner hr is a marina, with all facilities and visitors' berths; gate opens at approx HW −2 until HW −1.

Slip and grid at base of E wall, fuel from barge moored to W wall. All facilities except sailmaker. Owing to rabies regulations, there are strict prohibitions regarding animals in the entire area of the port. Rly (London 2h), all stores, R Temple YC. EC Thurs.

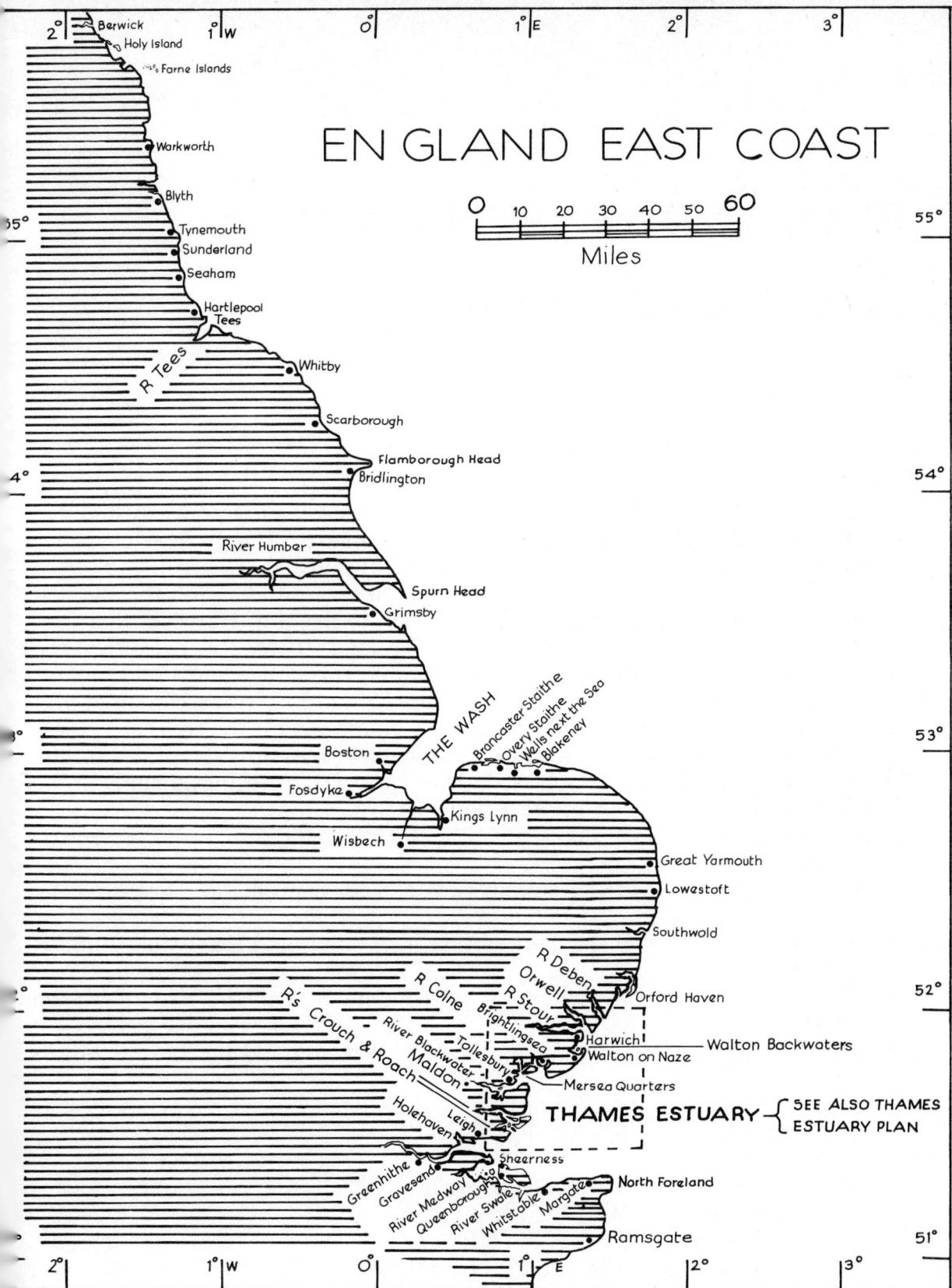

ENGLAND EAST COAST

0 10 20 30 40 50 60
Miles

- Berwick
- Holy Island
- Farne Islands
- Warkworth
- Blyth
- Tynemouth
- Sunderland
- Seaham
- Hartlepool
- Tees
- R Tees
- Whitby
- Scarborough
- Flamborough Head
- Bridlington
- River Humber
- Spurn Head
- Grimsby

THE WASH
- Brancaster Staithe
- Overy Staithe
- Wells next the Sea
- Blakeney
- Boston
- Fosdyke
- Kings Lynn
- Wisbech
- Great Yarmouth
- Lowestoft
- Southwold

R Deben
Orwell
R Colne
R Stour
Brightlingsea
R's Crouch & Roach
River Blackwater
Tollesbury
Maldon
Orford Haven
Harwich ———— Walton Backwaters
Walton on Naze
Mersea Quarters

THAMES ESTUARY { SEE ALSO THAMES ESTUARY PLAN

- Holehaven
- Leigh
- Greenhithe
- Gravesend
- Sheerness
- River Medway
- Queenborough
- River Swale
- Whitstable
- Margate
- North Foreland
- Ramsgate

55°
55°
54°
53°
52°
51°

2° 1° W 0° 1° E 2° 3°

ENGLAND, EAST COAST

North Foreland to Berwick

Charts BA 1607, 1975, 2052

In the Thames Estuary sandbanks are extensive and change frequently and it is essential to carry up-to-date and fully corrected charts. The N Kent coast has chalk cliffs as far as Westgate and is backed by hills; there are low cliffs at Warden Pt on the Is of Sheppey. From the Is of Grain to Clacton the shore is low. From Clacton to the Naze and at Bawdsey, to the N of Harwich, there are low sandstone cliffs. Conspic objects are N Foreland Lt Ho, Reculvers twin trs, the power stn chy at the mouth of the R Medway, two lattice masts on Foulness Is, the nuclear power stn at Bradwell, the Naze Tr and Felixstowe container port at the entrance to Harwich Hr. The estuary is notorious for the short steep seas raised in wind over tide conditions, particularly bad in NE winds in the Mid-Barrow area and off Clacton. Tides run up to 3kn at springs, mainly in the direction of the chans, those in the S being rotary.

Tides The interaction of the Estuary and Downs tides off N Foreland is summarised as follows.

(a) From −1.20 to +0.45 the stream runs N and W from the Downs to the Estuary.

(b) From +0.45 to +4.40 the Downs tide is N-going and the Estuary tide is E-going.

(c) From +4.40 to −4.50 the stream runs E and S from the Estuary to the Downs.

(d) From −4.50 to −1.20 the Estuary tide is W-going and the Downs tide is S-going.

At the N extremity of the Estuary:

DS Sunk LV	SW −5.40; NE +0.30

At intermediate points:

DS Tongue LV	W −5.00; E +1.25
Great Nore	W −4.35; E +1.45
Mid Barrow	SW −4.55; NE +1.15
Barrow Deep	SW − 5.25; NE +0.50

THAMES ESTUARY PASSAGES
Depths in Metres

Miles 0 ——— 5 ——— 10

HARWICH

Landguard Pt

(2)

Cork Hole

Cork Sand

(07)

Roughs Tr

R. STOUR

R. ORWELL

Walton Ch

Pye Sand

Walton Backwaters

WALTON-ON-NAZE

R. Colne

Brightlingsea

CLACTON

Medusa Ch

N. MERSEA

MERSEA QUARTERS

Tollesbury

R. Blackwater

Nuclear Power Stn

Bradwell

Sales Pt

St Peters Flats

KNOLL

Dengie Flats

WALLET

GUNFLEET SAND

Gunfleet Old Lt Hn (13m)

Sunk Hd. Tr (Ruins (5m))

EAST SWIN

Bn

Bn

Bn

Bn

Bn

LONG SAND

KNOCK DEEP

Bn

BUXEY SAND

Ray Sand

Whitaker Bn

E. BARROW

SUNK SAND

BLACK DEEP

DEEP

Fishermans Gat

FOULNESS SAND

Burnham on Crouch

R. CROUCH

Paglesham

FOULNESS. I.

Lattice Trs

R. Roach

Swatchway

WEST BARROW

WEST SWIN

BARROW

Knock John Tr (conspic)

Knock John Channel

S. LONG SAND

N. LONG SAND

Shingles Patch

W. Edinburgh Ch

S. Edinburgh Ch

Tongue Lt Vessel

Tongue Sand Tr (11m) (Conspic)

Havengore Crk

MAPLIN SANDS

THE WARP

Mouse

Oaze

OAZE DEEP

Knob Channel

SHINGLES

Shivering Sand Tr (17m)

Girdler

PRINCES CHANNEL

Tongue Sand

QUEENS CHANNEL

R. THAMES

Great Nore

Sand

Red Sand Tr (conspic) (17m)

Red Sand

Pan Sand

MARGATE SAND

Medway

The Cant

E. Spaniard

Warden Pt

R. Swale

Black Rk

Westgate

Margate

Capel Hill

Shell Ness

Whitstable Street

Reculvers

N. Foreland Lt Ho

Broadstairs

whitstable

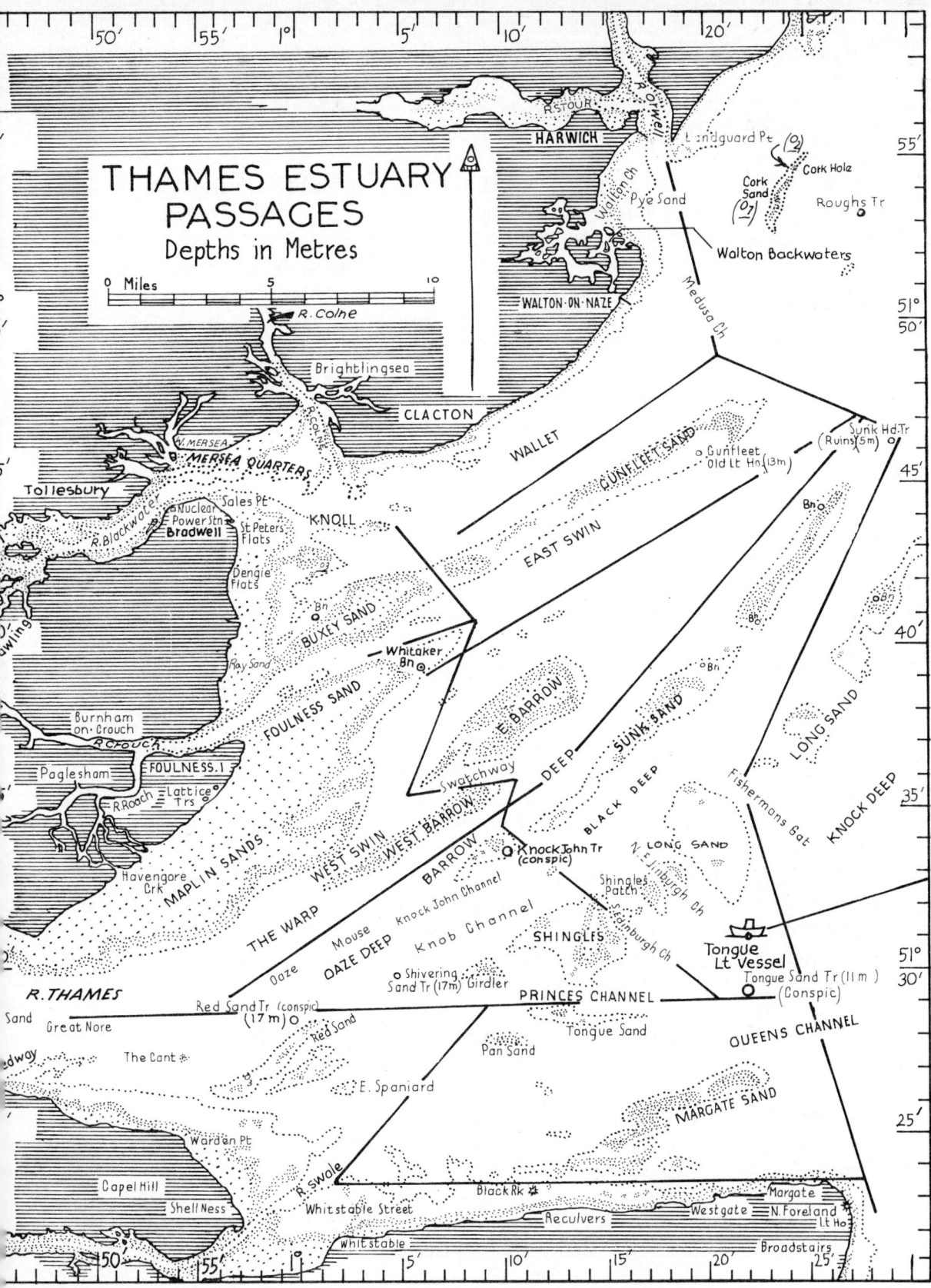

d on British Admiralty Charts (nos. in text) with the permission of the Controller of H.M. Stationery Office and of
Hydrographer of the Navy, and on other sources.

The Passage Notes are arranged as follows: (1) inwards and cross-Estuary from the S; (2) inwards from the N.

When traversing swatchways across the tide, a careful check must be maintained on soundings. For efficient passage-making in the Thames Estuary tides must be used to their best advantage: coming from the S this necessitates stemming an adverse tide in the Downs to make the first of the flood at N Foreland.

(1) N Foreland to the Swale, Rs Medway and Thames.

(a) Through the Horse and Gore chans, S of Margate Sands to the Spile in Four Fathoms chan. This passage is buoyed and lit but there are unmarked shallows and drying patches from the Margate Hook Spit to the Spile. In onshore winds there are no secure anchs other than the E Swale and R Medway.

(b) E of Margate Sand and through the Princes Chan.

DS Tongue LV W −5.00; E +1.25 (no slack, tide rotary). Princes Chan W −4.45; E +1.55.

This chan is well buoyed and lit; there is considerable commercial traffic.

(2) N Foreland to Rs Crouch, Blackwater and Colne.

From N Foreland pass E of Margate Sand and through the S Edinburgh Chan, marked only at the inner and outer ends, crossing the Knob and Black Deep Chans where extreme caution is necessary as tides run athwart the course. The swatchway across the Knock John Chan may be followed by keeping the Knock John and Knock John No. 1 buoys in transit astern, carefully watching soundings. (In 1980 there was a least depth of 1.5m at MLWS, 2.5m MLWN, on this line.) In the Barrow Deep proceed to Barrow Deep No. 9 lt buoy, thence through the Barrow Swatchway to the Maplin Bank lt buoy, and follow the E Swin Chan to the Whitaker Chan into the R Crouch or N across the Swin Spitway into the Rs Colne and Blackwater. An alternative route is to follow the Barrow Deep from Barrow Deep No. 9 lt buoy to Barrow Deep No. 3 lt buoy thence to the Whitaker lt buoy.

(3) N Foreland to Harwich.

(a) The direct route is E of the Margate Sands and the Tongue LV, through the Fisherman's Gat, entering the Black Deep between Nos. 8 and 10 buoys. Leave the Black Deep at the Sunk Head trs and proceed towards Harwich past the Gunfleet Spit buoy, entering Harwich from the Medusa Chan. When on passage N, continue N past the Sunk Head trs towards the Shipway or Sledway.

(b) As in (2) to Barrow No. 3, thence to the Gunfleet Spit buoy.

(c) Outside the sandbanks via the Kentish Knock, Longsand Head and Sunk LV.

(4) Sunk LV to Rs Medway and Thames.

The main chans are the Barrow and Black Deeps. To avoid the main shipping chans use the E and W Swins which are well buoyed and lit.

(5) Sunk LV to R Crouch.

Through the E Swin to the Whitaker buoy, thence as for R Crouch.

(6) Sunk LV to the Rs Colne and Blackwater.

DS Wallet, N end: SW −5.30; NE +0.45; S end: WSW −5.00; ENE +1.15.
Past the NE Gunfleet buoy into the Wallet, thence SW to the Knoll after which follow directions for R Colne or Blackwater.
(7) Harwich to the Whitaker buoy.
DS Naze: SW −5.30; NE +0.45; WSW −5.00; ENE +1.15.
(a) Through the Medusa Chan to the NE Gunfleet buoy and through the E Swin.
(b) Through the Medusa Chan giving the Naze an offing of at least 1M into the Wallet and across the Swin Spitway with a least depth of 1.2m. Soundings are irregular: after passing the Stone Banks buoy course should not be altered towards Walton Pier until the coast beyond is well open.
(8) Whitaker buoy to E Swale.
DS Whitaker: WSW −5.00; ENE +1.15; Columbine: W −4.00; E +1.30.
   Through the E and W Swins to the SW Barrow buoy, then given sufficient rise of tide, to the Spaniard buoy 2½M N of the Columbine buoy at the entrance to the E Swale. To avoid the Red and Middle Sands, from the SW Barrow buoy a course should be made to pass the Shivering Sand trs and make the Girdler bn, thence to the Spaniard.

MARGATE   Chart BA 1607
HW +0.55.   DS: E +2.00; W −4.30.
MHWS 4.8; MHWS 0.5; MTL 2.6; HWN 3.9; MHWN 1.4.
Hr is open to the NW, has 1.2m MHWS and dries 2.7m. Bottom sand and mud. This hr is not recommended for use without special reason and care must be exercised in avoiding the unmarked ruins of the pier.
Anchorage   In ordinary conditions reasonable shelter can be found just W of Margate, or N of Margate Pier.
   All stores. EC Thurs.

WHITSTABLE   Chart BA 2571   (Plan p98)
HW +1.20.   DS (Spaniard by): W −4.30; E +1.45.
MHWS 5.4; MLWS 0.5; MTL 2.9; MHWN 4.3; MLWN 1.5.
Approach   There are drying patches at LW in Whitstable Bay. Care should be exercised to avoid oyster beds, marked by flag buoys.
   To find the best water the approach should be made on a course of 155° from the Columbine Spit G con buoy or 182° from the Whitstable Street N Card (Q) buoy, taking care to avoid the Whitstable Street drying spit 3 ca to the W. By night approach in the G sector of the Fl WRG 5s lt at the end of the W pier, until the R ldg lts are in line. The tide runs across the entrance at a maximum speed of 2kn, W on flood and E on ebb. Ebb begins approx 1h before HW.
Entrance   The hr dries to 1.2m at LAT with shingle between the piers and mud inside, best water close alongside the W pier.
   Traffic sigs from E side of hr: F R lt by night or B ball by day signifies no entry. Tidal sigs on mast on E quay; R flag indicates more than 3m in the hr.

Based on British Admiralty Charts (nos. in text) with the permission of the Controller of H.M. Stationery Office and the Hydrographer of the Navy, and on other sources.

Berthing   Only permitted for a limited length of time for Customs clearance or other essential services. A mooring in the bay may be obtained from the Secretary of the Whitstable YC (tel Whitstable (0227) 272343).

Anchorage   Good anch in the bay for drafts up to 1.5m close by the yacht moorings W of the hr entrance and clear of fairway; also in Tankerton Bay 1m E of hr.

E SWALE AND HARTY FERRY   Charts BA 2571, 2572   (Plan p98)
HW +1.20.   MHWS 5.7; MLWS 0.6; MTL 3.1; MHWN 4.8; MLWN 1.5.

Approach and entrance   To maintain the best depth of water (2m) through the entrance, approach from the Columbine G con buoy on 234° to close N of the Pollard Spit R can buoy (QR), thence 227° leaving the Sand End G con buoy (Fl G 5s) wide to stb. Thence 237° towards Faversham Creek N Card buoy which may be lying dried out in the creek entrance, altering course to pass close N of the line of moorings.

Berthing   A mooring may be obtained from Tideway Services boatman operating from a fishing boat moored at the E end of the moorings. Uncomfortable in strong NE winds.

Anchorages   (1) At the W end of and in line with the moorings, clear of the fairway used by barges and fishing boats, in 3m. More comfortable shallow-draft anchorages may be found in the South Deep. Inn close by the hard on N side, some food obtainable. Fresh water can be taken from a spring at the head of the hard on the S side, from which Oare and Faversham are accessible. Boatyard and inn at junction of Faversham and Oare Creeks.

   (2) In the South Deep between Fowley Is and the S shore in 1m. To approach follow the S bank for approx 1M from Harty Ferry hard leaving a small Is marked by a perch with can top to stb until the moorings are sighted.

   Conyer with all facilities may be reached on the tide; the tortuous channel is well marked with perches, triangular tops to stb, round tops to port. Limited space. Conyer Marine if previously contacted will assist vessels on VHF.

RIVER MEDWAY   Charts BA 1834, 1835, 3683   (Plan p101)
HW (Sheerness) +1.30.   DS (Sheerness narrows): S −4.35; N +1.45.
Sheerness: MHWS 5.7; MLWS 0.6; MTL 3.1; MHWN 4.8; MLWN 1.5.
Upnor: HW +1.45. MHWS 5.9; MLWS 0.5; MTL 3.2; MHWN 4.9; MLWN 1.4.
The Medway is accessible at all times; it is well marked and navigable within limits to Tonbridge.

Approach   A traffic warning lt Fl 7s is exhibited from Garrison Pt on the E side of the entrance when tankers of 6,000 dwt and over are moving. A chy 74m conspic on the E end of the Isle of Grain is a good landmark for the entrance.
(1) Main chan app from the E marked by the Medway safe water Iso 5s buoy. The chan is deep and well marked. It should be avoided when shipping movements are taking place; ample water outside the chan for small craft.
(2) From Sea Reach through the Nore Swatchway leaving the Nore Swatch R

can Fl(4)R 15s buoy to stb, thence join the main chan at No. 11 G con buoy (Fl G 10s). (3) From the SE a course may be steered in 2m from the Spile G con (Fl G 2.5s) in the Four Fathom Channel to join the Medway Channel at No. 8 R can buoy (Fl R 5s). (4) An inshore passage (0.6m LAT) may be taken on a rise of tide from the Spile buoy leaving the tripod post E of the Cheyney Rks (drying) to port entering the Medway at the West Cant.

Entrance Stream runs at 3kn. On the ebb considerable advantage may be gained from an inflowing eddy that runs close in by the seaward side of Garrison Pt, or the main strength of stream avoided by keeping to the W. Sheerness is a busy commercial port unsuitable for small craft. There are two small boat basins: (1) boat basin to N within the bonded area, and to be avoided; (2) the S basin; normally open to small craft and can be used to obtain Customs clearance, but dangerous. The entrance is frequently blocked by the mooring lines of the Ro-Ro ferry and should be checked before attempting entry. Better to clear in at Queenborough.

From Garrison Pt to Rochester the chan is well buoyed and lit. Beware numerous unlit buoys outside chan. 8 ca upriver from Sheerness the entrance to the West Swale is marked by the Queenborough Spit E Card buoy (Q(3)10s). A further 1½M on in Saltpan Reach the entrance to Stangate Creek on the S side of the river is marked by the Stangate Spit E Card buoy (VQ(3)5s) which lies S of the fourth of the mooring buoys off the oil wharves on the Isle of Grain shore (N side of the Reach). These wharves extend from Victoria to Elphinstone Pt. Large tanker movements take place in this area and small craft must keep well clear. A Medway Ports Authority Notice to Mariners prohibits any unauthorised vessel from coming within 100ft of the jetties or the vessels moored there.

From Kethole Reach inwards the river appears deceptively wide towards HW, but the deep-water chan is only about 2 ca wide, buoyed. Speed limit of 6kn from Gillingham Reach inwards. At the S end of Chatham Reach a sharp lookout should be kept for vessels and their attendant lighters proceeding to and from Rochester. Navigation for vessels with high fixed masts stops at Rochester Bridge, headroom under the middle span 5.96m above MHWS giving 11.8m at MLWS but with depths of less than 1m in places. Passage under Rochester Bridge should not be attempted by vessels of over 0.8m draft at MLWS. Centre arch has least water, is subject to difficult tidal eddies and leads directly on to shoal patch. When depth is critical take Strood arch obliquely, lining up buttress on Strood side with esplanade pier on Rochester bank above bridge; straighten up into chan along outside line of RCC moorings. If heading for MPA visitors' buoy on Strood side, follow same approach, cross river when above these moorings and fall back onto them.

Progress beyond this point to Allington Lock 12M, the end of the tidal part of the river, is inadvisable before half flood. Navigation from Allington Lock is only suitable for motor cruisers. The lock is operated from 3h before to 2h after HW and manned at all times (tel Maidstone (0622) 52864). Maximum draft from Allington Lock to Maidstone is 2m; craft proceeding upriver against the stream

RIVER MEDWAY
Depths in Metres

5 Cables 0 1

0 1 2 3 Miles

N

CONTINUATION
OF MEDWAY RIVER

MAIDSTONE

STROOD
ROCHESTER
Tower Reach
Borstal
Wouldham Marshes
Wouldham Reach
Cuxton
North Halling
Halling
Ferry
Holborough
Snodland
Larkfield
Ditton
East Malling
New Hythe
Aylesford
Allington Marina
Lock Sanding
Scarborough
Burham
Horseshoe Reach
Boundary Stone
Cement Works
Eccles
Cobdown

Yacht Moorings
Hoo Marina
Marina YC
Lower Upnor
Upper Upnor
St Mary's
RN DD
Chatham
Gillingham
Rochester Bridge
Gun Whf
Anchor Whf
Brompton
Clock Tr
Naval Sailing Centre
Gillingham Marina

Hoo I
Kingsnorth Power Stn
Kingsnorth Jetty
SLEDE OOZE
MUSSEL BANK
BISHOP OOZE
DARNET NESS
Nor Marsh

Isle of Grain
Grain Power Stn
BP Oil Refinery (Numerous Tanks)
Radio Tr
Grainhard
Garrison Pt
Sheerness
SWATCHWAY
NORE SAND
West Nore Sand
Grain Spit
Jetty
Lees Tr
Water Tr
London Stone
YANTLET FLAT
Yantlet Creek
All Hallows
Landing Stage
Stoke Ness
KETHOLE REACH
SALTPAN REACH
Queenborough
Queenborough Pt
SWALENESS
STANGATE CR
West Garrison
HALSTOW
Windmill
Wind Pumps
Hard
Causeway
Pier

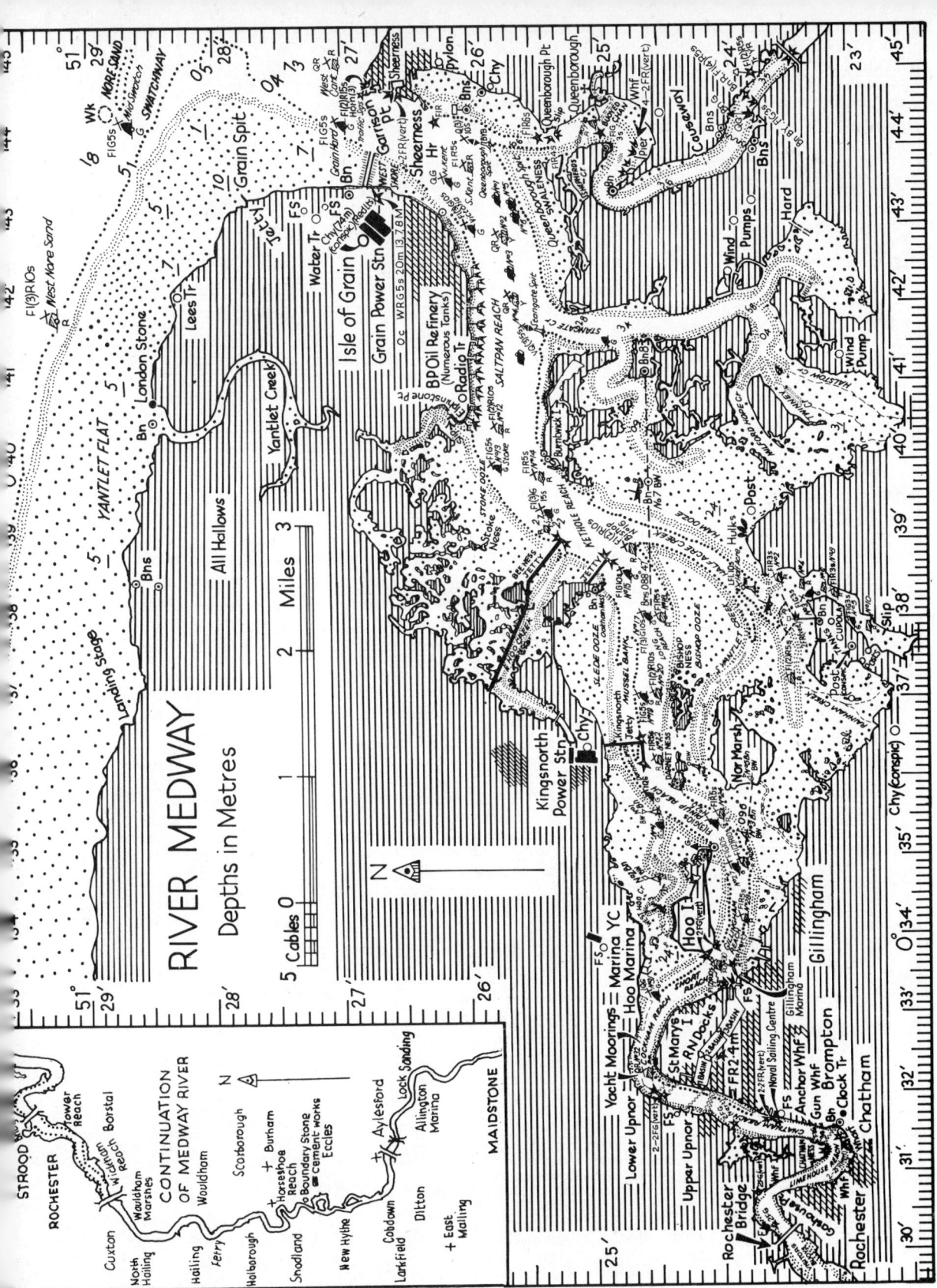

...ed on British Admiralty Charts (nos. in text) with the permission of the Controller of H.M. Stationery Office and of ...Hydrographer of the Navy, and on other sources.

I of Grain
43'
Grain Tr (Martello Tr)
Fl G 5s
Grain Hard
QR
W Cant
Q
29
46'
0°
47'
E
48'
2
Bn
D
PYLON
Bns
O Tripod Post
chy (conspic) 24m
Bn
2 FG (vert)
Fl R
Fl R
Fl (2) R 15s 4M Horn (3)
0·3
0·6
(Red Lts)
WEST SHORE
2 FR (vert)
Radio Mast (conspic)
JACOBS BANK
CHEYNEY ROCKS
0·3
51'
Grain Power Stn
Oc WRG 5s 20m 13/8M
White
S
SHEERNESS
GREEN BANK
SWING BANK
0·6
·26
·21
Horse Shoe Pt
Bn
3·2
SHEERNESS HARBOUR
Chys
Stn
Marine Town
Yacht moorings
QG
N Kent
Fl R
Fl R 5s
Lapwell Bank
Chys
Sheerness
HORN
Fl (3) G 10s
Victoria
Q (3) 10s
R
0·9
Pylon
THE LAPPEL
2 FG (vert)
QR
DN 2
Queenborough Spit
BYB
NW
Chy
West Minster
Minster Abbey (conspic)
Y
No 6
No 5
QUEENBOROUGH SPIT
SWALE NESS
Fl R 6s
DN
Queenborough Pt
Fl R 4s
2 FR (vert)
Yacht Moorings Y
51°
SHEERNESS Hr
N
QR
W. Cant
Minster
Tailness Marshes
Deadmans Island
HARD
Fairway
Queenborough
27 Depths in Metres
R
0
2
Cables
3
·24
Shepherds Cr
West Pt
THE HARD
FS
Fl (2) R 15s 13m 4M Horn (3) 30s
25'
LODEN HOPE
R
Fl G 3s
The Creek
QUEENBOROUGH FLATS
4·2 FR (vert)
Whf
Fl R
Garrison Pt
RO-RO BERTH
Bn Sig Stn. Traffic Sig
Radio Mast (conspic) (Red Lts)
25'
WEST SWALE
28
Water Tr
11·6
Slip
No 5
No 4
2 FR (vert)
Lower Camber
Port Authority
Rushenden Marshes
FS
8·8
Clock Tr
Custom Ho
Chy
Causeway
12·6
Cornwallis Steps
South Gate
24'
SWR
Lts
HORSE REACH
113°
Fl (4) R 5s 6m
Fl (2) R 5s 10m (Tr, Or, R)
26·5
Obscd
CRANES
Being reclaimed
Blue Town
24'
QG 7m
Fl G 3s 10m
3·5
2 FR (vert)
Kingsferry Bridge
2 FR (vert)
Causeway
Stn
Chy
N
Ferry Marshes
2-2 FG (vert)
Dn
Ramp
6
Tr
Chy
Fl R (Dn)
The Lappel
51°
23'
Wind pump
(Tr RW) 2 FG (vert) 9·7m
(Tr, BY) 2 Fl 11·9m
FS
0·44·5
E
2
Ridham Marshes
Wind pump
RIVER SWALE
Depths in Metres
Wind pump
Isle of Elmley
Jetty (ruins)
Wind Pump
Sharfleet Cr
Wellmarsh Cr
5
Cables
0
Mile
1
Elmley Hills
2 FG (vert)
Elmley Ferry
Cockleshell
Grovehurst Coal Jetty
Bn (R)
North Ferry
ELMLEY REACH
SWALE
Kelmsley Marshes
South Ferry
The Lilies
22'
Kelmsley Paper Mill
Chys
Tr
2-2 FG (vert)
Milton Cr
Whf
43'
44'
45'
46'
47'
R
R
0·48'
E
R

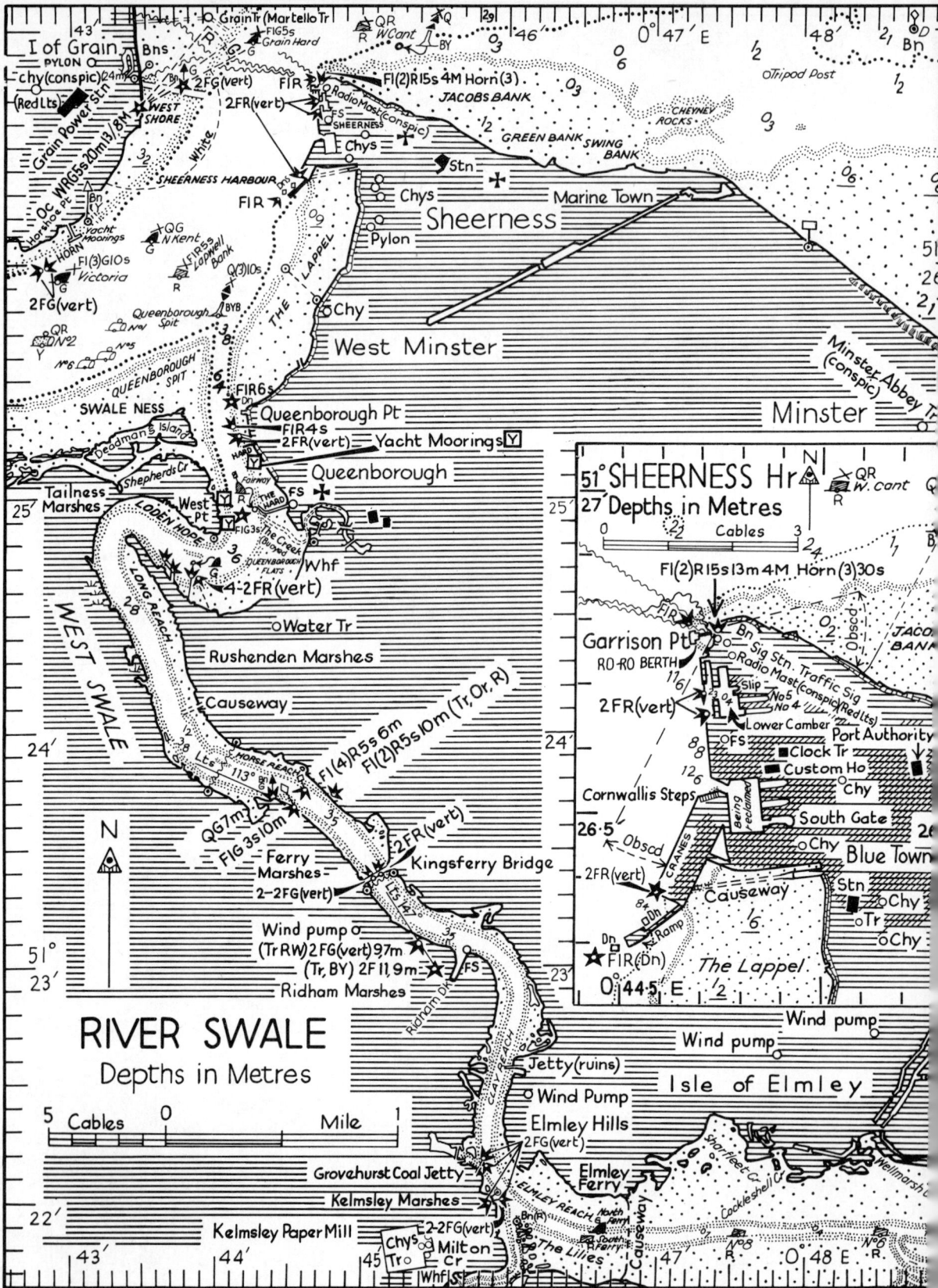

should give way to craft going downriver. Headroom under Maidstone Bypass Bridge is 9.45m at MHWS.

Medway Ports Authority maintains a Port Operation Service at Garrison Pt (tel Sheerness (07956) 3025/6) for the purpose of providing radio and radar assistance to all vessels navigating in the River Medway. Medway Radio maintains a constant watch on VHF chans 16 and 14, the latter being the port operation chan.

Anchorages (1) *Stangate Creek* (see *Entrance*) affords a quiet sheltered anch clear of traffic, in among the marshes. No facilities. To enter the creek leave the Stangate Spit E Card VQ (3) 5s buoy to stb. At night if the refinery flare is visible keep to mid chan of the Medway until the flare bears 002°. Maintain this back bearing to the entrance and then steer 179° up the creek. Anch well clear of this line and use riding lt: barges use chan day and night. Avoid a G con buoy on the W mud flats ½M from the entrance, also the mud flats on the E side for ¾M from the entrance to the first headland, after which the creek is clear of wreckage with good anch on either side.

(2) *Sharfleet Creek* leads out of Stangate on the stb hand ½M from the entrance. Good anch on the S side just inside, or on either shore further in clear of oyster beds. Landing places at public piers: in Limehouse Reach, Ship Pier and Blue Boar Pier, Bridge Reach, Strood Pier, and in Tower Reach, Esplanade Pier. Other landing places: Commodore Hard, Gillingham Strand (suitable for launching), Gillingham Pier steps just downstream of the dockyard entrance, Upnor Causeway upstream of the Arethusa shore establishment, Sun Pier, Chatham (dinghy landing only at downstream pontoon), Town Quay steps downstream of Rochester Bridge (suitable for dinghies), Strood esplanade steps upstream of Rochester Bridge, and the Medway Bridge Marina. Medway Ports Authority maintains six visitors' buoys above Rochester Bridge on the Strood side. There is a marina by the motorway bridge on the S side of the river. Fuel and supplies can be obtained from all the above places.

The wreckage of HMS Bulwark in Kethole Reach is marked by a R can buoy. It may be passed on either hand but vessels should not anch in the vicinity.

QUEENBOROUGH
Chart 2572 (Plan p102)

HW +1.30.   DS: S −4.00; N +2.30.

MHWS 5.7; MLWS 0.6; MTL 3.1; MHWN 4.8; MLWN 1.5.

A convenient and sheltered port easily accessible by day and night.

Approach and entrance From the R Medway leaving Queenborough Spit E Card buoy (Q(3)10s) close to stb. Further into the creek two dolphins (Fl R 6s and FR) marking the ruins of the rly pier must be left to port. The area of the derelict pier is dangerous and stumps are exposed at half-tide. Do not attempt to land at remains of pier with rly footbridge over. A course of 178° from the Queenborough Spit leads up the fairway.

Berthing At two large W mooring buoys immediately S of causeway for up to six yachts each, or at two orange and yellow visitors' buoys. The E side of the concrete barge opposite the causeway may be used by large vessels. Diesel in creek, chandlery, stores. Rly to London.

PASSAGE NOTES: QUEENBOROUGH TO HARTY FERRY THROUGH THE SWALE

Least depth at MLWS 1m.

DS: from −4.30 to −4.00, slack everywhere. Queenborough: S −4.00; N +2.30. Kingsferry: SE −4.00; NW +3.30 (i.e. in from Medway for 7½h, out towards Medway for 4½h.

Fowley Is: from −4.00 to +1.30 streams run in at both ends and meet here. From +1.30 to +5.00 the stream is E-going. From +5.00 −4.30 streams separate here and run out at both ends.

Harty Ferry: E +1.30; W −4.00.

Streams are strongest soon after they begin and the greatest rates, about 4kn at sp, occur near Kingsferry. It is easier to carry a fair tide when bound E.

Directions Just beyond Queenborough the chan turns to stb and the deepest water is close to the wharves on the port hand. A G con buoy marks the Horse Shoal (dries). Leave this to stb, passing S of the shoal. Approx 1M further on there is a wreck on the port hand: keep well clear. A further ½M beyond the wreck electric cables run across the river bed marked by beacons on either bank; a drying bank lies in mid-chan hereabouts: avoid by keeping to the stb side. Kingsferry Bridge lies ¾M further on. The br lifts on request, rly traffic permitting. Clearance at MHWS: closed 3.35m; lifted, up to 28.96m. To request opening, if possible telephone bridge keeper in advance (Sittingbourne (0795) 3627) giving ETA at bridge. A listening watch is maintained on VHF chan 10 or a message may be passed through Medway Radio on chan 14. A flag or round object in the rigging or 1 long followed by four short blasts indicates that passage is requested. Traffic lts R or G are shown for bridge closed or open; amber indicates no immediate prospect of opening.

There is a good hard here and anch for a short stay on S shore taking the mud. Beware of sizeable commercial vessels using the fairway on way to and from Ridham and Grovehurst docks, also Milton Creek.

From Kingsferry Bridge to Milton Creek the banks are a fair guide: keep near to the two wharves just before this creek and follow the outside curve of the river. From between the N (G con) and S (R can) ferry buoys steer to pass between the two noticeboards; when exactly between them turn to stb and pass close N of R can buoys 8, 6, 4, 2, laid at ½M intervals. At LW the chan is only a few metres wide here and bounded by large areas of mud which cover at half-tide. Least water (nearly dry at LAT) is near Fowley Is and at Elmey, where the causeway stands ½m above the river bed. A bar exists approx ½ ca beyond No. 2: sound along the edge of the spit off Fowley Is towards a post marking the stb hand entry to Conyer Creek, thence make good 097° until No. 1 G con buoy is abeam (this buoy dries and should be given a good offing), thence 123° to Harty Ferry anch. Distances: Queenborough to Kingsferry Bridge 2½M; Kingsferry Bridge to Harty Ferry 7M.

GRAVESEND   Chart BA 1186
HW +1.50.   MHWS 6.5; MLWS 0.5; MTL 3.5; MHWN 5.4; MLWN 1.6.
Approach   Care is required when passing through the outer ship moorings as the
tide runs very hard.
Berthing   In Canal Basin. To enter apply Lock Foreman (tel Gravesend (0474)
2392) on the port side of the lock. Entrance is at the E end of the promenade,
app by a narrow gut between drying banks. Sound in carefully as chan is subject
to continuous alteration. Vessels drawing over 2m should seek assistance from
the YC. The gates are opened from 1h before to HW if HW is between 0700 and
2100; otherwise the Lock Foreman will attend if given 24h notice. The basin is
owned by the Council and charges are for a minimum of 7 days. The moorings
within the basin are maintained by Gravesend SC; visitors may on request be
allocated a mid-basin mooring instead of lying against the dock wall. The Club
welcomes visitors and may assist, by prior arrangement, with masts (up to 40ft).
Small crane. Water, tel at Club. Rly, ferry. EC Wed.
Anchorage   Strangers should anch off the E end of the promenade well clear of
all moorings; tripping line essential. Close inshore the stream is weaker, but on
springs the shore dries out to the inner line of YC moorings. Two orange YC
buoys marked 'GCS 5' tons may be picked up by visitors waiting to enter the
basin. Constant traffic and heavy wash.

GREENHITHE   Chart BA 2151
HW +2.00.   MHWS 6.2; MHWN 4.9.
Sheltered in SE through S to SW winds; most exposed to NW. Anch off
causeway, end marked by a buoy which indicates the drying edge of the mud.
Sound carefully, as mud is steep-to in places, and it is advisable to rig tripping
line.

THE LONDON RIVER OR RIVER THAMES   Charts BA 1185, 1186, 2484,
                                                        2151, 3337, 3319
See also Cruising Association *Visiting Yachtsman's Guide to the London River*,
and PLA *Guide to Users of Pleasure Craft on the Thames Tideway*.
To make reasonable passage times in the River Thames it is essential to use the
tides, running at 3–4kn, to the best advantage, beginning the upriver passage at
LW in Sea Reach.
Approach   The Sea Reach deep-water chan is marked by safe water and special
buoys. It is restricted in width to 150m either side of the buoys and is maintained
at a depth only just sufficient for the deepest draft vessels using the port, so their
passage must not be impeded in any way. The N and S navigable margins of the
Reach are well marked and should be used by all small craft.
Thames Barrier   During the construction of the River Thames Barrier in
Woolwich Reach, a buoyed chan 122m wide leads through the works. Passage of
all craft is strictly controlled and permission must be obtained by tel (01–855 6956)
from Barrier Control or from PLA patrol launch, River Police, PLA Jetty in

Galleon's Reach, or via Woolwich Radio VHF chan 14. No stopping, turning or anch. Lt Fl R on control building prohibits all navigation.

Entrance Bound up-Thames from the R Medway, where Queenborough provides a convenient stopping-over point, a start can be made using the last hour of ebb to clear Garrison Pt and standing well clear of the Grain Spit start the inward passage through the Nore Swatch. A fair tide can then be held with reasonable speed as far as Richmond. Outward bound from Richmond, the best time to leave is as soon as the weir is drawn, sounding to maintain a sufficient depth of water outside the strongest of the stream. A fair tide should be found from London Bridge onwards. With no more than average speed a foul tide will be met long before comfortable shelter can be found outside the Thames, so it is preferable to bring up and await the next favourable tide before reaching Gravesend.

Ship signals used in the River Thames additional to those required by the International Regulations:

. . . . .   Turning short round to stb
. . . .   Turning short round to port

Bridge lights Navigable arches of Thames bridges carry 2 amber lts close together. A R triangle point down by day, or 3 R lts point down at night, denote bridge closed to navigation, except at Richmond Weir where 1 R shape or lt is shown when it is closed.

Berthing Not allowed at the privately owned piers and those belonging to the PLA or GLC, except perhaps for a short period with the express permission of the Piermaster.

Gravesend Canal Basin by prior arrangement (tel Gravesend (0474) 2392). At Grays Thurrock a YC mooring buoy may be obtained by prior arrangement. St Katharine Yacht Haven: entrance through lock on N bank just below Tower Bridge (tel 01–488 2400). The HQ of the Cruising Association overlooks the basin. All facilities. Avoid securing alongside groups of barges on swinging moorings which on the turn of tide may well foul each other, crushing craft lying between them.

Anchorages *Greenhithe* (see previous entry). *Erith* on S bank below jetties and Erith YC moorings, below and inside the lighter roads. *Margaret Ness* to *Cross Ness*, inside the lighter roads on the S bank. *Greenwich*, below the pier in line with it and abeam of the Naval College. It is always advisable to buoy the anch.

NOTES ON THE RIVER THAMES ABOVE HAMMERSMITH

Between Hammersmith and Richmond the tide remains at a low level for several hours, making practically the whole of the flood in the final 2h before HW. The ebb is more or less normal. Flood water running down the Thames can affect this behaviour considerably and strong winds at sea can cause fluctuation in the tides.

Between Richmond and Teddington, for the first 2h after the weir is drawn the tide flows up to Teddington, at other times a very weak tide, if any, flows downriver. At exceptional springs the tide may flow over Teddington Weir and one can sometimes carry it as far as Kingston or Hampton Court. In winter, Richmond Weir is sometimes left drawn and the tide above Richmond behaves in the same manner as that below. When the river is swollen the flow of water under Richmond Bridge can be dangerous.

Shooting bridges   The stream swirls round the buttresses of all bridges and to avoid being swept into them, arches should be taken squarely. They should be approached from a distance, so that the insides of both sides of the arch to be taken can be seen. Hammersmith is the lowest bridge with a headroom of 4.4m at HW.

The lock for the Grand Union Canal, Brentford, is normally open from 2h before to 3h after local HW, which is London Bridge +1h.

NOTES ON THE RIVER THAMES ABOVE TEDDINGTON

Above Teddington the river is controlled by the Thames Conservancy and all craft must have TC licences. There are special rates for power-driven craft visiting the Upper Thames for either 14 days or a calendar month.

The Conservators do not register vessels capable of being driven at high speed. All vessels must be navigated with caution and in such a manner as not to endager lives or cause injury to persons, other vessels, moorings, river banks or property.

Sound signals on power vessels are compulsory. Vessels are required to have port, stb and stern lts visible 2M and masthead lts visible 5M. International rules of the road and sound signals apply.

No waste, litter or sewage may be discharged into the river above Teddington Lock. Kingston Corporation (sewage pumping station near rly bridge), Shiplake, Temple, Boveney, Shepperton, Days and Abingdon Locks provide facilities for refuse disposal. TC inspect and if necessary seal pipes discharging into river.

TC have regulations regarding fire risk which are available from Head Office, 15 Buckingham St, London WC2 (tel 01–839 2441).

The river is dredged so that in summer it can be navigated as follows:

	Draft (m)	miles from Teddington
Teddington to Staines	2	17
Staines to Windsor	1.7	25
Windsor to Reading	1.4	55
Reading to Oxford	1.2	$93\frac{1}{2}$
Oxford to Lechlade	0.9	$124\frac{1}{2}$
Key bridge heights are:	(m)	
Teddington Lock Cut	5.8	
Desborough Chan	5.2	
Windsor	4	
Cookham	3.8	

Height (m)

Clifton Lock Cut	3.6
Folly (Oxford)	3.1
Osney	2.3

These are heights in dry weather with the water level at datum. In times of winter flow or flood they will be less. Lock-keepers will advise whether the water level is above or below datum.

The best navigational guide to the Upper Thames is that published by the Association of Thames Motor Boat Clubs and the best charts those published by Stanford, and Salter. The latter also publish a good guide.

Dredgers: pass on side showing W flag.

Yachts may moor to the towpath for not more than one day. For available moorings consult local boatmen.

Near all the larger towns small self-drive motor launches are for hire and their occupants seldom have any knowledge of the rules of navigation.

In summer there is no tide above Teddington and the river flow is under 1kn. In winter spring tides may flow as far as Molesey Lock, and in flood (usually Nov and Feb) the stream can run up to 12kn.

Locks operate till dusk except Molesey and Teddington which are always manned.

During winter months locks may be closed for repairs. TC will advise.

HOLEHAVEN   Charts BA 1186, 1185
HW +1.40.   MHWS 6.2; MLWS 0.5; MTL 3.3; MHWN 5.2; MLWN 1.4.
Approach and entrance   Approaching from Sea Reach the entrance to the creek (0.3m at LAT) lies immediately W of the last oil jetty on Canvey Is, the fourth from seaward and well inside the large new jetty running out from Holehaven. ½M inside the creek a bridge crosses it, connecting this new jetty to the Canvey shore. It has 9m headroom at MHWS and a navigable opening 30m wide. S of the pier crowded moorings lie in 2m at LAT, one of these may at times be available with permission from the Piermaster.

Tel outside Lobster Smack Inn close to causeway. Canvey village 1M, shops, PO, bus to Benfleet (3M), rly.

LEIGH   Chart BA 1185
HW +1.25.   MHWS 5.7; MLWS 0.5; MTL 3.1; MHWN 4.8; MLWN 1.4.
Approach   From the Leigh Chan: 8 ca WNW of Southend Pier lies the Leigh G con buoy marking the W side of the entrance to the Ray Gut which has 2.4 to 4m. This buoy should be left to port. Silting occurs and the approach should be made with caution.
Entrance   The Ray Chan is marked by port buoys. Approx 2 ca past No. 2 buoy a G con buoy marks the entrance to Leigh Creek. Offshore from Leigh the sands dry 4m for a distance of 7 ca to the Ray Chan.

Drying moorings off Two Tree Is in Hadleigh Creek are approached after the Ray Chan buoys leaving a large spher BWHS buoy to stb, then N to leave the next spher buoy to stb, then W to pass between two spher buoys and immediately N keeping the next spher G buoys to stb. The chan from the W end of the moorings to Canvey Bridge is marked by buoys to be passed close to.

Anchorage   In the Ray Gut in 2½ to 4m.

Fresh water from a water pump on Bell Wharf, all facilities at Leigh, EC Wed.

HAVENGORE CREEK   Chart BA 1185

This HW short-cut runs between the R Thames and the R Crouch and is available for shoal-draft vessels only. Navigate in daylight only, approx 1½h before and up to HW. The route has 2m at MHWS and 0.9m at MLWS. The height of tide may be reduced by up to 1m by S winds or high barometric pressure.

Approach   The Maplin Sand is a Min of Defence heavy artillery firing range; at times the passage of all vessels through this area is strictly controlled. For the latest information tel Shoebury (037 08) 2271.

Leaving the Warps 1½ to 1h before HW, to ensure that some rise remains, pass E of the wooden survey platform which lies ½M W of the E Shoebury G con buoy and make good a course of 337° leaving the H topmark beacons to port. These mark the Broomway, which runs approx at right angles to the course line, and lie some 3 ca from Havengore Creek entrance.

Entrance   The entrance may be located by sighting the swing bridge which crosses the creek. To contact the bridgekeeper for opening times tel Shoebury (037 08) 68184. When the sea wall is reached the chan deepens to 0.6 or 0.9m with steep sides. It may be marked by withies. Sounding in between the entrance pts, the bottom is mud to the SW side of fairway and sand to the NE. All this part dries 2½ to 3h after HW. Passing through the bridge, take great care if the flood is still making, as the tide does not run true. Once inside the line of the land the chan gradually deepens. To go to the R Roach and Burnham take the first turning on the stb hand after entering the Haven and continue N till reaching the Roach, then turn E for the Crouch.

To go through the Haven from Burnham, stand up the Roach. Take first creek on port hand and then the third on port hand again, the first and second branches leading to Shelford and New England respectively, obstructed by fixed bridges. If the branch to stb is taken, the Roach may be reached once more and Potton Is circumnavigated at MHWS. The nearest berth to the Haven where a vessel can lie afloat is just before entering the third turning, where there is 1.2 to 1.5m at MLWS. When the mud on the banks of the chan at this pt is covered there is 1m of water at the entrance to the Haven.

Streams at Havengore run strongly; the ebb and flood part and meet about ½M inside. There is more water at the entrance in NW winds, less in SE or SW. At slack neaps the waters sometimes fail to meet. Road over the Maplin Sands available at LW leads to Shoebury.

RIVER CROUCH   Charts BA 1975, 3750   (Plan p111)
HW (Burnham) +1.05.
MHWS 5.3; MLWS 0.5; MTL 2.4; MHWN 4.5; MLWN 1.4.

Accessible at all times. The coastline is low and there are few distinguishing marks; the spire of Foulness ch may be seen well inland in good visibility and there are two conspic lattice trs well to the S at Eastness on Foulness. The tides run hard, up to 3kn on a sp ebb, and follow the line of the chan. The river has a least depth of 2m in or close by the chan at the Sunken Buxey. The chan is narrow in places and shoals rapidly at the edges. Vessels drawing up to 2m can reach Battlesbridge, the upper limit of the river at MHWS, but the upper reaches are crowded making passage difficult.

Approach   (1) From the Whitaker safe water bell buoy (L Fl 10s) leave the S Buxey G con buoy to stb thence to the Sunken Buxey N Card buoy (Q), entering the river between the Outer Crouch G con buoy and the Crouch R can buoy where the chan narrows. Sound along 5m line either side in bad visibility. (2) Across the Swin Spitway (1.2m), from the Swin Spitway safe water Iso 10s bell buoy to the S Buxey G con buoy, across a least depth of 1.5m nearing the S Buxey. (3) From the Wallet through the Raysand Chan. This chan dries 1.2m at the S end; seasonal variations in the line of deepest water occur. Passage should only be attempted on a rising tide taking care to avoid being set upon the Knoll and the Bachelors Spit by the flood, sounding across into the Crouch chan.

Entrance   Inside the entrance the river is clear of dangers for approx 2M as far as the mouth of the R Roach. In this area neither bank should be approached too closely. During the summer two Y race buoys laid on the N side indicate the line of safe limit to the N. A further Y race buoy laid off Wallasea Ness on the W side of the Roach entrance marks the NE extremity of Branklet Spit which should be left to port proceeding up the Crouch. After Burnham, Wallasea Yacht Stn is situated on the S bank closely followed by Baltic Wharf at which timber ships berth. Between Creeksea and Fambridge, Bridgemarsh Is is completely covered at HW making identification of the chan difficult. Keep to the centre of the chan and do not enter bights in the river bank: the line of the S bank indicates the chan. About ½M E of Fambridge on the N bank there is a sunken sea wall, which is deceptive at HW owing to a bight in the new sea wall at this position. At Fambridge moorings line both sides of the river; the entrance to Stow Creek lies on the N side of the river leading to W Wick Marina.

Berthing   (1) At Burnham on mooring buoy, by arrangement with the boatman of one of the clubs (usually afloat in launches). Do not leave boat unattended on buoy until permission secured. (2) At Wallasea Is on application to the Wallasea Yacht St. Fuel barge. Stow Creek on the N bank leads to W Wick Marina, limited accommodation with slipway, water and diesel.

Anchorages   *Note:* Crouch Harbour Authority Bye-laws prohibit any vessel from anch in such a manner as to obstruct any fairway. Riding light should be shown. (1) Burnham, ½M below the town, clear of power cables marked by bns on banks. (2) In any clear berth on the N shore ½M above the town. Do not anch

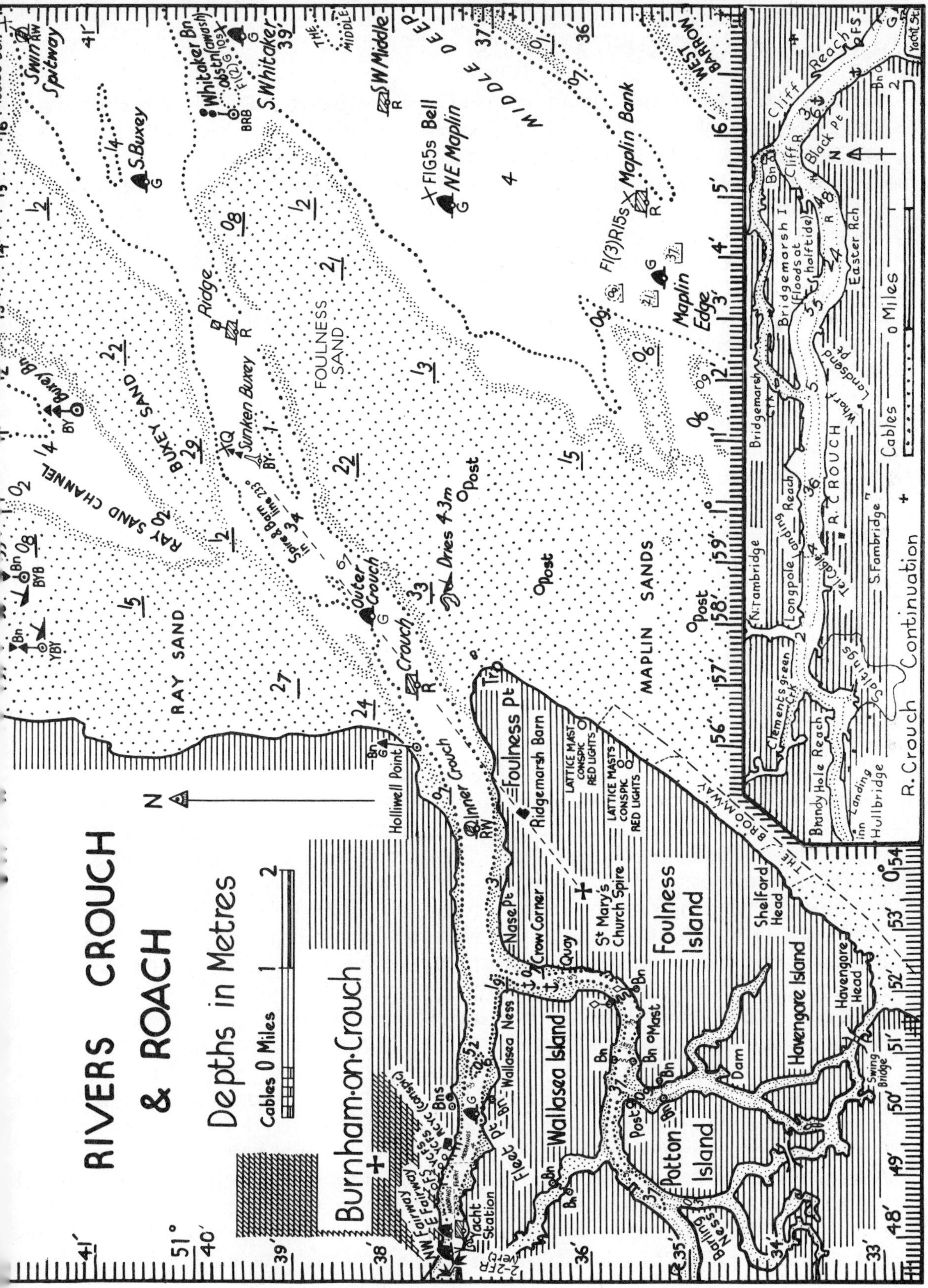

RIVERS CROUCH & ROACH

Depths in Metres

Cables 0 Miles

Burnham-on-Crouch

N

Swin Spitway

Whitaker Bn
S.Whitaker
S.Buxey
SW Middle
NE Maplin
FI(3)R15s Maplin Bank
FIG5s Bell
Maplin Edge
WEST BARROW
MIDDLE DEEP

Ridge
Buxey
BUXEY SAND
Sunken Buxey
RAY SAND CHANNEL
RAY SAND
Outer Crouch
Crouch
Dries 4·3m
Post
FOULNESS SAND
MAPLIN SANDS
Holliwell Point
Inner Crouch
Foulness Pt
Ridgemarsh Barn
LATTICE MASTS CONSPIC RED LIGHTS
Nase Pt
Crow Corner
Quay
St Mary's Church Spire
Foulness Island
Shelford Head
Havengore Head
Havengore Island
Wallasea Island
Potton Island
Barling Ness
Swing Bridge
Dam
Fleet Pt
Wallasea Ness
THE BROOMWAY
Yacht Station
NW Fairway
NE Fairway

R. Crouch Continuation

Cliff Reach
Easter Rch
Bridgemarsh I (Floods at halftide)
Bridgemarsh
Black Pt
Landsong
Longpole
Hamford
N.Fambridge
S.Fambridge
Clements green
Brandy Hole Reach
Hullbridge
R. CROUCH
Cables 0 Miles

on British Admiralty Charts (nos. in text) with the permission of the Controller of H.M. Stationery Office and of
ydrographer of the Navy, and on other sources.

among moorings as the ground is foul. All facilities, rly. EC Wed. (3) Cliff Reach. Keep well over to the S bank abeam of Baltic Wharf to avoid a spit which extends from the N bank a quarter of the way across the river. Anch in the bay of the S bank beyond the moorings in 5½m if the wind is W, and off the red cliff further upriver on the N bank in 3½m if the wind is E. Lion Creek has 2.4m in centre at MHWN. (4) Fambridge. Good anch in 2½ to 3m; avoid telegraph cable near the steps on S bank. Hard, slipway, rly to London. EC Wed.

RIVER ROACH   Chart BA 3750   (Plan p111)

Entrance   From seaward do not cut the corner at Nase Pt as the mud is extensive and unmarked. From Burnham do not pass inside Branklet Spit near LW. 1½M beyond the entrance is Horseshoe Corner where the river turns W; on the port hand in this reach is Yokefleet Creek leading to Havengore. ½M further on the river bears away SW and the moorings at Paglesham will be seen. Landing on Foulness Is prohibited. Beyond Paglesham the river shoals rapidly.

Anchorages   (1) Close under the W bank under the high sea wall in the bay above Wallasea Ness in W winds, and off the quay on the E side ¾M further up in E winds. (2) Inside the entrance to Yokefleet Creek in 2m. (3) Off Paglesham clear of the moorings. Landing at boatyard hard on N shore. Inn at Paglesham, 1M.

RIVER BLACKWATER   Chart BA 3741   (Plan p113)

HW (Bradwell) +0.50; HW Osea Is +1.10; HW Maldon +1.20.
DS: Knoll buoy   W −5.00; E   +1.55
    Osea Is   in −4.45, out +1.25
    Maldon   in −4.15, out +1.35

Accessible at all times, the river is navigable as far as Maldon on the tide.

Approach   From the Wallet the app may be made from the Knoll N Card buoy (Q) or the North Eagle N Card buoy. Both chans are clearly marked with a least depth of 3.8m but the N Eagle is unlit.

Entrance   From the Bench Head G con buoy (Fl G 5s) make good a course of 290° keeping the Bench Head and NW Knoll buoys in transit astern. When the Bradwell Power Station barrier wall stands well clear of the land, alter course to make good 275° until the barrier wall is in line, after which the chan runs in a direction of 235° towards Stone Pt, conspic and easily seen, on the S shore with moorings laid off it. Large laid-up vessels are often moored in the deepest water and serve to indicate the chan. With Osea Is ahead, to be passed to the S, stand in towards the Stone shore which is fairly steep-to. A narrow shoal patch 0.4m lies off Osea Pier from 2 ca E of the pier, W to No. 3 G con buoy. From midstream off Stangate Pt a course of 247° made good will clear this shoal. Numerous moorings, owned by the Marconi YC, extend well into the chan off the pt. The chan is buoyed above Osea Is.

Between the first and second R can buoys above Osea is Latchingdon Hole. After rounding Northey Isle turn into Colliers Reach, when Heybridge Basin

Rivers Colne & Blackwater

Depths in Metres

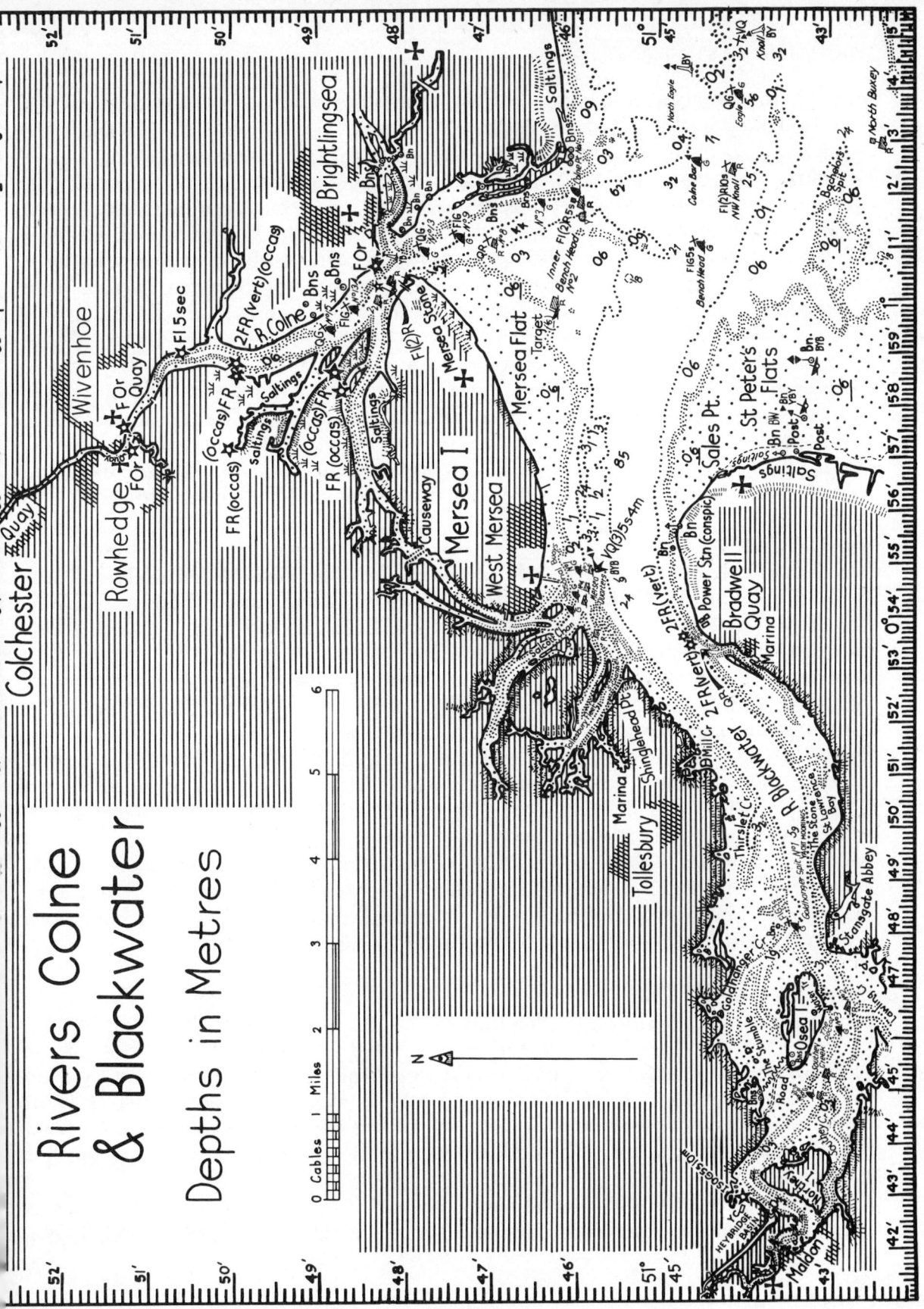

Colchester

Wivenhoe

Rowhedge

Brightlingsea

R. Colne

Mersea I

West Mersea

Mersea Stone

Causeway

Saltings

Mersea Flat

St Peter's Flats

Sales Pt.

Bradwell Quay

Marina

Power Stn (conspic)

Saltings

Tollesbury

Shinglehead Pt

Marina

Thirslet Cr.

R. Blackwater

The Stone

St. Lawrence Bay

Stansgate Abbey

Goldhanger Cr.

Osea I

Maldon

North Eagle

Eagle

Knoll

Colne Bar

NW Knoll

Bachelors Spit

North Buxey

Inner Bench Head No.2

Bench Head

Target

Bn

Saltings

Fl 5 sec

2FR (vert)(occas)

FR (occas)

(occas) FR

FR (occas)

2FR (vert)

2FR (vert)

Quay

Bn. Post

Goldmers Sd

Goldhanger Spit

The Stumble

Southey Cr.

N

0 Cables 1 Miles 2 3 4 5 6

lock will be seen on the stb side halfway down the reach. The chan dries with a hard bottom for ½M below the lock. At night a G lt Iso 5s is shown from the Blackwater SC clubhouse at Heybridge showing the chan from the Doctor buoy.

Berthing (See also entries for Bradwell and Mersea Quarters.) *Lawling Creek*, opposite Osea Pier; moorings may be available on application to Dann, Webb & Feesey. *Heybridge Basin*; there is a depth of 4m in the approach chan at MHWS. The lock opens from 1h before HW to HW; vessels up to 3.6m can enter at HW. Lock keeper is not obliged to attend at night: prior notice of arrival then advisable. Canal navigable to Chelmsford for 3.6m beam, 0.6m draft, 2m air draft. *Maldon*: a drying berth on staging may be obtained at the boatyard. There is 3m at MHWS and 1.5m at MHWN in the chan. EC Wed.

Anchorages (1) In Latchingdon Hole in 2m. (2) E of Osea pier-head. (3) Thirslet Creek, good anch in 3.3m or less. (4) Goldhanger Creek, anch in 2m. Goldhanger Spit is marked by a G con buoy to be left to port entering the creek. (5) Lawling Creek, opposite Osea Pier; good anch in 2 to 2½m, within 2 ca of the entrance. (6) Off Osea Pier and for ½M downstream. (7) Off the Stone.

BRADWELL   Chart BA 3741   (Plan p115)
HW +0.50.   MHWS 5.3; MLWS 0.5; MTL 2.8; MHWN 4.2; MLWN 1.3.
A small inlet on the S side of the R Blackwater, with approx 0.6m at MLWS. Situated inside Pewit Is, the creek is full of small craft moorings and also contains the approach chan to Bradwell Marina.

Approach From the E approach from close S of the Power Stn barrier wall, then alter course to leave entrance by approx 3m to stb. From the W turn onto this line from close to the W end of the barrier wall.

Entrance The narrow entrance chan is marked by a prominent square pile (QR) surmounted by a box. Follow line of withies round leaving them about 3m to stb until triangular leading marks on sea wall come into transit. Turn to stb immediately on passing G con buoy.

Berthing Bradwell Marina can accept visitors. Leading marks on S side of basin. Fuel and water. Customs clearance. Buoy sometimes available in creek. Do not anch: bottom foul with mooring chains. Stores, inn, chandlery, club with restaurant and bar at marina, also Bradwell Creek YC nearby.

MERSEA QUARTERS   Chart BA 3741   (Plan p115)
HW +0.55.   MHWS 5.2; MLWS 0.5; MTL 2.8; MHWN 4.0; MLWN 1.4.
Mersea Quarters has 2 to 7m and is reached by a chan to the N of the R Blackwater and separated from it by the Nass spit. The spit is marked by a bn with E Card topmark, VQ(3)5s, 4.6m above MHWS. The Nass dries 1 ca W of the bn and only 1.2m will be found close E of the bn. Vessels rounding the Nass at LW should exercise caution and keep well to the E and N of the bn, as the spit is extending.

Approach From the NW Knoll buoy it is 288° 4½M to the Nass bn. This is difficult to pick up from a distance and the black shed on Packingmarsh Is is a

Nuclear Power Stn

2FR(vert)
2FR(vert)
QR
Bn
Pewit I.

Marina
Cables
Depths in Metres

MERSEA QUARTERS

Depths in Metres
o Cables

N

West Mersea

Stonehill Hard
Strood Chan
Saltings
The Ray
RAY CHAN
Feldy Marshes
Kings Hard
Packingmarsh I.
Cobmarsh I.
SALCOTT CHAN.
Sunken I.
Saltings
Old Hall Marshes
Saltings
OLD HALL CR.
TOLLESBURY FLEET
Tollesbury Marina
Mill
Depth gauge
Mooring
Lit. Cob. I.
Gt. Cob. I.
North Chan
South Chan
Shinglehead Pt.
The Nass
MERSEA QUARTERS
(Seasonal Buoys)
G. No 1
R. No 2
G No 3
R. No 4
G. No 5
Osea I.
Pier
Inn

o Cables

Osea I.
Goldhanger Cr.
Saltings Cottages
the Pier
The Stumble
Bn
Road at LW
Bn
Northey I.
Jetty
IsoG.5s10m
YC
Heybridge Basin
Canal
MALDON
Colliers Reach
South Reach

Depths in Metres
o Cables

N

Stansgate Abbey
Caravan Park
Nayland Cr.
Wharf
Mundon Stone
Coopers Cr.
Lawling Cr.
Osea I.
Pier

d on British Admiralty Charts (nos. in text) with the permission of the Controller of H.M. Stationery Office and of lydrographer of the Navy, and on other sources.

115

useful mark till the bn is sighted. Coming from the R Colne, the shed on Packingmarsh Is well open of the W end of Mersea Is clears the Cocum Hills shoal. At night the lt on the Nass cannot be seen far.

Entrance   Pass 2 ca to the NE of the Nass Bn and make good course 285° up buoyed chan.

Berthing   (1) *Tollesbury Marina.* Tollesbury Fleet carries about 2m for 2M. There is a horse in midstream within the entrance, marked by R can buoys about 1 ca apart. A G drum marks the E end of Gt Cob Is. To proceed to Tollesbury via the S Channel, leave this G buoy to stb and follow chan which is marked by four G can buoys to stb and one R buoy to port marking Shingle Hills. The chan is also marked by withies. There are some deep-water moorings in S Channel near the entrance to Woodrolfe Creek and there is a rough hard where one can land by dinghy. It is advisable to keep as close as practicable to the moorings. The entrance to Woodrolfe Creek is marked by a small GWHS buoy to be left to stb and there is a tide gauge to indicate depth of water on harbour sill. While waiting for the tide it is possible to pick up a boatyard mooring marked WB. The marina is at the head of the ¾M Woodrolfe Creek, reached over a sill which has 1.8m at HW neaps. Inside, the hr is dredged to about 2.4m below sill level.

(2) *Thorn Fleet*, W of Packingmarsh Is which can be identified by its conspic B shed, carries 2.7m. *Mersea Fleet*, the chan between Cobmarsh Is and Packingmarsh Is and extending N to the Gut, is locally called the Creek and has 1.5m, but 1m on bar abreast shed. These creeks are too crowded with moorings to anch, but a vacant buoy can usually be found on enquiry. The best bet is between the mooring posts in the upper part of Thorn Fleet and lower Ray Channel, or ask advice from the WMYC boatman, usually cruising in the club launch during working hrs (look for a large ensign at stern).

Land at wooden jetty opposite the Gut and about 180m N of WMYC, or at the hard just below Clarke & Carter's shop. Water, fuel and stores, yacht chandlers and yards, scrubbing posts (apply to WMYC), wet dock (enquire at C & C), PO, tel. Store at end of causeway and more extensive shopping facilities in Mersea town, 1M. EC Wed.

Anchorages   (1) In the outer Quarters SE of the moorings, 2 to 7m. Uncomfortable in SE winds, buoy the anch. (2) Salcot chan S entrance marked by bns carries 1.8m to Sunken Is. Avoid this Is and anch below oyster notice board.

Strood chan may be sailed in a dinghy up to the causeway. Anch prohibited owing to oyster beds.

RIVER COLNE   Chart BA 3741   (Plan p117)
HW Brightlingsea +0.45; HW Wivenhoe +1.10.

Approach   From seaward as for the R Blackwater. Given sufficient rise of tide allowing for drying at LAT, a course may be made good from the N Eagle buoy to the Inner Bench Head R can buoy (Fl (2) R 5s). By night the Inner Bench Head buoy should be approached from the NW Knoll R can buoy (Fl R 10s), making good a course of 347° allowing for a flood tide set of 1½kn W, and a

BRIGHTLINGSEA
& R. COLNE
Depths in Metres

Rowhedge

Wivenhoe

Quay

F Or

F Or

Quay

F Or

Fl G 5s

2 FR (vert)(occas)(occas)

FR (occas)

(occas) FR

Pier

Saltings

R. Colne

Alresford Creek

Cables   0   Mile   1

Saltings

Geedon Cr

FR (occas) FR (occas)

Rat I

Saltings

Saltings

Saltings

Bns

QG

N°15

N°14

N°13A

Fl G

Bns

Brightlingsea

Batemans Tr

Westmarsh Pt

Pond

ROYAL HOTEL (CUPOLA)(CONSPIC)

Colne YC

Bn

Bn

Dewit

Saltings

Marsh

Saltings

Saltings

Pyefleet Chan

N°12

Fl(2)R

F Or

Cindery I

Hard

Bn

Martello Tr

N°1 (12)

Saltings

Water Tr (11)

St Osyth Stone Pt

YB

Bn

Bn

Mersea
Stone

Hard

Bn

N°3

QG

Mersea Island

Fl G

N°9

G

N°8

QR

Mersea Flat

West
Mersea

Target

Ray Creek Saltings

N°3

G

Colne Pt

Fl(2)R 5s

Inner Bench Head

Colne Pt

Fishery

Y

R

G

Bns

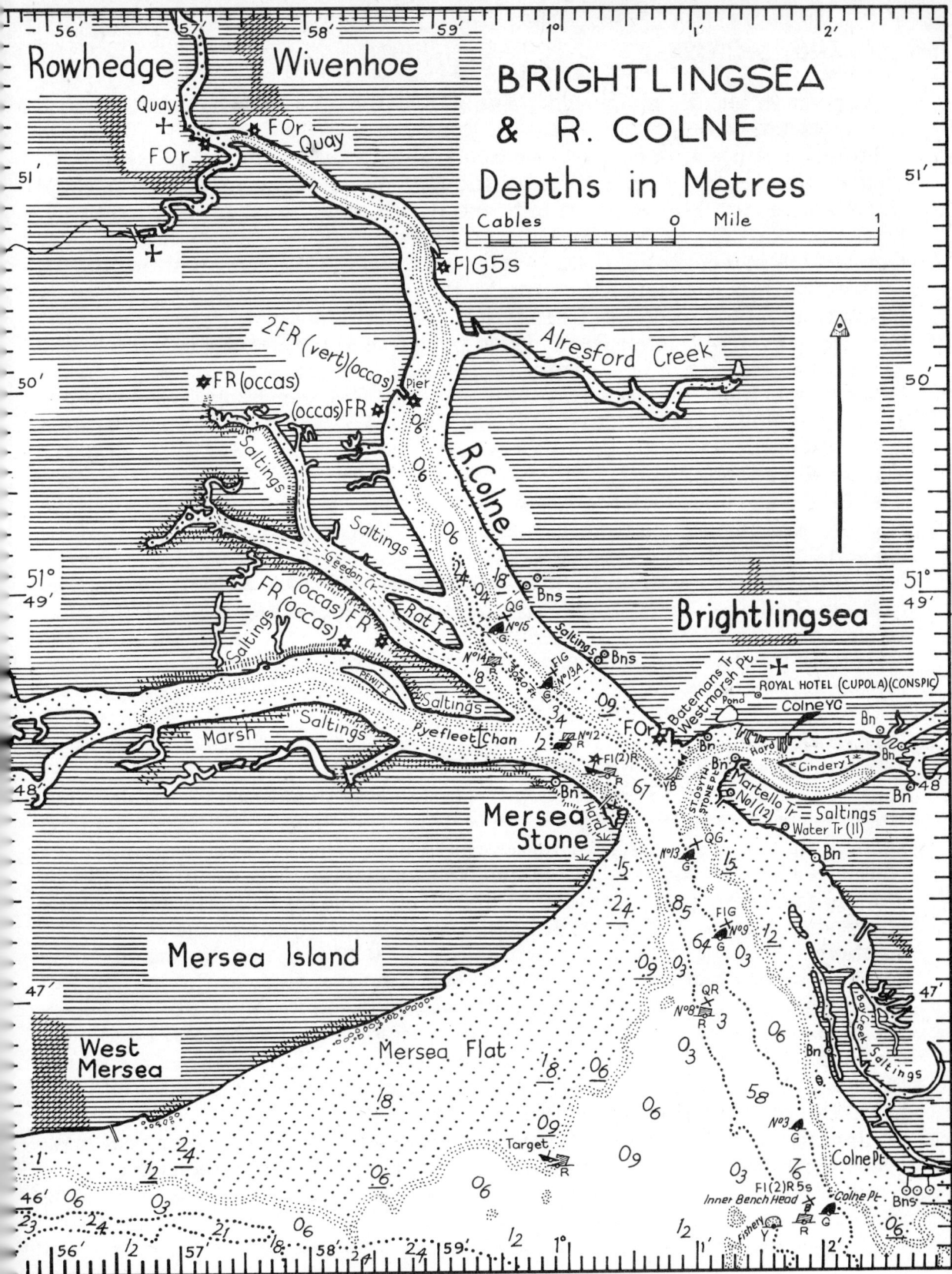

...sed on British Admiralty Charts (nos. in text) with the permission of the Controller of H.M. Stationery Office and of
... Hydrographer of the Navy, and on other sources.

similar set to the E on the ebb. The Colne Bar G con buoy is fitted with light-reflecting panels.

From the R Blackwater leave the Bench Head G con buoy (Fl G 5s) to port, thence make good a course to enter the R Colne S of the Inner Bench Head buoy, taking care not to be set onto the Bench Head shoal by the flood tide. From the Nass Bn in Mersea Quarters, given sufficient rise of tide to clear Cocum Hills in 0.6m LAT, make good 090° until the R can buoy marking the wk on Mersea Flats is abeam ½M to the N, thence make good 040° to enter the R Colne chan S of No.8 R can buoy (QR).

Entrance   From the Inner Bench Head buoy four G con buoys mark the E side of the chan through a least depth of 1.6m LAT (deeper water can be found between the Inner Bench Head buoy and No. 8 R can buoy (QR)), thence crossing to No. 13 G con buoy (QG). By night a FY light on Bateman's Tr kept 10° to stb of the bow from the Inner Bench Head buoy will clear the unlit No. 1 and No. 3 G con buoys.

Anchorages   (1) Between Mersea Stone and the R can buoy marking a wk to the N. Keep well clear of the chan as coasters anch and carry a riding lt. (2) Pyefleet chan in 2m E of Pewit Is and clear of oyster beds marked by withies.

Landing at Mersea Stone Pt or after half flood at E Mersea hard, and on the beach at Bateman's Tr ½M from Brightlingsea. Water at standpipe behind huts at Bateman's Tr, all facilities at Brightlingsea.

Vessels drawing 4.6m can reach Wivenhoe on springs, and drawing 3.6m the Hythe at Colchester.

BRIGHTLINGSEA   Chart BA 3741   (Plan p117)
HW +0.45.   MHWS 5.0; MLWS 0.4; MTL 2.7; MHWN 3.8; MLWN 1.2.

Entrance   From No. 13 G con buoy (QG) stand out in mid-chan until abeam of Brightlingsea Creek S Card buoy, close with it in 0.6m and proceed on 047° keeping the orange rectangular ldg marks in line. These can be seen under the conspic cupola of the Anchor Hotel. In summer keep close to the line of moorings and clear of the shallows to stb. By night FR ldg lts are shown; two FR lts are shown at the end of Brightlingsea hard on the N side of the chan.

Berthing   Apply to HM (tel Brightlingsea (020 630) 2200) for the use of a swinging mooring or the trots or piles. There is little water at the W range of mooring piles at LWS: do not attempt to pass between the W side of the pilings and the shore near LW. There are posts for scrubbing on the N shore. Landing at the hard. Colne YC have a pontoon connected to the shore by catwalk E of the hard; water hose. The club is well equipped and friendly. All facilities close by hard. HM office in Shipyard Estate. EC Thurs.

Alresford and Geeton Creeks dry. Navigable by shallow draft barges at HW. When the E banks up-river are covered there is approx 2m in the chan.

51°
53'

52·5'

Beaumont Quay

Landermere Quay

Water Tr

Lt Ho (disused)

Lt Ho (disused)

3

HALLIDAY
ROCK FLATS

1/2

Pye
End

SUNKEN PYE RW

1/2
2/1

55'

FS

FS

0/3

Saltings

1/2

1/2

No2
R

0/6

Crab Knoll
No3

2/7

G

1/2

0/6

0/3

51°
54'

WALTON

Depths in Metres

0   Cables   6

N

No5

High Hill
No4

G
R

0/9

2/1

Boat
Creek

0/6

6/1

No6

0/9

1/2

2/4

Dugmore

No7

R

G

0/9

0/9

Bramble . I

Pewit

1

(Covers at HW)

Island Pt

No9

No8

R

By

Mussel Scarfe

Walton Stone Pt

1/5
53'

Oakley Creek

Withies

R

4/2

6/1

Stone
Pt

0/6

HAMFORD WATER

8/5

WEST OR

3/6

Stone Creek

Dardanelles

Cormorant Creek

0/9

Skippers

I

Lndg

Lndg

Horsey
Island

3/4

Walton Chan

The Naze

KIRBY CREEK

Wharf

SALT

FLEET

CG
FS

Naze Cliff

52'

Boathouse
creek

Twizzle Creek

Hedge End

1

The Naze
Tr (49)

FORD

1/5

3

Lndg
Steps

1/5

HORSEY
The Wade
MERE

Titchmarsh
Marina

3

Foundry
Reach

CG
FS
LB

Kirby Quay

W & F YC

Sewer

Yacht Basin

Tr

13'   1°14'W   15'   17'

sed on British Admiralty Charts (nos. in text) with the permission of the Controller of H.M. Stationery Office and of
e Hydrographer of the Navy, and on other sources.

WIVENHOE
HW +1.10

Commercial traffic in the river is heavy around HW. There is 4½m in the chan at MHWS, and over 3m at MHWN.

Berthing A berth may be obtained on application to Colne Marine & Yacht Co, tel Wivenhoe (020 622) 2147. Landing at Wivenhoe SC hard, water available. EC Thurs.

WALTON BACKWATERS
Chart BA 2052   (Plan p119)

HW Walton-on-Naze +0.20.   HW Stone Point +0.30.

MHWS 4.2; MLWS 0.4; MTL 2.3; MHWN 3.4; MLWN 1.1.

Approach   The app is marked by the Pye End safe water buoy which lies in 1.2m 335° 2M from the Stone Banks R can and topmark buoy coming from the S. From the N, 240° 6 ca from the Landguard North Cardinal buoy (Q) at the entrance to Harwich Hr. The buoy is small and often difficult to pick out. The conspic Naze Tr is situated on the E side of the Naze. From the Stone Banks buoy a course maintained with Harwich ch spire ahead will lead close E of the Pye End buoy.

Entrance   7 ca SW of the Pye End buoy, No. 2 R can buoy marks the NE extremity of the Pye Sand and the entrance to the chan which deepens and runs in a SW direction for 1½M, marked on the shelving W side by G con buoys Nos. 3 to 7 and on the steep-to seaward side by R can buoys Nos. 2 to 8. At No. 8 buoy the chan becomes very narrow. Bound into Hamford Water leave Island Pt N Card buoy to port. When bound into the Walton Chan keep close to the R can buoys to avoid the spit running out from Island Pt. A R can buoy is laid off Stone Pt. The remainder of the chan is marked to port and stb by withies; the line of moorings indicates the best water. Approx 1.2M past Stone Pt the entrance to the Twizzle running E lies to stb and Foundry Creek, which dries, carries on to the S, leading to the Walton and Frinton YC.

Berthing   A mooring buoy may be obtained on application to the CA boatman. At the WFYC quay, which dries out, limited to 2h for visitors. There is a basin behind the YC with sluice opening an h or two before HW, by arrangement with Bedwell & Co. tel Frinton (025 56) 5873; craft up to 2m can lie afloat. In the Twizzle there are piles and a marina (1M from town) operated by Titchmarsh Marina, tel Frinton 2185.

Anchorages   Off Stone Pt, or elsewhere in Walton Channel or Hamford Water clear of moorings. The latter uncomfortable in NE winds. Landing at the WFYC hard approx 2h either side of HW, Shops ½M, all facilities. EC Wed.

HARWICH
Chart BA 2052, 2693   (Plan p121)

HW +0.45.   MHWS 4.0; MLWS 0.4; MTL 2.2; MHWN 3.4; MLWN 1.1.

DS: Cork buoy: SW −6.05; NE +0.10. Naze: S +6.10; N −0.15. Landguard Pt: flood (2kn) +5.30.   Across Beach End −0.30 to +0.30.   Ebb 0.30.

Accessible at all times. Rapidly developing as a premier container port: small

HARWICH

Depths in Metres

Cables 0 Miles 1

CONTINUATION OF R. ORWELL on the same scale

CONTINUATION of R. STOUR on the same scale

Ipswich Dock — Power Station — Alnesbourn Priory (ruins) — Cliff Quay — Halifax — Fox's Marina — Bridge under construction 1980 — Works in progress 1980

Felixstowe Pier — Storage tank (conspic) — Felixstowe Dk — Martello Tr — Landguard Pt — Wadgate Ledge — Rolling Ground — Platters — Inner Ridge — Pitching Ground — R Ground — Pye End

Fagbury Pt — Trimley — Walton — Shotley Spit — Shotley Pt — Water Tr — Mast — Parkeston Quay — Erwarton Ness — Harkstead Pt — Copperas Bay — Stutton Ness

HARWICH — Dovercourt — Water Tr (conspic) — Lt ho (disused) — Cliff Foot — Landguard — R. Beach End — N. Beach — N.W. Beach — Cliff End

Suffolk Yacht Hr — Collimer Pt — S. Mile Mks — N. Mile Mk — PinMill Yacht yard — Wolverstone Marina — Wolverstone Hall Pt — Freston

Seafield Bay — Works — channel marked by buoys — Mistley — Manningtree

N

...sed on British Admiralty Charts (nos. in text) with the permission of the Controller of H.M. Stationery Office and of
...e Hydrographer of the Navy, and on other sources.

craft should keep clear of the very large vessels manoeuvring inside or approaching the hr. Harwich Hr maintains a listening and information service on VHF chan 14.

Approach Well marked. From the S by night make good a course of 355° from the Medusa G con buoy (Fl G 5s) towards the Rolling Ground G con buoy (QG) to avoid the unlit Stone Banks and Outer Ridge buoys. From the E the Cork lighthouse buoy Fl 10s 22M 30s (horn) leads into the main chan. From the N at or near LW stand out to leave the Wadgate Ledge G con buoy (Fl G 10s) to stb, avoiding the shallow patches and wrecks in the vicinity.

Entrance The main chan entrance into the hr is marked on the stb side by the Rolling Ground buoy; thence as the chan turns N by G con lt buoys. On the port side it is marked by a N Card lt buoy and R can lt buoys. Ample water outside the chan for small craft. From the Cliff Foot R can buoy (Fl R 5s) steer N across the Shelf where coastal vessels may be at anch; when abeam of the N Shelf R can buoy (QR) make to leave the Grisle R can buoy (Fl R 2½s) broad to port. If crossing for the R Orwell proceed on the shortest chan crossing distance to the Shotley Spit S Card buoy (Q). If proceeding up the R Stour cross to the N side of the chan when clear of shipping, thence keep to the N until above Parkeston Quay.

Berthing It is possible to lie alongside Harwich Quay for approx 1h either side of HW. Good fendering is essential and vessels should not be left unattended as considerable wash may be experienced from passing vessels.

Anchorages Well inshore immediately to seaward of the moorings on the Shelf, otherwise upstream of Parkeston Quay in the R Stour. Landing at Harwich Quay where Customs' clearance may be obtained, or on the beach beside the HTSC. Shops in Harwich, EC Wed.

RIVER STOUR   Chart BA 2693   (Plan p121)
HW (Mistley) +1.10.
MHWS 4.2; MHWS 0.3; MTL 2.2; MHWN 3.4; MLWN 1.0.
Entrance Leaving Parkeston Quay to port proceed upriver in a W direction. The river is broad and straight for a distance of 2.5M until approaching Wrabness; the chan is buoyed and lit as far as Mistley. There is approx 0.6m at Mistley. The R Stour is navigable as far as Manningtree, 5M upriver of Wrabness, for 1.2m draft at HW.
Berthing A vacant buoy may be found at Wrabness for a short period.
Anchorages In the R Stour clear of the chan, riding lt essential.

RIVER ORWELL   Chart BA 2693   (Plan p121)
HW (Ipswich) +1.05.   MHWS 4.2; MHWN 3.4; MTL 2.3.
Entrance Between the Shotley Spit S Card buoy (Q) to port and Walton G con buoy (Fl (3) G 10s) to stb. The chan is dredged to 5.8m as far as Ipswich, the navigable limit 9½M from Harwich. It is well marked with lt buoys. The chan runs fairly in the middle as far as Collimer Pt. Above No. 4 buoy the mud extends

a long way out on the stb hand. The flood and ebb run at up to 3kn and pleasure craft must keep clear of commercial shipping. It is essential to pass the correct side of No. 5 buoy off Potters Pt as this spit dries extensively at LW. Anch in the chan is prohibited. Work is in progress (1981) on the Orwell Bridge which will cross the R in the vicinity of Nos. 10 and 11 buoys: it is essential to exercise caution in the vicinity while work is in progress.

Berthing   (1) Suffolk Yacht Hr (tel Nacton (047 388) 465 or VHF chan 37 during normal daytime hrs). Entrance marked by spher Y buoy, 1.2m in chan marked by port and stb bns. Immediately on entering hr turn to stb and berth at visitors' pontoon adjacent to fuel berth, contact HM for berth. All facilities. (2) Pin Mill. A mooring may be available: apply to CA Boatman. (3) Woolverstone Marina have pontoon berths and swinging moorings: apply CA Boatman. All facilities including repairs. (4) Fox's Marina at the W side in Ostrich Creek near No. 12 buoy. Enter chan S of No. 12 buoy, marked by port and stb bns, 1m. Limited number of berths (tel Ipswich (0473) 215091). All facilities including repairs and Renner hoist. (5) Ipswich New Cut, Debbage Yacht Services, tel Ipswich 50169. Enter New Cut on port hand when close to Dock Gates leaving spher R buoy close to port to avoid spit on stb hand. Access from half-tide for 1.2m draft; limited number of pontoon berths but boats dry out in soft mud. All facilities including repairs and 20 ton crane.

Anchorages   (1) Above Shotley Pt on W side opposite Fagbury buoy. Shore is steep-to, beware tel cable. Landing on isolated beaches at HW, good shelter in W winds. (2) In Long Reach on S side, well clear of main chan, show riding lt. (3) In Pin Mill bay below moorings, riding lt.

PASSAGE NOTES: HARWICH TO SOUTHWOLD

Charts BA 2693, 1543

Leaving Harwich round Landguard Pt keep close N of the buoyed chan and stand on as far as the Platters buoy to avoid numerous shifting shoals E of the Pt. Proceed NE from the Platters leaving the Wadgate Ledge buoy to port. A least offshore distance of ½M will thereafter clear all outlying dangers as far as Orfordness.

ORFORDNESS
DS: SW −6.00; NE +0.20.
The Ness is steep-to. An eddy runs close inshore N and S. Tides run hard and with wind over tide a steep, confused sea is raised. To avoid the Aldeburgh Ridge 7 ca offshore, stand close inshore or pass outside E of the Aldeburgh Ridge buoy.

SIZEWELL AND DUNWICH BANKS
To pass inside the banks from the S, make a position with Thorpe water tr in line with a grey churchlike building close N of the conspic tr 263° 2 ca, and with

Sizewell Nuclear Power Stn main buildings bearing 330°. Thence make good 348° on Minismere ex CGS (W cottages on S end of Cliff N of Minismere Level, 52°15'.1N, 1°37'.8E). Maintain this course, passing 2 ca inside the shallowest part of the bank until Southwold Lt Ho comes in line with Southwold Hr pier-heads: this leads clear inside Dunwich Bank. The shore is sand and shingle, steeply shelving; from N of Shingle Street no inshore shoals, except for the rocky reef projecting from Thorpeness (many lobster pots), to about ¾M S of Southwold Haven entrance. Inshore hazards are clearly visible.

Anchorage With winds between SW and NW there is good anch in 3½ to 5m, sand, anywhere between Sizewell and Dunwich.

RIVER DEBEN   Chart BA 2693   (Plan p125)

HW +0.20.   DS (offing): NE + 0.10; SW −6.05.
MHWS 3.7; MLWS 0.5; MTL 2.0; MHWN 2.9; MLWN 1.0.

Bar 0.3 to 1m, varying in depth and position. The banks are liable to shift at any time.

Approach The entrance lies between Felixstowe and Bawdsey Cliff. Prominent shoreline features are two Martello trs (marked T and U on chart BA 2693) to the W, and a radio tr N of the entrance. The lie of the chan alters frequently; there is a safe water offshore buoy (WE Haven) from which the Bar G con buoy can usually be seen. The entrance is rough in onshore winds, especially on the ebb: under these conditions entrance should not be attempted without local knowledge. Except in good conditions strangers are advised to arrange for pilotage (Mr Charles Brinkley acts as unofficial pilot for the entrance, and can be contacted on Felixstowe (039 42) 3469), or to follow in a local vessel of suitable draft and experience: hail to confirm.

Entrance If in settled weather and on a rising tide entry is attempted unaided, the following directions will help, however the chan can and does often change and any chart must be used with caution. Ldg marks may be in position, the rear a R disc and the front one a W spade shape. Beware strong cross-sets in outer entrance. A R can buoy marks a spit running out from the W bank and must be left to port. Keep to the centre of the chan between the ferry jetties on each side, then keep to the E side of the river leaving the Horse R can buoy close to port. Thereafter keep to the centre, giving pts a wide berth as far as Shottisham Reach. From the middle of this reach the chan is buoyed, R barrel buoys to port, G to stb; or triangular topmarked perches, those point up being left to stb.

Berthing (1) Ramsholt: a mooring may be obtained from the boatman. (2) Woodbridge, Tide Mill Yacht Hr (tel Woodbridge (039 43) 4222), on the port hand just beyond Woodbridge Docks. Dredged entrance chan marked by bns carries 2m at MHWN, 3m at MHWS, with 2m inside. In general, if a yacht has enough water to reach Woodbridge there is enough water to enter the Yacht Hr. Tide gauge. All facilities. Rly. EC Wed.

Anchorages Off the E bank at Felixstowe Ferry above the ferry. Ramsholt, clear of the moorings. Off Waldringfield: provisions.

RIVER DEBEN
Depths in Metres

Channel marked by buoys

Cables 0 Miles

N

Woodbridge

Marina

Kingston Quay

Robert Sham Ca.

Ferry Cliffs

Troublesome Reach

Methersgate Quay

Quay

Waldringfield

Boat Yard

YCFS

The Tips

Stonner Pt

Saltings

Rocks

Shottisham Creek

Landing

Reach

Inn

Ramsholt Quay

Ramsholt Marshes

Falkenham Marshes

Horse

Radio Tr (conspic) Red Lts (13)

Bawdsey Manor

Woodbridge Haven

QRW

Felixstowe Ferry

Martello Tr U

Martello T

SOUTHWOLD
Depths in Metres

Gp Fl (4) WR 20s 37m 22, 20M Lt Ho

SOUTHWOLD

SOUTHWOLD COMMON

Water Trs (conspic)

Footpath (old Railway)

(Not Navigable)

Buss Creek

Obsn

River Blyth

Sluice

Bailey Bridge

W Post

Storm Signal FS

CG

Ch (conspic) & CGFS 353°

North Pier Lt. & Water Tr in line 347°

THE DENES

Bns. in line 298°

Windmill

Harbour open through 305°

FS

Bns

Bns

Toilets

Piles

QR2M

N.Pier &

Lt Ho. 015°

Fl G or R 15s

THE FLATS

ROAD

Footpath

Harbour Inn

Blackshore

Inshore Rescue Boat

SC

County Sailing Centre

Visitors Pontoon

Chandlery & Boatman

Fisherman's huts

Slip

Bns

Tel Bns

Ferry

Dinghy Beach

Fisharman's Huts

MARSHES

Footpath on Flood Bank

HM

LB

Derelict Stage

Walberswick

Car Park

Garage Hotel

Store

The

Street

P.O

Inn

Cables

SOUTHWOLD
Depths in Metres

N

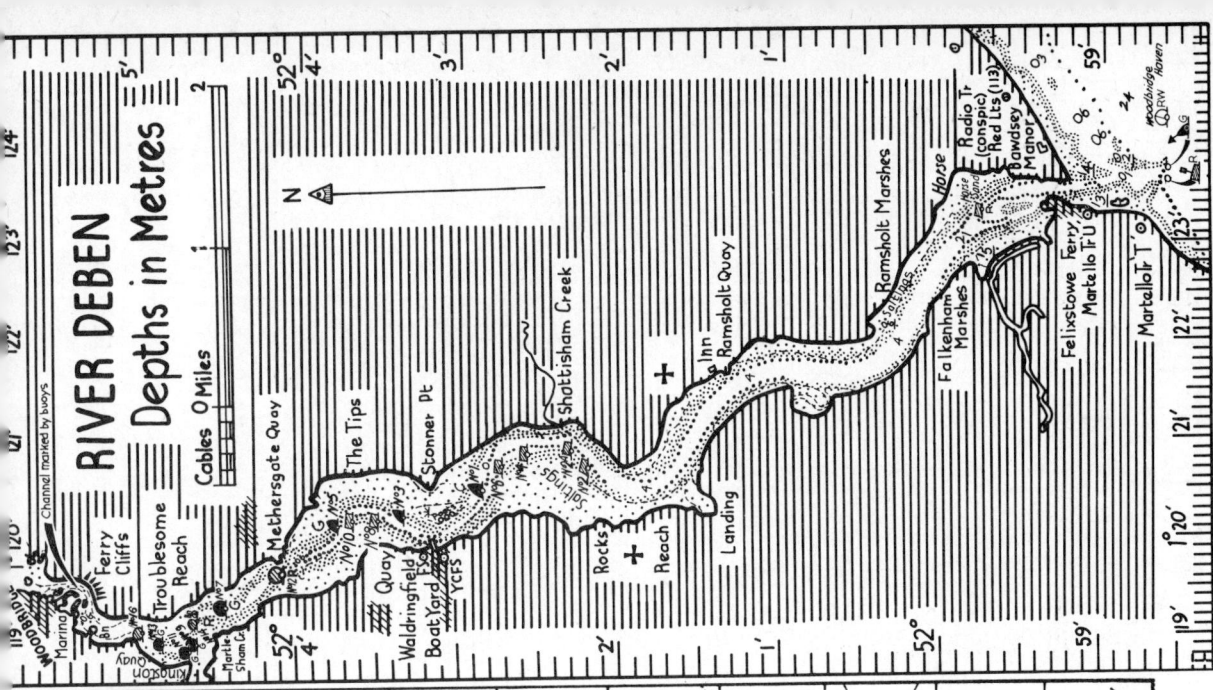

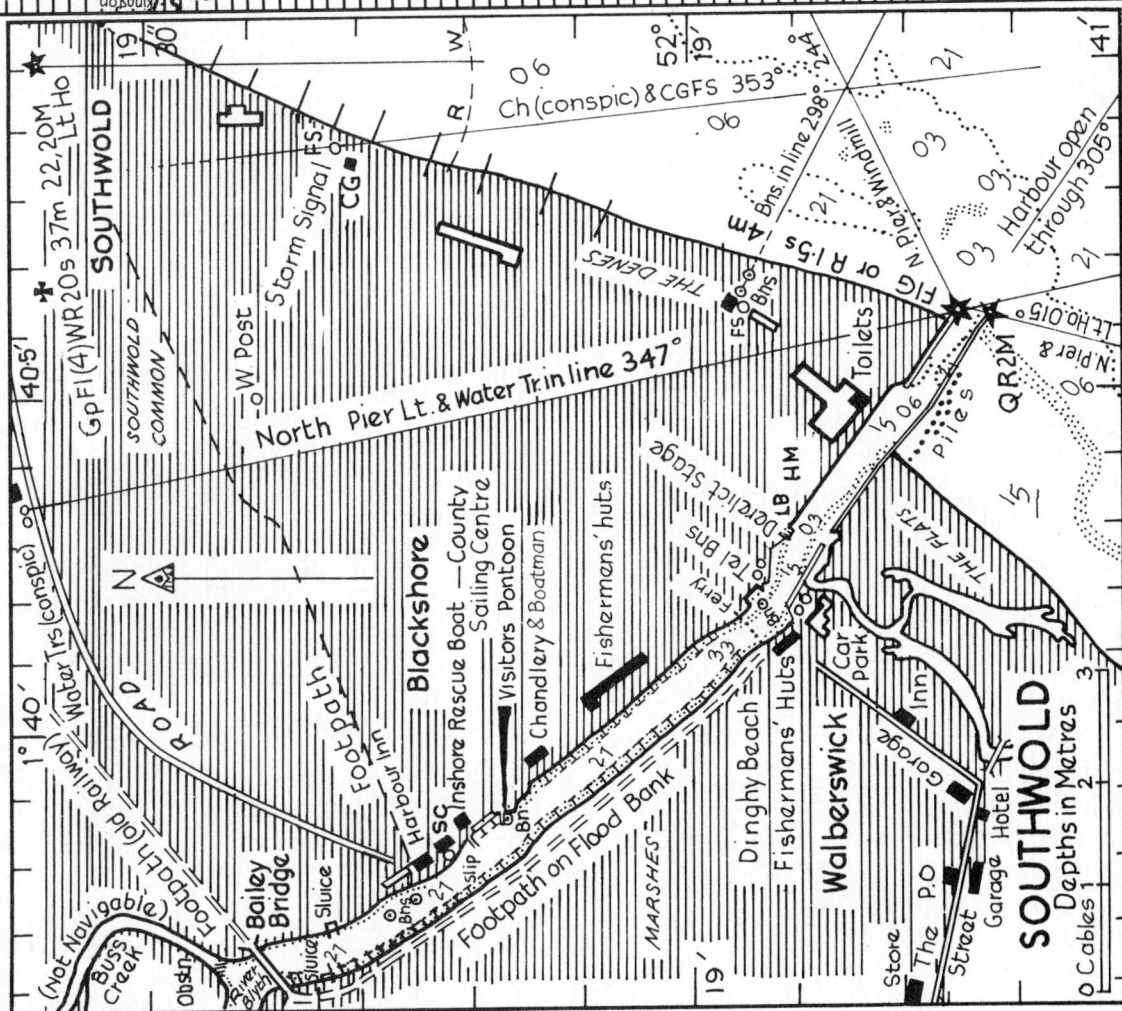

Based on British Admiralty Charts (nos. in text) with the permission of the Controller of H.M. Stationery Office and of the Hydrographer of the Navy, and on other sources.

RIVER ORE
Depths in Metres

One Mile

RIVER ORE

ORFORD
Castle (conspic)
Inn
Quay
Bn
Chantry Pt
Chantry Marshes
Cuckolds Pt
Havergate I
UPPER GULL
Gedgrave Marshes
Bn
Dove Pt
LOWER GULL
THE NARROWS
Bn
Flybury Pt
Boyton Marshes
Dock
Hard
The Cliff
Butley River
Burrow Hill
Butley Mills
Boyton
N

HOLLESLEY BAY
Green
Red
12
8
7
9
6
8
North Weirpt
Hollesley Bay Colony
Hollesley
Shingle Street
Martello Tr
Bn Y
C.G.
Orford Haven
LONG REACH
RIVER ORE

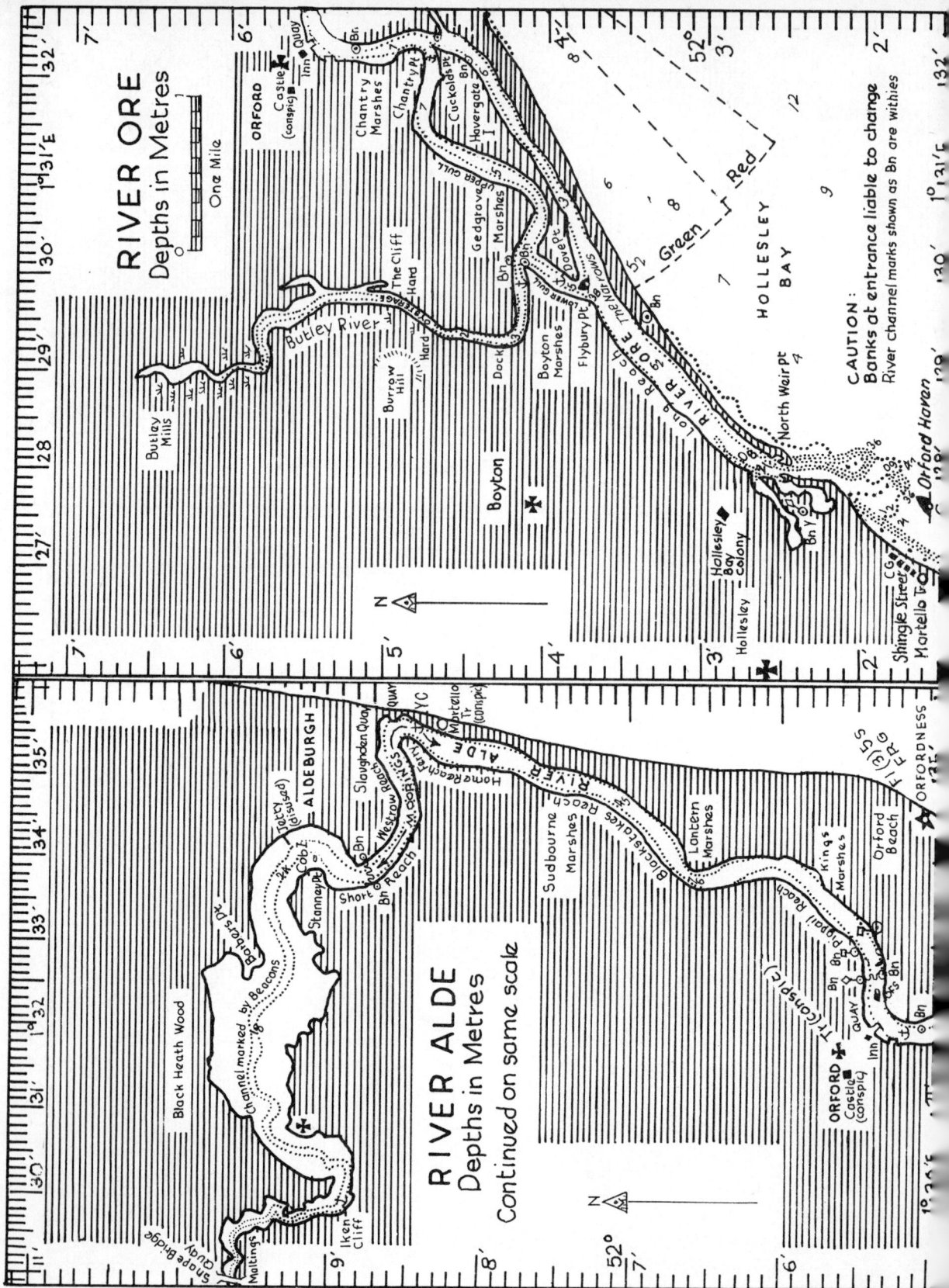

CAUTION:
Banks at entrance liable to change
River channel marks shown as Bn are withies

RIVER ALDE
Depths in Metres
Continued on same scale

ALDEBURGH
Slaughden Quay
Westrow Reach
Short Reach
Bn Reach
Cob (disused)
Stanny Pt
Barbers Pt
Black Heath Wood
Channel marked by Beacons
Iken Cliff
Snape Bridge Quay
Maltings
MOORINGS
Quay
A.Y.C.
Martello Tr (conspic)
ALDE RIVER
Home Reach
Blackstakes Reach
Lantern Marshes
Sudbourne Marshes
Kings Marshes
Orford Beach
Pigpail Reach
Tr (conspic)
ORFORD
Castle (conspic)
Inn
QUAY
Bn
ORFORDNESS
FERRY
FLS(3) 55
N

Based on British Admiralty Charts (nos. in text) with the permission of the Controller of H.M. Stationery Office and the Hydrographer of the Navy, and on other sources.

ORFORD HAVEN — Chart BA 2693 (Plan p126)

HW (Bar) +0.05. HW (Orford Quay) +1.00.
Bar: MHWS 3.2; MLWS 0.2; MTL 1.7; MHWN 2.6; MLWN 0.9.
DS in offing: N +0.15; S −6.00. The flood stream runs upriver for 1h after HW by the shore and the ebb runs down 1h after the water begins to rise at the entrance.

Bar 1.2m but liable to shift after a gale. Streams run fast, the ebb attaining 5kn or over at springs. Entrance during ebb requires reliable power, and should never be attempted in strong onshore winds. Entrance or departure should be at least half-tide.

There are good anch outside in Hollesley Bay with deep water close in to the beach in the G sector of Orfordness Lt during NW winds, and S of the Shingle Street martello tr in NW to SW winds.

Approach Shingle Street, marking the entrance to Orford Haven, may be located from seaward by a martello tr, old CGS, and a cluster of small houses situated 1M S of entrance. The tr is the fourth N from Bawdsey Cliff when app from the SW and the first after passing Orfordness when coming from the NE. When coming from the SW keep ½M offshore (watch out for nets) to avoid shingle banks lying off conspic cottage N of old CGS, until G con Orford Haven buoy has been identified and brought into line with ldg bn on shore with fluorescent Or diamond topmark. From NE, keep ½M off to avoid a shingle bank coming out from the N entrance head.

Entrance Wind against tide at entrance causes a heavy sea near and on the bar. Half-tide, preferably rising, is the safest time. Stand off until Orford Haven buoy has been identified and brought into line with ldg bn on shore (see above). The Orford Haven buoy lies off the entrance, its position being altered as often as surveying is possible, to suit changes in the chan: the bn is fixed. The buoy in line with the bn leads across the bar which lies almost ½M offshore. The line must be treated with caution and may not always show the best water all the way in. Do not close the N pt in the entrance as a shingle bank extends ½ of the distance across.

Once inside the best water is close to the seaward side of the river up to the N of Havergate Is. The chans here may be marked by bns (see plan). Water skiing is carried out in Long Reach. The Ore/Alde has 2.7 to 7.6m to Slaughden except in Pigpail Reach and over the horse 4 ca S of Aldeburgh martello tr. Deepest water is just W of centre. Above Slaughden Quay from Cob Is, chan is marked by bns with R cans and G flags (unreliable). Explore only on rising tide above half-tide. A ferry service using tank landing craft operates from Orford Quay, normally very cooperative with yachts.

The W side of Havergate Is has more room for beating up, the E side is straighter but more commercial traffic.

Berthing On a visitors' buoy, stay limited to one night only, S of Aldeburgh YC.

Anchorages Avoid the mouth where streams run hard. (1) Approx 1M above N Weir Pt close to the E bank. Streams still run strong and holding unreliable,

4.5m. (2) In the Gulls, $3\frac{1}{2}$M from entrance on the W side of Havergate Is and E of the entrance to Butley Creek in $7\frac{1}{2}$m. (3) Just S of Orford, $4\frac{1}{2}$M from entrance in $4\frac{1}{2}$m. (4) Off Slaughden in Westrow Reach (9M) in 4.5m. (5) For a short time in fine weather between martello tr and YC in 2m. (6) At Iken Cliff, 1.5m in chan at LW. Keep clear of fairway. It is very narrow above the Black Heath Reach. Riding lts advisable.

Landing prohibited (1) on Havergate Is, a bird sanctuary; (2) on E side of river from NE corner of Havergate to 1M S of Aldeburgh martello tr, Ministry of Defence.

Landing at Orford and Slaughden quays, most facilities at Aldeburgh. Lay ashore on S side of Slaughden Quay. Hotels and shops at Aldeburgh and Orford. EC Wed.

SOUTHWOLD   Chart BA 1543   (Plan p125)
HW -0.55.   DS: N $+0.15$; S -6.00.
MHWS 2.5; HLWS 0.4; MTL 1.5; MHWN 2.2; MLWN 0.9
The hr is formed by the mouth of the R Blyth which enters the sea approx $\frac{3}{4}$M S of Southwold, between two piers 137m long and 36m apart. The banks at the entrance are liable to change with E gales or a period of E winds, and during winter months sand and shingle banks may build up to reduce entry to near HW only or close the entrance for several weeks. Visitors should not attempt entry at night or in poor visibility, or with the wind more than moderate from S through E to N, when the entrance is dangerous. It is sheltered in SW to NW winds. Altogether a difficult and potentially dangerous entrance, to be approached with caution and only by experienced yachtsmen.

Approach   Arrival should be timed for $\frac{1}{2}$h either side of local HW when the entrance is slack and there is the best water. If carrying the ebb from the S, plan to take the new foul flood close inshore off Minismere ex-CG cottages, or anch 1–2 ca SE of pier-head in 5 to 6m, sand. Entry should not be attempted before 2–3h after LW. From S and even more from N, keep at least 3 ca offshore for the last mile before the entrance.

Entrance   Contact HM Roger Trigg, RNLI coxwain, for latest information on depths and chan. Tel Southwold (0502) 723502 (day) or 722638 (night) or on VHF Ch 16. If no answer try boatyard, 722593.

By night three Fl R lts ($1\frac{1}{2}$s) indicate port closed. Otherwise N pierhead shows Fl G $1\frac{1}{2}$s, S Pierhead QR. It is essential to have the vessel under full command before being committed to entry. The chan is narrow and there is little room to manoeuvre inside; the tide runs up to 4kn at half flood and 7kn after half ebb. There is a drying sandbank along the outside of the S Pier and a large shoal spreading N and seaward from the N pier. The chan is narrow; its edge with the N shoal can usually be seen from close to. The exact location and direction can change overnight, especially during E winds. Day-to-day information is essential during November to March. During May to September it usually settles down and can be expected to lie somewhere between transits N Pier lt on with

Southwold Lt Ho, 015°, and hr fully open on heading 305°. Least depth at MLWS is then usually about 2m, with least water in the last 50–100m to pier-heads. Concrete blocks lie up to 5m out from S pier-head.

Entrance is between the two piers. Unless previously advised otherwise, enter at least 5m clear of S pier-head but within S half of the entrance to avoid shoals inside N pier-head. Steer for the knuckle at inner root of N pier, pass close to posts marking concrete blocks sunk off knuckle, and continue close to wall below caravan site. S bank here is shoal. Stand out to mid-river after clearing derelict stage above 4kn speed restriction sign. Follow stb side of river, but keeping well out toward middle until after ferry, to Corporation visitors' pontoon outside Harbour Inn, Blackshore.

Berthing   On visitors' pontoon below Harbour Inn, only 1m alongside at LWS. Bottom is steeply shelving, hard mud. Or secure temporarily alongside N wall and contact HM at Caravan Park.

All facilities except repairs. EC Wed.

PASSAGE NOTES: SOUTHWOLD TO GREAT YARMOUTH
Chart BA 1543

From Southwold to Lowestoft there is an inshore passage in 6m approx 1½–2 ca offshore. In poor conditions use the outside route. To keep to the E of Barnard Shoal off Benacre Ness from the S, keep Southwold Lt Ho bearing nothing less than 218° until Kessingland ch bears 297°. This leads ½M clear of the end of the shoal. If Southwold ch is not visible, Covehithe ch bearing 240° leads to the same position, but across the S end of the shoal in less than 5.5m.

From Lowestoft to Great Yarmouth a safe distance of ½M offshore can be maintained.

LOWESTOFT   Charts BA 1543, 1536   (Plan p130)
HW −1.30.   MHWS 2.4; MLWS 0.5; MTL 1.5; MHWN 2.1; MLWN 1.0.
DS (S Channel): N +0.10; S −6.10.
Accessible at all times, least depth in entrance 4.3m.
Approach   Beware of shallow patches on the bank E of the N Road. With wind against tide a nasty sea gets up off Lowestoft Ness opposite the Lt Ho. Approach only from the N via the Hewitt Chan as the Newcome Chan has silted and become unreliable. Vessels should remain inside the buoyed chans as the banks are continually changing and deep water shown on charts outside the chans may have silted.
Entrance   With foul wind and ebb tide make the entrance from S pier. Keep N pier just shut in by S pier, enter carrying good way past the S pier-head, and be prepared for eddy. The yacht basin is a cul-de-sac at the SW corner of the hr. The turreted building on the promenade pier makes a wind eddy and often causes vessels to gybe. Inside the basin there is no room to come about.

A Fl W traffic control lt, which must be obeyed, is shown below the F R lt on

LOWESTOFT HARBOUR

1° 45' E

52° 28.5'

CG

WK /8

Spire

HAMILTON DOCK

WAVENEY DOCK

3·4 3 3 3·3 3·1

2FR(vert)

Silo (49) (conspic)

2FG (vert)

Customs & HM

Sladden's pier

North Europe Quay

FS

TRAWL BASIN
2FY (vert)

2FG (vert)
Jackamans Groyn

5·3

LAKE LOTHING

INNER HARBOUR 3·2 3

INNER PIER

E JETTY

River

4

Mooring Posts o

South Quay YC

LB

INNER S PIER ('8)

2FR (vert)
OUTER
HARBOUR

Or F

3·7 3·3

North Pier
OcG5s12m8M

KIRKLEY HAM

Chy O

Memorial

FS

2·5

3·9

OcR5s12m6M. Horn(4)60s
Traffic Sig

2·4

LOWESTOFT HARBOUR

Pavilion

SOUTH PIER

3·1

5·8

5·4

0·5

3·6

LOWESTOFT BANK

Depths in Metres

N

28'

2·8

2·4

1·4

5·6 0

Cables

0·5

Claremont Pier (ruins)
2FR 5,4m4M (vert)

1° 45'

2

GREAT YARMOUTH HAVEN

44'

44·5'

34·5

4·3

Landing

LB

Depths in Metres

0 1 Cables 2

N

Slips

34·4

Spending Beach

The Point

North Pier
OcG8s 8m6M

3

Lts in line 264°

3·8

Mooring Posts

2FG (vert)

52°

Oc 3s6m10M

3·1

3FG

2FG (vert)

0·7

3·5

CG

F11m

34·3

FR20m 6M &
Oc 6s7m 10M

Brush quay

South Pier

FS O

F Bu

Traffic Sig
HM

F1R3s11m11M
Tidal sig Traffic sig

Horn(3)60s

1° 44' E

44·5'

130

Based on British Admiralty Charts (nos. in text) with the permission of the Controller of H.M. Stationery Office and of the Hydrographer of the Navy, and on other sources.

the S Pier Lt Ho. When this lt is flashing vessels may leave the hr but none may enter. At all other times vessels may enter but must not leave the hr. Yachts may pass through the first bridge into the inner hr when it is opened for commercial traffic. Do not approach without G lt on N wall.

Berthing Yachts should secure to inner S pier pending allocation of a club mooring. Yachts lie in five tiers on the port side of S basin. Wire hawsers have been run between the three dolphins in centre of basin and S pier, with lines of buoys in between. Secure warps to hawser and appropriate buoy. Port VHF Chans 14, 16. Docks Manager tel (0502) 2286, Customs (NW side of bridge) tel 3213, CG tel 5365. Weather reports RAF Honington tel 03596 466. There is a dry dock and slipway. Land at steps at town end of basin. The YC has private steps where water may be obtained. All facilities. EC Thurs.

Lowestoft Hr bridge opens for yachts 0645 and 0930 daily, also 2100 weekdays. 1345 and 1730 Sundays. The rly swing bridge opens on request if clear. Mutford Locks open Wed 1300–1600 on 48h notice and summer Sats 0800–1200. These allow access to Oulton Broad and the southern Norfolk Broads.

GREAT YARMOUTH
Charts BA 1543, 1536   (Plan p130)

HW −2.05.   MHWS 2.4; MLWS 0.5; MTL 1.5; MHWN 2.0; MLWN 1.0.

This port is the busiest offshore industry support base in the UK. Visiting yachts are welcome, but it is essentially a commercial port and no special facilities exist. Published navigational directions must be strictly observed, particularly the one-way traffic system at the hr entrance; F amber lt on Port Control tr on S pier (or at night the extinguishing of ldg lts and various others) prohibits entry; 2 horizontal R oc or F lts on HM office, or 3 vert R balls, prohibit downstream movement beyond slipway. There are Fl amber and mauve tidal signals. Port Control (tel Great Yarmouth (0493) 63476, Yarmouth Radio chan 16, 12) is manned continuously and will advise on tidal and weather conditions. Radio-equipped yachts should make contact before entering or shifting berth and prior to departure.

Entrance There is 4.3m in the entrance and 4.8m up to the town with up to 1m less during strong SE winds. Small craft can enter at most times, but preferably at slack water; the stream runs up to 4kn. It makes up the hr until 1½h after HW at the pier head, and out of the hr until 1½ hr after LW at the pier-head. Entering with the flood, beware of the eddy which sets across the S pier-head towards the N pier. Entrance should not be attempted in strong SE winds, when a dangerous sea occurs especially on the ebb tide. Passage under sail within the port limits is not normally permitted. Anch in the hr prohibited except in emergency. Vessels are strongly advised to keep an anch cleared ready to drop especially if navigating up-tide of the bridges.

Berthing If clearing Customs, report to the Waterguard on the Fish wharf. Visitors should berth on Bunns Quay, opposite the Town Hall Quay close S of Haven Bridge. Space may sometimes be found at the S end of the fish-wharf among the local workboats, or on W Quay, but both are subject to heavy wash and risk of damage by manoeuvring ships. There are boatyards and marinas above Haven Bridge.

Port dues and Norfolk Broads temporary licences at The Haven Commissioners, 21 South Quay. All facilities and stores. EC Thurs.

Up-river. Great Yarmouth is the northern gateway to the Norfolk Broads via the R Bure (two fixed bridges, headroom about 2m at HW) and R Yare. To enter, the lifting Haven Bridge (headroom closed 4.2m at MLWS, 2.4m at MHWS) must be passed, preferably at slack water. Yachts are expected to fit in with booked openings for commercial shipping if possible: contact the Bridge Officer (VHF Chan 12 or 16 or tel Great Yarmouth 55151 in office hrs). Bridge signals Bu flag for N-bound traffic, R flag for S-bound; yachts must keep clear of ships.

NORFOLK COAST   Chart BA 108

DS Yarmouth Road	S +6.00; N −0.20
Cromer	ESE +4.30; WNW −1.15
Smith's Knoll	SE −5.45; NW +0.30

Inshore, the tidal streams run parallel to the coast and they run true in the chans parallel to the coast. In the outer chans the streams run true when they are strongest, but there is a set across the shoals towards the begining and end of each stream. The SE stream changes through SW to NW, and the NW stream changes through NE to SE. On this coast generally the NW stream is strongest at LW by the shore, and the SE stream strongest at HW.

DS Blakeney Overfalls: W −2.00; E +3.00.

The inshore Wash streams and the Norfolk coast streams meet and separate near Scolt Head.

DS E of Scolt Hd: E +4.10; W −2.00.

W of Scolt Hd: E −6.00; W +0.15.

Caution *North Norfolk* Before starting on passage to the N Norfolk coast, consider that no hr there is accessible during fresh onshore winds (anything appreciably N of E or W) and some become dangerous before this. Under bad conditions the outer entrances are a mass of broken water, and marks and buoys become very difficult to see. Grounding can easily result in the loss of the vessel. Conditions in entrances are rapidly worsened when the ebb begins or if there is any swell running from a past or coming onshore blow. Under these conditions entrances may be unsafe even in a light breeze. The most dangerous conditions are when there is a lot of water running out, i.e. at spring and surge tides. The nearest alternative safe hrs are 50M or more away and call for accurate navigation among the sands to reach them. Passage should not be started, even in fine weather, without preparing for this possibility.

It is difficult to assess conditions in the entrances from outside. Blakeney, Wells and Overy are all very exposed to onshore winds and conditions in the entrances deteriorate quickly. Brancaster is more sheltered and usually has appreciably less sea while its long chan is well sheltered once past the entrance.

In poor conditions avoid Blakeney and Overy. The choice is between Wells or Brancaster, or staying outside. Wells is lit far enough in to reach a safe anch if the bar can be crossed and its marks are fairly easy to see, but the sea builds up in the entrance much quicker than at Brancaster. At Brancaster the greater shelter is largely offset by the difficulty of sighting the small buoys, and entry after dark is not possible. If in doubt it is wiser to attempt neither.

In safe conditions, boatmen will pilot vessels in by prior arrangement. Telephone description of vessel, or, better, advise CG of intended passage so that pilot can check passage past Cromer for ETA.

BLAKENEY   Chart BA 108

HW (bar) −4.50; (town) −4.30.   Bar MHWS 5.7; MHWN 4.5.
DS: NW and W −1.00; E and SE +6.00.
14M W of Cromer, 5M E of Wells. Very exposed to onshore winds and conditions in the entrance deteriorate quickly. A poor hr for cruising yachts: most of it dries and any craft drawing more than 1.5m must expect to take the bottom at LW. Without local knowledge this hr should only be approached under ideal and settled conditions.

Approach   Conspic marks are Blakeney ch with large and small trs, Langham ch tr, turret and FS above trees on skyline 3¾M inland. A G con buoy lies close to the edge of the sand ½ ca NE of a wk.

From the E the shore may be kept close to until abeam of the CG lookout, whence hold a course 295°, keeping the whole length of beach along N side of Blakeney Pt well open until the G con buoy is sighted.

From the W give the Binks, the low sandy pt with clump of fir trees ½M E of Wells LB Ho, a berth of 1M and make G con buoy.

Entrance   Unmarked, shallow, frequently varies in position and depth. Impassable in fresh onshore winds and in lighter ones during the ebb or if a swell is running. In these conditions stranding will probably lead to the loss of the vessel. Should not be attempted by strangers without a pilot except under ideal conditions in a shallow-draft vessel, within 1h before HW at the entrance, in calm weather with good visibility, and with full understanding of the risk of stranding in an exposed position. If notified in advance Maj Andrew, Chairman Blakeney Boatmens' Association (tel Cley (0263) 740306) or Mr Stratton-Long, CA Boatman (tel Cley 740362), will provide pilotage.

Without up-to-date reliable knowledge of its current position, the stranger's only guide to the entrance is the appearance of the sea. The bottom is steep-to, soundings reducing abruptly from more than 7m to nothing, so that the sounder is of little help. Locally used transits are not easily identified and vary. Beware tidal set across the entrance during the last quarter flood. Within the entrance the chan usually trends first towards the SSE then in a SW direction thence towards the S.

Orange floats laid by fisherman on the W side of the chan should be left close to stb. Shallow flats run off a long way NW and W of Blakeney Spit, which should be left to port. The chan is obstructed by mussel lays standing up to 0.8m above the sand and drying at half-tide. The lays are protected by several Fishing Orders and vessels must be certain of sufficient water to pass over without touching. Soundings and the perch to stb marking the entrance to Simpool are the best guides here. Hammond's wk, 1 ca N of Simpool, is $\frac{1}{2}$ ca up on the sand. Past Simpool the chan curves to the E to pass approx 1 ca S of Blakeney Spit, which continually alters in shape. The chan inside the hr is marked by bns.

Berthing   The CA Boatman may be able to provide a mooring in the Pit, SE of old LB Ho, in 1m, 2M to village. The flats inside the hr cover approx 1.5m to 1m at neaps. Shallow-draft craft able to sit upright can anch and dry out, but it is a long way from the village, and muddy. Avoid narrow and crowded gut at quay, land from dinghy at hard near quay or in Morston Creek at HW.

Water, stores, petrol, diesel, chandlery, gas at Blakeney; launching hard, hotel. Water, stores and pub at Morston.

WELLS-NEXT-THE-SEA   Chart BA 108
HW (Bar) −5.00.   MHWS 6.0; MHWN 4.8; MHWS (Town) 3.6; MHWN 2.3. DS Offing: E +4.10, W −2.00; at Fairway buoy: In +1.10, out −5.10.

Wells is 5M W of Blakeney and the only lit hr in N Norfolk. The hr dries but the quay is accessible to 3m draft at MHWS, 2m MLWS. As with all hrs on this coast, it should only be attempted by strangers in fine, settled weather.

Approach   From E, pass Blakeney and leave the Binks, a low sandy pt with a clump of fir trees on it, 1M to port; sounding to keep clear of the shallows which lie up to 2M from the low coastline, to the Wells Fairway buoy. From W, make Bridgirdle R can buoy from whence the Wells Fairway spher safe water buoy lies 166° 4$\frac{1}{4}$M, 1$\frac{1}{2}$M from the hr entrance, and from which Holkham Obelisk and ch tr are visible among the trees approx 3M SW.

Entrance   Drying sands varying in position and impassable to small craft in fresh onshore winds lie $\frac{1}{4}$M S of the Wells fairway buoy. It is dangerous to attempt crossing the sands in moderate onshore winds, or in lighter ones against the ebb, also if a swell is running. Strangers should not attempt to enter under these conditions without a pilot. For pilotage and mooring contact the CA Boatman Mr F. Taylor tel Fakenham (0328) 710291, or Capt C Smith (HM), tel Fakenham 710727.

Most of the chan across the sand dries out; the outer part is liable to shift. The time to cross is within 2h of HW, preferably on the flood and only under ideal conditions. A small B buoy sometimes lies on the E side of the entrance chan: these outer buoys are liable to shift.

The hr mouth has a conspic W LB Ho with a R roof on its W pt. Close W of this is a conspic CG lookout with an Or balcony. A long line of trees on sandhills with beach-huts below extends W of the CG lookout. The fir trees on the Binks lie 1$\frac{1}{2}$M E of the LB Ho.

From the Wells fairway buoy lying in line 169° with the ldg lts (rear Y diamond topmark, Oc 4s, obscured by trees, off near line; front on foreshore, iron tripod, Or triangle topmark, QR) showing over the entrance to the chan but not through it, stand away from the W Sands high to the W and SW of the chan and leave the outer bn (tripod, small W diamond topmark Fl 10s) 1 ca to stb. If early on the tide with light surf on the ldg line, there may be a smooth further to the W with the inner bn (tripod, small W diamond topmark Fl 5s) between the CG lookout and the rear ldg lt. Crossing on this line make good a course of 128° and proceed as previously.

The chan thence is marked by G con buoys (one Fl, unreliable) which should be left fairly close to stb. The inner bn should be left ½–1 ca to stb. The front ldg lt is far out of the chan to stb. A R spher buoy, staff, Fl (unreliable), lying NNW of CG may be passed close on either hand. A R can buoy lying E of LB Ho should be left close to port. A G con buoy SSE of the LB Ho marks a spit round which the chan bends to stb and should be left to stb; the chan here is narrow. The steep-to mud on the outside of this bend has six R bns with triangle topmarks to be left to port. Do not borrow on the line of six W bns with W diamond topmarks on the W side of the straight chan leading to the town, the E side of which has gently shelving sand backed by steep-to saltings.

Berthing Alongside quay (car park) or take up mooring as directed, and take the ground. All facilities except repairs.

BURNHAM, OVERY STAITHE   Chart BA 108
HW −4.20.   MHWS 3.7; MHWN 2.8.   DS: E +4.10; W −2.00.
A small unlit drying hr 4½M E of Brancaster, 2½M of W of Wells. Not to be attempted without local knowledge except in fine, settled weather in shoal-draft craft with the tides making up towards springs.

Approach Conspic marks are Scolt Hd, high sandhills to the W, and Gun Hill, a high, steep-sided, flat-topped sandhill close to the E. The highest part of the rising ground inland lies to the W of the hr.

The entrance lies about 255° 2½M from the Wells buoy and 149° 3M from the Bridgirdle buoy. This latter course passes close E of the shallow part of Bridgirdle shoal and E of the shallow patch which extends ¾M offshore N and NW of Gun Hill. The inner part of Bridgirdle Shoal may also be crossed in suitable conditions in about 2m by following the shoreline of Scolt Hd Is at 4 ca off, but then stand off to ¾M round the shallows before approaching entrance.

Entrance Banks, chan and buoyage are so variable that no entry directions can be recommended as safe. Pilotage and mooring can be arranged by the CA Boatman.

Berthing Craft to be left unattended or in care of boatman should moor as directed off the staithe, accessible to 2m draft at MHWS, 1m MHWN, dries with a hard bottom. All facilities except repairs.

BRANCASTER STAITHE   Chart BA 108
HW (Bar) −4.25.   MHWS 5.9; MHWN 4.6.   DS: W +1.15; E −6.00.
An unlit hr 10M E of Hunstanton, 12M W of Wells. Not to be attempted by

strangers except in fine, settled weather, even then preferably with local assistance.

Approach Conspic marks are Scolt Hd, high sandhills, to E; golf clubhouse close to foreshore near entrance. The wk shown on the plan is in three parts, not usually visible at HW; it is marked to the N by a R buoy which dries. The highest part of the rising ground inland lies to the S of the hr.

From seaward make Bridgirdle R can buoy whence the entrance lies about 236° 4½M. In poor visibility, shallowing after passing deeper in Brancaster Road warns that the coast is near. From E, either make Bridgirdle buoy or, in suitable conditions, after passing the entrance to Overy Hr close the coastline of Scolt Hd Is to 4 ca and follow it at this distance to pass over the inner part of the shoal in about 2m, continuing on this course until the clubhouse bears 187°.

Entrance Banks, chan and buoyage are so variable that no entry directions can be recommended as safe. Pilotage essential. Pilotage and moorings can be arranged by CA Boatman.

Berthing A visitors' mooring may be available: anchored vessels must be prepared to take the ground. Small boatyard, all facilities.

PASSAGE NOTES: CROMER TO THE RIVER HUMBER

Charts BA 107, 108

DS Inshore along Lincolnshire coast: S and SW +2.00; NE and N −5.00.
   Inner Dowsing LV: W turning S +3.00; E turning N −3.00.
From the Blakeney Overfalls buoy pass between the Docking and Race buoys, leaving the Inner Dowsing LV approx 1M to port. From a position with the Protector Overfalls buoy 1M to port, the Rosse Spit buoy marking the approach to the R Humber will be sighted.

YORKSHIRE COAST   Charts BA 121, 129, 134
DS Spurn Pt to Bridlington: S +1.15; N −4.45.
   Flamborough Hd: S +0.10; N −6.00.
Flamborough Hd to Tees, streams are weak. As the streams turn offshore first 1½ to ½h may be gained by carefully watching the time of change and closing or standing offshore. The ebb sets N and the flood S. In poor visibility sound continuously, as an indraft into all the small bays is likely to set vessels into Bridlington and Filey Bays.

Bound N from Spurn, one may coast as far as Flamborough Hd at a safe offshore distance of ½M, and may anch anywhere between Spurn and Flamborough Hd in offshore winds. With onshore wind do not attempt to anch except in Bridlington Bay, as a sea is quickly raised.

Anchorages (1) *Bridlington Bay.* With the wind from NNW to SSW anch approx ¼M off the pier end, from NNW round to NE bring up under Danes' Dyke or near the S landing. (2) *Filey Bay.* Proceeding round Flamborough Hd keep the Lt Ho lantern open above the cliff tops and stand off Filey Brig marked by Filey Brig E Card buoy. The bottom is clay covered with sand, with foul ground beginning with Scarborough Rk appearing outside Car Naze. Do not remain in the bay with the wind E of NNE. In winds from W of S, anch 4M S of Filey under Speeton Cliffs. From Filey Brig buoy stand 1M offshore to avoid numerous wks. (3) *Scarborough Bay,* smooth bottom sand over blue clay with good holding ground. Open to winds from NNE to SSE. Anch with the Castle bearing 332° and Spa House from 260° to 290° in 5 to 7m. (4) Leaving Scarborough proceeding N, anch in *Whitby Bay*, or in *Sandsend Bay*. Beware of Up Gang Rks lying ¾M offshore midway between Whitby and Sandsend with 1.5m over them and 11m close by. (5) *Runswick Bay*. When entering to anch give Kettleness a wide berth.

THE WASH Charts BA 109, 1157, 1177 (Plan p138)

The spring tides range about 7m and neaps 2.7m, so that it is safe to expect to find 2m more than charted at MLWN.

DS in main chans: in +1.35; out −4.45. Sp rate 2kn.

Approach From the E: (1) Docking Chan, the ship route and well buoyed, but a long way round. (2) To the Woolpack R can buoy N of the Middle Bank, thence to the Lynn Well Lt Ho buoy (Fl 10s, horn (2)). This passage is narrow and seas break on both sides in NE winds. (3) Through the Bays, between Middle Bank and Sunk Sand. There is approx 5m at LW between the banks but less than 2m in the approach from the E. The chan is not buoyed and is difficult to follow. (4) Inside the Sunk Sand. At MLWS approx 1.5m of water can be found, more than shown on chart. At LW keep 2–3 ca off W sands and follow the coast round Gore Pt. Approx 1M N of Hunstanton Pier there is a mussel bank which runs out from the land and stands out black when uncovered. Sound outside to the W of this tongue. As the pier is approached keep close to the land and pass approx 1 ca from the end. Get the water tr on with the junction of the middle and outer third of the pier, make good 240° with these marks in line astern until Lynn No. 1 N Card bell buoy (VQ) bear 277°. Then steer for this buoy if bound for Boston or Sutton Bridge, and thence on 190° down the Daseleys Sled buoyed chan if bound for Lynn.

From the N, Lynn Well is the best approach.

In general the Wash is not easy once out of the main chans. It is best to wait until half flood before entering any of the rivers, unless a smack is followed. (Boston smacks draw approx 2m.)

KING'S LYNN Chart BA 1177 (Plan p139)

HW −4.45. MHWS 6.9; MLWS 1.0; MTL 3.7; MHWN 5.1; MLWN 1.8.

The chan is constantly changing, but it is well buoyed. 1.5m draft can get up about 2h after LW. In Lynn Cut and the river 9–10h ebb and 2–3h flood is usual; ebb in river can run up to 5kn. The hr is open at all times subject to draft. The dock is normally open about 1½h before HW and closes about HW and this is the best place to stay (accommodation limited, substantial entry charges). Yachts

THE WASH

Depths in Metres

Boston

RIVER WITHAM

Approaches to BOSTON

Based on British Admiralty Charts (nos. in text) with the permission of the Controller of H.M. Stationery Office and the Hydrographer of the Navy, and on other sources.

Left panel:

20′ 21′ 0° 22′ E 24′
52′ 52′

No7
FI G5s

DASELEYS SAND

PANDORA SAND

PB PETER BLACK SAND
R

IQ R10s
R

51′ 51′

3

8
0·8

4 5

Channel marked by
Lightbuoys & buoys
Subject to constant change

52° 50′

FI Y4s
Y
WEST DUMP

FI(3)G10s West Stones Bn

Barrier Wall

BULL DOG SAND

BnA

Training Wall
(dries 3·2m)

FI Y2s
Bn B

5 9

52° 49′ 49′

Bn C

VINEGAR MIDDLE

Bn D

Target

Bn E
FI Y6s

Water Tr

48′ 48′

N

Tr

FI Y2s
West Bank

CUT

47′ 47′

FI 1m 4M

F 16m 4M

Pylon (conspic)   Pylon (conspic)

46′ 46′

FI G3s

APPROACHES
to
KINGS LYNN
Depths in Metres

Kings Lynn

45′

Gt Ouse

20′ 0° 21′ E 22′ 23′ 24′

Right panel:

20′ 21′ 0° 22′ E 23′ 24′

59′ 59′

N

52° 58′

Q. Bell
Roaring Middle
BY

FI(2)R10s
Sunk
R

52° 57′

VQ. Bell
No1
BY

56′ 56′

27

3 6

4 5

5

Q(3)10s
No3
BYB

55′ 55′

3 3

7 7

DASELEYS SLED

OLD BELL MIDDLE

0·9

0·1

23

54′

6

Blackguard Sand

BULLDOG CHANNEL

FI G5s
No3A
G
CORK HOLE

SEAL SAND

STYLEMANS MIDDLE

No2
IQ R10s
R

53′ PA Bn

3 2

6 4

Q(3)10s
No5
BYB

FERRIER SAND

3 5

3 5

52′

No7
FI G5s
G

DASELEYS SAND

PANDORA SAND

0·1

PB SAND
PETER BLACK
R

0·1

Bottom:

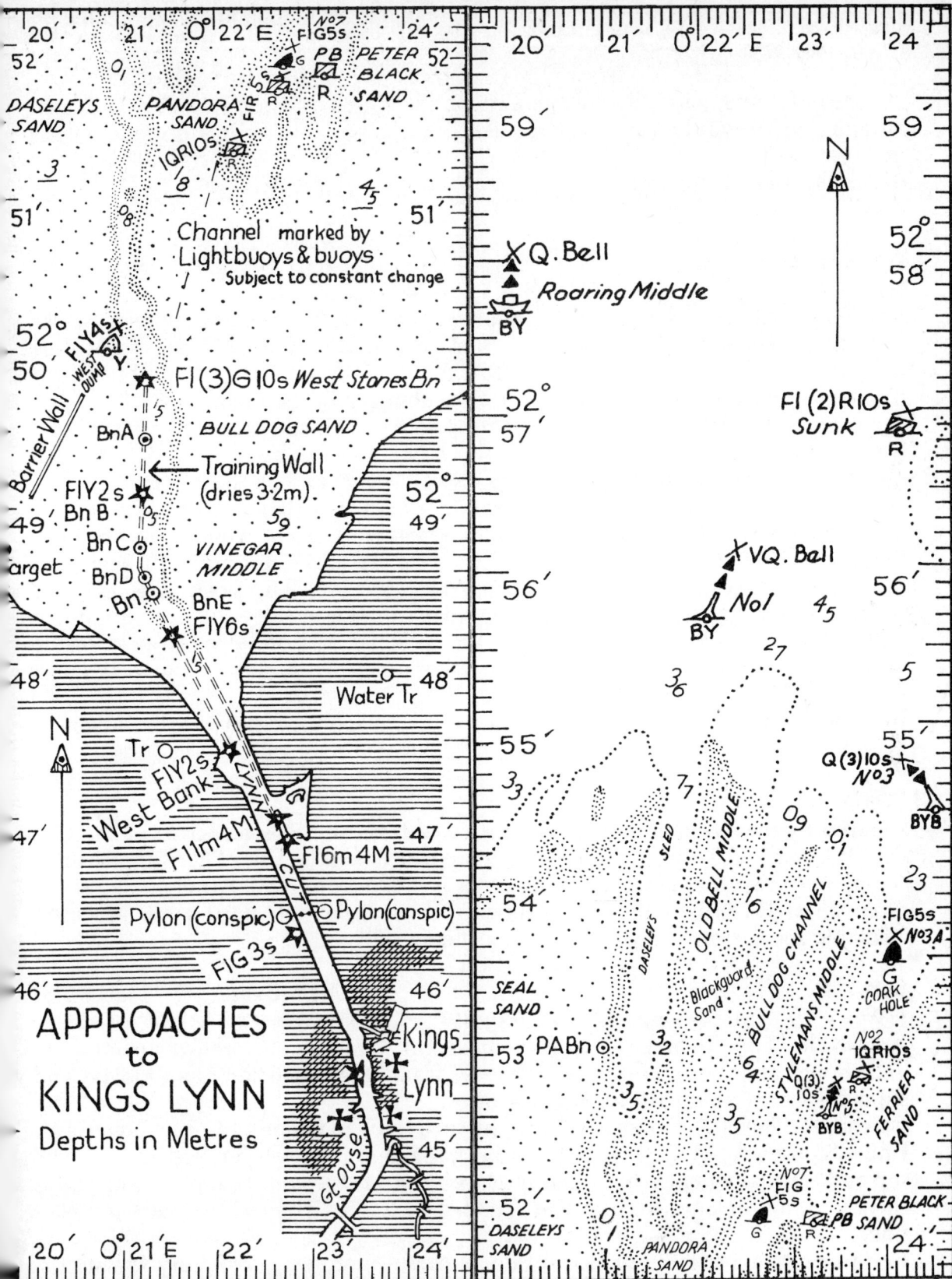

...d on British Admiralty Charts (nos. in text) with the permission of the Controller of H.M. Stationery Office and of
...Hydrographer of the Navy, and on other sources.

can be left here with the permission of the Dock Master (tel (0553) 2638). Bringing up in the river is not permitted but it is possible to lie alongside barges upstream at the sugarbeet factory or quays. Between the training walls and the docks the river is spanned by electric cables 47m above MHWS.

All facilities. EC Wed.

WISBECH

Chart BA 1177 (Plan p138)

HW −4.50.   MHWS 7.4; MHWN 5.5; MLWN 2.2.

Vessels of 4.8m draft springs and 3.4m neaps can reach Wisbech. The least water is 0.6m springs and 1.8m neaps, with 3.6m at half-tide. The entrance is not easy for a stranger. The Outer Gat tends to extend to the E. The bns and buoys are frequently moved without notice to follow changes in the chan.

Approach   The Wisbech chan leaves the Old Lynn chan S of the Bar Flat G con buoy; from there it is 225° 2.6M to Wisbech No. 1 G con buoy (Fl G 5s). Thence inwards West Mark Knock R can (Fl (2) R 6s) to port and on the stb hand E Card buoy (VQ), 178° leads to Fenland G con buoy (Fl (3) G 10s). Leave this 2–3 ca to stb and the perches after it a good ca to stb since they are well up on the mud.

Entrance   The chan passes between two 19m trs and enters the Wisbech cut, whence it is 3½M to Sutton Br, 12M to Wisbech. Fl lts R to port, W to stb, are shown from posts along the cut. Spring tides run 4kn in the R; neaps very much less. There is a swing br at Sutton Br, letter 'B' (− · · ·) on horn to open. Radio watch from −3.00 to HW Sutton Br: Chan 16, 9, 6, 8, 12, 14 on VHF, also 2182/2246kHz.

Berthing   Sutton Bridge: if intending to use the port contact HM in advance. Wisbech: moor at quay on port hand opposite grain elevator and contact HM.

FOSDYKE

Entered by the Welland Cut which runs SW from the Boston River at the Cut end. It is marked by bns on both sides at approx 64m intervals. There are no lts in summer. Access for vessels drawing up to 1.3m 2h from HW. Bring up at a small quay about ½M NE of the br on the stb hand, dries out, hard sand. Mooring available for vessels drawing 1.2m, short stay only.

BOSTON

Chart BA 1157 (Plan p138)

HW −4.10.   MHWS 6.6; MLWS 0.0; MTL 3.3; MHWN 4.8; MLWN 1.8.

Approach   The Freeman Chan is the best app. Wainfleet Swatchway needs care and should only be attempted in clear weather. Parlour Chan is unbuoyed and should only be used with local knowledge.

Entrance   The chan leading from High Horn (No. 14 G con Fl G 3s) buoy to Cut End G con buoy, Fl G 3s, is constantly changing but is well buoyed and lit. The top end is shoaling each year, and in places almost dries out at LW. Half flood is the best time for entering the Cut. Anch 5 ca SW of High Horn buoy to await tide.

Berthing   Not available in Boston dock except in emergency. Very few moor-

RIVER HUMBER
Depths in Metres

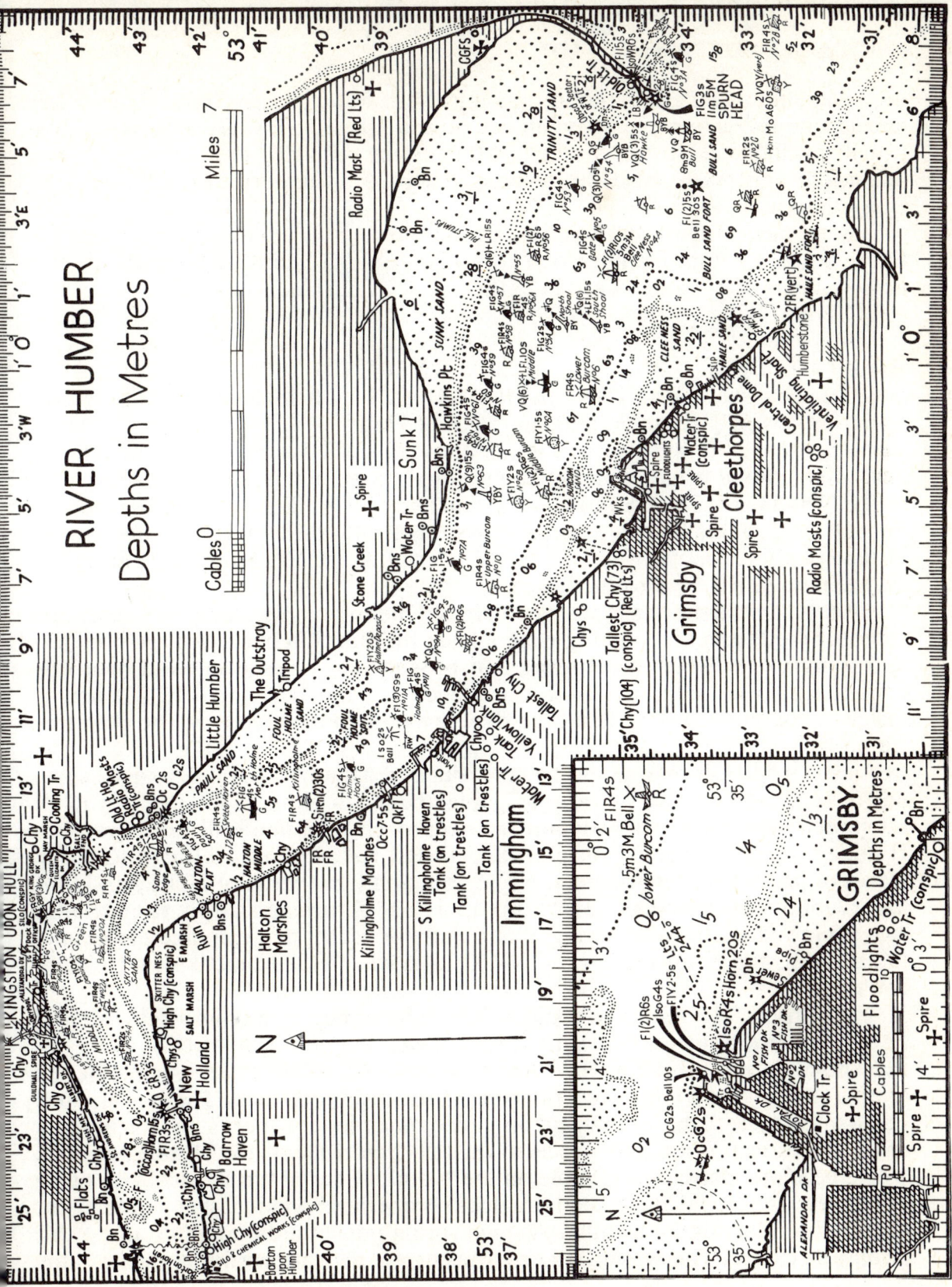

Miles 7

Cables 0

Radio Mast (Red Lts)

SPURN HEAD

TRINITY SAND

SUNK SAND

Hawkins Pt

BULL SAND FORT

Bull Sand

HAILE SAND

CLEE NESS

Central Dome

Cleethorpes

Grimsby

Radio Masts (conspic)

Tallest Chy (73) (conspic) (Red Lts)

Chys

Spire

Water Tr (conspic)

FLOODLIGHTS

Stone Creek

Spire

Sunk I

Water Tr

The Outstray

Tripod

Little Humber

PAULL SAND

FOUL HOLME SAND

FOUL HOLME SAND

Old Lt Ho Masts Radio Mast (conspic)

Cooling Tr

KINGSTON UPON HULL

Killingholme Marshes

S Killingholme Haven

Tank (on trestles)

Tank (on trestles)

Immingham

Water Tr

Yellow Tank

Tallest Chy

HALTON FLAT

HALTON MIDDLE

Halton Marshes

SKITTER SAND

SKITTER NESS

E MARSH

SALT MARSH

New Holland

Barrow Haven

High Chy (conspic)

Flats

High Chy (conspic)

Barton upon Humber

SILO & CHEMICAL WORKS (conspic)

N

GRIMSBY.
Depths in Metres.

N

Lower Burcom

FISH DK

ALEXANDRA DK

Water Tr (conspic)

Clock Tr

Spire

Cables

Floodlights

Spire

Spire

...ased on British Admiralty Charts (nos. in text) with the permission of the Controller of H.M. Stationery Office and of
...e Hydrographer of the Navy, and on other sources.

ings available in hr, advisable to pass into fresh water at the Grand Sluice, first and second levels being approx 2½h before and 2½h after HW Boston. A berth is usually available at Boston Marina. After passing the swing br there is restricted headroom and masts must be lowered. There is an underwater cable near St Botolph's ch.

Due to variability of levels in the Grand Sluice, it is advisable to contact the Sluice Keeper before planning a visit, tel Boston (0205) 5563. If in difficulty on arrival secure if possible near HM office at dock entrance and seek advice.

EC Thurs.

RIVER HUMBER Charts BA 107, 109, 1188, 3497 (Plan p141)
HW Grimsby −5.30. MHWS 7.0; MLWS 1.0; MTL 4.0; MHWN 5.5; MLWN 2.7;
Spring tides run 4½kn at Immingham, 5kn at Hull.
From S after sighting Rosse Spit R can buoy, Fl (2) R 5s, care should be taken if early on the flood to avoid being set into shoal water on the port hand. Keep well to the N and leave No. 2 Sand Haile R can buoy Fl(3) 10s, to port. The Chequer Shoal lt float should then be seen, and passed on either side. Entering the fairway of the Humber, pass between the Bull N Card lt float (VQ Horn (2)) and Spurn Pt, keeping fairly close to the latter.

From N, if at first hour of flood abeam of Dimlington high land or Kilnsea trs, steer for the Spurn LV keeping well outside the Binks, a bank of large boulders and shingle over which a confused and broken sea is raised in wind over tide conditions. Give outer Binks E Card buoy a good berth to stb. Thence to Grimsby, Immingham and Hull, the river is well lit and buoyed and the chan free from obstructions.

Berthing (1) Half-tide moorings of Humber Mouth YC on S bank. Chan narrow and steep-to hard sand, navigable about 2½h either side HW: not to be attempted until buoys can be identified. Approach W of line Bull Sand Fort with Humberston radio masts (conspic). Six stb RB barrel buoys (difficult to see in waves or against sun) mark chan, No. 2 about halfway between Haile Sand Fort and Cleethorpes Sewer bn; chan runs approx N–S turning sharply to port after No. 6 buoy when line of moorings clear. Safe for yachts that can take the ground (hard sand), can be uncomfortable in NE gales when Haile Sand covers 1h about HW.

(2) Grimsby. The entrance is marked by a hydraulic tr, ht 94m. Vessels enter hr by lock on stb side of hydraulic tr (available 2½h either side of HW, but gates may not be opened after HW for a yacht). At other times yachts tie up temporarily in or on left of the entrance to the disused E lock. The Royal Dock Basin may be used, but is tidal and only recommended for short stay. Yachts may enter the Royal Dock and proceed via the Union Dock to Alexandra Dock where accommodation is available on the N and S sides of the W arm. The swing br between the Royal and Alexandra docks is operated nominally on request, but opening is in fact unpredictable. At high spring tides, the flood-gates above this br may be closed. The Assistant Dock Master will allocate berths to yachts in the

basin or dock. Up river from Hull above Read's Is visitors should obtain a copy of chart 'Barton Haven to Burton Stather' published by the British Transport Docks Board at Kingston House Tower, PO Box 1, Bond St, Hull, updated or reissued at least monthly.

(3) At South Ferriby: apply to lock keeper for berth. (4) Visitors are welcome at Humber Yawl Club moorings in Brough Haven. (5) The HYC are developing a basin at Winteringham Haven on the S bank. Buoyed entrance availabe for 1.5m draft 1½h either side of HW neaps to 2½h either side of MHWS. Beware of submerged saltings downstream of entrance at high springs.

Anchorages   At the entrance to the river in the N chan, a good anch situated inside Spurn Pt; completely sheltered in N and E winds, secure in other winds if well inside. Bring up in 2 to 3½m opposite the Lt Ho.

Off Cleethorpes about 1M offshore in fine weather; untenable in strong winds.

RIVER TRENT   Chart BA 109
British Transport Docks Board Chart 'Barton Haven to Burton Stather'. R Trent (tidal) chart available from V. Sissons Esq. Guardian Offices, Worksop, Notts.
Navigable to Keadby Br. Lock on the W Bank below br gives access to canal. Crane available; with mast unstepped navigable to Nottingham. Depth at MLWN 1.6m, air draft at MHWS 4.2m.

HULL   Chart BA 3497
HW −5.00.   MHWS 7.3; MLWS 0.8; MTL 4.1; MHWN 5.8; MLWN 2.4.
Hull is a commercial port. Berths are strictly limited, there are no moorings and it is now virtually closed to yachts. Old Hr: yachtsmen are advised not to enter without special reason and local knowledge.

Anchorages   To the E of the mouth of the R Hull, above the entrance to Victoria Dock basin. At Paull, 130m off the end of the wooden jetty. Landing at the Corporation Pier.

PASSAGE NOTES: HUMBER TO BERWICK

For most of its length this passage offers no navigational difficulties, with no offshore hazards to affect a yacht. The poor supply of harbours available in strong onshore winds must always be borne in mind. In bad weather no attempt should be made to take the passage inside the Farne Is, where tides are strong and sea conditions can be very difficult. In such circumstances keep at least one mile E of the Longstone Lt Ho.

BRIDLINGTON   Chart BA 1882   (Plan p144)
HW +5.55.   MHWS 6.1; MLWS 1.1; MTL 3.6; MHWN 4.7; MLWN 2.3.
DS in offing: SE +2.00.
Bar   Sand bar across hr entrance: approx 0.6m at LAT. Hr dries.

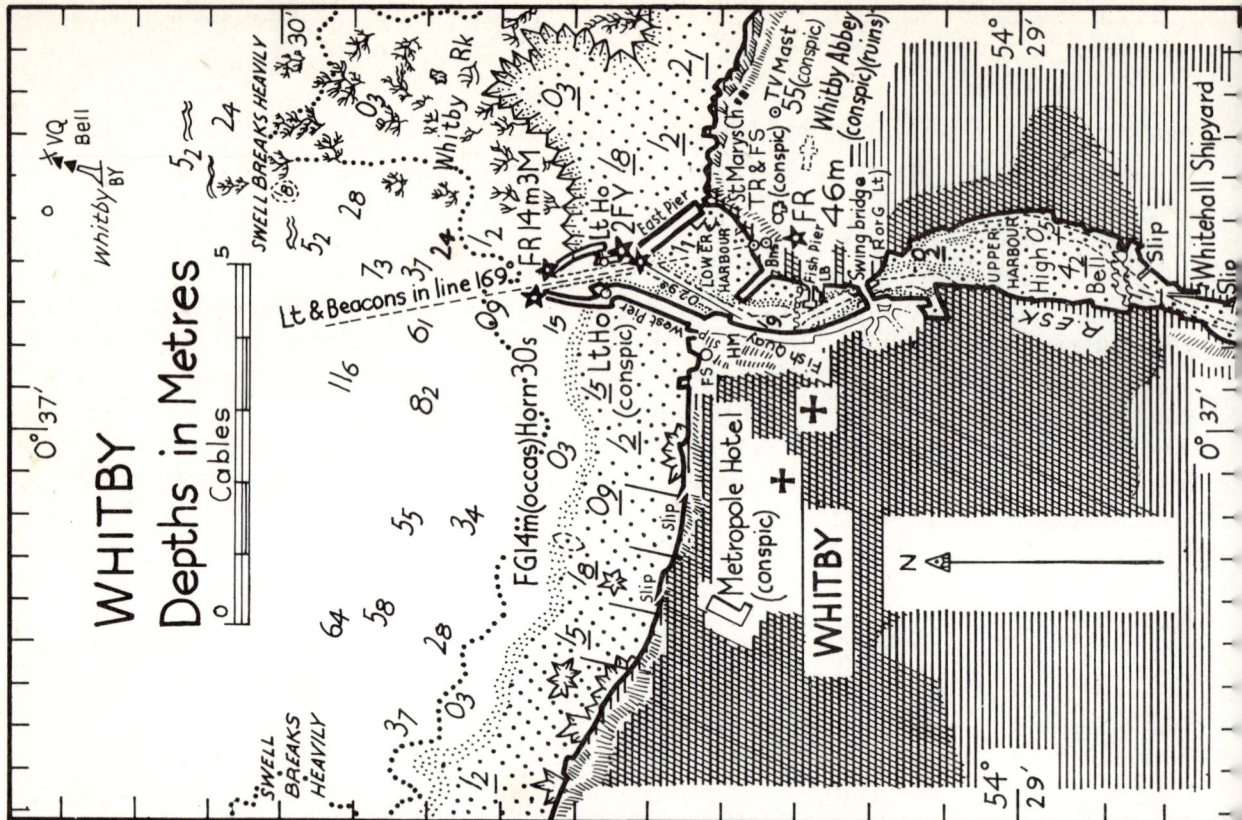

WHITBY
Depths in Metres

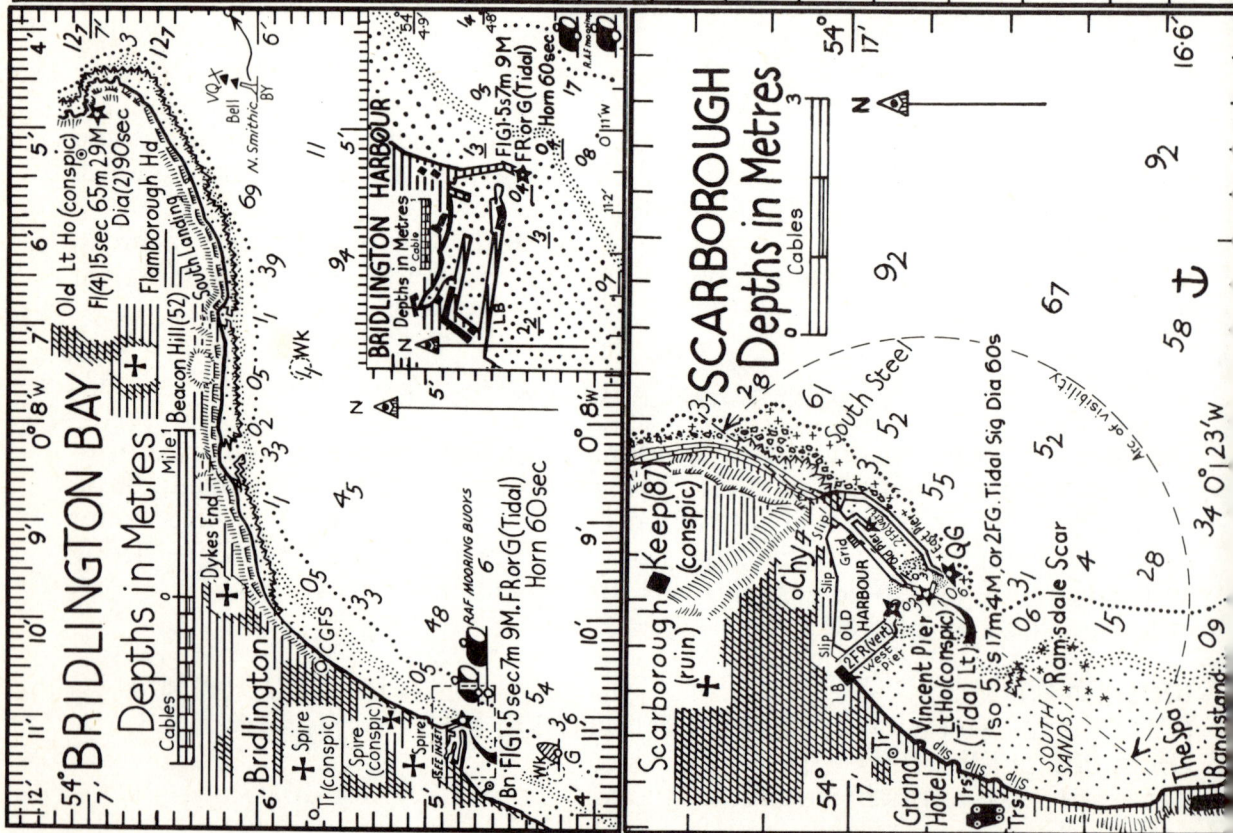

BRIDLINGTON BAY
Depths in Metres

BRIDLINGTON HARBOUR
Depths in Metres

SCARBOROUGH
Depths in Metres

Approach   App from the S so that hr entrance is open. N pier-head Fl G 1.5s, horn 60s. East end of fish quay S pier shows FR at night when depth available is 2.7m or over, when less water FG. A W flag with a B ball indicates entrance not clear.

Anchorage   Anch in Bridlington Bay approx ½M SE from piers.

Berthing   Against quays or on mud: anchor outside and enquire for berth. Fresh water can be obtained from points along S pier on request to the watchkeeper at the fish quay. Fuel is delivered by road tanker from a local garage.

The Royal Yorkshire YC is situated at the approach to the S pier.

SCARBOROUGH   Chart BA 1612   (Plan p144)
HW +5.40.   MHWS 5.7; MLWS 0.9; MTL 3.4; MHWN 4.6; MLWN 2.3.
DS in offing: SE +2.00

The Old Hr is reserved for the fishing fleet. The E Hr, available from half flood to half ebb, dries out completely at MLWS. No vessel should attempt to enter in onshore gales (NE through E to SSE).

Approach   When a B ball is hoisted at the Lt Ho FS or by night W Oc 5s is shown, there is more than 3.6m depth available in the Old Hr. The E Hr entrance has a concrete sill liable to silting and carrying approx 1.5m less water over it.

From the S give the shore a berth of somewhat less than ½M, closing in fine weather to 45m as the pier wall comes abeam. An eddy from the S bay sets round the pier-head and along the outer wall of the hr from quarter flood to HW. It runs NE at 1½ to 2kn (sp), increased by E and SE winds. Make allowance, especially coming from S. Beware isolated rocks drying 0.6m, in an area SSW of E pier-head up to a distance of 23m.

Entrance   Small craft run a great risk taking the entrance from the E and NE in bad weather, as the sea breaks for some distance outside piers.

Berthing   Yachts take up a quay berth if one is vacant or as directed in E Hr. The E Hr is entered between E pier and Vincent Pier (very narrow). Yachts are only allowed in the Old Hr in an emergency: anch off and go ashore for instructions. A fender plank is necessary when lying alongside: vessels should not be left unattended. The hr is safe but there is a good deal of swell in strong NE and E winds. There are three visitors' berths at Vincent Pier and Old Pier close to Lt Ho, secure and seek instructions from Lt Ho keeper. Spars available on loan.

Anchorage   Anch 1 to 3 ca from outer pier E of a line Scarborough Castle–Vincent Pier Lt Ho.

All facilities. Water at Lt Ho. EC Wed.

WHITBY   Chart BA 1612   (Plan p144)
HW +5.15.   MHWS 5.4; MLWS 0.8; MTL 3.1; MHWN 4.3; MLWN 2.0.
DS in offing: SE +2.00; NW −4.00.

Harbour available from 3h flood to 3h ebb for 2m draft. When the concrete ledge round foot of pier-heads is awash there is 2.4m on bar, 2m between the pier-heads, 1m within the inner pier and 2m at quay side on W side of hr.

Approach   Leave the Whitby N Card bell buoy (VQ) to the E and bring the first pair of ldg marks shown from buildings NNW of St Mary's ch on E side of hr in line 169°, front W triangle, rear W circle with B vert line. This line leads between the piers. Alternative ldg marks lt on E pier-head on with the square tr of the ch on the headland next to Abbey ruins. Vessels app from Scarborough should not make for the hr entrance after passing Whitby high lt but should first pass N of Whitby buoy.

Entrance   Near the piers a strong E set is encountered on the flood; the ebb runs in a N direction. The hr cannot be entered or left in a heavy swell from the N to the E. If conditions are marginal entry can be made during the flood, but ebb produces dangerous wind over tide conditions.

A ball is shown on W pier Lt Ho or FG by night, when vessels are expected and there is not less than 3m on the bar.

Berthing   In lower hr on W side on the quay between bridge and Marine Hotel, dries, mud. For a short stay, on the fish quay S of HM's office, busy with fishing boats. Advice from HM. Pass through the br (to open sound three blasts or contact bridge keeper on VHF Ch 16), and berth at pontoon on stb side with approx 1.5m at N end to 0.7 at S end, less on inshore side of pontoon; or secure to piles on port hand. Beware of stone causeway approx 20m upstream of S end of pontoon extending across the R and drying at LW.

Anchorage   Outside ¼–½M NNW of W pier opposite spa buildings in 5m, sand. All facilities. EC Wed.

RIVER TEES   Chart BA 2566   (Plan p147)
HW (entrance) +5.00.
MHWS 5.5; MLWS 0.4; MTL 3.2; MHWN 4.3; MLWN 2.0.
DS in offing: NW −4.30; SE +1.30.

Approach   In heavy weather, Hartlepool with more sea room is preferable to the Tees. Tees Fairway safe water pillar buoy, Iso 4s whis, marks the approach to the main chan dredged to 15.4m, marked by port and stb lt buoys.

Entrance   210° leads up fairway, to abeam of Seaton chan turning. Chan buoyed and lit to beyond Middlesbrough. Advice obtainable from Hartlepool Radio: VHF Chan 16, 12, 11, 8.

Berthing   In unsettled weather proceed to HM office at Tees Dock, 1½M after passing front ldg lt, for instructions. In fine settled weather small craft may berth in Seaton Snook or Greatham Creek and take ground. The bottom should be examined for slag. Seaton Snook is dangerous in W gales.

Buses to Middlesbrough, 2M walk to Seaton Carew; hotel, shops.

Anchorages   (1) Paddy's Hole, 202° 6 ca from S Gare Breakwater N end, on E side of entrance, up to 1.2m draft. The approach is buoyed: a mooring may be obtained from Dorman Long Marine Club. (2) Near Pilot jetty on either side of

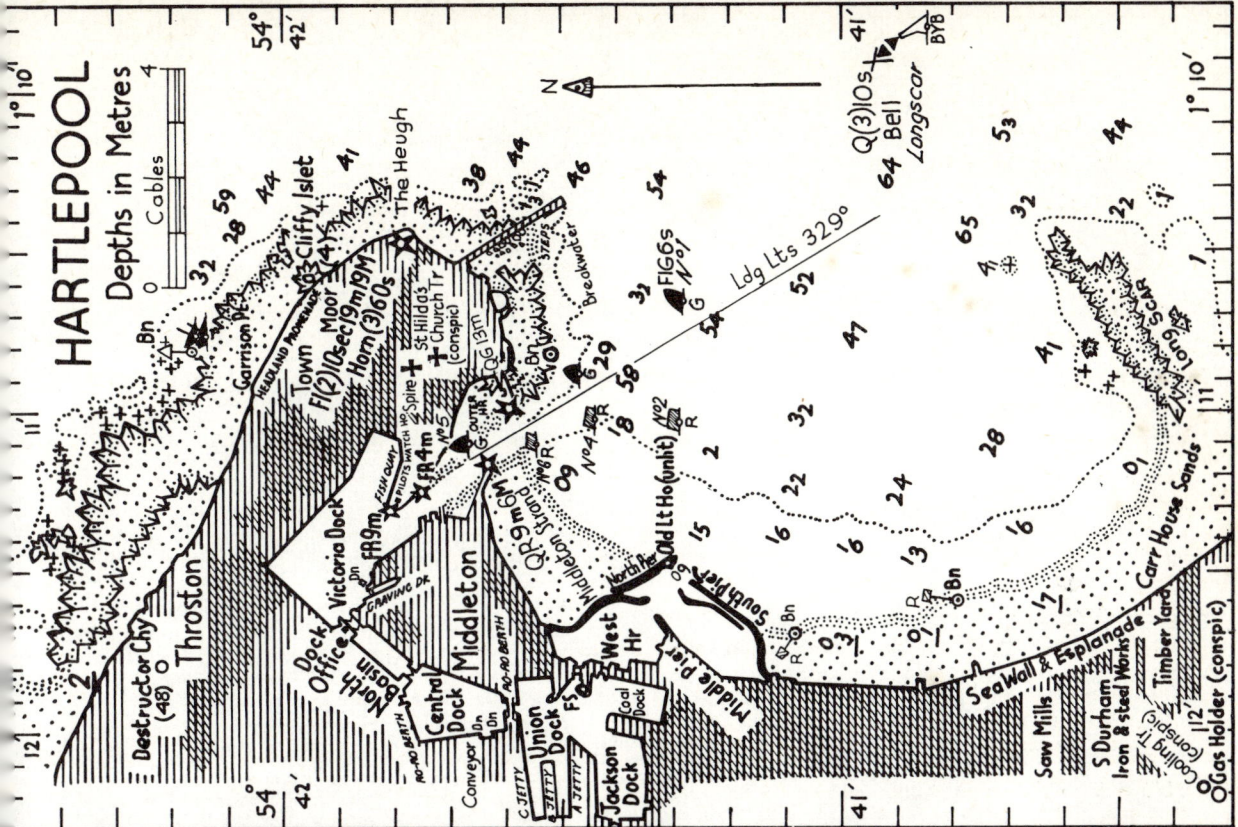

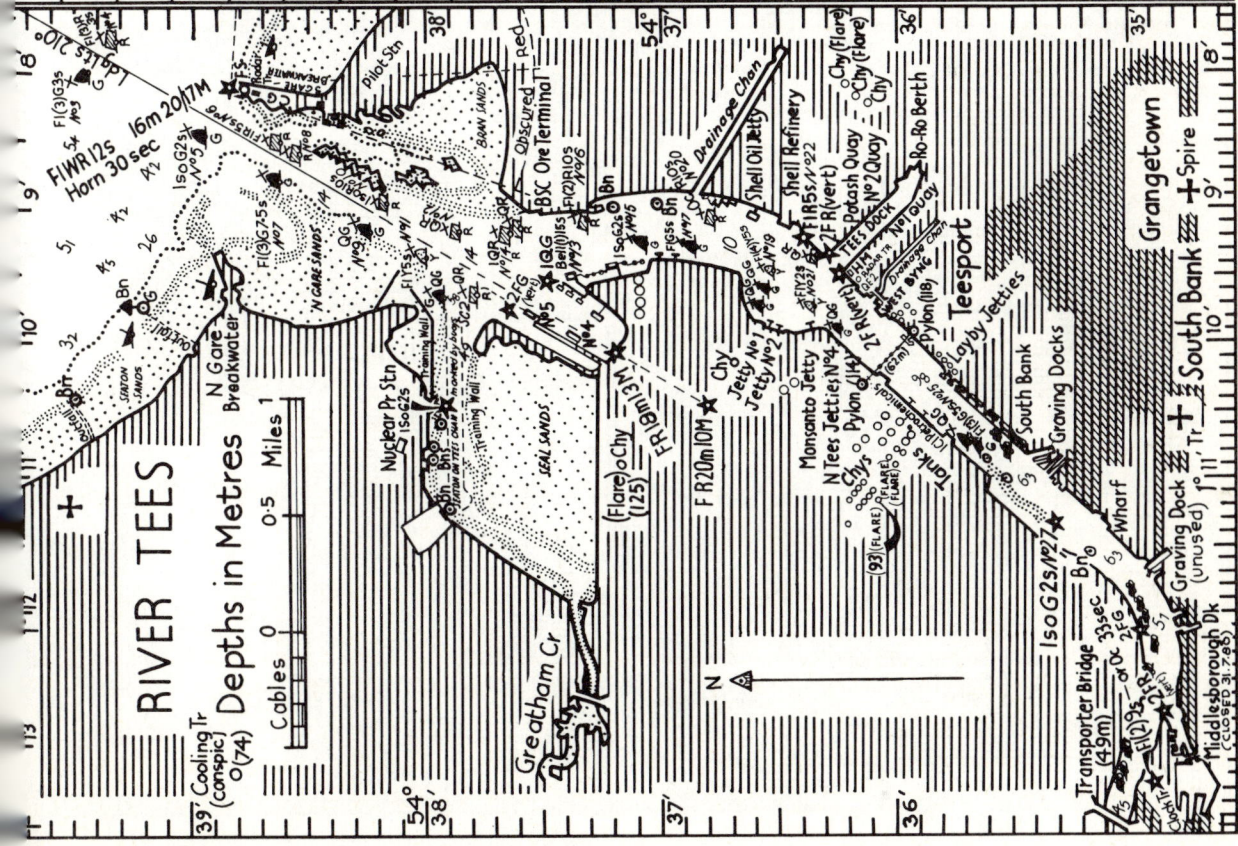

HARTLEPOOL
Depths in Metres

Throston
Destructor Chy (48)
Bn
Garrison Pt
Cliffy Islet
Headland Promenade
Town Moor Fl(2)10sec19m9M
The Heugh Horn(3)60s
St Hilda's Church Tr (conspic)
Spire
PILOT'S WATCH HO
FR4m FISH QUAY
FR9m
Graving Dk
Victoria Dock
Dock Office
North Basin
Central Dock
Conveyor
Union Dock
Jackson Dock
Coal Dock
West Hr
Middleton
Middleton Strond
QR9m6M
North Pier
South Pier
Middle Pier
Old Lt Ho(unlit)
Ldg Lts 329°
Longscar Q(3)10s Bell BYB
64 Bell
Fl G6s No1
SCAR No1
Carr House Sands
Sea Wall & Esplanade
Saw Mills
S Durham Iron & steel Works
Cooling(conspic)
Timber Yard
Gas Holder (conspic)

RIVER TEES
Depths in Metres

Ldg Lts 210°
Cooling Tr (conspic) (74)
Fl WR12s 16m 20/17M Horn 30 sec
N Gare Breakwater
N Gare Sands
Radar
S. Gare
Pilot Stn
BRAN SANDS
Obscured
BSC Ore Terminal
Nuclear Pr Stn
Training Wall
SEAL SANDS
Greatham Cr
Transporter Bridge (49m)
Middlesborough Dk (CLOSED 31.7.85)
Shell Oil Jetty
Shell Refinery
Brainope Chan
Chy (Flare)
Chy
Potash Quay
No2 Quay
Ro-Ro Berth
TEES DOCK
Pylon(118)
Grangetown
Spire
South Bank
Lay by Jetties
South Bank
Graving Docks
Monsanto Jetty
N Tees Jetties No4
Teesport
Graving Dock (unused)
Wharf
Tonks
(Flare) Chy (125)
FR20m10M
FR18m13M

SEAHAM

Depths in Metres

0 Cables 2

3.5

3.2

Feather.bed Rocks

2.9 5.9

0.4

0.1

1 3.2 4

N Breakwater

Fl G 10s.Dia 30s(occas)

FSO

FSO

North Dock

Outer Harbour

3.8 3.2

HM Traffic sigs

FS

1.5 2FR(vert) 2FR(vert)

1.4 2.1

S Breakwater 2FR(vert)

South Dock

LB

2M 4M

0.9 2.2

1 1 3.5

LIDDLE

0.1

0.2 0.4

SCARS

0.4 1.6 2.2

54° 50'

Well Rocks

1

1.6 2.7

Liddle Stack 1.3

(9)

N

1.6 2.9

1.5

Trs (conspic) 87 Nose Pt

0.3

1°19'

1°22' 21' 6.9

Tr & FS

CG

Roker

North Rocks

4.4 1.8

3.8 5.6 7

0.6 4.6 6

2.6 5.8

7

Monkwearmouth

Roker 1.2 Pier

Lt Ho (conspic) Fl 5s 25m 23M Siren 20s

3.7 4.6 6.5 8

0.8 0.6 1.9

North Dock

2FG(vert)

FS

Old North Pier QG 12m 8M Horn 10sec

WORKS IN PROGR

4.3 Fl 10s 14m 10M

DREDGED TO 5.0m

Arc of vis

55'

Fl 5s 3 2.2 1.7

Old South Pier

Old Lt Ho (18) New South Pier 0.7

2FR(vert) 2 Fl R 5s 2M LB

5.7m No 2 Dry Dk

Slip No 1 Gate No 1 Dry Dk

Slips Half tide Basin

Quay River Wear

Customs No 3 Gate

Port of Sunderland Authority

Swing Br

Coal Stns

Hudson Dock

Ship Bldg Yard

Slips

Flats (conspic) (61)

Flats (conspic) (53)

22 Staith Swing Bridge Old Lt Ho

23 Staith

S Outlet (closed)

Lift Br

Sunderland

Hendon Dock

SW Breakwater

54° 54'

N

Hendon Banks Barrier

SUNDERLAND

Depths in Metres

0 Cables 3

Breakwater

Groyne

Chy

1°22'

21'

148

Based on British Admiralty Charts (nos. in text) with the permission of the Controller of H.M. Stationery Office and the Hydrographer of the Navy, and on other sources.

piles. Water from Pilot Station or CG cottages. In emergency contact HM Tees Dock.

Navigation up River   ½M above Middlesbrough Dock (closed) is a Transporter br, 49m at MHWS. 2M further is Newport Br, 36m with span raised (6.4m closed: 24h notice to open), closely followed by the A19 road br (18m). 2M beyond this are the Stockton-Victoria Br (5.5m) and Rly Br (6.3m). Between Stockton and Yarm there is a pipe br and a HT electric cable; lowest has 7m at MHWS.

Proceed up Yarm R at half flood and descend early on the ebb. EC Wed.

HARTLEPOOL   Chart BA 2566   (Plan p147)
HW +4.50.   DS in offing: N −4.42; S +1.18.
MHWS 5.1; MLWS 0.8; MTL 2.9; MHWN 4.0; MLWN 1.8.
Tidal stream at entrance is rotary: ¼kn NW at −1.05; 1kn 200° at +1.55; ¼kn SE at +4.55; ¾kn 010° at −4.00.
Approach   Conspic landmarks are St Hilda's ch 2½ ca WSW of the head of Heugh breakwater, Durham Paper Mills chimney in the centre of W Hartlepool, and Durham Steel Works 6¼ ca SSE of the chimney. Heugh Lt Ho lies N of the hr entrance.

In heavy weather approach towards the Long Scar E Card buoy (Q) and give the Heugh a very good clearance to avoid the backwash which upsets the swell for some distance E and S of it. From the S, make for the Long Scar buoy to avoid the Long Scar shoal lying 8 ca SW of the buoy.
Entrance   The chan is marked to stb by three G con buoys, the outer one Fl G 6s, and to port by three R can buoys. By night ldg lts FR are shown from the E side of the hr entrance on 329°, by day R fluorescent boards.
Berthing   (1) Temporarily in the W hr by arrangement with Dockmaster. Unbuoyed, unlit and dries, suitable only for shoal-draft boats able to take ground. (2) For a few hrs on arrival tie up immediately to port on entering Old Hr alongside moored yachts or timber rafts. (3) At No. 5 Graving Dock which is tidal; apply to Hartlepool YC for mooring. Basin sill 0.7m MLWS, berths up to 10m (4) At Victoria Basin, moorings available by arrangement with Dockmaster.

Small craft may be slipped on Fish Sands or by arrangement with Dockmaster on grid near Pilots' pier.

All facilities. Old Hartlepool YC on small promontory at landward end of Stone Pt to port when entering. Tees SC on S corner of W Hr. EC Wed.

SEAHAM   Chart BA 1627 (Plan p148)
HW +4.45.   DS N −5.00; S +1.00.
MHWS 5.2; MLWS 0.7; MTL 3.0; MHWN 4.1; MLWN 2.0.
Approach   Keep ½M offshore until E of hr entrance, FS at NE corner of S Dock in line with N Lt Ho leads in clear of E Tangle Rk, 1.9m.
Entrance   There is 5m in the entrance with a 5m chan dredged to the South

Dock and 1m elsewhere in the Outer (tidal) Hr. The S dock is available 3h before to 1h after HW. Yachts lie along the quay as directed by HM.

The hr is large, well protected, has limited berthing and the entrance is normally easy. Extensive improvements in hand. Water on quay, limited facilities.

In severe NE and E winds the hr may be closed.

SUNDERLAND Chart BA 1627 (Plan p148)

HW +4.45. DS: N −5.00; S +1.00. MHWS 5.2; MLWS 0.8; MTL 3.0; MHWN 4.2; MLWN 2.0.

Approach The entrance to the R Wear is ¾M N of the S dock entrance (permanently closed) and is protected by crescent shaped granite piers. A R can buoy 139° 1.4M from Roker Pier Lt Ho marks Hendon Rk 0.9m: pass to E of buoy. There is a wreck almost awash at LW 1M N of river entrance at Whitburn Steel; Sunderland YC endeavour to maintain a buoy approx 1 ca to seaward, marked 'SYC'.

Entrance The uncompleted outer end of the New South Pier is marked by a R can buoy. Enter between Roker Pier and the R can buoy and then on a course between the inner piers, depth 5m.

Berthing On Sunderland YC moorings in North Dock basin, or by permission pick up a mooring N or S side of R beyond dock entrances or enter N dock.

Anchorage Clear of fairway inside N breakwater in 3m. All facilities. EC Wed.

TYNEMOUTH Chart BA 1934

HW +4.40. DS N −5.00; S +1.00. MHWS 5.0; MLWS 0.7; MTL 2.9; MHWN 3.9; MLWN 1.8.

The chan of the R Tyne from the sea to Jarrow Quay Corner is dredged to depth of 9m.

Approach Bring the ldg lts F W in line 258°.

Entrance Pass between the piers in mid-chan. Streams run hard and raise a steep sea in E winds: keep to N side entering, S side leaving.

Berthing For short stay, alongside the fish quay. For a longer stay, 2M upriver in the Albert Edward Dock.

Anchorage 100m NW of the G con buoy W of the N pier-head. All facilities. EC Wed.

BLYTH Chart BA 1626 (Plan p151)

HW +4.40. MHWS 5.0; MLWS 0.8; MTL 2.9; MHWN 3.9; MLWN 1.7. DS: N −5.00.

Approach The hr may be easily located at night by the industrial lts. The entrance opens to the S with sands to W and rks to E abreast of breakwaters. From S, when past St Mary's Is bring ldg lts 2 F Bu in line 321°. From the N, to clear the Sow and Pigs Rks leave the Sow and Pigs R can buoy to port and

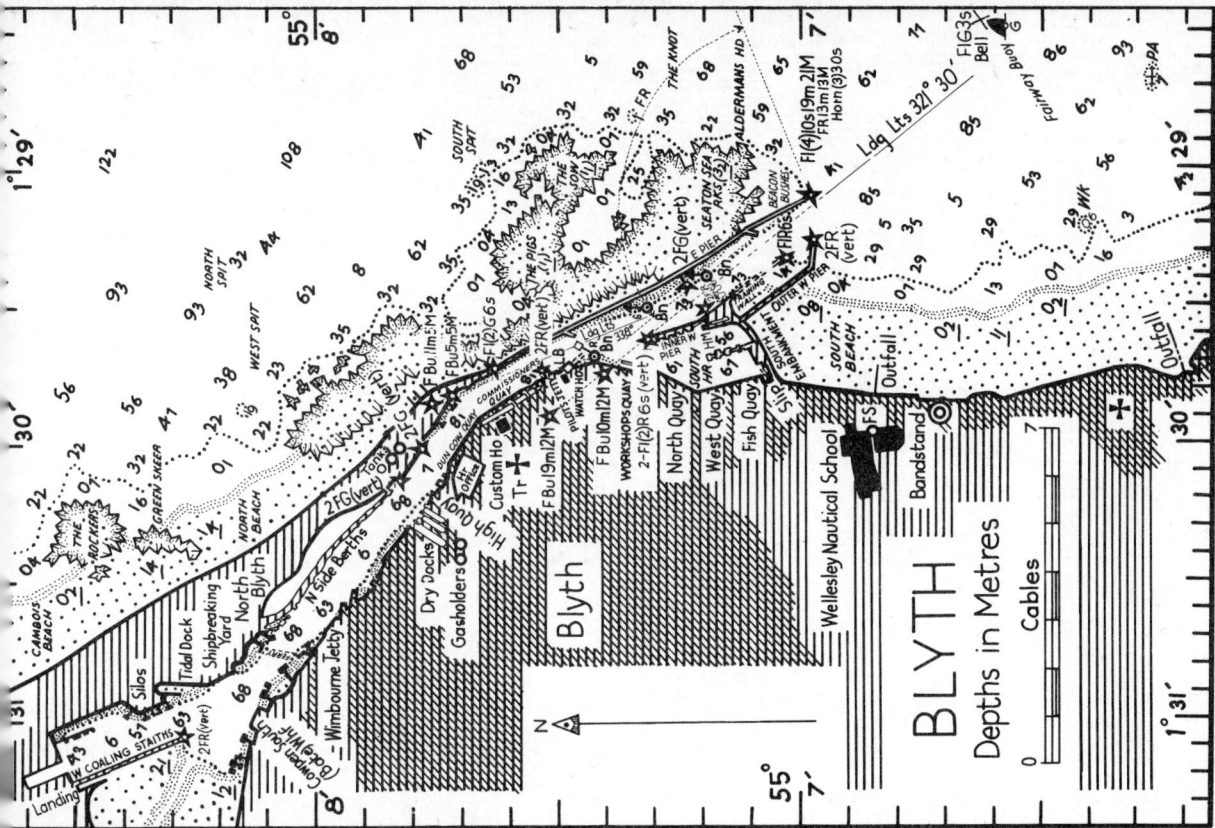

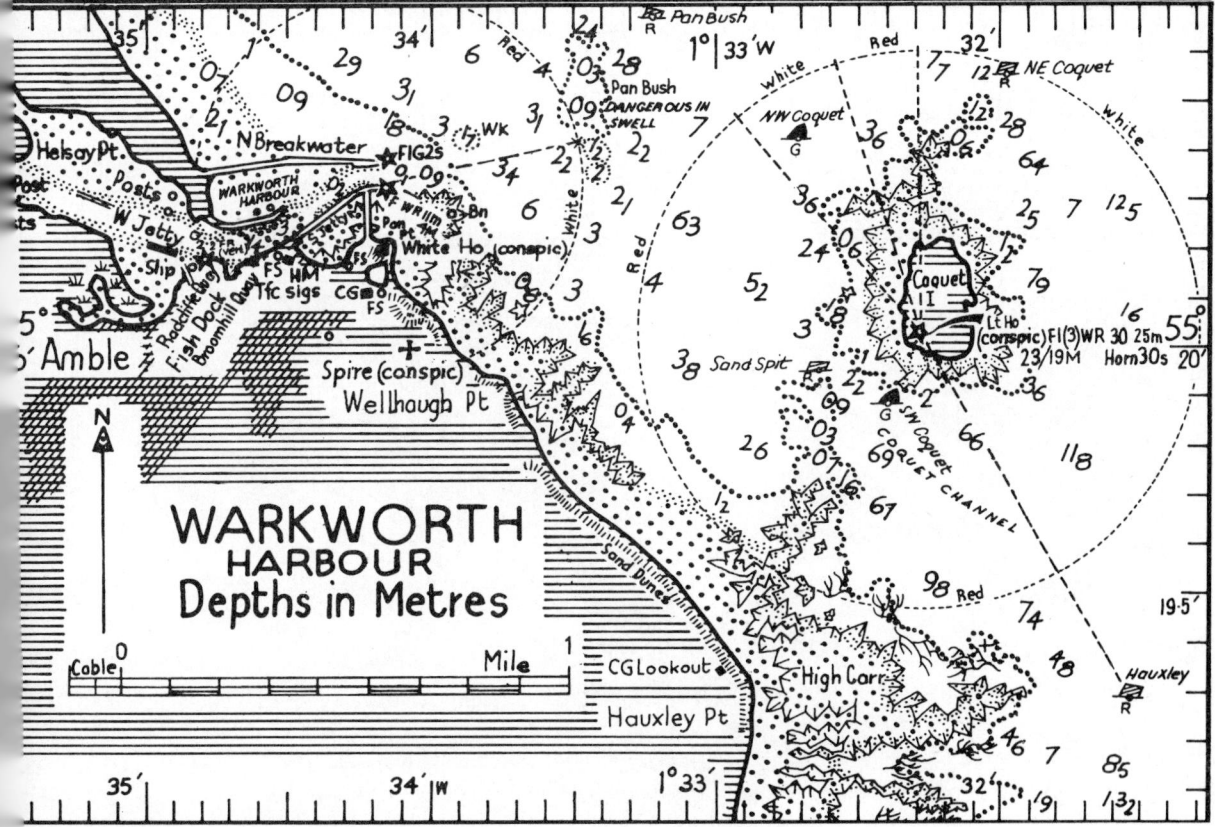

BLYTH
Depths in Metres

Cables

Blyth

North Blyth

Wellesley Nautical School
Bandstand

Custom Ho
Dry Docks
Gasholders
Silos
Tidal Dock
Shipbreaking Yard
Wimbourne Jetty
N Side Berths
Commissioners Quay
North Quay
West Quay
Fish Quay
Workshops Quay
Watch Ho
High Ho
Tr

SW COALING STAITHS
Landing

SOUTH SPIT
NORTH SPIT
WEST SPIT
NORTH BEACH
GREEN SKEER
THE ROCKERS
CAMBOIS BEACH
SOUTH BEACH
SEATON SEA

THE PIGS
THE KNOT
ALDERMANS HO
FAIRWAY BUOY
NE PIER
E PIER
SOUTH PIER
OUTER PIER
INNER PIER
BEACON
Outfall

Fl(4)lOs19m 21M
FR13m 13M Horn(3)30s
Ldg Lts 321° 30'
2FR(vert)
2FG(vert)
F.Bu.1m 1M
F.Bu.5m 5M
Fl(2)G 6s
2-FR(vert)
F.Bu.10m 12M
F.Bu.9m 12M WORKSHOPS QUAY
2-Fl(2)R 6s(vert)
Tfc sigs
2FG(vert)
2FR(vert)
Cable (Ladder)

WARKWORTH
HARBOUR
Depths in Metres

Cable 0   Mile 1

Amble
Helsay Pt
N Breakwater
WARKWORTH HARBOUR
W Jetty
Slip
Radcliffe Quay
Fish Dock
Braemill Quay
Post
Posts
White Ho (conspic)
FS HM
Tfc sigs
CG
FS
Spire (conspic)
Wellhaugh Pt
CG Lookout
Hauxley Pt
High Carr
Sand Dunes

Pan Bush
DANGEROUS IN SWELL
Wk
Bn

FlG2s
WR11m
Red
White

NW Coquet
G
NE Coquet
R
SW Coquet
G
Coquet
Lt Ho (conspic) Fl(3)WR 30 25m
23/19M Horn 30s
Sand Spit
COQUET CHANNEL
Hauxley
R
Red
White

HOLY ISLAND
Depths in Metres

Shell Road
Causeway
49'
48'
47'
1° 46'
45'

o Old Lime Kiln
The Links
The Lough
Brides Hole
Sheldrake

Chare Ends
Lough Hd

Lindisfarne, or
Holy Island

C G

St Mary's Ch
Belfry
F S
Lindisfarne Priory (ruins)
C G
Bn

Sandeel Beds

0·4
0·4
0·7
Bible Law
Castle (conspic) (11)
F S
The Ouse
Steps
Piers (ruins)
Castle Pt

St Cuthbert's I
slip
Steel End
0·1
The Yares
Stone Ridge
Hole Mouth
Ridge End
Ridge
B Y B
Ldg Bns 260°

0·1
3·2
6·2
1·3
Belfry & Bn in line 310°
0·4
0·7
Triton Shoal
Ridge
G Triton

55°
40'

0·7
0·9
4·1
0·1
3·5
2·5
3·5
1·3
2·2
3·2

1·1
2·8
0·4
Black Law
2·9
1·7
1·3
1·1
2·8

4·1
East Beacon (conspic) 21
West Beacon (conspic) 25
Old Law
Parton Stiel
1·3

2·6
2·2
7·4
4·1
Plough Seat
3·8
Plough Seat Reef
R

Plough Rk ♦ Bn
4·4
5·3

4·1
8
11 7·5
4

3·5
6·5
8

1·6
6·8
8

E Bn 21·3m
Beacons on Old Law
W Bn 25·3m

Cables
0   6

FARNE ISLANDS
Depths in Metres

39'
41'
1° 40'
39'
38'
37'
36'

Whirl Rks (breaks
23
6·2
1·1
1·9
(3·6) Kniveston
2·7
4·4
2·2
3·2

Fl 20s 23m 29M Siren (2) 60s
Lt Ho (conspic)
Longstone
1·9
Crafords Gut

N Wamses
13·8
Little Harcar
2·7

S Wamses
6·5
Big Harcar
13·5

Tr (conspic)
13·5
Brownsman I
Staple I
27
Callers (2·3) 2·3

Oxcar or S Goldstone (1·7)
5·6
13·8

17·8

55°
38'

Gun Rks (3·6)
1·7 (conspic)
21
16
Crumstone

1·1
Elbow
2·5
1·69
1·99
Staple Sound
31
32

Swedman
6·5 (0·5)
3·8
Megstone (5)
1·4·4
1·1
Knocks Reef
7·4

Swedman (0·5)
(0·2)
0·9 9
Forne Sound
2
The Kettle
W Wideopen (2)
The Bush (0·8)

White
1·6·3
Forne I
E Wideopen
6·8
5·6

37'
4·1
Fl (2) WR 15s 27m, 13, 9M
3·9
3·8

N

Cables
0   10

152
Based on British Admiralty Charts (nos. in text) with the permission of the Controller of H.M. Stationery Office and the Hydrographer of the Navy, and on other sources.

proceed in a S direction towards the Fairway G con bell buoy, Fl G 3s, from whence steer midway between the piers.

Entrance   Enter between the piers, round the N end of the inner pier (Fl(2) R 6s) into S Hr.

Berthing   Visiting yachts are usually accommodated by the Royal Northumberland YC in the S Hr, or berth temporarily and contact HM on inner W pier for instructions. All facilities. EC Wed.

WARKWORTH HARBOUR   Chart BA 1627   (Plan p151)

HW (Coquet Rd) +4.30.   MHWS 5.1; MLWS 0.8; MTL 2.9; MHWN 4.0; MLWN 1.8.

DS: N −5.00.

Bar   1m or less MLWS.

Approach   Clear the Pan Bush shoal marked on its N side by a R can buoy. From the S, there is a passage between the Coquet and the Hauxley R can buoy on the port hand; pass between SW Coquet G con and R can Sand Spit buoys. Local knowledge is desirable. From the N, pass between Pan Bush R can buoy and NW Coquet G con buoy till Pan Pt Bn comes over middle of S Pier, then approach hr. By night keep in W sector of Coquet Lt till breakwater lt, exhibited when 3m on bar, turns W, then app hr.

Entrance   Lies between two breakwaters which must be approached with care as the S-going stream sets straight across.

Berthing   Yachts lie at S quay in 2.4m. Further up the R Coquet beyond quays the YC may have moorings, approx 1m at MLWS, soft mud.

   All facilities. Bus to Newcastle and Alnwick.

HOLY ISLAND   Chart BA 1612   (Plan p152)

HW +4.00.   MHWS 4.8; MLWS 0.6; MTL 2.6; MHWN 3.7; MLWN 1.5.

DS in offing: SE HWD; NW +6.00; In hr entrance: flood −2.45; ebb +3.45.

A natural hr with 3 to 7m inside. Strong streams and eddies.

Approach   From the S keep Plough Bn open to E of Emmanuel Hd till the bns on the Old Law are in transit, then steer in on 260°. Least depth on line 1.3m. From the N through Goldstone Chan, leaving the E Card Ridge buoy off Castle Pt well to stb. Strangers should avoid the passage W of Plough Rk. Entry under sail is only possible with a fair stream or leading wind.

Entrance   Bring bns in line and steer in on 260°, leaving the Triton G con buoy to stb, until the triangular bn on the Heugh (which must not be confused with the tall narrow stone War Memorial further to the W) comes in line with St Mary's ch belfry 310°, then steer on this bearing to anch.

   The ebb runs at 4kn in the chan. The entrance is long and narrow, but is easy in fine weather with the help of the ldg marks. The Old Law Bns are conspic stone obelisks; the Heugh is a little cliff with a ch behind it. At LW the Law Bns must not be opened to N until Emmanuel Bn is closed behind Castle Pt. The marks are unlit and it is unwise to enter unless they can be seen.

Anchorages   Vessels exceeding 2m draft bring up off Heugh bn; those drawing 2m can lie 1 ca S of Steel End. In W gales vessels should lie to two anchs owing to the scend at HW. Small craft able to take the ground are more secure in the Ooze, soft mud, except in S and SE breezes when it should be avoided.

Water from tap in the square, stores at PO.

BERWICK   Chart BA 1612   (Plan p155)
HW +3.50.   DS: N −4.40; S +1.20.   MHWS 4.7; MLWS 0.6; MTL 2.6; MHWN 3.8; MLWN 1.3.
Bar   0.6 to 1.8m. Inside hr 2.4m.
Approach   From S, to clear the shoals in Berwick Bay keep Megstone and Farne Is lt tr in line astern, 142°. From N stand off from the shore ¾M. Approach pier-head with Lt Ho in line with Town Hall spire, or to S of this line.
Entrance   Enter parallel with pier, approx 10m off. Keep steering for bn after pier turns NNW, until Spittal ldg marks come in line 207°. Maintain this line until SE of second G con buoy, then steer for NW end of fish jetty. Do not keep too close to the G buoys which are laid in shoal water outside the chan. From here steer for the end of the pier at Tweed Dock.
Berthing   Temporarily at fish jetty: do not leave boat unattended. Otherwise Tweed Dock is normally left open and yachts can enter or leave at most states of tide except for 2h either side of LW. There is 0.6m in entrance. Berth as directed, usually alongside another vessel. Depth approx 1m at MLWS, bottom soft mud.

All facilities. EC Thurs.

EYEMOUTH
Depths in Metres

Hairy Ness

0 Cables 4

1, 7, 7, 12₂

3, 5

Lts 174°

Luff Hard Rk

Buss Craig

2, 2₄ 12₆

Hurcars

59 2₇

Inner 2, Buss

Dulce Craig

2, 5₃

3₆ 5

6₅

NESS END

5₆ 6

2₄

0₆

1/4

FS

N

CG

0₆

FIG

FIG

QG

FS

3

HM

Fog Horn

GUNSGREEN Pt.

QR

QR

Gasholder

Ch vane

Lifting Bridge

Quay

Eyemouth

Soltgreens Quay

B afloat

Eye Water

Slip

2° 5'

DUNBAR
Depths in Metres

Outer Bush

The Yetts

Castleford Rk

The Gripes

Oliver's Ship

Half Ebb Rk

Scart Rk

Perch

Wallaces Head Perch

Flint

97

T

Ldg line 198°

5

2₃

9₁

57

Old Hr.

VICTORIA Hr.

1₃ 1₃

Fort (ruin)

Broad Haven Br

Dunbar

QR

OcG6s 15m 3M

Swimming Pool

W

Dod Rk

3₇

OcG6s 22m 3M

N

2° 31'W

o Cable 1

30·8'

55° 9·9'

56

BERWICK
Depths in Metres

Spire 2°

Spire

Berwick upon Tweed

59

1₈

3

ROYAL BORDER BRIDGE

Town Hall spire (conspic)

Tfc sig

Meadow Haven

24

1/5

55'

BERWICK BRIDGE (LOW)

CGFS

Jetty

HM

Bns

2FG(vert)

·46

2₇

09

2

0₆

1₈

QG

FIG

Bn

Dn

FR

FS

2FR (vert)

spire

1/2

Tweed mouth

Fish Jetty

2FR (vert)

Spire

hy (conspic)

Spittal Pt

Lt Ho (conspic) Fl 5s 15m 10M & FG 8m Reed (occas)

2₄

0₆

1/2

0₆

2₄

0·3

N

0 Cables 7

2° 59'

St ABBS
Depths in Metres

o Half Cable

N

2° 8'w

55° 55'

55° 54'

5₅

Hog's Nose

Shoal

Ldg Lts

Maw Carr

NW Pier

Concrete Apron

FR

FR

Village Hall

Northfield House

2° 7·9'w

2° 8'

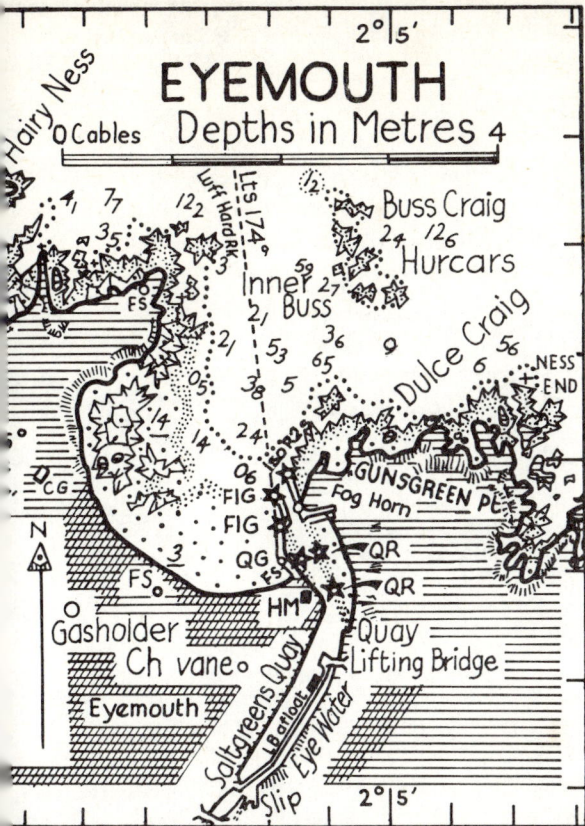

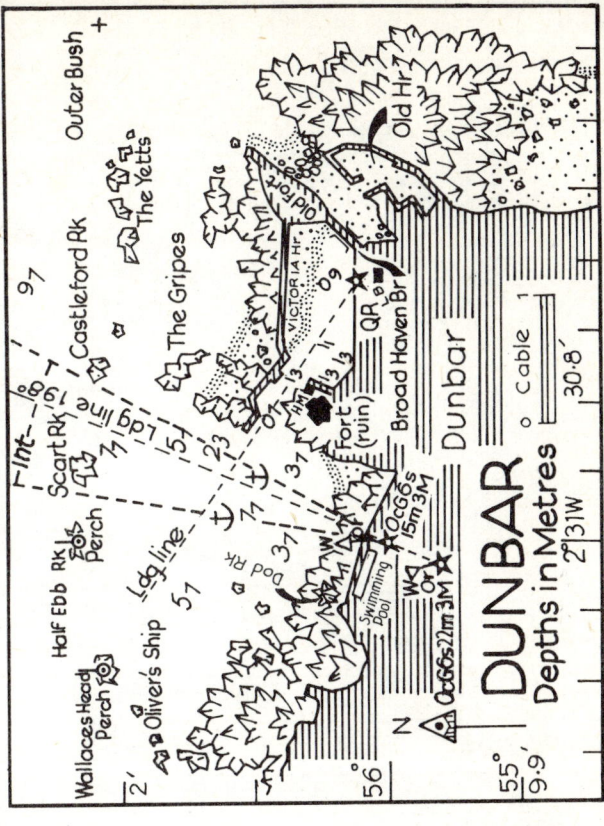

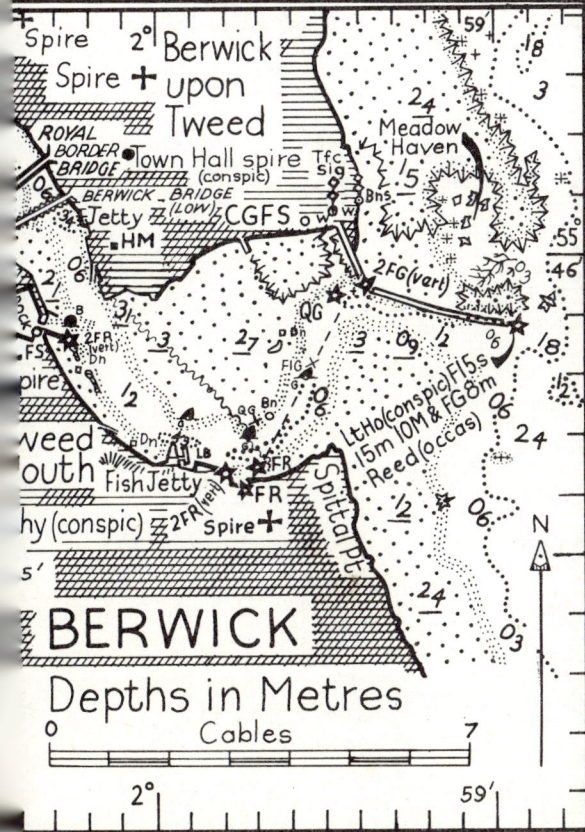

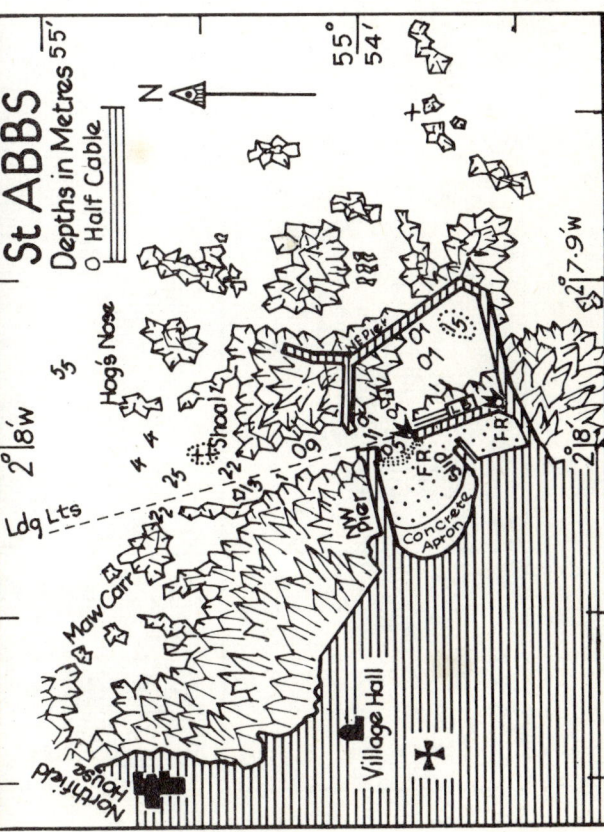

on British Admiralty Charts (nos. in text) with the permission of the Controller of H.M. Stationery Office and of ydrographer of the Navy, and on other sources.

155

SCOTLAND EAST COAST

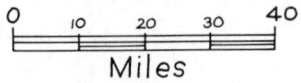

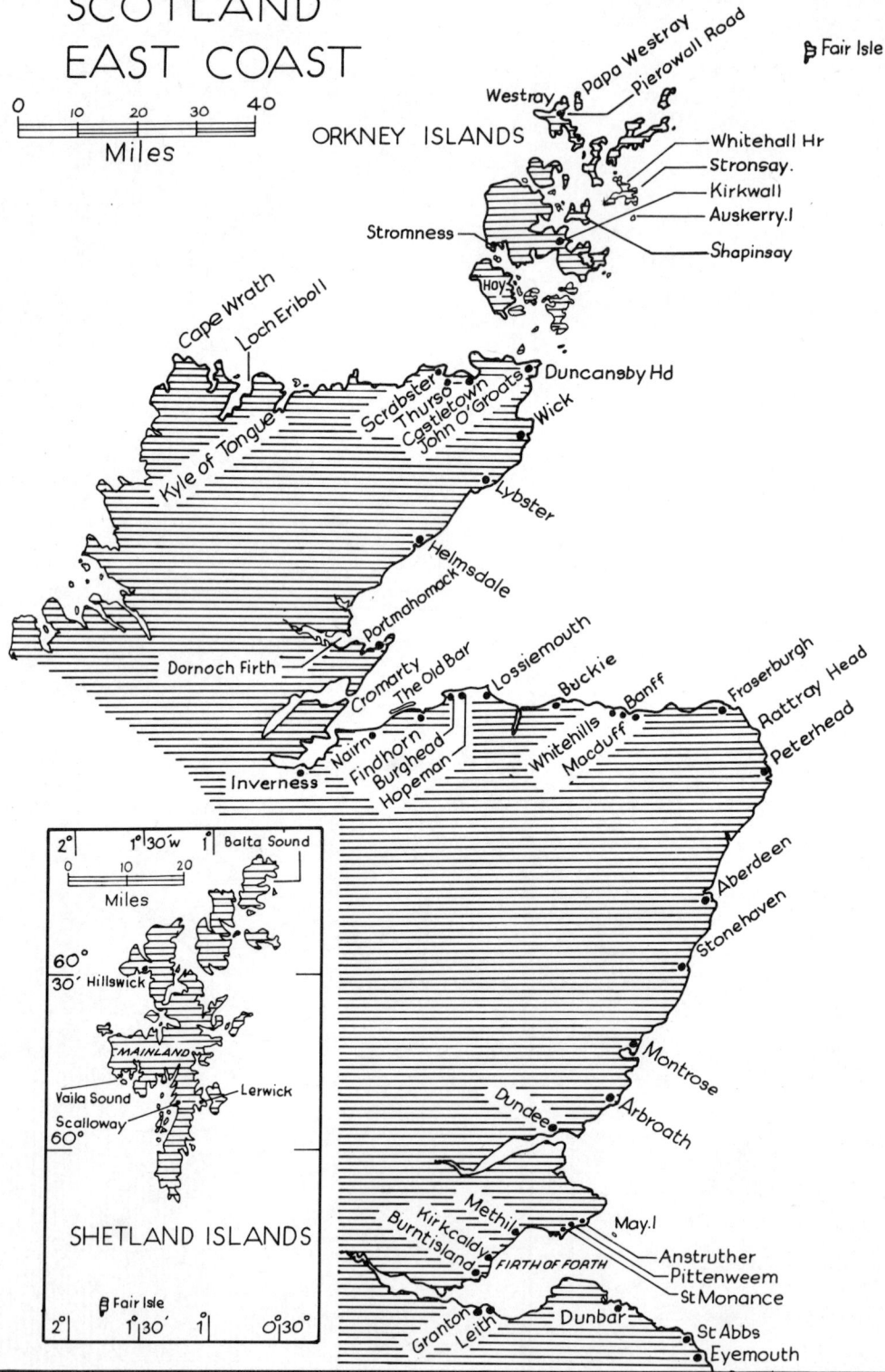

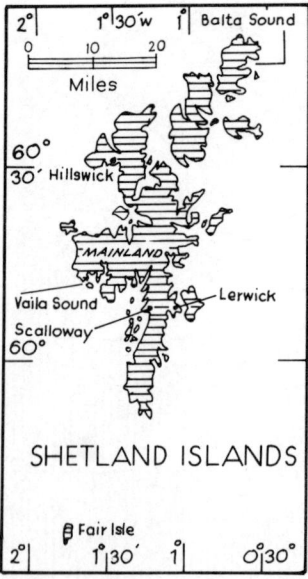

0 10 20 30 40
Miles

ORKNEY ISLANDS

Sumburg Hd
(Shetland I's)

Fair Isle

Papa Westray
Pierowall Road
Westray
Whitehall Hr
Stronsay.
Kirkwall
Auskerry.I
Shapinsay
Stromness
HOY

Cape Wrath
Loch Eriboll

Duncansby Hd
Scrabster
Thurso
Castletown
John O'Groats
Wick

Kyle of Tongue

Lybster

Helmsdale

Portmahomack

Dornoch Firth

Cromarty
The Old Bar
Lossiemouth
Buckie
Banff
Fraserburgh
Rattray Head
Peterhead
Nairn
Findhorn
Burghead
Hopeman
Whitehills
Macduff
Inverness

Aberdeen

Stonehaven

Montrose

Dundee
Arbroath

Methil
Kirkcaldy
Burntisland
May.I
Anstruther
Pittenweem
St Monance
FIRTH OF FORTH
Granton
Leith
Dunbar
St Abbs
Eyemouth

SHETLAND ISLANDS

2° 1° 30'w 1° Balta Sound
0 10 20
Miles

60°
30' Hillswick

MAINLAND

Vaila Sound
Scalloway
60°
Lerwick

Fair Isle
2° 1° 30' 1° 0° 30'

156

SCOTLAND

East Coast – Eyemouth to Wick

This passage involves the crossing of the estuaries of the Forth and Tay. Neither of these presents any great problems, but bad seas can be experienced across the mouth of the Forth, particularly in E winds against the ebb. The Tay is shoal for several miles out from the land, and if not being visited should be given a wide berth.

EYEMOUTH   Chart BA 1612   (Plan p155)
HW +3.30.   MHWS 4.7; MLWS 3.7.   DS: SE +0.30; NW −5.00.
A tidal hr 3½M S of St Abbs Hd. The entrance is 16m wide and faces W. The hr is safe in any weather, but it should not be approached in strong winds between N and E. The bar varies but normally 1m MLWS. If hr is closed, a R flag is shown (FR lt at night).
Approach   It is possible to approach either N or S of the Hurcar Rks, but the S passage has no ldg marks. To pass N, keep ½M offshore until the ldg marks come in line. These are: front, Y pole on W pier-head (Fl G); rear, Y pole 90m behind front (FG); 174°. E pier-head has lt Iso R 2s. If there is any sea, approach only at HW; if smooth, after half flood.
Entrance   Follow the ldg line until the hr is well open, then pass E pier fairly close keeping rather to the E of the centre of the chan, and proceed into hr between piers. On the port side there are 2 QR lts on cheq poles, and on the stb side 1 QR lt on cheq pole. This lt shows outside the hr but should be ignored until entry.
Berthing   As directed, or as space allows. Beware strong current from river after heavy rain. Soft mud. Fresh water on quay. Stores. All repairs. EC Thurs. HM tel Eyemouth (0390) 50223.

ST ABBS HARBOUR   Chart BA 160   (Plan p155)
HW +3.30.   MHWS 4.7; MLWS 3.7.   DS (St Abbs Head): ESE HWD; WNW −6.00.
This small hr about 1M S of St Abbs Hd has an inner hr which dries and an outer

157

hr in which there is 2m in places at LW. It should not be attempted in strong winds between N through E to SE.

Bar 1m in entrance chan.

Approach From S: steer on St Abbs Hd until Bird Cliff has been identified. It is a high reddish cliff facing SE and much whitened by bird droppings. When the hr (identifiable by conspic Y LB ho) comes abeam, steer for this cliff. Next identify Maw Carr, a prominent reddish rk 15m high with vertical sides about ¾ ca NNW of the hr entrance. Steer towards this rk. From N: follow the land round St Abbs Hd which is steep-to.

Entrance From a position off Maw Carr get the E edges of NW pier and centre pier in line and steer on this line exactly. The chan is narrow.

There are two ldg lts at night, a low R lt on the centre pier and a higher R lt behind.

Anchorage Berth as directed in outer hr. Local fishing boats mostly use inner hr. Water from tap on quay. Good grocer's shop. Strong warps needed in bad weather. Best berth S end of E wall.

DUNBAR   Chart BA 734   (Plan p155)
HW +3.40.   MHWS 5.2; MLWS 0.7; MTL 3.0; MHWN 4.2; MLWN 2.0.
There is about ½m at MLWS in the entrance but good anch just outside in reasonable weather while awaiting the tide. The entrance to the hr is a narrow cleft 10m wide in the cliffs to port of the ldg line, 2 Orange columns with W triangular topmarks, Oc G 6s. It is not visible until it is almost time to turn in. Berth as directed, probably on N quay where vessels ground at LW; bottom uneven. Uncomfortable if there is any swell outside. In bad weather yachts go into Old Hr through a bridge which the HM opens. All stores. EC Wed.

FISHERROW   Chart BA 734
HW +3.45.
A drying hr 5M ESE of Leith, with about 1½m MHWN, 2½m MHWS. Mainly used by pleasure craft. There is an Oc 6s lt on the E pierhead: approach over smooth sand and pass to W of pier-head when hr opens up. Approach dangerous in strong onshore winds. Berth on E pier; exposed to NW. All stores, good bus service to Edinburgh.

LEITH
The Forth Ports Authority has banned Leith to yachts since the new lock at the entrance was put into operation. No yacht would be turned away in emergency, but otherwise use Granton instead.

GRANTON   Chart BA 735   (Plan p159)
HW +3.50.   MHWS 5.6; MLWS 0.8; MTL 3.0; MHWN 4.5; MLWN 2.1.
Entrance Has 3m. Hr is divided into E and W arms. Information regarding entry available from Forth Navigation Service (VHF 16 and 12).

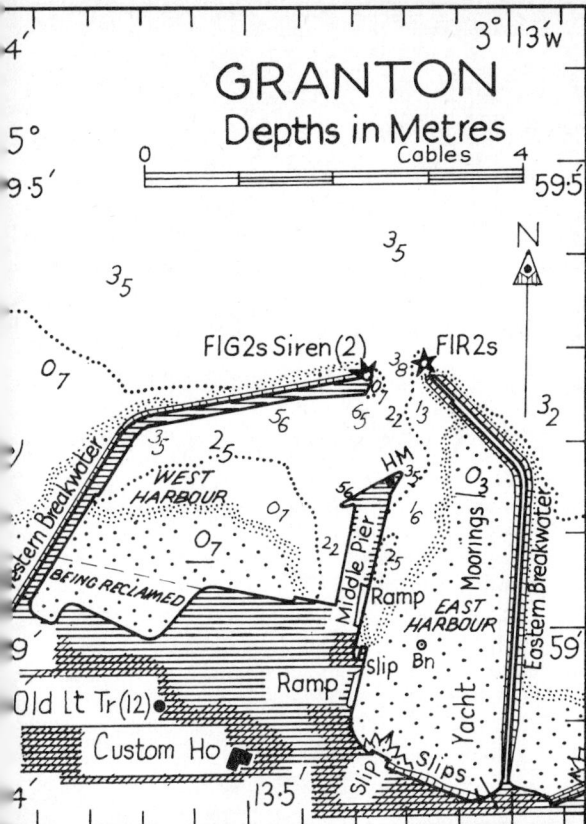

GRANTON
Depths in Metres

Cables
0   4

3° 13'w

4'

5°

9.5'

59.5

N

3.5   3.5

3.5   3.2

FlG2s Siren(2)   FlR2s

3.8

0.7   2.2   1.3   0.3   3.2
6.5   5.6

3.5   2.4   2.5

WEST HARBOUR   0.1   HM

BEING RECLAIMED   0.7

0.7   2.2

Middle Pier   Moorings

Ramp   EAST HARBOUR

Slip   Bn

Ramp   Yacht

Old Lt Tr (12)   Slip   Slips

Custom Ho

9'

4'

13.5   59

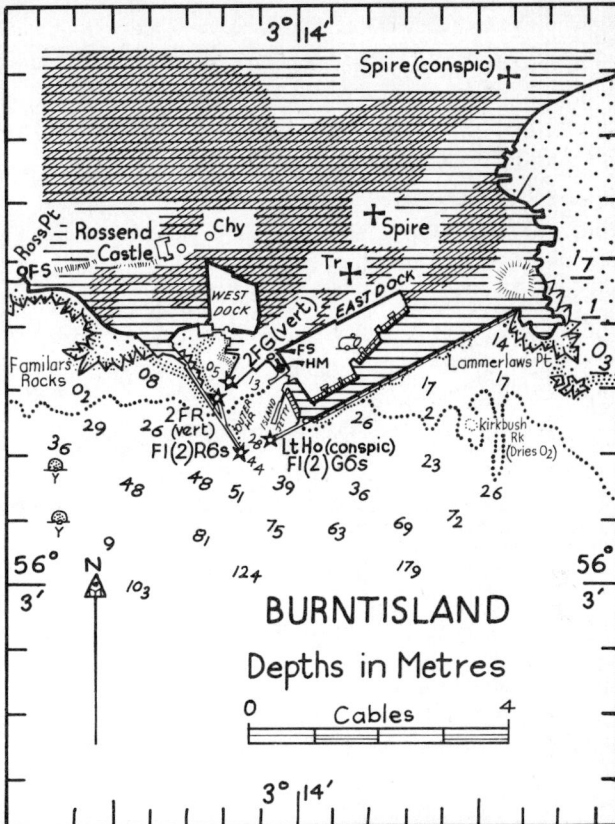

3° 14'

Spire (conspic)

Ross Pt   Chy   Spire
FS   Rossend Castle   Tr

WEST DOCK   EAST DOCK

Familars Rocks   0.8   2FG(vert)   FS HM   Lammerlaws Pt

0.2   1.3   14

0.5   kirkbush Rk (Dries 0.2)

2FR (vert)

29   2.6

3.6   Fl(2)R6s   4.4   Lt Ho (conspic)
    4.8   5.1   39   Fl(2)G6s   23   26

48   36

9   75   63   69   72

56°   N   81

3'   124   179   56° 3'

103

BURNTISLAND
Depths in Metres

0   Cables   4

3° 14'

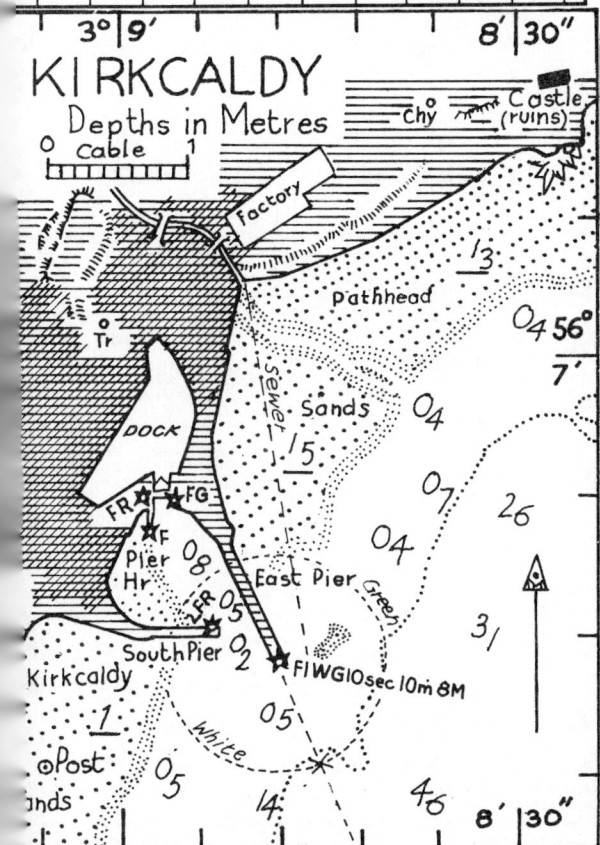

3° 9'   8' 30"

KIRKCALDY
Depths in Metres

Chy   Castle (ruins)

0   cable   1

Factory

1.3

Pathhead

Tr   0.4   56°

Sands   0.4   7'

DOCK   sewer   1.5

0.7   2.6

FR   FG   0.4

F   0.8   East Pier (green)

Pier Hr   3.1

FR   0.5

South Pier   0.2   FlWG10sec 10m 8M

Kirkcaldy   1   white

Post   0.5

nds   0.5   1.4   4.6   8' 30"

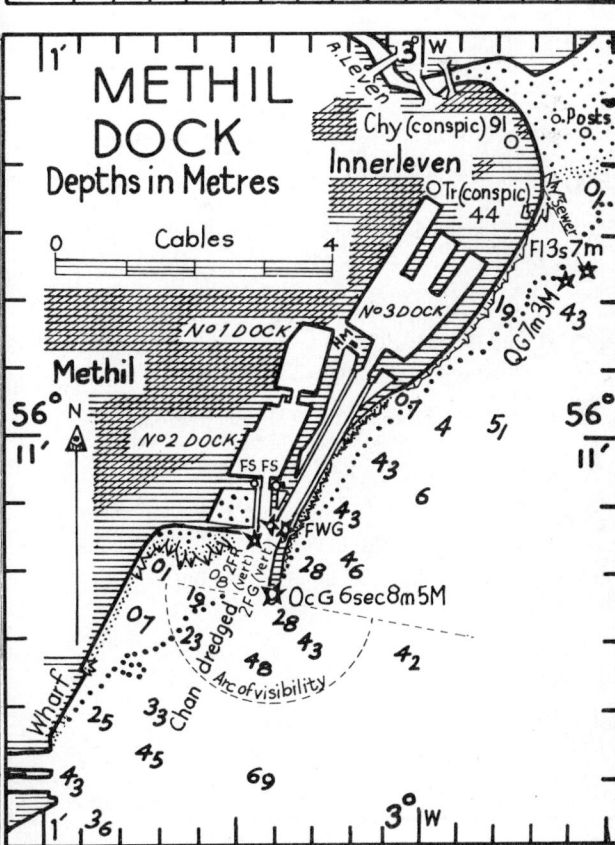

1'   3' W

METHIL DOCK
Depths in Metres

a Leven

Chy (conspic) 91   Posts

Innerleven   Tr (conspic) 44

Cables

0   4

Fl3s7m

N°3 DOCK

N°1 DOCK   19   QG7m3M   43

Methil   0.7   4   51   56° 11'

56° 11'   N   N°2 DOCK   43

FS FS   43   6

FWG

0.7   28   46

Wharf   0.1   2FR (vert)   43

1.9   2FG(vert)   OcG 6sec8m 5M

0.7   23   28   43   42

2.5   3.3   Chan dredged   48   Arc of visibility

4.5   69

4.3   3.6   1'   3° W

n British Admiralty Charts (nos. in text) with the permission of the Controller of H.M. Stationery Office and of
drographer of the Navy, and on other sources.

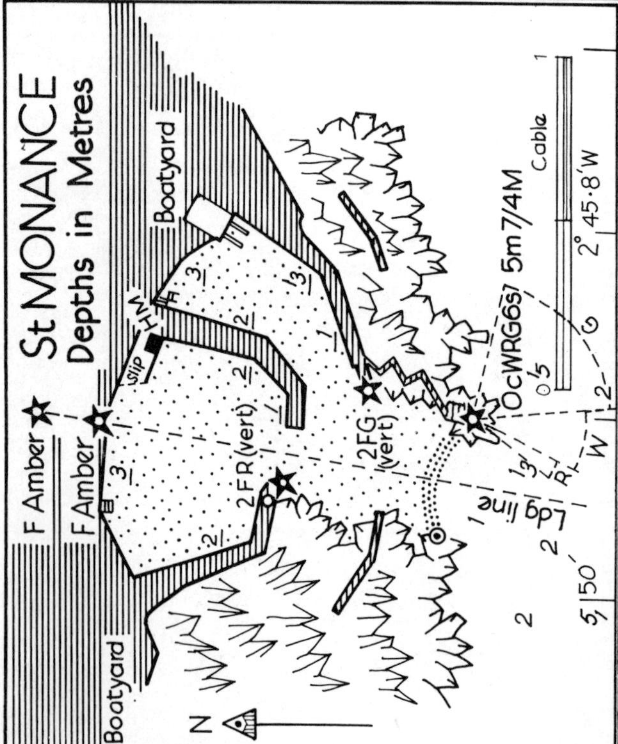

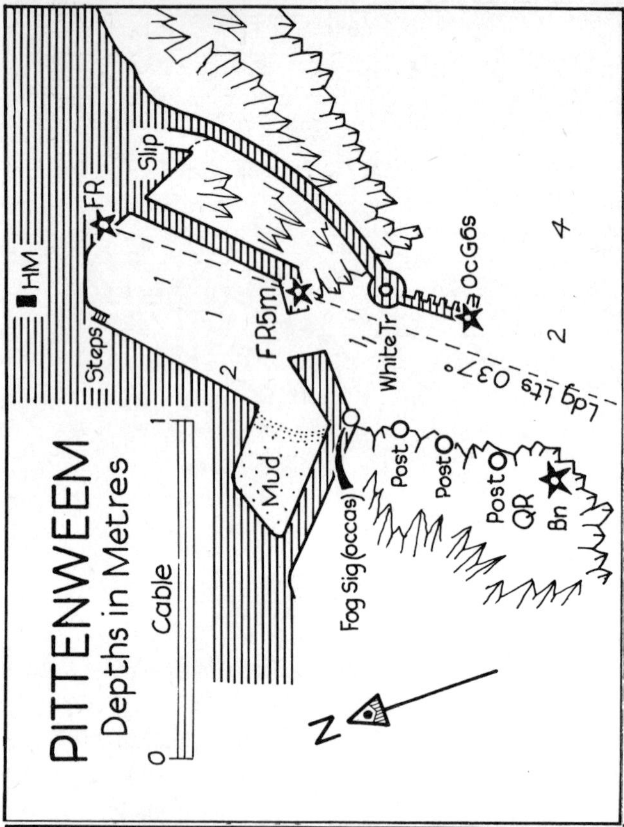

PITTENWEEM
Depths in Metres

■ HM

Steps

FR

Slip

Lk 1

1

Mud

Fog Sig (occas)

White Tr

F R5m

O Oc G6s

Post
Post
Post
QR

Bn

2

4

2

1

Lag Lts 037°

Cable

0 ⎯⎯ 1

N

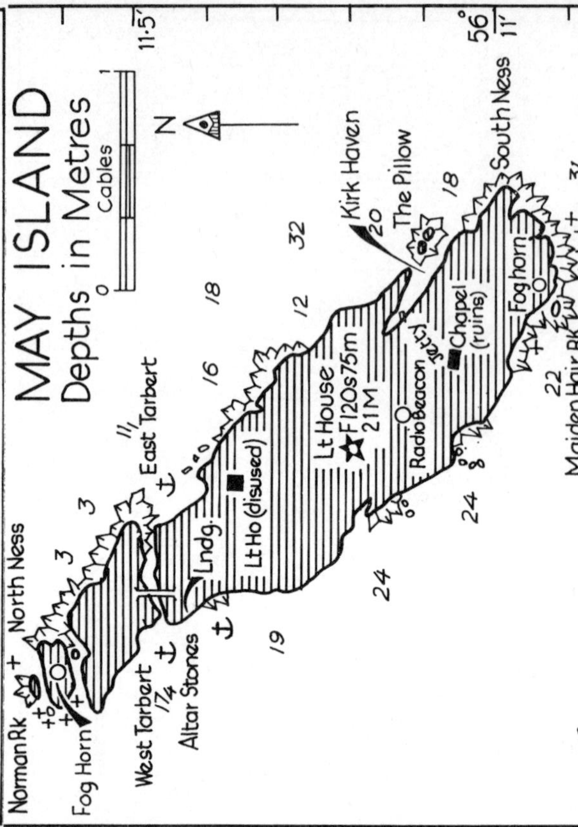

MAY ISLAND
Depths in Metres

Cables

0 ⎯⎯ 1

N

11·5

56°
11′

Kirk Haven

The Pillow

20

18

32

18

12

16

Radio Beacon

Chapel (ruins)

Fog horn

South Ness

Maiden Hair Rk

133′

8·9

22

24

8

24

East Tarbert

Lt House
Fl 2 Os 75m
21M

Lt Ho (disused)

Lndg.

11¼

3

3

3

19

24

North Ness

Norman Rk

Fog Horn

West Tarbert

Altar Stones

17¼

2°34′W

St MONANCE
Depths in Metres

56°
12′·2

F Amber ✶

F Amber ✶

F Amber

Boatyard

Boatyard

HM

Slip

2 FR (vert)

2 FG (vert)

Oc WRG 6s 5m 7/4M

1
3
2
2
3
3
1
2
2
2
2
1
1
0·5

W
R
R
G

Lag line

Cable

0 ⎯⎯ 1

N

5 | 50′

2° 45·8′ W

12′·1

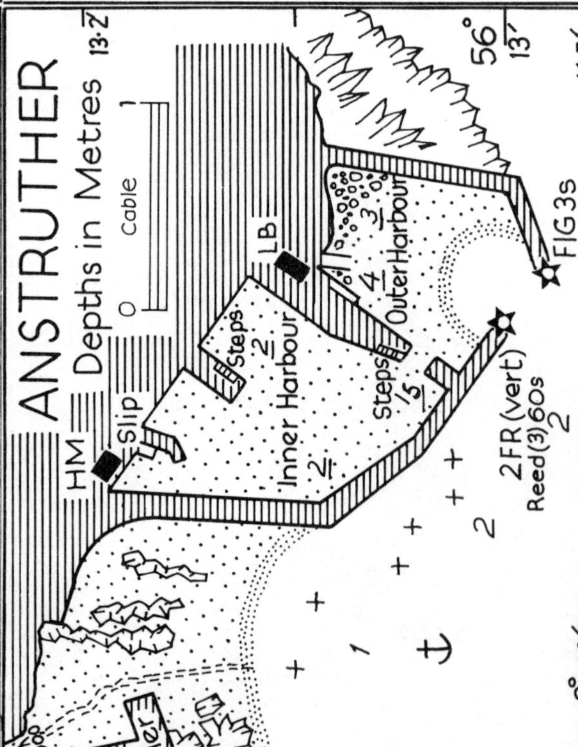

ANSTRUTHER
Depths in Metres

HM ■ Slip

13·2

56°
13′

·5′

LB

Steps

Inner Harbour

Steps

Outer Harbour

2
3
4
1
5
2
3

FIG 3s

2 FR (vert)
Reed (3) 60s

Old Pier

1

2

2°42′N

Cable

0 ⎯⎯ 1

N

Visiting yachts should moor on E side of middle pier and report to hr office on pier end. Entry prohibited when R flag with W diagonal cross is flown on signal mast at middle pier-head. All facilities and stores. Local clubs: Royal Forth and Forth Corinthian. Buses from gate to Edinburgh and Leith.

BURNTISLAND   Chart BA 739   (Plan p159)
HW +3.50.   MHWS 5.6; MLWS 0.8; MTL 2.9; MHWN 4.5; MLWN 2.1.
Consists of tidal outer hr and two wet docks: W dock prohibited to yachts.

Outer hr unsuitable for yachts in strong winds. Keep well clear of slipway near LW. E dock can be entered from approx HW −2 to HW; only short stay allowed. *Warning*: E dock is wide open to W winds and yachts should not be left unattended. Water and stores available. Trains to Edinburgh and Dundee from station adjacent to dock.

KIRKCALDY   Chart BA 739   (Plan p159)
HW +3.45.   MHWS 5.5; MLWS 0.7; MTL 3.0; MHWN 4.4; MLWN 2.0.
Bar $\frac{1}{2}$m.
Approach   This hr should not be approached in strong E winds as the sea breaks a long way out. Beware of shoal water off entrance. Except in emergency approach only after arrangements made: Methil Hr radio (VHF 16 and 14) will relay messages.
Entrance   Keep close to the E pier: the W side of the hr is shallower. It may be possible to berth alongside the E pier in depths of $\frac{1}{2}$ to $1\frac{1}{2}$m. Wet dock can be entered from HW −2 to HW, but this is not often allowed as there is little room. Water and stores available. Trains to Edinburgh and Dundee. Buses to all parts.

METHIL   Chart BA 739   (Plan p159)
HW +3.35.   MHWS 5.5; MLWS 0.7; MTL 3.0; MHWN 4.4; MLWN 2.0.
Bar $\frac{1}{2}$m off main Lt Ho.
Entrance and berthing   With sufficient rise of tide entrance is straightforward, but avoid in strong SW winds. Entrance is, however, practicable in strong E-SE winds, when other hrs on this coast are dangerous to enter. Yachts use No. 1 or 2 Dock on W side of hr; short stays only. Methil Hr has VHF, chans 16 (calling) and 14 (working).
Anchorage   Small vessel anchorage off hr: see chart BA 734.

ST MONANCE   Chart BA 190   (Plan p160)
HW +3.35.
A pleasant fishing hr, now little used. The hr dries and has about $3\frac{1}{2}$m MHWS; $2\frac{1}{2}$m MHWN.
Approach   Should not be attempted in bad weather or below half-tide.
Entrance   Enter between E breakwater and pole bn on rks to W of entrance. Berths available in E hr on outer pier. Dries, hard sand and mud. Water and stores. Local bus services. Boatbuilder and engineering firm. EC Wed.

PITTENWEEM
Chart BA 190 (Plan p160)

HW +3.35.

The busiest fishing hr of the East Neuk of Fife. Liable to be congested. Entrance chan is 15m wide with 2m at MLWS. Water, stores and local bus services.

ANSTRUTHER
Chart BA 190 (Plan p160)

HW +3.30. MHWS 5.5; MLWS 0.7; MTL 3.0; MHWN 4.4; MLWN 2.0.

Hr dries. Approach entrance (conspic lt tr at end of W breakwater) from S and enter from SSW when piers open to reveal ldg lts (FG) above root of E pier. Berth in inner hr alongside W pier or as directed. Best berth just above first knuckle. Dries, mud, shoals to N. All facilities. EC Wed.

Do not attempt entry in heavy weather from E to S. Inner hr soft mud.

OFFSHORE ANCHORAGES
Largo Bay Good anch N and E winds.

St Andrew's Bay Good anch S winds through W to NW. Anchor in suitable depth E of hr pier. Avoid rks to SE of pier-head.

RIVER TAY
Chart BA 1481 (Plan p163)

HW (bar): +3.35; (Dundee): +4.05. DS off bar: SW −1.15; NE +4.45; both 1¼kn.

W of Broughty Castle the ebb sets more strongly on N side and the flood more strongly on the S side. The river is navigable on the tide to the deep-water hr at Perth. Strict rabies control enforced.

Bar 5½m, between Gaa Spit and the Elbow. The bar should not be attempted in strong E winds or heavy onshore swell.

Entrance The chan is well buoyed. Passage across Abertay sands is prohibited because of stakes. With a draft of 1½m and approaching from N or S the chan is entered from outside the 10m line between the middle buoys. At half-tide in smooth water the chan may be joined from SE near the Abertay G con buoy Fl 6s, keeping the disused lt trs on Buddon shore in transit. Caution should be exercised as depths are liable to change.

Temporary anch may be found out of the main ebb stream on the N side close inshore S and W of Buddon high and low lts (disused), and on the S side close inshore by Lucky Bn.

Anchorage (1) S side. There is a good anch clear to W of Tayport hr entrance and to N of line of Tayport high and low lt trs (low tr disused). The hr dries except for dredged trench along W side of NE pier about 15m wide, used for berthing ships. The S side of the hr is encumbered with yacht moorings and anchors. Swell in W and NW gales. Stores and fuel in village, bus to Dundee. (2) N side. Broughty Hr is not recommended. Anch in W Ferry Bay by River Tay YC moorings 8 ca WNW from Broughty Castle, exposed to long SW fetch and strong ebb. The clubhouse is on the main road close by. Water from the beach hut opposite the moorings. Bus to Dundee. EC Dundee Wed. Yachts requiring

RIVER TAY
Depths in Metres

DUNDEE DOCKS
Depths in Metres

R. TAY (continuation)
Depths in Metres

Dundee

Monifieth

Broughty Ferry

West Newport

Woodhaven

Tayport

Spinning Mill

Tentsmuir Pt

MONIFIETH SANDS

BARRY SANDS

GAA SANDS

GAA SPIT

ABERTAY SANDS

ABERTAY SPIT

LADY BANK

MIDDLE BANK

THE BAR

Middle

Inner

Abertay

Elbow

Buddon Ness

Old High Lighthouse

Old Low Lighthouse

War Memorial (conspic)

Broughty Castle

Lucky Scalp

Larick Scalp

Horse Shoe

Tentsmuir

West Haven

Fairway LFl.10s

Camperdown Dock

Queen Elizabeth Wharf

King George V Wharf

Caledon West

Caledon Jetty

Victoria Dock

HMS Camperdown

TAY ROAD BRIDGE

Camperdown Rk

Colman Rk

Fowler Rk (4)

Beacon Rk (3.5)

Drummond Rk

FWR 6m 5M

FR 6s 5m 5M

TAY RAILWAY BRIDGE

Kingoodie

Inchture

Powgavie

Seaside

Errol

Port Allen

Glencarse

INVERGOWRIE BAY

DOG BANK

CARTHAGENA BANK

Carrie

Channel buoys

Newburgh

FlR 3s 8m 2M

2F.G (vert)

Chy (36)

Cables

Miles

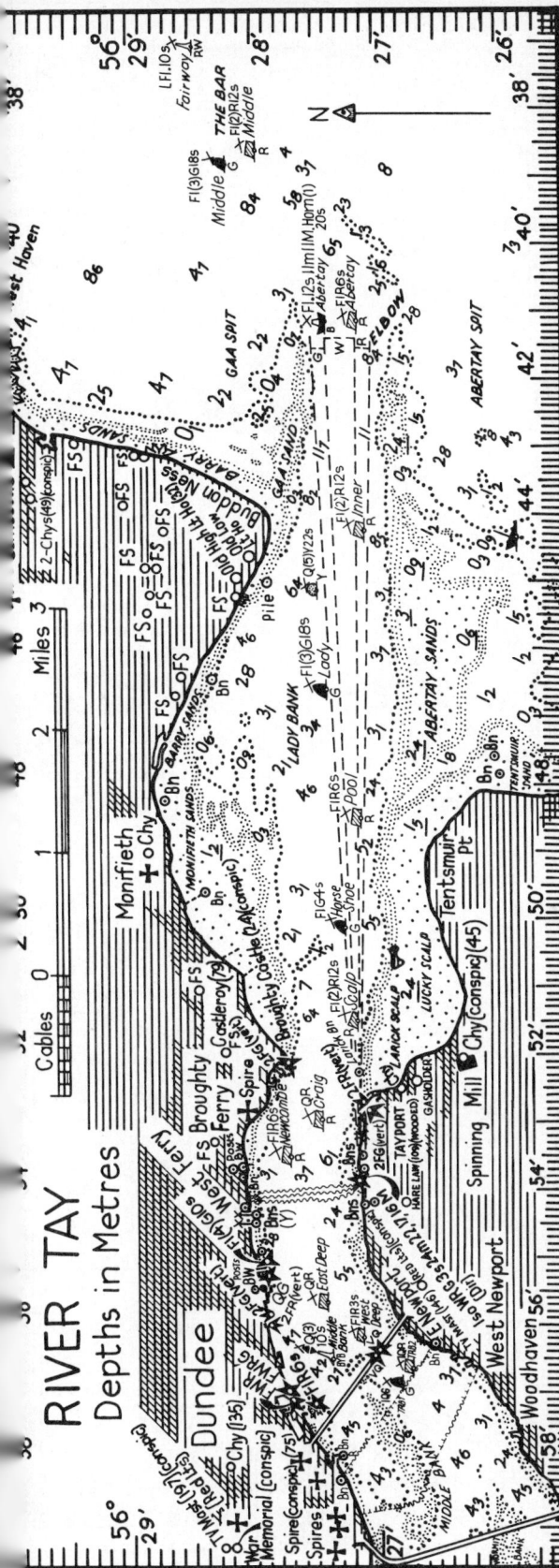

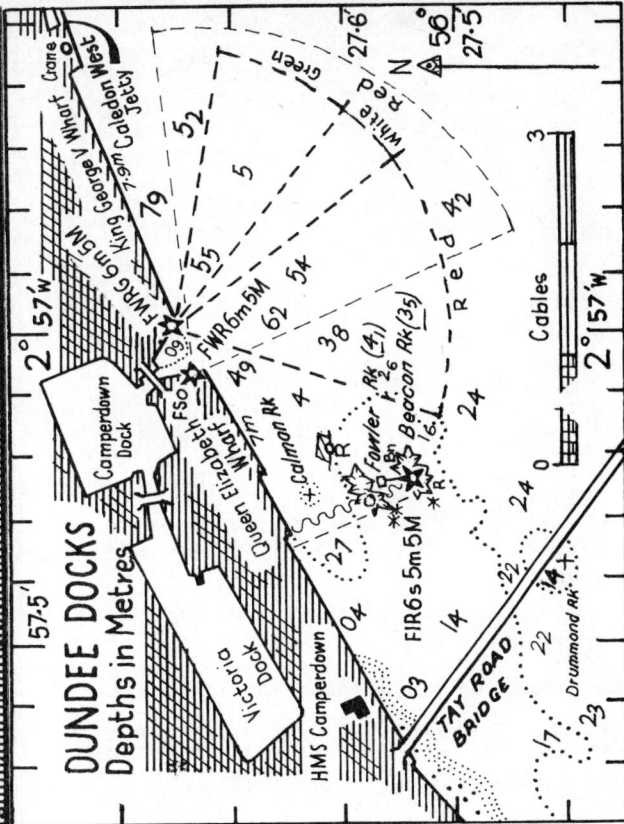

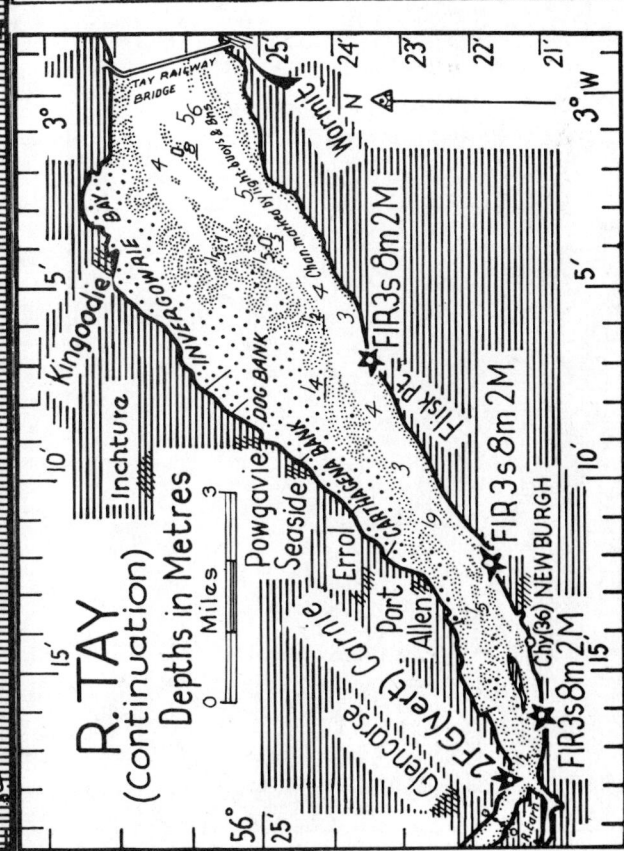

Based on British Admiralty Charts (nos. in text) with the permission of the Controller of H.M. Stationery Office and of the Hydrographer of the Navy, and on other sources.

163

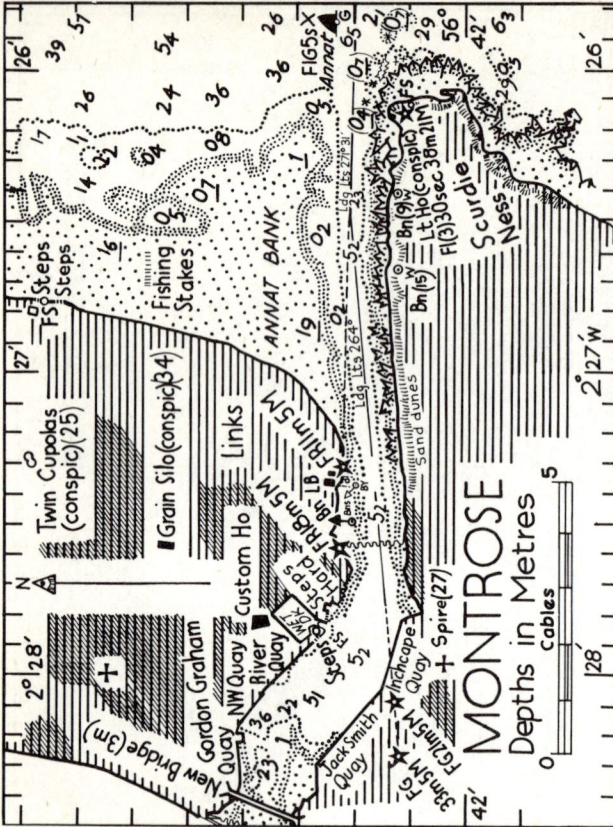

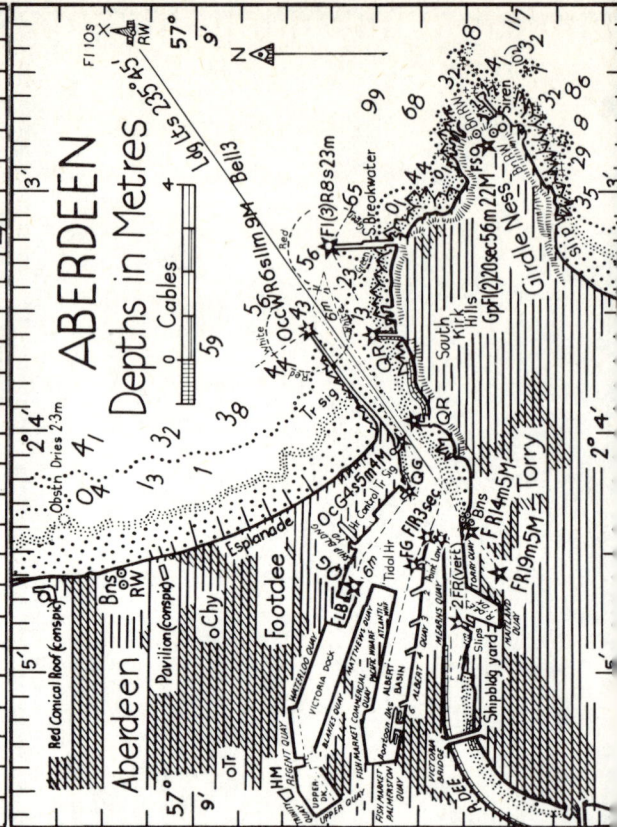

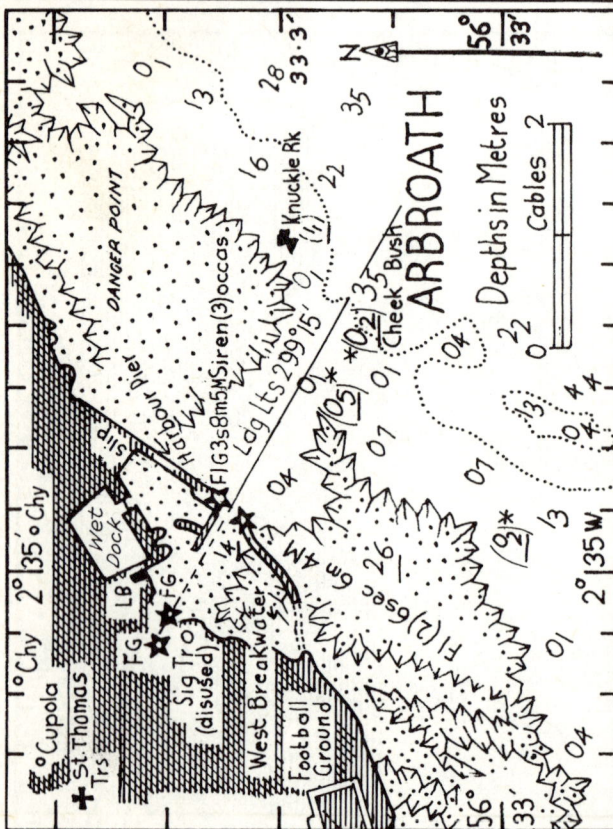

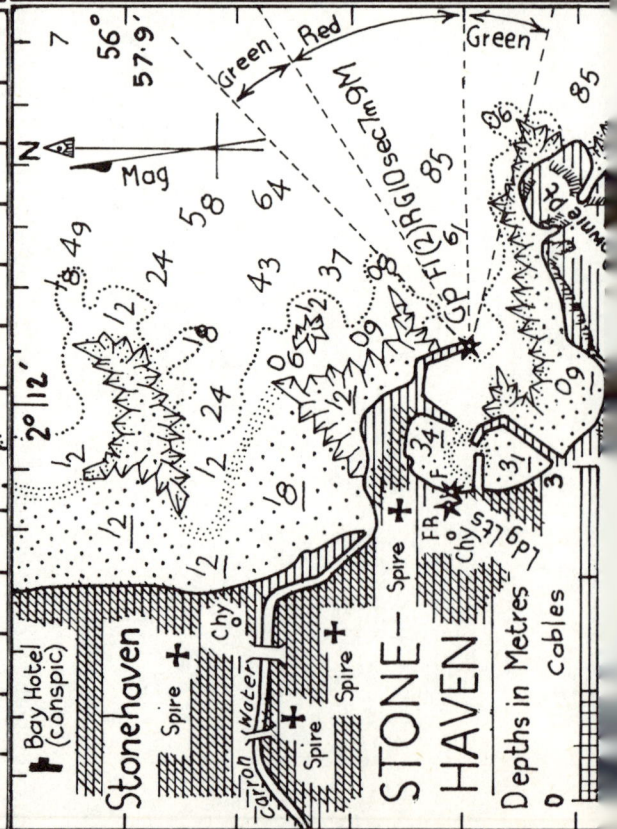

clearance should call at the Customs Ho at SW end of King George V Wharf (conspic W lt tr). The ebb sets strongly into the piles supporting the wharf. Clearance can also be obtained less conveniently in Tayport.
Dundee Docks (plan p163)   There is accommodation in docks under direction of the HM. Dock gates open 2h before HW and close at HW Dundee. Entrance about 4 ca E of road bridge. Heavy penalties for smoking.

ARBROATH   Chart BA 1438   (Plan p164)
HW +3.20.   MHWS 5.0; MLWS 0.7; MTL 2.9; MHWN 4.1; MLWN 1.8.
Bar ½m. Moderate SE swell causes scend in entrance: dangerous unless adequate power is available.
Approach   A round clump of trees 1.9M 036° from hr is a conspic seamark. It is most important to identify the white concrete pillars of the FG ldg lts and keep them strictly in line on entering to avoid rks approx 10m to port and stb of the line, 299°.
Anchorage   The hr consists of a tidal outer hr which dries and a wet dock which is frequently left open when vessels take ground. HM advises against vessels left unattended. All facilities. EC Wed.

OFFSHORE ANCHORAGE
Lunan Bay   In offshore winds, in suitable depths. Best landing, Ethie Haven at S end of bay.

PASSAGE NOTES: ARBROATH TO FRASERBURGH

The main part of this passage presents no difficulty except for the usual problem on the east coast of Britain that there is a serious lack of safe harbours in onshore gales. Tides run strongly round the Great Cape between Kinnairds Hd and Buchan Ness, and very heavy seas can be experienced in this area, especially in wind over tide conditions.

MONTROSE   Chart BA 1438   (Plan p164)
HW +3.35.   MHWS 4.8; MLWS 0.7; MTL 2.8; MHWN 3.9; MLWN 1.9.
Bar   Chan dredged to 5½m.
Entrance   Tidal streams are very strong, up to 6kn except during the first hour of the flood, which is the best time to enter. Enter on ldg marks, 271½°, front WR Tr 11m FR, rear W Tr 18m FR, and then follow middle of river. Consult dockgateman on VHF 16 and 12, or hail him for instructions at W knuckle of wet dock. The lock gates open HW −3 to HW.
   Do not attempt entrance in strong onshore winds during ebb as there are heavy overfalls. All facilities and fuel. EC Wed.

STONEHAVEN   Chart BA 1438   (Plan p164)
HW +2.45.   MHWS 4.5; MLWS 0.6; MTL 2.6; MHWN 3.6; MLWS 1.7.
A small hr in the SW corner of Stonehaven Bay, well sheltered from the S. There

is 1.5m in the outer hr; the inner hr, sand and mud, dries. Prominent marks are the War Memorial on Black Hill ¼M to the S, and the ruins of Dunnottar Castle about 9 ca S.

Entrance Give Downie Pt a berth of at least ½ ca, bring the head of the breakwater (Fl(2)RG 10s) to bear 267° and steer in. Leading lts 265° FG visible only when inside hr.

Berth alongside outer breakwater (swell in E winds), or take the ground in S inner basin, keeping close round the E wall for best water. Stores, water, fuel ½M. EC Wed.

ABERDEEN   Chart BA 1446   (Plan p164)
HW +2.35.   DS: SE −2.15; NW +3.45 (approx 1kn).
MHWS 4.3; MLWS 0.6; MTL 2.5; MHWN 3.4; MLWN 1.6.
A busy oil port: should be avoided except in emergency. In general use Stonehaven or Fraserburgh. The hr is protected from the S by Girdle Ness, but is open to the NE and should not be attempted on the ebb in gales from that quarter. Buchan Ness gives some protection when the wind is N of NNE. Yachts must comply with traffic signals and have name clearly displayed. Berthing instructions given by loudhailer from Control tr.

Approach On leading line (FR when ent safe, FG when dangerous) or by day keeping S face of N pier just open.

Entrance Pass between the N Pier and the S breakwater. Once inside, the River Dee is ahead, with the tidal hr opening out on the N side.

Berthing As instructed at Traffic Control office (VHF 16, 12) at root of N Pier. Temporary berth to seek instructions may be available at quay just beyond. All stores. EC Wed/Sat.

PETERHEAD   Chart BA 1438   (Plan p167)
HW +1.55.   DS (offing): S −2.00; N +3.30; both about 2kn.
MHWS 3.8; MLWS 0.5; MTL 2.2; MHWN 3.1; MLWN 1.5.
A busy oil and fishing port with no facilities for yachts, best avoided except in emergency. Available in any weather. The bay is now completely enclosed by breakwaters and this makes a safe port of refuge: anch behind the breakwaters in 3 to 7m in Brickwork Bay N of HM Prison (conspic), at least 3 ca clear of oil jetty. If requiring alongside berth, pass through basins to the far NW basin and berth alongside a boat on N wall, avoiding ice factory; CG HQ is adjacent. Entrance to N hr now permanently closed to shipping.

All facilities, rly, EC Wed.

RATTRAY HEAD
DS: S −2.00; N +3.30; both 3kn.
Dangerous seas can build up in the vicinity and it should be given a wide berth in fresh to strong winds.

FRASERBURGH

N

Depths in Metres

Cable

The Brothers

41·8

7

3₁ 3₃
3₃
5₂ 7₃
3₁

Lockie Hd

Fl.15s 37m 25M

Chy

WINTER BASIN

BALACLAVA

Slip

Dn
Booms
LB HARBOUR

SOUTH HR

QR10m5M

2FG or R Hor

QcR6sR12m5M

Middle Jetty

Inch Rocks

2₄

4

2₁

3₁

5₂
4₉

2₄

2₁

2₄

3₄

Balaclava Breakwater

FIG

Lts 291° 6s5m5M

2FG(vert)
23m4M
Siren(1) 20s
58

Arc of vis

57
41·5'

FlR6s6m5M

4₆
3₁
2₁

5₅

3₇

Burnett Buss
0₃ 4
2₄

59·8W

2₁

3₄

South Breakwater

FIG3 FIGFAITHLIE
2₀m 5M

FlR3S
8 FG or RHor

Boich Hd

Fishie Jetty

S Pier Drawbridge
Middle Jetty drawbridge

2°

PETERHEAD

N

30·5'

Roan Head

Roanheads Village
Chy

Memorial

Chy

Kirktown
FlR17m
FR13m

Spire(conspic)
Chy
Chy(conspic)

Spire
(conspic)33

Green
Hill

HARBOUR

HENRY HARBOUR
PORT HARBOUR
CG

LB
FG
FG

NORTH HD

85
2₇
11₉
12₈

13
6₀
6₁
13₄

SOUTH HEAD
13₁
57°
30'

Red
N Breakwater

2FR(vert)

Peterhead Bay

Ldg Lts 058·45°

Green

Iso RG6sec19m7M
Horn(1)30s

Fl(2)R12s24m7M
Lt Ho(conspic)

8₂
6₄
3₁

11

186

2₇
2₇

57°

25

9₈
12₈

8₅
98

6₀

0·60

3₁

Brickwork Bay
M.3

OcRG4S 7m1M

HM Prison

Salthouse Hd

Ldg Lts 314°

22

19₈

22

5

S Breakwater

ANCHOR

4·2FR(vert)

HORN

N
0
Red   Green

18₃
14₆
13₁
12₈

2₄
8
2₁
4₇
5

Depths in Metres

Cables

17₄
14₉

7₃ 13₁

19₅

1°46'W

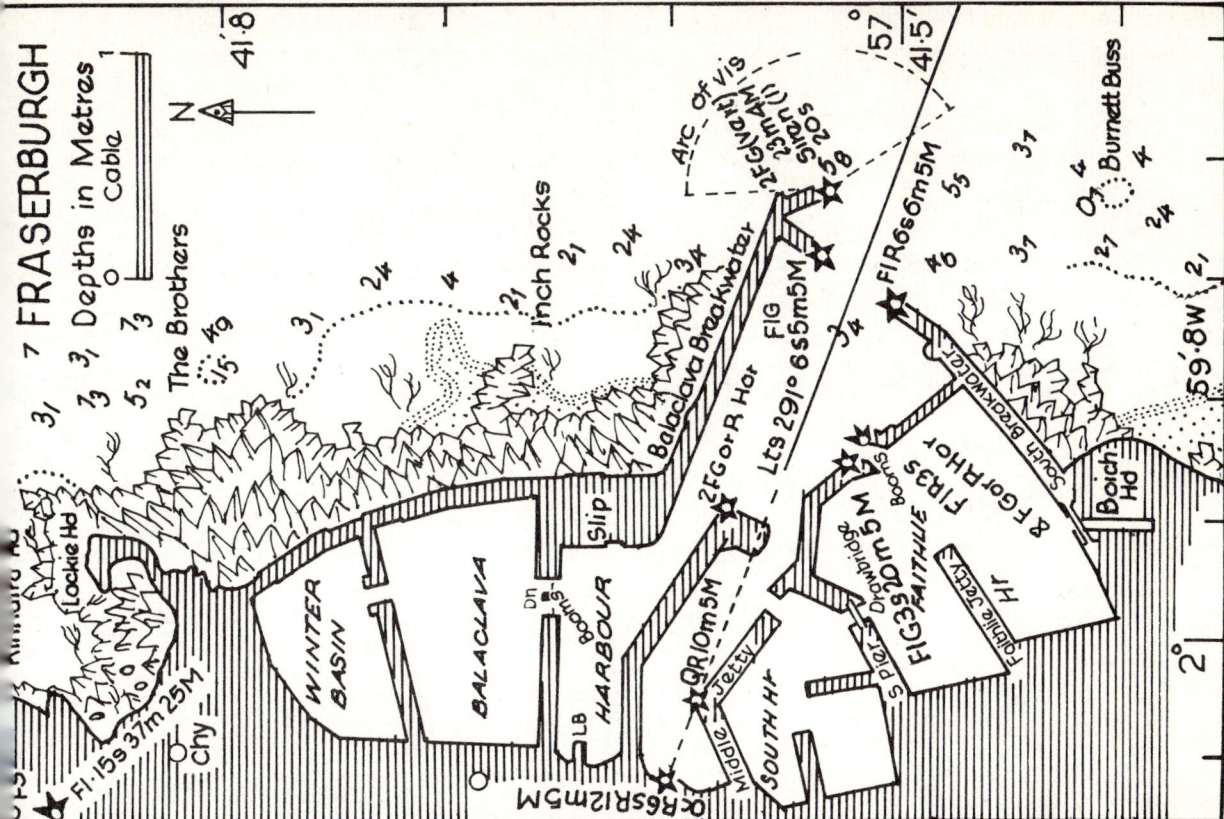

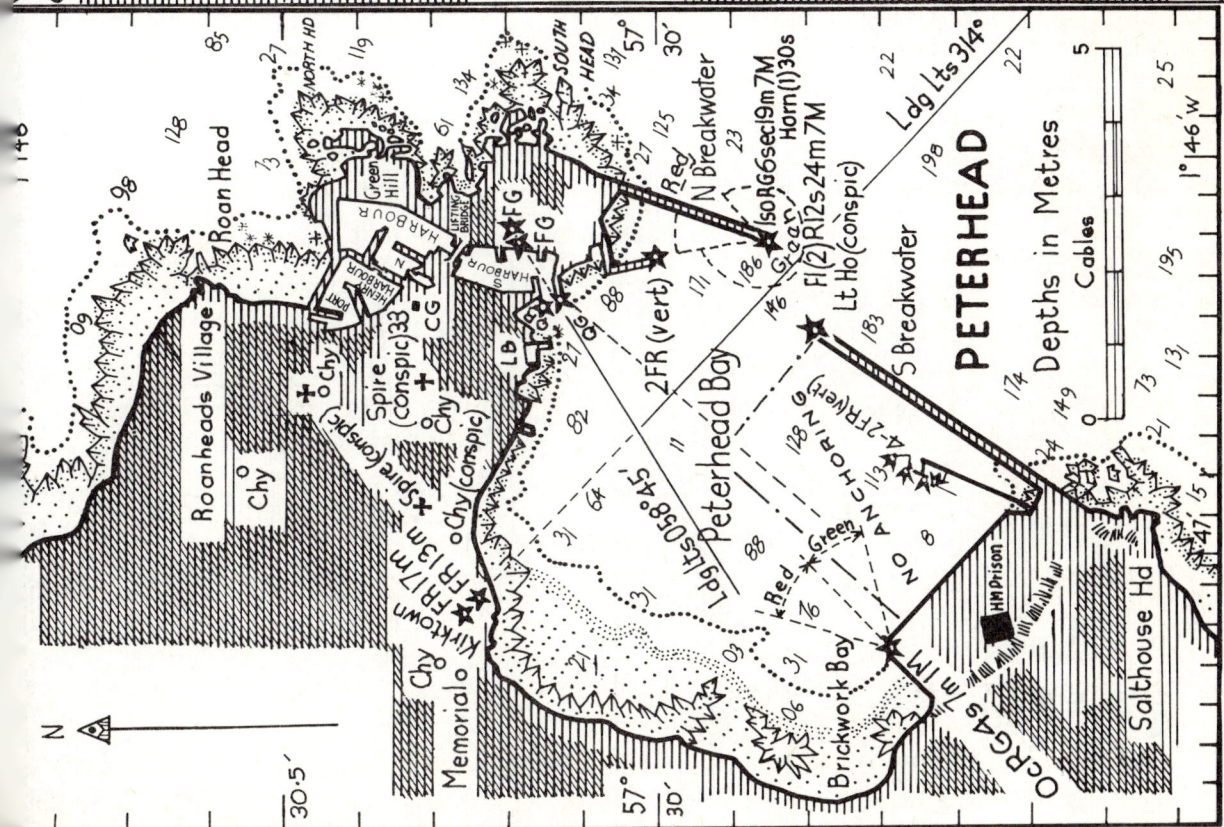

d on British Admiralty Charts (nos. in text) with the permission of the Controller of H.M. Stationery Office and of
Hydrographer of the Navy, and on other sources.

167

WHITEHILLS
Depths in Metres

N

Fl WR 3s (Siren)

BANFF & MACDUFF

Depths in Metres

2 Cables

Ldg Lts 127°

Red

2° 30′

12

Collier Rks

88

The Faw

30·5

White

Green

Macduff

Q G 4m 5M

FR 55m 3M

FR 44m 3M

Cross †

Tr & Dome

O War Memorial (Conspic)

Palmer Cove

N

BANFF BAY

Fl(2)WRG 6s12m9/7M Horn(2)20s

38

06

34

29

34

3·4

2·4

43

Slip

Meavie Pt

40·5

66

38

CG

Sea Town

Banff

57 40′

BUCKIE
Depths in Metres

N 41′

57°

40·9′

2 57w 47′

2° 57w 47′

Bents Pt.

Jetty

Slip

Slip

Slips

QR

No 4

LBZ

HM

No 3

Pier 4

Pier 3

Tr(3)

No 2

No 1

Pier 2

Pier 1

Fl G

Iso WG 2s 30m 16/12M

N Breakwater

Oc R10s 15M Siren(2)6 0s

Fl R 2s

OUTER

HF

West Pier

2 FR(vert)7m 11M

2 FG(vert)

THE NOOK

Green(G)

Fl R 5s 5m 3M

West Muck

Middle Muck

83

8

25

56

56

White

77

38

47

5

44

29

41

32

32

23

29

41

Ldg Lts 125°

1 Cables 2

PORTKNOCKIE
Depths in Metres

N

F

Cable

1

0

Based on British Admiralty Charts (nos. in text) with the permission of the Controller of H.M. Stationery Office and the Hydrographer of the Navy, and on other sources.

FRASERBURGH   Chart BA 1462   (Plan p167)
HW +1.35.   MHWS 3.9; MLWS 0.6; MTL 2.3; MHWN 3.1; MLWN 1.5.
Bar   None: 3½m in the entrance, but it can be dangerous in onshore gales. This is
a very busy fishing port by night and day, but there is usually plenty of room for
visiting yachts, and it is the first good port of call N of Stonehaven.
Approach   The old Parish ch spire just open S of Balaclava Pier 290°, or at night
the FR ldg lts (291°), lead in between the piers.
Berthing   Call HM on VHF 16/12 for instructions, otherwise berth in S hr
alongside SE pier and obtain instructions from HM, office in NE corner.

PASSAGE NOTES: FRASERBURGH TO WICK

Although apparently sheltered, surprisingly heavy seas can be encountered in the
Moray Firth in strong W or NW winds. On the direct passage, a sharp lookout
must be kept for oil rigs and their numerous support vessels. Large-scale charts
are needed if approaching Inverness, but otherwise the area presents no
particular navigational problems.

MACDUFF   Chart BA 1462   (Plan p168)
HW +1.10.   MHWS 3.5; MLWS 0.4; MTL 2.0; MHWN 2.8; MLWN 1.1.
The hr consists of three basins with an entrance 18m wide. Least depth in
entrance chan and basins is 2m. Sheltered in all conditions, but entrance can be
very rough in winds from W to N (see below). Banff then becomes a possible hr
of refuge.
Entrance   A W tr 19m high, Fl(2) WR 6s, is conspic on the head of N pier. Ldg
lts on B and W masts 127° lead through entrance to W basin. This hr should not
be attempted in onshore gales or in heavy swell. When hr is closed a B ball by day
and a G lt by night are shown over breakwater lt.
Berthing   In N-most basin, beyond the line of slipways. VHF 16/14/12. Water on
quays. A busy fishing port and crowded at times. All facilities. EC Wed.

WHITEHILLS   Chart BA 222   (Plan p168)
HW +1.05.   MHWS 3.9; MLWS 0.7; MTL 2.4; MHWN 3.1; MLWN 1.7.
A good hr on the W side of Knock Hd. The entrance faces NW, lt FRG on a W tr
on the pier-head. At night the R sector is the safe approach. Keep close SW of
the pier, leaving two unlit bns to stb, then turn sharply to port into hr.
   There is an outer and inner hr, both with 1.8m in most parts. Berth alongside
as space allows. The outer hr is subject to swell in bad weather. All facilities and
provisions.

PORTKNOCKIE   Chart BA 1462   (Plan p168)
HW +1.00.
Hr has two basins: inner one mostly dries. Entrance 9m wide faces W and has less

than 2.7m. Caution needed in N-ly winds above force 5. Often considerable surge inside.

Berthing Hr much silted especially in middle, quays dilapidated. Moor with long warps across NW or NE corners of outer hr. Check bottom before taking ground.

A FW lt is shown on the S pier and FR ldg lts, Aug to April only. When it is unsafe to enter, an ensign is flown by day and at night the front ldg lt changed from R to G. All stores.

BUCKIE   Chart BA 1462   (Plan p168)
HW +0.55.   MHWS 4.1; MLWS 0.7; MTL 2.4; MHWN 3.2; MLWN 1.6.
A busy fishing port, which can be entered safely in all weathers.

There is usually at least 2.2m in the entrance and inside there is 3m alongside in the four basins, where one should berth as directed (usually in No. 4 basin) or as opportunity offers. Flagpole on S side of entrance shows B ball, or FG and Fl G lts, when depth is less than 3m. Port has VHF chan 16/12, 0900–1700 Mon–Fri, and from 05 to 15 every hour outside these times. All facilities. EC Wed.

LOSSIEMOUTH   Chart BA 1462   (Plan p171)
HW +0.50.   MHWS 4.1; MLWS 0.6; MTL 2.4; MHWN 3.2; MLWN 1.6.
A busy fishing hr easily identified by Covesea Lt Ho at W of town. The hr entrance, 18m wide, faces ESE and should never be approached in bad weather from E or NE. Ldg lts (FR 292°) are shown when entry is safe. B ball on S pier (R over G at night) signifies entrance unsafe.

There is 1.8 to 2.4m in the hr, S basin deepest. After prolonged E-lies, less than 1.8m may be found at entrance.

When entering beware of a current of fresh water from the R Lossie which sets across the hr entrance in a N-ly direction causing confused conditions in bad weather.

HM tel (034-381) 3066. All facilities. EC Wed.

HOPEMAN   Chart BA 1462   (Plan p171)
HW +1.00.   MHWS 4.1; MLWS 0.6; MTL 2.2; MHWN 3.2; MLWN 1.6.
This hr dries to about 0.3m at LWS and entrance is not safe in strong winds. The hr is very popular, and berths are scarce during the season. Beware lobster pot floats and salmon nets in hr approaches.

Approach as shown on plan (2 FG ldg lts at night, 081°, Aug 1 to Apr 30 only) and enter the SW basin, free from swell under all conditions. Or anch about half a ca off, on a line along the S line of the entrance, unsuitable in fresh wind from W or if a big sea is running. Good holding, sand. Excellent chandler at the hr. The town has two hotels, PO and stores. Petrol or diesel from garage.

BURGHEAD   Chart BA 1462   (Plan p171)
HW +1.00.   MHWS 4.1; MLWS 0.6; MTL 2.2; MHWN 3.2; MLWN 1.6.
Hr offers shelter in all winds. Minimum 1.5m LWS at entrance. Berth as directed

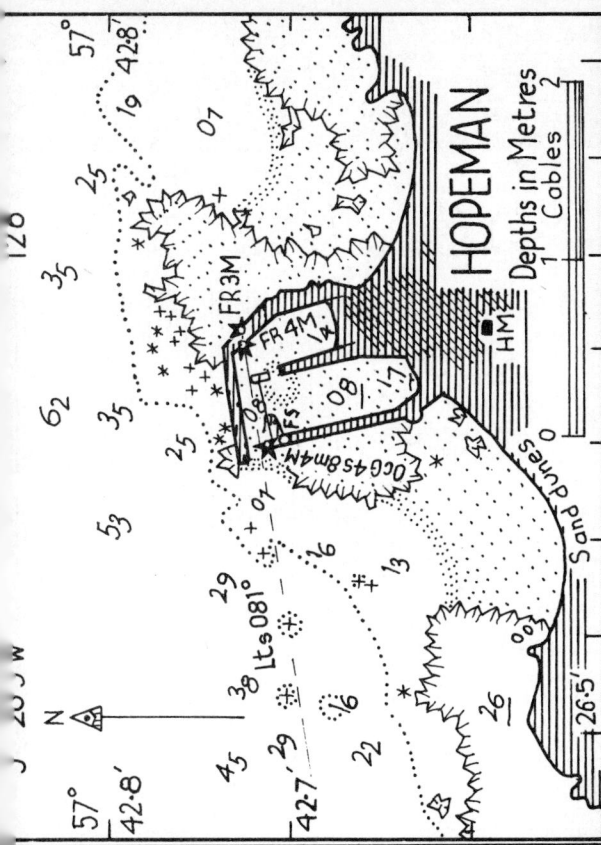

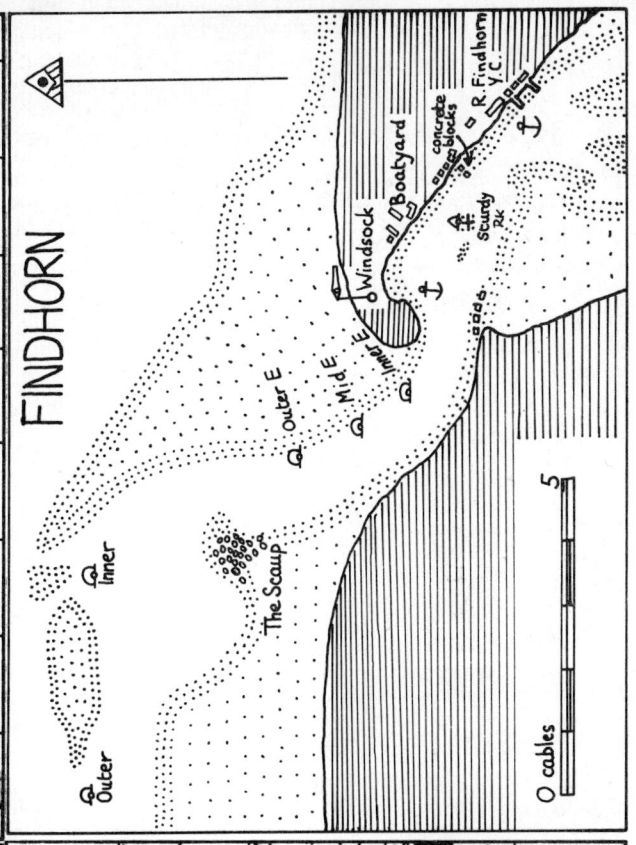

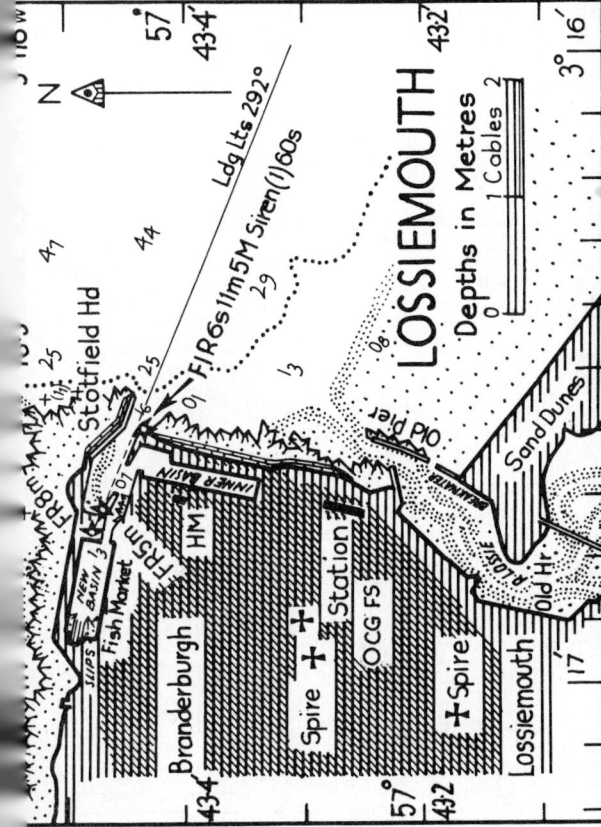

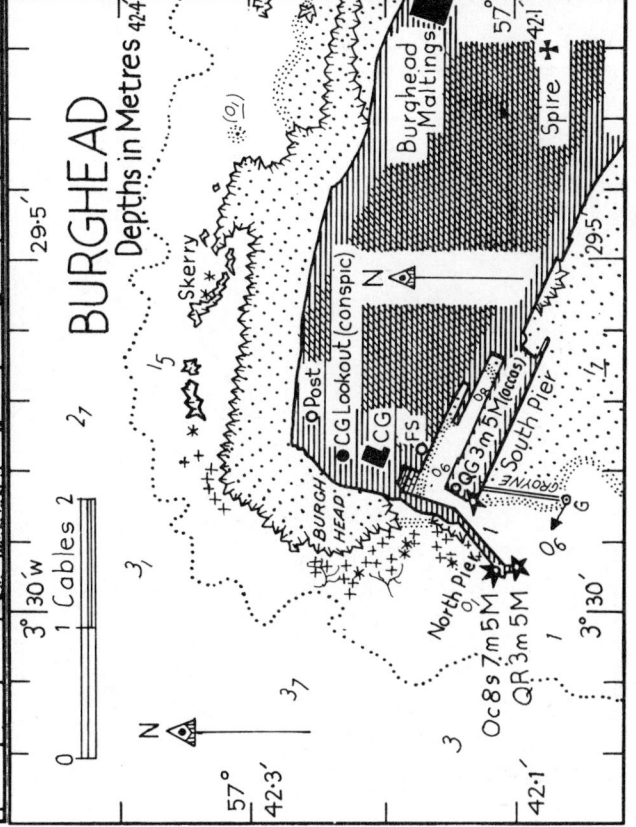

HOPEMAN

FR3M
FR4M
FS
OcG 4s 8m 4M
Lts 081°
Depths in Metres
Cables
Sand dunes
57° 42·8'
57° 42·8'

FINDHORN

R. Findhorn Y.C.
Boatyard
Windsock
Scurdy Rk
Outer E
Mid E
Inner E
Inner
The Scaup
Outer
concrete wavebreaks
5
O cables

LOSSIEMOUTH

Depths in Metres
Cables
Stotfield Hd
Fl R6s 11m 5M Siren(1)60s
Ldg Lts 292°
Old pier
Sand Dunes
Branderburgh
Spire
Station
OcG FS
Spire
Lossiemouth
Fish Market
FR8M
FR5M
HM
INNER BASIN
NEW BASIN
SLIPS
R. LOSSIE
Old Hr
57° 434'
57° 432'
3° 16'

BURGHEAD

Depths in Metres
Burghead Maltings
Spire
Skerry
Post
CG Lookout (conspic)
CG
FS
QG 3m 5M (occas)
South Pier
GROYNE
BURGH HEAD
North Pier
Oc 8s 7m 5M
Q R 3m 5M
Cables
57° 42·3'
57° 42·1'
3° 30' W
3° 30'

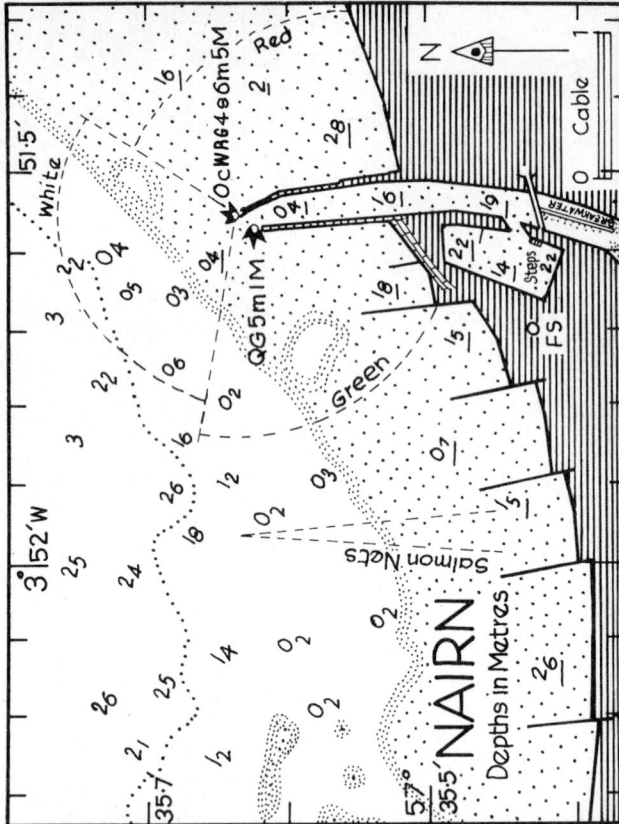

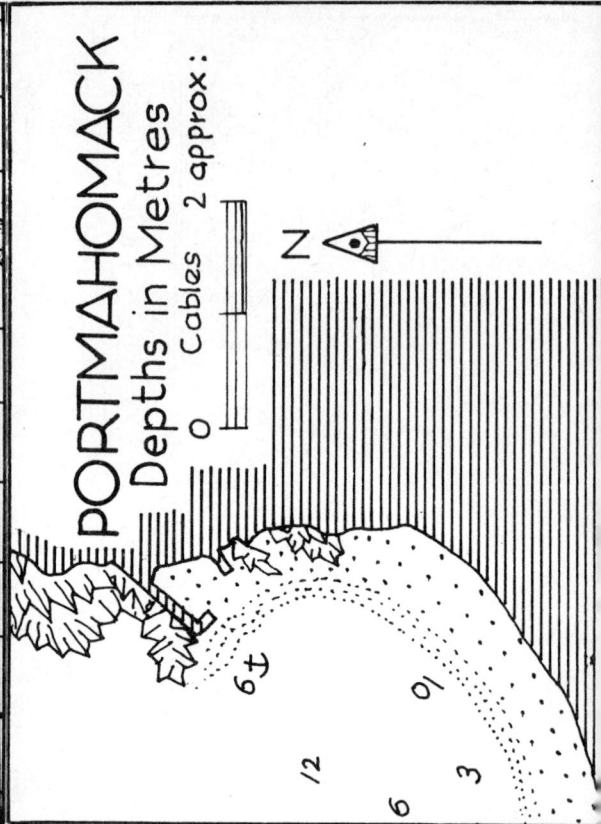

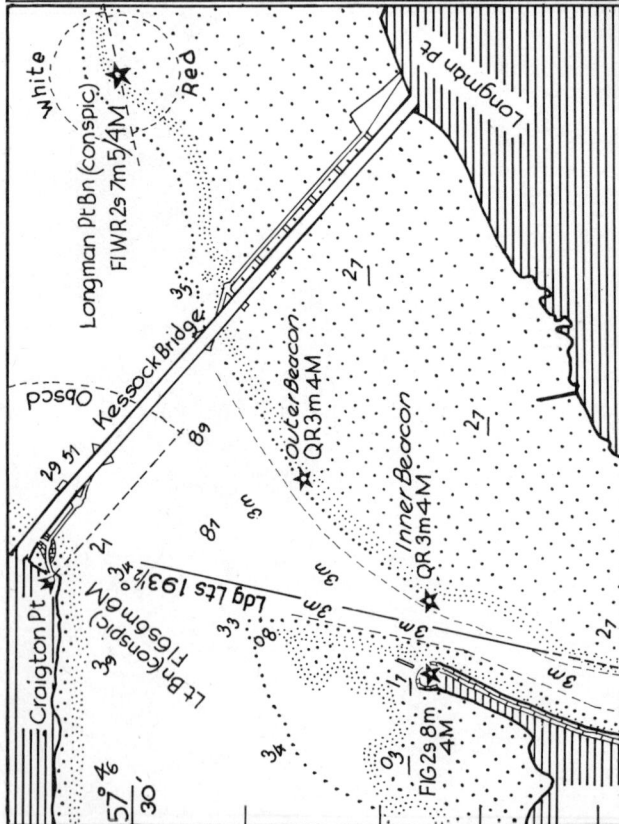

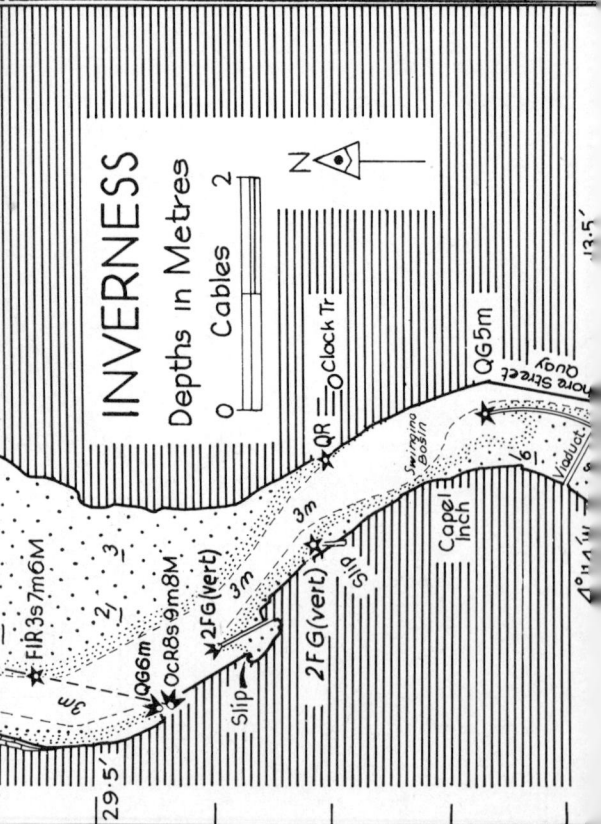

Based on British Admiralty Charts (nos. in text) with the permission of the Controller of H.M. Stationery Office and the Hydrographer of the Navy, and on other sources.

or as far up basin as possible but never on N side of S pier, reserved for large vessels. On entering hr keep 15m off wooden extension to N pier-head, then turn in and keep in mid-chan. At night, identify outer pier lts, then keep the G lt on S pier open S of the R on N pier-head extension. Tide gauge at side of entrance shows depth in main basin. Swell can be considerable at times.

Stores, hotels, chandlers, water, diesel, petrol. Bus to Elgin and Forres. HM may agree to keep an eye on vessels left in hr. HM tel (034-361) 337 (nights 317).

FINDHORN
Chart BA 223   (Plan p171)

HW +1.10.   MHWS 4.1; MLWS 0.6; MTL 2.2; MHWN 3.2; MLWN 1.6.
Caution   In view of frequent changes to the entrance, intending visitors are advised to ring Royal Findhorn YC, tel Findhorn (030 93) 247, for advice.
The village is conspic at the W side of Burghead Bay. There is a windsock E of ent.
Bar   Shifts constantly, tending to extend to W. Buoyage is unreliable.
Approach   Do not attempt in N winds above force 4. Outer Bay buoy, orange with W vertical stripes, lies nearly a mile WNW of the windsock.
Entrance   Leave Outer Bar buoy close to port and make for Inner, curving a little S of the direct line as chan is shoal right out to this line. Leave Inner close to port, and steer approx 148° for three buoys off E point of entrance (but appearing beneath W point). Leave them close to port, and a final buoy, marked 'Danger' to stb, to avoid the Sturdy bank. Do not turn off before coming close to the Inner Bar, to be sure of missing the Scaup bank.
Anchorage   Off boatyard in deep pool E of line between windsock and the Sturdy. Early ebb runs strongly, NW eddy for most of flood. Boats prepared to take ground can anch off piers or dry alongside. *Caution:* a line of concrete blocks runs out to LW line between boatyard and piers; outermost blocks cover at HW. Anchorage prohibited between these blocks and the piers.
Stores, PO, boatyard, water from tap by clubhouse near N pier. EC Wed.

NAIRN
Chart BA 1462   (Plan p172)

HW +1.00.   MHWS 4.3; MLWS 0.7; MTL 2.2; MHWN 3.3; MLWN 1.6.
Bar   Sand bar at entry to river. Shingle bar in chan. Yachts up to 0.9m draft can remain afloat at neaps at river jetties near mouth except with winds from NW through N to E. Complete shelter in drying basin under any conditions for vessels up to 3m draft. The chan entrance faces NNE. Beware lobster pot floats and salmon stake nets in approaches.
Approach   There is a conspic W octagonal lt tr on end of breakwater. Enter closer to W breakwater. When well inside cross to E breakwater until abreast W square mark on pile face. Thence into basin, hugging N side of chan. Do not attempt entry within 2h of LW. Entering over the sand bar with little water to spare, moor to the E breakwater and wait for tide. No anch inside jetties or basin. Deepest water at root of yacht mooring pontoon just inside N side of basin entrance.
Stores, diesel, chandlery, PO, YC. EC Wed.

INVERNESS
Charts BA 1077, 1078   (Plan p172)

HW +1.15.   MHWS 4.8; MLWS 0.7; MTL 2.7; MHWN 3.7; MLWN 1.8.

Approach   Moray Firth is crowded: vigilance essential at all times especially in bad visibility. Pass under bridge $\frac{1}{3}$ of its length from NW end. Get W triangle on pole in river in line with W triangle behind warehouse. Entry is very narrow but deep. Beware strong cross-sets, violent near springs. Once past the G Fl lt on the point, keep about 10 to 15m off the W bank, then cross diagonally to E bank once past the jetty on the W bank.

Entrance and berthing   After crossing to the E bank keep close inshore and pass E of jetty projecting N from the bridge – i.e. leave it to stb, in spite of its Fl R lt – proceed past moored coasters and moor 20–30m short of the bridge, alongside or to another vessel. Keep as far as possible off the training wall, especially near HW, as it slopes outwards under water. HM office is just over the br. Most helpful and will ring the canal if proceeding there. All stores within 1M. EC Wed.

PORTMAHOMACK
Chart BA 223   (Plan p172)

HW +0.50.   MHWS 4.1; MLWS 0.7; MTL 2.4; MHWN 3.3; MLWN 1.7.

This anch and hr lie on the S side of the entrance to Dornoch Firth. The hr dries out but anch off the pier in 2m offers shelter from E to SW winds. The anch is uncomfortable in SW to W winds when shelter may be obtained on the other side of the bay off the rks. Avoid patches of kelp as in some instances they hide large boulders marked on the anch chart. These boulders have 0.3m at LWS. The Curach Rk (dr 0.8m) lies WSW of the pier 2 ca out and is opposite the last house W of the Caledonian Hotel. A large boulder lies about $\frac{1}{2}$ ca off the pier with the NW corner of the pier in line with the small observation hut on the hill. Poorly marked stake nets are set about 2 ca NE of the hr from February until end of August. During these months it is advisable to bring the hr abeam before closing it. Two hotels, PO keeps most stores. Petrol or diesel $\frac{3}{4}$M on the Tain road.

HELMSDALE
Chart BA 1462   (Plan p175)

HW +0.35.   MHWS 3.7; MLWS 0.6; MTL 2.2; MHWN 2.9; MLWN 1.5.

A very good hr but should not be entered in E gales.

Bar   There is a sand bar at the entrance with about $2\frac{1}{2}$m at half-tide.

Entrance   Ldg marks (313°) are two W poles near the base of the W pier. At night Monday to Saturday inclusive, when boats drawing 1.2m can enter, a G lt on the seaward pole and a R lt on the landward pole will be shown by arrangement. (HM tel Helmsdale (043 12) 274). When there is enough water for larger vessels a R lt is shown on each pole.

Berthing   Berth in new hr alongside wall. All facilities. EC Wed.

LYBSTER
Chart BA 115   (Plan p175)

HW +0.20.   MHWS 3.5; MLWS 0.5; MTL 2.1; MHWN 2.8; MLWN 1.4.

A pier hr with inner and outer basin $2\frac{1}{2}$M WSW of Clyth Ness. Excellent refuge

HELMSDALE
Depths in Metres

E PIER
CG(FS)
Horn(1)30s
NEW HARBOUR
N.W PIER
FG(R.W.Fl.R)
N
(conspic)
Breakwater (ruins)
Post pillar
Old Stone Quay
Old Hr
6·9
21
09
0·2
18
15
24
18
21
Ldg Lts 313°
31
313°

58°
67'
58°
67'
38·5'
39'

Cables
0   1   2
1 Cables   2'

3°
3'

LYBSTER
Depths in Metres

INNER HARBOUR
1·8m
Basin
OUTER Hr
OcR6s
N
0   1
Cables

WICK
Depths in Metres

N
North Head
Proudfoot Rk
14·3
4·3
Memorial Tr(conspic)
Green
White
125
Bell(2)10S (Fishing)
Fl.WRG 12m 5/3M
Ldg Lts 234°
234°
FR
31
27
8
Bn(1)
3
24
3
3
3
27
21
0·3
Water of wick
River Pier
River Hr
Louisburgh
Slip
Jetty (ruins)
NORTH PIER
Inner Hr
1·8
1·8 Bn
4
Harbour
Quay
HM
Customs
Outer Hr
FR5m
FR8m
2FR (vert)
Spire(28) (conspic)
Burn Quay
Weir
2·4
1·2
2·4
1·8
Cables
0   1   2

58°
26·5
26·5'
26·3'
3°4'W
3°5'W
4'

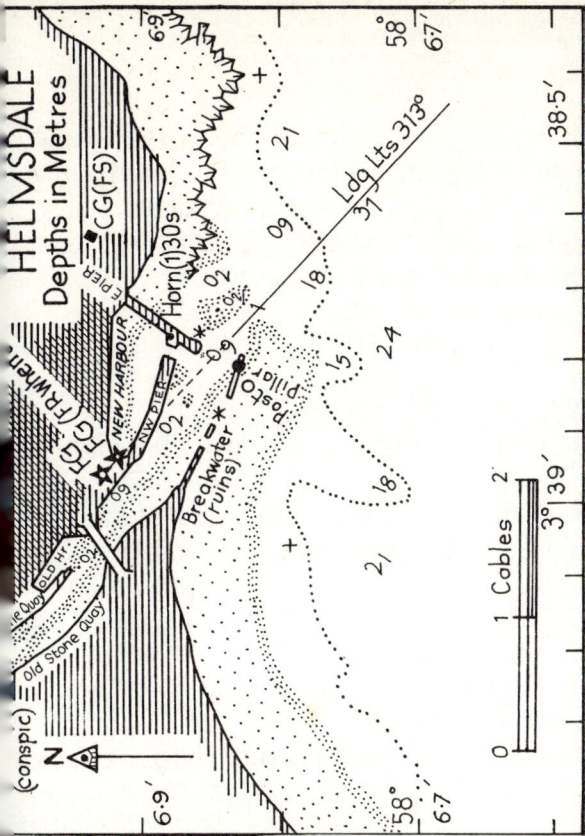

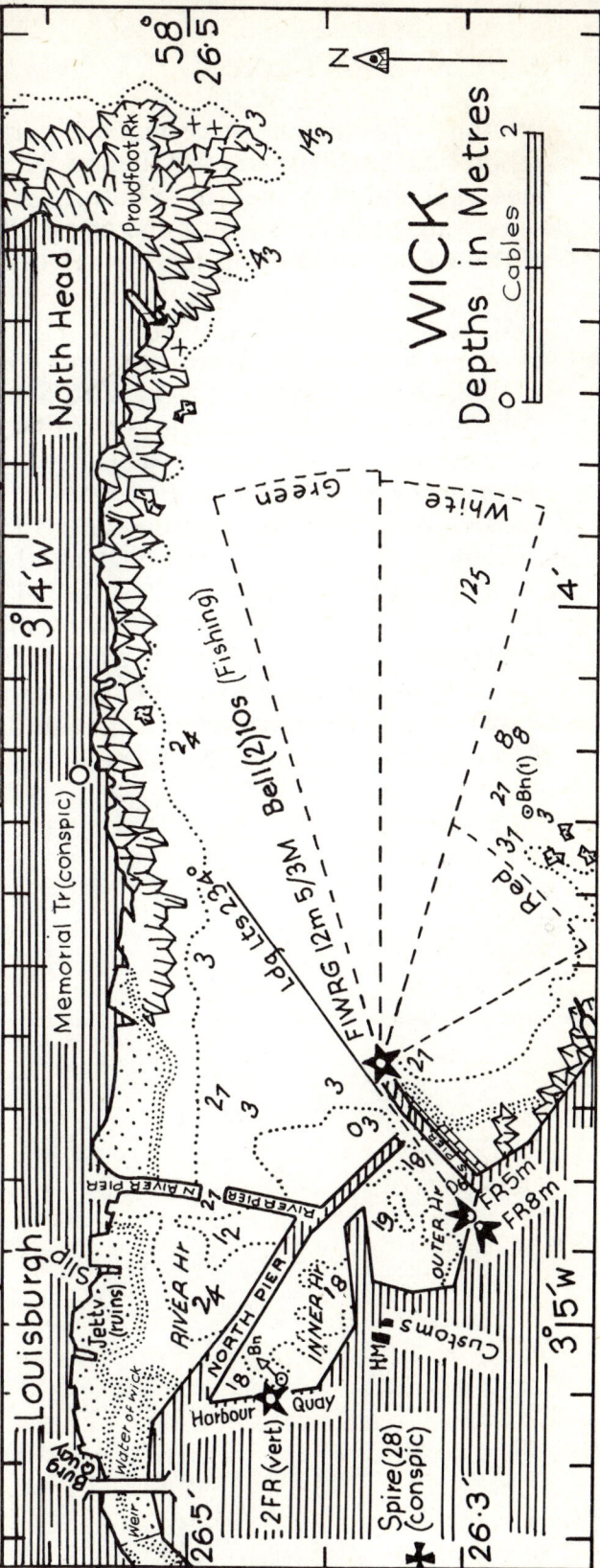

British Admiralty Charts (nos. in text) with the permission of the Controller of H.M. Stationery Office and of

rographer of the Navy, and on other sources.

175

although entrance must be made accurately. Approach W pier-head (FR on W tr) on between 350° and 005°T, and keep close in to this pier into hr. Berth on E side of N end of W pier, or in better shelter in SE corner of basin (W part dries).

Beware of being swept into rks on stb side of entry and first pier on stb side. Entry can be difficult in E gales. Hotel, stores ½M, EC Thurs.

WICK   Chart BA 1462   (Plan p175)
HW +0.30.   DS off Wick Bay: S −5.00; N +1.10.
MHWS 3.4; MLWS 0.5; MTL 2.0; MHWN 2.7; MLWN 1.4.
A busy oil and commercial as well as fishing port, without much room for yachts. Charges are high for the area. Entrance dangerous in strong E winds.
Approach and entrance   The hr lies at the hd of Wick Bay and is not seen until the bay is opened up. Approach the Lt Ho on the S pier (W tower) on between 285° and 270° (in W sector at night) and pass close N of it, then enter parallel with the N face of the S pier (ldg lts FR, 234°). Three B balls (or FG lt at night) from FS at Lookout House on S Head signifies hr closed.
Berthing   As space allows or as directed. Outer hr uncomfortable in E winds; over 2m in both. Avoid River Hr: dries, rough bottom.

All stores and fuel, water from standpipe opposite HM's office. Slip, repairs. EC Wed.

Orkney

The Clyde Cruising Club publish extensive *Sailing Directions* for Orkney and Shetland, detailing many anchs not included in this *Handbook*, and these SDs should be carried by anyone intending to cruise the islands. The anchs included here have been selected on the basis of accessibility and suitability as passage ports. In general, avoid western entrances during W-going stream against tide; eastern entrances become difficult with SE wind against tide.

STROMNESS   Chart BA 2568   (Plan p178)
HW −1.30.   MHWS 3.4; MLWS 0.4; MTL 2.0; MHWN 2.6; MLWN 1.4.
One of the most sheltered ports in the North of Scotland. Least water in hr 4.3m. No tidal stream in hr.
Approach   Through Hoy Sd from the W or from Scapa Flow, passing E of Switha and through Switha Sd. Very strong tides in approaches: entrance should not be made in bad weather with wind against tide. Easiest entrance from W with flood tide and keeping slightly to Hoy side. Ensure bn (Fl 4s) is well open to clear Kirk Rks. Keep Hoy Sd (low) and Is of Graemsay (high) Lt Hos in transit until Holms and chan buoys sighted.
Entrance   There are two ldg marks in the centre of the town, painted W and showing FR lts at night 317°. These lead up the hr between a pair of chan buoys.
Anchorage   As directed, or just to E of Ro-Ro ferry terminal, or moor alongside on of the piers if space available. Fuel and water. Good shopping centre. Orkney Hr Radio listens Ch 16, working 20, 9, 11.

KIRKWALL   Chart BA 1553   (Plan p178)
HW −0.15.   MHWS 2.9; MLWS 0.4; MTL 1.7; MHWN 2.2; MLWN 1.1.
Principal town of Orkney. Spire of St Magnus Cathedral conspic.
Approach and entrance   When entering by String hold course until Cathedral bears 190° when turn and enter on this bearing. By night via String, navigation is straightforward using lt sectors. Tide negligible in Kirkwall Bay.
Berthing   Berth in inner hr, well sheltered although there is a surge at the entrance in W-ly gales. Fl lt on outer pier-head, R and G lts at entrance to inner hr. Plenty of water at N end of W pier and N end of E side of inner basin. Deep water along whole of main pier outside. Safe anch for small yachts between the W pier-head and Crowness Pt to the W.
  All facilities. Flights to mainland. EC Wed.

SHAPINSAY   Chart BA 2584
HW −0.15.   MHWS 2.9; MHWN 2.2.
An easily accessible alternative anch to Kirkwall, and much more peaceful, is to be found in Ellwick Bay off the village of Balfour.

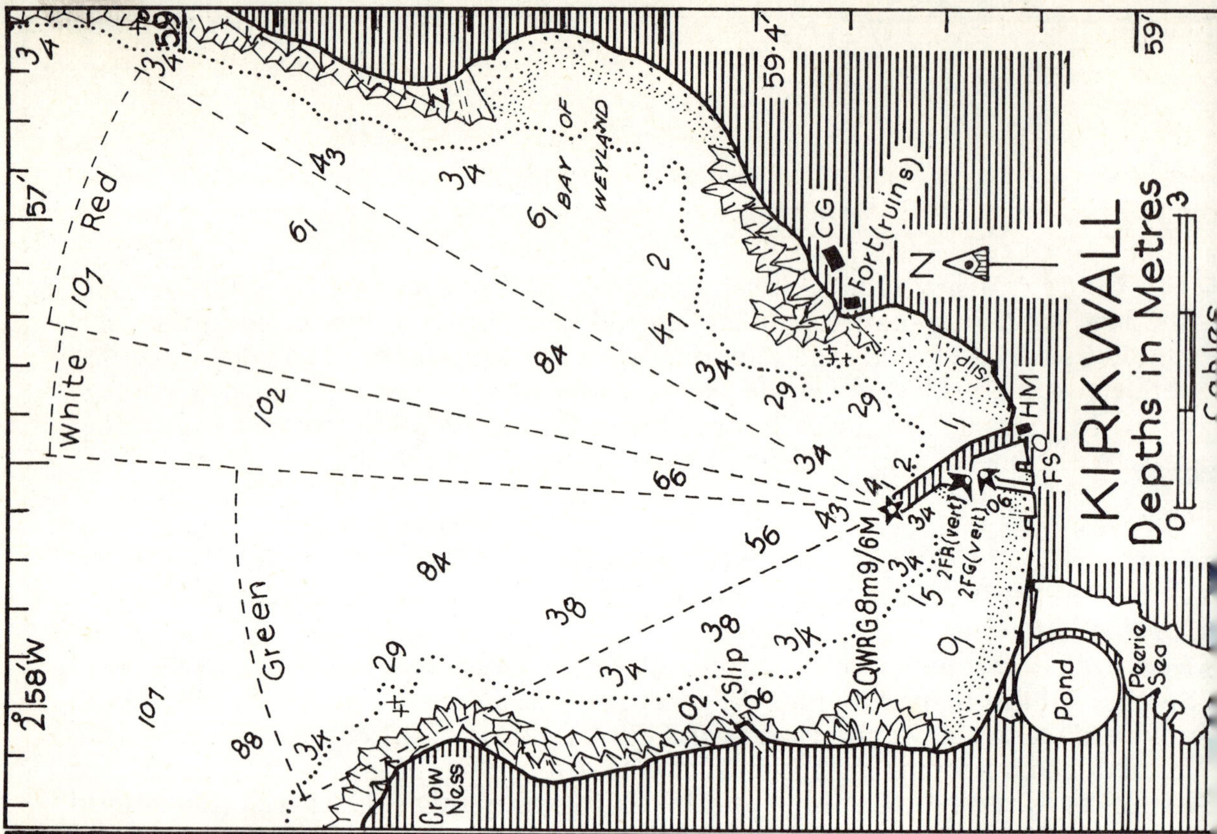

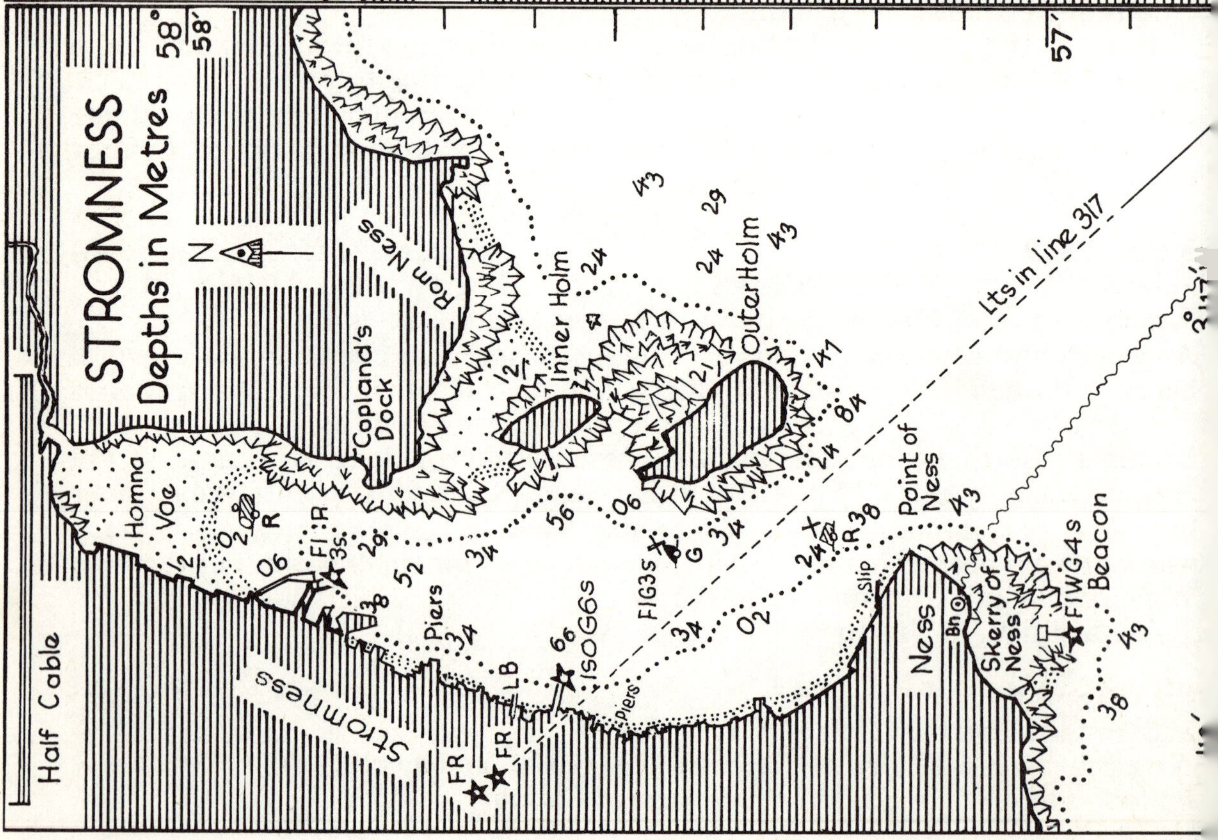

KIRKWALL
Depths in Metres

59·4

BAY OF WEYLAND

Red

White

Green

QWRG 8m9/6M

2FR(vert)
2FG(vert)

CG

Fort(ruins)

N

HM

FS

Peerie Sea

Pond

Slip

Crow Ness

Cables

STROMNESS
Depths in Metres

58°
58'

N

Rom Ness

Copland's Dock

Homna Voe

R

FI R
3s

Piers

Stromness

FR

FR FI LB

ISO G 6s

6s

FI G 3s

G

Inner Holm

Outer Holm

Point of Ness

Ness

Skerry of Ness

Slip

Bn

FI W G 4s
Beacon

Lts in line 317

Half Cable

Based on British Admiralty Charts (nos. in text) with the permission of the Controller of H.M. Stationery Office an the Hydrographer of the Navy, and on other sources.

WHITEHALL Hr, STRONSAY

Depths in Metres

0 Half Cable 0·5

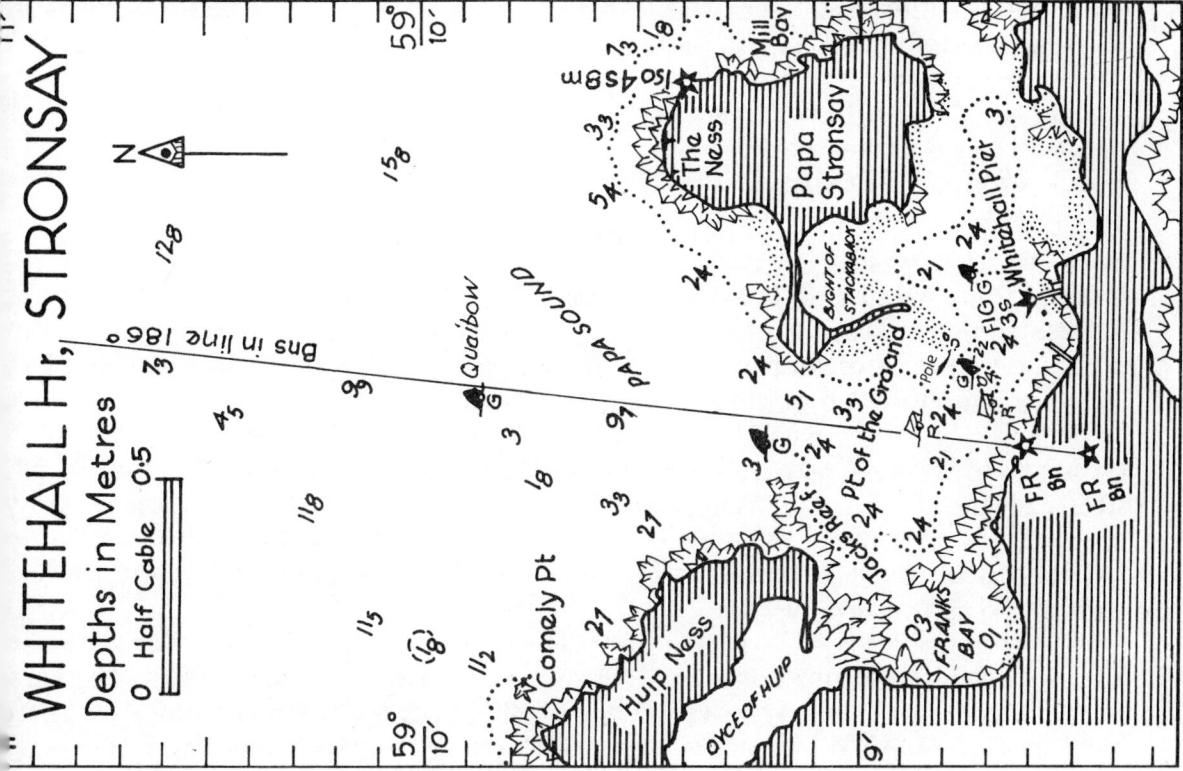

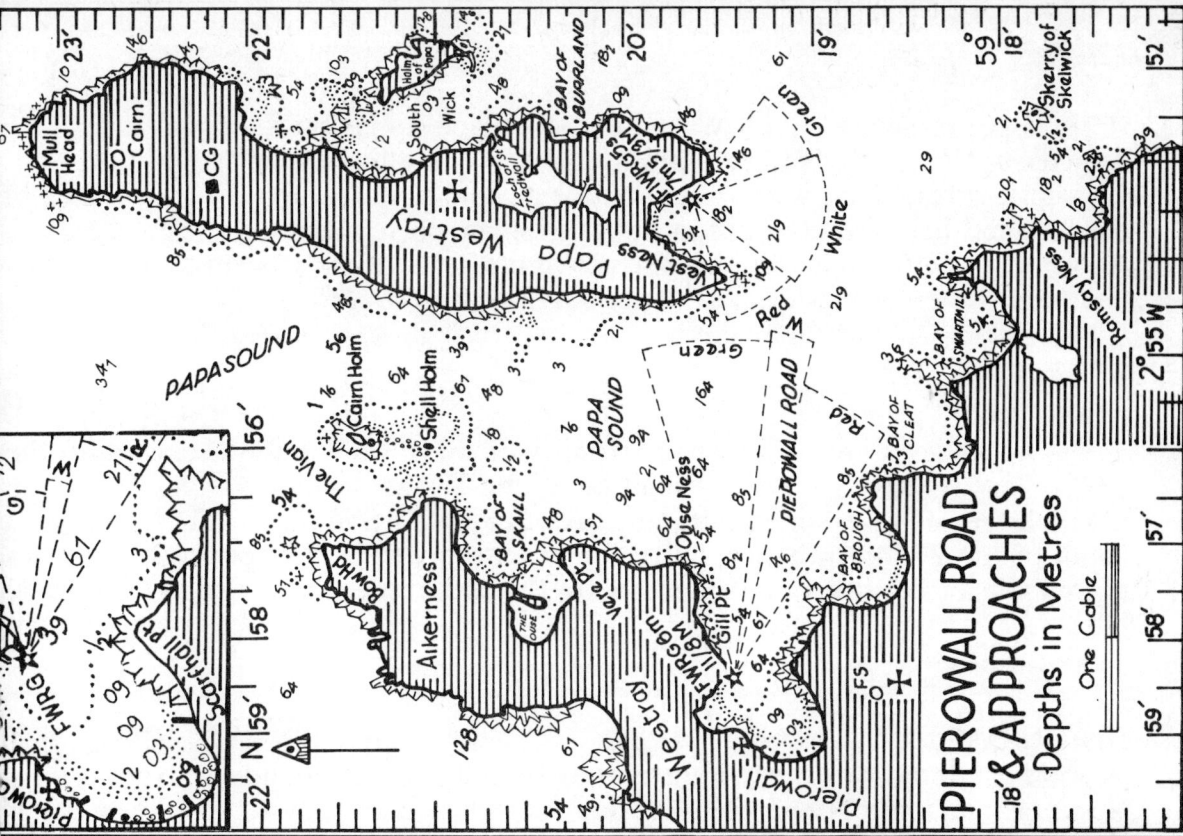

N

PAPA SOUND

Bns in line 186°

Quaiebow

Comely Pt

Huip Ness

OYCE OF HUIP

FRANKS BAY

Iso 45 8m

The Ness

Papa Stronsay

Mill Bay

BIGHT OF STACKABACK

Whitehall Pier

FlG G

Pole

So 24 Pt of the Ground

Westray Pt Rocks

FR Bn

FR Bn

PIEROWALL ROAD & APPROACHES

Depths in Metres

One Cable

Mull Head

Cairn

CG

South Holm Wick

BAY OF BURRLAND

West Ness

Papa Westray

Fl WRG 5s 7m 5·9M

Graand

White

Red

Green

PIEROWALL ROAD

BAY OF SWARTMILL

BAY OF CLEAT

BAY OF BROUGH

Skarry of Skelwick

Rapness

PAPA SOUND

Cairn Holm

Shell Holm

The Vian

BAY OF SKAILL

THE HOLE

Aikerness

Bowmore

Oyse Ness

Gill Pt

Fl WR G 8m

Westray

Pierowall

FS

Scarthill

FWRG

---

on British Admiralty Charts (nos. in text) with the permission of the Controller of H.M. Stationery Office and of ...drographer of the Navy, and on other sources.

179

Tides in the String (flood W and ebb E) reach a maximum of 5kn at sp.
Approach Entering from Shapinsay Sd leave Helliar Holm (Lt Ho) to stb. Balfour Castle and the wood behind it are a prominent feature. The bay is free of dangers and has a sandy bottom but there is much seaweed on the fringes.
Anchorage Off village in 2½–3m, or anywhere in bay according to wind direction. Berth alongside pier depending on draft.

PO, petrol from garage, shop.

AUSKERRY   Chart BA 2179
This small Is lies in the entrance to Stronsay Firth. It is uninhabited except for the Lt Ho keepers and has a very small hr on the W side.

The hr is safe to enter in summer except in strong SW winds. There is a least depth of 1.2m alongside pier, and 3.7m in entrance. The best berth is with lines to ringbolts either side of entrance and to the end of pier. No room to turn inside hr.

No facilities.

STRONSAY   Chart BA 2622   (Plan p179)
A good sheltered hr off the village of Whitehall, at the N end of Stronsay.
Approach By the N chan leaving Jacks Reef G con buoy to stb; keep the R shore bns in line, 186°. Leave the next R buoy to port and head towards hr leaving Grampie Bank G con buoy to stb. The hr is made up of two piers, E pier lit. Do not attempt the E entrance without local knowledge.
Anchorage In 3m between seaward ends of piers. Suitable anch may be found around bay. Refer to HM.

PO. Provisions in village. Petrol from garage. Hotel.

PIEROWALL, WESTRAY   Chart BA 2622   (Plan p179)
HW −1.20.   MHWS 3.7; MLWS 0.6; MTL 2.1; MHWN 2.8; MLWN 1.4.
Fairly strong tides run through Papa Sd between Westray and Papa Westray, but at the open mouth of Pierowall Bay the tide is negligible. Tides in Westray Firth are approximately 2 h behind those at Pierowall.
Approach *From W, via Papa Sd* Clear Noup Head Lt by 1M, then steer 070° for Mull Hd, Papa Westray. When Bow Hd on Westray bears 190° distant 0.7M, steer 122° for Old Kirk on W shore of Papa Westray. When Fitty Hill on Westray bears 215° alter course onto this bearing. When Pierowall Bay opens and Noup Hd bears 280° enter on this bearing. *Note*: Papa Sd is slightly tricky; safer to err on Papa Westray side of chan.

Via Weather Ness Clear Brough Hd Lt by 1M, then steer 065°. When Sacquoy, Saviskaill and Faraclett Hds are in transit, steer 083°. There are very strong tides here. When Wart Holm bears 280°, steer 044°. Pass through Weather Ness in mid-chan. When clear, steer 338° for Moclett Hd on Papa Westray. Continue course till Noup Hd bears as above. If wind is strong N or NE, Weather

Ness chan can be rough. Good anch in lee of Weather Ness near small boat moorings on W side of bay.

Anchorage   50m off Gill pier, close to moorings, depth never less than 3.7m, or on W side of bay off moorings least depth 1.8m (nearer village). Deep water alongside Gill pier but steamer lies in the W berth on Wed nights and at weekends. (*Note*: lt on Gill pier is very weak in comparison with other lts nearby.)

Village is on W shore of bay. All facilities, hotel. Flights to Kirkwall. Water at Gill pier from fish factory. Every assistance from Norman Cooper, Schoolhouse, Pierowall, tel 53.

Shetland

The Clyde Cruising Club *Sailing Directions* detail over 50 anchs and should be carried by anyone cruising the islands. The anchs described in this *Handbook* have been selected as passage ports giving ease of access and facilities for yachtsmen.

The Shetland Islands form an excellent cruising ground but certain precautions have to be taken that would not be necessary further S. A close watch must be kept on the barometer and weather indications and forecasts, as it is easy to anchor in an idyllic bay on a fine evening, and wake to find that it has turned into a lee shore overnight, with a howling SE wind increasing every minute.

Many anchorages have heavy weed, where a Fisherman or Bruce tends to hold better than a CQR, unless the latter is of 30kg or more. There is very little mud, most anchs having sand, gravel or clay bottom. Fortunately the water is usually so clear that it is easy to drop the anchor on a suitable spot.

FAIR ISLE (Plan p182)
The island has the good and secure hr of North Haven on its NE side. In NE winds it is uncomfortable, but quite safe in summer. (*Note*: the so-called South Hr is full of rks and should not be approached at any time without expert local knowledge, nor should the place marked on the chart as 'Usual landing place'.) Lie alongside the lee of the pier, best outside a fishing boat, 2m, or anch between the pier and stack, clear of the moored mail boat *Good Shepherd*. The ldg marks for entering are the Stack of North Haven in transit with the top of Sheep Craig, 199°.

When approaching Shetland keep at least 3M off Sumburgh Hd to clear the notorious 'roost' (race), which is worse by far than anything to be found in English waters. Even the Vikings were in dread of it and mentioned it in their sagas. A 7kn tide running in the face of a NW swell coming from Greenland is not to be trifled with. However, if proceeding from Lerwick 'round the heads' to Scalloway it is possible to dodge the roost by keeping inside it, close under Sumburgh Hd.

LERWICK
Depths in Metres

Cables

N

1°18'W

Bressay

Gardie Ho (conspic)

OcWRG 6s6m5M

Green

Red

Anchoring Prohibited

SOUTH HARBOUR

White

SOUND

Q 6+LFl.15s

LOOFA BAA

VB

F13S

QR

Ldg Bn 027°

BAY OF HEOGANES

Bn Pier (Bollards)

oFS

(Ruins)

Bn

Bn

Bn (Bollards)

MIDDLE GROUND

BRESSAY

NORTH GROUND HARBOUR

FR & FIR 3s (vert)

Fl(2)G.10s

6 G

L Flg

G

Fl(2)R.8s

FIR3S

FIR3S

QG

53

4

Bn

B

OcWR6s27m8M

(Ruins)

Pt of Sodland

QR

A

R

B

QG

G

W

R

Green

White

2FR(vert)

2FR(vert)

QR5m1M

F13S

FIR3S

2FG(vert)

2FG(vert)

Iso WG 6s4m3M

HM

po'ts

Housa (conspic)

FS

Clock Tr (conspic)

Radio Mast

F S CG

CG

South Ness

Fl(6s8m6M)

146

The Knab

Spire (Grand Hotel) (conspic)

Lerwick

BREI WICK

1°16'W

9'

FAIR ISLE
Depths in Metres

N

Cables

1°37'W

1°36'

Stacks of North Haven in line with Sheep Craig 199°

Skerry of Grindoline

The Nizz

274

Cristal Kame

Mopul

256

Cubbi Skerry

438

Stacks of Wirvie

North Haven

128

91

11

5

N.Gavel

274

Bu Ness

493

S. Gavel

3347

Goorh

Ramni Geo 493

SOUTH HAVEN

Bn

8

24

181

23

37

Sheep Craig

274

365

7 The Ruff

9

9

29

Stack of N. Haven

Radio Mast (216)

Fl(2)30s80m23M

SKROO

Oa Stack

25

31

164

Stacks of Skroo

31

274

48

Stack of North Haven in transit with Sheep Craig

59 33'

32'

Based on British Admiralty Charts (nos. in text) with the permission of the Controller of H.M. Stationery Office and the Hydrographer of the Navy, and on other sources.

URA FIRTH
(or HILLSWICK)
Depths in Metres

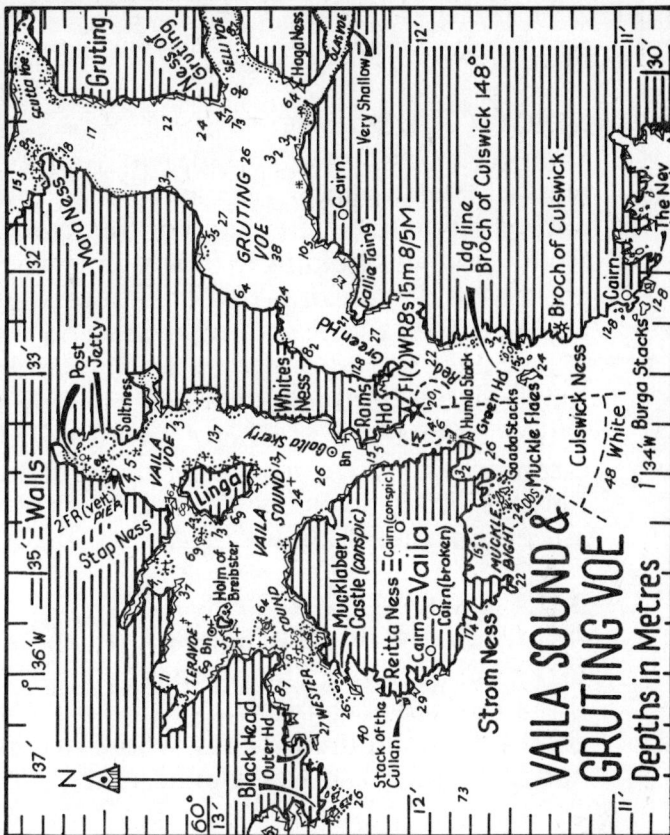

VAILA SOUND & GRUTING VOE
Depths in Metres

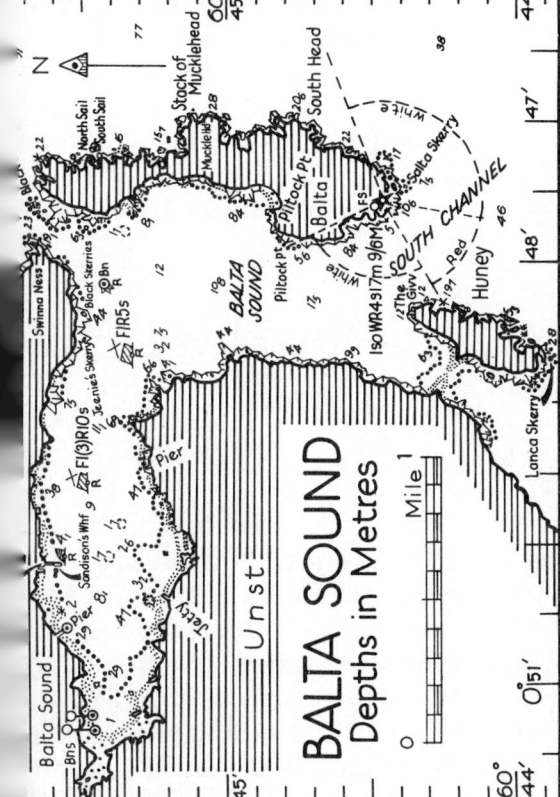

BALTA SOUND
Depths in Metres

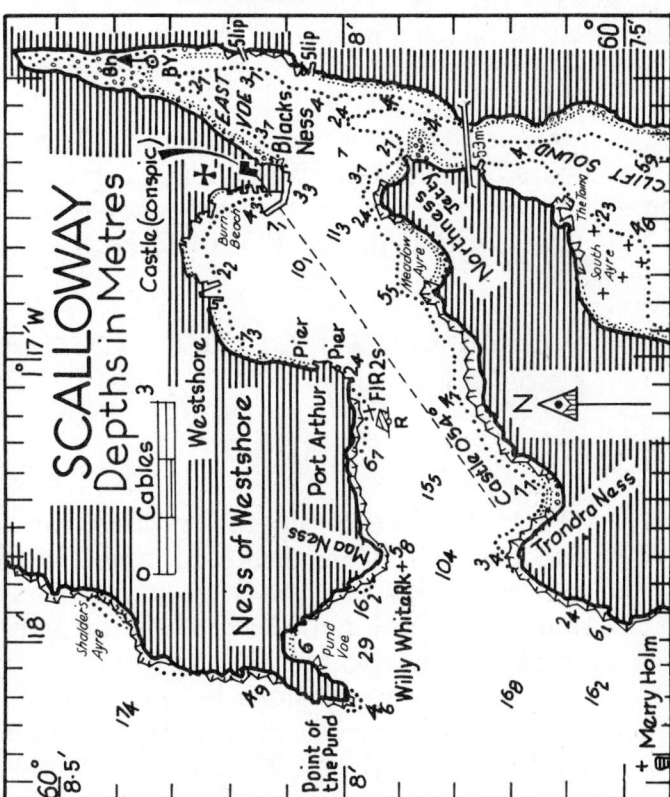

SCALLOWAY
Depths in Metres

British Admiralty Charts (nos. in text) with the permission of the Controller of H.M. Stationery Office and of
grapher of the Navy, and on other sources.

183

LERWICK HR   (Plan p182)

Convenient and easy to enter as the approach is funnel-shaped and the 183m cliffs of Bressay and Noss can be seen from a long way off. Although temporary anch is possible off the S end of the town, the bottom is a thin layer of sand over stones and the holding is not good. The HM usually berths yachts in a quiet corner inside the breakwater where they are safe and unlikely to drag their anchors. Best to tie up temporarily on arrival and seek his advice.

If forced to run down on to Shetland with a NW-ly gale it is wiser to take refuge in one of the hrs leading off St Magnus Bay rather than attempt Yell Sd with its fierce tides. The *Admiralty Tidal Atlas* for Orkney and Shetland is essential. There are good slips and repair facilities at Lerwick and Scalloway. EC Lerwick Wed, Scalloway Thurs. Yachtsmen are welcomed everywhere. Cranes at Lerwick and Scalloway.

BALTA SOUND (UNST)   Chart BA 1122   (Plan p183)

Approach by the S Channel, which is 3 ca wide and clear of dangers in mid-channel, though heavy seas occur in the ent in strong SE winds. Turn W into Balta Hr, and anch off the N shore a cable or so W of Sandison's Wharf in 4–8m, good holding in mud, or elsewhere according to wind. Water, diesel, boatyard, hotel. Shop, PO at Baltasound ($\frac{1}{4}$M).

URA FIRTH   Chart BA 606   (Plan p183)

The S-facing entrance at the NE end of St Magnus Bay is wide and clear, and can be entered in all weathers. Keep well to the middle of the Firth, then turn into Hamar Voe or Hills Wick. The former is best anch but no supplies; anch in main pool after narrow $\frac{1}{2}$M ent chan, 4–10m. Do not attempt to go further without chart BA 606. For Hills Wick, keep in mid-Firth until the bay is well open, then enter steering W for the middle of the bay. Anch in 4–6m, poor holding. Hotel, stores, water, diesel, PO, engineer and radio repairs.

North Coast of Scotland – Duncansby Head to Cape Wrath

PASSAGE NOTES

The N coast of Scotland stretches for some 60M in a more or less E to W direction. There are three prominent headlands along the coast: Dunnet Hd, the most northerly pt of the Scottish mainland, Strathy Pt and Whiten Hd. There are numerous small sandy bays along the coast which can be used for temporary anch in offshore winds, but they are highly dangerous if the wind moves towards to N and a careful watch must be maintained since wind changes are often sudden.

In winds above force 7, only two anchs are approachable with safety: Loch Eriboll in the W and Thurso Bay (Scrabster) in the E. The latter is difficult to enter with winds from the NE, when shelter can be obtained in Dunnet Bay, behind Dunnet Hd. The Clyde Cruising Club *Sailing Directions (N and NE Scotland)* offer excellent advice, and should be carried if cruising in the area.

THE PENTLAND FIRTH   Chart BA 2162

The passage from the E coast through the Pentland Firth is hazardous, and must only be attempted in winds of force 4 or less (not above 3 if W-ly), with good visibility and nowhere near spring tides (i.e. less than 5m range at Dover). Local advice should be sought: the RNLI coxwains at Wick and Scrabster are always helpful.

When approaching from the E coast, keep close to the Caithness shore northward of Freswick Bay: along this shore to Duncansby Hd there are 10h of slack water.

HW Duncansby Hd −0.45.   DS: W +1.00; E −5.45.

Round Duncansby Hd just before the W-going stream begins, about HW to +0.30 Dover, keeping so close to Duncansby Ness that Dunnet Hd is a little open of St John's Pt. Least depth is still 30m less than 50m off the cliffs.

Then keep within half a mile of the Caithness shore until up to St John's Pt, where the Rocks of Mey off its end should be passed 100m off. This keeps the boat out of the severe 'Merry Men of Mey' race, which otherwise stretches across to Tor Ness on Hoy. On no account try to pass through this race. In the main channel the W-going stream runs from half an hour after until 6h before HW Dover. Close inshore between Dunnet Hd and Torness the W-going stream runs until 4 or 4½h before HW Dover.

The E-going passage is somewhat easier, as no race forms across the strait and the wind is more likely to be with tide. Leave Scrabster at HW Dover +4.30, which will bring the boat off Dunnett Hd at about Dover +5.30, when the stream is just turning E-ly. Pass midway between St John's Pt and Stroma, steering well S to avoid being set onto the rocks S of Stroma (bn, unlit). Then steer out through the middle of Inner Sound, and round Duncansby Hd giving it a wide berth.

Gills Bay   The tidal stream sets towards St John's Pt from 3h before HW Dover and runs for 9h.

Brough Bay   The W-going stream runs NW from HW Dover until 2h before LW Dover. With the E-going stream there is an eddy running NW.

Brimsness   W-going stream runs from HW Dover until 6h after at up to 8kn during spring tides.

Cape Wrath   Close inshore, between the Stag Rock and the land, the tidal stream always runs to the W, but ½ off Cape Wrath the W-going stream begins 1¾h before HW Dover and runs up to 3kn at spring tides.

Stag Rock   Often difficult to see if there are any breaking crests, so it is best avoided by keeping close to the cliffs which are quite steep-to.

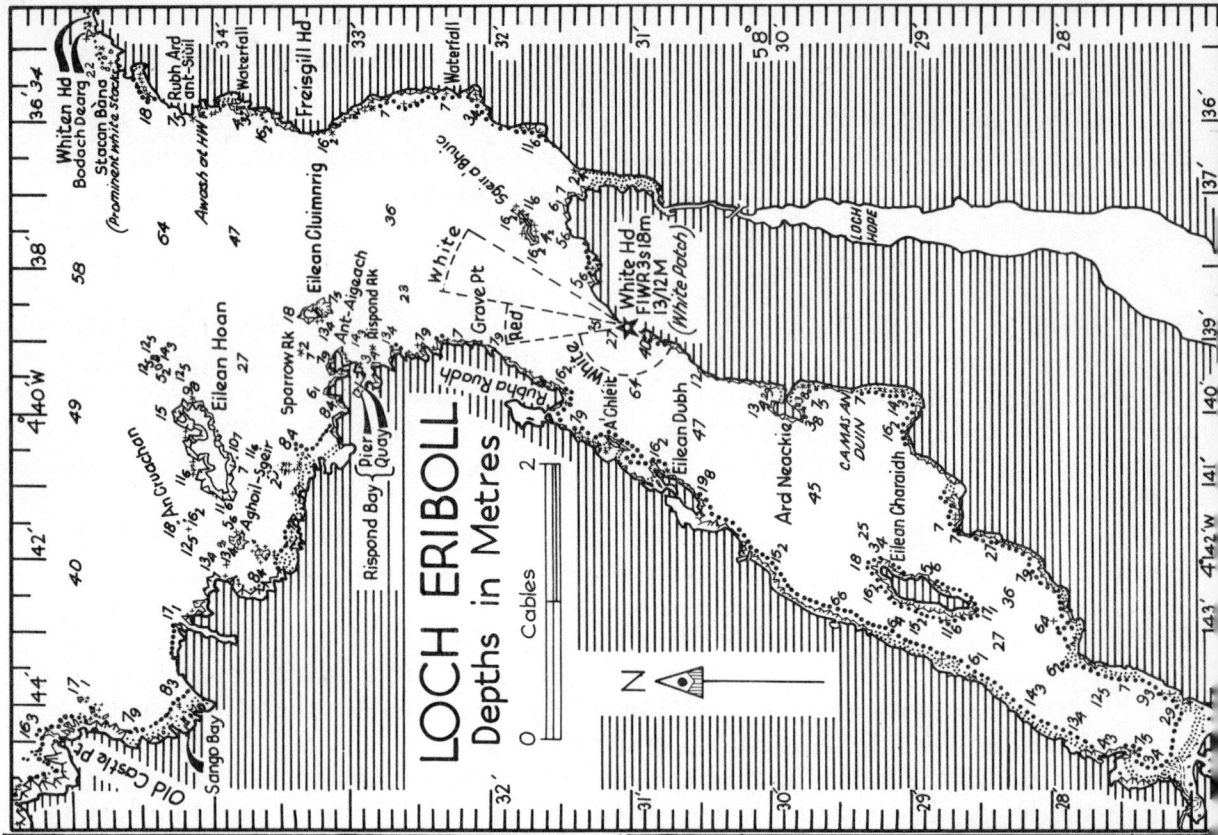

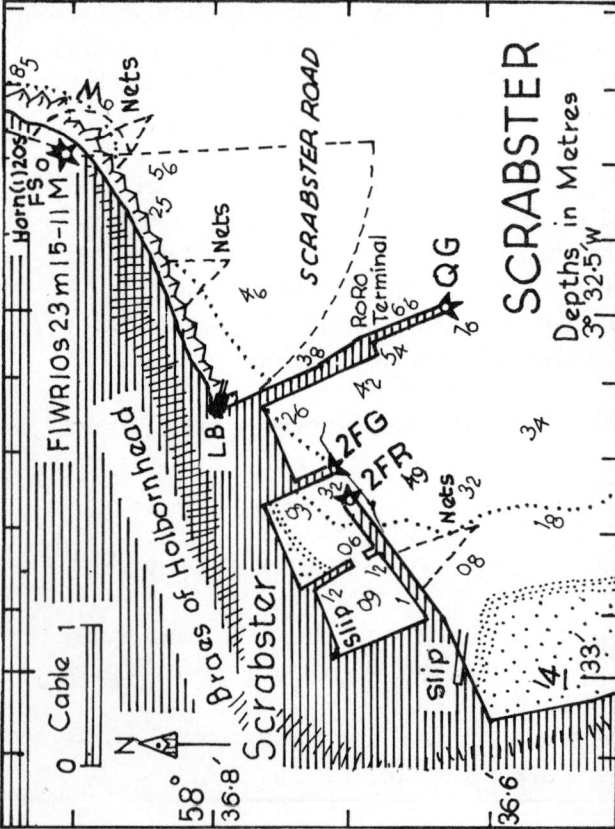

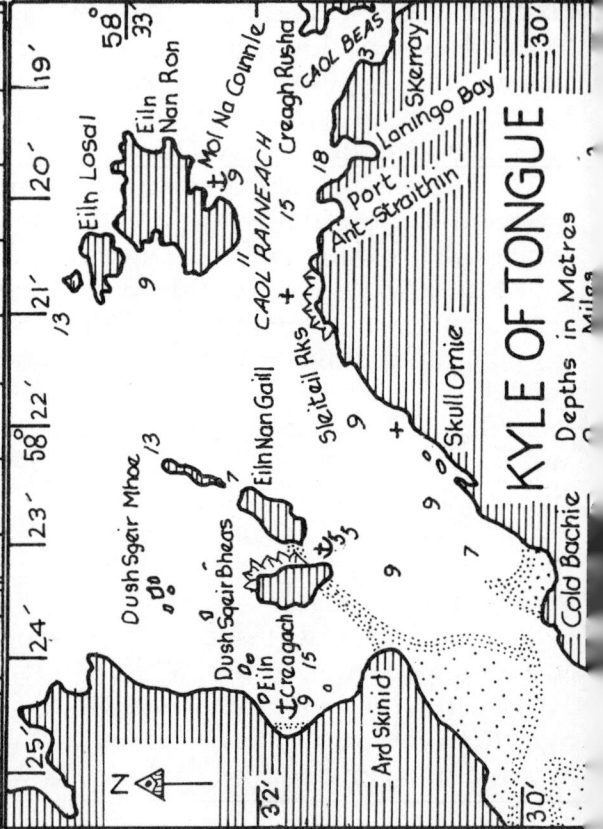

Based on British Admiralty Charts (nos. in text) with the permission of the Controller of H.M. Stationery Office and the Hydrographer of the Navy, and on other sources.

JOHN O'GROATS   Chart BA 2162
HW (Duncansby Hd) −0.45. MHWS 3.1; MHWN 2.4. DS: E −5.45;
W +1.00.
This enclosed hr now has 2m at MLWS in the appr and W part of the hr.
Approach from the N: there are no offlying dangers once clear of Duncansby
Ness. Berth as space allows alongside the W jetty; the E is used by the Orkney
ferry. The hr is crowded and should only be used in emergency, or to wait for an
hour or two for the tide through the Pentland Firth. Limited supplies and petrol.
Hotel.

THURSO   Chart BA 1783
HW and Rise, approximately as for Scrabster.
Difficult to enter if there is any swell or wind from the N. Ent has 1.8m MLWS.
The hr dries, stony, pebble bottom: only use after half-tide. It is situated on the
R Thurso and care must be taken in entering when the river is in spate. Keep
between the bns, which mark the outer edge of rocky ledges (see plan). The ldg
line consists of two G lts on poles. If using poles as ldg line beware of confusion
with third pole nearby.
   Tie up on W side of hr. Supplies. EC Thurs.

SCRABSTER   Chart BA 1783   (Plan p186)
HW −2.25.   MHWS 5.0; MLWS 0.8; MTL 2.9; MHWN 3.7; MLWN 2.1.
This hr can be entered at all states of the tide; there is no bar and it provides
complete shelter. There are two basins: the outer one dries in the NW corner but
there is at least 4.2m alongside the NE wall; the inner basin has at least 1.8m over
most of it. The bottom of the hr is sandy and provides a clean, comfortable berth.
It is used by the ferry to Orkney and also fishing boats and coasters. Pentland
Firth YC has its headquarters here with a number of moorings in the inner basin.
Visitors tie alongside the NE wall of the inner basin and contact the HM. Anch
not recommended.
   Limited stores. Diesel can be arranged. Repairs and slip Water at pier.
Infrequent bus service to Thurso.

SANDSIDE BAY   Chart BA 1954
This bay, about 8M W of Thurso Bay, contains a small hr in fair condition on the
W side of the bay. It affords shelter from winds from SE through W to N; it is
uncomfortable in winds from the NE. The hr almost dries at LW on a sp tide, but
the bottom is sandy and if care is taken to avoid isolated stones on the bottom
near the hr wall a boat can dry alongside quite comfortably.

KYLE OF TONGUE   Chart BA 1954   (Plan p186)
HW −3.30.   MHWS 4.7; MHWN 3.6.
The Kyle of Tongue contains a number of sheltered anchs. Entry during gales
and strong winds from the N is not recommended. Anch at Talmine, behind

Rabbit Is, gives protection from all except N to E winds; in E-lies shelter may be obtained at Skullomie Hr.

Talmine affords shelter from SE through W to N. Anch in 5m off the end of the slip. Entering from the W, do not turn in until the more W-ly of the two Rabbit Is closes Ard Skinid, the main headland on the W side of the Kyle. Close its W side to about 2 ca off its W-most point, then steer to anch S of Eilean Creagach in 5m. The whole area has a sandy bottom. Supplies at shop in Talmine, 10 min walk from slip.

Shelter from W-ly and NW-ly winds off Mol na Coinnle, a small bight on the E side of Eil na Ron. The anch can be recognised by the tin-roofed hut near the foreshore. Landing on the Is can be effected here. Uninhabited.

On the E side of the Kyle there is a small hr at Skullomie. The entrance, difficult to identify, is best seen from Rabbit Is. On looking SE, a house can be seen on the hillside: the hr is directly below this. The bottom is sandy and anch can be effected just outside the entrance. To enter, keep well clear of the broken wall to stb and keep towards the E shore. Limited supplies at Coldbachie, about 1½M.

Shelter from W to N winds by anch in 5m off the beach at the S side of Rabbit Is.

LOCH ERIBOLL   Chart BA 2076   (Plan p186)
HW Rispond −3.45.   MHWS 4.6;   MLWS 0.6;   MTL 2.6;   MHWN 3.5;
MLWN 1.8.
Loch Eriboll lies on the W side of Whiten Hd. Anch in the bays just N and S of Ard Neckie on the E side of the loch, well sheltered from the S and N respectively, or in 7m in the bay off the W house a mile to the S. Because of funnelling effects, SW winds are extremely fierce and anchs in other parts of the loch can give trouble.

An excellent anch for winds from the S through W to N is in Rispond Bay on the W side of the ent to the loch, in about 5m. The bottom is sandy but swinging room is a little restricted. The hr at Rispond has a sandy bottom but can only be entered after about half-tide; there is about 3.7m alongside at MHWS. It gives perfect shelter and boats can dry alongside quite comfortably.

Scotland, West Coast

Introduction

There are several hundred anchs available to yachts between Cape Wrath and the Mull of Galloway, many in beautiful rock-protected lagoons or beneath rugged mountains. The sailing can be sheltered or extremely exposed, conditions often changing within a small distance. Long hours of summer daylight mean that night sailing is seldom a necessity. This book can cover only a small fraction of the available anchs and therefore the principle that has been adopted is to select: (1) passage ports or anchorages 20 to 40 miles apart, relatively easy to enter, offering as far as possible water, stores, fuel, communications for crew changing; (2) secondary ports or anchorages between the main ports, offering fairly easy access and shelter but not necessarily stores etc; (3) interesting ports or anchorages which yachts on a limited visit may wish to explore, but for which additional information will need to be carried.

A yacht should have the Admiralty *West Coast of Scotland Pilot* and relevant charts aboard. If detailed exploration is intended, or visits to interesting anchorages listed in this volume proposed, the Clyde Cruising Club's *Sailing Directions* and sketch charts for the W Coast of Scotland and Outer Hebrides should be regarded as essential requirements for safe and enjoyable navigation. They can be obtained from the Clyde Cruising Club (SV *Carrick*, Clyde St, Glasgow G1 4LN). Holders of older copies should ensure they have all up-to-date amendments. (The *Sailing Directions* are referred to hereafter as CCC SD.) Mark Brackenbury's *Scottish West Coast Pilot* (Stanford Maritime) also provides detailed coverage from Troon to Ullapool.

Weather and Other Hazards

A yacht on passage from N to S will pass through three distinct areas separated by headlands: Cape Wrath to Ardnamurchan Pt (220 miles); Ardnamurchan Pt to Mull of Kintyre (90 miles); and Mull of Kintyre to Mull of Galloway (60 miles). Within each of these areas, alternative outer, middle, inner passages are available and are described in that order. Uncharted rocks can still be present, especially in less-used channels, and this should be borne in mind when using them.

Bad weather is not uncommon even in summer, and boats and crews must be ready to meet sudden gale conditions, sometimes unforecast. Conditions become less adverse further south, and protected passages are usually available. Do not anch for the night in anchs exposed to wind between W and S unless ready to shift if need arises.

Fierce squalls may be experienced in the lee of mountains, often exceeding the general wind level by two forces. Ground tackle should be chosen having regard

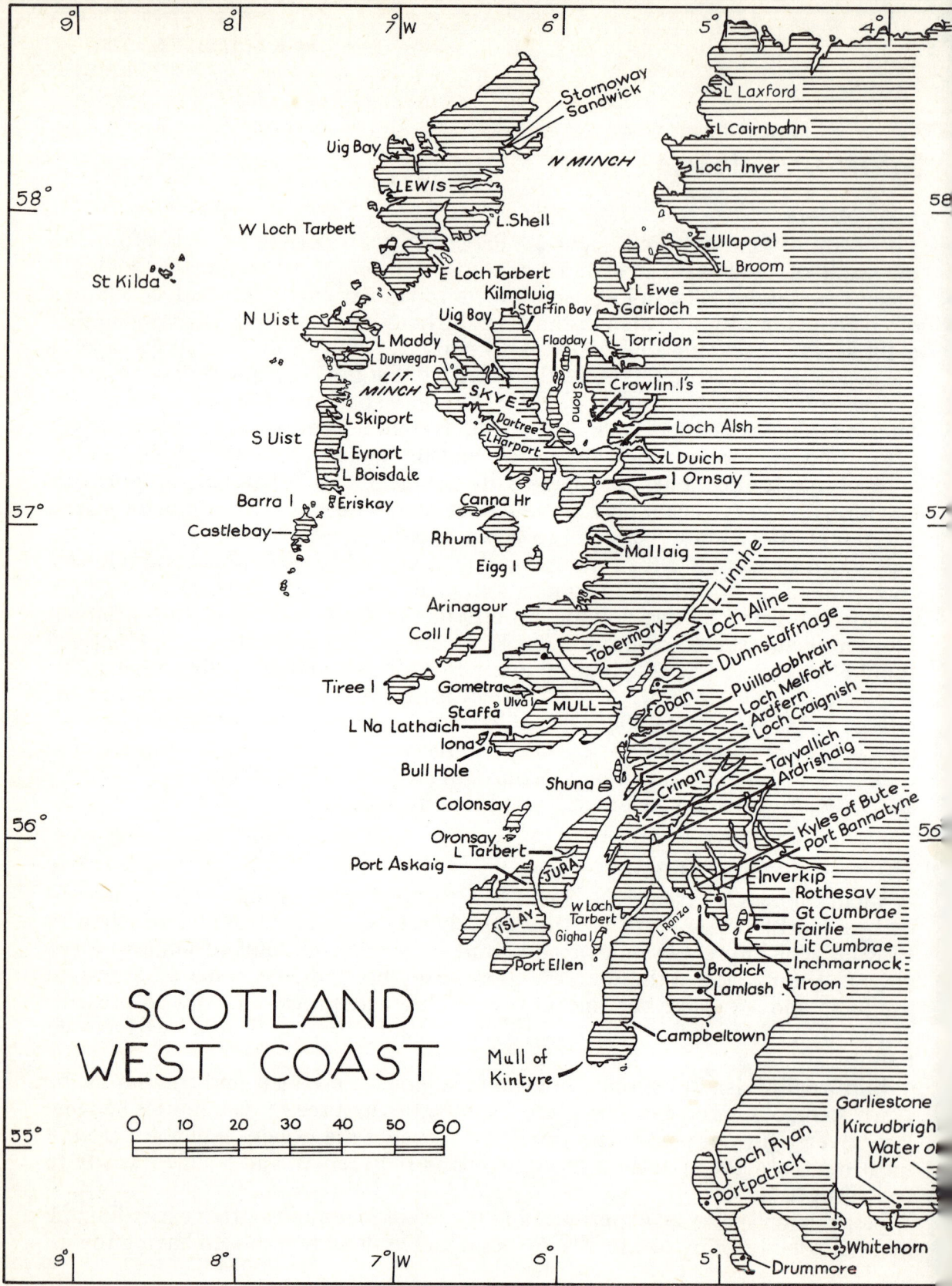

SCOTLAND WEST COAST

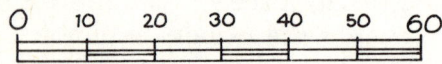

Stornoway
Sandwick
Uig Bay
LEWIS
N MINCH
L. Shell
W Loch Tarbert
St Kilda
E Loch Tarbert
Kilmaluig
Uig Bay
Staffin Bay
N Uist
L Maddy
Fladday I
L Dunvegan
LIT. MINCH
SKYE
S Rona
Crowlin I's
S Uist
L Skiport
Portree
L Harport
L Eynort
L Boisdale
Loch Alsh
L Duich
I Ornsay
Barra I
Eriskay
Canna Hr
Castlebay
Rhum I
Mallaig
Eigg I
L Linnhe
Arinagour
Loch Aline
Coll I
Tobermory
Dunstaffnage
Tiree I
Gometra
Puilladobhrain
Oban
Loch Melfort
Staffa
Ulva I
MULL
Ardfern
L Na Lathaich
Loch Craignish
Iona
Bull Hole
Tayvallich
Shuna
Ardrishaig
Crinan
Colonsay
Kyles of Bute
Oronsay
Port Bannatyne
L Tarbert
Port Askaig
Inverkip
JURA
Rothesay
Gt Cumbrae
ISLAY
W Loch Tarbert
L Ranza
Fairlie
Gigha I
Lit Cumbrae
Inchmarnock
Port Ellen
Brodick
Troon
Lamlash
Campbeltown
Mull of Kintyre
Garliestone
Kircudbrigh
Water o
Urr
Loch Ryan
Kircudbrigh
portpatrick
Whitehorn
Drummore

L Laxford
L Cairnbahn
Loch Inver
Ullapool
L Broom
L Ewe
Gairloch
L Torridon

0 10 20 30 40 50 60

to the strength of wind that can be encountered. Thick layers of kelp are frequently found and prevent some types of anchor from digging in. Plough type anchors of under 30kg frequently choke with weed and fail to dig in: the Fisherman often serves best, and the Bruce is well thought of in some quarters. Particularly in the N the yachtsman must be self-sufficient since aid, services, medical assistance and supplies may not be readily available.

In a number of places among the inner and outer islands local magnetic anomalies occur: close visual watch is essential in these areas.

PASSAGE NOTES: CAPE WRATH TO ARDNAMURCHAN POINT, OUTSIDE PASSAGE

Outer Hebrides – West Side
The navigation of the W side of the Outer Hebrides should not be attempted without a crew capable of handling the boat in extreme conditions. Heavy seas are common along the whole 100 miles of the W seaboard. The coast should not be closed except in settled weather and only with large-scale charts aboard. Shelter can be found by sailing round the N or S of the chain into the lee of the Is. Off North Harris and particularly at the S end of the isles, along North and South Uist, a vessel should stand off for several miles. The land on the W is so low that the vessel may be in difficulties before an accurate position is ascertained.

The general direction of the tidal stream offshore is NE on a rising tide, SW on a falling tide. Inshore the streams are variable and inset should be suspected. DS Butt of Lewis: NE +5.30; SW HWD; Barra Hd: NE +3.00; SW −2.30.

WEST LOCH TARBERT, HARRIS   Chart BA 2841   (Plan p193)
HW −5.15.   MHWS 4.2; MLWS 0.4; MTL 2.1; MHWN 3.2; MLWN 1.3.
A refuge offering comparative shelter once inside.
Approach   May be made either N or S of Taransay Is, the N approach being clearer. From the S, Middle Bo and Bo Usbig can be cleared by keeping Toe Hd and summit of Coppay Is in line. Keep in mid-sound to the narrows.
Entrance   From the N approach entrance should be made by shaping a course to the S shore of the loch. Coming from S of Taransay avoid sand spits on both sides at the narrows, and keep to the S shore of the loch. There are a number of rocks and islands on the N shore beyond the entrance.
Anchorage   Anch at the head of the loch in 10m off Tarbert. Stores. Water at head of loch. Steamer to mainland and Skye from East Loch Tarbert, dist 1M.

ST KILDA   Chart BA 2524
Approach   Usually made from Sd of Harris (see CCC SD) in settled conditions only, a distance of 42M.
Anchorage   Anch at head of Village Bay off Army depot and pier. If the wind comes between S and E do not attempt to anch: if already there, leave immediately.

THE MINCH AND LITTLE MINCH   Charts BA 1794, 1795

In strong winds in the Minches nasty seas may develop. Avoid areas charted 'Overfalls' or 'Breakers', particularly in the area of the Shiant Isles 12M N of Skye, during bad weather when the seas are dangerous. Large-scale charts are required for navigation inshore because of the numerous reefs and rocks. Low cloud may often hamper visibility making landfalls and identification difficult. Fog is rare.

The W side of the Minch is free from outlying dangers beyond $\frac{1}{2}$M offshore from the Butt of Lewis as far as the Shiant Islands. Submarine irregularities cause heavy overfalls and tides run 2 to 4kn. HW −4.20. Ox Rock dries 1m. Between the Shiant Is and the Little Minch, care is needed to avoid the numerous rocks between Harris and Skye; many overfalls. DS here SW −1.30; NE +4.20. The Sound of Harris needs large-scale charts and CCC SDs. Tides run up to 6kn. Daylight navigation only. Between Sound of Harris and S end of North Uist the coast is clean beyond $\frac{1}{2}$M offshore, but Benbecula and its islets should be given an offing of at least 1M. Further S dangerous rks exist up to 2M offshore S of Barra. Passage S of Barra Is is exposed to the full Atlantic swell.

The E side of the Minch and Little Minch is open for the first 30M to winds from W through NW to N. In bad weather give the N section of coast a good offing as seas can be heavy. At Cape Wrath (HW −4.00) the flood sets E and the ebb W 3kn sp at 1½h after local LW and HW. Beware Stag Rk covering ½ flood ¾M ENE of Lt Ho. **Danger:** *there is a Firing Area E of Cape Wrath (see Admiralty N Scotland Pilot)*. Numerous rocks and islets occur well offshore in this area: large-scale charts needed if closing the shore.

At Vaternish Pt and Neist Pt W of Skye there are tideraces up to 4kn with heavy overfalls. Offing of 2 to 4M is recommended. Canna should be given a wide berth and care taken to avoid rks which extend for 10M to the SW. In the vicinity of Canna, Rhum and Muck abnormal magnetic variations may be encountered. Around Muck there are outlying dangers, particularly in the Sound of Eigg. Tides run 2–4kn over Maxwell Bank, 3M S of Eigg, and tend to be deflected by the Is.

There are no outlying dangers at Ardnamurchan Pt but, being very exposed from W to NW and also to SW, heavy seas may be encountered even in moderate weather, and an offing of 1M is advisable.

West Side of The Minches − Butt of Lewis to Barra Head

STORNOWAY − LEWIS   Chart BA 2529   (Plan p193)

HW −4.30.   MHWS 4.8; MLWS 0.7; MTL 2.9; MHWN 3.7; MLWN 2.0

The main port of the Outer Hebrides, 20M S of the Butt of Lewis. Much used by ferries and fishing fleets. Uncomfortable with a swell from S, and often crowded.

W. LOCH TARBERT (HARRIS)
Depths in Metres

N

Miles

North Harris

South Harris

Bunaveneadar
Loch Meavaig
O.Chy
Ardhasaig
Tarbert
Geb Aird Stioclett
Pier
LOCH BUN
Duisker
Duisker (2)
Isay
Ben Luskentyre
Luskentyre
TRAIG LUSKENTYRE
SOUND OF TARANSAY
Aird Groadnish
Sgeir Tarcall
Soay Beag
Soay Mór
O.Cairn
O.Cairn
Cairn
Loch Leosavay
Rubha nan Tocag
Bo Usbig
Middle in weather bad weather
Taransay

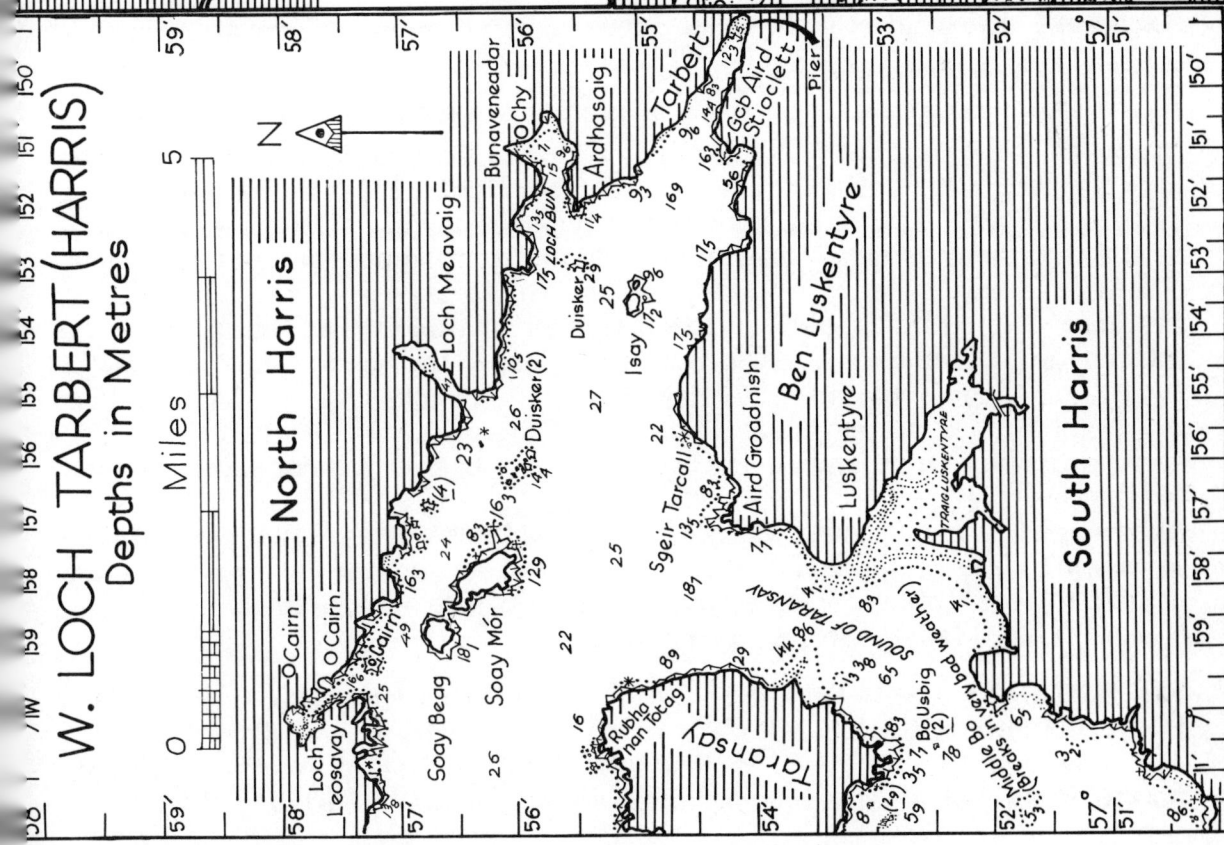

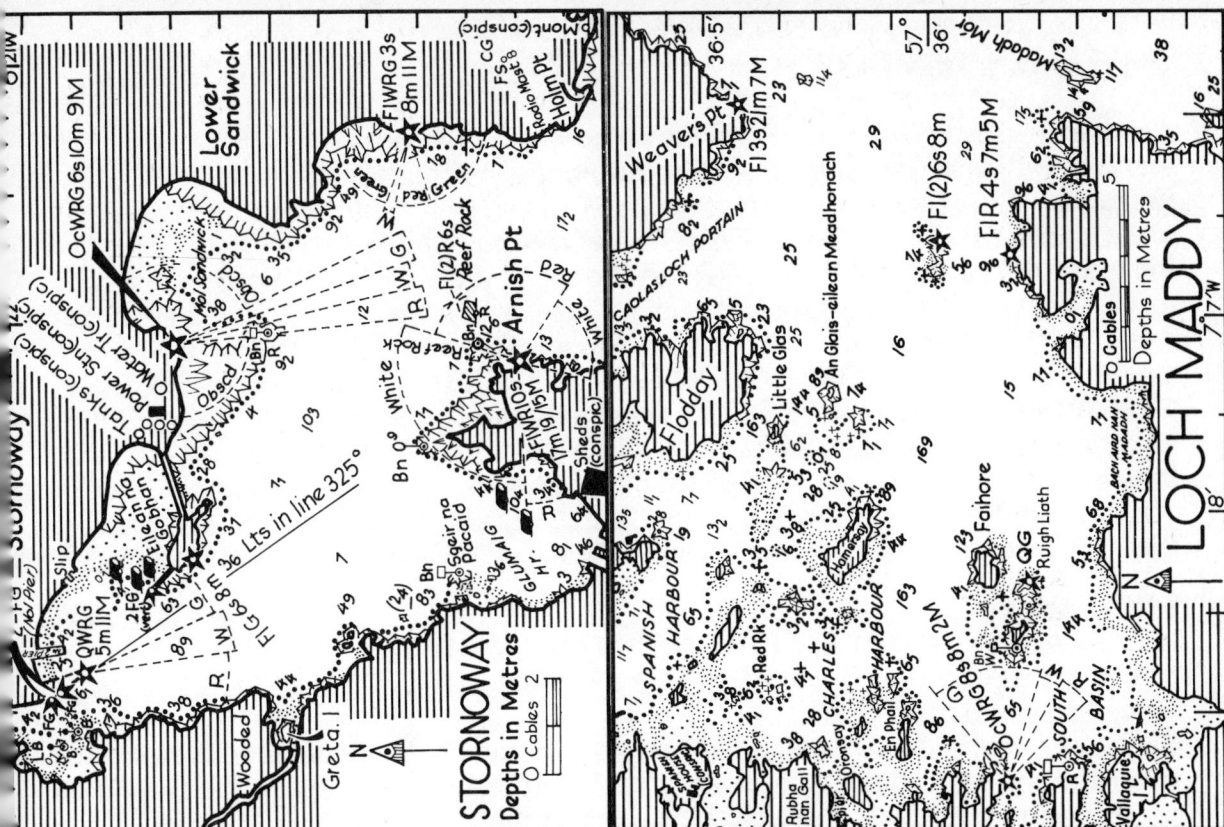

Based on British Admiralty Charts (nos. in text) with the permission of the Controller of H.M. Stationery Office and of the Hydrographer of the Navy, and on other sources.

193

STORNOWAY
Depths in Metres
O Cables 2

N

Stornoway
Fish Pier
Slip
Wooded
Greta I.
Glumaig Hr.
Sgeir na Pacaid
Sheds (conspic)
Arnish Pt
Reef Rock
Holm Pt
Radio Mast
CG
FS
Lower Sandwick
Holm Sandwick

OcWRG 6s10m 9M
Fl WRG 3s 8m 11M
Fl(2)R 6s Reef Rock
Fl WR10s15M
Fl(2)R 6s
QWRG 5m 11M
Fl G 3s
Lts in line 325°
Tanks (conspic)
Power Stn (conspic)
Water Tr (conspic)
D.Mont (conspic)

LOCH MADDY
Depths in Metres
O Cables

N

Weavers Pt
Fl 3 92l m 7M
CAOLAS LOCH PORTAIN
An Glas-eilean Meadhonach
Little Glas
Floddy
Madadh Mór
Fl(2)6s 8m
FlR 4s7m5M
SPANISH HARBOUR
CHARLES HARBOUR
SOUTH BASIN
Faihore
Ruigh Liath
QG
OcWRG 8s 8m 2W
Rubha nan Gall
Eri Phail
Vallaquie
BAGH AND NAN MADADH

Approach Enter from E, S of Eye Peninsula. Dangers are above water or marked by bns or perches which should be given a reasonable berth.

Entrance Enter between Arnish Pt Lt Ho Fl WR 10s and Holm Pt with R bn (unlit). Entrance is 4 ca wide. There is a R can buoy Fl(2)R 6s on the NE end of the reef off Arnish Pt and lt Fl WRG 3s 8m opposite showing W over the fairway to the W. Leave Eil na Gobhail well to stb on entering and keep clear of the shoals to the W of the inner hr and the Parson Rks marked by two iron perches. The pier has a lt QWRG showing W over the fairway to the S after passing Eil na Gobhail. FG lts 325° on the Ro-Ro terminal lead to the inner hr.

Anchorages (1) Private moorings below castle by walled structure beyond Parson Rks. (2) In the bay NW of Eil na Gobhail (Coul Is), more comfortable in suitable conditions. To take on stores, tie alongside E wall of inner hr. Stores, fuel, slip, steamer to Ullapool, flights to Glasgow, Inverness and inter-island.

LOCH SHELL   Chart BA 1794
HW −4.40.   MHWS 4.8; MLWS 0.7; MTL 2.8; MHWN 3.6; MLWN 1.9.
15M S of Stornoway, exposed to E, reasonably easy of access. High cliffs at entrance may baffle winds.

Entrance Between Streanach Hd and Ru Ailltenish. Streanach Hd is steep-to. Iuvard Is and Sgeir nan Caorach lie in the centre of the fairway. Leave these ½ ca to stb and take mid-chan course until past Orinsay. The S shore is clean.

Anchorage At head of loch. Dries out for some distance. Water at burns.

EAST LOCH TARBERT – HARRIS   Chart 2905   (Plan p196)
HW −4.50.   MHWS 5.0; MLWS 0.8; MTL 2.9; MHWN 3.7; MLWN 2.1.

Approach The chan to the N of Scalpay is clearer than the S chan. In the N chan the only danger up to Rubha Crago is Sgier an Daimh 1M NE of Rubha Crago and ½M offshore, 3.5m high, which must be given a wide berth. The chan S of Scalpay has many dangerous rks and should not be attempted without large-scale charts.

Entrance Note that the ebb sets inwards from 3h after HW at 2kn sp: the flood sets outward. Keep to N side which is fairly clear to the head of the loch. Rocks run ½ ca off the pt of the first bay on the N shore of the chan, but the island side at this point is steep-to and clean. Oban Rks, drying 1.1m LW, lie N of a line between Rubha Dubh and Sgeir Urgha. Tarbert Lt, Oc WR 6s, shows W over the fairway.

Anchorage In the extreme NW corner of East Loch Tarbert is an inlet ½M long 1½ ca wide, free of hidden dangers. Anchor in 4m off the pier just past the church, to avoid cable running across loch from W side of pier. Steamers to Skye, N and S Uist, Mallaig. Stores, water, fuel.

LOCH MADDY – NORTH UIST   Chart BA 2825   (Plan p193)
HW −5.00.   MHWS 5.6; MLWS 0.7; MTL 2.9; MHWN 3.6; MLWN 1.9.
This anch is not entirely free of obstruction and the bottom is soft giving only poor holding, but it is the nearest to a passage port on N Uist.

Approach   From N, the chan lies S of Maddy Beg off Weaver Pt. From S, approach outside Maddy More and clear Leac Maddy by 1 ca to avoid rks. Approach can be difficult in strong onshore winds when the seas can be heavy.
Entrance   Giving Glas More a reasonable berth to N or S and avoiding rks for 1 ca to its W, the loch is clear for ¾M to Fanore and Ree Lee Is. Take mid-chan between Ree Lee Is and S shore to clear rks to stb and shoals to port. Stream runs hard at entrance.
Anchorage   In 8m off the pier ½M WNW of Ree Lee Is. Poor holding. Stores, water, fuel, gas. Ferry to mainland and Skye.

LOCH SKIPORT – SOUTH UIST   Charts BA 2904, 2825
HW −5.15.   MHWS 4.6; MLWS 0.5; MTL 2.5; MHWN 3.3; MLWN 1.7.
This loch offers ease of access and a choice of three anchs, two of which are landlocked.
Approach and entrance   Pass N of Ornish Is taking mid-channel between this Is and N shore.
Anchorages   (1) McCormack Bay. Take mid-chan, N of Shillay More; avoid the two reefs on W side of McCormack Bay. Anch in 10m where Mannoch Arm bends SE. (2) Little Kettle Pool. Enter round NW end of Shillay More, 4m LW at entrance. Keep close in to Is to avoid rks in the SW three-quarters of pool. Anch in small bay, in 6m. (3) Wizard Pool. Approach E of Shillay More and Beg. Avoid reefs stretching N and NW from Ornish Pt by keeping Wizard Is just open of Shillay Beg to clear Float Rk. Alter course to stb when lagoon opens out to avoid the rk that dries, but give E pt of Shillay Beg reasonable clearance. A rk, dries 0.3m, N of Wizard Is. The anch lies through the gap between the two in 6m.

LOCH EYNORT   Chart BA 2825
HW −5.10.   MHWS 4.4; MLWS 0.5; MTL 2.4; MHWN 3.1; MLWN 1.7.
Exposed to E.
Approach   The N shore is clear except for Bo Coilenish 1 ca S of Coilenish Pt. The S shore is foul for at least 2 ca out.
Anchorages   (1) ½M along N shore NW of Coilenish Pt, just before the narrows, in 6m. (2) In Ceardal Bay in 6m on S shore, ¾M from entrance to loch after clearing the offlying rks.

LOCH BOISDALE   Chart BA 2770   (Plan p196)
HW −5.10.   MHWS 4.3; MLWS 0.5; MTL 2.4; MHWN 3.0; MLWN 1.6.
Fairly easy of access given reasonable care in navigation.
Approach   From N there are no difficulties if a course of 245° is shaped to pass between Rubha na Cruibe and Calva Is. From the S keep clear of Clan Ewan Rk, dries 1m, and McKenzie Rk marked by R buoy.
Entrance   Mid-chan between Gasay Is (avoiding rk 1 ca off E end) and N shore which is steep-to. Then keep rks (marked by G buoy Fl 6s) to stb.

NORTH HARBOUR
E. LOCH TARBERT
Depths in Metres

N

0 cable 1

57° 53'

52·8'

46
58
7·2
38
7·2
168
24
24·5
13·4
12·6
28
66
3
18·6 4·6 4
24
Aird an Aiseg
Mac Queans Rk
NORTH HARBOUR
Pier
8
7·4
FlG2·5s
4·6
18
1·9
3·2
FG
14
14
Pier
Rubha nan Cudaigean
23·0
24 8·6
5·4
9·4 Eileann na Praise
18·8
6·5
38

6° 43'W
42'

CASTLEBAY
Depths in Metres

0   3
Cables

N

BAGH & BEAG
0·7
6·2 9·9
3·2 6·2
62
Fl R 2s 7m 8M (occ·9)
Klessimul Castle
Rubha Glas
FR 22m 4M
FR 9m 4M
108
8·3
FERRY
Ldg Lts 295°
Ldg Lts 283°
Orosay
92
Fl 3s 7m 8M
Sgeir Liath
7·4
3·8
2·2
35 13
2·5 2·6
2·2
3·2 2·8
Bn (2)
Sgeir na Treanne
28
190 4 96m 7M
Sgeir Dubh
25
SOUND of VATERSAY
0·7
0·7
1·9 2·5
1·6
Sg na Rhon
Caragrich
3·2
Bn
Jetty
28
Vatersay

31'
7 30'W
29'

18'
17'
7 16'W

LOCH BOISDALE
Depths in Metres

0   Mile 1

57° 9'

N

21
198
16
41
3 BUN AN UILLT
14
47
36
Rubha na Cruibe
41
Creag Spuir
17
Pier in line with Hollisgeir 245°
29
8·8
Lochboisdale
Police Stn (conspic)
160 Rk
G4·3
FlG3s
Sgeir Rk
15
51 6
41
QG
43
8·4
7·9
41 43
25
White
34
Rhuba Bhuailt
2·9
Fl(2) 5s Gasay
38
Gasay Rk
29
23
Iasgaich
18
17
107
Mid Rk 2
Hut Shoal
Store Rk
Hollisgeir
13·4
41
13·4
Castle Calvay
13
12·5
Calvay
Fl WR 3s 11m 6/5M
125
Pier (ruins)(conspic)
29
125
Red
17
13·4
CALVAY SOUND
25
101

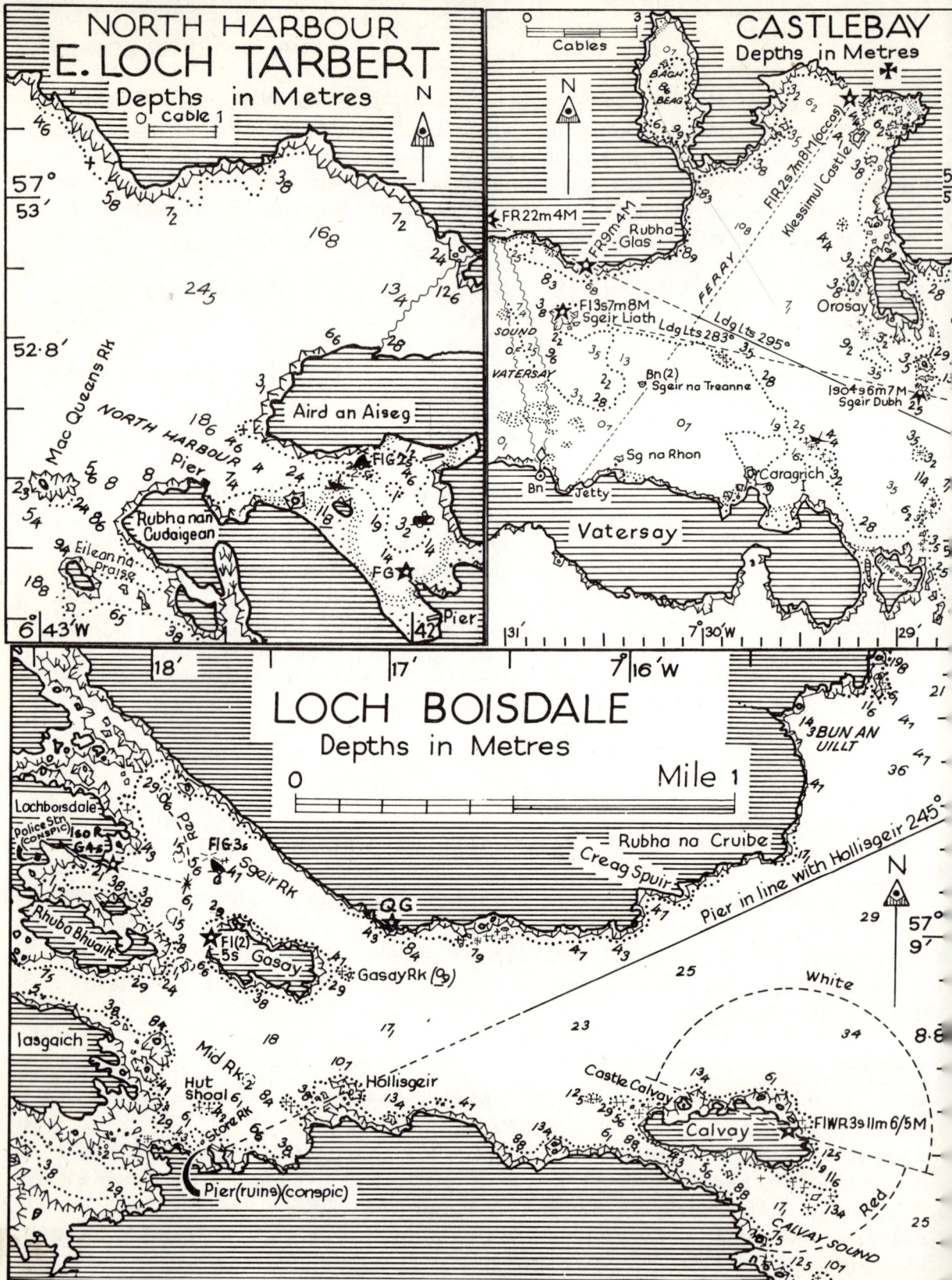

Based on British Admiralty Charts (nos. in text) with the permission of the Controller of H.M. Stationery Office and
the Hydrographer of the Navy, and on other sources.

Anchorage   Anch in 4m off pier clear of Ro-Ro terminal. Further in there is a reef close to the S side of the quay. Do not anch W of the pier-head. Stores, fuel, water. Ferry to mainland and other islands.

CASTLEBAY BARRA   Chart BA 2769   (Plan p196)
HW −5.25.   MHWS 4.3; MLWS 0.6; MTL 2.3; MHWN 3.1; MLWN 1.7.
Approach   From Bo Vich Chuan buoy: keep R buoy Fl(2) 12s, ¾M N of Muldonach Is, close to port to avoid reef marked by broken perch, covers half-tide, 2 ca to N of buoy. Approach Dubh Sgeir bn Fl 2s and leave it close to stb.
Entrance   Continue NW for ¼M to clear rks to NNW of Dubh Sgeir bn. Turn to stb when pier to N opens W of castle.
Anchorage   NW of castle in 6 to 10m. The bay is foul to N and E of castle. Stores, water, fuel, gas. Steamer to mainland.

East Side of The Minches

Passage notes: Mainland – Cape Wrath to Loch Ewe

DS: SSW +1.00; NNE −6.00.
Often an exposed lee shore. No attempt should be made to close the shores of the mainland or islands without large-scale charts because of the rocks and reefs which abound and are too numerous to describe in this volume. Bad seas in strong wind over tide conditions off Pt of Stoer.

LOCH LAXFORD   Chart BA 2503   (Plan p199)
HW −4.10.   MHWS 4.9; MLWS 0.7; MTL 2.7; MHWN 3.5; MLWN 1.9.
A good passage port, easy of access and useful when on passage round Cape Wrath.
Approach   Handa Is 15M S of Cape Wrath is a good landmark. The entrance lies 2M N of Handa. Rubha Ruadh is steep-to and recognisable by its red colour.
Entrance   The entrance to the loch is 6 ca wide. Keep to the N side of the chain of Is along the S shore, holding slightly to the Is side of mid-channel.
Anchorages   At the head of the loch or in the bays behind the Is on the S shore.

LOCH INVER   Chart BA 2504
HW −4.25.   MHWS 5.0; MLWS 0.8; MTL 3.0; MHWN 3.9; MLWN 2.1.
A useful passage port. In clear weather the sugar loaf mountain of Suilven is a first-class landmark for the entrance.

Approach   1½M offshore lies Clette Is which should be given a wide berth. On its E side there are rks for 1 ca. 1M NE of Clette Is lies Soya Is, also with rks off its E end. A red perch marks shoal water between Soya Is and the N shore.

Entrance   Between Soya Is and Kirkaig Pt on the S shore. Avoid the rk drying 1½m off Kirkaig Pt by keeping toward the S side of Soya Is and the R perch. Keep just S of the islet, 1M further up, to avoid rks on its N side. A sectored WRG lt on this islet shows W over the fairways. ¾M further in, keep the perch, marking a rk off a small pt on the S shore, to stb.

Anchorage   Anchor in 6m in the bay at the head of the loch beyond the perch. Stores, fuel, gas, hotel.

ULLAPOOL, LOCH BROOM   Chart BA 2500   (Plan p199)
HW −4.20.   MHWS 5.2; MLWS 0.7; MTL 3.0; MHWN 3.9; MLWN 2.1.
In Loch Broom 15M SE of Rubha Coigeach past the Summer Isles (in which there are a number of attractive anchs but for which large-scale charts and CCC SD are necessary).

Approach   The approach is best made round Cailleach Hd on the S entrance to Loch Broom, between Loch Broom and Little Loch Broom.

Entrance   Keep at least 2 ca off Carn Dearg, a headland 1½M E of Cailleach Hd, to clear a rock 1m high. A WRG 6s lt 4M further E stands on a beacon 11m high on the NE side of the entrance to the loch proper, at Rubha Cadail: it shows W over the fairways. The passage is then straightforward to Ullapool River about 1M NW of Ullapool Pier. An extensive area marked by a R can buoy (QR) dries for over 2 ca where Ullapool R joins the loch. The tide runs 2kn in the narrows. There is a FR lt on Ullapool pier.

Anchorage   In 6m in the bay just beyond Ullapool Pt, clear of moorings. Stores, water, fuel, gas. Bus to Inverness.

LOCH EWE   Chart BA 3146   (Plan p199)
HW −4.15.   MHWS 5.1; MLWS 0.7; MTL 2.9; MHWN 3.8; MLWN 2.0.
Anchorage easy of access and well protected from all quarters except N.

Approach   Providing a reasonable offing is kept from the coast there are no dangers in the approach. There is a MOD pier at the E side of the entrance and some mooring dolphins. There are also a number of unlit mooring buoys in the loch.

Entrance   The entrance is 1M wide and the shores are clear in the loch. Ewe Is and the islets ½M to the NW of it can be passed on either hand keeping to mid-chan.

Anchorage   In Poolewe Bay at the extreme S of the loch. There are submerged rks lying 1 ca N and S of Boor Rk on the W shore. Boor Rk stands 3m above HW ¾M from the loch head. Anchor in 4½m off the first white ho about ½M beyond Boor Rk. Stores, fuel, hotel, bus to Inverness.

ULLAPOOL
Depths in Metres

Cables 0   6

White House (conspic)

Bridge (conspic)

Carry Pt

2FR (vert)
Ullapool Pt

Ullapool
CG
Bn
QR
R

OTTER BANK

LOCH   BROOM

Ferry

Rubha Buidhe

123   196   41   73   16   8₂   9   23   105   27   29   25   13   22   32   105   68   10   7

57° 54'·38

5°10'W

53'

DUNVEGAN
Depths in Metres

One Mile

N

Jetty
Fl(3)G s
FlWG 3s 14m 7·5M
Uiginish Pt

Garbh Eilein

Fiadhairt Peninsula

Black Rk

Eilean Grianal

Eilean Dubh

Eilean Mòr

LOCH   MORE

Leinish Pt
Slip

Green
White
Obscd

6°36'W   37'   38'   39'   40'

57° 27'

26'

LOCH LAXFORD
Depths in Metres

N

Loch A'Chadh-Fi

Ardmore

Meall an Ulbhaidh

Rubh' na h-Airde Bige

Eilean Mhadaidh

Rubh' an Aiseig

Laxford Bay

Cnoc

Eilean Ard

Fanagmore Bay

Bàgh na Fionndalach Mòire

Ardmore Pt

Glas Leac

Sgeir Ruadh

Rubha Ruadh

En an Sìthein

LOCH DUGHAILL

One Mile   0   1

58° 24'

25'

5°7'W   6'   5'   8'   9'

23'

LOCH EWE
Depths in Metres

Cables   0   6

N

An Sagart
An Fraochlachan
AWASH AT HW

Wooded

Creagan nan Ondaagean

Port na Cloiche Gile

Boor Rocks

Pier
Hotel (conspic)
Poolewe

5°38'   39'   36'

57° 47'

46·5'

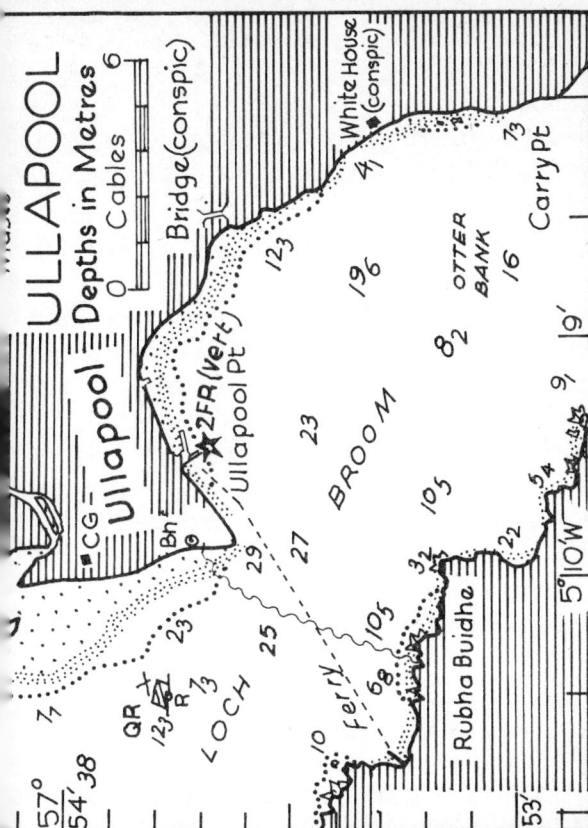

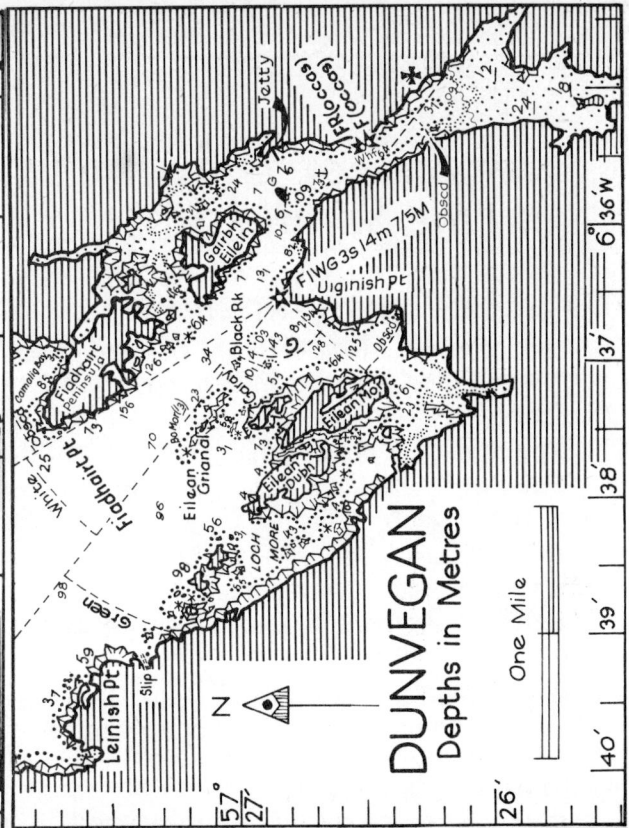

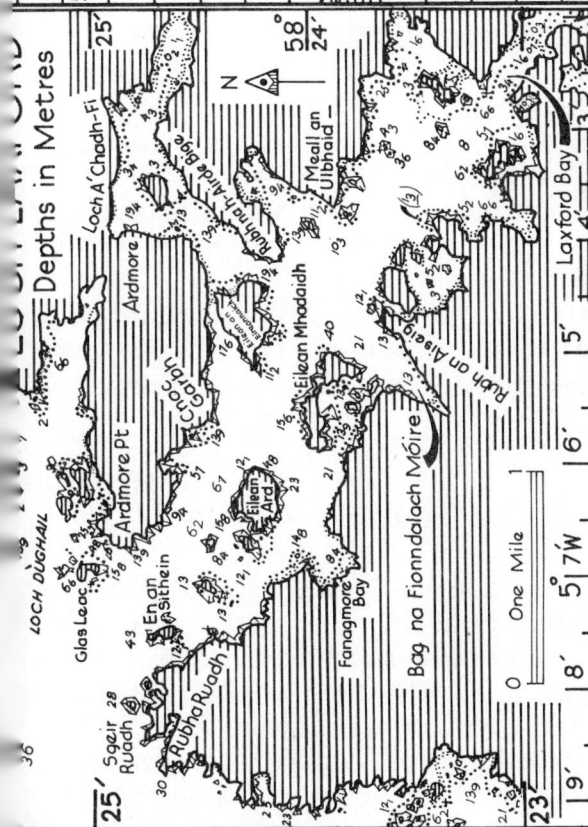

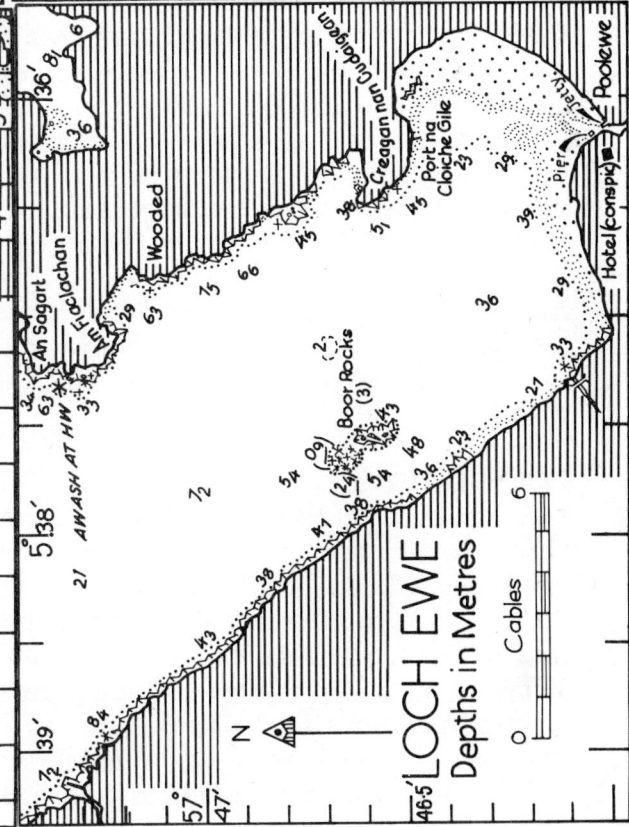

...d on British Admiralty Charts (nos. in text) with the permission of the Controller of H.M. Stationery Office and of ...ydrographer of the Navy, and on other sources.

East Side of The Minches–Isle of Skye (West) and the Small Isles

UIG BAY, LOCH SNIZORT   Chart BA 2533

HW −5.00.   MHWS 5.1; MLWS 0.6; MTL 2.8; MHWN 3.7; MLWN 2.0.

A small bay on the E side of Loch Snizort 8M from the N end of Skye, easy access.

Approach   Between Eil Trodday and the N tip of Skye the tide runs up to 3½kn. The flood sets E and the ebb sets W 2¾h after LW and HW respectively. From the W the Ascrib Is should be given a reasonable berth: otherwise no dangers in the approach.

Entrance   If coming from N round Ru Idrigil, avoid the spit running out 1 ca southwards from it, and the shoal running out from Rubha Dubh, just before the pier.

Anchorage   In 5m just NE of the pier-head (FRG). Swell in W to SW winds. Stores, water, gas. Steamer to Outer Isles, bus to Portree.

LOCH DUNVEGAN   Chart BA 2533   (Plan p199)

HW −5.10.   MHWS 5.2; MLWS 0.7; MTL 2.9; MHWN 3.8; MLWN 2.1.

Easy of access. Care needed approaching the head of the loch.

Approach and entrance   Tiderips will be encountered off Vaternish Pt to the N and Neist Pt to the W: keep a good offing from both, at least 2M. 3½M up the loch, Lampay Is 3 ca offshore is very foul and requires a wide berth. Thereafter no dangers until the head, which dries. A lt Fl WR 3s on Uignish Pt shows W over the fairway, R over dangers to the W. Course 128° on church tr clears all dangers to Gairbh Eilean. A G con buoy marks a rk 0.9m 1½ ca SE of Gairbh Eilean.

Anchorages   (1) Under the Castle. Leave G buoy to stb. (2) W of the church, in mid-chan, 6m. Pass N of G con buoy or keep 50m off W shore. Head of loch dries to a line not much further than this (see plan). Stores, fuel, gas, water, inn, steamer.

LOCH HARPORT   Chart BA 1795

HW −5.15.   MHWS 5.1; MLWS 0.8; MTL 2.9; MHWN 3.8; MLWN 2.1.

Offers shelter in bad weather from W.

Approach   Keep 2M off Neist Pt to avoid the race, and give Ru Ruadh 3M W of the entrance to L Bracadale a similar berth to clear the reef marked at its outer end by Dubh Sgeir Rk 5m above HW. McLeod's Maidens, three basalt columns 33m (outer) to 66m (inner), are a landmark ½M W of Ru Idrigill. The approach is exposed and surf breaks heavily in the vicinity of Dubh Sgeir.

Entrance   Enter between Wiay Is, clean to within 1½ ca, and Ru na Clach, giving the SE shore a fair berth. Pass well S of Oronsay Is, and give a good berth to

Ardtreck Pt (lt Iso 4s). Beyond here the loch is clean but dries for 1M at the head.
Anchorage   Off Carbost on the SW shore 1½M from the head, in 7m between distillery and pier. Mud. Shoal off burn. Stores, water.

Loch Scavaig   Close under the Cuillin Hills, magnificent scenery. Exposed to SW and fierce squalls off mountains. Entrance tricky. Take warps ashore. Visit in settled weather only. Use CCC SD.

CANNA
Chart BA 2208   (Plan p202)

HW −5.00.   Rise (est) MHWS 4.8; MHWN 3.7.
A very sheltered refuge, easy of access.
Approach   There are groups of rks extending 10M SW of Canna. Magnetic variation is abnormal in the vicinity. Approaching from SE, keep 2M off Rhum in swell from SW to avoid reflected seas.
Entrance   The entrance lies between Canna and Sanday at the E end of the Is. There are rks which cover only at HWS, 3 ca N of Sanday, which should be left to port going in. Approach entrance on a SW course for Rubha Carrinnis. Round it 100m off and steer 260° to avoid the drying rk near the pier.
Anchorage   In 3–4m on a line between the two churches on Canna to N and Sanday to S, just beyond the drying rk. Further up, the bay dries out. Very limited stores, water. Ferry to other islands and mainland three to four times a week.

RHUM
Chart BA 2208

HW −5.00.   Rise (est) MHWS 4.8; MLWS 3.7.
The anch is in Loch Scresort, on the E side of the Is, exposed to E. Approach rather to N of centreline of loch: a reef runs out 2 ca from the S shore at the entrance. Anch in 4m near head of loch before reaching the jetty. Limited provisions. Steamer.

EIGG
Chart BA 2207

HW −5.00.   MHWS 4.7; MLWS 0.5; MTL 2.6; MHWN 3.5; MLWN 1.6.
The two linked anchs are at the SE of the Is. Shelter can be had from any wind; subject to swell. Approach from S between Eiln Chathastail (Castle Is) and shore of Eigg, or from NE between bns marking Flad Sgeir and Garbh Sgeir (the latter covers only MHWS and above). Anch as directed E of the jetty, or in NE winds go through narrows mid-chan and anch SW of Galmisdale Pt. There is a reef off the pt by the jetty. Strong ebb starts 2h before HW in the chan. Holding not good. Limited stores, water, gas. Eigg Harbour (or 'flagship' *Eilean ban Mora*) listens on Chan 16.

PASSAGE NOTES: LOCH EWE TO KYLE OF LOCHALSH AND ARDNAMURCHAN

In the Inner Sound between Skye and the mainland DS is S −1.00; N +3.00. The passage is clear of danger to Cow Is. Between the Crowlin Is. and the mainland

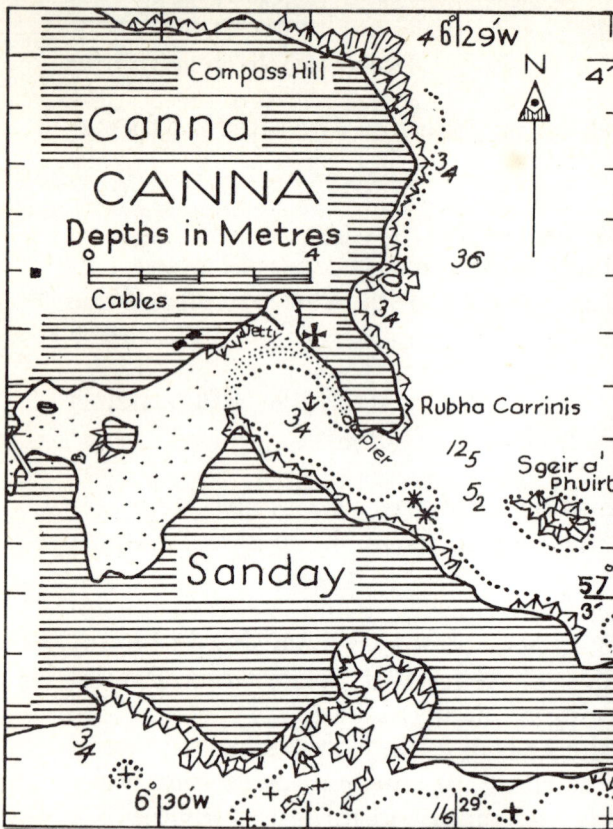

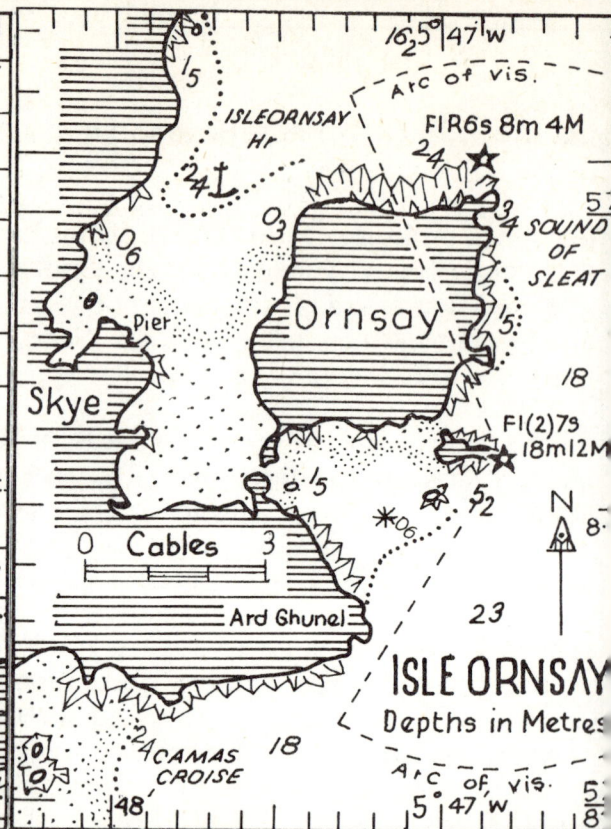

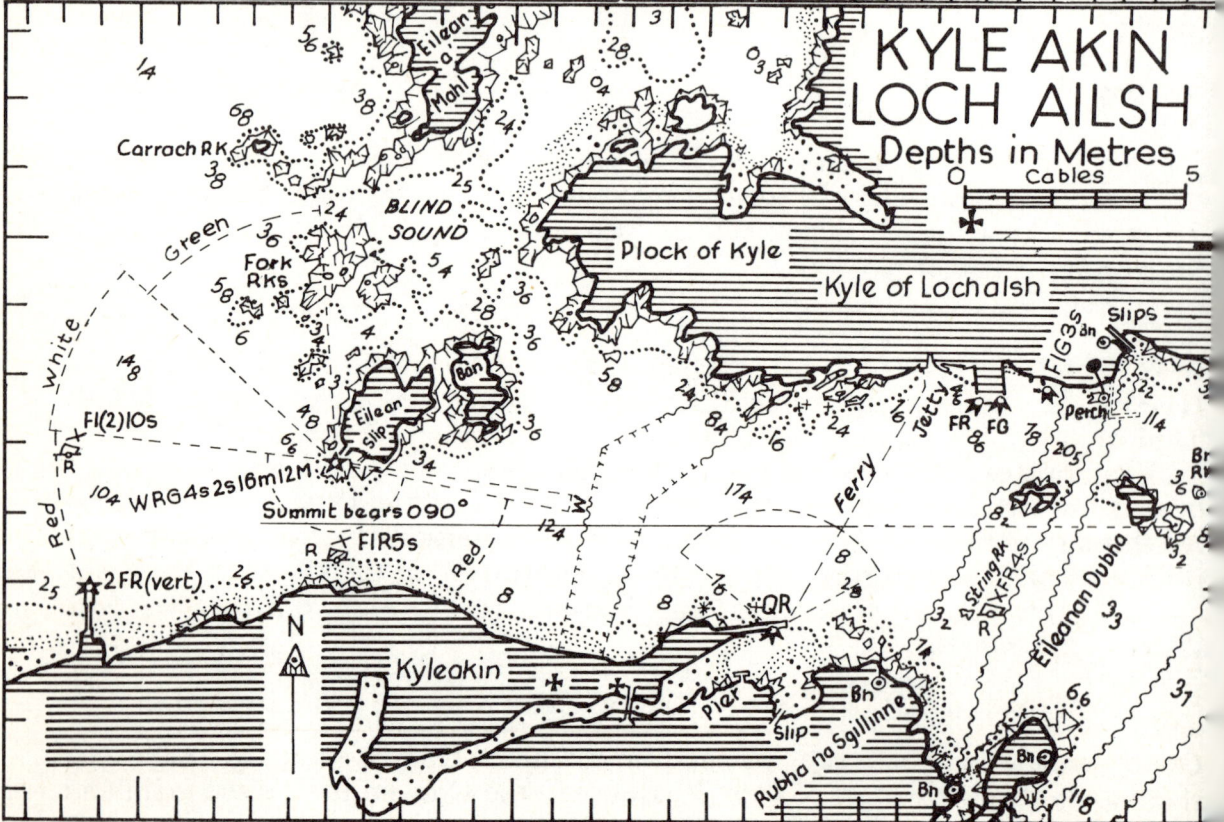

Canna
CANNA
Depths in Metres

Compass Hill

46|29'w

N
4'

36

Cables

Jetty

34

34

34

Rubha Carrinis

Pier

12₅

5₂

Sgeir a' Phuirt

Sanday

3₄

57
3₇

6°|30'w

16|29'

16.5 | 47'w

Arc of vis.

ISLEORNSAY Hr

Fl R6s 8m 4M

24

15

24

34

SOUND OF SLEAT

06

03

Pier

Skye

Ornsay

15

18

34

Fl(2)7s 18m12M

15

5₂

06

Cables

0   3

Ard Ghunel

23

ISLE ORNSAY
Depths in Metres

N
8'

8.

CAMAS CROISE

18

Arc of vis.

5°47'w

5

KYLE AKIN
LOCH AILSH
Depths in Metres

Cables
0   5

5₆

14

Eilean Mahl

28

04

03

68

38

Carrach Rk

Green

36

24

BLIND SOUND

25

Fork Rks

58

54

6

Plock of Kyle

Kyle of Lochalsh

Fl G 3s 8m
Slips

White

14₈

48

Eilean Slip

Ban

36

58

2₄

FR FG
86

Jetty

Perch

Fl(2)10s

6₅

34

84

6

174

Ferry

20₅
114

Red

WRG4s2s16m12M

Summit bears 090°

Fl R5s

12₄

Red

8

8

String Rk
X FR 4s
R

Eileanan Dubha

2FR(vert)

2₅

8

16

QR

3₂

33

N

Kyleakin

Pier

Bn

Slip

6₆

31

Rubha na Sgillinne

Bn

118

the chan is clean towards the island side. There are a number of dangerous rocks in the narrows between Kyle Akin and Kyle of Lochalsh.

If making for Portree between Raasay and Scalpay, note that at the narrows the tidal streams change. The flood sets S ¼h after LW, the ebb sets N ¾h before HW, −4.45, at 2 to 3kn. In this passage there are dangerous rks and reefs.

The tide runs 6–8kn in Kyle Rhea (pron. Ray), turning at HW and LW Ullapool. Flood runs N, ebb S. Strong eddies. Heavy overfall off Glenelg, particularly in S wind over ebb.

From here to Ardnamurchan Pt the passage is straightforward having due regard to charted dangers. Keep 2M offshore between Mallaig and Arisaig if large-scale charts not carried. Bo Faskadale Rk 3M N of Ardnamurchan marked by a G con lt buoy should be passed to the N. A big sea builds up off Ardnamurchan in westerly weather: small craft should preferably choose settled weather and stand a mile off when rounding it.

ISLE OF SKYE (EAST)
Care is required in the vicinity of Trodday Is and the N tip of Skye. There are rocks and the tide runs 3½kn, with race conditions.

STAFFIN BAY
HW −4.50
Exposed to N. Entrance clear. Anch in 6m 1 ca off Stenchol Is between its centre and the shore. Limited stores.

SOUTH RONA
Difficult of access. Excellent shelter. Use CCC SD.

FLADDAY (RAASAY)
Very snug. Use CCC SD.

PORTREE   Chart BA 2534
HW −4.45.   MHWS 5.3; MLWS 0.7; MTL 2.9; MHWN 3.7; MLWN 1.9.
The principal town on Skye. Anch subject to strong squalls.
Approach   Keep 300m off Am Tom Pt and the N and S shores to avoid rks; otherwise there is no difficulty.
Anchorage   NE of the pier (R lt) in 5m but not near the burn to N where holding is poor. Stores, water, fuel in 5 gal amounts, gas.

ISLE ORNSAY   Chart BA 2209   (Plan p202)
Excellent anchorage 8M SW of Kyle of Lochalsh in Sound of Sleat. Also useful while awaiting tide through Kyle Rhea. Approach clean from N between Isle Ornsay and Skye. Anch in 5m in the centre of bay. Sound carefully, as the bay is shoal a long way out from the hd. Limited stores, water, hotel.

Mainland–Loch Gairloch to Ardnamurchan Point

LOCH GAIRLOCH   Charts BA 2528, 2210
HW −4.40.   MHWS 5.2; MLWS 0.6; MTL 2.9; MHWN 4.0; MLWN 1.8.
Rather exposed to W.
Approach   Approach S of Long Is where the chan is 2M wide and clean.
Entrance   Straight up the loch, which is clean except for the branch into Loch Shieldaig (not to be confused with the one in Loch Torridon).
Anchorages   (1) In the N branch of the three lochs (bays ½M long) at the head, called Flowerdale Bay. The bay is clean. Anch in 6m in the centre of the bay no further than the outer end of the pier. Pier QR lt. Stores 1M, fuel, water. Pier dues reported high. (2) Badachro Hr, W of Eil Morrisdale. Keep to E side of chan entering, anch N of more E-ly of two main islets. Stores, hotel. CCC SD needed.

CROWLIN ISLES   Chart BA 2209
HW −4.45.   MHWS 5.3; MLWS 0.7; MTL 3.1; MHWN 4.0; MLWN 2.2.
Off the tip of Applecross, 5M NW of Kyle of Lochalsh.
Approach   A spit runs N from Eil Beg which must be cleared when approaching from N or W. The approach from the NE is clear.
Entrance and anchorage   Enter from N steering for chan between Eil More and Eil Meadhonac, keeping closer to Eil More. Anch in 4m before the first narrows. The S channel is not navigable. Good shelter, no supplies.

KYLE OF LOCHALSH   Chart BA 2540   (Plan p202)
HW −4.50.   MHWS 5.3; MLWS 0.8; MTL 3.1; MHWN 3.9; MLWN 2.2.
Useful hr for changing crews.
Approach   From NW and E the narrows have several hazards, but these are well marked, and Lt Ho has W sectors over clear water (see plan).
Berthing   (1) Anch off the hotel in 11m clear of the ferry. Exposed and disturbed. Stores, water, gas, trains to Inverness. (2) Temporarily alongside E side of pier, to provision etc. Stores, water, fuel from hose. (3) In small pool S of ferry pier at Kyle Akin (Skye), alongside as space allows.

MALLAIG   Chart BA 2534   (Plan p207)
HW −5.20.   MHWS 5.0; MLWS 0.7; MTL 2.9; MHWN 3.8; MLWN 2.1.
One of the largest ports on the W coast of Scotland, much used by ferries and fishing fleets.
Approach   From the N the strong tides in Kyle Rhea must be borne in mind, otherwise approach from N and S is straightforward.
Entrance   Enter W or E of Sgeir Dhearg (conspic W bn Iso 2s). Care required at night to locate bn against town lts. Ldg lts at pier.

Berthing   Controlled by HM. Anch in 6m in centre of hr just past second pier if room allows. Tripping line essential. Usually room to lie alongside during day. Stores, water, fuel, gas, chandlers. Trains to Glasgow, steamer to Small Is and Outer Hebrides.

PASSAGE NOTES: ARDNAMURCHAN POINT TO MULL OF KINTYRE

Ardnamurchan Pt is the westernmost pt of the Scottish mainland. Vessels southbound may take the exposed outer route through the Passage of Tiree, or the protected inner route through the Sound of Mull, Firth of Lorne and Sound of Jura. At the N end of the Sound of Jura, the Crinan Canal provides a short-cut to the Clyde Estuary. This can be useful in bad weather, avoiding heavy seas in the North Channel between the Mull of Kintyre and the NE coast of Ireland.

COLL TO ISLAY
The Passage of Tiree is entirely open to the SW, and small craft are advised against its use if strong SW-lies are forecast, because of the dangerous rocks and overfalls S of Iona and elsewhere. In settled weather, however, the islands, hills and small hrs make this an enchanting cruising ground.

ARINAGOUR – COLL   Chart BA 2474
HW −5.30.   MHWS 4.4; MLWS 3.2.
Sheltered hr on the W of the Passage of Tiree, halfway down the Is of Coll. Some swell from S/SE.
Approach   From the N avoid the Cairns of Coll, a group of rks extending 2M to the N of Coll; marked by a lt Fl 12s, but the outermost rk is unmarked. The shore is clean from this pt to Loch Eatharna in which lies Arinagour. From the S beware of unmarked rk halfway between Skerryvore and the S end of Tiree. Along the E coasts of Tiree and Coll, keep an offing of at least 1½M passing outside Roan Bogha, RW buoy Fl(3) 12s, at the E entrance to Gunna Sound.
Entrance and anchorage   The anch is best located by the new pier to the NW of the G buoy (lt). The pier is prominent; steer for it leaving G buoy to stb. Continue along the W of the loch towards the old pier. Anch in 4m just before the pt which marks rks to stb. Loch shoals rapidly beyond. Stores, water, fuel, gas. Launderette, hotel. Steamer.

GOMETRA – MULL   Chart BA 2652   (Plan p207)
HW −6.00.   MHWS 4.4; MLWS 0.6; MTL 2.5; MHWN 3.2; MLWN 1.8.
A perfectly protected hr between the Is of Gometra and Ulva on the W coast of Mull. Care needed in heavy weather.
Approach   The SW tip of Gometra Is should be given an offing of 1M to clear the reefs extending SE of Maisgear. From the S keep W of Little Colonsay avoiding the reefs extending 1½ ca offshore.
Entrance   Sgeir na Skeineadh, a rk drying 3.2m, lies 4 ca due S of the entrance.

Keep an offing of between 1 to 2½ ca from the islets off Rubha Brisdeadhrumh, the pt, to the narrows. This clears the rks to the W of the entrance and Sgeir na Skeineadh to the E. Enter the narrows (1 ca wide) slightly E of mid-chan to avoid spur projecting from W.

Anchorage Anch in 6 to 10m on the E side opposite the cottages on Gometra. Find a sandy patch without weed for the anchor. The W side has submerged reefs. No supplies.

STAFFA   Chart BA 2652

A fascinating island, famous for Fingal's Cave, to be visited in calm settled weather only. The anch is difficult and exposed. Landing is dangerous if a swell is running. CCC SD essential.

LOCH NA LATHAICH   Chart BA 2617   (Plan p207)
HW −5.55

An excellent place of shelter in an exposed sea area; 4M E of Iona on the N coast of the Ross of Mull, easy of access.

Approach From the N approach is straightforward. From the S there are many dangers, and this approach should not be attempted without chart 2617.

Entrance and anchorage At the W side of the entrance a group of islets Eil Liathaniac with a W bn Fl WR 6s can be passed on either hand, giving a fair berth. Hold to the W side of the loch, the E side being foul. Keep Eil nam Mean and Eil Ban at the head of the loch to port. Anch in 4m S of Eil Ban. Good shelter, some swell in NW gales. Stores, water, fuel 3M, bus.

IONA

BA chart 2617 and CCC SD are required for navigating the Sound of Iona which is shoal in the middle and has several rocks. Well worth a visit for its historical and religious connections.

ORONSAY – COLONSAY   Chart BA 2169
HW −6.00.   MHWS 3.9; MLWS 0.5; MTL 2.2; MHWN 2.7; MLWN 1.6.

Reasonable shelter from winds from S through W to NE can be found in the bay on the E side of Oronsay.

Approach An offing of ½M is advised if coming down the E shore from the N, until the bay opens up at Eil Treadhrach off the E tip of Oronsay. Continue almost to the N point of Eil Ghaoidmeal before turning NW into the bay.

Entrance and anchorage Enter the bay from the E 2 ca N of Eil Ghaoidmeal to avoid the reef running S of Eil Treadhrach. Supplies at Scalasaig, a good hr but open to E and NE (Plan p207).

ISLAY, SW COAST – LOCH INDAAL   Chart BA 2168
HW −5.00   MHWS 2.3; MLWS 0.8; MTL 1.5; MHWN 1.5; MLWN 1.4.

Exposed to winds from S to SW: not recommended when blowing from that direction. Note the small tidal range, imperceptible at neaps.

MALLAIG HARBOUR

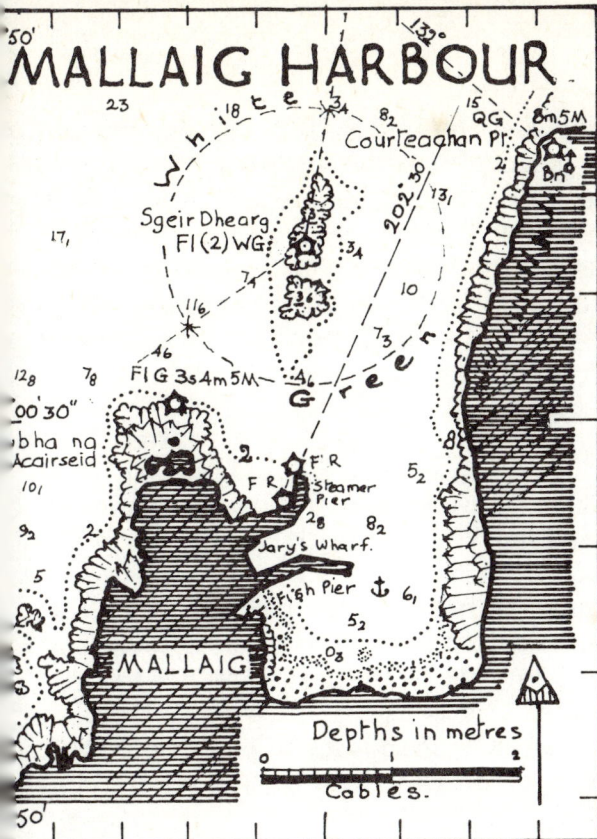

50'

13°

23 18'te 3·4 8·2 15 QG 8m5M

Courteaghan Pt.

Sgeir Dhearg
Fl(2)WG

202°3

13₁

17₁

3·4

10

73

Bn°

46

Gree

12₈ 7₈ Fl G 3s4m5M 4·6

·00'30"

·bha na
Acairseid

10₁

2·9

2

5·2

F R
Steamer
Pier
F R
2·8 8·2

Jary's Wharf.

5 9·2 2

Fish Pier 6₁

5·2

MALLAIG 0·3

Depths in metres

0 ... 1 ... 2

Cables.

50'

GOMETRA

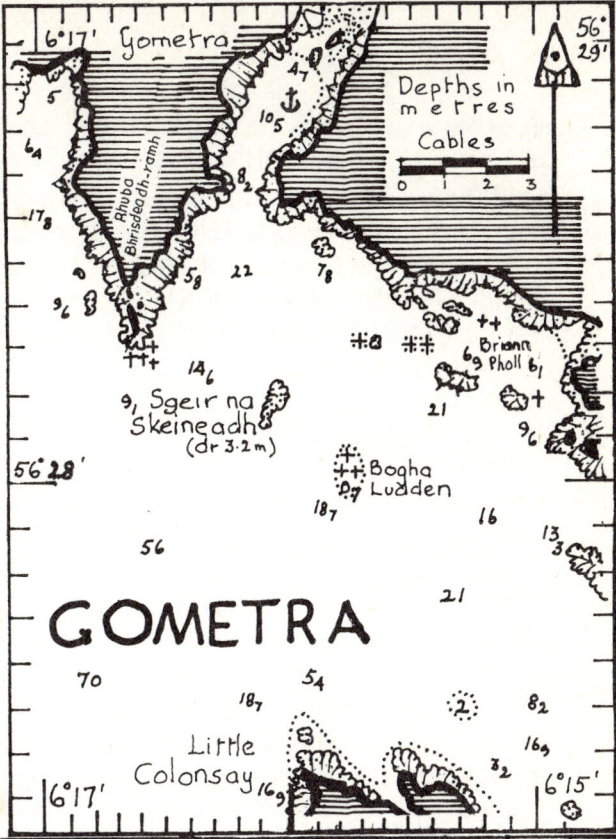

6°17' Gometra

56°
29'

5 47

Depths in
metres

Cables

0 1 2 3

6·4 105

17₈ 0 82

5·8 22

9·6

7₈

++

+₀ ** 6·9 Brian
Pholl 6₁

9₁ Sgeir na
Skeineadh
(dr 3·2m)

14·6

21 9·6

56 28'

++ Bogha
Ludden

18₇

9·7

16

13₃

56

21

GOMETRA

70

5·4

18₇

2₁ 8·2

Little
Colonsay 16·9

8

16·9

3·2

6°15'

6°17'

LOCH NA LATHAICH

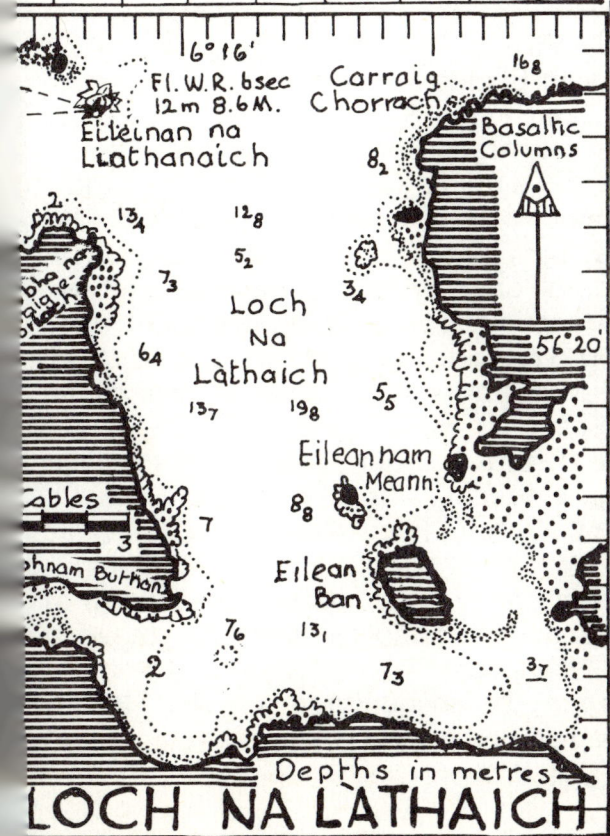

6°16'

Fl.W.R. 6sec
12m 8.6.M.

Carraig
Chorrach

16·8

Eilean na
Liathanaich

8·2

Basaltic
Columns

2 13₁ 12₈

73 5·2 3·4

56°20'

·bha
·laigh

6·4

Loch
Na
Làthaich

13₇ 19₈ 5·5

Eilean nam
Meann

8·8

Eilean
Ban

Cables

3 7

·hnam Buthan

7·6 13₁

2 37

73

Depths in metres

LOCH NA LATHAICH

SCALASAIG

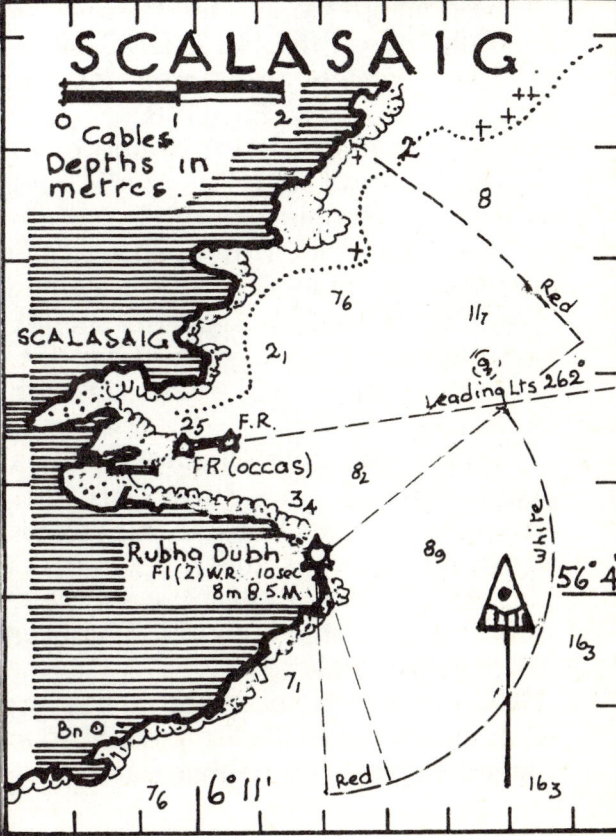

++

0 Cables 2 +

Depths in
metres

2

8

+

SCALASAIG

7·6

1·7

Red

2₁

3 Leading Lts 262°

2·5 F.R.

F.R.(occas) 8·2

3·4

Rubha Dubh
Fl(2)W.R. 10sec
8m 8.5.M.

8·9

56° 4'

White

7₁

16₃

Bn °

7·6 6°11' Red 16₃

·d on British Admiralty Charts (nos. in text) with the permission of the Controller of H.M. Stationery Office and of
·lydrographer of the Navy, and on other sources.

207

Approach   The W coast of Islay is exposed to N, W and S. Tides attain 8 to 9kn and numerous overfalls in the area are a hazard for small vessels.
Entrance   The entrance is straightforward providing the reef extending ½M W of Laggan Pt on the E side of the entrance to Loch Indaal is given a wide berth.
Anchorage   (1) In 5m beyond the pier at Bowmore on the E side of the loch. Subject to bad swell from SW. Stores, water at houses, gas. Steamer and plane to mainland. (2) Off Bruichladdich Pier on W side of loch; better in W-lies, but still uncomfortable.

TOBERMORY TO MULL OF KINTYRE   Charts BA 2171, 2169, 2168
The Sound of Mull gives a protected passage between the NE coast of Mull and the mainland. Dangers in the sound are well marked, and with careful use of the proper charts there are no problems. The tide runs up to 3kn.

At Duart Pt, E end of Mull, the tide runs 3kn between the pt and Lady's Rk, SW of Lismore. Lady's Rk covers at highest tides. It is marked by a bn Fl 6s 12m, not to be confused with Lismore lt Fl 10s 32m, ½M to the NE.

Turning S, Dubh Sgeir and Bogha Nuadh rks lie 1½ to 2M WSW of Kerrera Is. Kerrera Sound may be entered from N or S. The N chan is narrow and care must be taken to avoid Corran Ledge in the N of Oban Bay. The S chan is wide and well buoyed.

The tidal stream accelerates and runs strongly through Fladda Narrows with overfalls and whirlpools. Chart 2169 of the Firth of Lorne is essential, because of the many dangers in the area. Pass through Fladda Narrows roughly mid-chan with Fladda Lt Ho Fl(3)WR 18s to W, and Dubh Sgeir Lt Fl 6s to E. Once through the narrows, the Sound of Luing is straightforward, but the whole of Fladda Narrows and Sound of Luing are subject to overfalls and swirling currents. Loch Shuna to the E has a number of excellent anchs. See CCC SD.

Bound for Crinan or Loch Craignish, pass S of Coiresa and Craignish Pt; otherwise continue S, W of Reisa an t-Sruith. The passage to Craignish is subject to swirls and overfalls: CCC SD should be carried. If keeping W, beware of being swept through the dangerous Gulf of Corryvreckan, whose current reaches 8½kn W at spring floods, and where seas with tide against wind or swell can overwhelm an average yacht.

If proceeding down the Sound of Jura there is a submerged reef of irregular depth, parts of which surface as islands, extending 4M SSW of Craignish Pt, terminating at Ruadh Sgeir, lt Fl 6s 13.5m. Without large-scale charts the whole of this line of reef should be avoided.

Further S do not close the shores without large-scale charts. The SE end of Islay and the whole area of Gigha Is are heavily encumbered with rks extending 2M or more offshore.

There is a bad race, and heavy seas may be encountered, off the Mull of Kintyre. Small vessels are advised to await settled weather before attempting to round it, or use the Crinan Canal.

TOBERMORY
Chart BA 2474   (Plan p210)

HW −4.55.   DS: SE −5.20; NW −0.20.
MHWS 4.4; MLWS 0.7; MTL 2.5; MHWN 3.3; MLWN 1.8.
Entrance   Round N of Calve Is, no hazards.
Anchorages   (1) In 7m $\frac{3}{4}$ ca off pier-head at Tobermory. (2) Off Aros in SE corner of bay in 7m, restricted by fish farming. (3) In Doirlinn: chan between Calve Is and Mull. Do not go beyond point where depth falls to 5m, as there is a ruined bn in the chan. Stores, water, fuel in cans from behind steamer pier, gas, steamer.

LOCH ALINE
Chart BA 2390

HW −5.00.   MHWS 4.5; MHWN 3.2.
10M SE of Tobermory on the mainland side. Very sheltered.
Entrance   The tide runs fast in the entrance. Give the pts a good berth. Ldg marks 356° on quarry buildings, just inside on W shore, lead up the entrance marked by port and stb hand buoys. Keep ldg mks in line until abreast village, thence mid-chan.
Anchorage   Inside E pt of entrance in 7m, out of the stream. Stores from village.

LOCH LINNHE AND THE CALEDONIAN CANAL
Charts BA 2378, 2379, 2380

HW (Corpach) −4.50.   MHWS 4.1; MLWS 0.9; MTL 2.5; MHWN 3.1; MLWN 1.9.
Loch Linnhe provides access to the Caledonian Canal, thence to the Moray Firth on the NE coast of Scotland. Detailed charts of Loch Linnhe and the Caledonian Canal and the CCC SD are advised. The tide runs through Corran Narrows at 6kn and there are shoals to avoid in the vicinity. Beyond Corran, navigation presents no difficulty as far as Fort William (anch). The canal is entered at Corpach in the SW, and Clachnaharry, Inverness in the NE. The canal is 60M long of which 38M are through lochs. There are 29 locks. It can accommodate vessels of length 55m× beam $11\frac{1}{2}$m × draft $4\frac{1}{4}$m. Only sea locks open on Sunday, subject to staff availability and extra fee. Latest information obtainable from the Manager, Caledonian Canal, Clachnaharry, Inverness. Chart obtainable at either end. Passage of the canal takes a minimum of two days owing to speed limits and limited lock working hours (0800–1200 and 1300–1700).

Fixed bridge, clearance 18.2m at entrance to Loch Leven.

DUNSTAFFNAGE
Chart BA 2378

A useful sheltered anch 5M N of Oban when winds in Sound of Kerrera (Oban) are strong. Easy of access. Enter between Dunstaffnage Is and the pt. Anch in 6m near castle. Numerous moorings.

OBAN – ARDENTRAIVE BAY
Chart BA 1790   (Plan p210)

HW −5.15.   MHWS 4.0; MLWS 0.7; ML 2.4; MHWN 2.9; MLWN 1.8.

TOBERMORY HARBOUR

Cables
Depths in metres

Fl 3s 17m 15M
Rubha nan Gall
19₂
27

S O U N D   O F   M U L L

Rubha na Leip 19 43
23
40
4₃
TOBERMORY C.C.hut (white)
Pier Pier 43
2 FG
25
3
1₅ white mark
19₇
14₃ (9₇)
14
8₃
23
Eilean na Beithe
White post
Calve Island
Sgeir Calve (dr1·8m) 47
10₇
56° 37' (dr12m)
white mark 19₄
Dairlinn A Chailbhe 17 7₈
19₁
38'
56° 37'

LOCH CRAIGNISH

Shuna 5°36'
14
Culbhale + (·15) 6₇
22
46 2₁
34
Ardfern Yacht Centre Pier 7₃
Eilean Inshaig 13₄
17 8₇
Eilean + 6 Mhic Chrion
Hutcheson Rk + 18₉
12₅ ¾ Fort
24
22
13₁
Eilean Ona (·15) +
3₂
Eilean Dubh
Eilean Righ
Black Rks + 6₇ +
33
82 (0·2) +
14₅ Jetty
56°
+
Loch Beag
Mast
42 10
10₄
27
L o c h   C r a i g n i s h
Eilean Macaskin 7₆
Craignish Pt. 6₇
31
33
25
(·3)
+ (18)
Garbh Reisa 7₃
55
31
N
Cables Depths in metres

OBAN

cables
Depths in metres

25
5°30' 12₁ 23
Obscured 29' Carraig Mhichell
17₁
31 46 38
Fl.R 3sec 7m 4M
4
Rubha Bhearnaig
white
12₅
23
Wilson Rk
37
Dunollie Fl W.G. 3sec 7m. 5A M Memorial
14
Hutchesons Monument (conspic)
7 2₈
14₆
Rubha Chruidh
Sewer outfall
9₂
2₄
7
Q.G × G
18₉
white
13₇ 2₈ 9₂
Yacht moorings
17₇
30
18₃
Ardantrive Bay
38
Green
56°24'
OBAN
2₅
32
38
119
Obstn
2 FG (vert)
×Q
41
BY
40
39
14₃
QG+LFl 15₂ 3 18₃
(1₁)
4₉
34
Oc.G 6sec 10m 3M
43
YB 11 3₁ 6₁ 18₉ 27 (vert)
17₄ 27 13₁ 2 FG (vert)
7₉ 2₁
4 12₈

Based on British Admiralty Charts (nos. in text) with the permission of the Controller of H.M. Stationery Office and the Hydrographer of the Navy, and on other sources.

Approach   There are a number of dangers in the Sound of Kerrera but these are mostly well marked and should present no difficulty if the navigation marks are correctly used.

Entrance and anchorage   The centre of Oban Bay has the Sgeir Rathaid Bank lying in the middle of the fairway, which dries 1.2m. Yachts moor in Ardentraive Bay: go alongside pontoon and ask at boatyard. No room to anch. No satisfactory anch at Oban: yachts can lie to rly pier but it is exposed and boat should not be left unattended. Water, fuel, boatyard at Ardentraive; all stores, hotels, trains to Glasgow at Oban.

PUILLADOBHRAIN   Chart BA 2387
(Pron. 'pulldoran'.) A beautiful sheltered lagoon, 8M SW of Oban, at the N of Seil Is near Clachan Bridge ('the bridge over the Atlantic'). Use CCC SD.
   Easdale Sd, Cuan Sd, Scarba Sd also provide access to anchs worth visiting.

LOCH MELFORT AND LOCH SHUNA   Chart BA 2326
There are a number of excellent anchs in this loch, of which the following are recommended. (1) Craobh Is. Very secluded and snug, in 9m behind Eil Arsa. Restricted by fish farming. (2) N end of Shuna Is in 4m. A small bay just inside the pt. Marina at Loch Melfort in Loch na Cille. Slip, shipyard, all repairs.

LOCH CRAIGNISH – ARDFERN YACHT CENTRE
                                          Chart BA 2326   (Plan p210)
Toward the head of the loch a yacht centre with all facilities for yachtsmen has been developed, providing a much needed facility on this otherwise sparsely provided coast.

Approach   Straightforward, but this is an area of strong tides (8kn in Dorus Mor between Craignish Pt and Garbh Reisa) and CCC SD should be carried. Above all, avoid being swept through Corryvreckan if going N on the flood.

Entrance   The entrance to Loch Craignish by the main chan is clear if the shores and islands are given a berth of 1½ ca. Sg Dubh lies 2¼M up the loch, 2 ca S of the first two Is, Eil Buidhe and Eil Dubh, on the W side. Enter Ardfern Yacht Centre hr between Eil Mhic Chrion and Eil Inshaig, keeping well over to the Mhic Chrion side of the chan (the chart is misleading).

Berthing   Pick up a mooring and confirm ashore. In light or E winds one can also anch in the E end of the loch, 7–8m. Stores, chandlery, repairs, fuel, hotel etc at Ardfern.

LOCH CRINAN   Charts BA 2320, 2326
HW +5.50
Entrance to the Crinan Canal, 7½ (sea) miles long, providing a short-cut to the Firth of Clyde. In spite of its comparatively short length, the bridges, 15 locks and short working hours mean that a prompt start is needed to be sure of getting through in one day.

Approach The warnings for Loch Craignish apply also to Loch Crinan.
Entrance There are no difficulties in entering Loch Crinan if the shores are given a berth of 1½ ca, and care is taken to avoid Black Rk 2 ca N of Crinan Lt Ho.
Berthing (1) Anch in Crinan Hr W of the entrance to the Canal, between the hotel and Eil da Mheinn in 3 to 4m. Many private moorings. (2) Moor in either of the two basins of the Canal just through the sea lock. Limited stores, water, fuel, gas, chandlery, yacht yard.

CRINAN CANAL

The Crinan Canal runs from Crinan on the mainland, opposite the N end of the Isle of Jura, to Ardrishaig on Loch Fyne. The passage through the canal is 7½NM long, saving a coastwise passage round the Mull of Kintyre of 80M. The sea locks, which normally open at all states of the tide, and bridges are manned, but for locks in the canal one of the crew must be put ashore to take warps and operate the locks, so the passage can be tiring if short-handed. Working hours are strictly observed. Warning blasts on the horn must be given when approaching bridges. A fast time for transit is 6h. Max. vessel size 26.8m × 6.1m × 2.7m.

In very dry weather limitations on the supply and use of water for operating locks may be imposed, and the sea locks may only operate between HW −3 and +3. It is recommended that up-to-date information be obtained beforehand from the Crinan Canal Office at Ardrishaig or the lock-keeper at Crinan. Assistance through the canal can sometimes be obtained at either end at mutually agreed rates. There is almost 5h difference in the tidal constants for Crinan and Ardrishaig at the ends of the canal. Yachts going W have right of way. The W part of the canal is narrow and rock-sided, and great vigilance is needed particularly when rounding corners.

TAYVALLICH   Chart BA 2397   (Plan p213)

An extremely attractive, sheltered and popular anch in Loch Swen.
Approach and entrance From the S the chan between Eilean nan Leac and Corr Eilean is clear. From the N avoid Keills Rk and Danna Rk by keeping ¾M W of Danna Is. Once Sgeir Bun an Locha is visible clear of Sgeir Dhonncha, it is safe to cut across and into the loch entrance. Watch out for tidal sets. At the entrance keep over toward the E side of the loch. 3M up the loch, keep W of Sgeirean a Mhain (0.3m): the loch is then clear to the head.
Anchorage Tayvallich lies in a bay on the W shore near the head of the loch. The bay narrows to 100m with a rk in the middle of the narrows. Anch outside this dividing barrier, or enter keeping to the SW side and enter the inner hr. Many moorings, but anch allowed close to the central reef which nearly cuts this inner lagoon into two. Best pick up a mooring and ask advice ashore. Stores, water, gas, fuel, occasional bus conns. Good inn-restaurant.

LOCH SWEEN
Depths in Metres

TAYVALLICH

N

Tayvallich Quay
Turbiskill
Oib Rks
10.4
18.9
23
23
Eilean Loain
21
16.2
56
19.8
18.9
18.6
LOCH SWEEN
18.3
27.8
59
Kintallan
Rubha Cool
Quay
5.4
Oib Rks
CABLES 3
Rubha na Airde
12.8
29
11
Strong tidal streams
Taynish I
12.2
113
14
15.2
14
N
55°
58'
55°
Port Keills Jetties
18.3
19.3
Causeway
Rubh Breatanich
23.3
23
Jetty
LOCH NA CILLE
na no Cille
13.1
7
13.1
57'
Island of Danna
6.7
6.1
th Eilean
6.7
5
Castle Sween (ruins)(conspic)
Dhonnchai
10.7
10.1
2.7
6.1
6.7
7.3
8.1
Rk
7
5°42'W
40'
39'
38'
37'
36'
56'

0   1   Miles   2

PORT ELLEN
Depths in metres

6°13'
Imreual
White house (Red Roof)
PORT ELLEN
Port Im'ereaual
Kilnaughton Bay
3.7
7
Rubha Glas
Dr .2.3
5.2
3.4
Bn
Ro-Ro Terminal
The Ard
C.G
Rubha a Chuinniein
6.4
8.5
12.2
White
8.2
(4)
Fl.W.R.G. 19m 8&6 M
Ceann nan Ribheann
3.7
(5)
Carraig Fhada Lt Ho (conspic)
7
Green
4
(dr.9)
Sgeir Thraghaidh
11.5
7
12.2
55°
37'
QG
Red
White
G
7
Am Plodan (0.6)
4.3
15.2
8.5
The Gander (5)
14.5
N
14.3
5.5
5.8
Depths in metres
12.2
Cables
0 1 2 3 4 5

WEST LOCH TARBERT
Depths in metres
Cables

Jetty
6.4
16.5
Pier
6.1
QG 3m 3M
7.6
Rubha nan Leacag
32
9.6
3.1
Pier
9
Ardpatrick Pt.
27
(0.3)
Eilean Traighe
3.7
4.6
QR 3m 3M
10.7
Q(2)10s 11m8M
12.8
Dunskeig Bay
12.2
N
55°45'
14
10.4
4.3
Ronachan Pt.
5°35'

0   5

GIGHA ISLAND / GIGHA

0   5
Cables
41'
6.7
Bhanarach Rocks
Dr 1.5 4.6
Ardminish
Ardminish Bay
5.8
18.3
(0.6)
Sgeir Dhubh
22
Eilean a Chuil
5.2
Carraig nam Ban
18
GIGHA ISLAND
Sgeir Gigalum
.4.6
33
Eilean Liath
11.9
7.6
27
35
Pier
Coolas Gigalum
Y.B.Y
Wee Rocks
5.2
Dr 1.2
Gigalum Rocks
46
7.6
Gigalum
GIGHA
6.1
55°39'
45'
5°43'

---

n British Admiralty Charts (nos. in text) with the permission of the Controller of H.M. Stationery Office and of trographer of the Navy, and on other sources.

PORT ASKAIG, SOUND OF ISLAY   Chart BA 2481
HW −6.00.   MHWS 2.1; MLWS 0.4; MTL 1.1; MHWN 1.5; MLWN 1.0.
A village halfway up the Sound of Islay.
Approach   Keep to the Islay side of the sound, keeping to W of Black Rocks
(buoy). The Jura side is not entirely clear. A large-scale chart is advised to avoid
the various dangers in the sound.
Berthing   Alongside the new quay. Beware strong tides when manoeuvring.
Very small rise and fall at neaps. Stores, inn, water from ferry pier.

PORT ELLEN, ISLAY   Chart BA 2474   (Plan p213)
HW −5.45 sp; +1.35 np.   MHWS 1.9; MLWS 0.3; MTL 0.6; MHWN 0.8;
MLWN 0.5.
Exposed to S. Note the virtual lack of rise and fall at neaps.
Approach and entrance   Having rounded Texa Is and its outlying rks hold 270°
until the Fl WRG 3s lt on Carraig Fhada, on the W coast of the bay, bears 315°.
Make for the G con buoy, QG, in entrance of the bay. Then proceed 360° for
5 ca to clear the reef to the NE of the buoy.
Anchorage   In 4m midway between the pier in the NE corner of the bay and the
pt opposite to the S, but yachts are liable to be in the way of the ferry. If the ferry
is expected there is generally room to tie up against the NE side of the pier. The
bay shoals rapidly beyond this line and vessels should not go further in, though
shallow-draft yachts can dry inside the hr, or stay afloat at neaps. In W-ly
weather more shelter may be obtained off Kilnaughton Beach, ¼M N of Carraig
Fhada. All stores, water.

WEST LOCH TARBERT   Chart BA 2477   (Plan p213)
Approach   There are no difficulties in the approach. Dun Skeig, an isolated hill
142m high on the SE shore ¼M inland, is a good landmark for the entrance.
Entrance   Coming from the N stand off shore for ½M until the loch opens S of
Eil Traighe at the entrance. Stand over to the E of the entrance outside the bn,
QR, because Eil Traighe shoals extensively to the S for at least 2 ca. Keep to the
SE shore for approx 1M till Ardpatrick Ho on the N shore is clearly visible. Chart
2477 is required for safe navigation beyond this point because of rk patches in the
fairway.
Anchorage   When Ardpatrick Ho is well open cross over to NW side. Anch in
6m E of pier, mud and weed. No supplies. Other anchs available further up and
NE of Eilean da Ghallagain in 3m, toward the head of the loch. Perfect shelter at
head. 1M by road from here to E Loch Tarbert, stores, water, fuel, gas,
shipyard.

GIGHA   Chart BA 2475   (Plan p213)
HW +6.00 sp; +2.20 np.   MHWS 1.5; MLWS 0.6; MTL 0.9; MHWN 1.3;
MLWN 0.8.
Gigha Sound can only be navigated safely using large-scale charts. It is

encumbered with dangerous rks but with careful pilotage difficulties can be avoided. Tide runs 2–3kn. Use CCC SD.

Anchorage   Anch in Ardminish Bay to the S of Druimyeon avoiding the reefs extending off each pt and Kiln Rk off the jetty. Excellent holding, exposed to E. See plan. Stores, water in CG hut near landing jetty, gas, hotel.

CAMPBELTOWN   Chart BA 1864   (Plan p218)

HW +0.45.   MHWS 3.0; MLWS 0.4; MTL 1.7; MHWN 2.5; MLWN 0.9.

Well sheltered loch, especially useful when awaiting favourable conditions for rounding Mull of Kintyre.

Approach   From N avoid Otterard Rk, marked by E Card buoy Q(3) 10s, 1M off shore to N. After approx 1M S, after rounding the buoy, shape course 240° for two Y ldg bns (FY). From the E or S, Davarr Is should be given a berth of 1 ca. All between Davarr Is and the shore dries at LW.

Entrance   Pass between Millbeg G con buoy (Fl G 2s) and R can buoy 'A' (Fl R 10s) after which the loch is clear to the hr at its W end. Beware unlit mooring buoys at night.

Berthing   (1) Alongside the outer side of the N pier, SW of the elbow. (2) Anch off the S shore, opposite the quarry and jetty SE of ldg lts. Stores, water, fuel, gas, steamer and air conns.

EAST LOCH TARBERT – LOCH FYNE   Chart BA 2381   (Plan p218)

HW +1.20.   MHWS 3.4; MLWS 0.3; MTL 1.9; MHWN 2.9; MLWN 1.1.

An excellent sheltered hr, with good facilities for yachts.

Approach   Pass N of the bn (Fl R 2½s) marking the reef off Madadh Maol, then S of a second bn (QR) S of Eil a Choic. Do not approach either bn too close.

Entrance   After the second bn has been passed, steer straight for the main quay; keep it open to avoid the shoals that run ENE in line with it.

Berthing   Alongside the quay as space allows, or as directed. There are numerous moorings all over the inner loch: it may be possible to arrange to use one of these.

All facilities and stores. Fuel and water alongside. Steamer. Bus to Ardrishaig and Campbeltown.

ARDRISHAIG   Chart BA 2381

HW +1.20

Mainly used when waiting to enter the Crinan Canal: not a good anch outside.

Approach   Leave R can buoy Fl R 4s at entrance to Loch Gilp to port, G con buoy further in to stb, to clear shoals at entrance of loch. W sector of S pier-head lt leads in at night.

Anchorage   3 ca N by W of S pier-head in 3m. Sometimes possible to spend a night in the open sea lock; much better to lock in if possible. Provisions and fuel. Buses to Glasgow.

East Loch Tarbert to Mull of Galloway: Western Passage
Charts BA 2131, 2126, 2198

The passages of Lower Loch Fyne, Inchmarnock Water and Kilbrennan Sound are straightforward and generally well protected. Strong winds may occasionally funnel through the latter. Abnormal magnetic variation reported off Loch Ranza. DS Kilbrennan Sound: N −5.30; S +0.30.

Tides run up to 4kn at springs at S end of Mull of Kintyre and there is a dangerous race off Sron Uamha, the pt 2M SE of the Lt Ho. Exceptionally high seas occur with wind against tide. In such conditions the Mull should be given a berth of at least 3M.

LOCH RANZA   Chart BA 2221
HW +1.05.   MHWS 3.0; MLWS 0.4; MTL 1.7; MHWN 2.6; MLWN 0.9.
A loch on N end of Arran, affording shelter from all but NW to N winds, but subject to violent squalls in strong southerlies.
Entrance   Keep towards the S shore of the loch when entering to avoid extensive shoal running out from N shore.
Anchorage   1 ca N of the castle in 5m, or elsewhere as space allows. Sound carefully: S shore and head of loch are shoal. Heavy squalls in S gales: use heavy anch and ample scope. Vessels have been known to be blown out to sea.

Provisions and paraffin available. Water from PO. Hotel.

East Loch Tarbert to Mull of Galloway: Eastern Passage

These waters contain excellent cruising areas and are very popular with Clyde yachtsmen because of their beauty and relative shelter. The W Kyle of Bute is straightforward, dangers well marked and tides not strong. At the N end of Bute, at the Burnt Is, care is needed for negotiating the N or S chans, and tides run 3kn for a short distance. Chart BA 1906 essential. The E Kyle of Bute to Toward Pt is straightforward. The flood runs up the E Kyle and down the S Kyle.

The Cumbrae Is may be passed either W or E, dangers in the latter being well marked. Off the Ayrshire coast isolated patches of danger will be found inshore in the bight between Ardrossan and the Heads of Ayr. There is a race off the Mull of Galloway: in bad weather it should be taken close in at slack water.

ROTHESAY   Chart BA 1867
HW +1.05.   MHWS 3.4; MLWS 0.4; MTL 1.9; MHWN 2.9; MLWN 1.0.
Approach   In rough weather pass to S of Toward bank, G con buoy Fl G 3s. N and E winds open the anch in the bay; Port Bannatyne, the next bay N, is to be preferred in NNW winds.
Berthing   (1) Alongside the pier in the outer hr entered round the E end of the pier. Although the S quay dries, small yachts can lie afloat in 2m alongside the N quay. (2) Drying berths alongside in inner hr. (3) Anch in 6 to 8m N of the steamer pier-heads; uncomfortable owing to steamer wash.

Water at E pier-head. All stores. Steamers to Greenock and Glasgow. Repairs and yachtyard at Port Bannatyne. EC Wed.

RIVER CLYDE

A number of worthwhile cruising anchs exist in the Clyde and neighbouring lochs:

Kyles of Bute Famous beauty spot. Anch opposite Tighnabruaich. Large-scale chart BA 1906 needed for Burnt Is.

Holy Loch Anch off Hunters Quay or off Ardnadam 1M further in on the S shore.

Loch Long Anch at Cove on E side of loch just past Baron's Pt. Steep-to further up.

Loch Goil (off Loch Long) Good anch at Carrick Castle in 6m.

Gareloch Anch at Garelochhead. The CCC SD give full details.

INVERKIP

Marina, 3M SE of Dunoon. Facilities for leaving boats, changing crews, chandlery and repairs. Advance warning advisable. Entry at all states of tide and weather. Locate from Power Stn chimney (conspic): entrance lies $\frac{1}{2}$M to the N.

Channel marked by G buoy 'Kip' (QG); follow buoyed chan 2 ca to entrance. Trains to Glasgow.

GT CUMBRAE – MILLPORT   Chart BA 1867
HW +1.00

Pleasant anch on Gt Cumbrae Is. Swell with winds in S quarter. Unless using CCC SD enter round Farland Pt on the SE corner, and immediately enter the bay between the pt and the two Is named the Eileans lying 4 ca to the NW. Anch in 6m just E of the N end of the Eileans. Stores, water, gas, steamer.

TROON   Chart BA 1866   (Plan p218)
HW +0.50

A major marina development on the Ayrshire coast, where yachts can be left or crews conveniently changed. Accessible at all states of tide.

Approach From the S and W keep an offing of at least 2 ca to W of the spur of land behind which the hr lies until due W of the W pier with FWR lt. The line in is marked by G con buoys. From the N, Mill Rk, drying 0.4m, lies $\frac{1}{2}$M NNE of the entrance and is unmarked.

Entrance A R can buoy lies between the two pier-heads and Mill Rk. Keep W of this buoy. Enter between the pier-heads. There is between 2m and $3\frac{1}{2}$m in the outer hr, except off the slips toward the SE corner where there is less than 1m. The marina lies in the inner hr.

Stores, water, fuel, gas, repairs etc. Trains to Glasgow, buses, Prestwick airport nearby.

CAMPBELTOWN LOCH

Depths in metres

Cables
0 1 2 3 4 5

KILCHOUSLAND BAY
Yellow Rocks (dries 0.5m)
ISLAND DAVARR
Fl 5sec 21m Siren
KILDALLOG BAY
FlR 10sec
FlG 2sec
Millbeg Bank
Methe Bank
Oc.W 30.10sec
2QR 1m
New Pier
FlG 6sec
Trench Pt
2QR(vert)
2F R(vert)
Lifeboat House
F.Or.7m
F.Or.2R
CAMPBELTOWN

LOCH RYAN

Depths in metres

N

Cables
0 1 2 3 4

Cairn Pt
GpFl(2)R 10sec 4m 12M
Cairnryan
Ferry Term.
2FG(vert)
2FR
Jetty
FlR 5sec 5M
2FG(vert)
Prohibited anchorage
Foul area
FlG(10sec)
Dredged 5.0m
OccG16s
The Scar
The Wig Yacht anchorage
Wig sands
Kirkcolm Pt
Marian Port

EAST LOCH TARBERT

Depths in metres

Cables
0 1

Garbhaire
Port Ban
16.8
8.2
5.2
26
FlR 2.5sec 4m
Eilean a Choic
QG 3m
Hotel (conspic)
Leac Bhuidhe
Small Craft moorings
Perch G
FlR(2)
Harbour Office
FlG 5sec 4m
Landing Jetty
Slip
House (on) (red roof)
Small Craft moorings
Slip
TARBERT

TROON HARBOUR

Cables
0 1 2

obscured
2 FR (vert) 6m 6M
FlWG 3s
Sheerlegs
Crane
Dry Dock
Outer Harbour
Bldg
Harbour Office
Pilot Ho P.S.
Tidal Sig
Oc.WR 6sec 11m 5M Siren(3)30sec
Tidal 8.3in
Troon Pt
Ramp
Troon Marina

Depths in metres

Based on British Admiralty Charts (nos. in text) with the permission of the Controller of H.M. Stationery Office and the Hydrographer of the Navy, and on other sources.

LAMLASH HARBOUR   Chart BA 1864
HW +0.50.   MHWS 3.2; MLWS 2.7.
A natural hr on the SE side of Arran.
Approach and entrance   Round either the N or S ends of Holy Is, buoyed. The flood runs into the S ent and out of the N, the ebb vice versa.
Anchorage   (1) SE of Brodick pier in 6 to 8m, swell in E or strong S winds. (2) Off the farm ho on the NW of Holy Is in 7m. Do not land on Holy Is: private. (3) Off the SW shore of hr in 6 to 10m, giving good protection from S to W gales. Good shelter near S entrance in S gales. Stores, water, steamer from Brodick to mainland.

LOCH RYAN   Chart BA 1403   (Plan p218)
HW (Stranraer) +0.55.   DS in offing: N +1.00.
MHWS 3.0; MLWS 0.2; MTL 1.6; MHWN 2.5; MLWN 0.6.
Approach   The loch lies 2½M E of Corsewall Lt Ho. Milleur Pt N Card buoy (Q) marking ent should be left to stb.
Entrance   Having opened Cairn Pt Lt Ho Fl(2) R 10s, bring it 138° to clear Forbes shoal, 4.8m, 2M inside, to W. A sand spit runs out 1½M to SE from the W shore opposite Cairn Pt Lt Ho, 3½M inside the entrance, reducing the deep chan to 2 ca. The spit buoy Fl G 6s marks the SE end of the spit.
Anchorages   (1) The Wig. ½M S of Spit buoy, turn W at No. 1 bn to pass behind the sand spit which will be cleared in about ¾M. Anch in 3m, W of steamer pier. Sand and weed: CQR or Danforth may not hold. (2) Stranraer; anch restricted by steamer fairway. Anch in 3m NE of steamer pier. Open to N. (3) Lie alongside quay (dredged) well out of way of steamers. Stores, water, fuel, gas, rly. Steamer to Larne.

PORTPATRICK   Chart BA 2198
HW +0.35.   DS: N +0.15; S +6.10.
MHWS 3.8; MLWS 0.3; MTL 2.1; MHWN 3.0; MLWN 0.9.
15M from the Mull of Galloway, this small hr is no longer officially maintained, and should not be approached in strong onshore winds.
Entrance   Enter on 060° (at night 2 G ldg lts are sometimes visible): there is about 1½–2m in entrance, more inside. Keep midway between (damaged) piers. Do not turn to port until inner hr is well abeam, as there is a rock SE of the Is.
Berthing   Alongside as space allows. Stores, water, fuel, bus to Stranraer.

SOLWAY FIRTH
Great care must be taken in navigating the harbours, rivers and waters in the Solway Firth. Much of the area dries and the sandbanks and flats are subject to continuous change.

DRUMMORE
Chart BA 2198

HW +0.40

Hr dries out at LW. Vessels of 1.5m draft can enter after half-flood and lie along the quay. Good shelter from all winds. A breakwater extends E from pier-head.
Approach Shingle bank in middle of hr dries out at half-tide, but there is deeper water close to pier where gap is cut through bank. Enter on course 270° until inside face of pier is open, then turn parallel keeping 3 to 5m out. Ldg Lts FR on groyne lead in.
Berthing Berth alongside, or anch off in the bay, Mull Lt Ho on with Killiness farm. Heavy swell in SE winds. Provisions and fuel. Bus to Stranraer.

ISLE OF WHITHORN
HW +0.35.   MHWS 7.2; MLWS 0.8; MTL 4.0; MHWN 5.7; MLWN 2.3.
Hr dries at LW. 2½m at half-flood.
Entrance Keep well over towards W watchtower to the E side of the entrance. The stream flows SW across the entrance of the bay at all times when there is 2m or more in the hr, and sets on to the Skerries, a ledge marked by a thin iron rod on the W of entrance. Keep well away from both sides of the entrance. QR on pier.
Berthing Alongside quay. Stores, water.

GARLIESTON
HW +0.35.   MHWS 6.5; MHWN 4.9.
Hr dries at LW; 2m half-flood; complete shelter.
Approach and entrance Leave the pier-hd lt bn to port. Proceed with caution, space limited. Bn lt shown only Oct–Mar.
Berthing Deep-keel boats in stream bed alongside wall; bilge-keelers etc can dry on firm mud 20m out from wall.
   There are rocky patches in the inlet on the W side, marked by a perch, and a rk in the middle which dries 0.6m. Stores, water.

KIRKCUDBRIGHT
HW +1.00.   MHWS 7.5; MLWS 0.8; MTL 4.7; MHWN 5.9; MLWN 2.4.
Bar ¾M N of Torr Pt and 2M below Kirkcudbright, has 0.9m; hence to Kirkcudbright there is about 2m in the chan.
Approach For 2M from its head the bay, which is 3½M long and 1M wide, is occupied by two banks, the Millton and Manxman, which dry about 1½m. Keep Little Ross Lt Ho at the W point of the entrance open E of W bn 150m to the NE of it, till abreast of Torr Pt, which bears 038° from the Lt Ho. Then pass 1 ca from the pt.
Entrance The river is buoyed: CCC SD helpful.
Anchorage (1) In middle of river 100m below warehouses at Kirkcudbright. (2) In Fish pool abreast St Mary's Is, in complete shelter in 2½ to 3m, letting go in the stream and hauling into the W side with kedge; stream strong. (3) In Cutters pool

above the first buoy, in 1.8m; avoid LW rk below the buoy. (4) Just above Ross Is in 6m, exposed to the SE. Strangers should make the river before the banks are covered. Springs flow 3½kn; ebb much harder when there is a spate. FR lt on E pier when vessels expected. Stores in town, water. Rly. EC Thurs.

WATERS OF URR   Chart BA 1346

HW (Hestan Is) +0.40.   DS: W +1.00; E −5.00.

MHWS 8.3; MLWS 0.9; MTL 4.5; MHWN 6.3; MLWN 2.4.

This is a charming and beautiful estuary for boats of moderate draft capable of taking the ground, but strangers should seek local advice before a first visit. The entrance should be approached from the SW, as there are dangerous banks S and E of it. The chan is marked by a spher buoy, and then runs W of Rough Is marked by stb buoys and perches. Well worth a visit, but keelboats only by previous arrangement as suitable berths are extremely restricted. There is about 3m on the bar at half-tide. Water, stores and slip at Kippford. EC Thurs.

ENGLAND WEST COAST

8° 7°W 6°W 4° 3°

Corsewell Pt
Silloth
Maryport
Workington
Harrington
Whitehaven
St Bees Head
Belfast Lough
ISLE OF MAN
Ramsey Bay
St John's Pt
Barrow-in-Furness
Peel
Laxey
Ravenglass
Morecambe
Port Erin
Douglas
R Duddon
Piel Hr
Morecambe Bay
R Lune
54°
Derby Haven
Port St Mary
Heysham
Fleetwood
Castletown
R Ribble
R Mersey
R Alt
The Swellies
Menai Strait NE
R Dee
Holyhead
Conwy
Dun Laoghaire
Menai Strait SW
53°
Dinllaen
Pwllheli
Portmadoc
Abersoch
Bardsey I
St Tudwall's Road
Barmouth
Aberdovey
Aberystwyth
Rosslare
Cardigan
Newquay
Fishguard
Carnsore Pt
52°
Strumble Hd
Ramsey I
R. Cleddau
Carmarthen
Solva
Saundersfoot
Burry Port
Skomer I
Tenby
Llanelli
Porthcawl
Newport
St Ann's Hd
Milford Haven
Burry Inlet
Swansea
Penarth
Bristol
Stackpole Quay
St Govan's Head
Barry Dock
Pill
Portishead
Watermouth
Weston-S-Ma
Ilfracombe
R Axe
Lundy I
Appledore
Minehead
Watchet
Burnham
Hartland Pt
Barnstaple
Porlock Weir
51°
Bideford
Bude
Boscastle
Padstow
Hayle
St Ives
50°

0 10 20 30 40 50 60
Miles

7° 6°W 5° 4° 3°

ENGLAND, WEST COAST AND WALES

PASSAGE NOTES: NORTH CHANNEL TO MILFORD HAVEN

Chart BA 1824a

Unlike the S and E coasts, the W coast of England (including Wales) has large indentations and bays. The passage southbound from the North Channel thus consists of a series of offshore passages, the landfalls being headlands which extend far out into the Irish Sea.

The direct route from Corsewall Pt (off Loch Ryan) on the E side of North Channel is roughly due S, the straight line passing some 25M to the W of harbours in the Isle of Man (Peel or Port St Mary), Holyhead, and further S, Bardsey Is at the N end of Cardigan Bay and Fishguard at the S.

In bad weather both Holyhead and Fishguard would offer complete protection. The ports of the IoM offer shelter according to wind direction but those on the E coast of the island mean a considerable detour, and there is a race round Point of Ayre (N point of the IoM).

On the Irish side, roughly 25M to the W of the direct course there are not many harbours of refuge: Belfast Lough and Dublin Bay being the best.

In good visibility land can be seen on both sides simultaneously at some points as the coasts of IoM, Wales and Ireland are high. Tidal streams in the Irish Sea are moderate except off headlands. On direct passage, it is more important to time the tide in North Channel than anywhere else.

PASSAGE NOTE: SOLWAY FIRTH TO ST BEES HEAD

It is not possible to make the direct passage from Hestan Is to Maryport, nor should any attempt be made higher up the Firth where tidal streams are strong, sands are hard and seas can be steep. When leaving Hestan Is for the English shore keep off Barnhourie Sand, Dumroof Bank and Robin Rigg by making 170° over the ground until due W of Maryport before turning E. Workington is the only port of refuge which can be entered at all states of the tide. Wind against tide can raise a difficult sea over Workington Bank but the passage inside the Bank is safe.

Going S to Liverpool Bay the ebb will help to St Bees Hd: aim to get there 1h after LW and pick up the S-going flood from the Head onwards.

SILLOTH

HW +0.50.   DS: NE at −4.00 (4kn) in Catherine Hole.
MHWS 9.2; MLWS 0.8; MTL 4.8; MHWN 6.9; MLWN 2.3.
Bar   2.1m N of Ellison Scar.
Approach   From the S only. Navigation N of Silloth should only be attempted with local knowledge because of fast tidal streams in the estuary. Leave 'SO' G con bell buoy Fl(3)G 10s close to stb, then make 015° to pass close outside G con buoy Fl(2)G 5s. From here make 045° to pass Silloth Beckfoot G con buoy Fl (4)G 10s. The ldg lts (048°) should be in view (front Fl 1½s, rear FR) on W structures, and thence the stb side of the chan is marked by buoys shifted to meet channel changes but usually close to the line of the ldg lts.
Entrance   4 cables NE of front ldg lt. S Pier has white mast (8m) with F lt. Entrance dries.
Anchorage   (1) 1½ ca NW of front ldg lt off Lees Scar in about 6m. (2) Temporarily in outer harbour, which dries. (3) The wet innermost New Dock is commercial: see HM. Water on quays. All stores in town. EC Tuesday.

MARYPORT

HW +0.40.   DS: NE at −4.30 for 5½h (2kn) across entrance. Eddies off.
MHWS 8.6; MLWS 0.9; MTL 4.7; MHWN 6.6; MLWS 2.5.
Bar   Harbours and entrance chan dry for some distance W of S Pier. There is 1.8m over the bar at S Pier at half flood.
Approach   Keep at least 1M off coast until in the offing because shelving bottom is clay, foul with large rocks.
Entrance   Lt Fl 1½s on tr on S pier-head. Keep closer to N pier-head on entry until abreast first set of steps, then hold over to the end of the jetty with a small square bldg near its N end. Make fast here and seek advice. Port is officially 'closed' but vessels drawing up to 2.4m can enter at HW ± 2h at their own risk. Entrance last dredged in 1975 to combat silting on S side.
Berthing   (1) In offshore winds anch up to 1M NW of S pier-head in the Roads. (2) Berths alongside extensive quays all dry 5.2m. Water at quays. All stores in town. EC Wed.

WORKINGTON   Chart BA 1346

HW +0.25.   DS: NE across entrance −4.30 for 5½h (2kn). Eddies off.
MHWS 8.4; MLWS 0.9; MTL 4.6; MHWN 6.4; MLWN 2.5.
Bar   Extends for 3 ca N of R brick CGS (lt Fl 5s) near end of S pier. Localised steep seas occasionally.
Approach   Clear if S pier-head bears between 010° and 180°. From the S and W pick out Q lt on end of S pier and head northward until the leading lts FY are in

line 131° clearly framed between two pairs of FG lts. This line leads into the dredged chan and to the Turning Basin.

Entrance   Avoid shoal, marked by Fl R lt on perch, N of dredged chan. When 2 FR (vert) on end of N jetty is abeam, round up to port N into Turning Basin.

Berthing   (1) In offshore winds, anch 2 ca NW or SW of CGS. (2) In Turning Basin, sheltered from all winds, but do not leave unattended here as large ships pass through. (3) Vanguard SC may have a half-tide mooring free in the Tidal Dock, S of the Riverside Wharf. Note that trawlers, and Pilot and Fishery Protection vessels take all the Tidal Dock's quay berths. (4) With short or lowering mast, possible drying moorings on berths in tidal hr, inside rly br, which no longer opens.

HARRINGTON

HW +0.25.   DS: N −4.00 for 5h; S +2.00 for 6h.

Approach   No obstructions. From S Workington S Card buoy VQ(6)+L Fl 10s bill the hr bears 095° 2½M. W clubhouse prominent. Port only used by local fishing and sailing club, is marked by lt bn Fl G 5s.

Entrance   Small hr formed by stone pier on S side. Keep close to this in entry. Inner hr dries.

Berthing   (1) In offshore winds in settled weather, anch up to 2 ca W of entrance. (2) Contact Fishing and SC for temporary moorings or berths in inner hr.

WHITEHAVEN   Chart BA 1346   (Plan p232)

HW +0.15.   DS: E across entrance −5.00 for 4½h. Eddies off.

Bar   1 ca N of W pierhead.

Approach   Easily identified from N by tall chimney and tall monument on cliffs just S of hr. No obstructions.

Entrance   If tide serves, even during a gale. Keep close to W pierhead in W gales.

Berthing. (1) Outer hr dries 1.5 to 2m and inner hr 3 to 4m but both offer excellent shelter in all winds to vessels that can lie aground. (2) Queen's Dock (wet) is used by vessels up to 3000 tons. Consult HM. All stores in town. Diesel at Fish Quay. EC Wed.

Isle of Man

Chart BA 2094

Direction of tidal streams

Calf of Man to Langness   E −6.00; W +0.15.

Race of Chicken Rk, eddies and a race on both sides of Langness.

Langness to Maughold Head   NE +5.30 for 3¼h; SW −3.45 for 9¼h.

Manghold Head to Ayre Pt   N −3.30 for 9h; S +5.30 for 3½h.

Ayre Pt   E +6.00; W −0.15; race.

Based on British Admiralty Charts (nos. in text) with the permission of the Controller of H.M. Stationery Office and the Hydrographer of the Navy, and on other sources.

Contrary Head to Calf Sound   N −1.15; S +4.45.
S of Nyarbyl Pt   Stream nearly continuously N.
Calf Sound   S +4.00; N −1.30.
With SW winds and low barometer the rise of tide is increased by up to 1m. With high barometer and E and N winds the tides are lowered to the same extent.

None of the hrs where yachts can lie afloat is safe in all winds. There is some commercial activity, and some ports, particularly Peel and Douglas, are fairly crowded with fishermen from June to September inclusive. If HMs are warned in advance of a yacht's probable time of arrival, they take endless trouble in allotting suitable berths. Except at Douglas, where a continuous service is maintained, it is the general practice for HMs to be on duty 2h on either side of HW, and to meet incoming vessels and direct them to their berths. Yachts racing are excused dues in certain circumstances. Harbour staff are extremely helpful. Harbour dues moderate.

During August and September there may be concentrations of up to 100 fishing vessels between Chicken Rock and Douglas.

In good weather, vessels coming from the W can find shelter in Peel Hr, when there is sufficient rise. From the S, make first for Port St Mary. From the N, find a good temporary anch at Ramsey at all states of the tide. These anchs are all exposed to winds from certain directions and further details are given under the separate port headings.

PORT ST MARY   Chart BA 2696   (Plan p226)
HW +0.25.   MHWS 5.9; MLWS 0.6; MTL 3.2; MHWN 4.7; MLWN 1.7.
The hr dries, has 3m at MHWN, 2m when the Carrick covers; bottom sand and mud. Good shelter off the entrance in 2 to 3½m in NE through NW to SW winds. The bay should not be approached in strong S winds.
Approach   To clear the Carrick (lt bn QR 6m high) which dries 4.3m, keep Langness Lt Ho well open of Scarlett Pt stack, or at night when nearing the bay bring the lts of the harbour in line 303°. Approaching from E during the first part of the ebb, from Stack of Scarlett to S of the Carrick small craft should avoid standing too close inshore, until the Carrick shows, when the sea steadies. From SW give the shore a berth of 2 ca and round in to N of the Alfred Pier-head lt Oc R 10s.
Berthing   Anch 50 to 100m NW of Alfred Pier just inside the line of the two Lt Hos (one on Alfred Pier and the other on the inner pier). Larger craft may safely anch between the Carrick and hr entrance (5 to 7m) when wind is offshore. Rocks dry out between the LB mooring and the inner pier. There is a good mooring alongside in up to 1.2m with good wall ladders and steps. The outer part of pier is often occupied by fishing vessels.

Keep well in to pier to avoid reefs (marked by beacons with N cones) that lie parallel. Inner hr dries to chan, hard sand: centre is full of local moorings but yachts taking the ground can lie alongside. Six visitors' moorings off Chapel Bay.

There is a landing below the clubhouse of the IoM YC which has excellent facilities and is welcoming to visitors.

All stores. Bus to Castletown and Douglas. EC Thurs.

CASTLETOWN
Chart BA 2696 (Plan p226)

HW +0.25.

The bay affords good shelter in NNW through NE to SE winds. The bottom is not good and the tidal streams are felt. The hr dries.

Approach   To avoid the race off Langness Pt, give it a good berth in all winds. Approaching from E in heavy weather keep Clay Hd well open of Douglas Hd (E coast of Is just S of Douglas Hr), to clear rough ground 8 ca SE of St Michael's Is.

Entrance   Keep Spanish Hd (SW tip of island) open of the Stack till past the R can buoy Fl R 3s which marks the Lheeah Rio Rk and should be left to port. From abreast the buoy steer 022° till the inner jetty comes open N of the pier-head Lt Ho when steer 317° for the entrance. At the end of the breakwater the ground consists of rocky ledges and large boulders. Beware of confusing hr bns with Ronaldsway Airport landing lts.

Berthing   In 5.5m off the entrance, King William's College bearing 022°. The hr has 2.7m MHWN; there is a basin between the outer swing and inner fixed bridges. A hard runs down from the Lt Ho towards the LW mark and stands above the level of the bottom. Yachts may also berth in basin inside breakwater, bottom sand and shingle.

All stores. Bus to Port Erin and Douglas. EC Thurs.

DERBY HAVEN
Chart BA 2696 (Plan p226)

HW +0.25.

The bay affords shelter on a good bottom of sand and mud in 2 to 5m inside St Michael Is, Fort Is, and is available in N to S winds through W. Inside the breakwater the hr dries and affords complete shelter in all winds. Bottom mud and sand, 2m MHWN.

Entrance   With the S-going stream, which runs for 9h give N point of St Michael Is a good berth as the stream sets hard across a shelving rk at the entrance point. To enter, bring the lt Iso G 2s on SW end of breakwater to bear 262° and pass between it and the perch marking a rk to S of it. Anch 2 or 3 ca from the S end of the breakwater: bottom is foul 1 ca out from breakwater.

Stores at Castletown 2M. No supplies at Derby Haven but two pubs serving good meals if booked.

DOUGLAS
Chart BA 2696 (Plan p226)

HW +0.20.   MHWS 6.9; MLWS 0.8; MTL 3.9; MHWN 5.4; MLWN 2.4.

The outer hr has 4 to 7m, inner hr dries. A heavy sea runs in during SE gales. The inner hr has 2 to 4m at MHWN. There is a swing bridge 1¼ ca inside the inner hr which is opened as required 2h either side of HW.

Approach Keep Battery Pier Lt Ho W of 243° to clear Conister and other rks. In W breezes keep as close to Douglas Hd as is prudent: beware gusts. The early flood runs N close inshore from Santon Hd to Douglas Hd. Keep clear of car ferries entering or leaving.

Entrance Enter between the piers and steer about 247°.

Berthing Outer harbour: only a limited number of vessels are permitted to anch, between the LBS and Fort Anne Jetty, and HM's permission must first be obtained. Exposed to E. Three mooring buoys are laid during summer for visiting yachts. Inner harbour: tidal, available from HW −2 to +2. Extensively used by local pleasure craft, commercial vessels and coasters, and it may be difficult to find a convenient berth during the summer. The bay affords secure anch especially at the N end in 10m with shelter from N through W to S.

All facilities. EC Thurs.

LAXEY
HW +0.25.

Laxey Bay affords good anch in N to SW winds through W. The hr dries and has about 2m MHWN. It is available for small yachts only.

Approach Approaching from N and E FR lt on old pier is obscured when bearing less than 317°. Do not steer for entrance until Oc R 3s lt on old pier is open of breakwater hd lt Oc G 3s.

Entrance Care should be exercised in entering. The hr is narrow and there is risk of running onto rks on N side. These are marked by bns (W discs on BW spars).

Berthing Alongside the pier, if room. Offshore anchorage: anywhere in bay to S of hr as convenient, in 4 to 9m. Shops and pubs. Buses and trains to Douglas, Ramsey and top of Snaefell.

RAMSEY BAY   Chart BA 2696   (Plan p226)
HW +0.20.   MHWS 7.3; MLWS 0.8; MTL 4.1; MHWN 5.8; MLWN 2.4.

The bay affords secure anch and good holding ground, and is sheltered with winds from NNW through W to S but not necessarily in one position from all these winds. The Queen's Pier extends 685m from the shore to the S of the hr and vessels waiting to enter hr should anch between this pier and the S Hr Pier. It is dangerous to land at the steps on Queen's Pier: the timber at the sea end of the pier is rotten and use is discouraged. The hr lies within two piers, the ends of which are 90m inside LW mark. The hr dries and has up to 5.5m at MHWS, 4m at MHWN. Vessels are advised not to attempt the entrance earlier than 2½ to 2h before HW, or later than 1½ to 2h after HW.

Approach From N rounding Pt of Ayre (N point of Is) keep close inshore to avoid Whitestone Bank (7 ca E of pt). The stream sets round the pt into Ramsey Bay at about LW at Douglas, and runs for 3h. Watch for lobster pot buoys.

Berthing Berth alongside quay as instructed by HM, usually in the chan between the piers. When entering watch the stream, which sets N across the entrance for 9h from half-flood to LW approx.

Most facilities. Buses to Peel and Douglas, tram to Douglas in summer. EC Wed.

PEEL
Chart BA 2696 (Plan p226)

HW +0.15.   MHWS 5.3; MLWS 0.5; MTL 2.9; MHWN 4.2; MLWN 1.5.

The hr dries and has 3.3m at MHWN. During the fishing season (June to October) it is rather crowded. Anch sheltered from E through S to SW between the end of the breakwater and the R bn. The breakwater should be given good clearance and vessels should not stand in too far towards the shore as a shoal lies between the breakwater and the shore and depths on it are variable. Yachts which can take the ground safely are advised to moor alongside the S wall of the inner hr where it is cleaner than at most other quays and there are usually no fishing vessels. Entry to Peel should not be attempted in strong N to NW winds. All stores. Buses to Ramsey and Douglas. EC Thurs.

PORT ERIN
Chart BA 2696 (Plan p226)

HW +0.20.   MHWS 5.2; MLWS 0.4; MTL 2.8; MHWN 4.2; MLWN 1.6.

This inlet affords secure anch in 4 to 9m and shelter in winds from N through E to SW. Raglan Pier, lt Oc G 5s, on S side of bay forms a drying hr with sandy bottom, having 3.6m MHWN alongside.

Approach Rounding the Calf of Man and Chicken Rk in strong winds and weather-going stream, the race off the Lt Ho should be given a good berth. Close along the SW shore the tidal stream is slight, and vessels of moderate draft may avoid the strength of the stream, when weather permits, by standing in. Calf Sd should on no account be attempted without local knowledge by any but small craft in good weather, which pass through from N with a fair tide by keeping over to the rk on port hand after passing the bn on the stb hand. Chart 2696 essential.

Entrance A demolished breakwater covered at HW runs out N from the SW arm of the bay and is marked off its N end by a G con buoy. In the middle of the head of the bay are two lts, FR 099°, which lead into the middle of the bay.

Berthing Anch according to draft as convenient. A good berth is close to S shore between the old breakwater and the pier. A telegraph cable runs roughly E–W across the bay: care necessary when anchoring – position shown on chart 2696. Good landing at jetty shown on plan.

All stores. Buses to Castletown and Douglas. EC Thurs.

St Bees to Duddon
Chart BA 1961

The tidal stream within 3M of the coast runs S for 9h from +2.00. $\frac{1}{2}$M off Whitehaven flood and ebb streams run until 1h after local HW and LW respectively, but 2 to 3M off until 2h after.

RAVENGLASS

Chart BA 1961

HW +0.20.   DS: N at −1.00; S at +2.00.

Tarn Pt: MHWS 8.3; MLWS 0.9; MTL 4.5; MHWN 6.4; MLWN 2.5.

The harbour, formed by estuaries of Rivers Irt, Mite and Esk, dries out; it provides good shelter for vessels which can take the ground.

There is a gun testing range from Eskmeals on S side of inlet out to sea in a 5M quadrant bearing from 230° to 320° from inlet. R flags are shown on flagstaffs on S shore when firing about to begin or in progress; passage through this area is permitted.

Bar   About 0.6m.

Approach   From S avoid Selker Rks, 3M from entrance. They lie 1¼M out from shore, dry at MLWS and are marked by a G con bell buoy (Fl(3)G 15s) outside them. From N, avoid Drigg Rk (1.8m) lying 1M offshore and 2M 288° from entrance.

Entrance   Take the entrance about HW −2 when there is approx 2 to 2½m in the chan. Keep about ¼M from shore; turn up for the village of Ravenglass, keeping nearer the S shore.

Berthing   Anchor as convenient in the estuary either in the R Mite or the R Eske below rly bridges, near centre of estuary for best water. PO and village shop. Water in village. Facilities at Whitehaven 16M or Millom 14M. EC Wed.

RIVER DUDDON

Chart BA 1961

HW Duddon Bar −0.10.   MLWS 8.5; MLWS 0.9; MTL 4.6; MHWN 6.6; MLWN 2.6.

The chan is unmarked and constantly changes. Anch at Haverigg. Pier at Askam, where yachts lie aground. Pier and small hr at Hodbarrow on W side dries, ground foul off pier. Water and stores. At HW a small yacht can sail almost anywhere within the estuary.

PIEL HARBOUR and BARROW-IN-FURNESS   Chart BA 3164   (Plan p232)

HW Barrow +0.30.

MHWS 9.1; MLWS 1.0; MTL 5.0; MHWN 7.1; MLWN 2.8.

Bar   2.1m over Piel bar, chan dredged to 3.7m. Piel Hr has 1.8 to 3.7m.

Approach   Strangers should take the entrance at half flood. Flood runs from NW, ebb from S. Pick up Lightning Knoll RWVS Sph bell buoy Fl 10s, and leaving it close to stb steer 041° on first ldg lts (No. 1 Q, No. 2 Iso 2s). Keep on this line for just over 3M leaving Halfway R can buoy Fl R 5s and Outer Bay R can buoy Fl(4)R 10s to port until Bar R can buoy, Fl(2)R 5s is reached. Then bring Nos. 3 and 4 ldg lts in line 006° (No. 3 Q, No. 4 Iso 2s) and follow line for 1¼M till abreast of Piel.

Berthing   Anch clear of fairway. Chan to Barrow 3M is well marked, lateral buoyage. Landing at Piel Is and Roa Is. All facilities at Barrow. Water from HM. EC Thurs. Comfortable inn at Piel Is. Ferry to mainland.

FLEETWOOD
Depths in Metres

Ldg Lts 156°

Q Horn(3)15s
Fairway. N°1

Wyre Lt Ho
(disused)

FI R3s N°6

QR N°8

N°2 QG
N°0.

N°7 QG

GREAT
FORD
N°9

N°2
QG(Horn)

N°11 G

N°13 QR N°4

QR N°6

QR N°8

2FR(vert)

Iso6s

FIY2s

FIY4s

2FG(vert)
2FG(vert)
2FG(vert)

Dome

Custom Ho
Wyre Dock
Fish Dock

Fleetwood

CG

IOM Berth 1.4 cables W of N°20buoy

BLACK SCAR

NORTH
WHARF

KING
SCAR

King Scar
FI2G5s

Rossall Pt.

KNOTT END

KIRK
SCAR

o Cables 5
N

WHITEHAVEN
Depths in Metres

0 Cable 1
N

Chy o

4 FI R5s16m13M

THE BAR

Tom Hurd

Little Hurd

NORTH
SPIT

W Pier

North Pier
2FR(vert) 8m 9M

Stn.

Silo
HM

QUEEN'S
DOCK

NORTH WALL
NORTH

INNER
Hr.

New Tongue

OUTER
Hr.

2FR(vert)8m2M.

OLD QUAY

SOUTH
Old Tongue

FS

Customs

Chy

PIEL HARBOUR
Depths in Metres

0 Mile 1
N

Foulney I.

Iso 2s 14m6M.
Distant 4 cables

IsoR2s11M
Or. Bn A1/4

Iso 2s12m6M
Bn No2

Q 6m6M.
Bn No.1
BW

No.4 Bn Qk FI6m6M.
BW No.3 Bn

QR6M
Bn A1/3

FOULNEY TWIST

LITTLE FOULNEY SCAR

PIEL SCAR

INNER
CHAN.

PIEL
CHAN.

Lts 298°15

FI R3s Lts No 443 006°15

Coup Scar Pt.

Ridge Pt.

North West Pt.

MAWS
SCAR

Castle(ruins)

Pier (ruined)

North
East Pt

South East
Pt

Southend

Snab Pt.
Sheep I.

Foulmey Dr.

CG oFS
South End Haws

Hillsford Pt.

QR 8m 6M

Piel I.

Roa

Tr. Slip
B Slip

Based on British Admiralty Charts (nos. in text) with the permission of the Controller of H.M. Stationery Office and the Hydrographer of the Navy, and on other sources.

MORECAMBE BAY
Chart BA 2010

HW Morecambe +0.15.   DS in offing: W +1.00.
Streams run hard, 5kn max, and raise a short steep sea on the ebb with W winds.
Morecambe Bay lt buoy lies 17½M 250° from Wyre Lt Ho off Fleetwood.
   During Apr and May large concentrations of fishing vessels may occur up to 25M W or SW from lt buoy. Smaller concentrations Aug–Oct.

MORECAMBE

HW +0.15.   MHWS 9.5; MLWS 1.1; MTL 5.2; MHWN 7.2; MLWN 2.9.
The shallowest part dries 1.5m. Anch is exposed in rough weather. The chan shifts and should be taken at half flood. There is a pier hr which dries and affords good shelter.

HEYSHAM
Chart BA 1552

HW +0.15.   MHWS 9.5; MLWS 1.1; MTL 5.3; MHWN 7.4; MLWN 3.1.
Hr affords good shelter, depth 5.2m, but should not be used by yachts without special reason.
Approach   As Fleetwood, till past the Fairway buoy which is left to stb. Make No. 1 Heysham buoy and then make good 045° to No. 5 G con buoy Fl G and thence to the hr entrance, 4¼M.
Entrance   The chan is marked by lit lateral buoys. There are 2 FG (vert) lts on end of S jetty and ldg lts in line, 102°, lead up centre of dredged chan to the hr.
Berthing   Good anch inside as directed. All stores at Morecambe, 2M. Water. No hard. Steamers to Belfast, train to Morecambe.

RIVER LUNE
Approach   As for Fleetwood, then continue to Lune No. 1 W Card lt buoy.
Entrance   The Lune chan as far as Abbey Lt (on Plover Scar Rk) is marked by lateral buoys, some lit. Wait at No. 3 buoy until 4h flood and then run right up. Abbey Lt (Fl 2s) has a tide gauge showing the depth over the sill at Glasson Dock. Cockersand Lt FW and Abbey Lt in line 083° lead up the chan only between Nos. 2 and 4 buoys. After passing No. 6 buoy leave Abbey Lt to stb, Baithaven R can buoy to port, the G buoy marking Crook Scar to stb, then follow the line of R spher and can buoys moored to the training wall on the port hand to Glasson Dock entrance. (**Note:** *There are three wrecks on Bernard Wharf 2½M eastwards from No. 4 and No. 8 Fleetwood buoys.*)
Berthing   Glasson Dock. The shallowest part of the chan dries 2.1m and dock gates open from 1h before HW to HW. Boatyard, Good laying-up quarters. All facilities.
   Lancaster, 5M above Glasson Dock, can be reached by small craft near HW, but strangers are advised to take a pilot. The chan is narrow, well sheltered and pretty. Interesting town and has all facilities. The bed of the R Lune has 1.5m at the town at HW.

FLEETWOOD and SKIPPOOL   Chart BA 2010 (Plan p232)

HW (Wyre Lt Ho) +0.20. MHWS 9.5; MHWN 7.4.

HW Fleetwood +0.15. MHWS 9.5; MLWS 1.2; MTL 5.3; MHWN 7.6; MLWN 3.1.

DS in offing: W +1.00.

Bar 2.7m to 3.7m in main chan to Isle of Man Quay.

Approach and Entrance Make the Lune S Card YB lt buoy (Horn and Whis) and set course directly for No. 1 Fairway N Card lt buoy, leaving King Scar G con buoy (Q(2) G) to stb and Danger Patch R can buoy (Fl(3)R 10s) to port. Thence SE, leaving No. 2 R can buoy to port. The chan entrance has six G con buoys to stb, nine R can buoys to port. Nos. 3 and 7 QG and No. 5 Fl G 3s, Nos. 4 and 8 QR, and No. 6 R can Fl R 3s. Be careful of flood tide which sets strongly to E of these buoys.

Fleetwood is now used by Pandora Ro-Ro ships: keep clear when they are manoeuvring.

Wyre pile Lt Ho is on the NE elbow of the N wharf bank at the entrance to the river. Fleetwood ldg lts, 156°, only lead up the part of the chan from inside Wyre Lt Ho to abreast of No. 9 buoy. Then course must be altered slightly to stb to leave No. 16 R can buoy, (QR) to port. Then alter course to port and follow the Fleetwood shore leaving LB slipway dolphin FG to stb.

Berthing Watch out for car ferries which turn inside buoys Nos. 20 and 22. A flashing yellow lt is lit on top of staging on Fleetwood side when they are manoeuvring. Do not anchor in this area.

Land at jetty at Knott End or at landing stage used by local yachts ½M S of Knott End ferry slip. Anchor Knott End side of buoys or S of upstream buoy. All facilities at Fleetwood, water from quay in docks. Land on beach opposite No. 2 IoM berth. Ferry, Knott End to Fleetwood. Tram and bus to Blackpool. EC Wed.

Skippool is 5M above Fleetwood, the headquarters of the Blackpool and Fleetwood YC. Starting an h before HW, from midstream between Fleetwood ferry dock and Knot End pier steer 180° to the NW end of the ICI pier at Burn Naze, leaving a small G stb buoy abreast of cooling trs and a large unlit G con buoy close to stb. Alter course gradually to port and steer 135° from the ICI pier to midstream at Wardleys. There is no marked chan above the ICI pier and there are sandbanks in the river which shift, mostly just covered at half flood.

In the narrows between Wardleys and Skippool Creek the banks in mid-river are awash at 5m rise. Course to Skippool is 210°.

RIVER RIBBLE

Approach and Entrance From Nelson Preston RWVS spher buoy L Fl 10s (bell) steer 070° for Gut G con buoy Fl G 5s. Alter course to 060° and make for wall and G con buoy QG which marks the beginning of the chan. From here the chan is buoyed and lit about every ½M until just before the docks at Preston.

Berthing Near boatyard to port at Lytham, or at entrance to R Douglas on stb side, or at Freckleton on port side. All berths dry.

RIVER ALT
For yachtsmen wishing to visit the Liverpool area without encountering the commercial activity of the River Mersey, the River Alt is available to vessels drawing 1.8m for about 1½h either side of HW. The river cuts a winding course through the foreshore, which dries 4.5m. Chan shifts: it is advisable to obtain the latest information before attempting to enter.

Entrance   Enter from the Crosby Chan between buoys C12 and C16, passing either side of C14 and crossing Crosby E training bank behind which there is a wide sandbar which dries over 2m. Steer 076° for a can buoy surmounted by a short staff, moored off the N side of a prominent groyne between Crosby and Hall Road beach marks. The course of the river is then close to the N side of the groyne and is marked by spars maintained by the Blundellsands SC. About 1 ca from the sandhills the river turns sharply to port and continues on a course parallel to the coastline, forming a safe and sheltered anch known locally as the Lagoon, about 7 ca long. About 1m at LW, firm sand. It is possible to go further upriver to Hightown, but local knowledge is essential.

Berthing   Anch in the Lagoon where there are no moorings: local yachts use single oversize anch on a short scope. Landing at Blundellsands SC clubhouse on foreshore. Rly to Liverpool and Southport: good service, stations at Hightown, Hall Rd, Blundellsands and Crosby.

RIVER MERSEY   Charts BA 1951, 3490, 3477   (Plan p237)
HW Liverpool +0.15.
MHWS 9.3; MLWS 0.9; MTL 5.1; MHWN 7.4; MLWN 2.9.

Approach   Tides are strong, 5kn in some places, and wind against tide raises a steep sea in the outer reaches. There are training banks on both sides of the fairway, and yachts should take care not to go or be set outside the buoys, which are numerous and lit. Enter by the Bar, Queen's and Crosby chans and not by the Horse chan which is no longer officially recognised or buoyed.

Berthing   There are no facilities for anch or berthing yachts on the Liverpool side of the river. On the Birkenhead side there are the following anchs. (1) New Brighton. Anch only outside the fairway. Good holding, but tides run hard and this anch is only tenable in quiet weather. Heavy swell in W and N winds. Rly and bus to Birkenhead, rly to Liverpool. EC Wed. (2) Rock Ferry. Limited anch S of oil tanker piers. Holding good, but rig tripping line. Dinghies can land at Rock Ferry slip. Rly and bus to Birkenhead, rly to Liverpool. EC Thurs. (3) New Ferry. Limited anch, not recommended if any other berth available.

PASSAGE NOTE: LIVERPOOL TO CONWY

Chart BA 1978

Tidal streams between Gt Ormes Hd and Formby Pt run as follows: W: +1.00 to +5.00; E: −5.00 to −1.00.

Do not attempt short-cuts as seaward edges of some sandbanks are not buoyed. Do not attempt short-cut from Gt Ormes Hd to Conwy without local knowledge.

ESTUARY OF RIVER DEE
Large tidal estuary mostly drying at LW. Tidal streams run strongly in chans, which shift. Suitable for shallow draft vessels which can take the ground. Navigable up to Chester but local knowledge essential and masts must be lowered.

Approach   From W via buoyed chan between N Wales coast and outlying banks leading to Dee R can buoy Fl(2) R. From N via Hilbre Swash buoyed chan entering at R can buoy HE 2, QR, leading to Welshman buoy, E Card Q(3) 10s. Chans shift. Contact Harry Jones at West Kirby SC (tel (051) 625 5579), boatman and LB Cox, for up-to-date information. Strangers are recommended to call Liverpool Coastguard on VHF who will usually alert Harry Jones who will then make contact on VHF.

Berthing   Choice depends on direction of wind. In Hilbre Swash, adjacent to Hilbre Is, Hilbre Pool close to the E dries, sheltered S to W, good holding or close to W Hoyle Bank (covered at MHWS). Drying-out anch in N chan by W Kirby moorings S of Marine Lake and further E at Caldy: in SW chan immediately N of the Point of Air close into the bank in Mostyn Pool, $\frac{1}{4}$M E of mole forming E entrance to Mostyn Hr. Yachts are not welcome inside Mostyn Hr, but it can be used in case of need.

   Stores at W Kirby and Mostyn by dinghy at HW.

Wales

CONWY
Chart BA 1978   (Plan p237)

HW (Trwyn Du) −0.30. MHWS 7.6; MLWS 0.7; MTL 4.1; MHWN 5.9; MLWN 2.3.

DS on E side of Beaumaris Bay: E −5.00; W −0.30 to +7.00.

Bar   About 0.6m at MLWS. The Scabs dry. Flood runs 5h, ebb 7h. Vessels drawing 1.8m may enter at 2½h flood. The chan shifts.

Entrance   Make the Fairway RWVS spher buoy, which lies on a line NE of Puffin Is and the road tunnel entrance on Penmaenbach Hill, and also on a line Great Ormes Hd and the cut-away top of Penmaenbach Hill. The chan is marked by G con buoys Nos. 1, 3, 5; and R can buoys Nos. 2, 4 and 6. The chan is very shallow to seaward of No. 4 buoy, 1m LWS. To avoid shoal patches and the Scabs, keep stb hand buoys close aboard till S of No. 4, then head for No. 6 buoy. Leave Conwy Bn (B column, Fl WR 5s 46m) well to stb and steer up river keeping Bodlondeb Pt (wooded to water's edge) in line with centre of new Conwy Road Br.

Berthing   (1) Off Bodlondeb Pt near G sewer buoy. Buoy anch. (2) Pick up suitable vacant mooring and inform HM, Conwy (049263) 6253 or Prestatyn

CONWY
Depths in Metres

Llandudno • Bh
Chyo 19'
Tremlyd Pt
Pier
Tr
Tywyn
R. CONWY
Castle 17'
53° 18'
Green Bank
Burllingau Rk
CONWY
Red
Red
Channel
buoyed
Fl WR5s 5.5M
Fl WR5s 5.2M
SANDS
Conwy Morfa
Bodlondeb Pt
Penmaen-bach Pt
Penmaen-bach
Conwy
238
37
6½
Y
2
5
34
3
31
Penmaen-bach Pt
Llys Elisedd
Clynnog
Fairway RW
26
25
N
Mile 1
0

BARMOUTH
Depths in Metres

Barmouth Bridge
Quay
FERRY
Barrage Fl(4)R 20s
Fl(4)R 20s
LB F
Penrhyn Pt
FS
FS
37
N
3'
QR2M
Y PERCH
R
R
BAR BEACH
NORTH BANK
19
THE BAR
SOUTH BANK
15
0·9
0·9
0·5
1·6
0·5
2·7
Barmouth Outer
Fl 10s
Bar R
THE BAR
39
39
RW
52° 43'
42·5'
4° 4' W
5'

RIVER MERSEY
Depths in Metres

Seaforth
White Tr
Bootle
Training Wall
Rock Lt Ho(unlit)
New Brighton
Wallasey
Seacombe
Birkenhead
Dome (Town Hall)
Memorial
Liverpool
Stanley Dock
Car Ferry
Royal Liver Bldg (N spire)
Liverpool Landing Stage
Port of Liverpool Bldg (Dome)
Toxteth
Dingle
Algburth
DEVIL'S BANK
EASTHAM CH
Rock Ferry
New Ferry
Bromborough Dk
Cooling Tr
Tall Chys
Chys
26'
25'
24'
53° 23'
26'
25'
24'
53° 23'
22'
21'
3'
2'
1'
3'
N
Miles 2
Cables 0

...d on British Admiralty Charts (nos. in text) with the permission of the Controller of H.M. Stationery Office and of
...ydrographer of the Navy, and on other sources.

237

(07456) 6491 (house) to confirm use. N Wales Cruising Club premises with usual facilities are at Lower High St (Conwy 3481); they listen on VHF Ch M 1000–2230. All facilities and stores in town, EC Wed during season.

MENAI STRAIT   Chart BA 1464   (Plans p240, 241)

The Menai Strait between Anglesey and the mainland offers good shelter, excellent facilities and fine scenery. It can be entered at either end and with due care it is possible to pass right through. Two brs cross the Strait, the Britannia rly br and ¾M further E the Menai suspension br. There is a clearance of at least 24m beneath both at MHWS. An overhead cable with a clearance of 24m spans the strait W of Britannia br.

The following directions serve for craft up to 60T, and are arranged on the following plan: (a) inwards from the NE; (b) both ways between the bridges where the chan is encumbered with rks and is known as the Swellies; (c) inwards from the SW. Coasters drawing 4.6m use SW entrance at MHWS; the maximum length of craft to negotiate the Swellies is 70m. Caernarvon is the head of navigation inwards from both entrances and the changeover in the buoyage is marked by a Y con buoy.

Good anchs outside are: (1) 8M NW of the N entrance in NW corner of Red Wharf Bay off Moellfre LB slip, sheltered from winds between SSW and NNW. (2) 13M from SW entrance at Port Dinlleyn. (3) Cemaes Bay at the N end of Anglesey. Good anch for small craft inside the entrance pts, sheltered from NW, in 3.7m abreast the LB slip. Round Wylfa Hd shelter may be had from NE. There is a pier at the S end of the bay; a boat of 1.8m draft would ground inside it at 2h ebb. Race off Wylfa Hd. Water and stores in the village. (4) Cemlyn Bay. Inside Harry Furlong Reef is good anch to wait for tide at Carmel Hd, out of stream and fair shelter, used by coasters. Anch in 1.8m with Harry Furlong Bn on with end of Trwyn Cemlyn.

SAILING DIRECTIONS

(a) NE entrance to Menai Suspension Bridge

HW Trwyn Du −0.30.   MHWS 7.6; MLWS 0.7; MTL 4.1; MHWN 5.9; MLWN 2.3.
Menai Bridge −0.10.   MHWS 7.3; MLWS 0.8; MTL 4.0; MHWN 5.7; MLWN 2.3.
Beaumaris −0.10.   MHWS 7.6; MLWS 0.9; MTL 4.1; MHWN 5.8; MLWN 2.1.
DS in offing: E +6.00; W −0.15. In entrance, at Trwyn Du; inward −6.00; outward −1.15. Off Beaumaris: SW −4.25; NE +1.35.

Enter W of Puffin Is between Trwyn Du, Anglesey (Menai Lt Tr Fl 5½s) to stbd and Perch Rk Bn SW of Puffin Is to port. The entrance on E side of Puffin Is is not recommended for strangers. Inside, the ebb sets towards the bn. The first buoy (No. 2 lt float Fl R 5s) is ½M S of entrance and from there the chan runs in a

SW direction and is well buoyed as far as No. 7 G con buoy, off Gallows Pt SW of Beaumaris. At night lts at the LB slip nr Trecastell Pt 2FG (vert), Mountfield Bn (Fl WG 2s) and Beaumaris Pier FWG are useful guides. From Gallows Pt to Menai Bridge there are no navigation buoys; keep 1 ca from the Anglesey shore. **Anchorages** (1) Beaumaris, between the pier-head and Gallows Pt clear of fairway and moorings in 3½m, sand. The bight dries. Land at pier-head or Gallows Pt, yard at Gallows Pt, bus, all facilities and stores, EC Wed. (2) Bangor pier-head, between fairway and mudflats (dries) in 3½m, good holding but uncomfortable with tide against strong SW wind. Dickie's yard, slip and sheds; good shops at Bangor, buses and rly 1M; EC Wed. (3) Garth Ferry, opposite Bangor Pier, in 5½m clear of fairway and moorings; good shelter. Gazelle Hotel, bus. (4) Off Ynys y Big (islet midway between Garth and Menai Bridge) in 3½m. This affords the best shelter and there are shops at Menai Bridge, 1M.

(b) The Swellies (Plan p240)

DS: SW −1.35 (for 6½h); NE: +4.55 (for 5½h).

The flood runs NE here, and the ebb SW. Both streams run at 4 to 6kn, except for a short slack at HW and LW. Before making the passage it is advisable to check all the marks referred to in the following directions and to assess the tide accurately. It is not wise to rely on predicted times: strong SW winds postpone HW and strong NE winds have the reverse effect. If travelling SW, start when boats are swinging at their moorings near Menai Br Pier. If in any doubt consult local boatman at Port Dinorwic or Garth Ferry, or take a pilot.

Passage from SW: (1) From midstream pass under middle of S span of Britannia Br and steer on W bn on S shore till fixed lts (G) at base of S tr of bridge are in line. (2) Keep lts in line astern and Swelly Rk G con buoy just open of stb bow till Price's Pt bn is close abeam to stb. (3) Pass midway between Swelly Rk buoy and Price's Pt till Price's Pt begins to shut out centre tr of Britannia Br. (4) Then steer on NW tr of Menai Suspension Br till on a line between Swelly Rk buoy and middle of Suspension Br. (5) Then steer to pass under middle of Suspension Br.

Passage from NE: (1) Keep in midstream past Menai Br (St George's) Pier, Fl G 10s, and rk with bn on W side. (2) Pass under Menai Suspension Br centre. (3) Keep Swelly Rk buoy just open of port bow till Price's Pt bn is on with centre of Britannia Br. (4) Then steer on to Price's Pt bn till Swelly Rk buoy is abeam to stb; then steer to pass midway between Price's Pt and Swelly Rk buoy with bow on Gored Goch W Ho till past Price's Pt and Swelly Rk buoy astern to stb. (5) Steer on F lts at foot of S end of Britannia Br till bn (W) on S shore is abeam to port. (6) Then steer to pass under centre of S span of Britannia Br until in midstream W of bridge. (7) Keep on N side of fairway past Nelson Monument to Port Dinorwic.

(c) SW entrance of Strait to Britannia Rly Br

HW Fort Belan −1.05. MHWS 4.7; MLWS 0.6; MTL 2.7; MHWN 3.6; MLWN 1.8.

HW Caernarvon −1.05. MHWS 5.3; MLWS 0.6; MTL 3.0; MHWN 4.1; MLWN 1.9.

MENAI STRAIT N E
Depths in Metres

THE SWELLIES
Depths in Metres

Puffin I

CONWY

BAY

DUTCHMAN BANK

THE POOL

RUSHMAN SPIT

Perch Rk Bn(8)(conspic) Fl(2)R5s

NW ENTRANCE

Pilot Staff

Cross

Chy

Penmaenmawr Channel

Radio Mast (76)(conspic)(Red Lt)

Trecastell Pt

Spire

Castle (ruins)

Beaumaris

FlWG2s 8m 6M

FlWG5m 6M

Gallows Pt

Garth Pt

BANGOR FLATS

Port Penrhyn

Bangor

Castle

FS

Pen-y-coed Pt

Bath Pt

TRAETH LAFAN (LAVAN SANDS)

White

Weir

Tall Bldg

Spire

Menai Suspension Br (30·5m)

Tr (conspic)

2FR (vert)

Bn

Spire

Slip

Menai Suspension Bridge (30·5)

Boat Ho

Boat Ho

Wooded

Wooded

Price Point

FlWR2s 5m 3M

Britannia Br (27·4)

Bn Wooded

Platters

Swelly Rk

White

Pier

Bn

QR4m

G

Bn

Wooded

Spire

Slip

Weir

Menai Bridge

The Swellies

QR4m

Column (68) 0 (30·5m)

Spire

Britannia Bridge (27·4m)

SEE INSET

Miles

2

5 Cables 0

N

N

53° 15'

53° 14'

13'

19'

18'

17'

16'

15'

14'

13'

2'

3'

4'

5'

6'

10'

11'

4° 11'

30"

4°

240

MENAI STRAIT SW PART

Depths in Metres

Anglesey

Caernarvon

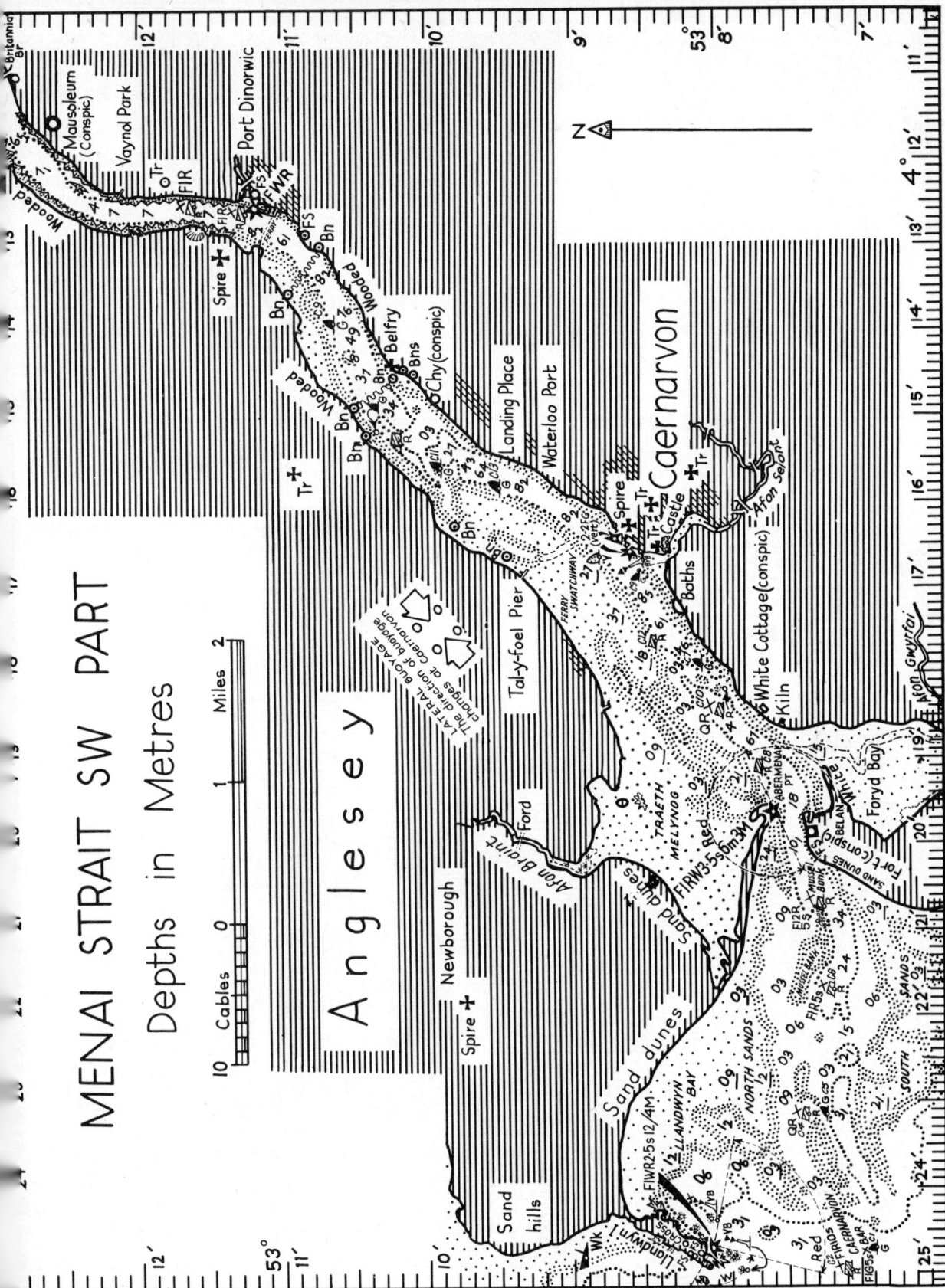

...d on British Admiralty Charts (nos. in text) with the permission of the Controller of H.M. Stationery Office and of Hydrographer of the Navy, and on other sources.

HOLYHEAD
Depths in Metres

38'   4° 37'W

Clipera Buoy, 2·5 cables E
(Red can)

0   Cables   5

N

16₅

11₃ 14₁

Fl(3)15s 21m 14M Siren (1)20s

8₆ 2

8 6

15

W

4₄

Red

8

Green

FAIRWAY

8₃
3₁

12₉
2₂

7₄
4₃

15₃

8₁

11m

Q Horn (1) 10s

10₇ 7
2₇

5₆

10₇

Steps (as marked)

9₅

Fl(4)R15s
R

(vert) 2FR

2FG (vert)

(vert) 2FR

2FG (vert)

SWAMPED MOORINGS
NO ANCHORING

Fl Y
2·5
Salt

10₁
2₂

6₂

Ts(5)

2₈

No1₃

NEW HARBOUR

6₃

10₅

7₆

2₈
6
G

5₆
G
R

Red

6₅

7

Ochy

Soldiers Pt

0₄

7

No2 2₈

No 4

3₄

5

2₂

Perch
R

YACHT MOORINGS

(occas) Dir Oc WRG

Perch
R

2₈

6₂

3

3

ALUMINIUM JETTY

LB

Salt.1

4₃

Fl Y 3s

3
4

7

FS

2FR (vert)

Sailing Club

Porth-y-felin

CG mast

CraigDdu

Lndg
FS

FAIRWAY

Old Lighthouse

2FR 7m 1M & FW or R10M Traffic sig

NO ANCHORING

Customs

Admiralty Pier

Dolphin
2FG (vert) Bell (occas)

CAR FERRY

FOUL

5m 2FG (vert) 5m

2FR (vert) float
R

Spire (conspic) ✠

✠

Belfry (conspic) ✠ Holyhead

Tr (conspic)

(vert) 2FG

OcG5s

OcG3s Bell(1)5s
(occas)

(vert) 2FR

5

5

(vert) 2FR

INNER HARBOUR

No1 Dock

Old Hr

No2 Dock

South Quay

2₇

1₃

2₇

Inys Peibic

2₂

1₉

(vert) 2FG
Ro-Ro

2FR (vert)

2FR (vert)

Station

Black Bridge

Mont

TOWYN BAY

4° 38'W

37'

Based on British Admiralty Charts (nos. in text) with the permission of the Controller of H.M. Stationery Office and the Hydrographer of the Navy, and on other sources.

HW Port Dinorwic −0.55.   MHWS 5.7; MLWS 0.8; MTL 3.2; MHWN 4.5; MLWN 2.0.

DS in offing: N +5.00; S −1.00. At Fort Belan: E +4.40; W −1.30.

Bar 1m. Should not be attempted in onshore winds of force 5 or more. Most buoys are lit and are shifted as necessary. Up-to-date information from HM Caernarvon (tel Caernarvon (0268) 2118).

Approach To find the outer pair of buoys marking the bar (C1, G con Fl G 5s and C2, R can Fl 10s) make a position 11½ ca S of Llanddwyn Is circular Tr (Fl WR 2½s). A S Card buoy marks rks off Llanddwyn.

Entrance The direction of the stream changes in different parts of the Strait at different times, but by half-flood it sets fair right through to Caernarvon, Port Dinorwic and the Swellies. Proceed across the bar by the buoyed chan (C1, 3, 5 G con; C2, 4, 6 R can). Then leave Mussel Bank buoy Fl(2) R to port, and the entrance is immediately ahead with Aber Menai Pt (W mast 4.6m, Fl RW 3M) to port and Belan old fort to stb. Inside, the buoyed chan is on the mainland side as far as 1½M NE of Caernarvon and it is particularly narrow and near to this shore between buoys C10 (R can QR) and C7 (G con). Sandbanks extend from the Anglesey shore. Afon Seiont buoy, a N card buoy SE of C9, marks the chan to Caernarvon Hr (dries). The head-of-navigation buoy (special Y con) is ¼M NE of C9, and from here to Port Dinorwic the buoyage is reversed: i.e. proceeding NE, R can buoys are stb hand buoys and G con buoys are port hand buoys and the numbers decrease. The head-of-navigation buoy and C13 (G con) mark the SE side of Traeth Gwyllt sandbank (dries) and C11 (G con) marks its NE corner. Steer midway between these buoys and the mainland shore. Pass close on the Anglesey side of C14 (R can), then in midstream to C9 (G con) and Port Dinorwic. Between Port Dinorwic and the brs there are no buoys; keep on the W side of midstream.

Berthing (1) Abermenai Creek, convenient for departure to the SW. Enter close to E side of point and anch in 5½m close to NE side, opposite a hut. Sheltered except in strong NE winds. No facilities. (2) Caernarvon. Anch in 7½m N of town and 2 ca NE of oil wharf wooden jetty with the head-of-navigation buoy bearing WNW; deep-water mooring also available, apply HM. Or go into hr S of town, mud, dries. HM allots berth. Signal for swing bridge to open is 1 long and 3 short blasts. All facilities, buses, EC Thurs. (3) Port Dinorwic. Anch in 4½m SW of village near moorings or go into basin, soft mud, dries. All facilities, bus, EC Wed.

SKERRIES and CARMEL HEAD   Chart BA 1413
DS between Skerries and Carmel Hd: NE +5.00; SW −1.00; 5–6kn in both directions. 1M NW of Skerries: NE −5.55; SW +0.30; 4–5kn in both directions.

HOLYHEAD   Chart BA 2011   (Plan p242)
HW −0.35.   MHWS 5.7; MLWS 0.7; MTL 3.2; MHWN 4.5; MLWN 2.0.
The hr of Holyhead lies between Holyhead Mountain, a conspic landmark,

213m, and Carmel Hd. It can be entered in all conditions. The depth inside the New Hr is generally 5–15m shoaling to 2m and under near the shore and with the Platters, just under 1m, on the E side of the hr. The Old Hr entrance is 1¼ ca wide 5m deep. A jetty from the N end of Salt Is. is for large tankers, which have right of way.

Approach From N, give the Skerries a berth of at least 1M, and keep S Stack well open of N Stack till breakwater Lt Ho bears SSE to avoid the race over Langdon Ridge. Thence steer for breakwater. From SW, give N and S Stacks a berth of at least 1M. Conspic chimney (Anglesey Aluminium Smelter) is a good mark.

Holyhead race extends 1½M offshore and is worst N of the Stacks in NW winds. At breakwater W-going stream runs for 9h, from half-flood to LW by the shore. At 1M off the Stacks the stream runs at 5kn max.

Entrance Between the breakwater and Clipera Rks, R can bell buoy, Fl(4) 15s. The R can N Platters buoy, Fl R 15s, marks entrance to New Hr. Give breakwater ½ ca clearance as there is foul ground close in from outer Platter rks; entrance marked by buoys.

Berthing In New Hr only. Apply for temporary mooring from Holyhead SC (tel (0407) 2496). NE winds cause a chop. Area of foul ground between aluminium jetty and N end of Salt Is. Land on beach between Trinity Ho buildings and Mackenzie Pier or at YC slip. Fully equipped boatyard with 30T lift and all repair facilities. Fuel and water on quay. All stores in town within ¼M, EC Tues.

NORTH and SOUTH STACKS   Chart BA 1970
DS: NNE +5.30; SSW −0.30; 5kn in both directions.
Race up to 1½M NW of S Stack and ½M W of N Stack on NNE stream.
Race up to ½M W of S Stack with SSW stream.

PORT DINLLEYN   Chart BA 1971
HW −1.55.   MHWS 4.6; MLWS 0.6; MTL 2.6; MHWN 3.4; MLWN 1.7.
DS in offing: N +6.00; S HWD. Stream runs out of bay to W for 9h at up to 2kn. This fine bay on the N side of the Lleyn peninsula, 15M SW of Caernarvon, affords the only safe anch between there and Pwllheli in S to W winds and settled weather. With strong NW winds some shelter can be found by shallow-draft boats close to the pt, but strong winds from NNW to NNE send in a heavy sea.

Approach From W, keep Yr Eifl (twin peaks 561m conspic) open of Porth Dinlleyn Pt to clear Careg-y-Chad, dries 2m, ¾M W of Pt. Give the rks off the pt a fair berth. Chwislen Rk (bn) is steep-to all round. From seaward, steer for Bodfean, a rounded wooded mountain 275m high, 1M S of Nevin.

Anchorage About 1 ca S of LB Ho in 1½ to 3m. Better holding further out in the bay but less shelter.

Groceries at Morfa Nevin, EC Wed. For petrol and general stores, Nevin, 2M or in Nevin Bay, 1M to E. Anch in Nevin Bay not recommended.

ABERSOCH and ST TUDWAL'S ROAD — Chart BA 1484 (Plan p247)
HW St Tudwal's Road −3.00.   MHWS 4.7; MLWS 0.6; MTL 2.5; MHWN 3.6; MLWN 1.3.   DS: NE +2.00; SW −4.00.
Hr is small with hard bottom and dries out ½M from shore. It is a very popular yachting centre. The anch offshore in St Tudwal's Road is protected from SSE through SW to NE. A heavy sea comes in with winds near E.

The S Caernarvon YC on Penbennar is open from July to September, landing slip and water. All stores in Abersoch, EC Wed.

PWLLHELI — Chart BA 1971
HW −3.00.   MHWS 4.9; MLWS 0.6; MTL 2.7; MHWN 3.7; MLWN 1.5.
DS: W by S −4.20; E +2.40; S at HWD.
A small secure crowded hr lying in Tremadoc Bay.
Bar   Varies in position and depth; has less than 0.3m.
Approach   Gimlet Rk (30m, quarried) lies just E of conspic row of white houses on the promenade. The hr entrance is E of this rk. Fresh E to SW winds cause a breaking sea offshore.
Entrance   Buoyed, with over 2½m at half-tide. Keep close to the buoys. The chan is narrow and follows S shore.
Berthing   Anch off YC W of Gimlet Rock and confirm with HM. All facilities and stores, boatyard, slips. Rly. EC Wed.

PORTHMADOG — Chart BA 1971
Note: The Admiralty spells this hr Portmadoc on charts and in Tide Tables.
HW −2.50.   MHWS 5.1; MLWS 0.7; MTL 2.8; MHWN 4.0; MLWN 1.6.
DS: S at HW.
Bar   About ½m, variable: there is 0.6m in chan at town. Hr affords complete shelter.
Approach   From St Tudwal's Road steer 068°, to make the Fairway buoy, RWVS Fl 4s.
Entrance   The chan is buoyed with unlit lateral buoys with reflectors (April through October only). Enter between Nos. 1 and 2 buoys in line with the Fairway buoy. Within the bar the chan has varying depths, 0.6m or more, and from Fechan Pt hugs the NW shore. Safest to allow 2h either side of HW for 1.3m draft. Chan shifts.
Berthing   Take the ground below the br. Moorings usually available for visitors, apply to HM G. M. Bicks, tel Porthmadog (0766) 2927. Temporary anch below Borth Pt in fine weather.

Rly. Extensive supplies and facilities, sailing school. EC Wed.

BARMOUTH — Chart BA 1484 (Plan p237)
HW −2.50.   MHWS 4.9; MLWS 0.6; MTL 2.8; MHWN 3.9; MLWN 1.7.
DS: S at HWD; N +5.00.
Bar   About ½m, 1M off the town. Hr is unapproachable in strong SW winds and should only be visited in fine weather. A very beautiful estuary.

Approach   Bring Fegla Fawr hill, a low turtle-back shaped hill inside S side of entrance, in line with house inside Penrhyn Pt. From Barmouth Outer buoy (spher RWVS L Fl 10s) leave R can Bar and inner buoys to port, and steer for entrance which has 3½ to 5½m in chan.

Berthing   Anch near rly bridge in 2 to 7m as close to shore as draft permits, to avoid strong stream (3–4kn on the ebb). Cables crossing the river are indicated by shore marks. There is a better berth with less stream above the bridge between two quays. Strangers should seek local advice. EC Wed.

ABERDOVEY   Chart BA 1484   (Plan p259)
HW −3.00.   MHWS 4.8; MLWS 0.5; MTL 2.7; MHWN 3.8; MLWN 1.7. DS: S −1.30; N +4.30.

This hr is in the first major inlet S of Cader Idris. It is unlit and daylight with good visibility is essential for the approach. The problem is to locate the Outer buoy: strangers are best advised to contact the Pilot, Mr J A Benbow, office tel Aberdovey (065 472) 626, home 247, or contact hr on VHF Ch 16 or 12.

Bar   About ¼m, shifts continually. There is about 3m at half-tide: it is unwise to enter with less water than this except in calm weather. In such conditions entry is possible on the ebb, but in W winds a bad sea gets up quickly on the ebb and entrance may be impossible.

Approach   First make the Aberdovey Outer RWVS spher buoy, moored in 9–11m at 52°32′N, 4°06′W. About 1M to the E lies the Bar G con buoy, and if no dangerous seas are breaking W of this buoy it is safe to enter. If in doubt wait till 1h before HW: if still impassable, shelter can be found in St Tudwal's Road.

Entrance   All buoys are G con and are left to stb. From Aberdovey Outer buoy steer for the Bar buoy, thence for South Spit buoy and then for the Inner buoy. Then steer for the wooden jetty. The buoys are frequently moved. At half flood the stream sets ENE across the entrance.

Berthing   Alongside jetty. Local advice needed before anch. *Note:* bns with Y diamond top marks E of jetty mark a submarine cable and prohibited anch. There is also a submerged cable approx 2½ ca W of jetty. Water at jetty. All stores, rly, EC Wed.

ABERYSTWYTH   Chart BA 1484   (Plan p247)
HW −3.15.   MHWS 4.8; MLWS 0.5; MTL 2.7; MHWN 3.7; MLWN 1.8. DS: S −1.00; N +5.00.

The hr may be located by Pendinas, a conspic 120m hill with Wellington monument, S of entrance.

Bar   1m off the pier. The hr mostly dries, but affords good shelter. Narrow entrance with right-angle turn inside the pier-head.

Approach   Wellington Monument on with lt mast will clear Castle Rks which lie N of entrance, which has 3m at half-tide.

Entrance   At night within W sector of S pier-head lt Fl(2) WG 10s (shows G to SW), crossing the bar 20m from N pier-head. When abreast the S pier-head steer

St Tudwal's Road

Depths in Metres

0 Cables 5

N

28
4
2
1
28
0.9
Bn Penbennar
St Tudwal's Shoal
3R
Bn (YC Jetty)
0.9
4
3,
St TUDWAL'S ROADS
19
28
INNER ROAD
5,3 Red
22
BORTH FAWR
59
OUTER ROAD 49'
obscd
Slip
86
Bn
R
Penrhyn Du
Porth Bach
5,3
5,3
East.I
Carreg-Trai
W
68
Cross
19
Bell
St Tudwal's Is
Carreg
Trai
(24)
R
R
83
48'
Lookout
196
White
St Tudwal's Sound
FIWR 20s 46m 15, 13M
12
62
Pistyll Cim
West.I
196
Trwyn yr Wylfa
24
heeiriad
Red

30'   29'   28'W   4°27'

52° 50'

52° 48'

2° 8'

ABERYSTWYTH

Depths in Metres

5.9w
THE WEG
4
5'
Hotel (white)
Spire 52°
Spire 25'
52° 25'
Pen Cwningen
52
3,3
0,4
Pier (ruins)
LB
48
06
Slip
63
University College
76
Aberystwyth
Castle Pt
64 4,2 Castle Rk
Castle (ruins)
Ldg Lts 138°
QWR
89
28
05
09
Fl(2)WG10s 12m10M
FR (occas)
FR (occas)
36
09
24.5'
8
G 3,5 obscd
0 Cables 3
Pendinas
Wellington Mont
4°5 (124)

N

FISHGUARD

Depths in Metres

0 Cables 6

N

Calf
Cow (2)
8
13,8
Pen Cw
N Breakwater
4,5
13,6
Bns
4,5
FIG5s 18m13M Bell(1)10s
FG 89m 5M
66
12
Anchoring
Q
FG 77m 5M
6
68
BY
Fishguard Bay Hotel
RAILWAY Sºⁿ
Ro-Ro Terminal
Lts 282°
10,8
9
LB
Prohibited
WK
Q(6)+LFl.15s
Boat Pier
3,3
YB
7
13
53
6
FIR 3s 10m 5M
7
58
GOODWICK
3
3
Needle Rk
Slip
0,5
Castle Pt
3,1
E Breakwater
19
24
4,4
5
SANDS
1,4
Fort (ruins)
Saddle Pt
0,4
(conspic) CGFS
YC
Chy (68)
59' FISHGUARD
58' Lower Town
4° 57'

1'

2°

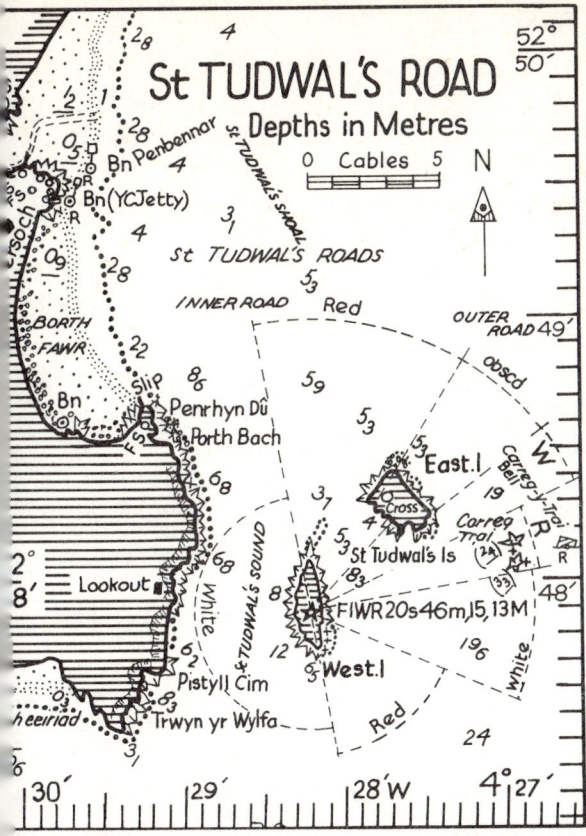

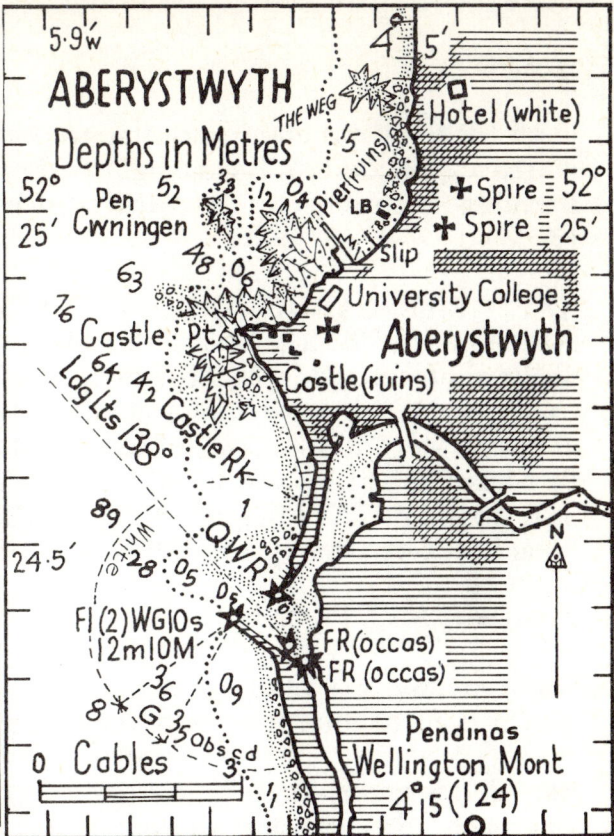

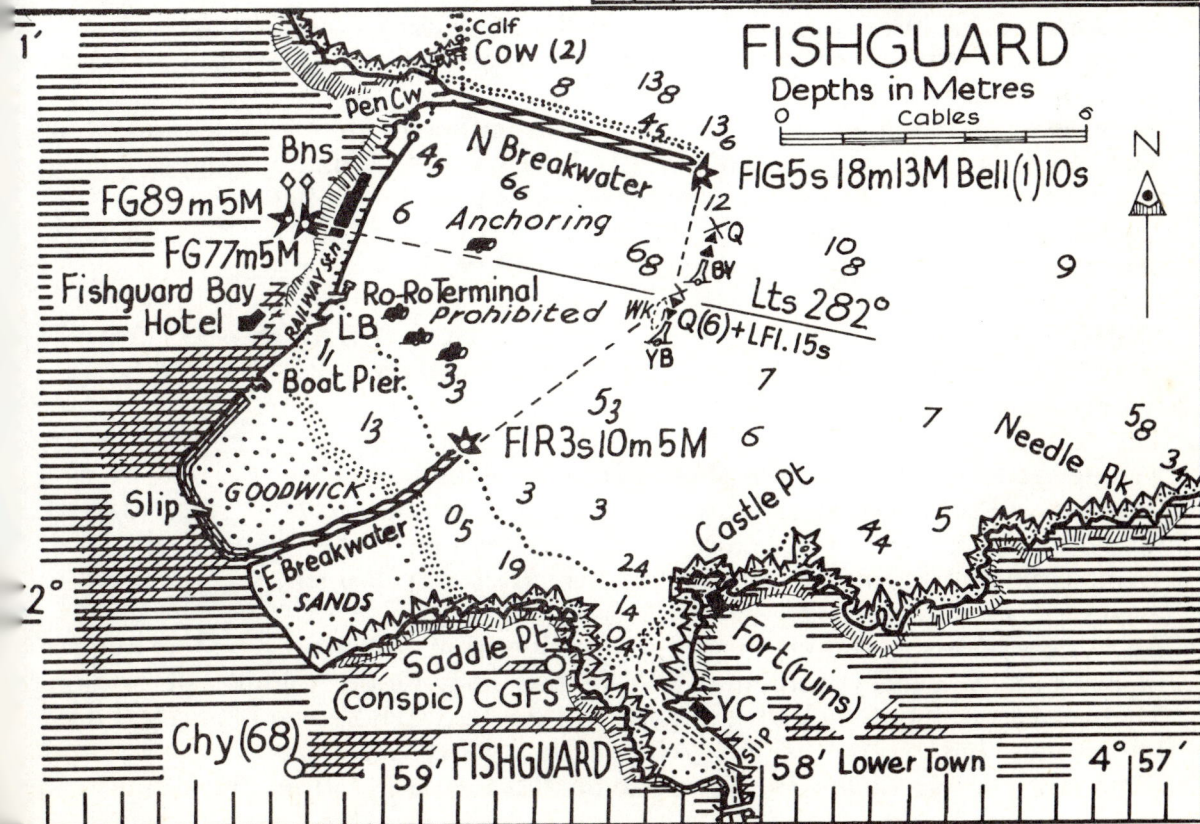

in on FR ldg lts, then alter course to port to head up river to Aberystwyth. Ldg marks are painted W for daylight entry.

Berthing   Alongside quays. HM's office inner end of Town Quay. All supplies, EC Wed.

NEW QUAY, CARDIGAN   Chart BA 1484

HW −3.30.   DS: S −1.00; N +5.00.

Sheltered from winds W through S to NE; with wind N or NW a dangerous sea comes in. Hr dries, bottom sand and clay. In fine weather vessels can lie head to anch and stern to pier, or outside the pier. The E side of bay off Ina Pt is foul. Pier-head has Fl WG 3s lt, W 135°–252°, G 252°–295°. A groyne runs out 45m SSE from the end of the pier and is marked by a bn with Y ball topmark. End of breakwater by LB slip has QWR lt, R 193°–230°, W 230°–099°.

CARDIGAN   Chart BA 1484

HW −3.50.   MHWS 4.7; MLWS 0.6; MTL 2.7; MHWN 3.5; MLWN 1.9. DS: S −1.00; N +5.00.

The hr is at the mouth of the R Teifi. Entrance difficult and dangerous in strong W to NW winds, but good shelter within. No special outlying dangers.

Bar   Dries and shifts. There is over 2½m at MHWS, and about 1½m MHWN.

Approach   Straightforward on a course approx SE.

Entrance   Prior inspection of the chan or the services of a pilot strongly advised. Leave R can buoy to port and steel bn with crossbar to stb, passing it about 6m off.

Berthing   (1) Good anch in soft mud with sufficient depth in several pools between St Dogmaels and Cardigan. (2) Take ground on muddy sand alongside Spillers Quay on rt bank, good shelter. Land on the beach below br.

 Pilot at Penrhyn. Chandlery, blacksmith. Provisions, hotels, PO and launderette in town, mainly on N side of river. EC Wed.

FISHGUARD   Chart BA 1484   (Plan p247)

HW −3.55.   MHWS 4.8; MLWS 0.8; MTL 2.8; MHWN 3.5; MLWN 2.1. DS in offing: N +6.00; S HWD.

The only hr between Milford Haven and Holyhead that can be entered in any weather at any time. Provides shelter from all winds.

Approach   From NW after passing Pen Anglas on coast to NW, steer to leave the N breakwater lt Fl G 5s close to stb. This will clear the rks off Pen Cw, dr 1.2m. Hold course until E breakwater lt Fl R 3s is well open, then proceed to anch.

Anchorage   Vessels should anch SE of the line from end of breakwaters to large mooring buoy. Anch prohibited NW of this line. Good holding, no stream. There is a convenient anch for drafts up to 1.8m between Saddle Pt and R lt on E breakwater, but exposed to NE. All facilities, water. Rly.

Fishguard Old Harbour   Between Saddle and Castle Pts, dries 1.2m, mud and clay. Hr shoals to 1m 1 ca inside the pts, bottom very stony. Heavy scend in N and NE gales, and entrance is dangerous then. Pwll Gwaelod ¾M inside Dinas Hd affords shelter to small craft in E gales.

PASSAGE NOTE: FISHGUARD TO STRUMBLE HEAD

Chart BA 1973

Bound S from Fishguard, advantage can be taken of an inshore eddy by keeping fairly close to the land until off Porthgain. This helps to get through Ramsey Sd before the full strength of the tide develops and causes overfalls at the S end.

PASSAGE NOTE: STRUMBLE HEAD TO ST ANN'S HEAD

Charts BA 1973, 1478

DS Strumble Head	SW −1.00; NE +5.00
Bishops and Clerks	SW −1.30; NE +4.30
Between Skomer and Grassholm	S −1.00; N +5.00
Smalls	S +0.15; N −5.45
Between Skokholm and St Ann's Hd	SE −0.30; NW +5.30
Inshore W of St Ann's Hd	SE −1.30; NW +4.30

This is an area of strong tides and turbulent seas. The streams run at 5kn near the Bishops, 4kn between Skomer and Grassholm, and up to 6 or 7kn in the narrow parts of the inner sounds. 2 or 3M W of the Bishops and Smalls the streams are much weaker (2 to 3kn). Eddies and races form off the rks, banks and Is during the strength of each stream: there is a particularly dangerous race called the Wild Goose Race, W of Skomer and Skokholm.

Four routes are available. (1) Outside the Smalls clear of all dangers; this is much the longest but avoids the worst of the tidal stream. (2) Outside the Bishops and between Skomer and Grassholm. (3) Inside the Bishops along the W coast of Ramsey Is and between Skomer and Grassholm. (4) Inshore through Ramsey and Jack Sounds.

For route (2) pass N Bishop which is unlit and 37m above HW, but do not turn southwards for S Bishop Lt Fl 5s until at least 1¼M W of N Bishop to clear heavy overfalls. Then steer to pass midway between Grassholm and Skomer and afterwards through Broad Sound between Skomer and Skokholm to avoid the Wild Goose Race. Steer to pass clear of St Ann's Hd Fl WR 5s.

Route (3): from N pass between St David's Hd and Carreg-trai (dries 4m) and steer to leave Gwahan to port. Pass down W coast of Ramsey Is between it and Llech Uchaf and continue S across entrance of St Bride's Bay to pass W of Skomer Is. Continue as for route (2). Route (3) should not be attempted at night but tides are less strong than in the sounds. Route (4) is a valuable short-cut but should be used by strangers only in good visibility, with a fair tide and reasonable weather. Chart 1482 is absolutely essential. Directions for the two sounds follow. In each case go through on slack water or with a fair tide.

Ramsey Sound   Chart BA 1482 essential. DS: S − 2.00; N +4.00; 6kn in the narrowest part.

From N, pass close to St David's Hd and steer to leave Carreg Gafeiliog, a bold rk 3m high off Pt St John, ½ ca to port. Steer towards a point midway between the E end of the Bitches and Pen Maen Melyn being careful to leave Horse Rk (dr 1m) to port. When Pen Dal-aderyn is abeam steer to keep St David's Hd in sight astern so as to clear the Shoe Rk (dr 2.7m). If broken water is seen ahead in the vicinity of Sylvia Rk calmer water will be eastward.

From S, Leave Sylvia Rk to the W and after passing it open St David's Hd of Pen Dal-aderyn to clear Shoe Rk. Steer midway between the E end of the Bitches and the mainland Pen Maen Melyn and continue due N being careful to leave Horse Rk about ¼ ca to stb. Steer midway between Gwahan to port and Carreg Gafeiliog to stb.

There is an anch in the sound just N of the Bitches. Permission to land on the island should be obtained from Mr R Pratt. To wait for tide or make short expedition ashore, safer to anch in Whitesand Bay.

Jack Sound   DS: S −3.00; N +3.00; 6–7kn.

BA chart 1482 is essential. From N, before entering the Sound identify Tusker Rk (1.5m) ¾ ca W of Wooltack Pt and the Blackstones 2 ca S of Midland Is. Pass W of Tusker Rk and immediately bring the Blackstones on with the W end of Skokholm. Approach the Blackstones, then pass close E of them. Rough water will be encountered on leaving this sound with a strong S wind against tide.

From S, while still to the S of the Blackstones identify them and also Tusker Rk. Pass close E of the Blackstones and steer for Tusker Rk. When Garland Stone opens N of Midland Is the vessel is clear of all dangers W of Tusker Rk.

SOLVA

HW −4.50.   MHWS 5.5; MLWS 0.7; MTL 3.2; MHWN 4.2; MLWN 2.3.

A small creek on N of St Bride's Bay, 4m inside the entrance. Dries 100m inside entrance rk: complete shelter for small craft which can dry, though nasty swell in extreme weather.

Entrance   50m wide. Black Rk, which dries approximately 4m, lies in centre; it is steep-to on its E side. Leave it close to port and proceed up the harbour keeping to outer side of bend. Beware of a spit of stones just inside entrance on W side at Trwyn Caws.

Anchorage   Temporary anch in calm weather may be found in 3m just behind the rk, but there is little room. In N winds better to anch outside. Small craft taking the ground can go further in and lie alongside the quay or in midstream off the LB Ho, or can go up further at HW. Strong winds from the S render the entrance impassable.

Some facilities and stores.

250

ST BRIDE'S BAY   Chart BA 1478
HW (Little Haven) −4.50.   MHWS 5.9; MLWS 0.7; MTL 3.3; MHWN 4.4; MLWN 2.3.

It is possible to anch in fine weather at various places in St Bride's Bay, especially with offshore winds. Avoid if any chance of strong winds from the W, as although the tides in the bay are weak, to get out of the bay one has to go either through the sounds or round Skomer Is in the S or Ramsey Is in the N, either way encountering strong tides.

Anchorage   With S or E winds, anch close in between Little Haven and Borough Hd. In N or E winds better anch between the entrance to Solva and Dinas Fawry. In S winds one can also anch in North Haven on Skomer Is, in about 6m. Chart 1482 is advisable. Beware of the reef on the E side of the entrance.

SKOMER ISLAND, SOUTH HAVEN   Chart BA 1482
HW −4.55.   MHWS 6.6; MLWS 0.7; MTL 3.7; MHWN 5.1; MLWN 2.5.

A small bay on the SE side of Skomer, giving shelter in winds from W through N to E. This is a most beautiful anchorage, and although it is exposed to S winds it is an easy fetch down to Milford Haven if it should blow up from that direction.

Entrance   If coming from Milford Haven aim for the Mew Stone, a prominent rk 48m high off the S-most tip of Skomer. Beware of rks extending S from the E part (The Neck) of Skomer Is, awash at MLWS.

Anchorage   Right up towards the head of the bay in about 6m, sand. Do not go further in at neaps as the ground becomes rocky.

   Land on The Neck or on the main part of the Is but not on the E side. Landing charge payable to the warden. Care should be taken on the Is to respect the wild life particularly where birds' nests are marked. No facilities.

MILFORD HAVEN   Charts BA 2878, 3274, 3275   (Plans p252–4)
HW −5.00.   MHWS 7.0; MLWS 0.7; MTL 3.8; MHWN 5.2; MLWN 2.5.

One of the finest natural harbours in the British Isles. From Dale in the W to Lawrenny in the E is about 12M, while the width varies from 1¾M to ½M. It is a major oil port with four terminals for very large tankers. There are two deep-water channels and small boats must keep out of the way of deep-draft vessels which are restricted to these channels. However, there is plenty of room to manoeuvre and tack between the deep-water channels and the shore.

   The Port Authority is the Milford Haven Conservancy Board whose jetty and office is at Hubberston Pt, with a Port Operations Centre with VHF radio, and a protected boat hr from which the Board's patrol and Pilot launches operate. These have green hulls and white upperworks and fly a blue flag with the word 'Harbourmaster' in white letters, or Pilot flag depending on duties. They are very helpful to yachts and their instructions must always be obeyed. Yachts should not approach within 300 ft of terminals or tankers.

   Attention is particularly drawn to the fact that Byelaws exist which make it mandatory for small vessels, including sailing vessels, to keep out of the way of

MILFORD HAVEN (1)
Depths in Metres

One Mile

N

Esso Terminal
3 For (vert) passage Boat
3 For (vert)
3FR (vert)
6F Bu (vert)
3FR (vert) Horn (2) 30s
Q X see note on chart
Q see note on next... Lt Bns 080
Fl(3)G10s East Angle G
Esso BY

South Hook Pt
Radio mast
Chys Q(121) Q(121) Q(121)

Stack Rock Loading Masts
Fort (conspic)

Montreal Rk YB
Bull Rk

Sandy Haven Pill
SANDY HAVEN
SANDY HAVEN BAY

Little Castle Hd
Oc 8s 5 3m 15M (Lt Bn)
Behar YB
Arc of vis Arc of vis

DALE ROADS

Watch House Pt
Great Castle Hd
Oc 4s 23m 15M & FWRG 25m 5/3M (Lt Bn)

Q(3)10s Dakotian BYB

Q6+?
LFl 15s South Hook YB
FIR 2·5s Stack Rk
Ldg Lt Bns 095°

Fl G 5s Chapel
Thorn Rk
Q(9)15s
Angle X BY
VQ
Thorn I. YBY
Fort (23)(conspic)
(15m) Chapel

WEST ANGLE BAY

Fl G 10s West Chapel G
FIR 5s East Chapel R
Fl G 5s Rot G

CHAPEL BAY
Ellens Well
OFS
Thorn Pt
Bns BW
Water Tr
East Blockhouse Pt
Trs
Angle
Slip Bn G
Angle Pt Slip (disused)
ANGLE BAY
Slip

CASTLES BAY
Sheep I.
Fl(3) G7s 18m
Lookout Houses

Dale
DALE FLATS
Yacht moorings Slip
F1(2) WR 5s 20m 5/3M Dale Pt
Castlebeach Bay
WATWICK BAY
F 80m 15M Watwick Pt

Ldg Lt Bns 039·45°
Q WR 2m 9·7M West Blockhouse Pt
Fl(2) R 5s Mill Bay
West Chapel
East Chapel
MILL BAY
WEST CHANNEL
W R G vis

LIGHTS :
FR 53m 12M
FR 53m 12M
F 54m 13M
St Anns Hd
Fl WR 5s 48m 23,22,19M
Horn (2) 6s

Q(9)15s Mid Channel/Rks R
FIR 2·5s St Anns R
YBY
Lt. Ho
White
W

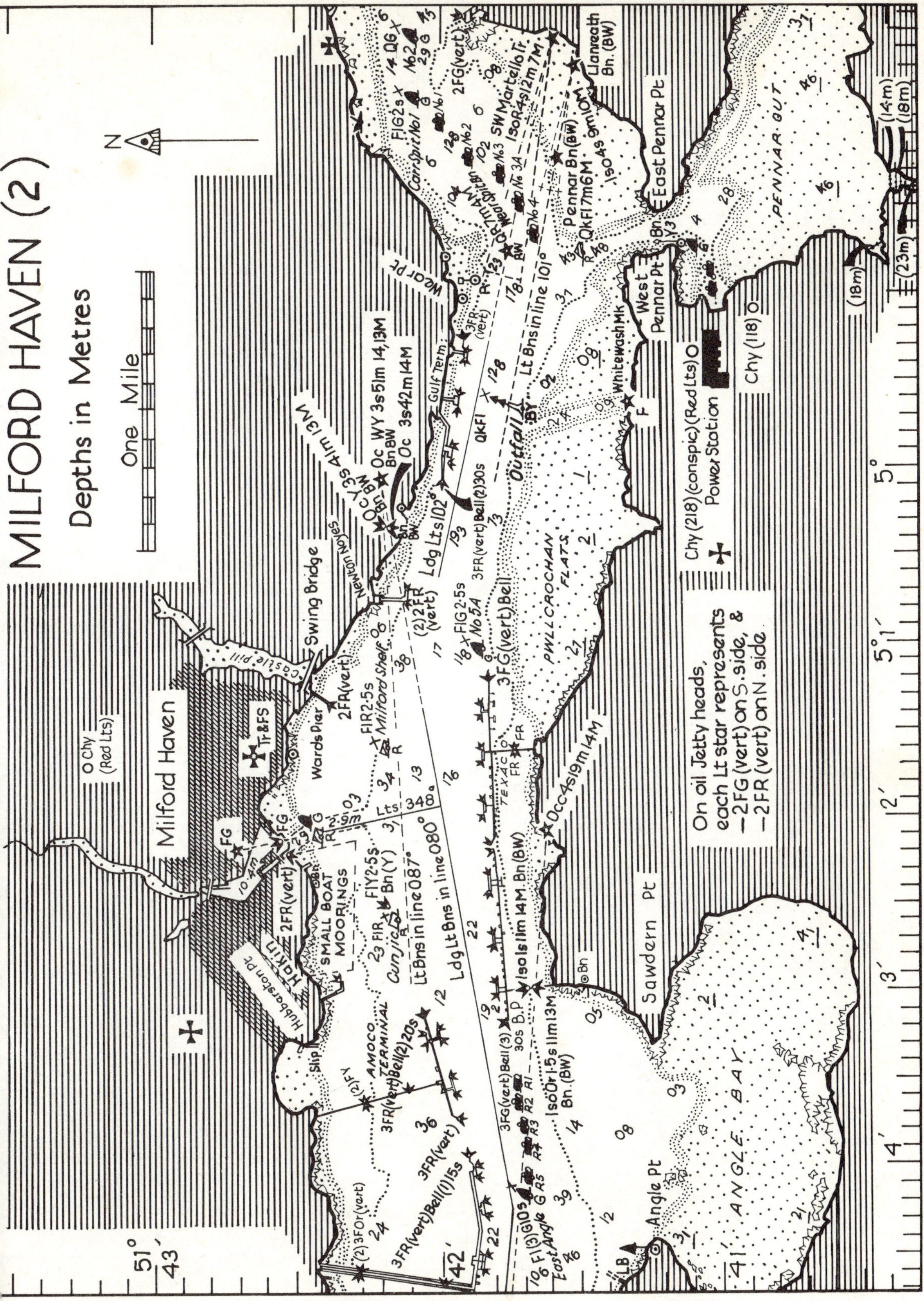

MILFORD HAVEN (2)

Depths in Metres

One Mile

N

Milford Haven

O Chy (Red Lts)

Swing Bridge

Castle Pill

Tr & FS

Wards Pier

2FA(vert)

FIR 2·5s

Milford Shelf

2FR(vert)

FG

SMALL BOAT MOORINGS

Hakin

Hubberston Pt

AMOCO TERMINAL

3FR(vert)Bell(2)20s

(2)FY

Slip

2·3 FIR FIY2·5s

Cunjic Bn(Y)

Lt Bns in line 087°

Ldg Lt Bns in line 080°

Lts 348°

3FR(vert)

3·6

3FR(vert)Bell(1)15s

(2) Fl(3)G10s

East Angle GR5

R4 R3 R2 R1

3FG(vert)Bell(3)

30s B.P.

Iso G r 1·5s 11m13M

Bn.(BW)

2·4

42'

3FOr(vert)

Newton Noyes

Oc WY 3s51m 14,13M

BnBW

Oc 3s42m14M

B2 BW

Bn BW

Ldg Lts 102°

Gulf Term.

QKFl

3FR(vert)Bell

Wear Pt

FIG2·5s

No 5A

3FG(vert)

TEXACO

FR

Occ4s9m14M

Sawdern Pt

Angle Pt

ANGLE BAY

PWLLCROCHAN FLATS

Outfall

Car Spit No1

FIG2s

No 6 Q.6

No2

2·9

2FG(vert)

No2 N.Bn

Nun Shoal

No 3

QR7m7M

No 3A

No 4

Lt Bns in line 101°

Pennar Bn(BW)

QkFl7m6M

Iso R4s 12m7M

SW Martello Tr.

Iso4s

Llanreath Bn.(BW)

9m1OM

East Pennar Pt

West Pennar Pt Bn

Whitewash Mk

F

Power Station

Chy (218)(conspic)(Red Lts)

Chy (118)

PENNAR GUT

(14m)

(18m)

(23m)

(18m)

On oil Jetty heads, each Lt star represents
—2FG (vert) on S. side, &
—2FR (vert) on N. side.

51°
43'

5°
5·1'
5·2'
5·3'
5·4'

MILFORD HAVEN (3) & CLEDDAU RIVER
Depths in Metres
One Mile

0   1

N

Fowborough Pt

Sprinkle

Landshipping Quay (ruin

North Wood

Llangwm

Black Tar Pt

Power (9m)

LLANGWM PILL

Wooded

Bn

GARRON PILL

Bn

Lawrenn

Bns

Bns

(28m)

(14m)

(20m)

Slip

Bn

WESTFIELD PILL

Benton Castle

Castle

Lawrenny Quay Pontoon

Slip

Williamston Pill

Jenkins Pt

RIVER CLEDDAU

Whalecombe

Barnlake Pt

Cleddau Br

Bn

Bn

(26m)

Bns

Jetty (ruins)

Fl(3)G10s P5

2FR(vert)

2FG(vert)

Slip

Burton Pt

BARGE TROTS

Steps

Slip

QR R

Fl(2)R10s

Fl G10s   No
Dockyard Bank   3   Fl(2)R10s

Fl(3)G15s
Dockyard Bank   No4   R

2FG(vert)

Neyland Pt

R

Hobbs Pt

Wooded

Coseston Pt

LANION PILL

COSHESTON PILL

Based on British Admiralty Charts (nos. in text) with the permission of the Controller of H.M. Stationery Office the Hydrographer of the Navy, and on other sources.

large vessels constrained by reasons of draft in the deep-water channels of the Haven.

Approach The Turbot Bank 4M S of St Ann's Hd, marked on its W edge by a W Card buoy VQ(9) 10s, causes a heavy sea in bad weather. There is also a confused and sometimes dangerous sea close to St Ann's Hd especially in SW gales against the ebb. In these conditions quieter water will be found in the E Channel or near Sheep Is. In daytime with good visibility the first conspicuous mark likely to be seen especially from the S is the power stn chimney near Pennar Gut, which may be seen from 25M away.

Entrance The entrance offers no obstructions to shallow draft vessels in most weathers, but the Middle Channel Rks, 5m, and Chapel Rks, 3m, in the centre of the entrance should be avoided in very heavy weather.

Both E and W Channels, the latter being the deeper one, are well buoyed and the W Channel has outstanding leading marks including a bn on Middle Channel Rks just outside the line of the entrance between St Ann's Hd and Sheep Is. The entrance is well lit and in poor visibility the ldg lts on W Blockhouse Pt may be seen before St Ann's Lt.

Although there is never any necessity to go inside Thorn Is there is 3m in the channel between Thorn Is and the mainland, the overhead cables giving a least headroom of 15m at MHWS.

The course to be taken between the outer line of the entrance (St Ann's Hd to Sheep Is) to the inner line (Dale Fort to Thorn Is) will vary according to the anchorage eventually to be used and the need to keep out of the way of deep-draft vessels in the main shipping channels. The shores on both sides are steep-to and can be safely approached to within ½ ca.

For vessels going to Pembroke Dock and beyond the chan is well buoyed. The S shore between Thorn Is and Popton Pt outside the line of Angle Bay is clean and it is possible to keep out of the way of deep-draft vessels manoeuvring into the Esso terminal. After the Esso terminal the main chan must be taken, although except at MLWS there will be room between this chan and Milford shelf.

The main dangers after this which may not be apparent are Wear Spit, (S end marked by a bn, QR), and Carr Rks (strong cross-tidal set), N edge marked by two stb buoys. There are two more stb buoys off Dockyard Bank. If proceeding beyond Hobbs Pt, take care to keep in the chan passing under the Cleddau Br (37m) as indicated by the position of the stb buoy just before it. After the br there is deep water to Lawrenny, and nearly to Landshipping where the river divides into the E and W Cleddau at Picton Pt. Take care to avoid spits projecting from the outside of bends in the river: some are marked by buoys. Above Lawrenny abreast Benton Castle do not approach the Castle closer than midstream to avoid rocks. At night caution should be exercised as there are many unlit mooring buoys. Navigation is possible above Picton Pt to Haverfordwest and Slebech but only to vessels of suitable draft when there is sufficient rise of tide. *Note:* the bridge at Haverfordwest cannot be opened.

Milford Docks   Mudflats extend from the entrance to a distance of 2½ ca, but the gates may be approached from the fairway by a narrow cut in the mud with a depth of 2.4m MLWS, ldg lts FG 348°. After passing between the buoys steer for the entrance gates which open from 2h before HW to HW. Signal for dock gates open: blue flag by day, 2 G lts (vert) at night, displayed on E side of entrance. The dock is largely used by trawlers but a clear berth can usually be secured at the inner (NW) end. In view of the many available anchorages it is not recommended unless of necessity.

Anchorages   From W to E: (1) Dale, about 3 ca NW of Dale Pt close to moorings. Secure and comfortable anch in most winds, particularly S and W. In strong N winds anch off N shore or in Castle Beach Bay. In strong E winds it is somewhat exposed and landing may be difficult. Moorings may be available: apply Dale Sailing Co. where water, chandlery, fuel and slipway are available. Provisions at village PO, showers at YC. (2) Sandy Haven Bay, sheltered in N and E winds. (3) Off Ellens Well and Angle Pt on S shore. (4) With sufficient rise of tide Angle Bay may be entered. Yachts can lie alongside W side of pier on S shore at W end of Bay. (5) At Milford off Hakin Pt or MHCB jetty W of town. (6) Pennar Park on the S side 1M W of Pembroke Dock, entrance marked by a R can buoy. Sheltered anch in 4m: buoy anch. Water, fuel, shop and restaurant ashore. (7) At Pembroke Dock above Hobbs Pt close to moorings (the tide runs strongly). Watch out for Cork–Pembroke car ferry which enters and leaves by chan E of Dockyard Bank. Chandlery at Hobbs Pt, also grid on inside of slipway. Diesel from East Llanion Marine, MoD Rd off Cleddau Br approach. (8) Off and above Trinity House Pier. (9) Off Williamston Pill, E of Burton Common and opposite the entrance to Lawrenny. (10) Off the jetty at Lawrenny where moorings may be available. Secure temporarily to visitors' buoy at creek entrance or to pontoon and go ashore to arrange a berth. Supplies available.

   Yachts on passage requiring only a night shelter use (1) or (2), otherwise any of the anchorages according to choice, (6) and (9) being very peaceful. All stores and facilities at Milford; stores and facilities in varying degree at Dale, Hobbs Pt, Neyland and Lawrenny. Rly from Milford and Pembroke Dock. EC Milford Thurs, Pembroke Dock Wed.

Passage notes: Milford Haven to Land's End

Chart BA 1123

The tidal stream mainly runs at right angles to the course to be made good although there is a slight advantage in leaving Milford Haven on the flood for the first 10 miles. As the coast of Cornwall is closed so the tide will be more in line with the course, especially between Cape Cornwall and Land's End where the streams run at a maximum of 2½kn.

   It is 110M from Milford Haven to Land's End, and very little shelter offers in bad weather. Milford Haven itself is easy to enter in any weather or state of the tide. To the E of the direct track, shelter can be found in the lee of Lundy in W or SW winds; otherwise Padstow is the only harbour to offer shelter from the prevailing SW-lies, but entry over Doom Bar would not be possible for most vessels at LW, or at any time in a strong NW-ly. St Ives offers shelter in S or E winds only.

Notes on navigation in the Bristol Channel E of line Hartland Point – Lundy – St Govan's Head

Chart BA 1179

Tidal streams in the channel are generally strong, a spring rate of 1.8kn midway between Lundy and St Govan's Hd increasing eastwards to 6kn at the Severn Bridge. The streams in the inner parts of Carmarthen and Bideford Bays are weak but there are races off many headlands, in particular Hartland Pt and Bull Pt on the S side and St Govan's Hd, Oxwich Pt and Mumbles Hd on the N, together with dangerous races, the Hen and Chickens and White Horses, off the NW and NE of Lundy.

Overfalls are widespread, sometimes in mid-Channel, and a short steep sea sets up quickly with wind against tide, so a craft unable to stay out at sea should be considered unsafe in the Bristol Channel if far from an accessible hr.

STACKPOLE QUAY

HW −4.50.   MHWS 7.9; MLWS 0.8; MTL 4.4; MHWN 5.9; MLWN 2.9.

Bar   None. The hr dries out soon after half-tide; it is very small and little used. There is room for two or three small vessels to lie on hard sand inside the breakwater.

Approach   The coast around Stackpole Bay is steep-to. The bottom abreast of the hr is rk but there is good anch out of the tide off Little Haven which can be used while waiting to enter. The bay is well sheltered from W and N winds, but should not be entered in winds between E and S. A stranger should inspect the hr at LW before attempting to enter.

Entrance   Between a cliff on the stbd side and a low wall of stone blocks to port. The cliff slopes at an angle of about 45° from the level of MHWN downwards. The wall which runs out from the outer corner of the breakwater dries just before half-ebb: it must be carefully avoided when covered. The chan between the rks and the wall is almost straight; it dries and has a bottom width of about 6m.

Berthing   Turn sharp to port round the end of the breakwater and tie up near it. The bottom is foul close to the wall. Chains on the bottom can be picked up and used for making fast fore and aft. No bollards, but a few small rings on the quay can be used for mooring.

No facilities. Rly at Pembroke 4½M.

The hr and adjoining property are privately owned, but there is a public coastal path. This is an attractive place but it requires suitable weather, prior inspection and considerable care.

TENBY
Chart BA 1482 (Plan p259)

HW −5.15.   DS in offing: W −5.00; E +1.00.

MHWS 8.4; MLWS 0.9; MTL 4.6; MHWN 6.3; MLWN 3.0.

Harbour   Dries 1m at the pier-head; bottom hard sand.

Approach   From the W by day through Caldy Sd. Steer ENE for Giltar Pt giving St Margaret's Is a berth of at least 2 ca. Pass between Giltar Patch R can and Eel Pt G con buoys. Then pass N of North Highcliff N Card buoy, but keep Eel Pt buoy open of Caldy Is astern until Tenby promenade is open of St Catherine Is, when head for Tenby Roads, giving Sker Rk a berth of $\frac{1}{2}$ ca.

When approaching Tenby Roads it is advisable to keep outside a line of four RAF buoys as there are numerous small moorings for local boats. A vessel drawing over 1m should not enter the hr until $2\frac{1}{2}$h before HW. By night, best pass S of Caldy Is giving it a berth of $\frac{1}{2}$M with wind against stream. The streams run hard in Caldy Sd, power or a fair wind needed if stream is foul. A weather-going stream causes a tide-rip at the W end of the Sd.

From the S and E by day, vessels drawing not more than 2m have only the Woolhouse Rk (S Card) to avoid. From S by night, vessels drawing not more than 2m may pass 2 ca off E end of Caldy Is and thence steer 346° to Tenby Roads, remembering that the Woolhouse Rk buoy is unlit. Vessels drawing less than 3.7m will pass safely E and N of the Woolhouse Rk if they do not enter R sector of Caldy Lt until spher Y buoy DZ2 (Fl(2)Y 5s) has been rounded.

Berthing   (1) Anch NNE of slip on N side of Castle Hill to await tide. Safe except in SE winds. (2) To enter hr at sufficient rise, steer well towards an iron post on the shore S of Goskar Rk and when nearly on the line joining the rk to the pier-head round up and come alongside the pier; apply to HM for berth. There is a wooden landing jetty at the end of the pier. The pier-head can be rounded as close as desired. Hr always very crowded but water is quiet. Only one or two visitors' berths are available, contact HM (tel Tenby (0834) 2717) in advance. (3) Caldy Road: small craft can bring up in Priory Bay outside the motorboat moorings, but as close inshore as draft permits to avoid the tide. An uncomfortable anch in all winds, but safe.

Land at hr. All facilities, stores, water, petrol, grid. Diesel at some distance, no sailmaker. Rly. EC Wed.

SAUNDERSFOOT
Chart BA 1482 (Plan p259)

HW −5.10.   DS: W −5.00; E +1.00.

MHWS 8.4; MLWS 0.9; MTL 4.6; MHWN 6.3; MLWN 3.0.

Harbour dries at about 4h ebb, but there is at least $3\frac{1}{2}$m inside at MHWS and $1\frac{1}{2}$m at MHWN. Yachts drawing 1m can enter at half-tide. Waiting to enter, good anch in 2m $\frac{1}{2}$M SE of the hr lt about 3 ca offshore, keeping the glasshouses on the W shore of the bay well open. Well sheltered from winds from NNE through W to SSW, good holding. Scend in strong SW and W gales.

Approach   Keep about 100m NE of the entrance until the N pier-head is nearly

TENBY

Depths in Metres

0   Cables   3

51° 41'

40·5

4°41'W

Waterwynch Bay

Bowman's Pt

TENBY ROAD

TENBY

THE POOL

SMALL CRAFT MOORINGS

SANDS

NORTH

Second Pt

First Pt

Stn

Spire (conspic)

Castle Hill

St Catherine's I (28)

Skar Rk (1)

Goskar Rk

2FR (vert)

LB/SLIP

CGFS

F

SLIP

N

PENARTH

Depths in Metres

0   Cables   5

51° 26'

3°9'W

CARDIFF FLATS

Inner Wrach

Outer Wrach

CEFN-Y-WRACH

Reed Mo (BA)(occas)

1·2m

1·2m

FIG 2·5s

QG

G

2FR (vert)

CG

QR

R

Bn

PMB & SC HEADQUARTERS

Penarth Dk Basin

Penarth Head

Tr. (conspic)

Penarth

E/V Tidal Harbour

Moorings

No Jetty

SLIP

Stn

Pier

SC

Post

N

ABERDOVEY

Depths in Metres

0   Cables   5

52° 33'

4°16'

4°6'

Sand hills

Aberdovey

Spire

Bn

Bn

CG

Bn (conspic)

Afon Leri

TRAETH MAELGHYN

Breakwaters

Twyni Bach

Sandhills

BORTH SANDS

SOUTH BANK

NORTH BANK

ABERDOVEY BAR

Bar

G

R DOVEY

South Spit

Inner

Aberdovey Outer

RW

N

SAUNDERSFOOT

Depths in Metres

0   Cables   5

51° 42·5

4°40'W

4°43'

SAUNDERSFOOT BAY

Saundersfoot

Wooded

Fl R 5s 6m 7M

R

Sewer

N

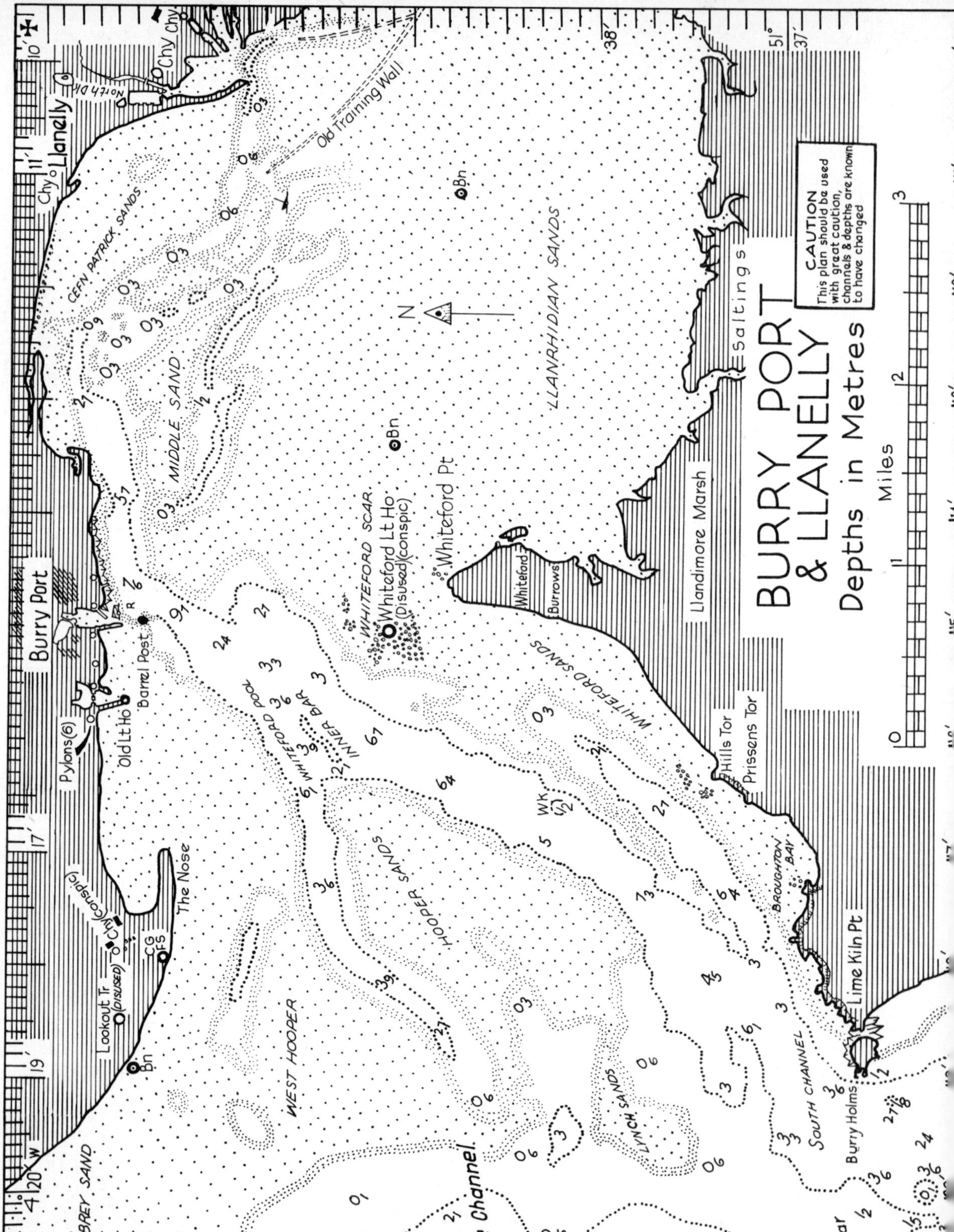
BURRY PORT
& LLANELLY
Depths in Metres
CAUTION
This plan should be used with great caution, channels & depths are known to have changed
Miles
Llanelly
Burry Port
Pembrey Sand
Cefn Patrick Sands
Middle Sand
Llanrhidian Sands
Whiteford Sands
Whiteford Scar
Whiteford Lt Ho (Disused)(conspic)
Whiteford Pt
Whiteford Burrows
Llandimore Marsh
Saltings
Old Training Wall
Barrel Post
Old Lt Ho
Pylons(6)
The Nose
Lookout Tr. (Disused)
Chy (conspic)
Whiteford Pool
Inner Bar
Hooper Sands
West Hooper
Lynch Sands
Middle Channel
South Channel
Outer Bar
Burry Holms
Lime Kiln Pt
Broughton Bay
Hills Tor
Prissens Tor

Based on British Admiralty Charts (nos. in text) with the permission of the Controller of H.M. Stationery Office and the Hydrographer of the Navy, and on other sources.

abeam, when steer for the hr leaving the N pier-head close to stb. A variable sandbank (about 3m at MHWS) extends about 50m from the S pier-head.
Berthing There may be room alongside sharp to stb inside the entrance against the NE pier, or alongside the SE wall. A limited number of moorings are available in the centre of the hr. Enquire first from HM, whose office is next to the SC at the NW end of the hr, tel Sandersfoot (0834) 3313. Bottom sand and mud. A lt Fl R 5s is exhibited from a cupola on the S pier-head. Yacht yard with repair and laying-up facilities. Fuel, chandlery and provisions. Water tap on the SW wall. Concrete slip for vessels up to 15m. Bus to Tenby and Haverfordwest, rly about 1M. EC Wed.

CARMARTHEN   Chart BA 1076
HW: Ferryside −5.05; Carmarthen −4.55.   MHWS Carmarthen 2.6; MLWS 0.4.
MHWS (Ferryside). 6.7; MLWS 0.1; MTL 3.1; MHWN 4.5; MLWN 0.8.
Bar Nearly dries; ground swell may break. Strong streams.
Approach Encumbered with shifting sandbanks: charts cannot be relied upon for the position of the fairway. The chan is not buoyed and entrance should not be attempted without either local knowledge or a Pilot. However, if swell is not heavy the bar can be crossed without any difficulty for 1½h on either side of HW by craft drawing 1.5m or less. Make towards St Ishmael ch, then to distinct B post in the centre of the river below Ferryside.
Entrance Once over the bar it is a delightful run as far as the brs just below Carmarthen, but there are no berths afloat above Blackpool. Various overhead cables cross the river, the least known ht being 15m. Except in a few pools the river is almost dry throughout at LW. It is difficult to tell where the chan lies.
Berthing Off (1) River Towy YC, a distinctive building on the foreshore at Ferryside, where the stream is strong. It is preferable to take the ground on the bank in the middle of the river: YC moorings give the lie of the stream and chan. (2) At HW one may proceed upriver to Blackpool below Green Castle, 2.4m at MHWN, water in pool at LW, good anch (3) Taf River. Laugharne, and for moderate drafts St Clears, but beware shallows off Laugharne.

BURRY PORT and LLANELLI   Chart BA 1167   (Plan p260)
Llanelli HW −5.05.   MHWS 7.8; MHWN 5.8.
Approach Free of dangers in Carmarthen Bay, but ground swell may break on the bar. Enter between 4 and 5h flood. Not advisable without special reasons, particularly as the chan is not buoyed; for shelter Swansea, Tenby or Saundersfoot are preferable. Strong stream.
Entrance Unlit. The chan through the sandbanks shifts. The entrance is close N of Burry Holm, a conspic detached rk (32m) off Limekiln Pt which separates Burry Inlet from Rhossili Bay. It passes through the S chan to the Lynch Pool, thence more or less straight towards Burry Port. There the dock is not available but vessels can lie in the outer hr, which dries. It can be approached 2½h either

side of HW and affords good shelter. The W-most of the three chimneys of the power stn provides an approach mark for the hr, being about 3 ca E of the entrance. A Y perch S of the hr Lt Ho (with Oc lt) marks the end of the breakwater, which covers 2h before HW: leave 1 ca to port. The tide runs across the entrance at 3½kn at springs.

From close off Burry Port the chan continues E to Llanelli, following the N-most chan shown on the chart, immediately S of Cefn Patrick Sand. This chan should not be attempted without local knowledge.

Berthing (1) The Kitchen, immediately N of Rhossili Pt, to await the tide and only in suitable winds. (2) Lynch Pool in 3½ to 5½m, exposed to winds from SW to N. (3) Just off Burry Port, 2 ca E of the hr entrance, in line with the perch. EC Tues.

SWANSEA   Chart BA 1161   (Plan p263)
HW −4.55.   MHWS 9.6; MLWS 1.0; MTL 5.3; MHWN 7.3; MLWN 3.2.
Available in all weathers, but accommodation for yachts is very limited. Permission to enter hr must be obtained from the HM before entering, except in emergency. Call Swansea Dock Radio on VHF Ch 14, or tel (0792) 50855/(26706 at night).

The approach chan is dredged to 1m to King's Dock outer sill. With 1.8m draft the King's Dock entrance jetty can usually be reached at any state of the tide. At LW vessels can wait here, but only with HM's permission. At very low spring tides vessels should not enter the river until the tide has made slightly.

Entrance Make the SW Inner Green Grounds S Card buoy Q(6) + L Fl 15s (Bell), and steer 020° for the Outer Fairway G con buoy QG (Bell) and the Inner Fairway G con buoy Fl G 2.5s, thence to the hr entrance. Local small craft lie in the river with HM's permission, but they dry out on mud at LW.

Good facilities, storage, yard, repairs. EC: Swansea Thurs, Mumbles Wed.

PORT TALBOT   Chart BA 1161
HW −5.00.   MHWS 9.6; MHWS 1.0; MTL 5.3; MHWN 7.3; MLWN 3.3.
Approach Difficult in strong onshore winds. Make for R can buoys marking dredged chan to new hr but leave to stb and proceed towards N breakwater (Fl(4) R 10s).
Entrance Leave N breakwater to stb and enter chan to old hr, in R Afan, keeping close to old S pier. Entry possible 1h after LW.
Berthing In chan up to the old wet dock, protected from E and N. Craft must not be left unattended due to high range of tide and steep-sided chan.

PORTHCAWL
HW −5.00.   MHWS 9.9; MLWS 1.0; MTL 5.4; MHWN 7.5; MLWN 3.3.
Approach From W, find Fairy W Card buoy. From E, Tusker R can buoy Fl(2) R 5s, and steer 315° to Fairy buoy making due allowance for tide and avoiding Fairy

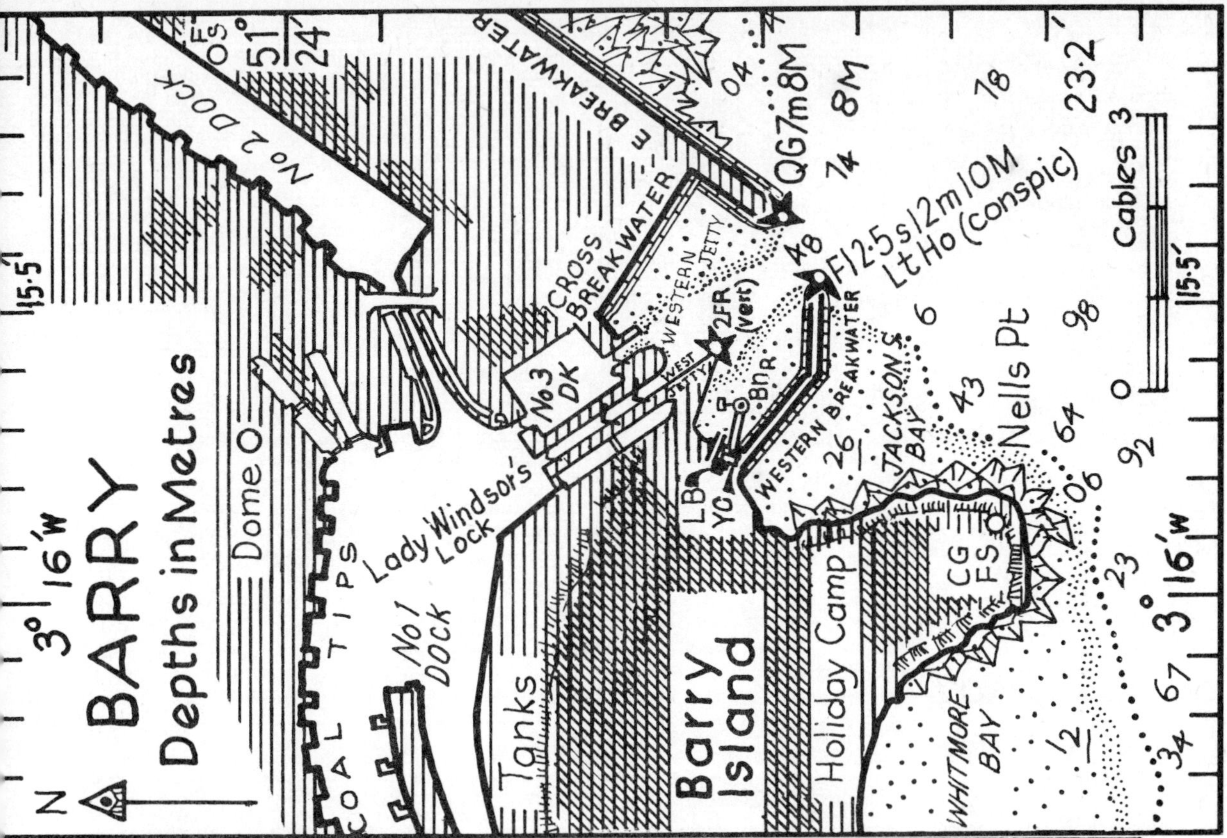

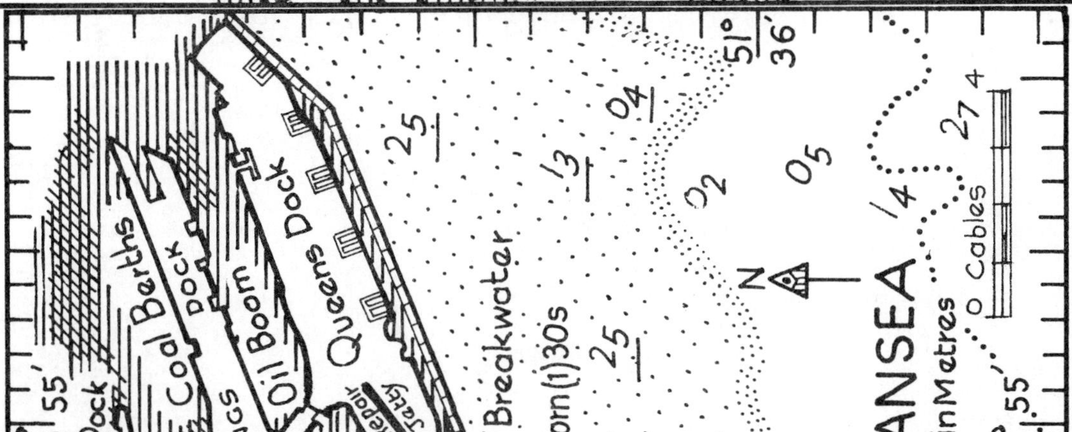

BARRY
Depths in Metres

N

3° 16'W

No 2 DOCK

Dome O

COAL TIPS

Lady Windsor's Lock

No 1 DOCK

Tanks

CROSS BREAKWATER

No 3 DK

E BREAKWATER

WESTERN JETTY

WEST BNr R

2FR (vert)

LB YG

WESTERN BREAKWATER

Q G 7m 8M

1k   8M

48

FI 2.5s 12m 10M
Lt Ho (Conspic)

78

23.2

Cables 3

6

98

JACKSON'S BAY

26

43

Nells Pt

64

92

O

Barry Island

Holiday Camp

CG FS

06

23

WHITMORE BAY

1·2

34   67

3° 16'W

51° 24'

51° 36'

SWANSEA
Depths in Metres

N

3° 55'

Prince of Wales Dock

Coal Berths

KINGS Dock

Oil Boom

Repair Jetty

Queens Dock

2FG (vert)

C 2FG (vert)

West Pier

R Tawe

4·4
FI(2)R 10s 9M

6

FG

Eastern Breakwater

2FG (vert) Horn (1) 30s

FIG 2·5s

X G

2·5

2·5

·3

·04

02

04

·08

·5

14

·7

1·1

DREDGED R 3·1

·5

23

X QG
Bell

G

05

27 4

O Cables

2   SWANSEA

3° 55'

Cables O

Based on British Admiralty Charts (nos. in text) with the permission of the Controller of H.M. Stationery Office and of the Hydrographer of the Navy, and on other sources.

263

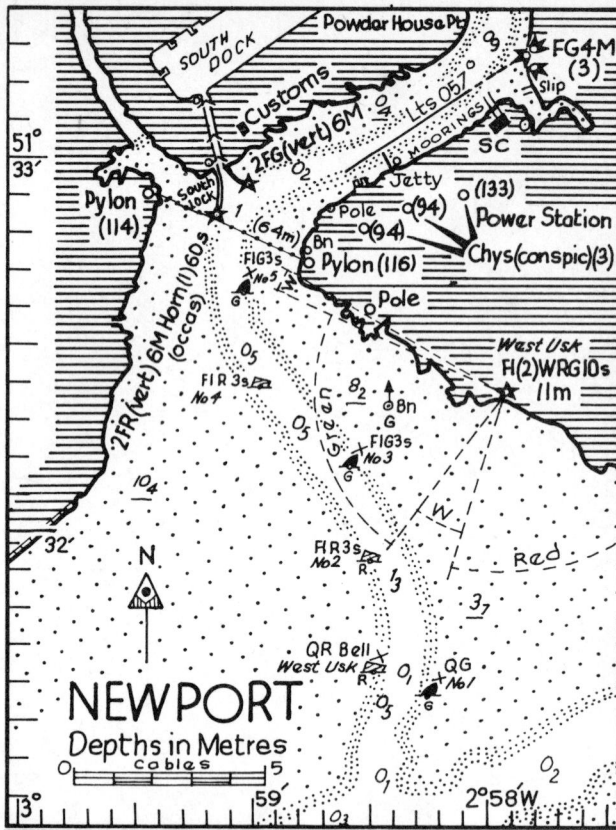

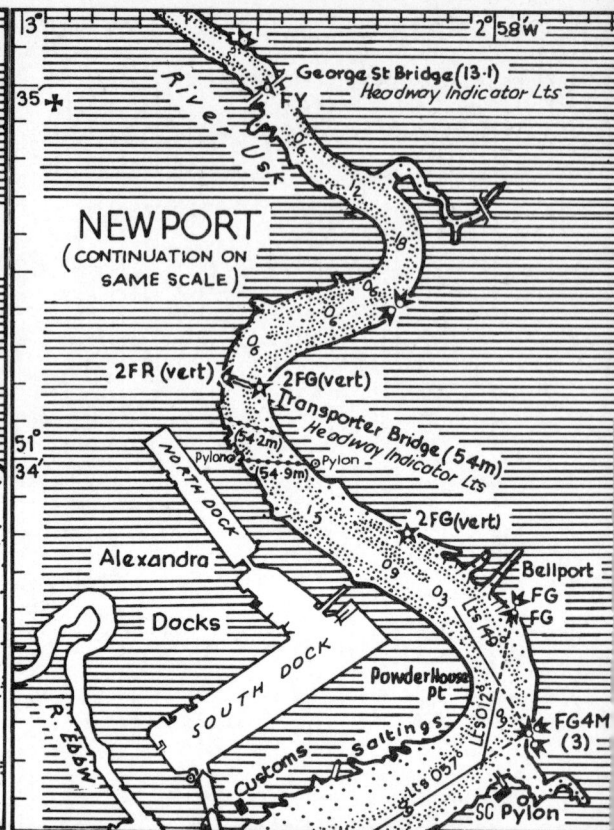

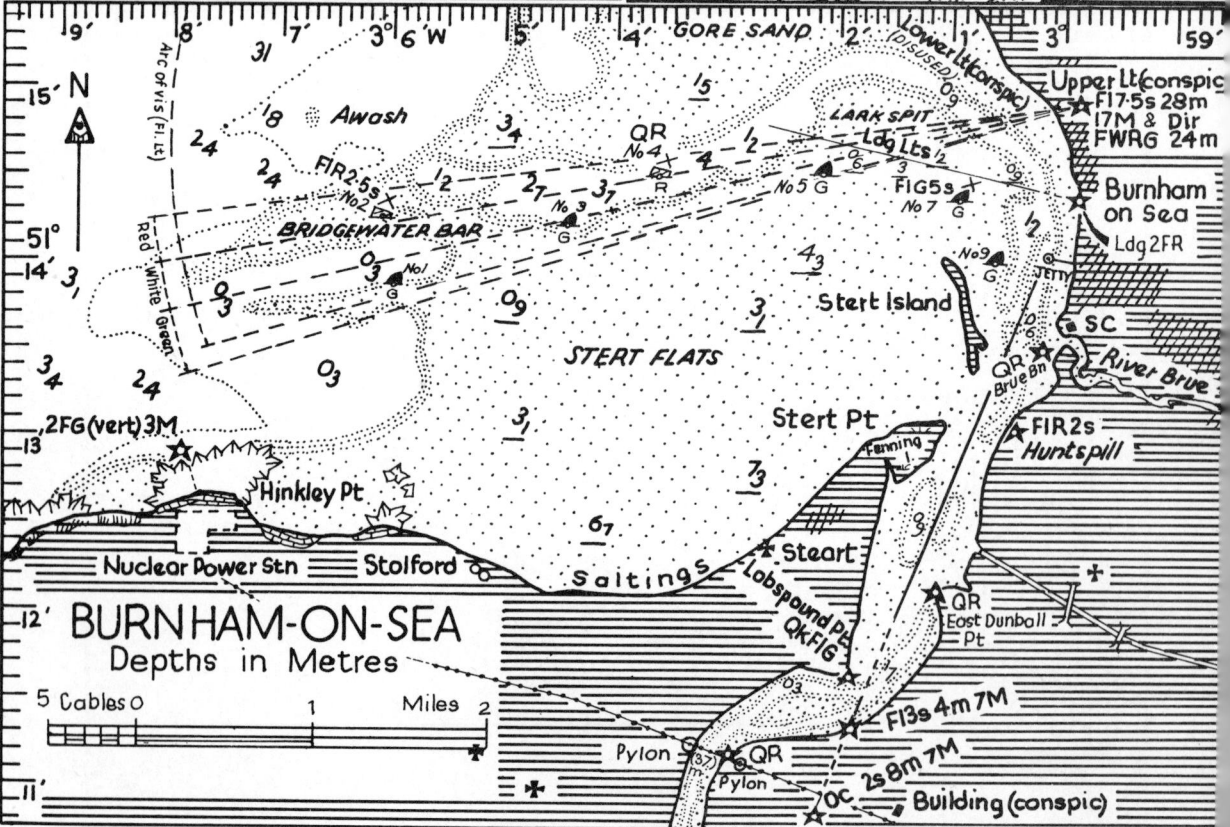

Based on British Admiralty Charts (nos. in text) with the permission of the Controller of H.M. Stationery Office and the Hydrographer of the Navy, and on other sources.

Rks. From Fairy buoy steer 010° to end of jetty (FWRG). Tide runs at 6kn (springs) off end of breakwater.
Berthing Harbour dries, soft mud. Or anch in 7m 3 ca SSE of Lt Ho, but poor holding.

BARRY   Chart BA 1182   (Plan p263)
HW −4.35.   MHWS 11.4; MHWS 0.9; MTL 6.2; MHWN 8.7; MLWN 3.7.
DS in offing: W −5.00.
The outer hr is always available. There is 4m at MLWS between the piers and to the docks. Great caution is necessary as traffic is often heavy. Give way to all merchant vessels entering or leaving.

At LW craft may anch in fairway but must move into yacht area as soon as tide allows. Keep clear of Pilot launch and Lifeboat on swinging buoys. Large yachts (over 11m or multihulls) cannot easily be accommodated.
Approach From the W, keep S of the line of the Nash Lts to clear the Scarweather and Nash Sands. From the E, give the shore a good berth.
Entrance The entrance lies between two breakwaters on the E side of Barry Is; turn hard to port inside. Due to silting the deep-dredged chan is only in line of entrance chan; steep sides. Beware cross-set in entrance.
Berthing Harbour crowded: apply to YC for berth. Anch may be dropped inside, tripping line advisable. The old hr W of Barry Is dries and is no longer of any use.

If strong S to SE winds are imminent or craft are to be left unattended, they are strongly advised to lock in at Lady Windsor Lock and proceed to Windway Marina.

All facilities, water at YC, outer hr free. EC Wed.

PENARTH   Chart BA 1182   (Plan p259)
HW (Cardiff) −4.27.   MHWS 12.3; MLWS 1.2; MTL 6.7; MHWN 9.6; MLWN 3.8.
Approach R lights on beacons are only lit when tanker due. Entrance dries 1m at LWS.
Berthing Harbour is crowded. Small yachts can anch anywhere below YC stages and well outside the end of steamer pier, others in Middle Pool. In strong winds between NE and SE, safest berth is to N of Penarth Dock; soft mud, legs useless. The inshore stream runs S 2h before HW. If early on tide anch in Ely R until tide allows, then moor at PMBSC pontoon on E side of river, Fl lt at night, and enquire for mooring.

All facilities and stores, water from YC. EC Wed.

NEWPORT   Chart BA 1176   (Plan p264)
HW −4.25.   MHWS 12.1; MLWS 0.2; MTL 6.0; MHWN 9.0; MLWN 2.9.
Bar There is about 0.5m on the bar between Newport Deep and West Usk buoy.

Approach   Make for Newport Deep G con buoy, Fl(3)G 10s, and leave it about ½M to stb steering 021° to pass between West Usk (QR) and No. 1 (QG) buoys at mouth of R Usk.

Entrance   Possible within 1h of LW but tide is strong, 4–5kn. Follow buoyed channel to South Lock after which keep slightly to stb of centre of river.

Berthing   Moorings on S side between jetty in front of power stn and SC dry 3½h after HW. Anch possible in 10m outside line of moorings.

England, West Coast

RIVER AVON, BRISTOL   Chart BA 1859

The booklet entitled 'Bristol City Docks – Information for Owners of Pleasure Craft' available from City Docks PBA Office, Underfall Yard, Cumberland Rd, Bristol BS1 6XG (tel (0272) 24797) will be found invaluable.

Approach   Find Cockburn R can buoy Fl(4)R 15s (Bell), and steer 098° for entry to R Avon at Swash Channel immediately S of South Pier of Avonmouth Docks, which just dries at MLWS.

Entrance   Proceed up R Avon taking care to keep in chan. Chart 1859 is essential. The chan is marked by ldg lts at many points along the banks. There are only two brs, the M5 Motorway Br (30m) and Clifton Suspension Br (73m), until Plimsoll swing br at the Cumberland Basin at the entrance to the City Docks. From the Swash Channel to the Cumberland Basin is 6.2M.

After entering R Avon inform Avonmouth Signal Stn that you are bound for the City Docks: call 'Avonmouth Radio' on Ch 16, working Ch 12 or 14, low power. Alternatively signal flag **R** or flash letter **R** (·−·). Wait for G signal light at Hotwells Pontoon before Dock entrance. Unless instructed to go directly into the lock, tie up at the Tongue Mead just upstream of the entrance.

If too late to be locked in, take the ground in soft mud in line with the entrance of the lock and not nearer than the iron ladder on port side 36m from lock gates.

Locking-in times are 2.35, 1.25 and 0.15h before HW, the lock gates remaining open for 30 mins after these times if other craft are expected.

Berthing   In the Floating Harbour, Feeder Canal or Netham Lock; visitors' moorings alongside Narrow Quay, turn N at end of Floating Hr on stbd side. All facilities. HM tel Bristol (0272) 25381.

PILL

Pill Creek is 3M upstream from R Avon mouth on stb hand. It dries out to soft mud: approach about HW. Visiting yachts lie against club jetty, but very crowded with local boats. There is a grid. Permission to use jetty or grid should be sought from the club. The clubhouse is a white rectangular building on the stb side at the entrance to the Pill.

PORTISHEAD

HW −4.15.   DS (offing): W −5.00.   MHWS 13.1; MHWN 9.9.

Approach The stream turns W close inshore 2h before HW and runs fast outside the Firefly buoy, which should be rounded close to. Then head for the pier, which should be given a good berth. Lights are Iso R 2s on pier end, and a port hand buoy Fl R 5s. An eddy on the flood sweeps towards the pier end.
Entrance The dock can be used as a harbour of refuge by arrangement with Avonmouth harbour authorities: call on VHF between HW −2.00 and +0.30.
Berthing Anch in 3½ to 7m between Firefly and Flatness Rks. Yachts can lie aground in the soft mud in the pool SE of the pier but the sides are steep. There is good anch in line with the lock gates and opposite the pier steps. Land at landing stage. Chan dries 1m at pier-head.

WESTON-SUPER-MARE
Chart BA 1152

HW −4.35.   DS in offing: W −5.00.
MHWS 12.0; MLWS 0.7; MTL 6.1; MHWN 9.0; MLWN 2.7.
Approach The causeway at the hr entrance is marked by a bn and there are two F G lts (vert) on the Grand Pier. The hr wall lies 2 ca N of Grand Pier.
Berthing Anch is available from 4h flood to 2h ebb except at dead neaps, but Knightstone Hr dries out and yachts normally use legs or make fast alongside two wooden dolphins. Shelter from all winds except S. Small yachts anch S of the old pier near the LB Ho in what is called the Cut or Sound; mainly dry at MLWS. Boatman will indicate the best berth. All stores, engine repairs. Rly EC Thurs.

RIVER AXE

A half-tide hr running into Weston Bay S of Weston. Fresh N-lies make the entrance difficult. To enter, bring Black Rk in line with W mark on Uphill Hill. Approach the rk to within 1 ca and leave it to port, then keep to mid-chan. A Weston Bay YC buoy 'Juicy' indicates the bar 4 ca from Brean Down about halfway along. There are withies on the N side of the chan. The river dries. No room to anch: take vacant mooring and enquire ashore.

   Further up at the E end of Brean Down a bend in the chan is buoyed and thereafter bns mark the chan upstream. In moderate winds anch in shallow bay under Brean Down.

   There is a boatyard at the top of Uphill Pill; chandlery, fuel and repairs. Craft up to 14m and 12T can be handled.

BURNHAM ON SEA
(Plan p264)

HW −4.35.   DS in offing: W −5.00.
MHWS 10.9; MLWS −0.2; MTL 5.2; MHWN 8.1; MLWN 2.1.
Lies at the head of Bridgwater Bay. Fairway crosses a bank inside which chan dries about 2 to 2½m. Shoals extend 5M out from the land which is flat and featureless except for Brent Knoll, a conical hill.
Bar 2.4m.

Approach and entrance   From W approach Brent Knoll on an E bearing ½M S of the Gore RWVS sph buoy (ISO 5s, Bell). Continue about E along buoyed chan. Buoyage is unreliable, particularly after heavy weather. No. 4 (R can) channel buoy also marks the swatchway through the Gore Sand to the N. The chan turns gradually to stb on nearing Burnham. From N and E within 2h of HW, steering S and keeping an eye on the depth, keep Flatholm Lt Ho on with the E end of Steepholm astern and cross the bank which dries about 2.4m, then pass close to the buoy join the former track.

By night, steer in on the W sector of Burnham lt (077°–079°). All the buoys are clear of the W sector. Continue until two R lts are in line 102°. The front lt is on the esplanade (daymark white vert stripe on sea wall) and rear lt on the SW corner of St Andrew's Church Tr. Continue on lts until Huntspill wall lt bears 185° and proceed on 185° to anch off Burnham or enter R Brue. A disused Lt Ho on piles on the foreshore, painted white with red stripe, is conspic by day and occasionally floodlit in summer.

After half-flood, craft drawing up to 1.8m have water over the sand to Burnham in moderate weather. In strong winds the whole area is a welter of broken water.

Berthing   A yacht can lie afloat 50m E of No. 4 buoy. The bottom off Burnham is hard sand, constantly shifting. There is a patch of mud between Nos. 7 and 9 buoys, too soft for legs and too hard for a keel yacht to sit upright.

Bridgwater Dock is now closed. Yachts drawing up to 1.8m may sit upright in soft mud in R Brue (unlit) which provides a sheltered anchorage or moorings. The banks are mostly steep-to and clearly visible at half-flood. The yard at Highbridge will assist visitors. All stores, fuel and facilities.

There is a small inlet at Combwich accessible near HW. Although coasters go up R Parrett to Dunball, there is no anch above Combwich. Shoal-draft yachts which can take the ground will find good shelter from W winds under Sterte Is and Pt.

WATCHET   Chart BA 1160
HW −4.55.   DS in offing: W −5.00.
MHWS 11.3; MLWS 1.0; MTL 6.1; MHWN 8.5; MLWN 3.6.
Available 2h either side of HW for average draft. The rks off the entrance dry ½M out.
Berthing   Inside, tie up alongside either breakwater, grounding on soft mud, and seek local advice. If early on the tide avoid the fishing stakes. The hr is used by small coasters. Anch outside in Blue Anchor Bay in 5 to 7m. Land at W pier, E pier, or town slip.

A B ball on the W pier-head (Fl G at night) and 2 FR (vert) lts on the E pier indicate at least 2.4m on the flood, 3m on ebb, at hr entrance. Hr office keeps VHF watch on ch 12, 14 and 16 from 2h before HW.

All facilities and stores. EC Wed.

MINEHEAD
HW −4.50

Hr is formed by a single pier curving E to SE and dries. It is dangerous to approach earlier than 2½h before HW, when there is 2.1m of water at the hr steps alongside the quay. No bar.

Approach From seaward, if tide too low to enter approach the W mark on shore abreast the hilltop 5 ca E of Greenaleigh Pt and about 5 ca NW of the column on the foundations of the old promenade pier, and anch abreast the mark 2 ca offshore in about 3½m. The column shows 3m above HW.

Entrance Round the pier-head at least 10m off. Go slow, little room inside. Two FG lts (vert) (vis 127°–262°) on pier-head.

Berthing As directed or as space allows, alongside pier or other vessels. Harbour is crowded. The bottom is an easy slope upwards from the entrance, sand with a layer of mud.

HM tel (0843) 2566.

All supplies. EC Wed.

PORLOCK WEIR
HW −5.00.

A delightful, privately owned hr in rural surroundings. Difficult entrance, Pilot advised, but completely safe once inside. Crowded in season: contact HM tel (064381) 523.

Bar Dries.

Entrance At the W end of Porlock Bay. Chan is very narrow (approx 15m) between a pebble bank to stb and a wooden-piled wall to port. The wall is marked by three withies and the entrance to the chan is between the outer of these and another to stb. Entrance 1h either side of HW for 1.8m draft.

Berthing In small pool inside the entrance, where a few shallow draft boats can lie afloat. Others go inside the piers and dry out. Anch in Porlock Bay only in very settled conditions; holding very poor except in a patch of sand to be found off the line of thatched cottages to the E of the entrance chan.

Two pleasant hotels, stores on quayside. Bus to Minehead. HM in white cottage at E end of village, opposite car park.

WATERMOUTH
HW −5.20

A small cove which dries, E of Ilfracombe. The entrance lies between Widmouth Hd and Burrow Nose. The sides are rocky but bottom is clear in between. Sheltered from all but N winds.

Berthing Anch on firm sand just inside entrance. When depth of water permits, motor in and pick up a visitors' mooring, red buoy with yellow handle, and contact HM in the local chandlery. Good protection behind breakwater.

ILFRACOMBE
Chart BA 1160 (Plan p271)

HW −5.25. MHWS 9.2; MLWS 0.7; MTL 4.9; MHWN 6.9; MLWN 3.0.

Half-tide drying hr, sandy bottom. There is 1.8m along outer pier, thence bottom shoals towards head of hr. Outer hr has about 1.5 and 1.2m at 2h flood, sp and np respectively. Ferry plying between hr and Lundy Is may return at HW day or night.

Berthing Go to the S side of the inner hr for directions but do not moor in line with the LB slip.

Water on pier and S side of the inner hr. Chandlery, diesel, marine engineer. Petrol 10 mins, stores 5 mins walk.

APPLEDORE
Chart BA 1160 (Plan p271)

HW −5.25. MHWS 7.5; MLWS 0.2; MTL 3.6; MHWN 5.2; MLWN 1.6.

Bar Bideford bar has about 1m. It is dangerous if heavy ground swell is running. Oc ldg lts are moved to suit the fairway.

If a sea is running on the bar, a good rise of tide should be awaited. Under bad conditions the entrance may be difficult and dangerous. The tide may be awaited in Clovelly Bay with wind S of W.

Approach In thick weather make Downend or Westward Ho! and thence shape a course for Bideford Fairway RWVS Spher bell buoy (Fl 10s) 3M N of Rock Nose, Westward Ho! Hence make good 110° to pass Bar G con buoy to stb, then proceed on ldg line 118° leaving Middle Ridge and Outer Pulley G con buoys to stb. After passing Outer Pulley buoy (QG), turn on to 160° to pass Pulley G con buoy to stb and continue to SE end of Grey Sand Hills. Then a course of 102° can be made good through Appledore Pool towards the LB, on a mooring buoy in the pool. After passing the slip on stb side watch out for three mooring buoys which may be partly submerged near HW.

Berthing Anch close above or below the LB and other two buoys in fine weather; buoy the anch, pool is full of old cables. The stream runs very strongly in this pool, uncomfortable in N winds during early ebb. Then better anch round the corner to NE with Crow Pt lt (Fl R 5s) bearing 240° and Appledore ch about 197°, but heavy anch needed in windy weather as holding only moderate. This position marks the limit of LW navigation inside the bar, 1.8m. At a sufficient rise Appledore may be rounded to the S and a drying berth picked up on the mud S of the village above the shipyard or at Appledore Quay.

Braunton Close inshore abreast the Ferry Ho on Broad Sands, a boat of 1.8m draft can berth in very soft sand. The vessel will make its own berth, sinking in several feet, but care should be taken not to get neaped. The position is excellent if a few days' stay is desired, but the soft berth should be located beforehand. Near midstream the sand is hard and anch likely to drag.

Bideford The passage from Appledore to Bideford is easy for 1.8m draft, 2h before HW or later. At Bideford berth along the W quay wall in the centre of the town, dries. The mud alongside the wall varies in consistency; soft in places and

APPLEDORE & BIDEFORD
Depths in Metres

0   Mile   1

4° 12' W
14'
13'
11'

5·9   3
3·6
4·2
0·6   Bar
(G)
0·6
(0·8)
3
Ldg Lts 117° 50'
(G)
2·1
Outer Pulley
SOUTH GUT
3·6
3
Pulley
3·2
0·1
4'
4·6
0·1
4·6
0·6
0·6

Airy Pt
Sand Hills
Ferry Ho
Horsey.I
Posts
Bn
Horsey Weir
Sand Dunes
BROAD SANDS
4·3   2·1
0·9
0·6
2·2FG (vert)
Chys
4'
Pole
FlR 5s 8m 4M
CROW RIDGE
Crow Pt
SPRAT RIDGE
1·2
2·2FG (vert)
Arc of vis
Oc 6s 22m 15M
INSTOW SANDS
Slip
Oc 10s 38m 15M
Tr
Slip
Slip
Slip
Instow
FS
North Devon YC
Yacht moorings
Ferry
3'

WESTWARD Ho! SANDS
Grey Sand Hills
Sand Hills
Northam Burrows
Bns
Posto
L.B
Slip
w
Oren
FS
Bns
Slips
Measured Distance
Slip
13·1
51° 13'

ILFRACOMBE
Depths in Metres

N
0   cables   3

10·5

THE RANGE
11
10·1
7·3
FR 39m 6M
7·8
5·9
5·9
6·4
BROAD
(occas)
(occas)
(occas)
Bullens Rk
Lantern Hill
FR
2·5
LB
Slip
Ilfracombe
Rapparee Cove

Appledore
Building (conspic)
Bn
Northam
4·1
2·3
F So
Slip
F So
Bideford
Southcott
East-the-Water
4° 11' W

Zeta Berth
Obelisk (ruins)
Westleigh
Bn
R.TORRIDGE
N
51° 2'

0·3
0·3
0·3

7' W   6·5'

d on British Admiralty Charts (nos. in text) with the permission of the Controller of H.M. Stationery Office and of Hydrographer of the Navy, and on other sources.

uneven. The tide often pushes the bow about a foot out from the wall just as the boat dries. Take a line ashore from the masthead.

Barnstaple Pilots at Appledore. Only approach near HWS. Beware neaping. EC Wed.

LUNDY ISLAND   Chart BA 1164
HW −5.30.   MHWS 8.0; MLWS 0.8; MTL 4.3; MHWN 5.9; MLWN 2.7.

The only reliable anch is that N of the SE point of the Is, as far in as draft permits. In winds between NW and SSW the shelter is good even in gales, owing to the height of the land, but the anch is exposed to winds with any E. Good holding. In strong winds from the E or N some shelter will be found on the W or S side of the Is. Anch is just possible very close in on the W side in about 10m.

From the anch in the SW part of the Is there is a landing place with a steep path and a rope to the top, or land on the beach nearby and walk up main track to top (145m). Landing may be difficult at HWS, particularly in N and E winds even when light.

BUDE
HW −5.40.   MHWS 7.7; MHWN 5.8.

Hr dries, available normally about 2h either side of HW; locking-in to canal requires minimum 5.5m rise. No outlying danger, but entry or exit impracticable in ground swell or breaking seas; lock may also then be inoperable. Sound in carefully: there may be no more than 1½m in the chan at HW neaps. Night entry not recommended. Notify expected arrival if possible to HM, tel Bude (0288) 3111 (Office), 3531 (home).

Approach The dish aerials above Bude are a conspic landmark. Coming from N or S, make the approach from the SW. Bring the outer ldg marks on cliff top on N side of hr (front, W spar with Y diamond topmark; rear, W flagstaff) in line 075° until Chapel Rk (linked to mainland by a breakwater) is abeam to stb.

Entrance Continue past Chapel Rk on 075° line of outer ldg marks. Barrel Rk marked by bn is ½ ca N of Chapel Rk. Leave this close to stb, and turn immediately onto the 131° line of the inner ldg marks (front, W pile with Y triangle topmark; rear, W spar with Y triangle topmark) ½ ca W of lock entrance. Lock is then clearly visible.

Berthing Berth in canal just inside lock. All stores. EC Thurs.

BOSCASTLE
HW −5.30.   MHWS 7.3; MLWS 0.9; MTL 4.1; MHWN 5.6; MLWN 2.7.

Approach All outlying dangers are visible. Enter only at or near HW in settled weather. While waiting for water it is possible to anch inside the Meachard Rk but usually preferable to heave-to outside.

Entrance Depth 4m MHWN. Leave the Meachard Rk either to port or stb and sail straight for the entrance, which is quite narrow. Go dead slow abreast the pier-head, as it is necessary to manoeuvre round an exceedingly sharp bend to stb. Berth against wall. Bottom hard sand overlying flat rk which outcrops in places. Vessels inside bump heavily in any ground swell.

PADSTOW
Chart BA 1168 (Plan p274)

HW −5.55.   MHWS 7.3; MLWS 0.8; MTL 4.1; MHWN 5.6; MLWS 2.6.

Bar   1m at MLWS, but liable to change.

Approach   The only dangers in Padstow Bay are shoal patches of rk close E and W of Newland Is. Stepper Pt, the W pt of the entrance, has a lt Fl 10s and also a W daymark 12.2m high and 83m above sea level.

Entrance   At HW sail straight in over Doom Bar keeping to the E centre of entrance. Leave a G con buoy Fl G 5s to stb, and R can Brea buoy to port. Make for a spher RWVS buoy Fl 10s marking N end of the pool. Thence steer S to the pool, or if bound for the hr turn to stb as soon as the shore immediately beyond St Saviour's Pt opens, thus leaving the Town Spit to port and a RW spar buoy close to stb. Turn into the dock entrance, lts FG on N jetty and FR on S.

Early on the tide keep a good ca W of Trebetherick Pt. In bad weather enter close round Stepper Lt; keep close to the rks till 1 ca inside Clouter Rk, dries 0.6m (12m from cliff), whence at sufficient rise cross straight across to abreast of Trebetherick Pt and then proceed as previously described.

The chan up to Wadebridge has many bends and is available for 1.2m draft at HWN.

Berthing   (1) In the pool as far S as possible, making sure of having water to float at LW. Second anch desirable as the pool is narrow. Fairly good holding, but avoid N end of pool as streams are strong there; sand bottom. (2) Just below the entrance to Padstow Dock. Good holding, but foul of the fairway at tide time. (3) Abreast the rly jetty in 1m at MLWS. Poor holding and tide fairly strong. (4) In the old dock, drying out against the quay or other craft. Bottom soft mud overlying rk. The new dock is full of fishing boats and the rly jetty is used by steamers which dry out. All facilities and stores. Rly. EC Wed.

HAYLE
Chart BA 1168 (Plan p274)

HW −6.05.   MHWS (St Ives) 6.6; MLWS 0.8; MTL 3.7; MHWN 4.9; MLWN 2.4.

Bar   Dries. Hr dries out and affords complete shelter.

Approach   Accessible only in fine weather.

Entrance   Bring RW pole lt bns on W of entrance in line 180°. Leave G bar buoy and G buoy on W spit to stb thence steer for W point of entrance, leaving half-tide training bank with five perches on it to stb.

At night F lts in line 180° lead in, in best water. They are lit only when there is 3.7m or more over bar.

Berthing   Vessels dry at LW, alongside quays. 300m inside the entrance the hr is divided by a long embankment which runs down to abreast the high lt bn and should be left to stb. The town and most of the wharves lie up the chan to SE.

RIVER CAMEL
Depths in Metres

Wadebridge
Treworran
Tr StBreock
Tregena Mill
Tregenna
Penquean
Cant Cove
West Cant
Cant Hill
Gentle Jane
Porthilly Cove
Porthilly
Trevorrick
Trevilgus
Little Petherick
Brea Hill
Cassock Hill
Rock
Stoptide
Dennis Cove
FR
PADSTOW
FG

5 Cable 0 Mile 1

HAYLE & ST IVES
Depths in Metres

Black Cliff
Hayle
Chys
EAST SPIT
WEST SPIT
Perch
Lelant
Carrack Gladden
Ldg Lts 180°
White or Green
Carrack Ch
Carracks
Baripliz Pt
HorRk
Red 28
2FG(vert)
PORTHMINSTER BEACH
Porthminster Pt
CARBIS BAY
CGFS
Tregenna Castle Hotel (conspic)
Viaduct (conspic)
Carbis Bay
Knill's Mont (conspic)
Tr
Carden Sand Dunes
St Ives
The Island St Leonard's
2FR(vert)
Comm Rk

5 Cables 0 Mile 1

PADSTOW
50° Depths in Metres

The Mouls
Roscarrock
Newland
Rainer Rks
Villiers Rk
Rumps Pt
Pentire Pt
Pentireglaze
Polzeath
Trebetherick Pt
CG
Brae Hill
Rock
FS
R Camel
PADSTOW BAY
Stepper Pt
HAYLE BAY
Clouter Rk
DOOM BAR
DAYMER BAY
Bar Buoy
HARBOUR COVE
Gun Pt
St Saviour's Pt
Mont
Gunver Hd
Daymark (conspic)
Buildings (conspic)
CGFS
2FG(vert)
2FR(vert)
Dock
Padstow

1 Mile 0

Nine perches in the E arm mark a long and narrow middle ground, above which to stb lies a reservoir for sluicing purposes.

All facilities. Pilot may be signalled when passing St Ives. Rly. EC Thurs.

ST IVES   Chart BA 1168   (Plan p274)
HW −6.05.   MHWS 6.6; MLWS 0.8; MTL 3.7; MHWN 4.9; MLWN 2.4.
A pier hr which dries 2m and is subject to heavy swell in onshore winds.
Approach and Entrance   Hoe and Merran Rks are cleared by keeping Knill's Monument on with Tregenna Castle Hotel. The ruins of the end of the outer breakwater are marked by a G con buoy. Round inner pier-head close to and moor alongside as convenient. At night the W pier shows 2 FR (vert) and the outer (Smeaton's) pier 2 FG (vert).

Alternatively, in onshore winds anch in 3m between the hr and the Carracks, or in Carbis Bay S of the Carracks.

All facilities. Rly. EC Thurs.

IRELAND
SW, S, & E COASTS

54°
53°
52°

5°W
7°
8°
9°W

Kilkeel
Carlingford
Clogher Hd
Skerries
Drogheda
Lambay I.
Malahide Inlet
Rogerstown
Dun Laoghaire
Dublin
Bray
Wicklow
Ardmore Pt
Arklow
Cahore Pt
Rosslare
Wexford
Tuskar Rk
Carnsore Pt
Bannow Bay
Coningbeg
Hook Hd
Waterford
Dunmore East
Helvick Hd
Youghal
Ballycotton
Cobh
Cork Hr
Cork
Oysterhaven
Kinsale
Old Head of Kinsale
Crosshaven
Galley Head
Castlehaven
Toe Head
Baltimore
Glandore
Fastnet
Valentia Hr
Port Magee
Gt Skellig
Kenmare R.
Sneem
Ardgroom
Kilmakillage
Glengariff
Bantry Hr
Berehaven
Bantry Bay
Gull Rk
Dursey I.
Sch
Castletown
Mizzen Head
Castletown Head
khaven

CONTINUATION
(Same Scale)

55°
5°W
10°
6°

Rathlin I.
Fair Head
Carnlough
Blackhead
Larne
Belfast Lough
Mew I.
Copeland I.
Donaghadee
Portavogie
Belfast
Strangford Lough
Ardglass
St John's Pt
Carlingford
Kilkeel

55°
54°W

0 10 20 30 40 50 60
Miles

IRELAND

Yachtsmen cruising to Ireland (certainly for anything more than a fleeting visit) are recommended to obtain the Irish Cruising Club Sailing Directions (referred to below as ICC). They are published in two volumes, one for the South and West Coasts and one for the East and North, and are obtainable from Mrs J H Guinness, Censure House, Baily, Co Dublin, Eire and also from nautical booksellers.

For the West Coast (between Bloody Foreland and Valentia) the relevant volume should be considered an essential part of the navigator's equipment. Accordingly, this section of the *Handbook* is restricted to brief passage notes and sailing directions for the most useful harbours from Valentia along the S, E and N coasts to Bloody Foreland, and only cruise planning notes for the W coast between Bloody Foreland and Valentia. ICC contain further information and cover many additional harbours and anchorages, of which a few are mentioned in the passage notes below.

Weather forecasts for Irish coastal waters are broadcast three times daily by Radio Eireann on 567 kHz at 0755, 1802 and approx 2355. There is also a Cork transmitter on 1188 kHz, and VHF gives the 0755 and 2355 forecasts. These are often more accurate than the BBC forecasts covering areas extending far to seaward. The BBC forecasts are, however, essential for tracking incoming weather.

Warnings   Salmon drift nets may be found all along the S, N and W coasts, often extending ½M to 1M in length. Frequently a fishing boat will mark one end, usually inshore, and a buoy the other, but sometimes there is no boat and the net is only marked by two buoys. This occurs most frequently on the Connemara and Mayo coasts. Most nets are taken in at night, but some may be left out. These are a serious danger to yachts under power, which should always keep a sharp lookout for them, particularly approaching a bay or estuary. Yachts with unprotected rudders might consider carrying a stout pole with a Y end or a suitable fitting for the spinnaker boom. This danger makes it inadvisable to cruise near the coast at night.

Lights   Another reason for avoiding making smaller ports by night is that the lesser navigational lights, which are operated and maintained by the local authorities, have all too frequently been reported not showing.

Gas Calor (Kosan) gas, though widely available, now comes in yellow containers different from the usual 10lb containers supplied in Britain. Though still holding 10lb the container is about 5in. taller when fitted with the supply tube, wider at the base and may not fit into existing gas lockers. It has a different connection which is provided for no extra charge if a British-type container is exchanged for the Irish container. Camping Gaz is widely available.

IALA BUOYAGE CHANGES

The IALA buoyage system will be introduced in the W of Ireland between Malin Head and the Old Head of Kinsale during 1981. Yachtsmen may have to use this *Handbook* in that area before the changeover has been completed.

Plans herein show buoys and other marks **as they are expected to be under the IALA system.** Any references in the text will also give the post-IALA description, enclosed in parentheses where the mark is going to be changed. This post-IALA description is preceded by a general description appropriate to both the old mark and the new. Where necessary, users of the *Handbook* should familiarize themselves from other sources with the old characteristics of a mark.

Ireland, Southwest Coast

PASSAGE NOTES: VALENTIA TO CROOKHAVEN

DS between Skelligs and the shore S +05.25, N −00.50; between Bull Rock and Dursey Hd S +02.45, N −03.15.
Dursey Sound is a useful channel between Dursey Is and the mainland, but the tides run up to 4kn. DS: S +01.45; N −04.15. Pass very close to Dursey Is.

In the Kenmare R above Sneem watch out for Maiden Rk in the middle, awash at LWS, marked by stb buoy (G con) 3 ca N of rk.

Between Three Castle Hd and Mizen Hd the streams run S and NW to N becoming E and W between Mizen Hd and Crookhaven; S and E +01.30, N and W −04.30. Off Mizen Hd the spring rate is 4kn, and off Three Castle Hd 3kn decreasing to 1½kn 4 to 5M offshore. The race off Mizen Hd is dangerous and may extend to Three Castle Hd; on S and E-going stream it extends SE in a crescent. If caught in the race steer straight out to sea, then parallel to the edge of rough water.

VALENTIA   Chart BA 2125   (Plan p279)
HW (Knights Town) +5.35.   DS: S −01.00; N +05.00.
MHWS 3.8; MLWS 0.5; MTL 2.1; MHWN 3.0; MLWN 1.2.
The hr affords shelter in all winds and may be entered from the NW at all states

VALENTIA HARBOUR

Depths in Metres

One Mile

N 56·5'

51° 56'

10°16'W   115'   117'   114'

CAHER RIVER

Quay
Landing
Cahirciveen
FG
FG
FG
FG
FG
FG
FG
FG
FG
FG
FG

Ballycarbery Castle (ruins)

Foughil I.

F(R)3s

Lts 034°
035°

Lts 076°

Lts 101°
09
09

Laght Pt.
Ballycarbery Pt.
Church

REENARD Pt.

CAHER BAR

09
11
31
37
31

Q(3)10s
BYB

FG Ferry
FG
13
610
58
24

Knights Town
Belfry (conspic.)
FG

QcMRG4s 11·8'9M

Enagh Pt.
Docairn Doulas Hd (conspic)

DOULUS BAY

Ballycoomin

LOUGH KAY
DOULUS BAR

Kay Rk
Og Rk

Black Rks
Lamb I.
Coarhacooin
Pilot Look-out
Beginish I.

Basalt Pt.
Fort Pt.
Red
Green
Red

FlWR2s16m

Fish Pt.
BYB
Harbour Rk

Occ4s 5M

LdgLts 141°

Cromwell Point

Cross

Red

22
88
85
9
85
3
34
85
49
24
21
2
58
85
98
20
7
31
8
8
A13
3

57'

PORTMAGEE Depths in Metres

N

51° 53'

10°20'W

Belle Ville
Waterview
Portmagee
Doory foot
Carhan pt
Swing Br

Quay Brack
Reencaragh Pt
Castle (run)

Foilhomurrum Bay
Scughaphort Reef
Deaf Rks
Foiltagarriff
Dohilla
Sig.Tr (run)
Long I.
Bull Rock
Beenhaboy Rks
Bray Hd

51° 53'
53·5'

123'   122'   Cables   One Mile

21
21
15
06
5
18
20
27
34
63
37
34

...d on British Admiralty Charts (nos. in text) with the permission of the Controller of H.M. Stationery Office and of
Hydrographer of the Navy, and on other sources.

279

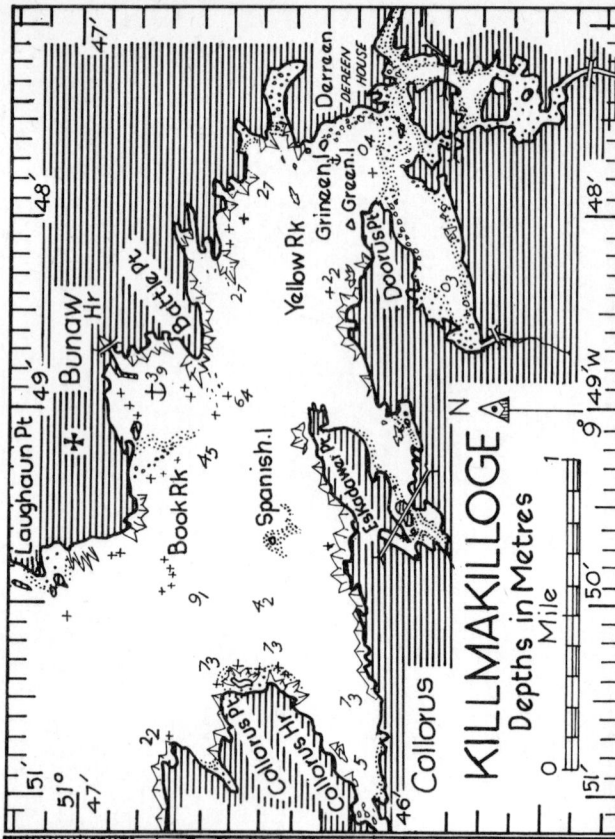

SNEEM
Depths in Metres

Cables 5

0

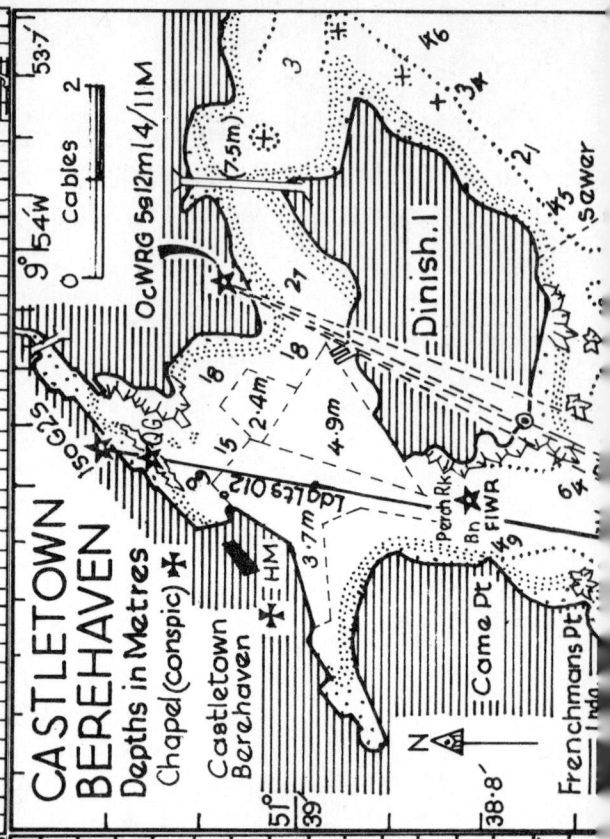

KILLMAKILLOGE
Depths in Metres

Mile

0

CASTLETOWN BEREHAVEN
Depths in Metres

Chapel (conspic) ✠

Castletown Berehaven

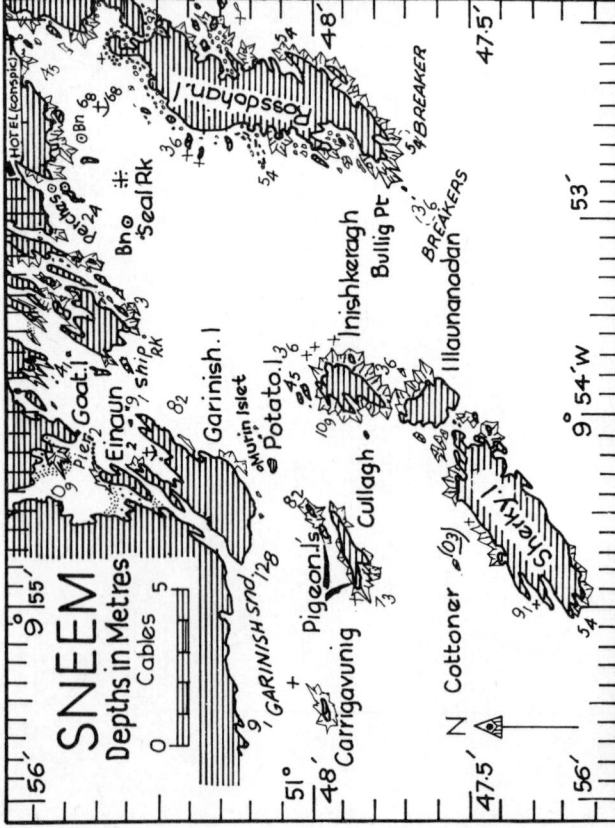

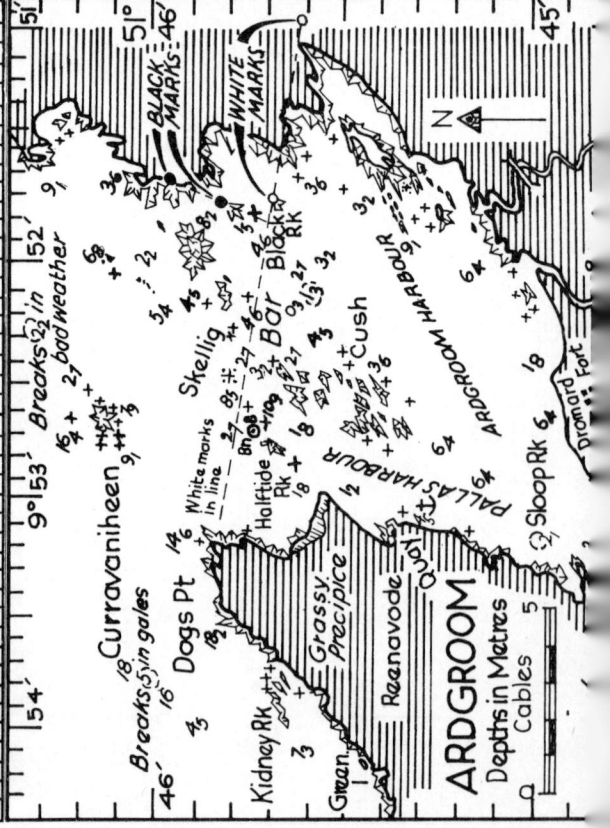

ARDGROOM
Depths in Metres

Cables 5

0

Based on British Admiralty Charts (nos. in text) with the permission of the Controller of H.M. Stationery Office and the Hydrographer of the Navy, and on other sources.

of the tide (exposed in NW gales), and, with sufficient rise, from SW through Portmagee chan. This has a bridge with opening span.

Bar   *By NW entrance:* the Cromwell Pt entrance has 7m on the ldg line. The Doulus bar has 3m. *By SW:* until inside Reencaragh Pt there is 8m; entrance chan 2m.

Approach   NW entrance: make Doulus Hd, avoiding the Coastguard patch in severe conditions.

Entrance   Having located Fort Pt, Fl WR 2s, bring W bns in line 141° or keep in W sector (141°–142°) of lt Oc WRG 4s leaving Harbour Rk bn to stb, and thence to anch as convenient, avoiding the Caher bar between E end of Beginish Is and Reenard Pt near LW.

Anchorages   In N winds, good anch off SE bight of Beginish Is, in 2 to 8m; or, according to wind, off Knights Town to S of jetty, or S of Reenard Pt, or as convenient in Portmagee chan. There is a pier at Reenard Pt with 3m on the SE side.

Caution   Do not anchor S and W of the pecked lines S of Knights Town owing to telegraph cables.

Caher River   If proceeding to Cahirciveen enter over Doulus bar, 3m, leaving Doulus Rks to stb and Kay Rk to port, thence SSE passing a full ca from E end of Beginish. From the hr, cross Caher bar, 0.3 to 1m, then close the S shore of the river till Ballycarberry castle comes abeam, when work towards N shore gradually till Cahirciveen barracks open and then proceed in midstream to the quay at Cahirciveen. There is a series of five ldg lines up the Caher R, FG lts on rather inconspic telephone-type poles. It is essential to use these leading marks. Streams run fast at springs. If lying afloat at Cahirciveen it is not possible to berth clear of the current.

Supplies at Knights Town, limited to bread and some general stores. Water on quay at Reenard Pt. Beginish Is, farm produce and home-made bread. Cahirciveen, all requirements.

PORTMAGEE   Chart BA 2125   (Plan p279)

Approach   Entrance inadvisable in heavy weather owing to violence of sea under Bray Hd and baffling winds. No dangers in approach.

Entrance   In strong SW winds the N entrance should be used. For 1¼M inside Reencaragh Pt, navigation requires great care and the chart should be studied carefully.

Anchorage   Below the bridge off the pier in 6m. To proceed through the bridge and through the 1m chan beyond, seek local advice. Bridge opening arranged by the postmaster, tel Portmagee 1.

SNEEM   Chart BA 2495   (Plan p280)
HW +5.40.   MHWS 3.5; MLWS 0.5; MTL 2.0; MHWN 2.8; MLWN 1.2.
A small hr on N side of the Kenmare R opposite Kilmakilloge; affords anch for small craft in 3 to 6m and upwards.

Approach   Close with the SE side of Sherky Is. To pass inside Sherky Is and avoid Cottoner Rk (dries 0.3m), keep nearer to Pigeon Is to port than to Sherky Is.

Entrance   Hence steer 013° on the hotel. When well past the third Is, Inishkeragh, steer 318° on the NE extreme of Garinish Is, leaving it close to port.

Anchorage   In 6m between Goat Is and the pier, or in 3m inside the bay at the N end of Garinish.

All necessities from Sneem, 2M but accessible at half-flood by dinghy. Water at Parknasilla Hotel.

KILMAKILLOGE   Chart BA 2495   (Plan p280)
HW +5.35.   MHWS 3.5; MLWS 0.5; MTL 2.0; MHWN 2.8; MLWN 1.2.

Inside Kilmakilloge, there are three separate harbours. Kilmakilloge, Bunaw and Collorus.

Approach   From E give Laughan Pt a berth of over 2½ ca; give W side of entrance a berth of 1½ ca.

Entrance   Book Rk, awash at LW, extends 3 ca off E shore, near a grassy precipice 53m high; off Collorus Pt on W side dangers extend 1½ ca. Enter on mid-channel course steering slightly W of Spanish Is. Thence according to anchorage. (1) For Kilmakilloge Hr, once past Collorus Pt alter course to 102° for the woods near Dereen Ho. Anchor in 4m SW of Yellow Rk, awash at HW. Landing at Dereen. No stores. (2) For Collorus Hr, round Collorus Pt keeping a good ca off, and passing between the Pt and Spanish Is slightly nearer the former. Anchor in middle of hr in 5m; holding soft with kelp and unreliable. No shops, but some provisions might be obtained from farms. (3) Bunaw Hr, on NE side of entrance, is entered through chan 1 ca wide between unmarked rks, with pier-head bearing 041°. There are poles with Y ldg lts on this bearing: front lt on pier-head. Anchor on ldg line in 4 to 6m. Limited stores and water available.

ARDGROOM   Chart BA 2495   (Plan p280)
HW +5.35.   MHWS 3.5; MLWS 0.5; MTL 2.0; MHWN 2.8; MLWN 1.2.

Approach and entrance   Enter between Dogs Pt at W of entrance and Curravaniheen, a rocky ledge 1m above MHWS. Leading marks across the bar are 2 W bns on E side of harbour: front bn on Black Rk, rear bn on shore. The rear bn could be mistaken for a chimney of a motel and is sometimes obscured by bushes. Entry should not be attempted unless these bns have been identified.

Steer to give Dogs Pt a full ca berth; when it bears about 166° round it towards SE and bring the W marks on the E shore in line bearing 099°; steer on them precisely, leaving Half Tide Rk bn to S. Continue so till Collorus marks, two unpainted concrete bns (one offshore and one on the shore, 2 and 3 ca respectively N of outer W bn), come in line 026°, being careful to alter course as they come on, and steer to keep them in line astern for ¼M, thence for Dromard fort, which is steep-to.

Anchorage   Anch in Pallas Hr to N of the fort, the latter bearing about 185°, 4 to 5 ca distant, or SE of Reenavode quay. Bottom weed on rather soft mud.

BEREHAVEN   Chart BA 1840
HW +6.05.   MHWS 3.5; MLWS 0.5; MTL 2.0; MHWN 2.7; MLWN 1.2.
Stream in offing is negligible. In entrance tide floods from HWD, ebbs from +06.10, max rate 2kn.
Approach and entrance   Berehaven is on N shore of Bantry Bay and can be approached E or W of Bere Is. The E entrance is wide but the W entrance, known as Piper's Sound, affords those coming from the S or W a shorter passage to Castletown, the best yacht anch. Ldg marks RW bn on SW shore of Dinish Is on with gable end of hut on mainland, W with VR stripe, 024°. W sector, 024° to 024½°, of lt on hut Oc WRG 5s leads in.
Anchorages   As alternatives to Castletown (see next entry): (1) In Dunboy Bay on W side of Piper's Sd, S of rk drying 1.5m; sheltered except in E winds. An oyster fishery uses floating lines and nets. (2) In Lawrence Cove on S side of Berehaven; sheltered except in N winds.

CASTLETOWN   Chart BA 1840   (Plan p280)
Bar   3m W of Dinish Is.
Entrance   The entrance channel is less than 50m wide abreast Came Pt immediately W of Perch Rk marked by G lt bn Fl WR 5s. Keep a little closer to this bn than to W shore. Ldg lts in line 012° on R marks with W stripe lead through the channel: rear Iso G 2s, front QG.
Berthing   (1) Anch in part dredged to 2.4m, or in a S blow closer to Dinish Is but clear of harbour works. (2) A berth may be available at W end of Quay (alongside a fishing boat) or at NE end: avoid central part. Water on quay. Petrol and diesel, shops, hotels, banks, PO.

GLENGARIFF   Chart BA 1838   (Plan p285)
HW (Bantry) +6.00.   MHWS 3.4; MLWS 0.5; MTL 1.9; MHWN 2.6; MLWN 1.2.
The hr is situated at the E end of Bantry Bay and affords complete shelter in beautiful surroundings.
Approach   Leave Corrid Pt (Four Heads Pt) about 3 ca to W and steer 015°, leaving Gun Pt a short ca to E.
Entrance   Give the inlet to NE within the Pt a sufficient berth to clear a patch of rks extending 1½ ca from its hd. Continue 015° within ¾ ca of the E side, leaving Ship Is and rks extending E of it well to port. There is an uncharted patch of rk, having 3m at MLWS, 30m E of Ship Rks.
Anchorages   (1) S of Bark Is. (2) NE of Bark Is. (3) For yachts of less than 1.8m draft, close to wooden pier N of Carrigeen Is. Pier has 1m LWS.
Note: the iron post of Pot Rock SW of Bark Is was missing in 1979.

Water on pier. PO, tel, bread, petrol and small stores in Glengariff village. Bus to Cork via Bantry.

BANTRY HARBOUR   Chart BA 1838   (Plan p285)
HW +6.00.   MHWS 3.4; MLWS 0.5; MTL 1.9; MHWN 2.6; MLWN 1.2.
Entrance   *North:* Whiddy Pt East may be rounded close in, but Is in hr are generally foul all round. Leave Horse and Chapel lt buoys to stb, Gurteenroe lt buoy to port. Beware unlit mooring buoys SE of Whiddy Pt East. *West entrance:* use only in good conditions. Bar has only 1.7m and sometimes breaks. Outside bar, Cracker Rk has only 1.8m.
Anchorages   (1) 1 ca NW of town pier; keep over 1 ca from demolished pier on N side. (2) About 3 ca W of (1), outside local yachts in 3½m. (3) ¼ ca SW of Rabbit Is in 2 to 3½m; oyster fisheries inside Rabbit Is. Anchs (1) and (2) subject to wash from Whiddy Is launches. Water on pier. Petrol, diesel, engineers, some repairs. Best shopping and transport centre on this coast. Bus to Cork, Glengariff, Castletownbere and (summer only) Kenmare, Killarney, Clonakilty.

Ireland, South Coast

CROOKHAVEN   Chart BA 2184   (Plan p286)
HW +6.05.   MHWS 3.3; MLWS 0.4; MTL 1.8; MHWN 2.7; MLWN 0.9.
The hr may be entered at all states of the tide, is 2M long, 2 ca wide. 10m at entrance, 3m off Crookhaven village, shoaling thence gradually to its head.
Approach   From the Fastnet Rock steer N to fetch the entrance. Give Alderman Rks and Black Horse Rks, which extend ½M to E of Streek Hd and are marked by a bn (N Card), a good berth, both shores being otherwise steep-to. Beware tidal set through Alderman Rks.
Entrance   At night do not steer for the W lt tr (Fl WR 8s) at N point of entrance till R sector covering Alderman Rks turns to W, when enter along N shore.
Anchorage   Anchor abreast village in 3m. In a SW blow shelter behind Granny Is; in E blow N of W point of Rock Is. Water from taps on both piers, PO, some stores from village shops. There is often kelp in this anchorage.

PASSAGE NOTES: CROOKHAVEN TO CORK
Charts BA 2424, 2129, 2092, 2184, 1765.
Tidal streams   In general the streams up to 5M offshore change at nearly the same time from Crookhaven to Old Head of Kinsale. E-going stream +0215; W-going stream −0400; spring rate 1 to 1½kn, but 2 to 2½kn off the Fastnet Rk and the main headlands. In Gascancue Sound: SE −0030; NW 0540; spring rate 3kn. Old Head of Kinsale to Cork Harbour: E +0045; W −0500.
    The channel between Fastnet Rk and Cape Clear is free of dangers apart from

BANTRY HARBOUR
Depths in Metres

Bantry

Whiddy I.

WHIDDY HARBOUR

Whiddy Pt. East

Reenydonagan Pt.

Roancarrig

Carrignagappul

Dunnamark

Reenbeg Pt.

Reenaour Pt.

Chapel I.

Hog I.

Rabbit I.

Castle Brackar

Falaun Rks.

House (White)

Aildnamarnagh Pt.

Eagle Pt.

Old Quay

E. Battery (disused)

Central Battery (disused)

Castle (ruin)

Cliffy Rk.

Horse I.

Tug Buoys

Saliboon Rk.

N

Miles

Cables

GLENGARIFF HARBOUR
Depths in Metres

Glengariff

Glengariff Br.

Reenmeenbridge

House (conspic)

Castle

Garranboy I.

Garvillaun I.

Ship I.

Tt (conspic)

Yellow Rks.

Calf I.

Bark I.

Bush

Quay

Pier

Carigeen I.

Illaunmuilline

Illauncraeveen

Gun I.

Obelisk

Portuguese Rk.

Carrigbuy

Big Pt.

Tinkar Rk.

Crowdy Pt.

N

Cables

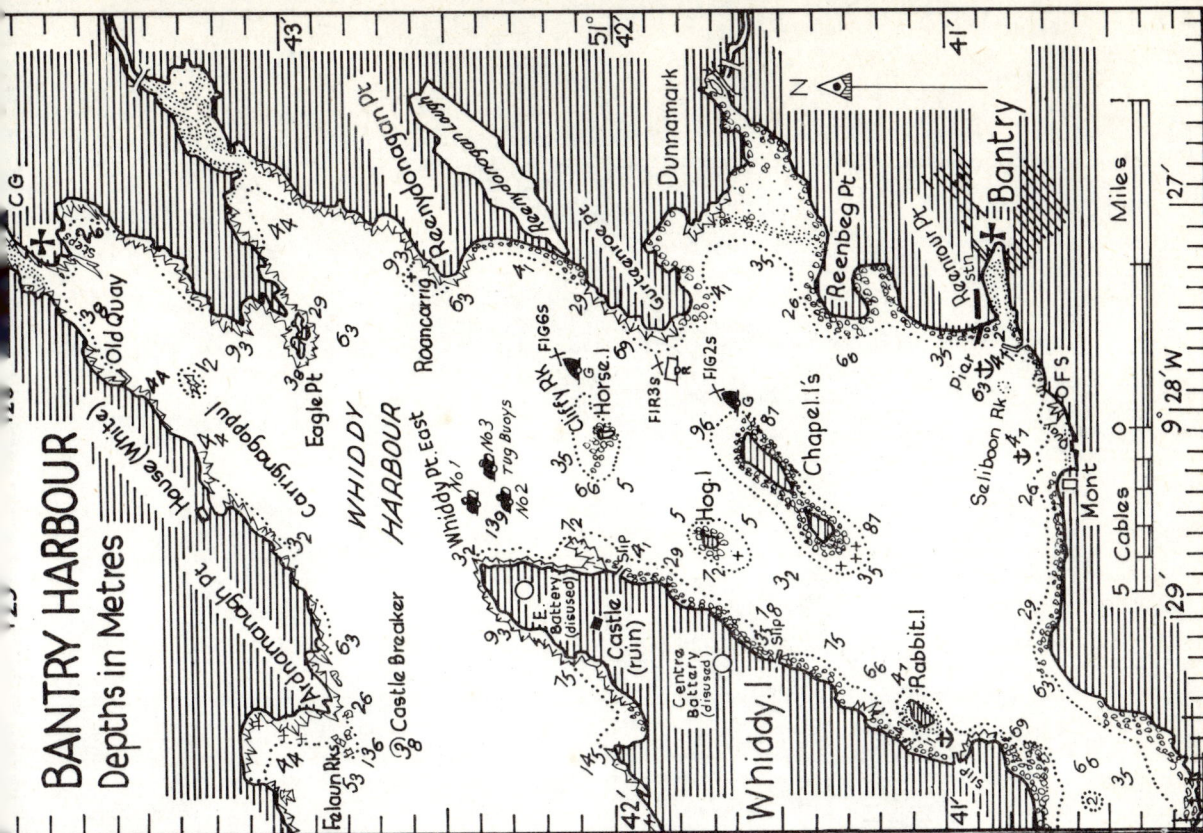

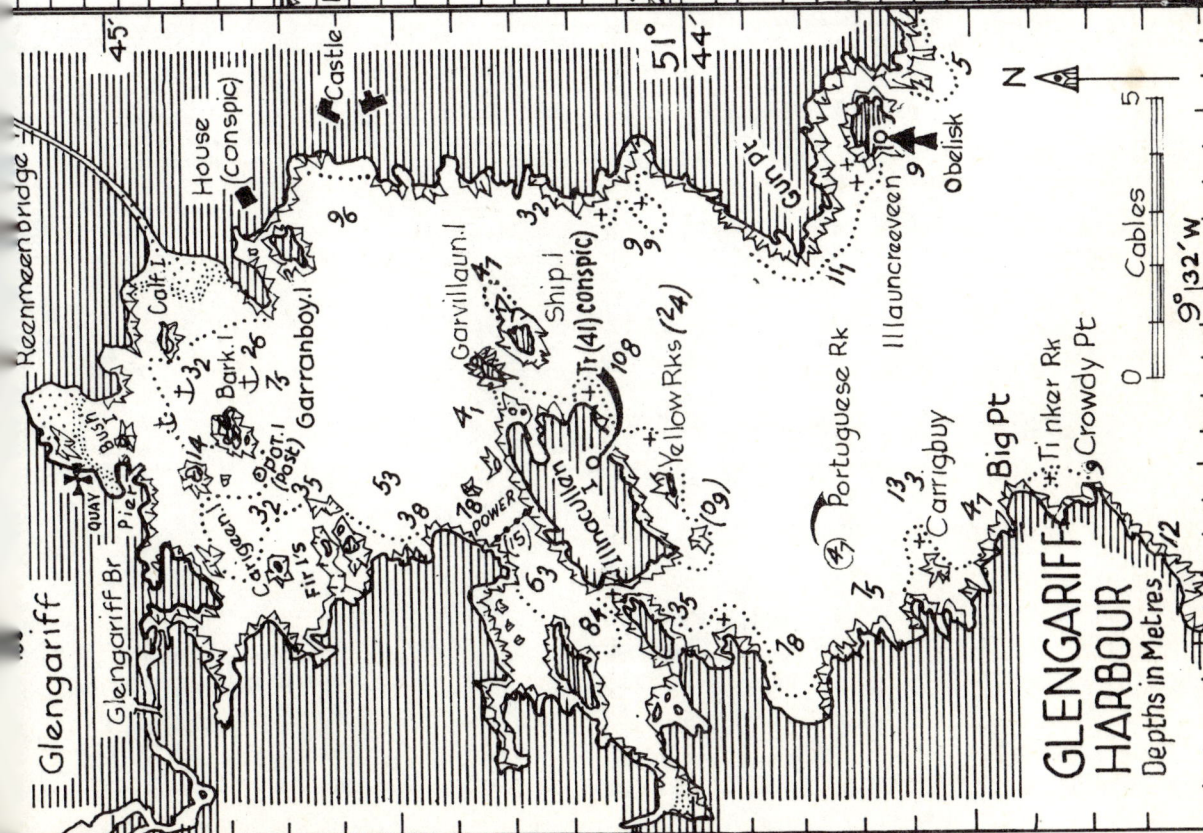

ed on British Admiralty Charts (nos. in text) with the permission of the Controller of H.M. Stationery Office and of
Hydrographer of the Navy, and on other sources.

CROOKHAVEN

MILE

Depths in Metres

ROCK I.

Tr (conspic) (38)
Tr (30)

Sheemon Pt
FS
FlWR 8s 13.11M (LtHo)
BY
Black Horse Rks

Streek Hd
Chy (conspic)
Tr (ruins) (conspic) (32)

Granny
Row Rk
Quays
Crookhaven

Gokane
Alderman Rks

N

51° 28′

FS

Quay (ruined)

Galley Cove
Reen Pt
Galley Cove

9° 43′ W

SCHULL HARBOUR

Oc 5 s11m11M
Oc 5 s8m11M

Schull
PIER
Steeple

Slip
Coshaan Pt

Schull Pt

Baker Rk
Perch R
Bull Rk

Depths in Metres

CASTLE ISLAND CHAN

Mweel Pt

GpFl(3)10s16m 8M
CASTLE GROUNDS
Fl G 3 s
Amelia Rk

Long Island Pt
LONG ISLAND

Ldg Lts 346°

N

Carthy's Pt

9° 32′ W

MUR RAYS CR

Ferry Pt
Harbour Rk
Oysterhaven
CG

N

Kinure Pt

Ballymacus Cr

Little Sovereign

51° 41′

Ballymacus Pt

OYSTERHAVEN

Depths in Metres

Big Sovereign

Cables

8° 26.5′ W

Based on British Admiralty Charts (nos. in text) with the permission of the Controller of H.M. Stationery Office and the Hydrographer of the Navy, and on other sources.

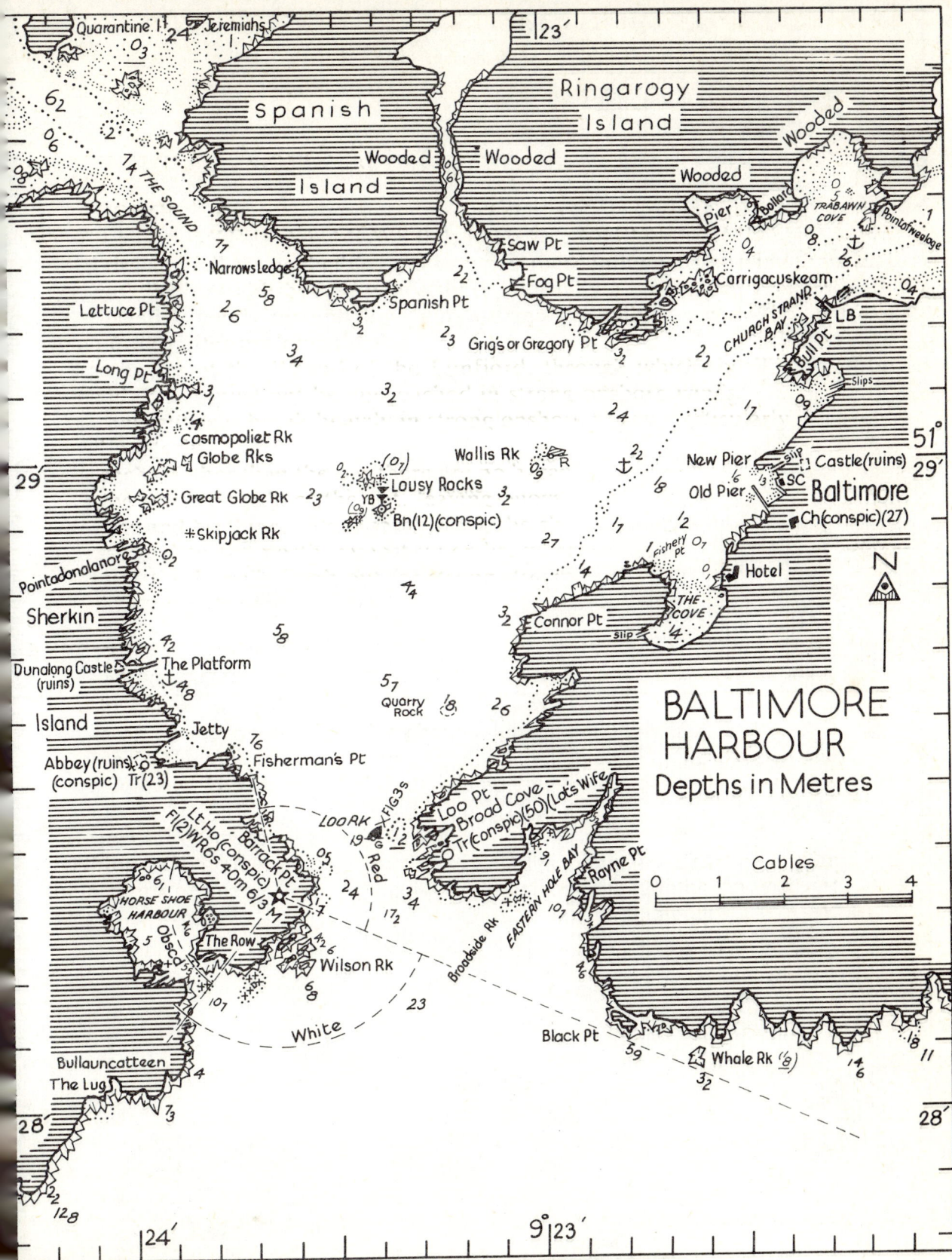

Quarantine I. Jeremiahs

24

0_3

6_2

0_6

0_9

THE SOUND

Spanish
Island

Wooded Island

Ringarogy
Island

Wooded   Wooded

Wooded

23'

Pier Bollard TRABAWN COVE Point of Wedge

0_5

0_4 0_8 0_4

Carrigacuskeam 3

Saw Pt

Fog Pt

CHURCH STRAND BAY

BUII PT LB

Slips

0_9

Narrows ledge

1_1

5_8

2_6

3_2

Lettuce Pt

Spanish Pt

Grig's or Gregory Pt

2_3

2_2

2_2

1_7

51° 29'

Long Pt

3_1

4_3

Cosmopoliet Rk
Globe Rks

3_4

3_2

2_4

New Pier Castle (ruins)
Old Pier SC Baltimore

1_8

Ch (conspic) (27)

Wallis Rk R

0_2 (0_7) Lousy Rocks

Great Globe Rk 2_3

YB

(0_9) Bn (12)(conspic)

3_2

2_7

1_7

1_2

Fishery Pt 0_7

Hotel

Skipjack Rk

Point adonalanore

0_2

1_4

1_1

1_4

THE COVE 4

Sherkin

4_2

5_8

A_4

3_2 Connor Pt

Slip

Dunalong Castle
(ruins)

The Platform

4_8

5_7

5_8 2_6

Island

Jetty

7_6

Quarry Rock

BALTIMORE
HARBOUR
Depths in Metres

Abbey (ruins)
(conspic) Tr(23)

Fisherman's Pt

LOO RK Fl G3s

Loo Pt
Broad Cove

Tr(conspic)(50)(Lot's Wife)

Lt Ho (conspic)
Fl(2)WRG5 40m 6_3

Barrack Pt

19 1_2

05

Red

Cables

0   1   2   3   4

6_1

HORSE SHOE HARBOUR

Obsc

5

24

3_4

17_2

9

Eastern Hole Bay Rayne Pt

10_1

The Row

4_6

Wilson Rk

6_8

23

Broadside Rk

4_6

Bullauncatteen

The Lug

4

White

Black Pt

5_9

Whale Rk (8)

1_4 1_8 11
6

2_2

12_8

7_3

3_2

24'   9° 23'   28'

Based on British Admiralty Charts (nos. in text) with the permission of the Controller of H.M. Stationery Office and of
the Hydrographer of the Navy, and on other sources.

287

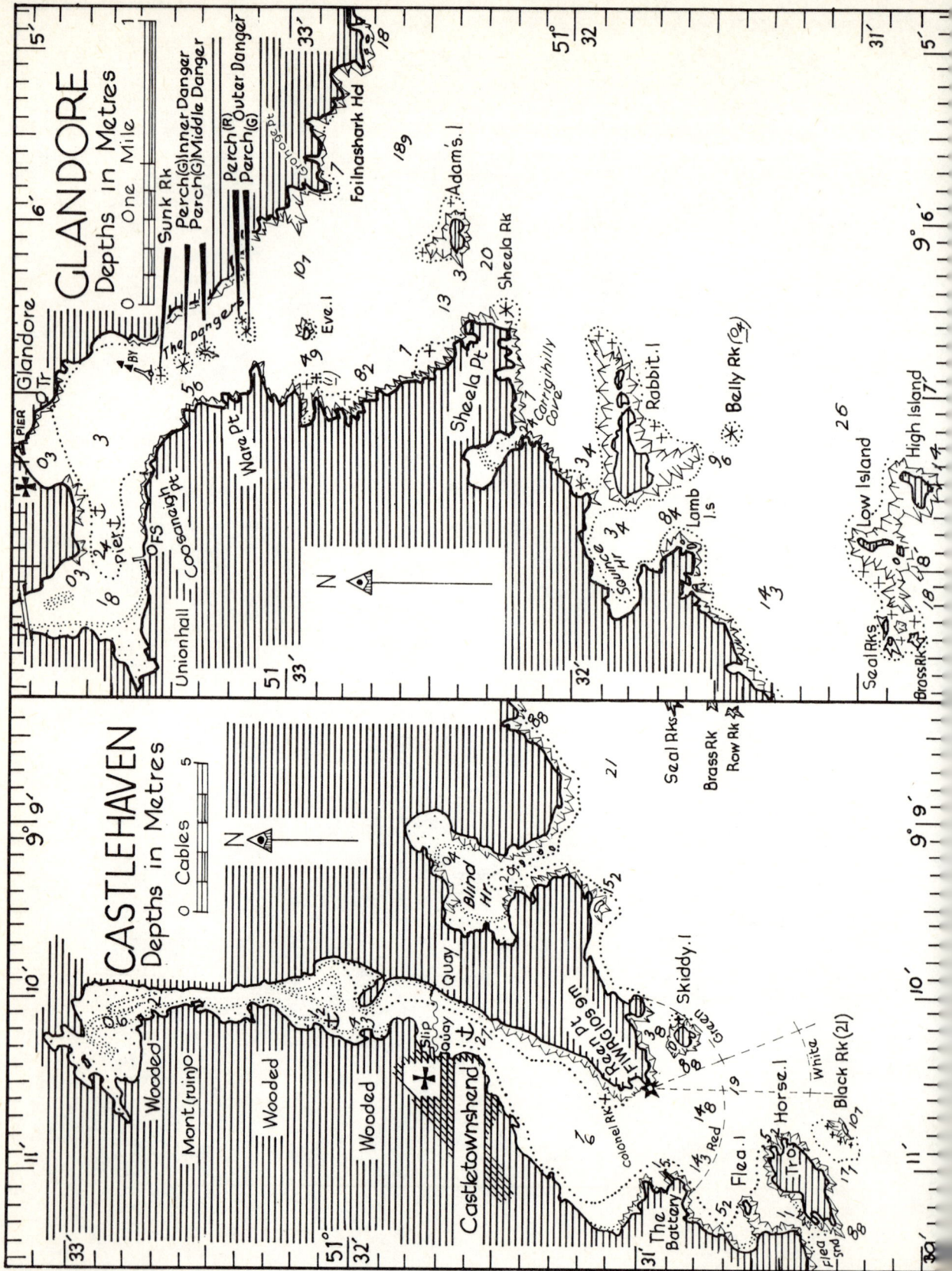

GLANDORE
Depths in Metres

One Mile

Sunk Rk
Perch (G) Inner Danger
Perch (G) Middle Danger
Perch (R) Outer Danger
Perch (G)

PIER
Glandore
Tr
FS
pier
Unionhall
Coosanagh pt.
Ware pt.
The Dangers
BY
Eve. I
Foilnashark Hd
Carrigologagh pt.
Adam's I.
Sheela Rk
Sheela pt.
Corrigihilly Cove
Rabbit. I
Source Hill
Lamb I.s
Belly Rk (0₄)
Low Island
High Island
Seal Rks
Brass Rk

N

CASTLEHAVEN
Depths in Metres

Cables

N

Mont (ruin)
Wooded
Wooded
Wooded
Wooded
Quay
Slip
Quay
Blind Hr.
Castletownshend
Reen pt.
FlW RG 109 9m
Colonel Rk
Skiddy. I
Green
Flea. I
The Battery
flea snd
Tra
Horse. I
White
Black Rk (2J)
Red
Seal Rks
Brass Rk
Row Rk

Based on British Admiralty Charts (nos. in text) with the permission of the Controller of H.M. Stationery Office and o the Hydrographer of the Navy, and on other sources.

a rock with 3m ¼M NE of Fastnet. Galley Hd is fairly steep-to; but ½M WSW is Dhulic Rk, dries 3.4m, with Sunk Rk, less than 1.8m, 1½ ca to SSW of it. Tides set across Dhulic Rk and it must be given a wide berth.

With wind against tide there can be a bad sea close to Galley Hd and to Seven Heads.

Off Old Head of Kinsale a potentially dangerous tide-race extends over 1M to SW on W-going stream, to SE on E-going stream. The race can be avoided by rounding the hd close up except in S winds or any strong winds; in these conditions give it a berth of over 2M.

SCHULL   Chart BA 2129   (Plan p286)
HW 6.10.   MHWS 3.2; MLWS 0.4; MTL 1.9; MHWN 2.7; MLWN 1.1.
The hr is situated between Schull Pt and Cosheen Pt and is protected by Long Is and other islands from S. It affords good shelter and may be preferred to Crookhaven in E winds and at other times. However, it is untenable in a S gale and then shelter should be sought behind Long Is; dig in the anchor with engine to ensure that it is clear of kelp. Heavy fishing boat traffic.
Approach   From S, when about 3 ca S of Amelia Rk buoy (G con, Fl G 3s) marking the rks W of Castle Is, steer 345° for entrance. From W, leave Cush Spit stb buoy (G con) to stb, thence for entrance.
Entrance   By day pass Bull Rk, dries at half-ebb, R perch, on either side: W shore is then clear apart from Baker Rk 1½ ca N of Schull Pt but E shore must be given a berth of at least 1 ca. By night ldg lts Oc 5s lead 346° to E of Bull Rk.
Berthing   Anch 1 ca off pier or lie alongside fishing boat on N side of pier. Water on pier, PO, all supplies.

BALTIMORE   Chart BA 3725   (Plan p287)
HW −6.05.   MHWS 3.6; MLWS 0.6; MTL 2.1; MHWN 3.0; MLWN 1.4.
Approach   The position of hr may be recognised by a conspic W tr called Lot's Wife on Beacon Pt, the E pt of entrance, and by the W Lt Ho (Fl (2) WR) on Barrack Pt, the W pt of entrance. S of the Lt Ho, give the W shore a berth of fully ¾ ca to clear Wilson Rk, awash at HW.
Entrance   Steer in 340° between entrance pts and give the inner E entrance pt, Loo Pt, a berth of ¾ ca, leaving stb buoy (G con) marking Loo Rk to stb. Steer N, leaving Quarry Rk, 1.8m, to stb till the northerly (new) pier comes open N of Connor Pt, 60°.
Anchorages   (1) N or W of New Pier. (2) In Church Strand Bay beyond the RNLI slip (the safest place in gales). (3) Off Skerkin Is under Dunalong Castle ruins. Yachts can also berth alongside NW face of New Pier (1.3m) in fine weather.
Rocks   Quarry Rk, 1.8m, lies 1¾ ca 004° from Loo Pt. Lousy Rks, situated in the W centre of the hr, dry, and are marked by a bn (S Card) on SE rock. Wallis Rk, 0.9m, in E centre of the hr, has a R can buoy E of the rk. Other rks obstruct NW corner of the hr along the shore.

Water on New Pier. Chandler and small yard, PO, general store, bus to Skibbereen, 8M.

CASTLEHAVEN   Chart BA 2092   (Plan p288)
HW +6.25.   DS: E +2.00; W −4.00.
MHWS 3.7; MLWS 0.4; MTL 2.0; MHWN 2.9; MLWN 1.0.
Can be entered at all states of tide, and affords a protected and excellent anch in all weathers, with some swell in SW winds.
Approach   Hr lies 3M NE of Stag Rks.
Entrance   Steer in halfway between Horse Is to port and Skiddy Is to stb. A lt is shown from W framework tr on Reen Pt, and at night the W sector leads in. Continue heading for NE shore until the Stags open through Flea Sd, to port, which line clears Colonel Rk, 1m, on SE shore. In hazy weather keep in mid-channel.
Anchorages   Anchor abreast of Castletownshend or lower down clear of fishing boats, which enter at night along SE shore. In SW winds better shelter will be found upstream just above the Fort, where the fishermen go.

A few general shops. Skibbereen, where all stores may be obtained, is 5M.

GLANDORE   Chart BA 2092   (Plan p288)
HW −6.10.   DS: E +2.00; W −4.00. MHWS 3.7; MHWN 3.0.
Approach   The entrance lies between Foilnashark Hd on W and Sheela Pt on E and is divided into two chans by Adam Is. From SW give High Is a berth of 1 ca; an alternative approach inside High Is is described in ICC but is not recommended for strangers. From E there are no dangers on the direct course from a position S of Dhulic Rk.
Entrance   Between Adam Is and Foilnashark Hd giving Adam Is a wide berth, or between Adam Is and Sheela Pt; then steer to pass 1 ca E of Eve Is. Pass midway between W shore and the Dangers, three separate rocks in the middle of the chan. The Outer Danger is marked by a stb perch (G, con topmark) on its W side and a port perch (R, can topmark) on its E side. The Middle Danger and the Inner Danger are each marked by one perch (G, con topmark). Sunk Rk, about 1 ca N of the Inner Danger, is marked by a buoy (N card). Strangers should not attempt to sail between the Dangers and should particularly note that the perches on the Outer Danger mark the ends of what is in effect one rock.
Anchorages   (1) In W or NW winds off Glandore pier in 2½m. (2) In S or SW winds off Unionhall in 2½m; give Coosaneigh Pt a good berth to avoid mudbank extending 1 ca from it. Water at both piers. Provisions and some fuel at Unionhall.

KINSALE   Chart BA 2053   (Plan p291)
HW −6.00.   MHWS 4.0; MLWS 0.5; MTL 2.3; MHWN 3.2; MLWN 1.4.
Bar   3m, 2 to 3 ca S of Charles Fort.
Approach   From E keep outside the Bulman Rk S Card lt buoy off Hangman Pt.

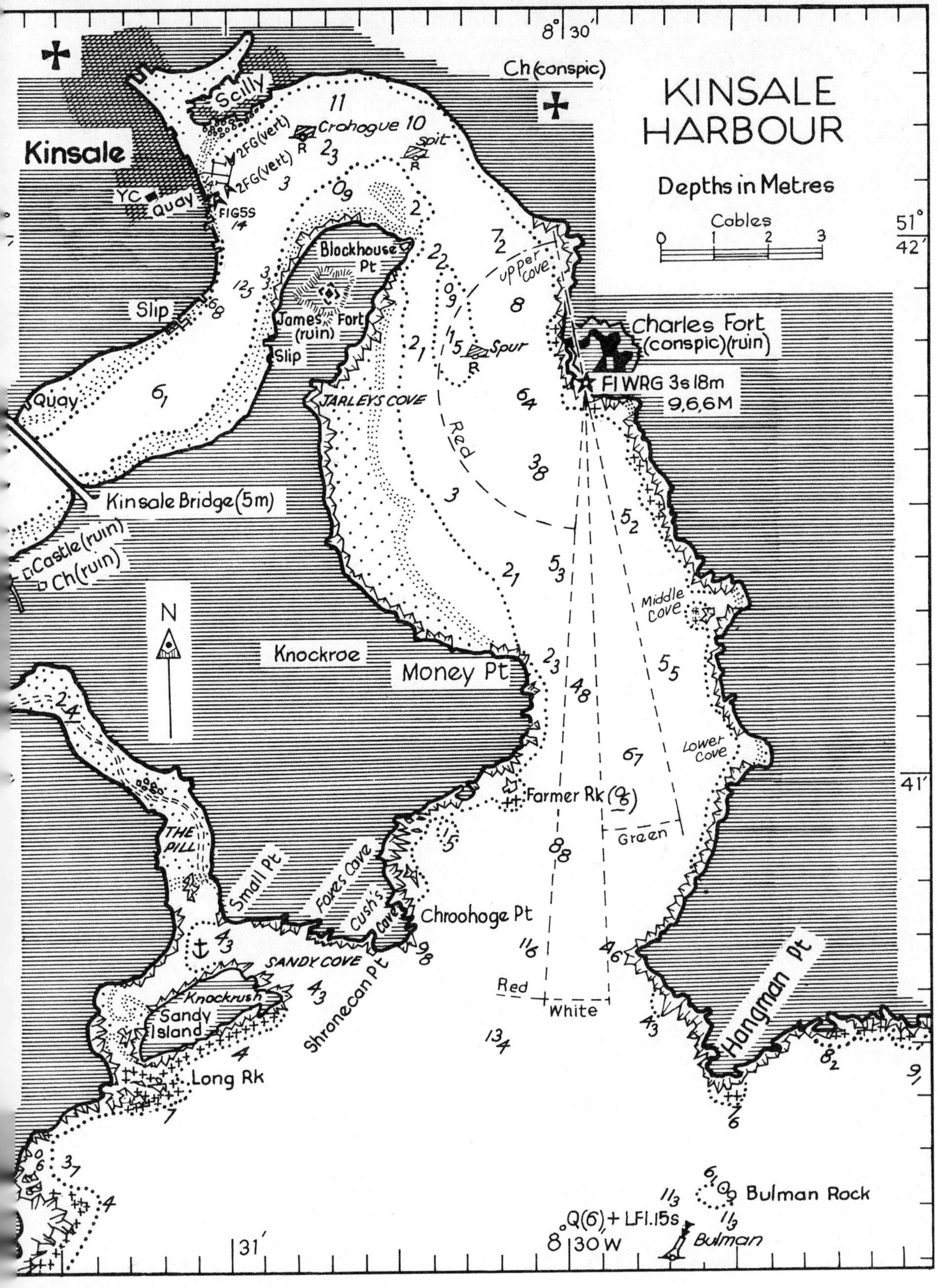

KINSALE HARBOUR

Depths in Metres

Ch (conspic)

Kinsale

Scilly

11

Crohogue 10

2FG(vert) R

2FG(vert)

spit

R

YC Quay

3

FIG5S

14

0.9

2

12.5

Blockhouse Pt

2.2

7.2

Upper Cove

Slip

3.3

0.9

8

Charles Fort
(conspic)(ruin)

Slip

6.8

James Fort
(ruin)

2.1

1.5

Spur
R

FI WRG 3s 18m
9,6,6M

6.1

Quay

Slip

JARLEYS COVE

Red

6.4

3.8

Kinsale Bridge (5m)

3

5.2

Castle (ruin)

Ch (ruin)

2.1

5.3

Middle Cove

N

Knockroe

Money Pt

2.3

4.8

5.5

Lower Cove

2.4

6.7

THE PILL

Farmer Rk (0.6)

8.8

Green

Small Pt

Foxes Cove

1.5

11.6

Chroohoge Pt

Cush's Cove

Red

White

4.3

SANDY COVE

Shronecan Pt

0.8

4.6

4.3

Hangman Pt

Knockrush

13.4

Sandy Island

4

8.2

9.1

Long Rk

3.7

6

6.1

Bulman Rock

4

Q(6) + LFI.15s

1.3

1.3

8° 30 W

Bulman

Cables
0 1 2 3

51°
42'

41'

31'

8° 30'

Glenbrook   Boatyard   Water Tr (conspic)   EAST PASSAGE continued in inset

Great Island

Radio Mast   Spire (conspic)   Customs   Shipyard   CUSKINNY BAY   Fair Rk   Perch

Summer Pt   Pylon   Spire (conspic)(91)

Cobh

FlR 2.5s 4m 4M. Tr R   Varolme Cork Dyd   Spire   FS   Chy   Rushbrooke   THE BAR   FAIRWAY   EAST CHANNEL
Spiros (conspic)   Monkstown   Y C Quay   COBH ROAD   FlR 5s No20   FlR 5s No18   FIG 2.5s No9   IsoWR4s10m 7M Spit Bank   East Spit
2-FR   2 FR (vert)   SPIT BANK   FIG 5s No91

2 FR (vert)   White Pt   FIG 5s No5   2 FR (vert)   Haulbowline Island   BEING RECLAIMED   FIG 5s No14   2 FG (vert)   Power Stn
2 FR (vert)   FIG 5s   Rocky I.   FIG 5s No12   2 FG (vert)
MONKSTOWN Cr   MAJOR HARBOUR WORKS IN PROGRESS 1980   Spike I.   FlR 5s No10   Black Rock   CORKBEG   WHITEGATE BAY   Quay
OYSTER BANK   Fort Mitchel   CAUTION NO YACHT TO APPROACH WITHIN 50 METRES OF OIL JETTY   Quays
Pfizer Chemical Factory   Ballybricken Pnt   Pier(ruins)   FIG 2.5s No7
Ringaskiddy I.   Ringaskiddy   Martello Tr   Pylon   CURLANE BANK   FIG 5s No8   Whitegate Oil Refinery   Mast(93)
Flare(71)(occas)(conspic)

LOUGH BEG   Concrete Block   FlG 5s No5   Dognose   Oc 5s14m 5M   Oc 5s 5m 5M   Fort Davis   Oc R 5s 21m 5M
Cl Lts 252°   C2   White House
F 15m 3M   Rams Head   Fort Meagher   RAMSHEAD BAY   Oc R 5s 11m 5M   Oc R 5s

Brown I.   8½ w   F 10m   TURBOT BANK   FIG 2.5s No6   WHITE BAY   FIG 2.5s No3
2 FR   Town Quay   Boatyard   Slip   FlR 5s W4   Ho (red Roof)
Boat Ho   Bagwell's Hill   Spire (conspic)   For CROSSHAVEN see separate plan   Weavers Pt   FIG 10s W1   Mast Canavan Pt   Oc WR 20s30m 20,16M, Dia. 30s

Great Island

EAST PASSAGE (Continued at same scale)   East Grove Trafalgar Tr   Quay   Spire (ruins)   POULNAGALLEE BAY   Roche's Pt   Tr
Belgrove   Quay   Pylon   Mast   Water Tr (conspic)   FIR 10s W2   FlR 2.5s   Outer Harbour Rock   Cow Rk   Calf Rk
Wooded   Pylon   Ch   Wooded   Marloag Pt   Slip   Gold Pt   Slip   MYRTLEVILLE BAY

Perch   Fair Rk.   RINGABELLA BAY

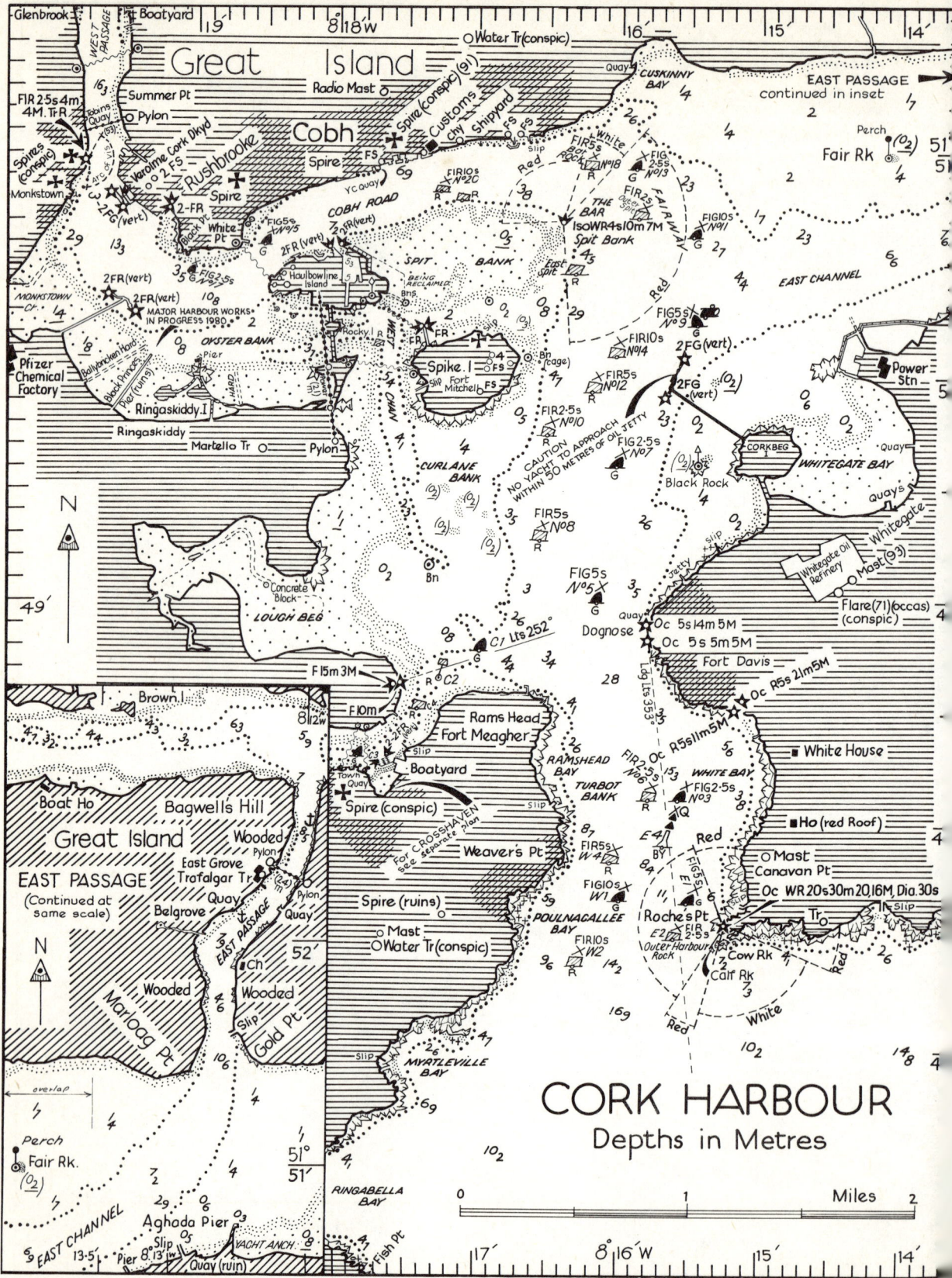

CORK HARBOUR
Depths in Metres

0   1   Miles   2

Aghada Pier   Slip   Pier   YACHT ANCH.   Fish Pt   Quay (ruin)
EAST CHANNEL

Based on British Admiralty Charts (nos. in text) with the permission of the Controller of H.M. Stationery Office and the Hydrographer of the Navy, and on other sources.

The hr will then open up to N and when Charles Fort is visible between Money Pt and Preghane Pt, steer for it. At night the W sector of Charles Fort lt leads in.
Entrance   Keep in mid-chan and cross the bar S of Charles Fort. The W side of the chan from the bar round Blockhouse Pt to the town is marked by three R can buoys which must be left to port.
Berthing   (1) At Kinsale YC marina N of Town Quay; visitors' berths on outer pontoon, but a finger berth inside marina may be available. Berths controlled by HM, office on pier-head. (2) Anch on bank N of James Fort, 2 to 4m. (3) Anch in river between Town Quay and bridge. Landing at Town Quay or on SE shore from (3). Water on quay, fuel, all stores, bus to Cork. EC Thurs. Cork airport 12M.

OYSTERHAVEN

Chart BA 2053   (Plan p286)

A quiet safe harbour 2M E of Kinsale.
Entrance   Approach either side of Big Sovereign and make for centre of entrance. Give Ballymacus Pt on W of entrance a berth of at least ¾ ca. Harbour Rk, 1m, is 1½ ca E of Ferry Pt and must be passed on its W side.
Anchorages   (1) N of Ferry Pt midway between N and S shore in 4 to 6m, soft mud and weed. Keep Kinure Pt on E side of entrance open of Ferry Pt. (2) In N branch of hr in 3m, sand.

CORK HARBOUR

Charts BA 1777, 1773   (Plan p292)

HW −5.50.   DS: E +1.00; W −4.30.
Hr is accessible at all times.
Approach   From Old Hd of Kinsale, Cork RWVS buoy, Fl 10s, off the entrance to the port of Cork bears 58°, 12½M. Hence Roche's Pt, the E pt of the entrance, 001°, 4¾M. The approach is clear of obstruction for small craft excepting Daunt Rk, 3.5m, marked by R buoy Fl(2)R 6s, 7 ca 140° from Roberts Hd: to leave this to W bring the high tr E of Roche's Pt Lt Ho on with tree clump in rear, 018°. By day, having left Daunt Rk about 4 ca to port, a course 009° made good will lead into the entrance between Weaver Pt and the Lt Ho. By night, a R sector from Roche's Pt Lt Ho covers Daunt Rk, and this sector should be shut in before rounding up for Roche's Pt Lt Ho. 016°.
Entrance   No dangers for small craft in entrance to Cork Hr. To make for Crosshaven, the main yachting centre, round Ram Pt at a distance of fully 2 ca and steer for the G con buoy at entrance to Carrigaline River. Leave this buoy to stb and R bn and R can buoy to port. FW ldg lts with W diamond daymarks lead S of G buoy and N of R bn 252°. (See separate plan on p295.) In the entrance the tidal streams follow the bends, the flood and ebb streams setting into White Bay.
Berthing   *Crosshaven:* (1) At W end of RCYC marina. (2) At Crosshaven Boat Yard (tel (021) 831161) marina. (3) Anch below Town Quay clear of tel cables. (4) Ask Crosshaven Boat Yard for a mooring. Good supplies, all facilities. Bus to Cork.
   Cobh: anch W of town. Garage, shops, hotels, PO, bank. EC Wed. *East Ferry:*

(1) Marina S of Belgrove Quay. (2) Anch on W side S or E of quay, 2 to 3m; (3) On E side ½M further up, 3 to 4m. *Cork:* a berth may be obtained by permission of Port Operations Office, Cobh.

In offshore winds, awaiting tide, anch will be found outside the entrance in Ringabella Bay.

Warning No yacht may approach within 50m of Whitegate oil jetty.

PASSAGE NOTES: CORK TO TUSKAR ROCK

Charts BA 2049, 2740

Tidal streams: Cork to Waterford less than 0.5kn starting progressively later towards Waterford where they begin ENE +05.15; WSW −1.00. Between the Saltees and Carnsore Pt ENE +05.25, spring rate 2.4kn; WSW −00.40, spring rate 2.6kn.

Off Hook Hd there is a dangerous tidal race extending 1M S of the Hd, especially in strong westerlies. To avoid this race keep outside the 20m line.

E of Hook Hd, Baginbun and Bannow Bays though exposed to SE give good shelter from westerlies. The recommended offshore anchorage is at the SW end of Bannow Bay just N of Ingard Pt.

A yacht proceeding from Waterford to the E coast has the choice of the offshore or inshore passage. Using the offshore passage make for the Coningbeg LV, and thence to a position S of South Rk buoy (S Card) and E of the Tuskar Rk. Give the Tuskar a good berth as the tide sets onto it. For the inshore passage, pass between the Saltees or N of them and about ¼M S of Carnsore Pt. Chart BA 2740 and directions in ICC are essential for this passage.

Warning: the sea area off the SE corner of Ireland is to be avoided in bad weather.

BALLYCOTTON   Chart BA 2049
HW −5.55.   DS: E +3.00; W −3.00
MHWS 4.1; MLWS 0.5; MTL 2.3; MHWN 3.3; MLWN 1.2.
A small pier hr, with 2 to 3m alongside pier.
Approach Hr lies behind Ballycotton Is at the W extremity of the bay, is free from swell except in S winds, and may be of use to small craft caught between Youghal and Cork Hrs. It is small and congested with fishing boats. Bottom a mass of mooring chains. Anch outside to NE of breakwater. Water on pier, hotels, village shops, PO. Bus to Cork.

YOUGHAL   Chart BA 2071   (Plan p295)
HW −5.45.   DS: W at HWD.
MHWS 4.1; MLWS 0.5; MTL 2.3; MHWN 3.3; MLWN 1.2.
The tidal stream sets into hr at +1.30, out at −4.20; 2½ to 3kn springs.
Bar Not to be attempted in a big sea. The approach is divided by Bar Rks, 0.6m and Blackball Ledge, 3.4m, into two chans, E Bar, having 2m, and W Bar 1.8m. In E Bar one may expect less sea and less stream. S winds cause a heavy sea in

CROSSHAVEN
Depths in Metres

20'
19'

1°
0 Mile 1

8.5'

F 10m 3M
F 15m 3M

Ldg Lts 252° Cl 17'44
C2 R Perch
C1 R

FS Bn
Scotchman's Pt
Fort Meagher

N

Moorings 3.5

Pier

2

2.3
2.2 Mooring
2.2FR (vert)

6.6

Slip
Drakes Pool 4.1

Wooded .5

Landing possible Quay
Slip

23
2.2
Moorings
Slip
YC FS
Quay

Slip
4
Slip

The Point
MARINA Boatyard

7.7'

Moorings

Crosshaven
Spire

8° 18'W

4.7'

20'
19'
17'

52'
50'
7° 49'W

2.7
2.7
2.7

3.4
3.7

Chy

Cross

Youghal

ClockTr (conspic)
Chy (conspic) Mall Dock

Tr (conspic)
FS

FIWR

Moll Goggin's Corner
Williamstown

Ferry
Pier
Ferry Pt

6.4

LB

1.9

1.6 White
8.2

5.8

DUTCHMANS BALLAST

YOUGHAL
Depths in Metres

0 Cables 6

7'

N

East Pt

Blackball Head
CALISO BAY
4

57'

Mast
FS

Sluice

1°
6'

.1
.6

5.5
2

5.1

EAST BAR
1.7

3.5
3.5

3.7

3

.1
2

1.7

1.8

1.8

1.5

3.7

51°
56'

.1
8

WEST BAR

1.8

3 Red

Blackball Ledge
3.4

Blackball

Bog Rk

2.7

.8

2.7

1.2

3.7
.8
.8
.8

Bar Rocks

Clonard Rk

0.9

.8

W

Bar Rocks
YB

6.7

55'

YOUGHAL BAY

52'
51'
7° 50'W
49'

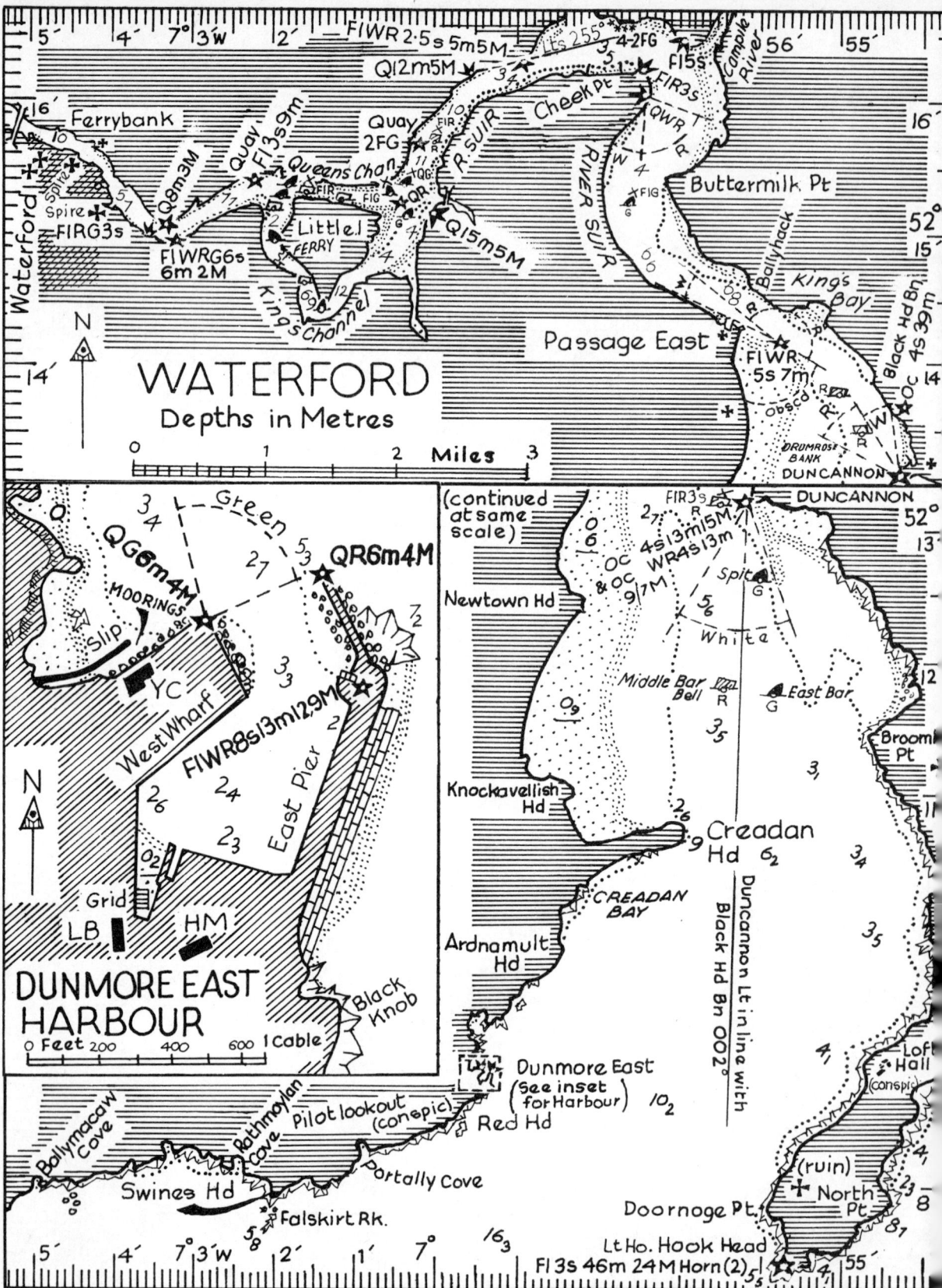

WATERFORD
Depths in Metres

Fl WR 2.5s 5m5M
Q 12m5M
Lts 25°
4-2FG
Fl 5s
FIR3s
QWR1r

Ferrybank
Quay
2FG
R.SUIR
Cheek Pt
River Suir
Camaha River
56'

Quay
Fl3s9m
Queens Chan
FIR
TQG
QR
Q15m5M
W6
FIG

Buttermilk Pt

Spire
FIRG3s
Q8m3M
Little I.
FERRY
Ballyhack

King's Bay

Fl WRG6s
6m 2M
King's channel

Passage East
Fl WR
5s 7m
Black Hd Bn
4s 39m
Oc

Obscd
R
W
DRUMROSE BANK
DUNCANNON

N

0   1   2   Miles   3

(continued
at same
scale)

DUNCANNON

FIR3s
Oc 4s13m15M
& Oc WR4s13m
9.7M
52°13'

Green
QG6m4M
MOORINGS
QR6m4M

Slip
Newtown Hd

Spit
White
52°12'

YC
West Wharf
Fl WR8s13m12.9M
East Pier

Middle Bar
Bell
R
East Bar
G
Broom Pt

N

Knockavellish Hd

Creadan Hd
6.2
3.4

Grid
LB
HM

CREADAN BAY
3.5

DUNMORE EAST HARBOUR

0 Feet 200   400   600   1 Cable

Black Knob

Ardnamult Hd

Duncannon Lt in line with Black Hd Bn 002°

Loft Hall
(conspic)

Bollymacaw Cove
Rathmoylan Cove
Pilot lookout (conspic)

Dunmore East
(see inset for Harbour)
10.2

Red Hd

Swines Hd
Portally Cove
Falskirt Rk.

Doornoge Pt.
(ruin)
North Pt

8

Lt Ho. Hook Head
Fl 3s 46m 24M Horn(2)

Based on British Admiralty Charts (nos. in text) with the permission of the Controller of H.M. Stationery Office and the Hydrographer of the Navy, and on other sources.

the bay. N winds reduce the tidal rise, S winds cause a sea outside, and SW gales a swell inside; the ebb sets on to W Bar.

Approach From W, using the W Bar chan leave Youghal Bar S Card buoy marking Bar Rks (0.6m) about 2 ca to stb, then steer direct for the entrance about N.

Using E Bar chan, coming from S, leave Blackwall Ledge R can buoy to port. From E, steer for Lt Ho when it comes well open of Blackball Hd and bears about 300°.

Entrance Having passed the Lt Ho, keep in towards the W shore. The E side of entrance on a transit between E Pt and Ferry Pt is shoal.

Anchorages (1) On a 3m bank off the most N-ly warehouse. (2) In 2 to 4m N of Ferry Pt, to NW of a dolphin.

All stores. EC Wed.

HELVICK   Chart BA 2049
HW −5.30.   MHWS 4.1; MLWS 0.5; MTL 2.3; MHWN 3.4; MLWN 1.1.

A very small fishing hr enclosed by a breakwater and a pier, with W Bn (FW) on pier-head, inside Helvick Hd; good shelter. Keep close to stb pier entering. Depth between piers 1m. Berth at N Pier, 2m, outer part. Water, limited supplies.

WATERFORD   Chart BA 2046   (Plan p296)
HW −5.30 at Dunmore East.   DS: W by N −2.00 to +5.00; SSE −6.00 to −3.00.

MHWS 4.5; MLWS 0.4; MTL 2.4; MHWN 3.6; MLWN 1.2.

Dunmore East is a small artificial hr on the W side of the entrance which affords a convenient port of call. Lt Ho on pier shows Fl WR 8s; lts QR at end of breakwater extension to E pier and QG at N end of W quay. There are yacht moorings in the bight N of NW quay. Berth alongside on E or NW side of hr and report to HM. Water from tap on W quay diesel on E quay, shops and PO in village. Bus to Waterford. YC.

Bar 4M inside Hook Hd, has 3m. The R Suir has 10 to 4m up to Waterford. Below Duncannon outgoing stream follows E side, the ingoing W side.

Approach The summit of Slieve Coiltia bears 360° from the entrance, which lies between Swines Hd, 60m, on the W side, and the long low-lying Hook Hd 4M to the E. It bears 296°, 11M from Coningbeg LV. In hazy weather care must be taken to distinguish Tramore Bay, which has three W trs on the W pt and two on the E pt of the bay, from the Waterford entrance.

The approach is clear of obstructions except Falskirt Rk, 2 ca S of Swines Hd, covers at ⅔ flood, and Brecaun reef, 2M NE of Hook Hd, 3 ca offshore (0.5m), to clear which keep Hook Lt Ho W of 233°. Tower Race extends 1M to the S of Hood Hd, and should be given a good berth. In fresh W winds over W-going stream conditions are severe.

Entrance Keep in buoyed chan. Abreast Duncannon the chan lies on E side, and the Drumroe bank to W (1m or less) must be avoided. Duncannon Ldg Lts lead in 002°. Ldg Lts show 255° over Cheek Pt bar. Ldg Lts, 097°, indicate fairway through Queen's chan.

Anchorages (1) Opposite Hell Pt 7½M above Hook Hd, just above Ballyhack in 5m on E side close in out of tidal stream. (2) W of Cheek Pt (avoid fish weirs) in 3m, ½ to 1 ca N of village quay, secure anch, good holding, little stream. (3) In W side of King's Channel just N of the W bank ferry stn. No facilities. The E side is silted up and there is no passage through the wires of the ferry. (4) Waterford town; berth at landing stage downstream of clock tr. Strong flood stream.

Beating up the river near HW, vessels must be careful to avoid old stumps of fish weirs, which extend over the mud flats toward the chan. R Suir has 2.5m at Fiddoum Is, and dries 3M below Carrick. There are two lifting brs at Waterford. R Barrow has plenty of water in the buoyed chan to New Ross but the chan is very narrow between Red Bank and the W side. Barrow Bridge at confluence has 7m clearance MHWS, 11m MLWN, opens for 3 blasts but preferably tel Campile 37. Pilots at Dunmore. EC Thurs.

Ireland, East Coast

Warning: A sharp lookout should be kept for lobster pots.

PASSAGE NOTE: CARNSORE PT TO DUBLIN BAY
Charts BA 1787, 1468, 1415

Tidal streams: DS in middle of St George's Channel: NE +6.00, SW HWD. Outside Tuskar Rk: NE −05.30, SW HWD, 2½kn; there is a set onto the rk. Streams change about 1½h earlier between the Irish banks and the shore; they set across these banks.

From Land's End it can be dangerous to come in W of the Tuskar Rk, but coming from the W yachts need not leave this rk to port.

The passage from Carnsore Pt to Rosslare should not be attempted at night.

From Tuskar to Dublin Bay the normal route is outside the Blackwater bank, inside the S Arklow Lt Ho buoy, thence past Wicklow Hd and through Dalkey Sound, quite clean except close to island side, or through Muglins Sd, but this has rks with under 2m on each side. By night go outside Muglins, Lt Fl 5s.

Keep away from Arklow Bank, a dangerous shallow ridge.

Approaching Dublin Bay from E make Kish Lt Ho Fl(2) 30s, Horn(2) 30s, thence to S Burford S Card lt buoy, Horn(1) 20s, leaving N Kish N Card lt buoy to port.

In Dublin Bay, yachts are required to keep out of way of commercial shipping.

ROSSLARE   Chart BA 1772   (Plan p299)
HW −5.10.   MHWS 2.0; MLWS 0.4; MTL 1.2; MHWN 1.5; MLWN 0.9.

WEXFORD
Depths in Metres

26'

6°21'W

52°21'

BUOYS
Buoys positioned
for Summer
months only.

CAUTION
Banks & depths
subject to change

Sand Dunes 9m high
The Raven Pt

Forestry Gap

(1.m high)

r. Slaney

Training Wall
Ballast Bank
Covers
Bn

5·8m
(conspic)

res

Trespan Rk

Large new
factory

Training Wall—marked by posts
(Awash at H.W)

Perch
Perch

Perch Ruins
(awash at HW)

Submerged ruins

Slaney Wk

Bar No 1

COAL CHANNEL

Rosslare Pt

Sand Dunes
1m high

Windmill
(ruin)

Remains of old Embankment

Sand Dunes
6m high

N

Chy Tall Chy
Chy Chys
Embankment

0 Mile 1

25' 24' 22' 6°21'W 19'

ROSSLARE Hr.
Depths in Metres

20·5' 6°20'W

0 Cables 4

Ldg Lts 124°

Fl WRG 5s 15m 13,10,10M

Green W Red

Ldg Lts 124°

Red

R 34 LB

No2

R R R

No1

FR 10M

24 steps

FR
12m

works in progress
(1980)

CG

WICKLOW
Depths in Metres

52°
59·2'

N

0 Red 1
Coble

59·1'

Fl.1·5s 5m 6M

West Pier

Fl WR 5s 11m 6M

Planet Rk

E Pier

Pogeen Rk

White

Fl WG 5m 6M

Slip

LB

Packet Quay

White Boathouse

Black Castle (ruins)

Leittrim River

N

2·3' 6°2'W

---

on British Admiralty Charts (nos. in text) with the permission of the Controller of H.M. Stationery Office and of drographer of the Navy, and on other sources.

The hr, opening NW, is formed by a curved breakwater and is a very busy commercial port in which yachts are not allowed to berth alongside. It is convenient for yachts bound from SW England to E coast of Ireland, however, and for yachts bound S along the Irish coast held up by headwinds. A new inner pier is being constructed and yachts may not anchor within 100m SW of it or in the approaches.

Anchorages (1) SW of the breakwater. (2) If (1) is fully occupied by local boats, anch further W beyond an area of rocky bottom in 2 to 5m; safe and comfortable in winds between WSW and SE but untenable in fresh winds between W and NE.

Petrol and diesel, small shop, PO, hotels. Car ferry to Fishguard.

WEXFORD HARBOUR   Chart BA 1772   (Plan p299)

HW −3.05 Sp, −6.25 Np.

MHWS 1.7; MLWS 0.2; MTL 1.0; MHWN 1.4; MLWN 0.5.

Once entered, this hr is completely safe, sheltered and charming.

Bar 1.5m (but 1m in inner chan).

Approach Dangerous in strong winds between S and E. In general visitors should not attempt to enter without local assistance (see below) but in offshore winds and settled weather a stranger with reliable power may attempt the entrance from a position about 1M E of the N end of the detached (Nly) part of Rosslare Pt. Slaney wreck, an unmarked dangerous wreck 1¼M SE of Raven Pt, lies close S of the approach to the bar.

Entrance Leave the ruins of a fort, awash at HW, to port and feel in on soundings, proceeding about NW until near the shore, then turning onto SW for the end of the S training wall, whence the water is deep to the quay. There are unlit lateral buoys laid by the Wexford Hr Boat Club (summer only) marking the chan.

Berthing Good holding in hr on E side, or lie alongside quay in centre of town, or by arrangement against disused LV, now a museum. Good shops, restaurants, boatyard, YC.

Warning The banks in the entrance are variable in depth and position and the information on the plan must not be relied upon in detail. Strangers should telephone John Sherwood, Rosslare (053) 22875 (shop hours) or 22713 (home), or the Boat Club (22039), who will give latest information and supply Pilot if thought necessary.

ARKLOW   Chart BA 633   (Plan p302)

HW −01.50.   DS: SSW −01.00.   MHWS 1.1; MHWN 1.0.

Bar and river to wharves dredged to not less than 3.5m. Dock mostly 1.7m but dries in E corner and either side of ship hoist. Note very small tidal rise.

Entrance Narrow and difficult under sail. Dangerous in gales from N through E to SW. S pier-head has 10m steel tr, Fl WR 6s; N pier-head Fl G 3s. Dock on S side provides perfect shelter against NE or SE quay with 10m wide entrance. Do not go beyond the old low quay W of Dock entrance as the river is then shallow with obstructions. All facilities, except sailmaker. EC Wed.

WICKLOW   Chart BA 633   (Plan p299)
HW: HWD.   DS: SE at HWD.   MHWS 2.7; MHWN 2.3.
The hr faces N and is exposed in NE winds; inner part offers complete shelter.
Entrance   For Inner Hr steer between outer piers towards W boathouse; when face of ferry quay opens turn sharp to stb. Keep front of RNLI boathouse open to avoid shallows on SE side.
Berthing   (1) Anchor in outer hr midway between ends of W pier and quay in 2 to 3m outside YC moorings. (2) In inner hr. The S side is being developed for use by fishing boats and yachts; if the quays there are not yet available a yacht may go alongside the steamer quay, beyond knuckle, with permission from HM office in middle of pier. Petrol on S quay. All stores and facilities except sailmaker. EC Thurs.

DUN LAOGHAIRE   Chart BA 1447   (Plan p302)
HW +0.45.   DS off entrance: SE −1.30; NW +5.00.
MHWS 4.1; MLWS 0.6; MTL 2.4; MHWN 3.4; MLWN 1.5.
A large artificial hr on S side of Dublin Bay, always available. Major yachting centre. Badly exposed to NE and E gales, when anchors may drag and no good berth available: then best make for Liffey.
Entrance   Allow for tide across hr mouth. Keep well clear of ferries, which have right of way.
Berthing   Anch outside moored yachts opposite entrance off RIYC; moorings often available. Royal St George YC has moorings inside E pier, quieter in E-ly winds. Berth alongside moored ships in coal hr, but subject to much traffic and scend in NE wind. Inner hr only for 4ft draft. Water in coal hr or tap at RIYC. All facilities. EC Wed.

PORT OF DUBLIN (RIVER LIFFEY)   Chart BA 1447
Not very suitable for yachts, but all facilities.
Entrance   Bar buoys may be ignored but beyond Lt Ho keep to chan between R buoys and G buoys and beacons.
Berthing   As directed or alongside quay or vessel just below bridge. Best not to leave yacht unattended.

PASSAGE NOTE: DUBLIN BAY TO FAIR HEAD
Charts BA 44, 2093, 2198, 2199, 3709

Tidal streams   Between Hill of Howth and St John's Pt: DS N +6.00; S HWD; strong S of Rockabill Pt, weak further N and negligible S of St John's Pt. Between St John's Pt and Fair Hd: N and NW HWD, S and SE +6.00; weak near St John's Pt, strong N of Belfast Lough, reaching 4½kn in entrance to North

DUN LAOGHAIRE HARBOUR
Depths in Metres

East Pier
YACHT MOORINGS
BOYD
Dia. or Bell
Fl(2)BGl6M 22M
QWR
W.711m75511M7M
Fl(3)G.75ssllM7M
FAIRWAY No 1
FAIRWAY No 2
Anchorage
YACHT MOORINGS
Fl R 3s
Moorings
HM Mail Boat Pier
Steps
Car Ferry Slip
National YC
2FR(vert)
Royal Irish Yacht Club
Royal St George YC
Station
JH
Moorings
Dun Laoghaire MC
Motor
N
53° 18'
6° 8w
0 Cables 1
17.6

ARDGLASS
Depths in Metres

Phennick Pt
Green
Fl R 3s 10m 5M Horn 20s (occas)
Red
Bn
Bn
R
Fl R 3s
Iso WRG 4s 10m 8-5M
N.Pier
HM
Ardglass
N
54° 15.5'
5° 36'
36.5'
16'
0 Cables 2

ARKLOW
Depths in Metres

N
52° 48.8'
Green
Red
White
Fl I WR 6s 10m 8M
Fl I G 3s
N.Pier
S.Pier
Bn
RW
(44)
Chys
(45)
Piles
Dock
Ship Hoist
LB
Boatyard
Tank
Sewers
52° Arklow 47.6'
6° 8.3w
0 Cable 1

KILKEEL
Depths in Metres

N
54° 3.7'
Maeeny's Pier
Breakwater
Tr
Pier
Tow Slip
INNER HARBOUR 1m
HM
CG
Spanish Breach
54° 3.6'
59.4'
59.6'w
6°
35'
35.5'
0 Cable 1

Chan. There is an inshore eddy on the SE stream between Torr Hd and Fair Hd, NW from −04.00 for 10h.

Ballyquintin Pt, E of the entrance to Strangford Lough, should be given a berth of ½M. There are extensive rks off Kearney Pt 3¼M NE of Ballyquintin Pt. South Rk LV is moored 2M E of South Rk, marked by a disused Lt Ho 18m high. North Rks, 1½M E of Ringboy Pt, must be passed at least 1½ ca to E.

Donaghadee Sound inside Copeland Is is the normal passage for yachts sailing along the coast; S entrance marked by buoys.

SE of Muck Is there is a race which should be taken with the stream. The Maidens are two dangerous groups of rks within 4M of Ballygalley Hd separated by a chan 1M wide.

Rogerstown Inlet in the bay facing Lambay Is provides sheltered anch for up to 1.7m draft. Drogheda, on R Boyne, provides good shelter for a night but has no special berths for yachts. Portavogie, some 8M N of Strangford Lough, is at present so congested that yachts should use it only in emergency.

Carnlough Hr, some 11M N of Larne, provides shelter for yachts drawing less than 1.5m, and for these is a useful port for a passage to or from the Scottish coast.

MALAHIDE INLET   Chart BA 633
HW +0.30.   MHWS 4.2; MLWS 0.5; MTL 2.4; MHWN 3.5; MLWN 1.5.
A safe anchorage for yachts drawing up to 2m.
Bar 0.3m.
Entrance During summer S bank is marked by a R buoy and N bank by a G buoy. A G buoy marks the middle of the chan 4 ca further in. Flood stream runs up to 3kn and ebb up to 3½kn. (*Note:* the buoys noted above as G were reported as still being B in late 1980.)
Anchorage The river is full of moorings. Anch 3 to 4 ca to seaward of the Grand Hotel, use tripping line. Shipwright, shops, chandler, restaurants. Train and bus to Dublin.

SKERRIES BAY
This bay affords shelter from SE through S to W.
Approach From S give Skerries Is a good berth, also Cross Rk, 4 ca NNE of pier-head and marked by R can buoy QR moored to NNW, occasionally absent. Pier-head lt Fl R 6s leads in. Anch in 5m NW of pier-head. Pier has 1m alongside outer part of extension.

CARLINGFORD LOUGH   Chart BA 2800   (Plan p305)
HW Cranfield Pt +0.25.   MHWS 4.8; MLWS 0.7; MTL 2.9; MHWN 4.3; MLWN 1.8.
HW Warren Pt +0.35.   DS: N −05.00; S +00.20.
Tidal streams Weak outside, 3½kn in buoyed approach chan, 4½kn just E of Lt Ho, 1½kn between entrance and Greenore, 5kn off Greenore, 2½kn between

Stalka and Watson rks, 1½kn off Carlingford, quiet above Killowen Pt. Between Lt Ho and No. 5 buoy the flood tends to N; there is a S-going eddy on flood along E side of Block House Is. Otherwise the streams follow chans. Small yachts cannot enter or leave against the tide and should have reliable power or leading wind even with fair tide.

Carlingford L lies 39M N of Dublin, 28M S of Strangford, and may be located by Carlingford Mt, 585m, some 5M NW of entrance and by the Mourne Mts to the N.

There are shoals E and W of the approach within 1M of the entrance pts, Ballagan on W and Cranfield on E. The whole entrance is blocked inside at LW by the Limestone Rks, except the cut, a narrow chan 100m long on NE side.

Approach From NE or SE, leave to stb Hellyhunter buoy, S Card QG + L Fl 15s. From S, keep a mile or more off Ballagan Pt. Cranfield Pt (not conspic) with houses bearing 016° or No. 2 buoy, R, bearing N will lead to entrance.

Entrance Steer on Vidal ldg lts, RW piles Oc 3s 1M inside the Pt, 310°, along buoyed and lit chan, leaving Haulbowline Lt Ho ¼M to port, till Greenore Lt, Iso 10s, bears 287°, when steer for it. Proceed between further lit lateral buoys till abreast Killowen Pt, hence 355° to anch off Wood House, or off Rostrevor quay, 1 to 4m.

Anchorages (1) Between quay and breakwater at Greenore just past end of old rly station in 3m. (2) ½M N of Carlingford Hr in 3m, or berth alongside either pier in hr, which dries. (3) Between Killowen Pt and Rostrevor. (4) In SW wind, off Greer's quay.

In S wind the lough is disturbed. Onshore gales render the bar impassable. Squalls from the hills. Landing is impossible at Rostrevor pier at LW, but Carlingford Lough YC just N of Killowen Pt has a slip where one can always land, though caution needed at LW. Water at Greenore and Warrenpoint; stores at Greenore and Carlingford, best at Warrenpoint.

Note: the NE shore of the lough is Northern Ireland, the SW the Republic. Customs formalities are observed. Newry commercial basin is accessible by canal entered near HW above Warrenpoint. EC: Carlingford Thurs, Warrenpoint Wed.

KILKEEL   Chart BA 2800   (Plan p302)

HW +0.15.   DS: S +1.00; N −5.00 (weak).

MHWS 5.3; MLWS 0.7; MTL 3.1; MHWN 4.4; MLWN 1.9.

A crowded fishing port 3¼M NNE of Hellyhunter buoy. Visitors are permitted to berth; useful alternative for small craft if tide into Carlingford is missed. Depth off quays is mostly 1.1m but parts of the basin and the outer end of the chan are shallower.

Approach From about 1M offshore with hr bearing between 340° and 350°, or steer first for CGS.

Entrance When 100m away from pier-head steer between 010° and 015° till inner side of pier is visible, then enter.

Cables

Cranfield Point

Soldiers Pt Tr (6)
IQG
FIR
Oc 3s12m 11M
Green I.
Oc 3s7m 11M
Oc 8
Block House

Sheep RK
(5)

LIMESTONE ROCKS

Northern Ireland

Cranfield Pt
Soldiers Pt
Tr (6)
IQR
FIR
Oc 3s 12m 11M
Occ3s
Wid RK
Block House
LIMESTONE ROCKS
New England Rks
Green I.
Occ3s7m 11M

Q(6)+LFl.15s Horn(2)20s
Hellyhunter
Ldg Lts 310°.VB
Fl(3)10s32m 20M FR21m 9M.Horn(1)30s
CARLINGFORD cut

HOSKYN CHANNEL
Bailagan Spit

FS
Greenore
Bailagan Pt

Earl Rk
Halpin RK
FRIOM
Greenore Point
Breakwater Iso 10s9m 14M F6m
Rostrevor
Rostrevor Quay
Wood House
Killowen Pt
Y.C.
No3 KILLOWEN BANK
QG
QR No2
Red

MILL BAY
Bn Stalka Rk
Bn Brdgh'l Rock
Watson RKs
Fl G3s
Occ3s
FRIOM
FG
Greenore Pt
Quay
White
CARLINGFORD BANK

Greencastle Pt
12m 11M
Iso 10s 9m

Republic of Ireland

Priory (ruins)
Carlingford
FWR5m 2M

CARLINGFORD LOUGH
Depths in Metres

spire

N

Warrenpoint
Dobbins Pt
Spire
Rostrevor
Fl3s3M
Gannaway Rk
QF No6
Ldg Lts 310°25
Greer's Quay
Landing
Fort
No7
ROSTREVOR BAY
IQG No5
IQR No4

5 cables 0   1   2   Miles 3

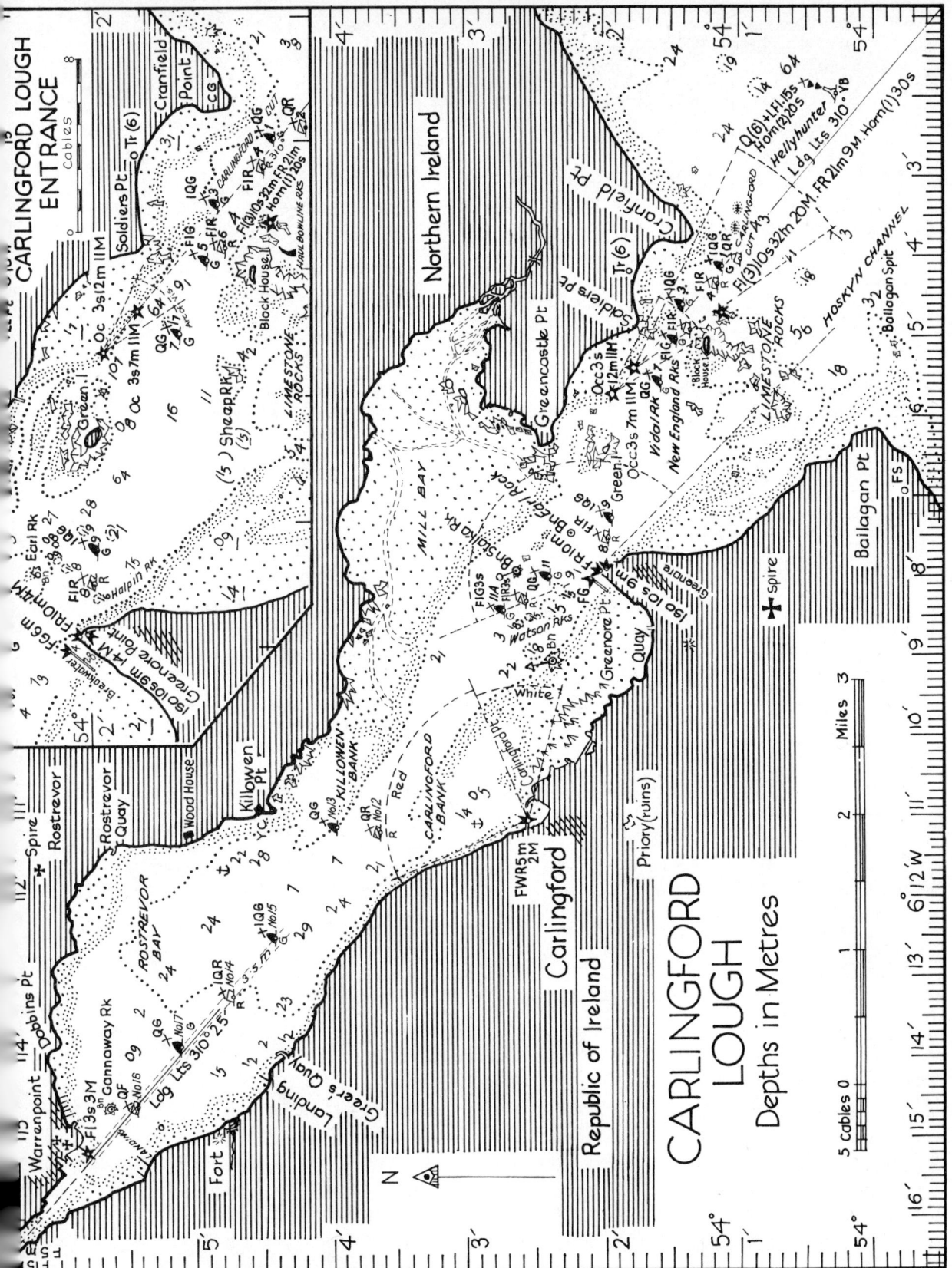

ed on British Admiralty Charts (nos. in text) with the permission of the Controller of H.M. Stationery Office and of Hydrographer of the Navy, and on other sources.

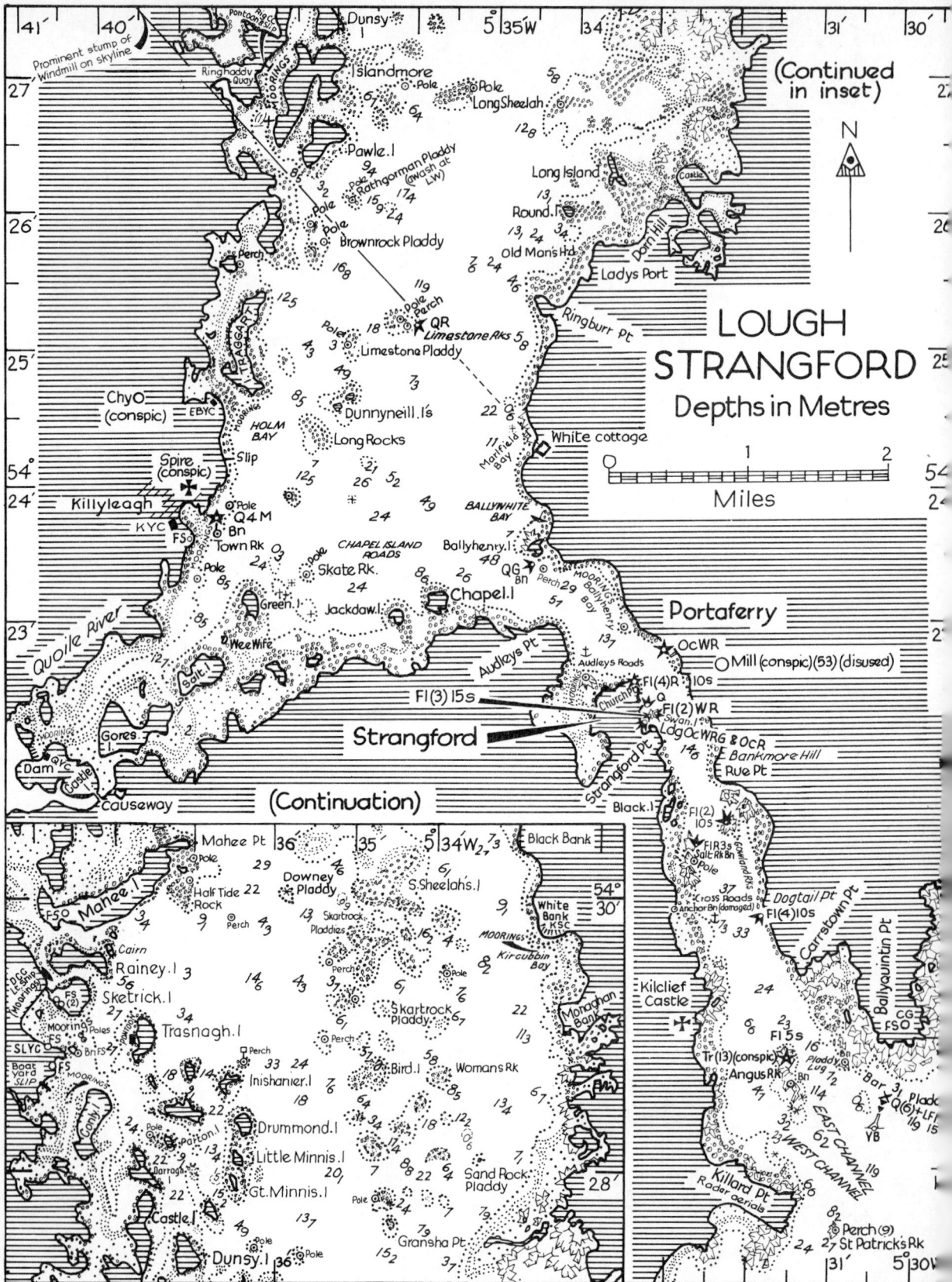

LOUGH STRANGFORD
Depths in Metres

Prominent stump of Windmill on skyline

Ringhaddy Quay

Dunsy

Islandmore

Pole

Pole Long Sheelah

Long Island

Castle

Pawle. I

Round. I

Rathgorman Pladdy (wash at LW)

Dom Hill

Old Man's Hd

Ladys Port

Pole

Pole

Brownrock Pladdy

Ringburr Pt

Pole Perch

QR Limestone Rks

Limestone Pladdy

Perch

ChyO (conspic)

EBYC

HOLM BAY

Slip

Spire (conspic)

Dunnyneill. Is

Long Rocks

Marlfield Bay

White cottage

(Continued in inset)

N

Killyleagh

KYC

Q 4 M

Bn

FSO

Town Rk

BALLYWHITE BAY

Pole

CHAPEL ISLAND ROADS

Ballyhenry. I

Skate Rk.

QG Bn

Perch

Ballyhenry Bay

Portaferry

Green. I

Jackdaw. I

Chapel. I

OcWR

Mill (conspic)(53)(disused)

Quoile River

WeeWife

Salt. I

Audleys Pt

Audleys Roads

Fl(4)R 10s

Q

Fl(2)WR

Gores. I

Dam

RYC

Castle

Strangford

Fl(3)15s

Churchbay

Strangford Pt

Ldg Oc WRG & OcR

Bankmore Hill

Rue Pt

Black. I

Fl(2)10s

Causeway

(Continuation)

(Miles scale 1 2)

Inset / Continuation

Mahee Pt

Pole

Black Bank

White Bank KSC

Half Tide Rock

Downey Pladdy

S.Sheelah's. I

Mahee I

FSO

Skartrock Pladdies

Perch

MOORINGS

Kircubbin Bay

Cairn

Rainey. I

Sketrick. I

Perch

Skartrock Pladdy

Monaghan Bank

Kilclief Castle

Fl IR3s Salt Rk Bn

Pole

Cross Roads

Anchor Bn (damaged)

Dogtail Pt

Fl(4)10s

Carrstown Pt

Ballyquintin Pt

CG FSO

FS(2)

Trasnagh. I

Poles

Bn FS

SLYG

FS

Perch

Bird. I

Womans Rk

Boat yard SLIP

Inishanier. I

Granby

Patton. I

Drummond. I

Little Minnis. I

Gt. Minnis. I

Sand Rock Pladdy

Narragh

Castle. I

Tr(13)(conspic)

Angus Rk

Fl 5s

Pladdy Lug

Bn

Bar

Q(6)+LFl

YB

EAST CHANNEL

WEST CHANNEL

Killard Pt

Radar aerials

Dunsy. I

Pole

Gransha Pt

Perch (9)

St Patrick's Rk

Berthing   Moor alongside in inner basin and seek HM's directions. Fuel, water, shipwrights. All stores in town, ½M. EC Thurs.

ARDGLASS   Chart BA 633   (Plan p302)
HW +0.25.   MHWS 4.8; MLWS 0.5; MTL 2.6; MHWN 4.0; MLWN 1.3.
Tidal streams are slight.
A pier hr 1M N of Ringfad Pt, a conical hill with tr, always available, has 2 to 3m. SE winds send in heavy swell. There is an inner basin with 3m at HW, bottom deep mud, affording perfect shelter at all times. Rks extend from both sides of the shore outside the hr entrance.
Approach   Give shore on either side a fair berth. At night: approach in the W sector of Iso 4s WRG lt on inner pier. Opposite the outer pier an iron tripod marks the rks on E side of fairway.
Entrance   Round end of outer pier close to, turn to SW and leave tripod bn marking rk NW of pier, to stb.
Anchorage   Between this bn and the quay. All supplies. Bus to Downpatrick.

STRANGFORD LOUGH   Chart BA 2156   (Plan p306)
HW Killard Pt +0.20; Strangford Quay +2.00; Killyleagh +2.10.
DS: E +2.00 for 3h; SW +5.00 for 8h.
MHWS Killard Pt 4.5; MLWS 0.5; MTL 2.5; MHWN 3.8; MLWN 1.2.
MHWS Strangford Quay 3.6; MLWS 0.4; MTL 2.0; MHWN 3.1; MLWN 0.9.
Lough Strangford is 12M long and 2M wide, a magnificent small craft area. Navigation near LW is obstructed by numerous shoals called 'pladdies'.
Bar   None in E chan.
Approach   In strong winds between SSW and E no yacht should approach or leave the entrance on the ebb, when the sea breaks heavily outside. In such conditions departure should be timed for the young flood. Otherwise enter with flood and leave with ebb.
   The stream runs true in and out of the Narrows at 2h after HW and LWD, except that immediately N of Angus Rk flood and ebb run NW and SE respectively. At Bankmore Pt the spring stream runs at 7kn.
   Guns Is, 30m high with W obelisk bn, is S of entrance. Angus Tr, Fl 5s, 13m with con topmark, is visible in the centre of the entrance, with Angus Bn, a truncated obelisk, to its left. N of entrance there is a conspic windmill above Portaferry.
   From S give St Patrick's Rk (bn), 3 ca off Killard Pt, a good berth. From N clear Bar Pladdy, 0.6m, S Card lt buoy, by keeping Ringfad Pt open of Guns Is. Alternatively, make for Strangford Fairway safe water buoy, Fl 10s; thence steer to leave Bar Pladdy buoy to stb.
Entrance   By E chan, when N end of Portaferry town comes open W of Bankmore Hill and Rue Pt steer 342°, leaving Bar Pladdy buoy to stb and Pladdy Lug W pile bn at least 1 ca to stb and Angus bn to port, into the Narrows till Kilclief castle bears 264°, when Meadows shoal has been left to port. Hence in

mid-chan to pass between Gowland Rks bn (Fl(4) 10s) to stb, and poles and bns marking shoal water to port. NW of Gowland Rks strong eddies in midstream Then anch as required. Strangers should not attempt other chans.

By night keep Dog Tail Pt (Fl(4) 10s) in line with Gowland Rks (Fl(2) 10s) 341° until Salt Rk bn (Fl R 3s) bears 330°. Keep Salt Rk bn on this bearing till Dog Tail Pt lt is abeam. Bring this lt on a bearing of 98° and sound into anchorage (1). It is risky for strangers to attempt to make other anchorages by night.

Anchorage (1) Cross Roads on W side is the nearest anchorage to the entrance, but no landing. W anchor bn on shore, and a W bn on Tully Hill (not on plan) in line 260° lead into the anchorage; anch in 3½m. (2) Ballyhenry Bay, ¼M from Portaferry town. (3) In Audleys Roads between small stone pier and perch. S and inside of this is all shoal. Other good anchs for small craft are: (4) Quoile R inside Gore's Is, 2 to 4m, and other places. (5) S of Killyleagh, 2m or more. (6) Inside Trasnagh Is, 2 to 4m off SLYC moorings. (7) S of Rainey Is, 2 to 6m. (8) S and W of Mahee Is, 4 to 6m. (9) in E winds in Kircubbin Bay, 4 to 8m. Water: taps at Ringhaddy CC pontoon and at SLYC; stores Killinchy village, 2M inland. Diesel from Morrow Marine, Killyleagh.

DONAGHADEE   Chart BA 3790

HW +0.25.   DS: N −3.00; S +6.00.
MHWS 4.0; MLWS 0.5; MTL 2.2; MHWN 3.4; MLWN 1.1.
A small pier hr, open to ENE, subject to swell in onshore winds; has 1 to 3m over E half of its area. The hr lies to S of Copeland Is. There is a small marina 3 ca S of Donaghadee Hr; visitors must first apply for permission to enter and arrange for a Pilot.

Approach Approach entrance with ch tr open to the N of S pier-head, to clear rks on either side of entrance. Allow particularly for S-going tide.

Berthing There is now little room for a visiting yacht to anchor and the hr can only be recommended for a temporary visit. Berth alongside SE quay and report to HM who can advise about entering the marina.

Petrol, stores in the town. Bus to Bangor. EC Thurs.

BELFAST LOUGH   Chart BA 1753

HW +0.05.   DS in offing: N +1.00.
MHWS 3.5; MLWS 0.4; MTL 2.0; MHWN 3.0; MLWN 1.1.
The lough is 10½M long, depths decreasing from 12 to 3m.

Approach Rounding Orlock Pt, avoid the Briggs Rks ¾M offshore, R can buoy, Gp Fl R (2) 10s.

Berthing (1) Bangor: (a) anch in Ballyholme Bay in 3½ to 5½m, or on a Ballyholme YC visitors' mooring (launch service), exposed to winds from NW to NE; (b) anch in Bangor Bay ½M to W, also exposed, or with up to 1.8m draft under lee of N pier of Bangor Hr. Shops, boatyard, chandlery, slipping facilities. (2) Cultra, 5M W of Bangor. Anch in offshore winds in 3½ to 4m outside yacht moorings. Water from RNIYC, stores nearby, boatyard and slipping facilities.

LARNE LOUGH
Depths in Metres

North Hunter Rock

Q

BY

HUNTER ROCK

Q(6)+LFl.15s

South Hunter Rock

Horn(3)30s

YB

Black Cave Hd(30)

Obscd

White

Red

White

Obscd

Red

N

52.5

Green

White

Ldg Lts 184°

DREDGED TO 9/m

Q(3)10s

No1
BYB

Barr Pt
Tr(12)Dia

Skernaghan Pt
(15)

BROWNS
BAY

Fl(2)G6s

Black Chy

Iso WRG 2s18m14.11.11M
Ferris Pt

No3

IsoWR5s 23m 11M
Chaine Tr(conspic)

Larne

FlR3s

Island
Magee

PORTRUSH
Depths in Metres
Cable

12.5

FG(vert)(occas)
FR(vert)(occas)

2FR
(vert)

Watch Tr(conspic)

FG

2FG(vert)

Fl(2)R6s

Boat
Moorings

Idn

Idn Idn

Ballylumford
Power Stn

LB

55°
12.4

2FR(occas)
(vert)
Oc8s(occas)

4 2FR(vert)

Yellow Stone

SOUTH PIER

Slip

Curran Pt

QG4

No5

QG

2FR
(vert)

61

FlG 3s 9m 6M
FlR

264°

G1

No7

Oc R10s

FIG

SOUTH
PIER

310°

0.3

A
G
R

6.1

Traffic Sigs

0.6

Oc6s(occas)

3.3

0.9

PORTRUSH BAY

0.6

0.3

3.9

5.5

39.6W

24

6 39.4'

0.3

0.6

5.3

2.1

0.9

/2

/2

/2

Glynn

Bn No 11

Oc 4s6m 12M

Artifical
Island

0.9

0.9

5°46'W

Oc 4s 14m12M

Bn No12

0.6

0.9

0.6

ased on British Admiralty Charts (nos. in text) with the permission of the Controller of H.M. Stationery Office and of
e Hydrographer of the Navy, and on other sources.

(3) Belfast Hr. Enter by dredged chan and berth as directed in Spencer Dock, past Milewater Basin on stb side of central chan (4) Carrickfergus. Alongside W pier in Carrickfergus tidal hr, or anch W of Carrickfergus Bank in 2m 2 ca offshore at Greenisland. All stores in Carrickfergus town.

LARNE LOUGH   Chart BA 1237   (Plan p309)
HW +0.10.   DS: N at HWD.
MHWS 2.8; MLWS 0.4; MTL 1.6; MHWN 2.5; MLWN 0.8.
Larne Lough affords the best shelter between Belfast and Foyle loughs. Tidal streams run strongly in the offing, 4½kn max, and raise big lop. The navigable area within the lough is considerably reduced by shoal banks on the W side. The chan carries 6m for 1½M, and 4m to 2m abreast Mill Bay.
Approach   The entrance lies 4M S of the Maidens. The approach is obstructed by Hunter Rk, 0.8m, marked by N and S card lt buoys, situated 2¼M 036° from Ferris Pt, the E pt of the entrance. On entering steer between quays to stb and two pile bns to port, Fl R 3s and Fl(2) R 6s respectively. By night ldg lts, Oc 4s, 184°, lead to the entrance.
Anchorage   (1) In 5m ¾M S of Ferris Pt Lt Ho, SW of the Yellow Stone (painted occasionally) 1 ca E of the L-shaped wharf opposite No. 7 buoy. Anch off Curran Pt is permitted NW of a line from the Pt to No. 5 buoy and SW of a line from No. 5 buoy to S end of ferry quays, but is not recommended for overnight as holding is poor. Useful for short visit to Larne. (2) Outside a shallow bay 1M SE of (1), ½ ca offshore in 2 to 3m NW of moored boats. Beware wreck ¾ ca off the shore of the bay and 1¼ ca SE of its NW tip.

Water at Wymers Pier, petrol and stores in town, diesel by arrangement with Hr office. Repairs. Ferry from Island Magee to Larne.

Ireland, North Coast

PASSAGE NOTE: FAIR HEAD TO BLOODY FORELAND

Note: A sharp lookout should be kept for salmon nets and lobster pots when navigating this coast.

Tidal streams   DS: Fair Hd to Malin Hd, WNW +01.00, ESE −0500. Malin Hd to Bloody Foreland, inshore, WSW −02.30, ENE +03.00. Malin Hd to Horn Hd, offshore, ENE, become E and SE −05.30; SW, becoming W −01.30; slack at −02.30 and from +03.00 to +06.00. Streams are strong near Fair Hd but get progressively weaker to W; 6kn in Rathlin Sound, 4kn in Inishtrahull Sound, 2kn in Tory Sound. Detailed tidal stream information and advice, beyond the scope of these notes, from ICC SDs.

Rathlin Sound, 2 to 3M wide, is the normal approach to the N coast. A fair tide is essential; the overfall SW of Rue Pt must be avoided from +01.00 to +0.300. Beware Carrickmannanon Rk, 3 ca NE of Kinbane Pt, across which the tidal streams set. Skerries Sd is convenient in moderate conditions but keep outside in swell or strong offshore winds.

Inishtrahull Sound should not be attempted if there is any sea running; in bad weather it is advisable to pass 3M N of Torr Rks.

Between Lough Swilly and Mulroy Bay the coast should be given a wide berth using the clearing marks on chart BA 2699.

Portstewart is a small hr 2½M SW of Portrush which in quiet weather is convenient for a temporary visit, and advice may be obtained about entering the Bann and a berth arranged at Coleraine Marina.

Culdaff Bay provides good anch in winds between SE and NNW, and is useful if awaiting favourable conditions for Inishtrahull Sound. Sheephaven offers fair-weather anch: see ICC.

The N coast of Ireland is most beautiful, with many interesting geological formations, including the famous Giant's Causeway, and in ideal conditions it can be an idyllic cruising ground. It must, however, never be forgotten that the whole length of the coast is completely exposed to the full weight of the Atlantic swell when the wind is from between W and N, and in established strong winds from this quarter, conditions can be such as to test even the most seaworthy and strongly crewed yacht. If conditions deteriorate suddenly there is no wholly satisfactory refuge from onshore gales, so boats cruising the coast should be prepared to keep the sea for some time before shelter can be reached. Indeed, if a strong SW-ly wind begins to show any sign of veering, it is wise to consider putting in straight away, to avoid the danger of being caught on a lee shore.

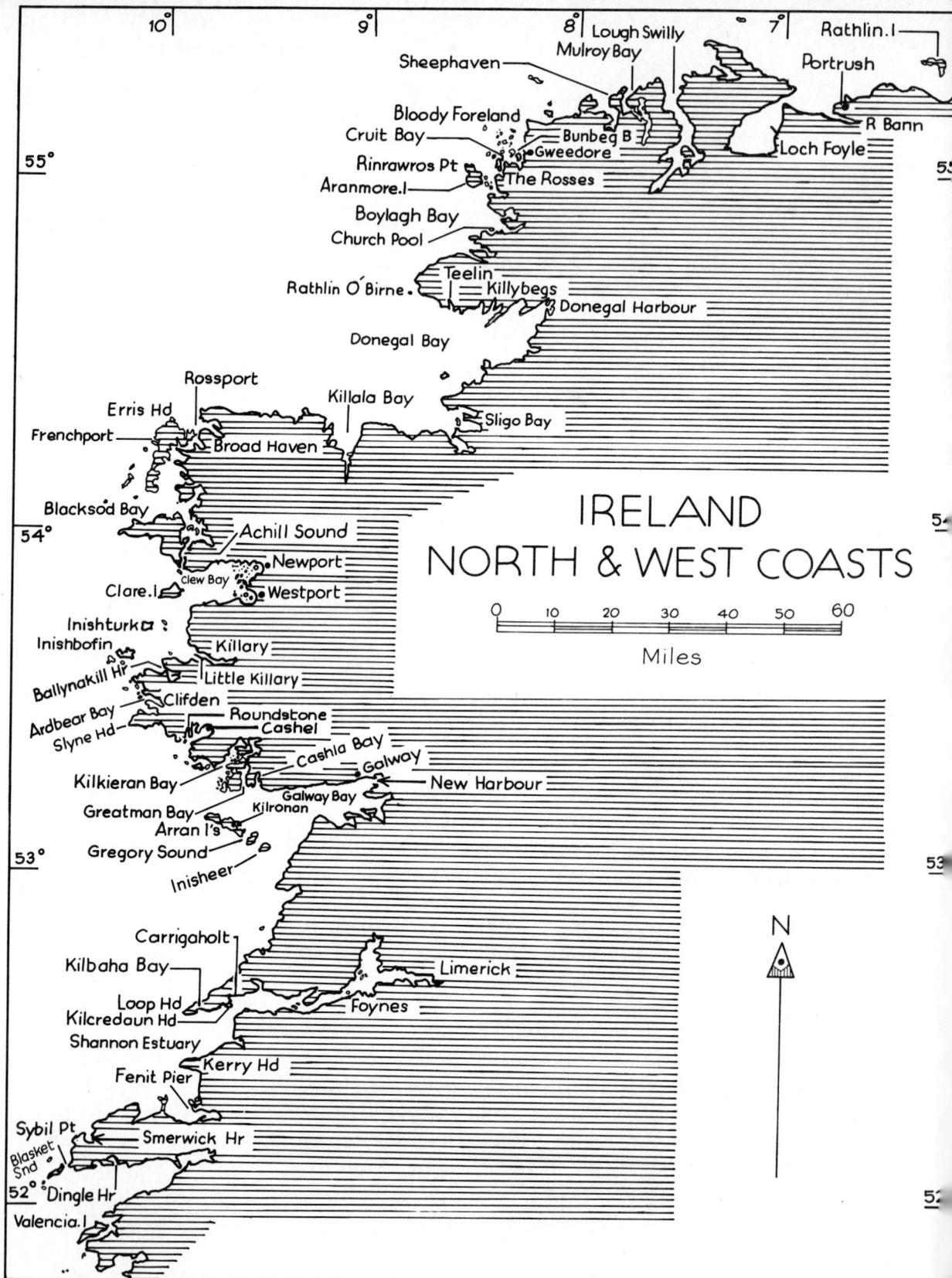

Rathlin.I

Lough Swilly
Mulroy Bay

Sheephaven

Portrush

Bloody Foreland
Cruit Bay

Bunbeg B
Gweedore

R Bann

Rinrawros Pt
Aranmore.I

The Rosses

Loch Foyle

55°

Boylagh Bay
Church Pool

Teelin

Rathlin O'Birne

Killybegs

Donegal Harbour

Donegal Bay

Rossport

Killala Bay

Erris Hd

Sligo Bay

Frenchport

Broad Haven

IRELAND
NORTH & WEST COASTS

Blacksod Bay

54°

Achill Sound

Newport

Clare.I

Clew Bay

Westport

0   10   20   30   40   50   60

Miles

Inishturk
Inishbofin

Killary

Ballynakill Hr

Little Killary

Ardbear Bay
Slyne Hd

Clifden

Roundstone
Cashel

Cashla Bay
Galway

Kilkieran Bay

New Harbour

Greatman Bay

Galway Bay
Kilronan

Arran I's

53°

Gregory Sound

Inisheer

N

Carrigaholt

Kilbaha Bay

Limerick

Loop Hd
Kilcredaun Hd

Foynes

Shannon Estuary

Kerry Hd

Fenit Pier

Sybil Pt

Smerwick Hr

Blasket
Snd

52°

Dingle Hr

Valencia.I

PORTRUSH
Chart BA 49   (Plan p309)

HW −4.10.   DS: E +6.00; W HWD.
MHWS 2.1; MLWS 0.4; MTL 1.2; MHWN 1.4; MLWN 1.1.
A small hr on W side of Ramore Hd, good shelter except in N gales.
Approach   Swell makes entrance difficult in onshore winds over force 4. Beware submerged breakwater projecting 20m SW from N pier.
Entrance   Hr has 2m in entrance, 3 to 5m inside.
Berthing   Berth alongside N quay and seek directions from hr office. Rly to Belfast and Derry; all supplies. EC Wed.

RIVER BANN
Chart BA 2723, 2798

HW (Coleraine) −3.45.   MHWS 2.1; MLWS 0.3; MTL 1.2; MHWN 1.6; MLWN 0.7.
Bar   3.7m.
Approach   River mouth is between stone training walls projecting 2 ca N from beaches. It must not be attempted in strong onshore winds or if swell is breaking noticeably on ends of training walls.
Entrance   Keep towards E wall as W side is foul with boulders. Chan 45m wide, dredged to 3m, is marked with perches, R to port, G to stb. Beware possible salmon nets across full width of river.
Berthing   (1) In Coleraine Marina on NE bank 4M from entrance. Water on pontoons, chandlery, 15T Travellift crane. Shops and fuel ½M away. (2) Anch on NE side ½M upstream of old CGS, clear of chan.

LOUGH FOYLE
Charts BA 2499, 2486.

HW −4.00 at Warren Pt; −3.20 at Moville.   DS in offing: W at HWD.
MHWS (Moville) 2.3; MLWS 0.3; MTL 1.3; MHWN 1.8; MLWN 0.8.
Approach   The big-ship approach is W of Tuns bank, leaving buoy Fl R 3s to port. A safe-water pillar buoy Fl 10s lies about 2M NE of Inishowen Hd. Yachts from E may pass between Tuns bank and shore, 4m. Approach this chan about 3 ca offshore and when ½M from Magilligan Pt move in to 2 ca offshore; beware tidal set towards Tuns bank on ebb.
Entrance   There is 3½kn springs past Magilligan Pt through the ½M wide entrance. The chan lies close to the NW shore throughout. 5M inside, the chan divides; the W chan, along N shore, is well marked by R lt bns to port and G buoys or bns to stb, some lit. The N Middle Bank, marked by bn, dries.
Anchorages   Poor and exposed to strong streams. (1) Opposite CGS at Greencastle with SW side of stn just open about ½ ca offshore in 2 to 3m. If wind comes onshore move up the lough or if this is not possible lie alongside a fishing boat in Greencastle Hr (in general unsuitable for yachts). Buoy anchor, sand. (2) Abreast Carrickarory pier in 2m; good shelter from SW, open to SE. Stream is strong outside line of pier-head. (3) At Londonderry at quay on W side below

Craigavon Br: ebb runs up to 6kn. All facilities at Londonderry apart from chandlery or boatyard.

LOUGH SWILLY   Chart BA 2697 (Plan p315)
HW (Rathmullan) −4.50. MHWS 4.3; MLWS 0.5; MTL 2.5; MHWN 3.2; MLWN 1.9.

The lough is entered between Fanad Head Lt and the bold Head of Dunaff. It is 26M long, 3½M wide, and has 15 to 20m up to Fort Stewart; bottom sand and mud.

Approach Care should be taken to carry tide through Inishtrahull Sound, where the W-going stream runs 3h only. Give W pt of entrance a berth of ½M and leave Swilly Rks G con stb buoy (Fl G 3s) to stb. By night, keep out of the R sector of Fanad Lt.

Entrance Off Dunree Hd up to Buncrana Bay, keep at least ½M clear to W, or keep Dunree Hd and Fanad Lt in line.

Anchorages (1) Portsalon Bay, 4½M inside Fanad Hd on W shore, excellent anch off the pier in 2 to 5m, large hotel. Exposed to E. (2) Fahan Creek is the most sheltered anch although uncomfortable in NW winds; the entrance is silting and the rise of the tide irregular. Yachts drawing over 1.8m should not attempt it; others are advised to enter 1–1½h before HW and leave if they ground. Anch SE of moored yachts in 2 to 5½m. Bus to Buncrana and Derry. (3) W of Macamish Pt sheltered from SE to N through W, 3 to 5m, sand. (4) Rathmullan Rd, N of pier off the town. The best place for visiting yachts; water at pier-head, small grocery, petrol, ferry to Fahan.

LOUGH MULROY   Chart BA 2699 (Plan p316)
HW (bar) −4.55. MHWS 3.9; MHWN 2.9.

Mulroy Lough affords 12M of navigable chan. A power cable across Moross Chan, clearance 10m, bars N water to yachts with higher fixed masts.

Bar 3.5m, breaks in onshore winds and big swell. It should be inspected before entering.

Approach The coast is foul on both sides of entrance. From W, Horn Hd Tr in line with Frenchman Rk (always visible), 250°, clears E and W breakers. From E, keep highest part of Dunaff Hd open of Magheraguna Pt, at W entrance to Lough Swilly, on 089°, until Melmore Hd (with ruins of tr), the W entrance to Lough Mulroy, bears 230°, when approach on that bearing.

Entrance Between Melmore Hd to W and Ballyhoorisky Pt to E. The chan now lies E of Bar Rks. High Rk only covers at highest springs, Low Rk covers at half-tide. Leave Low Rk 1 ca to stb or High Rk 2 ca. When past them, steer 207° for first narrows (4kn stream). After the narrows, keep in mid-chan till past Dundooan Rks, whence work along the W side.

Anchorage (1) N of Dundooan Rocks in 3½ to 5½m, sand. (2) Fanny's Bay on W side about 3M inside the bar in 2m affords complete shelter out of the stream at

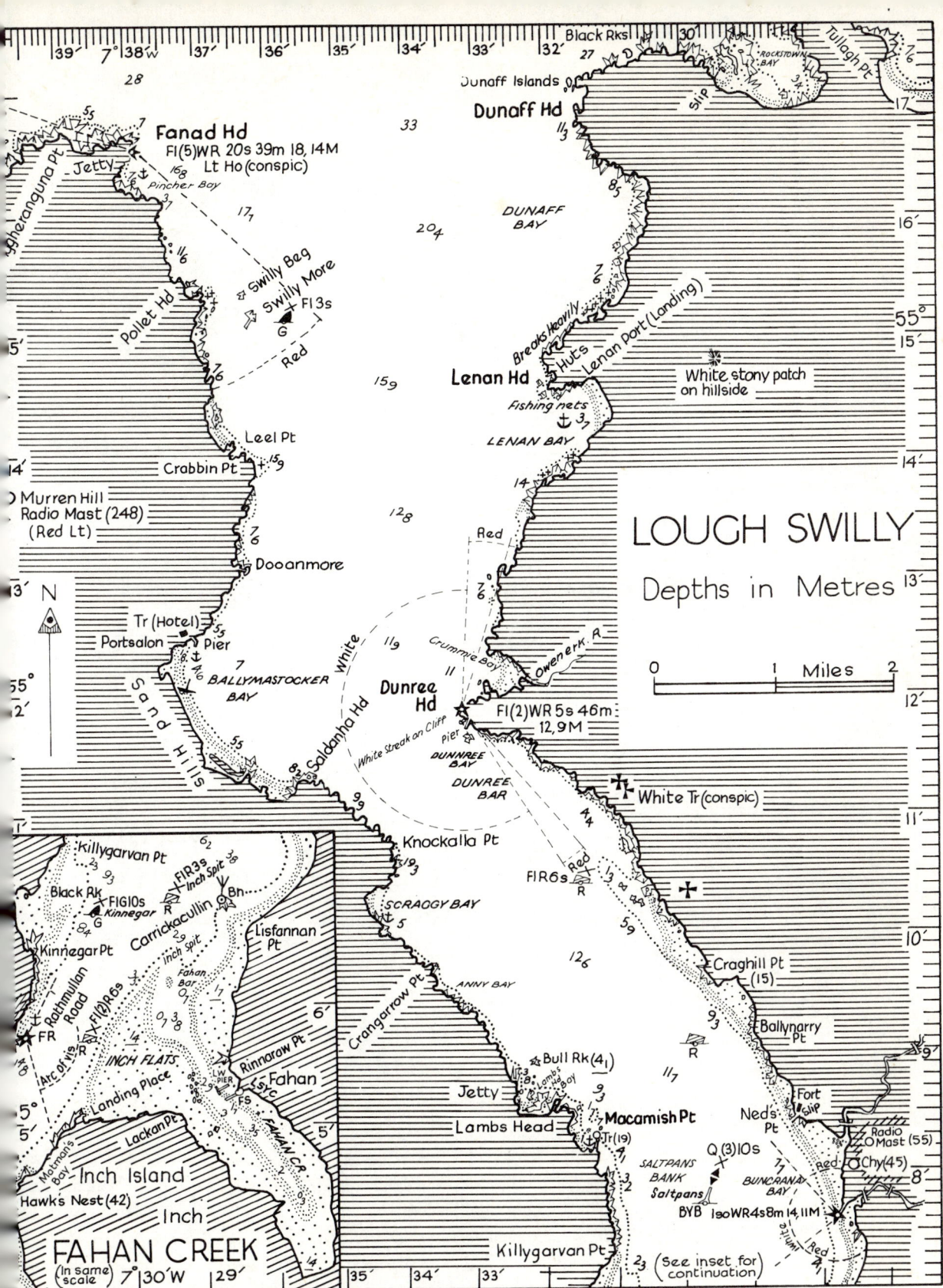

LOUGH SWILLY
Depths in Metres

39' 7°38'W 37' 36' 35' 34' 33' 32' 31' 30'

28

Black Rks
27
D
ROCKTOWN BAY
Tullagh Pt
17
34

Dunaff Islands
33

Dunaff Hd

Fanad Hd
Fl(5)WR 20s 39m 18, 14M
Lt Ho (conspic)

Gharanguna Pt
Jetty
16 8
Pincher Bay
3 7
17 1
11 6

DUNAFF BAY
204

Slip
17

16'

Pollet Hd
Swilly Beg
Swilly More
Fl 3s
G
Red

7 6

Breaks Heavily
Huts
Lenan Port (Landing)
White stony patch on hillside

159

55°
15'

5'

7 6

Lenan Hd
Fishing nets
3 7
LENAN BAY

Leel Pt
15 9

14'

Crabbin Pt
15 9

14

Murren Hill
Radio Mast (248)
(Red Lt)

128

7 6

Red

13'

3'

Dooanmore

7 6

LOUGH SWILLY
Depths in Metres

0   1   Miles   2

13'

Tr (Hotel)
Portsalon
Pier

119
White

Crummie Bay
Owen erk R
7 6

Red

55°
12'

7
5 5
4 6
BALLYMASTOCKER BAY

Soldanha Hd
White streak on Cliff

Dunree Hd
Pier
11
Fl(2)WR 5s 46m 12,9M

12'

Sand Hills

55

DUNNREE BAY
DUNREE BAR

White Tr (conspic)

11'

8 9
9 9

Knockalla Pt
9 3

4 4

Red
Fl R 6s
R

1'

Killygarvan Pt
6 2
2 3 9 3
Fl R 3s
Inch Spit
3 8
Bn

SCRAGGY BAY
5

5 9

Craghill Pt (15)

10'

Black Rk
Fl G 10s
R
Kinnegar
G
8 4
Carrickacullin
inch spit

Lisfannan Pt

12 6

ANNY BAY

9 3

Ballynarry Pt
R

Kinnegar Pt
Fahan Bar
Fl(2)R 6s
R
0 1
3 8

6'

Crangarrow Pt
Rinnaraw Pt

11 7

9'

FR
Arc of vis
R
INCH FLATS
LW PIER
Fahan
FS

6'

Bull Rk (4 1)
Lambs Boy

R

Fort Slip

Ned's Pt
Radio Mast (55)

Landing Place
Lackan Pt

5'

FAHAN CR

Jetty
Lambs Head

Macamish Pt
Tr (19)

Red
Chy(45)

8'

Matman's Bay

Inch Island
Hawk's Nest (42)

Inch

14

FAHAN CREEK
(In same scale)

Killygarvan Pt
2 3

Q(3) 10s
SALTPANS BANK
Saltpans
BYB IsoWR4s8m 14,11M
BUNCRANA BAY
Red

(See inset for continuation)

7°30'W 29' 35' 34' 33'

315

50'   **7°49'W**   **48'**   **47'**   **46'**   **45'**

Carrickannon ∘₉

Sunken Rk ₃
13₁ (BREAKERS)

8₉

Flughog Rk

28

11₃

Rinboy P

10₇

MELMORE BAY

9

East Breaker

West Breaker
4

Little Frenchman's Rk (2₄) ∘

6₇

6₈

Melmore Hd

17₁

Ballyhoorisky Pt

Tonogu

Tr (45) (ruins)

Fl3s9m 3M
Ravedy.I

Blind Rk

1₅

Quay

**55°
15'**

MELMORE ROADS

Ballyhoorisky

Shanlough Pt

12₂

8₉

Milgor Strand

Ballyhoorisky.I

3₇

10₇

5₈

18₂

BOYEECHTER BAY

11

Tormore (16)

Stowney

Long Rk

Rosses Pt

High Rk

Bar Rks

9₁

Doaghmore Pt

**55°
14'**

Carnabantry

TRANAROSSAN BAY

10₇ ROSSES STRAND

Glenoory Pt

Dualtys Isle

12

GORTNALUGHO BAY

7

FIRST NARROWS

SAND HILLS

R o s g u i l l

Dundooan Rks

10₄

Glinsk Pt

8n

13'

Knox Hole

8₅

Alcorns Hd

13'

Fl5s5m 2M

4₃

0₉

Murvan Hd

MULROY BAY

Depths in Metres

Crannoge Pt

GLINSK BAY

6₁

2₁

6₁

Drumnacraig Bay

Bullogfeme Bay

0   One Mile   1

Fanny's Bay

0₉ 2₁

7₆

6₁

Drumnacraig Pt

12'

6₁

6₁

Ardy Pt

6₁ 3₄

2₁

12'

Slip

Billy Moon's Pt

8n

5₈

Paddy's Pt

Second Narrows

Pier

Seedagh Pt

MILLSTONE BAY

2₇

CG

FR5m 2M

DONNIES BAY

F.15m 8M

Rinnoris

Hotel

Maslack Pt
(Landing at LW)

1

Island Roy

8₈

5₈

1₅

Ferry

Rawros Pt

9₈

4

Black Rk
(1₅)

7₆

6₁

2₇

Ferry pt

3₄

11'

Door of the Ship Creek

Binnanean Pt

2₁

5₈

CARRICK BAY

Marks P

7 49W   **48'**   **47'**   **46'**

Obscd

N

316

all times. PO and shop at Downings village, 1M across the peninsula dividing Sheep Haven from Mulroy. Excellent hotel at Rosapenna, ¾M. Bus to Derry. (3) In Bullogfemule, a land-locked basin on E side just above the second narrows. The third narrows or Hassans Pass has 8kn stream and should be taken at slack water. Flood begins at +4.00, ebb at −2.30.

Ireland, West Coast

This coast resembles the W coast of Scotland and the Scandinavian peninsula. In an uncharacteristically 'purple' passage, H J Hanson, who compiled the early editions of this *Handbook* almost singlehanded, wrote, 'The splendour of the mountains, their varying colours, whether in the rising or setting sunlight, by noonday or under the moon, the glory of the sea in fine weather at sundown, when it often resembles a lake of molten gold, the mighty cliffs, attaining in Donegal and Mayo to a height of nearly 2,000 ft, and the secure harbours scattered with few exceptions at easy intervals, will well repay the efforts required to reach these waters.' That is as true today as it was when it was written over fifty years ago.

Except when crossing the mouth of Donegal Bay and between Galway Bay and the Blaskets, there is usually an easily accessible hr close by. In unsettled weather a yacht may be held up to leeward of one or other of the headlands, but on such occasions most hrs afford facilities for dinghy sailing or excursions.

Although a careful and experienced skipper can in general navigate this coast with ease and confidence, it is fully exposed to the Atlantic swell. If overtaken by bad weather and poor visibility, unless a familiar anchorage is close at hand it may well be necessary to get clear of the land until the weather improves. This coast should therefore be cruised only by seaworthy yachts capable of making to windward and remaining at sea in any conditions.

Local opinion is that the sailing season starts well on in June and closes early in September, on account of the heavy swell which is usually running in the Atlantic at other times of the year. So long as there is swell in the offing, only a moderate onshore breeze is needed to bring it quickly into the coast, but from the end of June the coast is usually subject only to such seas as may be caused by local breezes or a summer gale.

Many W coast anchorages have heavy growths of kelp on the bottom, and the CQR anchor (at least in weights below 30kg) tends to clog and drag, as does the Danforth. A large fisherman is the traditional solution: the Bruce is also well thought of in some quarters. Whatever is used, it is wise to ensure that the anchor is holding, particularly in calm conditions, by reversing the motor. Vessels are advised to moor on two anchors when left unattended on such ground.

Streams are not extensively charted, but are apt to be considerably stronger off headlands giving rise to confused and possibly breaking seas with any weight of wind. Headlands such as Loop, Slyne, Achill and Erris Heads and Bloody

Foreland should be treated with the greatest respect and an offing of two to three miles lessens the chances of a shaking-up when rounding. Avoid, in all but calm periods, those areas in which the symbol for overfalls is indicated on the chart.

ICC give detailed advice on the Admiralty charts required. The Admiralty *Irish Coast Pilot* should also be carried.

The ensuing pages of this *Handbook* provide, in each of three sections of the coast between Bloody Foreland and Valentia, brief general notes followed by short notes on a selection of harbours. They indicate possible harbours of refuge for cruise planning purposes only: bad weather may make it unsafe to approach any harbour. Anyone cruising the area should regard the ICC *Sailing Directions* as essential.

PASSAGE AND CRUISING NOTES: BLOODY FORELAND TO ERRIS HEAD

The Rosses, extending 15M from the Bloody Foreland to Aranmore, afford a fascinating cruising area on the direct route for a yacht sailing round Ireland, sheltered by a string of islands and with several good anchorages. The Stag Rocks and more particularly the Bullogconnell shoals must be given a good berth.

The direct course between Rinrawros Pt on Aranmore and Rathlin O'Birne some 20M to S leads clear of dangers, but there is a strong set into Boylagh Bay.

Yachts proceeding S with insufficient time to explore Donegal Bay should make for Erris Hd (47M from Rathlin O'Birne) with the option of putting into Broadhaven or carrying on. Proceeding N on the direct passage, Rathlin O'Birne is the best landfall, with the options of making for Killybegs (or Teelin in favourable weather) or for Aranmore.

For those with more time Donegal Bay contains several interesting inlets between Sligo and Killybegs. Between Killala and Broadhaven there is a 24M stretch of inhospitable coast which should be given a wide berth in all but exceptionally calm and settled conditions.

The best harbours of refuge are Killybegs, and in S or E winds Rutland Hr inside Aranmore.

Anchorages

BUNBEG and **GWEEDORE HARBOUR** HW (Gweedore) −5.00. MHWS 3.8; MLWS 0.5; MTL 2.2; MHWN 2.9; MLWN 1.5.
Gweedore Hr, the channel to Bunbeg Quay, is sheltered by Inishinny and Carrickfin and a possible place to leave a yacht. Bar about 0.3m. The channel is lit, but as the lights cannot be relied on, strangers should not attempt to enter at night. Water at quays; shops and garage in village, ½M.

CRUIT BAY is easy of access and secure in all summer winds. Gortnasate Quay has 3m alongside; water on quay, some stores at Gortnasate ½M.

ARANMORE The island and its vicinity affords numerous anchs for small craft and, in fine weather, is a fascinating area for a prolonged visit. The best anch is in Rutland Hr between Duck Is and Inishcoo. Burtonport (2.5m alongside quay) can be reached at rise of tide from Rutland Hr. Shops, PO, water at Burtonport. There are many beacons and leading marks inside Aranmore; the lights are not absolutely reliable and strangers should not attempt the channels after dark.

CHURCH POOL   This bay, 4½M E of Dawros Hd, provides good shelter, except with wind between N and E, to the E of Inishkeel Is. No facilities on Inishkeel. Portnoo, to S of Inishkeel, provides better shelter from NE wind but is exposed to swell which can render it dangerous in any conditions of wind.

TEELIN   A picturesque natural harbour exposed to S and SW swell. Water from tap on quay; limited stores at Teelin village 1½M.

KILLYBEGS   HW −5.10.   MHWS 4.1; MLWS 0.6; MTL 2.3; MHWN 3.0; MLWN 1.5. A secure natural harbour on N side of Donegal Bay, 14M E of Rathlin O'Birne and 3M N of St John's Pt Lt Ho. Accessible by day or night in nearly all weather conditions. Its attraction for yachts has been diminished by its increasing use as a fishing port. All facilities except sailmaker.

DONEGAL HARBOUR   A reasonably accessible anch which provides shelter in pretty surroundings. Well water at house near Salthill Quay. Supplies at Donegal, accessible only by dinghy.

SLIGO HARBOUR   HW   −5.10.   MHWS   4.1;   MLWS   0.5;   MTL   2.3; MHWN 3.0; MLWN 1.5. A shallow estuary through which the Garavogue R runs from Sligo to the narrow entrance between Rosses Pt and Oyster Is. Overnight anch off Rosses Pt is possible in settled weather. Follow the directions in ICC up to the quays at Sligo. Strangers should not attempt to go beyond the E end of Oyster Is at night. All facilities at Sligo except boatbuilder and sailmaker. Rly to Dublin.

KILLALA   HW −5.10.   MHWS 3.8; MHWN 2.7. The SW corner of Killala Bay. It has a natural chan leading to a dredged chan up to the pier. The bar has 1m; although reasonably sheltered it should not be attempted in fresh NE wind. A safe but not ideal hr. Water on quay, shops and garage in Killala.

ROSSPORT   A narrow creek on E side of Broadhaven Bay affords anchorage in complete shelter but the entrance is across a bar with only 0.5m, exposed to the ocean swell: a calm sea is therefore essential. Not recommended for yachts drawing more than 1.4m. Some supplies.

BROADHAVEN   A large inlet with clear approach and a safe hr of refuge in most summer gales, but a bad NW or N gale can cause the entrance to break right across. Milk and water obtainable from cottages near Knockan Pt.

Passage and Cruising notes: Erris Head to Slyne Head

The coast from Erris Hd to Slyne Hd is deeply indented, with long stretches fronted by islands affording some protection from the swell. It is a fine day-cruising area, although not well enough lit for sailing inshore at night. There are many sheltered bays, the pick of the anchs being Broadhaven, Blacksod Bay, Clew Bay, Killary, Ballynakill, Inishbofin and Clifden. Frenchport is handy if pressed for time.

Achill Sound, given sufficient rise of tide, provides a sheltered short-cut for yachts with mast heights of less than 11m (subject to checking the clearance locally).

Blacksod Bay is a possible refuge in bad weather.

Anchorages

FRENCHPORT A small inlet providing a port of call on the direct route for yachts sailing round Ireland. Not recommended if the W-ly swell is running high. No facilities, no water.

BLACKSOD BAY HW (quay) −5.25. MHWS 3.9; MLWS 0.4; MTL 2.1; MHWN 2.9; MLWN 1.4. A good place to make for in bad weather with safe anchorages easily accessible by night or day. Shop, pub and PO at Blacksod Quay, but no fuel. Belmullet, best approached by hired car or bus from Blacksod Quay, is a good town for supplies; the quay at Belmullet dries and may have as little as 1.5m at HWN.

ACHILL SOUND at the NW corner of Clew Bay is shoal for much of its length but can be used by yachts with 1½m draft at HWN. The bridge across the sound can be opened by prior arrangement with Achill Sound Fire Brigade, but electricity cables span the opening at about 12m: local enquiries must be made about the height as it varies. Each end of the sound provides a natural haven.

CLEW BAY The head of this bay is filled with dozens of Is for a distance of 4M offshore with several good anchs between them as well as tidal chan to Newport and Westport. Do not attempt to sail among the Is at night.

NEWPORT may be made by a yacht drawing 1½m at half flood. Berth alongside quay; butcher, chemist, garage.

WESTPORT and approaches HW −5.35. There are anchorages in Dorinish Hr, Inishlyre Hr, and in the bay SE of Collanmore Is, where Mayo YC has moorings: landing on club pier N of Rosmoney Hill, 4T crane on pier which dries. The chan from Dorinish Hr to Westport, 5M, has 1.3m as far as Carricknakally, 3¾M; thence 0.6m to the quay and is marked by perches and buoys. Awaiting tide for Westport there is temporary anch S of Carricknakally. Shop, supermarket, restaurant, pub at quay. All shopping facilities at Westport town 1M. Train to Dublin.

CLARE IS. (to W of Clew Bay) and **INISHTURK** (5M further S) are well worth a visit. Both have drying hrs subject to surge in any sea or swell, and offshore anchorages sheltered from winds between SW and NW.

KILLARY BAY is a narrow inlet of great natural beauty, 8½M long. It affords secure anch according to draft, but W winds funnel up the inlet and make the usual anch at Leenane uncomfortable. Hotel, small shops, petrol at Leenane.

LITTLE KILLARY (SALRUCK) is an inlet close S of Killary Bay; its head provides a first-class yacht anch which can be entered in almost any weather given good visibility. No facilities.

BALLYNAKILL HR is a narrow bay easily entered by day which provides good refuge and excellent shelter. Among a number of anchs, Fahy Bay approached over a bar with 0.6m is one of the best in the W; water by permission at Ross Lodge, provisions at Moyand 2M by road. Barnadera Bay has a stone pier with 3.5m HWS; petrol and most supplies at Letterfrack ½M.

INISHBOFIN   HW −5.45.   MHWS 4.1; MLWS 0.5; MTL 2.3; MHWN 3.1; MLWN 1.6. Inishbofin Hr provides a secure and convenient anch but is inaccessible in strong SW wind or heavy swell. Kelp on bottom makes two anchors advisable. Some stores. Rusheen Bay on E of Inishbofin offers sheltered anch in W winds.

CLIFDEN BAY   This hr has secure anch in 4–12m in all winds, but although accessible at all times it is fronted by a large area full of rocky Is and shoals with many breakers. It is not prudent to stand into the bay unless the W bn on Carrickarone (11m) can be identified. Clifden is a good place to replenish stores. Bus to Galway. Clifden quay, 3m MHWS, can be reached at sufficient rise of tide. Further in, Ardbear Bay, across a bar with 1.1m, provides complete shelter. Boatyard with crane and slipway, engine repairs, visitors' moorings off yard, yachts looked after.

PASSAGE AND CRUISING NOTES: SLYNE HEAD TO VALENTIA

The South Connemara coast between Roundstone Bay, 15M E of Slyne Hd, and Cashla, 32M from Slyne Hd, affords a fascinating cruising ground with a wide choice of anchs among several bays.

For 20M between Cashla and Galway the N shore of Galway Bay is exposed with no safe harbours. The S side has a number of anchs between Galway and Black Hd. Thence the 45M of coast to Loop Hd has no safe anch and should be given a good offing. Passages to or from the S can be shortened by spending a night at Kilronan, Aran Is, in suitable weather conditions.

If making a direct passage between the Aran Is and Blasket Sound, note that the course from the Gregory Sound to Sybil Pt passes 7M W of Loop Hd. There is no light between Inisheer and Loop Hd (33M SW of Inisheer) and at night it is important not to get to the E of the direct course. Nor is there any major light between Loop Hd and Inishtearaight (39M). In the prevailing swell there is a pronounced set to the E for which it is wise to allow 5°.

Yachts bound between the Mayo, Sligo or Donegal coasts and the S should consider a direct Inishbofin-Valentia passage. This eliminates the inconvenience of seeking the mouth of the R Shannon with its strong ebb, dangerous when running against strong W and SW winds. The direct passage also brings one well off Slyne Head which nearly always provides a lumpy welcome to those venturing near.

There are, however, possible anchs between Loop Hd and Sybil Hd which, apart from Smerwick Hr, involve varying deviations from the direct course.

If passing through or outside the Blaskets, it is especially important to note and respect those areas where overfalls are indicated on the large-scale chart. The magnetic anomaly to the N of the Blaskets is to be treated seriously: its influence is reported as very localised but extreme enough to spin the card of a compass through 360°.

The best hrs of refuge are, in the N of the area, Roundstone and Cashla Bays, and S of Loop Hd, Dingle Hr. Yachts may also run for shelter in the R Shannon, notably at Carrigaholt.

Anchorages

ROUNDSTONE BAY and **BIRTERBUY BAY** (also known as **TRAGHBOY** or **CASHEL**) HW −5.55. MHWS 4.4; MLWS 0.5; MTL 2.5; MHWN 3.4; MLWN 1.7. These bays, which have a common approach, afford a number of secure anchs in all weathers and a fascinating sailing ground in fine weather. In heavy and thick weather from SW the whole approach is breaking water and should be avoided by strangers as the marks will probably be obscured. There is a bar 1.2m in the entrance to Roundstone. Water and provisions at Roundstone Quay and Cashel. Roundstone is a good base for cruising Connemara.

KILKIERAN BAY can be entered in almost any conditions and gives excellent shelter. Tide runs 2kn in narrows and 1½kn inland.

GREATMAN BAY may be entered at all times but has rather more rocks and slightly poorer shelter than Cashla Bay. Stream 2kn springs in narrows. Best anch is off Maurmeen Quay; a few groceries in village. Bealadangan at head of bay has anch and offers an attractive sail into the heart of Connemara at half flood; small supermarket.

CASHLA BAY is the easiest harbour in the area. There is a light at the entrance. Given sufficient visibility it is accessible at all times and affords secure anch in all winds in 4 to 6m off Struthan Quay on W side. Water at Rossaveal Quay on E side, no diesel. Shops at Carraroe 1M from Struthan Quay.

GALWAY and **NEW HARBOUR**   HW −5.55.   MHWS 5.1; MLWS 0.6; MTL 2.9; MHWN 3.9; MLWN 2.0. At Galway city there are wet docks, convenient for shopping, but Galway is now a busy commercial port. The dock gates open HW −1 to HW. For more peaceful surroundings, anch in Rinville Bay ('New Harbour' on chart BA 1984) where boats of the Galway Bay SC are based; visitors' moorings, no charge.

KILRONAN on Aran Is is a convenient port of call for yachts visiting Galway Bay and an interesting Is. to visit, but much development in recent years has made it a busy trawler port used by boats of up to 24m, which often enter or leave during darkness. The anch is uncomfortable in winds with E in them and could be untenable in E gales. There is a daily ferry to Galway and a frequent air service. Water on pier, some provisions.

KILBAHA, 3M E of Loop Hd on N shore of the entrance to the R Shannon, affords excellent temporary anch in 3m, sheltered with the wind N of W, open to S and SE. Farm produce and water obtainable.

CARRIGAHOLT   This bay 1½M N of Kilcredaun Hd gives good protection from W winds. The most convenient anch is exposed to wind and sea from S to NE; in winds between S and W a yacht can lie alongside New Pier (dries) in SW corner of bay. The Old Pier at village on N of bay is safe in all weather but has less than 2m MHWN. Groceries and petrol in village.

SHANNON ESTUARY   HW at Kilbaha Bay −5.50.   MHWS 4.3; MLWS 0.5; MTL 2.4; MHWN 3.3; MLWN 1.5. The Shannon is 50M long from Loop Hd to Limerick. The real mouth is between Kilcredaun Hd and Kerry Hd, some 11M E of Loop Hd. From there to the R Fergus, 25M, there is a stretch of sheltered water 1 to 2M wide with several good anchs protected from all but E winds and many quays and creeks for yachts that can take the ground. The best anch is in the natural hr of Foynes on the S side below the entrance to the R Fergus. Limerick Dock is inconvenient for more than a short stay as a yacht may be required to move frequently.

FENIT PIER, an artificial hr on E side of Tralee Bay, is the only place between the Blaskets and the Shannon where a yacht can lie safely in a gale from any direction. But there is no room to swing and the pier is unsuitable for lying alongside. Groceries, PO at Fenit village ½M. No petrol.

SMERWICK HR is an open bay facing NW. It is exposed to considerable ground swell but provides shelter from winds except those with N in them. There is a pier at the village of Ballynagal where there is shop, pub, phone and bus.

DINGLE HR HW +6.00. MHWS 3.8; MLWS 0.5; MTL 2.1; MHWN 2.9; MLWN 1.3. A land-locked hr with a safe entrance and free from swell, but most of it is shallow and the only alternative to berthing alongside a fishing boat at the pier is to anchor almost 1M from the pier and the town. Water and diesel on pier, all normal supplies in the town.

DENMARK AND THE SOUTHWEST BALTIC

It would be far beyond the scope of this book to attempt to deal with this magnificent cruising area in detail, but we have found it possible to include a cruise planning map together with brief entries on a number of ports and harbours. This list is by no means exhaustive, but provides basic information on a representative selection of ports covering the area most usually cruised by British yachts.

It is impossible to achieve a fully logical order in dealing with harbours in an area like Denmark, which is really a vast archipelego, and it will therefore be found that the harbours are all numbered on the cruise planning chart and a key to the numbers is provided opposite. The entries are listed in alphabetical order with German ports first, then Danish, then Swedish. This alphabetical listing facilitates looking up a harbour selected from a chart.

Routes to the Baltic
There are three main ways by which a yacht can reach the Baltic: round the Skaw; through the Limfjord, a narrow sound which runs through the northern part of the Jutland Peninsula between the North Sea and the Baltic; or by the Elbe and the Kiel Canal (Nord-Ostsee Kanal). It should be remembered that the West Jutland coast is a bleak lee shore with no really safe harbours in onshore gales, but in bad weather Helgoland is always a useful refuge. The outer part of the Elbe estuary can be extremely dangerous, particularly with an onshore wind over the ebb, and if using this route it is important to wait until the flood begins to make before attempting to go east of the Elbe 1 Light Vessel.

Charts and Pilot Books
Danish charts are excellent and easy for the English-speaking yachtsman to use. They can be obtained through J D Potter Ltd, 145 Minories, London EC3, or direct from Farvandsdirekdoratet, Esplanade 15, Ekspeditionen, 2100 Copenhagen. Other books which will be found useful are *Baltic Pilot*, by Stan Townsend, *Kommas Havnelods* and *Der Danske Havnelods*. The latter two are of course in Danish, but have valuable plans of harbours and much information

DENMARK & S.W. BALTIC
Cruise Planning Chart

SWEDEN

Lessø

KATTEGAT

29 Anholt

Limfjord   Limfjord

28

57°

25
24   23
26

27

N

JUTLAND

22   21

The Sound   59
58   60
57   61

56°

DENMARK

19
20

18   Samsø
17
16   34   33   30   32   31   62

15   **LITTLE BELT**
35   56

14   **GREAT BELT**   Copenhagen   64

Esbjerg   12   13   36   37   **Sjoelland**   55   65

Fyen I   39   38

11   41   49   54
42   40   52   53

10   43   50   51

55°   9   47
5   46   Lolland   48   **Moen**
4   44   45   **Falster**

LITTLE BELT   Langeland

3   **KIEL BAY**
2   Fehmarn

Kiel 1

Nord Ostsee kanal

Helgoland

54°   R. Elbe

GERMANY   **Miles**

R. Weser

8°   9°   10°   11°   12°

10   20   30   40   50   60

which can be easily puzzled out with the aid of a dictionary, or even without, given a basic knowledge of German. It is important to remember in this part of the Baltic that although there is no tide, the general water level can rise or fall as much as a metre as a result of weather conditions. It is therefore most dangerous to go into a harbour whose depth is shown as leaving the vessel with only a few inches to spare, as there is a danger of being 'neaped' by a change of wind and stuck for an unforseeable length of time.

Customs and other regulations change too often to be covered in this book: CA members will find up-to-date notes every year in the *Year Book*.

Southwest Baltic

CRUISE PLANNING CHART

It should be pointed out that the diphthong ae (æ) and the letter ø come at the end of the Danish alphabet. This should be noted when using Danish alphabetical lists. However, this is found difficult by English-speaking readers, particularly when occurring after a different initial letter, and we have therefore adopted the alphabetical order in English as though æ were simply those letters in an English list, while ø has been treated the same as o.

It is impossible to achieve a wholly logical order of dealing with harbours in an archipelago, but it may be worth pointing out that broadly speaking the order has been northwards from Kiel up the Little Belt to the Limfjord, on north to Skagen, south via the Great Belt, and then eastwards south of Sjælland and north up the Sound (Oresund) on the Danish side, then south down the Sound on the Swedish side.

The harbours are later listed in alphabetical order, so that they may be readily looked up from the chart, but for cruise planning purposes we have first provided a key in numerical order, so that the harbours can be readily found when using the cruise planning chart.

PORTS ON CRUISE PLANNING CHART IN NUMERICAL ORDER

1. Düsternbrook
2. Stickenhörn
3. Eckernforde
4. Marstal
5. Ærøskøbing
6. Fjællebroen
7. Søby
8. Faaborg
9. Sonderborg
10. Aabenraa
11. Assens
12. Kolding
13. Middelfart
14. Fredericia
15. Vejle
16. Kolby Kaas
17. Langør
18. Tunø
19. Aarhus
20. Ebeltoft
21. Grenaa
22. Randers
23. Hals
24. Aalborg
25. Løgstør
26. Nykøbing (Limsfjord)
27. Lemvig
28. Skagen
29. Anholt
30. Hundested
31. Frederickssund
32. Nykøbing (Sjælland)

Ports on Cruise Planning Chart in Numerical Order (*contd*)

33. Odden	44. Bagenkop	55. Køge
34. Sejerø	45. Rødby	56. København
35. Kalundborg	46. Nakskov	57. Helsingør
36. Odense	47. Spodsbjerg	58. Gilleleje
37. Kerteminde	48. Sakskøbing	59. Mölle
38. Korsør	49. Næstved	60. Viken
39. Nyborg	50. Vordingborg	61. Raa
40. Agersø	51. Stubbekøbing	62. Kyrkbacken
41. Omø	52. Kalvehave	63. Bäckviken
42. Svendborg	53. Stege	64. Limhamn
43. Rudkøbing	54. Præstø	65. Skanör

Alphabetical Key to Numbers on Chart

I German harbours

Düsternbrook	(1)	Eckernförde	(3)	Stickenhörn	(2)

II Danish harbours

Aabenraa	(10)	Kalvehave	(52)	Odden	(33)
Aalborg	(24)	Kerteminde	(37)	Odense	(36)
Aarhus	(19)	København	(56)	Omø	(41)
Ærøskøbing	(5)	Køge	(55)	Præstø	(54)
Agersø	(40)	Kolby Kaas	(16)	Randers	(22)
Anholt	(29)	Kolding	(12)	Rødby	(45)
Assens	(11)	Korsør	(38)	Rudkøbing	(43)
Bagenkop	(44)	Langelinie: see		Sakskøbing	(48)
Copenhagen: see		København		Sejerø	(34)
København		Langør	(17)	Skagen	(28)
Ebeltoft	(20)	Lemvig	(27)	Søby	(7)
Faaborg	(8)	Løgstør	(25)	Sønderborg	(9)
Fjællebroen	(6)	Marstal	(4)	Spodsbjerg	(47)
Fredericia	(14)	Middelfart	(13)	Stege	(53)
Frederikssund	(31)	Næstved	(49)	Stubbekøbing	(51)
Gilleleje	(58)	Nakskov	(46)	Svendborg	(42)
Grenaa	(21)	Nyborg	(39)	Thyborøn: see	
Hals	(23)	Nykøbing		Danish North Sea	
Helsingør	(57)	(Limfjord)	(26)	Tunø	(18)
Hundested	(30)	Nykøbing		Vejle	(15)
Kalundborg	(35)	(Sjælland)	(32)	Vordingborg	(50)

III Swedish harbours

Bäckviken	(63)	Limhamn	(64)	Raa	(61)
Kyrkbacken	(62)	Mölle	(59)	Skanör	(65)
				Viken	(60)

GERMAN HARBOURS

Düsternbrook (1). Large yacht hr near centre of Kiel. Visitors proceed to central pier Basin 1 and enquire for berths. Showers and meals at Kiel YC, buses to town.

Eckernförde (3). There is a new yacht hr between the naval base and the fishing hr. Visitors' moorings, YC. All stores, good bathing.

Stickenhörn (2). The home port of the British Kiel YC. Most friendly, all facilities and assistance, but yachts must not be left unattended for security reasons.

DANISH HARBOURS

Aabenraa (10). Busy commercial hr at W end of fjord. Entrance marked by spars, ldg lts at night. The SC have jetties on the E side of the New Hr (Nyhavn) (the N-most of the three) and there may be a berth there. Otherwise go alongside the end wall of the Old Hr (Gammelhavn), the centre of the three. All stores.

Aalborg (24), Limfjord. There is a marina just W of the two bridges, 2m. All stores, food from YC.

Aarhus (19). The second largest city in Denmark. The yacht hr is separate, with an entrance NW of that of the main hr. Three yacht clubs, fuel cheaper in main hr.

Ærøskøbing (5). On the island of Ærø: beautiful, but usually crowded. The town is a famous showpiece and well worth a visit. Stores, few facilities.

Agersø (40). The hr lies on the E side of the Is, 2.8m. Keep to the left or right after entering to avoid slipway running down the centre of the hr. Crowded but helpful.

Anholt (29). Hr lies near the NW point of the Is. The N side of the Is is all sand dunes, and it is a great mecca for visiting Danish yachtsmen. Yachts generally moor on the W mole of the inner basin, bows-on with a stern anchor. Good facilities, often crowded.

Assens (11). The yacht hr is in the SW corner of the area enclosed by the main breakwater, 2.5m. Good supplies, all facilities.

Bagenkop (44). The nearest Danish hr to Kiel. Yachts moor in the NE-most basin, No. 3. Some stores and facilities. Ldg lts 110°.

Ebeltoft (20). A charming town, and has a new marina S of the old hr. Follow the W quay of the commercial hr southwards, and the marina entrance is easily found. All facilities; the town is a showpiece and well worth a visit.

Faaborg (8). Yachts moor alongside on the NE wall, reported expensive. Approaches well buoyed. All supplies and facilities, interesting town.

Fjællebroen (6). A major yachting hr on the S coast of Fyn. Entrance is buoyed, important to keep in chan. Berth on the mole at either side of the entrance or as directed. All facilities.

Fredericia (4). Yachts berth in the old hr, the most E-ly basin. Highly industrial, and Middelfart (q.v.) is to be preferred.

Frederickssund (31). A busy hr in the Roskildefjord, just S of the Prince Frederick Br, which must be passed before entering the hr. Flag 'N' (or national ensign) at half-mast on the signal halyard, and **N** $(-\cdot)$ in Morse on the foghorn is the signal to open the br. Yachts moor in the small outer basin on the N side of the new hr, 2.7m. Some facilities.

Gilleleje (59). Crowded and busy hr. Yachts berth on E side of S basin. Rather dirty and not very attractive town, but a useful stopping place on the way to the Sound.

Grenaa (21). On the E coast of Jutland, and a useful staging point. Yachts berth in the N hr, or on the W wall of the S hr. All supplies.

Hals (23). A useful hr at the E end of the Limfjord. Entrance is narrow, beware cross-currents. There is a tidal range of up to $\frac{1}{2}$m. Berth in the SW basin, stores, few facilities.

Helsingør (57). This is Shakespeare's Elsinore, and the castle (Kronborg) can be visited. Yachts use the N hr, on the N side of the town, always crowded; berth as opportunity offers. All stores and facilities, YCs. Trains to Copenhagen.

Hundested (30). A busy hr on the E side of the entrance to the Isefjord, N Sjælland. Yachts berth in the S hr on the S or W side. Good supplies, yacht yard.

Kalundborg (35). An important ferry and commercial hr on W Sjælland. The yacht club can be approached by a buoyed channel. It lies outside the hr beneath two large radio masts to the W. Otherwise berth in W hr, all stores and facilities.

Kalvehave (52). A small and often shallow hr in the Ulvsund. Enter from the S, and moor on the E side of the basin. Some facilities.

Kerteminde (37). On the E side of Fyn. There is now a yacht hr with an entrance some 200m N of the commercial hr, although large yachts still moor on the N side of the latter. Easy approach, good stores, chandlery, YC.

København (*Copenhagen*) (56). The official city YC is Langelinie, almost in the middle of town, a few yards N of the Little Mermaid statue. Yachts berth between a buoy and the jetties. The hr is uncomfortable from the wash of passing ships: perhaps for this reason there is usually a berth, but if not it is worth trying Svanemølle, $2\frac{1}{2}$M by water along the chan to the N. This is a large marina; berth as opportunity offers. There is also a very small hr at Tuborg, which sometimes has room. All facilities, but Langelinie is surprisingly far from supplies as it is surrounded by parks and gardens.

Køge (55). A useful hr S of Copenhagen. Moor in the inner hr near the W end of the N quay. Good supplies, interesting town.

Kolby Kaas (16). On the W side of Samsø. Yachts moor on the W or S sides of the S basin. Keep W of the two buoys marking shoal water on their E side. Limited stores; the main village is a mile from the hr.

Kolding (12). The importance of this hr is mainly that it is only one hour by train from Esbjerg, which has regular ferry connections with Harwich. It is therefore useful for changing crews, etc. There is a marina immediately to the N after entering the hr, with fuel, and a good chandler. Limited toilets, and the main town and supplies is a 20 min. walk.

Korsør (38). A major commercial and naval hr on the W of Sjælland. Berth in the yacht hr, on the S side of the outer part of the main hr. Beware currents in approach, and heavy ferry traffic. All facilities.

Langør (17). On the NE side of Samsø. A pretty hr in beautiful surroundings, buoyed but not lit. Berth on the quays as space allows, 2.5m, but this may be lowered by as much as 1m in S winds. Modest stores.

Lemvig (27) has a dredged channel, buoyed, with ldg lts on 171½°. Moor in the fishing hr, although better shelter in bad weather in the middle hr. All facilities, beautiful town.

Løgstør (25). A large hr in the middle of the Limfjord. Moor in either of the two more western basins, as space allows. All stores.

Marstal (4). At the E end of Ærø, usually very crowded, mostly with German yachts. Moor as space allows at the S end of the hr, probably at jetties Nos. 2, 3, 6 or 8. A most beautiful town, with an interesting old ship museum. All facilities.

Middelfart (13). A useful small hr near Fredericia, and cleaner and more comfortable. Moor alongside as opportunity offers. Diesel from fishmonger, all stores.

Næstved (49). An industrial hr reached through a long dredged chan. Not normally used by yachts, but an interesting town. The W basin has 6m, the E basin 2m, yachts berth as space allows. All stores, usefully placed.

Nakskof (46). This large commercial hr is seldom visited by yachts, but is most interesting and worth the detour. The dredged chan is well marked. Berth near the E end of the N quay or as directed. All stores, interesting church.

Nyborg (39). A major ferry hr on the E coast of Fyn. The yacht hr has its own entrance W of the main hr, and the small E hr (at the NE end of the main hr) is also reserved for yachts. New marina with its own special buoyed channel. All supplies and facilities, interesting castle, well worth a visit.

Nykøbing (*Limfjord*) (26). One of three hrs of this name, it is a useful stop on passage to the Limfjord. There is a dredged channel, well buoyed, with 4.5m. Moor along the W wall by the hr office. All supplies and facilities, pleasant town.

Nykøbing (*Sjælland*) (32). In the Isefjord, entered by a well buoyed channel. Large yachts berth in the SW basin, small ones along the E jetty. Good stores.

Odden (33). Main importance to yachtsmen of this busy fishing town is that it fills a considerable gap between usable hrs. Deep-draft yachts moor in the outer hr alongside the N wall, small ones may find a berth in the inner basin. Considerable wash. Some supplies, few facilities. Diesel.

Odense (36) is Denmark's third city. Danish chart 115 is needed for entry. There is a yacht basin at Stige, or yachts can moor alongside the E wall of the middle basin. The town was the birthplace of Hans Andersen, and has impressive buildings and museums. An industrial hr, but worth a visit.

Omø (41). Very small, but good shelter once inside. Max depth 2.2m, but there are shallow patches on both sides of the hr. It is also possible to anchor nearby. Beautiful unspoilt island. Simple stores, some way away.

Præstø (54). There are considerable yacht moorings to the E of this hr, but depth is only 1.5m and deep-draft vessels berth at the yacht jetties in the hr. Excellent stores. An attractive town in beautiful surroundings.

Randers (22). A large commercial hr on the NE coast of Jutland, usefully placed. Yachts approach by the well buoyed chan and use the N basin, which has a yacht hr, or it may be possible to berth at the W end of the basin, considerably nearer the shops. Good supplies, few facilities.

Rødby (45). A usefully placed hr if going to the Sound by the outside route. Heavy ferry traffic. Yachts berth in N basin, on the E or N quays, 5m. A few shops, no facilities.

Rudkøbing (43). Largest town on Langeland, with a yacht hr NE of the two commercial hrs. It has 2.2m; visitors berth at the W end of the N mole. The town has some interesting old buildings. Good stores and facilities.

Sakskøbing (48). Approached through a dredged chan, which must not be attempted at night. Berth as space allows, modest supplies.

Sejerø (34). This hr lies on the S side of the island, NW of Sjælland. Keep well clear of the W mole when entering: there is a wreck off the end. Moor in the inner part of the main hr, bows to the jetty, stern to post, facing SE. There is a wooden jetty for small yachts in the NE corner. Good supplies, interesting village, 10 min. walk. Small yachts may be able to find space in the old hr, but its entrance is less than 10m wide. Only attempt with reliable power.

Skagen (28) is the most N-ly town in Denmark, and the first hr available after approaching via the Skaw. Current can set strongly across the entrance. Yachts enter the SW half of the inner hr and moor to the N side of pier 1 in the middle basin, or as directed. All facilities and supplies. Interesting museum.

Søby (7). Useful hr at the N end of Ærø. Yachts moor on the S side of the central mole, or in the SE corner of the inner basin. Store near hr, otherwise supplies in village, good bathing beach to the SW.

Sønderborg (9). A large crowded hr on the island of Als. There is a small yacht hr on the E side of the entrance, but it is usually full and it is best to berth at the N end of the long wooden quay on the E side of the main hr, usually several deep. All facilities.

Spodsbjerg (47). A useful hr on the E side of Langeland. Yachts berth in the S, fishing harbour, on the S mole just inside the entrance or as opportunity offers. Limited stores.

Stege (53). This hr is approached by a dredged channel and is lit. The yacht hr is the first entrance on the port (NE) side, 2.5m. Some supplies, interesting old houses in the town.

Stubbekøbing (51). A useful hr on the way to Copenhagen from the S. The approach is well lit and buoyed. Yachts berth in the E basin, at the W end of the S wall. Good supplies, welcoming YC.

Svendborg (42). The approach to this large town is intricate but well buoyed: Danish chart 170 is recommended. The current in the sound can run up to 5 or 6kn. The yacht hr lies between Taasinge Br and the town, 2.5m, but visiting yachts often use the commercial hr, berthing on wooden jetties in the NW corner. All supplies and facilities. A popular tourist resort.

Tunø (18). A small hr on a beautiful small island. Yachts berth on the N side of the outer hr, 3m, crowded in season. Usually necessary to use a stern anchor, which should be ready before entry. Limited supplies, and most attractive surroundings.

Vejle (15). A rather dull town at the end of a most beautiful fjord. The yacht basin is on the N side inside the entrance, supplies 10 min. walk. Visitors may also moor at the W end of the commercial hr. All stores.

Vordingborg (50). Yachts use the N hr, by the buoyed channel. The yacht basin has about 2m, but often less in good weather. Friendly clubhouse. Some supplies, castle and museum. If lack of space or water, proceed past yacht hr and moor alongside town quay.

SWEDISH HARBOURS

Bäckviken (63). On the E side of Ven, slightly exposed to E or NE winds. Berth as space allows (only 1½m at W end of S mole). The surrounding area is most beautiful.

Kyrkbacken (62). On the W coast of Ven, slightly open to strong W winds. Yachts berth on the W or N side of the hr, 3m. Some stores, no facilities. Beautiful area, good bathing.

Limhamn (64). A large new yacht hr, just to the S of the old commercial hr. The entrance is buoyed, and visitors' berths are at the end of jetty K. Provisions from block overlooking hr, bus to Malmö.

Mölle (59). This pleasant, clean little hr lies just S of the point of the Kullen. There are ldg marks by day, lit by night. Berth on the W mole, usually stern to anchor. Good stores, few yacht facilities.

Raa (61). A large yachting centre serving Halsingborg. The yacht hr is to the S immediately after the entrance, berths usually available for visitors. It has 2.5m; larger yachts can berth in the old hr. Good shops, but a long way from the yacht hr.

Skanör (65). A fishing hr with considerable provision for yachts. Moor along the outer end of the N mole or at the end of the central jetty. Smaller boats can berth between posts and jetty. Heavy swell in NW winds. Meals at SC, good stores, good bathing.

Viken (60). A pleasant hr for small yachts N of Halsingborg. There is just under 2m inside but less in some conditions. Berth on the W or N quays. Limited supplies, no facilities.

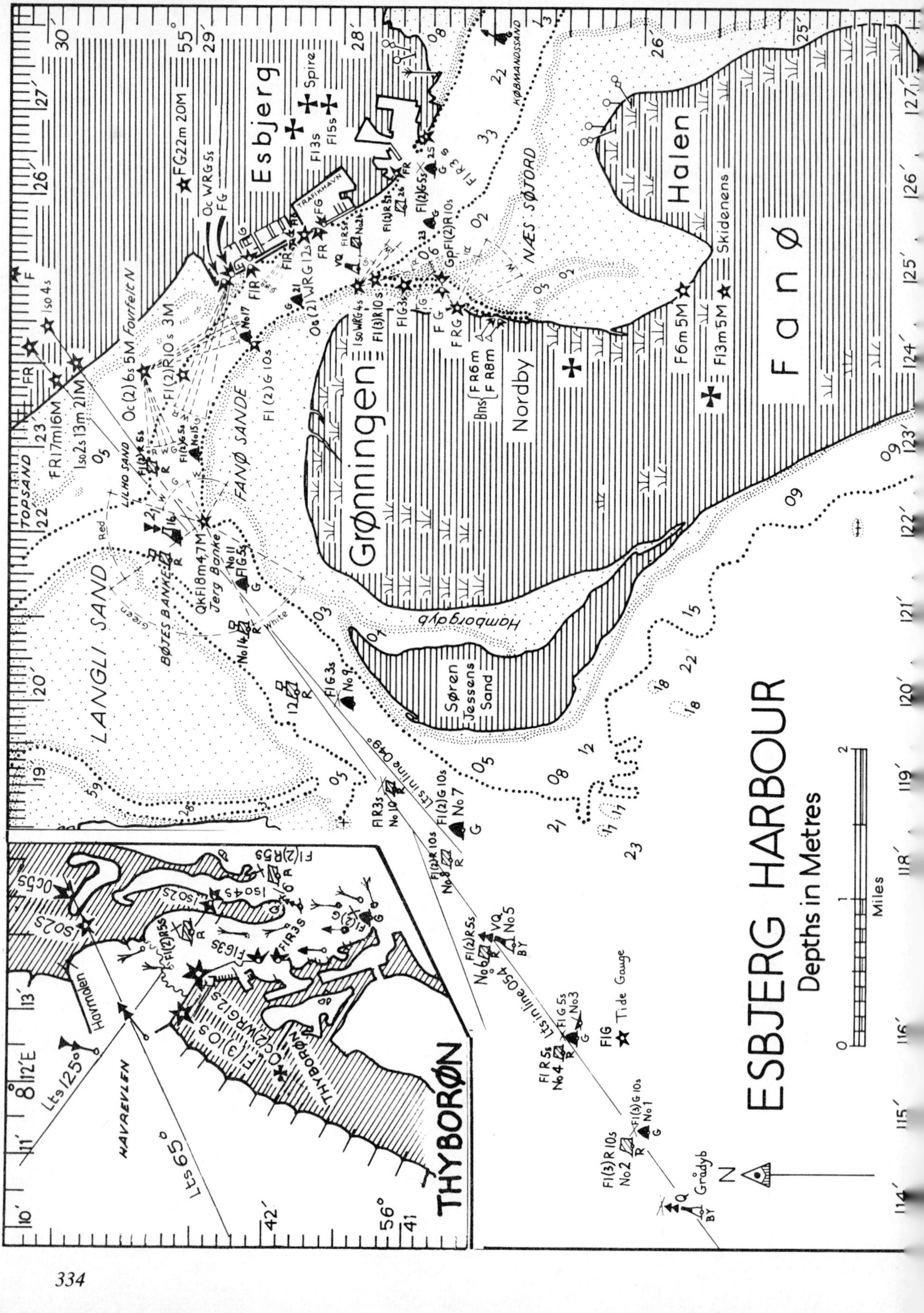

ESBJERG HARBOUR

Depths in Metres

Esbjerg

THYBORØN

Fanø

Halen

Nordby

Grønningen

LANGLI SAND

TOPSAND

FANØ SANDE

Søren Jessens Sand

NÆS SØTORD

Hamborgdyb

Skidenens

Kjøbmandssand

BØJES BANKE

LILHØ SAND

Jerg Banke

HAVREVLEN

Havmølen

Lts 125°
Lts 65°

Lts in line 049°

Grådyb

Tide Gauge

Miles

N

Denmark: North Sea Coast

THYBORØN   Chart BA 2325, Dan 104 (Plan p334)
HW +5.00.   MHWS 0.4; MLWS 0.0; MTL 0.2; MHWN 0.3; MLWN 0.1.
Tidal rise and fall are negligible, and stream is more influenced by wind than tidal
changes. With established W winds there is usually a current into the hr; with
established E winds current flows out. Currents usually run at 1–2kn, but can
reach 6–8kn after prolonged gales.
    The hr lies at the W end of the Limfjord, through which the Baltic can be
reached, but it must not be approached in strong onshore winds.
Bar   5m, but seas break heavily in strong onshore winds, particularly if current
is still westerly.
Approach   Other than the bar there are no hazards offshore. Steer to pass 500m
N of the southern side of the ent, leaving buoys with N cone topmarks to stb.
Entrance and berthing   Steer south along the chan, enter the hr by the first ent,
and proceed to the northernmost inner hr, where berths are usually available
alongside the E wall. Look out for strong stream in the chan and across the hr
ent. All stores, Customs.

ESBJERG   (Plan p334)
HW +2.00   MHWS 1.6; MLWS −0.1; MTL 0.8; MHWN 1.4; MLWN 0.2.
This hr has no special provision for yachts, but is included as the only port of
refuge on an otherwise bleak lee shore.
Approach   Heavy traffic passing in and out of the hr is usually the best
identification. The chan is well buoyed, and the first leading line is visible 16M
offshore.
Entrance   Follow the buoyed chan round to the E and SE.
Berthing   On arrival, proceed to the SW corner of the Trafikhaven and enquire
for a more permanent berth. The hr keeps a 24-hour watch on VHF 16. All
stores, Customs.

ESBJERG TO BLANKENBERGE AND THE FRENCH BORDER

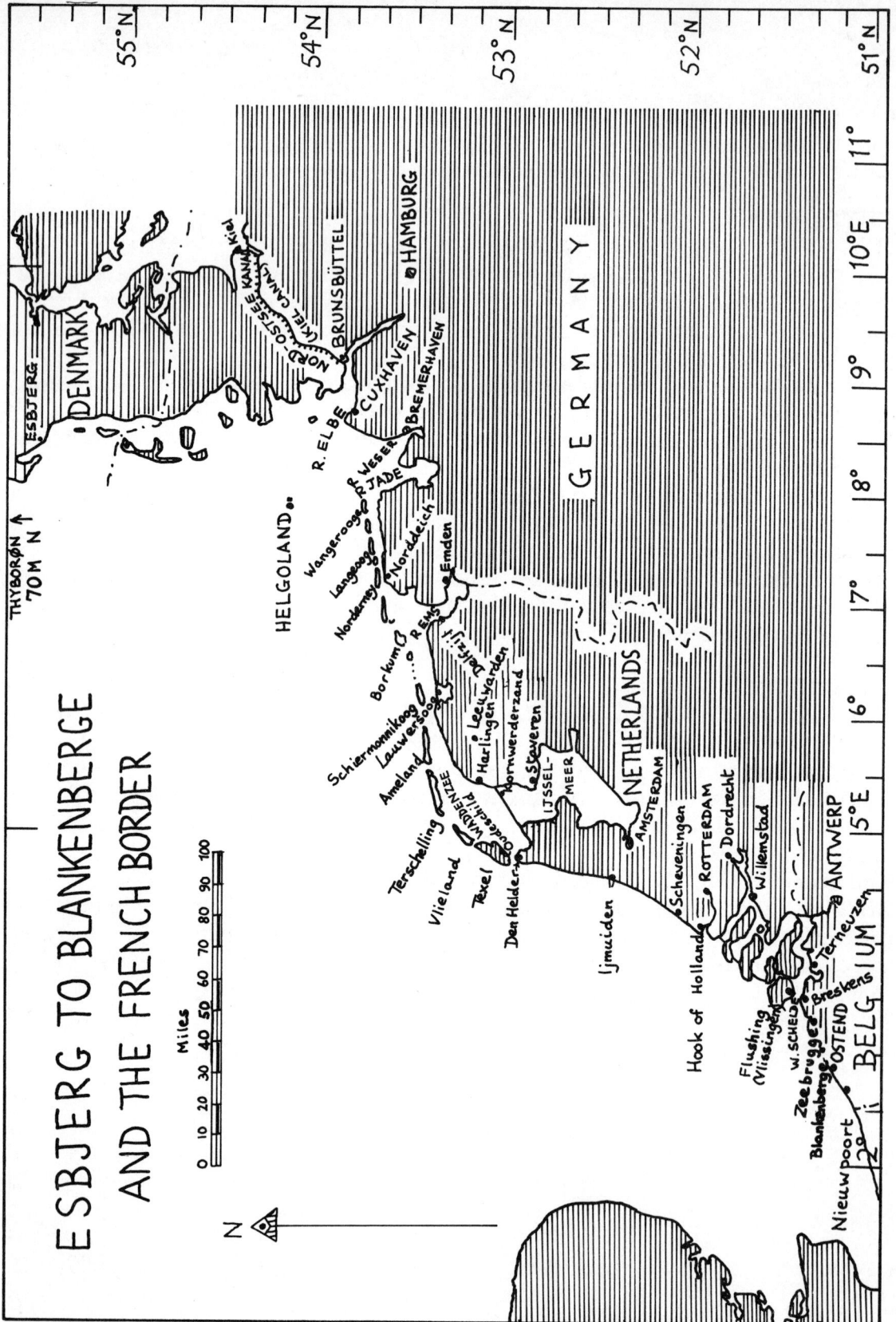

N

Miles
0 10 20 30 40 50 60 70 80 90 100

DENMARK

ESBJERG

THYBORØN
70 M N

NORD-OSTSEE KANAL / KIEL CANAL
Kiel

BRUNSBÜTTEL

HAMBURG

CUXHAVEN

R. ELBE

BREMERHAVEN

R. WESER

R. JADE

HELGOLAND

Wangerooge

Langeoog

Norderney

Norddeich

Emden

Borkum

R. EMS

Juist

Schiermonnikoog

Lauwersoog

Leeuwarden

Harlingen

Ameland

Dornwerderzand

Staveren

IJSSEL-MEER

Terschelling

Vlieland

WADDENZEE

Texel

Den Helder

Ijmuiden

AMSTERDAM

Scheveningen

ROTTERDAM

Hook of Holland

Dordrecht

Willemstad

ANTWERP

W. SCHELDE

Terneuzen

Flushing (Vlissingen)

Breskens

Zeebrugge

OSTEND

Blankenberge

Nieuwpoort

BELGIUM

NETHERLANDS

GERMANY

336

GERMANY

The German North Sea coast is an interesting but wild area, with strong tidal streams and few harbours that are accessible in all weathers. It is usually possible to enter the main ones in onshore gales, but impossible to put to sea from them in similar conditions, as the wind is then against the stream.

Passage notes: Brunsbüttel to the Ems

Going W, the problem is, as already stated, getting out of the River Elbe, as the seas become dangerous in strong winds against the tide, while few yachts have enough power to make headway against both wind and the stream, which can run up to 5kn. Helgoland provides the only all-weather hr in the German Bight until the R Ems is reached, passing round the N and W sides of Borkum. If caught in a NW gale in the E part of the Bight, it is possible to run for shelter into the R Jade, where Hooksiel provides a safe refuge. Like the Elbe, the Jade should only be entered on the flood in onshore gales.

KIEL CANAL (see also Brunsbüttel)   Chart G 42

The canal is known as the Nord-Ostsee Kanal in German. Instructions (*Merkblatt für die Sportschiffahrt auf den Nord-Ostsee Kanal*) and chart available at locks. Length 53M. Dues payable at locks either end (report at lock office with ship's papers). Duty-free stores obtainable at Gieselau staging berths and from fuel barge at Kiel locks. Sailing, except motor-sailing, not permitted. Yachts may not travel at night or in bad visibility. Speed limit 15 kph, less in branches. Berthing along banks prohibited, and precluded by wash. Permitted yacht staging berths: Brunsbüttel Yacht Hr (Km 1.8); by Dükerswisch Bridge (Km 21.5); by Gieselau Lock (turn off to N at Km 40.5); in the R Eider (turn off to N at Km 66) at Rendsburg in the official yacht hr past a small marina and yacht moorings; at Borgstedter Enge (Km 70); or in the Flemhudersee (turn off to S at Km 85.4). The Kiel-Holtenau YC (Km 98.5) is on the Baltic side of the lock at staging; outside for tugs etc, inside for yachts, all facilities on quay to E, key for showers from lock-keeper's office to W.

Light signals for entry into locks: W over G is for commercial traffic. Yachts must wait for single W lt. 3 R (vert) lts shown in the canal is the only signal applying to yachts: all movement prohibited while displayed.

BRUNSBÜTTEL   Chart G 45   (Plan p339)
HW +1.45.   MHWS 2.9; MLWS 0.0; MTL 1.4; MHWN 2.6; MLWN 0.3.
This is the entry port for the Kiel Canal, and if bound for the Canal it is best to lock in and proceed straight to the yacht hr on the N bank.
Approach   The approach is well buoyed: yachts should wait E of the E mole until the single side light for entry is shown, and not obstruct the manoeuvres of commercial ships entering or leaving the locks.
Entrance and berthing   Through the locks (dues) and into the yacht hr: berth as directed or as space allows. All facilities and supplies. Duty-free diesel about ½M along Canal. If passing through the Canal without visiting Germany, fly the International Code Flag 3rd Substitute. This also applies to the approach up the Elbe.
Altenhafen   Yachts visiting Brunsbüttel, but not intending to use the Canal, can save the expense of the locks by entering the Altenhafen, just W of the lock entrances. There is 1.7m at half-tide in the entrance. Moor alongside guest pontoon on the E bank, dries to soft mud; keelboats dry upright. All stores.

CUXHAVEN   Chart G44   (Plan p339)
HW +0.45.   MHWS 3.2; MLWS −0.1; MTL 1.5; MHWN 2.8; MLWN 0.3.
This hr now has one of the largest of all the German North Sea yacht fleets, and an excellent yacht hr.
Approach   The chan is well buoyed from both directions, and the yacht hr entrance lies immediately NW of the very conspicuous radar tower in front of the lighthouse. Up-river traffic should have no problem, but descending from Brunsbüttel the necessity to cut across the busy traffic in the river requires reliable power and steady nerves.
Entrance   Straightforward, but beware the strong stream across the entrance, which can reach 5kn.
Berthing   Pontoon berths as space allows. Water and showers; diesel in the Altenhafen, the next basin to the SE. Stores from town, long walk. YC, showers, toilets.

RIVER ELBE
HW (Scharhörn) −0.05   (Plan p339)
This river is bounded by shoals and sandbanks that run far out to sea. Very severe seas occur in wind over tide conditions, and with W or NW gales the river must on no account be entered until the flood has begun. Until then, keep W of the Elbe 1 LV. The chan is well buoyed, but traffic is very heavy and yachts must keep right over to the stb side of the chan. If passing through the Canal without visiting Germany, International Code Flag 3rd Substitute should be flown.

RIVER ELBE

Depths in Metres

...ed on British Admiralty Charts (nos. in text) with the permission of the Controller of H.M. Stationery Office and of Hydrographer of the Navy, and on other sources.

339

29 54 52 15 8 53' 54 (0₂) HÖV (0₃) 6 29
19 (0₁) WITKLIFF (0₁) (0₃)
65 09 NATHURN (0₁) (0₁) BRUNN 09
Inseldamm 08 BRUNN 6 (0₁) Kalberdans
28 07 06 8 (0₁) (0₃)
HENGST Nordhorn 06 No5 (0₂) 23
KASTEAL HORN WRW DÜNENDAMM WEST
FLAGGENBURG HORN GWR
GÖRTEL o Radio mast DÜNE
(50) DÜNEN IsoWRG 4s
11' HELGOLAND HAFEN G 14,11,10M
GpOcc(3)WRG FR
BLOCKHORN Nordost RC hafen
RC Fl5s WAL 21 09 07
82m 28M Oben m
Radio Mast(80) 06 28
19 OccR BY8
OccR FWG B3 SÜD AADE
FWG B8 RWG BRUNI
03 FWR B1 REEDE
Binnenhafen B6 B4 27
SATHURN SÜDHAFEN B2 No5 G
BRUNN 59 R
16 Westmole Südkaje Pontoons 64 Ostmole OcWG6s
27 VORHAFEN 81 FlG4s
GÖRTEL KANT Bn FG(Nauto) G No3
GpOcc(2)R Green
AFGANG 12s No6 DANSKERMANNS
54° Südmole R HORN
10' 42 34
(0₃) No1
HOG STEAN G

HELGOLAND

Depths in Metres

0   Mile   1

Hogstean
No4 R

No2
R Lights in Line 20°

VQkFl(3)5s
7° 52' E 53' BYB Helgoland 54'

340

HELGOLAND   Chart G88   (Plan p340)
HW −0.25.   MHWS 2.6; MLWS 0.0; MTL 1.3; MHWN 2.3; MLWN 0.4.
Once an English possession, this is the only truly all-weather hr in the SE part of
the North Sea. It can be approached from either the N or S, and one of these
approaches is always sufficiently sheltered to permit entry.
Approach   The chans from both directions are well buoyed.
Entrance   Yachts use the southernmost basin on the main Is, entered between
two pier-heads; no hazards.
Berthing   There are yacht pontoons (bows to pontoon, a moored barge, and
stern to a buoy) in the NE part of the Vorhafen. Alternatively, yachts can
proceed into the Südhafen immediately to the N, where there is another
pontoon. This gives better shelter and is a very much shorter walk from the shops
and facilities. All facilities, fuel and supplies, inexpensive as this is a low-tax
island. Safe, but severe swell in easterly gales.

RIVERS JADE AND WESER   Chart G2, 7, 4, 49
The buoyed chans into both these rivers begin at the Weser LV, N of
Wangerooge. There are good yacht hrs at Hooksiel and Wilhelmshaven on the R
Jade, and Bremerhaven on the R Weser. Both rivers can safely be entered in
strong onshore winds once the flood is running, but as with the Elbe it is almost
impossible to get out in these conditions.

THE GERMAN FRISIAN ISLANDS – INSHORE PASSAGES
After passing between the islands the flood stream fans out towards the mainland
and into chans parallel to the mainland between the Is and the shore. The chans
gradually become shallower and the tide becomes slacker until a place behind
each Is is reached where the tides round its two ends meet and there is never any
tidal stream to speak of. These regions tend to silt and banks form which dry
about a metre. These are called '*Hohe watts*' (high flats) in German waters and
'*wantij*' banks (weak tide banks) in Dutch waters. Owing to the timing of the
tides, the watershed behind each Is occurs at a point roughly two-thirds of its
length from the W end.

All the main watersheds behind the German Frisians between the Weser and
the Ems have 1½ to 2m at MHW. The Bants Balje chan between Norderney and
the Ems has 2½m. Passage is only possible in daylight with good visibility. Chans
are marked at intervals with withies (saplings) on the N side. Double withies
mark chan entrances and junctions. With the possible exception of the Baltrum–
Norderney and Langeoog–Spiekeroog watersheds, only one watershed can be
passed on a tide. The tide floods up to the watersheds from both sides. In an
emergency the mainland hrs (Harlesiel, Bensersiel, Norddeich) offer shelter.

Note: the sands change constantly and up-to-date German charts are essential.
Where possible obtain local advice before each passage. *Frisian Pilot* by Mark
Brackenbury gives detailed descriptions of all the inshore passages behind both
the German and Dutch Is. The German charts are essential, but tend not to give

the depth of water at the watersheds. However, boats of draft up to 1.5m can negotiate all the main chans at HW. Although it would be most unwise to attempt any of these passages at night without detailed local knowledge, it is worth mentioning that the withies marking all the main chans have bands of reflective tape round them, which enables them to be seen by torchlight.

WANGEROOGE   Chart G2   (Plan p343)
HW −0.25.   MHWS 3.1; MLWS 0.0; MTL 1.6; MHWN 2.7; MLWN 0.5.
This is a strategically placed hr at the SW tip of the Is. Entrance is through the Dove Harle from the seaward, or over the banks from inshore. The hr is uncomfortable, and sometimes dangerous, in strong winds from any direction except between NW and NE, in which circumstances it is safer to make for Harlesiel, the mainland hr to the S; however, there is only 0.4m at LWS in the approach to this hr. No facilities at Wangerooge, stores and water at Harlesiel.

LANGEOOG   Chart G89   (Plan p343)
HW −0.25.   MHWS 3.0; MLWS 0.0; MTL 1.5; MHWN 2.6; MLWN 0.5.
This well sheltered hr at the SW corner of the Is has recently had a small marina development, dredged to 1.2m. Enter between pier-heads and leave all withies to stb before steering for the pontoons. YC and restaurant at the hr, stores from town, a good 1½M walk.

NORDERNEY   Chart G89   (Plan p343)
HW −0.45.   MHWS 2.7; MLWS 0.0; MTL 1.3; MHWN 2.3; MLWN 0.4.
One of the best hrs in the German Frisians. Beware of strong cross-tides in the entrance; proceed northwards up the hr keeping towards the W side, when the extensive yacht moorings become visible. YC and some supplies at the hr; full supplies, hotels etc in town, 1M. Diesel, water.

NORDDEICH   Chart G89 (Plan p343)
HW −0.40.   MHWS 2.8; MLWS 0.0; MTL 1.4; MHWN 2.5; MLWN 0.5.
The mainland port S of Norderney, reached between two breakwaters more than a mile long. Proceed S between them and take the E arm where the chan divides. Yacht moorings at the E end of the hr. A new yacht hr with several hundred berths is under contruction W of the breakwaters. All stores and facilities.

BORKUM   Chart G90   (Plan p343)
HW −1.05.   MHWS 2.6; MLWS 0.0; MTL 1.3; MHWN 2.3; MLWN 0.4.
One of the few Frisian hrs that can safely be approached in onshore gales, although even here wind over tide conditions must be avoided. The hr is at the extreme S tip of the Is, approached by a buoyed chan running along the S side of a training wall which covers at HW. Yachts berth at the centre pontoon of the three on the W side of the hr. Fuel and all facilities, some stores; the main town is over 3M to the NW.

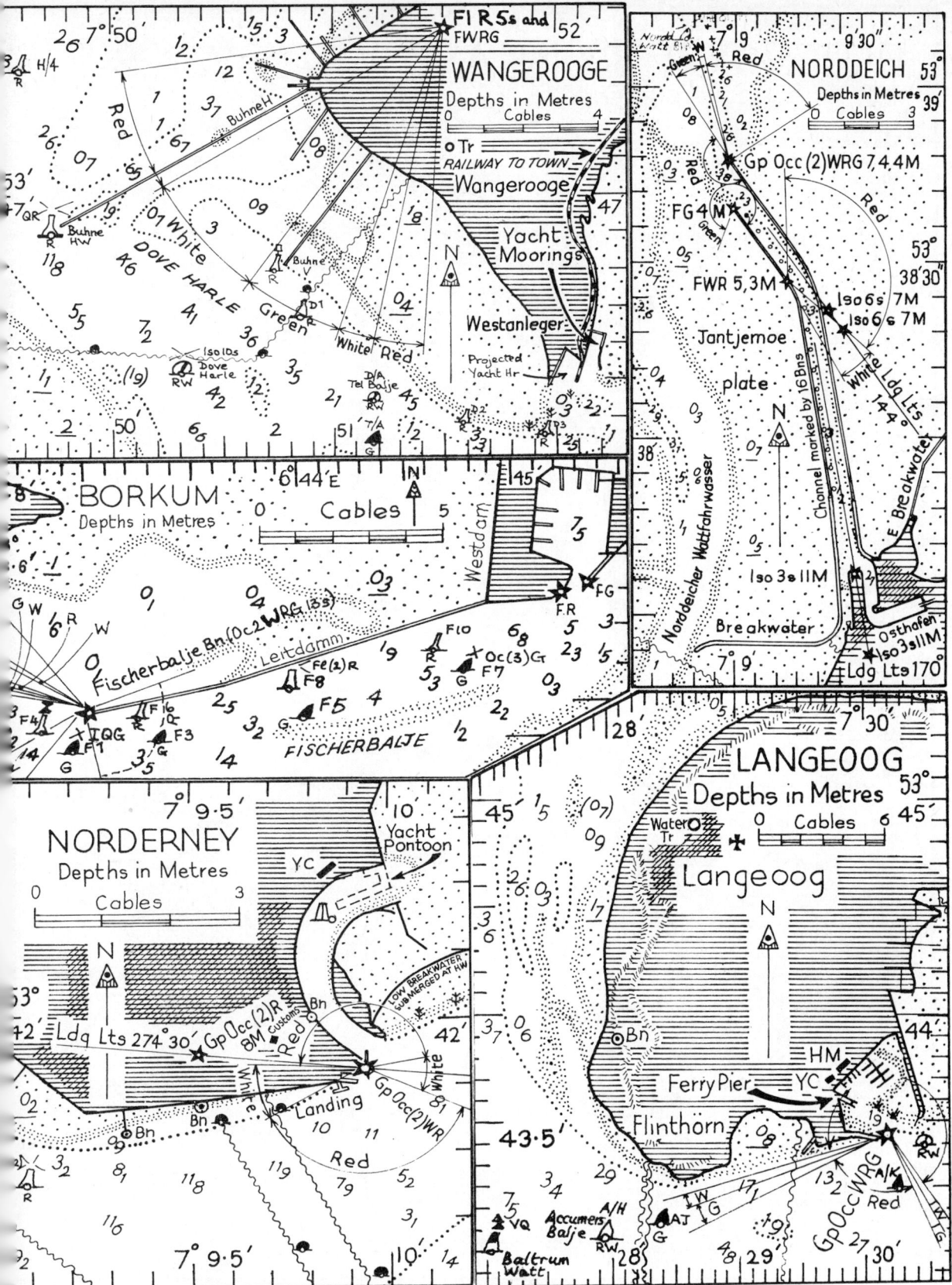

WANGEROOGE
Fl R 5s and FWRG
Depths in Metres
0 Cables 4
Tr
RAILWAY TO TOWN
Wangerooge
Yacht Moorings
Westanleger
Projected Yacht Hr
Red
White
Dove Harle Green
White Red
Iso IDs
Dove Harle
RW
Buhne H
Buhne HW
Buhne V
QR
R
H/4
R
N
7°50'
52'
47'
53'
50'

NORDDEICH
Depths in Metres
0 Cables 3
Gp Occ (2)WRG 7,4,4M
FG 4M
FWR 5,3M
Iso 6s 7M
Iso 6s 7M
Jantjernoe plate
White Ldg Lts 144°
Red
Green
Red
Norddeicher Wattfahrwasser
Channel marked by 16 Bns
Iso 3s 11M
Breakwater
Osthafen
Iso 3s 11M
E Breakwater
Ldg Lts 170°
N
Nordd (2) Watt B4
7°9'
9°30"
53'
39'
53°
38'30"
38'
7°9'

BORKUM
Depths in Metres
0 Cables 5
6°44'E
Westdam
Leitdamm
Fischerbalje Bn(Oc2 WRG 13S)
FE(1)R
F8
F5
F10
Oc(3)G
F7
FG
F.R
F1
IQG
F3
FISCHERBALJE
GW
R
W
G
N
45'

NORDERNEY
Depths in Metres
0 Cables 3
Yacht Pontoon
YC
LOW BREAKWATER SUBMERGED AT HW
Bn
Customs
BM
Gp Occ(2)R
Red
Gp Occ(2)WR
White
Red
Landing
Ldg Lts 274°30'
Bn
Bn
R
N
53°
42'
42'
7°9.5'
7°9.5'

LANGEOOG
Depths in Metres
0 Cables 6
Water Tr
Langeoog
Bn
HM
Ferry Pier
YC
Flinthörn
Accumers Balje
Baltrum Watt
A/H
AJ
RW
VQ
G
Gp Occ WRG
Red
W
G
RW
A/K
N
7°30'
53°
45'
44'
43.5'
28'
30'

343

DUTCH PORTS & INLAND WATERWAYS

KEY TO NUMBERS ON PLAN

1 Emden
2 Delfzijl
3 Lauwersmeer
4 Nes
5 W Terschelling
6 O Vlieland
7 Harlingen
8 Kornwerderzand
9 Den Oever
10 Oudeschild
11 Den Helder
12 Ijmuiden
13 Scheveningen
14 Hook of Holland
15 Rotterdam
16 Haringvliet
17 Grevelingen
18 E Schelde
19 W Schelde
20 Vlissingen
21 Breskens
22 Terneuzen
23 Veere
24 Hansweert
25 Willemstad
26 Dordrecht
27 Alphen
28 The Hague
29 Leiden
30 Oude Wetering
31 Schiphol
32 Amsterdam
33 Millingen
34 Nijmegen
35 Arnhem
36 Utrecht
37 Marken
38 Monickendam
39 Volendam
40 Hoorn
41 Enkhuizen
42 Medemblik
43 Muiden
44 Spakenburg
45 Harderwijk
46 Elburg
47 Kampen
48 Schwarzsluis
49 Urk
50 Lemmer
51 Staveren
52 Hindeloopen
53 Workum
54 Makkum
55 Sneek
56 Leeuwarden
57 Groningen

Juist
Borkum
Schiermonnikoog
Ameland
Terschelling
Vlieland
Texel
WADDENZEE
Dokkumer Ee
Reitdiep
Eemskanaal
R Em.
v Harinxma K
R van Starkenborgh kanaal (max height 6·80m)
Pr. Margrietkanaal
HOLLAND
IJSSELMEER
Noordhollands Kanaal
Ringvaart
Amstel
IJssel
IJSSEL
(Max: height, 10m.)
(THE NETHERLANDS)
Amsterdam Rijn
Neder Rijn
River Lek
Rijnk
R Waal
WAAL
Nieuwe Waterweg
Hollandse IJssel
Bergsche Maas
Zuid Willemsvaart
MAAS
RIJN
Duisberg
Dusseldorf
GERMANY
Koln (Cologne)
BONN
Maastricht
Albertkanaal
Antwerp
BELGIUM
GHENT
Kanaal Gent-Terneuzen

(10 Kilometres = 5·4 Sea Miles)

Scale of sea Miles

0   10   20   30   40   50   100

HOLLAND

The coastline of the Netherlands extends for about 250 miles, in addition to the offshore islands of the Dutch Frisians. For the most part it is flat and featureless, with only a dozen or so main ports of entry to the land. Yet within the country there are reputedly 8000 miles of navigable waterways, more boats per head than for any other people, great rivers and canal-superways, the extraordinary sea-lake of the Ijsselmeer (the old Zuider Zee), and a nation which has repeatedly fought against other nations for its right to be independent, and against the sea to exist at all.

Holland is not the Dutch name for the country and correctly describes only two of the eleven provinces. But Holland is the name most commonly used by English-speaking nations to embrace all the provinces of the Netherlands and is therefore used here.

Following the general layout of this *Handbook*, ports of entry are listed from N to S. However, many yachtsmen pass into Holland from the S, for a leisurely cruise through the central areas or around the Ijsselmeer, or to make a weather-free passage to the Baltic. There are therefore separate sections giving brief descriptions of fixed-mast inland routes and the ports of the Ijsselmeer.

The country divides into the following main cruising grounds:

(a) The W Schelde to Rotterdam – the area of the remarkable Delta scheme which has made non-or semi-tidal all the waterways of Zeeland except the R Schelde itself. Ideal for a family holiday.

(b) Central Holland – the most heavily populated area, and crossed by the Rhine in its various disguises and the R Maas. These great rivers and the linking system of super-canals carry huge tonnages in ocean-going ships (whose paths it can be unpleasant to cross). The area offers a view of the old and new Holland but is not really suitable for a fixed-mast boat.

(c) Amsterdam and Noord Holland. A visit to the Venice of the Northwest will not be forgotten.

(d) The Ijsselmeer and its ports (see the separate section).

(e) The lakes of Friesland in the hinterland of Stavoren and N towards Leeuwarden. Remarkable for the number of sailing craft, and a very relaxed cruising area.

(f) The Waddenzee and Frisian Islands – for the more experienced only, but a fascinating and attractive area.

Charts

There is a wide selection available of British, Dutch and German Admiralty Charts: of these the Dutch are to be preferred for coastal waters. There are also excellent Dutch yachting charts for all inland areas and the Waddenzee. These are invaluable, being designed for small boats with a wealth of extra information and port plans, and are very clearly presented. There are two categories:

(a) *Kaart voor zeil- en motorjachten 1800 Series*, published in folder form by the Dutch Hydrographic Office. These cover the Southern Estuaries (1803/05/07/09), the Waddenzee (1811/12), and the Ijsselmeer (1810). They are particularly good value.

(b) *Waterkaarts*, published by ANWB (with offices in the principal towns), covering all other inland waterways in 18 large-scale charts, showing bridge heights, yacht hrs, etc. (*Note:* measurements on the ANWB charts are all in decimetres.)

To equip with these charts is costly but the benefits are considerable. Most British chart agents will supply them to order, while J D Potter Ltd, 145 Minories, London EC3N INH usually carry a stock. Alternatively order direct from ANWB, Wassenaarseweg 220, the Hague. There is an excellent Dutch Admiralty Tidal Atlas, which can be ordered from the same sources, as can Born's Schipperskaart, a one-sheet map of the whole of Holland and its waterways, invaluable for cruise planning.

The *Almanak voor Watertoerisme, Vol II* produced annually, should also be carried. It contains the fullest information on bridges, locks, tides, facilities, tel nos., etc throughout the country with every town and village in alphabetical order. Obtainable from the same suppliers, or from larger bookshops in Holland. Although in Dutch, the essential information is quite easily understood. It will hereafter be referred to as AvW.

Regulations

It is a requirement that every boat shall have on board Vol I of the *Almanak voor Watertoerisme*. This contains general police rules for rivers and canals, and rules to prevent collisions. It is in Dutch and while its possession by a foreign yacht may not be insisted upon, a copy prominently displayed can help to give a good impression in any contact with authority. Also important if going there are the separate Rules applying to the Rhine with all its form and branches – the Rivers Waal, Neder-Rijn, Lek and Ijssel. These are called *Rynvaartpolitiereglement*.

From small boats the rules of the Dutch waterways are in fact straightforward:

(1) Keep well out of the way of all commercial vessels, even when under sail. They always have right of way. In any case wash and suction from a large barge can be very severe.

(2) Keep to starboard, even when under sail.

(3) Look out for vessels dodging the tide. They should show a BLUE flag (or blind) run out from the stb side of the wheelhouse, or a W Fl Lt at night, or give two blasts. This means that they are crossing to the 'wrong' side of the river and (exceptionally) a small boat with insufficient water may have to cross also to pass stb to stb.
(4) Look out for tows. R flag with W centre should be flown by tug and tow, and the towlines can be very long.
(5) Look out for dredgers: pass only on the side showing two balls, upper R lower B; alternatively a disc, or RW board. At night R and W lts replace balls.
(6) Look out for ferries of all types, especially cable ferries, and pendulum ferries riding to a cable moored in midstream.
(7) Avoid travelling at night, but if absolutely unavoidable show an all-round W masthead light. When lying alongside, always show a riding light.
(8) Speed limits apply on all lesser waterways.
(9) Anchoring is permitted almost anywhere, subject to normal prudence, but it is most unwise in busy waterways. Always rig a riding light when at anchor.

Bridges and Locks
Opening times AvW (2) gives all the details but there are some general guidelines. Most road bridges will open any weekday from dawn to dusk and on Saturday mornings but seldom (in Friesland never) on Sundays and public holidays. Busy road bridges will not open in rush hours nor for single yachts; and only briefly when they do: helmsmen and crew must be ready. Railway bridges open according to their timetables and long waits can occur.

There are two important bridges which are likely to continue to cause special trouble on the alternative fixed-mast routes from Rotterdam to Amsterdam. At Sassenheim the road bridge opens only 0600–0700 Mon–Fri and 1000–1100 Sat and Sun. And the railway bridge into the Ijssel and Amsterdam opens only at (about) 0100 (but this may vary). Dues are often charged at locks and sometimes at smaller bridges.

On bridges or locks a R lt means stop or not navigable, G means proceed, R and G means wait, W or Y means pass under. Y diamond means two-way traffic; two Y diamonds means compulsory one-way traffic. RWR striped board means no entry from this direction. Heights of fixed bridges are shown in metres.

Small boats usually go last into large locks but the keeper may direct otherwise. Beware of heavy propeller wash: never cast off when a barge moored ahead is preparing to leave.

Equipment
Extra warps, fenders, small tyres (in plastic bags), planks for pile mooring, ship-to-shore ladder, iron stakes for bank mooring, a mud weight, very long quants or boathooks, a powerful hooter, funnels and containers for water and fuel can all be useful. Dinghies should not be towed.

Weather Forecasts
In English from Scheveningen at 1040 and 2240 on 1862 and 2824 K/CS.

Fuel
Note especially the Dutch words: Petrol = *benzine;* paraffin = *petroleum;* diesel = *diesel;* lubricating oil = *olie;* two-stroke oil = *twee tact olie.*

Pilot Books
Useful books to carry aboard include:
Admiralty Pilot, North Sea (East); North Sea Harbours and Pilotage – Calais to Den Helder by E Delmar-Morgan, rev by Jack Coote; *Frisian Pilot* by Mark Brackenbury; *Barge Country – An Exploration of the Netherlands Waterways* by John Liley; *Through the Dutch Canals* by P. Bristow; *Waterways in Europe* by R. Pilkington; *Inland Waterways of the Netherlands* (3 vols) by E.E. Benest; *Inland Waterways of Holland* by W.E. Wilson.

Language
English is generally understood although much less so in Friesland. The following glossary may be helpful.

afval	= rubbish	oost (abbr O)	= east
bakboord	= port	sluis	= lock
betonning	= buoyage	vaarwater	= channel
beweegbare	= opening (bridge)	vast	= fixed (bridge)
brug	= bridge		
geen	= no, none	veer	= ferry
gesloten	= shut	verboden	= forbidden
havengeld	= harbour dues	wassalon	= launderette
havenmeester	= harbourmaster	zuid (abbr. Z)	= south

DELFZIJL   Charts D 1555, DY 1812   (Plan p350)
HW −0.20.   DS (offing): E +6.00; W HWD; (off hr): flood −5.10; ebb +0.40. MHWS 3.4; MLWS 0.3; MTL 1.8; MHWN 3.0; MLWN 0.7.
Important hr with good shelter and all facilities. The offices of chart agents Datema are at 11 Oude Schans. Direct access to the fixed-mast route to Belgium (about 6 days).
Approach   The main NW approach chans between Borkum and Rottumeroog are well buoyed. The N approach through German waters from Norderney has well under 1m at LWs, and the buoys are small.
Entrance and berthing   Note that since 1980 the only entrance is at the ESE end of the Zeehavenkanaal, 3M from the yacht hr. Enter between pier-heads (QG on W and FR on E) allowing for strong cross-tide. Proceed W up canal and berth in yacht hr on stb side past the locks to canal to Groningen and the S. All supplies and facilities, but considerable walk to town. HM tel (05960) 14966.

THE ZEEGATS

The principal Zeegats (gates to the sea) in the Dutch Frisians are the Westerems, leading to Delfzijl, Emden and the canal system; the Friesche Zeegat between Ameland and Schiermonnikoog for access to Lauwersmeer and canal system; the Zeegat van Terschelling to hrs at Terschelling and Vlieland, or 'overland' to Harlingen or Den Helder; and the Zeegat van Texel and Marsdiep, between Texel and the Dutch mainland, a direct access to Den Helder and Harlingen. All are well buoyed, but onshore winds over the ebb produce dangerous seas and the banks are constantly shifting. In general the waters of the Waddenzee are ill suited for deep-keel boats. To try to leave through any of the Zeegats except the Marsdiep in W or NW gales is dangerous, but most can safely be entered as long as the buoys are clearly visible at an hour before HW, when wind and stream are together. Note that the Zeegat between Texel and Vlieland, the Eirlandsche Gat, is unmarked and should not be attempted.

LAUWERSOOG   Chart D 1458, DY 1812
HW −1.45.   MHWS 2.9; MLWS 0.5; MTL 1.7; MHWN 2.7; MLWN 0.8.
All-weather hr with good facilities and YC. Direct access to fixed-mast routes.
Approach   The inside passages from E or W are marked by withies and are over watersheds. From the N the chan is well buoyed from 4M NW of Schiermonnikoog.
Berthing   The Visserhaven outside the lock is uncomfortable. Better to lock through (limited times on Sun and look out for a strong stream in the lock). The yacht hr lies to SE, all facilities and YC; or cross 2M to charming Oostmahorn YC (05193–1445) where there is a slipway and all facilities.

SCHIERMONNIKOOG   Chart D 1458, DY 1812
Hr lies in the SW of the Is. Difficult access with only about 1½m at mean HW, but good hr and beautiful Is. Reserve a berth in summer months (tel 05195–544).

AMELAND   Chart D 1458, DY 1811
HW −1.55.   MHWS 2.4; MLWS 0.2; MTL 1.3; MHWN 2.1; MLWN 0.7.
Hr lies in the mid-S of the Is at Nes. Difficult access and no proper hr, but shelter in all but E to S winds. Approach from the S is over watersheds. From seaward, there are extensive sandbanks in the Zeegat and the buoyed chan runs along the NE coast of Terschelling. This is a minor Zeegat and should only be attempted in good weather.

HARLINGEN   Chart D 1456, DY 1811   (Plan p350)
HW −2.05.   MHWS 2.2; MLWS 0.2; MTL 1.2; MHWN 1.9; MLWN 0.4.
Attractive town with all facilities.
Approach   From Ameland and the NE along the coast, there are two drying watersheds about midway. From the SSW, there is deep water in a narrow, well buoyed chan to a watershed (1.1m at LW) 1½M from the town. To the WSW, a

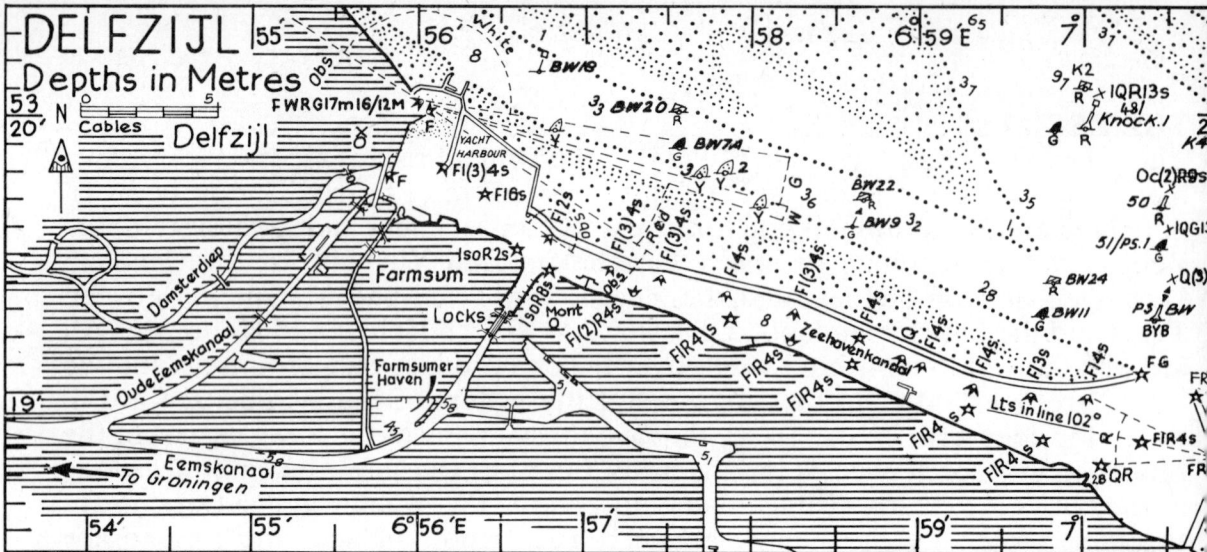

DELFZIJL
Depths in Metres

GRONINGEN

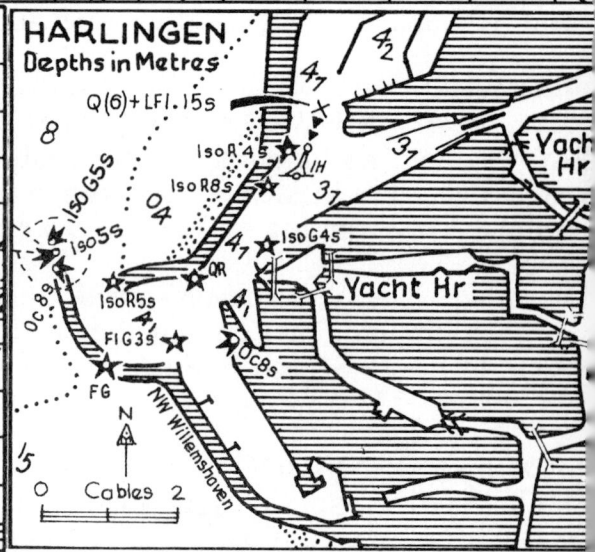

HARLINGEN
Depths in Metres

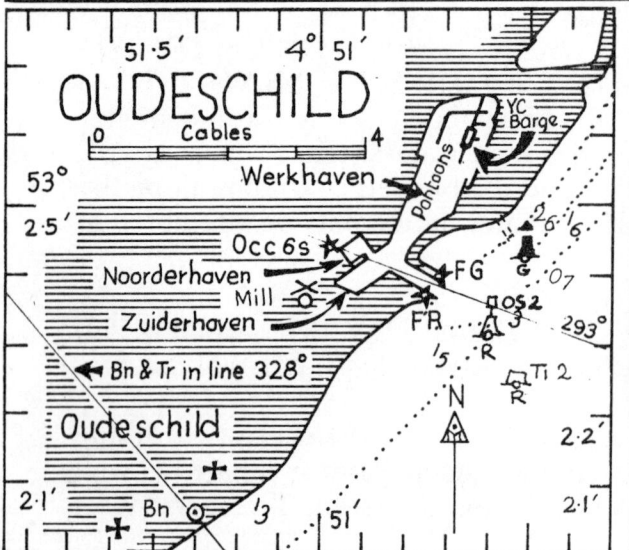

OUDESCHILD

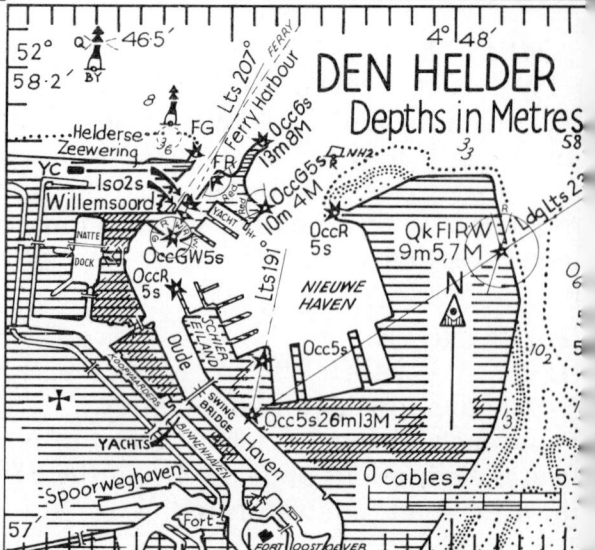

DEN HELDER
Depths in Metres

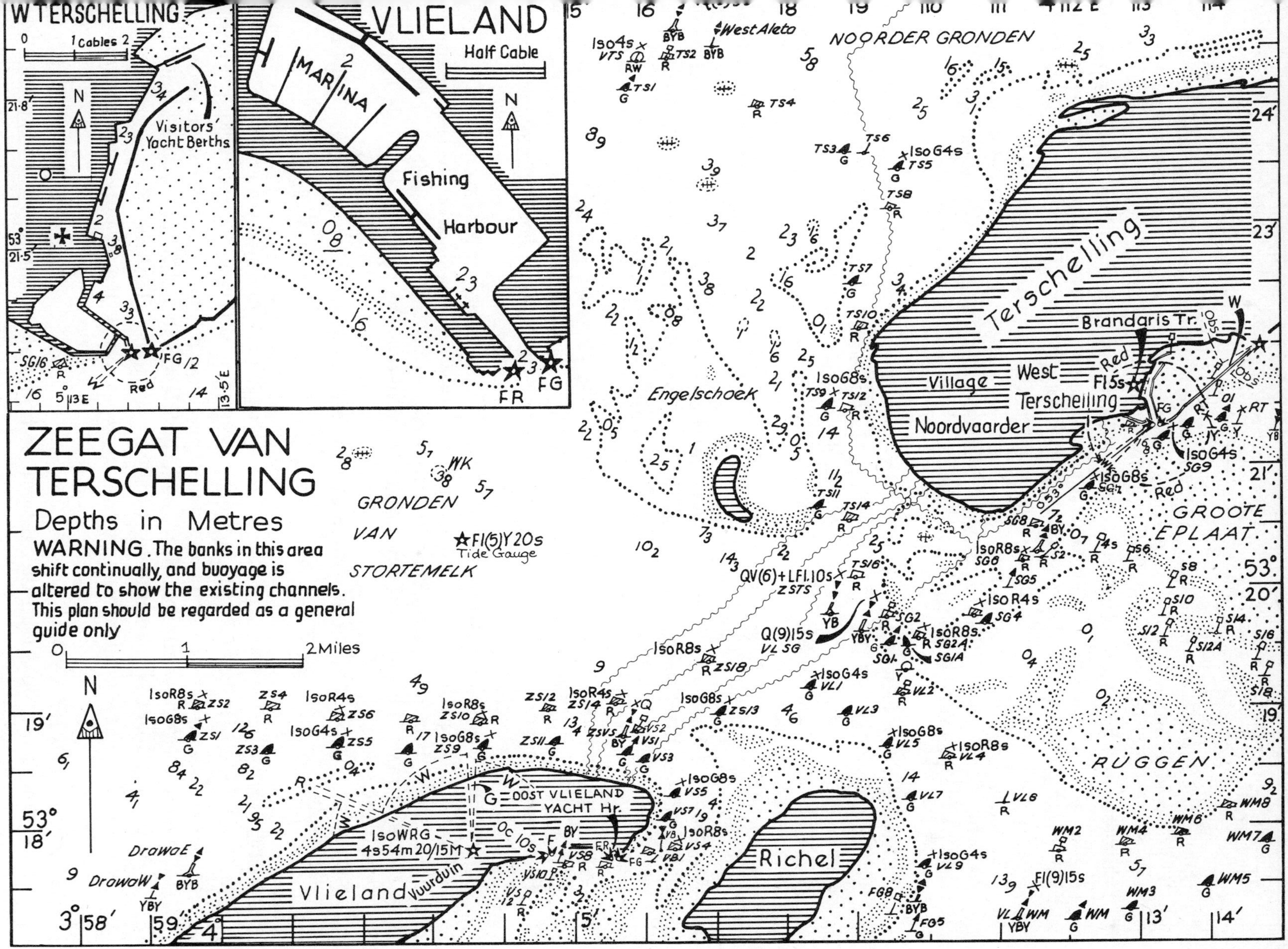

ZEEGAT VAN TERSCHELLING

Depths in Metres

WARNING. The banks in this area shift continually, and buoyage is altered to show the existing channels. This plan should be regarded as a general guide only

VLIELAND

W TERSCHELLING

Half Cable

MARINA

Fishing Harbour

Visitors Yacht Berths

N

Terschelling

West Terschelling

Village

Noordvaarder

Brandaris Tr.

Obs.

NOORDER GRONDEN

West Aleta

Engelschoek

GROOTE PLAAT

RUGGEN

Richel

OOST VLIELAND YACHT Hr.

Vlieland

Vlieland

STORTEMELK

GRONDEN VAN

Tide Gauge

Fl(5)Y20s

N

0   1   2 Miles

0   1 Cables 2

dam – the Pollendam – extends 3M; the chan is alongside to the S, well buoyed. There is a stream across the dam at HW. This chan continues in deep water to the hrs of Terschelling and Vlieland and the wide Zeegat to the North Sea.

Entrance and berthing   Entrance faces N in line with the Pollendam but masked from view by sea wall. Bear away to N to enter. Berth in Noorderhaven (brs open half past each hr), or pass through NE lock into van Harinxma Kanaal. This gives direct access to the fixed-mast routes and there is small yacht hr to stb. Excellent facilities, sailmaker etc at Noorderhaven, diesel from barge in Voorhaven. *Warning:* Noorderhaven is closed by floodgates for up to $1\frac{1}{2}$h either side of HW at very high springs.

ZEEGAT VAN TERSCHELLING   Chart D 1456   (Plan p351)
HW Stortemelke −4.25.   DS in offing: ENE +4.30; WSW −1.30.   Mid-chan (Stortemelke): ENE +3.20; WSW −2.50, 1.6kn.
To N (Thomas Smit): SE +4.10 NW −2.00, 1.5kn. To S (Vliestroom): SE +3.50 NW −2.30, 2.8kn.

In Stortemelke, the first of the ebb sets to N. In Thomas Smit, first of flood and ebb set to E and W respectively.

Approach   Chans are well buoyed and lit, but observe usual great care in navigating in the Frisians in strong winds. *Note* that the plan is an indication for use in planning or emergency only: banks and buoyage constantly change.

WEST TERSCHELLING   Chart D 1456, DY 1811   (Plan p351)
HW −2.55.   MHWS 2.1; MLWS 0.3; MTL 1.2; MHWN 1.9; MLWN 0.7.
Charming, busy holiday town in SW corner of Is with good town facilities. Magnificent beaches.

Approach   From Vliestroom at buoy VL–SG, following chan carefully to NE as banks shift frequently. At night keep to W sector of ldg lts from SG10, bearing 53°, until within the entrance. Note that the breakwater at E side of entrance covers at HW. The view of the banks from above the town at low tide is well worth the walk.

Berthing   At NE end of hr. Stagings near entrance are for ferries only. HM tel 05620–2515.

VLIELAND   Chart D 1456, DY 1811   (Plan p351)
HW −2.55.   MHWS 1.8; MLWS 0.1; MTL 1.0; MHWN 1.6; MLWN 0.5.
Port is at SE corner of the Is and was considerably enlarged in 1980 to provide new yacht hr. Well sheltered. Stores and hotels in town, 1M. Ferry to Harlingen.

   Approach from NE around tip of the Is through Vliesloot. Proceed through outer hr, reserved for fishing boats, into inner yacht hr and berth as directed.

KORNWERDERZAND   Chart D 1454, DY 1811
The E sealock of the Afsluitdijk is open 24 hours every day and affords refuge in

bad weather but only basic facilities. Makkum just to the SE in the Ijsselmeer is easily reached but may be crowded. HM 05177–232.

DEN OEVER   Chart D 1454, DY 1811
The W sealock to the Ijsselmeer has all-weather yacht hrs on either side. The N hr is convenient for provisioning but the area has little of interest. The lock is closed on Sundays and holidays, and open only 2h on Saturdays. HM 02271–1303.

OUDESCHILD   Chart D 1454, DY 1811   (Plan p350)
HW −3.40
Port lies in the mid-S of the Is of Texel and is busy in summer. Yacht hr is controlled from the club barge in NE. Good facilities (and bicycles).
Entrance   From ESE, buoy T12 in the Texelstroom, then bearing 293° to buoy OS2. Watch out for strong cross-tides. Ldg lt is Oc 6s between FR and FG on pier-heads. HM tel 02220–2710.

ZEEGAT VAN TEXEL   Chart D 1454, DY 1811
HW Schulpengat −4.55.   DS in offing: NE +4.00; SW −3.00.
But note: in the Zeegat, the ebb from +3.00 to +5.00 runs SW off Den Helder. The Dutch Tidal Atlas is strongly advised for all passages in and around the Waddenzee. By leaving Den Helder 5½h after HW Harlingen, it is possible to achieve an easterly run of 50 to 60M on a fair tide.
Approach   There are three buoyed channels from the North Sea: from the SW (S buoys), W (WG buoys), and NNW (MG buoys). Between the latter lies the Noorderhaaks sandbank, about 4M long, which is low-lying and is not well marked. All these chans (especially the W) are most unpleasant in strong winds against the ebb.
   Note that if approaching from W there are two lighthouses on the mainland 7M S of Den Helder: Grote Kaap (F) and Kleine Kaap (Iso 5s) which are in line with the most S-ly buoys SL, SG and S2. There are also ldg lts on Texel (front Iso 4s, rear Oc 8s) on a bearing of 026°. All of the Marsdiep and Texelstroom is an exercise area of the Royal Netherlands Navy. A good lookout should be kept for submarines.

DEN HELDER   Charts BA 191, D 1454, DY 1811   (Plan p350)
HW −4.20
This is the principal naval hr of Holland and is strictly controlled.
Approach   Watch out for cross-currents and for ferries to W of entrance and shoal water to E. Best line is on ldg line (Oc 5s), 191°. RWR lts forbid entrance.
Berthing   There are three yacht hrs. The Royal Naval (Officers) is to stb immediately on entering. Hospitable, but tidal and some distance from the town. Use of clubhouse restricted to showers and toilets. Alternatively, lock into the

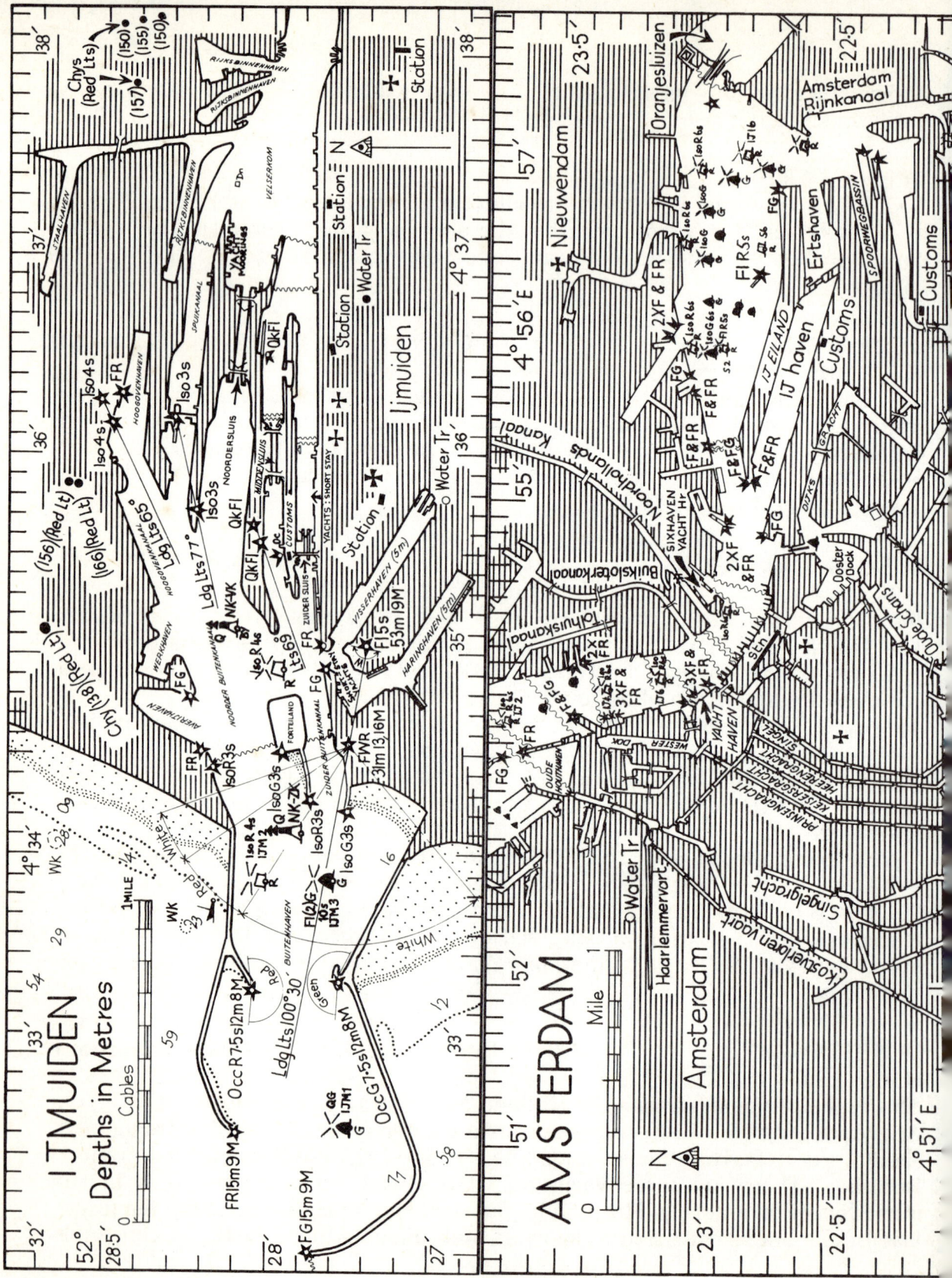

IJMUIDEN
Depths in Metres

Chys (Red Lts)   (157)● (150)● (155)● (150)●

RIJKS BINNENHAVEN
RIJKSBINNENHAVEN
STAALHAVEN
VELSEROM
☐ Dn

Station
N
Station
● Water Tr
Station

Iso4s   Iso4s   FR   Iso3s   QKFl   Iso3s

HOOGOVENHAVEN
MIDDENSLUIS
NOORDERSLUIS

IJmuiden

Yachts: short stay →
○ Water Tr
Station

Ldg Lts 77°
QKFl   QKFl
Customs
Zuider Sluis →
FR Lts 69
NK4K   Q
IsoR4s
FG

WEERHAVEN
HOOGOVENKANAAL

(56)(Red Lt)
(66)(Red Lt)
Chy(38)(Red Lt)

NOORDER BUITENHAVEN
AVERIJHAVEN
FR
IsoR3s
FORTEILAND
ZUIDER BUITENKANAAL

Q IsoG3s
NK-2K
IsoR3s
Iso G3s

FWR 31m 13,16M
VISSERHAVEN (5m)
Fl5s 53m 19M
HARINGHAVEN (5m)
○ Water Tr

1 MILE

Wk 28   Wk
White
Red
Green

IJM 2
IsoR4s
K5 IJM3   Fl(2)G
Iso G3s
R

FRl5m9M
OccR7·5s12m8M
Ldg Lts100°30'
R
QG IJM1
OccG7·5s12m8M
FGl5m9M

Cables   0

52°   28·5'   32'   33'   54   59   58   71   16   12   4° 34'   36'   37'   38'   29

AMSTERDAM

Oranjesluizen
Amsterdam Rijnkanaal

Nieuwendam

2XF & FR
IsoR6s   1716
IsoR6s   IsoG6s
IsoR6s   S4
Fl RSs
F&FR
F&FG   Fl RRSs
F&FR   IJ EILAND
5FG
Ertshaven
IJ HAVEN
Customs
SPOORWEGBASSIN

SIXHAVEN YACHT Hr
Noordhollands Kanaal
Buiksloterkanaal
Tolhuiskanaal

2XF
2XF & FR
3XF & FR
3XF & FR
DIJKSGRACHT
YACHT HAVEN
FG
FR
Oude Schans
Ooster Dock
Oude Houtmanskanaal

WESTER DOK
SINGEL
PRINSENGRACHT
KEIZERSGRACHT
HERENGRACHT
SINGELGRACHT

○ Water Tr
Haarlemmervoort
Amsterdam
Kostverloren voort

N

Mile   0

4° 51'E   52'   53·5'   22·5'   23'   23·5'   55'   4° 56'E   57'

354

Binnenhaven where the Petty Officers' Club and a private club adjoin each other. All facilities and the town is nearby.

From the Binnenhaven, there is access to the Noord-Hollands Kanaal to Amsterdam. *Note:* fixed-mast vessels must keep to the more W-ly chan N of Purmurend to avoid a fixed bridge (7m). HM 02230–14833 ext 322; CG 02230–12732.

IJMUIDEN   Chart BA 124   (Plan p354)
HW +3.50.   MHWS 2.1; MLWS 0.3; MTL 1.2; MHWN 1.7; MLWN 0.5.
DS: N +2.00; S −4.00.
Streams run hard across entrance, which is rough in onshore winds. There is a shoal to the W of the S mole: keep well to N of fairway. This is the largest fishing port in Holland.
Entrance   There are high chimneys, often producing bright yellow smoke, and prominent bldgs. Ldg lts are on the S side of the entrance, which is 350m wide, Fl 5 and FWR, 100°. There are four locks to the Noordzee Kanaal: yachts most often use the S, the Zuidersluis.
Berthing   Overnight or short daytime stay permitted on a pontoon in NW elbow of Haringhaven at S entrance (useful for awaiting tides, but do not leave boat unattended). Short stay, for clearing Customs etc, just inside the Zuidersluis is possible. Longer stay may be permitted in the yacht hr in the E approach to the N lock: can be uncomfortable. All stores in town, but few yacht facilities. Most people entering Ijmuiden will in any case be bound for Amsterdam (18M) where there are excellent yacht facilities. See separate entry on p354.

SCHEVENINGEN   Chart BA 3233   (Plan p357)
HW +3.05.   DS NE +2.00; SW −4.00.
MHWS 2.1; MLWS 0.2; MTL 1.1; MHWN 1.7; MLWN 0.6.
Extended seawalls have improved the entrance but great care is needed in strong onshore winds.
Entrance   Identifiable by tall buildings and by Lt Ho at N end of town; lts are FG and FR.
Berthing   YC and marina (rather expensive) is at S end of innermost basin. All facilities, and public transport to the Hague. There is no access to inland waterways. HM 070–514031.

HOOK OF HOLLAND (EUROPOORT)   Chart BA 132   (Plan p357)
HW +2.55.   MHWS 2.0; MLWS 0.3; MTL 1.1; MHWN 1.7; MLWN 0.4.
DS: Offshore and to the SW, the tidal streams are complex and the Pilot and Tidal Atlas should be consulted. At the entrance to the Hook the flood begins +0035 HWD and the ebb begins +0520. Mean tidal rates $3\frac{1}{2}$–4kn. DS becomes SW +0620 HWD and N −0025 HWD. E winds greatly affect the flood stream. The tidal set across the entrance is strongest at HW +$2\frac{1}{2}$h.

Traffic to Europoort and Rotterdam, the largest Dutch ports, is heavy at all times. There is direct access to France and Switzerland via the Rhine and Ruhr.
Approach   The entrance is between long moles and is dangerous in NW winds on the ebb. The coast is featureless and buoyage limited except from the W (Eurogeul), but within Europoort and at the Hook itself there are prominent chimneys, lts visible in daylight, mushroom-topped trs at pier-heads, etc. From the NE there are no dangers.

From the SW keep well offshore to avoid shoals. The Goeree lt platform is 30m high (Fl 4 20 s Horn 4) at 51° 56′N, 3° 40′E, from which the Hook bears 250°, 14½M.

The Eurogeul is buoyed 85° every 2M to Euro 7, the next buoy being Maas. Centre, Iso 4s, from which bearing is 112° 5M to the entrance. Keep at least ½M S of Maas Centre to avoid shipping.
Entrance   The N mole extends 1½M. Entrance lts are N mole head FR (and Al WR 8s in fog), S mole head FG (and Al WR 8s in fog). After a mile, the Nieuwe Waterweg divides. Keep to N channel for Rotterdam; S channel leads to Europoort, which yachts should not enter.
Berthing   There are no satisfactory facilities at the Hook. Berghaven (2½M from entrance) is a poor possibility, preferably at slack high or low water and avoiding the ebb. Berth alongside in W part. Useful for Harwich ferry (300m).

ROTTERDAM   Chart BA 133, DY 1809
HW +4.55.   MHWS 2.1; MLWS 0.3; MTL 1.2; MHWN 1.8; MLWN 0.4.
16M from the sea. Great care needed because of heavy traffic and tidal streams. Power is obligatory.
Berthing   There are yacht hrs at Maassluis (avoid in strong tides) and others at Vlaardingen and Schiedam on the N bank (12–14M from the sea). The Royal Maas YC is just behind the Euromast in Rotterdam itself and is recommended. Beyond the city centre (pass under the lifting brs in Koningshaven on S bank), there is a hr to port and 2M after the road br on the S bank a large yacht hr with repair yard, chandler, etc.

ZEEGAT VAN GOEREE–HARINGVLIET   (Plan p357)
HW (Locks) +3.30.   MHWS 2.2; MLWS 0.3; MTL 1.2; MHWN 1.9; MLWN 0.4.
The direct route to Dordrecht from the sea is through the lock at Haringvliet-sluizen between the 'islands' of Goeree and Voorne. The Zeegat is shallow, the channel narrow, the banks change often. Entry should not be attempted in strong W or NW winds. The duration of the flood in the entrance is only 5h and of the ebb 8h: but the tides are confused and adjacent streams may run in opposite directions.
Approach   Of the buoyed chans, that from W is lit. Pick up SG RW buoy Iso 4s, then course alterations are required at SG 10 (to 083°), at P1 (to 098°), at P4 (to

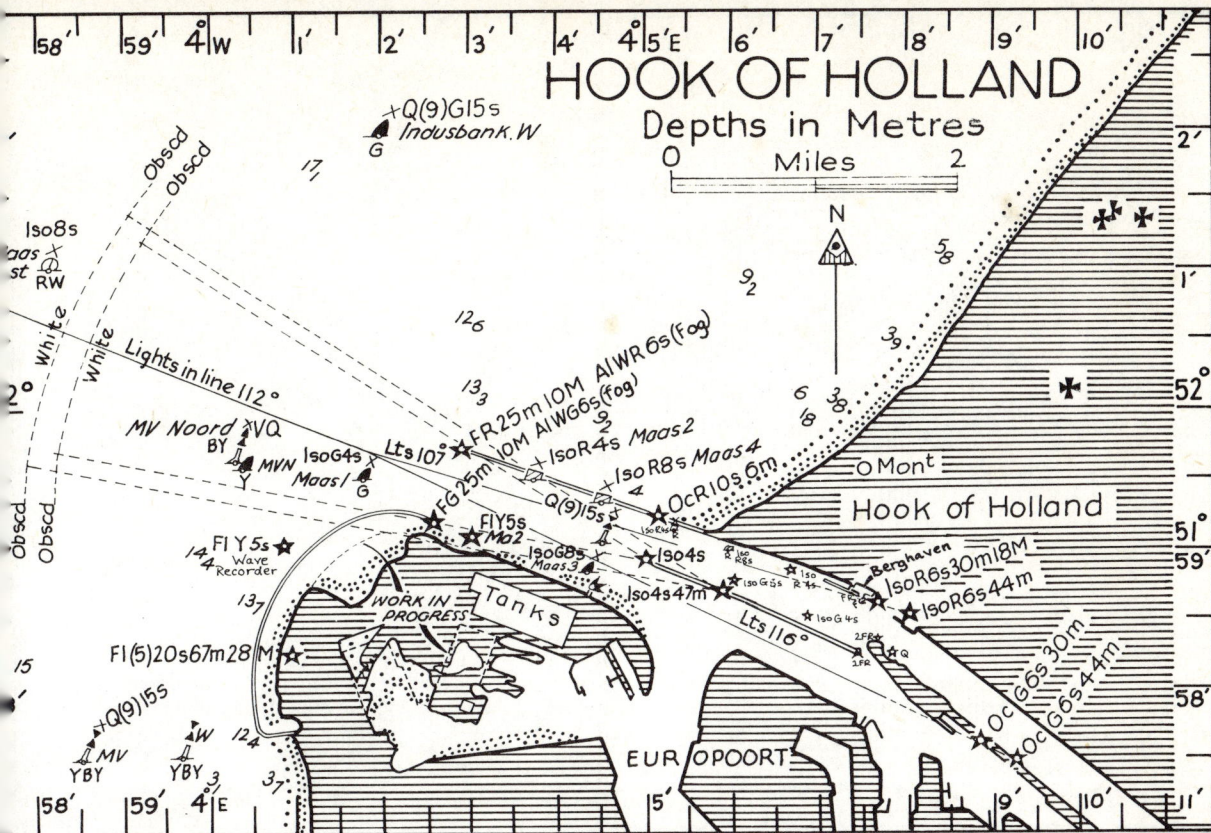

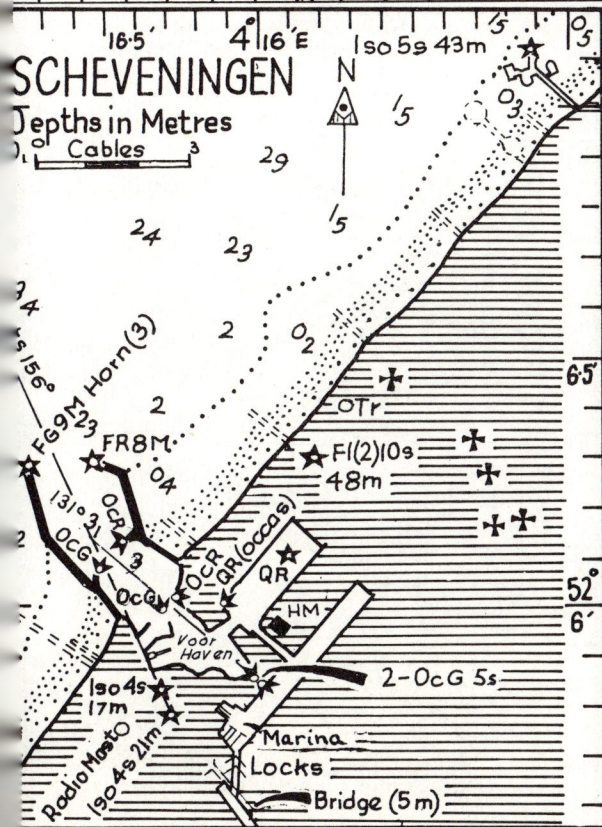

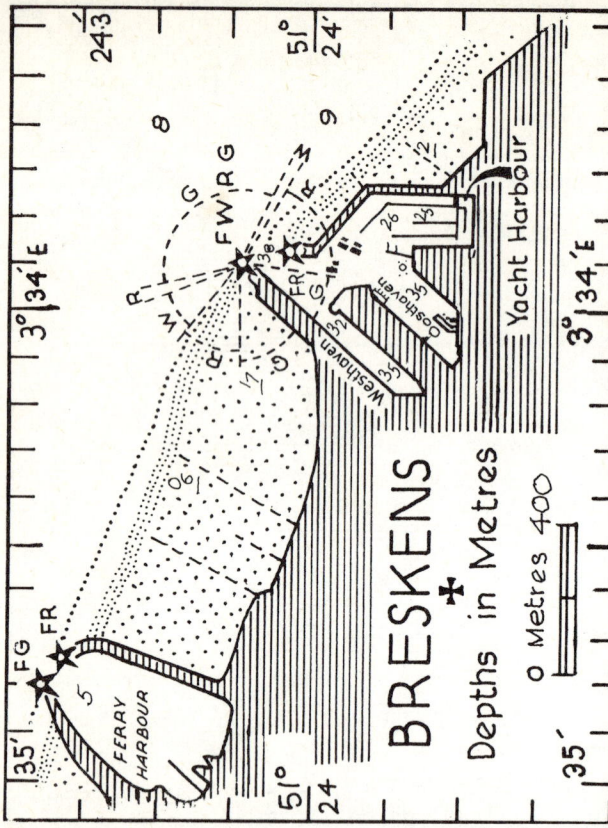

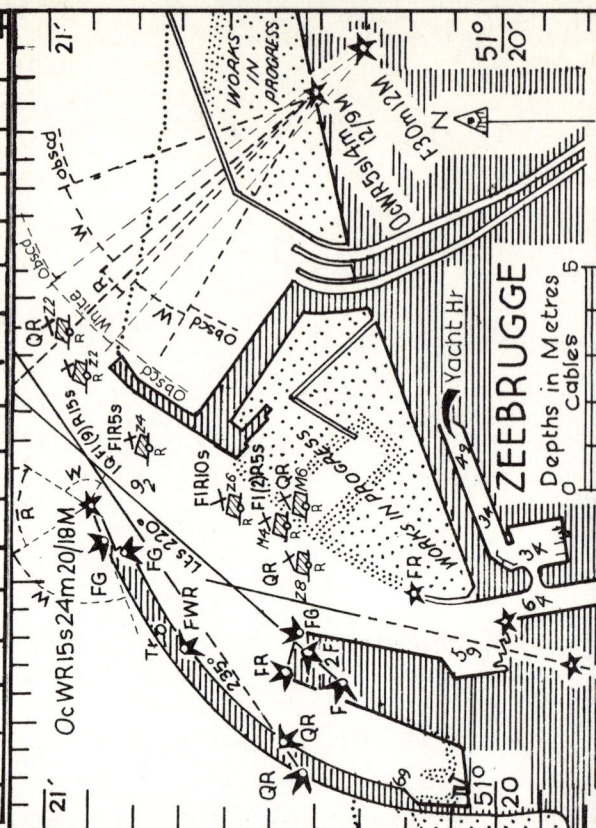

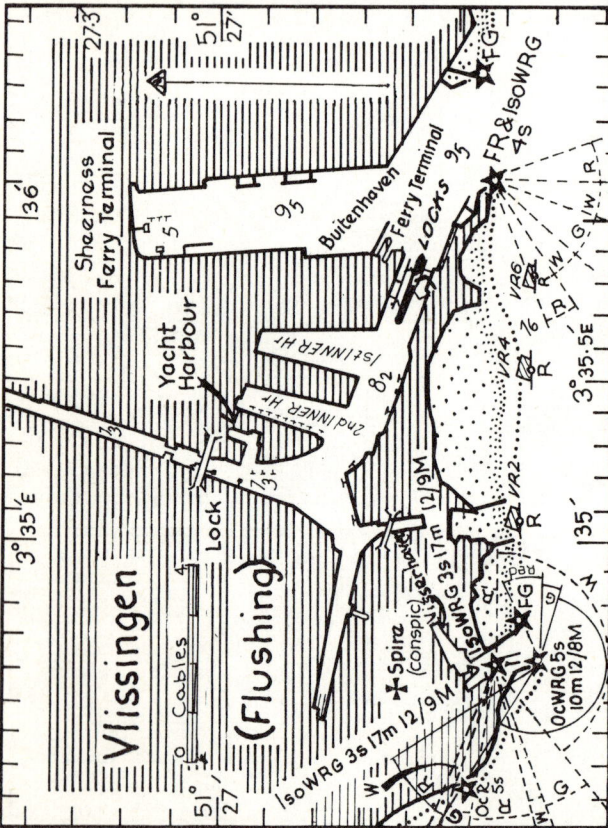

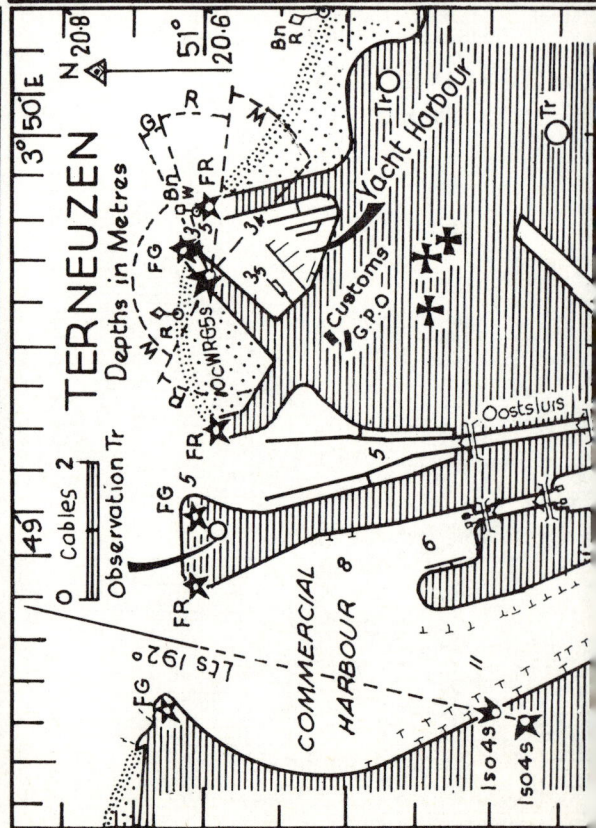

150°), and P7/P9 (into moles of Buitenhaven). The distance from SG is about 7½M.

The lock opens 24h Mon–Fri, but daylight only on weekends and holidays.
Berthing   There are three hrs at Hellevoetsluis, 3M E of the lock. The most convenient for all facilities and the old town is the centre hr. The Haringvliet has a number of Is and is about 20M long before it joins the Hollandse Diep via a lifting br giving access to all inland areas.

THE EAST SCHELDE
At the time of writing (late 1980), the exact plans for the new flood barrier and the effects that this will have on the channels in the approach are not known. The estuary should therefore not be approached from seaward without absolutely up-to-date information from reliable sources. In view of the works in progress and the probability of substantial changes before this *Handbook* is published, it would therefore be unwise to give any detailed sailing directions in the present edition: these will be included in *Corrections* as soon as possible.

THE WEST SCHELDE
There are two main approach channels, the Oostgat and the Wielingen. Both are well lit and buoyed, and present no problems. The most direct channel for a boat coming from England is the Deurloo, but this is dangerous in strong onshore winds and unlit. Once within the sandbanks, the river is sheltered from the full force of the North Sea swell, but conditions can still be rough for a yacht well up the estuary, particularly in wind over tide conditions.

FLUSHING (Vlissingen)   Chart BA 325, DY 1803   (Plan p358)
HW +2.10.   MHWS 4.8; MLWS 0.4; MTL 2.5; MHWN 3.9; MLWN 1.0.
The principal entry port in S Holland, and gives access to the inland waterway system.
Approach and entrance   Yachts are permitted to use the Visserhaven, but this is overcrowded and often uncomfortable. The main yacht harbour is inside the canal system, reached by locks in the main hr, 1M E of the Visserhaven. Entrance to both harbours is straightforward, but allow for powerful cross-set on the approach and keep a sharp lookout for heavy ferry and commercial traffic, which should be given right of way.
Berthing   The yacht hr is at the E side of the canal, just before a swing br and second lock, usually left open. Good shelter, few facilities, and stores some distance.

TERNEUZEN   Charts BA 120, DY 1803   (Plan p358)
HW +2.40.   MHWS 5.0; MLWS 0.3; MTL 2.6; MHWN 4.1; MLWN 0.9.
This port gives entry to the canal to Ghent and France. It lies some 12M up the R Schelde from Flushing, on the S bank.
Approach and entrance   The yacht hr is the most easterly of the three basins. Entrance is straightforward, but allow for strong cross-set.

Berthing   There are two sets of marina berths, each with its own small YC. Few facilities, but all stores in the attractive town, which lies behind the dyke and is usually invisible from sea level.

BRESKENS
Charts BA 325, DY 1803   (Plan p358)

HW +2.10.   MHWS 4.8; MLWS 0.4; MTL 2.5; MHWS 3.9; MLWN 1.0.

A small harbour on the S entrance to the R Schelde, well placed as a port of entry or departure.

Approach and entrance   There are two hrs about 1M apart: the W one is for ferries only. Yachts enter the E hr, taking care to approach from nothing E of N, as a sandbank extends to a line N by E of the entrance. The entrance is straightforward between the pier-heads, but beware of strong cross-sets.

Berthing   At pontoons in the SE part of the hr. All facilities, but inconvenient for stores, which are some distance.

FIXED-MAST INLAND ROUTES

(Plan p344)

The Netherlands can be crossed with a fixed mast by a number of different routes, with only the occasional inconvenience of waiting for a bridge to open. For yachts with lowering masts and for motor boats, there is a huge choice of routes including access to the hearts of most cities, but these are outside the scope of this book.

In this section the principal fast routes from SW to NE of the country are summarised. By the fastest routes and dawn-to-dusk motoring, the journey from Flushing to Delfzijl can be done with good luck on six weekdays (i.e. excluding Sat, Sun and holidays). But hardly anyone will want or need to do this. If the North Sea weather is bad the inland waterways can be entered easily from the Wester Schelde or the Hook, at Ijmuiden, Den Helder, or from the Waddenzee at Harlingen or Lauwersoog. If the weather turns fair, the fastest passage will be made by leaving the system from the nearest of the above ports and travelling along the coast.

The rest of this section is laid out schematically to give the skeletons of the main routes, with very brief notes on places not referred to elsewhere.

Wester Schelde to Delfzijl

Fast route
From Vlissingen to Veere into the Ooster Schelde and NE to the locks at Willemstad.

Alternatives
From Hansweert into the Ooster Schelde, turning W to rejoin the 'fast route' to avoid fixed bridges on the Schelde-Rijn Kanaal.

(Veere is recommended. Also St Annaland in the Krabbenkreek, between the Ooster Schelde and Grevelingenmeer, for a comfortable berth, beaches etc.)

From Willemstad turn E to Dordrecht (a busy centre, expect delays; bridges closed Sun, holidays). Dordrecht YC is third ent to stb above bridges.

From Dordrecht turn N to join Nieuwe Mass after 4M. Then W for 2M towards Rotterdam. Then sharp to stb into Hollandsche Ijssel (keep well clear of corner and try to take the tide upstream).

Ijsselmond YC is to port at ent to Ijssel, with all facilities.

On the Hollandsche Ijssel, turn W ½M before Gouda through the Julianasluis into the Gouwe.

To avoid Dordrecht, either (*a*) from Willemstad, turn W into Haringvliet and after 12M turn NE into Spui. No bridges. This leads into the Oude Maas; turn W to join Nieuwe Maas, to W or Rotterdam.

Or (*b*): 3M before Dordrecht turn W into Oude Maas and then as above. Bridges open Sun.
(Yacht hrs on Spui and on Oude Maas after 5M on stb side.)

These alternative routes then require passage through Rotterdam to rejoin the 'fast' route. The route through Leiden and Den Haag has a height limit of 7m.

Note: After 15M beyond Alphen all bridges remain closed on Sun and public holidays (1980). There is no alternative to this bottleneck except to exit at the Hook and re-enter at Ijmuiden.

At Alphen turn W into the Oude Rijn and N after 4M into the Helmans to Oude Wetering. Then NE into the Ringvaart, past Schiphol Airport (limited opening times), into the Schinkel. The last barrier is the notorious railway bridge opening approx 0100–0200. Entry to the Noordzeekanaal is just W of Amsterdam centre.

A route almost equal in distance, but with more bridges, is to turn W into Ringvaart after Oude Wetering. The immediate problem is the road bridge at Sassenheim which opens only in the early morning (0600–0700 weekdays, 1000–1100 weekends). After this bridge keep to port to Haarlem. The bridges and locks beyond have only limited opening on Sun and holidays. This leads to the Noordzeekanaal midway between Ijmuiden and Amsterdam.

Boats under approx 33ft can avoid Amsterdam to the E by turning E after Dordrecht to Arnhem direct or via Millingen and Nijmegen. Then down the Ijssel to Kampen and the Ketelmeer. These are picturesque routes.

From Amsterdam (through the Oranjesluis) enter the Ijsselmeer. Keep to the W side through the lock before Enkhuisen. Then cross direct to the sea-lock at Kornwerderzand on the E side. Re-enter at Harlingen. Then to Leeuwarden.

Then keep NE to Dokkum and across and into the Lauwersmeer. From the SE corner take the Reitdiep continuing in its main chan and skirting the centre of Groningen to the S. (See plan p350). There are twelve bridges to pass through – usually a long process – before emerging into the Eemskanaal with 20M to Delfzijl.

Note that only boats under 6.8m height can use the van Starkenborgh Kanaal into Groningen, and there is no alternative to the Lauwersmeer route for fixed masts.

Via Den Helder, take the Zijkanaal before the bridge to the W of Amsterdam. (Do not take Noord Hollands Kanaal because of fixed bridge at Purmurend.) *Via Kampen* (see Ijsselmeer Section – 12.7m fixed bridge). *Via Staveren* or Lemmer to Sneek, to rejoin the 'fast route' at Leeuwarden.

This final section can be completed faster in fair weather by locking out of the Lauwersmeer and taking the open sea route N of Schiermonnikoog and Rottumeroog. The channel is to the NW of Schiermonnikoog. The passage inside the islands has three watersheds and requires shallow draft and considerable power if a night is not to be spent at anchor en route.

AMSTERDAM
(Plan p354)

This of of course one of the major cities of Holland, and gives access through the Orange Locks to the Ijsselmeer, and also to the canal systems for S and N Holland. The main yacht hr for Amsterdam is the Sixhaven, NE of the conspic rly stn. It is on the N bank of the canal, and Amsterdam is on the S bank, but there are frequent free ferries. Alternatively, there is a small yacht hr NW of the stn below the conspic Havengebouw, much subject to swell from passing ships. Moorings here are bows to pontoon, stern to post, and for those who do not mind the motion it is very convenient for the city and usually less crowded than the Sixhaven. If proceeding to the Ijsselmeer it is often more convenient to lock out through the Orange Locks (Oranjesluizen) and use the small hr of Durgerdam on the N bank, 1M to the SE.

THE PORTS OF THE IJSSELMEER

The Ijsselmeer is a fascinating inland sea, roughly 40 miles by 20. Created by the completion in 1932 of the great Afsluitdijk, the dam across its mouth, fishing fleets still leave for the North Sea just as they did before, and there are also now huge nettings of the eel, pike, etc which flourish in its fresh waters. Most of the ports retain highly individual characters.

The water is of a depth generally of 2 to 2½m (but there are shoals and an up-to-date chart is essential). Gales blow up quickly and produce short steep seas that must be treated with great respect, but generally the area is excellent for sailing. Beware of fishing nets, not always well marked. There is a second dam across the Ijsselmeer from Enkhuizen to Lelystad with locks at either end.

The principal harbours – and there are many other refuges and marinas – are summarised below.

(1) W side of the Ijsselmeer
Volendam   As touristy as the Tower of London and catering for the charabanc trade. However, much of the port is quite genuine, especially away from the waterfront, and the fishing fleet is active. Very limited moorings. Worth a short visit.

Marken   Was an isolated Is and is distinguished by unique fishermen's houses. Marken is strictly Protestant while Volendam is Catholic, the differences between the communities being even more marked than in their different traditional costumes. Limited moorings. Keep closely to the buoyed chans in this area. Avoid Sunday visits.

Monnickendam   Also a tourist town but charming with some beautiful streets, excellent restaurants. Two marinas: try the stb one first, nearer the town and with good club facilities. Recommended for overnight.

Edam   The entrance is easily missed. River hbr, usually with limited moorings. The town is interesting, especially the Captain's House.

Hoorn   A splendid town with a long history and many fine buildings. It now has no fishing fleet, but Tasman came from here and Cape Horn is named after the town. For an overnight stop, mooring in the old hr in the town centre rather than in the marinas is possible. All facilities: somewhat expensive. Interesting museum, good restaurants. Recommended.

Enkhuizen   Once the largest town on the Ijsselmeer, the hrs remain and there is now a large marina to the N. Use the old hr (first left) for short stay and shopping, but the Werkhaven or the marina for overnight. Look out for fishing boats moving at speed. An interesting, busy town. Visit especially the Zuider Zee Museum.

Medemblik   A pleasant smaller town of interest and the nearest port to the Waddenzee on the W side of the Ijsselmeer. Many beautiful old buildings. The river hbr tends to be busy, the inner basin beyond the road br is large and peaceful. All facilities.

(2) Channel S and E of the Flevoland Polders
Note: this route passes under a 12.7m fixed br.

Muiden   A busy point of entry (leading to Utrecht and the great rivers) with an equally busy road br. In the outer hr is the hospitable Royal Netherlands YC, overlooked by the restored castle. Otherwise poor facilities.

Spakenburg   An interesting market town with two marinas and river hbr. Good for shipping and 'local colour'.

Harderwijk   Now a seaside resort. Marina by the lock; the old port is largely for industrial traffic. Europe's largest Dolphinarium; beaches and playground may provide a useful diversion. Good shops.

Elburg   The charming mediaeval moated town lies just beyond the end of the hr. Limited moorings but should on no account be missed.

Zwartsluis   Not strictly an Ijsselmeer port but with marina, alongside berths, and useful shops. Well sheltered and adjacent to the Zwartermeer.

Ketelmeer   Two useful refuges about 5M above the Ketelbrug are: Schokkerhaven on the N, no facilities at all in artificial hr but the old Is of Schokland, $\frac{3}{4}$h walk, is preserved as an interesting museum; and *Ketelhaven* on the S, no shops or fuel but showers and restaurant, and a comfortable hr.

If returning to the Ijsselmeer through the Ketelbrug, follow Section (3) from Urk onwards.

(3) Direct Route–Amsterdam to Friesland

Pass the old fortress Is of Pampus and follow the NE line of the dyke for 20M to Lelystad. There is one refuge just short of halfway, i.e.

Lelystad   Yachting facilities very limited. The town dates from the completion of the Polder dyke in 1956.

Urk   For 700 years until 1942 this was an Is in the middle of the Zuider Zee, and is still determinedly separate from the surrounding area. Traditional dress is generally worn by men and women. The fishing fleet is the largest on the Ijsselmeer. The architecture is simple but the town is unique. Limited moorings and facilities; avoid weekends when the fleet is in, and particularly Sun. Little English spoken. Unfriendly, but worth a visit.

Lemmer   Entry for the fixed-mast route across Friesland to Groningen via Leeuwarden. Yacht hr NW of town. Good boatyard.

Staveren   Once one of the cities of the Hanseatic League, but little remains. In addition to the old (stb hand) hr, there are large marinas on the Johan Frisokanal 1M to the S, which leads also to the principal Friesland lakes. This is now a major sailing centre. Note that there are shoals for 2–3M offshore, extending to a lesser extent as far round as Lemmer. Ferry service to Enkhuizen.

Hindeloopen   A small town of great charm with a 1200 year history. The hr is small but there is a 300-berth marina to port. Many German yachts are kept here.

Workum   Another old port of lesser interest, but sheltered and with all facilities.

Makkum   The nearest port to Kornwerderzand. The town is pleasant and notable for its excellent pottery. Small hr.

BELGIUM

North Sea Harbours and Pilotage (*Calais to Den Helder*) by E. Delmar-Morgan (revised by J. Coote) is a useful volume to have on board. The streams run in the direction of the coast, the E-going stream running its hardest at local LW and the W-going stream at local HW.

ZEEBRUGGE   Chart BA 97   (Plan p358)
HW +1.25.   MHWS 4.8; MLWS 0.3; MTL 2.5; MHWS 3.9; MLWN 1.1.
As well as being a yachting port in its own right, Zeebrugge gives access to the canal to Bruges.

Approach and entrance   The hr is protected by a 1½M mole, but the entrance can be very rough in strong onshore winds. There are extensive works in progress (1980) in and near the hr, and yachts should leave all R buoys to port when entering and inside the hr.

Berthing   The yacht hr is entered through a narrow gap in the E wall of the more easterly of the two main basins. It provides perfect shelter when alongside berths, but is usually overcrowded.

All facilities and several restaurants near the yacht hr, but main shops are some distance.

BLANKENBERGE   Chart BA 325   (Plan p366)
As a result of recent expansion, this is now one of the most important yacht hrs in Belgium.

Approach and entrance   The harbour is approached between two long piers, and the channel is dredged to 1.5m during the summer; but between Oct and Ap it silts up, and in early spring or at any time after onshore gales there is little or no water at LWS. Approach on the ldg line, two R St Andrew's Crosses by day, two FR vert neon tubes by night.

Berthing   The hr curves round to port, and the old yacht basin lies at the end of this limb. A new larger basin has been made to the SW, entered through a narrow passage on the stb hand just after the bend. Berth in either as space allows. All facilities and stores, good bathing. Two YCs.

BLANKENBERGE
Depths in Metres

Cables

0   3

N

19.2'

FR 14m 11M

Lts 134°

51°
19'

FG 16m 11M

E. Pier

W. Pier

Oc(2) 8s 32m 20M

Dunes

FR

FR

Sluice

OLD YACHT HARBOUR

NEW YACHT HARBOUR

3° 7'E

6.5'

6.5'

3° 7'E

Wk 5

FG 12m 9M Bell(2)

FR 12m 10M Horn Mo(K)

51°
10'

43'   44'   2° 45'

Leert de Ton 75m

o Water Tr
GpFl(2)R 14s 26m 21M

o Radar Sc

9'

Casino

LB

Nieuwpoort Bad

NIEUWPOORT

Depths in Metres

0   Mile   1

Lombardsij

Nieuwpoort

8'
Water Tr o

OOSTENDE
Depths in Metres

Q(3)10s

BYB

Binnenstroombank

62

Ldg Lts 128°

2° 55'

FR 13m Horn Mo(OE)

Fl Or (occas)

57'

N

14'30"

14'30"

63

62

FG 12m Bell(1)

Radar Scanner

FR
FR

Slip

GpFl(3)10s 63m

51°

14'

54

32

Yacht Berths

FG

FR

Tidal Basin

Fish Dock

51°
14'

Montgomery Dock

Tr o

Naval Basin

o Water Tr

Obscd

Twin Spires o

DREDGED TO 4.1

Ochy

Voorhaven

Mercator Yacht Basin

Fl Bu

De Mey Dock

HM

Customs

Yacht Berths

RYC Ostende

Achterhaven

Oostende Brugge Canal

Tr

Cables

0   1   2   3   4   5   6   7   8   9   1 MILE

o Water Tr

Houtdok

54'   2° 55'   56'   57'

OSTEND (OOSTENDE)   Chart BA 125   (Plan p366)
HW +1.15.   MHWS 5.0; MLWS 0.2; MTL 2.6; MHWS 4.1; MLWN 1.1.
A major town and important yacht hr.
Approach and entrance   There are no navigational hazards in the approach, although it is worth avoiding offshore shoals in heavy weather even if they appear to have plenty of water, as seas can be very much more severe in the shallower areas. Ostend is a busy commercial and ferry port: all ferries have absolute right of way. A flashing Y lt on the E pier-head and the entrance to the Montgomery Dock is the first entry on the stb hand inside the harbour.
Berthing   There are tidal yacht berths and a YC at the end of the Dock, but the main yacht hr is reached through a lock at the S end which gives access to the two basins of the Mercator Yacht Hr in the centre of the town. If staying longer than overnight, it is cheaper to lock in.
   An alternative berth is at the RYC Ostend pontoons at the SE end of the Voorhaven, quiet and comfortable but 2M from town. All facilities and stores.

NIEUWPOORT (NIEUPORT)   Chart BA 125   (Plan p366)
Approach and entrance   The hr entrance is dredged to 1.5m but it should be avoided in the latter part of the ebb and near LW in strong NW winds. The main Lt Ho is some way E of the pier-heads. Enter between the piers, beware cross-set off entrance.
Berthing   After a mile, the hr divides and there is a YC with marina moorings up each of the arms: the one in the E limb being mainly Flemish speaking, and that to the W mainly French. Both are large clubs with restaurants and good facilities, but shops are a long way.

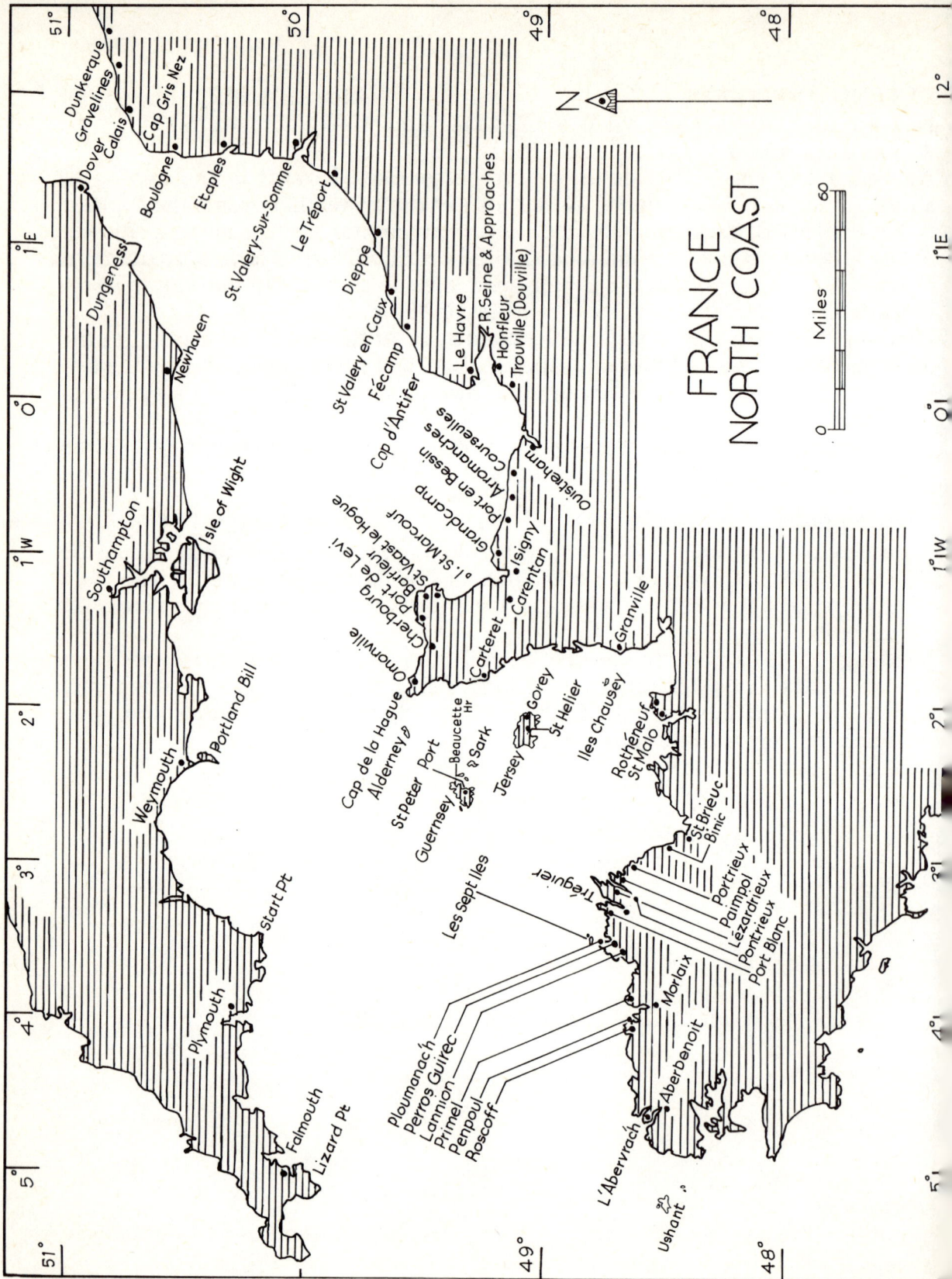

FRANCE
NORTH COAST

Miles 0 ... 60

N

Dunkerque
Gravelines
Calais
Cap Gris Nez
Dover
Boulogne
Etaples
St Valery-Sur-Somme
Le Tréport
Dungeness
Dieppe
Newhaven
St Valery en Caux
Fécamp
Cap d'Antifer
Le Havre
R. Seine & Approaches
Honfleur
Trouville (Douville)
Ouistreham
Courseulles
Arromanches
Port en Bessin
Grandcamp
Isigny
Carentan
Iles St Marcouf
Barfleur
St Vaast le Hougue
Port de Levi
Cherbourg
Omonville
Cap de la Hague
Alderney
St Peter Port
Beaucette Hr
Sark
Guernsey
Jersey
Gorey
St Helier
Iles Chausey
Granville
Carteret
Rothéneuf
St Malo
St Brieuc
Binic
Portrieux
Paimpol
Lézardrieux
Pontrieux
Port Blanc
Tréguier
Les Sept Iles
Ploumanac'h
Perros Guirec
Lannion
Primel
Penpoul
Roscoff
Morlaix
Aberbenoit
L'Aberrvrach
Ushant

Southampton
Isle of Wight
Portland Bill
Weymouth
Start Pt
Plymouth
Falmouth
Lizard Pt

FRANCE

Since the last edition of this *Handbook* was published, the popularity of yachting has greatly increased in France and a large number of new yacht harbours have been built. Older yachtsmen may regret the changes which these developments have brought to some formerly little-known coasts and estuaries, but many family cruising men welcome the security and convenience of the modern marinas. Along the French coast one is seldom far from shelter.

With the introduction of the IALA system of buoyage, navigational marks, for which the French authorities have always had a high reputation, have been further improved: however, the mariner must guard against becoming over-confident. The Normandy coast has shifting sands extending up to a mile or more offshore, and an onshore wind can produce dangerous conditions over a wide area. The north Brittany coast has tidal streams which in places run at 8 knots or more, and rocks which allow no margin for mistakes in navigation. Conditions are less tricky south of Ushant, but this is the Bay of Biscay and much of the coastline is open to the Atlantic.

Nevertheless with careful planning and good seamanship the coasts of France provide a highly enjoyable cruising area.

Charts
Entries for French harbours quote the numbers of the largest scale charts available, either French or British Admiralty. Smaller scale charts will of course also be needed, details of which can be obtained from chart agents. In addition to official charts, useful commercial charts of the French coast are available, published in England by Imray (Imray, Laurie, Norie & Wilson Ltd, St Ives, Cambridgeshire, England), by Stanford Maritime Ltd (12–14 Long Acre, London WC2E 9LP), and in France by EMOM (Editions Maritimes et d'Outre Mer, 17 rue Jacob, 75006 Paris).

Pilot Books
In addition to the Admiralty Pilots, useful books to have aboard when cruising the N coast of France include *North Sea Harbours* (*Calais to Den Helder*) by E.

Delmar Morgan (rev. Jack Coote), *Normandy Harbours and Pilotage* by E. Delmar Morgan (rev. Mark Brackenbury), and *North Brittany Pilot* by Adlard Coles, all published by Adlard Coles Ltd; and *Channel Island Pilot, French Pilot Vol. 1, Omonville to Tréguier* and *Vol 2, Port Blanc to Ile de Sein* by Malcolm Robson, and *Channel Harbours and Anchorages* by Adlard Coles, all published by Nautical Publishing Co. *Brittany and Channel Islands Cruising Guide* by David Jefferson, published by Stanford Maritime, covers the French coast from Cherbourg to St Nazaire, offshore islands and Brittany canals. Much useful information may also be found in *Annuaire Nautisme* published by Editions Chabassol, 30 rue de Gramont, 75002 Paris, covering all France or in regional booklets.

Port entry signals
Details of port entry signals can be found in *Reed's Nautical Almanac*. While in some ports it may not be compulsory for yachts to obey the entry and traffic signals shown, it is generally advisable to do so for their own safety unless directed by the Harbour Authority to ignore them.

Formalities
As always, these are subject to change: for latest information see the CA *Year Book*. Yachts may soon have to carry a Certificate of British Registry; until end-1983, HM Customs Form C1328 (Parts 2 and 3) is accepted.

For further information, see the leaflet 'Yachting and Boating in French Waters' obtainable from the French Government Tourist Office, 178 Piccadilly, London W1V 0AL.

French Inland Waterways (Plan p372)

GENERAL INFORMATION AND CRUISE PLANNING

The internal waterways system of France is an extensive and commercially important network which covers a great part of the country and connects with those of Belgium, Holland and Germany. From a yachtsman's point of view it has a twofold attraction; as a route between sea cruising areas and as an interesting cruising area in its own right.

The best months for navigating the inland waterways are April, May and June. Earlier, the rivers are liable to flood; after June the risk of water shortage increases. Works and repairs to canals are carried out throughout the navigable season and it is essential to obtain the current programme of closures (chômages), a list of which is available from the French Government Tourist Office, London W1V 0AL.

Dimensions The maximum dimensions for a yacht going from the U.K. to the Mediterranean via the main French canals are: length 38.50m, beam 5.05m, draft 1.80m, height 3.50m. On the Canal du Nivernais these dimensions are reduced to

30m × 5.05m × 1.20m × 2.7m. On the Canal de Bourgogne the headroom in the tunnel at Pouilly-en-Auxois is only 3.10m.

For the Canal du Midi between the Atlantic and the Mediterranean the dimensions are: length 30m, beam 5.50m, draft 1.60m, height 3.00m at the centre of bridge arches, reducing to 2.00m at the sides.

On the Brittany route between the Channel and the Atlantic, maximum dimensions are 25.80m × 4.50m × 1.30m × 2.50m.

Through routes

The popular route southwards through France is from Le Havre up the R Seine via Rouen to Paris; 368km, 7 locks. Thence to the Saône by one of the following routes:

The Bourbonnais (Western) route, 500km, 158 locks. Some commercial traffic. Probably the quickest route.

The Nivernais route, 555km, 227 locks. Beautiful and varied. Shallow. No commercial traffic but numerous hire boats.

The Burgundy route, 496km, 227 locks. Very beautiful but slow. Tunnel with restricted headroom. No commercial traffic except south of Dijon.

The Marne (Eastern) route, 578km, 155 locks. Quick. Agreeable country. Some commercial traffic.

All these routes involve the passage of the Rivers Saône and Rhône. From Chalon sur Saône to the mouth of the Rhône is 464km. Do not attempt to go out to sea through the Rhône delta: there are constantly shifting dangerous sandbanks. If eastbound, the best course is to lock out of the R at Port St Louis from where a short canal leads into the Golfe de Fos. Alternatively it is possible to leave the R at Arles and go direct to Fos through the Canal d'Arles à Fos. If westbound in the Mediterranean, it is possible to turn into the Petit Rhône about 2km above Arles: this leads into the Canal du Rhône à Sète and so into the sea either at Aigues Mortes or at Sète.

The Rhône is now completely canalised from Lyon to the sea and the current does not normally exceed 4kn. A pilot is no longer necessary. Any yacht with a reliable engine capable of maintaining a speed of 6kn should have no difficulty about returning upstream.

Other routes

Atlantic to the Mediterranean   From the mouth of the Gironde to Bordeaux is nearly 100km. From Bordeaux to Castets, 56km, where the canal begins, the river is still tidal and there are shallows. If possible arrange to follow a barge. From Castets the Canal Latéral à la Garonne leads to Toulouse, 193km, 53 locks, and from there the Canal du Midi runs to Sète.

On the Canal du Midi, just after Le Somail, is the junction with the Canal de la Nouvelle, 40km, 13 locks, which enters the Mediterranean at Port la Nouvelle.

Brittany Canals   From the English Channel to the Bay of Biscay via St Malo, Dinan, Rennes, Redon and the R Vilaine.

CANALS

ROUTES TO BELGIUM & HOLLAND

1	C. de Calais
2	C. de Dunkerque
3	C. de Bourbourg
4	C. de Furnes
5	C. D'Ypres
6	C. de Plasschendale
7	C. de Bruges
8	Zeebrugge Ship Canal
9	C. de Bruges à Gand
10	Terneuzen Ship Canal
	C. de Mons
12	C. de Charleroi à Bruxelles à Rupel
13	Albert Canal
14	Antwerp - Rotterdam Canal
15	C. de Dessel à Schoten
16	C. de Bocholt à Herentals
17	C. de Dessel à Kwaardmechelin
18	Zuidwillemsvaart
19	Maas-Vaal Canal

ROUTES TO GERMANY

20	C. de L'aisne à L'oise
21	C. des Ardennes
22	C. de L'est Br. Nord
23	C. de La Marne au Rhin
24	C. de Houilleres
25	C. d'Alsace
26	C. de L'est Br. Sud
27	C. Du Rhône au Rhin

ROUTES TO PARIS

28	C. du Nord
29	C. de St. Quentin
30	C. Sambre à L'Oise
31	C. de la Somme
32	Tancarville Canal
33	C. de L'Ourcq

ROUTES TO MEDITERRANEAN

(I) MARNE ROUTE

34	C. Lat. à La Marne
35	C. de la Marne à la Saone

(II) BOURGOGNE/NIVERNAIS ROUTE

36	C. de la Haute Seine
37	C. de Bourgogne
38	C. du Nivernais

(III) BOURBONNAIS ROUTE

39	C. du Loing
40	C. de Briare
41	C. Lat. à la Loire
42	C. Roanne à Digoin
43	C. du Centre

RIVER RHONE

44	C. d'Arles à Fos
45	C. du Rhône à Sete

BRITTANY CANALS

46	C. d'Ille et Rance
47	C. du Blavet
48	C. Nantes à Brest

GIRONDE/MIDI ROUTE

49	C. Lat. à la Garonne
50	C. du Midi

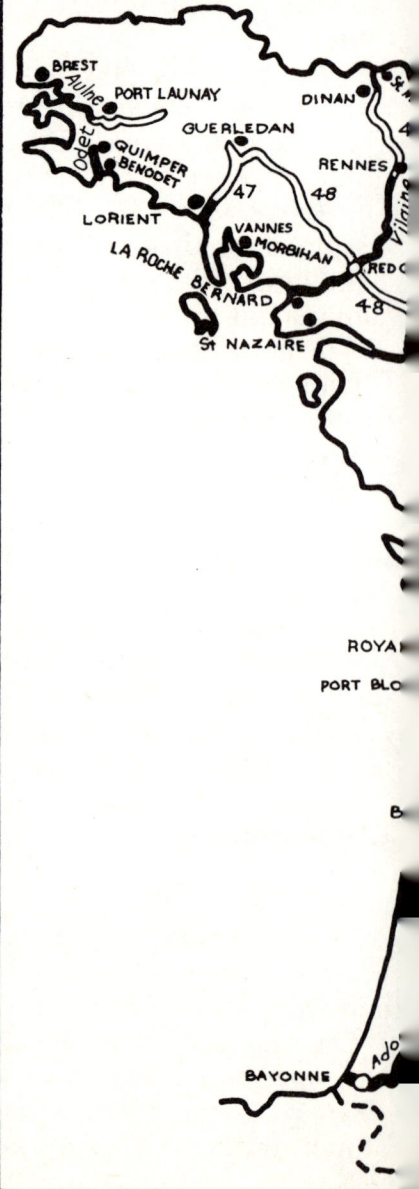

NAVIGABLE WATERWAYS
OF FRANCE

NAVIGABLE RIVERS

CANALS

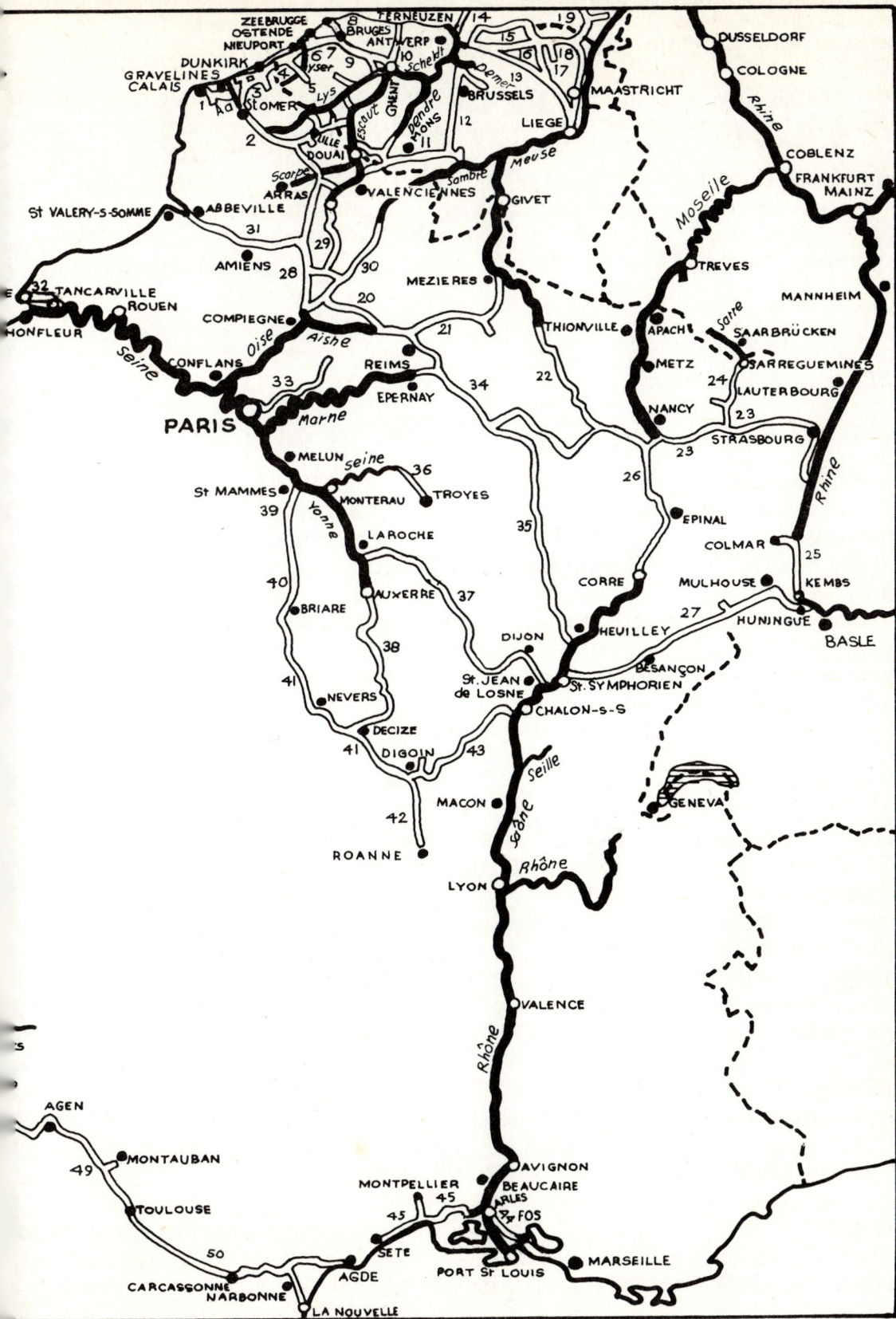

ZEEBRUGGE
OSTENDE
NIEUPORT
DUNKIRK
GRAVELINES
CALAIS
St VALERY-S-SOMME
TANCARVILLE
HONFLEUR
ROUEN
ABBEVILLE
AMIENS
COMPIEGNE
CONFLANS
PARIS
MELUN
St MAMMES
MONTEREAU
BRIARE
AUXERRE
NEVERS
DECIZE
DIGOIN
ROANNE
MACON
LYON
VALENCE
AGEN
MONTAUBAN
TOULOUSE
CARCASSONNE
NARBONNE
LA NOUVELLE
AGDE
SETE
MONTPELLIER
PORT St LOUIS
MARSEILLE
FOS
ARLES
BEAUCAIRE
AVIGNON
GENEVA
St SYMPHORIEN
BESANÇON
St JEAN de LOSNE
CHALON-S-S
DIJON
HEUILLEY
CORRE
MULHOUSE
KEMBS
HUNINGUE
BASLE
COLMAR
EPINAL
STRASBOURG
NANCY
LAUTERBOURG
SARREGUEMINES
METZ
SAARBRÜCKEN
APACH
SARRE
TREVES
THIONVILLE
MEZIERES
GIVET
VALENCIENNES
ARRAS
DOUAI
LILLE
HONS
MONS
LIEGE
MAASTRICHT
BRUSSELS
GHENT
ANTWERP
BRUGES
TERNEUZEN
St OMER
Aa
Yser
Lys
Scorpe
Escaut
Sambre
Dendre
Demer
Scheldt
Meuse
Oise
Aisne
Marne
Seine
Yonne
Seille
Saône
Rhône
Rhine
Moselle
DUSSELDORF
COLOGNE
COBLENZ
FRANKFURT
MAINZ
MANNHEIM
REIMS
EPERNAY
TROYES
LAROCHE

LILLE
DOUAI

1 2 5 6 7 8 9 10 11 12 13 14 15 16 17 18 19
3 4
31 29 30 28 20 21 22
33 34 24 23
36 26 25
35 23
39 37 27
40 38
41
41 43
42
49 45 45
50

373

Other through routes   There are other through routes. It is possible to enter the Belgian and French waterways at Zeebrugge, Dunkerque, Gravelines or Calais.

For detailed coverage of the above routes, see the separate Cruising Association publication 'Notes on French Inland Waterways'. When planning a cruise on the inland waterways it is essential to check both dimensions and depths and the programme of closures (*chômages*). Do not place too much reliance on published dimensions and depths: depths in particular can vary appreciably according to season.

French Channel Ports

DUNKERQUE   Charts BA 1352, F 6500   (Plan p375)
HW +0.55.   DS: E −2.00; W +4.00.
MHWS 5.8; MLWS 0.6; MTL 3.2; MHWN 4.7; MLWN 1.5.
A busy commercial hr, but with good facilities for yachts.
Approach   Must be along the coast by well buoyed channels from E or W. The offshore banks dry at LAT, and should not be crossed even at HW except in light winds.
Entrance   Straightforward, but allow for strong cross-set outside pier-heads. Keep along E breakwater into Avant Port, giving way to commercial shipping. Capitainerie listens on VHF Ch 12.
Berthing   Alongside yacht pontoons on the W side of the Avant Port (2m). Fuel, water, repairs. All stores from town, some distance.

GRAVELINES   Chart F 6501   (Plan p375)
HW +0.45.   DS: W −4.00; E −1.00. Slack +5.00 to −5.00.
MHWS 5.9; MLWS 0.5; MTL 3.2; MHWN 4.8; MLWN 1.4.
Bar   Variable, dries about 1.5m. Reported silting. Do not attempt in strong onshore winds.
Approach and entrance   The hr lies midway between Calais and Dunkerque, each distant 10M. It may be recognised by the villages Grand and Petit Port Philippe on either side of the entrance. Be careful to allow for the stream, which sets hard to the E across the entrance at HW.

Enter 1h before HW and hug W pier entering, E pier when inside. Port Philippe lt tr (Oc(4) WG 12s) has W sector 193°–200°, G sector 186°–193°.
Berthing   Vessels may take the ground in the tidal hr, soft mud, or berth in the basin, available HW −1 to +1. Quays are reserved for commercial and fishing craft.

Canals to Belgian and French waterways.

CALAIS   Charts BA 1352, F 6474   (Plan p376)
HW +0.35.   DS: E −2.00; W +3.30.
MHWS 7.2; MLWS 1.0; MTL 4.1; MHWN 6.0; MLWN 2.2.

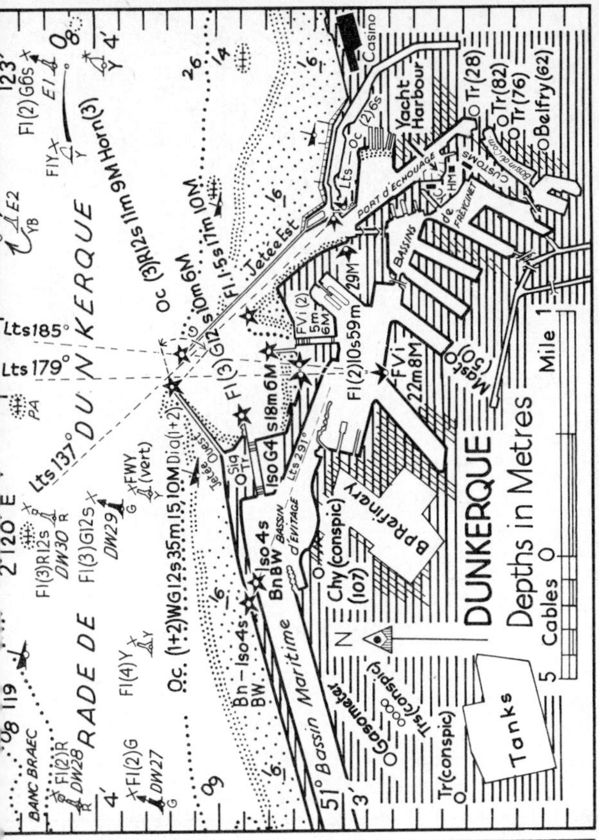

DUNKERQUE
Depths in Metres

Top-left panel (DUNKERQUE):

123'
Fl(2)G6s
El.4.0.8'
FlY
Y 4'
Y 8'

Casino
Yacht Harbour
Tr(28)
Tr(82)
Tr(76)
Belfry(62)

Oc(2)G6s

E2
YB

Lts185°

Lts179°
PA

RADE DE DUNKERQUE

Lts137°

2120 E

Oc(3)R12s11m9M Horn(3)

Oc(3)R12s10m6M

Fl.G12s10m6M

Fl.5s17m10M

Tete.fst.
PORT D'ECHOUAGE
CUSTOMS

Lts185°
Lts179° PA

Fl(3)G12s
FVl 5m 6M
Fl(2)10s59m24M
FVl 22m8M

Fl(3)R12s
DW28
Fl(3)G12s
DW29
G

FWY
Iso.G4s18m6M
Iso.4s
BnBW
BASSIN MARITIME

G.FWY
Y
G(vert)

Fl(4)Y
Y

Oc(1+2)WG12s35m.15.10MDig(1+2)

Bn.Iso.4s
BW

Chy(conspic)
Tr(conspic)

Fl(3)R12s
DW28
BANC BRAEC
Fl(2)R
DW27
G

N
Tks(conspic)
O.Gasometer

51° Bassin Maritime

TANKS

Mile 1
Cables 0
5

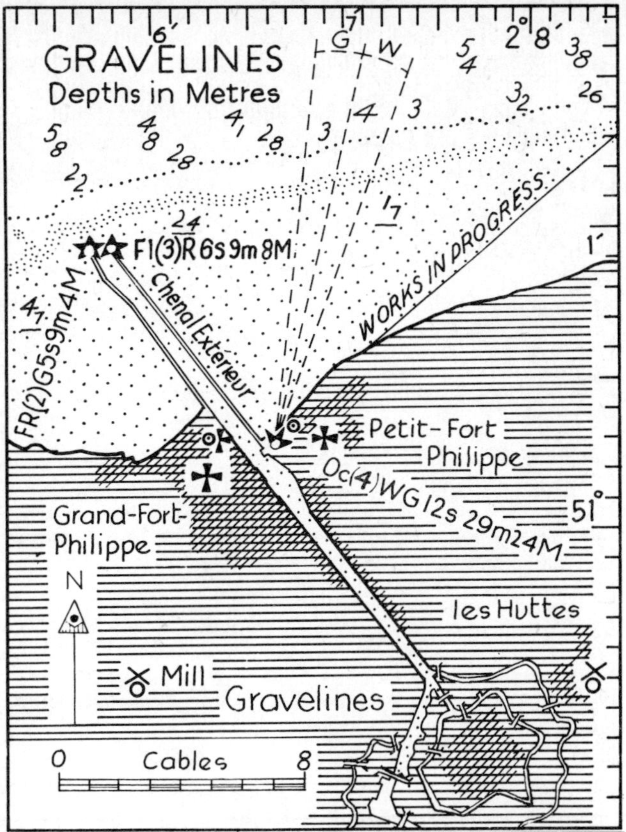

GRAVELINES
Depths in Metres

2°8'38

G W
6'
5 4

Chenal Exterieur

WORKS IN PROGRESS

Fl(3)R6s9m8M

FR(2)G6s9m4M

Petit-Fort Philippe

Oc(4)WG12s29m24M

51°

Grand-Fort-Philippe

les Huttes

N

Mill

Gravelines

0   Cables   8

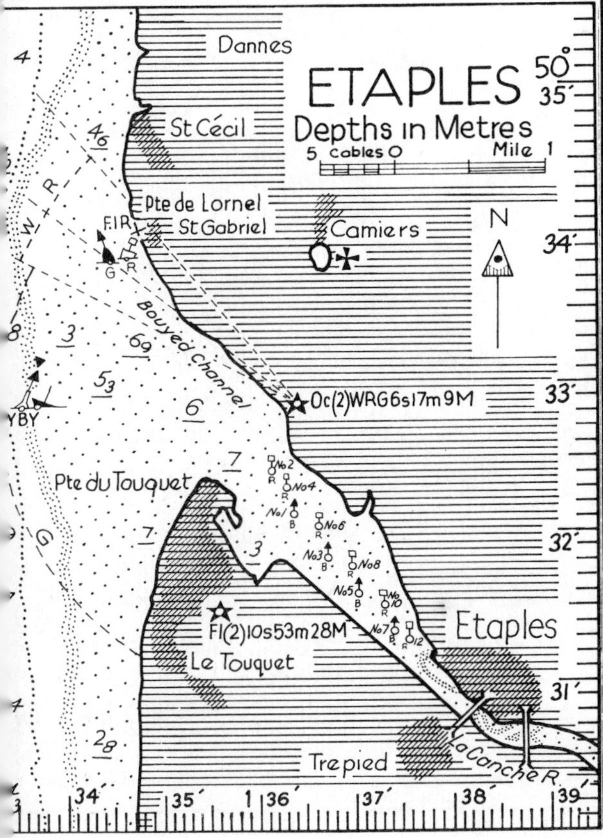

ETAPLES
Depths in Metres

Dannes

50°35'

5 Cables 0   Mile 1

St Cécil

Pte de Lornel
St Gabriel

Camiers

34'

N

F.l.R

Bouled Channel

YBY

Oc(2)WRG6s17m9M

33'

No2
R
No4
No1
No6

Pte du Touquet

7

No3
B
No8
No5B
No7
WD

32'

Fl(2)10s53m28M

No7
Di2

Etaples

Le Touquet

31'

Trepied

La Conche R

34'   35'   1 36'   37'   38'   39'

St VALERY sur SOMME
Depths in Metres

La Maye.R
St Firmin

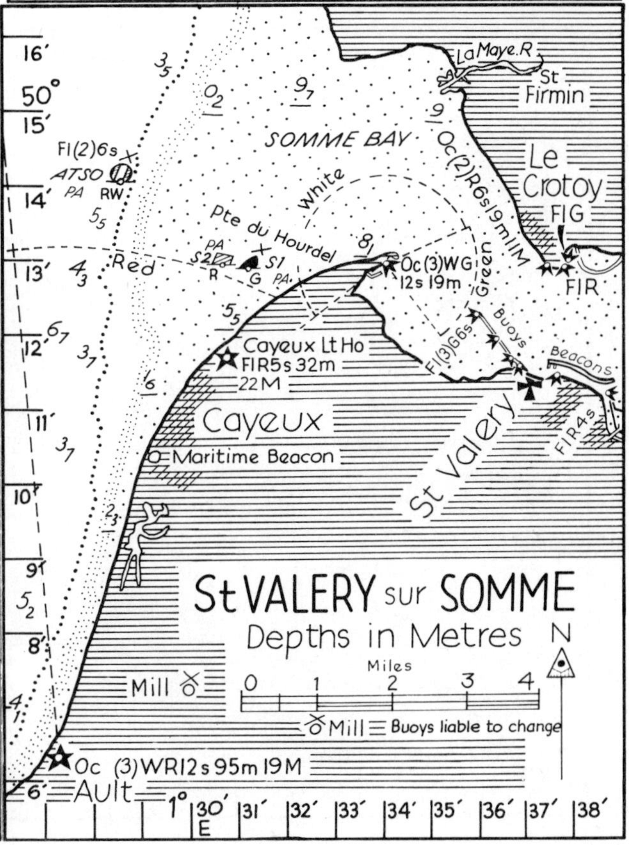

16'
50°
15'

SOMME BAY

Oc(2)R6s19m11M

Fl(2)6s
ATSO
PA RW

14'

Le Crotoy

Fl.G

Pte du Hourdel
PA
S2 S1
R G

white

13'

Red

Oc(3)WG12s19m

FlR

8'

Fl(3)G6s

buoys

beacons

12'

6,7

Cayeux Lt Ho
Fl.R5s32m 22M

Cayeux

St Valery

Fl.R4s

11'

Maritime Beacon

10'

9'

Miles
St VALERY sur SOMME
Depths in Metres   N

0 1 2 3 4

8'

Mill

Mill   Buoys liable to change

Oc(3)WR12s95m19M
Ault

6'

1°30'E 31' 32' 33' 34' 35' 36' 37' 38'

BOULOGNE
Depths in Metres

Cables

Pte de la Creche · Fort de la Creche · Old Fort (ruin) · Digue Nord · Old Battery · RD · PLAGE DES BAINS · Casino · TV Relay · Mast · Sig Stn · LB & Pilots · Quai d'échouage · PORT DE MARÉE · LA LIANE FLEUVE · Chanzy · Quai Chanzy · Quai Thurot · Bassin à flot · Quai Desire · Quai Desire Delmotte · Mole Sud · Quai Jean Voisin · Bassin Loubet · Yacht Harbour · Sig Mast · White Tanks · Quai Amiral Huguet · Tr(conspic) · Water Tr · High Chys · Tr(conspic) · DARSE SARRAZ BOURNET · Quai de l'Europe · PETIT PORT · Caisson (ruin) · Hovercraft Station · FR(occas)

FIR 1·5s 10m 7M · FI(2+1)5s 26m 19M Horn(2+1) 60s · Ldg Lts 123° · RADE CARNOT · FI(2)R6s · RC2 · RC1 · Iso G4s · Intensified sector · Digue Carnot · RD 101° · Ldg Lts 119° 30′

FR II m 8M · FI 11m 14M · FG · FR II m 4M · Iso G4s · FR64m II M

CALAIS
Depths in Metres

Cables

FI(3)Y (2 buoys) · Oc(2)R6s · CA10 · Oc(2)R6s · CA10 · Colais Main Lt 140° · Lts in line 118° 30′ · Iso G3s 12m 9M Bell · Jetée Ouest · Jetée Est · FG(occas) · FI(2)R10s 11M 18M Dia 2 · Sand Dunes · Digue Nord · BASSIN DES CHASSES DE L'EST · FR 14m 10M · Water Tr · Sig Stn · Pylon · HM · Quai de la Loire · BASSIN CARNOT · FI(4)5s 59m 22M · Bldg(conspic) · Old Belfry · Dry Dock · Chy · Moselle · Quai de la Moselle · Quai de la Meuse · Canal de la Meuse · Canal d'Asfeld · Quai de l'Iscaut · Quai du Rhin · Quai Tamise · Quai du Danube · Tr(82)(conspic) · Water Tr · Avant Port · Fort Risban · Le Grand Courant · YC · Yacht Harbour · BASSIN DE L'OUEST · Canal d'Asfeld

376

Based on British Admiralty Charts (nos. in text) with the permission of the Controller of H.M. Stationery Office and of the Hydrographer of the Navy, and on other sources.

Approach In winds over force 6 from NW to NE it is wiser to make for Boulogne. Calais hr lies 11¼M E of C Gris Nez Lt Ho (W tr, Fl 5s, siren) and 21½M from Dover pier-head.

From the W keep C Gris Nez well open of C Blanc Nez until abreast the entrance, when bring Calais Lt Ho (Fl(4) 15s) to bear between the jetty lts, 140°, and proceed on this bearing, remembering that the spring tide sets hard to E across the jetties at HW. From E keep at least 2M offshore until the pier-heads bear 185°, except in calm weather above half-tide, when it is safe to cross the Ridens shoal.

Entrance Beware of strong cross-set in outer part of entrance, as the stream flows straight through the piles of the piers at up to 4kn. Keep clear of heavy ferry traffic. Port Radio listens on Ch 12.

Berthing The YC du Nord de la France has a yacht hr in the Bassin de l'Ouest with all facilities. If not locking in or when waiting for gates to open one can lie alongside quay on E side of W arm of Avant Port (N two-thirds only) or pick up a mooring if available. If forced to anch, keep 20m from W and S sides on account of dredger's anch chain, and rig tripping line. There is a hard in corner to N of lock gates. Scend can be severe in Avant Port.

Only enter E arm of Avant Port if entering Bassin Carnot en route for the inland waterway system.

BOULOGNE   Charts BA 438, F 6436, 5526   (Plan p376)
HW +0.05.   DS: S +4.15; N −2.30.
MHWS 8.9; MLWS 1.1; MTL 5.0; MHWN 7.1; MLWN 2.8.

The entrance between the pier-heads is sheltered by the outer breakwater, so the hr is always available. This makes it particularly valuable as it is one of the few hrs on the coast that can be used at any state of the tide.

Approach The sea breaks heavily on the offshore shoals (Bassure de Baas) S and N of the entrance in gales from SW to NW, when it is best to keep 3M offshore until the entrance bears E. The town is easily identified by conspic landmarks. The Terres de Tourmont rise to a height of 175m 9M S of the town and are visible 25M to seaward. Overlooking the town itself are Mt Lambert surmounted by a fort, 184m, the tr of the cathedral, and further to N the conspic column of the Grand Armée, 137m. The N breakwater has a sunken outer part: its outer end is marked by a wooden tr, Fl R.

Entrance Enter between this tr and the outer end of the S breakwater. Steer S 1 ca inside the S pier until inner piers open up (ldg lts 123°), when steer for inner hr. Lts G over W over R (shown from S side of inner hr entrance) prohibit all movement in the inner hr: yachts must obey this signal. Once inside inner piers keep to N side until yacht pontoons come in sight beyond Gare Maritime.

Berthing At yacht pontoons as directed or as space allows. 2.4m at ends of pontoons, but no more than 1m LWS near quay. Grid. Water, no fuel. All supplies.

ETAPLES
Chart F 5526 (Plan p375)

HW HWD.   DS: N −2.45; S +3.20.

MHWS 8.8; MLWS 0.9; MTL 4.8; MHWN 7.1; MLWN 2.6.

A drying hr, only to be explored by shallow draft yachts in good weather. Approaches and hr dry: approach 1h before HW. In W winds and thick weather this coast should not be closed unless position is accurately known, as the sea breaks heavily several miles offshore and the stream at springs sets into the bays and violently across the banks, 4kn.

Bar   The banks between the pts of entrance dry to over a mile off the shoreline.

Approach   Only in good weather, preferably a few days before springs. The valley of the R Canche lies 12M S of Boulogne, between the Pte de Lornel and the Pte du Touquet, and may be located by its position S of the Terres de Tourmont, a conspic range 175m high, visible from 25M to seaward in clear weather. The S side is marked by a Lt Ho, R tr with brown band, Fl(2) 10s, 53m. The NW shore is marked by the Camiers Lt Ho, R metal framework tr, Oc(2) WRG, 6s, 17m; W over the best water, R and G over the highest banks.

Entrance   The chan is marked by buoys and bns, altered to meet changes. The first pair is usually about ½M W of Pte de Lornel. There is about 1m to Etaples at HWN; over 2½m at HWS.

Berthing   Vessels ground alongside quay on NW side of town. Some stores, no facilities.

SAINT VALERY-SUR-SOMME
Chart F 3800 (Plan p375)

HW (Le Hourdel) +0.15; (St Valéry) +0.25.   DS: NNE −2.10; SW +3.20.

MHWS (St Valéry) 9.8; MHWN 7.9.

The entrance to the R Somme lies between St Quentin Pt to N and the town of Cayeux to S.

Bar   The estuary dries 1½M to seaward of the shoreline. Strangers are advised to employ a local pilot or fisherman. The channel dries: there is 3m to St Valéry at HWN. The banks are constantly changing and various wrecks lie in the vicinity of the entrance.

Approach   The N Card Baie de Somme buoy, VQ, lies about 325° 2¾M from the Cayeux Lt Ho. The entrance to the chan is marked by a pair of buoys (A1, G con, and A2, R can) about 1 to 2M inshore of this buoy, their position varying but usually SE to SSE of it. Although tortuous and variable the chan is well buoyed from here. At least 2h at 4kn made good should be allowed for the passage between the outer buoy and St Valéry. In up to force 5, entry may often be difficult but not normally dangerous; above, especially in SW–NW winds and on the ebb, conditions can be hazardous. Good timing is essential: the stream can run at up to 5kn at springs. There is little water at neaps, especially if wind is E, and departure should be not later than HW −30 min.

Entrance   Cayeux Lt Ho, a W tr with R top, 32m high, Fl R 5s, lies about 2M WSW of the entrance. At Le Hourdel Pt a lt Oc(3) WG shows W to seaward, G to landward. The buoyed chan leads to the RWVS chan division buoy which lies about ½M E of Pte du Hourdel.

Berthing   From the division buoy one chan runs in a generally SE direction to St Valéry-sur-Somme. This chan is marked with buoys and bns. There are sea walls projecting some way from the land, submerged at HW, and it is essential to keep closely to the fairway. Continue to the marina where there are yacht berths, bow to pontoon and stern to buoy, about 1.5m at LW at the ends of the pontoon; roots dry. Haul stern lines very taut as streams are strong, especially on the ebb. Petrol from pontoon but no diesel. Canal to Abbeville. Good shops, hotels etc. Chandlery.

Le Crotoy   The other chan from the division buoy runs in a generally E direction to Le Crotoy. It has less water: only about 1m at MHWN. The buoy numbers are prefixed with letter C. From the last buoy steer for the fishing boat quay and keep well to port right round to the yacht hr, leaving a small G spher buoy to stb. Then turn to stb and berth on one of the pontoons. Berths dry. Shops and restaurants in Le Crotoy.

LE TREPORT   Chart BA 1351; F 934, 5928   (Plan p380)
HW −0.05.   DS: SW +2.00; NE −4.30.
MHWS 9.2; MLWS 0.6; MTL 4.9; MHWN 7.3; MLWN 2.3.

Bar   The sands dry 1½ ca off the mole-heads. The depth in the entrance is 5.8m at MHWN when vessels of 3m draft can enter the basin. Entrance is possible for medium draft within 3h of HW in good weather. Difficult in strong onshore winds, and severe scend in outer hr in such conditions.

Approach   Le Tréport lies 13½M from Dieppe and 3½M N of Mt Joli-Bois pyramid. From W keep the E pier-head, lt Oc R, signals, open of the W pier-head, lt Fl(2) G, to clear Les Granges and other rks.

Entrance   Allow for the NE set of stream: wind baffles and squalls in entrance. Flag 'P' or W lights means entrance open.

Berthing   Vessels may find a berth in NE corner of tidal hr, soft mud, heavy scend at times, or in the basin through the lock. To enter, sound three blasts. The dock opens about 1h before HW, closes at HW. Entry signal: G flag or G lt. Exit: R flag or R lt.

   Water, stores. No diesel. Crane (4½T). Boatyard (S quay).

DIEPPE   Charts BA 2147, F 934, 5927   (Plan p380)
HW −0.10.   DS: ENE −4.45; WSW +1.15.
MHWS 9.1; MLWS 0.6; MTL 4.8; MHWN 7.1; MLWN 2.4.
Hr is available at all states of the tide and is dredged to about 4m. Basin opens HW −2 to +1. Swell runs into hr.

Approach   Dieppe lies 5M E of Pte d'Ailly Lt Ho, a W square tr, Fl(3) 20s. Vessels should steer for the W jetty head; lt Iso WG, reed. The ldg lts, QR, lead in 138°: front W structure R top, rear W hut R top.

Entrance   The chan hugs the W jetty, is 75m wide and bears SSE; curves S and

LE TRÉPORT
Depths in Metres

50°
4·5'
1° 22'

FI(2) G 10s 15m 23M
Reed Mo(N)
OcR 4s 8m 7M
HM
Station
Casino
Crucifix
Yacht Moorings
Water Tr
Water Tr
N
0 Mile 1
3·5'
1° 23'

St VALERY EN CAUX
Depths in Metres

0° 42'
8 43'
Oc(2+1)G 12s13m14M
FI(2)R6s
St Leger
Customs
Parking
AVANT PORT (80 PLACE
Bridge & Lock
PORT DE PLAISANCE (650 PLACES)
Dieppe
0 Cables 3
N

DIEPPE
Depths in Metres

1° 4·7'
IsoWG4s11m12,8M
Reed 30s
Awash
Oc(4)R12s12m8M
Ldg Lts 138°
Red
A5
Pte de Femme Grosse
Sig Mast
QR 19m 6M
Sig Station 49°
Radio Mast
FI Vi
QR 35m6M 56'
Belfry
56'
Dieppe
Quai la Marne
Sig Mast
N
Quai
Avant Port
Visitors
LB
Belfry
Le Pollet
YC
Bassin Duquesne
Arrière Port
Gunremer
Bassin Canada
Larques R
Yacht Basin
Tr
55'·5'
1° 5'
5·5'
49°
55·5
0 1 Cables 2

FÉCAMP
Depths in Metres

0° 22E
22·5
Les Charpentiers
46·3'
Pte Fagnet
Semaphore
N D du Salut
FI(2)10s 14m 12M
T.V. Pylon
49°
46'
Quay
Avant Port
Arrière Port
Half-tide Basi
Bassin Bérigny
Bassin Freycine
Quay
Chy
Chy
Fécamp
Casino
N
0 1 2 3 4 5
Cables

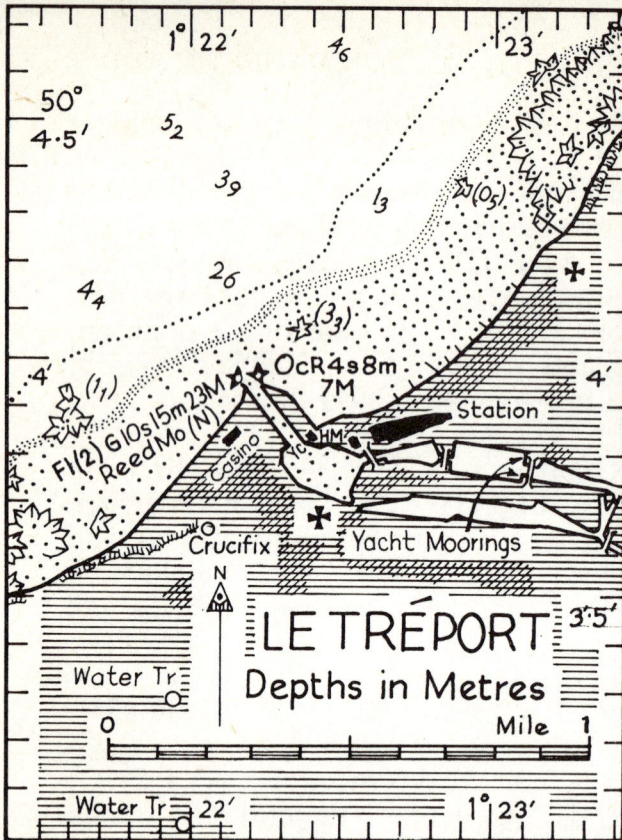

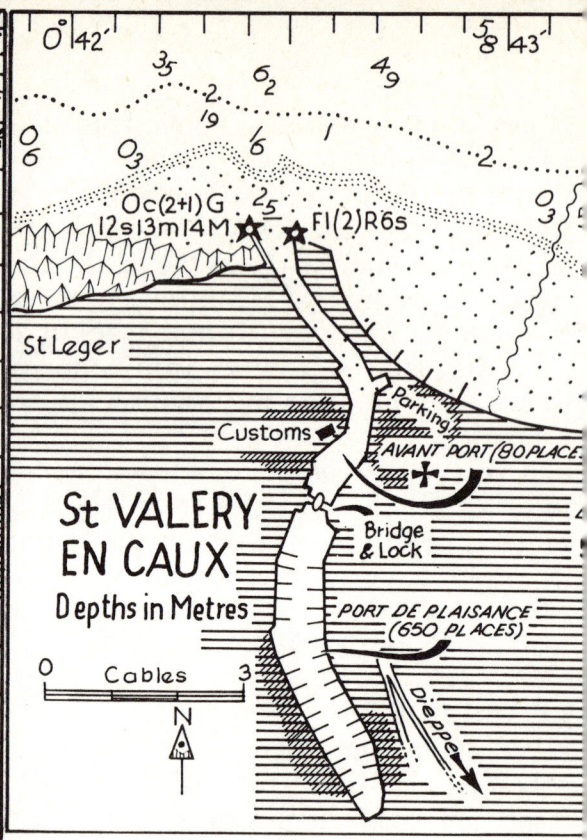

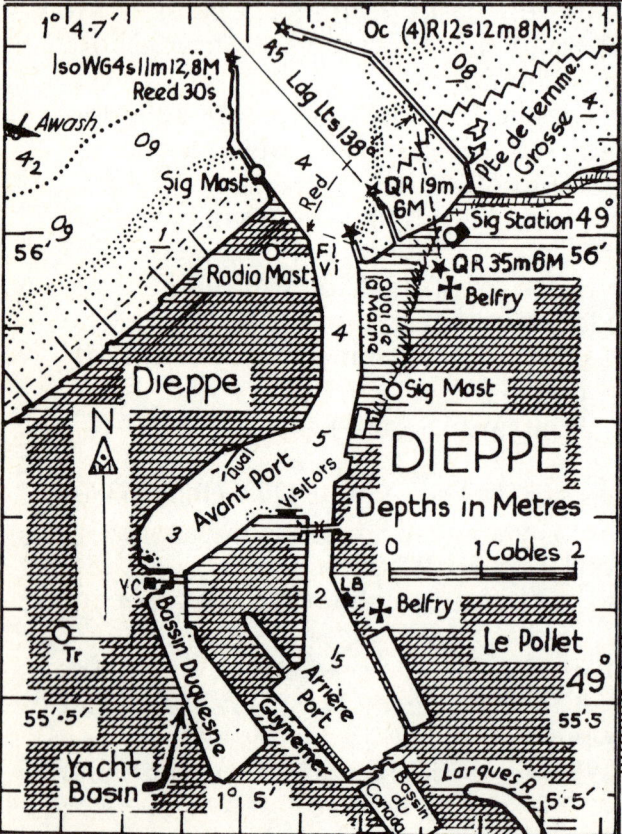

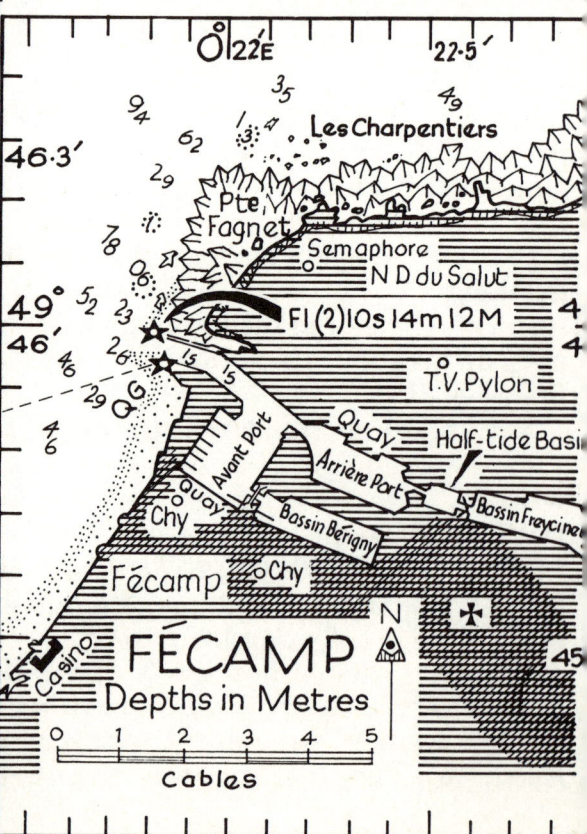

Based on British Admiralty Charts (nos. in text) with the permission of the Controller of H.M. Stationery Office and the Hydrographer of the Navy, and on other sources.

then turns to W into Avant Port. Yachts must obey traffic signals: R over W over R, no entry; G over W over G, no departure; G over W over R, no entry or departure. Keep clear of ferries and beware dredger cables. Port Radio Ch 12.
Berthing Vessels can take the ground in Arrière Port to SE, about 1m, soft bottom, entered through a drawbridge. Yachts usually lie at pontoon W of bridge into Arrière Port (a bad berth in onshore winds) until they can enter Bassin Duquesne. YC and pontoons on stb hand.

Heavy swell in outer hr with winds between SW and N. All facilities and stores. Good restaurants.

SAINT VALERY-EN-CAUX   Chart F 933   (Plan p380)
HW −0.25.   DS: ENE −5.00; WSW +1.00.
MHWS 8.7; MLWS 0.8; MTL 4.7; MHWN 7.0; MLWN 2.3.
A small tidal hr which has been converted into a marina with space for about 650 yachts. Entrance dangerous in winds from N to NE over force 5.
Approach   Care must be taken to avoid the Ridens, 1M ENE of entrance, 0.6m. The hr lies between two piers, 365m long, 55 to 35m apart. There is 2m in the entrance at half-tide: advisable to wait for more water if wind is onshore.
Entrance   Enter between piers, and keep over to E pier, leaving R posts marking wave-break ramp close to port, to avoid shingle bank off W pier. Then keep to mid-channel. There is an eddy across the entrance from E to W on the flood, continuing until ½h after HW.
Berthing   There are a few moorings on which one can wait until lock gates open (2¼h either side of HW). When gates open, tie up on visitors' pontoon just inside on stb side, and confirm with hr office on bridge. All stores, good restaurants, crane, repairs.

FECAMP   Charts F 932, 931   (Plan p380)
HW −0.35.   DS: SW +0.20; NE −5.00.
MHWS 7.7; MLWS 0.7; MTL 4.3; MHWN 6.4; MLWN 2.5.
Bar   Entrance chan is dredged to 1.5m. Approach shelves steeply and can be dangerous in strong winds from W or NW.
Approach   The Charpentiers rks which extend from Pte Fagnet at N of entrance should be given a good berth. Small craft will carry 3.7m if they keep the semaphore on top of Pte Fagnet in view. In strong W or NW winds yachts should only enter between HW −2 and +1. The tidal stream is slack at HW; strong cross-set onto the rocks during the flood. Under sail beware of sudden failure of wind due to baffling.
Entrance   The entrance lies between two jetties. N jetty has lt Fl(2), 10s; S jetty lt QG. R flag or lt on mast on S jetty means no entry, G flag or lt no departure. Enter in mid-channel: beware cross-sets and shingle spit running W from S jetty head.
Berthing   On pontoons in Avant Port. The outer half of pontoon C is reserved for visitors. Otherwise, if not directed by the HM take any vacant space and contact the Capitainerie at the top of the main ramp.

Water on pontoons, fuel from pontoon just NE of lock into Bassin Bérigny (gates open HW −2). For long stay or if leaving boat unattended, lock into Bassin Bérigny as there is considerable scend in Avant Port in certain conditions. Showers, bar etc at the YC which shares the Capitainerie buildings. Good shops, restaurants, chandlery etc.

PASSAGE NOTE: FECAMP TO LE HAVRE

It is important to give a good berth to the oil terminal S of Cap d'Antifer, and do nothing to impede the large tankers who can enter and leave at speed, and have to stick closely to the buoyed chan. The coast is clean from there to Cap de la Hève, from close off which a yacht can cut across into the entrance chan of Le Havre at buoy LH 14.

SEINE ESTUARY   Charts BA 2146, F 6683, 4937   (Plan p383)
Navigation of the Seine Estuary, especially at spring tides, requires extreme care owing to the numerous and shifting banks of hard sand. Early morning fog is very frequent in the estuary and in the river itself.

The Seine bore (le Mascaret), which used to cause dangerous conditions at times of exceptional height of tide in the river, officially no longer exists, but between Quillebeuf and La Mailleraye it can still be experienced in less violent form at high spring tides.

The stand of the tide at HW is very marked in the bay and particularly in the estuary, where the period during which the tide does not fall more than 20cm varies; about 3h and 2h at springs and neaps respectively.

The entrance to the river is either by the Chenal de Rouen or, in bad weather, by the Tancarville Canal.
Chenal de Rouen   This chan is subject to slight changes but is very well marked by buoys and beacons. The fastest passage will be made by leaving Le Havre in time to reach the main chan as the flood begins. Since the time of HW is progressively later as one ascends the river, a yacht of moderate speed can reach Rouen on one tide. Alternatively, from Honfleur or Deauville leave as soon as the gates open and go as far as possible upstream to anch or moor when the ebb starts.
Canal de Tancarville   Avoids the lower part of the estuary but is not recommended unless conditions there are exceptionally bad. There are two locks and many swing brs which may open only after a prolonged wait. From the yacht hr at Le Havre, enter by the small craft lock at the E end of the Arrière Port past the Thoresen ferry quay. Then cross the Bassin de la Citadelle into the Bassin de l'Eure. Turn sharp to stb and take the first opening on the port side through the bridge into the Bassin Fluvial. This leads into the Bassin Vétillart and so into the canal. Lock into the river at Tancarville; lock only operates near HW.

The Seine is tidal to the lock at Amfreville-Poses, 40km above Rouen. A yacht with mast stepped can get as far as the Bassin St Gervais on the N bank of the

SEINE ENTRANCE, LE HAVRE & HONFLEUR

Depths in Metres

Miles

0 Cables   1

NOTE
See also plans of
Le Havre & Honfleur

Canal de Tancarville

Canal Central Maritime

Harfleur

Le Havre

Honfleur

Water Tr
Chy
Chy
Tr
Fort
Fort
Spire
Water Tr
Fort

Bassin du Commerce
Bassin Vauban
Bassin Dock
Bassin Bellot
Bassin Fluvial
Bassin du Roi
Quai Hermann du Pasquier
Quai de la Flandre
Garage de Graville (Red Lts)
Chys
Chys (conspic) (Red Lts)
Retillart
Mole Central
Digue Charles Laroche
Digue Sud
Digue Ouest
Digue Nord

Tr (conspic)
F 78m 26M
F 36m 27M
FIR 5s15m 21M Raed

Bn

Banc d'Amford

Gambe d'Amford

works in progress (1978)

Green
Red

CHENAL DE ROUEN (Marked by light buoys)

Digue du Ratier (marked by beacons)

Banc du Ratier

LES RATELETS

DE L'A O

ESTUAIRE

SEINE

Grand Placard Sud

FI(3)Y4S
FI Y4S
Oc(2)R
Oc(2)R
ISOG
FI(4)R
FI(5)Y2O5
ISOG15s
FR
No6
Rotier
Ratelets
VBY
YB
YBY
Kannick 2.2 Wk

CAP DE LA HÈVE
FI5s123m 24M
Bn
FI GLH13
OcR LHI.4
R Ldg Lts
ISOG
107°
LYB
LHI.6
LHI5
Oc(2)R

Honfleur
Old Lt Ho
Villa (conspic)
Bn
Oc(2)R6s12M
FI(3)WRG12s15m 18,14,14M
QG
Q
QG
VQ(6)LFI.10s
FI(9)15s

N

Ratier S

Banc du Ratier
FI

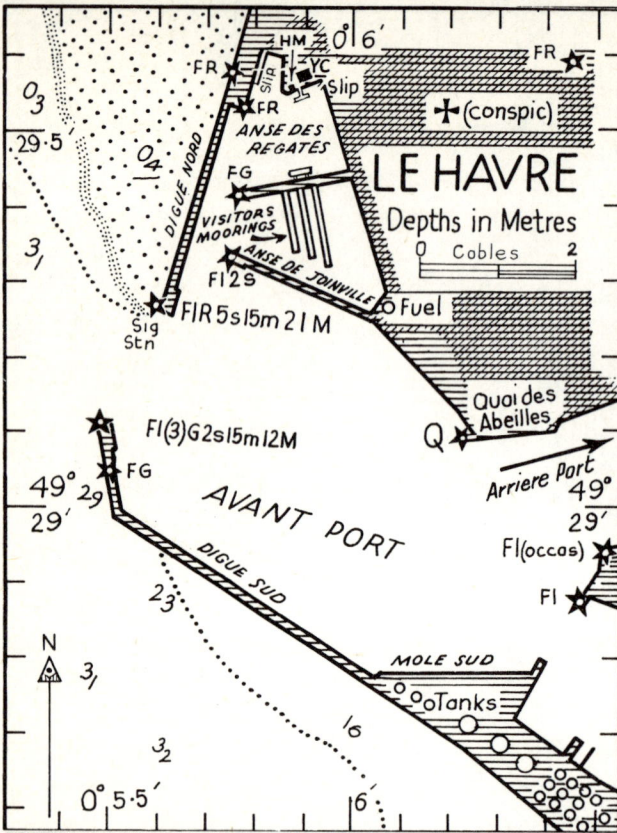

LE HAVRE
Depths in Metres

0 Cables 2

✠ (conspic)

DIGUE NORD
FR
HM
YC
Slip
FR
FR
FG
ANSE DES REGATES
VISITORS MOORINGS
ANSE DE JOINVILLE
Fl 2s
FlR 5s 15m 21 M
Sig Stn

O°6'
29·5'
0·3
0·4

49° 29·5'
FG
Fl(3)G 2s 15m 12M
AVANT PORT
DIGUE SUD
23
31
32
N
3·1
MOLE SUD
Tanks
16
16
0° 5·5'

Fuel
Quai des Abeilles
Q
Arriere Port
49° 29'
Fl(occas)
Fl

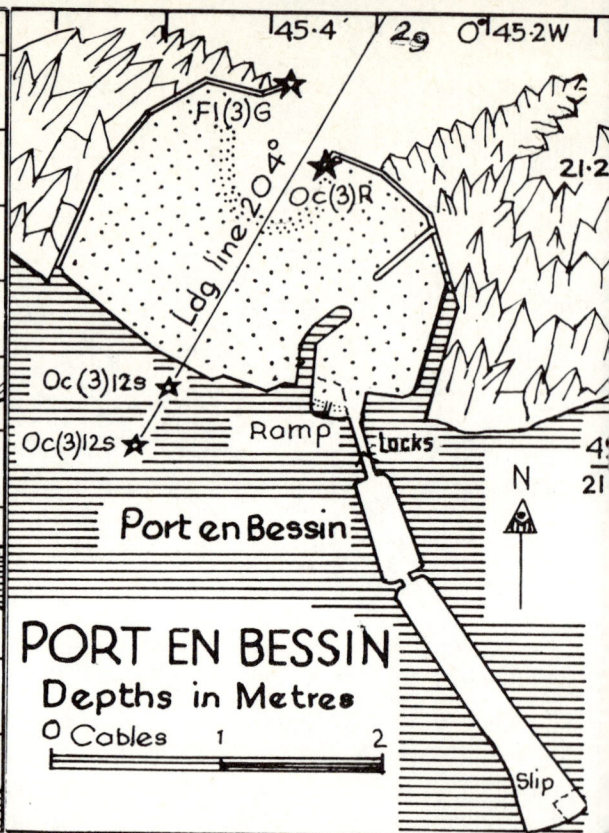

PORT EN BESSIN
Depths in Metres

0 Cables 1 2

0°45·2W
45·4' 29
Fl(3)G
Oc(3)R
Ldg line 204°
21·2
Oc(3)12s
Oc(3)12s
Ramp
Locks
N
21
Slip

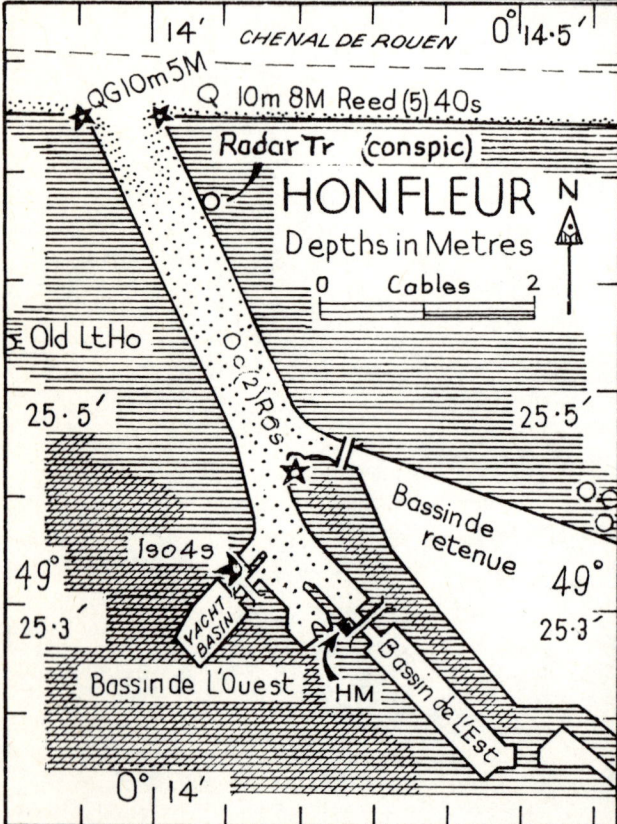

CHENAL DE ROUEN 0° 14·5'
QG 10m 5M
Q 10m 8M Reed (5) 40s
HONFLEUR
Depths in Metres

0 Cables 2

Radar Tr (conspic)
N
Old Lt Ho
Oc(2)R 6s
25·5'
25·5'
Bassin de retenue
49°
25·3'
Iso 4s
YACHT BASIN
Bassin de L'Ouest
HM
Bassin de L'Est
49° 25·3'
0° 14'

49° 25'
4' 1° 3' 2'
No 3 BY
No 5 BY
No 1 BY
Lts 146°
0·5
0·8
ROCHES DE GRANDCAMP
24
Oc(2)R 6s 10m 9M
2 Ldg Lts Q
Oc 4s 8m 10M
Pte de Maisy
Fl 6 4s 8m 5M
Grandcamp
Oc 4s 28m 12M
Tr (ruins)
Tr
Maisy
GRANDCAMP HARBOUR
Oc(2)R
FG
oil
Electric
GRANDCAMP
Depths in Metres
Mile

0 1

Based on British Admiralty Charts (nos. in text) with the permission of the Controller of H.M. Stationery Office and the Hydrographer of the Navy, and on other sources.

river 3km before the centre of Rouen. Masts can be unstepped there, but facilities are much better in the yacht hr at Le Havre.

For further details, and suggested mooring places in the river, see the CA publication 'Notes on French Inland Waterways'.

LE HAVRE   Charts BA 2990, 2146; F 6683   (Plan p384)
HW −1.05.   MHWS 7.8; MLWS 1.0; MTL 4.5; MHWN 6.4; MLWN 2.7.
There is slack water for 2 to 3h around HW; the tide flows about 5½h and ebbs about 7h. Le Havre is a major yachting centre, as well as being a large commercial port.
Approach   Cap de la Hève Lt Ho, W octagonal tr, R top, Fl 5s, 123m, is situated 2M NNW of the entrance. Shingle banks, awash at LW to N of approach and having 1m to S of approach, extend 2M from the entrance. Le Havre LV is generally off station in the summer and is replaced by a buoy, Fl(2) R 10s, RWVS.
Entrance   At LW enter from between LH9 buoy, G con, Oc(2) G 6s, and LH10, R can, Oc R 4s, with C de la Hève bearing 065° 2¾M, and follow the buoyed chan but keep well to the side to avoid hindering commercial shipping. Enter Avant Port between Digue Nord, Fl R 5s, and Digue Sud, Fl(3) G 2s. Port entry signals do not have to be observed by yachts but a constant stream of commercial traffic uses this port and a very careful lookout should be maintained. Ldg lts 107°.
Berthing   After entering, turn hard to port keeping at least 50m off the inner side of the Digue Nord, and enter yacht hr. Visitors berth on outer side of outer pontoon in outer basin, stern to buoys: have warps ready. Water at pontoons, fuel SE corner of outer basin. Grid, crane for unstepping masts. Chandlers on quay, all stores. Large YC with restaurant etc, also smaller one.

For a long stay the Bassin du Commerce may be used by yachts. It is comfortable, clean and more sheltered than yacht hr. Lock opens around HW.

HONFLEUR   Charts BA 2146, F 4937   (Plan p384)
HW −1.30.   MHWS 7.8; MHWN 6.4.
A drying hr with an inner yacht basin. Outer hr dries 1.5m. Entrance chan dries 1m; keep near middle. A beautiful and picturesque town.
Approach   From the N make the G Ratier NW buoy. From the S make the W Card Ratelets buoy. Thence leave the Digue du Ratier to the S and keep to the buoyed Chenal de Rouen up the Seine until Honfleur entrance bears SE.
Entrance   It can be identified by conspic W radar tr just to its E. It is on the S bank of the Seine, formed by jetties, partly stone, about 65m apart, their seaward ends being marked by pylons QG to stb and Fl to port. Inside the hr the chan forks. Take right fork and enter avant port.
Berthing   Yachts lock into Vieux Bassin (about 1h either side HW, opening times posted on lock gates), first basin on stb hand (swing br), or lie (soft mud bottom) alongside any quay in the avant port not occupied by fishing boats. Beware sill near swing br, rocks alongside quays and other obstructions. The

larger basin on the port hand may be found preferable. Capitainerie listens on VHF Ch 11.

Train to Rouen etc. Water from tap by museum. All stores. Repairs.

DEAUVILLE – TROUVILLE   Charts BA 2146; F 5530   (Plan p387)

HW −1.40.   DS: NE −4.35; SW +0.10.

MHWS 7.7; MLWS 0.8; MTL 4.3; MHWN 6.3; MLWN 2.5.

Bar   The sands dry 6 ca offshore from Deauville Pt on W side of R La Touques. The entrance chan is dredged in summer, when it dries about 1m: in winter or early spring it can dry as much as 1½m or more.

Approach   In good weather the entrance can be approached at all but 2h either side of LW: in strong onshore winds approach HW −2 to HW or avoid altogether. From N keep slightly W of the town (the casino at Trouville is conspic) to avoid the Banc du Ratier. From W keep an offing of about 1½M until Trouville SW buoy, W Card, is identified about a mile outside the pier-heads. From here a course may be set for the entrance. In any case steer so that the final approach can be made on about 150°. At night there is no problem: the W sectors of the two outer lts provide a safe angle of approach, and when closer in the ldg lts, Oc R 4s, provide a safe line through the outer pier-heads. Note, however, that the front ldg lt is obscured from anywhere NE of the line of the E outer breakwater, so that when approaching from the N it will not be seen until close in.

Entrance   At night keep on the ldg line, and by day look out for the posts marking the E and W training walls and the shoal off the end of the main Port Deauville breakwater. Leave the former to port and the latter close to stb if entering the lock for Port Deauville. For the old hr keep straight up the chan, avoiding the E side which is shoal.

Berthing   (1) In Port Deauville marina. All facilities available but often a long walk from the visitors' moorings, as indeed is the town. Locks operate whenever there is water outside: about 3h before to 5h after HW. Expensive. (2) In the old hr of Deauville-Trouville, locks open 2h before until 2½h after 'debut de plein mer'. For a list of times write to Deauville YC. Beautiful clubhouse and all facilities. The old hr is close to restaurants and shops. Charges considerably below Port Deauville. Fuel and water by hose.

Tides   The tide remains within ½m of its maximum rise for 3¼h at springs and 4½h at neaps. The stream runs up to 2½kn flood, 1½kn ebb, inside, but is slack for ⅓h either side of HW.

OUISTREHAM   Chart F 891   (Plan p387)

HW −1.30.   DS: ESE −6.00; WNW HWD.

MHWS 7.5; MLWS 0.7; MTL 4.2; MHWN 6.1; MLWN 2.5.

Bar   The sands dry 2M offshore but chan is dredged to 3.2m.

Approach   Make the RW whistle buoy, Iso 4s, moored in 6m 2½M N of the

DEAUVILLE-TROUVILLE
Depths in Metres

0°4'E

Lts in line
150°
Cables
0   5

white
Red
Red
W
FlWG4s10m10M
R
Fl(4)WR12s
15m 10/7M
Reed(2)30s
IsoG4s 9m5M
QG
G
QR
QCR4s9M
QCR4s10M

Trouville
Casino

R. La Touques

N

49°
22'

Port Deauville
DYC
BRB
0°4' **Deauville**   5'

49°
.5'

25
27
05

OUISTREHAM
Depths in Metres

0°14'   13'

No1 FIG4s
FlR4s No2
Lts 187
5   6
65
07
05
49°
18'
13
05
3,1 24 36
1
02 33
04 18'
Oc(2)R6s 7m
FG
Bn
R
Bn
R
BANCS DE MERVILLE
35
3
IsoG4s12m 6M Horn10s

Ouistreham
Oc G4s
Bn
R
Bn Bn Bn
R R R
43
• Old Fort
49°
17'

Pontoons
Oc(1+3)R12s 11M DE siege
FlR2s
Oc(1+3)R12s
Customs
YC
Oc WR4s 37m 16,12M
Yacht
Hr
Water Tr
+

La Roque
Cables
0   6

CANAL DE CAEN
15   0°13' 14

N

49°
18'

COURSEULLES
Depths in Metres

0°27'
Cables
0   6

78
38 45
54
Iso4s
4
RW Courseulles
15
3
FOSSE DE COURSEULLES
43 18   2
15
17 33
12
08
21
08
Rr DE LA MARGUERITE (01)
38 41
08
49°
21' 34 41 48
31 34
38
08
18 22
08
Bns in line 198°
2
(01)
2 31 24
Rocher Germain
02 08
15
04
05

IsoWG 4s 9m9M
Cross (9m)
Oc(2)R6s 9m10M 33
East Jetty
RIVER SEULLE
AVANT PORT
46 26
20·5
18
1
26

Courseulles

Bernières
49°
20'
27'   0°26'

N

COURSEULLES YACHT HARBOUR

LA MANCHE

Digue RIVER SEULLE
Quai Ouest
DRYING RAMP
AVANT PORT
Quai des Alliés
Nouveau Bassin
Swing bridge
Quai Est
Customs
HM YC
BASSIN A FLOT
Quai Est

Cables
0   2

N

D'après la carte marine française avec l'autorisation du Service Hydrographique et Océanographique de la Marine.   387

entrance. Thence to entrance, 187° (ldg lts Oc(1+3) R 12s) past R and G buoys marking the chan.

Entrance   The E dyke extension, which covers, has a lt Oc(2) R 6s at its head which is nearly 1M N of the head of the E jetty. Main lt from Lt Ho on E side of lock is Oc WR 4s, R 120°–151°, W elsewhere.

Leave G buoys close to stb. At the head of the W jetty is a B and G pylon, 12m, Iso G 4s. At the root of W jetty is a lt Oc G. Watch the stream at the pier-heads. A training wall marked by bns runs out 1M 000° from the root of the W jetty.

Berthing   Yachts can lie in the tidal basin alongside pontoons on either side of the chan (considerable wash), or lock into Caen Canal through locks on either side of control tr. These open HW −3 to +3¼ in July and Aug, −2 to +2¼ in other months. The entrance to the yacht hr is just inside locks on E side. Visitors' berths opposite entrance. YC. All stores.

Caen Canal   Yachts wishing to go to Caen (16km) should report to the lock control tr to pay dues and arrange for br openings. There is a yacht hr in Bassin St Pierre near the centre of Caen.

COURSEULLES   Charts BA 1821; F 5598   (Plan p387)
HW −2.30.   DS: E +5.35; W −1.10.
MHWS 7.0; MLWS 0.7; MTL 3.8; MHWN 5.5; MLWN 2.2.
A drying hr with yacht basins, entrance dangerous in strong onshore winds.
Bar   The shore dries over ½M beyond the pier-heads. Vessels of 2.4m draft can enter MHWN. HW stands for 1¾h at springs.
Approach   Courseulles lies 2½M E of Pte de Ver Lt Ho, Fl(3) 15s, and 1½M W of Bernières which has a ch spire. The coast from Arromanches on the W to Langrune on the E is fronted by the Calvados plateau, a shoal ledge extending 2M offshore. Give the shore a berth of 2M until the Courseulles pillar buoy, RWVS with spher topmark, lt Iso 4s, is identified and closed. Then identify the pier-heads, the W of which is marked by a dolphin with brown wooden tr and G top. A horn on this tr sounds every 30s from HW −2 to +2 during fog. Steer so as to approach on a course of 198°.

Vessels waiting for tide anch in 3 to 4m, 2 ca E of Roche de la Marguerite.
Entrance   Best between HW −2 and +1. Once between the jetties keep to the E side until the end of the wooden part of the E pier, thereafter in mid-channel.
Berthing   Yachts enter basin straight on through Avant Port (lock gates open HW −2 to +2), or turn to stb through small swing br and proceed to new basin (protected by sill with approx 1.2m at 2½h either side of HW). All facilities.

PORT-EN-BESSIN   Charts BA 2073, F 5513   (Plan p384)
HW −2.00.   DS: W −0.45; E +6.15.
MHWS 7.2; MLWS 1.0; MTL 4.1; MHWN 5.9; MLWN 2.5.
A small drying fishing hr protected by two breakwaters within which are two

basins. The shore dries ½M beyond the pier-heads. Do not attempt entrance in N to NE winds over force 5. Otherwise approach at half-tide or over.
Entrance   Pier-heads are painted W and are visible a long way off. Ro Bn 'BS' on 313.5kHz, 5M, continuous. Lts in line lead in 204°. Avant port dries 2m.
Berthing   Outer and inner tidal hrs dry, many rks and can be dangerous scend. Mooring possible along inner side of inner hr quays. Wet basin usually crowded with fishing boats. Take advice from HM. Stores, cranes (6T), repairs, water.

GRANDCAMP

Charts BA 2073, F 847   (Plan p384)

HW (est) −2.20.   MHWS (est) 6.8; MHWN (est) 5.5.
Approach   1M to E of Isigny chan bell buoy, a line of three N Card buoys, Nos. 1, 3 and 5, mark seaward limits of Roches de Grandcamp, dry 1.6m. Approach can be made within 2h of HW from any point between these buoys. Lts Fl G on W pier-head, Oc(2) R 6s siren 30s on RW column on E pier-head.
Entrance   Between breakwaters, keeping in mid-chan.
Berthing   Yachts enter wet basin, open approx 2½h either side of local HW. (Gates actually open LW, close HW Dunkerque.) Visitors berth on the outer half on the N pontoon. All facilities except diesel: there is a pump, but the fuel may only be sold to fishermen.

ISIGNY

Charts BA 2073, F 847   (Plan p390)

DS: in Rade de la Capelle off entrance to Chenal d'Isigny, SSW +4.55; S +5.55; NNE −1.30. In offing, 2½M 352° from Grandcamp lt tr: E +6.05; W HWD (E-going stream begins S and quickly changes direction E; W-going stream begins SW and quickly changes to W).
Approach   As for Carentan. Roches de Grandcamp are marked by buoys.
Entrance   The Isigny chan RWVS bell buoy lies 1½M SE of the Carentan chan buoy. Thence the chan is marked by R and G buoys and bns. Lts in line 173°, synchronised: front, W post, 7m, Oc(1+2) 12s; rear, W pylon, 19m, Oc(1+2) 12s. Turn to port up the R Aure where the R Vire joins. Hug the left bank to miss a spit on the corner and proceed in midstream to Isigny. There is about 2.7m water at half-tide.
Berthing   Berth on SW side about 200m N of town. Soft mud. Avoid concrete apron at foot of SW wall.
   Water on quay. Bank, shops.

CARENTAN

Charts BA 2073, F 847   (Plan p390)

DS: SSW and NNE in the approach S of the Cardonnet bank. Clear of this bank, it follows the shore line. See also under Isigny.
Bar   The whole indentation called Baie du Grand Vey, which gives access at HW to Carentan and Isigny, is full of sandbanks, which dry practically throughout at LW.
Approach   The Grand Vey may be located by its position 6M S of Iles St

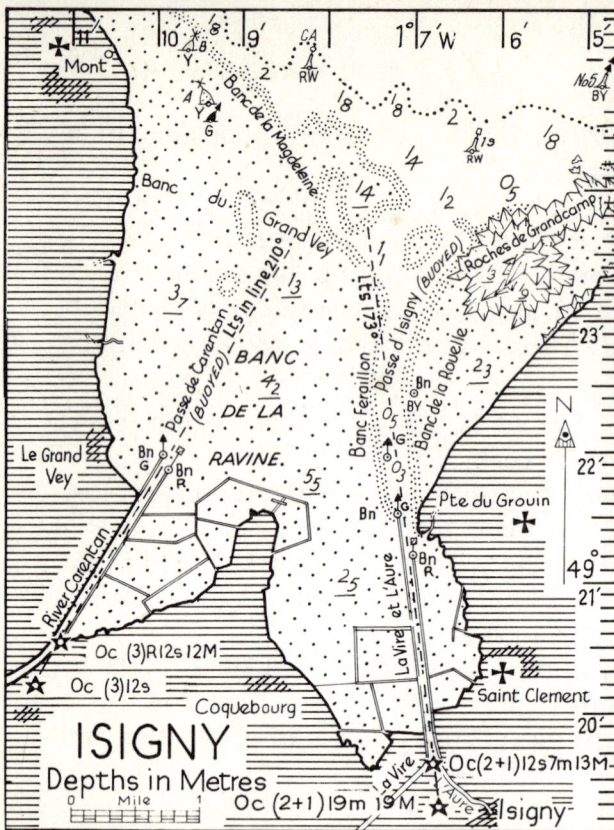

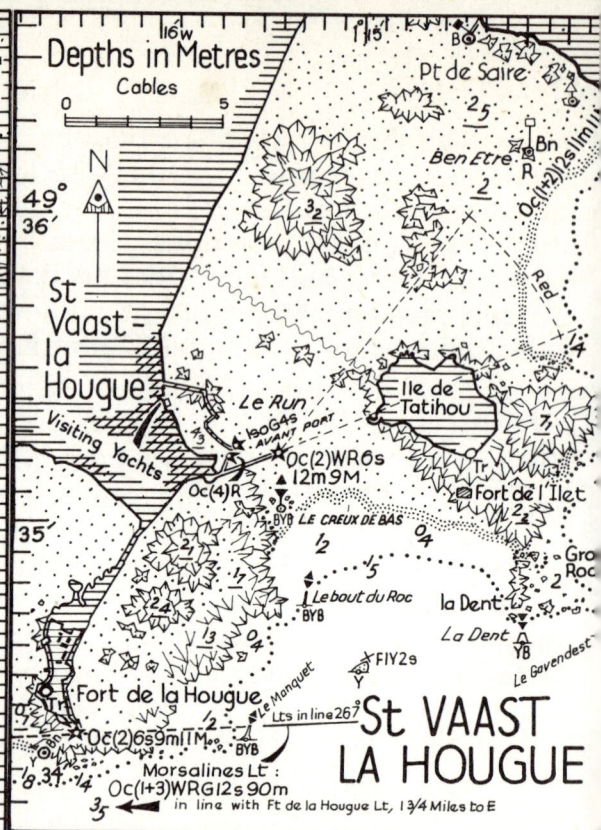

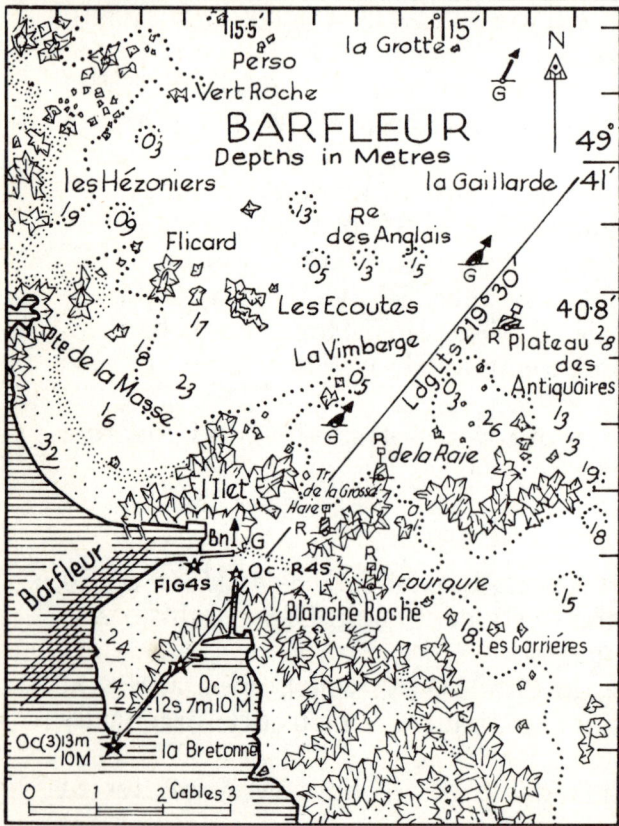

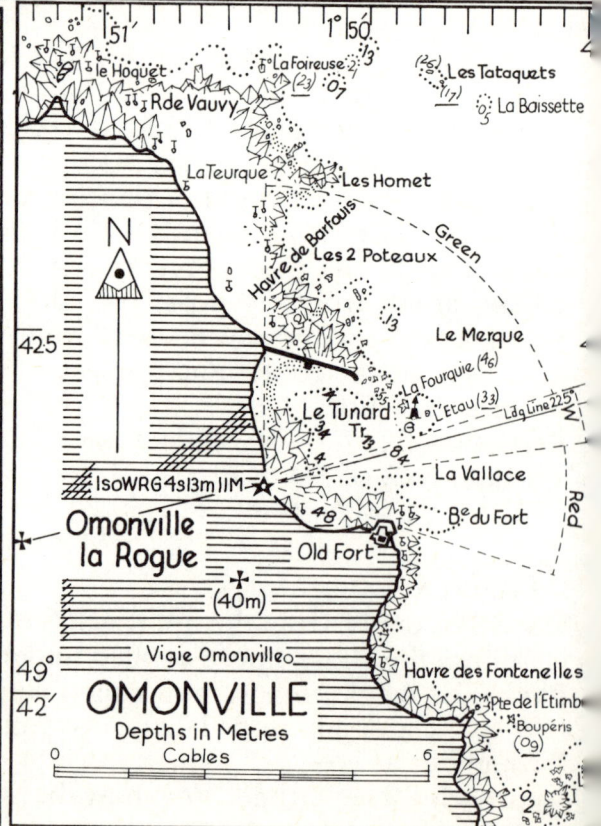

D'après la carte marine française avec l'autorisation du Service Hydrographique et Océanographique de la Ma

Marcouf, by the conspic ch of Ste Marie du Mont standing on a hill (28m) on W side of estuary, and by the spire of Maisy ch close to the shore on the E side.

Entrance   The entrance to the Carentan chan is marked by a RWVS bell buoy. The stream sets strongly towards the entrance buoy and across the banks beyond it. Thence keep between the R and G chan buoys and bns. The chan dries about 2m in places, and is tortuous: at half-tide it has about 1.2m. Lock gates are some 7M from bell buoy. Ldg lts 210°: front, W post, 6m, Oc(3) R 12s; rear, W column, 14m, Oc(3) 12s, synchronised. The port is available for 2m draft at MHWN. At high spring tides there may be a small bore in the chan and turbulence in the lock. It is only opened at sufficient rise of tide, and this may not occur at extreme neaps. From the lock proceed 1M to Carentan; grassy quays, quiet and clean.

Berthing   Vessels berth in the basin at Carentan. The lock sill is 1.8m above chart datum.

ILES SAINT-MARCOUF   Charts F 847, BA 2073

There is a S Card bn, 10.1m, on the rks 1 ca W of the larger Is, Is du Large. Usual anch is off SW of this Is. There is also an anch to SE opposite a small footbridge about 25m from shore. Buoy anch, stream strong.

   Land at boat hr. To enter, leave the first withy very close to stb, then approach second withy and leave it very close to port. Enter within about 2h of HW. When rocks near bn are just awash there is 1.3m in the entrance to the boat hr.

SAINT VAAST   Chart F 5522   (Plan p390)

HW −2.40.   DS in Grande Rade: SW −5.30; NE +0.30; 2½kn.
An eddy runs N during the English Channel E-going stream.
MHWS 6.0; MLWS 0.6; MTL 3.4; MHWN 5.1; MLWN 2.1.
The port lies 5M S of Barfleur and dries 2m. Useful if, with stormy W winds, a yacht is unable to make Cherbourg.

Approach   From the N, after passing Le Moulard and Roches Dranguet trs on the shore between Barfleur and St Vaast, locate two broad trs, each with a turret on one side of the top, one on S side of I de Tatihou, the other Fort de la Hougue. Giving I de Tatihou a clearance of 1M to the N, locate two spar buoys, Card S, ¾M S of it. Leave them to stb and sail in about NNW to round the outer jetty with the prominent lt structure at the end; Oc(2) WR, siren, R 219°–247°, W elsewhere. Half-tide or more needed.

Entrance   The entrance chan is wide, 1M across at the outer buoys and free of dangers. The port side is marked by buoys and bns.

Berthing   Very crowded during the season: visiting yachts may have difficulty in finding a satisfactory berth. May anch in the approach chan as close in as water allows. Good holding and shelter except in strong winds between E and S. At half-tide there is about 1.4m of water in inner hr (fishing boats). There is very restricted berthing for yachts at the N end of the quay here: pass between the inner breakwater head N of entrance, Iso G, and the Groyne head S of entrance,

FRANCE, NORTH COAST

Oc(4) R. Keep W of posts marking steep drying bank in NE part of inner hr. It is possible but often unpopular to lie along the outer jetty; untenable in E winds. Water, stores, restaurants, some facilities.

At night Morsalines lt in line with La Hougue lt, 267°, clears the rks (Gavendest) SE of I de Tatihou. Turn for lt on breakwater head when it bears 340°.

BARFLEUR   Charts BA 2073, F 5618   (Plan p390)
HW −2.40.   MHWS 6.4; MLWS 0.9; MTL 3.7; MHWN 5.1; MLWN 2.3.
The port lies 1½M S of Pte de Barfleur and dries about 1m between pier-heads, 2–4m inside. S of the pt eddies reduce the duration of the S-going stream to 3¼h beginning at +4½. The eddy is strong near Pte de Barfleur and causes overfalls where it meets the main chan streams. It is weaker ¾M S of the pt, 2kn.

At springs the Barfleur race extends 3 or 4M NE and E of the pt. Approaching from E or SE, vessels should keep SE of the line of Barfleur ldg lts until clear of the race. Montfarville ch spire on rising ground 1M S of Barfleur is conspic, as is the castle-like ch of Barfleur itself.
Approach   From a position about 1¼M ESE of Pte de Barfleur, steer 219° on the 7m W square lt tr (ldg lts Oc(3) R 12s at night), and between the buoys and bns which mark the chan from ½M off the entrance. In daylight, be careful not to confuse the front leading lighthouse with the hexagonal white tr on the S breakwater. The correct line leads about 50m S of the more conspic tr on the S breakwater. At sufficient water enter between the jetty heads.

If in the right conditions approach be made from the W around the Pte de Barfleur, the shorter approach which largely avoids the race is to change course when the beacon, W Card, on La Jamette E of Pte de Barfleur Lt Ho bears 152° to leave the bn a few metres to stb. Continue on same course to pass La Grotte G buoy to stb. Then approach the hr on the ldg line.
Anchoring   Near the ldg line in 5 to 6m, sand and mud, poor holding. Also in the bay N of the town, sheltered from all directions except E and NE. Approach 256° from La Roche à l'Anglais G buoy.
Berthing   Berth along NW quay, dries 2 to 3m, bottom level mud, sand and gravel; or W quay, dries 3 to 4m. E side is uneven and rocky.

There is a strong surge in the hr with fresh winds between NE and E. It may at times be crowded with fishing boats. Boatyard, supplies, buses to Cherbourg. *Note:* it was reported in 1980 that a major marina development was planned at Barfleur. If this goes ahead, it may well close the hr while the works are carried out.

CHERBOURG   Charts BA 1106, 2602; F 5627   (Plan p393)
HW −3.40.   DS: ENE +4.45; WSW −2.00.
MHWS 6.2; MLWS 0.8; MTL 3.5; MHWN 4.8; MLWN 2.3.
The hr may be entered at all times and is secure in all winds. The yacht hr is one of the largest in the area, and a major yachting centre.

CHERBOURG
Depths in Metres

Mile

0   Mile   1

PASSE DE L'EST
(swept to 6·6m)

ÎLE PELÉE

Bn (Tripod) (ruins)

Tromet

Digue de l'Est

Oc(2)WR6s18m11·07M

White   Red

Fl(4)R12s

Fort de l'Est

White   green   G

IsoWG4s19m12/9M

PASSE DE L'EST

Arc of vis

Fort Central   Bn

VQ(6)+LFl.10s4m

Digue Centrale

GRANDE RADE

La Tenarde

Digue du Homet

Fort du Homet

Fl(3)WR15s19m   Reed(3)60s

White

Fort de l'Ouest   Oc.R.4s

Red

PASSE DE L'OUEST

Gare Maritime Lt between Fort du Homet Lts 141°

Fort de Chavagnac

Obstn(2)

Oc(1·2)WG12s8m11/8M

White   Green

Digue de Querqueville   Bn

Ldg Lts 124°

Lts in line 196°

PETITE RADE

Jetée des Flamands

Fort des Flamands

Pylon

Port des Flamands

ChyO   ChyO   ChyO

IsoG4s16m

Fl(2)R9s5m

Fl(2)R6s   Fl.G

Fl10m11s

Fl.G.4s2m Horn10s

QR9m

FR3m

FVi   QG 8m

Iso G.4s7m

Yacht Hbr

YC

Belfry

Hôtel de Ville   Statue

Cherbourg

Twin spires

QkFl.G6m

QkFl.G26m

QkFl.5m   CUPOLA (conspic)

ChyO

BASSIN NAPOLÉON III

HM

Water Tr

Tr (conspic)

CHERBOURG YACHT HARBOUR

Fl.G4s   Fl.G4s

QR   QR

Oc(2)G6s

Iso G4s

Fuel

Club Ho & Capitainerie

Gare Maritime

Cable

Slip

Toilets

N

Based on British Admiralty Charts (nos. in text) with the permission of the Controller of H.M. Stationery Office and of the Hydrographer of the Navy, and on other sources.

Approach The hr lies nearly midway between C de la Hague and Pte de Barfleur. Strangers should give the coast to E and W a berth of at least 2½M to avoid outlying dangers and the races off the headlands. The race off Pte de Barfleur in strong winds and weather-going tides vies in violence with that of Alderney. It should be remembered that the tidal stream changes 2 or 3h later in mid-chan than along the shore, so that by taking advantage of this fact a fair stream may be carried for 9h. CH 1 buoy, RWVS, Oc 4s, whistle, lies 3M NW of the W entrance.

Entrance The W entrance is marked on its E side by the Fort de l'Ouest, Fl(3) WR, reed, showing W from 122° over the centre breakwater to 355°, R elsewhere. A R buoy within the entrance must be left to port. The other side of the W entrance is marked by the Querqueville Lt Oc(1+2) WG (G to 120°, W elsewhere) on the W breakwater, from which a course 117° will lead to the entrance to the Petite Rade. Leave the FG lt on the Digue du Homet to stb.

Another entrance is by the Passe de l'Est, also easy but keep to W side to avoid shoals near I Pelée.

A third entrance is the Passe Cabart Danneville at E end of the Grande Rade. Entrance is narrow with strong streams. Large-scale chart necessary.

Berthing The yacht hr lies in the Petite Rade immediately to the W of the Gare Maritime. Enter between the NW corner of the Gare Maritime, lt QR, and the marina pier-head, lt Oc(2) G, 6s.

All possible facilities, 24-hour showers at Capitainerie. YC, chandlery, sailmaker etc. Duty-free stores convenient. Capitainerie listens on VHF Ch 9. Fuel except near LW.

Anchoring is no longer permitted in the Petite Rade. If wishing to anch, proceed to the W end of the Grande Rade (isolated, and considerable swell).

OMONVILLE-LA-ROGUE   Charts BA 1106, F 5631   (Plan p390)
HW −3.50.   DS (1M N): E −6.00; W −0.30.
MHWS 6.1; MLWS 0.8; MTL 3.5; MHWN 4.7; MLWN 2.4.
A small hr, 4M ESE of Cap de la Hague, sheltered from SSE through W to NNW. To the W, rks and shoals extend N about 6 ca offshore from Pte de Jardehou, 3½M E of Cap de la Hague, to the Basse Bréfort N Card whistle buoy. For 3½M to the E rks lie ½M offshore. Raz de Bannes tr, N Card, marks the edge of the shoal.

Approach From W keep at least 1M off until Omonville has been identified. The entrance is marked by Le Tunard G bn tr, and to the S are the ruined remains of an old fort. Keep well to the E of the transit of these (194°) in order to clear the rks of Les Tataquets, and to allow for the strong tidal stream usually running WNW.

From the E keep at least 1M offshore until well E of the above transit.

Entrance   ½ ca wide between a submerged rk off the old fort and Le Tunard bn marking the rks off the end of the breakwater. On the shore between these there is a white tr with R top, lt Iso WRG 4s. Bring this tr on with Omonville ch, 255°, and enter on this line. At night use white sector (same bearing).

Berthing   Two large visitors' buoys. Several boats moor bow to buoy, each with their own stern anch. Alternatively anch to SE of the short breakwater offshore in 5m, sand. Ground very foul. Beware of rks E of breakwater.

Café, a few shops.

There is good holding, sand and mud, in Anse St Martin, halfway between Omonville and Cap de la Hague. Sheltered from SE through S to W. Port Racine, on W side of Anse St Martin, dries and is very small.

CHANNEL ISLANDS

Chart BA 2669

The islands are situated in the bight to the SW of Cap de la Hague at the head of which is the Gulf of St Malo and bay of Mont St Michel. Cap de la Hague interferes with the Channel tides causing rotatory anticlockwise tidal streams with little slack and an exaggerated range at the head of the gulf. All obstructions should be given ample clearance as the streams run with great rapidity even at neaps. The Admiralty Tidal Stream Atlas 'The Channel Islands and Adjacent Coasts of France' or Stanford's *Tidal Atlases* should be carried as they give the strengths and directions of the streams. The range of mean spring tides varies from $5\frac{1}{2}$ to 12m within the area. Tides make and take off very rapidly: considerable variations from tidal predictions both in time and height occur due to meteorological conditions. Take care also when using tide tables to check the time zone in which times are expressed.

The islands afford secure shelter at St Peter Port in Guernsey, and at St Helier in Jersey, and offer many anchs in offshore winds. Avoid spring tides or unsettled weather for a first visit. If approaching from the W it should be noted that the N side of Jersey and the S side of Guernsey are high, Jersey sloping down to the S and Guernsey down to the N. Marine radio bns on the Casquets, St Helier Hr, Corbière (Jersey) and the Roches Douvres, also air bns in Alderney, Jersey (2) and Guernsey, give considerable approach assistance; but in fog or if becalmed among the islands, remember the streams and either anchor or use your engine while your position is still known to be safe.

St Peter Port Radio (Guernsey) and Jersey Radio keep continuous watch on 2182 kHz and VHF ch 16. Alderney Radio, ch 16, listens during office hours. Local weather forecasts are broadcast from Jersey simultaneously on 1726 kHz and VHF ch 25 at 0645, 1245, 1845 and 2245. More detail is given than in the BBC shipping forecasts for these waters.

Channel Harbours and Anchorages by Adlard Coles (Nautical Publishing) is an excellent volume to have on board, and the Royal Channel Islands YC Handbook gives much useful information. *Channel Islands Pilot* by Malcolm Robson (Nautical Publishing) is a comprehensive work containing charts and sailing directions for many approach and inshore passages, as well as descriptions of harbours and anchorages. The British and French Islands are covered in *Brittany and Channel Islands Cruising* Guide by David Jefferson (Stanford Maritime). *Alderney Sailing Directions* by Philip Spencer (available from Alderney SC) is a small but valuable pamphlet covering that island.

From Guernsey the islands of Sark and Herm merit a visit, while from Jersey the Ecrehous and Iles Chausey are worth visiting in fine weather at neaps.

PASSAGE NOTES: CHERBOURG AND THE CHANNEL ISLANDS

Between Cherbourg and the Channel Islands, Omonville 8M W of Cherbourg is a convenient port of call. From Omonville St Peter Port lies about 36M to the W through the Alderney Race, and about 42M by the Casquets. An eddy running W inshore from Omonville begins at HWD $-5\frac{1}{2}$. There is slack water in the Race at -1.00. A fair stream can be carried for longer on the passage to Guernsey by the Casquets than on that through the Race.

The Alderney Race is over 7M wide and presents no difficulty in reasonable weather, although there are overfalls, marked on the chart, which should be avoided so far as possible. The tidal streams at springs can run at up to 6 or 7kn or even more, and it is essential to time one's passage accordingly. Advantage can be taken of the eddies close inshore round Alderney, which are shown in the *Tidal Stream Atlas*.

On passage from Cherbourg to the Channel Is, leave Cherbourg yacht hr at about HWD -4 to catch the start of the inshore W-bound eddy. Note that the SW stream through the Race starts about $\frac{3}{4}$h before HWD. If bound for Alderney or the Casquets, a generous allowance must be made for tidal set. If bound through the Race for Guernsey or Jersey, the most comfortable passage will be at about HWD before the overfalls have built up.

Southbound from Alderney, the shortest route to Guernsey is through the Swinge. Leave Braye hr 2 to $2\frac{1}{2}$h after local HW to avoid the overfalls which build up S of Burhou. Leave Corbet Rk about 100m to port and then change course to keep Great Nannel just open E of Burhou until Les Etacs are on the port beam.

From St Peter Port to Jersey or Brittany The yacht hr at St Peter Port has a sill at the entrance and the most favourable tidal streams do not coincide with possible departure times. If bound for Jersey or St Malo it may be desirable to leave the yacht hr and anch or pick up a mooring to await the tide. If bound SW, leave as late as possible on a falling tide while there is still sufficient depth over the sill. Note that between the Channel Is and the N coast of Brittany the tidal streams run very strongly, especially those running E and W. It is essential to make full allowance for them, particularly in the neighbourhood of the Roches Douvres, Barnouic and the Minquiers.

Northbound from St Peter Port Leave as soon as the stream in the Little Russel turns N at about HWD $+4\frac{3}{4}$. This should give a favourable tide through the Swinge or the Alderney Race. If bound for Alderney, note that the tide runs NE

ALDERNEY HARBOUR
Depths in Metres

Cables

Admiralty Breakwater

SUBMERGED BREAKWATER

Ldg Lts 215°

Braye (0.5) Rk

Visitors — Fairway—Keep clear

Small Craft Moorings

Grosnez Pt

Little Crabby Hr

CRABBY BAY

Braye

Bn (White cone)

Iso 10s17m18M

Roselle Pt

Toulouse Rk

Visitors Moorings

BRAYE BAY

Bibette Hd

Fort Albert

Homet des Agneaux

Saye Bay

Château à l'Étoc

Int Sector

Iso WR4s10m7M

Iso WR4s10/M

HM SC

F13s WK BY

Safety Or

BW

BEAUCETTE MARINA

Grande Canupe

Petite Canupe

Grune Pierre

Grune la Passe

Y.B.

Pierre

Doyle Passage

Ldg Lts & Mark 276°

105

Fort Doyle Power Stn

Sill dries 2.4m

Cables

FERRN

GOREY
Depths in Metres

Cables

La Coupe Pt

Turret (conspic)

FLIQUET BAY

Verclut Pt

Martello Tr

Slip

St Catherine Bank

St CATHERINE BAY

Fl 1·5s18m8M
St Catherine

La Crête Pt
Slip

Mont Orgueil Castle (64)

OcR5s Spire
24m8M

Gorey

OcRG5s 8m12M

OcRG5s

Le Coupe Turret open East of
Verclut Pt

Lts 298°
QG

North Ridge

BANC DU CHATE

Green

INNER ROAD

OUTER ROAD

398

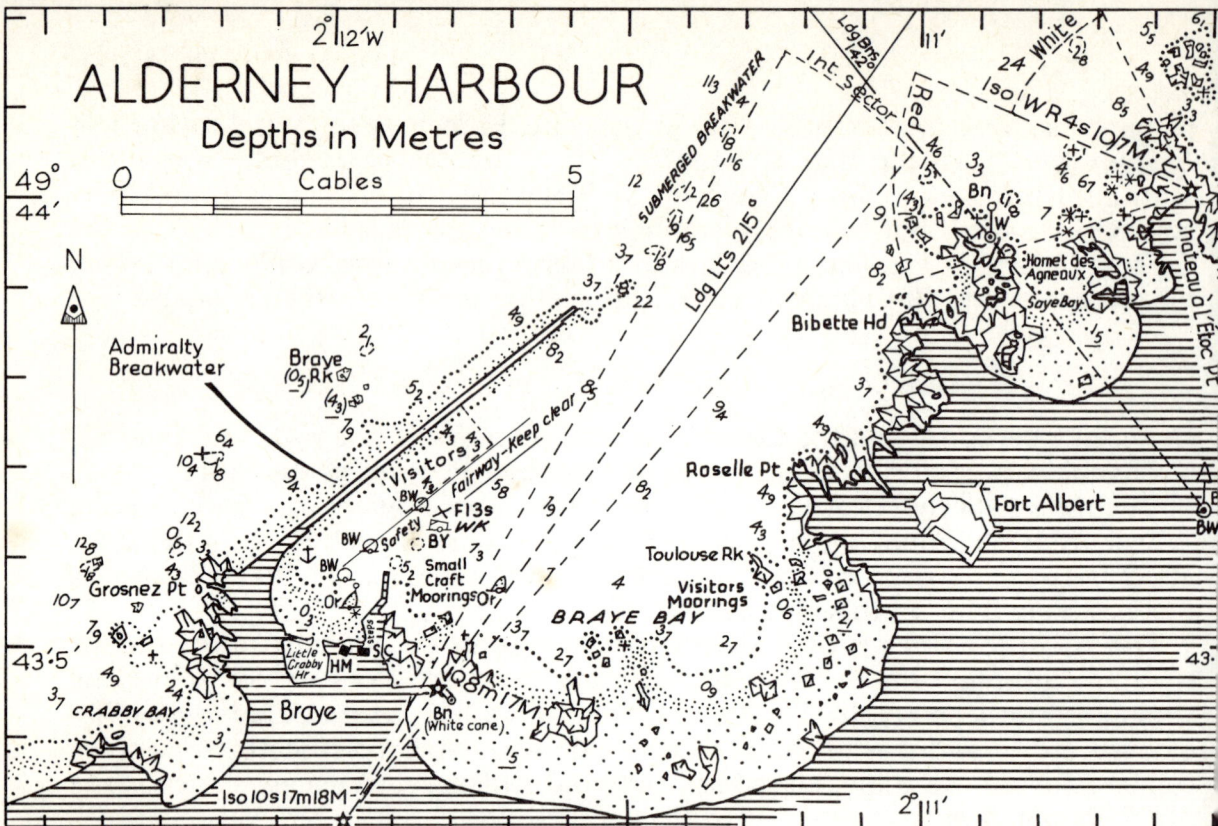

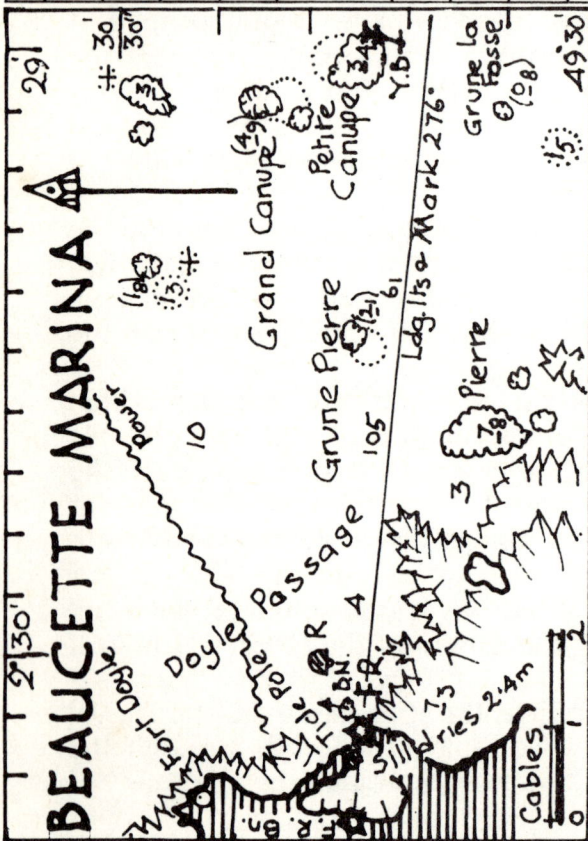

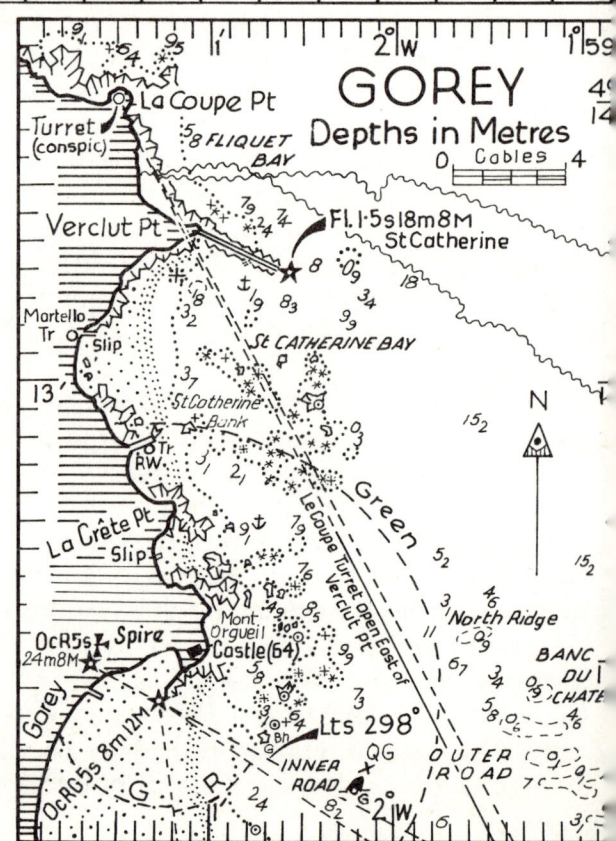

Based on British Admiralty Charts (nos. in text) with the permission of the Controller of H.M. Stationery Office and the Hydrographer of the Navy, and on other sources.

in the Race longer than in the Swinge and change course if you run out of tide before entering the Swinge. Approaching the Swinge keep the Great Nannel just open E of Burhou to clear Pierre au Vraic (rk which dries at extreme LWS) and to clear Les Etacs rks at SW extremity of Alderney. Avoid the worst of the overfalls in the Swinge by keeping to the E side of the chan, about 100m W of Corbet Rk.

To Cherbourg   From Alderney leave at about HWD +5 to catch the start of the NE-going stream. If coming from Guernsey or further afield, note that the early W-going stream along the N coast of the Cherbourg Peninsula is if anything stronger than the *Tidal Atlas* would suggest. Avoid it by keeping well offshore. The basic principle in these waters is to **let the tides work for you.**

BRAYE, ALDERNEY   Chart BA 60   (Plan p398)

HW −4.05.   DS (Race): SW −3.30; NE +5.15.
MHWS 6.3; MLWS 0.8; MTL 3.6; MHWN 4.7; MLWN 2.6.
The simplest approach to Alderney is from the NE.

For tidal streams in the vicinity of Alderney refer to the *Channel Pilot*, the tidal insets on Admiralty Chart 60, and *Tidal Stream Atlas Channel Islands and Adjacent Coast of France (NP264)*. There is least stream off the entrance to Braye Hr about HW Dover +5.00. In making the approach, bearings and transits should be observed carefully. At night the ldg lts must be kept in alignment 215° front Q, rear Iso 10s. The bn on Château à l'Etoc Pt shows R 071°–111° and W 111°–151°.

Entrance   Bring W con bn near hd of Old Hr pier on with St Anne's ch spire 210°. Beware of submerged extension of Admiralty Breakwater which extends over 3 ca NE beyond visible end. Clearance northwards is obtained by keeping triangular bn inland from hd of Saye Bay clear to N of bn on Homet des Pies. By night Quenard Lt Ho clear off Château à l'Etoc, 113°, gives a similar clearance. Align ldg lts until within the breakwater.

Moorings   Some 80 visitors' moorings, Y con buoys, in area SE of breakwater and S of Toulouse Rk. Leave buoyed fairway clear for steamers berthing alongside jetty. Berthing alongside or beaching requires prior permission from HM. All yachts must report to HM/Customs. Little Crabby hr is reserved for local boats except for fuelling, 2h either side of HW.

Yachts may anch clear of fairway and moorings. Some foul ground; use trip line on anchor. Anchor lights needed. Avoid area at SW end of hr occupied by store pots.

The iron jetty extension has been demolished but obstructions remain NE of end of quay. Area E of jetty is occupied by private moorings. Land by dinghy at steps (avoiding rk marked by orange pole) or at slipway below HM office; keep slipway clear. Anti-pollution regulations; strict anti-rabies regulations – no animals may be landed. Speed limit 4kn. Diesel, water, chandlery, CA boatman and ferry near HM. Stores, water, hotels, telephone and toilets near Old Hr.

Flights to England, Jersey and Guernsey. Diver, crane 10T. Alderney SC welcomes visitors.

GUERNSEY   Chart BA 3400
DS off E side: SW −1.30; NE +5.30.
At the NE end of Little Russel chan between the Braye Rks and Amfroque, the stream sets directly towards N end of Herm from +1.45 to +3.45. The course from the Casquets to a position off Les Hanois, the SW corner of Guernsey, is 224° and for those inexperienced in pilotage this approach, (3) below, is the easiest; in bad visibility it is strongly recommended.

ST PETER PORT   Chart BA 807   (Plan p401)
HW −4.40.   MHWS 9.0; MLWS 1.0; MTL 5.0; MHWN 6.7; MLWN 3.5.
St Peter Port is on the E side of the Is and has 4.6m in the entrance. There is 4–2m in the outer part of the hr: the inner part dries, apart from the marina, which is protected by a sill.
Approach   There are three lines of approach: (1) from N by Little Russel chan; (2) from NE by Great Russel chan; (3) from S by Grand Road.
(1) *Little Russel chan*   Do not approach Platte Fougère from W on a bearing less than 165°, or from E on a bearing greater than 255°. The Little Russel may be used even at LW by day with good visibility. At other times according to conditions, but the stream runs very fast at springs and it can be rough with wind over tide.

From the N, make for a position E of Platte Fougère grey octagonal lt tr, 15m, off the NE corner of the Is. From here the Little Russel chan runs S, with a 96m hill at the SE end of the Is above St Martin's Pt, and Brehou tr to E of it. Doyle's Column, a conspic square granite tr, stands on high ground about 4 ca NNW of St Martin's Pt. Bring Brehon tr open its width E of St Martin's Pt, 208°, and steer so till the high land at NE end of Sark shuts in with the northernmost bluff land of Herm. Then leaving Roustel, B and W cheq stone tr, 8m, well to stb, and Rousse bn well to port, bring Belvedere house, W, on the bluff abreast the lt tr E of Fort George, in line with the W patch just within the SE angle of Castle Cornet, 224°. Steer so and proceed into hr clear of all dangers.

By night approach on a safe bearing of Platte Fougère lt. When 3M from the lt, steer to gain the ldg line of Castle Breakwater lt and Belvedere lt, 220°.
(2) *Great Russel chan* is 2M wide and easy of access. Enter it from N with the W extreme of Little Sark open E of the E side of Brecqhou. When St Martin's Pt comes open S of Goubinière Rk steer 230°, allowing for tide. When the Lt Ho on S pier of St Peter Port old hr comes well S of Castle Cornet, 300°, keep it so to clear Sardrière and Têtes d'Aval (or Lower Heads) G con bell buoy Fl 5s to S, then enter hr.
(3) *From the W and S* the NW shore of Guernsey should be given a berth of 3½M and Les Hanois lt 1½M, and the S shore about a mile. Passing W of Guernsey at night do not bring Les Hanois lt to bear more than 164° until Casquet lt bears

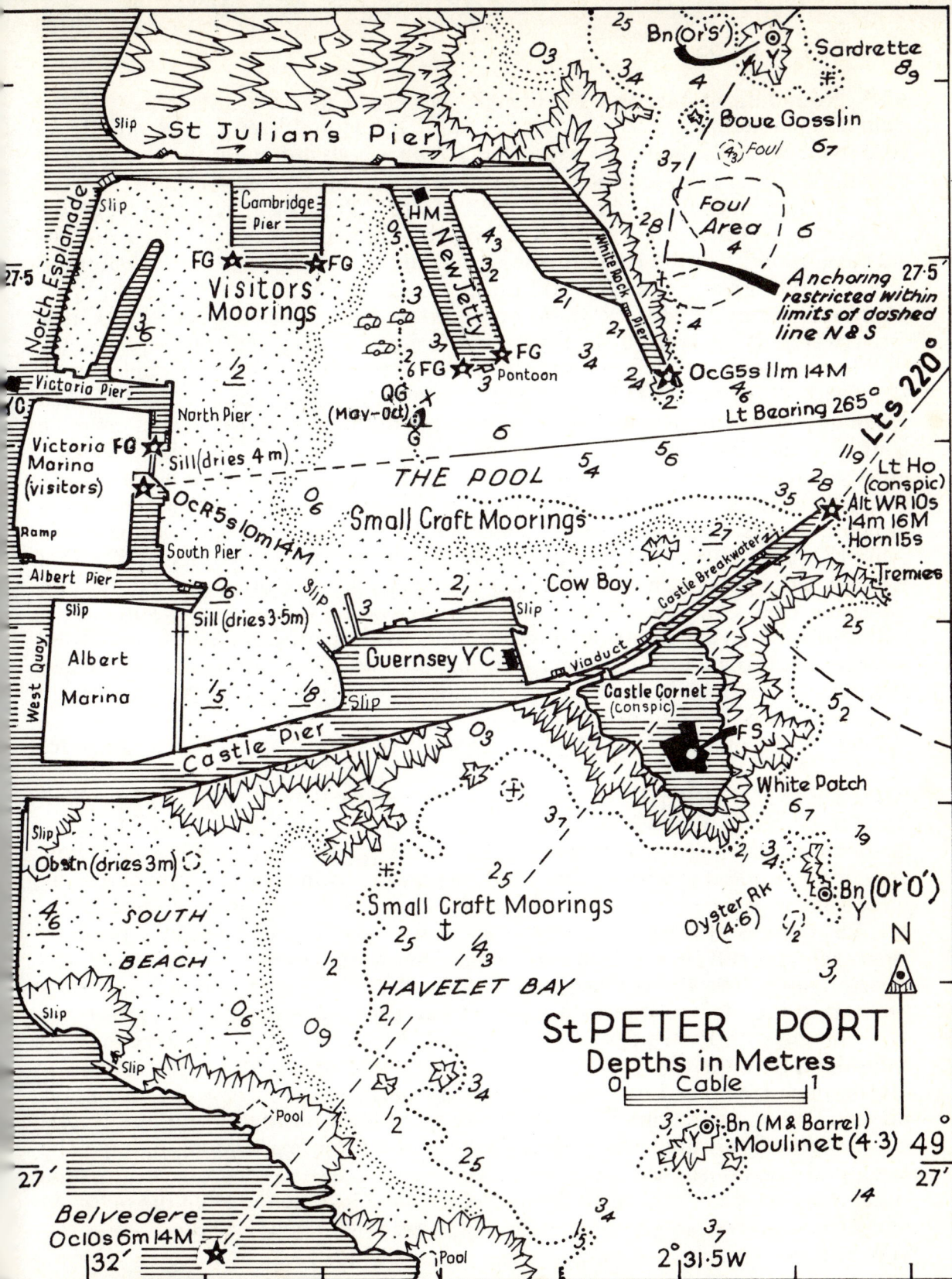

Bn (Or S')
Sardrette
8 9
0 3
2 5
3 4
4
Boue Gosslin
6 7
(4₃) Foul
3 7 1
2 8
Foul Area
4
6
Anchoring restricted within limits of dashed line N & S
27·5'

St Julian's Pier
Slip
Slip
Cambridge Pier
HM
New Jetty
4 3
3 2
2 1
White Rock Pier
2 1
3 4
2 4
OcG5s 11m 14M
4 6
Lt Bearing 265°
Lts 220°

North Esplanade
27·5'
FG
FG
Visitors' Moorings
3
0 3
2
2 6
6 FG
QG (May-Oct)
G
3 7
FG
Pontoon
3
6
5 4
5 6

Victoria Pier
FG
North Pier
Victoria Marina (visitors)
FG
Ramp
Sill (dries 4 m)
OcR5s 10m 14M
0 6
THE POOL
Small Craft Moorings
11 9
28
3 5
Lt Ho (conspic)
Alt WR 10s 14m 16M
Horn 15s

South Pier
Albert Pier
West Quay
Slip
Albert Marina
Sill (dries 3·5m)
1 5
0 6
Slip
3
2 1
1 8
Slip
Cow Boy
Castle Breakwater
2 7
Tremies
2 5
Guernsey YC
Viaduct
Castle Cornet (conspic)
5 2

Slip
Obstn (dries 3m)
SOUTH BEACH
4 6
Castle Pier
0 3
3 7
2 5
White Patch
6 7
2 1
3 4
1 9
Oyster Rk (4·6)
1 2
Bn (Or 'O')
Y
FS
N

Slip
Slip
Pool
0 6
0 9
1 2
Small Craft Moorings
2 5
1 2
2 1
3 4
1 4 3
HAVELET BAY
3 1

St PETER PORT
Depths in Metres
0 ——— Cable 1

Bn (M & Barrel)
Moulinet (4·3)
49°
27'
3
3 7
1 4

27'
Belvedere
Oc10s 6m 14M
32'
2 5
3 4
1 5
Pool
2° 31·5'W

051°. Rounding St Martin's Pt, the SE corner, at about a mile, steer on the Saumarez monument, 358°, and so to the hr. If beating, keep La Grande Braye well open W of Brehon tr to avoid the Great Russel indraught, and remember that the E-going tide does not set N round St Martin's Pt till 4h flood.

By night from S, from a position off St Martin's Pt lt (Fl(3) WR 10s), keep the old hr R lt just open of Terres Pt, 342°. When St Martin's Pt bears 215°, steer 015° till the G lt of the White Rk pier comes on with the W lt of Castle Breakwater (Al WR 10s, 308°) when steer 330° till the R lt bears 265°, then proceed into hr.

Entrance Bring Lt Ho, Oc R 5s, on end of S pier of old hr open N of Castle Breakwater, lt Al WR 10 sec, and steer 265°. A R flag or lt on N pier-head, visible from seaward, denies entrance: visible only from inside hr, similar signals deny exit. Port radio, VHF Ch 16 and 12 continuous, also 2182 and 1642.5kHz.

Berthing Instructions may be obtained by radio: otherwise yachts may be contacted by HM's launch on entering. Old hr marina has a sill which restricts entry or departure to approximately half-tide; gauge at entrance shows depth over sill. Visitors' moorings at pontoons on S side of the marina. Other moorings at pontoons just outside marina entrance or on buoys in the Pool. Marina in old Albert Dock is restricted to residents only. Customs and HM's office at N end of S pier where application can be made for yachts able to take the ground to moor alongside Coal Quay in old hr. Can be very crowded in summer season.

It is possible to anch outside or in one of the bays in offshore winds and settled weather. Alternatively moorings may be had at the Channel Islands Yacht Marina (see below). Royal Channel Islands YC (Guernsey HQ) at head of old hr; Guernsey SC at end of Castle Pier.

Fuel. Water on pontoons. Reparis, Charts. All stores, hotels, restaurants etc.

BEAUCETTE HARBOUR
Charts BA 807, 808 (Plan p398)

Tidal data: see St Peter Port

The Channel Islands Yacht Marina at Beaucette hr, close S of Fort Doyle, is now very popular and it is wise to check availability in advance. The entrance can be dangerous in strong winds from NE or E. A sill in the entrance dries 2.4m at MLWS, but has at least 1.7m depth except within 2½h of LW St Peter Port.

Approach and entrance Each side of the 18m wide entrance is painted W and clearly visible. The Petite Canupe S Card buoy SE of Petite Canupe Rk marks the start of the ldg line approach. Ldg marks: front, on N head of the entrance a W rectangle with R stripe; rear, a R rectangle with W stripe. Lts are exhibited from the ldg marks.

Approach from the Little Russel with ldg marks in line, 276°. The channel is marked during the summer months by two G buoys on the N side and two R buoys on the S. Owing to the nature of the bottom, these are liable to drag. The G-topped buoy just inside the entrance must be left to stb. There are tidal streams across the approach course, and care must be taken to keep the marks in line so as to avoid rks on either side. Tides are slack about 3h before and after HW St Peter Port.

From the N, keep well to the E of the Canupe rks in the Little Russel until the ldg marks are in line. From the S, proceed to Roustel bn, then alter course to make good 343° keeping Roustel in line with the S (right hand) edge of Jethou Is until the ldg marks are in line. Short-cuts are inadvisable except with local knowledge.

Berthing   Visitors' reception on port hand; sound horn on entry and departure. Berth at pontoons. Water and electricity on pontoons. Fuel, repairs.

SARK   Chart BA 808

HW −4.40.   MHWS 9.0; MLWS 1.0; MTL 5.0; MHWN 6.6; MLWN 3.5.
Tidal streams E and W of and close to Sark run up to 7kn at springs at HW and LW. The NE coast of Sark is slack at half-tide and HW, and the SW coast is slack at half-tide and LW, but there are many eddies so power is essential.

Creux Hr   Approach from S with Pt Robert Lt Ho in line with white tunnel arch in Creux Hr, 344°. When Creux beach fills the pier-heads, enter on 320°.

Anchorage   Outside in Les Laches, 5.5m, hard sand, but prohibited W of a line S from Creux jetty head. Lie against wall inside (prohibited against steps), dries 2.7m. Depth in entrance 4.0m at half-tide. Fuel, water, shops, crane, hotels.

   This hr is of use only in settled weather or with wind offshore. Streams set onto the dangers and power is essential.

Maseline Hr   Approach from NE with E side of L'Etac de Sark in line with W side of Les Burons, 211°. When Pt Robert Lt Ho opens to S of Grande Moie, alter course to leave Grand Moie maximum of 1 ca to the N; thence steer S for the pier.

Anchorage   W or NW of jetty in 5 to 8m, sand, no stream. Berthing at jetty prohibited at steamer times, and all other times unless attended. Uncomfortable in NE wind.

   Both Creux and Maseline jetties exhibit a FW lt on hd, vis ½M.

Dixcart and Derrible Bays   From SE with Sark mill (no vanes) open W of Pt Chateau in Dixcart Bay, 337°. Both are clear of danger in middle, sand 3 to 5m. No water. Path at Dixcart to hotels and village.

La Grève de la Ville   Approach with Noire Pierre (3.7m) midway between Grande Moie (30m) and the NE face of les Burons (22m), 153°. Noire Pierre is clean all round within 10m, so pass either side and anch anywhere in bay in about 5m, sand.

Havre Gosselin   Approach from N with W-ly rock of Little Sark seen through Gouliot Passage, 188° (half-tide is slack). When through Gouliot head E leaving Moie de Gouliot (50m) ½ ca to port. Hr is clear of dangers, no stream. Anch in 5m, shingle and sand, as near to stone landing steps as convenient.

JERSEY   Chart BA 3655

All vessels arriving at Jersey, unless from the Minquiers or Ecrehous, have come from outside the Bailiwick and must clear at either St Helier or Gorey.

   The SE and NE corners of Jersey are encumbered by outlying obstructions, but the Is may be readily approached from WNW and from the N between the Pierres de Lecq (or Paternosters) and Dirouilles groups.

Approaching St Helier it should be noted that at half flood all rks in the immediate offing in the entrance to St Aubin's Bay will have not less than 2m over them. Off Noirmont Pt, approaching the hr in thick weather, remember that the outset from St Aubin's Bay runs to SW for 9h round Noirmont Pt from half flood to LW excepting HW slack.

At night, approaching NE corner of the Is from N, St Catherine's Lt opening and closing behind La Coupe Pt will clear the Dirouilles to the W.

At the N and S of Jersey, it is slack water at HW and 6h after HW by the shore. At E and W ends of the Is, it is slack water at about half-tide by the shore.

ST HELIER
Chart BA 1137 (Plan p405)

HW −4.50. DS (2M S): W −4.30; E +2.10.
MHWS 11.1; MLWS 1.3; MTL 6.2; MHWN 8.1; MLWN 4.1.

Approach By NW passage, on nearing La Corbière Lt Ho at the SW pt of the Is keep the summit of Jersey high land in line with or above the lantern of the Lt Ho in order to clear the dangers off the pt. At night, the FR lt situated 4 ca ENE of the Lt Ho, in horizontal line with the lantern. Once round the Lt Ho steer 097° to pass 2½ ca S of La Moye Pt and continue on this until La Corbière Lt Ho is seen touching La Moye Pt, 290°. Then steer 110° to pass approximately 2 ca S of Noirmont Pt. When Noirmont Pt is abeam, steer 082° on the W passage ldg marks, that is La Grève d'Azette Lt Ho, Oc 5s; Mont Ubé lt, Al WR 6s; and /or Dog's Nest bn, in transit. This will pass N of Les Fours G buoy, QG; N of Ruaudière G bell buoy, Fl G 3s; and S of the RW Oyster Rk, bn. Soon after passing the Oyster bn, the Platte bn, Fl R 1½s, will be seen off the end of Elizabeth Castle breakwater. Alter course to port round the Platte bn to bring the ldg lts of St Helier in transit, 023°, W patches by day; front Oc G 5s 8m 11M, rear Oc R 5s 20m 12M, synchronised.

Other lines of approach are fully described in the *Channel Pilot*.

The Small Roads in the approach to the hr has 3m or more.

Entrance Power is advisable owing to the blanketing of the wind from quay walls if under sail, also strong set across pier-heads from half-flood to HW. Steer on ldg lts or marks until hr entrance is well open, then for entrance. Two G lts in line 078° give direction of hr ent.

Traffic signals Lt signals are shown from the roof of the pier-head control station at Victoria pier-head, fixed lts by day, Fl at night. Signals do not apply to vessels entering or leaving the marina but there is considerable commercial traffic and great care is essential in these narrow waters. Speed limit 5kn.

Berthing Visiting yachts are directed by Port Control to marina. Entrance, dredged to 1m, lies immediately S of hr entrance. Steer as to enter hr as above until marina entrance buoy, Q G, is abeam to stb; then turn following line of R port-hand buoys, QR. Entrance is narrow: great care necessary in cross-winds or at LW. Duty official directs yachts to a berth. Depth at pontoons is between 1.8m

JERSEY ST HELIER & STAUBIN

Depths in Metres

St Helier

St Aubin

ST AUBIN BAY

BELCROUTE BAY

PORTELET BAY

Martello Tr No 1

Martello Tr No 2

Mon Plaisir Ho

Pt Le Grouin

La Cotte Pt

Pt de Bût

Noirmont Pt

Castle Pier

St Aubin Fort

Grosse Rk Bn

Bn(pole)

Bathing Pool

Mark in line with Gros du Château 341°

Gros du Château

Baleine

Diamond Rk

Grosse Rk Bn

Ho in line with Tr 339°

Ho in line with Grosse Rk Bn 000

Tr in line with Grosse Rk Bn 000

Ldg Lts in line with Dogs Nest Bn 082°

Dogs Nest Bn

Dogs Nest Rk

Oyster Rk

Nipple Rk

Trois Grunes

SOUTH PASSAGE

MIDDLE PASSAGE

SILLETTE PASSAGE

WESTERN PASSAGE

Les Fours

QG

Sillette

Grande Vaudin

Les Grunes Vaudin

Danger Rk

Grunes aux Dardes

Ruaudière Rk

Mont Ubé Lt
Alt W R 6s 46m 14,12M

La Grève d'Azette
Oc.5s 23m 14M

La Motte (Island)

Bailhache

Fort Regent (conspic)

HM Sig Post

FS

Yacht Hr

Tr Harbour

Chy (95)(conspic)

NEW HR

OLD HR

Elizabeth Castle

Oc.G 11M

Oc. R 12M

Spire

Spire

Mo(D)W R 12s 4Nm 14,10M Horn(3)

Fl(4)R 15s

Fl(2)R 6s

Fl G 3s Ball

Fl(2)R 6s

Fl(4)R(15)18m 13M Tr (conspic)

Ldg Lts 023°

0 Mile 1

and 1m. Water on pontoons, showers and toilets. Fifteen or 20 min. walk to shops. A new marina between Albert Pier and New North Quay is expected to be in operation by end 1981.

The St Helier YC overlooks the hr. The Royal Channel Islands YC is at St Aubin.

Anch outside St Helier hr in the Small Roads is not recommended owing to shipping movements.

SAINT AUBIN   Chart BA 1137   (Plan p405)
Approach as for St Helier. When in the chan abreast of Ruaudière G bell buoy, Fl G 3s, turn N and leaving Diamond R buoy, Fl(2) R 6s, close to port, steer 332° for 1.3M. Then steer between small port and stb buoys marking the chan between moorings, 252°, and enter hr through pier-heads.

At night, bn on N pier-head has lt Iso R 4s and also Dir F WRG. Steer on the W sector, 252°, of the directional lt until the entrance.

Berthing   Drying berths for visitors alongside N quay. RCIYC has its HQ at The Bulwarks: showers, meals, visiting yachtsmen welcome. Water on N quay, fuel, all facilities. Buses to St Helier.

GOREY   Charts BA 1138, 3655   (Plan p398)
An attractive drying hr, but generally very crowded.

Approach   From the N, from ½M E of St Catherine's Breakwater the square stone Seymour tr (15.8m) will be seen 4M to the S with Little Seymour bn 3 ca N of the tr. Bring the two in line and steer on this course 184° to Gorey Roads G buoy, QG. Then alter course to stb with the hr ldg marks in line 298°: front, Lt Ho on pier-head, Oc RG 5s, 8m, 12M; rear, WR patch on stone wall, Oc R 5s, 24m, 8M.

From the SE, from a position 1M E of Grande Anquette Refuge bn, BW whence pier-head is in line with Gorey ch spire, 305°, and continue on that bearing until abeam of Le Giffard buoy, RW cheq, when course should be altered to the N in order to bring the ldg lights in line, 298°. Bns are generally iron poles with topmarks the initial letter of the name.

Anchorage   E of pier; or take the ground inside, hard sand, mooring bow and stern; or lie alongside pier inside staging at pier-head. Dries 3 to 4½m. Stream runs fast at anch E of pier and there is a sharp set to NE past pier-head between half flood and half ebb. St Catherine's Bay, inside the breakwater off Verclut Pt, affords anch in 3 to 9m, bottom sand and weed, moderate holding.

Buses to St Helier, launch to Carteret. Water from tap by landing stage, fuel from pumps nearby. Stores ½M.

Bound N, leave at half flood to catch the N-going eddy inshore.

France, North Coast

Chart BA 2669; F 880, 881

The W side of the Cherbourg Peninsula is an inhospitable and rocky coast, exposed to winds from between W and N. There is no sheltered anch. The marks are difficult to identify and fog, although not very frequent, may occur at any season. There are two chans leading S from the Alderney Race.

The Passage de la Deroute runs E of Les Ecrehou, between the Plateau de l'Arconie and les Boeufs, and between the Plateau des Minquiers and the Iles Chausey. In the narrow part of the chan the flood runs at 4 to 5kn, the ebb at $3\frac{1}{2}$ to 4kn.

Another chan, the Deroute de Terre, runs inshore from Carteret to Granville. Depths of no more than 0.9m exist at the S end of this chan.

Granville, the only hr on this coast where yachts can remain afloat, is accessible only at certain times.

Diélette   A small drying hr about 11M S of C de la Hague. Affords shelter from winds between ENE and S. Entrance dries 2.1m.
Carteret   A small fishing port 10M S of C de Flamanville. Only accessible near HW by day. Approach dries 4m $\frac{1}{2}$M to seaward of jetty heads. Entrance bordered by sandbanks liable to frequent change. Berth along quay at inner end of W jetty, dries 7 to 9m.

GRANVILLE
Chart BA 2669, F 5897   (Plan p409)

HW −5.05.   MHWS 12.8; MLWS 1.4; MTL 7.1; MHWN 9.6; MLWN 4.6.
Granville can be identified by the Pte du Roc which terminates in a steep cliff on which is a grey circular lt tr with R top, Fl(4) 15s. Up to 4M offshore there are depths of less than 5m with patches which dry.
Approach   From W make the W Card buoy, VQ(9) 10s, $3\frac{1}{4}$M W of Pte du Roc, marking the W side of La Videcoq rk (dries 1m).
Entrance   From this buoy, with sufficient water steer 090° for the BR lt tr, Le Loup, Fl(2) 6s, $2\frac{3}{4}$ ca S of W jetty head. Leave this to stb and the W jetty head, lt Iso R 4s, to port.
Berthing   Yachts berth in the half-tide marina (Port de Hérel) to the SE of the

Avant Port. Enter by standing on past the Avant Port entrance, then turning hard to port to round the new wall extending SE from the old E jetty head. On rounding the curved tip of this wall (Fl(2) R 6s), pass between it and the S tip of new detached breakwater (Fl G 4s) guarding the marina area, avoiding the line of R posts, lts Fl Bu, to the N marking the dinghy basin. Entrance is over a sill, depth shown on lit tide gauge on wall near entrance, through chan 16m wide marked by R and G bns. Sill dries about 6m, or 5.25m when gate lifted at certain tides. Least depth at pontoons 1.5m to N, 2.5m to S.

Fishing fleet occupies all inner berths in old hr. YC. All facilities.

ILES CHAUSEY
Charts F 829, 824

HW −5.05.   MHWS 12.9; MLWS 1.9; MTL 7.4; MHWN 9.8; MLWN 4.9.

A beautiful archipelago of islets and rocks. Grande Ile, the largest island, affords anch in the sound on its NE side.

Approach With large-scale chart the approach is straightforward from the S, and with some care it is possible to depart to the N near HW. Although the rise and fall is very great, the tidal streams are not excessively strong.

Entrance   From SE of Pte de la Tour Lt Ho, Fl 5s, keep RW bns (near the Lt Ho) to port and the Epiettes G con buoy, Fl G 2s, to stb. Steer towards La Crabière Est S Card bn, Oc WRG 4s, in line with L'Enseigne BW tr, 332°. Keeping La Crabière Est bn close to stb, alter course 30° to port for next RW bn and keep this to stb also.

Anchorage Visiting yachts anch between this bn and the next pair of bns beyond it. There are two lines of mooring buoys laid by the Granville YC each side of the deep chan and any free ones may be used. Choose a mooring according to the direction of the wind so that the boat lies in deep water. At springs the N part of the anch dries, but there is 2m in the S part. Close under the chapel there is a beach where vessels with bilge keels or legs may take the ground.

Landing stage for dinghies SW of moorings. Larger wharf by the hotel is for ferries; unattended craft or dinghies are strictly forbidden alongside.

ROTHENEUF
Charts BA 2700, F 5645   (Plan p409)

HW (St Malo) −5.10.   MHWS (St Malo) 12.1; MHWN 9.1.

DS (Chenal de la Bigne): NE +1.50; SW −4.55. Attains 3 to 4kn at sp and the approach near HW when the rks are covered can be dangerous.

A drying hr about 3½M E of St Malo. Entrance is narrow and should only be attempted in good conditions, but complete shelter inside for yachts with bilge keels or legs. Large-scale chart essential.

Approach and entrance   From St Malo depart by Chenal de la Bigne. After leaving La Petite Bigne G bn 50m to port, continue on course 042°. After leaving Le Durand (dries 10m) and Le Roger (dries 4.7m) to stb, the bn marking the entrance will be seen, distant about 7 ca. When this bn bears 175° steer on this

GRANVILLE
Depths in Metres

Granville

Casino

Port de Hérel

Port de Roche Gautier

Pte de Roche Gautier

Bassin de Mouillage

Bassin d'evolution

5 Lts. Bu

Oc G4s

FlR4s7M

IsoG4s11m6M

IsoR4s7m12M

BASSIN À FLOT

AVANT PORT

Le Roc

Pt du Roc (Cap Lihou)

Pt de la Fourche

la Fourche

Fl(4)15s49m23M

Fl(2)6s11M

Le Loup

BRB

59

N

48° 495'

50

1°37'

1°36'

ROTHÉNEUF
Depths in Metres

CHENAL DE LA BIGNE 222°-042°

les Haurets

les Houtieux

Le Roger

le Durand

La Petite Bigne

Bn G

le Benetin

les Fourchettes

Grand Chevreuil

Petit Chevreuil

Pte Benard

Sig Stn (disused)

Bn B G

La Brunette

ANSE du Val

Statue

Pte de Rothéneuf

Rothéneuf Tr

Entrance in line with Windmill Tr 162°

Windmill Tr

N

0 Cables 6

48°

42'

41'

1°58'

1°57'

St QUAY PORTRIEUX
Depths in Metres

Le Four Tr Bn & Moulières de Portrieux in line 168°

Ile Harbour Oc(2)6s15m11M

La Hergue W

Moulières de St Quay BY

Gremineu

Le Secret

Guengalnie

Guidlacre

Re Penn

Pte de St Quay

Moulières de Portrieux Tr Bn BYB

Chef de Ane

Les Poylins

Les Cognées

St Quay

Pte de Portrieux

Portrieux

IsoG4s10m11M

FlR4s

Pte de Porteleut

Les Noirs YB

Herflux YB

Réhan

Rochers Dean

Gd Aubert

Meidouze

RADE DE PORTRIEUX

les Moutons

Le Gourvelot

Bn W

G

Le Four W

LES ANES

Roche Houesse

N

0 Cables 7

2°47'W

48'

46'

48° 9'

48° 5'

2°

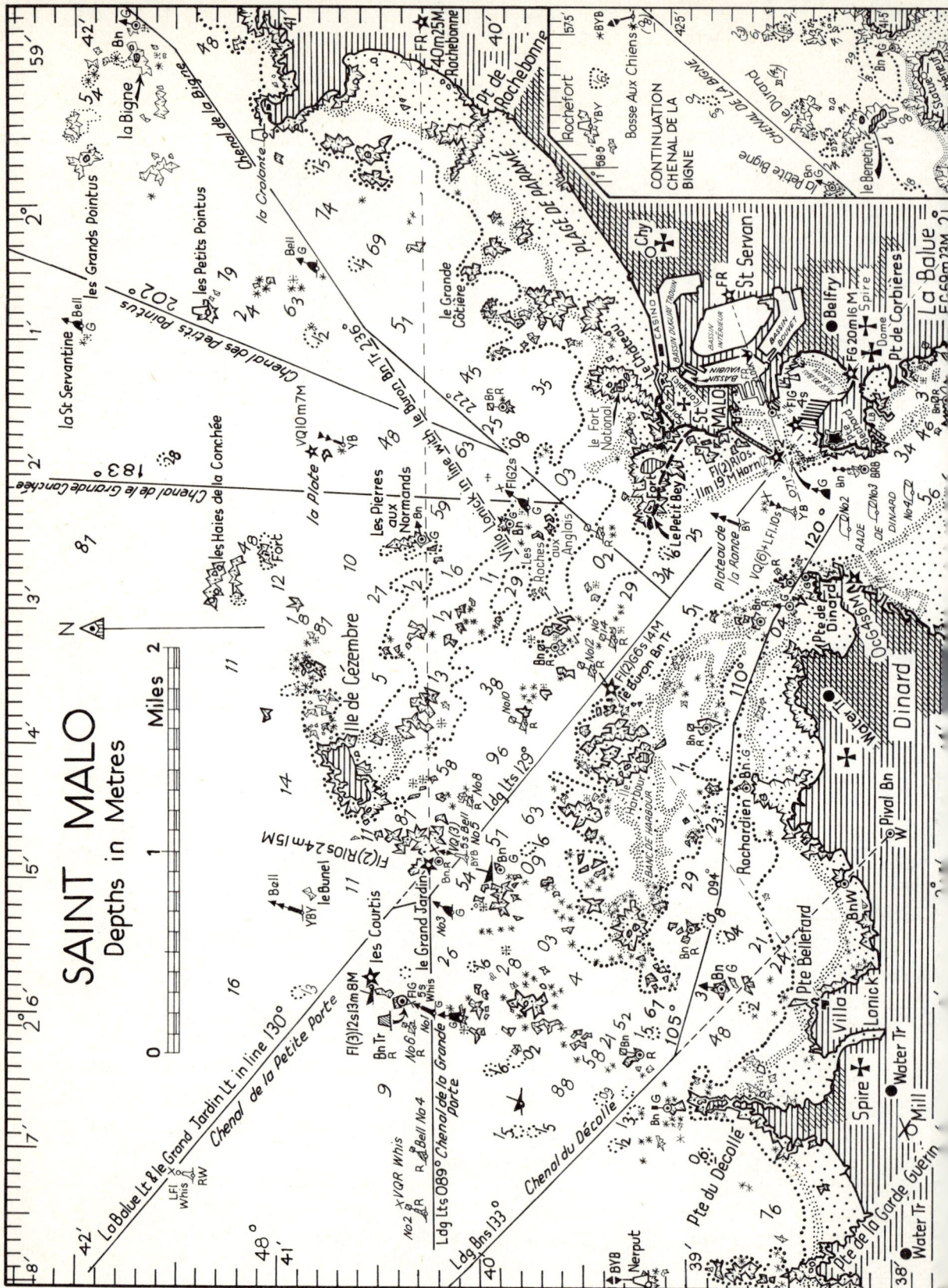

SAINT MALO
Depths in Metres

N

Miles
0   1   2

la Bigne
les Grands Pointus
les Petits Pointus
la St Servantine
Chenal de la Bigne
la Croûte
Pt. de Rochebonne
FR 40m25M Rochebonne
Pt. de Rochebonne
PLAGE DE PARAMÉ
CONTINUATION CHENAL DE LA BIGNE
Bosse Aux Chiens
la Petite Bigne
le Bénétin
St Servan
Chenal des Petits Pointus
Chenal de la Grande Conchée
les Haies de la Conchée
le Fort
la Plate
le Grande Côtière
le Fort National
le Grand Jardin
Île de Cézembre
Les Pierres aux Normands
les Roches aux Anglais
CASINO
Casino
BASSIN INTÉRIEUR
BASSIN BOUVET
ST MALO
Belfry
La Balue
le Petit Bey
Pte de Corbières
Dome
Spire
le Buron
Plateau de la Rance
Pte de Dinard
Dinard
le Bunel
les Courtis
le Grand Jardin
Chenal de la Petite Porte
BANC DE HARBOUR
Water Tr
Rochardien
Pte Bellefard
Villa
Lonick
La Balue Lt & le Grand Jardin Lt in line 130°
Chenal de la Grande Porte
Chenal du Décollé
Pte du Décollé
Spire
Villa
Water Tr
Mill
Nerput
Pte de la Garde Guérin
Ldg Bns 133
Ldg Lts 129°
Ldg Lts 089°

Based on British Admiralty Charts (nos. in text) with the permission of the Controller of H.M. Stationery Office and the Hydrographer of the Navy, and on other sources.

course and enter leaving it close to stb. Alternatively the ldg line is the W side of Pte Bénard just open with an old converted windmill, 163°, which leaves le Roger rk ½ ca to stb.

Anchorage There is a deep-water anch outside the hr immediately WNW of the entrance bn, only safe in settled weather. Inside, the whole hr dries about 8m with good sandy bottom in SW corner near village with shops and restaurants.

SAINT MALO   Charts BA 2700; F 5645   (Plan p410)

HW −5.10. MHWS 12.1; MLWS 1.4; MTL 6.7; MHWN 9.1; MLWN 4.4.

The safest approach route by day and night is to make Cap Fréhel, Lt Ho Fl(2) 10s, grey square tr 85m, whence steer for the Grand Jardin, 24m grey tr Fl(2) R 10s, by the Chenal de la Grande Porte to reach the Rance at HW. The N routes are subject to strong cross streams, and should only be used with a steady fair breeze under sail, or with reliable power.

Tidal streams In the chan between the Minquiers and Iles Chausey on the N, and the coast of St Malo Bay on the S, the flood sets ESE and the ebb WNW. Although generally not so strong as around the Channel Is, streams of over 3kn occur at springs and must be allowed for. The Admiralty Tidal Stream Atlas *The Channel Islands and Adjacent Coasts of France* is strongly recommended.

Approach From the W by the Chenal de la Grande Porte. The chan is well marked.

From the NW by the Chenal de la Petite Porte. Cross-tidal stream. Les Courtis (Lt Ho Fl(3) 12s) and Le Bunel (W Card buoy) are outlying rks.

From N and NE by the Chenal de la Grande Conchée, Chenal des Petits Pointus or Chenal de la Bigne.

Entrance By Grand Chenal from a position 1½ ca W of Grand Jardin lt tr, bring the St Malo ldg lts, both FG, in line, 129°. By day the chan is well marked on both sides.

Berthing New marina at St Servan, on the stb hand before the entrance to St Malo docks. Head towards the lock and turn to stb to cross the sill, dries 2m, between the ferry terminal forming the S approach to the lock, and a can buoy with R flag marking the extremity of the marina's protective sill. There is an inner sill, with illuminated tide gauge at its N end, visible on entering.

Alternatively there are yacht pontoons in the Bassin Vauban, close under the walls of St Malo. Entry by lock HW −2 to +1; first and last exits ½h later. Signals: R flag, no entry; G flag, no exit; R and G flags, lock not available. From lock turn to port to pontoons. All facilities. Crane for lowering masts for canal (or there is a free crane on the quay at Dinan).

Berths for larger yachts may be available in the Bassin Duguay-Trouin.

Anchorage Most suitable anchorages are now occupied by permanent moorings. Available positions are generally exposed to strong streams and wind. In fine weather a good berth may be found in the Rade de Dinard.

RIVER RANCE
Chart F 4233

The Rance is dammed above St Servan but is easily navigable up to Dinan by any yacht with a reasonable engine and drawing not more than 1.2m. There is normally little current, but when turbines are operating the level falls rapidly and currents can be strong.

Going upstream from St Malo, keep to the W side of the river and follow closely the R port-hand buoys leading to the lock in the barrage which opens every hour on the hour. Above the lock, port-hand buoys mark the danger area near the barrage. Navigation up to Le Chatelier lock is straightforward, but French chart 4233 is recommended; there are more buoys not shown on this chart which should be carefully observed, especially if the water is low. Detailed information about water levels can be obtained from the marinas at St Malo, or the lock-keeper at the barrage.

Above Le Chatelier lock follow the dredged chan, well marked with beacons. Pontoons at Dinan in beautiful situation. Free crane for lowering masts. Walk up steep hill to picturesque town.

BAIE DE SAINT BRIEUC
Charts BA 2669; F 832, 833

DS: 6M N of Grand Léjon; SE +2.00, 3 kn; NW −4.10, 2 kn. At 1½M N of Cap Fréhel; ESE +2.05; WNW −5.25; both streams attain 4kn.

The hrs in Baie de St Brieuc dry except Le Légué, a small port at the head of the bay, and Binic on the W side of the bay, both of which have wet docks. The best anch during W winds is in Anse de Bréhec, entered between Pte de Bréhec (about 1½M S of Pte de Minar) and Pte de Tour, about ¾M to the SSE (½M from which to NE is the tr bn marking Le Taureau rk: BRB, topmark 2 B spher (vert)).

ERQUY
Charts F 5724, 833

HW −5.10. MHWS 11.2; MLWS 1.3; MTL 6.3; MHWN 8.5; MLWN 4.1.

The rade and port is a mile S of C d'Erquy which lies 7M W of Cap Fréhel, and affords a useful anch bound W from St Malo. C d'Erquy has conspic W cliffs on its SW side, and the chapel on Ilot St Michel is 2½M to E.

Approach   From E, from a position 4M W of Cap Fréhel, steer 229° through the Chenal d'Erquy with Cap d'Erquy in line with Le Verdelet Rk, leaving two S Card buoys to stb. When within 4 ca of Les Châtelets, round Cap d'Erquy at 2 ca leaving a R buoy to port, until the jetty bears 090°.

From W, a course 100° made good from a ca S of Rohein YBY lt tr, Card W, leads on to Moulin Turquet. When the jetty, 10m W tr with R top, Oc(1+2) WRG, bears 090°, steer in keeping in the W sector.

Anchorage   There is good holding, sand and mud, about ½M W of the jetty which runs N and S, sheltered from NE through E to SE. With fresh SW winds this berth is not recommended. Berths alongside the jetty are rarely available.

ST BRIEUC (LE LEGUE) Charts BA 2669, F 833
HW −5.20. MHWS 11.2; MLWS 1.3; MTL 6.3; MHWN 8.5; MLWN 4.1.
The hr lies on the W side of the head of the bay. There is a disused sig stn on Pte du Roselier, 73m, and a W tr, 9m, Iso G 4s, on Pte à l'Aigle jetty.
Approach Pass W of Grand Léjon, R tr W bands 23m, Fl(5) WR 20s, and 1½M W of Le Rohein, YBY tr 14m, VQ(9) 10s, keeping at night in the W sector of Grand Léjon lt (350°–015°) which leads between Roches de St Quay and Le Rohein.
Entrance Dries as far as Pte du Roselier and as much as 5.5m. Pass 2 ca E of Pte du Roselier, steering S for the entrance. Pass the Lt Ho on Pte à l'Aigle at not more than 1 ca to avoid Les Galettes rks. Small buoys mark the chan. Hence keep in the middle of the fairway for 2 ca, and then 15m from the towpath to the lock, securing to a quay outside while waiting to enter. The sill is 5m above chart datum. Outer basin has about 5.5m, the inner somewhat less. The lock gates operate from HW St Malo −2 to +1 at springs, but only from −1 to HW at neaps.
  Water and shops at port. Rly, all supplies and bank at St Brieuc, 1M.

BINIC Chart F 833
HW −5.20. MHWS 11.2; MLWS 1.3; MTL 6.3; MHWN 8.5; MLWN 4.1.
The small port lies 2½M S of Portrieux and dries. 2h before local HW a 1kn counter-current sets E across the entrance for 1h.
  Anch to wait for raise 1½ to 2M off entrance, mud and clay.
  The hr, entered between two moles (N mole hd has a W tr, 12m, Oc(3) 12s), is in two parts. In outer hr, berth against N mole, dries 4m, bottom mud. Inner hr is a wet basin for about 150 yachts. Gates open 1h either side of HW, but only during HM's working hours. All supplies.

SAINT QUAY, PORTRIEUX Charts BA 2669, F 5725 (Plan p409)
HW −5.20. DS (W of Roches de St Quay): SSE +1.05, 2¼kn; NW −5.10, 2kn.
MHWS 11.2; MLWS 1.3; MTL 6.3; MHWN 8.5; MLWN 4.1.
The port lies ½M S of Pte de St Quay on which is a sig stn, W ho and FS. 3 ca W of Pte de St Quay is the pointed belfry of St Quay ch.
  With winds from N through E to SE there is a surge in the hr, though conditions have been improved by the building of a new mole to the S. The hr dries 3 to 5m along the W side of the jetties.
  A chan ½M wide separates the coast, which to the S of the hr dries for 1M offshore, from the Roches de St Quay, at the N end of which is the Ile Harbour Lt Ho, W square tr, 16m, Oc(2) 6s, WRG. La Madeaux bn tr, W Card, about ½M NNW of Ile Harbour, marks the NW end of the reef.
Approach From the Grand Léjon, Ile Harbour Lt Ho bears 229°, 7½M.
Entrance From N, from a position 1½M N of Ile Harbour Lt Ho steer for Moulières de Portrieux RW tr in line with the W tr on Le Four, 168°. Then get La Longue tr, S card, in line with Herflux tr, R and W, 119°. After ½M alter so as to

put Pordic ch on with Le Four W tr, 182°, until the jetty hd bears 270°. Jetty hd lt is Iso 4s, W 306°–312°, G elsewhere.

From S, bring La Hergue W tr in line with Le Pommier rk (3M beyond La Hergue) 317°. Leave La Roselière W Card buoy to stb and after 2M, when the jetty hd bears 270°, enter leaving Les Moutons E Card buoy ½ ca to stb. At night, remember that Rohein lt is VQ(9) 10s, while Cap Fréhal is Fl(2) 10s.

Anchorage   In the Rade, good holding but exposed from N through E to S when Roches de St Quay are covered. Berth well in against W side of jetty, two ladders. Hr crowded with small yachts and fishing boats on moorings which dry out.

Small holiday resort. Water on quay; all supplies and restaurants.

PAIMPOL   Charts BA 2557, F 3670   (Plan p415)
HW −5.15.   DS (anch W of La Jument): SE +1.00; NW −6.15. Both streams attain 2kn.
MHWS 10.3; MLWS 0.5; MTL 5.4; MHWN 7.8; MLWN 3.2.

Approach   *From E:* Chenal de la Jument. The Anse de Paimpol is entered between the I St Rion, 36.9m, with two pointed summits, and the grassy Is of Mez de Goelo (off Pte de Plouézec) with the W square L'Ost Pic Lt Ho, Oc WR 4s, 20m, at its E end. Bring the Château de Coniat and Paimpol clock tr in line with top of Pte Brividic, 260°, and steer on this line N of La Jument RW tr to the roads. Anch to await tide 1 ca SW of La Jument, sand and gravel.

From N: (1) Chenal du Denou. With sufficient water, from a position ¾M E of Men-Gam BYB tr, E Card, steer 193° with the Denou W tr in line with Plouézec ch spire. The chan is deep but rks dry close to the ldg line. When Valve Rk (painted W) is abeam to stb, alter course to pass W of Denou white tr at ¾ ca; thence for La Jument and the ldg marks for Paimpol. Alternatively pass to E of the dangers and enter from E. (2) Chenal de la Trinité is well marked by bns, and convenient when bound for Lézardrieux.

Entrance   With sufficient water continue on the ldg line of Pte Brividic on with Paimpol clock tr and Château de Coniat, 260°, dries 3.6m, until abreast Le Vahel bn, when bear to stb to pass midway between Mesquer R bn and El Bras B bn. Thence to the buoys and bns which lead to the jetty hd. Hr has FR ldg lts, 264°.

Anchorage   There is restricted sheltered anch between the mud banks about 1½M W of La Jument.

Berthing   The lock is open for at least 1h at HW; at night only when St Malo tide exceeds 10m. Moor to pontoons in wet basin.

Water, small yard, stores and rly. Chandler, sailmaker.

TRIEUX RIVER AND BREHAT ROADS (LEZARDRIEUX)
                                    Charts BA 2557, F 832   (Plan p418–19)
HW (les Héaux) −5.20; (Lezardrieux) −4.15.
DS near Plateau de la Horaine: SE +1.35; NW −4.40.
MHWS (Les Héaux) 9.8; MLWS 1.0; MTL 5.4; MHWN 7.5; MLWN 3.4.

PAIMPOL
Depths in Metres

PORT DE PAIMPOL

Paimpol

Pte du Minar
Pte de Plouézec
Ile Tamenaz
le Taurel
Mez de Goëlo
Lost Pic
Oc WR 4s 20m
White
Red
WR
Rk Govayan
La Jument
R. Denou
Ile St Rion
Les Charpentiers
la Cormorandière Pyr. Bn
Pilier de la Vierge
Spire
Pte de la Trinité
Chenal de la Trinité
CHENAL DE LA JUMENT
Paimpol ClockTr in line with summit of Pte Brividic 260°
MOUILLAGE DE PAIMPOL
Ile Blanche
Pte de Guilben
Le Vahel
El Bras
Mesquer
Lts in line 264°
Portz-Don Oc(2) WR 6s 11m
Pte Brividic
Paimpol Clock Tr
FR
Denou W Tr in line with Plouézec Ch 193°
Plouézec Ch

Glénans Sailing School
Slip
Lock
N
3° 2·5'W
48° 47'

2 Miles
Cables
0 1 2 Miles
0 Cable 1

48° 48'
48° 47'
48° 46'

57'
58'
59'
3°W

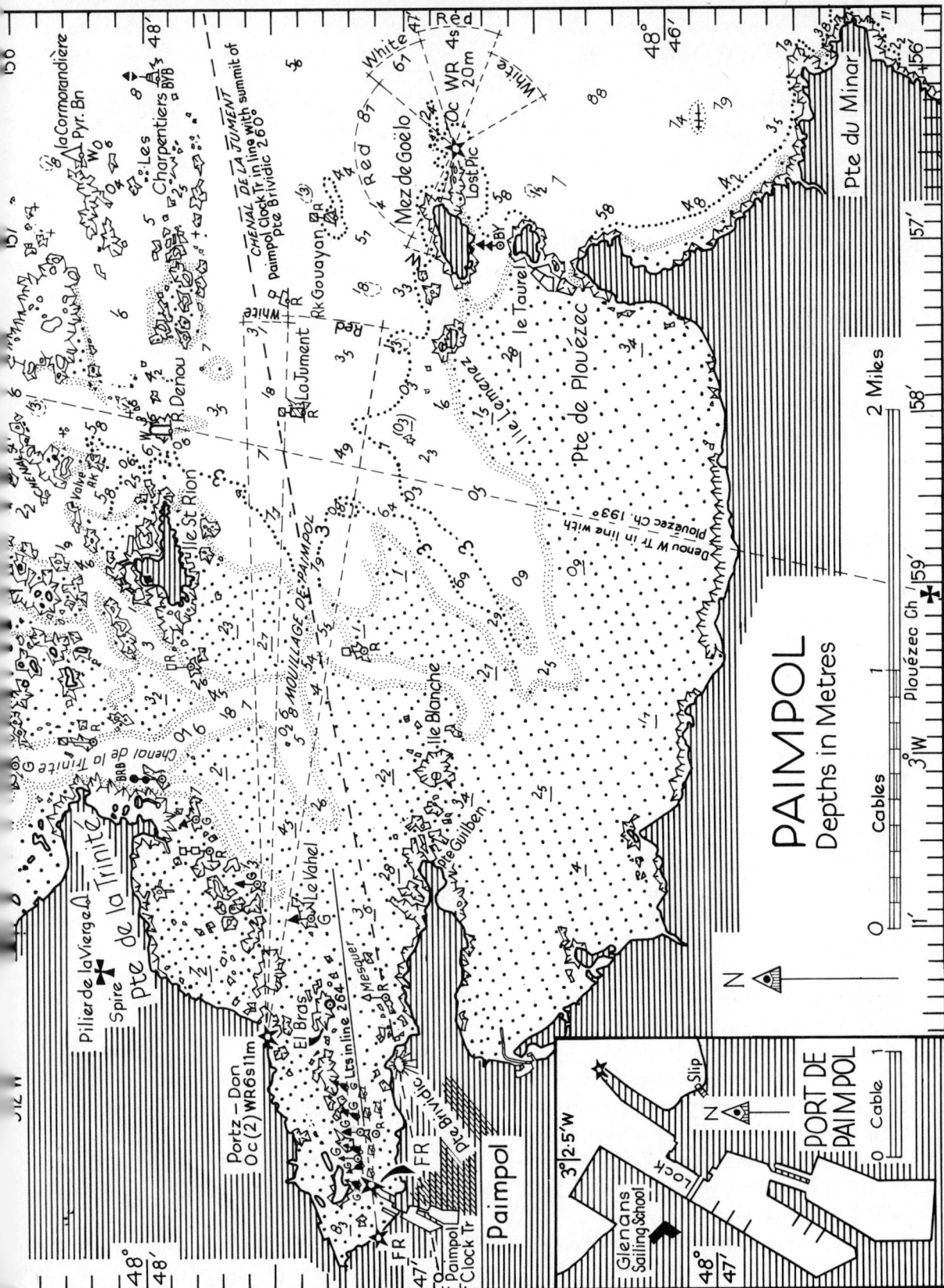

près la carte marine française avec l'autorisation du Service Hydrographique et Océanographique de la Marine.

MHWS (Lézardrieux) 10.0; MLWS 0.9; MTL 5.4; MHWN 7.5; MLWN 3.4.
The main entrance chan to Trieux R (also known as Pontrieux R) carries 6m at
LW and is lighted. Small vessels can enter from W by the Moisie chan, less than
2m, and by the Men du Castrec chan; from SE by the Ferlas chan, 2.4m; and
from N by the Bréhat chan.

The entrance to the river lies at the NW arm of St Brieuc Bay, between Les
Héaux to the NW and the Is Bréhat and Plateau de la Horaine to the SE. In clear
weather the distant Brittany hills, over 300m high, may be seen to S and SW,
20M inland from St Brieuc. On near approach the Lt Ho on les Héaux plateau
and the ch and spire of Plougrescan will be seen to the right, and to the left the
lofty spire of Plouézec, the I Bréhat with the chapel of St Michael, and the Lt
Hos of le Paon and Rosédo. Le Paon lt is situated 4¾M, 122° from Les Héaux lt.

Tidal streams   The flood stream off the entrance slacks 1h before HW by the
shore, the ebb 1h after LW. The flood stream outside sets hard on to La Horaine
plateau and into St Brieuc Bay at 4 or 5kn springs; the ebb in the reverse
direction. The tide is strongest at 1h after half flood and half ebb. The entrance
should not be attempted without power at spring tides except at slack water with
a good breeze, as the tidal streams set hard across the chan till past the entrance
to Le Kerpont. NW winds raise a heavy sea on the ebb.

Approach   The recommended approach is by the Grand Chenal from the NE.
The Moisie, Castrec and Bréhat chans lead into the Grand Chenal. Approaching
from the NE give the Barnouic plateau a good clearance. A bearing of 212° from
the Barnouic lt tr (BYB, VQ(3) 5s), making due allowance for the tidal stream,
will fetch the Basse du Nord buoy, RW pillar, staff and two globes, situated
about 1M N of La Horaine BW lt tr and about 6M E of Les Héaux lt tr off the
mouth of Le Tréguier R. Thence alter course SW to enter the Grand Chenal
marked on the port hand by a R can buoy, square topmark, and on stb hand by a
Les Sirlots G con buoy. From Les Sirlots the course is 225°, well marked with bns
to the R entrance. Marks continue to Lézardrieux.

Moisie chan   Keep the spire of St Michael's chapel, I de Bréhat, on with
Rosédo W pyramid, 159°, till the Croix and Bodic lts come in line, whence as for
Grand Chenal.

Men du Castrec chan   Bring the W pyramid on Arcouest Pt on with the G tr of
Vieille du Tréou, 174° and proceed thus till Croix and Bodic lts come in line,
whence as for Grand Chenal.

Bréhat chan   Bring Port Moguer tr in line with the Cormorandière W pyramid
168° and keep it so till the RW tr on Men Garo comes on with the W pyramid on
Quistillic Rk, a very conspic mark, 245°, when alter course and bring St Barbe
chapel open to W of summit of St Riom I, 202°, and then the spire of
Ploubazlanec on Men Gam, E Card tr, 235°. This bearing leads into Bréhat
roadstead where there is good holding in 5.5m upwards and good shelter from
NW to NE winds.

Ferlas chan   Bring the spire of the chapel of St Michael on the I Bréhat to bear
296° open to left of Quistillic pyramid. Continue on this bearing till La Croix Lt

Ho comes in line with the S side of Raguenez-Bras, 277°, when turn and continue on the new alignment through Ferlas chan which is well marked.

By night, the approach to the Grand Chenal and Trieux R is indicated by upriver ldg lts: Bodic (Q) rear, La Croix (Oc 4s) front, 225°. With good visibility the lts can easily be identified about 5M S of the Barnouic lt (VQ(3) 5s, unreliable). On this course the lt of Pte de la Horaine will be left about $1\frac{1}{2}$M to port and that of Les Héaux about $4\frac{1}{2}$M to stb.

Entrance On approaching La Croix Lt Ho leave it to port at a safe distance bringing the Coatmer lts in line 219°. When abeam of Bodic lt alter course for Perdrix lt tr, Iso G 4s, 6 ca distant; thence to berth.

The R is navigable, least depth 5.9m to Pte Coatmer and 3.2m thence to Lézardrieux, as far as Pontrieux, an attractive little town 16M from Paon lt. The chan is narrow and tortuous, and the stream very rapid, but presents little difficulty near HW.

Anchorage *In Trieux R.* (1) In Pomelin road, stream not very strong. (2) At neaps on mud SE of I de Bois, stream very strong at springs. (3) A little S or abreast of Feu d'Amant at W mooring buoys if available, or anch if room inshore of buoys, avoiding stakes at LW mark. There is a footpath to the village on the W bank.

I de Bréhat. (1) Port Clos W of Men Joliquet Lt Ho, or further in at neaps, strong tide and disturbed by launches from mainland. (2) La Corderie at N end of Kerpont. Anch at entrance between four bns. Available to deep-draft yachts at neaps only; good anch further in for small yachts with bilge keels or legs. (3) La Chambre. Delightful and popular anch at neaps, rocky scenery, but only 0.6 to 0.9m at MLWS.

Berthing There is a marina at Lézardrieux. All facilities including comfortable YC. Do not anch at Lézardrieux (poor holding).

It is possible to berth in the basin at Pontrieux. Sill of lock is 3.4m above datum.

TREGUIER RIVER   Chart BA 2668, F 967, 973   (Plan p420–1)
HW (Tréguier) – 5.45.   MHWS 9.7; MLWS 0.9; MTL 5.3; MHWN 7.4; MLWN 3.3.

The R Tréguier emerges 5M below the town of Tréguier, 3M W of Les Héaux Lt Ho (grey tr, 49m), $2\frac{1}{2}$M E of Pte du Château, and 5M W of Trieux R.

Tidal streams 5M N of Les Héaux: E +1.45; W −4.30; 4kn. La Jument buoy: E +1.15; W −5.00; 4kn. Grande Pass N of Les Renards: E +0.30; W −5.45; 4kn. In Passe de la Gaine between Les Héaux and mainland: ENE +0.15; WSW +4.45; 3kn. N of La Corne lt tr: SW-going stream +0.30; NE −5.45; 3kn.

Approach Closing from NW, from off the Pte du Château will be seen the belfrey of Plougrescant and wireless mast of Gonery, the spire of Tréguier cathedral 8M distant, and the SE corner of the I d'Er (W pyramid with B band). To E side of the chan are La Corne lt tr and Skeiviec W bn tr. To W side is Taureau Rk, B tr.

APPROACHES TO LEZARDRIEUX (1)

Depths in Metres

Miles

Cables

CAREC DONE

BASSE PLATTE

Men du Castrec

MEN DU CASTREC PASSAGE
Vieille du Tréou & Arcouest Trs in line 174°

MOISIE PASSAGE
Rosedo Pyramid & Chapel in line 160°

Ar Mesclek

Bn BYB

Moisie Rk Bn Tr

La Traverse

Noguejou Bihan

Ar Gazec Rk

PLATEAU DES SIRLOTS

Les Sirlots

Whistle G

Vieille du Tréou Bn Tr

GRAND CHENAL

Green

recommended track

Les in Line 225°

ENTRANCE TO PONTRIEUX RIVER

Basses des Pen Azen

Pen Azen

White

Petit-Pen Azen

Red

Paon Rk

FWRG

Rodello

Pen-ar-Rest

Beg an Marie

W Bn Tr

Carbouchö Rk

Bn

Moroch Rk

Brézellec Rk

Louet Rk

Stallio Bras

Toull Ahoult Rk

Men Buas

Men ar Goulan

Oc (3)WRG12s48m
17/13M

Red   White   Green

Basse de la Gaîne

Bn G

Les Héaux

White

Bréhatins Rk

BASSES DES HÉAUX

PASSE DE LA GAÎNE

G Bn

N

Bn G

Ile Blanche

Bras Rk

Ile Vierge

Les Soldats

BYB

ILE St MODE

Trogouerat

Runentraou

Lanneros

Le Sillon du Talbert

Le petite Grève

Sillon de Talbert

D'après la carte marine française avec l'autorisation du Service Hydrographique et Océanographique de la Ma

418

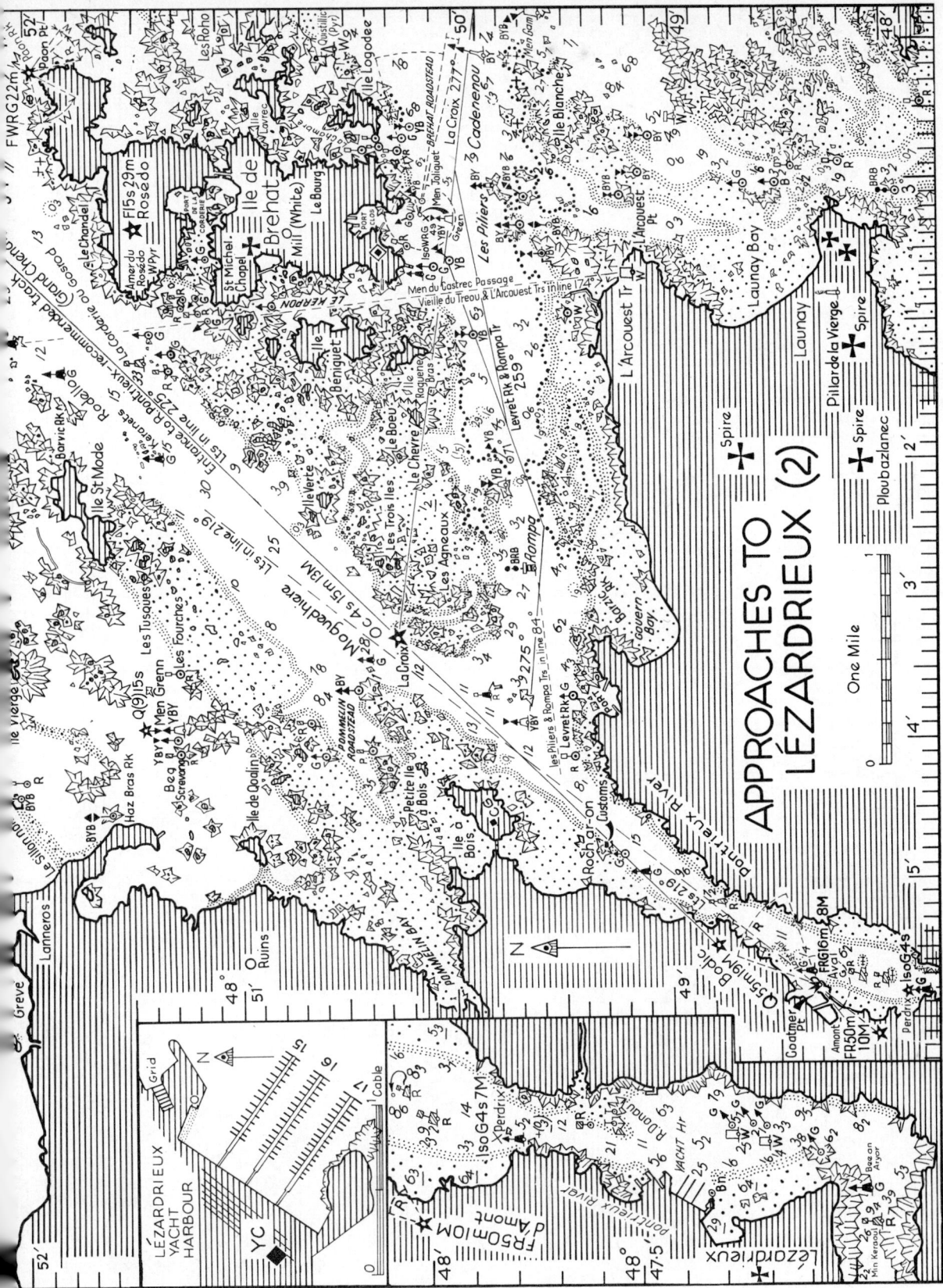

APPROACHES TO LÉZARDRIEUX (2)

One Mile

rès la carte marine française avec l'autorisation du Service Hydrographique et Océanographique de la Marine.

419

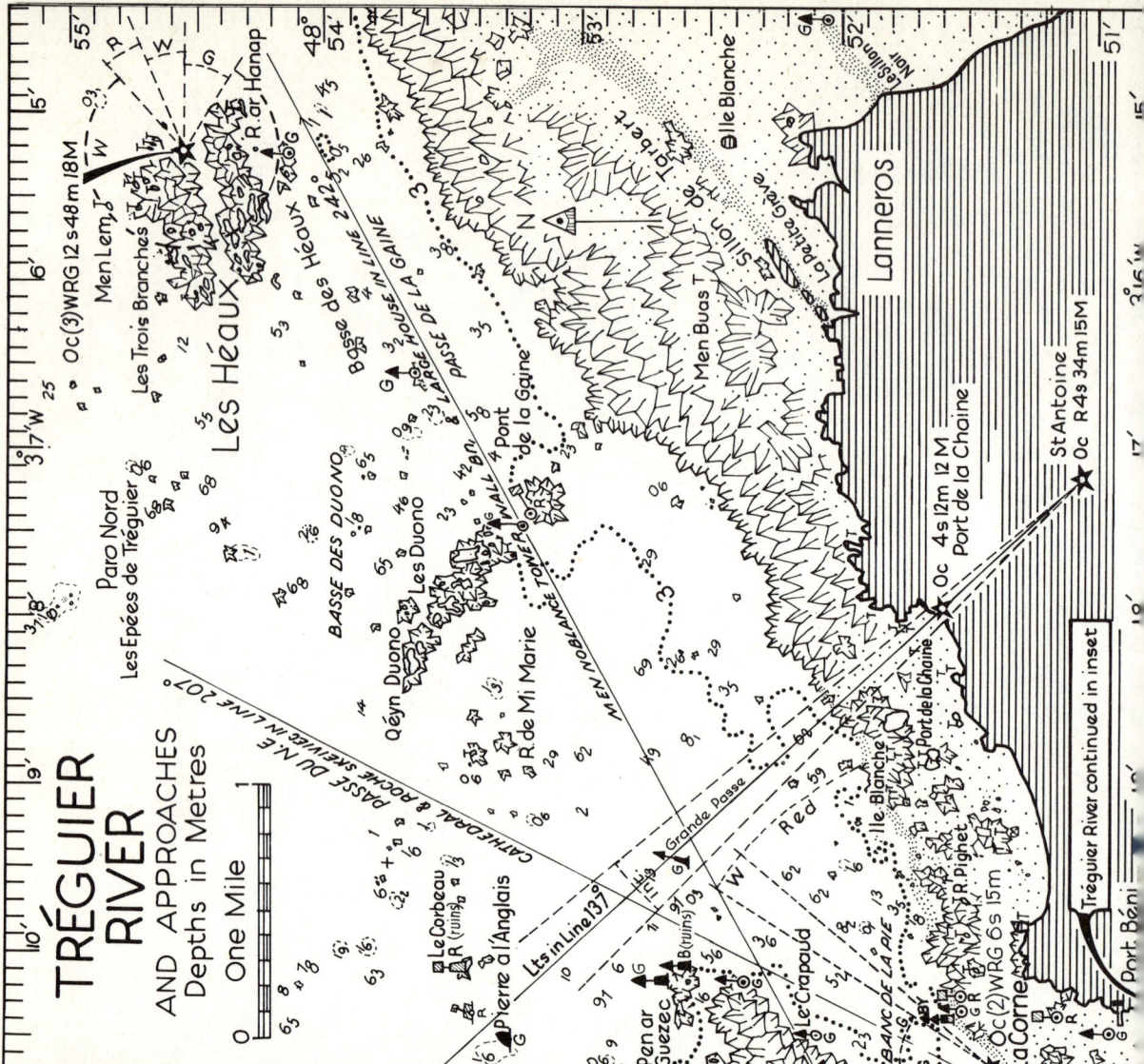

TRÉGUIER RIVER

AND APPROACHES
Depths in Metres

One Mile

Les Épées de Tréguier

Paro Nord

Les Trois Branches

Men Lem I

Oc(3)WRG 12s48m18M

R ar Hanap

Les Héux

BASSE DES DUONO

Les Duono

Qéyn Duono

R. de Mi Marie

Basse des Héux

House de la Gaine

LARGE HOUSE IN LINE 242°

PASSE DE LA GAINE

Pont de la Gaine

WALL END Pont

MEN NOBLANCE TOWER

CATHÉDRAL & ROCHE SKÉIVIÉE IN LINE 207°

PASSE DU N.E.

Le Corbeau R (ruins)

Pierre d'Anglais

Lts in Line 137°

Pen ar Guezec

B (ruins)

Le Crapaud

Grande Passe

Red

BANC DE LA PIE

Ile-Blanche

R Pignet

La Corne

Oc(2)WRG 6s 15m

Port Blanc... Ile Blanche

Men Buas

Sillon de Talbert

La Petite Gaîne

Ile Blanche

Est Sillon

Lanneros

St Antoine
Oc R4s 34m 15M

Oc 4s12m 12 M
Port de la Chaine

Port de la Chaine

Tréguier River continued in inset

Port Béni

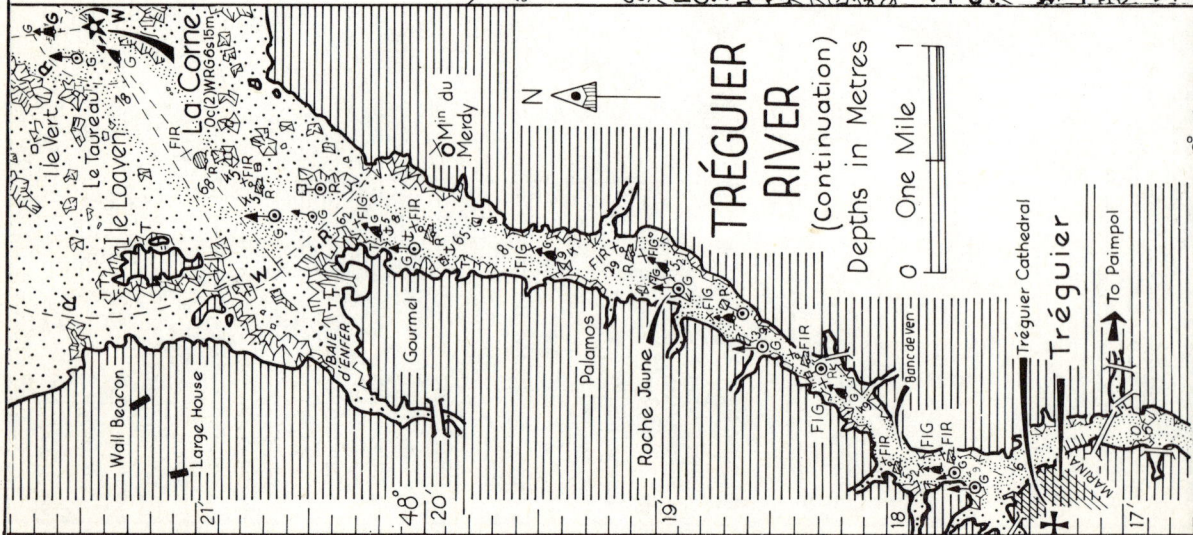

TRÉGUIER RIVER
(Continuation)
Depths in Metres

One Mile

N

Wall Beacon

Large House

Ile Loaven

Le Toureau

Le Vert

Ile Vert

La Corne

Oc(2)WRG6s15m

Min du Merdy

BAIE d'ENFER

Gourmel

Palamos

Roche Jaune

Banc de ven

Tréguier Cathedral

Tréguier

MARINA

To Paimpol

D'après la carte marine française avec l'autorisation du Service Hydrographique et Océanographique de la Ma

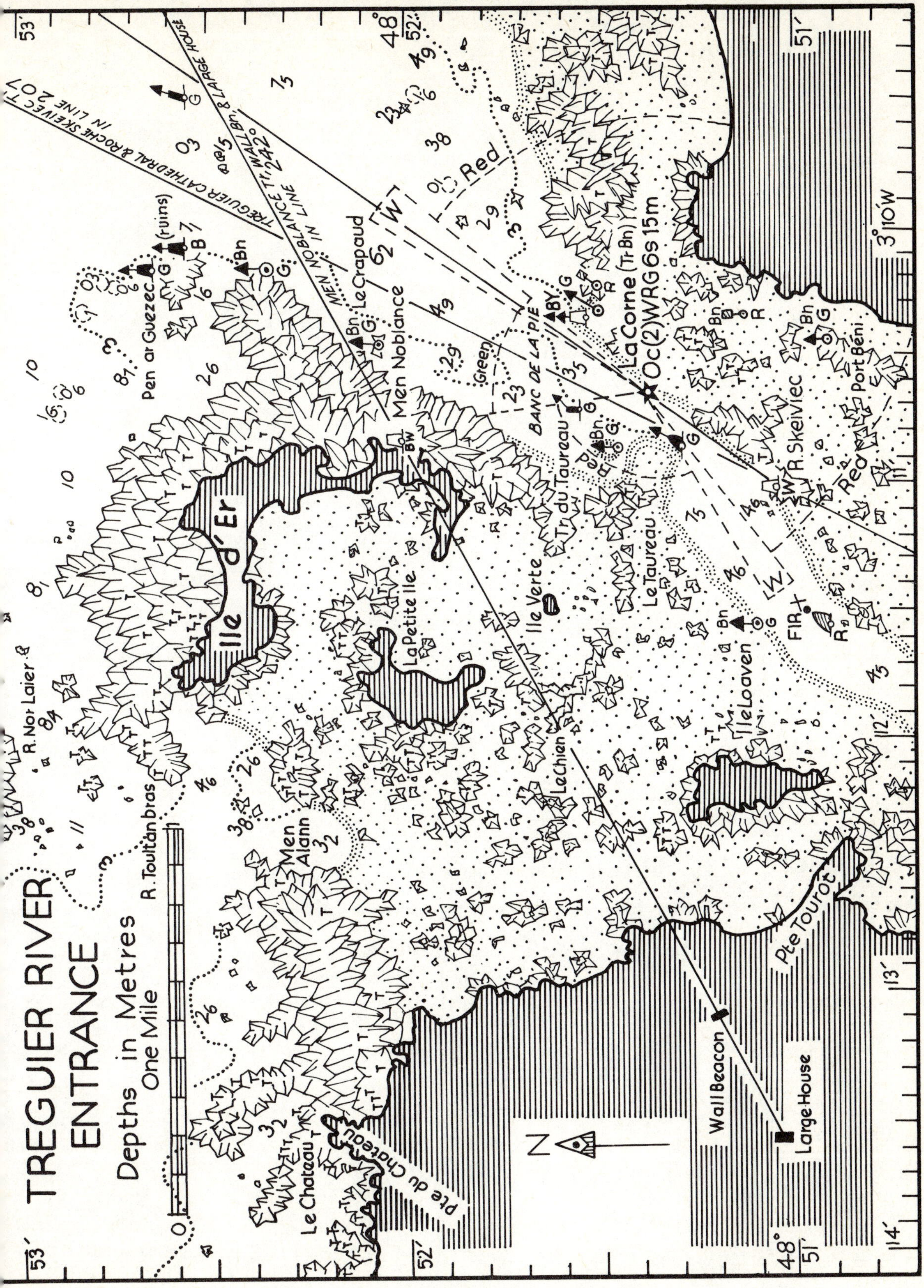

TREGUIER RIVER ENTRANCE

Depths in Metres

One Mile

0

Ile d'Er

La Petite Ile

Ile Verte

Le Chien

Le Taureau

Ty du Taureau

Ile Loaven

FIR

Men Alann

Le Chateau

Pte du Chateau

R. Toultan bras

R. Nor Laier

Pen ar Guezec

Men Noblance

Le Crapaud

MEN NOBLANCE Ty WALL Bn & LARGE HOUSE IN LINE 207°

TREGUIER CATHEDRAL & ROCHE SKEIVEC Ty IN LINE 207°

MEN NOBLANCE Ty & WALL Bn & LARGE HOUSE IN LINE 242°

BANC DE LA PIE

La Corne (Tr-Bn) Oc(2)WRG 6s 15m

W R Skeivlec

Red

Port Beni

Pte Tourot

Wall Beacon

Large House

N

48° 52'

48° 51'

53'

52'

51'

3° 10' W

13'

12'

14'

…rès la carte marine française avec l'autorisation du Service Hydrographique et Océanographique de la Marine.

PORT BLANC
Depths in Metres

Cables

N

White Tr & Mill inline 150°

Red

Green

W

48° 51'

Le Four

Pierre Rousse

I. des Levrette

I. St Gildas

Roho Douar

R. Ruz

R. louet

I. Milieu

I. des Genets

I. du Chateau Neuf

I. des Femmes

I. aux Marsouins

Vieux Chateau

I. Marquer

PORT BLANC

Le Voleur

La Petite Ile

Lou x Moutons

50

I. Bruc

White Tr FIWRG 17m 10M

ANSE PELLINEC

Pellinec

Mln de la Comtesse

LANNION RIVER
Depths in Metres

Red

W

Green

Pt de Becléguer
Oc(4)WRG 12s 60m

Servel Pte

CG

Traleguer

RIVER LANNION

Steps

Custo

Tr G

Tr G

Corvin

Le Yaudet (Guiodel)

Cables

O

Lannion

Fixed Bridge

32'   O   31'   30'   3° 29'W   28'

PENPOUL
Depths in Metres

Cables

48° 42'

N

Pte de Cléguer

Enez Toll

Les Vernes

Trebunnec

R. Noire

Caspari

Ile St Anne

le Four.

St Pol de Léon

Cathedral

41' Penpoul

Landing

Castle

BnTr

le Turc
les Chaines

Enez Ebel G

Pte de Jean

I. Blanche

PRIMEL
Depths in Metres

N

Pte de Primel

la Zamegues

WG

R. Cam

Pte du Diben

FIG 4s

ANSE DE PRIMEL

Trego

Primel

Chy (W)
FR35m 5

RW Mur Amer
FR 5 6m

(38m)

Le Diben

Cables

3° 50'W   49'

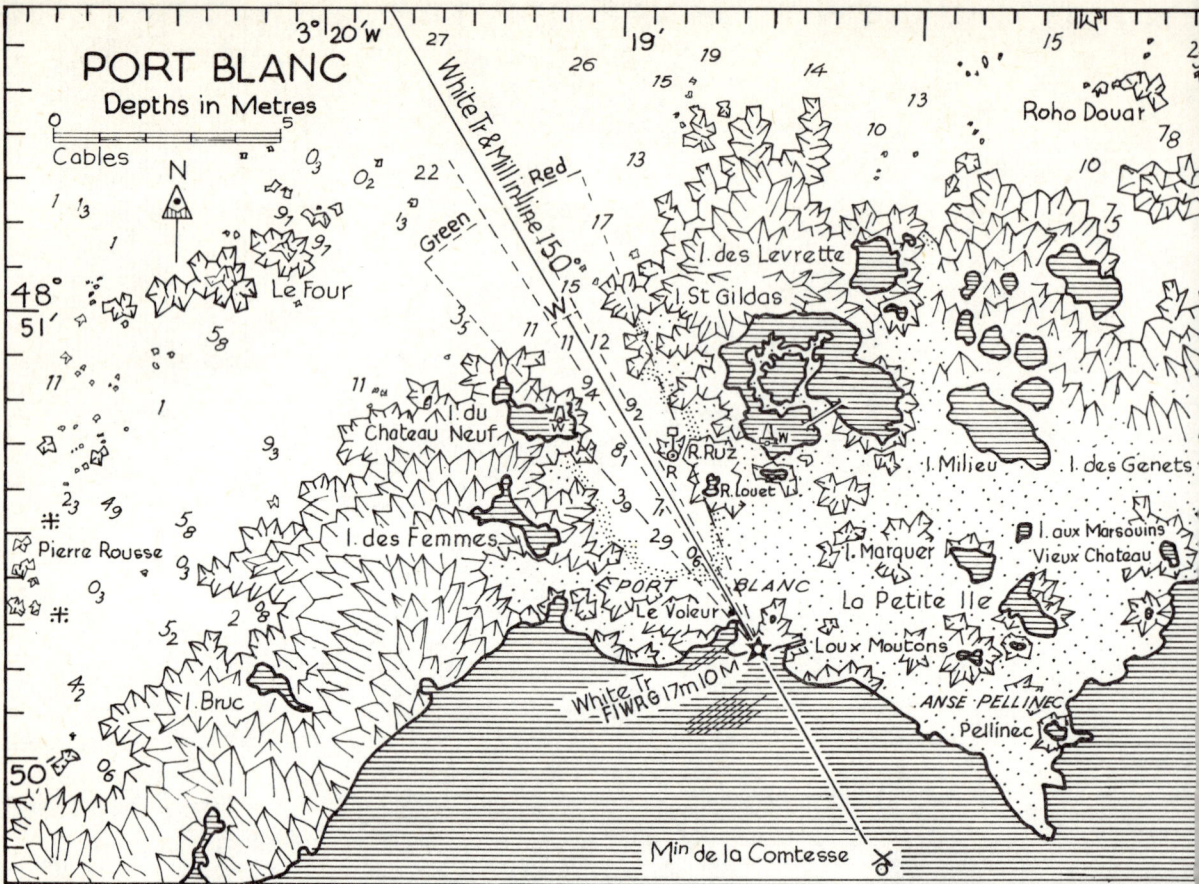

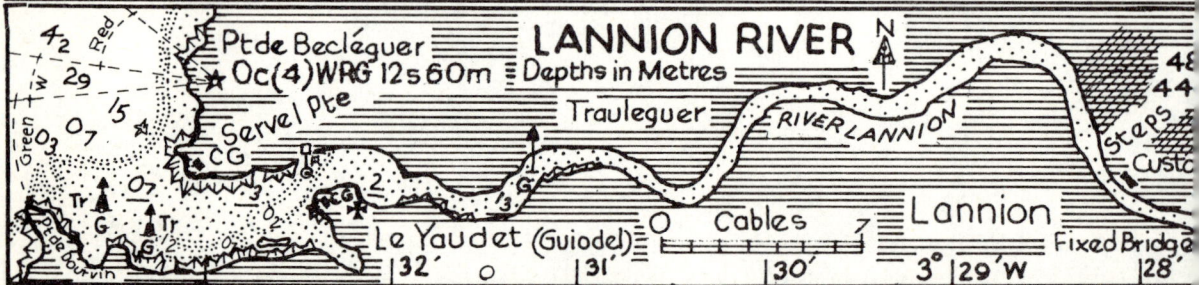

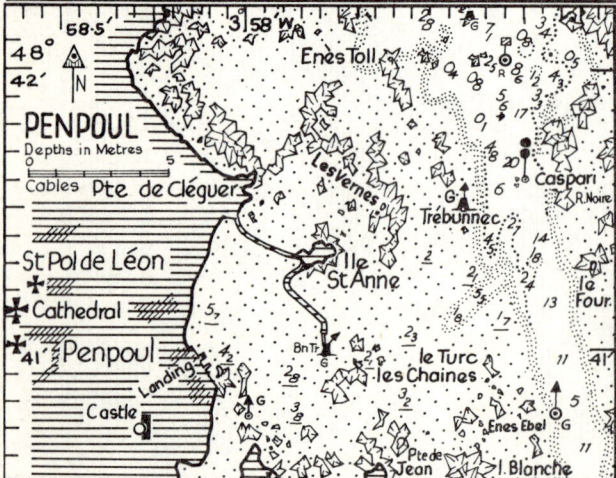

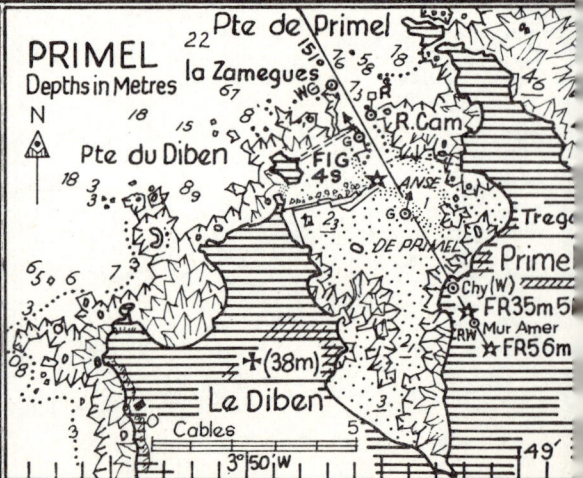

D'après la carte marine française avec l'autorisation du Service Hydrographique et Océanographique de la M

Entrance   There are three chans. (1) Grand Passe, 4.4m. With reasonable visibility can be taken by day or night at any state of the tide. Port de la Chaine in line with St Antoine lt, 137°. The W house of Port de la Chaine is hard to locate. Alternatively conspic water tr in line with Pleubian belfry, 154°, leads well to Pen ar Guezec buoy. Chan is well buoyed but allow for strong cross-set. (2) Passe NE, 1–4m W and NW seas break across this chan. Should only be attempted with large-scale French chart. Tréguier cathedral spire between the two Pen ar Guezec trs leads to the N Card La Jument buoy. From a position SW of La Jument bring Rocher Skeiviec in line with Tréguier cathedral spire, 207°. (3) Passe de la Gaine, 0.3m. Daylight and good visibility are necessary for this chan. The line should be exactly followed. To enter, identify Roch ar Hanap, 7m high, the outermost of the rks stretching out SSE from Les Héaux Lt Ho. 1¾ ca S of it, steer with Plougrescant wall bn in line with Men Noblance tr, 242°. There are two stb bns leading into the narrow part (150m wide) of the chan off the Duono rks, here marked with one port and three stb bns. The stb bns are about 8 ca apart.

   From La Corne to Tréguier the river chan is buoyed in addition to being marked by perches. Buoys are lit, R or G as appropriate, and passage by night up to Tréguier is possible with due care.

Anchorage   (1) SW of La Corne lt tr, exposed to NW and NE. (2) Off village of Roche Jaune. Landing, general store. (3) Abreast of Palamos, 4m, 2M above La Corne; if crowded try between next two stb-hand bns to S, 4m. Avoid small creek opposite Palamos, steep-to rk. (4) N of Banc de Ven, out of tide near W bank of river.

Berthing   In marina off quay at Tréguier. Streams are strong: moor securely. All facilities, good shops and restaurants.

PORT BLANC   Chart F 974   (Plan p422)
HW (est) −5.45.   DS: E +0.15; W −6.00; 2½kn.
MHWS (est) 9.5; MLWS 0.9; MTL 5.3; MHWN 7.3; MLWN 3.3.
Between Port Blanc and Pte du Château to E, rks extend 1½M offshore. Port Blanc is exposed to winds between NW and NE and fresh winds cause a dangerous swell and breaking sea in the narrow entrance. There is usually some swell in the anchorage.

Approach   From NW the Plateau du Four, W of entrance, is marked by a R buoy at its NW end. Bring Le Voleur W tr, Fl G, in line with Moulin de la Comtesse on top of hill, 150°, which leads in 7m to the entrance. Ldg marks in gap in trees are difficult to pick up except when on ldg line.

Entrance   Lies between I du Château Neuf to W and I St Gildas to E. Both have conspic W pyramids.

Anchorage   A little SW of the ldg line, SW of Roc'h Ruz, R bn, in 7m, or closer in in most tides, sand and shell.

   The cove is frequented only by local fishing boats and small yachts. Hotel and small shops.

PERROS-GUIREC   Chart F 974   (Plan p425)
HW (est) −5.50.   MHWS (est) 9.3; MLWS 0.9; MTL 5.2; MHWN 7.2; MLWN 3.4.

DS (1M NW I Tomé and in the chans): E +0.30; W −4.30.

E-going stream attains 4¾kn in E chan and 2¾kn in W chan at springs.

W-going stream attains 4¼kn and 2¾kn respectively. In the anch in Anse de Perros, W stream begins 1¼h earlier and attains 2kn.

I Tomé, high and rocky, lies off the entrance to the Anse de Perros; rks extend ¾M off its W side and 6 ca E of its N side.

Approach   The W chan, 0.9m, is entered with Kerjean bn bearing 143½°, directional lt Oc(3) WRG 12s, between Bilzic R tr and La Fronde B buoy. The E chan, 1.5m, marks are a white house with gable ¼M S of port, Oc(4) 12s, and Kerprigent W tr, Q, on top of hill, 225°. The R Guazer buoy marks the Plateau du Four. The tide sets slightly athwart this chan.

Anchorage   Anch with good shelter from SE through S to NW in 1.8 to 3m, ½ ca SW of RW Pierre du Chenal tr, ½M S of I Tomé.

Entrance   The alignment for the E chan leads to the hr. The best water is marked by trs as the banks dry 1.5 to 3.3m. Enter between quay heads, lts R and G, whence through a single gate at E end of sill which encloses N half of hr. The sill covers when the height of tide is 7m, and the gate is opened as long as the sill is covered. Gate is 7m wide. The sill is well marked with a continuous line of stakes painted in ½m RW bands to show the depth over it. One may also lie alongside the E wall before the sill; calm in N-ly and W-ly winds.

Berthing   After passing through gate, turn to port to pontoons with mooring for 150 yachts. Depth on pontoons 2.4m, decreasing to NW and towards shore.

Fuelling jetty on E side of hr. Shops and restaurants on quay. Buses to Lannion. Better shops and beaches at Perros (1M).

PLOUMANAC'H   Chart F 967
HW −5.50.   MHWS 8.9; MLWS 0.9; MTL 5.0; MHWN 7.0; MLWN 3.4.

A restricted but fascinating fair-weather anch surrounded by strange-shaped pink rocks and dominated by a lofty chateau. Large-scale chart essential.

Entrance lies 2 ca W of Mean Ruz Lt Ho and is well marked by bns. All deep-water positions are normally occupied by moorings, but there is room in the inner harbour for yachts which can take the ground on bilge keels or legs.

Shops and restaurants.

TREGASTEL   Chart F 967
About a mile W of Ploumanac'h, this hr provides moorings afloat even at springs. Entrance chan is marked by bns. Inner buoys dry but outer ones lie in 2m of water at LWS. Uncomfortable in strong winds between W and N, especially near HW when outer rks cover. Some shops.

PERROS-GUIREC
Depths in Metres

N

0 ——— 1 Mile

D'après la carte marine française avec l'autorisation du Service Hydrographique et Océanographique de la Marine.

425

Tréguignec

Keriec

X Mill

Kerjean Bn
Dir Oc(3)WRG 12s 78m

ANSE DE TRAESTEL

R.h Meg
R.Brue
PLATEAU DU FOUR
Guozer R
Pierre Rousse
B.Sam Holen
D'Gromm
R.Morville
Toc Guenn
R.du Moulin
La Petite
I.Sicre
Basse Nessa
Lights in line 22

Toull Garre

Le Noire de Tome
R.Keheddes
Les Couillons de Tome
pt du Carne
Île Tomé
Pierre Jean Rouzic
Bn R
La Durante
La Duranquiu

Pierre Marquer
Le Volet
R pp
Le Gouronhout
Pierre du Chenal
Bilzic
R
La Fronde
Green
du Sphinx
R Bernard
Y B Y

Perros-Guirec
Bassin à Flot
Fl(2) R6s
Oc(4)12s 28m5M
Fl(2)6s
Bn G
R

Le Taupeau
La Horaine
BY
Customs
BASSIN à FLOT
Sill (covers)
Gate
FIR R
Fl(2)G6s
Stakes RW
Fl(2)R6s
Bassin de Chasse

LES SEPT ILES   Chart F 967

A fair-weather open anch. Approach towards the E end of I aux Moines from the SE, avoiding isolated rks. Anch about E of Lt Ho on I aux Moines. Landing on steps at end of slip. Pathway to Lt Ho and old fort at W end of Is.

TREBEURDEN   Chart F 6056

HW −6.00.   MHWS 9.0; MLWS 1.2; MTL 5.2; MHWN 7.0; MLWN 3.5.
Trébeurden lies about 4M NW of the mouth of the Lannion R and provides a good deep-water anch in winds from NE through E to S. The key to the approach is the Basse Blanche buoy, W Card, which marks the W end of the Crapaud shoals. From a position about 1¼M S of this buoy a course of 070° leads to the conspic I de Milio (50m high). Alter course to leave the NW tip of this I about 1½ ca to stb and enter the anch which lies on its N side. Tidal streams slight, holding good. Landing slip for dinghies. Shops and restaurants.

LANNION RIVER   Charts F 6056, 5950   (Plan p422)

HW −6.05.   DS at Le Crapeau: ESE +1.00; WSW −5.00; 2kn.
MHWS (Trebeurden) 9.0; MLWS 1.2; MTL 5.2; MHWN 7.0; MLWN 3.5.
The bay is entered between Pte de Primel and I Grande, and is encumbered with numerous shoals and rks.

Conspic objects on the S side are Pte de Primel W watchtower and the pointed belfry of Plougaznou. On the E side S of I Grande hummock and tr are the belfries of Trébeurden on the cliff near the white disused Bihit sig stn, and Plemeur-Bodou 2M to E.

On the Pte de Becléguer, the Lt Ho, W ho 60m, shows Oc(4) WRG, 12s.

Approach   Make for Pte de Becléguer Lt Ho between the bearings of 084° and 098° (W sector). The entrance, covered by the G sector, is barred by a bank (dries 0.7m) extending about 2 ca N of Pte de Dourvin. Numerous Y buoys are connected with an anti-oil slick barrage: they have no navigational significance.

During winds from between WNW and NW, breaking seas prevent entry. Chan is marked by trs and bns, dries 2.6m to Le Yaudet (Guiodel) and 5m to Lannion, and is narrow and tortuous.

Anchorage   Off Trébeurden N of I Milliau in settled weather. Local boats winter on legs in the S bay of I Grande. Between Le Taureau and river mouth there is good holding in 4½–12m, sand and shell.

In river at Le Yaudet (Guiodel) there is a low quay, E of which shallow draft craft can dry out about 1.2m. Between 100m and ½M upstream of Le Yaudet there are pools in centre of river. They are easily found by sounding and provide good anch in 1–3m least depth. Landing at quay at Le Yaudet, short walk to village, two restaurants but no shops. Stores at Ploulec'h, 2M.

Port de Lannion   The river is marked with bns and presents no particular difficulties, but there is some commercial traffic by sand dredgers. Rough quay beside main road on N side opposite short quay on S side; always 2m at HW.

Bottom said to be level but mooring is not easy as bollards have been almost buried by road works.

All supplies. Buses, rly. Attractive town.

PRIMEL   Charts F 5950, 5827   (Plan p422)
HW −6.10.   MHWS (est) 8.8; MHWN 6.8; MTL 5.1.
The entrance lies 3 ca SW of the Pte de Primel, the E point of the Bay of Morlaix. The hr is frequented by fishing boats in the summer. In strong winds the sea breaks across the entrance and on-shore winds send considerable swell into anch.
Approach   From a position ½M NW from Pte de Primel steer on the line of the ldg marks, two W rectangles with VR stripes, FR lts, 151°, 2 ca N of the entrance. Rks dry ½ ca E of this line.
Entrance   Leave Zamégues Rk, W and R patch, to stb and enter between two prominent rks marked by bns. Here the chan is 27m wide, 7m. Abreast of the jetty head, Fl G 4s, the chan bears SE for ½ ca, then continues S for ½ ca more. The remainder of the hr dries 1 to 3m.
Anchorage   Moor in the chan in 2 to 9m near the ldg line but not more than 2 ca inside the entrance. It is also possible to lie against the S side of the quay where a chan has been dredged.
Caution: there are rks which dry, especially by the centre portion.

Good landing, water and stores at Le Diben on W side and Primel on E side.

MORLAIX ROADSTEAD AND RIVER   Charts BA 2744, F 5827 (Plan p428)
HW (Morlaix) −6.00.   DS: W +6.00; E −0.30.
MHWS 8.9; MLWS 1.2; MTL 5.1; MHWN 6.9; MLWN 3.5.
Morlaix Road, in the estuary of the Morlaix R, may be reached at all times and affords anch in 6 to 8m. The chan beyond the roadstead dries when nearing the entrance to the river, which carries 3m at MHWN up to Morlaix town where there is a wet dock. The river above the estuary may be entered at about 1h before HW to avoid the tidal stream, which is rapid at half flood.
Approach   The bay of Morlaix lies within Bloscon and Primel Pts, 6M apart. It is divided into two by the I de Callot and the Carentec peninsula, on the W side of which is the entrance to the Penzé R, while on the E side lies the approach to Morlaix R. The Penzé R is well marked with lateral and leading marks, and navigable to beyond Pte de l'Ingoz. Anch is possible S of the BR bn, and beyond Pte de l'Ingoz: little water off Carantec, but water at slip, and supplies from town.

There are three lines of approach to Morlaix. (1) By the Grand Chenal E of I Ricard, 2.0m on the ldg line. From E keep Les Triagoz lt bearing 063° astern to pass N of La Méloine bank; leave Les Trépieds buoy, W Card, whistle, to port; and carry on till I Louet and La Lande Lt Hos, 5 and 7M distant respectively, come into line 176° when round in on that bearing. The R Stolvezen buoy, 1M N

427

PLATEAU DES DUONS

Le Menk
YBY
R

Les Bisayers
Les Cochons Noir
P.te Vache
Le Paradis
W
La Vielle
G
Ile Verte

GRAND CHENAL
Lights in line 176°

Stolvezen
R
La Pierre Noire
G

CHENAL DE TREGUIER
Lights in line 190°

Lts in line 151°

Pte de Primel
18
Pte du Diben
WG R
Le Diben
TREGASTA
FR35m5
FR58m5

R. Jaunes

le Cerf
Ricard
G
le Beckem
Tourgi
I aux Dames
P.t Aremen
R

Green
Calhic
Ile de Sable
la Chambre
R

Ile de Callot

Gd Cochon
la Corbeau
Red
White
R

BRB

Roch Pigher
Ile Toull Hovarn
W

Barre de Flot
Château du Tourcau
I. Noire
Oc(2) WRG 6s
15m12M

Obs.
White
Ptc de Bamenez
Green

Carantec
Oc(3) WG 12s 17m 13M
Louet

FlR2s
No 2

Pte de Samson

51'

N

MORLAIX RIVER
(Continuation)
Depths in Metres
0   Cables   6

Rivière de Morlaix

R

N

FlG 2s
No 3

FlR 2s
No 4

MORLAIX
ROAD
Depths in Metres

Le Fransie

Fl 5s 85m 23M
La Lande

Locquénolé

FlG 2s
No 5
G

Bassin à flot

Le Dourdu River

La Jument
G

Morlaix River
BUOYED CHAN.

Miles
0   1   2

48°
38'
48°
37'

428

D'après la carte marine française avec l'autorisation du Service Hydrographique et Océanographique de la Mar

of I Ricard and lying between La Vieille and Pierre Noire trs, is the key to the entrance. From the I de Batz on W of approach carry on as if for Triagoz, leaving the Pot de Fer buoy, E Card, bell, to stb till the same lts come into line. Or from Chenal de Batz steer for the Stolvezen buoy, between Les Bisayers and Roches Duon. Keep the marks in line 176° till abreast of the Calhic rk, G tr, when steer 160°, leaving the Corbeau G tr to stb and passing between I Louet to stb and the Château du Taureau to port.

Hence keep the edge of Château du Taureau just on with W edge of I Ricard astern, and steer 153°, leaving La Barre de Flot buoy to stb, whence this course leads up the estuary in mid-chan. The chan shoals 1½M beyond La Barre de Flot and small craft may anch when abreast the Château de Lanoverte to await sufficient rise to enter the R. This approach is not recommended at night because various dangers are situated near the line of the ldg marks.

(2) By the Tréguier chan in E side of approach (dries 0.9m). Keep Le Triagoz lt 063° astern until the I Noire and La Lande lts are in line, 190°. Then round in on the latter bearing, and having passed between La Chambre G tr and I Blanche R tr, steer SW until E edge of Château du Taureau comes on with W edge of I Ricard, whence with the latter marks in line astern continue as above (see (1)). This chan is to be preferred at night and affords more room for beating in at sufficient rise of tide by day. The stream is very rapid at half flood.

At night keep the Lande and Noire lts in line, 190°, till the lt Oc(3) of I Louet turns to G, when steer for it till R lt of I Noire, Oc(2) WRG, turns to G, when round in, 180°. Carry on till lts turn to W and for a cable beyond, when the Barre de Flot will have been passed. Hence chan lies 153°. A berth may be chosen as convenient, either side of the fairway in 5m.

(3) The main chan, 5.8m, W of I Ricard is the big-ship chan but is unlit. Make the Stolvezen R buoy; thence the chan is well marked by G bns to stb.

Anchorage The banks are steep-to and stream runs 4kn at springs. Small craft will find 2.7m in the chan abreast of Lanoverte. When the oyster banks are covered a bearing should be taken on the Château du Taureau. Yachts may prefer to berth SE of Pen Lann Pt in 5.5m with Beclem hidden behind Château du Taureau.

Morlaix River Leaving Morlaix road about 1h before HW, follow the chan which is now well buoyed. At the bend above Loquénolé it is possible to anch, preferably W side. Thence the river is marked by buoys and posts fitted with cat's-eyes. It is 3¾M from the entrance to the town of Morlaix. Outside lock avoid W quay, rocky bottom. Berth in basin (pontoons) on right bank about halfway along. Lock normally functions from HW −1½ to +1 (sill dries 3.1m). HW at lock approx as at anchorage.

Leaving Morlaix, the roadstead should be reached before the ebb has set in hard.

Showers on quay. Bank and all supplies in town.

PENPOUL
Chart F 5827 (Plan p422)

HW (Roscoff) −6.10. MHWS 8.8; MHWN 6.8; MTL 5.0.

A drying hr on the W bank of the Penzé R, about 3M S of Roscoff. A modern breakwater gives good shelter for yachts that can take the ground on bilge keels or legs. Deep-water anch in about 10m in the R chan is uncomfortable in northerly winds.

Approach The entrance to the Penzé R from Basse de Bloscon buoy, N Card, VQ, is well marked by beacons but the chart above is recommended. After leaving Trébunnec bn tr about 2 ca to stb, the trumpet-shaped bn tr marking the end of Penpoul breakwater will be seen about ¾M SW, with the two ch trs of St Pol de Léon beyond. From a point about 3 ca S of Trébunnec, with sufficient rise of tide, make for the trumpet-shaped bn. This line leads across oyster beds marked by numerous withies, but there are no other hazards. Enter, leaving the bn to stb.

Anchorage There are rks at the S end of the anchorage, but a large area in the centre is flat sand drying 3 to 4m.

Dinghy landing at quay on W side. St Pol de Léon, interesting small town, shops, ½M.

PORT DE BLOSCON
Charts BA 2745, F 5828 (Plan p431)

HW (Roscoff) −6.10. MHWS 8.8; MLWS 1.2; MTL 5.0; MHWN 6.8; MLWN 3.0.

A new hr built primarily for car ferries and commercial shipping but which provides a satisfactory deep-water anch for yachts. It lies on the E side of the headland on which Roscoff lies, and is less than a mile from that town. It can be entered at any state of the tide and provides good shelter in winds from N through W to SE.

Approach From the N the W side of the chan is bounded by the I de Batz with a prominent Lt Ho, Fl(4) 25s, and the two Lt Hos in the sea, Ar-Chaden (S Card, Q(6) WR + L Fl WR 15s) and Men-Guen Bras (N Card, Q WRG 4s). The Basse de Bloscon buoy, N Card, VQ, marks a dangerous rk about 3 ca W of Men-Guen Bras and should be left to stb.

The jetty forming the N side of the hr lies ½M S of Basse de Bloscon and its end is marked by a W column with a G top, Fl WG, 4s. The W sector, 210°–220°, leads clear of all outlying dangers.

Entrance Enter between the jetty head and a N Card buoy, VQ, 2 ca to the SE.

Anchorage Anch on the S side of the hr as close inshore as possible while avoiding rks. Anch prohibited in an area N and W of the N Card entrance buoy.

ROSCOFF
Charts BA 2745, F 5828 (Plan p431)

HW −6.10. MHWS 8.8; MLWS 1.2; MTL 5.0; MHWN 6.8; MLWN 3.0.

Hr dries, is accessible to 4.8m draft at springs; 2.8m at neaps. Swell in onshore gales. There is a concrete pier about the same height as the N hr wall at Roscoff

PORT DE ROSCOFF

Depths in Metres

One Mile

N

SEE INSET

Lts in line 210°

Basse Astan
VQ(3)5s Whistle
BYB 17
Mean an gui bras

Charlezenned

Ile de Batz
Fl(4) 25s 69m 21M
& FR 66m 9M
Mill

Penven

Pte Occidentale

St Barbe Pyr Bn
Basse Platte Tr Bn
BY
Ar Conn

l'Oignon
in line with Le Loup 106°

la Croix
Malvoch
Bihan
Tehi6
Bn
Porz Kernoch
YB

Par Roc'h
Ar-Poloss

I. Tisaoson
White
Pyr.Bn(R), I.Pighet
Q(6)WR+LfiWR15s12m
Ar Choden (BnTr)
QWRG4s
12m12M Men-Guen Bras(BnTr)
Pte de Bloscon

Basse de Bloscon

Réd

le Menk
le Cordonnier
Guerhéon
Ar Pourven
VQ

St Barbe Pyr Bn
Pte de Bloscon

Roscoff

Water Tr

Oc(1+2)12s7m
Oc(1+2)12s 24m13M

I. Verte
FVi
BYB

ANCH?
PROHIBITED

(INSET)

I. Tisaoson
Pyr.Bn
Réd
Ar Choden
Q(6)WR+LfiWR15s 12m
QWRG4s 12m
Rannic
Men-Guen Bras
BY
Roc'h zu
Oc(1+2)12s
Dusian

Ile Verte
FVi
Bn
BYB
YBY
Bn
An Oan
Porz Roc'h
BY
Roscoff

après la carte marine française avec l'autorisation du Service Hydrographique et Océanographique de la Marine.

431

projecting N for approx 3.5 ca from the elbow of the N wall and terminating in a ramp to the chan at a point approx 1 ca SW of Duslen bn tr.

Approach   Recommended approach is by the Passe à l'Est de Benven, dries 2m. At night from E with sufficient rise of tide, approach in W sector, 197°–257° of Men-Guen Bras lt tr, N card, Q WRG 4s 12m, until S of a line I de Batz lt – Ar-Chaden lt, 290°. Then steer on I de Batz lt, Fl(4) 25s, leaving Ar-Chaden to N until Roscoff lts come into line, 210°.

Entrance   Steer on Roscoff lts, 210°, and round into the hr, lying against the jetty.

Berthing   There are good berths along the N and W sides of the outer hr. Berth by a ladder if possible, otherwise access to quay is awkward at LW. Bottom is level. Berthing is also possible in inner hr.

Anchorage   Just NE of intersection of the line Ar-Chaden tr and Duslen tr, 278°, and Ste Barbe ch just open E of Rannic tr, 175°, in about 1m (mooring buoy sometimes available).

Shops, restaurants, bonded stores, rly, hotels.

CHENAL DE L'ILE DE BATZ   Charts BA 2745, F 5828   (Plan p431)
HW −6.10.   MHWS 8.8; MLWS 1.3; MTL 5.1; MHWN 6.8; MLWN 3.5.
This chan is unlit. Approaching from the E, make a position about 1 ca NE of Basse de Bloscon buoy, N Card, VQ, and bring Malvoc'h and Duslen bn trs into line, 282°. Follow this line which leads close S of Ar-Chaden lt tr, S Card, and N of Men-Guen Bras lt tr, N Card. Before coming abreast Roc'h Zu bn, alter course to make good 270° to pass between Duslen bn tr and the mauve bn tr marking the extremity of the high concrete pier. Keep close to the latter as rks dry from Duslen to mid-chan. When Men-Guen Bras and Roc'h Zu bn are in line astern, 109°, continue so passing close S of An-Oan bn. Then alter course so as to bring An-Oan bn into line with Ile Pighet R pyramid astern 101°, and steer on this alignment to Malvoc'h bn tr.

From W, approach with Le Loup rk (W top) in line with the W pyramid at Ste Barbe, 106°. This leaves Basse Platte bn tr and l'Oignon bn close to stb. When abreast of the latter, steer 090° to a position 1 ca S of Malvoc'h bn tr.

Arriving at the Ile de Batz chan from the W near HW at nightfall there is good anch off Ar Skeul bn tr, I de Siec. S of this is Mogueriec, a trawler port with plenty of room for yachts that can take the ground, dries 4–5m.

Complete shelter at Porz Kernoch, dries 2–5m, on I de Batz. Level ground for bilge keels or legs N to NW of W pyramid on I Kernoch, or near hr entrance SE of W pyramid (dries 5.5m). The E wall to the hr projects about 2 ca in a S-ly direction from I aux Moutons Rk and is used as a landing slip by ferries from Roscoff. The end is marked by a single pole bn.

It is possible to anch outside, approx 2½ ca ESE of Malvoc'h bn tr in 4.5m. Stream runs fast.

Modest restaurants and shops in village.

PONTUSVAL (BRIGNOGAN)

HW +6.05.   DS (5M N of entrance): E +2.30; W −4.00; $2\frac{3}{4}$kn.

MHWS (est) 8.4; MHWN 6.4; MTL 4.8.

A small inlet which dries. Conspic objects are the square Lt Ho 13m, on the Pte de Beg-Pol, 1M NW of the entrance, a tall RW Ro mast about $\frac{1}{4}$M SW of the Lt Ho, and a water tr.

The W pyramid at Coatanguy on with the belfry of Plounéour 1M S, 178°, leads between the dangers to the entrance, marked by a R tr to port and W marks on rks to stb.

Hr dries about 2m halfway and 5m near its head; sand with rocky patches. Advisable to anch near fishing boat moorings and select a berth at LW at which to take the ground. Stores at Brignogan.

L'ABERVRAC'H

HW (Fort Cézon) +5.50.   MHWS 7.9; MLWS 1.0; MTL 4.4; MHWN 6.0; MLWN 2.9.

The approach to L'Abervrac'h lies 3M W of Ile Vierge Lt Ho, a grey granite tr (75m). There are four entrances of which the Grand Chenal is best for the stranger. The Malouine and Pendante have cross-tidal streams; La Fronde dries 3m.

Approach   To enter by the Grand Chenal, bring the Ile Vierge Lt Ho to bear 090°, 3M distant, and bring Ploudalmezeau steeple, 5M distant, open W of Lampaul steeple, 186°. This posn is clear W of the Libenter and Pendante reefs which bar the direct approach.

Steer 1M on 186° leaving the Libenter W Card buoy, Fl(9) 15s, which marks the Libenter shoal about 2 ca to port until Lanvaon and Vrach ldg lts come into line 100°. At this position the Petite Fourche BW buoy will be seen fine on the port bow, $\frac{1}{2}$M distant. Steer on the ldg line 100° leaving the Libenter buoy 2 ca to port, and then the RW tr of the Petit Pot de Beurre 100m to port. If the shore marks cannot be seen, steer 186° until abreast of the Libenter buoy; then steer to pass 2 ca S of it before coming on to 100°. The Petit Pot de Beurre will then indicate the direction of the chan until the ldg marks become visible.

The Malouine chan lies 2 ca E of the easily identified Pendante rk. Leading marks are the squat Petit Pot de Buerre tr and a W pyramid, $1\frac{1}{4}$M, in line 176°. Leave to port a R tr and when nearing the first R buoy leave the transit and the two R buoys $\frac{1}{2}$ ca to port.

If the white pyramid mark for the Malouine chan cannot be identified or if visibility is only $\frac{1}{2}$M, locate La Pendante, the most westerly outlying rk, 6m high, which leans unmistakably. Leave the rk $1\frac{1}{2}$ ca to port and, watching the stream, steer for a position 3 ca W of the Grand Pot de Buerre, 4 ca from La Pendante. This chan, a variation of the Pendante, is 3 ca wide and is used by fishermen.

Entrance   Just past the Petit Pot de Beurre, the Palue and St Antoine lts will be seen in line, 128°. If these cannot be identified by day, the run of the chan is sufficiently indicated by the Breach Ver B tr which is left to stb, and the tip of I

L'ABERVRAC'H
Depths in Metres

Mile 1

0

Q(9)

Le Libenter

YBY

Lights in line 100°

GRAND CHENAL DE L'ABERVRAC'H

p'te Fourche 48°

YBY

Rusven

YBY

I. Guenioc

Chenal de la Malouine

La Malouine

La Pendante

Gd pot de Beurre

p'it pot de Beurre

I. Vrac'h QR19m7M

Plateau Lezen

Ile Vierge Fl5s 77m 29M

Feu de Lanvaon Q55m 10M

Plouguerneau

St Antoine Oc(2)6s14m12M

La Palue FG9m7M

Presqu ile Marguerite

I. Bilou

I. d Ehre

R. aux Manes

Breach Ver

Br

I. Tariec

I. Goro

Le Chien

L'Aberbenoit

BRB

N

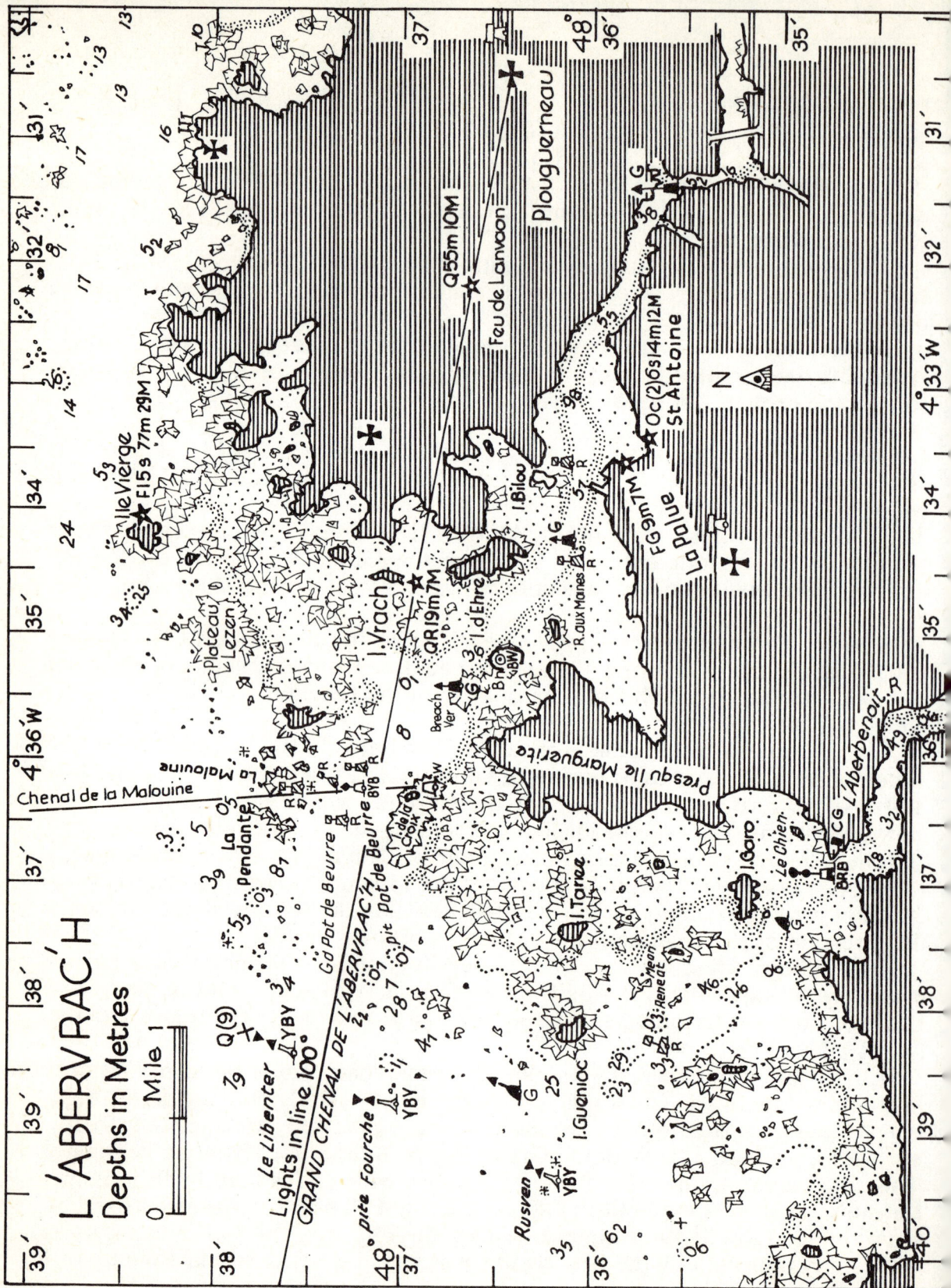

D'après la carte marine française avec l'autorisation du Service Hydrographique et Océanographique de la Marine

d'Ehre which is left fairly close to port. Steer so, keeping a little to S of the ldg line when 1 ca N of the BW mark on I Cézon to avoid a spit. The two trs, BW and R, on Roche aux Moines are left to stb, and two R buoys to port. Then alter course to 095° and steer for Touris RW tr.

Berthing There is a large quay off the village, and just above it a pontoon with berths for visiting yachts up to 30ft. In the season numerous mooring buoys for visitors are laid S of Touris tr. YC provides ferry service. Larger vessels may anch below the quay and above Roche aux Moines. This berth can be exposed.

Bus to Brest. Fuel at quay, water from tap. Bonded stores. Hospitable YC with showers. Sailing prohibited in hr area.

Paluden To enter the river, when past Touris tr and with the shore end of the quay astern, steer for the quay upriver on the N shore. Nearing the quay turn to stb up centre of river; stakes mark sides of chan. In the river continue in midstream, giving Beg-an-Toul B tr a wide berth, then keep a little to the W side of the chan until nearing the quays. Anch just inside the river or just above the quays, 1½m, in complete shelter.

Some shops near quay, more choice at Lannilis, 1M.

L'ABERBENOIT Chart F 964; BA 1432 (Plan (L'Abervrac'h) p434)
HW +5.45. MHWS 8.0; MLWS 1.1; MTL 4.6; MHWN 6.3; MLWN 3.1.
The entrance is nearly 3M from the Petite Fourche buoy at the W end of the approach to L'Abervrac'h.

Approach By the chan E of Rusven, not to be attempted in strong WNW weather.

Make the Petite Fourche W Card buoy. A course 170° made good from close W of this buoy will leave Rusven Est E Card buoy to W and will lead to a position about 1½ ca W of La Jument de Guénnioc, a rk off the W side of I Guénnioc. This rk is low, 4m, and from the direction of La Petite Fourche buoy just overlaps I Guénnioc, 13m, which can be recognised by the large boulder balanced on its E side.

At LW there are rks which dry 1m little more than ½ ca each side of this line, strangers should enter about 2h before HW. When La Jument de Guénnioc is abeam keep the E side of La Jument de Garo in line with Le Chien, RB bn tr, 143°. The latter is hard to locate, being covered at HW. La Jument de Garo, 7m, is a little W of I Garo, 12m.

Proceeding on 143°, leave Carrac ar Poul Doun (1m) to port, bear a little to port leaving Mean Reneat (0.3m, nearly on the ldg line) to stb, and then a little to stb leaving La Jument de Garo to port.

Entrance Leave Le Chien close to port, avoid the spit to port on the corner and carry on in midstream.

Anchorage Near the ferry; land either side. A little way up the hill to stb there is a restaurant and small shops. There is better anch off a chateau on the N bank opposite the first big bend of the R to stb.

PORTSALL ROCKS PASSAGE

A useful short-cut between L'Abervrac'h and the Four Channel in good visibility with leading wind or power. French chart 5772 is essential.

Westbound passage   From the Petite Fourche buoy off L'Abervrac'h steer 255°. When a small but conspic W tr with R top on the skyline of Pte de Landunvès is just open S of the conspic Petit Men Louet bn tr, steer 219° on this line to leave Plateau de Rusven and Trepied reef to port and Le Relec and Bosseven Amont to stb. Le Relec, dries 5.2m, is visible at half-tide.

When Ile Longue is abeam to port alter course to bring the S rk of Le Grem in line with Bosseven Creiz pyramid. Le Grem is a striking and obvious lump of rk. Bosseven Creiz is a rk with two peaks on one of which is a W pyramid with rounded top. Bosseven Aval has a similar W pyramid but only one peak.

When Le Four Lt Ho and Bosseven Aval pyramid are in line, 229°, alter onto this course. Pass not more than 50m to SE of Bosseven Aval.

When Men Ar Pic tr is abeam to port bring Bosseven Creiz and Bosseven Aval into line astern, 035°. Identify Le Lurch, a rk abeam to port. When this is in line astern with Grand Men Louet, 049°, keep them in line to come out S of Le Four. Le Taureau, a rk with a small W Card tr 6 ca E of Le Four, should be left to port. Grand Men Louet and Petit Men Louet are close to each other but can be distinguished as Petit Men Louet has a large masonry tr painted W on its N side. Grand Men Louet is a larger rk whose summit is rounded and painted W on its S side.

Eastbound passage   To pick up the Le Lurch – Grand Men Louet ldg line, identify the Grand Château rks 4 ca E of Le Four. The line passes about 1 ca S of these. Leave Le Taureau rk with its small tr to stb. The Grand Men Louet summit does not project above the higher parts of Le Lurch and can only be seen in the cleft of that rk. Another rk, Men Gouzaine, is easily distinguished, and open just W of Le Lurch, leads on the right line, 049°.

When Bosseven Griez and Bosseven Aval come in line, 035°, follow this until Men Ar Pic is abeam to stb. Now edge off the line to leave Bosseven Aval not more than 50m to port. When past Bosseven Aval bring Le Four Lt Ho in line astern with Bosseven Aval, 229°. Hold this line until the southernmost rk of Le Grem is in line with Bosseven Creiz on the port quarter, 249°. Follow this line until the W tr with R top on Pt de Landunvès and Pte Men Louet tr are in line astern, 219°. This leads out ½M W of Petit Fourches buoy. Strong tides may be encountered.

PORTSALL

HW +5.35.   MHWS 7.6; MLWS 1.3; MTL 4.5; MHWN 6.0; MLWN 3.0.

Approach   (1) From seaward: from a position 1M SW of the Basse Paupion buoy identify the spire of Ploudalmezeau ch and also Le Lurch, a large rk S of the Men Ar Pic tr. Keep the rk and spire in line, 108°. When Bosseven Aval rk with a single peak and a W conical bn bears 068°, alter course to keep in line with two large rectangular ldg marks ½M N of Portsall, front W, rear RW, 085°. This course leaves Men Ar Pic tr to stb and Ile Verte and both Men Louets to port. (2) From the Relec chan and chan du Raous: when Bosseven Amont bears N steer 191° with the large W pyramid of Caleroc (bottle-shaped with R top, not to be confused with Pte de Landunvès bn tr) and the smaller WY front pyramid of Losquée in line. The latter has a door in its base and stands close S of a house. These marks are not easy to see. It is necessary to borrow a few yards to the NW when Enes Scoune is abeam to avoid a rk which is awash at MLWS.

Anchorage   (1) At springs in the roads with 10m MLWS clear of the ldg line, with Petit Men Louet tr bearing N. Suitable only in settled weather. (2) At neaps or middle tides 100m S of La Pendante BY bn tr. Avoid the rks on which the bn stands and the small rk to the E of it. Sound carefully as the water shoals rapidly to the S. (3) Dry out on sand alongside the end of the quay. Surge in NW gales.

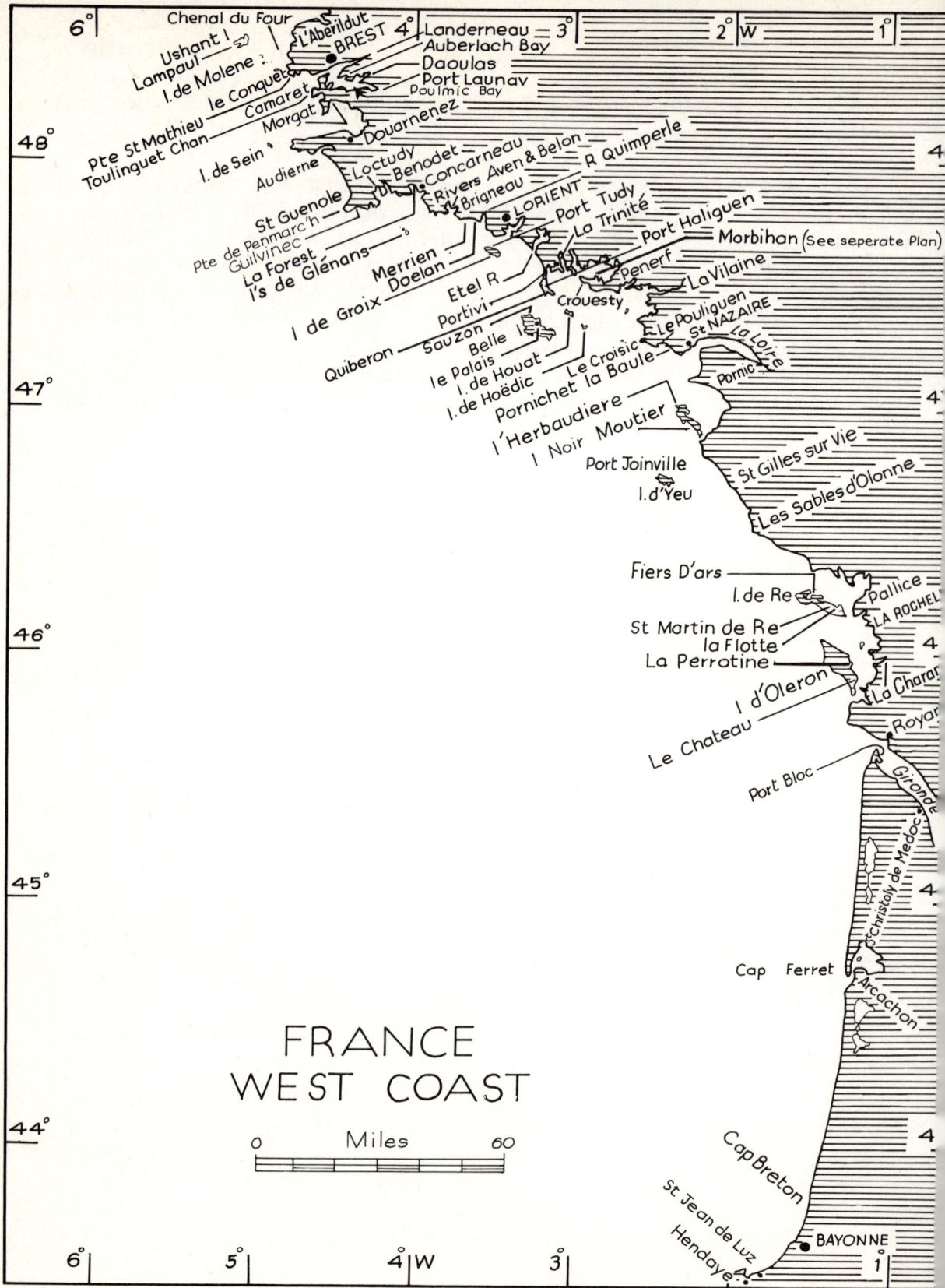

Ushant I
Lampaul
I. de Molene
L'Aberildut
BREST
Landerneau
Auberlach Bay
Daoulas
Port Launav
Poulmic Bay
le Conquet
Camaret
Pte St Mathieu
Toulinguet Chan.
Morgat
Douarnenez
48°
I. de Sein
Audierne
Loctudy
Benodet
Concarneau
Rivers Aven & Belon
Brigneau
R Quimperle
St Guenole
Pte de Penmarc'h
Guilvinec
La Forest
I's de Glénans
LORIENT
Port Tudy
La Trinité
Port Haliguen
Morbihan (See seperate Plan)
Merrien
Doelan
Etel R
Portivi
Penerf
La Vilaine
Le Pouliguen
St NAZAIRE
La Loire
I de Groix
Quiberon
Sauzon
Belle I
le Palais
I. de Houat
I. de Hoëdic
Crouesty
Le Croisic
Pornichet la Baule
Pornic
47°
l'Herbaudiere
I Noir Moutier
Port Joinville
I. d'Yeu
St Gilles sur Vie
Les Sables d'Olonne
Fiers D'ars
I. de Re
Pallice
LA ROCHEL
St Martin de Re
la Flotte
La Perrotine
46°
I d'Oleron
La Charan
Le Chateau
Royan
Port Bloc
Gironde
St Christoly de Medoc
45°
Cap Ferret
Arcachon

FRANCE
WEST COAST

0   Miles   60

44°
Cap Breton
St Jean de Luz
Hendaye
BAYONNE

France – West Coast

The flood stream up the coasts of Spain and Portugal flows SE into the Bay of Biscay, producing HW first in the SE corner and travelling thence to W and N. A feeble stream flows at all times in a N direction close along the shore from San Sebastian to within a few miles of the entrance to the Gironde R; and, from off the Gironde, a weak stream flows N about 50 to 60M offshore till approaching Penmarc'h, where it tends closer in. The inshore tidal streams extend about 12M off the coast. The flood stream in the rivers makes on the bottom an hour or more before the ebb stream has finished at the surface, and the rise frequently commences only 1h or more after LW.

North Biscay Pilot by K. Adlard Coles and A. N. Black, and *South Biscay Pilot* by Robin Brandon, are helpful volumes to have on board in these waters. *Brittany and Channel Islands Cruising Guide* by David Jefferson covers this coast as far as St Nazaire, with the Brittany canals. Details of all ports and harbours on the French coast can be found in the annual French publication *Annuaire Nautisme* (Editions Chabassol, 30 rue de Gramont, 75002 Paris), also published in the form of regional booklets.

FOUR CHANNEL (CHENAL DU FOUR)   Charts BA 2694, 3345; F 5287

HW(Ushant) +5.30. MHWS 7.4; MLWS 1.4; MTL 4.4; MHWN 5.7; MLWN 3.0.

Direction of streams   The offing stream between the N end of the Four Channel and the Ile de Batz, 43M to the E, turns ENE at +2.00; WSW at −4.00. Close inshore the stream turns 1½h earlier. The flood stream sets round Melgorne Pt and the Four Rk from the SW and across the Portsall plateau, and the ebb stream in the reverse direction.

DS at S end of Channel: N −0.40, 5½kn; S +5.25, 4¾kn. Off Pte de Corsen: N −1.25; S +4.40, 3kn. Abreast Les Platresses: NNE −0.25; SSW +5.40, 2kn; N of Les Platresses: NNE −0.10; SSW +5.40, 3kn.

Vessels bound for W France from the English Channel and vice versa usually avoid passing W of Ushant by using one or other of the chans between Ushant and the mainland. This shortens the passage and avoids the heavy swell often found W of Ushant. However, it is important to note that with strong winds against tide, severe steep seas build up in the Four Channel (Chenal du Four) which are quite beyond the capabilities of the average small yacht.

It was formerly usual to pass 6M or more to W when taking outside passage; the Traffic Separation Lanes off Ushant now apply, and S-bound vessels have to pass either within 2M or 20M off. The Four Channel carries 6½m of water, and may be navigated without difficulty in hazy weather so long as visibility is no less than 2M.

Approach Nearing the N end of the Four Channel from the N or NE the principal landmarks are as follows. To the SW, the cliffs of Ushant Is with the Stiff Lt Ho 83m high. To the E, the Lt Tr on the Ile Vierge, a circular granite tr 77m high; the ch and spire of Plouguerneau; the Corn Carhai Lt Tr, a W octagonal tr 16.4m high; and at the E side of the entrance to the chan itself the Four Lt, a circular grey stone tr 28m high, 10M from the Stiff Lt on Ushant.

There are three chans between the Is and the mainland: the Fromveur, where the streams run at 9kn at springs, the Helle, the chan of approach from NW, and the Four, which is the most frequented and best buoyed and lit, 13M long. At the N end of this chan the stream runs at 3 to 6kn at springs, while in the narrows at the S end it attains 6 to 7kn.

Entrance *From N by day*, having given the Portsall plateau a sufficient berth, leave the Four Lt Tr and keep it open to S of Portsall Lt Tr, till Kermorvan and St Mathieu Lt Trs come in line, bearing 158°. The Kermorvan W square Lt Tr rises from the rks at the foot of Kermorvan Pt and will be seen against the heights behind Le Conquet. The St Mathieu W circular Lt Tr stands high on the cliff against the skyline, and near it the old lt tr now used as a signal stn, and the ruins of the ancient abbey.

Enter the chan from N with these trs in line, 158°, leaving G marks to stb and R marks to port, and carry on so until: (a) the Petite Fourche rk appears to the W of La Goaltoch astern with the Grande Melgorne showing between the two, bearing 008°; or (b) Grand Vinotière Lt Tr, 15m, bears 180°. Then steer 180° to pass W of Grand Vinotiere and E of the G buoy (whis) Le Rouget, abreast of the tr. When past the tr bring it in line with Corsen Lt astern 011° and keep it so until: (a) Les Vieux Moines Lt Tr appears halfway between Cap la Chevre and the western Tas de Pois rock, 132°, then steer on this transit 132°; or (b) the lantern of St Mathieu secondary lt comes on with the main rear lt of St Mathieu, 128°, when steer with it so till Kermorvan and Trezien Lt Trs are nearly in line, 007°, then round out clear of the Pt of St Mathieu with them in line astern leaving Les Vieux Moines Lt to port.

From N by night, having made the Four Lt bring it to bear E astern till St Mathieu Lt (intensified sector $157\frac{1}{2}°$–$159\frac{1}{2}°$) and Kermorvan Lt are in line, $158\frac{1}{2}°$, then steer on them till the W sector of Corsen Lt to port is entered. Then steer 190° and be careful to remain in the W sector of Corsen Lt astern which will lead between the Grande Vinotiere Lt to port and the lt buoy to stb abreast of it. Continue 190° in the W sector of Corsen till the R sector of St Mathieu secondary lt is entered, when alter course according to stream and wind till the R sector of Corsen Lt comes on with Grande Vinotiere Lt bearing 010°. Then steer with Corsen and Grande Vinotiere Lts in line 010° astern, till the W sector of St Mathieu secondary lt is entered, when alter course and bring this lt in line with St Mathieu main rear lt, 118° or nearly so, leaving the Tournant lt buoy to port. Carry on with St Mathieu lts in line till Trezien Lt comes nearly on with Kermorvan Lt, 007°, when turn to bring them in line astern and keep them so till the lt of Les Vieux Moines comes abeam, when alter course for the SE, keeping within the visible sector of Les Vieux Moines until Portzic and Le Minou lts come in line, 068° for Brest.

From S at night, enter the chan with Kermorvan and Trezien Lts in line, 007°, and steer so until the G sector of St Mathieu secondary lt is entered. Then steer a point or two to stb, and continuing so enter the W sector of St Mathieu secondary lt and bring the main and secondary St Mathieu lts in line, 118° astern. Steer on this line, leaving the Tournant lt buoy to stb. Continue thus till the R sector of Corsen Lt is entered. Bring this lt on with Vinotiere Lt, 010° ahead. As soon as the Vieux Moines Lt or the R lt of St Mathieu are shut out, alter course to enter the W sector of Corsen Lt steering about 343° till this W sector is entered. Then steer on the lt, 013° leaving lt buoy to port and Grande Vinotiere Lt to stb till Kermorvan and St Mathieu lts come in line. Keep them in line astern, 158°, till Four Lt bears E, when take your departure.

Anchorages   (1) L'Aberildut. See separate entry, below. (2) Porzmoguer, a good fine weather anch in 4½m or more, 1M S of Corsen Pt. Bring the two houses inside the bay in line and anch on this transit, with the belfry of Le Conquet open to right of Pte Brenterch in 4½m, sand. (3) Blancs Sablons Bay, a good fine-weather anch in 7½m, sand, in N part of the bay, clear of stream but exposed to W and N. There is an eddy stream in S part of the bay. (4) Anch prohibited S of line Ushant to mainland and N of line Ile de Molène to mainland. (5) Ile de Molène (see plan 443), a rather desolate but attractive island, has an anch sheltered in winds from E through S to WSW. Numerous outlying rks and fierce currents. From ½M N of Le Faix Lt Bn (N Card) steer due W until N mill (RW) is in line with Les Trois Pierres Lt Ho. Leave Lt Ho 1 ca to port and steer on ldg line of SW mark with W mark on quay, leaving Bazou Real to stb. Watch shingle bar when S of quays and anch as far in as possible, or lie alongside quays. No fuel, water at 1600 daily. PO, small shops. Ferry and hydrofoil to mainland.

L'ABERILDUT   Charts BA 2694 F 5721 (Plan p443)
HW +5.25.   MHWS 7.6; MHWN 6.0; MTL 4.5 (est).
Bar   Dries 2m with hard bottom.
Approach   Keep Breles ch tr, 2M inland, on with Lanildut ch tr, 079°. Breles ch tr is 3M from Le Lieu Tr; the latter is easily identified, being shaped like a bottle. Abreast of Men Garo continue with the rectangular Lt Ho (Oc(2) WR) on the N side of the entrance bearing 083°. Await tide E of Men Garo. Enter with sufficient water (there is about 2½m on the bar at half-tide), and from a position 50m from the N shore steer to cross gradually towards the S shore and when over the bar round up for the quay. Halfway up the hr an obstruction runs out from the E shore to the middle of the chan.

Anch 1 ca off the quay (buoy anch), 8m, in line with telegraph poles running down to the root of pier on NW side of hr, keeping Lanildut ch well open of the prominent house on the N foreshore. Very crowded.

Shops, small restaurant, shipyard.

LAMPAUL, USHANT
Charts BA 2694; F5567 (Plan p443)

HW +5.25. MHWS 7.4; MLWS 1.4; MTL 4.4; MHWN 5.7; MLWN 3.0.

An interesting place to visit in good weather, but to be avoided in strong westerlies. Lampaul is Ushant's main ferry harbour.

Approach With Le Corce Is in line with the Stiff Lt Ho, then passing 100m S and E of Le Corce.

Anchorage (1) At E end of Lampaul Bay, near the mooring buoys. Completely exposed to the W. (2) In 2m just inside the outer hr, clear of the ferry. The inner hr dries.

Water, fuel from garage, PO, hotel, restaurants. Ferry to Brest.

LE CONQUET
Charts BA 2694, F 5159 (Plan p443)

DS: N −0.40 (6kn); S +5.25 (5kn).

MHWS 7.1; MLWS 1.3; MTL 4.2; MHWN 5.5; MLWN 2.9.

A picturesque inlet between Kermorvan and the Pte Sainte Barbe. It is the port for Ushant and Molène, and is frequented by coasters and kelp carriers; should be visited in fine weather, avoiding spring tides. Beware strong cross-tides in entrance.

The port dries inside the jetty and in heavy W-ly weather a keelboat is likely to sustain damage if it should remain in the port at LW. The swell enters the hr most on the flood. The outside anch between La Louve rk and the jetty hd is protected in winds from NE to SE through E, and is exposed and untenable in winds from other directions.

Hr is quiet in E winds. Mooring buoys in outer hr are safe, and comfortable in normal settled westerly weather. Fuel piped at jetty (5m at half-tide) by arrangement with supplier near LBS. All stores.

L'ANSE DE BERTHEAUME
Charts BA 2690, 2694; F 6678

Lying only 3½M ENE of Pte de St Mathieu and being sheltered from winds between N and SW, under suitable conditions the W side of this bay offers a useful passage anch. However, as it is unlit and there are offliers, it should only be entered in daylight. Should the wind shift, Camaret and the Rade de Brest are within a short distance.

On approaching from the W, keep clear of the offliers which run from E of Les Vieux Moines as far as the bay itself. Avoid also the drying rk close NE of Le Coq buoy.

The Chateau de Bertheaume on the W headland of the bay is conspic. Give the chateau a berth of 2 ca to avoid offliers, including the drying rk Le Chat to the NE. This rk will have been cleared before the sandy cove just N of the chateau bears W.

Anch in about 5m close in, outside local moorings. Beware the rocks stretching out 4 ca to the SE from the Trez Hir Hotel (on the seashore and marked on the chart); these lie among the N-ly moorings. Beware also rks and patches in other parts of the bay.

LE CONQUET
Depths in Metres

N

22

Opening 7 foot Br.

Le Conquet 48°
21·5'
Cables 3 0

Presqu'ile
de Kermorvan
Pte de Kermorvan

La
Louve R

Oc64s

Oc64s 4
TR Bn & end of Pier
079°
Fl G 9s 9
20·5m

Petite
Vinotière
Pors Babu

(26)

36
3·4

11

ILE DE MOLÈNE
Depths in Metres

48°
24·5
14·8
24·2
3 8

Lost
ar
Gog

Baz Wenn

Baz Druez
4·57'W

Gd. Ledenez de Molène
Pt. Ledenez da
Molène

Iso WRG 4s 15m 9M
Les Trois Pierres

R. Goulin

Bazou Real

Men Bliou Béhan

NORTH MILL
RW

Fl(3)WRG12s
Fl(2)WRG6s

Ile
de
Molène

SOUTH MILL

58

Les Deux
Menhirs

N

LABERILDUT
Depths in Metres

N

48°
28'

Cables 27·8

45·5'

Oc (2)
WR 6s 12m

Pools have
been dredged
inside & outside
Bar. The inner
pool is shown
on this plan.

4° 46'W

Men Garo

Bec Cléguar

Gato Belen

Roc'h Du

Descléo
Bras

le
Liou

Tr Bn

R

46·5'

LAMPAUL
Depths in Metres
Cables

N

48°
27'
27·5

5|7'w

6'

Lampaul

Le Gd. Truc

Ar Garn
(06)

Le Corce
22

15

25

près la carte marine française avec l'autorisation du Service Hydrographique et Océanographique de la Marine.

BREST

Depths in Metres

Brest

Cables

Zone Industrielle de St Marc

ANSE DU MOULIN BLANC

YACHT HARBOUR

IsoR4s

HM

Slip

Land Reclamation in progress 1980

BUOYED CHANNEL

Works in progress 1980

L. Moulin-Blanc

Oc(2)R6s

N

Pte Marloux

BANC DE PLOUGASTEL

FlG2s
No7
G

FlG2s
No5
G

FIR4s
No6
R

Oc(2)G6s7M

Oc(2)R6s5M

IsoR4s

MÔLE DE L'EST

Oc R4s
No4
R

Oc(2)R6s

BW

IsoR4s

BANC DU CORBEAU

FlG4s
No1
G

Fl(2)R6s
No2
R

PORT DU COMMERCE

MÔLE DE L'OUEST

IsoR4s

FlG4s
6M

Jetée du Sud

Zone Réservée

Oc WRG(1+3)12s 20m

IsoG

LA PENFELD

Vts 3)12s

IsoR

IsoR

Jetée Est

QG5M

ArcFl(v)s

QR5M

ArcFl(v)s

PROHIBITED ANCHORAGE

RADE ABRI

No8

No9

Jetée Sud

Obstructions

Jetée Ouest

BANC DE St PIERRE

Basse St Pierre

FlR(3)12s
R

Basse Pennou Pell
R

Brest

D'après la carte marine française avec l'autorisation du Service Hydrographique et Océanographique de la Ma

BREST Charts BA 3247, 3248; F 6542, 6427, 6426 (Plan p444)
HW +5.25. MHWS 7.4; MLWS 1.3; MTL 4.4; MHWN 5.8; MLWN 3.0.

Tidal streams in the Goulet In Passe Sud the flood stream begins ½h after local LW and flows E; the ebb soon after HW, to W. The ebb sets obliquely between Pte des Espagnols and Pte de Dellec. During the ebb an E-running eddy flows inshore along the S side of the Goulet, attaining its greatest strength during the latter half. In the Passe Nord the streams begin about ½h later. Contrary wind and tide kick up a steep sea.

Approach From W leave Les Vieux Moines to port, steer 100° for 3½M, passing S of Le Coq (3.6m) and Beuzec (1.8m), and carry on till Portzic Lt comes in line with Petit Minou Lt, 068°, when steer 070° up the pass, to leave Portzic Lt to port. From abreast Portzic continue 064° for the hr entrance. At night, from Les Vieux Moines steer 100° till Portzic Lt comes open N of Petit Minou Lt, when steer 070° as above.

From S, having rounded Toulinguet Pt, steer 010° till Portzic comes open N of Mengam, when steer to leave Portzic to port and continue as above; by night steer 010° from Toulinguet to Petit Minou till Portzic comes well open N of Mengam R sector, when head to pass of Portzic and continue so for hr entrance.

From Toulinguet, to pass S of Mengam, steer 037°. At night keep in W sector of Mengam Lt; R over shoals.

Entrance The breakwater heads are marked by R and G lts. Beware numerous large mooring buoys.

Berthing Visitors are expected to use the new marina about 2M E of the Port du Commerce in Anse du Moulin Blanc. Make for the first port hand buoy marking the entrance to the Anse de Landerneau and steer NNE for the marina breakwater head, entering between marker buoys. 2m. HM, diesel, no petrol. Restaurant, chandlery, water, toilets. Basic provisions only in village; poor bus to Brest, taxi recommended. Charts in Brest from Jouanneau, 75 rue de Siam.

Within the GOULET DE BREST

Landerneau River May be ascended at sufficient rise of tide as far as Landerneau, 12M. There is 24m clearance under the bridge; use the N arch. 4m least water as far as St Jean. 3m draft can reach Landerneau at HW. It is advisable to leave early on the ebb or before HW. There is much mud exposed at LW.

Entrance Leave the buoy off Moulin Blanc to port, buoy with con topmark close to stb. A buoy marks the rk off Pte Ste Barbe. To enter by S side of the Deraliou bank at sufficient rise, keep the fort of I Longue in line with Pte Marloux astern, 220°. This line nearly dries at LW.

Anchorage A good berth at Le Passage. Vessels anch also at St Jean and can lie alongside the quay at Landerneau.

Auberlach Bay Affords good anch, mud, in 3½m ¼M offshore S of jetty. Vessels of 1.8m draft can enter within 2h of HW and dry alongside the jetty. Bay exposed to W. At the head of the bay there is a lagoon, dries, soft mud. A shingle spit runs down from the N shore, leaving a narrow entrance close to the S shore, through which the tide runs hard. Enter at slack water, round the end of the spit and hug the spit on its inner side till close to the N shore. Keep close inshore till abreast the village; anch there in complete shelter.

Daoulas River Vessels of 2.7m draft can reach Daoulas at HWS. There is anch in 2.7m, mud, ¾M from entrance, close to S bank off a little cove where fishing boats lie. Stores 1M.

Bay of Poulmic Good anch to S of the shoal area, close inshore, with Plougastel on with the middle mill of Traoulior and Pte des Espagnols, to N of Penar Vir, in 3m.

Bay of Le Fret Anch in 3.6m, mud and clay, off quay.

Chateaulin River Vessels of 4m draft can reach Port Launay, 13M above Landevennec and Chateaulin, at HWS; 3m at HWN. Good shops at Port Launay. The chan is well marked by buoys. There is a lock at Guilyglas, 1M below Port Launay; the upper sill dries 2.7m. Lock opens HW −2. HW at Port Launay is ½h after HW Brest; the basin has 2.7m. A good berth will be found at Port Stivel (Landevel ½M walk), and in the bays N and S of Bay of Folgoat around the first bend of the river, in line with the horns of the bay, out of the stream; clay bottom, 4m, soft mud further in. There is a bridge at I de Terenez 29.9m above HW. Recognised anch at Tregarvan, and at Dineault, clear of the stream.

Passage notes: Biscay coast

HW throughout the length of the coast and along the N coast of Spain from Ushant to Cap Finisterre occurs approx 4.30 to 5.30h after HWD.

In spring and summer prevailing winds between Ushant and the Gironde are from between W and NE through N, but in the neighbourhood of Brest SW winds are frequently experienced. Gales are not frequent during June through August, but at no time can freedom from W gales be relied on, and in unsettled weather small craft are well advised not to stray too far from shelter. In the autumn, E winds are more frequent. Fog rarely lasts long on this coast.

CAMARET Charts BA 2690, F 6678 (Plan p447)
HW +5.10. MHWS 6.9; MLWS 1.2; MTL 4.0; MHWN 5.3; MLWN 2.8.
Hr is sheltered from all directions except E, but there is sometimes a swell. Yachts berth at pontoons which are situated under N breakwater in up to 5.4m. Water from tap, at top of pontoon gangway as well as at hd of slip alongside S mole, where fuel is also obtainable. This slip must be left clear. All facilities, public showers available at certain times daily on quay. Bonded stores.

THE TOULINGUET CHANNEL
The stream sets S about +5.30, N at about −0.30. The passage is narrow, but may be made with care by day or night with a fair tide, in clear weather, as the

CAMARET
Depths in Metres

4° 36'W

35'

34'

Cables   0   6

7_4

13_2

7_4

Pte du Gd Gouin

13_4

White

5

7_2

Green

Pte Ste-Barbe

7_4

5

7_4

48°

17'

14

9_9

G

Iso WG 4s 7m

7_4

Styvel

YACHT Hr 7_4 W 7_4

chain

1·5m

Fl(2)R6s 9m 5M

Camaret-sur-Mer

R
QR

16·5'

6·3'

(R)
(6) ▲ Ar-men
White   (4s)
4_2 Piper
2_6 Oc(3)WR 12s 35m

Q6

GRANDE PASSE

6_4 R. de l'Ermitage

Ile Tristan

4_2 Môle Est-Ouest

Iso G4s 9m4M

Arc of vis

3

Treboul

Ile St Michel

1_4

RADE DE GUET

5_6 G

48°

6'

Yacht Hr

Passe du Guet

Môle Men-léon

5m

Oc(2)R6s 6m 6M

1·5m

polidoire

R
R
R

5m

6_2

4_5

Pte de Beg-ar-Vir

OcG4s 5m 7M

3_6

5
m
PORT DE ROSMEUR

✠ Douarnenez

2_3

3

2_4

N

DOUARNENEZ
Depths in Metres

Port Rhu

0   Cables   5

20·2'

4° 19'W

près la carte marine française avec l'autorisation du Service Hydrographique et Océanographique de la Marine.

447

tide sets straight through the fairway at 2 to 3kn. From N, pass midway between La Louve rk tr and Pohen rk.

Chan has 4.5m. From the S make the W tas de Pois allowing for the inset into Douarnenez Bay. Hence steer for Toulinguet Lt with the Petit Minou Lt Ho a little open to W of Toulinguet Pt, 011°. When abreast of Toulinguet rks at night when St Mathieu Lt is hidden behind them, steer about 335° to pass between Pohen and La Louve tr. When clear to the N of them, round up to E as soon as Portzic Lt Ho comes open of the S side of the Goulet, but if bound for the N chan hold on for the Minou Lt till well clear to N of the Fillettes, onto which the flood tide sets.

MORGAT
Chart F 5186

After rounding Cap de la Chevre into B de Douarnenez, there is a pleasant anch at Morgat, some 3½M from the cape in a wooded bay with golden sands. The bay is sheltered from N and W but exposed between S and E; however, there is complete protection at the marina inside the new rounded mole N of Pte de Morgat. Although hr dries, with sandy bottom, the marina berths have at least 2m. Approach is straightforward to pontoons. HM, water, showers, fuel, stores.

DOUARNENEZ – TREBOUL
Charts BA 798, F 667   (Plan p447)

HW +5.10.   MHWS 6.9; MLWS 1.3; MTL 4.1; MHWN 5.4; MLWN 2.8.

A fascinating spot in fine weather, 16M inside Pte du Van. Marina at Treboul.
Approach   To clear the Basse Veur, 4.1m, keep the Millier Lt open of La Jument Pt until Ploare ch comes open to the E of Douarnenez ch. At night keep in the W sector of Millier Lt, Oc(2) WRG 6s, until the R sector of Ile Tristan Lt, Oc(3) WR 12s has been crossed.
Anchorage   Yachts are not allowed in the fishing hr but anch off Rosmeur S of the hr. There are lts Iso G 4s and Oc(2) R 6s on N and S sides of the hr entrance, and an Oc G lt on the end of Rosmeur mole.

There is an anch completely exposed from NW to NE in the Rade de Guet. The entrance to Pouldavid R is through the Grande Passe, dredged to be available at all tides. Past the Treboul jetty head, QG, turn to stb into marina in the Treboul inlet, dredged to 1.5m. There are some visitors' buoys just outside the marina. There are also drying quays further up the river at Port Rhu.

Water by tap at Port Rhu and Rosmeur, by hose with fuel nearby at Treboul. Good shops at Treboul, and all facilities at Douarnenez itself.

ILE DE SEIN
Chart F5252

A useful port of call if the weather is settled and a large-scale chart is available. Approach is best made by the N chan guarded by a whistle buoy, Iso G. Anch in lee of mole in clear water. Heavy swell at HW with NW wind.

RAZ DE SEIN   Charts BA 798, 2351, F 5252
Tidal streams   HW +5.00.   The stream runs 6–7kn at springs, 3–4kn at neaps.
In the middle of the Raz the NE-going flood begins at −1.30, the SW ebb +4.45,
attaining 7 and 6kn respectively. There is a period of slack water for about ½h at
the end of the flood stream.

The passage should be taken at slack water, except at neap tides and in fine
weather. With wind against tide, the passage is rough in moderate winds, but
when the wind and stream are together the sea is smooth in the Raz, though it
can then be rough outside. Between the Chaussee and Tevennec the stream runs
NW −1.45, SE +4.30, 3kn; at La Vielle NNW −1.30, SSE +4.30; there are
counter-currents inshore.

Directions   By day from S. When within 2M of La Vielle bring Tevennec rk five
times its own width to W of La Vielle and keep it so, till Ile de Sein bears about
280°, then round La Vielle at ½M or more. Keep La Vielle 180° astern till
Tevennec and Ile de Sein come in line, which clears to W. By day from the N,
steer for La Vielle 180°, round it and bring Tevennec rk five times its width open
W of La Vielle astern for 2½M, which clears to S. At night from S, approach La
Vielle Lt in its W (325°–355°) sector and, with the aid of Tevennec Lt, round it.
When the NW sector of La Vielle is reached steer 013°. Allowance should be
made for the tidal stream to avoid Le Vielle on the ebb and Les Barillets on the
flood. At night from the N, steer for La Vielle, 180°, pass close W of La Platte Lt,
bring Tevennec to bear 328°, and steer 148°.

AUDIERNE AND ST EVETTE ANCHORAGE
                                Charts BA 2351, F 5937   (Plan p450)
HW +4.55.   MHWS 5.2; MLWS 0.8; MTL 3.0; MHWN 3.9; MLWN 2.0.
Hr is 9M SE of La Vielle, and may be approached in all but established bad
weather from S; an attractive spot in fine weather. The river is only accessible
after half-tide and strong S winds produce a dangerous sea in the entrance.
However, the breakwater 3 ca NE of Le Sillon protects a useful anch, known as
the St Evette anch, to the W of the river entrance. It is safe in all but strong SE
winds though subject to some swell when there is any S in the wind. It is
accessible at any state of the tide and thus recommended for starting a passage
through the Raz towards the N.

Approach   From the E keep Kergadec Lt Tr (FR upper, QWRG lower) in line
with lt Oc (1+2) WG on pierhead at W of river mouth, 331°; from W after
rounding Pte de Lervily, Fl WR 12s, enter by the Grand Chenal and keep
Kergadec Lt Tr and the old Lt Ho W of entrance in line, 006°. When making for
St Evette anch keep on this until the end of the breakwater bears NW, then alter
course to round it ½ to 1 ca off to avoid the rks off its foot and the shallow patch to
the E. For the hr, whose entrance almost dries, keep on the transit till the
pier-head lt, Oc WG 12s, bears 034°, when steer 042° till the river comes open to
E of the pier-head, or at night till the pier-head lt turns W. Then steer 039° to
leave the pier-head lt fairly close to port and Le Corbeau rk, YBY tr, well to stb.

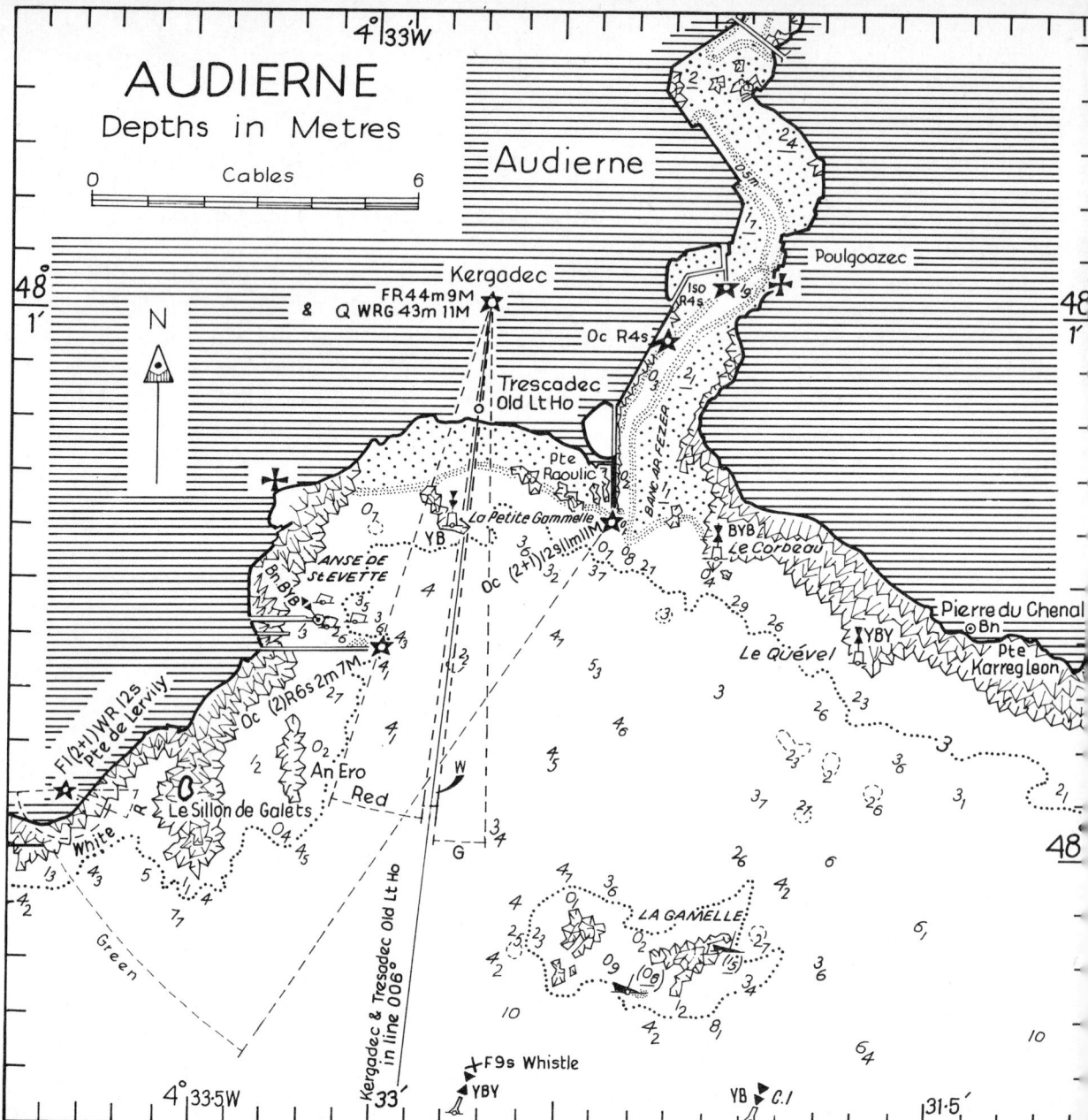

AUDIERNE
Depths in Metres

Cables
0   6

Audierne

N

48° 1′

Kergadec
FR 44m 9M
& Q WRG 43m 11M

Poulgoazec

Iso R4s

Oc R4s

Trescadec
Old Lt Ho

Pte Raoulic

La Petite Gammelle

YB

ANSE DE St EVETTE

Oc (2+1) 12s 11m 11M

Le Corbeau

BYB

Pierre du Chenal
Bn

Pte Karreglon

Le Quével

YBY

Fl(2+1) WR 12s
Pte de Lervily

Oc (2) R6s 2m 7M

An Ero
Red

W

Le Sillon de Galets

White

G

Green

Kergadec & Tresadec Old Lt Ho
in line 006°

LA GAMELLE

Fl 9s Whistle
YBY

YB C.I

48°
1′

48

33′

31·5′

4° 33·5′W   4° 33′W

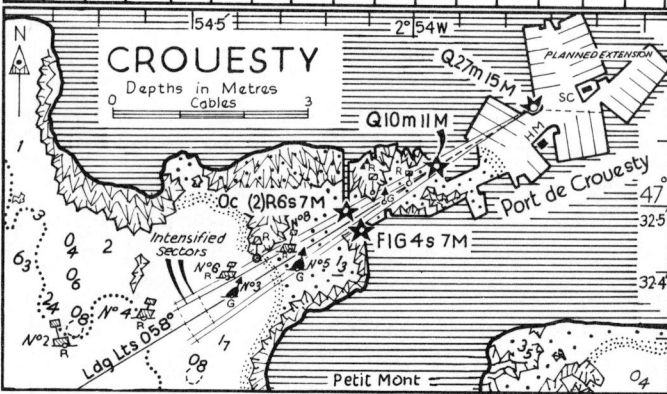

CROUESTY
Depths in Metres
Cables
0   3

N

545   2° 54W

PLANNED EXTENSION

Q 27m 15M

SC

Q 10m 11M

Oc (2) R6s 7M

Port de Crouesty

47′

Intensified
sectors

N°6
N°3
N°8
N°5

Fl 1G 4s 7M

32·5

32·4

N°4
N°7

N°2

Ldg Lts 058°

Petit Mont

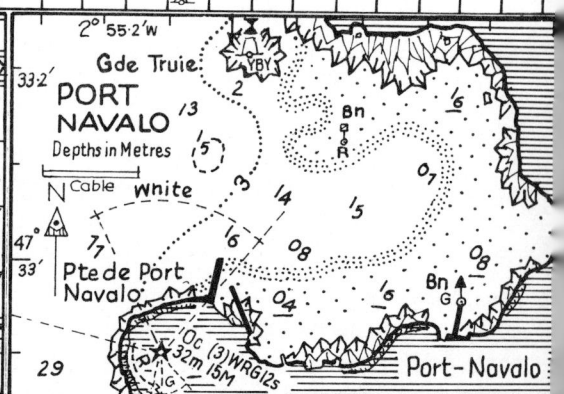

2° 55·2′w

Gde Truie

YBY

PORT NAVALO
Depths in Metres

Bn
R

N Cable   white

47′
33′

Pte de Port
Navalo

Bn
G

Oc (3) WRG 12s
32m 15M

29

Port-Navalo

D'après la carte marine française avec l'autorisation du Service Hydrographique et Océanographique de la Mari

450

St GUÉNOLÉ
Depths in Metres

47°|49'

N

0   Cables   5

Fl(3)G12s
G

Ldg Lts 123°

12₄

94 5

Pellenic

68

Baz Névez
12₆

16

29

I. Conq

82

53

18

38
Staviou

(6)
53

QkFlR12m4M
QkFlR 10m4M
St Guénolé

05

23

2·5m

Carrec Louet
Krugen

R&G
Fl(2)R5s
Fl(2)R 5s   G   FlG
R FlG
G FlG
Lts Q27

2

17

FlG2s
Scoëdec
34

04

04

05

04

N.D. de la Joie

45
5
3
05
34
5₂
Basse Plate

14 2·3

2 22 29 ·25
31
59

9₄
I.Men Menez
3
13

FG9m5M

FG13m5M
Pt de Penmarch

17
07

Bn(R)

Ile Garo

03

Cable (marked)
02 3 24
56 04
18

Cable (marked)

1
06 01
06

01

3
4₂

33
1m Quay

3·3

Loctudy

0   Cables   5

13

4

33

28

Ile Tudy

(5)

03
06

Bn
Bn(G)
Roches des Perdrix
G Fl4sWRG4s8M

08 R 07
83 56 53

Karek Croisic

1·3

Fl(4)WRG12s17M
de Langoz

R

04

04

01

W

W

R

LOCTUDY
Depths in Metres

N

04

01

05

03

07

02

04

05

08

15 50·5'

Men Audierne
(13)
G 15

15

33

3 13

18
294°

16

Karek Saoz
09

22

2

47°
50'

15

23

4°|9'W

10'

'après la carte marine française avec l'autorisation du Service Hydrographique et Océanographique de la Marine.

Inside, the chan runs along the W side, not far from the pier; then to midstream. From the Poalgoazec corner it lies along the W side of the bridge; in the apex of the angle 2 ca below the bridge there is less water.

Anchorage In the St Evette anch, the W mooring buoys are used by fishermen but may be picked up when not in use. The least swell will be found between these buoys and the breakwater, and as close to the LB slip as possible. At certain tides, the Ile de Sein ferry arrives at another slip with a bn at its end parallel to and N of the LB slip, and its line of approach is between the breakwater and the buoys. There is also a good anch between La Petite Gamelle, marked by a YB bn, and the mooring buoys outside the local small craft. Landing at steamer slip at all states of the tide. Audierne hr mostly dries below the bridge.

Best quay berth is where quay runs NW–SE. A berth may be available (if unobstructed: do not rely on it) with anch downstream and warp to E arch of the bridge. This hole is silting and there is little water at present. Great care is required. The pool is very near the bridge and the flood runs strongly.

At neap tides there may be a berth abreast the hotel in 1.8m. It is necessary to anch clear of the fishing boats, which fill the entire length of the quay at weekends. Good anch above the bridge in 3.6m. Hard below the bridge on W side. Vessels of 1.8m draft can reach village of Pont Croix, 3M above the bridge, but there is nothing but mud.

Warning: Buoyage changes Text and plans for the remaining ports in France describe the buoyage and lights as projected after the IALA changes. These are scheduled for 1981, but may not keep up with the timetable.

ST GUÉNOLÉ
Chart F 6645 (Plan p451)

HW (Audierne) +4.55. MHWS 5.2; MLWS 0.8; MTL 3.0; MHWN 3.9; MLWN 2.0.

Fishing hr just N of Pte de Penmarc'h, protected by breakwater on W side. Entrance just dries, but about 1.8m can be found inside.

Approach Locate the whistle lt buoy 9 ca N of Menhir Lt Tr. From just N of the buoy, steer 123° on the ldg lts on Pte de Penmarc'h, conspic bns with B and W bands. This course passes to N of Pellenic rks, dry 2.7m. When Scoedec G Tr is on with Notre Dame de la Joie on skyline, 096°, steer to port and leave the tr ½ ca to stb. Steer for a point 25m E of entrance to avoid submerged rks lying S of the W side of the entrance. Thence enter 027° between the bns on Conq and Krugen. Two inner ldg lts, QR (027°) are exhibited from concrete posts on N side of hr, but they are not easily identified by day.

Anchorages S of the LB slip in 0.9m, rock covered by muddy sand, or alongside jetty after inspecting bottom at LW. All facilities except petrol which is not available at a reasonable distance. Water from hose on quay on application at fish market.

Passage note: Penmarc'h Point to La Gironde River

Penmarc'h lies low and may be identified by the octagonal Lt Ho 60m high standing 120m from the old tr, which is shorter and smaller.

About 4M S of Penmarc'h Pt the stream is rotatory: WSW −1.00; N +1.45; E +4.50; S −4.30. About 2M SW of Penmarc'h Pt the stream is rotatory clockwise. The flood stream runs N changing to E through NE; the ebb is SE changing to W through S.

The general direction of the tidal streams offshore along the coast between Penmarc'h and the R Gironde is as follows:

Time (on HWD)	Direction	Time (on HWD)	Direction
HWD	N	−6.00	SW
+1.00	NE by N	−5.00	SW by W
+2.00	E	−4.00	W
+3.00	E	−3.00	W
+4.00	SE by E	−2.00	NW by W
+5.00	SE by S	−1.00	NW by N

At certain times the stream flows straight on and offshore.

GUILVINEC   Charts BA 2351, F 6646
The hr is dredged, bottom sand; very crowded when fishing boats are in. In fine weather there is a quiet anch in 3m, off entrance, which is protected by the outlying reefs, even from SW. Vessels of 2.4m draft can enter at any time.
Approach   The approach lies between the Etocs and Basse Spinec, and carries 2.7m. Bring the rectangular W rear Lt Ho, Oc R, 19.5m, and the cylindrical BHWS front Lt Ho, Oc WG, 7m, both with large R spher tops and easy to identify, in line 053° and keep them so. The Nevez N Card buoy, Q, E of Les Etocs rks, is left to stb. This transit leads over the Basse des Herbes, 1.8m, to avoid which at LW it is necessary to bear away to port before the old Penmarc'h Lt Ho comes in line with Locarec rk, 292°; afterwards return to ldg line.
Entrance   Continue on the ldg line, up buoyed chan. W mole head has FR lt; E mole head a FG lt.
Anchorage   The outside anch has 2.7m, sand and rock, with Lt Hos in line and Locarec on with Men Du bn, 272°. The N quay has 2.7m MHWS. Moor to mooring buoy or anch near W mole in 2.7m and take a line to mole, but do not haul too close as bottom is foul alongside W mole. Water hose, no fuel. Little room and no provision for yachts.

LOCTUDY   Charts BA 3645, F 6649   (Plan p451)
HW +5.05.   MHWS 5.0; MLWS 0.5; MTL 2.7; MHWN 3.6; MLWN 1.7.
Bar   Outside the entrance the S part of the bar has about 1.5m; the N part almost dries. Moorings in 3.6m inside; a charming spot. Shops, hotels, restaurant.

BÉNODET
Depths in Metres

Cables
0 — 5

N

47/53
52

4°7'W   6'

Lodet R.
Pte de Bâbord
FR
FG
FG
FR
9 7
10 2
2 7
4 7

Pte de Beg vir
ANSE DE PENFOUL
Port de Penfoul
Pte de Kergait

R
Bn
BW
W
8 8
8 2
G
12 6
NO ANCH
13
10
4

Oc (2+1)12s 48m 15M
Bénodet
Pte du Coq
Oc G(2+1)12s 11m 14M
G
2 2

Pte du Toulgoët
Ste-Marine
FIR
19
Arc of vis

Anse de Trez
28
13
14
0 4
0 6
7
3
12
8 6
5 6
0 3

Oc (3+1)12s 19m 12M
Pte de Combrit
NO ANCH
3
2 1
3 5
4 1
3 9
0 2
8
4 9
G
Le Four
1 4

Pte de Bénodet
1 9

NO ANCH
Lts 346°
6 5
6 6
R
Y
5 5
Arc of vis
La Rousse
7 3 R
G
Les Verres

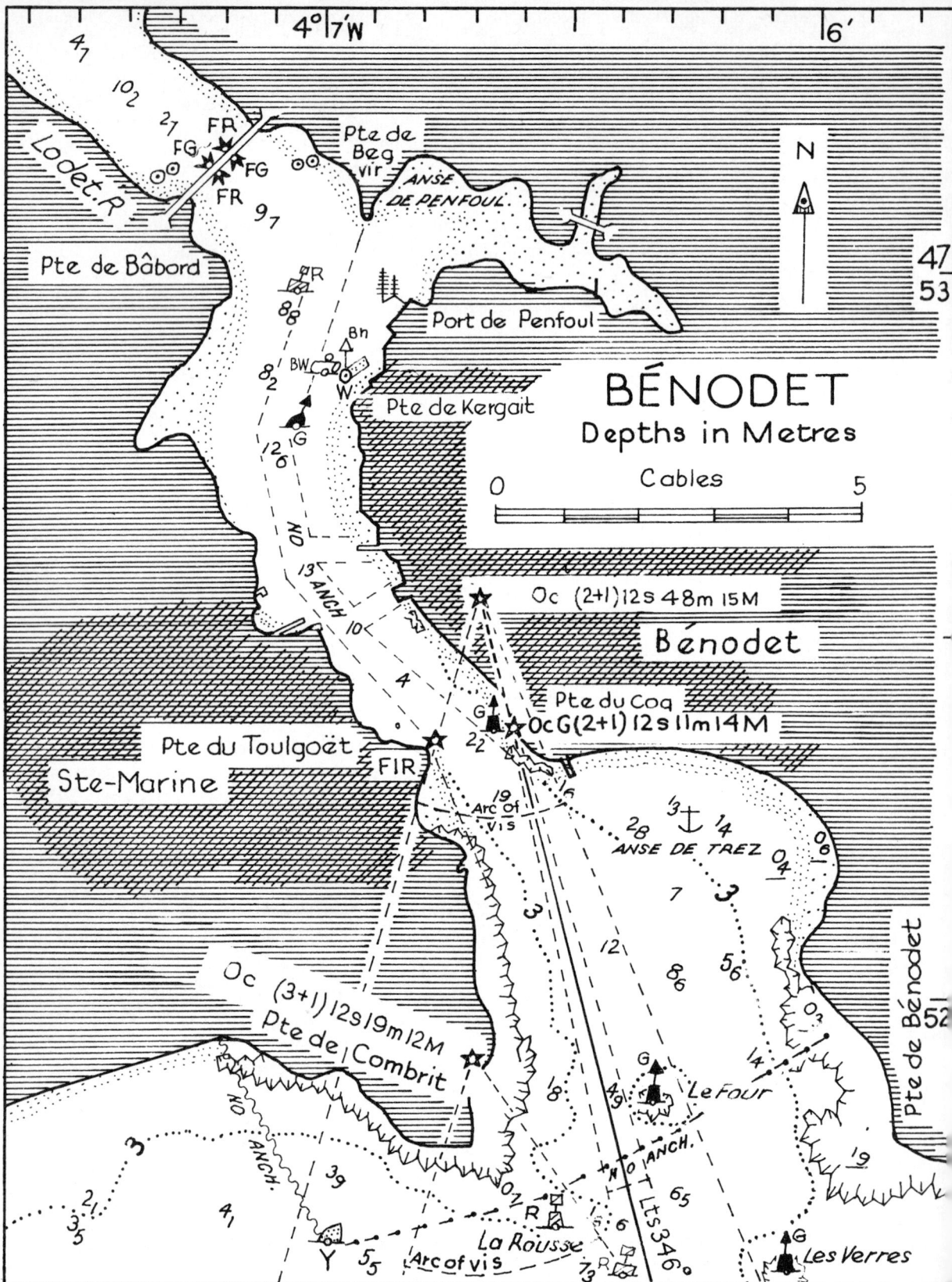

D'après la carte marine française avec l'autorisation du Service Hydrographique et Océanographique de la Mar...

454

Approach   As for Bénodet. After Basse du Chenal buoy is abeam to port, steer 312° for the entrance about 2M distant, leaving Basse Bilieu buoy to port.

Entrance   Leave Karek Saoz, R tr, to port, Men Audierne G bn to stb, and stand in with the Perdrix Tr bearing 294°, open to S of bn off Ile Tudy; and midway between Château Moc and Château Durumain (the two most E-ly buildings seen among the dark trees in the background). This transit clears Karek Croisic close on its S side. When the entrance comes fully open on nearing the Perdrix Tr, steer 274° on Château Laubrière, further westward among the dark trees, leaving the quay fairly close to port.

Anchorage   There are mooring buoys beyond the LB; or anch outside the moored boats NW of Loctudy quay. Kedge essential. Ebb runs 3kn. Or just above the quay at Ile Tudy. Water on quay or from fish market. Pont l'Abbe is 3M upriver: visit on the tide (vessels up to 3m draft sometimes get up). Rly to Quimper and buses from Pont l'Abbé, whose natives are called Bigoudens. There is a hotel at Ile Tudy. Outside anch sand, good in W winds.

BENODET   Charts BA 3645; F 6649, 6679   (Plan p454)
HW +5.05.   MHWS 4.8; MLWS 0.5; MTL 2.6; MHWN 3.6; MLWN 1.7.
The entrance to the Odet R is E and N from Menhir; 5.4m in chan.

Approach   From W having rounded Menhir, a course 135° made good for $4\frac{1}{2}$M will lead to a position S of Basse Spinec, whence steer 081°, $8\frac{1}{4}$M, on Ile Mouton Lt, leaving Ar Guisty, tr, Karek Greis and Rostolou buoys to port till Bénodet high lt comes in line with Combrit Lt, 000°; round in on this bearing about 5M till near approach, when bring Le Coq and Bénodet Lt Hos on E side of entrance in line, 346°, and keep them so till nearing Le Coq, whence proceed in midstream. At night, ldg lts and sectored lts make the approach simple.

Entrance   In the entrance leave two R buoys to port and two G bns to stb.

Anchorage   Outside the narrows in the Anse de Trez, open Bénodet Lt E of Le Coq Lt and anch when Loctudy Lt is hidden by Pte de Combrit, in about $5\frac{1}{2}$m. Anchorage is prohibited in the fairway between Pte de Coq and Anse de Kergos, and permanent moorings occupy all available space outside the chan. There are visitors' moorings (quite expensive) opposite and in Anse de Kergos, dries. Water from tap. Fixed bridge, clearance 30m, 2.5 ca NW of Anse de Kergos. Fuel in season from barge on E bank at entrance to Anse de Keradaon. Land at marina in the Anse de Keradaon. Regular flights to UK.

The Odet R is marked by bns in the upper reaches and dries above Lanros. Lower down the ebb runs strongly. At Pors Meillou, halfway to Quimper, berth alongside the quay near its W end, bottom sand and mud. The quay covers at MHWS, and there is about 1.3m at half-tide.

At Quimper the best berth is at the first quay to port, 3.6m MHWS. Water from hose. A Bailey bridge by Lochmaria ch makes access by river with fixed mast impossible. Anch in the river at Rosaves, Combrit, Keramblais and Lanros in 1.8m S of detached rk.

ILES DE GLENAN
Charts BA 2352; F 6647, 6648

HW (Concarneau) +5.05.   MHWS 4.9; MLWS 0.7; MTL 2.8; MHWN 3.8; MLWN 1.9.

A most picturesque archipelago, well sheltered in summer and having the only coral beaches in Europe. It is the home of the famous Cercle Nautique des Glénans Sailing School, whose boats are in evidence everywhere among the Is.

Approach   There is no safe approach from the S. Approach should be made from the N to Ile Penfret, the eastern Is (easily recognised by the Lt Ho) which has no dangers until within ½ ca at the N end. If proceeding to St Nicholas follow the coast of Ile Penfret until off the coral beach about halfway down the W side, whence steer for the houses on Ile St Nicholas, about 276°.

Anchorage   Outside the CNG moorings off SW of Ile Penfret, 1.8m; off coral beach on Penfret; La Chambre off St Nicholas, 3.6m; at neaps, midway between chimney on Ile du Loc'h and fort on Ile Cigogne (2½m LWN).

If leaving La Chambre for Bénodet, steer for the middle of Ile Penfret 096° and when about 2½ ca SE of Ile de Barrenec steer to pass between the two western Pierres Noires, 355°, two steep-to rks; the eastern one is said to resemble a crouching lion.

Chenal des Bluiniers from La Chambre to W dries 0.6m.

Small cafe on St Nicholas, no other facilities. Charts F 6647 and 6648 essential.

PORT LA FORET
Charts BA 3645, F 6650

HW (Concarneau) +5.00.   MHWS 4.9; MLWS 0.7; MTL 2.8; MHWN 3.8; MLWN 1.9.

A picturesque village with a marina of 300–400 berths.

Approach   Stand in with the end of Cap Coz breakwater, Fl(2) R 6s, bearing about 345°, and enter the approach chan which is marked by buoys outside and bns inside. Leave Cap Coz breakwater head to port and Kerleven breakwater, Fl G 4s, to stb. At head of the chan turn to stb leaving the dock head, Iso G 4s, to stb and enter marina. Depth in approach chan 1.2m; no anch in chan, speed limit 3kn.

Berthing   Yachts are normally met by HM's launch and allotted a berth. Visitors' berths at heads of alternate pontoons marked in green. Depth in marina 2m. Fuel, electricity and showers. Bus service to Concarneau and Quimper; shops and hotel.

CONCARNEAU
Charts BA 2352, 3645; F 6650   (Plan p457)

HW +5.00.   MHWS 4.9; MLWS 0.7; MTL 2.8; MHWN 3.8; MLWN 1.9.

A fishing hr with a major yacht marina. Some swell in onshore winds.

Approach   From S, to clear the Corven de Trevignon and Soldats do not let Pte de la Jument W pyramid bear less than 365°; at night keep in the intensified sector of the ldg lts.

When Pte de la Jument is abeam bring the ldg lts (front Oc(3) 12s, rear Q) in line, 029°. This leads between Basse du Chenal bn to port and Le Cochon Tr,

CONCARNEAU
Depths in Metres

0   Cables   2

Concarneau

Beuzec Cong Lt 0.8M

Arrière Port 3m

5m

Slip

Fl(2)G6s

La Ville Close

Fl(2)R6s

Fl R4s

OC(2)WR

Fl G4s

AVANT PORT

Môle de la Croix

La Croix Lt Ho

× Fl R4s 4M

La Médée

☆ FG 7M

Men Marque

Ar Gazec

28

Oc(3) 12s 14m 12M

Beuzec Cong & La Croix Lts in line 28° 40'

Beuzec Cong Lt Q 87m 2M

6.5

6.4

Arc of vis

R   W

Kersos

G

Men Gren

× Fl G4s
Men Fall

G

Fl(3)WRG 12s 9m 10M

Le Cochon

Be du Chenal

Barzic

ANSE DE KERSOZ

0.2

0.2

RIVERS AVEN & BELON

Depths in Metres

0   Cables   7

Rosbras

Pylon

Belon

49'

Aven River

Belon River

Lanriot

Pt de Riec

Bn

N

Port Manech

Oc(4) RG 12s 8m

Beg-ar-Vechen

Pt de Kerhermain

47'

48'

Bn

W   R   W   G

PORT TUDY
Depths in Metres

0   Cables   4

N

47'

39'

38.9'

Arc of vis

Bn R

(4)

Iso G4s 6M

3.8

Fl(2)R6s 12M

Port Tudy

---

d'après la carte marine française avec l'autorisation du Service Hydrographique et Océanographique de la Marine.

Fl(3) WRG 12s, to stb. Continue until past Men Fall buoy, or until Lanriec Lt becomes visible, then enter between Lanriec Lt and La Medee R Tr, Fl R 4s.

Entrance   A 0.9m rk lies abreast the N Lanriec pyramid.

Berthing   The Avant Port is a yacht marina; visitors moor at the E end of the second last pontoon going S, or as space allows. Fuel, water, showers. Double-ended mooring buoys on N side of La Ville Close in inner hr 2.4m; quays reserved for fishing and commercial boats. Anch in Anse de Kersos or outside off La Croix mole in 5½m; ebb runs hard, mud is strong.

The old walled town is worth a visit. All facilities.

RIVER AVEN   Charts BA 2352, F 5479   (Plan p457)
HW +4.50.   MHWS 4.9; MHWN 3.9.

The mouth of the river is situated inside Beg-ar-Vechen. The bar in the entrance dries 0.9m, but being sheltered from SW rarely breaks. The Aven offers anch at Port Manec'h, outside the bar, in 2½m, and at Rosbras 1¼M upriver in 2m. The river is very beautiful up to Pont-Aven, 3¾M, but is not well marked above Rosbras.

Approach   Having rounded Beg-ar-Vechen, Port Manec'h will be seen to port, and the bn of the bar rks, Le Roch, will be seen ahead.

Entrance   Leaving Le Roch to port, a midstream course will lead to Rosbras. When the base of the bn of Le Roch is covered, 1.8m of water will be found over the inner bar abreast Le Poulguen. Going upstream, deepest water tends to be close to the port hand perches: sounding advisable. Pools crowded with moorings, so anch is virtually impossible.

Anchorage   At Port Manec'h, about 1 ca off the small breakwater; sound in. At Rosbras, between or up to 1 ca below the quays, which dry; flood 2kn, ebb 3kn. At Pont-Aven, a picturesque town, a long quay affords berths drying 2–3m. The best quay to use is round the corner, on the last straight before the footbridge. Moorings in 2½m.

Approaching Beg-ar-Vechen after dark, keep in the W sector of the lt and anch in 3.6m to SE, or inside, according to draft.

RIVER BELON   Charts BA 2352, F 5479   (Plan p457)
HW +4.50.   MHWS 4.9; MLWS 0.5; MTL 2.7; MHWN 3.9; MLWN 1.5.

The entrance is open to SW, and the bar which dries 1.5m is much more exposed than that of the R Aven, and impassable in bad weather. There is an inner bar, same depth, abreast the first bend in the river, ½M inside the entrance. Attractive scenery as far as Bélon.

Approach   Leave the bn on Bec-Lerzou rk off Pte Kerhermain to stb, and steer to pass 100m off the next point on the stb side.

Entrance   The chan then crosses to the N shore, whence bring Beg-ar-Vechen Lt to bear 240° astern till abreast next pt to stb, where the chan turns somewhat S of E and then 030°; when the next bend comes open to stb, round the pt and proceed thereafter in midstream.

Anchorage Below the moorings, between the quays at Bélon and Lanriot, in 2 to 3½m. Quay dries 1.8m. Oyster beds above Bélon. Stream runs 2kn on the flood and 3kn on the ebb. Restaurant at Lanriot.

BRIGNEAU   Charts BA 2352, F 5479
HW +4.50.   MHWS 4.9; MLWS 0.5; MTL 2.7; MHWN 3.7; MLWN 1.7.
A sardine port, ½M NNE of Beg Morg. The inlet is protected by a mole with a W Lt Ho with R top, Oc(2) WRG 6s, but is not tenable in onshore weather; it dries 1.2m, mud.
Approach From the buoy or S card bn 3½ ca to the NNW, make for the stb side of entrance. A W board on with the Lt Ho on the breakwater leads in on 335°. Round the breakwater into midstream.
Berthing Alongside the quay to port, dries 1.2m.
  Water on quay; shops, cafés in village.

MERRIEN   Charts BA 2352, F 5479
HW +4.50.   MHWS 4.9; MLWS 0.5; MTL 2.7; MHWN 3.7; MLWN 1.7.
The creek dries 0.6–0.9m, soft mud bottom in pool; complete shelter. It is 1½M E of Beg Morg, identifiable by a conspic W bn on the hillside ½M W of the entrance. Beautiful scenery. The port is protected from W by the reef which extends ½M S from the W pt of the entrance, S Card bn, and may be entered when Brigneau and Döelan are not accessible.
Approach Leaving the Pte de Bali 1½ ca to stb, bring the guardhouse, a long low building on the right bank within the creek, in line with the E pt of entrance, W bn con topmark, bearing 005°, when a W Lt Ho (Q) with R top will be seen against the trees on the skyline to the left of the guardhouse. When this Lt Ho is visible one is clear of the outer rks, so keep it open of and in middle of the entrance.
Entrance Hence proceed in midstream till the Lt Ho is abeam and then keep nearer to the port hand quay, R bn, from where the chan leads to the stb quay.
Anchorage A berth afloat at neaps may be found above in a pool abreast the SW end of stb quay.

DOELAN   Charts BA 2352, F 5479
HW +4.50.   MHWS 4.9; MLWS 0.6; MTL 2.7; MHWN 3.8; MLWN 1.7.
A sardine port; dries 1.5m to abreast the quays and 2.4m at the head. The inner quay affords good berth with bollards and flat bottom. Picturesque, good shelter in ordinary weather. In heavy onshore weather Merrien is better, and more easily approached.
Approach Leave the Basse de la Croix, R bn, to port, and steer in on the line of the ldg lts, front W tr G band, Oc(1+2) WG 12s, rear W tr R band, QR, 014°, leaving Le Four G tr to stb and La Vache bn to port.
Entrance Having passed the point bear to port, and keep in midstream to the Quai de la Meyriere, 350m above the lower lt, which dries, bottom mud; or further up the creek.

LORIENT
Depths in Metres
One Mile

0 _____ 1

Yacht Hr

Avant Port de Commerce

HM

YC

Pte de l'Espérance
QWRG 9M

Fl(4)12s7M

N°2

N°13

RN°10

Le Blavet

FlR 2s 6₂ 6₃

2 Lts (Oc (3) G12s 14m 10M
       Oc (3) G12s 12m 11M

QR 28m 15M

RADE DE PEN MANE

Réd

N°3

Pen-Mane

N°11

Pengarne

Bn

QR 16m 12M

Oc (2)R 6s 31m 15M

Ter River

Fl4s 7m

Pte de Kéroman
Oc (2)R.6s 25m 14M

Lts in line 2.17°

NG

Île St Michel

St Catherine

Oc (3)G12s 18m 10M

Fl(3)G12s
Banc du Turk

M5

M4

N°6

N°4

Int

Bn
R 9

Lts 356°

M2 M3

M1

Oc (4)R12s 10m 10M   Kernével

Oc (4)R12s 15m 12M

RADE DE PORT-LOUIS

YBY

Pte de Kerzo

N°1

D2

FlR 4s 5M
Le Cochon

N°1

Bn

La Jument Oc R 4

N°2

Oc G4s 6m
le pain de Sucre

Iso 4s 7m

Citadelle

YC

Q 30m 15M

Roche de Toulhars

BWO

Port Louis

Larmor

Fort de Lacqueltas

Bns

la Potée de Beure

Q 7 m 9M

p.t Belorch

Ile aux Souris
le Cabon

Gd. Belorc'h

BAIE DE LOCMALO

BRB
la Paix

Le Soulard

BRB

Bn

Basse Kaléri

Int Sctor

Lts 060°

la Pesquerez

Ban Gâvres

WORKS IN PROGRESS 1979

3°22'W

21'

460

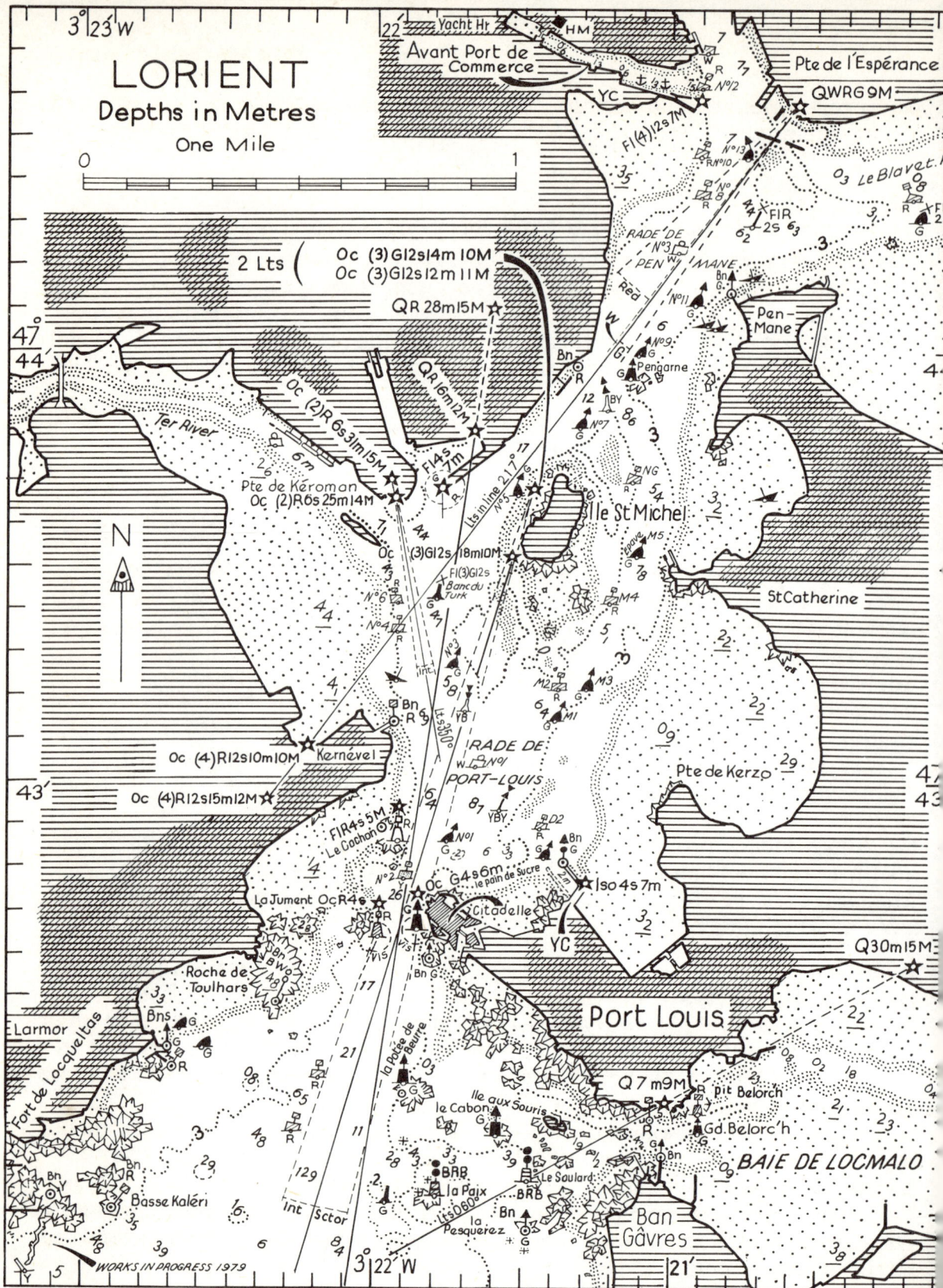

D'après la carte marine française avec l'autorisation du Service Hydrographique et Océanographique de la Mar

Anchorage A berth may be found to lie afloat at ordinary tides in the outer part of the creek, considerable swell in S winds. Outside the hr vessels anch on the ldg line in 6m, bottom sand and rock, just inside breakwater, slightly W of ldg line and just outside sardine boats.

Stores, hotel.

RIVER QUIMPERLE Charts BA 2352, F 5479
HW +4.50. MHWS 5.0; MLWS 0.6; MTL 2.8; MHWN 3.9; MLWN 1.7.
Bar dries 1.8m, and sea breaks heavily in onshore winds. Sandbanks shift every tide. Stream runs at 6kn on ebb, when entrance is impossible. Flood begins 2h after LW. A beautiful river.
Approach Make W pt of entrance, best about an hour before HW.
Entrance Leave Kergoranton Tr (R) close to port, and two bns to port, then sound way into Pouldu.
Anchorage Pouldu, anch in holes. Anch outside with Kergoaranton Tr bearing about 044°. Buses to Quimperlé.

PORT TUDY, ILE DE GROIX Charts BA 2352, F 5912 (Plan p457)
HW +4.50. MHWS 5.0; MLWS 0.6; MTL 2.8; MHWN 3.9; MLWN 1.7.
A small hr affording shelter in 3m, but some swell in NE winds.
Approach Approaching the N side of the Ile de Groix, the W end, with Pen Men W square Lt Ho, Fl(4) 25s, should be given a berth of about 1M. From E keep the semaphore of Beg Melen, Pen Men Pt, open N of the Grognon battery.
At night, beware of large unlit mooring buoys close inshore NW of entrance.
Entrance Nearing the port, bring the spire of St Tudy ch in line with the W end of the N jetty, 220°. This leads between the rks which lie on either side of the approach.
Berthing Steer in between the pier-heads, Lt Ho on each, and proceed to marina in inner hr. Cafés, stores, PO in village.

LORIENT Charts BA 304, F 6470 (Plan p460)
HW +5.10. MHWS 5.0; MLWS 0.8; MTL 2.9; MHWN 3.9; MLWN 2.0.
A major commercial and naval hr with considerable yachting development. The approach is sheltered from the SW by the Ile de Groix.
Approach By the W passage, give the N shore a berth of about 1M, bring the Lohic and Kerbel ldg lts (Q) in line 060½°, and steer so until N of Les Trois Pierres bn tr. For the S passage, leave the two buoys off Les Bastresses 100m to stb, then steer to pass close E of Les Trois Pierres bn tr. From here, steer to pass close W of the Citadel NW of Port Louis (ldg lts 008½°, QR) and take the buoyed chan into the town.
Berthing Anch NE of the citadel and towards the mole of Port Louis in about 3½m; above yacht moorings at Kernevel (recommended); opposite Penmané on W side of chan in 3½m; or off the N end of Penmané, S of the large mooring buoys. Lock (−2.00 to +1.00 HW) into the wet basin in middle of town

(marina). Entrance to port just above R Blavet. There are also marina-type berths outside the lock. All facilities.

ETEL RIVER   Charts BA 2352, F 5560
HW +5.05.   MHWS 5.0; MLWS 0.6; MTL 2.8; MHWN 3.9; MLWN 1.7.
The entrance is midway between Lorient and Belle Ile.
Bar   Variable in depth and position, dries, and may be crossed in quiet weather after half flood with 1.8m draft. Entrance requires great caution, and is best taken 1½ to 1h before HW. It should not be attempted at night nor on the ebb. The flood stream sets across the bar to NE. The streams inside turn 1½h after HW and LW, and attain 4–5kn at springs.
Approach   Keep two water trs in line, 050°, after leaving Rohen Tr to port. Hoist ensign to masthead for directions for crossing the bar from the Fenoux semaphore (mast over shed and W gable end 1 ca W of Lt Ho). Semaphore arm revolved or moved side-to-side indicates acknowledgement; B ball or arm held horizontal – no entry; R flag – wait for more water; arm vertical – proceed; arm tilted – steer in direction of upper end.
Entrance   Leave Chaudronnier Tr ½ ca to port and keep the W bank well aboard to avoid the midriver bank Le Banc du Stang. When nearing Etel town, the chan is in midriver.
Berthing   Anch just S of LB Ho on SW end of quays. Alongside inside of quay 1½ to 2½m, but the dredged part is narrow and the end of the quay must be left for ferries. Anch above town on either side of river but tides are very strong. Do not go much above Vieux Passage. All facilities.

PORTIVI   Chart BA 2353, F 5420
HW +5.00.   MHWS 5.3; MLWS 0.7; MTL 3.0; MHWN 4.1; MLWN 1.9.
A pretty corner in fine weather and moderate winds from W and offshore. On the N end of the W side of Quiberon.
Approach   Bring Carnac spire in line with Pen Goc'h, 052°, and keep it so leaving Men Melein to N and Roch-Vidic-Bras to S, till Portivi mill comes on with end of jetty, 127°, when keep it so, passing S of Guedic (bn) and Keroustaing (bn). Having passed the two bns, turn to port a little to pass N of jetty.
Anchorage   Between Keroustaing bn and Roch-Vidic-Bihan in 1½ to 3m, or at mooring buoy abreast bn. Inside, at the end of the slip, bottom dries 1.2m.

PORT MARIA, QUIBERON   Charts BA 2353, F 5352
HW +5.05.   MHWS 5.1; MLWS 0.7; MTL 2.9; MHWN 3.9; MLWN 1.8.
Artificial hr, sheltered from all winds, at S end of Quiberon Peninsula. Used by many fishing vessels and the ferries to Belle Ile and Houat. Half the hr dries so there is not much room.
Approach   Approach in W sector of main Lt Ho (W tr, Q WRG, 28m), until ldg

PORT HALIGUEN
Depths in Metres

Oc (2)WR 6s12M
FlG2s
FR
FlVi2s
Fl(3)G12s
PORT DE PÊCHE
Cable
0
Reception Pontoon
Périchéren
Red
R Red
YB
8
47° 29.3'
29.1'
15.5'
3° 6'W
3° 6.2'W

LE PALAIS
Depths in Metres
Cables

Môle Bourdelle
FlG (2+1)12s
Oc(2)R6s 11M 11M
Môle Bonnelle
Q. Bonnelle
AVANT PORT
Visitors
Visitors
N
(3)
Citadelle
HM
Customs
Grill
Drying Basin
Quai Leblanc
WET BASIN
20.9
47° 20.8'
3° 9.5'W
3° 9.3'
29
6
23

LA TRINITÉ
Depths in Metres
Cables
N

R DE CRACH
QWRG
Pte de Menhalenn
R Vasière
R Vaneresse
FlRG
FlG
FlG
FIR
Yacht Harbour
Oc(2)WR 6s
La Trinité
Bridge
15QR
4s
Red

Iso 4s 20m 13M
Pte kerneves
IsoWR64s 8m 10M
Lts 347°
W G
R
White
Fl(4)R12s
Pte de Makau
01 Red 4
Pte de Kerbihan
Pte Mare
Oyster Beds
Mouskar
Green
35.4'
35'
47°
3°
3° 1.5W

près la carte marine française avec l'autorisation du Service Hydrographique et Océanographique de la Marine.

463

lts, two BW trs, QG, E of breakwater come into line, 006°, and steer on this.
Entrance   Between S mole, Oc(2) R 6s, and E mole, Iso G 4s.
Anchorage   Anch in 1–2m on S side of hr, but not too near S mole, which has rks
at its base. E mole is reserved for ferries and landward side of hr is rocky.
   Hotel, restaurants, shops, buses. Water at E quay. Rly at Quiberon, ½M.

PORT HALIGUEN, QUIBERON   Charts BA 2353, F 5352   (Plan p463)
HW +5.15.   MHWS 5.2; MLWS 0.6; MTL 2.9; MHWN 3.9; MLWN 1.9.
Pleasant yacht hr with moorings and marina, 3.5m in entrance, to E of old drying
hr and village on E side of Quiberon Peninsula. Sheltered in all but strong NE to
E winds. Complete shelter will be provided by projected breakwater; in
meantime approach and entrance may be altered by construction works.
Approach   No difficulties except in heavy SE-ly weather. From about 1M ESE,
steer approximately 300° on Lt Ho, Oc(2) WR 6s, keeping in W sector. Avoid line
of unlit naval buoys and floats in line NW to SE 6 ca from entrance. Leave S
Card buoy SW of these to stb; RB buoy marks a wreck about ½ ca from entrance.
Entrance   Leave R buoy to port and enter between breakwater heads.
Berthing   Report to pontoon A (Ponton d'Acceuil) at end of W pontoon, or
HM launch in outer hr. All facilities. Met reports daily. No bonded stores.
Customs, shops, hotels, restaurants, buses, rly and flights from Quiberon (1M,
no transport but pleasant walk).

LE PALAIS, BELLE ILE   Charts BA 2353, F 5911   (Plan p463)
HW +5.00.   MHWS 5.1; MLWS 0.7; MTL 2.9; MHWN 3.9; MLWN 1.9.
Entrance has 2m. The inner hr dries. Swell in E winds.
Entrance   Midway between pier-heads, W Lt Hos on pier-heads; S: Oc(2) R 6s;
N: Fl(2+1) G 12s.
Anchorage   Vessels lie to anch with a warp to the wall in 3m. There is a wet
basin approached through the inner hr. Outside anch to E clear of fairway; heavy
sea in NW and SE blows, sheltered from W and SW. Anch between the N jetty at
Le Palais and the approaches to Sauzon is prohibited. Ferry to Quiberon (rly).

SAUZON, BELLE ILE   Charts BA 2353, F 5911
HW +5.00.   MHWS 5.1; MLWS 0.7; MTL 2.9; MHWN 3.9; MLWN 1.9.
Port de Sauzon is entered 3 ca S of Pte du Cardinal, which is 1½M SE of Pte des
Poulains. Steer in, 224°, on the 9m W circular Lt Tr (Oc(3+1) 12s). At night,
enter in W sector.
   Anch inside N part of outer hr, sheltered by breakwaters except from strong
E-lies. Inner hr entrance has 1.8m at half-tide. Best berth inside, which dries, is
inside the outer quay to port on entering, bottom flat sand; clean.

LA TRINITE, CRAC'H RIVER   Charts BA 2353, 2358; F 5352   (Plan p463)
HW +5.15.   MHWS 5.3; MLWS 0.6; MTL 3.0; MHWN 4.1; MLWN 2.0.
The river provides good shelter off La Trinité in 2–2½m.

Approach   Carnac ch spire and nearby water tr are conspic. Keep the road bridge on about 344° until the outer buoy is reached. At night, ldg lts rear Iso 4s, front Iso WRG 4s, 347°.

Entrance   From the outer buoy the entrance is well buoyed and lit by Dir Q WRG, and then Oc(2) WR 6s lt at La Trinité; keep in W sectors. Oyster beds are marked with perches.

Berthing   Moor behind slatted jetty and report to marina office. Marina depth up to 3m. All facilities.

THE MORBIHAN (INLAND SEA)

Charts BA 2358, 2359; F 3165, 5554   (Plan p466)

HW (Pt Navalo) +5.20.   MHWS 4.9; MLWS 0.5; MTL 2.7; MHWN 3.7; MLWN 1.7.

Off Pte de Port Navalo, the flood stream runs N at +0.30 and the ebb S at +6.00, spring rate for both 7½kn. In Auray R, the flood stream begins at HWD, the ebb at +5.30; both attain about 3kn at springs.

HW (Ile aux Moines) +6.00. The flood stream starts 1¾h after LW, and the ebb 1½h after HW.

Approach   The E pt of the entrance to the Morbihan may be identified by the tall W tr of the Navalo Lt Ho, Oc(3) WRG 12s. From S keep Crac'h steeple in line with the E end of Méaban Is, 335°, to clear the Plateau du Grand Mont. From W steer 055° for the Butte de Thumiac, a mound-shaped hill 30m high, about one-third of the way between Navalo and Grand Mont, semaphore. Bring Bàdene spire (conspic on a hilltop N of entrance) just open W of Pt Navalo and in line with Petit Veisit, 001°, W wall, which shows low near the waterline W of Navalo. Continue so, 6½m least water, rounding Navalo Pt a reasonable distance off. Between Méaban and Petit Mont, more water will be found to E of this transit.

Entrance   Slack water may be awaited in the bay SE of Petit Mont. Entering on the flood, the W side should be kept aboard till well within the river, as the stream sets strongly on to the Grand Mouton, G bn. Past Navalo Pt at slack water, bring the tr of Le Grégan on with middle of Ile Radenec, 011°, and leave the Lieu buoy Fl 2s on this transit well to port.

Anchorages   *Note:* other than Port du Crouesty or Port Navalo, the BA or Fr large-scale chart must be carried if visiting the Morbihan anchorages.

Port du Crouesty (plan p450)   Large and useful marina in the next inlet to the SE. From the W after rounding Méaban, the entry is just to the N of Petit Mont. From the S the Marina Lt Ho (W tr) is clearly visible over the beach S of Petit Mont. Entrance and chan into the hr (minimum depth 4m) is marked by G and R buoys. Pass between the breakwaters and watch for G and R bns marking ends of obstacles. Continue past fuel pontoon to stb and crane, to pontoon marked 'Visiteurs'. All facilities, stores at Arzon.

Port Navalo (plan p450)   Some moorings and space to anch in the bay out of the

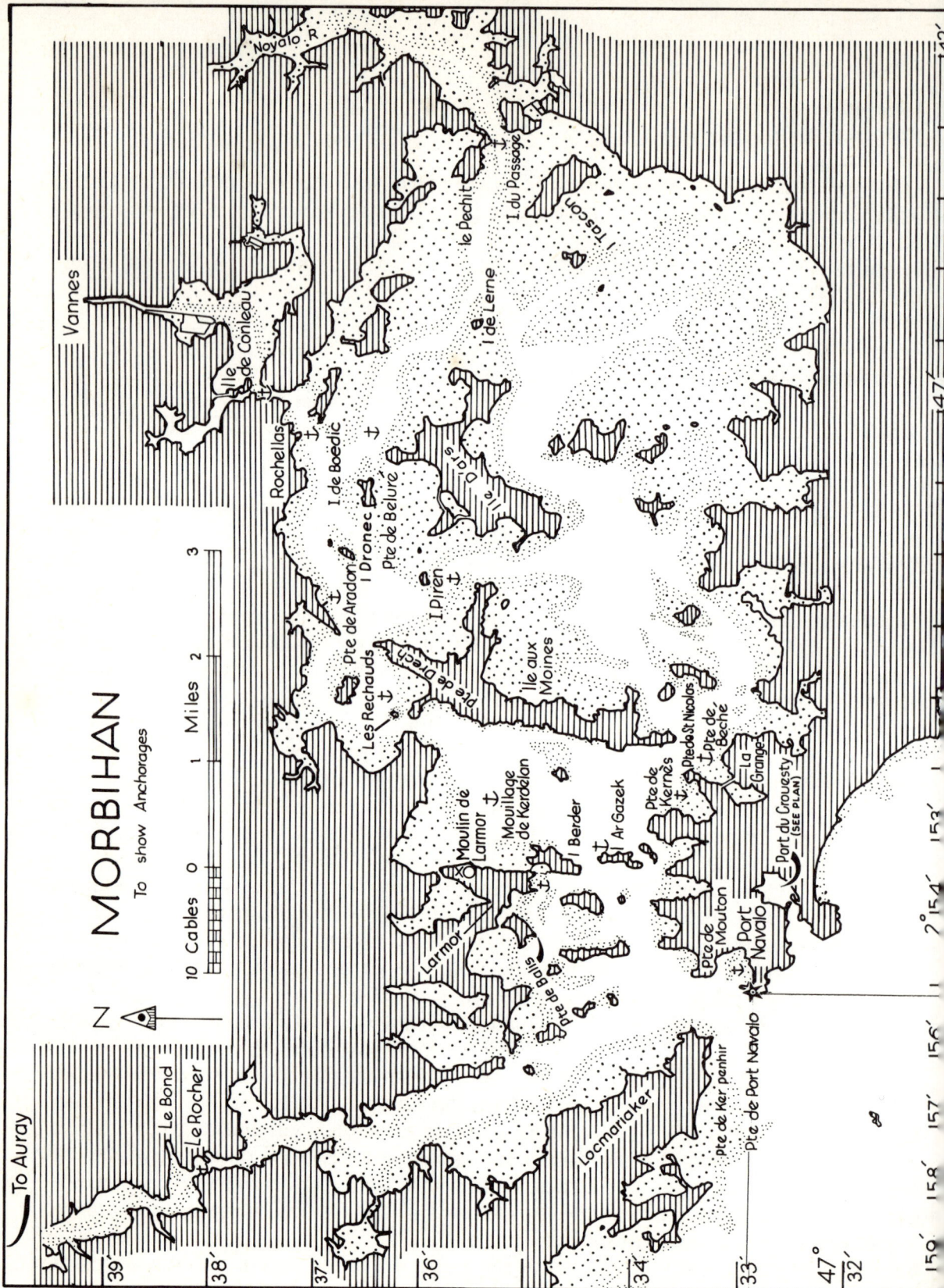

MORBIHAN

To show Anchorages

N

10 Cables 0   1 Miles 2   3

To Auray

Le Bond

Le Rocher

Larmor

Pte de Kar penhir

Pte de Port Navalo

Locmariaker

Moulin de Larmor

Mouillage de Kerdalon

Pte de Bois

Pte de Mouton

Port Navalo

I Berder

Ar Gazek

Pte de Kernès

Pte St Nicolas

Pte de Boche

La Grange

Port du Crouesty (SEE PLAN)

Ile aux Moines

I Piren

Pte de Drech

Les Rechauds

Pte de Aradon

I Dronec

I de Boedic

Pte de Belure

Rochellas

Ile de Conleau

Vannes

Noyalo R

Ile de Lerne

I de Lerne

le Pechit

I du Passage

Tascon

39'

38'

37'

36'

34'

33'

47° 32'

2° 15.4'

153'

156'

157'

158'

159'

10'

147'

D'après la carte marine française avec l'autorisation du Service Hydrographique et Océanographique de la Mar

tide. All facilities, but the port is exposed to W and NW winds which can raise a very steep sea quickly.

River Auray   HW(Auray) +5.45. MHWS 5.2; MLWS 0.7; MTL 2.9; MHWN 4.0; MLWN 1.9. The R Auray runs into the W end of the Morbihan. Bring Pte Espagnol open of Pte du Bler, 335°, and pass E of Le Grand Harnic and a R bn. Past Pte du Bler keep the spire of Arzon on with the Château of Ile Renaud astern, 141°. After passing R buoy to port, and the Catis buoy to stb, steer in a gradual curve round the mud on stb hand until heading midway towards the narrows off Pte Espagnol. From Pte Espagnol keep to E side till Anse de Kerdreau opens, when keep W bank well aboard. LW navigation ceases 2M below Auray above which the chan is well marked.

Anchorage   Secure anch at Le Rocher, 6M up the river, 2M below Auray, 2–5m. Café and shops at Le Bono, ½M by dinghy. At Auray, 3.6m in centre of river opposite low quay at St Goustan, which dries alongside. All facilities. Fast trains to Quimper for flights to UK.

Larmor   SE of Pte de Balis close to village of Larmor. Anch in 2–4½m; perfect shelter from wind and tide, but bottom foul in places.

Kerdelan Roads   NE of Ile Berder, 3½ to 5½m.

Ile aux Moines (off N end)   Perhaps the best anch in the Morbihan, in 3 to 6m, halfway between Les Réchauds and Pte de Drech, with Le Petit Logoden just hidden behind Pte de Drech; or to N of W buoy near Les Réchauds. Landing at Pte de Drech or Pte des Réchauds, handy for Le Bourg. Good holding, sand and mud, close to but out of tideway. Or at Port Blanc, opposite, to NW, good anch but no facilities. Restaurant on Ile aux Moines.

Ile Piren   To S of Is in 3 to 6m, but tidal stream cannot be avoided. Landing Ile aux Moines at Pte de Brouhel within easy reach of Le Bourg.

Aradon   Opposite the mainland village ½M NE of Pte d'Aradon.

Ile de Boedic opposite Rochellas, also nearer Penbock.

N of Ile d'Ars   NE of Pte de Beluré in 2m with E side of Ile Lerne on with W side of Ile Tascon, and Roche d'Aradon on with N pt of Dronec. Landing at Pte de Beluré.

Conleau   In the bight on W side of chan just S of Conleau.

Vannes   HW −5.05. MHWS 4.6; MLWS 1.2; MTL 2.9; MHWN 3.9; MLWN 2.1. Proceeding to Vannes, care is required rounding the Réchauds where the stream is fierce: keep in the W centre of the running stream and avoid the eddy streams; see chart F 3165 or BA 2358. LW navigation ceases above Conleau. Vannes, 10M above Navalo, can be reached by vessels of 3m draft at springs, 2.5m at neaps. Lock gates open 2h either side of HW, into town basin now a marina. All facilities. Water by hose at ferry quay to port.

Noyalo River   Good anch in Anse de Trucattee and between Le Passage and Le Pechit Is.

La Grange   In 1.8m with mill of Larmor twice its width open of Pte de Nicholas, 1 ca, or more N of Pte de Beché. The overhead cable to Ile aux Moines is at height of 21.6m.

Kernés   E of Pte de Kernés off the Anse in 3 to 6m with S end of Ile Berder on with Pte de Kernés and its NE end on with mill of Larmor.
Ar Gazek (Ile de Jument)   ½ ca E of the Is in 3 to 6m. Perfect shelter.

ILE DE HOËDIC   Charts BA 2353; F 135, 5482
HW +5.10.   MHWS 5.1; MLWS 0.5; MTL 2.8; MHWN 3.9; MLWN 1.9.
The W of the N coast of Hoëdic is a prohibited area. Enter between the two moles which enclose a delightful sandy bay available at all states of the tide. Turn to stb and anch in 2–4m. Water from pump. Only a small village ashore.

ILE DE HOUAT   Charts BA 2353, F 135
HW +5.05.   MHWS 5.2; MLWS 0.6; MTL 2.9; MHWN 4.0; MLWN 1.8.
Towards the E end of N coast of the Is, La Vieille rk is very conspic and the hr is ¾M from it bearing 200°. Approach from either side of La Vieille, a good transit from W being breakwater Lt Ho in line with ch. Turn sharply around end of breakwater, leaving it 20m to stb, and anch in fairway, taking stern lines to breakwater. Keep the stern about 6m off breakwater which protrudes under water and avoid a rocky patch between third and fourth vertical ladder from end of breakwater. Once clear of the shallow 0.9m patch near outer end, there is 1.8 to 2.4m most of the way along. Good shelter. Pier-head lt Iso WG 4s. Two small shops, hotel.

PENERF   Charts BA 2353, F 5418
HW +5.10.   MHWS 5.4; MLWS 0.6; MTL 3.0; MHWN 4.1; MLWN 1.9.
The river enters Quiberon Bay 3M W of Vilaine R.
Approach   Between R buoy off Pte de Penvins to W and Borenis G con buoy to E. The conspic W Tour de Penerf will be seen to NE.
Entrance   There are three passes. (1) E pass, marked but narrow and winding, has 1.8 to 3.6m. (2) Central pass, La Traverse, has 0.3m and is not safe with any swell. (3) W pass has 4.5m, narrow and poorly marked with a bar inside (dries).
   E pass: from 2 ca W of Borenis buoy steer 352° 6 ca for the R La Traverse Bn (opposite Viodec rk); the G La Traverse Bn is 1 ca further W. Continue NW and N leaving the Pignon Tr and Men Drean Bn (R) to port, and the G Bayonelle beacon and two other bns to stb, whence round in, 066°, past a G bn and the R bn on the rk du Chenal for the Penerf Quay, bn with triangle.
   Central pass: at sufficient rise leave G bn on La Traverse to stb and join E pass at Pignon Lt Tr.
   W pass: not before half-tide, pass close E of l'Artimon, leave two G bns to stb, and curve eastward onto 066°, to Penerf Quay.
Anchorage   Outside in 7m between the buoys. Inside near the quay, 3½m, mud, clear of oyster beds. Small hotel.

LA VILAINE
Charts BA 2353, F 5482

HW +5.10.   MHWS 5.5; MLWS 0.8; MTL 3.2; MHWN 4.4; MLWN 2.0.
The river is 135M long, and is dammed at Arzal where one can lock into a tideless lake as far as Redon. Entry to the Brittany canal system can be made at Bellions Lock, shortly below Redon. The bar has 0.9m.

Approach   Good visibility essential. In strong onshore winds it is best to approach by the Varlingue passage, 2m, with the mill of Avalac, the Prières Tr and the W wall of Port des Barques (E of Penlan Pt) in line 023° (the latter two marks are difficult to pick out from seaward). When Basse Kervoyal Tr comes on with the mill of Bile ($4\frac{1}{2}$M E of Penerf) 273°, steer with it so astern, till the Tréhiguier lts come in line, 112°. Then steer on them leaving Petit Sécé Tr to stb. From W, Penlan lt open S of the Prières Tr 052°, leads towards entrance in 1.5m, whence proceed as above.

At night, keep in the W sector of Penlan lt until R Tréhiguier lt bears 106°, then steer 090° until on the transit of the Tréhiguier lts: front Oc(4) 12s, rear Oc(4) R 12s. Then continue with them in line.

Anchorage   Off Tréhiguier in soft mud, exposed to W and NW. At Vieille Roche, just below the dam, outside the moorings on S bank, complete shelter. Lock into river. Lock opens on request irrespective of tide 0630–1930, except public holidays. There is a pleasant berth up at St Antoine Quay, La Roche Bernard. Good buoys in river and pontoons for small yachts. Laundry and showers at camp site. Deep water to Pont Tournant de Cran and marina at Redon. Canal connections with Nantes and St Malo.

LE CROISIC
Charts BA 3216 F 139   (Plan p473)

HW +5.05.   MHWS 5.6; MLWS 0.9; MTL 3.2; MHWN 4.2; MLWN 2.0.
A popular holiday resort and fishing hr which dries but has good though crowded anchs off it in the pool. Yacht hr in Chambre Hervé Rielle (see below). The entrance chan is dredged to 1.2m but the tides are strong, exceeding 4kn at springs, when entry should be made 1h before HW. At neaps entry possible at any time. There is a gauge (difficult to read) at the head of Tréhic jetty indicating depth of water at quayside.

Approach   The port may be located by its position S of La Turballe and by the XVth century walled town of Guérande, with its spire, on the heights 3M behind, and by the ch trs of Le Croisic and Batz, 46m and 55m respectively. Keep Le Croisic ch bearing 157° until it is possible to identify the ldg marks: W pylons, front with BW cheq topmark, rear with rectangular board dark G and W chevrons, both Oc(1+2) 12s. Keep these in transit on 156° until the elbow in Tréhic jetty.

Entrance   Turn a little to stb on to second ldg marks, GW, QG. Keep these in transit 174° until the final ldg marks come into line, RW tanks with RW cheq openwork topmarks, both Oc R 4s. Steer on this transit, 131°, until well past the first front ldg mark and leave quays about 50m to stb.

At sufficient rise of tide to clear rks which dry, the second transit can be disregarded provided the R tr, Oc(2) R, on Grand Mabon rk is left to port.
Anchorage The pool has 1.5m and a 2.1m hole, and good shelter, with end of Penbron jetty on with E middle of the Hospital and the signal mast on with the quay, but streams are strong and holding only fair, sand. Best berth is under Penbron jetty in about 2–3m on E edge of the Penbron chan, where the stream is not so strong, 3kn; sound carefully, and do not go too far up. Alongside the Croisic quays are drying-out berths, about 1.2m above datum, called *chambres*; these are formed and protected by islets called *jonchères*. Enter beyond Gde Jonchères (the second). Visitors berth in the last (fifth) one, Chambre Hervé Rielle. Great care is required in approaching the quay if the stream is running. The fishing boats ground at the entrance to the *chambres* on the flood and haul in as the tide rises.

All facilities. Rly.

Outside anchorage: N of transit of W seamark on shore and Trévaly mill, 058°, and on line of ldg lts.

LE POULIGUEN Charts BA 3216, F 4902
HW +5.00.   MHWS 5.3; MLWS 0.5; MTL 2.9; MHWN 4.0; MLWN 1.8.
The hr is exposed to the SE and a S-ly swell breaks in the shallow water. The 1M chan leading to the port dries 1.5m. While 1.2m draft can enter at half-tide, yachts drawing 1.8m should enter just before HW and only when swell is absent.
Approach Make the R Penchâteau buoy, Oc R, ½M SE of Pte de Penchâteau (the W-ly pt of the bay), and 6M E of Le Croisic. Thence steer N to leave the R Basse Martineau buoy to port. A cable NW of this buoy there is anch in 2½–3m.
Entrance From Basse Martineau leave R bns to port and G to stb. Then enter with the ch spire open between the pier-heads (lt on S pier-head QR), keeping a little to the W of the middle to avoid a high bank of sand on E side. It is not advisable to enter at night.
Anchorage Apply to YC boatman, who acts as HM, mooring alongside stb quay to enquire for berth. The Le Pouliguen (W) side either dries or is very shallow. Bottom hard sand. Yacht yards, marine engineers, shops. Trains, bus from La Baule to St Malo, airport.

PORNICHET–LA BAULE Charts BA 3216, F 4902
HW +5.00.   MHWS 5.3; MLWS 0.5; MTL 2.9; MHWN 4.0; MLWN 1.8.
This large new artificial harbour 4M E of Le Pouliguen is available for drafts up to 4½m at all states of the tide in any conditions. The entrance is absolutely straightforward, having been built out beyond all inshore hazards. 1100 berths. Fuel and all marina facilities.

ENTRANCE TO RIVER LOIRE, ST NAZAIRE
Charts BA 3216; F 5456, 4882
HW +5.25.   MHWS 5.4; MLWS 0.5; MTL 2.9; MHWN 4.0; MLWN 1.6.

Bar   4.8m: in strong W winds should only be approached during second half of the flood. The approach is divided into two chans by La Banche bank.

Approach   From NW bring Le Four lt, 293° astern, and pass about a mile S of Gd Charpentier lt, Q WRG. Then with the three ldg lts QR in line, steer 025° for the bar. From SW, having left the Pilier Lt Ho a good berth to SE bring the ldg lts in line 025°.

At night, do not enter the R sector of La Banche lt till past the G sector of **Gd Charpentier**. The topmost ldg lt is Kerlédé, which shows through the trees on the hilltop, next the high Portcé lt, a rectangular building with gable at the edge of the cliff, and the low lt is close to it at the foot of the cliff, its lt being visible only on a narrow sector close to the ldg line.

Entrance   The entrance hugs the NW shore. Having passed between three pairs of lt buoys, keeping on the ldg line, Aiguillon lt is left to port. Carry on 025° till within 2 ca of Trébézy buoy, then steer 048°, leaving the Trébézy buoy to port and a G buoy to stb. Having left the latter about 80m astern, steer 095° towards Les Morées Tr for 5 ca. Thence 064° past the buoy off Villéz-Martin Pt, bearing 070°. Good temporary anch at Bonne Anse between La Rougeole and the Lt Ho in about 3m. No stream, but 2M from St Nazaire.

Berthing   The docks are not available to yachts, but a short stop is generally allowed alongside the E Péreire quay (NE corner of St Nazaire basin), entering by the E (old) lock, which opens as demanded by traffic. The outer hr, Penhoet basin and the main S lock and the drydock are reserved exclusively for large commercial vessels. A good anch, somewhat out of the stream, is midway between No. 16 (Chantier) buoy and Roche de Penhoet bn tr in 4m, opposite the Chantiers Atlantique.

The passage from St Nazaire to Nantes, 30M, can easily be completed on the flood tide. There is a ship canal between Ile Carnet and La Martinière 9M upriver, and a canal runs from Nantes N and W, affording connection with the Vilaine and St Malo through Redon, and with Lorient by the Blavet at Pontivy.

At Nantes there is a quiet and sheltered anch in 5½m in the Bras de Pirmil just below rly br at Houte Ile. From Trentemoult along the S bank of Bras de Pirmil there are moorings and a yacht yard. A more convenient mooring for the city of Nantes is on the N bank of the N arm of the river, where there is a visitors' pontoon. All facilities at St Nazaire and Nantes.

PORNIC   Charts BA 3216, F 5039   (Plan p473)
HW +4.55.   MHWS 5.3; MLWS 0.7; MTL 2.9; MHWN 4.1; MLWN 1.6.
The old port dries 1.8m, sand and mud. The N side is rocky and there is a breakwater off Goumalon Pt, which covers at HW. The end is marked by a bn.

Anch offshore in fine weather in 3½m W or SE of Noveillard jetty. The extended breakwater off Noveillard encloses a large modern marina. Least depth 2m: up to 3m. Access from SE: safe under most conditions, little swell inside. Chan marked by port hand buoy and perch, and R and G Fl lts on piles either side of entrance. Visitors' pontoon is the nearest to the entrance. Full marina facilities. Customs.

BOIS DE LA CHAISE, NOIRMOUTIER   Charts BA 2547, F 5039
HW +5.05.   MHWS 5.3; MLWS 0.4; MTL 2.8; MHWN 3.9; MLWN 1.6.
Small craft anch in 3m, mud, with Pte des Charniers open to S of Le Cobe rk and with Fort St Pierre bearing 187°; sheltered from a NW blow but a good deal of swell comes round the pt. The hr of Noirmoutier dries 1.8 to 2.4m. The chan is marked by bns; there is a lt Gp Occ at the jetty head.

L'HERBAUDIERE, NOIRMOUTIER   Charts BA 2647, F 5039   (Plan p473)
HW +5.05.   MHWS 5.3; MLWS 0.4; MTL 2.8; MHWN 3.9; MLWN 1.6.
An excellent passage hr with well sheltered modern marina, depth 2–3m. Approach and entrance least depth 1m marked by R and G buoys and bns. Keep E end of breakwater in line with L'Herbaudiere ch clock tr (if not obscured by trees). Reporting point at first pontoon to port. Water and power at berths; fuel, showers, chandlery, caretaking. Shops, PO in village. First three nights free for foreigners.

PORT JOINVILLE (or BRETON) ILE D'YEU
                              Charts BA 2647, F 6613   (Plan p474)
HW +5.05.   MHWS 5.2; MLWS 0.7; MTL 2.9; MLWN 4.0; MLWN 1.9.
The hr, which dries, is exposed to NW, N and NE, and winds from these directions bring in a heavy swell. The high water tr just W of the town is more conspic than the Lt Ho. The marina has 2.5m.
Approach   Ch bearing 202° lined up with W Lt Tr (G top) on NW jetty head, Oc(3) WG 12s, or at night there are ldg lts QG, 202½°, W trs with G tops.
Entrance   Keep on these ldg marks, 0.9m, until it is necessary to turn to port halfway between first lt tr and E quay to enter main hr.
Anchorage   Outside in Anse de Ker Chalon, 3½m, 6 ca SE of entrance, or in marina in E hr, 2.5m, well sheltered. W inner hr is reserved for ferries and fishing boats. Anch in outer hr forbidden except to wait for tide. All facilities. Ferries to mainland (Fromentine).

ST GILLES SUR VIE   Charts B 2647, F 6613
HW +5.05.   MHWS 5.2; MLWS 0.7; MTL 3.0; MHWS 4.1; MLWN 2.0.
A small tidal hr which may be located by the two spires of La Croix and St Gilles, the high Lt Ho at Croix de Vie, and the low rock headland of Gross Terre off which lie the Pilours, a conspic rk marked by a S Card lt buoy. Swell breaks heavily in the entrance. Ebb runs 6kn springs, 4kn neaps. Channel dredged to 1.5m. Enter after half flood except in fine weather. Swell can be dangerous. Sheltered outside between N and E.
Approach   Give the Pilours, off Pte de Grosse Terre, a good berth.

LE CROISIC

Depths in Metres

Ldg Lts 156°

Green

Green white 1·3

WG4s16M *Le Trehic*

Les Medecins (0₃)

Les Picresses (2)

Jetée du Trehic

174°

131°

Oc(2)R6s

R R

Chy

QG
QG

GpOcc(2+1)12s 10m 10M
GpOcc(2+1)12s 14m 12M

Oc R4s
Oc R4s

0   Cables   5

2°31·5'   31'

Yacht Hr
(Visitors)

PORNIC

Depths in Metres

2°7'w   6·5'

47°7'

N

0   Cables   2

La Noëveillard

Oc(3+1) WRG12s 22m 14M

HM

Ch'enal

Fl(2)G6s

Bn
G

Pte de
La Noëveillord

Fl(2G)2s
Fl R5s

Fl(2+1) 7s

Pte Gourmalon

Green

47°18'

2°7'w   6·5'

L'HERBAUDIÈRE

Depths in Metres

0   Cables   5

Green

3·5   3·5   W   3·5

3₂

3·5

Green

3   2   Fl G

G l 3

0₆   Fl G

Fl(2)R5s

Bn

Bn
G ll   R
R

Oc (2+1)WG12s
7m 10M
(Fog Sig)

Fl(2)R6s

0·5m 1m

Yacht
Hr

l'Herbaudière 1·5'

2°18W   17·5'

StMARTIN DE RÉ

Depths in Metres

1°22'W

N

0   Cable   1

46°12·7'

46°12·6'

Le Chenal

IsoG4s10m7M

Oc (2)WR6s
18m13M

Red

HM   YC

(4m) WET BASIN
Pontoons
G lll

21·7'

47°2'

---

après la carte marine française avec l'autorisation du Service Hydrographique et Océanographique de la Marine.

D'après la carte marine française avec l'autorisation du Service Hydrographique et Océanographique de la Mari

PORT JOINVILLE

Depths in Metres

Green W G

La Galiota

MARINA
Jetée de l'Est
Rocher du Port
R Bn

WHARF QG

Lts 202°

White

Pte de Bouet

Oc (3) WG 12s 6m 9M

Chy

QG

N

2° 20·5'W
20·5'W

46° 44'

46° 43·7'

2° 21'

LES SABLES-D'OLONNE

Depths in Metres

Cables

N

HM

WET BASIN

Customs

Water Tr

La Chaume

Oc (2+1) 12s 33m 13M

FR FR

Fl (2+1) 42m 17M

Fort St-Nicholas

Le Bois Marine

La Baleine

L'Armandèche

Oc R 2·5s 33m 9M

Oc R 2·5s 11m 9M

Oc R 2·5s 11m 9M

L'Estacada

Jetée des Cables

PETITE RADE

QG 11m 11M

BRB

Lts 327°

Lts 320°

Fl (2) R 1s 10m 10M

LE NOURA

Obscd

46° 30'

46° 29·9'

1° 47'

1° 48'W

PORT BLOC

Depths in Metres

Cables

N

Pte de Grave
BnY

Phare de Grave

Fl G 4s 8m 5M

Iso R 4s 8m 8M

Oc W/R 6s 49m 14M/11M

Port Bloc

Fort

Red

1° 3'W

45° 34·5'

45° 34'

ROYAN

Depths in Metres

Cable

N

YC

Customs

HM

Fl G 2s

Oc (2) R 6s 8m 7M

Fl (2) R 1s 11m 11M

Conche de Foncillon

1° 1'W

1·5'

45° 37·5'

45° 37'

Entrance At sufficient rise pass between the pier-heads, with lts (Oc(1+3) R 12s) in line, 041°, and continue so till beyond the Gd Mole. At N end of the Garenne jetty steer to pass between the buoys off Croix-de-Vie; then the chan bears 132° for 3½ ca to the R buoy marking the Bank de l'Adon. Bear to port to St Gilles. Flood sets hard on to Mole de L'Adon and ebb on to La Rotonde.

Berthing Moor at new marina on Adon Bank (1.5m). Access near HW, sheltered, or alongside quays (0 to ½m) outside Adon hr, or at quay (dries ½m) to stb at St Gilles sur Vie just below the bridge, where the streams are not so strong. Anch in the chan is prohibited and Adon hr is reserved for fishing vessels. All facilities at Croix-de-Vie. Rly.

LES SABLES D'OLONNE   Charts BA 2648, F 6551   (Plan p474)
HW +5.15.   MHWS 5.2; MLWS 0.7; MTL 3.0; MHWN 4.1; MLWN 2.0.
An important fishing port and popular holiday resort. The hr has 1.5m throughout.

Approach In strong SE, S or SW winds, especially when there is a swell, the shoals make the approaches rough. In bad weather the SE approach is safer. Keep the GW tr on the hd of Jetee des Sables (QG) in line with grey square Tour de la Chaume with W turret top (Oc(1+2) 12s) until W jetty hd is abeam to port, when bear to port.

Entrance Bring the two inner bns, FR, near La Chaume Lt Ho in line and steer on them, 327°, until well inside the jetties and then keep to stb.

Anchorage The wet basin is limited to commercial traffic. New yacht hr (beyond main hr) in Bassin Des Chasses available all states of tide. Safe but inconvenient for town and expensive. Water and power. All facilities. Rly.

ST MARTIN, ILE DE RÉ   Charts BA 2641, F 6668   (Plan p473)
HW +4.50.   MHWS 6.2; MLWS 0.6; MTL 3.4; MHWN 4.6; MLWN 2.2.
DS: in Pertuis Breton the flood or ESE stream begins about 6h before HW Pte de Graves; the ebb stream begins at or shortly after HW there. (HW Pte de Grave approx +5.25 HWD.) A battlemented fortress port, most picturesque, with wet dock 3m. Approach and entrance dry 1.5m about 1 ca from mole head.

Approach From NW to clear Rocha bank and leave it to W, leave lt buoy to S and W, and bring ch and Lt Ho of St Martin in line 210°. From SE give St Martin shore a berth of 1M, pass well N of Le Couranneau N Card buoy and bring mole head to bear 213°, rounding it at 5 or 6m.

Entrance Proceed in mid-chan between bastions. When the hr opens out the cut to the lock will be seen to stb. Tie up in the cut to await locking. Inside the dock, 3m, proceed to port, and tie up alongside the low wall in the W corner of the basin. The lock opens approx 1h either side of HW. A blackboard by the gates shows times of opening of bridge on each tide. Lock cut dries. Pontoons inside, usually very crowded.

Anchorage The outside anch in the Little Road is well sheltered from S and SW, 2 to 4m, with Le Fier upper lt on the Pte du Loix, 274°, and St Marie and La

Flotte chs in line, 163°. The outer hr dries. There is a grid between a pair of petrol pumps and the causeway linking the Is with the town. Steamer to La Rochelle.

LA FLOTTE, ILE DE RÉ   Charts BA 2641, F 6668

HW +4.50.   MHWS 6.2; MLWS 0.6; MTL 3.4; MHWN 4.6; MLWN 2.2.
The basin dries, mud. Good anch offshore sheltered from S to SW wind, 1.8 to 3m. Bring La Flotte and Chassiron lts in line, 204°, and Baleines lt open of St Martin lt, 282°.
Approach   Keep La Flotte Lt Ho 215°. If approaching from E leave bn off Pte de Barres at least 1 ca to port until Lt Ho bears 215°.
Entrance   Leave R can buoy to port and steer straight for centre of narrow entrance between jetties.
Berthing   Moor alongside jetty (dries 2.1m) immediately to stb on entering inner hr. Provisions, hotels, fuel in town. Water from tap on E quay near YC.

FIERS D'ARS, ILE DE RÉ   Charts BA 2641, F 6521

HW +4.50.   MHWS 6.2; MLWS 0.6; MTL 3.4; MHWN 4.6; MLWN 2.2.
A very agreeable summer anch, with strong tides.
Approach   After half-tide, on transit of two Lt Hos on Pte du Fier in line 265°. The Lt Hos are not conspic, but appear in a nick in the trees: rear, G turret on a pink house; front, a square board on a pylon, which can be moved as and when the chan shifts. Be careful not to confuse with Les Baleines Lt Ho. Approaching on the transit, a stb buoy marks the end of the Banc du Bucheron.

½M further in the chan shoals and dries 0.6m, then deepens again to a hole about ¼M long with up to 3m. This is the outer anch, exposed to N and E but sheltered from S and W. In another ½M on the transit, just before the Roche Eveillon bn (port), Ars en Re ch spire will be seen bearing 231° and open of L'Abbesse bn. A conspic chimney bears 232° of the bn. Following this alignment, leave the bn 1 ca to port over a rock bottom, dries 1.5m, running parallel to the Pte du Fier shore, at the inshore end of which there is a landing slip. The second deep pool of the main anch begins here, with 1.8m. After leaving L'Abbesse bn close to port, the chan is buoyed until the hr entrance, dries 3m.
Berthing   Outer or inner anchs as above, latter exposed to NE at HW. Hr has quays both sides, being shallower in centre, but is crowded. Water, restaurant and yard at hr; shops ½M.

LA PALLICE   Charts BA 2746, F 6468

HW +5.10.   MHWS 6.2; MLWS 0.9; MTL 3.6; MHWN 4.8; MLWN 2.5.
La Pallice is now entirely commercial and unsuitable for yachts. The outer hr has 4.8m and gives access to the wet dock, which may be entered by small craft ½h before HW, or at other times by permission when a large vessel is entering.
Approach   The hr is opposite the SE end of the Ile de Re, 1½M, 022°, from Lavardin Lt Ho.

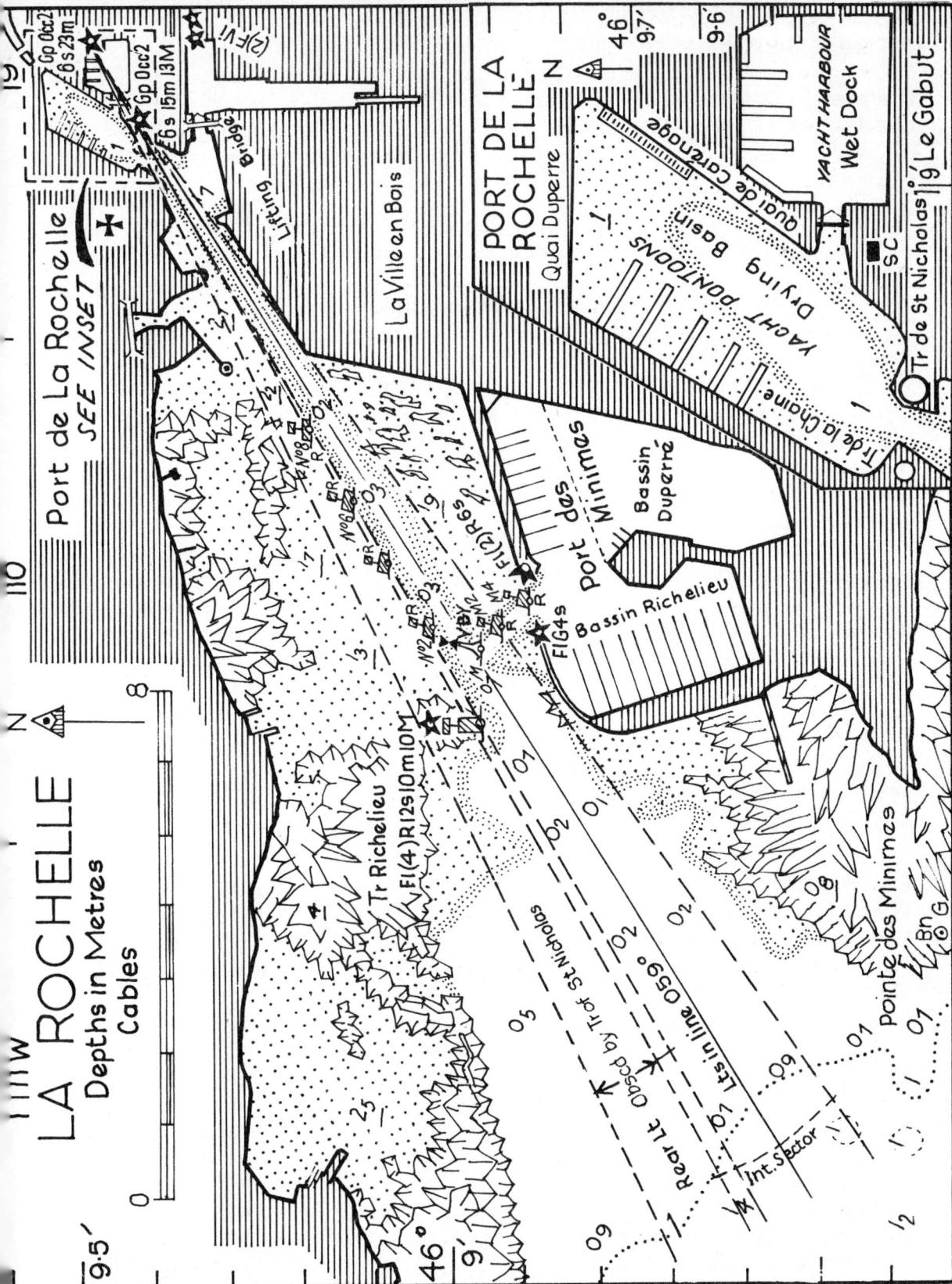

LA ROCHELLE

Depths in Metres
Cables

Port de La Rochelle
SEE INSET

Port de La Rochelle

PORT DE LA ROCHELLE

Gp Occ2
6s 23m

Gp Occ2
6s 15m 13M

(2)F.V!

La Ville en Bois

Lifting Bridge

Quai Duperre

Quai de Carénage

YACHT HARBOUR
Wet Dock

YACHT PONTOONS

Drying Basin

Tr de St Nicholas 19 Le Gabut

SC

Tr de la Chaîne

Port Minimes

Bassin Duperré

Bassin Richelieu

Fl G 4s

Tr Richelieu

Fl(4)R12s10m10M

Pointe des Minimes

Bn
(Q)G

Rear Lt Q50cp Tr of St Nicholas

Int Sector

Ldg line 059° Tr of St Nicholas

Front Lt Q50cp

après la carte marine française avec l'autorisation du Service Hydrographique et Océanographique de la Marine.

Entrance   Between the pier-heads.
Anchorage   In NE part of outer hr.
   Application to leave the dock must be made before 6 p.m.

LA ROCHELLE   Charts BA 2746, 2641, 2648; F 6468   (Plan p477)
HW +5.10.   MHWS 6.2; MLWS 0.9; MTL 3.6; MHWN 4.8; MLWN 2.5.
There is 0.3m in chan to the main hr; the outer hr dries and the basin has 3m.
Chan to Port des Minimes marina has 1m; 2m inside.
Approach   From a position 1M S of Le Levardin Tr steer 059°; from off Pte de
Chef de Baie continue on ldg lts, RW tr front, W rear, Oc(2) 6s, 059°. E of Tr
Richelieu (Fl(4) R 12s) the chan is narrow. Rocky flats dry to N, mud banks to S.
Anch to await tide just S of Pte de Chef de Baie. See (3) below for approach to
Port des Minimes marina.
Entrance   Between the old trs, St Nicholas and de la Chaine.
Berthing   (1) Visitors' pontoons (1.2m) on N side of outer (tidal) hr. (2) Lock in
(HW −1½ to +1½) to wet basin on E side. Footbridge opened as required and
berths allocated by bridge keeper. While waiting for lock, moor temporarily
between dock entrance and Tour St Nicholas, alongside fishing boats if necessary. (3) In new Marina, at Port des Minimes on stb hand immediately after
passing Tr Richelieu, with 1m least depth in chan and 2m inside. Entrance chan
on 133° is 160m E of Tr Richelieu before first R main chan buoy (LR2) marked
by three buoys: 'M' W Card, 'M2' and 'M4' both R, all to be left to port.
Entrance is marked by bns with R and W posts: square R topmarks with W
borders to port, B triangle topmarks with W borders to stb. By night lts Fl(2) R
to port, Fl G to stb. As construction continues marks may be changed. Inside,
limits of dredged areas are marked by W buoys. Full marina facilities, bonded
stores. Transport to town difficult. Rly in town.

LA CHARENTE RIVER, ROCHEFORT   Charts BA 2746, F 4333
HW +5.25.   MHWS 5.5; MLWS 1.3; MTL 3.5; MHWN 5.1; MLWN 2.2.
Bar   Fouras bar, outside entrance, has about 0.9m. In the river there are bars at
Lupin and Charras which do not affect the 50m wide dredged chan, 1.8m.
   In the river, tidal streams attain 4kn at springs, where it is confined between
embankments, and 2kn elsewhere. There is a bore at high spring tides.
Entrance   The river is entered between Fouras Tr and Sig Stn on the N bank and
Ile Madame. Steer 115° with the RW square trs (QR) 2M SE of Fouras in line
until nearly abreast Fouras when ldg lt trs on the S bank E of Port des Barques
come in line, 135°. Front is W square tr, rear has black gable and band, both Iso
G 4s. Thence pairs of bns mark the dredged chan when it does not run in
midstream.
Anchorage   In Rade de l'Ile Aix, good holding in 5 to 10m, mud; sheltered
except from W to NW. In the river at Martrou or Soubise, out of the chan. There
is a lift bridge at Martrou open for yachts HW −1 and +2 (times on La Rochelle)

for 10 min: three W lts indicate passage open. Yacht hr in dock. Shops and hotel at Soubise, 5 min walk.

LE CHATEAU, ILE D'OLERON   Charts BA 2648, F 6037
HW +5.10.   MHWS 6.0; MLWS 0.9; MTL 3.5; MHWN 4.9; MLWN 2.3.
A busy fishing hr. The 17th century town lies entirely within the walls. **The first Maritime Laws, the basis of laws adopted later by Europe, originated on the Is.**

A 2M bridge connects the Is at Pte d'Ors to the mainland SW of **Bourcefranc**, centre span 80m long gives a clearance at HAT of 12.15m between spans 14–34 with 15.10m between spans 20–24. The principal chans are marked both from the N and S by a W triangular board with G triangle to stb, and a W rectangular board with R rectangle to port. Both are marked at night by FW lts.
Approach   From N, the Juliar Tr, Lt Hos and walls of the town are conspic, and the chan is marked by bns and buoys.
Entrance   Leave the outer bn and the withies close to stb and steer straight ahead for the ldg lt structures to proceed up the dredged chan, 40m wide; 0.7m at MLWS, 2.1 at MLWN.
Berthing   Tie up immediately to port in inner hr, 1.2m soft and deep mud (2.2m draft will sit upright), but this may be in the way of the fishing boats. The quay on the stb side dries 2.7m near the seaward end, bottom soft mud, with plenty of ladders and mooring rings.

An alternative is to anch off Pte Gatseau out of tide and close to sandy beach, sounding to find the hole.

Petrol and diesel from garage nearby. Small yard; shops and restaurants 5 min. Water scarce and brackish. Bus and ferry.

LA PERROTINE (BOYARDVILLE), ILE D'OLERON
                                          Charts BA 2746, F 3711
HW +5.05.   MHWS 6.1; MLWS 0.8; MTL 3.5; MHWN 4.9; MLWN 2.3.
A small tidal port, with drying bar. A few yachts based here but only a few berths for those which cannot take the ground. A wet dock has been established.
Approach   The entrance is about 2M, 200° from Fort Boyard. Leave the buoy well to port and approach the end of the jetty keeping the NW side open, until about 50m from its end, when keep close to it until the river is entered.
Entrance   Keep to stb of mid-chan, once in the river.
Berthing   There are four short quays to stb: take the second or fourth. The first is wooden and unsuitable, the third is reserved for ferries and bn maintenance boats. Yachts take the ground but do not dry completely. HM's office on quayside. Small shops, restaurant, yard, chandlery, water on quay.

SEUDRE RIVER, MARENNES AND LA TREMBLADE
                                          Charts BA 2648, F 6037
HW +5.20.   MHWS 5.8; MLWS 1.2; MTL 3.5; MHWN 4.7; MLWN 2.4.

La Seudre R runs into Coureau d'Oleron near the S end and offers secure anchs in deep water once in the river. The new bridge gives a clearance at HAT between spans 3–9 of 12.5m with 15.10m between spans 5–7. The principal chan is marked by W boards and by a Fl W lt in the centre between spans 6 and 7.

Approach Well marked, but narrow chans with markings rather far apart. La Soumaille, N of Barat Bank, and La Garrigue, to its S, join at the river entrance.

Entrance After passing middle ground buoy where chans meet, keep to mid-chan. There is 18m at HW under power cables.

Anchorages (1) Off La Cayenne de Seudre, on N side near ferry. (2) By canal, dries 2.4m and lock in (HW −1 to +1) to the basin at Marennes, used only by yachts. (3) Off La Grève, ½M upstream from La Cayenne, on S side near the ferry. (4) By canal, dries 2.4m, to crowded drying-out stone piers, soft mud, at La Tremblade.

All facilities, including yards at Marennes and La Tremblade, but limited at ferry wharves.

Passage note: Ile d'Oleron to Gironde River

With wind against tide the Pertuis de Maumusson can be dangerous, breaking right across. Even in calm weather, on approach from seaward the outer buoys are not identifiable in the confused seas, and the broken water is not apparent until one is committed. The flood stream sets into and the ebb stream out of Coureau d'Oléron at both ends; the streams meet and separate in the strait and differ greatly according to their position. Details are given in the *Bay of Biscay Pilot*.

La Mauvaise bank, N of the Gironde R entrance, should be given a wide berth. Enter by Grand Passe de l'Ouest (7.7m), well marked, or Passe Sud, adequately marked. It is inadvisable to enter with a strong NW wind. In Rade de Royan the flood, SE, begins approx +0.30; the ebb, NW, at +6.00; 3.8kn springs. There are eddies.

Offshore anch inside Pte de la Chambrette is preferred to that under Pte de la Coubre, inside Barre à l'Anglais.

GIRONDE RIVER Charts BA 2910, 2916; F 6336, 6141, 6139
HW +5.35. DS (main ent): SE +0.35; NW −5.25. Flood 2½kn (sp); Ebb 4kn. MHWS 5.2; MLWS 0.9; MTL 3.0; MHWN 4.1; MLWN 1.9.

From the mouth of the Gironde R to Bordeaux is 50M. Above St Christoly, Pauillac and Lamarque are possible stopping places. The Gironde becomes the R Garonne above the junction with the R Dordogne.

Anchorages Possible in many places in soft mud but the current is strong. (1) *Mortagne-sur-Gironde*. Entrance is buoyed but dries 0.6m to quay. Lock in whenever water permits. Water, yacht yard, fuel in village, diesel by lorry. Locks open 1h before HW in daylight. Pontoons. Wintering possible. (2) *Rade de Trompeloup*. Anch in up to 7m, mud, about ½M W of Ile Pauillac. Berth alongside pontoons off jetty, or inner side of moored barges. Provisions in town. (3) *Blaye.* Mooring buoys off town near ferry jetty, or berth alongside. Provisions in town, water, fuel. (4) *Pauillac.* New marina. 4m at pontoons.

ROYAN
Charts BA 2916, F 6141 (Plan p474)

HW +5.30. MHWS 5.2; MLWS 0.8; MTL 3.0; MHWN 4.0; MLWN 1.9. Entrance and hr dredged to 1.5m. Although generally packed, full marina facilities at E end of hr. Berth temporarily at first pontoon across hr and report to YC in basement of Casino for a permanent berth. Water at pontoon; petrol and diesel. Crane for masts. Most recommended staging post. Clear police and Customs here rather than at Bordeaux. Visitors' pontoon at entrance is exposed.

PORT BLOC
Charts BA 2910, F 6141 (Plan p474)

HW +5.15. MHWS 5.3; MLWS 1.0; MTL 3.1; MHWN 4.2; MLWN 2.0. A well sheltered hr with 2.7m.

Entrance About 4 ca S of Pte de Grave. Very strong streams and currents may be encountered between the Pt and the hr.

Berthing Moor between buoys on W side of hr. Small marina-type pontoon, with water hose.

Bus to Verdun-sur-Mer, 1M; ferry to Royan, ½h; train to Bordeaux. Basic provisions, restaurant. Good base for exploring vineyards.

ST CHRISTOLY DE MEDOC
Charts BA 2196, F 6139

A small inlet 16M up the R Gironde, dries, mud. The entrance is just S of a prominent disused pier and is marked by perches. There is about 1.8m at HW springs. Moor to stone quay. Facilities as for a very small village.

BORDEAUX
Charts BA 2916, F 6139

HW −4.30. MHWS 5.2; MLWS 0.0; MTL 2.4; MHWN 4.0; MLWN 0.4. Anch or berth at marina, Point du Jour (suspension bridge) 4M outside city on W bank opposite Lormont; berth inside pontoons, quite secure and landing easy. Rly (10 min). YC, water by hose. Disused gantry operable, but not recommended, for masts.

The dock basin at Bordeaux is dirty and charges are high.

PASSAGE NOTE: BORDEAUX TO CASTETS

At Castets is the first lock into the Canal Lateral à la Garonne which joins the Canal du Midi at Toulouse.

The R Garonne to Castets, 35M, is unbuoyed with extensive mudbanks. Garonne pilots do not operate above Bordeaux. Without a chart or a pilot a barge should be followed; barges moor just above the Bordeaux bridge. Castets can generally be reached on one tide. The flood comes up at over 5kn, the water suddenly rising a foot with a 1.5m wave; the last of the ebb goes down at 2kn.

The lock at Castets is to stb. If, with the Garonne in spate and the upstream current therefore weakened, it should prove impossible to make Castets on one tide, ask permission to tie to a sand barge (they do not move overnight) or go alongside the pontoon at Cadillac securing also to the mooring buoy upstream.

ARCACHON   Charts BA 2664, F 172   (Plan p483)
HW +6.20.   MHWS 4.3; MLWS 0.2; MTL 2.2; MHWN 3.1; MLWN 1.1.
Fairway entrance is about 7M S of Cap Ferret, thence 9M into the basin. Hr is not accessible in heavy onshore weather or at night. It is advisable to enter at half flood.
Entrance   Chan varies in depth and position, usually running E then turning N with about 3m. It is marked by lateral buoys, moved as the banks change. Application should be made to the Service Maritime at Royan for latest information on buoyage.
Berthing   In the marina at the E end of the town (report to the Bureau de Port de Plaisance), or anch E of Cap Ferret. There are half a dozen small ports within the basin accessible on the tide to local craft of shallow draft.
   Rly, first class yards, all facilities. Water, petrol and diesel at marina.
Warning   Care must be taken of the FIRING DANGER AREA that lies off the coast between Cap Breton and La Négade bns. Yachts must keep beyond 30M or inside 3M from the coast. The areas that are dangerous and forbidden are broadcast each day after each weather bulletin by Bordeaux-Arcachon Radio.

CAP BRETON   Charts BA 2665, F 6586   (Plan p484)
A hr with three marinas, two not yet completed. Entrance is possible at half-tide, but impracticable in strong onshore weather.
Entrance   Enter between wooden pile to S and stone jetty to N. Tides run strongly. At the beginning of the canal to Hossegor, turn to stb through narrow gap to enter the river.
Berthing   Marina immediately to stb, and two more a little way up by the YC Landes. All facilities. Deep-water moorings available.

BAYONNE   Charts BA 1343, F 6536   (Plan p484)
HW (Boucau) +5.00.
MHWS 4.3; MLWS 0.7; MTL 2.5; MHWN 3.3; MLWN 1.8.
A large town and surprisingly clean for a commercial port, about 3M up R Adour. Large marina at Port D'Anglet (see plan).
Entrance   Close to breakwater, then midstream between jetties. Traffic signals from conspic tr to stb. After first bend, keep to stb.
Berthing   (1) At Port d'Anglet marina, all facilities, bus to Bayonne. (2) Alongside small wooden piers on stb hand just short of bridge, near conspic town hall. HM's office is ½M downstream. Rly. (3) YC Adour Atlantic ½M above traffic signal tr welcomes visitors, and may allocate pontoon berth or mooring. Water, fuel on pontoons. Showers, shops and chandlers nearby. Bus to Bayonne.

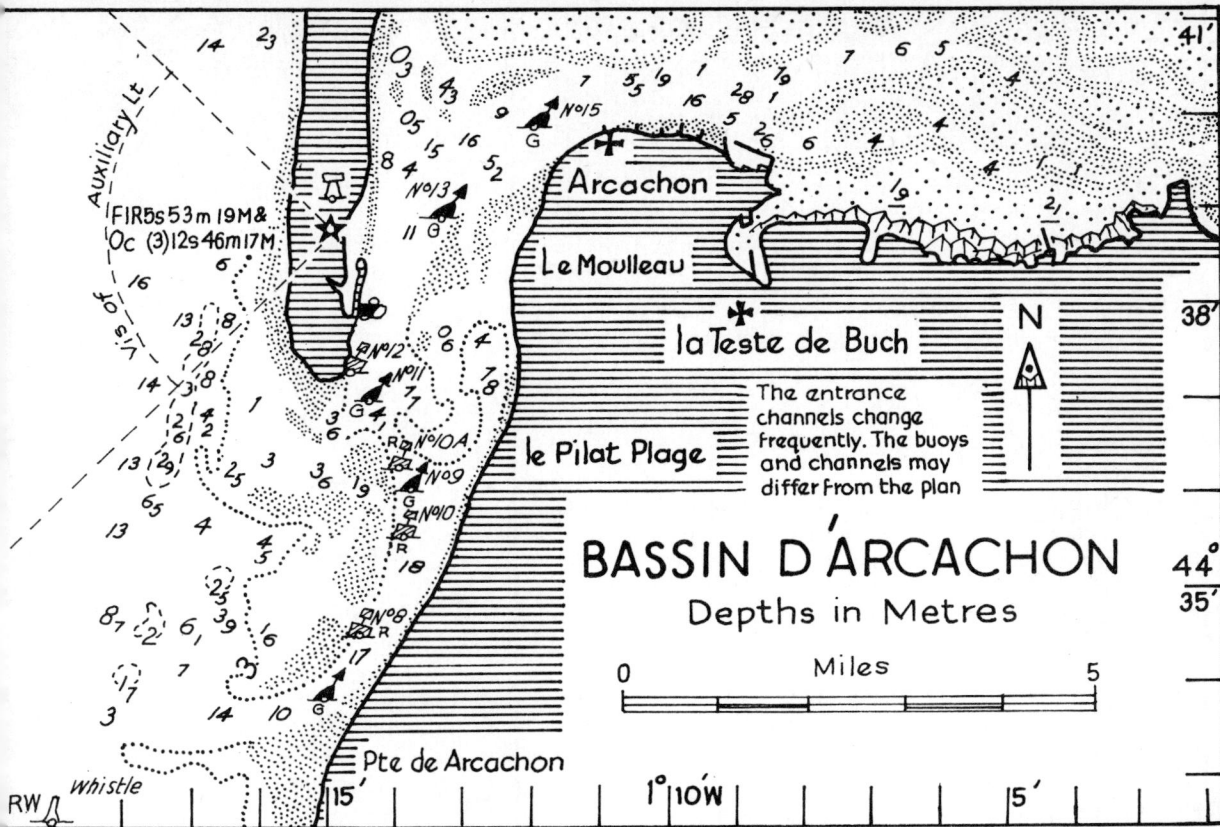

BASSIN D'ARCACHON
Depths in Metres

Arcachon

Le Moulleau

✠ la Teste de Buch

le Pilat Plage

The entrance channels change frequently. The buoys and channels may differ from the plan

N

Auxiliary Lt

FlR5s53m19M&
Oc (3)12s46m17M

Vis of

Pte de Arcachon

Whistle

RW

N°15 G
N°13 G
N°12 G
N°11 G
R N°10 A.
N°9 G
N°10 R
N°8 R

44°
35'

41'

38'

0   Miles   5

15'   1°10'W   5'

PORT D'ARCACHON
Depths in Metres

N

SIIP

HM

YC

0   Cables   3

44°
39.7'

39.6'

9.5'   1°9'W

après la carte marine française avec l'autorisation du Service Hydrographique et Océanographique de la Marine.

483

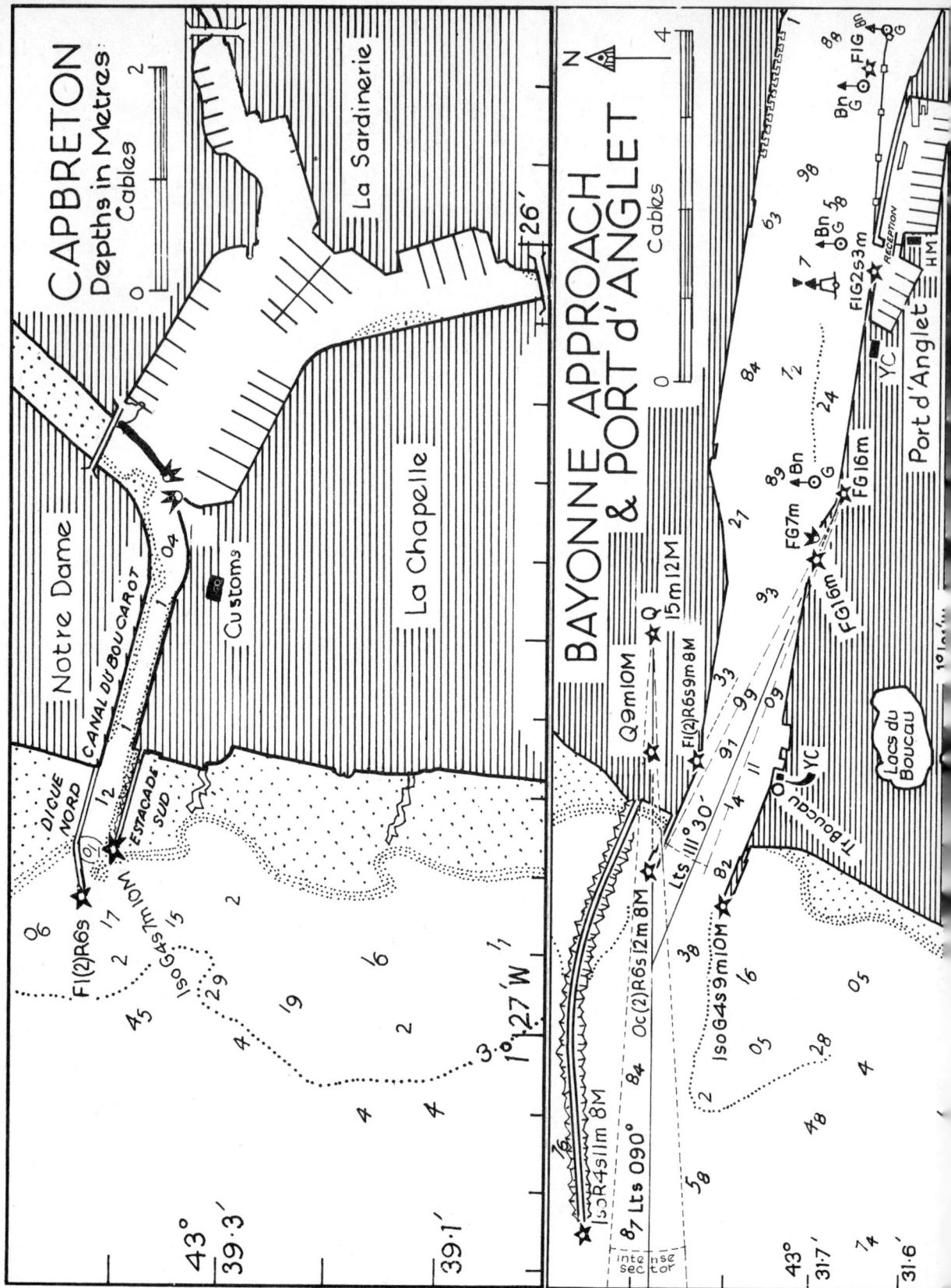

CAPBRETON

Depths in Metres

Cables

La Sardinerie

Notre Dame

CANAL DU BOUGAROT

Customs

La Chapelle

DIGUE NORD

ESTACADE SUD

Fl(2)R6s

IsoG4s7m10M

26'

43° 39·3'

39·1'

1°27'W

3°

BAYONNE APPROACH & PORT d'ANGLET

N

Cables

Q9m10M

Q

15m12M

Fl(2)R6s9m8M

Lts 111°30'

Oc(2)R6s12m 8M

IsoR4s11m 8M

Lts 090°

Intense sector

IsoG4s9m10M

Tr Boucau

YC

Lacs du Boucau

Port d'Anglet

FG16m

FG16m

FG7m

Bn

FIG2s3m

RECEPTION

HM

YC

Bn

FIG

43° 31·7'

31·6'

1°30'W

D'après la carte marine française avec l'autorisation du Service Hydrographique et Océanographique de la Mar...

ST JEAN DE LUZ   Charts BA 1343, F 6526
HW +5.00.   MHWS 4.4; MLWS 0.5; MTL 2.4; MHWN 3.2; MLWN 1.6.
Yachts may not stay in fishing port; small crowded marina alongside Quai Maurice Rave in inner hr. Anch off Socoa, hr dries. YC Basque is now at Laraidenia Marina at Ciboure; all facilities.

HENDAYE   Charts BA 1343, F 6551
HW +5.05.   MHWS 4.3; MLWS 0.4; MTL 2.3; MHWN 3.1; MLWN 1.5.
Approach is impracticable in heavy weather.
Entrance   Keep close to stb (W) training wall until its root at Roca Punta, where turn to port, following line of deep-water moorings and passing 75m S of large con bn to yacht anch S of landing stage. YC on landing stage, with limited facilities. Reporting to Customs (next to YC) essential as this is the frontier between France and Spain.

Water and diesel on quay, petrol nearby. Good restaurants and shops, 1M.

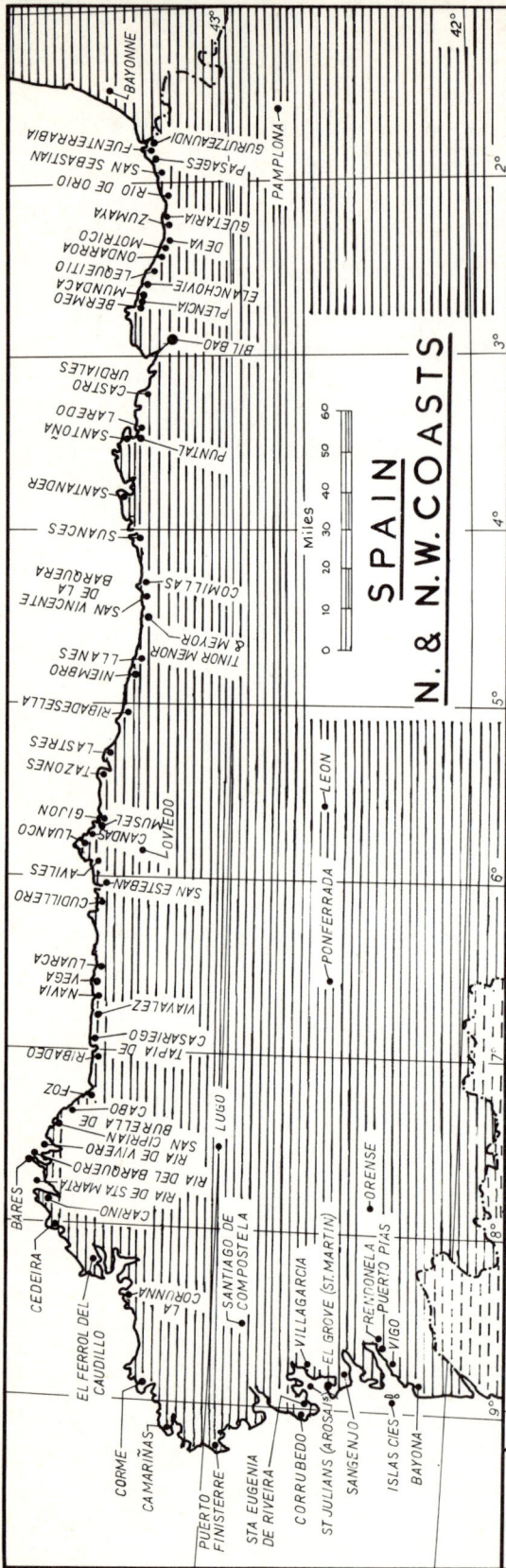

SPAIN
N. & N.W. COASTS

Miles
0 10 20 30 40 50 60

BAYONNE
FUENTERRABIA
SAN SEBASTIAN
PASAGES
GURUTZEAUNDI
PAMPLONA
RIO DE ORIO
GUETARIA
ZUMAYA
DEVA
MOTRICO
ONDARROA
LEQUEITIO
ELANCHOVIE
MUNDACA
PLENCIA
BERMEO
BILBAO
CASTRO URDIALES
LAREDO
SANTOÑA
PUNTAL
SANTANDER
SUANCES
COMILLAS
SAN VINCENTE DE LA BARQUERA
TINOR MENOR & MEYOR
LLANES
NIEMBRO
RIBADESELLA
LASTRES
TAZONES
GIJON
LUANCO
CANDAS
MUSEL
OVIEDO
SAN ESTEBAN
AVILES
CUDILLERO
LUARCA
VEGA
NAVIA
VIVALEZ
CASARIEGO
TAPIA DE
RIBADEO
FOZ
CABO
BURELLA DE
SAN CIPRIAN
RIA DE VIVERO
RIA DEL BARQUERO
RIA DE STA MARTA
CARIÑO
BARES
CEDEIRA
EL FERROL DEL CAUDILLO
CORME
CAMARIÑAS
PUERTO FINISTERRE
STA EUGENIA DE RIVEIRA
CORRUBEDO
ST JULIANS (AROSA)
SANGENJO
VILLAGARCIA
EL GROVE (ST.MARTIN)
REDONDELA
PUERTO PIAS
ISLAS CIES
VIGO
BAYONA
LA CORUNNA
SANTIAGO DE COMPOSTELA
LUGO
ORENSE
LEON
PONFERRADA

LUGO

PORTUGAL

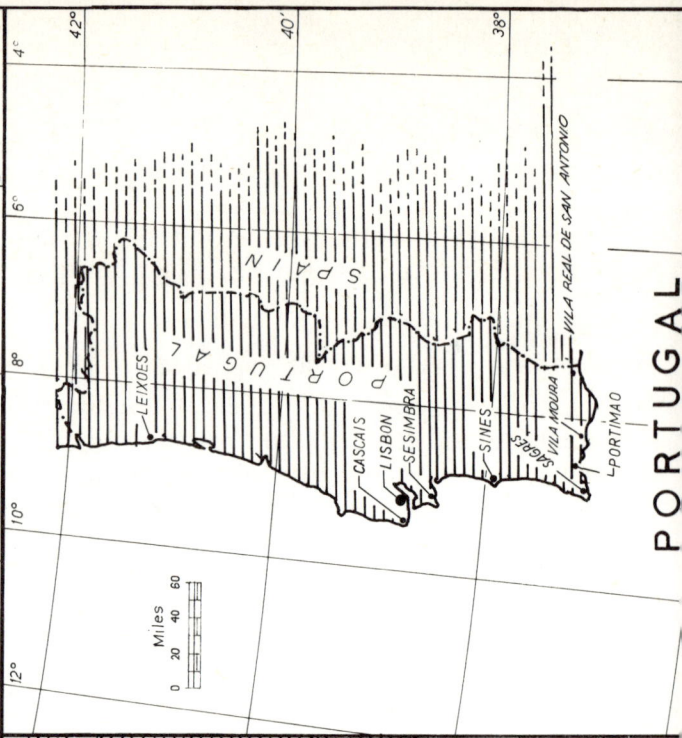

SPAIN
PORTUGAL

LEIXOES
CASCAIS
LISBON
SESIMBRA
SINES
VILAMOURA
FARO
VILA REAL DE SAN ANTONIO
PORTIMAO

Miles
0 20 40 60

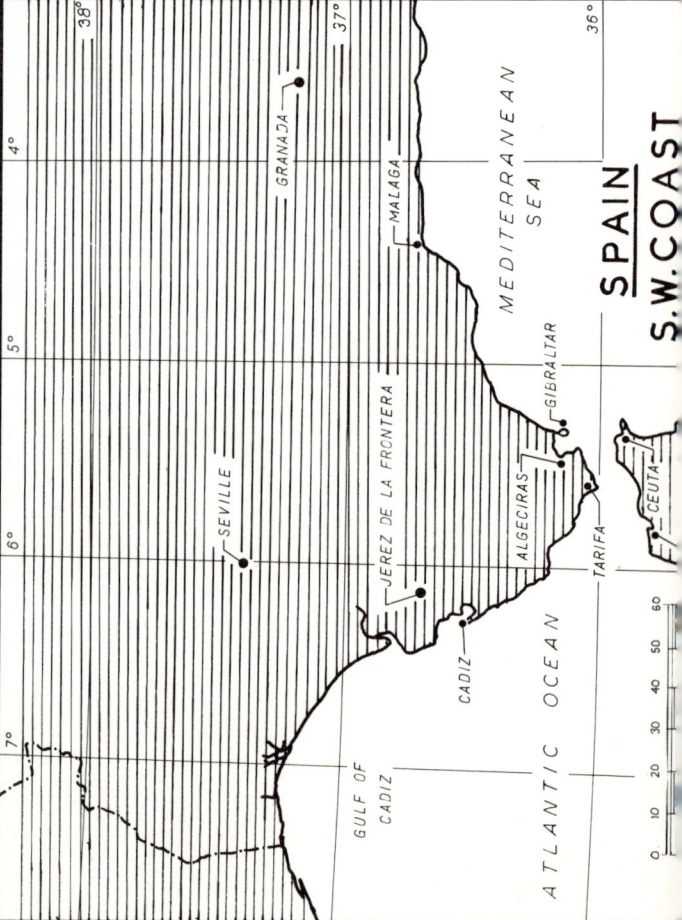

SPAIN
S.W. COAST

MEDITERRANEAN SEA

ATLANTIC OCEAN

GULF OF CADIZ

GRANAJA
MALAGA
GIBRALTAR
ALGECIRAS
CEUTA
TARIFA
CADIZ
JEREZ DE LA FRONTERA
SEVILLE

Miles
0 10 20 30 40 50 60

SPAIN AND PORTUGAL

Formalities   Officialdom is not troublesome in Spain and is less so than it used to be in Portugal. In both countries there are International Police who check the ordinary police. Passports are now inspected by officials in most ports. Numerous duplicates of a prepared list giving: name of yacht, port of registry, tonnage, length in metres, names and passport numbers of crew, are a great help. Crews returning by train or air should ensure that when their entry formalities are completed, all their passports are stamped. Otherwise, there may be difficulties when leaving the country.

Swimming costumes, bare backs and brief costumes should not be worn away from the beach or boat by men or women (this is true in both countries). In Portugal a clean Bill of Health will allow disembarcation of crew. Individual passports may remain in possession of their owners. Contact the marine authorities immediately after arrival, preferably through Pilot's Service, if any.

Books   It is essential to take the Admiralty *List of Lights* as this is the only place where details of the characteristics of the lights can be found: BA charts do not give the full details of some lights. The Admiralty *Pilots* are also useful and the latest Supplements must be obtained. *South Biscay Pilot* (La Coruna to the Gironde Estuary) by R. Brandon (A. Coles Ltd) is an excellent volume to have on board.

Spain, North Coast

In summer the winds are largely between NW and NE. Fifty miles offshore the winds are usually more W-ly in direction. In fine sunny weather land and sea breezes are experienced along the coast. At times, a heavy swell runs there even in fine weather. Under these conditions it is not possible to enter many shallow hrs.

Fuenterrabia   The Spanish town opposite Hendaye, an attractive old fortified town. Do not divert at Roca Punta; anchor some ½M further on near large fishing boats.

Gurutzeaundi   A tiny hr in the shelter of Cabo Higuer; no facilities except water and fuel. Enter from S keeping well clear of breakwater heads. Anchor, moor or berth alongside.

Pasages   43°30′N, 1°54′W. A hr with deep water and sheltered in all weathers. Make fast to mooring buoys off villages of Pasages de San Juan and San Pedro, on port and stb sides. Deep water inshore. This is a busy port used by large vessels.

San Sebastian   43°19′N, 2°00′W. A large landlocked bay. Enter on 158°, anchor to stb behind Isla de Santa Clara, or berth in small yacht hr to port. All facilities.

Rio de Orio   Enter only at HW with no swell. Anchor below bridge or berth alongside at sea end of wharf. Limited facilities, unspoilt.

Guetaria   43°18′N, 2°12′W. New breakwater running SE from Club Nautico gives shelter for anch outside (6–8m). Inside, lie alongside if draft allows or anch inside stb breakwater in 6–8m, buoying anch. Diesel, restaurants, basic supplies.

Zumaya   Enter at top half of tide in good weather. Berth to stb just above a small hard. Limited facilities, rather commercial.

Deva   Enter at HW in calm conditions. Anchor just below bridge. A holiday centre, limited facilities.

Motrico   Enter near HW. Anchor or moor to stb just inside entrance. Limited facilities. An attractive place.

Ondarroa   Enter at top half of tide. Moor to large buoys in outer or inner hr. Inner hr tends to be oily. Limited facilities. Commercial fishing port.

Lequeitio   43°22′N, 2°30′W. Enter on 212° close to breakwater heads. Inner hr crowded, swell in outer hr. Good facilities, a very pleasant place.

Elanchove   Moor to buoys in outer hr, or alongside S mole taking stern line to large buoy to keep off ledge especially near steps. A beautiful and unspoilt port. Very limited facilities.

Mundaca   A very small port. Enter at HW in good conditions. Anch just inside the entrance. Very attractive with limited facilities.

Bermeo   43°25′N, 2°44′W. A good hr with everything one can need, but smelly. Deep water alongside the S pier immediately to port of the entrance.

Plencia   A drying estuary. Enter at HW. Alternatively, anch behind breakwater on E side of the bay. Limited facilities.

Bilbao   43°20′N, 3°02′W. Large breakwaters enclose Bilbao Bay and form a large area of sheltered water. Yachts may anch on E side; the anch is safe but can be rough in strong winds which precludes landing from a small dinghy. The Club provides a launch, late trips by negotiation. Land at pier on the E shore. Real Sport Club have marina nearby, with raft. Visitors' berths at end of W pontoon, showers. Buses and electric trains to Bilbao. The main commercial port is up the Ria Nervion; not recommended. Diesel can be bought from the fishing hr at Santuree or by can from the garage up the hill in Algorta.

Castro Urdiales   43°25′N, 3°13′W. An artificial hr enclosed by breakwaters. In winds between NE and SE it is somewhat exposed and subject to swell. Anchor in NW corner of hr or off the YC on the W shore. Moorings may be available but do not use large W buoys in middle of hr. Swell in E winds. Moderate sized seaside resort; clean and interesting town with Roman remains, arcades along cobbled streets, cathedral, etc.

Laredo   A charming town on steep hillside. Drying hr with fair facilities. Enter at top half of tide and berth alongside to port just inside main hr. Alternatively, good anch can be found with N or NW winds in deep water in lee of Pto del Emballo.

Santona   43°27′N, 3°26′W. A fine natural hr behind a high rocky peninsula. Very fine scenery in approaches. Enter artificial hr W of the town or anch on N side of hr. Visitors' moorings are the group of five S of the others. It may be more convenient to overnight at El Puntal.

Santander   43°28′N, 3°48′W. A considerable port and attractive town on a large estuary that can be entered in all weathers at any state of tide. There is good anch in the river off the YC, safe but somewhat exposed in bad weather; buoy anchor. One can also make fast in the Molnedo basin on the SW side with stern to the quay, but often overcrowded. Diesel available in fishing port or in Molnedo basin when tide allows, water by hose. Good market for all foods. New marina, safe but inconvenient for town. YC.

Suances   43°26′N, 4°02′W. Anch in lee of Pto del Dichose in N and NW winds, subject to swell. Alternatively, cross bar near HW (may be fierce) and enter estuary close to port hand training wall. Anch above jetty about 20ft from training wall with stern line to jetty or on port side opposite jetty. Avoid jetty, which is rough and much used by fishing craft. Limited facilities. Ships use river more than might be expected.

Comillas   A small drying hr, enter at HW following two sets of ldg marks/lts. Dry out beside wall to E. Limited facilities.

San Vincente de la Barquera   43°23'N, 4°23'W. A beautiful place. Enter near HW. A tricky chan near to stb bank. Anchor near bridge with warp to ring on first arch from E, or to one of two large mooring buoys 200m from slip. Fair facilities, water from café.

Tina Menor and Tina Meyor   43°24'N, 4°31'W. Two delightful deserted *rias*. Enter near HW close to stb side. Anchor about 400m inside. No facilities.

Llanes   A drying port; approach in good weather from a position with the radio trs in line. Enter the inner hr through a narrow entrance near a tall tr. Not recommended except with W and S winds. Good holding ground. Attractive but dirty town with primitive resources.

Niembro   A small drying *ria* with a quay. Enter at HW in good conditions and dry out alongside the quay. Quite deserted and very beautiful.

Ribadesella   43°28'N, 5°04'W. A good small port but with a bar, dangerous in strong onshore winds. Keep close to the quay on N side and continue until within 100m of the concrete bridge over the R. Moor to the quay on the port hand, close to shops. Water behind fish market. Fine mountains all round. Delightful hill walks.

Lastres   Little room for yachts, but berths alongside possible at N corner of NE pier; beware shelf and overhangs at outer end of pier. An attractive, clean and unspoilt village. Conspic TV tr on Pt Misiera. Numerous mooring lines in hr. Heavy swell. Diesel from fish quay, usual facilities.

Puntal   Enter river at HW in good conditions, near stb training wall. Hr is on stb side after ½M. Anchor at N end of hr. No facilities.

Tazones   A small unspoilt village with a little hr which almost dries. Anchor just inside the mouth. Limited facilities.

Gijon   43°33'N, 5°40'W. A commercial hr, being developed into a major tanker port. On entry, keep outside all works, then steer for C de Santa Catalina. Yacht hr lies inside the Diguede Liguerica, shallow, soft mud. Also possible to anchor in the outer hr. YC at end of Darsena No. 1 jetty; good showers and bar. All facilities, diesel available at sufficient rise of tide. A dirty and unattractive hr and town, but easy to enter and secure.

Musel   43°34'N, 5°42'W. A commercial port. Anchor to SE of entrance to Puerto Pesquero, or berth alongside inside. Good shelter. Very oily; alongside berths always busy with trawlers. Poor shopping. Extensive hr works.

Candas   A small fishing hr that almost dries. Anch just behind the breakwater in fair weather only. Limited facilities.

Luanco   43°37'N, 5°47'W. A small fishing hr and holiday resort. In fair weather only, anch just behind the outer breakwater. Provisions in village 1M.

Aviles   43°36'N, 5°57'W. A major commercial port, easy entrance. Anch just round bend of river on port hand opposite Club del Mar, sheltered and calm. Buoyage is constantly altered as hr works proceed, but port can be entered in almost any weather. Good facilities.

San Esteban   43°34'N, 6°05'W. Difficult bar in offshore winds. Keep on the line of ldg marks until the entrance to the basin is open to stb. Enter basin and keep about 50m from quays on W side. Berth as directed. Excellent shelter. A commercial port; coal dust. Fair shopping.

Cudillero   A traditional fishing port. Enter with care at HW, fine weather only, on 200°. Dry out alongside wall on E side of hr.

Luarca   43°33'N, 6°32'W. A beautiful hr and town. Enter on 170° and follow chan; turn 90° to stb and moor against W side of inner hr (dredged) avoiding end of ramp to stb at inner end of chan. Anch possible but uncomfortable, clear of fairway just inside and to port of outer entrance. Good facilities, fuel, water.

Vega   Very small port for small yachts only. Use only in fair weather. Enter near HW with end of breakwater in line with centre gable of long low ho; turn sharp to stb. Dry out on S wall of hr. Limited facilities.

Navia   A pleasant fishing hr and town. Enter at HW in good weather near stb bank, cross over after 100m to port bank. Hr entrance is on port side after 1M. Berth alongside fishing boat or wall. Good facilities.

Viavelez   Small. Enter on 125° near HW in fair weather. Dry alongside stb quay. Few facilities.

Tapia   Charming fishing hr and village. Enter above half-tide and anch near fishing boat moorings. Fair facilities.

Ribadeo   43°32'N, 7°02'W. A wonderful great *ria* which can be entered in most conditions. Follow two sets of ldg marks, then follow the stb shore to quay on Punta Mirasol; berth alongside. Good facilities including good yard. Diesel, water from hose on quay.

Foz   Enter only at HW in good weather. Follow local fishing craft as the chan changes. Berth either inside or outside hr wall. Fair facilities.

Burela   A fishing hr. Berth alongside a fishing boat or dry out against the wall further up the hr. Rather commercial. Fair facilities.

San Ciprian   An extraordinary and very attractive sandy anch behind a drying reef. Enter on ldg marks and anch close S behind the reef; few facilities. Do not use in strong winds from N. One simple restaurant.

Ria de Vivero   43°33′N, 7°36′W. A beautiful *ria*. Easy entrance. The two lts either side of the entrance are on distinctive W columns. Anch behind breakwater at Cillero and at many other places, or go up river at HW and dry out against wall on port hand just short of bridge.

Ria del Barquero   Another beautiful *ria* with easy entrance and many places to anch, especially near fishing boats at Bares and between the bridge and Puerto del Barquero in Rio Sor.

Bares   Safe anch in all winds, good holding in sand. Primitive village, one cafe/shop.

Ria and *Ensenada Santa Marta*   43°31′N, 7°51′W. A large and very beautiful *ria* with easy entrance. Anch behind the breakwater at Carino (safe but dirty, poor facilities), in the bay at Espante, or berth alongside further up the *ria* at Santa Marta de Ortiguera. Pilot advisable for entrance to *ria* itself. Limited facilities.

Cedeira   The most beautiful and unspoilt *ria* on the coast. Very clean and quiet. Beware submerged rocks at entrance, especially half-tide rock near hr entrance. New large breakwater extending SSW from Punta del Castillo makes huge enclosed secure hr; anch almost anywhere, best opposite pier outside fishing boat moorings. Large and busy fishing fleet. Fair facilities. Diesel from pump on quay. Excellent walks above town. Fisherman anchor best due to thick kelp.

El Ferrol   43°28′N, 8°14′W. A large *ria* with a considerable naval base. Very clean. All facilities. Enter in any weather on ldg line. Berth alongside near ferry hard on far side of commercial hr. Much wash. Petrol and diesel on jetty, water from tap at the ice plant. Good chandler and shops. Much preferable to La Coruna.

Spain, West Coast

The coast from Finisterre to Isla Salvora can be dangerous in bad weather as there are unmarked rocks a long way out. The headlands are well lit, but many of the lights are high and can be obscured by mist. There is little information regarding tidal streams, but S of Finisterre the current at times sets towards the land. N winds seem to predominate in summer and can be strong at times, NE gales occurring quite often off Finisterre.

La Coruna   43°22'N, 8°23'W. Pleasant and interesting city but very oily water. Entrance easy by day or night. Berth alongside YC near root of Dique de Adrigo, the cleanest berth in the hr. Diesel, petrol; or make use of the small marina just behind, water, showers. All facilities.

Castilla de San Anton   In strong SW wind sheltered anch may be found in a small bay NW of Punta de Oza in 5 to 7m, sand. All facilities. In suitable conditions, pleasanter anch will be found in the *ria* at Mera Ares San Filipe or La Redonda.

Corme   43°16'N, 8°57'W. Picturesque but primitive village. Enter the Ensenada de Corme and steer for the mooring buoys S of the village. When the village ch bears N, head for the northern of the two sandy beaches. Anchor in 7m, sand. Do not attempt the basin W of village. Anch exposed to W to SW. Simple stores only.
   Alternative is Lage: more shelter, diesel on quay. Pleasant anch and unspoilt village; lie outside hr or alongside fishing boat inside.

Camarinas   43°07'N, 9°13'W. Pleasant and safe anch in all but S to SW winds. Possible to dry out or anch in hr or outside. Picturesque town with most facilities. Fuel from quayside pump by ferry landing, water from fish market quay opposite. The *ria* has other pleasant anchs off sandy beaches.

Puerto Finisterre   42°54'N. A busy crowded fishing port. Picturesque village. Restaurant, diesel on quay. Useful port of call. Anchor behind breakwaters among fishing boats or off sandy beaches N of port. Protected from SW through W to N. If crowded, *Puerto Corcubion* anch is recommended (water, fuel and shipyard).

Corrubedo   42°34'N. Clean and pleasant village. Safe in all but SW winds. Good holding in sand. Beware rks extending about 15m off breakwater head.

El Grove (St Martin) 42°30'N. Very busy mussel fishing port, clean with all facilities. Good holding. There are many pleasant anchs giving complete safety inside the Ria de Arosa. Main entrance is between Isla Salvora and Pta de Grove.

St Julians (Arosa Is) 42°26'N. Anch off town among fishing boats. Quaint primitive village with no cars. Several bars/shops.

Sta Eugenia de Riveira Large, well sheltered fishing port. Easy access day or night. All berths belong to returning fishing boats. Anch not permitted inside hr, but possible outside, in shelter of outer jetty, just off the beach out of the fairway. All facilities.

Villagarcia Pleasant town. Moor alongside small YC on jetty with FS. All facilities, but diesel only in cans from garage. Good water from hose from YC. Good supermarket at end of jetty.

Sangenjo 42°24'N. Clean safe port in all but S or SW winds. Smart YC. Anchor in middle of hr, or bow to breakwater and stern to anch.

Islas Cies Sheltered bay on E of Is. Almost uninhabited, clear water and W sand.

Vigo 42°15'N, 8°44'W. By far the best port in N Spain. Steer for the Guia chapel until abreast of the NE end of the Transatlantic mole. The buildings and jetty of the Real Club Nautico lie SW from here. The two club buildings are cream-coloured; the one on the jetty head is rounded on its NE end. Anchor NW of the club jetty or enter the basin SW of jetty. In the basin secure head to buoy and stern to quay; berth is well sheltered but water is dirty. Most convenient for city centre. Hr crowded: if no room try first berth to stb at entrance. YC sees to formalities. Water on jetty. Larger yachts lie on outside of basin mole, not recommended for lighter craft. Fuel in quantity from CAMPSA oil jetty W of fish hr, or CANGAS or MAONA. Otherwise diesel must be fetched from roadside garage nearby. Magnificent YC with good swimming pool. Wonderful view of *ria* and city from castle, about 20 min walk from YC. Superb sailing and fine bays with clean beaches in *ria*.

Puerto Pias, Vigo Bay Small sheltered drying hr. Very remote. One primitive shop 10 min walk over rly to S jetty, which is submerged at HW.

Redonela, Vigo Bay Unmarked entrance which dries to its mouth between two training walls. Electric cables and very low overhead tel cables just short of town quay.

Bayona, Vigo Bay   42°08'N, 8°50'W. Make for the W con tr in the centre of Bayona Bay (Cabezo de San Juan), thence steer SSW for E end of stone jetty which extends E from Pinta Tenaza and lies N of the town. Shelter from all winds. Village primitive but charming, old fortress overlooks bay. Land at stone causeway at SW end of the town, or at jetty off Monte Real YC. Club offers all facilities, and deals with formalities. Anch (6m, sand) outside YC moorings, take YC buoy, or berth at YC pontoon at jetty. Water and diesel on jetty. Buses to Vigo. All stores including fresh foods. More convenient than Vigo on passage.

Portugal

Note: Separation Schemes now operate off Cape Roca and Cape St Vincent, also in the Straits of Gibraltar.

Leixoes 41°11'N, 8°42'W. Completely modernised and very busy. Four large chimneys of an oil refinery just E of Leca Lt Ho are visible by day for 15 to 20M. The new Esporarao breakwater affords good shelter from seaward when entering the outer hr. The only place for yachts is in the inner basin in the NE corner of the port where two YCs have their premises and some moorings are available. Clubs welcome visitors and offer facilities. Authorities issue Portuguese Green Card to expedite formalities elsewhere.

Cascais 38°42'N, 09°25'W. On N side of estuary of R Tagus. W-going stream starts shortly after LW Cascais. Anchor only close to YC, sand and mud, or use a club mooring. Bottom shelves from YC deeper to S and E to accommodate the largest of yachts. Open to S and E; swell and wash likely. Boatmen in attendance until about 6 pm. Night approach confused by brilliant lts in bay. In strong onshore winds when sea breaks over club jetty and along beaches making landing from dinghy difficult, better go upstream to yacht hr at Belem. YC deals with all official formalities, and provides all assistance. Good shopping for food at supermarket. Morning market. Fuel. A good place from which to visit Lisbon, frequent trains. Sandy beaches. Yachts cannot go alongside due to depth but this is not inconvenient either for landing or for stores, thanks to boatman service. Water clean.

Lisbon 38°44'N, 9°08'W. Visiting foreign yachts are expected to find a berth in Doca de Bon Successo (immediately upstream of the Belem Tr) and not in the Doca de Belem which is nearest to the facilities of the Associacao Naval de Lisbon (and second dock upstream of the Belem Tr). Basin accommodates the largest yachts, but is very crowded and dirty. Moor bow to buoy, stern line to quay; do not anch, bottom foul. Land at slipway SW end of jetty, or steps NW end. HM calls on arrival, skipper is taken by car into Lisbon for issue of Green Card and passport examination; this takes about an hour. HM office displays notices and weather bulletins. Showers at YC; chandlers, provisions, fuel, water. Tram to city centre.

Sesimbra 38°26'N, 09°06'W. Useful anch with jetties for fishing boats and affords shelter against winds from W to NE. Approaching, beware fishing nets extending S of Cape Espichel. Anchor as close in as draft allows for protection from prevailing offshore winds, often strong in the evenings. Dinghy to jetty or to shore (nearer for shops). No YC or officials. Stores and restaurants, no special facilities for yachts. LB and storm signals.

Baia de Sines 37°57′N, 8°52′W. Useful anch mainly used by fishing boats, sheltered from winds from NW to NE; now being developed as major port. Fishing nets extend 6 ca seawards each side of the bay so it is essential to approach on line of ldg lts. Anch 100m E of end of LB slip in 3½m or more. Easy row ashore. No YC or officials. Fresh provisions in one to two very simple restaurants.

Baia de Sagres 36°59′N, 8°57′W. Simply a useful place to anch under the lee of Cape St Vincent. Beware of strong offshore winds when rounding Cape. No dangers (or marks) in the Bay. Anch as near to end of bay as draft will allow; gradually shelving sand. Landing on beach by dinghy. Shelter from prevailing winds between W and NE, usually strong in the evenings. Swell may enter after a Levanter and prevent landing.

Portimao 37°06′N, 8°31′W. Entrance, difficult against a strong ebb with a S-ly, is between two BW trs, at end of two moles, affording good protection for anch in outer hr. If not proceeding to the fishing port of Portimao (crowded and shallow), best anch is about halfway along, and 50m off the W mole (3½m at MLWN). In a Levanter, move to other side in deeper water under lee of land.

If proceeding to town of Portimao, best water is indicated by two circular ldg marks, front W, rear R, higher one difficult to pick up. The lower one is on top of the cliff below the ch and the upper at the E end of the ch. There are no buoys. When the town of Ferragudo is abeam turn NW and steer on the inner ldg line of two R huts astern (easy to see) and so to the town of Portimao, mooring securely (strong current) on E side of river; W side is fully occupied by fishing boats at night. Water and diesel on quay, repair yard above br, most facilities. Pilot available.

Vilamoura 37°04′N, 8°11′W. Major yacht hr ½M W of Quarteira, 6M E of Albufeira. 4.5m in outer hr, 2.3m inside. Enter between quays and report to visitors' pontoon at entrance to inner hr. All facilities, caretaking, 40T slipway, Customs. At heart of the Algarve development.

Vila Real de San Antonio 37°14′N, 7°25′W. One of the safest, best and most pleasant hrs on the S coast of Portugal. Use Admiralty hr plan or follow fishing boat in and proceed to small dock above the commercial and fishing boat wharf. Fuel in dock, slipway, shipwright. Town, still unspoilt, about ½M. Approach can be difficult in onshore winds. Shifting bar. New moles either side of chan at entrance.

Spain, Southwest Coast, to Gibraltar

Cadiz 36°32'N, 6°18'W. From the end of the San Felipe mole, steer for the yacht hr at the root of the mole. Entrance (unlit) is at SE corner of this basin. Anch inside in mud/sand (exposed in Levanter) or moor stern to YC pontoons. Fuel, water at pontoons. All facilities. Port is attractive, with interesting chs and fine restaurants.

Tarifa 36°0'N, 5°37'W. Allow for strong tide when entering. Berth alongside at inmost end of basin protected against all winds. Strict police formalities for landing. Stores, bathing.

Algeciras 36°07'N, 5°26'W. Round the end of the main breakwater, obtain clearance at ferry boat quay to stb, then make for the SW corner of the basin. Bow to anch, stern to YC quay. Club Ho projects into the water and is readily identified by a verandah shaded with matting. Good shelter except in strong Levanter; then anch in lee of main breakwater. All supplies.

Gibraltar This is a British Admiralty port with strict regulations. It is a convenient and well sheltered port of call on passage to and from the Mediterranean. It is unnecessary to signal for permission to enter. Berth at marina N of 'F' Head, about 500m S of frontier, or at Destroyer Pens for larger yachts. All facilities, inexpensive provisioning, BA chart agent.

BIBLIOGRAPHY

The following books may be recommended as useful when cruising the appropriate areas, in addition to the relevant Admiralty Pilots, tidal atlases etc. Publishers are abbreviated as follows: Imray Laurie Norie & Wilson Ltd: Imray; Stanford Maritime Ltd: Stanford; Adlard Coles Ltd (Granada Publishing Ltd): Coles; Faber & Faber Ltd: Faber; James Laver Printing Co. Ltd: Laver; Nautical Books (Macmillan): Nautical; Yachting Monthly: YM; Royal Northumberland Yacht Club: RNYC; Clyde Cruising Club: CCC; Irish Cruising Club: ICC; Bristol Channel Yachting Conference: BCYC; Cruising Association: CA. Books are listed in the order in which the areas appear in the *Handbook*.

Title	Author	Publisher
Shell Pilot to the South Coast Harbours	Adlard Coles	Faber
Visiting Yachtsman's Guide to the London River		CA
East Coast Rivers (Humber to Swale)	Jack Coote, Henry Irving	YM
Sailing Directions, Humber Estuary to Rattray Head		RNYC
Sailing Directions, North and East Coasts of Scotland		CCC
Sailing Directions, Orkneys		CCC
Sailing Directions, Shetland		CCC
Sailing Directions, West Coast of Scotland		CCC
Scottish West Coast Pilot, Troon to Ullapool	Mark Brackenbury	Stanford
Sailing Directions, Outer Hebrides		CCC
Irish Sea Cruising Guide	Robert Kemp	Coles

499

Cruising Guide to the Isle of Man	Robert Kemp	Laver
Cruising Guide, Anglesey and Menai Strait	Robert Kemp	Laver
Bristol Channel Handbook		BCYC
Sailing Directions, South and West coasts of Ireland		ICC
Sailing Directions, North and East coasts of Ireland		ICC
Norwegian Cruising Guide	Mark Brackenbury	Stanford
Baltic Pilot	Stan Townsend	Coles
Frisian Pilot, Den Helder to Brunsbüttel	Mark Brackenbury	Stanford
Barge Country (Dutch and Belgian canals and rivers	John Liley	Stanford
North Sea Harbours, Calais to Den Helder	Jack Coote after E. Delmar-Morgan	Coles
Normandy Pilot, Calais to Cherbourg	Mark Brackenbury	Coles
Notes on French Inland Waterways		CA
France – the Quiet Way (French canals and rivers)	John Liley	Stanford
Brittany and Channel Islands Cruising Guide	David Jefferson	Stanford
Channel Islands Pilot	Malcolm Robson	Nautical
French Pilot Vol. I (Omonville to Tréguier)	Malcolm Robson	Nautical
French Pilot Vol. II (Port Blanc to Ile de Sein	Malcolm Robson	Nautical
North Brittany Pilot	A. Coles/RCC	Coles
North Biscay Pilot	A. Coles/A. N. Black	Coles
South Biscay Pilot	Robin Brandon	Coles

It should be pointed out that the above list is not intended to be exhaustive, but only a selection of recommended pilot books. Most if not all are available through J. D. Potter Ltd, 145 Minories, London EC3N 1NH, or major nautical booksellers.

INDEX

Notes on the use of the Index Page numbers given in *italic* type refer to plan pages. All entries are indexed under their individual names; geographical descriptions such as Loch, River, etc are put after the name, as are words such as le, de etc. Entries are in alphabetical order of *all* letters, including those in second or subsequent words in the entry e.g. Portivi, Port Joinville, Portknockie, Port la Forêt, Portland Bill). Passage Notes are listed in geographical (i.e. *Handbook*) order at the end of the Index.

Aabenraa, 329
Aalborg, 329
Aarhus, 329
Aberbenoit, L', *434*, 435
Aberdeen, *164*, 166
Aberdovey, 246, *259*
Aberildut, L', 441, *443*
Abersoch, 245, *247*
Abervrac'h, L', 433, *434*, 435
Aberystwyth, 246, *247*, 248
Achill Sound, 320
Ærøskøbing, 329
Agersø, 329
Alde R, *126*, 127–8
Aldeburgh, *126*, 127–8
Alderney, *398*, 399–400
Algeciras, 498
Aline, Loch, 209
Alt R, 235
Ameland, 349
Amsterdam, *354*, 362
Angle B, *252*, 256
Anholt, 329
Anstruther, *160*, 162
Appledore, 270, *271*
Aranmore, 318–19

Arbroath, *164*, 165
Arcachon, 482, *483*
Ardentraive B, 209, *210*, 211
Ardglass, *302*, 307
Ardgroom, *280*, 282–3
Ardrishaig, 215
Arinagour (Coll), 205
Arklow, 300–1, *302*
Arosa Is, 494
Arundel, 80, *82*, 83
Ashlett Creek, 62, *64*
Askam, 231
Assens, 329
Auberlach B, 445–6
Audierne, 449, *450*
Auray R, 467
Auskerry, 180
Aven R, *457*, 458
Aviles, 491
Avon R (Bristol), 266
Avon R (Christchurch), 54
Axe R, 267

Babbacombe, 26
Bäckviken, 333
Badachro, 204

Bagenkop, 329
Ballycotton, 294
Ballynakill Hr, 321
Balta Sound, *183*, 184
Baltimore, *287*, 289–90
Banff, *168*, 169
Bangor (N Ireland) 308, *309*, 310
Bangor (N Wales), 239, *240*
Bann R, 313
Bantry, 284, *285*
Bares, 492
Barfleur, *390*, 392
Barmouth, 245-6, *237*
Barnstaple, 272
Barquero, Ria del, 492
Barra, *196*, 197
Barrow-in-Furness, 231, *232*
Barry, *263*, 265
Batz, Ile de *431*, 432
Bayona, 495
Bayonne, 482, *484*
Beaucette (Guernsey), *398*, 402–3
Beaulieu R, 50, 60, *61*
Beaumaris, 239, *240*

Beer Roads, 26
Belfast Lough, 308–10
Belle Ile, *463*, 464
Belon R, *457*, 458–9
Bembridge IoW, 51, 68, *69*
Bénodet, *454*, 455
Berehaven, *280*, 283
Bermeo, 488
Bertheaume, Anse de, 442
Berwick-upon-Tweed, 154, *155*
Bideford, 270, *271*, 272
Bilbao, 489
Binic, 413
Birdham Pool, 75, *77*
Birkenhead, 235, *237*
Birterbuy B, 322
Blacksod B, 320
Blackwater R, 112, *113*, 114
Blakeney, 133–4
Blancs Sablons B, 441
Blankenberge, 365, *366*
Blaye, 481
Blundellsands, 235
Blyth, 150, *151*, 153
Boisdale, Loch, 195, *196*, 197
Bois de la Chaise, 472
Bordeaux, 481
Borkum, 342, *343*
Borough Is, 26
Boscastle, 272–3
Bosham, 75, *77*
Boston, *138*, 140, 142
Boulogne, *376*, 377
Bournemouth, 50
Boyardville, 479
Bradwell, 114, *115*
Brancaster Staithe, 135–6
Braunton, 270, *271*
Braye (Alderney), *398*, 399–400
Bréhat Roads, 414, 416–17
Bremerhaven, 341
Breskens, *358*, 360
Brest, *444*, 445
Bridlington, 143, *144*, 145

Bridlington B, 136
Bridport, 39–40
Brightlingsea, *117*, 118
Brighton, *82*, 83–4
Brigneau, 459
Brignogan, 433
Bristol, 266
Brixham, 33, *34*, 35
Broadhaven, 319
Broom, Loch, 198, *199*
Brough Haven, *141*, 143
Brunsbüttel, 338, *339*
Bryher (Scilly), 5, 6
Buckie, *168*, 170
Buckler's Hard, 60, *61*
Bude, 272
Bunbeg, 318
Burela, 492
Burghead, 170, *171*, 173
Burnham-on-Crouch, 110, *111*, 112
Burnham-on-Sea, *264*, 267–8
Burnham Overy, 135
Burntisland, *159*, 161
Burry Port, *260*, 261–2
Burtonport, 318–19

Cadillac, 482
Cadiz, 498
Caen, 388
Caernarvon, *241*, 243
Cahirciveen, 281
Calais, 374, *376*, 377
Caledonian Canal, 209
Calstock, *22*, 23
Camaret, 446, *447*
Camarinas, 493
Carmarthen, 261
Camber Hr, 70, *71*
Campbeltown, 215, *218*
Canal de Tancarville, 382
Canal du Midi, 371
Canal du Nivernais, 370–1
Canche R, *375*, 378
Candas, 491
Canna, Is of, 201, *202*
Cap Breton, 482

Cardigan, 248
Carentan, 389, *390*, 391
Cargreen, *22*, 23
Carlingford Lough, 303–4, *305*
Carnlough, 303
Carrickfergus, 310
Carteret, 407
Carrigaholt, 323
Cascais, 496
Cashel, 322
Cashla B, 322
Castets, 481–2
Castilla de San Anton, 493
Castlebay, Barra, *196*, 197
Castlehaven, *288*, 290
Castletown (Berehaven), *280*, 283
Castletown IoM, *226*, 228
Castro Urdiales, 489
Cawsand, 19
Cedeira, 492
Cemaes B, 238
Cemlyn B, 238
Chapman's Pool, 44
Charente R, 478–9
Château, Le (I d'Oleron), 479
Chateaulin R, 446
Chausey, I, 408
Cherbourg, 392, *393*, 394
Chichester Hr, 74–5, *76*–7, 78–9
Christchurch, 51, *52*, 54
Church Pool, 319
Clare Is, 321
Clew B, 320
Clifden B, 321
Clovelly B, 270
Cobh, *292*, 293
Colchester, 118
Coleraine, 313
Coll, Is of, 205
Colne R, *113*, 116, *117*, 118
Colonsay, 206, *207*
Comillas, 489
Concarneau, 456, *457*, 458
Conquet, Le, 442, *443*

Conwy, 236, *237*, 238
Conyer Creek, 104
Copenhagen, 330
Cork, *292*, 293–4
Corme, 493
Corrubedo, 493
Coruña, 493
Courseulles, *387*, 388
Cowes IoW, 60, 62, *63*
Crac'h R, *463*, 464–5
Craignish, Loch, *210*, 211
Creux Hr (Sark), 403
Crinan, Loch, 211–12
Crinan Canal, 212
Croisic, Le, 469–70, *473*
Crookhaven, 284, *286*
Crosshaven, 293, *295*
Crotoy, Le, *375*, 378–9
Crouch, R, 110, *111*, 112
Crowlin Is, 204
Cruit B, 318
Cudillero, 491
Culdaff B, 311
Cultra, 308
Cuxhaven, 338, *339*

Dale, *252*, 256
Daoulas R, 446
Dartmouth, *30*, 31, 33
Deauville, 386, *387*
Deben R, 124, *125*
Dee R, 236
Delfzijl, 348, *350*
Dell Quay, 75, *77*
Den Helder, *350*, 353, 355
Derby Haven, *226*, 228
Derrible B, 403
Deva, 488
Diélette, 407
Dieppe, 379, *380*, 381
Dingle Hr, 324
Dittisham, 31, *32*
Dixcart B, 403
Doelan, 459
Donaghadee, 308
Donegal, 319
Dordrecht, 361
Douarnenez, *447*, 448

Douglas, *226*, 228–9
Dover, 89, *90*
Drogheda, 303
Drummore, 220
Dublin, 301
Duddon R, 231
Dunbar, *155*, 158
Dundee, *163*, 165
Dungeness Roads, 85
Dunkerque, 374, *375*
Dun Laoghaire, 301, *302*
Dunstaffnage B, 209
Dunvegan, Loch, 200
Düsternbrook, 329

East Ferry, Cork, *292*, 293–4
Ebeltoft, 329
Eckernförde, 329
Edam, 363
Eigg, Is of, 201
Elanchove, 488
Elbe R, 338, *339*
Elburg, 364
Elbury Cove, 33
Emsworth, *77*, 78
Enkhuizen, 363
Eriboll, Loch, *186*, 188
Erith, 106
Erquy, 412
Esbjerg, *334*, 335
Etaples, *375*, 378
Etel R, 462
Ewe, Loch, 198, *199*
Exeter, 39
Exmouth, 26, 36, *38*, 39
Eyemouth, *155*, 157
Eynort, Loch, 195

Faaborg, 329
Fair Isle, 181, *182*
Falmouth, 12, *14*
Fambridge, 110, *111*, 112
Fareham, 73
Fécamp, *380*, 381–2
Felixstowe Ferry, 124, *125*
Fenit Pier, 323
Ferriby, *141*, 143

Ferrol, 492
Fiers d'Ars (I de Ré), 476
Filey B, 136–7
Findhorn, *171*, 173
Fishbourne, *59*, 66–7
Fisherrow, 158
Fishguard, *247*, 248–9
Fjællebroen, 329
Fleetwood, *232*, 234
Flotte, La (I de Ré), 476
Flushing, *358*, 359
Folkestone, 88, *90*
Fosdyke, 140
Four Channel, 439–41
Fowey, 15, *17*, 18
Foyle, Lough, 313–14
Foz, 492
Fraserburgh, *167*, 169
Freckleton, 234
Fredericia, 329
Frederickssund, 330
Frenchport, 320
Fuenterrabia, 487

Gairloch, Loch, 204
Galway, 323
Gareloch, 217
Garlieston, 220
Gibraltar, 498
Gigha, *213*, 214–15
Gijon, 490
Gillan Creek, 10, 12
Gilleleje, 330
Gironde R, 480–1
Glandore, *288*, 290
Glasson Dock, 233
Glénans, Is de, 456
Glengariff, 283–4, *285*
Goil, Loch, 217
Gometra, 205–6, *207*
Gorey, *398*, 406
Gorran, 15
Gosport, 70, *71*
Grandcamp, *384*, 389
Granton, 158, *159*, 161
Granville, 407–8, *409*
Gravelines, 374, *375*
Gravesend, 105

Great Cumbrae, 217
Greatman B, 322
Great Yarmouth, *130*,
    131–2
Greencastle, 313
Greenhithe, 105
Greenore, 303–4, *305*
Greenwich, 106
Grenaa, 330
Grève de la Ville, La, 403
Grimsby, *141*, 142–3
Groix, I de, 461
Grove, El (S Martin), 494
Guernsey, 400–3
Guetaria, 488
Guilvinec, 453
Gurutzeaundi, 487
Gweedore, 318

Hals, 330
Hamble R, 65–6, *67*
Hamoaze, *21*, 23
Harderwijk, 364
Harlingen, 349, *350*, 351
Harport, Loch, 200–1
Harrington, 225
Hartlepool, *147*, 149
Harty Ferry, *98*, 99
Harwich, 120, *121*, 122
Havengore Creek, 109
Havre, L, *384*, 385
Havre Gosselin, 403
Hayle, 273, *274*, 275
Hayling B, 51
Hayling Is, *72*, 73–9
Helder, Den, *350*, 353, 355
Helford R, 10, *11*
Helgoland, *340*, 341
Helmsdale, 174, *175*
Helsingør, 330
Helvick, 297
Hendaye, 485
Herbaudière, L', 472, *473*
Heybridge Basin, *113*, 114
Heysham, 233
Hindeloopen, 364
Hodbarrow, 231
Höedic, I de, 468

Hoek van Holland, 355–6,
    357
Holehaven, 108
Holyhead, *242*, 243–4
Holy Is, *152*, 153–4
Holy Loch, 217
Honfleur, 384, 385–6
Hook of Holland, 355–6,
    357
Hook Rocks, 85
Hooksiel, 337, 341
Hope Cove, 26
Hopeman, 170, *171*
Hoorn, 363
Houat, I de, 468
Hull, 143
Humber R, *141*, 142–3
Hundested, 330
Hythe, 62, *64*

Ijmuiden, *354*, 355
Ilfracombe, 270, *271*
Indaal, Loch, 206, 208
Inishbofin, 321
Inishturk, 321
Inver, Loch, 197–8
Inverkip, 217
Inverness, *172*, 174
Iona, 206
Ipswich, 123
Isigny, 389, *390*
Isleornsay, 202, 203
Itchenor, 75, *77*

Jack Sound, 250
Jade R, 341
Jersey, 403–6
John O'Groats, 187

Kalundborg, 330
Kalvehave, 330
Kerteminde, 330
Keyhaven, *53*, 54
Kiel Canal, 337–8
Kilbaha, 323
Kilkeel, *302*, 304, 307
Kilkieran B, 322
Killala, 319

Killary B, 321
Killybegs, 319
Killyleagh, *306*, 307–8
Kilmakilloge, *280*, 282
Kilronan, 323
Kingsferry, 104
King's Lynn, 137–8, *139*
Kingston-upon-Hull, 143
Kingswear, *30*, 31
Kinsale, 290, *291*, 293
Kircaldy, *159*, 161
Kircudbright, 220–1
Kirkwall, 177, *178*
Knott End, 234
København, 330
Køge, 330
Kolby Kaas, 330
Kolding, 330
Kornwerderzand, 352–3
Korsør, 331
Kyle Akin, *202*, 204
Kyle of Lochalsh, *202*, 204
Kyle of Tongue, *186*, 187–8
Kyrkbacken, 333

Lamlash, 219
Lampaul (Ushant), 442,
    443
Lancaster, 233
Landerneau R, 445
Langeoog, 342, *343*
Langør, 331
Langstone Hr, *72*, 73
Lannion R, *422*, 426–7
Laredo, 489
Largo B, 162
Larne Lough, 310
Lastres, 490
Lauwersoog, 349
Lawling Creek, *113*, 114
Laxey, 229
Laxford, Loch, 197, *199*
Lawrenny, *254*, 256
Legue, Le, 413
Leigh-on-Sea, 108–9
Leith, 158
Leixoes, 496
Lemmer, 364

Lemvig, 331
Lequeitio, 488
Lerwick, *182*, 184
Lézardrieux, 414, 416–17, *418–19*
Limhamn, 333
Linnhe, Loch, 209
Lisbon, 496
Littlehampton, 80, *81*
Little Killary, 321
Liverpool, 235
Lizard, The, 8–9
Llanelli, *260*, 261–2
Llanes, 490
Lochranza, 216
Loctudy, *451*, 453, 455
Loe Pool, 9
Løgstør, 331
Loire R, 470–1
Londonderry, 314
London River, 105–8
Long, Loch, 217
Looe, *16*, 18–19
Lorient, *460*, 461–2
Lossiemouth, 170, *171*
Lowestoft, 129, 130, 131
Luanco, 491
Luarca, 491
Lulworth Cove, 44
Lunan B, 165
Lundy Is, 272
Lune, R, 233
Lybster, 174, *175*, 176
Lyme B, 24–5
Lyme Regis, 39
Lymington, 50, 54–5, 56

Macduff, *168*, 169
Maddy, Loch, *193*, 194–5
Maidstone, 100, 103
Makkum, 364
Malahide Inlet, 303
Maldon, *113*, 114
Mallaig, 204, 207
Malpas, 13, *14*
Marennes, 479–80
Marken, 363
Man, Is of, 225–30

Manningtree, 122
Margate, 97
Marstal, 331
Maryport, 224
Maseline Hr, 403
Medemblik, 363
Medway R, 99–100, *101*, 103
Melfort, Loch, 211
Menai Strait, 238–9, *240–1*, 243
Mengham Rythe, *77*, 78
Merrien, 459
Mersea, West, 114, *115*, 116
Mersey R, 235, *237*
Methil, *159*, 161
Mevagissey, 15, *16*
Middelfart, 331
Middlesborough, 146, *147*, 149
Milford Haven, 251, *252–4*, 255–6
Millport, 217
Mill Rythe, *77*, 78–9
Minehead, 269
Moléne, I de, 441, *443*
Mölle, 333
Monnickendam, 363
Montrose, *164*, 165
Morbihan, 465, *466*, 467–8
Morecambe, 233
Morgat, 448
Morlaix Roads and R, 427, *428*, 429
Mortagne-sur-Gironde, 480
Mostyn, 236
Motrico, 488
Mousehole, 6, 7
Muiden, 363
Mullion, 9
Mulroy, Lough, 314, *316*, 317
Mundaca, 488
Musel, 490

Næstved, 331
Nairn, *172*, 173

Nakskov, 331
na Lathaich, Loch, 206, *207*
Navia, 491
Nes, 349
Netley, 62, *64*
Nevin B, 244
New Brighton, 235, *237*
New Harbour, 323
Newhaven, *81*, 84–5
Newlyn, 6, 7
Newport, *264*, 265–6
New Quay, Cardigan, 248
Newtown R (IoW), 57, *59*, 60
Niembro, 490
Nieuwpoort, *366*, 367
Noirmoutier, 472, *473*
Norddeich, 342, *343*
Norderney, 342, *343*
Nord-Ostsee Kanal, 337–8
Nyborg, 331
Nykøbing (Limfjord), 331
Nykøbing (Sjælland), 331

Oban, 209, *210*, 211
Odden, 331
Odense, 331
Oleron, I d', 479
Omø, 331
Ore R, *126*, 127–8
Orford Haven, *126*, 127–8
Omonville-la-Rogue, *390*, 394–5
Ondarroa, 488
Orio, Rio de, 488
Orkney, 177–81
Oronsay, 206
Ornsay, Is, *202*, 203
Orwell R, *121*, 122–3
Osborne B, 50
Ostend, *366*, 367
Oude Schild, *350*, 353
Ouistreham, 386, *387*, 388
Oysterhaven, *286*, 293

Padstow, 273, *274*
Paglesham, *111*, 112
Paignton, 33

Paimpol, 414, *415*
Palais, Le (Belle I), *463*, 464
Pallice, La, 476–7
Pasages, 488
Passage Notes *see list after Index*
Pauillac, 481
Peel, *226*, 230
Pegwell B, 86, 89
Pembroke Dock, *253*, 256
Penarth, *259*, 265
Penerf, 468
Penpoul, *422*, 430
Pentland Firth, 185
Penzance, 7, 8
Perros-Guirec, 424, *425*
Perrotine, La (I d'Oleron), 479
Peterhead, 166, *167*
Piel Hr, 231, *232*
Pierowall, *179*, 180
Pill Creek (R Avon), 266
Pin Mill, *121*, 123
Pittenweem, *160*, 162
Plencia, 488
Ploumanac'h, 424
Plymouth, 19, *20*, 23
Polkerris, 15
Polperro, 18
Polruan, 15, *17*, 18
Pontusval, 433
Poole Hr, 45, *46–7*, 48–9
Poolewe, 198, *199*
Porlock Weir, 269
Pornic, 471–2, *473*
Pornichet–La Baule, 470
Pouliguen, Le, 470
Præstø, 332
Port Askaig, 214
Port Bannatyne, 216–17
Port Blanc, *422*, 423
Port Bloc, 481
Port Breton, 472, *474*
Portchester Lake, 70
Port de Bloscon, 430, *431*
Port Dinlleyn, 244
Port Dinorwic, 239, 243

Port du Crouesty, *450*, 465
Port Ellen, *213*, 214
Port-en-Bessin, *384*, 388–9
Port Erin, *226*, 230
Port Haliguen, *463*, 464
Porthcawl, 262, 265
Porthleven, 9, 10
Porthoustock, 9
Porthmadog, 245
Portimao, 497
Portishead, 266–7
Portivi, 462
Port Joinville, 472, *474*
Portknockie, *168*, 169–70
Port la Forêt, 456
Portland Bill, 25–6
Portland Hr, 40, *41*, 42
Portlemouth, 28
Portmagee, *279*, 281
Portmahomack, *172*, 174
Port Maria, 462–3
Port Mellin, 15
Port Navalo, *450*, 465, 467
Portpatrick, 219
Portsall, 436–7
Portree, 203
Portrieux, *409*, 413–14
Portrush, *309*, 313
Port St Mary, *226*, 227–8
Portstewart, 311
Portsmouth, 68, 70, *71*
Port Talbot, 262
Port Tudy (I de Groix), *457*, 461
Portzmoguer, 441
Poulmic, B of, 446
Preston, 234
Primel, *422*, 427
Puerto Finisterre, 493
Puerto Pias, 494
Puilldobhrain, 211
Puntal, 490
Pwllheli, 245

Queenborough, *102*, 103–4
Quimperlé R, 461

Raa, 333

Ramsey B, *226*, 229–30
Ramsey Sound, 250
Ramsgate, 86, *91*, 92
Ramsholt, 124, *125*
Rance, R, 412
Randers, 332
Ranza, Loch, 216
Ravenglass, 231
Ré, Ile de, *473*, 475–6
Redonela, 494
Rendsburg, 337
Rhum, Is of, 201
Ribadeo, 491
Ribadesella, 490
Ribble, R, 234
Richborough, 89, 92
Roach, R, *111*, 112
Rochelle, La, *477*, 478
Rochester, 100, 103
Rødby, 332
Rogerstown Inlet, 303
Roscoff, 430, *431*, 432
Rosslare, 298, *299*, 300
Rossport, 319
Rotheneuf, 408, *409*, 411
Rothesay, 216–17
Rotterdam, 356
Rouen, 382, 385
Roundstone B, 322
Rudkøbing, 332
Runswick B, 137
Ryan, Loch, *218*, 219
Ryde, 51
Rye, 86, *87*, 88

Sables D'Olonne, Les, *474*, 475
St Abbs, *155*, 157–8
St Andrew's B, 162
St Aubin, *405*, 406
St Austell B, 15
St Bride's B, 250–1
St Brieuc (Le Legue), 413
St Brieuc, B de, 412
St Christoly de Medoc, 481
St Evette, 449, *450*
St Germans R, *21*, 23
St Gilles sur Vie, 472–3

St Guénolé, *451*, 452
St Helier, 404, *405*
St Ives, *274*, 275
St Jean de Luz, 485
St Julians (Arosa Is), 494
St Kilda, 191
St Malo, *410*, 411
St Marcouf, Is de, 391
St Martin, Ile de Ré, *473*, 475–6
St Martin's Is, Scilly, 5
St Mary's Is, Scilly, *3*, 5
St Mawes, 12, *14*
St Monance, *160*, 161
St Nazaire, 470–1
St Peter Port, 400, *401*, 402
St Quay, Portrieux, *409*, 413–14
St Tudwal's Road, 245, *247*
St Vaast-la-Hougue, *390*, 391–2
St Valéry-en-Caux, *380*, 381
St Valéry-sur-Somme, *375*, 378–9
Sagres, B de, 497
Sakskøbing, 332
Salbuck, 321
Salcombe, 28, *29*, 31
Saltash, *22*, 23
San Ciprian, 492
Sandsend B, 137
Sandside B, 187
Sandy Haven, *252*, 256
San Esteban, 491
Sangenjo, 494
San Sebastian, 488
Sta Eugenia de Riveira, 494
Santa Marta, 492
Santander, 489
Santona, 489
San Vincente, 490
Sark, 403
Saundersfoot, 258, *259*, 261
Sauzon, Belle Ile, 464
Scalasaig, 206, *207*
Scarborough, 137, *144*, 145
Scavaig, Loch, 201

Scheveningen, 355, *357*
Schiermonnikoog, 349
Schull, *286*, 289
Scilly Is, 1, *2–4*, 5–6
Scrabster, *186*, 187
Scresort, Loch (Rhum), 201
Seaford Road, 85
Seaham, *148*, 149–50
Seaview, 51
Sein, I de, 448
Sein, Raz de, 449
Seine, R, 382, *383*
Sejerø, 332
Sept Iles, Les, 426
Sesimbra, 496–7
Seudre R, 479–80
Shannon R, 323
Shapinsay, 177, 180
Sharfleet Creek, *101*, 103
Shell, Loch, 194
Shetland, 181–4
Silloth, 224
Sines, B de, 497
Skagen, 332
Skanör, 333
Skerries B, 303
Skiport, Loch, 195
Skippool, *232*, 234
Skomer Is, 251
Sligo, 319
Small Downs, 86
Smerwick Hr, 324
Sneem, *280*, 281–2
Snizort, Loch, 200
Søby, 332
Solva, 250
Solway Firth, 219
Sønderborg, 332
Southampton Water, 62, *64*, 65
South Ferriby, *141*, 143
Southwold, 124, *125*, 128–9
Spakenburg, 364
Spodsbjerg, 332
Stackpole Quay, 257
Staffa, 206
Staffin B, 203

Stangate Creek, *101*, 103
Starhole B, 28
Start B, 24, 26
Staveren, 364
Stege, 332
Stickenhörn, 329
Stokes B, 50
Stonehaven, *164*, 165–6
Stornoway, 192, *193*, 194
Stour, R, *121*, 122
Stranraer, *218*, 219
Strangford Lough, *306*, 307–8
Stromness, 177, *178*
Stronsay, *179*, 180
Stubbekøbing, 332
Studland B, 45, *46*
Suances, 489
Sunderland, *148*, 150
Svendborg, 332–3
Swale R, *98*, 99
Swanage, 44
Swansea, 262, *263*
Swilly, Lough, 314, *315*

Taf R, 261
Tamar R, *22*, 23
Tancarville Canal, 382
Tapia, 491
Tarbert, E Loch (Harris), 194, *196*
Tarbert, W Loch (Harris), 191, *193*
Tarbert, E Loch (Kintyre), 215, *218*
Tarbert, W Loch (Kintyre), *213*, 214
Tarifa, 498
Tay R, 162, 163, 165
Tayvallich, 212, *213*
Tazones, 490
Teddington, 107
Teelin, 319
Tees R, 146, *147*, 149
Teignmouth, 35–6, *37*
Tenby, 258, *259*
Terneuzen, *358*, 359–60
Terschelling, *351*, 352

Thames R, 105–8
Thorney, 75, *77*, 78
Thurso, 187
Thyborøn, *334*, 335
Tina (Menor and Meyor), 490
Titchfield Haven, 66
Tobermory, 209, *210*
Tollesbury, 116
Topsham, 39
Torbay, 24, 26, 33, 35
Torquay, *34*, 35
Totland B, 50
Totnes, *32*, 33
Toulinguet Channel, 446–7
Towy R, 261
Trébeurden, 426
Tréboul, *447*, 448
Trégastel, 424
Tréguier R, 417, 420–1, 423
Tremblade, La, 479–80
Trent R, 143
Tréport, Le, 379, *380*
Tresco (Scilly), 5–6
Trieux R, 414, 416–17, *418–19*
Trinité, La (Crac'h R), *463*, 464–5
Trompeloup, 480–1
Troon, 217, *218*
Trouville, 386, *387*
Truro R, 13, *14*
Tunø, 333
Tynemouth, 150

Uig B, Skye, 200
Ullapool, 198, *299*

Ura Firth, *183*, 184
Urk, 364
Urr, Waters of, 221

Valentia, 278, *279*, 281
Vannes, 467
Vega, 491
Vejle, 333
Viavelez, 491
Vigo, 494
Viken, 333
Vilaine, La, 469
Vilamoura, 497
Vila Real de San Antonio, 497
Villagarcia, 494
Vivero, Ria de, 492
Vlieland, *351*, 352
Vlissingen, *358*, 359
Volendam, 363
Vordingborg, 333

Waldringfield, 124, *125*
Wallasea, 110, *111*
Walton Backwaters, *119*, 120
Wangerooge, 342, *343*
Warkworth, *151*, 153
Warsash, 65–6, *67*
Wash, The, 137, *138*
Watchet, 268
Waterford, *296*, 297–8
Watermouth, 269
Wells-next-the-Sea, 134–5
Weser, R, 341
West Bay, 24–5, 39–40
West Kirby, 236

West Mersea, 114, *115*, 116
Weston-super-Mare, 267
Westport, 320
West Terschelling, *351*, 352
Wexford, *299*, 300
Weymouth, *41*, 42
Whitby, 137, *144*, 145–6
Whitehaven, 225, *232*
Whitehills, *168*, 169
Whitesand B, 15
Whithorn, Is of, 220
Whitstable, 97, *98*, 99
Wick, *175*, 176
Wicklow, *299*, 301
Wilhelmshaven, 341
Winteringham Haven, *141*, 143
Wisbech, *138*, 140
Wivenhoe, 120
Woodbridge, 124, *125*
Woolverstone, *121*, 123
Wooton (IoW), 50–1, *59*, 66–7
Worbarrow B, 43–4
Workington, 224–5
Workum, 364
Wrabness, 122

Yarmouth (IoW), 50, 55, 57, *58*
Yarmouth (Norfolk) *see* Great Yarmouth
Yealm R, 26, *27*, 28
Yeu, Ile d', 472, *474*
Youghal, 294, *295*, 297

Zeebrugge, *358*, 365
Zumaya, 488

Index of Passage Notes

Arranged in geographical (i.e. *Handbook*) order

Scilly Is to Penzance 1
Penzance to Falmouth 9
Falmouth to Plymouth 13, 15
Plymouth to Weymouth 23–6
Weymouth to Poole 43–4
Poole to Chichester 49–51
Chichester to Newhaven 79
Newhaven to Ramsgate 85–6
North Foreland to Harwich 94–7
Queenborough to Harty Ferry by the
    Swale 104
Harwich to Southwold 123
Southwold to Great Yarmouth 129
Cromer to the Humber 136
Humber to Berwick 143
Berwick to Arbroath 157
Arbroath to Fraserburgh 165
Fraserburgh to Wick 169
Duncansby Head to Cape Wrath 184–5
Cape Wrath to Ardnamurchan (Offshore
    Passage) 191
Cape Wrath to Loch Ewe (Inshore) 197
Loch Ewe to Ardnamurchan (Inshore)
    201, 203
Ardnamurchan to Mull of Kintyre 205

East Loch Tarbert to Mull of Galloway
    216
North Channel to Milford Haven 223
Solway Firth to St Bees Head 223–4
Liverpool to Conwy 235–6
Menai Strait 238–43
Fishguard to St Ann's Head 249–50
Milford Haven to Land's End 256–7
Valentia to Crookhaven 278
Crookhaven to Cork 284, 289
Cork to Tuskar Rock 294
Carnsore Point to Dublin Bay 298
Dublin Bay to Fair Head 301–2
Fair Head to Bloody Foreland 310–11
Bloody Foreland to Ern's Head 318
Ern's Head to Slyne Head 320
Slyne Head to Valentia 321
Brunsbüttel to the Ems 337
Fécamp to Le Havre 382
Cherbourg and the Channel Islands 397–8
Cherbourg Peninsula, West Coast 407
Ushant to Cape Finisterre 439
Penmarc'h Point to the Gironde 453
Ile d'Oleron to the Gironde 480
Bordeaux to Castets 481–2